THE Kaleidoscope OF Gender

4th edition

THE Kaleidoscope OF Gender

Prisms, Patterns, and Possibilities

4th edition

Joan Z. Spade

*The College at Brockport,
State University of New York*

•

Catherine G. Valentine

Nazareth College

Los Angeles | London | New Delhi
Singapore | Washington DC

Los Angeles | London | New Delhi
Singapore | Washington DC

FOR INFORMATION:

SAGE Publications, Inc.
2455 Teller Road
Thousand Oaks, California 91320
E-mail: order@sagepub.com

SAGE Publications Ltd.
1 Oliver's Yard
55 City Road
London EC1Y 1SP
United Kingdom

SAGE Publications India Pvt. Ltd.
B 1/I 1 Mohan Cooperative Industrial Area
Mathura Road, New Delhi 110 044
India

SAGE Publications Asia-Pacific Pte. Ltd.
3 Church Street
#10-04 Samsung Hub
Singapore 049483

Printed in the United States of America

Library of Congress Cataloging-in-Publication Data

Spade, Joan Z. The kaleidoscope of gender : prisms, patterns, and possibilities / Joan Z. Spade, The College at Brockport, State University of New York, Catherine G. Valentine, Nazareth College—Fourth Edition.

pages cm
Includes bibliographical references.

ISBN 978-1-4522-0541-0 (pbk.)
ISBN 978-1-4833-0179-2 (web pdf)

1. Sex role. 2. Sex differences (Psychology) 3. Gender identity. 4. Man-woman relationships. 5. Interpersonal relations. I. Valentine, Catherine G. II. Title.

HQ1075.K35 2013
305.3—dc23   2013013953

This book is printed on acid-free paper.

Acquisitions Editor: Diane McDaniel
Editorial Assistant: Lauren Johnson
Production Editor: Libby Larson
Copy Editor: Megan Granger
Typesetter: C&M Digitals (P) Ltd.
Proofreader: Jennifer Thompson
Cover Designer: Candice Harman
Marketing Manager: Erica DeLuca

13 14 15 16 17 10 9 8 7 6 5 4 3 2 1

CONTENTS

PREFACE

This fourth edition of *The Kaleidoscope of Gender: Prisms, Patterns, and Possibilities* provides an overview of the cutting-edge literature and theoretical frameworks in the sociology of gender and related fields for understanding the social construction of gender. Although not ignoring classical contributions to gender research, this book focuses on where the field is moving and the changing paradigms and approaches to gender studies. *The Kaleidoscope of Gender* uses the metaphor of a kaleidoscope and three themes—prisms, patterns, and possibilities—to unify topic areas. It focuses on the prisms through which gender is shaped, the patterns gender takes, and the possibilities for social change through a deeper understanding of ourselves and our relationships with others, both locally and globally.

The book begins, in the first part, by looking at gender and other social prisms that define gendered experiences across the spectrum of daily lives. We conceptualize prisms as social categories of difference and inequality that shape the way gender is defined and practiced, including culture, race/ethnicity, social class, sexuality, age, and ability/disability. Different as individuals' lives might be, there are patterns to gendered experiences. The second part of the book follows this premise and examines these patterns across a multitude of arenas of daily life. From here, the last part of the book takes a proactive stance, exploring possibilities for change. Basic to the view of gender as a social construction is the potential for social change. Students will learn that gender transformation has occurred and can occur

and, consequently, that it is possible to alter the genderscape. Because prisms, patterns, and possibilities themselves intersect, the framework for this book is fluid, interweaving topics and emphasizing the complexity and ever-changing nature of gender.

We had multiple goals in mind as we first developed this book, and the fourth edition reaffirms these goals:

1. Creating a book of readings that is accessible, timely, and stimulating in a text whose structure and content incorporate a fluid framework, with gender presented as an emergent, evolving, complex pattern—not one fixed in traditional categories and topics

2. Selecting articles that creatively and clearly explicate what gender is and is not and what it means to say that gender is socially constructed by incorporating provocative illustrations and solid scientific evidence of the malleability of gender and the role of individuals, groups, and social institutions in the daily performance and transformation of gender practices and patterns

3. Including readings that untangle and clarify the intricate ways gender is embedded in and defined by the prisms of culture, race/ethnicity, class, sexuality, age, ability/disability, and cultural patterns of identities, groups, and institutions

4. Integrating articles with cross-cultural and global foci to illustrate that gender is a continuum of categories, patterns, and expressions whose relevance is contextual and continuously shifting, and that gender inequality is not a universal and natural social pattern but, rather, one of many systems of oppression

5. Assembling articles that offer students useful cognitive and emotional tools for making sense of the shifting and contradictory genderscape they inhabit, its personal relevance, its implications for relationships both locally and globally, and possibilities for change

These goals shaped the revisions in the fourth edition of *The Kaleidoscope of Gender*. New selections in this edition emphasize global and intersectional analyses throughout the book. More readings focus on masculinities, and the final chapter highlights new contemporary social movements for gender justice. We continue to explore the role of institutions in maintaining gender difference and inequality. Across the chapters, readings examine the individual, situational, and organizational bases for gendered patterns in relationships, behaviors, and beliefs. Additionally, many readings illustrate how multiple prisms of difference and inequality, such as race and social class, create an array of patterns of gender—distinct but sometimes similar to the idealized patterns in a culture.

As in the third edition, reading selections include theoretical and review articles; however, the emphasis continues to be on contemporary contributions to the field. A significantly revised introduction to the book provides more extensive and detailed descriptions of the theories in the field, particularly theories based on a social-constructionist perspective. In addition, the introduction to the book develops the kaleidoscope metaphor as a tool for viewing gender and a guide for studying gender. Revised chapter introductions contextualize the literature in each part of the book, introduce the readings, and illustrate how they relate to analyses of gender. Introductions and questions for consideration precede each reading to help students focus on and grasp the key points of the selections. Additionally, each chapter ends with questions for students to consider and topics for students to explore.

It is possible to use this book alone, as a supplement to a text, or in combination with other articles or monographs. It is designed for undergraduate audiences, and the readings are appropriate for a variety of courses focusing on the study of gender, such as sociology of gender, gender and social change, and women's studies. The book may be used in departments of sociology, anthropology, psychology, and women's studies.

We would like to thank those reviewers whose valuable suggestions and comments helped us develop the book throughout four editions, including the following.

Fourth edition reviewers:

Nancy Ashton; Allison Alexy, Lafayette College; John Bartkowski, University of Texas at San Antonio; Beth Berila, St Cloud State University, Women's Studies Program; Ted Cohen, Ohio Wesleyan University; Francoise Cromer, Stony Brook University; Pamela J. Forman, University of Wisconsin—Eau Claire; Ann Fuehrer, Miami University; Katja Guenther, University of California, Riverside; William Hewitt, West Chester University of PA; Bianca Isaki, University of Hawai`i at Manoa; Kristin J. Jacobson, The Richard Stockton College of New Jersey; Brian Kassar, Montana State University; Julia Mason, Grand Valley State University; Janice McCabe, Florida State University; Kristen McHenry, University of Massachusetts Dartmouth; Elizabeth Markovits, Mount Holyoke College; Jennifer Pearson, Wichita State University; Sara Skiles-duToit, University of Texas, Arlington; Mary Nell Trautner, University of Buffalo, SUNY; Julianne Weinzimmer, Wright State University; and Lori Wiebold, Bradley University.

Third edition reviewers:

ChaeRan Freeze, Brandeis University; Patti Giuffre, Texas State University; Linda Grant, University of Georgia; Todd Migliaccio, California State University, Sacramento; J. Michael Ryan, University of Maryland, College Park; and Diane Kholos Wysocki, University of Nebraska at Kearney.

Second edition reviewers:

Patti Giuffre, Texas State University, San Marcos; Linda Grant, University of Georgia; Minjeong Kim, University at Albany, SUNY; Laura Kramer, Montclair State University; Heather Laube, University of Michigan, Flint; Todd Migliaccio, California State University, Sacramento; Kristen Myers, Northern Illinois University; Wendy Simonds, Georgia State University; Debbie Storrs, University of Idaho; and Elroi Waszkiewicz, Georgia State University.

Finally, we would like to thank students in our sociology of gender courses for challenging us to think about new ways to teach our courses and making us aware of arenas of gender that are not typically the focus of gender studies books.

INTRODUCTION

This book is an invitation to you, the reader, to enter the fascinating and challenging world of gender studies. Gender is briefly defined as the meanings, practices, and relations of femininities and masculinities that people create as we go about our daily lives in different social settings. Although we discuss gender throughout this book, it is a very complex term to understand and the reality of gender goes far beyond this simple definition. While a more detailed discussion of what gender is and how it is related to biological maleness and femaleness is provided in Chapter 1, we find the metaphor of a kaleidoscope useful in thinking about the complexity of the meaning of gender from a sociological viewpoint.

THE KALEIDOSCOPE OF GENDER

A real kaleidoscope is a tube containing an arrangement of mirrors or prisms that produces different images and patterns. When you look through the eyepiece of a kaleidoscope, light is typically reflected by the mirrors or prisms through cells containing objects such as glass pieces, seashells, and the like to create ever-changing patterns of design and color (Baker, 1999). In this book, we use the kaleidoscope metaphor to help us grasp the complex and dynamic meaning and practice of gender as it interacts with other social prisms—such as race,

ethnicity, age, sexuality, and social class—to create complex patterns of identities and relationships. Three themes then emerge from the metaphor of the kaleidoscope: prisms, patterns, and possibilities.

Part I of the book focuses on prisms. A prism in a kaleidoscope is an arrangement of mirrors that refracts or disperses light into a spectrum of patterns (Baker, 1999). We use the term *social prism* to refer to socially constructed categories of difference and inequality through which our lives are reflected or shaped into patterns of daily experiences. In addition to gender, when we discuss social prisms, we consider other socially constructed categories such as race, ethnicity, age, physical ability/disability, social class, and sexuality. Culture is also conceptualized as a social prism in this book, as we examine how gender is shaped across groups and societies. The concept of social prisms helps us understand that gender is not a universal or static entity but, rather, is continuously created within the parameters of individual and group life. Looking at the interactions of the prism of gender with other social prisms helps us see the bigger picture— gender practices and meanings are a montage of intertwined social divisions and connections that both pull us apart and bring us together.

Part II of the book examines the patterns of gendered expressions and experiences created by the interaction of multiple prisms of difference and inequality. Patterns are regularized, prepackaged ways of thinking, feeling, and acting in society, and gendered patterns are present in almost all aspects of daily life. In the United States, examples of gendered patterns include the association of the color pink with girls and blue with boys (Paoletti, 2012). However, these patterns of gender are experienced and expressed in different ways depending on the other social prisms that shape our identities and life chances. Furthermore, these patterns are not static, as Paoletti illustrates. Before the 1900s, children were dressed similarly until around the age of 7, with boys just as likely as girls to wear pink—but both more likely to be dressed in white. In addition, dresses were once considered appropriate for both genders in Europe and America. It wasn't until decades later, in the 1980s, that color became rigidly gendered in children's clothing, in the pink-and-blue schema. You will find that gendered patterns restrict choices, even the colors we wear—often without our even recognizing it is happening.

Another example of a gendered pattern is the disproportionate numbers of female nurses and male engineers (see Table 7.1 in this book). If you take a closer look at engineers and nurses (as discussed in Chapter 7), you will note that engineers are predominately White men and nurses White women. Consequently, the patterns of gender are a result of the complex interaction of multiple social prisms across time and space.

Part III of the book concerns possibilities for gender change. Just as the wonder of the kaleidoscope lies in the ever-evolving patterns it creates, gendered patterns are always in flux. Each life and the world we live in can be understood as a kaleidoscope of unfolding growth and continual change (Baker, 1999). This dynamic aspect of the kaleidoscope metaphor represents the opportunity we have, individually and collectively, to transform gendered patterns that can be harmful to women and men. Although the theme of gender change is prominent throughout this book, it is addressed specifically in Chapter 10 and in the Epilogue.

One caveat must be presented before we take you through the kaleidoscope of gender. A metaphor is a figure of speech in which a word ordinarily used to refer to one thing is applied to better understand another thing. A metaphor should not be taken literally. It does not directly represent reality. We use the metaphor of the kaleidoscope as an analytical tool to aid us in grasping the complexity, ambiguity, and fluidity of gender. However, unlike the prisms in a real kaleidoscope, the meaning and experience of social prisms (e.g., gender, race, ethnicity, social class, sexuality, and culture) are socially constructed and change in response to patterns in the larger society. Thus, although the prisms of a real kaleidoscope are static, the prisms of the gender kaleidoscope are shaped by the patterns of society.

As you step into the world of gender studies, you'll need to develop a capacity to see what is hidden by the cultural blinders we all wear at least some of the time. This capacity to see into the complexities of human relationships and group life has been called sociological imagination or, to be hip, "sociological radar." It is a capacity that is finely honed by practice and training both inside and outside the classroom. A sociological perspective enables us to see through the cultural smokescreens that conceal the patterns, meanings, and dynamics of our relationships.

GENDER STEREOTYPES

The sociological perspective will help you think about gender in ways you might never have considered. It will, for example, help you debunk *gender stereotypes*, which are rigid, oversimplified, exaggerated beliefs about femininity and masculinity that misrepresent most women and men (Walters, 1999). To illustrate, let's analyze one gender stereotype that many people in American society believe—women talk more than men (Anderson & Leaper, 1998; Swaminathan, 2007; Wood, 1999).

Social scientific research is helpful in documenting whether women actually talk more than men, or whether this belief is just another gender stereotype. To arrive at a conclusion, social scientists study the interactions of men and women in an array of settings and count how often men speak compared with women. They almost always find that, on average, men talk more in mixed-gender groups (Brescoli, 2011; Wood, 1999). Researchers also find that men interrupt more and tend to ignore topics brought up by women (Anderson & Leaper, 1998; Wood, 1999). In and of themselves, these are important findings—the stereotype turns reality on its head.

So why does the stereotype continue to exist? First, we might ask how people believe something to be real—such as the stereotype that women talk more than men—when, in general, it isn't true. Part of the answer lies in the fact that culture, defined as the way of life of a group of people, shapes what we experience as reality (see Chapter 3 for a more detailed discussion). As Allan Johnson (1997) aptly puts it, "Living in a culture is somewhat like participating in the magician's magic because all the while we think we're paying attention to what's 'really' happening, alternative realities unfold without even occurring to us" (p. 55).

In other words, we don't usually reflect on our own culture; we are mystified by it without much awareness of its bewildering effect on us. The power of beliefs, including gender beliefs, is quite awesome. Gender stereotypes shape our perceptions, and these beliefs shape our reality.

A second question we need to ask about gender stereotypes is: What is their purpose? For example, do they set men against women and contribute to the persistence of a system of inequality that disadvantages women and advantages men? Certainly, the stereotype that many Americans hold of women as nonstop talkers is not a positive one. The stereotype does not assume that women are assertive, articulate, or captivating speakers. Instead, it tends to depict women's talk as trivial gossip or irritating nagging. In other words, the stereotype devalues women's talk while, at the same time, elevating men's talk as thoughtful and worthy of our attention. One of the consequences of this stereotype is that both men and women take men's talk more seriously (Brescoli, 2011; Wood, 1999). This pattern is reflected in the fact that the voice

of authority in many areas of American culture, such as television and politics, is almost always a male voice (Brescoli, 2011). The message communicated is clear—women are less important than men. In other words, gender stereotypes help legitimize status and power differences between men and women (Brescoli, 2011).

However, stereotypical images of men and women are not universal in their application, because they are complicated by the kaleidoscopic nature of people's lives. Prisms, or social categories, such as race/ethnicity, social class, and age, intersect with gender to produce stereotypes that differ in symbolic meaning and functioning. For example, the prisms of gender, race, and age interact for African American and Hispanic men, who are stereotyped as dangerous (as noted in Adia Harvey Wingfield's reading in Chapter 7). These variations in gender stereotypes act as controlling images that maintain complex systems of domination and subordination in which some individuals and groups are dehumanized and disadvantaged in relationship to others (see Bonnie Thornton Dill and Marla H. Kohlman's article and other readings in Chapter 2).

DEVELOPMENT OF THE CONCEPT OF GENDER

Just a few decades ago, social scientists assumed that gender encompassed two discrete categories described as sex roles—masculine/men and feminine/women. These sex roles were conceptualized in a biological "essentialist" framework to be either an automatic response to innate personality characteristics and/or biological sex characteristics such as hormones and reproductive functions (Kimmel, 2004; Tavris, 1992) or a mix of biological imperatives and learning reinforced by social pressure to conform to one or the other sex role (Connell, 2010). For example, women were thought to be naturally more nurturing because of their capacity to bear children, and men were seen as prewired to take on leadership positions in major societal institutions such as family, politics, and business. This "sex roles" model of women and men was one-dimensional, relatively static, and ethnocentric, and it is *not* supported by biological, psychological, sociological, or anthropological research.

The concept of gender developed as social scientists conducted research that questioned the simplicity and accuracy of the "sex roles" perspective. One example of this research is that social scientists have debunked the notion that biological sex characteristics cause differences in men's and women's behaviors (Tavris, 1992). Research on hormones illustrates this point. Testosterone, which women as well as men produce, does not cause aggression in men (see Robert M. Sapolsky's reading in Chapter 1), and the menstrual cycle does not cause women to be more "emotional" than men (Tavris, 1992; see Aaronette M. White and Tal Peretz's reading in Chapter 6).

Another example is that social scientific research demonstrated that men and women are far more physically, cognitively, and emotionally alike than different. What were assumed to be natural differences and inequalities between women and men were clearly shown to be the consequence of the asymmetrical and unequal life experiences, resources, and power of women compared with men (Connell, 2010; Tavris, 1992). Consider the arena of athletics. It is a common and long-held belief that biological sex is related to physical ability and, in particular, that women are athletically inferior to men. These beliefs have been challenged by the outcomes of a recent series of legal interventions that opened the world of competitive sports to girls and women. Once legislation such as Title IX was implemented in 1972, the expectation that women could not be athletes began to change as girls and young women received the same training and support for athletic pursuits as did men. Not surprisingly, the gap in physical strength and skills between women and men decreased dramatically. Today, women athletes regularly break records and perform physical feats thought impossible for women just a few decades ago.

Yet another example of how the "sex roles" model was discredited was the documentation of inequality as a human-created social system. Social scientists highlighted the social origins of patterns of gender inequality within the economy, family, religion, and other social institutions that benefit men as a group and maintain patriarchy as a social structure. To illustrate, in the 1970s, when researchers began studying gender inequality, they found that women made between 60 and 70 cents for every dollar men made. Things are not much better today. In 2010, the median salary for women was 81.8% of men's median salary (Bureau of Labor Statistics, 2012).

The intellectual weaknesses of "sex roles" theory (Connell, 2010), buttressed by considerable contradictory evidence, led social scientists to more sophisticated theories and modes of studying gender that could address the complexities and malleability of sex (femaleness and maleness) and gender (femininities and masculinities). In short, social science documented the fact that we are made and make ourselves into gendered people through social interaction in everyday life (Connell, 2010). It is not natural or normal to be a feminine woman or a masculine man. Gender is a socially constructed system of social relations that can be understood only by studying the social processes by which gender is defined into existence and maintained or changed by human actions and interactions (Schwalbe, 2001). This theory of gender social construction will be discussed throughout the book.

One of the most important sources of evidence in support of the idea that gender is socially constructed is derived from cross-cultural and historical studies as described in the earlier discussion of the gendering of pink and blue. The variations and fluidity in the definitions and expressions of gender across cultures and over time illustrate that the American gender system is not universal. For example, people in some cultures have created more than two genders (see Serena Nanda's reading in Chapter 1). Other cultures define men and women as similar, not different (see Christine Helliwell's reading in Chapter 3). Still others view gender as flowing and changing across the life span (Herdt, 1997).

As social scientists examined gender patterns through the prism of culture and throughout history, their research challenged the notion that masculinity and femininity are defined and experienced in the same way by all people. For example, the meaning and practice of femininity in orthodox, American religious subcultures is not the same as femininity outside those communities (Rose, 2001). The differences are expressed in a variety of ways, including women's clothing. Typically, orthodox religious women adhere to modesty rules in dress, covering their heads, arms, and legs.

Elaborating on the idea of multiple or plural masculinities and femininities, Australian sociologist Raewyn Connell coined the terms *hegemonic masculinity* and *emphasized femininity* to understand the relations between and among masculinities and femininities in patriarchal societies. Patriarchal societies are dominated by privileged men (e.g., upper-class White men), but they also typically benefit less privileged men in their relationships with women. According to Connell (1987), hegemonic masculinity is the idealized pattern of masculinity in patriarchal societies, while emphasized femininity is the vision of femininity held up as the model of womanhood in those societies. In Connell's definition, hegemonic masculinity is "the pattern of practice (i.e., things done, not just a set of role expectations or an identity) that allowed men's dominance over women to continue" (Connell & Messerschmidt, 2005, p. 832). Key features of hegemonic masculinity include the subordination of women, the exclusion and debasement of gay men, and the celebration of toughness and competitiveness (Connell, 2000). However, hegemony does not mean violence per se. It refers to "ascendancy achieved through culture, institutions, and persuasion" (Connell & Messerschmidt, 2005, p. 832). Emphasized femininity, in contrast, is about women's subordination, with its key features being sociability, compliance with men's sexual and ego desires, and acceptance of marriage and child care (Connell, 1987). Both hegemonic masculinity and emphasized femininity patterns are "embedded in specific social environments" and are, therefore, dynamic as opposed to fixed (Connell & Messerschmidt, 2005, p. 846).

According to Connell, hegemonic masculinity and emphasized femininity are not necessarily the most common gender patterns. They are, however, the versions of manhood and womanhood against which other patterns of masculinity and femininity are measured and found wanting (Connell & Messerschmidt, 2005; Kimmel, 2004). For example, hegemonic masculinity produces marginalized masculinities, which, according to Connell (2000), are characteristic of exploited groups such as racial and ethnic minorities. These marginalized forms of masculinity may share features with hegemonic masculinity, such as "toughness," but are socially debased (see Wingfield's reading in Chapter 7).

In patriarchal societies, the culturally idealized form of femininity, emphasized femininity, is produced in relation to male dominance. Emphasized femininity insists on compliance, nurturance, and empathy as ideals of womanhood to which all women should subscribe (Connell, 1987). Connell does not use the term *hegemonic* to refer to emphasized femininity, because, she argues, emphasized femininity is always subordinated to masculinity. James Messerschmidt (2012) adds to our understanding of femininities by arguing that the construction of hegemonic masculinity requires some kind of "buy-in" from women and that, under certain circumstances and in certain contexts, there are women who create emphasized femininities. By doing so, they contribute to the perpetuation of coercive gender relations and identities. Think of circumstances and situations—such as within work, romantic, or family settings—when women are complicit in maintaining oppressive gender relations and identities. Why would some women participate in the production of masculinities and femininities that are oppressive? The reading by Karen D. Pyke and Denise L. Johnson in Chapter 2 is helpful in answering these questions, employing the term *hegemonic femininity* rather than *emphasized femininity*. They describe the lives of young, second-generation Asian women and their attempts to balance two cultural patterns of gender in which White femininity, they argue, is hegemonic, or the dominant form of femininity.

Another major source of gender complexity is the interaction of gender with other social categories of difference and inequality. Allan Johnson (2001) points out,

> Categories that define privilege exist all at once and in relation to one another. People never see me solely in terms of my race, for example, or my gender. Like everyone else's, my place in the social world is a package deal—white, male, heterosexual, middle-aged, married . . .—and that's the way it is all the time. . . . It makes no sense to talk about the effect of being in one of these categories—say, white—without also looking at the others and how they're related to it. (p. 53)

Seeing gender through multiple social prisms is critical, but it is not a simple task, as you will discover in the readings throughout this book. Social scientists commonly refer to this type of analysis as intersectionality, but other terms are used as well (see Chapter 2 for a discussion of this). We need to be aware of how other social prisms alter life experiences and chances. For example, although an upper-class African American woman is privileged by her social class category, she will face obstacles related to her race and gender. Or consider the situation of a middle-class White man who is gay; he might lose some of the privilege attached to his class and race because of his sexual orientation.

Finally, gender is now considered a social construct shaped at individual, interactional, and institutional levels. If we focus on only one of these levels, we provide only a partial explanation of how gender operates in our lives. This idea of gender being shaped at these three different levels is elaborated in Barbara J. Risman's article in Chapter 1 and throughout the book. Consider these three different ways of approaching gender and how they interact or influence one another. At the *individual* level, sociologists study the social categories and stereotypes we use to identify ourselves and label others (see Chapter 4). At the

interactional level, sociologists study gender as an ongoing activity carried out in interaction with other people, and how people vary their gender presentations as they move from situation to situation (see Betsy Lucal's reading in Chapter 1). At the *institutional* level, sociologists study how "gender is present in the processes, practices, images and ideologies, and distributions of power in the various sectors of social life," such as religion, health care, language, and so forth (Acker, 1992, p. 567; see also Joan Acker's reading in Chapter 7).

THEORETICAL APPROACHES FOR UNDERSTANDING GENDER

Historically, conflict and functionalist theories explained gender at a macro level of analysis, with these theories having gone through many transformations since first proposed around the turn of the 20th century. Scholars at that time were trying to sort out massive changes in society resulting from the industrial and democratic revolutions. However, a range of theories—for example, feminist, postmodernist, and queer theories—provide more nuanced explanations of gender. Many of these more recent theories frame their understanding of gender in the lived experiences of individuals, what sociologists call microlevel theories, rather than focusing solely on a macrolevel analysis of society, wherein gender does not vary in form or function across groups or contexts.

Functionalism

Functionalism attempts to understand how all parts of a society (e.g., institutions such as family, education, economy, and the polity or state) fit together to form a smoothly running social system. According to this theoretical paradigm, parts of society tend to complement each other to create social stability (Durkheim, 1933). Translated into separate sex role relationships, Talcott Parsons and Robert Bales (1955), writing after World War II, saw distinct and separate gender roles in the heterosexual nuclear family as a functional adaptation to a modern, complex society. Women were thought to be more "functional" if they were socialized and aspired to raise children. And men were thought to be more "functional" if they were socialized and aspired to support their children and wives. However, as Michael Kimmel (2004) notes, this "sex-based division of labor is functionally anachronistic," and if there ever was any biological basis for specific tasks being assigned to men or women, it has been eroded (p. 55).

The functionalist viewpoint has largely been discredited in the social sciences, although it persists as part of common culture in various discourses and ideologies, especially conservative religious and political thought. It is also replicated in the realms of neuroscience and evolutionary psychology. In brief, the former tries to explain gender inequality by searching for neurological differences in human females and males assumed to be caused by hormonally induced differences in the brain. The hypothesized behavioral outcomes, according to neuroscientists such as Simon Baron-Cohen (2003), are emotionally tuned in, verbal women in contrast to men who are inclined to superior performance in areas such as math and music (Bouton, 2010). The latter, evolutionary psychology, focuses on "sex differences" (e.g., high-risk-taking male behaviors) between human females and males that are hypothesized to have their origins in psychological adaptations to early human, intrasexual competition. Both approaches, which assume there are essential differences between males and females embedded in their bodies or psyches, have been roundly critiqued by researchers (e.g., Fine, 2010) who uncovered a range of problems, including research design flaws, no significant differences between female and male subjects, overgeneralization of findings, and ethnocentrism.

Conflict Theories

Karl Marx and later conflict theorists, however, did not see social systems as functional or benign. Instead, Marx and his colleague Friedrich Engels described industrial societies as systems of oppression in which one group, the dominant social class, uses its control of economic resources to oppress the working class. The economic resources of those in control are obtained through profits gained from exploiting the labor of subordinate groups. Marx and Engels predicted that the tension between the "haves" and the "have-nots" would result in an underlying conflict between these two groups. Most early Marxist theories focused on class oppression; however, Engels (1942/1970) wrote an important essay on the oppression of women as the earliest example of oppression of one group by another. Marx and Engels inspired socialist feminists, discussed later in this introduction under "Feminist Theories."

Current theorists, while recognizing Marx and Engels's recognition of the exploitation of workers in capitalist economies, criticize early conflict theory for ignoring women's reproductive labor and unpaid work (Federici, 2012). They focus on the exploitation of women by global capitalism (see articles by Bandana Purkayastha in Chapter 2 and Jie Yang in Chapter 5). Conflict theories today call for social action relating to the oppression of women and other marginalized groups, particularly within this global framework.

Social Constructionist Theories

Social constructionist theories offer a strong antidote to biological essentialism and psychological reductionism in understanding the social worlds (e.g., institutions, ideologies, identities) constructed by people. This theory, as discussed earlier, emphasizes the social or collective processes by which people actively shape reality (e.g., ideas, inequalities, social movements) as we go about daily life in different contexts and situations. The underpinnings of social constructionist theory are in sociological thought (e.g., symbolic interactionism, dramaturgy, and ethnomethodology), as well as in anthropology, social psychology, and related disciplinary arenas.

Social constructionism has had a major impact on gender analysis, invigorating both gender research and theoretical approaches (e.g., discussions of doing gender theory, relational theory, and intersectional analysis). From a social constructionist viewpoint, we must learn and do gender (masculinities and femininities) in order for gender differences and inequalities to exist. We also build these differences and inequalities into the patterns of large social arrangements such as social institutions. Take education. Men predominate in higher education and school administration, while women are found at the elementary and preschool levels (Connell, 2010). Theories rooted in the fundamental principles of gender social construction follow.

"Doing Gender" Theory

Drawing on the work of symbolic interactionism, specifically dramaturgy (Goffman) and ethnomethodology (Garfinkel), Candace West and Don H. Zimmerman in 1987 published an article simply titled "Doing Gender." In this article, they challenged assumptions of the two previous decades of research that examined "sex differences" or "sex roles." They argued that gender is a *master identity*, which is a product of social interactions and "doing," not simply the acting out of a role on a social stage. They saw gender as a complicated process by which we categorize individuals into two sex categories based on what we assume to be their sex (male or female). Interaction in contemporary Western societies is based on "knowing the sex" of the individual we are interacting with. However, we have no way of actually knowing an individual's sex (genitalia or hormones); therefore, we infer sex categories based on outward characteristics such as hairstyle, clothing, etc. Because we infer sex categories of the individuals we meet, West and Zimmerman argue that we are likely to question those who break from expected gendered behaviors for the sex categories we assign to them. We are also accountable for our own gender-appropriate behavior. Interaction in most societies becomes particularly difficult if one's sex category or gender is ambiguous, as you will read in Lucal's article in Chapter 1.

Thus, this process of being accountable makes it important for individuals to display appropriate gendered behavior at all times in all situations. As such, "doing gender" becomes a salient part of social interactions and embedded in social institutions. As they note, "Insofar as a society is partitioned by 'essential' differences between women and men and placement in a sex category is both relevant and enforced, doing gender is unavoidable" (West & Zimmerman, 1987, p. 137).

Of course, they recognize that not everyone has the same resources (such as time, money, and/or expertise) to "do gender" and that gender accomplishment varies across social situations. In considering the discussion of who talks more, "doing gender" might explain why men talk more in work groups, as they attempt to portray their gendered masculinity while women may be doing more gender-appropriate emotion work such as asking questions and filling in silences. As such, when men and women accomplish gender as expected for the sex categories they display and are assigned to by others, they are socially constructing gender.

This concept of "doing gender" is used in many articles included in this book, but the use of the concept is not always consistent with the way the authors originally presented it (West & Zimmerman, 2009). The article by Nikki Jones included in Chapter 2 is part of a 2009 symposium considering the original 1987 article and its implications, in which she examines the challenges of doing gender for young, poor Black girls. Doing gender is a concept that helped move the discussions of sex/gender to a different level where interactions (micro) and institutions (macro) can be studied simultaneously and gender becomes a more lived experience, rather than a "role."

Performative Theory

Judith Butler, a philosopher, conceptualizes gender as a performative act. Like West and Zimmerman, she emphasizes that gender is not a performance, or "a certain kind of enactment"

(Butler, 2009, p. i). Instead, she argues that gender identities are understood and agreed on by self and others through bodily acts (e.g., walk and gestures) and speech acts. She argues that gender is always negotiated in a system of power that establishes norms within which it is reproduced or, when the norms are challenged, altered (Butler, 2009). As such, performative theory focuses on the intersubjective creation of gender in relationship to the larger social structure.

Postmodern Theories

Postmodernism focuses on the way knowledge about gender is constructed, not on explaining gender relationships themselves. To postmodernists, knowledge is never absolute—it is always situated in a social reality that is specific to a historical time period. Postmodernism is based on the idea that it is impossible for anyone to see the world without presuppositions. From a postmodernist perspective, then, gender is socially constructed through discourses, which are the "series of stories" we use to explain our world (Andersen, 2004). Postmodernists attempt to "deconstruct" the discourses or stories used to support a group's beliefs about gender (Andersen, 2004; Lorber, 2001). For example, Jane Flax argues that to fully understand gender in Western cultures, we must deconstruct the meanings in Western religious, scientific, and other discourses relative to "biology/sex/gender/nature" (cited in Lorber, 2001, p. 199). As you will come to understand from the readings in Chapters 1 and 3 (e.g., Nanda and Helliwell), the association between sex and gender in Western scientific (e.g., theories and texts) and nonscientific (e.g., films, newspapers, media) discourses is not shared in other cultural contexts. Thus, for postmodernists, gender is a product of the discourses within particular social contexts that define and explain gender.

Queer Theories

Queer theories borrow from the original meaning of the word *queer* to refer to that which is "outside ordinary and narrow interpretations" (Plante, 2006, p. 62). Queer theorists are most concerned with understanding sexualities in terms of the idea that (sexual) identities are flexible, fluid, and changing, rather than fixed. In addition, queer theorists argue that identity and behavior must be separated. Thus, we cannot assume that people are what they do. From the vantage point of this theory, gender categories, much like sexual categories, are simplistic and problematic. Real people cannot be lumped together and understood in relationship to big cultural categories such as men and women, heterosexual and homosexual (Plante, 2006).

Relational Theory

The relational theory of gender was developed in response to the problems of the "sex roles" model and other limited views of gender (e.g., categoricalism, as critiqued by queer theory above). Connell (2000) states that a gender relations approach opens up an understanding of "the different dimensions of gender, the relation between bodies and society, and the patterning of gender" (pp. 23–24). Specifically, from a relational viewpoint, (1) gender is a way of organizing social practice (e.g., child care and household labor) at the personal, interactional, and institutional levels of life; (2) gender is a social practice related to bodies and what bodies do but *cannot* be reduced to bodies or biology; and (3) masculinities and femininities can be understood as *gender projects* that produce the *gender order* of a society and interact with other social structures such as race and class (pp. 24–28).

Feminist Theories

Feminist theorists expanded on the ideas of theorists such as Marx and Engels, turning attention to the causes of women's oppression. There are many schools of feminist thought. Here, we briefly introduce you to those typically covered in overviews (see Chapter 10 for discussion of feminist theories such as "do-it-yourself" feminism). One group, socialist feminists, continued to emphasize the role of capitalism in interaction with a patriarchal family structure as the basis for the exploitation of women. These theorists argue that economic and power benefits accrue to men who dominate women in capitalist societies. Another group, radical feminists, argues that patriarchy—the domination of men over women—is the fundamental form of oppression of women. Both socialist and radical feminists call for far-reaching changes in all institutional arrangements and cultural forms, including the dismantling of systems of oppression such as sexism, racism, and classism; replacing capitalism with socialism; developing more egalitarian family systems; and making other structural changes (e.g., Bart & Moran, 1993; Daly, 1978; Dworkin, 1987; MacKinnon, 1989).

Not all feminist theorists call for deep, structural, and cultural changes. Liberal feminists are inclined to work toward a more equitable form of democratic capitalism. They argue that policies such as Title IX and affirmative action laws opened up opportunities for women in education and increased the number of women professionals, such as physicians. These feminists strive to achieve gender equality by removing barriers to women's freedom of choice and equal participation in all realms of life, eradicating sexist stereotypes, and guaranteeing equal access and treatment for women in both public and private arenas (e.g., Reskin & Roos, 1990; Schwartz, 1994; Steinberg, 1982; Vannoy-Hiller & Philliber, 1989; Weitzman, 1985).

Although the liberal feminist stance may seem to be the most pragmatic form of feminism, many of the changes brought about by liberal varieties of feminism have "served the interests of only the most privileged women" (Motta, Fominaya, Eschle, & Cox, 2011, p. 5). Additionally, liberal feminist approaches that work with the state or attempt to gain formal equal rights within a fundamentally exploitive labor market fail to challenge the growth of neoliberal globalism and the worsening situation of many people in the face of unfettered markets, privatization, and imperialism (Motta et al., 2011; e.g., see discussion of the Great Recession in Chapter 5). In response to these kinds of issues and problems, 21st century feminists are revisiting and reinventing feminist thinking and practice to create a "more emancipatory feminism" that can lead to "post-patriarchal, anti-neoliberal politics" (Motta et al., 2011, p. 2; see readings in Chapter 10).

Intersectional or Prismatic Theories

A major shortcoming with many of the theoretical perspectives just described is their failure to recognize how gender interacts with other social categories or prisms of difference and inequality within societies, including race/ethnicity, social class, sexuality, age, and ability/disability (see Chapter 2). A growing number of social scientists are responding to the problem of incorporating multiple social categories in their research by developing a new form of analysis, often described as intersectional analysis, which we also refer to as prismatic analysis in this book. Chapter 2 explores these theories of how gender interacts with other prisms of difference and inequality to create complex patterns. Without an appreciation of the interactions of socially constructed categories of difference and inequality, or what we call prisms, we end up with not only an incomplete but also an inaccurate explanation of gender.

As you read through the articles in this book, consider the basis for the authors' arguments in each reading. How do the authors apply the theories just described? What observations, data, or works of other social science researchers do these authors use to support their claims? Use a critical eye to examine the evidence as you reconsider the assumptions about gender that guide your life.

THE KALEIDOSCOPE OF GENDER: PRISMS, PATTERNS, AND POSSIBILITIES

Before beginning the readings that take us through the kaleidoscope of gender, let us briefly review the three themes that shape the book's structure: prisms, patterns, and possibilities.

Part I: Prisms

Understanding the prisms that shape our experiences provides an essential basis for the book. Chapter 1 explores the meanings of the pivotal prism—gender—and its relationship to biological sex. Chapter 2 presents an array of prisms or socially constructed categories that interact with gender in many human societies, such as race/ethnicity, social class, sexuality, age, and ability/disability. Chapter 3 focuses on the prism of culture/nationality, which alters the meaning and practice of gender in surprising ways.

Part II: Patterns

The prisms of the kaleidoscope create an array of patterned expressions and experiences of femininity and masculinity. Part II of this book examines some of these patterns. We look at how people learn, internalize, and "do" gender (Chapter 4); how gender is exploited by capitalism (Chapter 5); how gender acts on bodies, sexualities, and emotions (Chapter 6); how gendered patterns are reproduced and modified in work (Chapter 7); how gender is created and transformed in our intimate relationships (Chapter 8); and how conformity to patterns of gender is enforced and maintained (Chapter 9).

Part III: Possibilities

In much the same way as the colors and patterns of kaleidoscopic images flow, gendered patterns and meanings are inherently changeable. Chapter 10 examines the shifting sands of the genderscape and reminds us of the many possibilities for change. Finally, in the Epilogue, we examine changes we have seen and encourage you to envision future changes.

We use the metaphor of the gender kaleidoscope to discover what is going on under the surface of a society whose way of life we don't often penetrate in a nondefensive, disciplined, and deep fashion. In doing so, we will expose a reality that is astonishing in its complexity, ambiguity, and fluidity. With the kaleidoscope, you never know what's coming next. Come along with us as we begin the adventure of looking through the kaleidoscope of gender.

REFERENCES

Acker, J. (1992). From sex roles to gendered institutions. *Contemporary Sociology, 21*(5), 565–570.

Andersen, M. L. (2004). *Thinking about women: Sociological perspectives on sex and gender* (6th ed.). Boston: Allyn & Bacon.

Anderson, K. J., & Leaper, C. (1998). Meta-analysis of gender effects on conversational interruption: Who, what, when, where, and how. *Sex Roles, 39*(3–4), 225–252.

Baker, C. (1999). *Kaleidoscopes: Wonders of wonder.* Lafayette, CA: C&T.

Baron-Cohen, S. (2003). *The essential difference: The truth about the male and female brain.* New York: Basic Books.

Bart, P. B., & Moran, E. G. (Eds.). (1993). *Violence against women: The bloody footprints.* Newbury Park, CA: Sage.

Bouton, K. (2010, August 23). Peeling away theories on gender and the brain. *New York Times.* Retrieved January 24, 2013, from http://www .nytimes.com/2010/08/24/science/24scibks.html

Brescoli, V. (2011). Who takes the floor and why: Gender, power, and volubility in organizations. *Administrative Science Quarterly, 56*(4), 622–641.

Bureau of Labor Statistics. (2012). *Current Population Survey, Table A-26: Usual weekly earnings of employed full-time wage and salary workers by detailed occupation and sex, annual average 2011.* Retrieved from http://www.bls.gov/cps/earnings .htm

Butler, J. (2009). Performativity, precarity, and sexual politics. *AIBR, 4*(3), i–xii.

Connell, R. W. (1987). *Gender and power: Society, the person and sexual politics.* Stanford, CA: University of Stanford Press.

Connell, R. W. (2000). *The men and the boys.* Berkeley: University of California Press.

Connell, R. W. (2010). Retrieved from www.raewyn connell.net/

Connell, R. W., & Messerschmidt, J. W. (2005). Hegemonic masculinity: Rethinking the concept. *Gender & Society, 19*(6), 829–859.

Daly, M. (1978). *Gyn/ecology, the metaethics of radical feminism*. Boston: Beacon Press.

Durkheim, E. (1933). *The division of labor in society*. Glencoe, IL: Free Press.

Dworkin, A. (1987). *Intercourse*. New York: Free Press.

Engels, F. (1970). *Origin of the family, private property, and the state*. New York: International Publishers. (Original work published in 1942)

Federici, S. (2012). *Revolution at Point Zero: Housework, reproduction, and feminist struggle*. New York: PM Press.

Fine, C. (2010). *Delusions of gender: How our minds, society, and neurosexism create difference*. New York: W. W. Norton.

Herdt, G. (1997). *Same sex, different cultures*. Boulder, CO: Westview Press.

Johnson, A. (1997). *The gender knot*. Philadelphia: Temple University Press.

Johnson, A. (2001). *Privilege, power, and difference*. Mountain View, CA: Mayfield.

Kimmel, M. S. (2004). *The gendered society* (2nd ed.). New York: Oxford University Press.

Lorber, J. (2001). *Gender inequality: Feminist theories and politics*. Los Angeles: Roxbury.

MacKinnon, C. A. (1989). *Toward a feminist theory of the state*. Cambridge, MA: Harvard University Press.

Messerschmidt, J. (2012). Engendering gendered knowledge: Assessing the academic appropriation of hegemonic masculinity. *Men and Masculinities, 15*(1), 56–76.

Motta, S., Fominaya, C. F., Eschle, C., & Cox, L. (2011). Feminism, women's movements and women in movement. *Interface, 3*(2), 1–32.

Paoletti, J. B. (2012). *Pink and blue: Telling the boys from the girls in America*. Bloomington: Indiana University Press.

Parsons, T., & Bales, R. F. (1955). *Family, socialization, and interaction process*. Glencoe, IL: Free Press.

Plante, R. F. (2006). *Sexualities in context: A social perspective*. Cambridge, MA: Westview.

Reskin, B. F., & Roos, P. A. (1990). *Job queues, gender queues: Explaining women's inroads into male occupations*. Philadelphia: Temple University Press.

Rose, D. R. (2001). Gender and Judaism. In D. Vannoy (Ed.), *Gender mosaics: Social perspectives* (pp. 415–424). Los Angeles: Roxbury.

Schwalbe, M. (2001). *The sociologically examined life: Pieces of the conversation* (2nd ed.). Mountain View, CA: Mayfield.

Schwartz, P. (1994). *Love between equals: How peer marriage really works*. New York: Free Press.

Steinberg, R. J. (1982). *Wages and hours: Labor and reform in twentieth century America*. New Brunswick, NJ: Rutgers University Press.

Swaminathan, N. (2007). Gender jabber: Do women talk more than men? *Scientific American*. Retrieved March 10, 2012, from http://www.scientific american.com/article.cfm?id=women-talk-more-than-men&print=true

Tavris, C. (1992). *The mismeasure of woman*. New York: Simon & Schuster.

Vannoy-Hiller, D., & Philliber, W. W. (1989). *Equal partners: Successful women in marriage*. Newbury Park, CA: Sage.

Walters, S. D. (1999). Sex, text, and context: (In) between feminism and cultural studies. In M. M. Ferree, J. Lorber, & B. B. Hess (Eds.), *Revisioning gender* (pp. 193–257). Thousand Oaks, CA: Sage.

Weitzman, L. J. (1985). *The divorce revolution: The unexpected social and economic consequences for women and children in America*. New York: Free Press.

West, C., & Zimmerman, D. H. (1987). Doing gender. *Gender & Society, 1*(2), 125–151.

West, C., & Zimmerman, D. H. (2009). Accounting for doing gender. *Gender & Society, 23*(1), 112–122.

Wood, J. T. (1999). *Gendered lives: Communication, gender, and culture* (3rd ed.). Belmont, CA: Wadsworth.

PART I

PRISMS

1

THE PRISM OF GENDER

In the metaphorical kaleidoscope of this book, gender is the pivotal prism. It is central to the intricate patterning of social life and encompasses power relations, the division of labor, symbolic forms, and emotional relations (Connell, 2000). The shape and texture of people's lives are affected in profound ways by the prism of gender as it operates in their social worlds. Indeed, our ways of thinking about and experiencing gender, and the related categories of sex and sexuality, originate in our society. As we noted in the introduction to this book, gender is very complex. In part, the complexity of the prism of gender in North American culture derives from the fact that it is characterized by a marked contradiction between people's beliefs about gender and real behavior. Our real behavior is far more flexible, adaptable, and malleable than our beliefs would have it. To put it another way, contrary to the stereotypes of masculinity and femininity, there are no gender certainties or absolutes. Real people behave in feminine, masculine, and nongendered ways as they respond to situational demands and contingencies (Glick & Fiske, 1999; Tavris, 1992).

To help us think more clearly about the complexity of gender, two questions are addressed in this chapter: (1) How does Western culture condition us to think about gender, especially in relation to sex and sexuality? (2) How does social scientific research challenge Western beliefs about gender, sex, and sexuality?

WESTERN BELIEFS ABOUT GENDER, SEX, AND SEXUALITY

Most people in contemporary Western cultures, such as the United States, grow up learning that there are two and only two sexes, male and female; two and only two genders, feminine and masculine; and two and only two sexualities, heterosexual and homosexual (Bem, 1993; Lucal, 2008; Wharton, 2005). We are taught that a real woman is female-bodied, feminine, and heterosexual; a real man is male-bodied, masculine, and heterosexual; and any deviation or variation is strange, unnatural, and potentially dangerous. Most people also learn that femininity and masculinity flow from biological sex characteristics (e.g., hormones, secondary sex characteristics, external and internal genitalia). We are taught that testosterone, a beard, big muscles, and a penis make a man, while estrogen, breasts, hairless legs, and a vagina make a woman. Many of us never question what we have learned about sex and gender, so we go through life assuming that gender is a relatively simple matter: A person who wears lipstick, high-heeled shoes, and a skirt is a feminine female, while a person who plays rugby, belches in public, and walks with a swagger is a masculine male (Lorber, 1994; Ridgeway & Correll, 2004).

The readings we have selected for this chapter reflect a growing body of social scientific research that challenges and alters the Western view of sex, gender, and sexuality. Overall, the readings are critical of the American tendency to explain virtually every human behavior in individual and biological terms. Americans overemphasize biology and underestimate the power of social facts to explain sex, sexuality, and gender (O'Brien, 1999). For instance, Americans tend to equate aggression with biological maleness and vulnerability with femaleness; natural facility in physics with masculinity and natural facility in child care with femininity; lace and ribbons with girlness and rough-and-tumble play with boyness (Glick & Fiske, 1999; Ridgeway & Correll, 2004). These notions of natural sex, gender, and sexuality difference, opposition, and inequality (i.e., a consistently higher valuation of masculinity than femininity) permeate our thinking, color our labeling of people and things in our environment, and affect our practical actions (Bem, 1993; Schilt & Westbrook, 2009; Wharton, 2005).

We refer to the American two-and-only-two sex/gender/sexuality system as the "pink and blue syndrome" (Schilt & Westbrook, 2009). This syndrome is deeply lodged in our minds and feelings and is reinforced through everyday talk, performance, and experience. It's everywhere. Any place, object, discourse, or practice can be gendered. Children's birthday cards come in pink and blue. Authors of popular books assert that men and women are from different planets. People love PMS and alpha-male jokes. In "The Pink Dragon Is Female" (see Chapter 5), Adie Nelson's research reveals that even children's fantasy costumes are predictably gendered as masculine or feminine. The "pink and blue syndrome" is so embedded within our culture and, consequently, within individual patterns of thinking and feeling that most of us cannot remember when we learned gender stereotypes and expectations or came to think about sex, gender, and sexuality as natural, immutable, and fixed. It all seems so simple and natural. But is it?

What is gender? What is sex? What is sexuality? How are gender, sex, and sexuality related? Why do most people in our society believe in the "pink and blue syndrome"? Why do so many of us attribute one set of talents, temperaments, skills, and behaviors to women and another, opposing set to men? These are the kinds of questions social scientists have been asking and researching for well over 50 years. Thanks to the good work of an array of scientists, we now understand that gender, sex, and sexuality are not so simple. Social scientists have discovered that the gender landscape is complicated, shifting, and contradictory. Among the beliefs called into question by research are

- the notion that there are two and only two sexes, two and only two genders, and two and only two sexualities;
- the assumption that the two-and-only-two system is universal; and
- the belief that nature, rather than nurture, causes the "pink and blue syndrome."

USING OUR SOCIOLOGICAL RADAR

Before we look at how social scientists answer questions such as, "What is gender?" let's do a little research of our own. Try the following: Relax, turn on your sociological radar, and examine yourself and the people you know carefully. Do all the men you know fit the ideal of masculinity all the time, in all relationships, and in all situations? Do all the women in your life consistently behave in stereotypical feminine fashion? Do you always fit into one as opposed to the other culturally approved gender category? Or are most of the people you know capable of "doing" both masculinity and femininity, depending on the interactional context? If we allow ourselves to think and see outside the contemporary American cultural framework, we will observe that none of the people we know are aggressive all the time, nurturing all the time, sweet and submissive all the time, or strong and silent all the time. Thankfully, we are complex and creative. We stretch and grow and develop as we meet the challenges, constraints, and opportunities of different and new situations and life circumstances. Men can do mothering; women can "take care of business." Real people are not stereotypes.

Yet even in the face of real gender fluidity, variation, and complexity, the belief in sex/gender/sexuality dichotomy, opposition, and inequality continues to dominate almost every aspect of the social worlds we inhabit. For example, recent research shows that even though men's and women's roles have changed and blended, the tendency of Americans to categorize and stereotype people based on the simple male/female dichotomy persists (Glick & Fiske, 1999; Shields, Garner, Di Leone, & Hadley, 2006). As Glick and Fiske (1999) put it, "We typically categorize people by sex effortlessly, even nonconsciously, with diverse and profound effects on social interactions" (p. 368). To reiterate, many Americans perceive humankind as divided into mutually exclusive, nonoverlapping groups: males/masculine/men and females/feminine/women (Bem, 1993; Lucal, 2008; Wharton, 2005). This perception is shored up by the belief that heterosexuality or sexual attraction between the two, and only two, sexes/genders is natural. *Heteronormativity* (see Chapter 6 for detailed discussion) is now the term commonly used by sociologists to refer to the "cultural, legal, and institutional practices" that maintain a binary and unequal system (Schilt & Westbrook, 2009, p. 441). The culturally created model of gender, as well as

sex and sexuality, then, is nonkaleidoscopic: no spontaneity, no ambiguity, no complexity, no diversity, no surprises, no elasticity, and no unfolding growth.

SOCIAL SCIENTIFIC UNDERSTANDINGS OF SEX, GENDER, AND SEXUALITY

Modern social science offers a rich and complex understanding of gender, sex, and sexuality. It opens the door to the diversity of human experience and rejects the tendency to reduce human behavior to simple, single-factor explanations. Research shows that the behavior of people, no matter who they are, depends on time and place, context and situation—not on fixed sex/gender/sexuality differences (Lorber, 1994; Tavris, 1992; Vespa, 2009). For example, just a few decades ago in the United States, cheerleading was a men's sport because it was considered too rigorous for women (Dowling, 2000), women were thought to lack the cognitive and emotional "stuff" to pilot flights into space, and medicine and law were viewed as too intellectually demanding for women. As Carol Tavris (1992) says, research demonstrates that perceived gender differences turn out to be a matter of "now you see them, now you don't" (p. 288).

If we expand our sociological examination of sex/gender/sexuality to include cross-cultural studies, the real-life fluidity of human experience comes fully alive (see Chapter 3 for a detailed discussion). In some cultures (e.g., the Aka hunter-gatherers), fathers as well as mothers suckle infants (Hewlett, 2001). In other cultures, such as the Agta Negritos, women as well as men are hunters (Estioko-Griffin & Griffin, 2001). Among the Tharus of India and Nepal, marriage is "woman-friendly" and women readily divorce husbands because each woman "enjoys a more dominant position and can find another husband more easily" (Verma, 2009, pp. 2–3). As Serena Nanda discusses in-depth in her reading in this chapter, extraordinary gender diversity was expressed in complex, more-than-two sex/gender/sexuality systems in many pre-contact Native American societies.

In addition, the complex nature of sex/gender/sexuality is underscored by scholarship on multiple masculinities and femininities, as discussed in the introduction to this book. There is no single pattern of masculinity or femininity. Masculinities and femininities are constantly in flux (Coles, 2009). Recall that Connell (2000), in her analysis of masculinities, argued that hegemonic masculinity produces complicit, marginalized, and subordinated masculinities. The chapter reading by Akihiko Hirose and Kay Kei-ho Pih extends Connell's work through study of the negotiation of hegemonic and marginalized masculinities in the arena of mixed martial arts.

Let's use sociological radar again and call on the work of social scientists to help us think more precisely and "objectively" about what gender, sex, and sexuality are. It has become somewhat commonplace to distinguish between gender and sex by viewing sex, femaleness and maleness, as a biological fact unaffected by culture and thus unchanging and unproblematic, while viewing gender as a cultural phenomenon, a means by which people are taught who they are (e.g., girl or boy), how to behave (e.g., ladylike or tough), and what their roles will be (e.g., mother or father) (Sorenson, 2000). However, this mode of distinguishing between sex and gender has come under criticism, largely because new studies have revealed the cultural dimensions of sex itself (Schilt, 2010). That is, the physical characteristics of sex cannot be separated from the cultural milieu in which they are labeled and given meaning. For example, Robert M. Sapolsky's chapter reading debunks the widely held myth that testosterone causes males to be more aggressive and domineering than females. He ends his article by stating firmly that "our behavioral biology is usually meaningless outside the context of the social factors and environment in which it occurs." In other words, the relationship between biology and behavior is reciprocal, both inseparable and intertwined (Yoder, 2003).

Sex, as it turns out, is not a clear-cut matter of DNA, chromosomes, external genitalia, and the like, factors that produce two and only two sexes—female and male. First, there is considerable biological variation. Sex is not fixed in two categories. Biologist Fausto-Sterling (1993) suggests that sex is more like a continuum than a dichotomy. For example, all humans have estrogen, prolactin, and testosterone but in varying and changing levels (Abrams, 2002). Think about this: In American society, people tend to associate breasts and related phenomena, such as breast cancer and lactation, with women. However, men have breasts. Indeed, some men have bigger breasts than some women, some men lactate, and some men get breast cancer. Also, in our society, people associate facial hair with men. What's the real story? All women have facial hair, and some have more of it than do some men. Indeed, recent hormonal and genetic studies (e.g., Abrams, 2002; Beale, 2001) are revealing that, biologically, women and men, female and male bodies are far more similar than different.

Second, not only do femaleness and maleness share much in common, but variations in and complexities of sex development produce *intersexed* people whose bodies do not fit either of the two traditionally understood sex categories (Fausto-Sterling, 2000; Fujimora, 2006). Until recently, intersexuality was kept a secret and treated as a medical emergency (Grabham, 2007). Now that activists and researchers are challenging the marginalization and medicalization of intersexuality, we understand that intersexed people are not a rarity. Scientists estimate that up to 2% of live births are intersexual. Among intersex births are babies born with both male and female characteristics and babies born with larger-"than-average" clitorises or smaller-"than-average" penises (Lucal, 2008). Fujimora (2006) examined recent research on sex genes and concluded that "there is no single pathway through which sex is genetically determined" and we might consider sex variations, such as intersex, as resulting from "multiple developmental pathways that involve genetic, protein, hormonal, environmental, and other agents, actions, and interactions" (p. 71). Lorber and Moore (2007) argue that intersexed people are akin to multiracial people. They point out that just as scientists have demonstrated through DNA testing that almost all of us are genetically interracial, similarly, "if many people were genetically sex-typed, we'd also find a variety of chromosomal, hormonal, and anatomical patterns unrecognized" in our rigid, two-sex system (p. 138). Sharon E. Preves's reading in this chapter offers exciting insights into the meanings and consequences of contemporary and historical responses to individuals who are intersexed.

Biology is a complicated business, and that should come as no surprise. The more we learn about biology, the more elusive and complex sex becomes. What seemed so obvious—two opposite sexes—turns out to be a gross oversimplification.

Then, what is gender? As discussed in the introduction to this book, gender is a human invention, a means by which people are sorted (in our society, into two gender categories), a basic aspect of how our society organizes itself and allocates resources (e.g., certain tasks assigned to people called women and other tasks to those termed men), and a fundamental ingredient in how individuals understand themselves and others ("I feel feminine"; "He's manly"; "You're androgynous").

One of the fascinating aspects of gender is the extent to which it is negotiable and dynamic. In effect, masculinity and femininity exist because people believe that women and men are distinct groups and, most important, because people "do gender," day in and day out. It is now common for gender scholars to refer to gender as a performance or a masquerade, emphasizing that it is through the ways we present ourselves in our daily encounters with others that gender is created and re-created. The chapter reading by Betsy Lucal illustrates vividly how gender is a matter of attribution and enactment.

We even do gender by ourselves, and sometimes quite self-consciously. Have you ever tried to make yourself look and act more masculine or feminine? What is involved in "putting on" femininity or masculinity? Consider *transvestism,* or cross-gender dressing. "Cross-dressers know that successfully being a man or a woman simply means convincing others that you are what you appear to be" (Kimmel, 2000, p. 104). Think about the emerging communities of *transgender* people who are "challenging, questioning, or changing gender from that assigned at birth to a chosen gender" (Lorber & Moore, 2007, p. 139). Although most people have deeply learned gender and view the gender category they inhabit as natural or normal, intersex and transgender activists attack the boundaries of "normal" by refusing to choose a traditional sex, gender, or sexual identity (Lorber & Moore, 2007). In so doing, cultural definitions of sex and gender are destabilized and expanded.

You may be wondering why we have not used the term *role,* as in *gender role,* to describe "doing gender." The problem with the concept of roles is that many social roles, such as those of teacher, student, doctor, or nurse, are situation specific. However, gender, like race, is a status and identity that cuts across situations and institutional arenas. In other words, gender does not "appear and disappear from one situation to another" (Van Ausdale & Feagin, 2001, p. 32). In part, this is a consequence of the pressures that other people exert on us to "do gender" no matter the social location in which we find ourselves. Even if an individual would like to "give up gender," others will work hard to define and interact with that individual in gendered terms. If you were an accountant, you could "leave your professional role behind you" when you left the office and went shopping or vacationing. Gender is a different story. Could you leave gender at the office? What would that look like, and what would it take to make it happen?

So far, we have explored gender as a product of our interactions with others. It is something we do, not something we inherit. Gender is also built into the larger world we inhabit in the United States, including its institutions, images and symbols, organizations, and material objects.

For example, jobs, wages, and hierarchies of dominance and subordination in workplaces are gendered. Even after decades of substantial increase in women's workforce participation, occupations continue to be allocated by gender (e.g., secretaries are overwhelmingly women; men dominate construction work) and a wage gap between men and women persists (Bose & Whaley, 2001; Steinberg, 2001; see also the introduction to this book and the introduction to Chapter 7). In addition, men are still more likely to be bosses and women to be bossed. The symbols and images that surround us and by which we communicate are another part of our society's gender story. Our language speaks of difference and opposition in phrases such as "the opposite sex" and in the absence of any words except awkward medical terms (e.g., hermaphrodite) or epithets (e.g., fag) to refer to sex/sexual/gender variants. In addition, the swirl of standardized gendered images in the media is almost overwhelming. Blatant gender stereotypes still dominate TV, film, magazines, and billboards (Lont, 2001). Gender is also articulated, reinforced, and transformed through material objects and locales (Sorenson, 2000). Shoes are gendered, body adornments are gendered, public restrooms are gendered, ships are gendered, wrapping paper is gendered, and deodorants are gendered. The list is endless. The point is that these locales and objects are transformed into a medium for gender to operate within (Sorenson, 2000). They make gender seem "real," and they give it material consequences (p. 82).

Just as culture spawns the binary and oppositional sex and gender template (Grabham, 2007), sexuality, too, is socially constructed (see discussion in Chapter 6). It is not "a natural occurrence derived from biological sex" (Schilt & Westbrook, 2009, p. 443). But in the United States, the imperative to do heterosexuality dominates and is bound to privilege and power. Schilt and Westbrook state that our gender system "must be conceived of as heterosexist, as power is allocated via positioning in the gender and sexual hierarchies" (p. 443). Masculinity and heterosexuality are privileged, while femininity and homosexuality are denigrated. Other sexualities (e.g., bisexuality and pansexuality) are relegated to the margins.

In short, social scientific research underscores the complexity of the prism of gender and demonstrates how gender/sex/sexuality are constructed at multiple, interacting levels of society. The first reading in this chapter, by Barbara J. Risman, is a detailed examination of the ways our gender structure is embedded in the individual, interactional, and institutional dimensions of our society, emphasizing that gender cannot be reduced to one level or dimension: individual, interactional, or institutional. We are literally and figuratively immersed in a gendered world—a world in which difference, opposition, and inequality are the culturally defined themes. And yet, that world is kaleidoscopic in nature. The lesson of the kaleidoscope is that "nothing in life is immune to change" (Baker, 1999, p. 29). Reality is in flux; you never know what's coming next. The metaphor of the kaleidoscope reminds us to keep seeking the shifting meanings as well as the recurring patterns of gender (Baker, 1999).

We live in an interesting time of kaleidoscopic change. Old patterns of sex/gender/sexuality difference and inequality keep reappearing, often in new guises, while new patterns of convergence, equality, and self-realization have emerged. Social science research is vital in helping us stay focused on understanding the prism of gender as changeable and helping us respond to its context—as a social dialogue about societal membership and conventions and "as the outcome of how individuals are made to understand their differences and similarities" (Sorenson, 2000, pp. 203–204). With that focus in mind, we can more clearly and critically explore our gendered society.

REFERENCES

Abrams, D. C. (2002, March–April). Father nature: The making of a modern dad. *Psychology Today,* pp. 38–42.

Baker, C. (1999). *Kaleidoscopes: Wonders of wonder.* Lafayette, CA: C&T.

Beale, B. (2001). The sexes: New insights into the X and Y chromosomes. *The Scientist, 15*(15), 18. Retrieved from http://www.the-scientist.com/?articles.view/articleNo/13499/title/The-Sexes--New-Insights-into-the-X-and-Y-Chromosomes/

Bem, S. L. (1993). *The lenses of gender.* New Haven, CT: Yale University Press.

Bose, C. E., & Whaley, R. B. (2001). Sex segregation in the U.S. labor force. In D. Vannoy (Ed.), *Gender mosaics* (pp. 228–239). Los Angeles: Roxbury.

Coles, T. (2009). Negotiating the field of masculinity: The production and reproduction of multiple dominant masculinities. *Men and Masculinities, 12*(1), 30–44.

Connell, R. W. (2000). *The men and the boys.* Berkeley: University of California Press.

Dowling, C. (2000). *The frailty myth.* New York: Random House.

Estioko-Griffin, A., & Griffin, P. B. (2001). Woman the hunter: The Agta. In C. Brettell & C. Sargent (Eds.), *Gender in cross-cultural perspective* (3rd ed., pp. 238–239). Upper Saddle River, NJ: Prentice Hall.

Fausto-Sterling, A. (1993, March–April). The five sexes: Why male and female are not enough. *The Sciences,* pp. 20–24.

Fausto-Sterling, A. (2000). *Sexing the body: Gender politics and the construction of sexuality.* New York: Basic Books.

Fujimora, J. H. (2006). Sex genes: A critical sociomaterial approach to the politics and molecular genetics of sex determination. *Signs, 32*(1), 49–81.

Glick, P., & Fiske, S. T. (1999). Gender, power dynamics, and social interaction. In M. Ferree, J. Lorber, & B. Hess (Eds.), *Revisioning gender* (pp. 365–398). Thousand Oaks, CA: Sage.

Grabham, E. (2007). Citizen bodies, intersex citizenship. *Sexualities, 10*(29), 28–29.

Hewlett, B. S. (2001). The cultural nexus of Aka father-infant bonding. In C. Brettell & C. Sargent (Eds.), *Gender in cross-cultural perspective* (3rd ed., pp. 45–46). Upper Saddle River, NJ: Prentice Hall.

Kimmel, M. S. (2000). *The gendered society.* New York: Oxford University Press.

Lont, C. M. (2001). The influence of the media on gender images. In D. Vannoy (Ed.), *Gender mosaics.* Los Angeles: Roxbury.

Lorber, J. (1994). *Paradoxes of gender.* New Haven, CT: Yale University Press.

Lorber, J., & Moore, L. J. (2007). *Gendered bodies.* Los Angeles: Roxbury.

Lucal, B. (2008). Building boxes and policing boundaries: (De)constructing intersexuality, transgender and bisexuality. *Sociology Compass, 2*(2), 519–536.

O'Brien, J. (1999). *Social prisms: Reflections on the everyday myths and paradoxes.* Thousand Oaks, CA: Pine Forge Press.

Ridgeway, C. L., & Correll, S. J. (2004). Unpacking the gender system: A theoretical perspective on gender beliefs and social relations. *Gender & Society, 18*(4), 510–531.

Schilt, K. (2010). *Just one of the guys? Transgender men and the persistence of gender inequality.* Chicago: University of Chicago Press.

Schilt, K., & Westbrook, L. (2009). Doing gender, doing heteronormativity: "Gender normals," transgender people, and the social maintenance of heterosexuality. *Gender & Society, 23*(4), 440–464.

Shields, S., Garner, D., Di Leone, B., & Hadley, A. (2006). Gender and emotion. In J. Stets & J. Turner (Eds.), *Handbook of the sociology of emotions* (pp. 63–83). New York: Springer.

Sorenson, M. L. S. (2000). *Gender archaeology.* Cambridge, UK: Polity Press.

Steinberg, R. J. (2001). How sex gets into your paycheck and how to get it out: The gender gap in pay and comparable worth. In D. Vannoy (Ed.), *Gender mosaics.* Los Angeles: Roxbury.

Tavris, C. (1992). *The mismeasure of woman.* New York: Simon & Schuster.

Van Ausdale, D., & Feagin, J. R. (2001). *The first R: How children learn race and racism.* Lanham, MD: Rowman & Littlefield.

Verma, S. C. (2009, October). Amazing Tharu women: Empowered and in control. *Intersections: Gender and Sexuality in Asia and the Pacific, 22.* Retrieved June 1, 2011, from http://intersections.anu.edu.au/issue22/verma.htm

Vespa, J. (2009). Gender ideology construction: A life course and intersectional approach. *Gender & Society, 23*(3), 363–387.

Wharton, A. S. (2005). *The sociology of gender.* Malden, MA: Blackwell.

Yoder, J. D. (2003). *Women and gender: Transforming psychology.* Upper Saddle River, NJ: Prentice Hall.

Introduction to Reading 1

Barbara Risman is a sociologist who has made significant contributions to research and writing on gender in heterosexual American families. In this article, she argues that we need to conceptualize gender as a social structure so we can better analyze the ways gender is embedded in the individual, interactional, and institutional dimensions of social life. You will want to pay special attention to Table 1.1, in which Risman summarizes social processes that create gender in each dimension.

1. Why does Risman include the individual dimension of social life in her theory of gender as a social structure?

2. What are the benefits of a multidimensional structural model of gender?

3. Define the concept "trading power for patronage," and discuss at least two examples from your experience or observations of heterosexual relationships.

GENDER AS A SOCIAL STRUCTURE

THEORY WRESTLING WITH ACTIVISM

Barbara J. Risman

In this article, I briefly summarize my . . . argument that gender should be conceptualized as a social structure (Risman 1998) and extend it with an attempt to classify the mechanisms that help produce gendered outcomes within each dimension of the social structure.

GENDER AS SOCIAL STRUCTURE

With this theory of *gender as a social structure,* I offer a conceptual framework, a scheme to organize the confusing, almost limitless, ways in which gender has come to be defined in contemporary social science. Four distinct social scientific theoretical traditions have developed to

explain gender. The first tradition focuses on how individual sex differences originate, whether biological (Udry 2000) or social in origin (Bem 1993). The second tradition . . . emerged as a reaction to the first and focuses on how the social structure (as opposed to biology or individual learning) creates gendered behavior. The third tradition, also a reaction to the individualist thinking of the first, emphasizes social interaction and accountability to others' expectations, with a focus on how "doing gender" creates and reproduces inequality (West and Zimmerman 1987). The sex-differences literature, the doing gender interactional analyses, and the structural perspectives have been portrayed as incompatible in my own early writings as well as in that of others

From Risman, Barbara, "Gender as a Social Structure." *Gender & Society 18*(4), p. 429. Copyright © 2004. Published by SAGE Publications on behalf of Sociologists for Women in Society.

(Epstein 1988; Kanter 1977; Ferree 1990; Risman 1987; Risman and Schwartz 1989). England and Browne (1992) argued persuasively that this incompatibility is an illusion: All structural theories must make assumptions about individuals, and individualist theories must make presumptions about external social control. While we do gender in every social interaction, it seems naive to ignore the gendered selves and cognitive schemas that children develop as they become cultural natives in a patriarchal world (Bem 1993). The more recent integrative approaches (Connell 2002; Lorber 1994; Ferree, Lorber, and Hess 1999; Risman 1998) treat gender as a socially constructed stratification system. This article fits squarely in the current integrative tradition.

Lorber (1994) argued that gender is an institution that is embedded in all the social processes of everyday life and social organizations. She further argued that gender difference is primarily a means to justify sexual stratification. Gender is so endemic because unless we see difference, we cannot justify inequality. I share this presumption that the creation of difference is the very foundation on which inequality rests.

I build on this notion of gender as an institution but find the institutional language distracting. The word "institution" is too commonly used to refer to particular aspects of society, for example, the family as an institution or corporations as institutions. My notion of gender structure meets the criteria offered by Martin (forthcoming). . . . While the language we use may differ, our goals are complementary, as we seek to situate gender as embedded not only in individuals but throughout social life (Patricia Martin, personal communication).

I prefer to define gender as a social structure because this brings gender to the same analytic plane as politics and economics, where the focus has long been on political and economic structures. While the language of structure suits my purposes, it is not ideal because despite ubiquitous usage in sociological discourse, no definition of the term "structure" is widely shared. Smelser (1988) suggested that all structuralists share the presumption that social structures exist outside individual desires or motives and that social structures at least partially explain human action. Beyond that, consensus dissipates. Blau (1977) focused solely on the constraint collective life imposes on the individual. Structure must be conceptualized, in his view, as a force opposing individual motivation. Structural concepts must be observable, external to the individual, and independent of individual motivation. This definition of "structure" imposes a clear dualism between structure and action, with structure as constraint and action as choice.

Constraint is, of course, an important function of structure, but to focus only on structure as constraint minimizes its importance. Not only are women and men coerced into differential social roles; they often choose their gendered paths. A social structural analysis must help us understand how and why actors choose one alternative over another. A structural theory of action (e.g., Burt 1982) suggests that actors compare themselves and their options to those in structurally similar positions. From this viewpoint, actors are purposive, rationally seeking to maximize their self-perceived well-being under social-structural constraints. As Burt (1982) suggested, one can assume that actors choose the best alternatives without presuming they have either enough information to do it well or the options available to make choices that effectively serve their own interests. For example, married women may choose to do considerably more than their equitable share of child care rather than have their children do without whatever "good enough" parenting means to them if they see no likely alternative that the children's father will pick up the slack.

While actions are a function of interests, the ability to choose is patterned by the social structure. Burt (1982) suggested that norms develop when actors occupy similar network positions in the social structure and evaluate their own options vis-à-vis the alternatives of similarly situated others. From such comparisons, both norms and feelings of relative deprivation or advantage evolve. The social structure as the context of daily life creates action indirectly by shaping actors' perceptions of their interests and directly by constraining choice. Notice the phrase "similarly situated others" above. As long as women and men see themselves as different kinds of people, then women will be unlikely to compare their life options to those of men. Therein lies the power of gender. In a world where sexual anatomy is used to dichotomize human beings into types, the differentiation itself diffuses both claims to and expectations for gender equality. The social structure is not experienced as oppressive if men and women do not see themselves as similarly situated.

While structural perspectives have been applied to gender in the past (Epstein 1988; Kanter 1977), there has been a fundamental flaw in these applications. Generic structural theories applied to gender presume that if women and men were to experience identical structural conditions and role expectations, empirically observable gender differences would disappear. But this ignores not only internalized gender at the individual level . . . but the cultural interactional expectations that remain attached to women and men because of their gender category. A structural perspective on gender is accurate only if we realize that gender itself is a structure deeply embedded in society.

Giddens's (1984) structuration theory adds considerably more depth to this analysis of gender as a social structure with his emphasis on the recursive relationship between social structure and individuals. That is, social structures shape individuals, but simultaneously, individuals shape the social structure. Giddens embraced the transformative power of human action. He insisted that any structural theory must be concerned with reflexivity and actors' interpretations of their own lives. Social structures not only act on people; people act on social structures. Indeed, social structures are created not by mysterious forces but by human action. When people act on structure, they do so for their own reasons. We must, therefore, be concerned with why actors choose their acts. Giddens insisted that concern with meaning must go beyond the verbal justification easily available from actors

because so much of social life is routine and so taken for granted that actors will not articulate, or even consider, why they act.

This nonreflexive habituated action is what I refer to as the cultural component of the social structure: The taken for granted or cognitive image rules that belong to the situational context (not only or necessarily to the actor's personality). The cultural component of the social structure includes the interactional expectations that each of us meet in every social encounter. My aims are to bring women and men back into a structural theory where gender is the structure under analysis and to identify when behavior is habit (an enactment of taken for granted gendered cultural norms) and when we do gender consciously, with intent, rebellion, or even with irony. When are we doing gender and re-creating inequality without intent? And what happens to interactional dynamics and male-dominated institutions when we rebel? Can we refuse to do gender or is rebellion simply doing gender differently, forging alternative masculinities and femininities?

Connell (1987) applied Giddens's (1984) concern with social structure as both constraint and created by action in his treatise on gender and power (see particularly chapter 5). In his analysis, structure constrains action, yet "since human action involves free invention . . . and is reflexive, practice can be turned against what constrains it; so structure can deliberately be the object of practice" (Connell 1987, 95). Action may turn against structure but can never escape it.

A theory of gender as a social structure must integrate this notion of causality as recursive with attention to gender consequences at multiple levels of analysis. Gender is deeply embedded as a basis for stratification not just in our personalities, our cultural rules, or institutions but in all these, and in complicated ways. The gender structure differentiates opportunities and constraints based on sex category and thus has consequences on three dimensions: (1) At the individual level, for the development of gendered selves; (2) during interaction as men and women face different cultural expectations even when they fill the identical structural positions; and (3) in institutional domains where explicit regulations regarding resource distribution and material goods are gender specific.

Advantages to Gender Structure Theory

This schema advances our understanding of gender in several ways. First, this theoretical model imposes some order on the encyclopedic research findings that have developed to explain gender inequality. Thinking of each research question as one piece of a jigsaw puzzle, being able to identify how one set of findings coordinates with others even when the dependent variables or contexts of interest are distinct, furthers our ability to build a cumulative science. Gender as a social structure is enormously complex. Full attention to the web of interconnection between gendered selves, the cultural expectations that help explain interactional patterns, and institutional regulations allows each research tradition to explore the growth of their own trees while remaining cognizant of the forest.

A second contribution of this approach is that it leaves behind the modernist warfare version of science, wherein theories are pitted against one another, with a winner and a loser in every contest. In the past, much energy . . . was devoted to testing which theory best explained gender inequality and by implication to discounting every alternative possibility.[1] Theory building that depends on theory slaying presumes parsimony is always desirable, as if this complicated world of ours were best described with simplistic monocausal explanations. While parsimony and theory testing were the model for the twentieth-century science, a more postmodern science should attempt to find complicated and integrative theories (Collins 1998). The conceptualization of gender as a social structure is my contribution to complicating, but hopefully enriching, social theory about gender.

A third benefit to this multidimensional structural model is that it allows us to seriously investigate the direction and strength of causal relationships between gendered phenomena on each dimension. We can try to identify the site where change occurs and at which level of analysis the ability of agentic women and men seem able at this, historical moment, to effectively reject habitualized gender routines. For example, we can empirically investigate the relationship between gendered selves and doing gender without accepting simplistic unidirectional arguments for inequality presumed to be either about identities or cultural ideology. It is quite possible, indeed likely, that socialized femininity does help explain why we do gender, but doing gender to meet others' expectations, surely, over time, helps construct our gendered selves. Furthermore, gendered institutions depend on our willingness to do gender, and when we rebel, we can sometimes change the institutions themselves. I have used the language of dimensions interchangeably with the language of levels because when we think of gender as a social structure, we must move away from privileging any particular dimension as higher than another. How social change occurs is an empirical question, not an a priori theoretical assumption. It may be that individuals struggling to change their own identities (as in consciousness-raising groups of the early second-wave women's movement) eventually bring their new selves to social interaction and create new cultural expectations. For example, as women come to see themselves (or are socialized to see themselves) as sexual actors, the expectations that men must work to provide orgasms for their female partners becomes part of the cultural norm. But this is surely not the only way social change can happen. When social movement activists name as inequality what has heretofore been considered natural (e.g., women's segregation into low-paying jobs), they can create organizational changes such as career ladders between women's quasi-administrative jobs and actual management, opening up opportunities that otherwise would have remained closed, thus creating change on the institutional dimension. Girls raised in the next generation, who know opportunities exist in these workplaces, may have an altered sense of possibilities and therefore of themselves. We need, however, to also study change and equality when it occurs rather than only documenting inequality.

Perhaps the most important feature of this conceptual schema is its dynamism. No one dimension determines the other. Change is fluid and reverberates throughout the structure dynamically. Changes in individual identities and moral accountability may change interactional expectations, but the opposite is possible as well. Change cultural expectations, and individual identities are shaped differently. Institutional changes must result from individuals or group action, yet such change is difficult, as institutions exist across time and space. Once institutional changes occur, they reverberate at the level of cultural expectations and perhaps even on identities. And the cycle of change continues. No mechanistic predictions are possible because human beings sometimes reject the structure itself and, by doing so, change it.

Social Processes Located by Dimension in the Gender Structure

When we conceptualize gender as a social structure, we can begin to identify under what conditions and how gender inequality is being produced within each dimension. The "how" is important because without knowing the mechanisms, we cannot intervene. If indeed gender inequality in the division of household labor at this historical moment were primarily explained (and I do not suggest that it is) by gendered selves, then we would do well to consider the most effective socialization mechanisms to create fewer gender-schematic children and resocialization for adults. If, however, the gendered division of household labor is primarily constrained today by cultural expectations and moral accountability, it is those cultural images we must work to alter. But then again, if the reason many men do not equitably do their share of family labor is that men's jobs are organized so they cannot succeed at work and do their share at home, it is the contemporary American workplace that must change (Williams 2000). We may never find a universal theoretical explanation for the gendered division of household labor because

universal social laws may be an illusion of twentieth-century empiricism. But in any given moment for any particular setting, the causal processes should be identifiable empirically. Gender complexity goes beyond historical specificity, as the particular causal processes that constrain men and women to do gender may be strong in one institutional setting (e.g., at home) and weaker in another (e.g., at work).

The forces that create gender traditionalism for men and women may vary across space as well as time. Conceptualizing gender as a social structure contributes to a more postmodern, contextually specific social science. We can use this schema to begin to organize thinking about the causal processes that are most likely to be effective on each dimension. When we are concerned with the means by which individuals come to have a preference to do gender, we should focus on how identities are constructed through early childhood development, explicit socialization, modeling, and adult experiences, paying close attention to the internalization of social mores. To the extent that women and men choose to do gender-typical behavior cross-situationally and over time, we must focus on such individual explanations. Indeed, much attention has already been given to gender socialization and the individualist presumptions for gender. The earliest and perhaps most commonly referred to explanations in popular culture depend on sex-role training, teaching boys and girls their culturally appropriate roles. But when trying to understand gender on the interactional/cultural dimension, the means by which status differences shape expectations and the ways in which in-group and out-group membership influences behavior need to be at the center of attention. Too little attention has been paid to how inequality is shaped by such cultural expectations during interaction. I return to this in the section below. On the institutional dimension, we look to law, organizational practices, and formal regulations that distinguish by sex category. Much progress has been made in the post–civil rights era with rewriting formal laws and organizational practices to ensure gender neutrality. Unfortunately, we have often found that despite changes in gender socialization and gender neutrality on the institutional dimension, gender stratification remains.

What I have attempted to do here is to offer a conceptual organizing scheme for the study of gender that can help us to understand gender in all its complexity and try to isolate the social processes that create gender in each dimension. Table 1.1 provides a schematic outline of this argument.[2]

Cultural Expectations During Interaction and the Stalled Revolution

In *Gender Vertigo* (Risman 1998), I suggested that at this moment in history, gender inequality between partners in American heterosexual couples could be attributed particularly to the interactional expectations at the cultural level: the differential expectations attached to being a mother and father, a husband and wife. Here, I extend this argument in two ways. First, I propose that the stalled gender revolution in other settings can similarly be traced to the interactional/cultural dimension of the social structure. Even when women and men with feminist identities work in organizations with formally gender-neutral rules, gender inequality is reproduced during everyday interaction. The cultural expectations attached to our sex category, simply being identified as a woman or man, has remained relatively impervious to the feminist forces that have problematized sexist socialization practices and legal discrimination. I discuss some of those

processes that can help explain why social interaction continues to reproduce inequality, even in settings that seem ripe for social change.

Contemporary social psychological writings offer us a glimpse of possibilities for understanding how inequality is reconstituted in daily interaction. Ridgeway and her colleagues (Ridgeway 1991, 1997, 2001; Ridgeway and Correll 2000; Ridgeway and Smith-Lovin 1999) showed that the status expectations attached to gender and race categories are cross-situational. These expectations can be thought of as one of the engines that re-create inequality even in new settings where there is no other reason to expect male privilege to otherwise emerge. In a sexist and racist society, women and all persons of color are expected to have less to contribute to task performances than are white men, unless they have some other externally validated source of prestige. Status expectations create a cognitive bias toward privileging those of already high status. What produces status distinction, however, is culturally and historically variable. Thus, cognitive bias is one of the causal mechanisms that help to explain the reproduction of gender and race inequality in everyday life. It may also be an important explanation for the reproduction of class and heterosexist inequality in everyday life as well, but that is an empirical question.

Schwalbe and his colleagues (2000, 419) suggested that there are other "generic interactive processes through which inequalities are created and reproduced in everyday life." Some of these

Table 1.1 Dimensions of Gender Structure, by Illustrative Social Processes[a]

	Dimensions of the Gender Structure		
	Individual Level	*Interactional Cultural Expectations*	*Institutional Domain*
Social Processes	Socialization Internalization Identity work Construction of selves	Status expectations Cognitive bias Othering Trading power for patronage Altercasting	Organizational practices Legal regulations Distribution of resources Ideology

a. These are examples of social processes that may help explain the gender structure on each dimension. They are meant to be illustrative and not a complete list of all possible social processes or causal mechanisms.

processes include othering, subordinate adaptation, boundary maintenance, and emotion management. Schwalbe and his colleagues suggested that subordinates' adaptation plays an essential role in their own disadvantage. Subordinate adaptation helps to explain women's strategy to adapt to the gender structure. Perhaps the most common adaptation of women to subordination is "trading power for patronage" (Schwalbe et al. 2000, 426). Women, as wives and daughters, often derive significant compensatory benefits from relationships with the men in their families. Stombler and Martin (1994) similarly showed how little sisters in a fraternity trade affiliation for secondary status. In yet another setting, elite country clubs, Sherwood (2004) showed how women accept subordinate status as "B" members of clubs, in exchange for men's approval, and how when a few wives challenge men's privilege, they are threatened with social ostracism, as are their husbands. Women often gain the economic benefits of patronage for themselves and their children in exchange for their subordinate status.

One can hardly analyze the cultural expectations and interactional processes that construct gender inequality without attention to the actions of members of the dominant group. We must pay close attention to what men do to preserve their power and privilege. Schwalbe et al. (2000) suggested that one process involved is when superordinate groups effectively "other" those who they want to define as subordinate, creating devalued statuses and expectations for them. Men effectively do this in subversive ways through "politeness" norms, which construct women as "others" in need of special favors, such as protection. By opening doors and walking closer to the dirty street, men construct women as an "other" category, different and less than independent autonomous men. The cultural significance attached to male bodies signifies the capacity to dominate, to control, and to elicit deference, and such expectations are perhaps at the core of what it means for men to do gender (Michael Schwalbe, personal communication).

These are only some of the processes that might be identified for understanding how we create gender inequality based on embodied cultural expectations. None are determinative causal predictors, but instead, these are possible leads to reasonable and testable hypotheses about the production of gender. . . .

NOTES

1. See Scott (1997) for a critique of feminists who adopt a strategy where theories have to be simplified, compared, and defeated. She too suggested a model where feminists build on the complexity of each others' ideas.

2. I thank my colleague Donald Tomaskovic-Devey for suggesting the visual representation of these ideas as well as his usual advice on my ideas as they develop.

REFERENCES

Bem, Sandra. 1993. *The lenses of gender.* New Haven, CT: Yale University Press.

Blau, Peter. 1977. *Inequality and heterogeneity.* New York: Free Press.

Burt, Ronald S. 1982. *Toward a structural theory of action.* New York: Academic Press.

Collins, Patricia Hill. 1998. *Fighting words: Black women and the search for justice.* Minneapolis: University of Minnesota Press.

Connell, R. W. 1987. *Gender and power: Society, the person, and sexual politics.* Stanford, CA: Stanford University Press.

———. 2002. *Gender: Short introductions.* Malden, MA: Blackwell.

England, Paula, and Irene Browne. 1992. Internalization and constraint in women's subordination. *Current Perspectives in Social Theory* 12:97–123.

Epstein, Cynthia, Fuchs. 1988. *Deceptive distinctions: Sex, gender, and the social order.* New Haven, CT: Yale University Press.

Ferree, Myra Marx. 1990. Beyond separate spheres: Feminism and family research. *Journal of Marriage and the Family 53*(4): 866–84.

Giddens, Anthony. 1984. *The constitution of society: Outline of the theory of structuration.* Berkeley: University of California Press.

Kanter, Rosabeth. 1977. *Men and women of the corporation.* New York: Basic Books.

Lorber, Judith. 1994. *Paradoxes of gender.* New Haven, CT: Yale University Press.

Martin, Patricia. Forthcoming. Gender as a social institution. *Social Forces.* Myers, Kristen A., Cynthia D. Anderson, and Barbara J. Risman, eds. 1998. *Feminist foundations: Toward transforming society.* Thousand Oaks, CA: Sage.

Ridgeway, Cecilia L. 1991. The social construction of status value: Gender and other nominal characteristics. *Social Forces 70*(2): 367–86.

———. 1997. Interaction and the conservation of gender inequality: Considering employment. *American Sociological Review 62*(2): 218–35.

———. 2001. Gender, status, and leadership. *Journal of Social Issues 57*(4): 637–55.

Ridgeway, Cecilia L., and Shelley J. Correll. 2000. Limiting inequality through interaction: The end(s) of gender. *Contemporary Sociology* 29:110–20.

Ridgeway, Cecilia L., and Lynn Smith-Lovin. 1999. The gender system and interaction. *Annual Review of Sociology* 25:191–216.

Risman, Barbara J. 1983. Necessity and the invention of mothering. Ph.D. diss. University of Washington.

———. 1987. Intimate relationships from a microstructural perspective: Mothering men. *Gender & Society* 1: 6–32.

———. 1998. *Gender vertigo: American families in transition.* New Haven, CT: Yale University Press.

Risman, Barbara J., and Pepper Schwartz. 1989. *Gender in intimate relationships.* Belmont, CA: Wadsworth.

Schwalbe, Michael, Sandra Godwin, Daphne Holden, Douglas Schrock, Shealy Thompson, and Michele Wolkomir. 2000. Generic processes in the reproduction of inequality: An interactionist analysis. *Social Forces 79*(2): 419–52.

Scott, Joan Wallach. 1997. Comment on Hawkesworth's "Confounding Gender." *Signs: Journal of Women in Culture and Society 22*(3): 697–702.

Sherwood, Jessica. 2004. Talk about country clubs: Ideology and the reproduction of privilege. Ph.D. diss., North Carolina State University.

Smelser, Neil J. 1988. Social structure. In *Handbook of sociology,* edited by Neil J. Smelser. Beverly Hills, CA: Sage.

Stombler, Mindy, and Patricia Yancey Martin. 1994. Bring women in, keeping women down: Fraternity "little sister" organizations. *Journal of Contemporary Ethnography* 23:150–84.

Udry, J. Richard. 2000. Biological limits of gender construction. *American Sociological Review* 65: 443–57.

West, Candace, and Don Zimmerman. 1987. Doing gender. *Gender & Society* 1:125–51.

Williams, Joan. 2000. *Unbending gender: Why family and work conflict and what to do about it.* New York: Oxford University Press.

Introduction to Reading 2

By analyzing the challenges she faces in the course of her daily experience of negotiating the boundaries of our gendered society, sociologist Betsy Lucal describes the rigidity of the American binary gender system and the consequences for people who do not fit. Since her physical appearance does not clearly define her as a woman, she must navigate a world in which some people interact with her as though she is a man. Through analysis of her own story, Lucal demonstrates how gender is something we do, rather than something we are.

1. Why does Lucal argue that we cannot escape "doing gender"?

2. How does Lucal negotiate "not fitting" into the American two-and-only-two gender structure?

3. Have you ever experienced a mismatch between your gender identity and the gender that others perceive you to be? If so, how did you feel and respond?

WHAT IT MEANS TO BE GENDERED ME

Betsy Lucal

I understood the concept of "doing gender" (West and Zimmerman 1987) long before I became a sociologist. I have been living with the consequences of inappropriate "gender display" (Goffman 1976; West and Zimmerman 1987) for as long as I can remember. My daily experiences are a testament to the rigidity of gender in our society, to the real implications of "two and only two" when it comes to sex and gender categories (Garfinkel 1967; Kessler and McKenna 1978). Each day, I experience the consequences that our gender system has for my identity and interactions. I am a woman who has been called "Sir" so many times that I no longer even hesitate to assume that it is being directed at me. I am a woman whose use of public rest rooms regularly causes reactions ranging from confused stares to confrontations over what a man is doing in the women's room. I regularly enact a variety of practices either to minimize the need for others to know my gender or to deal with their misattributions.

I am the embodiment of Lorber's (1994) ostensibly paradoxical assertion that the "gender bending" I engage in actually might serve to preserve and perpetuate gender categories. As a feminist who sees gender rebellion as a significant part of her contribution to the dismantling of sexism, I find this possibility disheartening.

In this article, I examine how my experiences both support and contradict Lorber's (1994) argument using my own experiences to illustrate and reflect on the social construction of gender. My analysis offers a discussion of the consequences of gender for people who do not follow the rules as well as an examination of the possible implications of the existence of people like

me for the gender system itself. Ultimately, I show how life on the boundaries of gender affects me and how my life, and the lives of others who make similar decisions about their participation in the gender system, has the potential to subvert gender.

Because this article analyzes my experiences as a woman who often is mistaken for a man, my focus is on the social construction of gender for women. My assumption is that, given the gendered nature of the gendering process itself, men's experiences of this phenomenon might well be different from women's.

THE SOCIAL CONSTRUCTION OF GENDER

It is now widely accepted that gender is a social construction, that sex and gender are distinct, and that gender is something all of us "do." This conceptualization of gender can be traced to Garfinkel's (1967) ethnomethodological study of "Agnes."[1] In this analysis, Garfinkel examined the issues facing a male who wished to pass as, and eventually become, a woman. Unlike individuals who perform gender in culturally expected ways, Agnes could not take her gender for granted and always was in danger of failing to pass as a woman (Zimmerman 1992).

This approach was extended by Kessler and McKenna (1978) and codified in the classic "Doing Gender" by West and Zimmerman (1987). The social constructionist approach has been developed most notably by Lorber (1994, 1996). Similar theoretical strains have developed outside of sociology, such as work by Butler (1990) and Weston (1996). . . .

Given our cultural rules for identifying gender (i.e., that there are only two and that masculinity is assumed in the absence of evidence to the contrary), a person who does not do gender appropriately is placed not into a third category but rather into the one with which her or his gender display seems most closely to fit; that is, if a man appears to be a woman, then he will be categorized as "woman," not as something else. Even if a person does not want to do gender or would like to do a gender other than the two recognized by our society, other people will, in effect, do gender for that person by placing her or him in one and only one of the two available categories. We cannot escape doing gender or, more specifically, doing one of two genders. (There are exceptions in limited contexts such as people doing "drag" [Butler 1990; Lorber 1994].)

People who follow the norms of gender can take their genders for granted. Kessler and McKenna asserted, "Few people besides transsexuals think of their gender as anything other than 'naturally' obvious"; they believe that the risks of not being taken for the gender intended "are minimal for nontranssexuals" (1978, 126). However, such an assertion overlooks the experiences of people such as those women Devor (1989) calls "gender blenders" and those people Lorber (1994) refers to as "gender benders." As West and Zimmerman (1987) pointed out, we all are held accountable for, and might be called on to account for, our genders.

People who, for whatever reasons, do not adhere to the rules, risk gender misattribution and any interactional consequences that might result from this misidentification. What are the consequences of misattribution for social interaction? When must misattribution be minimized? What will one do to minimize such mistakes? In this article, I explore these and related questions using my biography.

For me, the social processes and structures of gender mean that, in the context of our culture, my appearance will be read as masculine. Given the common conflation of sex and gender, I will be assumed to be a male. Because of the two-and-only-two genders rule, I will be classified, perhaps more often than not, as a man—not as an atypical woman, not as a genderless person. I must be one gender or the other; I cannot be neither, nor can I be both. This norm has a variety of mundane and serious consequences for my everyday existence. Like Myhre (1995), I have found that the choice not to participate in femininity is not one made frivolously.

My experiences as a woman who does not do femininity illustrate a paradox of our two-and-only-two gender system. Lorber argued that "bending gender rules and passing between genders does not erode but rather preserves gender boundaries" (1994, 21). Although people who engage in these behaviors and appearances do "demonstrate the social constructedness of sex, sexuality, and gender" (Lorber 1994, 96), they do not actually disrupt gender. Devor made a similar point: "When gender blending females refused to mark themselves by publicly displaying sufficient femininity to be recognized as women, they were in no way challenging patriarchal gender assumptions" (1989, 142). As the following discussion shows, I have found that my own experiences both support and challenge this argument. Before detailing these experiences, I explain my use of my self as data.

MY SELF AS DATA

This analysis is based on my experiences as a person whose appearance and gender/sex are not, in the eyes of many people, congruent. How did my experiences become my data? I began my research "unwittingly" (Krieger 1991). This article is a product of "opportunistic research" in that I am using my "unique biography, life experiences, and/or situational familiarity to understand and explain social life" (Riemer 1988, 121; see also Riemer 1977). It is an analysis of "unplanned personal experience," that is, experiences that were not part of a research project but instead are part of my daily encounters (Reinharz 1992).

This work also is, at least to some extent, an example of Richardson's (1994) notion of writing as a method of inquiry. As a sociologist who specializes in gender, the more I learned, the more I realized that my life could serve as a case study. As I examined my experiences, I found out things—about my experiences and about theory—that I did not know when I started (Richardson 1994).

It also is useful, I think, to consider my analysis an application of Mills's (1959) "sociological imagination." Mills (1959) and Berger (1963) wrote about the importance of seeing the general in the particular. This means that general social patterns can be discerned in the behaviors of particular individuals. In this article, I am examining portions of my biography, situated in U.S. society during the 1990s, to understand the "personal troubles" my gender produces in the context of a two-and-only-two gender system. I am not attempting to generalize my experiences; rather, I am trying to use them to examine and reflect on the processes and structure of gender in our society.

Because my analysis is based on my memories and perceptions of events, it is limited by my ability to recall events and by my interpretation of those events. However, I am not claiming that my experiences provide the truth about gender and how it works. I am claiming that the biography of a person who lives on the margins of our gender system can provide theoretical insights into the processes and social structure of gender. Therefore, after describing my experiences, I examine how they illustrate and extend, as well as contradict, other work on the social construction of gender.

GENDERED ME

Each day, I negotiate the boundaries of gender. Each day, I face the possibility that someone will attribute the "wrong" gender to me based on my physical appearance. I am six feet tall and large-boned. I have had short hair for most of my life. For the past several years, I have worn a crew cut or flat top. I do not shave or otherwise remove hair from my body (e.g., no eyebrow plucking). I do not wear dresses, skirts, high heels, or makeup. My only jewelry is a class ring, a "men's" watch (my wrists are too large for a "women's" watch), two small earrings (gold hoops, both in my left ear), and (occasionally) a necklace. I wear jeans or shorts, T-shirts, sweaters, polo/golf shirts, button-down collar shirts, and tennis shoes or boots. The jeans are "women's" (I do have hips) but do not look particularly "feminine." The rest of the outer garments are from men's departments. I prefer baggy clothes, so the fact that I have "womanly" breasts often is not obvious (I do not wear a bra).

Sometimes, I wear a baseball cap or some other type of hat. I also am white and relatively young (30 years old).[2] My gender display— what others interpret as my presented identity— regularly leads to the misattribution of my gender. An incongruity exists between my gender self-identity and the gender that others perceive. In my encounters with people I do not know, I sometimes conclude, based on our interactions, that they think I am a man. This does not mean that other people do not think I am a man, just that I have no way of knowing what they think without interacting with them.

Living With It

I have no illusions or delusions about my appearance. I know that my appearance is likely to be read as "masculine" (and male) and that how I see myself is socially irrelevant. Given our two-and-only-two gender structure, I must live with the consequences of my appearance. These consequences fall into two categories: issues of identity and issues of interaction.

My most common experience is being called "Sir" or being referred to by some other masculine linguistic marker (e.g., "he," "man"). This has happened for years, for as long as I can remember, when having encounters with people I do not know.[3] Once, in fact, the same worker at a fast-food restaurant called me "Ma'am" when she took my order and "Sir" when she gave it to me.

Using my credit cards sometimes is a challenge. Some clerks subtly indicate their disbelief, looking from the card to me and back at the card and checking my signature carefully. Others challenge my use of the card, asking whose it is or demanding identification. One cashier asked to see my driver's license and then asked me whether I was the son of the cardholder. Another clerk told me that my signature on the receipt "had better match" the one on the card. Presumably, this was her way of letting me know that she was not convinced it was my credit card.

My identity as a woman also is called into question when I try to use women-only spaces. Encounters in public rest rooms are an adventure. I have been told countless times that "This is the ladies' room." Other women say nothing to me, but their stares and conversations with others let me know what they think. I will hear them say, for example, "There was a man in there." I also get stares when I enter a locker room. However, it seems that women are less concerned about my presence, there, perhaps because, given that it is a space for changing clothes, showering, and so forth, they will be able to make sure that I am really a woman. Dressing rooms in department stores also are problematic spaces. I remember shopping with my sister once and being offered a chair outside the room when I began to accompany her into the dressing room. Women who believe that I am a man do not want me in women-only spaces. For example, one woman would not enter the rest room until I came out, and others have told me that I am in the wrong place. They also might not want to encounter me while they are alone. For example, seeing me walking at night when they are alone might be scary.[4]

I, on the other hand, am not afraid to walk alone, day or night. I do not worry that I will be subjected to the public harassment that many women endure (Gardner 1995). I am not a clear target for a potential rapist. I rely on the fact that a potential attacker would not want to attack a big man by mistake. This is not to say that men never are attacked, just that they are not viewed, and often do not view themselves, as being vulnerable to attack.

Being perceived as a man has made me privy to male-male interactional styles of which most women are not aware. I found out, quite by accident, that many men greet, or acknowledge, people (mostly other men) who make eye contact with them with a single nod. For example, I found that when I walked down the halls of my brother's all-male dormitory making eye contact, men nodded their greetings at me. Oddly enough, these same men did not greet my brother.

I had to tell him about making eye contact and nodding as a greeting ritual. Apparently, in this case I was doing masculinity better than he was! I also believe that I am treated differently, for example, in auto parts stores (staffed almost exclusively by men in most cases) because of the assumption that I am a man. Workers there assume that I know what I need and that my questions are legitimate requests for information.

I suspect that I am treated more fairly than a feminine-appearing woman would be. I have not been able to test this proposition. However, Devor's participants did report "being treated more respectfully" (1989, 132) in such situations. There is, however, a negative side to being assumed to be a man by other men. Once, a friend and I were driving in her car when a man failed to stop at an intersection and nearly crashed into us. As we drove away, I mouthed "stop sign" to him. When we both stopped our cars at the next intersection, he got out of his car and came up to the passenger side of the car, where I was sitting. He yelled obscenities at us and pounded and spit on the car window. Luckily, the windows were closed. I do not think he would have done that if he thought I was a woman. This was the first time I realized that one of the implications of being seen as a man was that I might be called on to defend myself from physical aggression from other men who felt challenged by me. This was a sobering and somewhat frightening thought.

Recently, I was verbally accosted by an older man who did not like where I had parked my car. As I walked down the street to work, he shouted that I should park at the university rather than on a side street nearby. I responded that it was a public street and that I could park there if I chose. He continued to yell, but the only thing I caught was the last part of what he said: "Your tires are going to get cut!" Based on my appearance that day—I was dressed casually and carrying a backpack, and I had my hat on backward—I believe he thought that I was a young male student rather than a female professor. I do not think he would have yelled at a person he thought to be a woman—and perhaps especially not a woman professor.

Given the presumption of heterosexuality that is part of our system of gender, my interactions with women who assume that I am a man also can be viewed from that perspective. For example, once my brother and I were shopping when we were "hit on" by two young women. The encounter ended before I realized what had happened. It was only when we walked away that I told him that I was pretty certain that they had thought both of us were men. A more common experience is realizing that when I am seen in public with one of my women friends, we are likely to be read as a heterosexual dyad. It is likely that if I were to walk through a shopping mall holding hands with a woman, no one would look twice, not because of their open-mindedness toward lesbian couples but rather because of their assumption that I was the male half of a straight couple. Recently, when walking through a mall with a friend and her infant, my observations of others' responses to us led me to believe that many of them assumed that we were a family on an outing, that is, that I was her partner and the father of the child.

Dealing With It

Although I now accept that being mistaken for a man will be a part of my life so long as I choose not to participate in femininity, there have been times when I consciously have tried to appear more feminine. I did this for a while when I was an undergraduate and again recently when I was on the academic job market. The first time, I let my hair grow nearly down to my shoulders and had it permed. I also grew long fingernails and wore nail polish. Much to my chagrin, even then one of my professors, who did not know my name, insistently referred to me in his kinship examples as "the son." Perhaps my first act on the way to my current stance was to point out to this man, politely and after class, that I was a woman.

More recently, I again let my hair grow out for several months, although I did not alter other aspects of my appearance. Once my hair was about two and a half inches long (from its original quarter inch), I realized, based on my encounters with strangers, that I had more or less passed back into the category of "woman." Then, when I returned to wearing a flat top, people again responded to me as if I were a man.

Because of my appearance, much of my negotiation of interactions with strangers involves attempts to anticipate their reactions to me. I need to assess whether they will be likely to assume that I am a man and whether that actually matters in the context of our encounters. Many times, my gender really is irrelevant, and it is just annoying to be misidentified. Other times, particularly when my appearance is coupled with something that identifies me by name (e.g., a check or credit card) without a photo, I might need to do something to ensure that my identity is not questioned. As a result of my experiences, I have developed some techniques to deal with gender misattribution.

In general, in unfamiliar public places, I avoid using the rest room because I know that it is a place where there is a high likelihood of misattribution and where misattribution is socially important. If I must use a public rest room, I try to make myself look as nonthreatening as possible. I do not wear a hat, and I try to rearrange my clothing to make my breasts more obvious. Here, I am trying to use my secondary sex characteristics to make my gender more obvious rather than the usual use of gender to make sex obvious. While in the rest room, I never make eye contact, and I get in and out as quickly as possible. Going in with a woman friend also is helpful; her presence legitimizes my own. People are less likely to think I am entering a space where I do not belong when I am with someone who looks like she does belong.[5]

To those women who verbally challenge my presence in the rest room, I reply, "I know," usually in an annoyed tone. When they stare or talk about me to the women they are with, I simply get out as quickly as possible. In general, I do not wait for someone I am with because there is too much chance of an unpleasant encounter.

I stopped trying on clothes before purchasing them a few years ago because my presence in the changing areas was met with stares and whispers. Exceptions are stores where the dressing rooms are completely private, where there are individual stalls rather than a room with stalls separated by curtains, or where business is slow and no one else is trying on clothes. If I am trying on a garment clearly intended for a woman, then I usually can do so without hassle. I guess the attendants assume that I must be a woman if I have, for example, a women's bathing suit in my hand. But usually, I think it is easier for me to try the clothes on at home and return them, if necessary, rather than risk creating a scene. Similarly, when I am with another woman who is trying on clothes, I just wait outside.

My strategy with credit cards and checks is to anticipate wariness on a clerk's part. When I sense that there is some doubt or when they challenge me, I say, "It's my card." I generally respond courteously to requests for photo ID, realizing that these might be routine checks because of concerns about increasingly widespread fraud. But for the clerk who asked for ID and still did not think it was my card, I had a stronger reaction. When she said that she was sorry for embarrassing me, I told her that I was not embarrassed but that she should be. I also am particularly careful to make sure that my signature is consistent with the back of the card. Faced with such situations, I feel somewhat nervous about signing my name—which, of course, makes me worry that my signature will look different from how it should.

Another strategy I have been experimenting with is wearing nail polish in the dark bright colors currently fashionable. I try to do this when I travel by plane. Given more stringent travel regulations, one always must present a photo ID. But my experiences have shown that my driver's license is not necessarily convincing. Nail polish might be. I also flash my polished nails when I enter airport rest rooms, hoping that they will provide a clue that I am indeed in the right place.

There are other cases in which the issues are less those of identity than of all the norms of interaction that, in our society, are gendered. My most common response to misattribution actually is to appear to ignore it, that is, to go on with the interaction as if nothing out of the ordinary has happened. Unless I feel that there is a good reason to establish my correct gender, I assume the identity others impose on me for the sake of smooth interaction. For example, if someone is selling me a movie ticket, then there is no reason to make sure that the person has accurately discerned my gender. Similarly, if it is clear that the person using "Sir" is talking to me, then I simply respond as appropriate. I accept the designation because it is irrelevant to the situation. It takes enough effort to be alert for misattributions and to decide which of them matter; responding to each one would take more energy than it is worth.

Sometimes, if our interaction involves conversation, my first verbal response is enough to let the other person know that I am actually a woman and not a man. My voice apparently is "feminine" enough to shift people's attributions to the other category. I know when this has happened by the apologies that usually accompany the mistake. I usually respond to the apologies by saying something like "No problem" and/or "It happens all the time." Sometimes, a misattributor will offer an account for the mistake, for example, saying that it was my hair or that they were not being very observant.

These experiences with gender and misattribution provide some theoretical insights into contemporary Western understandings of gender and into the social structure of gender in contemporary society. Although there are a number of ways in which my experiences confirm the work of others, there also are some ways in which my experiences suggest other interpretations and conclusions.

WHAT DOES IT MEAN?

Gender is pervasive in our society. I cannot choose not to participate in it. Even if I try not to do gender, other people will do it for me. That is, given our two-and-only-two rule, they must attribute one of two genders to me. Still, although I cannot choose not to participate in gender, I can choose not to participate in femininity (as I have), at least with respect to physical appearance. That is where the problems begin. Without the decorations of femininity, I do not look like a woman. That is, I do not look like what many people's commonsense understanding of gender tells them a woman looks like. How I see myself, even how I might wish others would see me, is socially irrelevant. It is the gender that I appear to be (my "perceived gender") that is most relevant to my social identity and interactions with others. The major consequence of this fact is that I must be continually aware of which gender I "give off" as well as which gender I "give" (Goffman 1959).

Because my gender self-identity is "not displayed obviously, immediately, and consistently" (Devor 1989, 58), I am somewhat of a failure in social terms with respect to gender. Causing people to be uncertain or wrong about one's gender is a violation of taken-for-granted rules that leads to embarrassment and discomfort; it means that something has gone wrong with the interaction (Garfinkel 1967; Kessler and McKenna 1978). This means that my nonresponse to misattribution is the more socially appropriate response; I am allowing others to maintain face (Goffman 1959, 1967). By not calling attention to their mistakes, I uphold their images of themselves as competent social actors. I also maintain my own image as competent by letting them assume that I am the gender I appear to them to be.

But I still have discreditable status; I carry a stigma (Goffman 1963). Because I have failed to

participate appropriately in the creation of meaning with respect to gender (Devor 1989), I can be called on to account for my appearance. If discredited, I show myself to be an incompetent social actor. I am the one not following the rules, and I will pay the price for not providing people with the appropriate cues for placing me in the gender category to which I really belong.

I do think that it is, in many cases, safer to be read as a man than as some sort of deviant woman. "Man" is an acceptable category; it fits properly into people's gender worldview. Passing as a man often is "the path of least resistance" (Devor 1989; Johnson 1997). For example, in situations where gender does not matter, letting people take me as a man is easier than correcting them.

Conversely, as Butler noted, "We regularly punish those who fail to do their gender right" (1990, 140). Feinberg maintained, "Masculine girls and women face terrible condemnation and brutality—including sexual violence—for crossing the boundary of what is 'acceptable' female expression" (1996, 114). People are more likely to harass me when they perceive me to be a woman who looks like a man. For example, when a group of teenagers realized that I was not a man because one of their mothers identified me correctly, they began to make derogatory comments when I passed them. One asked, for example, "Does she have a penis?"

Because of the assumption that a "masculine" woman is a lesbian, there is the risk of homophobic reactions (Gardner 1995; Lucal 1997). Perhaps surprisingly, I find that I am much more likely to be taken for a man than for a lesbian, at least based on my interactions with people and their reactions to me. This might be because people are less likely to reveal that they have taken me for a lesbian because it is less relevant to an encounter or because they believe this would be unacceptable. But I think it is more likely a product of the strength of our two-and-only-two system. I give enough masculine cues that I am seen not as a deviant woman but rather as a man, at least in most cases. The problem seems not to be that people are uncertain about my gender, which might lead them to conclude that I was a lesbian once they realized I was a woman. Rather, I seem to fit easily into a gender category—just not the one with which I identify. In fact, because men represent the dominant gender in our society, being mistaken for a man can protect me from other types of gendered harassment. Because men can move around in public spaces safely (at least relative to women), a "masculine" woman also can enjoy this freedom (Devor 1989).

On the other hand, my use of particular spaces—those designated as for women only—may be challenged. Feinberg provided an intriguing analysis of the public rest room experience. She characterized women's reactions to a masculine person in a public rest room as "an example of genderphobia" (1996, 117), viewing such women as policing gender boundaries rather than believing that there really is a man in the women's rest room. She argued that women who truly believed that there was a man in their midst would react differently. Although this is an interesting perspective on her experiences, my experiences do not lead to the same conclusion.[6]

Enough people have said to me that "This is the ladies' room" or have said to their companions that "There was a man in there" that I take their reactions at face value. Still, if the two-and-only-two gender system is to be maintained, participants must be involved in policing the categories and their attendant identities and spaces. Even if policing boundaries is not explicitly intended, boundary maintenance is the effect of such responses to people's gender displays.

Boundaries and margins are an important component of both my experiences of gender and our theoretical understanding of gendering processes. I am in effect both woman and not woman. As a woman who often is a social man but who also is a woman living in a patriarchal society, I am in a unique position to see and act.

I sometimes receive privileges usually limited to men, and I sometimes am oppressed by my status as a deviant woman. I am, in a sense, an outsider within (Collins 1991). Positioned on the boundaries of gender categories, I have developed

a consciousness that I hope will prove transformative (Anzaldua 1987). In fact, one of the reasons why I decided to continue my non-participation in femininity was that my sociological training suggested that this could be one of my contributions to the eventual dismantling of patriarchal gender constructs. It would be my way of making the personal political. I accepted being taken for a man as the price I would pay to help subvert patriarchy. I believed that all of the inconveniences I was enduring meant that I actually was doing something to bring down the gender structures that entangled all of us.

Then, I read Lorber's (1994) *Paradoxes of Gender* and found out, much to my dismay, that I might not actually be challenging gender after all. Because of the way in which doing gender works in our two-and-only-two system, gender displays are simply read as evidence of one of the two categories. Therefore, gender bending, blending, and passing between the categories do not question the categories themselves. If one's social gender and personal (true) gender do not correspond, then this is irrelevant unless someone notices the lack of congruence.

This reality brings me to a paradox of my experiences. First, not only do others assume that I am one gender or the other, but I also insist that I *really am* a member of one of the two gender categories. That is, I am female; I self-identify as a woman. I do not claim to be some other gender or to have no gender at all. I simply place myself in the wrong category according to stereotypes and cultural standards; the gender I present, or that some people perceive me to be presenting, is inconsistent with the gender with which I identify myself as well as with the gender I could be "proven" to be. Socially, I display the wrong gender; personally, I identify as the proper gender.

Second, although I ultimately would like to see the destruction of our current gender structure, I am not to the point of personally abandoning gender. Right now, I do not want people to see me as genderless as much as I want them to see me as a woman. That is, I would like to expand the category of "woman" to include people like me. I, too, am deeply embedded in our gender system, even though I do not play by many of its rules. For me, as for most people in our society, gender is a substantial part of my personal identity (Howard and Hollander 1997). Socially, the problem is that I do not present a gender display that is consistently read as feminine. In fact, I consciously do not participate in the trappings of femininity. However, I do identify myself as a woman, not as a man or as someone outside of the two-and-only-two categories.

Yet, I do believe, as Lorber (1994) does, that the purpose of gender, as it currently is constructed, is to oppress women. Lorber analyzed gender as a "process of creating distinguishable social statuses for the assignment of rights and responsibilities" that ends up putting women in a devalued and oppressed position (1994, 32). As Martin put it, "Bodies that clearly delineate gender status facilitate the maintenance of the gender hierarchy" (1998, 495).

For society, gender means difference (Lorber 1994). The erosion of the boundaries would problematize that structure. Therefore, for gender to operate as it currently does, the category "woman" is expanded to include people like me. The maintenance of the gender structure is dependent on the creation of a few categories that are mutually exclusive, the members of which are as different as possible (Lorber 1994). It is the clarity of the boundaries between the categories that allows gender to be used to assign rights and responsibilities as well as resources and rewards.

It is that part of gender—what it is used for—that is most problematic. Indeed, is it not *patriarchal*—or, even more specifically, *heteropatriarchal*—constructions of gender that are actually the problem? It is not the differences between men and women, or the categories themselves, so much as the meanings ascribed to the categories and, even more important, the hierarchical nature of gender under patriarchy that is the problem (Johnson 1997). Therefore, I am rebelling not against my femaleness or even my womanhood; instead, I am protesting contemporary constructions of femininity and, at least indirectly, masculinity under patriarchy. We do not, in fact, know what gender would look like if it were not constructed around heterosexuality in the context of patriarchy. Although it is possible that the end of patriarchy would mean the end of gender, it is at least conceivable that something like what we now call gender could exist in a postpatriarchal future. The two-and-only-two categorization might well disappear, there being no hierarchy for it to justify. But I do not think that we should make the assumption that gender and patriarchy are synonymous.

Theoretically, this analysis points to some similarities and differences between the work of Lorber (1994) and the works of Butler (1990), Goffman (1976, 1977), and West and Zimmerman (1987). Lorber (1994) conceptualized gender as social structure, whereas the others focused more on the interactive and processual nature of gender. Butler (1990) and Goffman (1976, 1977) view gender as a performance, and West and Zimmerman (1987) examined it as something all of us do. One result of this difference in approach is that in Lorber's (1994) work, gender comes across as something that we are caught in, something that, despite any attempts to the contrary, we cannot break out of. This conclusion is particularly apparent in Lorber's argument that gender rebellion, in the context of our two-and-only-two system, ends up supporting what it purports to subvert. Yet, my own experiences suggest an alternative possibility that is more in line with the view of gender offered by West and Zimmerman (1987): If gender is a product of interaction, and if it is produced in a particular context, then it can be changed if we change our performances. However, the effects of a performance linger, and gender ends up being institutionalized. It is institutionalized, in our society, in a way that perpetuates inequality, as Lorber's (1994) work shows. So, it seems that a combination of these two approaches is needed.

In fact, Lorber's (1994) work seems to suggest that effective gender rebellion requires a more blatant approach—bearded men in dresses, perhaps, or more active responses to misattribution.

For example, if I corrected every person who called me "Sir," and if I insisted on my right to be addressed appropriately and granted access to women-only spaces, then perhaps I could start to break down gender norms. If I asserted my right to use public facilities without being harassed, and if I challenged each person who gave me "the look," then perhaps I would be contributing to the demise of gender as we know it. It seems that the key would be to provide visible evidence of the nonmutual exclusivity of the categories. Would *this* break down the patriarchal components of gender? Perhaps it would, but it also would be exhausting.

Perhaps there is another possibility. In a recent book, *The Gender Knot,* Johnson (1997) argued that when it comes to gender and patriarchy, most of us follow the paths of least resistance; we "go along to get along," allowing our actions to be shaped by the gender system. Collectively, our actions help patriarchy maintain and perpetuate a system of oppression and privilege. Thus, by withdrawing our support from this system by choosing paths of greater resistance, we can start to chip away at it. Many people participate in gender because they cannot imagine any alternatives. In my classroom, and in my interactions and encounters with strangers, my presence can make it difficult for people not to see that there *are* other paths. In other words, following from West and Zimmerman (1987), I can subvert gender by doing it differently.

For example, I think it is true that my existence does not have an effect on strangers who assume that I am a man and never learn otherwise. For them, I do uphold the two-and-only-two system. But there are other cases in which my existence can have an effect. For example, when people initially take me for a man but then find out that I actually am a woman, at least for that moment, the naturalness of gender may be called into question. In these cases, my presence can provoke a "category crisis" (Garber 1992, 16) because it challenges the sex/gender binary system.

The subversive potential of my gender might be strongest in my classrooms. When I teach

about the sociology of gender, my students can see me as the embodiment of the social construction of gender. Not all of my students have transformative experiences as a result of taking a course with me; there is the chance that some of them see me as a "freak" or as an exception. Still, after listening to stories about my experiences with gender and reading literature on the subject, many students begin to see how and why gender is a social product. I can disentangle sex, gender, and sexuality in the contemporary United States for them. Students can begin to see the connection between biographical experiences and the structure of society. As one of my students noted, I clearly live the material I am teaching. If that helps me to get my point across, then perhaps I am subverting the binary gender system after all. Although my gendered presence and my way of doing gender might make others— and sometimes even me—uncomfortable, no one ever said that dismantling patriarchy was going to be easy.

Notes

1. Ethnomethodology has been described as "the study of commonsense practical reasoning" (Collins 1988, 274). It examines how people make sense of their everyday experiences. Ethnomethodology is particularly useful in studying gender because it helps to uncover the assumptions on which our understandings of sex and gender are based.

2. I obviously have left much out by not examining my gendered experiences in the context of race, age, class, sexuality, region, and so forth. Such a project clearly is more complex. As Weston pointed out gender presentations are complicated by other statuses of their presenters: "What it takes to kick a person over into another gendered category can differ with race, class, religion, and time" (1996, 168). Furthermore, I am well aware that my whiteness allows me to assume that my experiences are simply a product of gender (see, e.g., hooks 1981; Lucal 1996; Spelman 1988; West and Fenstermaker 1995). For now, suffice it to say that it is my privileged position on some of these axes and my more disadvantaged position on others that combine to delineate my overall experience.

3. In fact, such experiences are not always limited to encounters with strangers. My grandmother, who does not see me often, twice has mistaken me for either my brother-in-law or some unknown man.

4. My experiences in rest rooms and other public spaces might be very different if I were, say, African American rather than white. Given the stereotypes of African American men, I think that white women would react very differently to encountering me (see, e.g., Staples [1986] 1993).

5. I also have noticed that there are certain types of rest rooms in which I will not be verbally challenged; the higher the social status of the place, the less likely I will be harassed. For example, when I go to the theater, I might get stared at, but my presence never has been challenged.

6. An anonymous reviewer offered one possible explanation for this. Women see women's rest rooms as their space; they feel safe, and even empowered, there. Instead of fearing men in such space, they might instead pose a threat to any man who might intrude. Their invulnerability in this situation is, of course, not physically based but rather socially constructed. I thank the reviewer for this suggestion.

REFERENCES

Anzaldua, G. 1987. *Borderlands/La Frontera.* San Francisco: Aunt Lute Books.

Berger, P. 1963. *Invitation to sociology.* New York: Anchor.

Butler, J. 1990. *Gender trouble.* New York: Routledge.

Collins, P. H. 1991. *Black feminist thought.* New York: Routledge.

Collins, R. 1988. *Theoretical sociology.* San Diego: Harcourt Brace Jovanovich.

Devor, H. 1989. *Gender blending: Confronting the limits of duality.* Bloomington: Indiana University Press.

Feinberg, L. 1996. *Transgender warriors.* Boston: Beacon.

Garber, M. 1992. *Vested interests: Cross-dressing and cultural anxiety.* New York: HarperPerennial.

Gardner, C. B. 1995. *Passing by: Gender and public harassment.* Berkeley: University of California.

Garfinkel, H. 1967. *Studies in ethnomethodology.* Englewood Cliffs, NJ: Prentice Hall.

Goffman, E. 1959. *The presentation of self in everyday life.* Garden City, NY. Doubleday.

———. 1963. *Stigma.* Englewood Cliffs, NJ: Prentice Hall.

———. 1967. *Interaction ritual.* New York: Anchor/ Doubleday.

———. 1976. Gender display. *Studies in the Anthropology of Visual Communication* 3:69–77.

———. 1977. The arrangement between the sexes. *Theory and Society* 4:301–31.

hooks, b. 1981. *Ain't I a woman: Black women and feminism.* Boston: South End Press.

Howard, J. A., and J. Hollander. 1997. *Gendered situations, gendered selves.* Thousand Oaks, CA: Sage.

Johnson, A. G. 1997. *The gender knot: Unraveling our patriarchal legacy.* Philadelphia: Temple University Press.

Kessler, S. J., and W. McKenna. 1978. *Gender: An ethnomethodological approach.* New York: John Wiley.

Krieger, S. 1991. *Social science and the self.* New Brunswick, NJ: Rutgers University Press.

Lorber, J. 1994. *Paradoxes of gender.* New Haven, CT. Yale University Press.

———. 1996. Beyond the binaries: Depolarizing the categories of sex, sexuality, and gender. *Sociological Inquiry* 66:143–59.

Lucal, B. 1996. Oppression and privilege: Toward a relational conceptualization of race. *Teaching Sociology* 24:245–55.

———. 1997. "Hey, this is the ladies' room!": Gender misattribution and public harassment. *Perspectives on Social Problems* 9:43–57.

Martin, K. A. 1998. Becoming a gendered body: Practices of preschools. *American Sociological Review* 63:494–511.

Mills, C. W. 1959. *The sociological imagination.* London: Oxford University Press.

Myhre, J. R. M. 1995. One bad hair day too many, or the hairstory of an androgynous young feminist. In *Listen up: Voices from the next feminist generation,* edited by B. Findlen. Seattle, WA: Seal Press.

Reinharz, S. 1992. *Feminist methods in social research.* New York: Oxford University Press.

Richardson, L. 1994. Writing: A method of inquiry. In *Handbook of Qualitative Research,* edited by N. K. Denzin and Y. S. Lincoln. Thousand Oaks, CA: Sage.

Riemer, J. W. 1977. Varieties of opportunistic research. *Urban Life* 5:467–77.

———. 1988. Work and self. In *Personal sociology,* edited by P. C. Higgins and J. M. Johnson. New York: Praeger.

Spelman, E. V. 1988. *Inessential woman: Problems of exclusion in feminist thought.* Boston: Beacon.

Staples, B. 1993. Just walk on by. In *Experiencing race, class, and gender in the United States,* edited by V. Cyrus. Mountain View, CA: Mayfield. (Originally published 1986)

West, C., and S. Fenstermaker. 1995. Doing difference. *Gender & Society* 9:8–37.

West, C., and D. H. Zimmerman. 1987. Doing gender. *Gender & Society* 1:125–51.

Zimmerman, D. H. 1992. They were all doing gender, but they weren't all passing: Comment on Rogers. *Gender & Society* 6:192–98.

Introduction to Reading 3

Sharon E. Preves, a sociologist, has done groundbreaking research on what it is like to live in contemporary America with an intersexed body that doesn't conform to "standard" medical definitions of male and female. She recruited subjects for her study by contacting established intersex support groups in the United States and Canada, yet finding willing interviewees was difficult because intersexuality is largely invisible and intersexed people generally don't self-identify as intersexed. Despite this challenge, Preves interviewed 37 intersexed adults in a private, face-to-face format, largely in participants' homes. Her book, from which this excerpt is taken, is built on her subjects' personal narratives.

1. Why does the author state that "bodies that are considered normal or abnormal are not inherently that way"?

2. Why is intersexuality a social, not medical, problem?

3. What themes are shared between this reading and the piece by Betsy Lucal?

BEYOND PINK AND BLUE

Sharon E. Preves

Recently I participated in a cultural diversity fieldtrip with twenty-two second graders in St. Paul, Minnesota. When I arrived at their school, the kids were squirrelly with anticipation. They were a colorful and varied bunch—some were tall and thin, others short and stout. Moreover, they were from a variety of racial and ethnic backgrounds and spoke nearly a half dozen native languages. When it was time to begin our community walking tour, the teachers attempted to bring the busy group to order quickly. How did they go about doing so? They told the children to form two lines: one for girls and the other for boys. The children did so seamlessly because they had been asked to line up in this manner countless number of times before. Within moments, the children were quiet and attentive. I was struck then, as I had been many times before, by how often and in the most basic ways societies are organized by a distinction between sexes. Even with children of every shape and color, the gender divide worked as a sure way to bring order to chaos. "Girls in one line, boys in the other." But sometimes the choice between the lines—and sexes—isn't so easy.

Which line would you join? Think about it seriously for a minute. How do you know whether to line up with the girls or the boys? For that matter, what sex or gender *are* you and how did you *become* the gender you are? Moreover, how do you *know* what sex and gender you are? Who decides? These questions may seem ridiculous. You may be saying to yourself, "Of course I know what gender I am; forget this book." But really stop to think about how you know what sex you are and how you acquired your gender. Most of us have been taught that sex is anatomical and gender is social. What's more, many of us have never had the occasion to explore our gender or sexual identities, because neither has given us cause for reflection. Much like Caucasians who say they "have none" when asked to explore their racial identity, many women and men find it difficult to be reflective about how they know and "do" gender.[1]

This article explores what happens to people who, from the time of their birth or early adolescence, inhabit bodies whose very anatomy does not afford them an easy choice between the gender lines.[2] Every day babies are born with bodies that are deemed sexually ambiguous, and with regularity they are surgically altered to reflect the sexual anatomy associated with "standard" female or male sex assignment. There are numerous ways to respond to this plurality of physical type, including no response at all. Because sex and gender operate as inflexible and central organizing principles of daily existence in this culture, such indifference is rare if not nonexistent. Instead, interference with sex and gender norms are cast as a major disturbance to social

order, and people go to remarkable lengths to eradicate threats to the norm, even though they occur with great regularity.

Recent estimates indicate that approximately one or two in every two thousand infants are born with anatomy that some people regard as sexually ambiguous. These frequency estimates vary widely and are, at best, inconclusive. Those I provide here are based on an exhaustive review of recent medical literature.[3] This review suggests that approximately one or two per two thousand children are born with bodies considered appropriate for genital reconstruction surgery because they do not conform to socially accepted norms of sexual anatomy. Moreover, nearly 2 percent are born with chromosome, gonad, genital, or hormone features that could be considered "intersexed"; that is, children born with ambiguous genitalia, sexual organs, or sex chromosomes. Additional estimates report the frequency of this sexual variance as comprising approximately 1 to 4 percent of all births.[4]

These estimates differ so much because definitions of sexual ambiguity vary tremendously.[5] This is largely because distinctions between female and male bodies are actually on more of a continuum rather than a dichotomy. The criteria for what counts as female or male, or sexually ambiguous for that matter, are human standards. That is, bodies that are considered normal or abnormal are not inherently that way. They are, rather, classified as aberrant or customary by social agreement.[6] We have, as humans, created categories for bodies that fit the norm and those that don't, as well as a systematic method of surgically attempting to correct or erase sexual variation. That we have done so is evidence of the regularity with which sexual variation occurs.

Melanie Blackless and colleagues suggest that the total frequency of nongenital sexual variation (cases of intersexed chromosomes or internal sexual organs) is much higher than one in two thousand.[7] They conclude that using a more inclusive definition of sexual ambiguity would yield frequency estimates closer to one or two per one hundred births, bringing us back to the 1 to 2 percent range.

To put these numbers in perspective, although its occurrence has only recently begun to be openly discussed, physical sexual ambiguity occurs about as often as the well-known conditions of cystic fibrosis and Down syndrome.[8] Since there are approximately four million babies born annually in the United States, a conservative estimate is that about two to four thousand babies are born per year in this country with features of their anatomy that vary from the physical characteristics typically associated with females and males.[9] Some are born with genitalia that are difficult to characterize as clearly female or male. Others have sex chromosomes that are neither XX nor XY, but some other combination, such as X, XXY, or chromosomes that vary throughout the cells of their bodies, changing from XX to XY from cell to cell. Still others experience unexpected physical changes at puberty, when their bodies exhibit secondary sex characteristics that are surprisingly "opposite" their sex of assignment. Some forms of sexual ambiguity are inherited genetically, while others are brought on by hormonal activity during gestation, or by prescription medication women take during pregnancy. Regardless of its particular manifestation or cause, most forms of physical sexual anatomy that vary from the norm are medically classified and treated as forms of intersexuality, or hermaphroditism.

Take Claire's experience as an example.[10] Claire is a middle-class white woman and mother of two teenage daughters who works as a writer and editor. She was forty-four years old when she conveyed the following story to me during a four-hour interview that took place in her home. Claire underwent a clitorectomy when she was six years old at her parents' insistence, after clinicians agreed that her clitoris was just "too large" and they had to intervene. The size of her clitoris seemed to cause problems not for young Claire, but for the adults around her. Indeed, there was nothing ambiguous about Claire's sex before the surgery. She has XX chromosomes, has functioning female reproductive organs, and later in life went through a physically uneventful female puberty. Claire's experience illustrates that having a large clitoris is perceived as a physical trait dangerous to existing notions of gender and sexuality, despite the sexual pleasure it could have given Claire and her future sexual partners. In fact, doctors classify a large clitoris as a medical condition referred to as "clitoral megaly" or "clitoral hypertrophy." Conversely, small penises for anatomical boys are classified as a medical problem called "micropenis."

Reflecting on the reasons for the clitorectomy she underwent at the age of six, Claire said, "I don't feel that my sex was ambiguous at all. There was never that question. But I'm sure that [clitorectomies] have been done forever because parents just [don't] like big clitorises because they look too much like a penis." Even more alarming are the physical and emotional outcomes of genital surgery that might be experienced by the patient. About the after effects of her surgery, Claire said,

> They just took the clitoris out and then whip stitched the hood together, so it's sort of an odd-looking thing. I don't know what they were hoping to preserve, although I remember my father thinking that if someone saw me, it would look normal because there's just a little skin poking out between my lips so it wouldn't look strange. I remember I was in the hospital for five days. And then it just got better and everything was forgotten, until I finally asked about it when I was twelve. [There was] total and complete silence. You know, it was never, never mentioned. I know you know what that does. I was just in agony trying to figure out who I was. And, you know, why . . . what sex I was. And feeling like a freak, which is a very common story. And then when I was twelve, I asked my father what had been done to me. And his answer was, "Don't be so self-examining." And that was it. I never asked again [until I was thirty-five].

During the course of my research I spoke with many other adults across North America who had childhood experiences remarkably similar to Claire's. Their stories are laden with family and medical secrecy, shame, and social isolation, as well as perseverance and strength of spirit, and eventual pride in their unique bodies and perspectives.

Personal Narratives

Being labeled as a misfit, by peers, by family members, or by medical diagnosis and treatment, is no doubt a challenge to one's identity development and stability. This is especially true for children whose bodies render traditional gender classification ineffective, for there is seemingly no place to belong without being gendered, especially during childhood. Negotiating identity, one's basic sense of place and self, is a challenge for many of us, and is potentially far more challenging for people whose sex is called into question. The social expectation for gender stability and conformity is prevalent across social spheres. Nearly every aspect of social life is organized by one's sex assignment—from schooling and relationships, to employment and religion, sports and entertainment, medicine and law. Because North American cultures are structured by gender, successful participation in society's organizations and personal relationships requires gender categorization. Many of us negotiate questions of sex and gender with little effort. Others, however, do not have the luxury or ease of fitting neatly into a dual-gendered culture.

In an attempt to understand how intersexuals experience and cope with their marginality in a society that demands sexual conformity, I turned to them directly for answers. In the end, I interviewed thirty-seven individuals throughout North America whose bodies have been characterized by others as intersexed.

Intersex Is a Social, Not Medical, Problem

While being born with indeterminate sexual organs indeed problematizes a binary understanding of sex and gender, several studies show—and there seems to be general consensus (even among the doctors performing the "normalizing" operations)—that most children with ambiguous sexual anatomy do not require medical intervention for their physiological health.[11]

Nevertheless, the majority of sexually ambiguous infants are medically assigned a definitive sex, often undergoing repeated genital surgeries and ongoing hormone treatments, to "correct" their variation from the norm.

It is my argument that medical treatments to create genitally *unambiguous* children are not performed entirely or even predominantly for the sake of preventing stigmatization and trauma to the child. Rather, these elaborate, expensive, and risky procedures are performed to maintain social order for the institutions and adults that surround that child. Newborns are completely oblivious to the rigid social conventions to which their families and caregivers adhere. Threats to the duality of sex and gender undermine inflexibly gendered occupational, education, and family structures, as well as heterosexuality itself. After all, if one's sex is in doubt, how would they identify their sexual orientation, given that heterosexuality, homosexuality, and even bisexuality are all based on a sexual binary? So, when adults encounter a healthy baby with a body that is not easily "sexed," they may understandably experience an inability to imagine a happy and successful future for that child. They may wonder how the child will fit in at school and with its peers, and how the child will negotiate dating and sexuality, as well as family and a career. But most parents don't find a real need to address these questions until years after a child's birth. Furthermore, it is my contention that parents and caregivers of intersexed children don't need to be so concerned about addressing the "personal troubles" of their children either. Rather, we should all turn our attention to the "public issues" and problems wrought by unwavering, merciless adherence to sex and gender binarism.[12]

That medical sex assignment procedures could be considered cosmetic raises several important questions, including the human influences in constructing definitions of health and pathology. Bodies are classified as healthy or pathological (or as normal and abnormal) through social expectations, human discourse, and human interaction. As a result, what is seen as normal or standard in one culture and time is seen as aberrant and strange in another. Indeed, deviance itself is created socially through human actions, beliefs, and judgments.[13] Consider Gilbert Herdt's anthropological research in Papua New Guinea. The Sambia males of Papua New Guinea believe that they become masculine by ingesting the semen of adult men. In order to become virile, therefore, Sambian boys perform oral sex on and ingest the semen of adult men.[14] According to Herdt, such activity is considered a standard rite of passage to manhood among the Sambia in Papua New Guinea, much like a bar or bat mitzvah is seen as a customary ritual of young adulthood among Jews.

I offer the above example to illustrate that definitions of normal and abnormal vary tremendously by culture. That said, there is no reason to consider intersex as necessarily problematic in itself. In fact, since physical sexual ambiguity has been shown to be a cause of health problems in only very rare cases, sexual ambiguity could be considered a *social* problem, rather than a physical problem. Rare physical problems do occur in cases where eliminating bodily waste, such as urine and feces, is difficult because of internal physiological complications or infrequent cases of salt-wasting congenital adrenal hyperplasia, which is a condition where children have hyperactive adrenal glands and hormone therapy is required to regulate the endocrine system.[15] Because Western cultures place such strong emphasis on sexual (and other forms of) categorization, intersex ambiguity causes major social disruption and discomfort. If there were less concern about gender, there would be less concern about gender variation. Because intersex is often identified in a medical setting by physicians during childbirth or during a pediatric appointment in later childhood, the social response to intersex "deviance" is largely medical.

A BRIEF HISTORY OF SEXUAL AMBIGUITY IN MEDICINE

According to one theory, sex distinctions were based on a continuum of heat, with males' bodies being internally hotter than females', thus creating the impetus for external male reproductive organs and colder, internal female organs.[16] In Thomas Laqueur's analysis, this differential temperature theory actually provided the basis for a one-sex conceptual model, with females being seen as the inverse of males.[17] (That is, female and male anatomy was viewed as identical, although the vagina was viewed as an inverted penis, the uterus as an internalized scrotum, the fallopian tubes as seminal vesicles, the ovaries as internal testicles, and so on.)

In their historical review of medical literature, Myra Hird and Jenz Germon demonstrate that based on this humoral theory, sixteenth-century philosophers and physicians regarded hermaphroditism as evidence of two sexes existing in one body.[18] With the invention of microscopy and surgery on *living* patients at the beginning of the twentieth century (rather than upon autopsy after death), the notion of anatomical hermaphroditism was transformed. Hird and Germon argue that the newer concept of one "true sex" being hidden by sexually ambiguous anatomy didn't enter the fray until Klebs's classification system. Klebs identified five categories of sexual classification: female, male, female pseudohermaphrodite, male pseudohermaphrodite, and true hermaphrodite. Klebs identified people as true hermaphrodites only if they had the very rare combination of ovarian and testicular tissue in the same body. All other cases of hermaphroditism, for example people who had ambiguous genitalia but no combination of gonadal tissue, were identified as pseudohermaphrodites. Klebs's classification system served to drastically decrease the number of people who were defined as hermaphrodites, and thus reinforced the newly popular thought that there were two and only two sexes: female and male, with a very rare and unusual exception in the case of true hermaphroditism.

Early surgical attempts to regulate the appearance of sexual anatomy, such as lowering abdominal testicles, appeared in the beginning of the nineteenth century.[19] A primary motive for the social insistence upon outward displays of gender clarity was an underlying fear of homo-sexuality, or "hermaphroditism of the soul," a threat that was present in the sexually ambiguous (or, quite literally, *bisexual*) body of the her-maphrodite. By appearing, outwardly, to be of the "other" sex, it was feared hermaphrodites would tempt heterosexual partners into "homo-sexual" relations.[20]

As Alice Dreger, Myra Hird and Jenz Germon, and others point out, medical methods of response to physical sexual ambiguity have changed yet again in more recent times.[21] Unlike eighteenth- and nineteenth-century medical attempts to reveal a "true sex" that is disguised by pseudohermaphroditic (or false) sexual ambi-guity, the current medical model relies on mak-ing a sex assignment that is most appropriate for heterosexual capacity. Hird and Germon refer to this as the "best sex" mentality in medical sex assignment.

UNANSWERED QUESTIONS

Despite the recent mobilization and activism of thousands of intersexuals worldwide, the social focus on gender categorization and genital regularity continues to be strong, in both medical and nonmedical sectors. In order to improve the quality of life not just for those labeled intersexed, but for us all, we must remove or reduce the importance of gender categorization and the need for gender catego-ries, including the category of intersex itself. A more realistic and tangible goal is to respond far less to sexual variance. That is, to focus on the health of children born with genital varia-tion, not on their difference. An outcome of this philosophy would prevent physicians from cutting into the bodies of intersexed patients unless a clear physiological need presents its necessity. Moreover, this philosophy would ask us to hold off on rushing kids into a patient mentality and instead send them to speak with counselors or other kids with divergent sexual anatomy. We should refrain from identifying

them as different in any way, unless a child demonstrates a need and a desire for such spe-cial attention. Pushing the label of sexual ambiguity, sexual difference, or "sexual prob-lem" onto children through medicalization, or remedicalization via social services, leads to stigmatization of the self. What's more, there is no inherent need for children to have therapy unless a need presents itself. We shouldn't restigmatize intersexuals by assuming a need for therapy or "preventative treatment" on the basis of physical variation alone. While these support resources are invaluable for people who have already been adversely affected by negative socialization—and family members and clinicians should be prepared to call on support services if necessary—we shouldn't assume that genital variation itself creates a pathological need.

Will the category and identity "intersex" disappear altogether if doctors stop treating, studying, and classifying children in this way, or will this category continue to expand further into academic and social realms until its presence is solidified in a way similar to the presence of transgender, gay, or alcoholic identities? Focusing less on articulating the category "intersex" may indeed be a step in the right direction toward the ultimate goal of focusing less on gender and sexual categoriza-tion. After all, returning to the elementary school children and the "gender lines" to which they are socialized to adhere, the clear message from my research is to decrease sex and gender categorization rather than to create yet a third rigid sex or gender line for us all to ponder. Instead, we should focus on loving and accepting children as they are, not because of or in spite of their differences, but rather just because they are terrific kids in their own right with or without bodies that vary from some mythical standard.

While my research addresses many ques-tions about the construction and negotiation of contested sex, several important issues related to assessing and revising the treatment of sexual ambiguity remain untouched. Future research in this area should include intensive research on two additional groups: parents of intersex children and clinicians who specialize in intersex management. This research should focus on parents' and clinicians' personal and professional experiences with intersexuality and their perspectives on genital variation and the management thereof. Additional research should include observation of family consultations with medical staff and follow-up visits regarding the "sexing" of intersexed infants, in order to offer further insight into the interactional aspect of the social construction of sex and gender. Timely research in this area may provide further empirical data to inform the current debate and potential shift in intersex clinical management.

Despite my systematic analysis of former patients' experiences with medical sex assignment, the void remains for a rigorous analysis of the experiences of those with variant sexual anatomy who are not associated with intersex support and advocacy organizations and those who did not undergo medical sex assignment. This research is critical because proponents of surgical sex assignment will most likely resist clinical reform until the experiences of these populations are better understood. Until then, critics of my research and that of others will continue to shrug off the overwhelming dissatisfaction and trauma reported by intersex activists as representative of a disgruntled but vocal minority.

Far more could also be learned about the impact of peer social support as a means of reframing sexual ambiguity in a more positive light. In order to develop effective recommendations for clinical practice as they relate to peer advocacy, further investigation is needed that focuses specifically on the role of social support in coping with difference. Clinical mandates should also be informed by further research on the impact of age-appropriate disclosure of information to intersexuals and their family members. Developing a longitudinal research

program with this focus is possible now that some children deemed sexually ambiguous are being raised in a new era of social support and have access to complete and accurate diagnostic information.

Finally, the strategies and efforts of intersex activists warrant further attention, as does the overall concept of the intersex social movement. Due to their prolific appearances in print, film, and radio media, substantive content analysis of their activism efforts is possible. This analysis could inform a more nuanced understanding of models of coming-out and community empowerment rather than assimilation to an existing social norm. This research is now possible because there are already substantial archives related to this area, and because intersex patient, parent, and doctor communication, education, and support networks continue to emerge.

NOTES

1. West and Zimmerman 1987.

2. While there is tremendous cross-cultural variation in responding to physical sexual variation, I explore how North American intersexuals experience and cope with being labeled sexually ambiguous in a culture that demands sexual conformity.

3. Blackless et al. 2000.

4. Money 1989; Edgerton 1964; Fiedler 1978.

5. Dreger 1998b; Kessler 1998.

6. Hird 2000.

7. Blackless et al. 2000.

8. See Dreger 1998b:43; Desai 1997; and Roberts et al. 1998.

9. National Center for Health Statistics (2001). Note that others project an annual birthrate of 1,500–2,000 intersexed children in the United States (Beh and Diamond 2000).

10. Most research participants chose pseudonyms for themselves to be used in the study. Perhaps as evidence of their desire to overcome the secrecy and shame they associated with attempts to erase their intersexuality, 27 percent of those I interviewed chose to use their real names. I do not distinguish here or elsewhere between those who chose pseudonyms and those who did not.

11. Diamond and Sigmundson 1997b; Dreger 1998a; Kessler 1998.
12. Mills 1959:8.
13. Newman 2002; Becker 1963.
14. Herdt 1994, 1998.
15. Wilson and Reiner 1998; Kessler 1998; Diamond and Sigmundson 1997b.
16. Note that Aristotle valued "male" heat over "female" cold and viewed females' lack of heat as a sign of inferiority and even deformity (Cadden 1993).
17. Laqueur 1990.
18. Hird and Germon 2001.
19. Pagliassotti 1993.
20. Hekma 1994; Dreger 1995.
21. Dreger 1998b; Hird and Germon 2001.

REFERENCES

Becker, Howard. 1963. *The Outsiders.* New York: Free Press.

Blackless, Melanie, Anthony Charuvastra, Amanda Derryck, Anne Fausto-Sterling, Karl Lauzanne, and Ellen Lee. 2000. "How Sexually Dimorphic Are We?" *American Journal of Human Biology* 12(2): 151–166.

Cadden, Joan. 1993. *Meanings of Sex Differences in the Middle Ages: Medicine, Science, and Culture.* New York: Cambridge University Press.

Desai, Sindoor S. 1997. "Down Syndrome: A Review of the Literature." *Oral Surgery, Oral Medicine, Oral Pathology, Oral Radiology, and Endodontics.* September. *84*(3): 279–285.

Dreger, Alice Domurat. 1995. *Doubtful Sex: Cases and Concepts of Hermaphroditism in France and Britain, 1868–1915.* Ph.D. dissertation, Indiana University.

———. 1998a. "'Ambiguous Sex'—or Ambivalent Medicine? Ethical Issues in the Treatment of Intersexuality." *Hastings Center Report 28*(3): 24–36.

———. 1998b. *Hermaphrodites and the Medical Invention of Sex.* Cambridge, Mass.: Harvard University Press.

Hekma, Gert. 1994. "A Female Soul in a Male Body: Sexual Inversion as Gender Inversion in Nineteenth-Century Sexology." In *Third Sex, Third Gender: Beyond Sexual Dimorphism in Culture and History,* ed. Gilbert Herdt, 213–239. New York: Zone Books.

Herdt, Gilbert. 1994. "Mistaken Sex: Culture, Biology and the Third Sex in New Guinea." In *Third Sex, Third Gender: Beyond Sexual Dimorphism in Culture and History,* ed. Gilbert Herdt, 419–445. New York: Zone Books.

———. 1998. *Same Sex, Different Cultures: Exploring Gay and Lesbian Lives.* Boulder, Colo.: Westview Press.

Hird, Myra J. 2000. "Gender's Nature: Intersexuality, Transsexualism and the 'Sex'/'Gender' Binary." *Feminist Theory 1*(3): 347–364.

Hird, Myra J., and Jenz Germon. 2001. "The Intersexual Body and the Medical Regulation of Gender." In *Constructing Gendered Bodies,* ed. Kathryn Backett-Milburn and Linda McKie, 162–178. New York: Palgrave.

Kessler, Suzanne J. 1998. *Lessons from the Intersexed.* New Brunswick, N.J.: Rutgers University Press.

Laqueur, Thomas. 1990. *Making Sex: Body and Gender from the Greeks to Freud.* Cambridge, Mass.: Harvard University Press.

Mills, C. Wright. 1959. *The Sociological Imagination.* New York: Oxford University Press.

Money, John. 1989. *The Geraldo Rivera Show.* "Hermaphrodites: The Sexually Unfinished."

National Center for Health Statistics. 2001. "Births: Preliminary Data for 2000." NVSR 49, No. 5. 20 pp. (PHS) 2001–1120.

Newman, David. 2002. *Sociology: Exploring the Architecture of Everyday Life.* 4th ed. Thousand Oaks, Calif.: Pine Forge Press.

Pagliassotti, Druann. 1993. "On the Discursive Construction of Sex and Gender." *Communication Research 20*(3): 472–493.

Roberts, Helen E., Janet D. Cragan, Joanne Cono, Muin J. Khoury, Mark R. Weatherly, and Cynthia A. Moore. 1998. "Increased Frequency of Cystic Fibrosis among Infants with Jejunoileal Atresia." *American Journal of Medical Genetics* 78: 446–449.

West, Candace, and Don H. Zimmerman. 1987. "Doing Gender." *Gender & Society 1*(2): 125–151.

Wilson, Bruce E., and William G. Reiner. 1998. "Management of Intersex: A Shifting Paradigm." *Journal of Clinical Ethics* 9(4): 360–369.

Introduction to Reading 4

Robert M. Sapolsky is professor of biology and neurology at Stanford University and a research associate with the Institute of Primate Research, National Museums of Kenya. He is the author of *The Trouble With Testosterone, Why Zebras Don't Get Ulcers,* and, most recently, *A Primate's Memoir.* Sapolsky has lived as a member of a baboon troop in Kenya, conducting cutting-edge research on these beautiful and complex primates. In this article, he uses his keen wit and scientific understanding to debunk the widely held myth that testosterone causes aggression in males.

1. Why do many Americans want to believe that biological factors, such as hormones, are the basis of gender differences and inequalities?

2. Sapolsky says that hormones have a "permissive effect." What does "permissive effect" mean in terms of the relationship between testosterone and aggression?

3. How does research on testosterone, male monkeys, and spotted hyenas help one grasp the role of social factors and environment in behavioral biology?

THE TROUBLE WITH TESTOSTERONE

Robert M. Sapolsky

Face it, we all do it. We all believe in certain stereotypes about certain minorities. The stereotypes are typically pejorative and usually false. But every now and then, they are true. I write apologetically as a member of a minority about which the stereotypes are indeed true. I am male. We males account for less than 50 percent of the population, yet we generate an incredibly disproportionate percentage of the violence. Whether it is something as primal as having an ax fight in an Amazonian clearing or as detached as using computer-guided aircraft to strafe a village, something as condemned as assaulting a cripple or as glorified as killing someone wearing the wrong uniform, if it is violent, males excel at it. Why should that be? We all think we know the answer. A dozen millennia ago or so, an adventurous soul managed to lop off a surly bull's testicles and thus invented behavioral endocrinology. It is unclear from the historical records whether this individual received either a grant or tenure as a result of this experiment, but it certainly generated an influential finding—something or other comes out of the testes that helps to make males such aggressive pains in the ass.

That something or other is testosterone.[1] The hormone binds to specialized receptors in muscles and causes those cells to enlarge. It binds to similar receptors in laryngeal cells and gives rise to operatic basses. It causes other secondary sexual characteristics, makes for relatively unhealthy blood vessels, alters biochemical events in the liver too dizzying to even contemplate, has a profound impact, no doubt, on the workings of cells in big toes. And it seeps into the brain, where it binds to those same "androgen" receptors and influences behavior in a way highly relevant to understanding aggression.

What evidence links testosterone with aggression? Some pretty obvious stuff. Males tend to have higher testosterone levels in their circulation than do females (one wild exception to that will be discussed later) and to be more aggressive. Times of life when males are swimming in testosterone (for example, after reaching puberty) correspond to when aggression peaks. Among numerous species, testes are mothballed most of the year, kicking into action and pouring out testosterone only during a very circumscribed mating season—precisely the time when male–male aggression soars.

Impressive, but these are only correlative data, testosterone repeatedly being on the scene with no alibi when some aggression has occurred. The proof comes with the knife, the performance of what is euphemistically known as a "subtraction" experiment. Remove the source of testosterone in species after species and levels of aggression typically plummet. Reinstate normal testosterone levels afterward with injections of synthetic testosterone, and aggression returns.

To an endocrinologist, the subtraction and replacement paradigm represents pretty damning proof: this hormone is involved. "Normal testosterone levels appear to be a prerequisite for normative levels of aggressive behavior" is the sort of catchy, hummable phrase that the textbooks would use. That probably explains why you shouldn't mess with a bull moose during rutting season. But that's not why a lot of people want to understand this sliver of science. Does the action of this hormone tell us anything about individual differences in levels of aggression, anything about why some males, some human males, are

exceptionally violent? Among an array of males—human or otherwise—are the highest testosterone levels found in the most aggressive individuals?

Generate some extreme differences and that is precisely what you see. Castrate some of the well-paid study subjects, inject others with enough testosterone to quadruple the normal human levels, and the high-testosterone males are overwhelmingly likely to be the more aggressive ones. However, that doesn't tell us much about the real world. Now do something more subtle by studying the normative variability in testosterone—in other words, don't manipulate anything, just see what everyone's natural levels are like—and high levels of testosterone and high levels of aggression still tend to go together. This would seem to seal the case—interindividual differences in levels of aggression among normal individuals are probably driven by differences in levels of testosterone. But this turns out to be wrong.

Okay, suppose you note a correlation between levels of aggression and levels of testosterone among these normal males. This could be because (a) testosterone elevates aggression; (b) aggression elevates testosterone secretion; (c) neither causes the other. There's a huge bias to assume option a, while b is the answer. Study after study has shown that when you examine testosterone levels when males are first placed together in the social group, testosterone levels predict nothing about who is going to be aggressive. The subsequent behavioral differences drive the hormonal changes, rather than the other way around.

Because of a strong bias among certain scientists, it has taken forever to convince them of this point. Behavioral endocrinologists study what behavior and hormones have to do with each other. How do you study behavior? You get yourself a notebook and a stopwatch and a pair of binoculars. How do you measure the hormones? You need a gazillion-dollar machine, you muck around with radiation and chemicals, wear a lab coat, maybe even goggles—the whole nine yards. Which toys would you rather get for

Christmas? Which facet of science are you going to believe in more? Because the endocrine aspects of the business are more high-tech, more reductive, there is the bias to think that it is somehow more scientific, more powerful. This is a classic case of what is often called physics envy, the disease among scientists where the behavioral biologists fear their discipline lacks the rigor of physiology, the physiologists wish for the techniques of the biochemists, the biochemists covet the clarity of the answers revealed by the molecular biologists, all the way down until you get to the physicists, who confer only with God.[2] Hormones seem to many to be more real, more substantive, than the ephemera of behavior, so when a correlation occurs, it must be because hormones regulate behavior, not the other way around.

As I said, it takes a lot of work to cure people of that physics envy, and to see that interindividual differences in testosterone levels don't predict subsequent differences in aggressive behavior among individuals. Similarly, fluctuations in testosterone levels within one individual over time do not predict subsequent changes in the levels of aggression in that one individual— get a hiccup in testosterone secretion one afternoon and that's not when the guy goes postal.

Look at our confusing state: normal levels of testosterone are a prerequisite for normal levels of aggression, yet changing the amount of testosterone in someone's bloodstream within the normal range doesn't alter his subsequent levels of aggressive behavior. This is where, like clockwork, the students suddenly start coming to office hours in a panic, asking whether they missed something in their lecture notes.

Yes, it's going to be on the final, and it's one of the more subtle points in endocrinology— what is referred to as a hormone having a "permissive effect." Remove someone's testes and, as noted, the frequency of aggressive behavior is likely to plummet. Reinstate precastration levels of testosterone by injecting that hormone, and precastration levels of aggression typically return. Fair enough. Now this time, castrate an individual and restore testosterone levels to only 20 percent of normal and . . . amazingly, normal precastration levels of aggression come back. Castrate and now generate twice the testosterone levels from before castration—and the same level of aggressive behavior returns. You need some testosterone around for normal aggressive behavior—zero levels after castration, and down it usually goes; quadruple it (the sort of range generated in weight lifters abusing anabolic steroids), and aggression typically increases. But anywhere from roughly 20 percent of normal to twice normal and it's all the same; the brain can't distinguish among this wide range of basically normal values.

We seem to have figured out a couple of things by now. First, knowing the differences in the levels of testosterone in the circulation of a bunch of males will not help you much in figuring out who is going to be aggressive. Second, the subtraction and reinstatement data seem to indicate that, nevertheless, in a broad sort of way, testosterone causes aggressive behavior. But that turns out not to be true either, and the implications of this are lost on most people the first thirty times you tell them about it. Which is why you'd better tell them about it thirty-one times, because it is the most important point of this piece.

Round up some male monkeys. Put them in a group together, and give them plenty of time to sort out where they stand with each other— affiliative friendships, grudges and dislikes. Give them enough time to form a dominance hierarchy, a linear ranking system of numbers 1 through 5. This is the hierarchical sort of system where number 3, for example, can pass his day throwing around his weight with numbers 4 and 5, ripping off their monkey chow, forcing them to relinquish the best spots to sit in, but, at the same time, remembering to deal with numbers 1 and 2 with shit-eating obsequiousness.

Hierarchy in place, it's time to do your experiment. Take that third-ranking monkey and give him some testosterone. None of this within-the-normal-range stuff. Inject a ton of it into him, way higher than what you normally see in a rhesus monkey; give him enough testosterone to grow antlers and a beard on every neuron in his brain. And, no surprise, when you then check the behavioral data, it turns out that he will probably be participating in more aggressive interactions than before. So even though small fluctuations in the levels of the hormone don't seem to matter much, testosterone still causes aggression. But that would be wrong. Check out number 3 more closely. Is he now raining aggressive terror on any and all in the group, frothing in an androgenic glaze of indiscriminate violence? Not at all. He's still judiciously kowtowing to numbers 1 and 2, but has simply become a total bastard to numbers 4 and 5. This is critical: testosterone isn't *causing* aggression, it's *exaggerating* the aggression that's already there.

Another example just to show we're serious. There's a part of your brain that probably has lots to do with aggression, a region called the amygdala.[3] Sitting right near it is the Grand Central Station of emotion-related activity in your brain, the hypothalamus. The amygdala communicates with the hypothalamus by way of a cable of neuronal connections called the stria terminalis. No more jargon, I promise. The amygdala has its influence on aggression via that pathway, with bursts of electrical excitation called action potentials that ripple down the stria terminalis, putting the hypothalamus in a pissy mood.

Once again, do your hormonal intervention; flood the area with testosterone. You can do that by injecting the hormone into the bloodstream, where it eventually makes its way to this part of the brain. Or you can be elegant and surgically microinject the stuff directly into this brain region. Six of one, half a dozen of the other. The key thing is what doesn't happen next. Does testosterone now cause there to be action potentials surging down the stria terminalis? Does it turn on that pathway? Not at all. If and only if the amygdala is sending an aggression-provoking volley of action potentials down the stria terminalis, testosterone increases the rate of such action potentials by shortening the resting time between them. It's not turning on the pathway, it's increasing the volume of signaling if it is already turned on. It's not causing aggression,

it's exaggerating the preexisting pattern of it, exaggerating the response to environmental triggers of aggression.

This transcends issues of testosterone and aggression. In every generation, it is the duty of behavioral biologists to try to teach this critical point, one that seems a maddening cliché once you get it. You take that hoary old dichotomy between nature and nurture, between biological influences and environmental influences, between intrinsic factors and extrinsic ones, and, the vast majority of the time, regardless of which behavior you are thinking about and what underlying biology you are studying, the dichotomy is a sham. No biology. No environment. Just the interaction between the two.

Do you want to know how important environment and experience are in understanding testosterone and aggression? Look back at how the effects of castration were discussed earlier. There were statements like "Remove the source of testosterone in species after species and levels of aggression typically plummet." Not "Remove the source . . . and aggression always goes to zero." On the average it declines, but rarely to zero, and not at all in some individuals. And the more social experience an individual had being aggressive prior to castration, the more likely that behavior persists sans cojones. Social conditioning can more than make up for the hormone.

Another example, one from one of the stranger corners of the animal kingdom: If you want your assumptions about the nature of boy beasts and girl beasts challenged, check out the spotted hyena. These animals are fast becoming the darlings of endocrinologists, sociobiologists, gynecologists, and tabloid writers. Why? Because they have a wild sex-reversal system—females are more muscular and more aggressive than males and are socially dominant over them, rare traits in the mammalian world. And get this: females secrete more of certain testosterone-related hormones than the males do, producing the muscles, the aggression (and, as a reason for much of the gawking interest in these animals, wildly masculinized private parts that make it supremely difficult to tell the sex of a hyena). So this appears to be a strong vote for the causative powers of high androgen levels in aggression and social dominance. But that's not the whole answer. High up in the hills above the University of California at Berkeley is the world's largest colony of spotted hyenas, massive bone-crunching beasts who fight with each other for the chance to have their ears scratched by Laurence Frank, the zoologist who brought them over as infants from Kenya. Various scientists are studying their sex-reversal system. The female hyenas are bigger and more muscular than the males and have the same weirdo genitals and elevated androgen levels that their female cousins do back in the savannah. Everything is in place except . . . the social system is completely different from that in the wild. Despite being stoked on androgens, there is a very significant delay in the time it takes for the females to begin socially dominating the males—they're growing up without the established social system to learn from.

When people first grasp the extent to which biology has something to do with behavior, even subtle, complex, human behavior, there is often an initial evangelical enthusiasm of the convert, a massive placing of faith in the biological components of the story. And this enthusiasm is typically of a fairly reductive type—because of physics envy, because reductionism is so impressive, because it would be so nice if there were a single gene or hormone or neurotransmitter or part of the brain that was it, the cause, the explanation of everything. And the trouble with testosterone is that people tend to think this way in an arena that really matters.

This is no mere academic concern. We are a fine species with some potential. Yet we are racked by sickening amounts of violence. Unless we are hermits, we feel the threat of it, often as a daily shadow. And regardless of where we hide, should our leaders push the button, we will all be lost in a final global violence. But as we try to understand and wrestle with this feature of our sociality, it is critical to remember the limits of the biology. Testosterone is never going to tell us much about the suburban teenager who, in his after-school chess club, has developed a particularly aggressive style with his bishops. And it certainly isn't going to tell us much about the teenager in some inner-city hellhole who has taken to mugging people. "Testosterone equals aggression" is inadequate for those who would offer a simple solution to the violent male—just decrease levels of those pesky steroids. And "testosterone equals aggression" is certainly inadequate for those who would offer a simple excuse: Boys will be boys and certain things in nature are inevitable. Violence is more complex than a single hormone. This is endocrinology for the bleeding heart liberal—our behavioral biology is usually meaningless outside the context of the social factors and environment in which it occurs.

NOTES

1. Testosterone is one of a family of related hormones, collectively known as "androgens" or "anabolic steroids." They all are secreted from the testes or are the result of a modification of testosterone, they all have a similar chemical structure, and they all do roughly similar things. Nonetheless, androgen mavens spend entire careers studying the important differences in the actions of different androgens. I am going to throw that subtlety to the wind and, for the sake of simplification that will horrify many, will refer throughout to all of these related hormones as "testosterone."

2. An example of physics envy in action. Recently, a zoologist friend had obtained blood samples from the carnivores that he studies and wanted some hormones in the sample assays in my lab. Although inexperienced with the technique, he offered to help in any way possible. I felt hesitant asking him to do anything tedious but, so long as he had offered, tentatively said, "Well, if you don't mind some unspeakable drudgery, you could number about a thousand assay vials." And this scientist, whose superb work has graced the most prestigious science journals in the world, cheerfully answered, "That's okay, how often do I get to do *real* science, working with test tubes?"

3. And no one has shown that differences in the size or shape of the amygdala, or differences in the numbers of neurons in it, can begin to predict differences in normal levels of aggression. Same punch line as with testosterone.

FURTHER READING

For a good general review of the subject, see E. Monaghan and S. Glickman, "Hormones and Aggressive Behavior," in J. Becker, M. Breedlove, and D. Crews, eds., *Behavioral Endocrinology* (Cambridge, Mass.: MIT Press, 1992), 261. This also has an overview of the hyena social system, as Glickman heads the study of the Berkeley hyenas.

For technical papers on the acquisition of the female dominance in hyenas, see S. Jenks, M. Weldele, L. Frank, and S. Glickman, "Acquisition of Matrilineal Rank in Captive Spotted Hyenas: Emergence of a Natural Social System in, Peer-Reared Animals and Their Offspring," *Animal Behavior* 50 (1995): 893; and L. Frank, S. Glickman, and C. Zabel, "Ontogeny of Female Dominance in the Spotted Hyaena: Perspectives from Nature and Captivity," in P. Jewell and G. Maloiy, eds., "The Biology of Large African Mammals in Their Environment," *Symposium of the Zoological Society of London* 61 (1989): 127.

I have emphasized that while testosterone levels in the normal range do not have much to do with aggression, a massive elevation of exposure, as would be seen in anabolic steroid abusers, does usually increase aggression. For a recent study in which even elevating into that range (approximately five times normal level) still had no effect on mood or behavior, see S. Bhasin, T. Storer, N. Berman, and colleagues, "The Effects of Supraphysiologic Doses of Testosterone on Muscle Size and Strength in Normal Men," *New England Journal of Medicine* 335 (1996): 1.

The study showing that raising testosterone levels in the middle-ranking monkey exaggerates pre-existing patterns of aggression can be found in A. Dixson and J. Herbert, "Testosterone, Aggressive Behavior and Dominance Rank in Captive Adult Male Talapoin Monkeys *(Miopithecus talapoin),*" *Physiology and Behavior* 18 (1977): 539.

For the demonstration that testosterone shortens the resting period between action potentials in neurons, see K. Kendrick and R. Drewert, "Testosterone Reduces Refractory Period of Stria Terminalis Neurons in the Rat Brain," *Science* 204 (1979): 877.

Introduction to Reading 5

Akihiko Hirose and Kay Kei-ho Pih offer a rich intersectional analysis of the co-construction of multiple masculinities. Their research is based on ethnographic observations in two mixed martial arts (MMA) settings: the Ultimate Fighting Championship (UFC) and its Japanese counterpart, PRIDE Fighting Championship (PRIDE). They attended MMA events and also gathered data at public Pay-Per-View venues. The two settings allowed Hirose and Pih to observe actual matches and audience responses. In addition, they analyzed MMA advertisements, print media, and Internet content. The UFC and PRIDE settings provided the authors with the opportunity to observe the uses and meanings of two technical styles—striking and submission—in the negotiation of hegemonic and marginalized masculinities.

1. "Selective authorization of the marginalized" is a central concept in Hirose and Pih's analysis. In your own words, define this concept and give an example from the reading.

2. What is the relationship between White American and Asian masculinities in MMA and in the larger relationship between the "West" and the "Orient"?

3. Why do the authors state that conventional masculine behaviors benefit an individual even if he or she prefers to do otherwise?

MEN WHO STRIKE AND MEN WHO SUBMIT

HEGEMONIC AND MARGINALIZED MASCULINITIES IN MIXED MARTIAL ARTS

Akihiko Hirose and Kay Kei-ho Pih

onnell ([1995]2005) theorizes that hegemonic masculinity usually develops relationships with three other forms of masculinity. *Complicit* masculinity is located on the same side as hegemonic masculinity, in that it benefits from the superiority of a hegemonic form. For instance, reliance on conventional masculine behavior usually benefits an individual when participating in sports, such as American football, even if he or she prefers to do otherwise. *Subordinated* masculinity, however, is positioned at the complete opposite of what hegemonic masculinity represents. Empirically, Connell uses homosexual men's status as an example that consists of "the repository of whatever is symbolically expelled from hegemonic masculinity" ([1995]2000, p. 78). This subordination is established because of what masculinity generally embodies in its "external" relation to femininity (Demetriou 2001). *Marginalized* masculinity, according to Connell, is "always relative to the *authorization* of the hegemonic masculinity of the dominant group" (Connell [1995]2000, 80–81).[1] Connell illustrates the position of marginalized masculinity by referring to the appropriation of black masculinity by whites in which "black sporting stars become exemplars of masculine toughness, while the fantasy figure of the black rapist plays an important role in sexual politics among whites" (p. 80). Although empirical examples, not theoretical explanations, tend to characterize the relationships of these three forms to hegemonic masculinity in Connell's writing, they are connected relationally and structurally. That is, identifiable attributes of each type are formed

only in relation to other forms. . . . The hegemonic form of white American masculinity is not hegemonic because of its substantive attributes commonly understood as men's qualities (e.g., assertiveness, strength, lack of emotion). Rather, it is the "other" that is relationally contrasted with the "self," and therefore, constructed as such, forms the relationship with the hegemonic self. In the case of white American and Asian masculinities, as Ishii-Kuntz (2003) puts it, "it is the formation of others or marginalized masculinities that in Western societies assists a white, middle-class and heterosexual native-born male in defining his own masculinity" by presenting marginalized masculinities of Asian American males "as either hypermasculine or effeminate" (p. 199).

Furthermore, the defining concept of the process of authorization suggests that the relationships between hegemonic and marginalized forms of masculinity are interactive rather than oppositional and mutually exclusive (Demetriou 2001). In criticizing the undertheorized nature of Connell's hegemonic masculinity, Demetriou argues, "hegemonic masculinity is not a purely white or heterosexual configuration of practice but it is a hybrid bloc that unites practices from diverse masculinities to ensure the reproduction of patriarchy" (2001, 337). . . . In the next section, by looking at the interaction between the forms of masculinity that have emerged in the newly instituted sport of MMA, the formation of hegemonic masculinity in a given institutional setting is argued to be a more reciprocal and dialectic process that involves the practice of selectively authorizing seemingly oppositional elements.

Mixed Martial Arts

Mixed martial arts[2] is a newly institutionalized genre of spectator combat sports that integrates various forms of martial arts and sports such as boxing, kickboxing, judo, and jujitsu. . . .

As the name indicates, MMA involves heterogeneous styles of sports and various arts that have already developed their own histories, traditions, techniques, and rules. The "mixing" of diverse athletic cultural backgrounds makes MMA rather unique compared to many other sports. . . . After a period of exploring and developing its own "identity" in the market and institutionalization in dealing with the environments of its organizational fields (DiMaggio and Powell 1983), MMA now presents a relatively coherent image and can be identified as an "industry" that has generated its own norms and standards. In other words, both external and internal to its social organization, MMA has developed its own distinctive culture. The elements of MMA that have an external connection tend to involve hypermasculine and hyperheterosexual discourse. Although cultural variations are easily observed among various regional markets, there is a fairly coherent public image that MMA is dangerous, violent, and thus only for "real" men.[3] Internally, the two major styles that athletes exhibit in MMA—striking and submission—have contrastingly emerged and can be commonly traced back in their technical origins to the training backgrounds of the athletes (Wertheim 2009).[4] These two styles are used to characterize every participant of an MMA match: those who rely on the style of striking to punch and kick an opponent or those who submit to an opponent using various grappling and submission techniques. Furthermore, the two major styles that athletes display are open to interpretations in cultural discourse and a differential assignment of masculine status.

Men Who Strike and Men Who Submit

In MMA, the group of various techniques that has been developed in boxing, kickboxing, karate, and kung-fu demonstrates a relatively coherent style that involves the striking of opponents through the use of kicks, punches, and hitting with the knees and the elbows. Fighters who rely on striking techniques are necessitated by technical effectiveness to maintain a certain distance from their opponents. Because of their distance and upright standing position, the style echoes the traditional "fight" style of the West. It easily resembles images of "bar fights," or "fist fights," which are not so foreign to those who are familiar with the simple yet stylized idea of two men fighting each other. Physical contact between the fighters is generally limited to brief moments of impact, ensuring fast-paced matches. There are several common ways to end a fight in MMA such as a knock out (i.e., KO), a referee stoppage, and a "tap out" (admission of loss by one of the fighters). When striking is the main competition technique of the fighters in a given match, a KO is the expected and preferred way to end the fight. A KO presents a very dramatic and sudden ending to the fight, and appears particularly more popular in North America than in other regions such as Japan.

By contrast, a fighting style that employs techniques from judo, jujitsu, sambo, and wrestling in the process of taking opponents down to the ground and uses various submission techniques faces a less enthusiastic reception from North American fans. When a fight goes to the "ground" from the "standing" sequences of exchanging punches and kicks, it easily and quickly generates booing from spectators. Fights between those who employ submission techniques, often called grapplers or submission specialists, may not end with a quick and sudden KO. Rather, the sequence may involve a more complex exchange of grappling techniques, and knowledge of such techniques can help fans "appreciate" the fight more than matches between strikers. Unlike the maintenance of certain physical distance by strikers, grapplers prefer close proximity between the two fighters for their skills to be effective. Constant and prolonged physical contact between fighters is, therefore, common. Technical exchanges of submission or grappling skills seem to appear less "violent" compared to the exchanges of punching and kicking between fighters. By contrast, striking matches are seen as being more "violent."[5] Thus, striking is viewed as a more manly way of fighting. A famous boxing trainer who also coaches MMA fighters commented on the opponent his trainee faces: "If we can keep the fight standing up, if he chooses to fight us like a man, we'll dominate him" (quoted in Hamlin 2009). Even if a fighter loses by being knocked out, his masculinity is preserved since he "did not quit."

Contrary to such hegemonic, John Wayne-like images of striking fights, submission fighters suffer from impressions of being "less violent." . . . Being seen as less violent in a sport in which physical strength and domination of an opponent is the fundamental goal can be damaging to one's masculine image by being labeled "less masculine." Because of this somewhat less "manly" and often feminized image of the submission technique, a win by submission can sometimes even be seen as "cheating" although it is a perfectly rule-bound way of achieving a victory.[6] The defeated not only lost because the winner used refined techniques but the opponent also cheated using an "unmanly" way of fighting. Occasionally, postfight comments include disappointment felt by the defeated striker on how his opponent "didn't fight like a man." In addition, submission is considered a more humiliating way to lose since the fighter is forced to admit, verbally or by "tapping" that he is giving up. To avoid such humiliation, some fighters actually refuse to tap, sometimes causing a loss of consciousness or bodily injury. Hence, there is a common expression in MMA, "tap or snap," which suggests the ultimate choice the fighter has to make when facing a voluntary admission of loss—a choice that does not exist for a fighter who is knocked out or defeated by striking.

A differential cultural reception based on the distinction between striking and submission seems more apparent to the UFC and other North American MMA organizations than those in Japan or Brazil. Following the commercial success of the UFC in the United States, Japan also professionalized and commercialized MMA as a sport, and the PRIDE fighting Championship (PRIDE) began in 1997 and lasted ten years until it became defunct in 2007.[7] Information on both MMA organizations on both sides of the Pacific was readily available due to active marketing, the use of Pay-Per-View, and the Internet. The Japanese MMA scene also shares the institutionalization of the two major fighting styles. Yet, the cultural reception and assignment of meanings to the two styles differ significantly from those of North America. Particularly, the submission fighting style in Japan does not show any sign of feminization compared to the American setting. The fights, even by two submission fighters who do not use striking and so long as they are technically refined, rarely receive booing from the audience as a sign of disapproval or dissatisfaction. Victories by submission are often viewed as being equally, if not more, legitimate compared to KOs by strikers. The exhibition of a form of masculinity based on technicality is not feminized.

Many submission and grappling techniques require relatively prolonged physical contact with one's opponent and often resemble culturally recognizable postures of homosexuality in America and Japan alike. Kimmel argues that "homophobia is a central organizing principle of our cultural definition of manhood" (Kimmel 1994, 131). . . . Thus, "the fear of being seen as a sissy dominates the cultural definition of manhood" in America (Kimmel 1994, 131). For wrestling (the dominant grappling sport in America[8]), being on the top of an opponent is technically preferred. A man on top symbolizes the sexually penetrating position as opposed to a man on bottom who is vulnerable of being signified as the penetrated and thus, the submitted. However, for many combat forms derived from East Asian martial arts such as judo or jujitsu, neither being on top nor on the bottom has a clear decisive advantage. Therefore, technically speaking, each position can be equally advantageous depending on the fighting style. In fact, one of the most common finishing moves in MMA using jujitsu submission techniques has often been initiated from the athletes who are at the bottom. . . .

SELECTIVE AUTHORIZATION OF THE MARGINALIZED

When MMA is seen as an arena in which different types of masculinity compete against one another, winning a match emasculates one's opponent and grants the winner the status of being a "real man." However, the chance of winning using submission skills is technically no greater than that of striking; therefore, well-trained grapplers can reverse the masculine ascendancy of strikers by submitting them. They can likewise be defeated in the process by being knocked out. It is true that rules do not limit fighters to choose either way of fighting; however, the general cultural trends seem to remain relatively unchanged. Striking is still extremely popular in the United States; men who submit are feminized. If so, why do feminized forms of MMA technique persist? The answer, we argue, lies in the relational nature of hegemonic masculinity, rather than technical superiority of certain styles. Relationally, the form of hegemonic masculinity embodied by the striking fighting style cannot generate and sustain its hegemonic status by itself. It needs and relies upon marginalized forms of masculinities. If strikers in MMA embody a specific, institutionalized form of the hegemonic "self," the "other" that is feminized and marginalized may be the grapplers and submission specialists. The relationship constructs and maintains the status of MMA hegemonic masculinity, not the other way around. At the same time, the relationship involves "the formative process of hegemonic masculinity as a reciprocal one, as a dialectic of appropriation/marginalization" (Demetriou 2001, 346).

If winning a match and eventually becoming a champion grants the status of being the strongest, toughest man in MMA, losing a match is clearly an effective form of emasculation. It then follows that losing to a feminized man who submits is particularly emasculating to a striker embodying hegemonic MMA masculinity. How can a striker maintain hegemonic status? The boundary between striking and submission in MMA masculinities is never clear cut. Empirically, there always emerge "hybrid" types in which the boundaries of technical styles become ambiguous. In fact, the process of hybridization is not necessarily a result of technical inevitability, but "a strategy for the reproduction of patriarchy" by the hegemonic form of masculinity (Demetriou 2001, 349). However, hegemonic masculinity tends to justify the primacy of the technical necessity of a gendered hierarchy just as all social structures empirically do. Hybridization is a type of domestication of otherness by the hegemonic form through the selective authorization process of marginalized elements. In fact, the marginalization of nonhegemonic elements by way of feminization comes with the process of appropriation of the elements into a hegemonic self as a form of selective authorization. As such, strikers in MMA adopt various submission techniques as the institutionalization of MMA further advances. Feminized and exotic techniques serve technically to advance their combat skills. The selective authorization process, however, often appears to legitimize the formerly less recognized elements to fulfill technical necessity. Here, when authorized, feminized elements can work as a type of cultural capital for hegemonic masculinity within the MMA field (Bourdieu [1986]2002).

A popular and exemplary striker in MMA, Mirko Filipović of Croatia, began his MMA career after moving from the sport of kickboxing where he was extremely successful. Filipović continued to be successful in MMA with his striking skills, including his signature move of a left high kick. However, after losing a well-publicized match to a skilled Brazilian jujitsu submission specialist, he incorporated submission into his training menu by inviting another Brazilian submission specialist as a training partner. His example is not unusual for contemporary

MMA fighters who start out primarily as strikers. While many of them, including Filipović, still maintain striking as their primary form of fighting and perhaps their identity, learning submission techniques has become increasingly common among them largely for the purpose of defending themselves from submission specialists and occasionally for incorporation into their offense. Obviously, the mastering of submission skills as cultural capital does not happen overnight, especially for those who have been trained as strikers. It is an embodying *practice*. . . .

According to Gitlin, the hegemonic process is developed by "domesticating opposition, absorbing it into forms compatible with the core ideological structure" (Gitlin 1979, 263). Thus, consent that is crucial in maintaining hegemonic forms is "managed by absorption as well as by exclusion" (p. 263). When exotic ways are learned and conquered by the hegemonic masculinity of strikers, the hegemonic form strengthens the core practice and adjusts to changing environments. Selective authorization of the marginalized elements involves the domestication process of foreign, oppositional attributes by the hegemonic form. At the same time, striking techniques are also learned and practiced by submission specialists to counter the accumulation of cultural capital by strikers. For instance, Kazushi Sakuraba, a popular Japanese fighter who made his career in MMA as a submission specialist, went to learn striking skills at a Brazilian gym that houses a striker who defeated Sakuraba more then once using striking skills.

Even if both the feminized and the hegemonic elements are attributionally shared by both forms, the relational position of the hegemonic form does not change and the otherness of the marginalized form also remains the same. In fact, counterappropriation by the marginalized form makes it almost indistinguishable from the complicit form of masculinity in terms of their content (Connell [1995]2000). Similarly, female MMA fighters, who have started to frequent fights and are gaining popularity with both audiences and athletes, also rely on the hegemonic

forms of MMA techniques. To be sure, in the American MMA scene, there are many female submission specialists, but among women fighters, the hegemonic form is undoubtedly that of striking which involves the culturally institutionalized attitudes and practices of their male counterparts. In this way, MMA masculinity, be it hegemonic or marginalized, is an emergent institutional structure that is relatively independent from the attributional contents of the individual athletes. Therefore, it has less to do with the actual individual fighters who may show "feminine" attributes or may be "sincerely" interested in studying Asian culture and martial arts with "respect," but more to do with the structural autoproduction of institutional practices and discourse. Agents of hegemonic structure may also be the agents of the marginalized form, and the contrary is also true. Yet, their structural positions remain the same.

There are structural parallels to the relationship between white hegemonic masculinity and Asian American marginalized masculinity and striking MMA hegemonic and marginalized MMA submission forms of masculinity. One always presupposes another, and the seemingly oppositional elements are, in fact, constitutive of another. Just as marginalized Asian American masculinities serve the hegemonic status of white American masculinity, the feminization of MMA men who submit also serves to maintain a hegemonic counterpart. This logic mirrors Edward Said's conception of Orientalism (1978, 1): "The Orient is not only adjacent to Europe; it is also the place of Europe's greatest and richest and oldest colonies, the source of its civilizations and languages, its cultural contestant, and one of the deepest and most recurring images of the Other." European representations of the Orient constructed the seemingly oppositional relationship. The supposed opposition then "presented the West as, for example, rational, progressive, adult, and masculine, and the East, in turn, as irrational, backward-looking, childish, and feminine" (Klein 2003, 10). The representations of cultural uniqueness of the

East and its exotic incompatibility with the West are also a way to legitimize the impenetrability of the Western self. However, the structural relationship that grants the West its positional superiority is maintained, not by internally coherent and mutually exclusive traits of each opposition, but by constant interaction between the two. As such, the Orient and Europe are not mutually exclusive: "The Orient is an integral part of European *material* civilization and culture" (Said 1978, 2).[9] The elements of the Orient are often incorporated into the West without the negative intention of rejection by the actors who are interested in learning about the other. Said further argues that "neither the term Orient nor the concept of the West has any ontological stability; each is made up of human effort, partly affirmation, partly identification of the Other" (Said 2004, 870). Similarly, the relationship between the hegemonic and marginalized masculinity in MMA is predicated on the process of the identification of the other, or the *othering* of "feminized" elements, which grants opposing masculine attributes to those who practice and embody hegemonic masculinity and authorize or domesticate the same exoticized elements. The distance between the hegemonic and the marginalized is measured by the strategic willingness of the hegemonic form to authorize and incorporate elements of the other. At the same time, just because they interact in the process of *othering* does not mean the elements of the other become less different from the self. The differences may, in fact, be accentuated.

CONCLUSION

As an exploratory theoretical discussion, this article examined the marginalization and authorization of certain forms of masculinity by looking at a particular institutional setting of the sport of MMA. We have argued that the boundaries between hegemonic and marginalized forms of masculinity—a distinction empirically embodied

by techniques and styles involving striking and submission in MMA—are not as rigid and restrictive in terms of their attributional characteristics that seemingly appear mutually exclusive. In upholding its superior position over their marginalized counterparts, hegemonic forms do not necessarily oppose and reject marginalized elements entirely. Rather, hegemonic masculinity structures and maintains a relationship with marginalized forms that is interactive and mutually constitutive. Just as white hegemonic masculinity in North America rejects certain elements of Asian masculinity (e.g., caricatured foreignness and unassimilability) and at the same time strategically incorporates some of the favored elements (e.g., martial arts, exotic primitiveness), the MMA hegemonic form of masculinity similarly selectively authorizes the marginalized form to its advantage. In this way, the marginalized status is maintained not only by exclusion but also by inclusion.

NOTES

1. Emphasis in the original.

2. It is also commonly known as no holds barred fighting, ultimate fighting, or *vale tudo* (Bottenburg and Heilbron 2006).

3. To be sure, there has been a notable increase in female athletes in MMA.

4. It is becoming less common that a fighter's technical background determines his main style since there seem to be more new MMA fighters who start out as MMA fighters. This was not possible at the inception of MMA for obvious reasons. At the time, all fighters emerged from their own specialized disciplines.

5. Since it is permitted to punch an opponent even when he is on the ground, the image of MMA being a "barbaric event"—two bloody men punching each other—was used in an attempt to ban MMA following initial public outcry against the UFC, the first major, and probably most famous professional MMA organization in America.

6. When the UFC first organized MMA events, many of the first winners such as Royce Gracie used submission techniques, particularly from jujitsu,

which did not fit the advertised image of two grown men punching each other.

7. There are currently about four major MMA organizations in Japan.

8. Now, the practice of jujitsu may be more popular in America, following the popularization of jujitsu gyms throughout the country.

9. Emphasis in the original.

REFERENCES

Connell, R. W. [1995]2005. *Masculinities*. Berkeley: University of California Press.

Demetriou, Demetrakis Z. 2001. Connell's concept of hegemonic masculinity: A critique. *Theory and Society* 30:337–61.

DiMaggio, Paul, and Walter Powell. 1983. The iron cage revisited: Institutional isomorphism and collective rationality in organizational fields. *American Sociological Review* 48:147–60.

Gitlin, Todd. 1979. Prime time ideology: The hegemonic process in television entertainment. *Social Problems* 26:251–66.

Hamlin, Tom. 2009. Freddie Roach Predicts Arlovski to KO Fedor. *MMA Weekly* http://www.mmaweekly.com/absolutenm/templates/dailynews.asp?articleid=7910&zoneid=3 (accessed January 20, 2009).

Ishii-Kuntz, Masako. 2003. Balancing fatherhood and work: Emergence of diverse masculinities in contemporary Japan. In *Men and masculinities in contemporary Japan: Dislocating the Salaryman Doxa*, ed. J. Roberson and N. Suzuki, 198–216. London: Routedge.

Kimmel, Michael S. 1994. Masculinity as homophobia: Fear, shame, and silence in the construction of gender identity. In *Theorizing masculinities*, ed. H. Brod and M. Kaufman, 119–41. Thousand Oaks, CA: Sage.

Klein, Christine. 2003. *Cold War Orientalism: Asia in the Middlebrow Imagination, 1945–1961*. Berkeley, CA: University of California Press.

Said, Edward W. 1978. *Orientalism*. New York: Vintage Books.

———. 2004. Orientalism once more. *Development and Change* 35:869–79.

Wertheim, L. Jon. 2009. *Blood in the cage*. Boston: Houghton Mifflin Harcourt.

Introduction to Reading 6

The anthropologist Serena Nanda is widely known for her ethnography of India's Hijaras, titled *Neither Man nor Woman*. The article included here is from her more recent book on multiple sex/gender systems around the world. Nanda's analysis of multiple genders among Native North Americans is rich and detailed. As you read this piece, consider the long-term consequences of the failure of European colonists and early anthropologists to get beyond their ethnocentric assumptions so they could understand and respect the gender diversity of North American Indian cultures.

1. Why does Serena Nanda use the term *gender variants* instead of *two-spirit* and *berdache*?

2. What was the relationship between sexual orientation and gender status among American Indians whose cultures included more than two sex/gender categories? How about hermaphroditism and gender status?

3. Why was there often an association between spiritual power and gender variance in Native American cultures?

— Multiple Genders Among North American Indians —

Serena Nanda

The early encounters between Europeans and Indian societies in the New World, in the fifteenth through the seventeenth centuries, brought together cultures with very different sex/gender systems. The Spanish explorers, coming from a society where sodomy was a heinous crime, were filled with contempt and outrage when they recorded the presence of men in American Indian societies who performed the work of women, dressed like women, and had sexual relations with men (Lang 1996; Roscoe 1995).

Europeans labeled these men "berdache," a term originally derived from an Arabic word meaning male prostitute. As such, this term is inappropriate and insulting, and I use it here only to indicate the history of European (mis)understanding of American Indian sex/gender diversity. The term berdache focused attention on the sexuality associated with mixed gender roles, which the Europeans identified, incorrectly, with the "unnatural" and sinful practice of sodomy in their own societies. In their ethnocentrism, the early European explorers and colonists were unable to see beyond their own sex/gender systems and thus did not understand the multiple sex/gender systems they encountered in the Americas. They also largely overlooked the specialized and spiritual functions of many of these alternative sex/gender roles and the positive value attached to them in many American Indian societies.

By the late-nineteenth and early-twentieth centuries, some anthropologists included accounts of North American Indian sex/gender diversity in their ethnographies. They attempted to explain the berdache from various functional perspectives,

that is, in terms of the contributions these sex/gender roles made to social structure or culture. These accounts, though less contemptuous than earlier ones, nevertheless largely retained the emphasis on berdache sexuality. The berdache was defined as a form of "institutionalized homosexuality," which served as a social niche for individuals whose personality and sexual orientation did not match the definition of masculinity in their societies, or as a "way out" of the masculine or warrior role for "cowardly" or "failed" men (see Callender and Kochems 1983).

Anthropological accounts increasingly paid more attention to the association of the berdache with shamanism and spiritual powers and also noted that mixed gender roles were often central and highly valued in American Indian cultures, rather than marginal and deviant. These accounts were, nevertheless, also ethnocentric in misidentifying indigenous gender diversity with European concepts of homosexuality, transvestism, or hermaphroditism, which continued to distort their indigenous meanings.

In American Indian societies, the European homosexual/heterosexual dichotomy was not culturally relevant and the European labeling of the berdache as homosexuals resulted from their own cultural emphasis on sexuality as a central, even defining, aspect of gender and on sodomy as an abnormal practice and/or a sin. While berdache in many American Indian societies did engage in sexual relations and even married persons of the same sex, this was not central to their alternative gender role. Another overemphasis resulting from European ethnocentrism was the identification of berdache as *transvestites*. Although berdache often cross-dressed, transvestism was not consistent within or across societies. European descriptions of berdache as *hermaphrodites* were also inaccurate. Considering the variation in alternative sex/gender roles in native North America, a working definition may be useful: the berdache in the anthropological literature refers to people who partly or completely take on aspects of the culturally defined role of the other sex and who are classified neither as women nor men, but as genders of their own (see Callender and Kochems 1983:443). It is important to note here that berdache thus refers to variant gender roles, rather than a complete crossing over to an opposite gender role.

In the past twenty-five years there have been important shifts in perspectives on sex/gender diversity among American Indians and anthropologists, both Indian and non-Indian (Jacobs, Thomas, and Lang 1997:Introduction). Most current research rejects institutionalized homosexuality as an adequate explanation of American Indian gender diversity, emphasizing the importance of occupation rather than sexuality as its central feature. Contemporary ethnography views multiple sex/gender roles as a normative part of American Indian sex/gender systems, rather than as a marginal or deviant part (Albers 1989:134; Jacobs et al. 1997; Lang 1998). A new emphasis on the variety of alternative sex/gender roles in North America undercuts the earlier treatment of the berdache as a unitary phenomenon across North (and South) America (Callender and Kochems 1983; Jacobs et al. 1997; Lang 1998; Roscoe and Murray 1998). Current research also emphasizes the integrated and often highly valued position of gender variant persons and the association of sex/gender diversity with spiritual power (Roscoe 1996; Williams 1992).

A change in terminology has also taken place. Berdache generally has been rejected, but there is no unanimous agreement on what should replace it. One widely accepted suggestion is the term *two-spirit* (Jacobs et al. 1997; Lang 1998), a term coined in 1990 by urban American Indian gays and lesbians. Two-spirit has the advantage of conveying the spiritual nature of gender variance

as viewed by gay, lesbian, and transgendered American Indians and also the spirituality associated with traditional American Indian gender variance, but the cultural continuity suggested by two-spirit is in fact a subject of debate. Another problem is that two-spirit emphasizes the Euro-American gender construction of only two genders. Thus, I use the more culturally neutral term, variant genders (or gender variants) and specific indigenous terms wherever possible.

DISTRIBUTION AND CHARACTERISTICS OF VARIANT SEX/GENDER ROLES

Multiple sex/gender systems were found in many, though not all, American Indian societies. Male gender variant roles (variant gender roles assumed by biological males) are documented for 110 to 150 societies. These roles occurred most frequently in the region extending from California to the Mississippi Valley and upper-Great Lakes, the Plains and the Prairies, the Southwest, and to a lesser extent along the Northwest Coast tribes. With few exceptions, gender variance is not historically documented for eastern North America, though it may have existed prior to European invasion and disappeared before it could be recorded historically (Callender and Kochems 1983; Fulton and Anderson 1992).

There were many variations in North American Indian gender diversity. American Indian cultures included three or four genders: men, women, male variants, and female variants (biological females who by engaging in male activities were reclassified as to gender). Gender variant roles differed in the criteria by which they were defined; the degree of their integration into the society; the norms governing their behavior; the way the role was acknowledged publicly or sanctioned; how others were expected to behave toward gender variant persons; the degree to which a gender changer was expected to adopt the role of the opposite sex or was limited in doing so; the power, sacred or secular, that was attributed to them; and the path to recruitment.

In spite of this variety, however, there were also some common or widespread features: transvestism, cross-gender occupation, same sex (but different gender) sexuality, some culturally normative and acknowledged process for recruitment to the role, special language and ritual roles, and associations with spiritual power.

Transvestism

The degree to which male and female gender variants were permitted to wear the clothing of the other sex varied. Transvestism was often associated with gender variance but was not equally important in all societies. Male gender variants frequently adopted women's dress and hairstyles partially or completely, and female gender variants partially adopted the clothing of men; sometimes, however, transvestism was prohibited. The choice of clothing was sometimes an individual matter and gender variants might mix their clothing and their accoutrements. For example, a female gender variant might wear a woman's dress but carry (male) weapons. Dress was also sometimes situationally determined: a male gender variant would have to wear men's clothing while engaging in warfare but might wear women's clothes at other times. Similarly, female gender variants might wear women's clothing when gathering (women's work), but male clothing when hunting (men's work) (Callender and Kochems 1983:447). Among the Navajo, a male gender variant, nádleeh, would adopt almost all aspects of a woman's dress, work, language and behavior; the Mohave male gender variant, called alyha, was at the extreme end of the cross-gender continuum in imitating female physiology as well as transvestism. . . . Repression of visible forms of gender diversity, and ultimately the almost total decline of transvestism, were a direct result of American prohibitions against it.

Occupation

Contemporary analysis emphasizes occupational aspects of American Indian gender variance as a central feature. Most frequently a boy's interest in the implements and activities of women and a girl's interest in the tools of male occupations signaled an individual's wish to undertake a gender variant role (Callender and Kochems 1983:447; Whitehead 1981). In hunting societies, for example, female gender variance was signaled by a girl rejecting the domestic activities associated with women and participating in playing and hunting with boys. In the arctic and subarctic, particularly, this was sometimes encouraged by a girl's parents if there were not enough boys to provide the family with food (Lang 1998). Male gender variants were frequently considered especially skilled and industrious in women's crafts and domestic work (though not in agriculture, where this was a man's task) (Roscoe 1991; 1996). Female gender crossers sometimes won reputations as superior hunters and warriors.

Male gender variants' households were often more prosperous than others, sometimes because they were hired by whites. In their own societies the excellence of male gender variants' craftwork was sometimes ascribed to a supernatural sanction for their gender transformation (Callender and Kochems 1983:448). Female gender variants opted out of motherhood, so were not encumbered by caring for children, which may explain their success as hunters or warriors. In some societies, gender variants could engage in both men's and women's work, and this, too, accounted for their increased wealth. Another source of income was payment for the special social activities of gender variants due to their intermediate gender status, such as acting as go-betweens in marriage. Through their diverse occupations, then, gender variants were often central rather than marginal in their societies.

Early anthropological explanations of male gender variant roles as a niche for a "failed" or cowardly man who wished to avoid warfare or other aspects of the masculine role are no longer widely accepted. To begin with, masculinity was not associated with warrior status in all American Indian cultures. In some societies, male gender variants were warriors and in many others, men who rejected the warrior role did not become gender variants. Sometimes male gender variants did not go to war because of cultural prohibitions against their using symbols of maleness, for example, the prohibition against their using the bow among the Illinois. Where male gender variants did not fight, they sometimes had other important roles in warfare, like treating the wounded, carrying supplies for the war party, or directing postbattle ceremonials (Callender and Kochems 1983:449). In a few societies male gender variants become outstanding warriors, such as Finds Them and Kills Them, a Crow Indian who performed daring feats of bravery while fighting with the United States Army against the Crow's traditional enemies, the Lakota Sioux (Roscoe and Murray 1998:23).

GENDER VARIANCE AND SEXUALITY

Generally, sexuality was not central in defining gender status among American Indians. But in any case, the assumption by European observers that gender variants were homosexuals meant they did not take much trouble to investigate or record information on this topic. In some American Indian societies same-sex sexual desire/practice did figure significantly in the definition of gender variant roles; in others it did not (Callender and Kochems 1983:449). Some early reports noted specifically that male gender variants lived with and/or had sexual relations with women as well as men; in other societies they were reported as having sexual relations only with men, and in still other societies, of having no sexual relationships at all (Lang 1998:189–95).

The bisexual orientation of some gender variant persons may have been a culturally accepted expression of their gender variance. It may have resulted from an individual's life experiences, such as the age at which he or she entered the gender variant role, and/or it may have been one aspect of the general freedom of sexual expression in many American Indian societies. While male and female gender variants most frequently

had sexual relations with, or married, persons of the same biological sex as themselves, these relationships were not considered homosexual in the contemporary Western understanding of that term. In a multiple gender system the partners would be of the same sex but different genders, and homogender, rather than homosexual, practices bore the brunt of negative cultural sanctions. The sexual partners of gender variants were never considered gender variants themselves.

The Navajo are a good example (Thomas 1997). The Navajo have four genders; in addition to man and woman there are two gender variants: masculine female-bodied nádleeh and feminine male-bodied nádleeh. A sexual relationship between a female nádleeh and a woman or a sexual relationship between a male-bodied nádleeh and a man were not stigmatized because these persons were of different genders, although of the same biological sex. However, a sexual relationship between two women, two men, two female-bodied nádleeh or two male-bodied nádleeh, was considered homosexual, and even incestual, and was strongly disapproved of.

The relation of sexuality to variant sex/gender roles across North America suggests that sexual relations between gender variants and persons of the same biological sex were a result rather than a cause of gender variance. Sexual relationships between a man and a male gender variant were accepted in most American Indian societies, though not in all, and appear to have been negatively sanctioned only when it interfered with child-producing heterosexual marriages. Gender variants' sexual relationships varied from casual and wide-ranging (Europeans used the term promiscuous), to stable, and sometimes even involved life-long marriages. In some societies, however, male gender variants were not permitted to engage in long-term relationships with men, either in or out of wedlock. In many cases, gender variants were reported as living alone.

There are some practical reasons why a man might desire sexual relations with a (male) gender variant: in some societies taboos on sexual relations with menstruating or pregnant women restricted opportunities for sexual intercourse; in other societies, sexual relations with a gender variant person were exempt from punishment for extramarital affairs; in still other societies, for example, among the Navajo, some gender variants were considered especially lucky and a man might hope to vicariously partake of this quality by having sexual relations with them (Lang 1998:349).

BIOLOGICAL SEX AND GENDER

Transformations

European observers often confused gender variants with hermaphrodites. Some American Indian societies explicitly distinguished hermaphrodites from gender variants and treated them differently; others assigned gender variant persons and hermaphrodites to the same alternative gender status. With the exception of the Navajo, in most American Indian societies biological sex (or the intersexedness of the hermaphrodite) was not the criterion for a gender variant role, nor were the individuals who occupied gender variant roles anatomically abnormal. The Navajo distinguished between the intersexed and the alternatively gendered, but treated them similarly, though not exactly the same (Thomas 1997; Hill 1935).

And even as the traditional Navajo sex/gender system had biological sex as its starting point, it was only a starting point, and Navajo nádleeh were distinguished by sex-linked behaviors, such as body language, clothing, ceremonial roles, speech style, and work. Feminine, male-bodied nádleeh might engage in women's activities such as cooking, weaving, household tasks, and making pottery. Masculine, female-bodied nádleeh, unlike other female-bodied persons, avoided childbirth; today they are associated with male occupational roles such as construction or firefighting (although ordinary women also sometimes engage in these occupations). Traditionally, female-bodied nádleeh had specific roles in Navajo ceremonials.

Thus, even where hermaphrodites occupied a special gender variant role, American Indian gender variance was defined more by cultural than biological criteria. In one recorded case of an interview with and physical examination of a gender variant male, the previously mentioned Finds Them and Kills Them, his genitals were found to be completely normal (Roscoe and Murray 1998).

If American Indian gender variants were not generally hermaphrodites, or conceptualized as such, neither were they conceptualized as transsexuals. Gender transformations among gender variants were recognized as only a partial transformation, and the gender variant was not thought of as having become a person of the opposite sex/gender. Rather, gender variant roles were autonomous gender roles that combined the characteristics of men and women and had some unique features of their own. This was sometimes symbolically recognized: among the Zuni a male gender variant was buried in women's dress but men's trousers on the men's side of the graveyard (Parsons quoted in Callender and Kochems 1983:454; Roscoe 1991:124, 145). Male gender variants were neither men—by virtue of their chosen occupations, dress, demeanor, and possibly sexuality—nor women, because of their anatomy and their inability to bear children. Only among the Mohave do we find the extreme imitation of women's physiological processes related to reproduction and the claims to have female sexual organs—both of which were ridiculed within Mohave society. But even here, where informants reported that female gender variants did not menstruate, this did not make them culturally men. Rather it was the mixed quality of gender variant status that was culturally elaborated in native North America, and this was the source of supernatural powers sometimes attributed to them.

Sacred Power

The association between the spiritual power and gender variance occurred in most, if not all, Native American societies. Even where, as previously noted, recruitment to the role was occasioned by a child's interest in occupational activities of the opposite sex, supernatural sanction, frequently appearing in visions or dreams, was also involved. Where this occurred, as it did mainly in the Prairie and Plains societies, the visions involved female supernatural figures, often the moon. Among the Omaha, for example, the moon appeared in a dream holding a burden strap—a symbol of female work—in one hand, and a bow—a symbol of male work—in the other. When the male dreamer reached for the bow, the moon forced him to take the burden strap (Whitehead 1981). Among the Mohave, a child's choice of male or female implements heralding gender variant status was sometimes prefigured by a dream that was believed to come to an embryo in the womb (Devereux 1937).

Sometimes, by virtue of the power associated with their gender ambiguity, gender variants were ritual adepts and curers, or had special ritual functions (Callender and Kochems 1983:453; Lang 1998). Gender variants did not always have important sacred roles in native North America, however. Where feminine qualities were associated with these roles, male gender variants might become spiritual leaders or healers, but where these roles were associated with male qualities they were not entered into by male gender variants. Among the Plains Indians, with their emphasis on the vision as a source of supernatural power, male gender variants were regarded as holy persons, but in California Indian societies, this was not the case and in some American Indian societies gender variants were specifically excluded from religious roles (Lang 1998:167). Sometimes it was the individual personality of the gender variant rather than his/her gender variance itself, that resulted in occupying sacred roles (see Commentary following Callender and Kochems 1983). Nevertheless, the importance of sacred power was so widely associated with sex/gender diversity in native North America that it is generally agreed to be an important explanation of the frequency of gender diversity in this region of the world.

In spite of cultural differences, some significant similarities among American Indian societies are particularly consistent with multigender systems and the positive value placed on sex/gender diversity (Lang 1996). One of these similarities is a cosmology (system of religious beliefs and way of seeing the world) in which transformation and ambiguity are recurring themes. Thus a person who contains both masculine and feminine qualities or one who is transformed from the sex/gender assigned at birth into a different gender in later life manifests some of the many kinds of transformations and ambiguities that are possible, not only for humans, but for animals and objects in the natural environment. Indeed, in many American Indian cultures, sex/gender ambiguity, lack of sexual differentiation, and sex/gender transformations play an important part in the story of creation. American Indian cosmology may not be "the cause" of sex/gender diversity but it certainly (as in India) provides a hospitable context for it (Lang 1996:187). . . .

As a result of Euro-American repression and the growing assimilation of Euro-American sex/gender ideologies, both female and male gender variant roles among American Indians largely disappeared by the 1930s, as the reservation system was well under way. And yet, its echoes may remain. The current academic interest in American Indian multigender roles, and particularly the testimony of contemporary two-spirits, reminds us that alternatives are possible and that understanding American Indian sex/gender diversity in the past and present makes a significant contribution to understandings of sex/gender diversity in the larger society.

REFERENCES

Albers, Patricia C. 1989. "From Illusion to Illumination: Anthropological Studies of American Indian Women." In *Gender and Anthropology: Critical Reviews for Research and Teaching,* edited by Sandra Morgen. Washington, DC: American Anthropological Association.

Callender, Charles, and Lee M. Kochems. 1983. "The North American Berdache." *Current Anthropology* 24(4): 443–56 (Commentary, pp. 456–70).

Devereux, George. 1937. "Institutionalized Homosexual of the Mojave Indians." In *Human Biology,* 9:498–597.

Fulton, Robert, and Steven W. Anderson. 1992. "The Amerindian 'Man-Woman': Gender, Liminality, and Cultural Continuity." *Current Anthropology* 33(5): 603–10.

Hill, Willard W. 1935. "The Status of the Hermaphrodite and Transvestite in Navaho Culture." *American Anthropologist* 37: 273–79.

Jacobs, Sue-Ellen, Wesley Thomas, and Sabine Lang, eds. 1997. *Two-Spirit People: Native American Gender Identity, Sexuality, and Spirituality.* Urbana and Chicago: University of Illinois.

Lang, Sabine. 1996. "There Is More than Just Men and Women: Gender Variance in North America." In *Gender Reversals and Gender Culture,* edited by Sabrina Petra Ramet, pp. 183–96. London and New York: Routledge

———. 1998. *Men as Women, Women as Men: Changing Gender in Native American Cultures.* Trans. from the German by John L. Vantine. Austin: University of Texas Press.

Roscoe, Will. 1991. *The Zuni Man-Woman.* Albuquerque: University of New Mexico Press.

———. 1995. "Cultural Anesthesia and Lesbian and Gay Studies." *American Anthropologist,* 97: 448–52.

———. 1996. "How to Become a Berdache: Toward a Unified Analysis of Gender Diversity." In *Third Sex, Third Gender: Beyond Sexual Dimorphism in Culture and History,* edited by Gilbert Herdt, pp. 329–72. New York: Zone (MIT).

Roscoe, Will, and Stephen O. Murray, eds. 1998. *Boy-Wives and Female-Husbands: Studies in African Homosexualities.* New York: St. Martins.

Thomas, Wesley. 1997. "Navajo Cultural Constructions of Gender and Sexuality." In *Two-Spirit People: Native American Gender Identity, Sexuality, and Spirituality,* edited by Sue-Ellen Jacobs, Wesley Thomas, and Sabine Lang, pp. 156–73. Urbana and Chicago: University of Illinois.

Whitehead, Harriet. 1981. "The Bow and the Burden Strap: A New Look at Institutionalized Homosexuality in Native North America." In *Sexual Meanings: The Cultural Construction of Gender and Sexuality,* edited by Sherry B. Ortner and Harriet Whitehead, pp. 80–111. Cambridge: Cambridge University Press.

Williams, Walter. 1992. *The Spirit and the Flesh: Sexual Diversity in American Indian Culture.* Boston: Beacon.

❦ Topics for Further Examination ❧

- Visit the website of the Intersex Society of North America (http://www.isna.org) and read the organization's mission statement and tips for parents. The blog posts are also interesting. In addition, you will find websites on male lactation and men breastfeeding to be helpful in expanding your understanding of biological overlap between males and females.
- Locate research on gender bending in the arts (e.g., performance art, literature, music videos). For example, visit Diane Torr's website (http://www.dianetorr.com).
- Google "doing gender" and explore the many websites that discuss the concept and its application.

2

THE INTERACTION OF GENDER WITH OTHER SOCIALLY CONSTRUCTED PRISMS

Afeter considering what gender is and isn't, we are going to complicate things a bit by looking at how other socially constructed categories of difference and inequality, such as race, ethnicity, social class, religion, age, ability/disability, and sexuality, shape gender. As is the case with prisms in a kaleidoscope, the interaction of gender with other social prisms creates complex patterns of identity and relationships for people across groups and situations. Because there are so many different social prisms that interact with gender in daily life, we can discuss only a few in this chapter; however, other social categories are explored throughout this book. The articles we have selected for this chapter illustrate three key arguments. First, gender is a complex and multifaceted array of experiences and meanings that cannot be understood without considering the social context within which they are situated. Second, variations in the meaning and display of gender are related to different levels of prestige, privilege, and power associated with membership in other socially constructed categories of difference and inequality. Third, gender intersects with other socially constructed categories of difference and inequality at all levels discussed in the introduction to this book—individual, interactional, and institutional.

PRIVILEGE

In our daily lives, there usually isn't enough time or opportunity to consider how the interaction of multiple social categories to which we belong affects beliefs, behaviors, and life chances. In particular, we are discouraged from critically examining our culture, as will be discussed in Chapter 3. People who occupy positions of privilege often do not notice how their privileged social positions influence them. In the United States, privilege is associated with white skin color, masculinity, wealth, heterosexuality, youth, able-bodiedness, and so on. It seems normal to those of us who occupy privileged positions and those we interact with that our positions of privilege be deferred to, allowing us to move more freely in society. Peggy McIntosh (1998) is a pioneer in examining these hidden and unearned benefits of privilege. She argues that there are implicit benefits of privilege and that persons with "unearned advantages" often do not understand how their privilege is a function of the disempowerment of others. For example, male privilege seems "normal" and White privilege seems "natural" to those who are male and/or White.

The struggle for women's rights in the United States also has seen the effects of privilege, with White women historically dominating this movement. The privilege of race and social class created a view of woman as a universal category, which essentially represented White women's interests. While many women of color stood up for women's rights, they did so in response to a universal definition of womanhood derived from White privilege (hooks, 1981). This pattern of White dominance is not a recent phenomenon and has been recognized within the African American community for some time, as discussed in the first reading in this chapter, by Bonnie Thornton Dill and Marla H. Kohlman. For example, in 1867, former slave Sojourner Truth responding to a White man who felt women were more delicate than men, described the exertion required of her work as a slave and asked, "Ain't I a woman?" (Guy-Scheftall, 1995). One hundred years later, women of color, including Audre Lorde (1982), bell hooks (1981), Angela Davis (1981), Gloria Anzaldúa (1987), and others, continued to speak out against White privilege within the women's movement. These women, recognizing that the issues facing women of color were not always the same as those of White women, carried on a battle to make African American women visible in the second wave of feminism. For example, while White feminists were fighting for the right to abortion, African American women were fighting other laws and sterilization practices that

denied them the right to control their own fertility and bear their own babies. Women of color, including Thornton Dill (in this chapter) and others, some of whom are listed in this introduction, continue to challenge the White-dominated definitions of gender and fight to include in the analysis of gender an understanding of the experience of domination and privilege of all women.

UNDERSTANDING THE INTERACTION OF GENDER WITH OTHER CATEGORIES OF DIFFERENCE AND INEQUALITY

Throughout this chapter introduction, you will read about social scientists and social activists who attempt to understand the interactions between "interlocking oppressions." Social scientists develop theories, with their primary focus on explanation, whereas social activists explore the topic of interlocking oppressions from the perspective of initiating social change. Although the goals of explanation and change are rarely separated in feminist research, they reflect different emphases (Collins, 1990). As such, these two different agendas shape attempts to understand the interaction of gender with multiple social prisms of difference and inequality. Much of this research on intersectionality is written by women, with a focus on women, because it came out of conflicts and challenging issues within the women's movement. As you read through this chapter and book, it is important to remember that the socially defined gender categories in Western culture intersect with other prisms of difference and inequality. And, as Collins (1998, 2001) has argued, consider how the meanings of gender and other categories of difference and inequality are embedded in the structure of social relations within nations.

The effort to include the perspectives and experiences of *all* women in understanding gender is complicated. Previous theories had to be expanded to include the interaction of gender with other social categories of difference and privilege. These efforts to refine or redefine the concept of intersectionality continue. Yet, as Davis (2008) argues, the ambiguity and open-endedness of the concept makes it successful as a feminist theory because it is more accessible and, thus, applied more meaningfully. To better understand the development of the concept of intersectionality, we group these efforts into three different approaches. The earliest approach is to treat each social category of difference and inequality as if it were separate and not overlapping. A second, more recent approach is to add up the different social categories that an individual belongs to and summarize the effects of the social categories of privilege and power. The third and newest approach attempts to understand the simultaneous interaction of gender with all other categories of difference and inequality. These three approaches are described in more detail in the following paragraphs because they help us understand the complexity of applying an intersectional approach.

Separate-and-Different Approach

Deborah King (1988) describes the earliest approach as the "race–sex analogy." She characterizes this approach as one in which oppressions related to race are compared with those related to gender, but each is seen as a separate influence. King quotes Elizabeth Cady Stanton, who in 1860 stated, "Prejudice against color, of which we hear so much, is no stronger than that against sex" (p. 43). This approach, the race–sex analogy, continued well into the late 20th century and can get in the way of a deeper understanding of the complexity of gender. For example, in the race–sex analogy, gender is assumed to have the same effect for African American and White women, while race is defined as the same experience for African American men and women. However, the reading by Karen D. Pyke and Denise L. Johnson in this chapter, which explores Asian American women's definitions of "femininity," illustrates how we cannot assume that gender will mean the same thing to different women from the same society. Although these Vietnamese American and Korean American women were born and

raised in the United States, they live with two different cultural definitions of femininity, an idea we will consider in more depth in the next chapter. Although they may try, the reality is that Asian American women cannot draw a line down their bodies separating gender from ethnicity and culture. As these women's words suggest, the effects of prisms of difference on daily experience are inextricably intertwined. For example, African American females cannot always be certain that the discrimination they face is due to race or gender, or both. As individuals, we are complex combinations of multiple social identities. Separating the effects of multiple social prisms theoretically does not always make sense and is almost impossible to do on an individual level.

Looking at these individual challenges, King (1988) argues that attempting to determine which "-ism" (e.g., sexism, racism, or classism) is most oppressive and most important to overcome does not address the real-life situations. This approach pits the interests of each subordinated group against the others and asks individuals to choose one group identity over others. For example, must poor, African American women decide which group will best address their situations in society: groups fighting racial inequality, gender inequality, or class inequality? The situations of poor, African American women are more complex than this single-issue approach can address.

The race–sex analogy of treating one "-ism" at a time has been criticized because, although some needs and experiences of oppressed people are included, others are ignored. For instance, Collins (1990) describes the position of African American women as that of "outsiders within" the feminist movement and in relations with women in general. She and others have criticized the women's movement for leaving out of its agenda an awareness of the experiences and needs of African American women (e.g., King, 1988). This focus on one "-ism" or another—the formation of social action groups around one category of difference and inequality—is called identity politics.

Additive Approach

The second approach used by theorists to understand how multiple social prisms interact at the level of individual life examines the effects of multiple social categories in an additive model. In this approach, the effects of race, ethnicity, class, and other social prisms are added together as static, equal parts of a whole (King, 1988). Returning to the earlier example of poor, African American women, the strategy is one of adding up the effects of racism, sexism, and classism to equal what is termed *triple jeopardy*. If that same woman was also a lesbian, her situation would be that of *quadruple jeopardy*, according to the additive model.

Although this approach takes into account multiple social identities in understanding oppression, King and others reject it as too simplistic. We cannot simply add up the complex inequalities across social categories of difference and inequality, because the weight of each social category varies based on individual situations. McIntosh (1998) argues that privileges associated with membership in particular social categories interact to create "interlocking oppressions" whose implications and meanings shift across time and situations. For example, for African American women in some situations, their gender will be more salient, while in other situations, their race will be more salient. The article by Nikki Jones in this chapter helps illustrate this fact. As Jones found, the behavior of the young woman she followed through life on the streets of San Francisco reflected both social and local expectations for multiple identities, including race, sex, class, and sexuality—to the point that her behavior was constantly changing.

Interaction Approach

The third approach to understanding the social and personal consequences of membership in multiple socially constructed categories is called multiracial feminist theory. Various terms are used by multiracial feminist theorists to describe "interlocking oppressions," including *intersectional analysis* (Baca Zinn & Thornton Dill, 1996), *interrelated* (Weber, 2001), *simultaneous* (Collins, 1990; Weber, 2001), *multiplicative* or *multiple jeopardy* (King, 1988), *matrix of domination* (Collins, 1990), and *relational* (Baca Zinn, Hondagneu-Sotelo, & Messner, 2001; Baca Zinn & Thornton Dill, 1996). The first article in this chapter, by Thornton Dill and Kohlman, provides an overview of the meaning of intersectional analysis. For the purposes of this book, we describe this approach as consisting of "prismatic" or intersectional interactions, which occur when socially constructed categories of difference and inequality interact with other categories in individuals' lives. A brief discussion of some of these different models for explaining "interlocking oppressions" is useful in deepening our understanding of the complex interactions of membership in multiple social prisms.

King (1988) brings these interactions to light, discussing the concept of multiple jeopardy, in which she refers not only "to several, simultaneous oppressions, but to the multiplicative relationships among them as well" (p. 47). As a result, socially constructed categories of difference and inequality fold into individual identities, not in an additive way but in a way in which the total construction of an individual's identity incorporates the relationship of the identities to one another. King's model includes both multiple social identities and situational factors to understand individual differences. For example, being a submissive woman might matter more in certain religious groups where women have more restricted roles, while race or class may be less salient in that situation because the latter social prisms are likely to be similar across the religious group.

Baca Zinn et al. (2001) emphasize that gender is relational. Focusing on gender as a process (Connell, 1987), they argue that "the meaning of *woman* is defined by the existence of women of different races and classes" (Baca Zinn et al., 2001, p. 174). As Pyke and Johnson's reading in this chapter illustrates, the fact that the Asian American women they interviewed were confused about whether to accept Asian standards of gender or American standards "normalizes" and makes White femininity dominant.

Collins (1990), on the other hand, conceptualizes oppressions as existing in a "matrix of domination" in which individuals not only experience but also resist multiple inequalities. Collins argues that domination and resistance can be found at three levels: personal, cultural, and institutional. Individuals with the most privilege and power—White, upper-class men—control dominant definitions of gender in this model. Collins discusses how "White skin privilege" has limited White feminists' understandings of gender oppression to their own experiences and created considerable tension in the women's movement. Tensions occur on all three levels—personal, within and between groups, and at the level of institutions such as the women's movement itself—all of which maintain power differentials. Furthermore, as she has since argued, these intersections of inequality are embedded in national identity systems of gendered social organizations (Collins, 1998, 2001).

As you can see, this third approach does not treat interlocking oppressions as strictly additive. The unequal power of groups created by systems of inequality affects interpersonal power in all relationships, both within and across gender categories. The articles in this chapter illustrate how multiple socially constructed prisms interact to shape both the identities and opportunities of individuals. They also show how interpersonal relationships are intricately tied to the larger structures of society or nations, as Collins (2001) argues, and how gender is maintained across groups in society.

These efforts to understand gender through the lens of multiple social prisms of difference and inequality can be problematic. One concern is that gender could be reduced to what has been described as a continually changing quilt of life experiences (Baca Zinn et al., 2001; Connell, 1992). That is, if the third approach is taken to the extreme, gender is seen as a series of individual experiences and the approach can no longer be used as a tool for explaining patterns across groups, which is meaningless in generating social action. Thus, the current challenge for researchers and theorists is to forge an explanation of the interaction of gender with other socially constructed prisms that both recognizes and reflects the experiences of individuals, while at the same time highlighting the patterns that occur across groups of individuals.

The application of intersectional analyses continues to be riddled with debates over how it should be done. An article in this chapter by Bandana Purkayastha adds to this discussion by elaborating on the ways intersectionality can be applied in transnational or global spaces. This piece clearly points to the fact that intersectional analysis is a dynamic and lively addition to the study of gender difference and inequality.

Another current debate addresses the methods or the way we do research on intersectionality (Choo & Ferree, 2010). As you will see, much of the research applying intersectional analysis uses qualitative research. However, Leslie McCall (2005) carefully laid out an argument that considered why this was so. She argued that the methodology of intersexuality research is complicated by the need to define "categories" of difference and inequality. But when defining categories, such as gender or race, to individuals you are studying, you take away the meanings they bring to those categories and the way they experience them. McCall argues for using categories such as gender, race, and social class, even though they are imperfect, in quantitative research to study the complexity associated with examining multiple categories of difference and inequality.

Since we live in a world that includes many socially constructed categories of difference and inequality, understanding the ways social prisms come together is critical for understanding gender. How we visualize the effects of multiple social prisms depends on whether we seek social justice, theoretical understanding, or both. How can we use these experiences to better understand the lived lives of individuals and work to make those lives better, such as that of Kiara in the Jones article in this chapter? If multiple social categories are linked, then what are the mechanisms by which difference is created, supported, and changed? Are multiple identities multiplied, as King (1988) suggests; added, as others suggest; or combined into a matrix, as Collins (1990) suggests? Or, as Purkayastha suggests in this chapter, must we also consider nation in our analysis as we examine the interactions of gender with other categories of difference and inequality (see also Collins, 2001)? We raise these questions not to confuse you, but rather, to challenge you to try to understand the complexity of gender relations.

PRISMATIC INTERACTIONS

We return now to the metaphor of the kaleidoscope to help us sort out this question of how to deal with multiple social identities in explaining gender. Understanding the interaction of several socially constructed identities can be compared to the ray of light passing through the prisms of a kaleidoscope. Socially constructed categories serve as prisms that create life experiences. Just as the kaleidoscope produces a flowing and constantly changing array of patterns, we find individual life experiences to be unique and flowing. However, similar colors and patterns often reoccur in slightly different forms. Sometimes, when we look through a real kaleidoscope, we find a beautiful image in which blue is dominant. Although we may not be able to replicate the specific image, it would not be unusual for us to see another blue-dominant pattern. Gender differences emerge in a similar form—not as a single, fixed pattern but as a dominant, broad pattern that encompasses many unique but similar patterns. However, introducing the notion of category of gender adds questions relating to how these categories are defined. Are categories of gender based in individual identities, symbolic representations, or social structures (Choo & Ferree, 2010; Winker & Degele, 2011)?

The prism metaphor offers an avenue for systematically envisioning the complexity of gender relations. We would argue that to fully understand

this interaction of social influences, one must focus on power. The distribution of privilege and oppression is a function of power relations (Baca Zinn et al., 2001). All the articles in this chapter examine differences defined by power relations, and power operates at every level of life, from the intimate and familial (see the reading by Pyke and Johnson in this chapter) to the global (see the reading by Purkayastha in this chapter). It is difficult to explain the combined effects of multiple social prisms without focusing on power. We argue that the power one accrues from a combination of socially constructed categories explains the patterns created by these categories. However, one cannot add up the effects from each category one belongs to, as in the additive approach described earlier. Instead, one must understand that, like the prisms in the kaleidoscope, the power of any single socially constructed identity is related to all other categories. The final patterns that appear are based on the combinations of power that shape the patterns. Individuals' life experiences, then, take unique forms as race, class, ethnicity, religion, age, ability/disability, body type, and other socially constructed characteristics are combined to create patterns that emerge across contexts and daily life experiences.

Consider your own social identities and the social categories to which you belong. How do they mold you at this time, and how did they, or might they, frame your experience of gender at other times and under different circumstances? Consider other social prisms such as age, ability/disability, religion, and national identity. If you were to build your own kaleidoscope of gender, what prisms would you include? What prisms interact with gender to shape your life? Do these prisms create privilege or disadvantage for you? Think about how these socially constructed categories combine to create your life experiences and how they are supported by the social structure in which you live. Keep your answers in mind as you read these articles to gain a better understanding of the role prisms play in shaping gender and affecting your life.

REFERENCES

Anzaldúa, G. (1987). *Borderlands/La Frontera: The new mestiza.* San Francisco: Aunt Lute Book Company.

Baca Zinn, M., Hondagneu-Sotelo, P., & Messner, M. A. (2001). Gender through the prism of difference. In M. L. Andersen & P. H. Collins (Eds.), *Race, class, and gender: An anthology* (4th ed., pp. 168–176). Belmont, CA: Wadsworth.

Baca Zinn, M., & Thornton Dill, B. (1996). Theorizing difference from multiracial feminism. *Feminist Studies, 22*(2), 321–327.

Choo, H. Y., & Ferree, M. M. (2010). Practicing intersectionality in sociological research: A critical analysis of inclusions, interactions, and institutions in the study of inequalities. *Sociological Theory, 28*(2), 129–149.

Collins, P. H. (1990). *Black feminist thought: Knowledge, consciousness, and the politics of empowerment.* New York: Routledge.

Collins, P. H. (1998). Intersections of race, class, gender, and nation: Some implications for Black family studies. *Journal of Comparative Family Studies, 29*(1), 27–36.

Collins, P. H. (2001). It's all in the family: Intersections of gender, race, and nation. *Hypatia, 13*(3), 62–82.

Connell, R. W. (1987). *Gender and power: Society, the person, and sexual politics.* Stanford, CA: Stanford University Press.

Connell, R. W. (1992). A very straight gay: Masculinity, homosexual experience, and the dynamics of gender. *American Sociological Review, 57,* 735–751.

Davis, A. Y. (1981). *Women, race, and class.* New York: Random House.

Davis, K. (2008). Intersectionality as buzzword: A sociology of science perspective on what makes a feminist theory successful. *Feminist Theory, 9*(1), 67–85.

Guy-Scheftall, B. (Ed.). (1995). *Words of fire: An anthology of African-American feminist thought.* New York: New Press.

hooks, b. (1981). *Ain't I a woman: Black women and feminism.* Boston: South End Press.

King, D. (1988). Multiple jeopardy: The context of a Black feminist ideology. *Signs, 14*(1), 42–72.

Lorde, A. (1982). *Zami: A new spelling of my name.* Trumansberg, NY: Crossing Press.

McCall, L. (2005). The complexity of intersectionality. *Signs, 30*(3), 1771–1800.

McIntosh, P. (1998). *White privilege and male privilege: Unpacking the invisible knapsack.* Wellesley, MA: Wellesley College Center for Research on Women.

Weber, L. (2001). *Understanding race, class, gender, and sexuality: A conceptual framework.* Boston: McGraw-Hill.

Winker, G., & Degele, N. (2011). Intersectionality as multi-level analysis: Dealing with social inequality. *European Journal of Women's Studies, 18*(1), 51–66.

Introduction to Reading 7

Intersectionality: A transformative paradigm in feminist theory and social justice

—Thornton Dill and Kohlman

Intersectional theory is not an easy concept to define for many of the reasons described in the introduction to this chapter. In this piece, Thornton Dill and Kohlman discuss some of the key issues relating to intersectional theory today. They look at the roots and history of intersectionality from the perspective of Black feminists and also review some debates about methodological issues surrounding intersectionality. While their focus was also on social justice, we were not able to include that discussion in this excerpt, but we encourage you to be sensitive to issues of social justice and intersectionality that they weave throughout this piece, particularly in their conclusion to this reading. They end by contrasting "strong intersectionality" with "weak intersectionality," further illustrating the various ways this paradigm has been applied. This reading helps us understand the value of thinking deeply about differences and the need for intersectional analyses.

1. How have Blacks, particularly Black women, helped shape the development of intersectional analyses?

2. What are the problems of studying intersectionality using quantitative methodology, and what are the advantages of doing so?

3. Explain what they mean by the difference between "strong intersectionality" and "weak intersectionality."

INTERSECTIONALITY

A TRANSFORMATIVE PARADIGM IN FEMINIST THEORY AND SOCIAL JUSTICE

Bonnie Thornton Dill and Marla H. Kohlman

As a Black scholar writing about women's issues in the mid-1980s, Thornton Dill joined with several colleagues in calling for a feminist theoretical paradigm that would expose the disconnect between experience and theory in the often untold stories of women of color and those without economic privilege (Baca Zinn, Cannon, Dill, & Higginbotham, 1986). They understood that feminist theory was quite limited without the purposeful integration of the notion of difference, beginning with race, ethnicity, class, and culture. They also understood that the integration of race and class into the gendered discourses extant at that time would change the nature of feminist discourse in important and powerful ways.

More than two decades later, one of the first things students learn in women's studies classes is how to look at women's and men's lives through multiple lenses. The concept of *intersectionality* has been a key factor in this transition. This conceptual tool has become integral to both

theory and research endeavors, as it emphasizes the interlocking effects of race, class, gender, and sexuality, highlighting the ways in which categories of identity and structures of inequality are mutually constituted and defy separation into discrete categories of analysis. Intersectionality provides a unique lens of study that does not question difference; rather, it assumes that differential experiences of common events are to be expected.

As scholars producing intersectional work began to apply their insights to institutional dynamics, they began to speak and write about the challenges and opportunities that exist within and through the academy and the labor market, and in law and public policy. Thus, intersectional scholarship is engaged in transforming both theory and practice across disciplinary divides, offering a wide range of methodological approaches to the study of multiple, complex social relations. In her widely cited 2005 article, "The Complexity of Intersectionality," sociologist

From Thornton Dill, Bonnie, and Marla H. Kohlman. 2011. "Intersectionality: A Transformative Paradigm in Feminist Theory and Social Justice." Pp. 154–174 in *Handbook of Feminist Research, 2e.*, edited by Sharlene Hesse-Biber. Thousand Oaks, CA: SAGE Publications.

Leslie McCall states that "intersectionality is the most important theoretical contribution that women's studies, in conjunction with related fields, has made so far" (p. 1771).

In this chapter, we [map] the developments in intersectional theorizing and institutional transformation in the past decade while also offering our views on the future of intersectionality for feminist theory and methodology.

ROOTS AND HISTORY

Intersectional scholarship emerged as an amalgamation of aspects of women's studies and race and ethnic studies. Its foundations are in the scholarly tradition that began in the 19th century with Black women such as Sojourner Truth, Maria Stewart, and Anna Julia Cooper and men like W. E. B. DuBois—intellectuals who first articulated the unique challenges of Black women facing the multiple and simultaneous effects of race, gender, and class. What distinguished this early work on Black women was that it argued forcefully and passionately that the lives of African American women could not be understood through a unidimensional analysis focusing exclusively on either race or gender.

Intersectional scholarship, as we know it today, fused this knowledge from race and ethnic studies with aspects of women's studies and refined it in the debates and discourse that informed the civil and women's rights activism of the 1960s and 1970s. Before that time, women's studies emphasized the importance of gender and sexism while Black and Latino studies focused on race and racism as experienced within these respective communities. Each field sought to interrogate historical patterns of subordination and domination, asserting that we live in a society that is organized around complex and layered sets of inequalities. . . .

Categories of race/ethnicity, class, and gender were defined as major markers and controllers of oppression in the earliest discussions of intersectionality, with limited attention given to other categories such as sexuality, nation, age,

disability, and religion, which have been discussed in more recent years. One result of this historical trajectory is a perspective asserting that individuals and groups can simultaneously experience oppression and privilege. Mere recognition of this history is not sufficient to form a complete understanding of the extensive ranges of "structures and experiences produced by intersecting forms of race and gender"; neither does it ensure proper acknowledgment of the "interlocking inequalities, what Patricia Hill Collins calls the 'matrix of domination'" (Baca Zinn & Dill, 1996, p. 326).

Collins explains that "the matrix of domination is structured on several levels. People experience and resist oppression on three levels: the level of personal biography; the group or community level of cultural context created by race, class, and gender; and the systemic level of social institutions" (Collins, 1990, p. 227). Collins distinguishes her conceptualization of interlocking theories, or oppressions, from the traditional additive models of oppression found in much traditional feminist theory. . . .

By noting the ways in which men and women occupy variant positions of power and privilege across race, space, and time, intersectionality has refashioned several of the basic premises that have guided feminist theory as it evolved following the 1950s. Many have explicitly recognized that the prototypical model for feminist theory post-1950s was based on the lives of White women whose experiences as wives, daughters, and mothers were to be strictly differentiated from the experience of Black women as informed by historical precedent. "Judged by the evolving nineteenth century ideology of femininity, which emphasized women's roles as nurturing mothers and gentle companions and housekeepers for their husbands, Black women were practically anomalies" (Davis, 1981, p. 5). Indeed, "one cannot assume, as have many feminist theorists and activists, that all women have had the same experience of gender oppression—or that they will be on the same side of a struggle, not even when some women define that struggle as 'feminist' . . . [F]or peoples of color, having children and maintaining families have been an essential part of the struggle against racist oppression. [Thus, it is not surprising that] many women of color have rejected the white women's movement's view of the family as the center of 'women's oppression'" (Amott & Matthaei, 1991, pp. 16–17), which many find to be the decisive message of books regarded as pivotal foundations of the second wave of the feminist movement such as *The Feminine Mystique* by Betty Friedan or *Of Woman Born* by Adrienne Rich. We do not mean to imply, either, that all women of color would renounce the accounts offered in the pages of these books. We offer these textual examples as evidence that intersectional scholarship has been able to highlight the myriad ways in which the experiences of some White women and women of color differ in the nuances of the maintenance of family. More specifically, these differences are to be found within the inextricable lines of racial ethnicity and gender that were influential in the fomentation of a feminist consciousness for some women that was both distinct from and dependent upon the experiences of other women.

Indeed, the family has been for many women of color a sort of "haven in a heartless world" of racism that provides the needed support to fight against oppression of many types (Dill, 1979; hooks, 1984). Drawing on the work of a number of the pioneering Black feminist intersectional scholars, Landry (2000) argues in his book on Black middle-class women that this support enabled Black women to produce a new ideology of womanhood that permitted the formation of the modern dual-career and dual-earner family. This model of womanhood rejected the notion that "outside work was detrimental to [Black women's roles] as wives and mothers" (Landry, 2000, p. 73). Indeed, Black women of the late 19th and early 20th centuries realized that "their membership in the paid labor force was critical to achieving true equality with men" (p. 74) in the larger U.S. society in a way that was not available to White women under the cult of true womanhood that constrained them to the exclusive domains of hearth and home. Women of

color, having always been regarded as a source of labor in the United States, were never the beneficiaries of this ideology of protectionism and were not, therefore, hampered from developing an ideology that saw beyond the dictates of traditional feminist principles based in the experience of gender subordination perceived as endemic to all women (see, for example, Davis, 1972).

Winifred Breines (2006) provides an interesting reflection on the role and relationship of early intersectional thinking that promoted an understanding of mutually constituted structures of difference and inequality in feminist experiences. As she argues in *The Trouble Between Us: An Uneasy History of White and Black Women in the Feminist Movement,*

> In the development of the feminist movement, one of the most dramatic political shifts was from a desire to overcome difference to its promotion. Integration or interracialism as a goal migrated toward difference and an embrace of identity that precluded togetherness. This was a disturbing process but, in retrospect, probably inevitable. Postwar young people, especially whites, knew very little about racism and sexism. They had to separate to learn who they were in the race, class, and gender terms constructed by American society. . . . Just as identity politics divided the society that created such politics in the first place, they divided the movements. (Breines, 2006, p. 16)

Breines (2006) concludes her text on the differences that emerged between Black and White women in the feminist movement with words from several young feminists, one of whom contends that "unlike second wave feminism, which has operated from a monolithic center, multiplicity offers the power of existing insidiously and simultaneously everywhere. 'Women' as a primary identity category has ceased to be the entry point for much young activist work" (p. 196). Breines (2006) follows this with the admonition that young feminists have come to this knowledge having read the experiences of those who struggled before them: "They may not be aware of it, but the racial learning curve that began in the early 1960s continues among younger—and older—feminists in the twenty-first century" (p. 199). Similar to the project embarked upon by Breines, the research and writing of feminist scholars of color continues the tradition of theorizing the experience of women of color who have been ignored in the scholarship on both race and gender. These scholars have produced landmark studies based on lived experience at the intersections of race, gender, ethnicity, class, and sexuality.[1]

GROWTH AND DISSEMINATION: EMERGING INQUIRIES AND CONTROVERSIES

As an approach to creating knowledge that has its roots in analyses of the lived experiences of women of color—women whose scholarly and social justice work reveals how aspects of identity and social relations are shaped by the simultaneous operation of multiple systems of power—intersectional scholarship is interdisciplinary in nature and focuses on how structures of difference combine to create a feminist praxis that is new and distinct from the social, cultural, and artistic forms emphasized in traditional feminist paradigms that focus primarily upon contrasting the experiences of women in society to those of men. Intersectionality is intellectually transformative not only because it centers the experiences of people of color and locates its analysis within systems of ideological, political, institutional, and economic power as they are shaped by historical patterns of race, class, gender, sexuality, nation, ethnicity, and age but also because it provides a platform for uniting different kinds of praxis in the pursuit of social justice: analysis, theorizing, education, advocacy, and policy development.

The people who engage with this work do so out of strong commitments to diversity, multiculturalism, and human rights, combined with a desire to create a more equitable society that recognizes, validates, and celebrates difference. The social justice agenda of this scholarship is crucial to its utility in fomenting theory and praxis specifically designed for analyzing inequalities of power and privilege, and, consequently, intersectionality is of interest to persons outside the academy who share concerns that underlie this scholarship. As Catherine MacKinnon contends, "What is important about intersectionality is what it is doing in our world, how it is traveling around the world and being used in defense of human rights, not just what it says" (MacKinnon, 2010).

The intellectual vibrancy within and around intersectional theory is yielding new frontiers of knowledge production that include, but are not limited to, scholarship on identity and the applicability of intersectionality to groups in other social locations or in multiple social locations simultaneously (Browne & Misra, 2003; Henderson & Tickamyer, 2009; Kohlman, 2010). Discussions about methodologies, language, and images most accurately convey the complexities of these interrelationships. For example, the development of the queer of color critique (Ferguson, 2003; Johnson & Henderson, 2005) as an intervention into sexuality studies establishes race and ethnicity as critical dimensions of queer studies, scholarship on globalization and international human rights moves intersectionality beyond the U.S. context (Davis, 2008; Knapp, 2005; Mohanty, 2003; Yuval-Davis, 2006), and work that continues explicitly to link theory and practice provides an analytical foundation for social justice and critical resistance. Within each of these topics, there are disagreements about approach and perspective, . . . and the debates and discussions contribute to the vibrancy of the topic and thus to advancing this scholarship and producing knowledge that illuminates the many factors that shape processes of experiencing multiple identities and social locations.

Because the contemporary growth of intersectionality as a theoretical approach is relatively recent and has developed in a number of different fields, future growth is largely defined by the trajectory of current debates and inquiries.

* * *

Methodological Concerns

Debates around methodologies center on the concern of remaining grounded in the questions, struggles, and experiences of particular communities that generate an intersectional perspective. At the same time, methodological debates about intersectionality often extend this approach to identify common themes and points of connection between specific social locations and broader social patterns. Stated somewhat differently: How do we benefit from comparisons and interrelationships without negating or undermining the complex and particular character of each group, system of oppression, or culture? Answers to this question are embedded in discussions about the language and metaphors that most effectively convey the concept of intersectionality as well as in debates about the use of qualitative and historical versus quantitative research methodologies.

Central to the discussion of language have been disputes about the adequacies and limitations of the term "intersectionality" and the metaphors associated with it. Scholars working with these ideas continue to seek ways to overcome an image that suggests that these dimensions of inequality, such as race, class, and gender, are separable and distinct and that it is only at certain points that they overlap or intersect with one another. This concern was specifically articulated by Deborah King in 1988 when she called for a model of analysis permitting recognition of the "multiple jeopardy" constituted by the interactive oppressions that circumscribe the lives of Black women and defy separation into discrete categories of analysis. The modifier "multiple" refers not only to several simultaneous oppressions but to the multiplicative relationships among them as well (King, 1988, p. 47). It is now widely recognized that intersectionality is more than a car crash at the nexus of a set of separate roads (Crenshaw, 1989). Instead, it is well understood that these systems of power are mutually constituted (Weber, 2009) such that there is no point at which race is not simultaneously classed and gendered or gender is not simultaneously raced and classed. How to capture this complexity in a single term or image has been an ongoing conversation.

Recent work by Ivy Ken (2007) provides a useful overview of a number of the conceptual images in use: that is, the notion of "intersecting versus interlocking" inequalities, which has been expressed in metaphors such as crossing roads or a matrix or the importance of locating oppressions within "systems versus structures versus institutions." She then moves on to analyze the limitations of these analytical approaches and suggests aspects of intersectionality that remain unexplained. She further proposes an innovative and promising approach to thinking about these ideas using the processes of producing, using, experiencing, and digesting sugar as a metaphor for describing, discussing, and theorizing intersectionality (Ken, 2008). For example, she addresses the importance of context-specific relationships in understanding how race, class, and gender oppression is "produced, what people and institutions do with it once they have it in their hands, what it feels like to experience it, and how it then comes to shape us" (Ken, 2008, p. 154). Ken argues that the relationships among sources of oppression, like race, class, and gender, start with production—every aspect of race, class, and gender has been and is produced under particular social, historical, political, cultural, and economic conditions.

Given the intersectional argument that race, class, gender, and other axes of inequality are always intertwined, co-constructed, and simultaneous (Weber, 2009), questions and debates have arisen about how quantitative approaches that rely on the analysis of separate and distinct variables can account for such interactivity. Two issues frame this debate. The first is the idea that these axes of inequality are not simply characteristics of individuals to be used as variables, isolated from the particular histories, social relations, and institutional contexts that produced them (Amott & Matthaei, 1996; Stacey &

Thorne, cited in Harnois, 2009). The second is the task of developing quantitative approaches that address and reveal the overlapping differences present in intersectional analyses in a way that will yield important, generalizable results.

The work of Leslie McCall (2001, 2005) with regard to race, class, and gender in different types of labor markets has been particularly important in efforts to rethink the use of quantitative tools so that they can reveal the differential ways race, class, and gender interact within different social contexts. Her *Signs* article (2005) has been an important tool in efforts to provide empirical evidence of the value of intersectional analysis in the quantitative social sciences. Specifically, McCall applies an intersectional approach to an examination of the impact of economic restructuring on wage inequalities (see also Hancock, 2008; Simien, 2007; Valentine, 2007). To do this, she studies the effect of multiple factors on different racial/ethnic, class, and gender groups and on the relationships both within and between those groups in different regional economies. What she finds is that the patterns are not the same: that a single economic environment may create advantages for some in a group and disadvantages for others in the same group relative to other groups, thus making some environments more appropriate for one set of social policies while a different set may be more appropriate for another. She states: "different contexts reveal different configurations of inequality [and] no single dimension of overall inequality can adequately describe the full structure of multiple, intersecting, and conflicting dimensions of inequality" (McCall, 2005, p. 1791).

Kohlman (2006, 2010) has utilized intersection theory to illustrate how the experiences of men and women who report having experienced sexual harassment in the U.S. labor market differ because of the interaction of several forces of oppression that influence behavior simultaneously. She employs quantitative methods to illustrate successfully that it is both possible and imperative to deconstruct commonly used additive models of analysis, which mask the intersectional effects shaping the experiences of those embedded within them. Catharine Harnois (2005, 2009), by applying multiracial feminist theory in the design of a quantitative analysis of women's paths to feminism, has both revealed and offered meaningful explanations for variations among women by race and ethnicity, differences within racial-ethnic categories that had not been thought to exist.

Because empirical findings from quantitative analyses dominate the social sciences, are seen as authoritative and generalizable, and often provide the documentation upon which social policy is built, quantitative research that demonstrates the importance of intersectionality offers the opportunity to expand the framework's applicability and impact. The danger, however, is that these axes of inequality may be read as a reductive analysis of the interaction of a set of individual characteristics, thus diluting the power and full meaning of the experiential theory these interactions have been constructed to illustrate. Quantitative methodologies, when read in conjunction with findings produced from the qualitative studies that continue to dominate research within the intersectional paradigm, provide analytic frames that complement, apply, and extend the impact and understanding of intersectionality.

It is also important to note that debates about methodology are not limited to a quantitative versus qualitative discussion, but, rather, embrace the idea that we must continue to explore and expand the approaches we use to address an even broader range of questions that can be generated by this scholarship. These should include applied and theoretical and interdisciplinary and transversal modes of inquiry, among others. Interdisciplinary research must embrace multiple methodological approaches to capture the complexities and nuances in the lives of individuals and the experiences of groups of people (see also Hancock, 2007). A key criterion is to avoid essentializing people's experiences by burying intragroup diversity within isolated analytical categories.

* * *

CONCLUSION

In 1979, Audre Lorde stood before an audience at a conference devoted to Simone de Beauvoir's book *The Second Sex* in New York City and spoke these words:

> Those of us who stand outside the circle of this society's definition of acceptable women; those of us who have been forged in the crucibles of difference—those of us who are poor, who are lesbians, who are Black, who are older—know that *survival is not an academic skill.* It is learning how to stand alone, unpopular and sometimes reviled, and how to make common cause with those others identified as outside the structures in order to define and seek a world in which we all can flourish. It is learning how to take our differences and make them strengths. (Lorde, 1984, p. 112)

More than three decades later, Lorde's clear mandate for social justice resonates at the very core of what intersectionality was, is, and must continue to be in order to serve the aims of those individuals who have found themselves to be situated in different social locations around the margins of feminist debates and inquiries. Just as Lorde called for feminists to turn difference into strengths, the theoretical paradigm of intersectionality has provided a voice and a vision to scholars seeking to make visible the interlocking structures of inequality to be found within the academic and everyday concerns that shape both our livelihoods and our experiences of the world.

Intersectionality has traveled a long distance, and, indeed, we recognize that it has taken many forms across academic disciplines and life histories. Intersectionality has now reached the point where it may be regarded as a member of the theoretical cannon taught in courses on law, social sciences, and the humanities. Intersectionality has, thus, increased in strength and, perhaps alternatively, suffered significant dilution in application as often happens when any theoretical tool is either misinterpreted or misapplied. As to the evidence of intersection theory's increasing strength, we know that intersectionality has been the practice of Black feminist scholars for

generations; in that respect, this paradigm is not at all new. It has just been a long time coming into its own, and now, having been newly embraced as a powerful tool of social justice, social thought, and social activism by a larger population of feminist researchers, it has become more visible than ever before.

As to the evidence of its misapplication, we caution scholars to be mindful of what we consider to be "strong intersectionality" and "weak intersectionality." "Strong intersectionality" may be found in theoretical and methodological rubrics that seek to analyze institutions and identities *in relation to one another.* That is, "strong intersectionality" seeks to ascertain how phenomena are mutually constituted and interdependent, how we must understand one phenomenon in deference to understanding another. On the other hand, "weak intersectionality" explores differences without any true analysis. That is to say, "weak intersectionality" ignores the very mandate called for by Audre Lorde and seeks to explore no more than how we are different. "Weak intersectionality" eschews the difficult dialogue(s) of how our differences have come to be—or how our differences might become axes of strength, fortification, and a renewed vision of how our world has been—and continues, instead, to be socially constructed by a theory and methodology that seeks only occasionally to question difference, without arriving at a deep and abiding understanding of how our differences are continuing to evolve.

Part of the proliferation of "weak intersectionality" may be found in the interdisciplinary narratives advancing the argument that this paradigmatic tool operates in different ways in different institutional spaces. This argument is also reminiscent of the contention that intersectional theory has been individualized within separate fields of knowledge. We can only reply to such arguments by, first, acknowledging that intersectionality has developed disparately within different spheres of knowledge because of the way in which intersectional theorizing is applied across disciplinary fields. For example, some might encounter intersectionality as a concrete reality that hinders effective litigation under the law because whole people are literally required to split their identity(ies) in order to be properly recognized in a court of law. But when this same legal phenomena is read and discussed in the social sciences or humanities, the scholars at issue might study it as a structural impediment or analytic frame that defies discrete analysis. That being said, this dilemma has the very real potential of diverting one's attention away from the theoretical imperative of intersectionality as source of illumination and understanding to one that distorts and misrepresents lived experiences of the law, social norms, and social justice.

But we also recognize, as a second proposition, that intersectionality has developed differently across spheres of knowledge because of the differing experiences and privileges we enjoy as scholars and everyday citizens of the world. We noted previously, for example, that intersectionality has benefited tremendously from differing methodological applications and transnational discourses, even as we remain steadfast in our contention that this paradigm was born of the experiences of Black women in the United States that could not be properly understood using the unidimensional lens of race or of gender in academic and legal discourses.

Having established the foregoing premises of "strong intersectionality" and "weak intersectionality," we now see intersectional theorizing developing into a paradigm of analysis that defies separation into distinct fields of knowledge because of its explanatory power as a theoretical tool that does not require tweaking "to make it fit," so to speak. This is because the primacy of the basic core principles of intersectionality—that is, mutually constituted interdependence; interlocking oppressions and privileges; multiple experiences of race, gender, sexuality, and so forth—are now more widely recognized as such and scholars are more apt to hold one another to these basic rules of application, whatever methodology is employed. In fact, the debates occurring within intersectional scholarship today reflect the growth and maturation of this approach and

provide the opportunity to begin, as Lynn Weber says, to "harvest lessons learned" (as cited in Dill & Zambrana, 2009, p. 287).

Among the lessons learned and knowledge produced is a broader and more in-depth understanding of the notion of race, racial formation, and racial projects. Another is a broader understanding of the concept of nation and of notions of citizenship both in the United States and globally. Concepts such as situated knowledge (Lorde), oppositional consciousness (Sandoval), and strategic essentialism (Hurtado) offer ways to theorize about difference and diversity. A third lesson is the knowledge that there is no single category (race, class, ethnicity, gender, nation, or sexuality) that can explain human experience without reference to other categories. Thus we have and will need to continue to develop more nuanced and complex understandings of identity and more fluid notions of gender, race, sexuality, and class. The work relies heavily on a more expanded sense of the concept of social construction and rests much of its analysis on the principle of the social construction of difference. Organista (2007) contests the dominant culture's imperialism and resistance to discussion of human differences within and across cultures and calls for a discussion of difference "beyond the kind of defensive and superficial hyperbole that leaves social oppression unchallenged" (p. 101). And, although the scholarship still struggles with the pull to establish either a hierarchy of difference or a list that includes all forms of social differentiation, both of which are antithetical to the specific objectives of intersectionality, a body of knowledge is being produced that provides a basis for understanding the various histories and organizations of these categories of inequality. This evolving body of knowledge is helping us better understand what differences render inequalities and how to resist reductionist impulses. As a theoretical paradigm,[2] intersectionality is unique in its versatility and ability to produce new knowledge. We remain optimistic about the future of intersectionality, particularly if this scholarship respects its crucial commitments to laying bare the roots of power and inequality, while continuing to pursue an activist agenda of social justice.

NOTES

1. This list is not meant to be exclusive or exhaustive but a reflection of the breadth of early intersectional scholarship: Patricia Hill Collins (1990), Kimberlé Crenshaw (1989), Gloria Anzaldúa (1987), Maxine Baca Zinn and Bonnie Dill (1996), Audre Lorde (1984), Angela Y. Davis (1981), Cherríe Moraga (1983), Chela Sandoval (1991), Chandra Talpade Mohanty (1988), and bell hooks (1984).

2. In 1998, Collins referred to intersectionality as an "emerging paradigm." In 2007, Hancock argues it has become a normative and empirical paradigm.

REFERENCES

Amott, T. L., & Matthaei, J. A. (1991). *Race, gender and work*. Boston: South End Press.

Amott, T. L., & Matthaei, J. A. (1996). *Race, gender and work* (New ed.). Boston: South End Press.

Anzaldúa, G. (1987). *La Frontera/Borderlands: The new Mestiza*. San Francisco: Aunt Lute Books.

Baca Zinn, M., Cannon, L. W., Dill, B. T., & Higginbotham, E. (1986). The costs of exclusionary practices in women's studies. *Signs: Journal of Women in Culture and Society, 11*, 290–303.

Baca Zinn, M., & Dill, B. T. (1996). Theorizing difference from multi-racial feminism. *Feminist Studies, 22*(2), 321–331.

Breines, W. (2006). *The trouble between us: An uneasy history of white and black women in the feminist movement.* New York: Oxford University Press.

Browne, I., & Misra, J. (2003). The intersection of gender and race in the labor market. *Annual Review of Sociology, 29*, 487–513.

Collins, P. H. (1990). *Black feminist thought: Knowledge, consciousness, and the politics of empowerment.* Boston: Unwin Hyman.

Crenshaw, K. (1989). Demarginalizing the intersection of race and sex: A black feminist of antidiscrimination doctrine, feminist theory, and antiracist politics. *University of Chicago Legal Forum*, 139–167.

Davis, A.Y. (1972). Reflections on the black woman's role in the community of slaves. *The Massachusetts Review, 13*(1/2), 81–100.

Davis, A.Y. (1981). *Women, race, and class.* New York: Random House.

Davis, K. (2008). Intersectionality as buzzword: A sociology of science perspective on what makes a feminist theory successful. *Feminist Theory, 9*(1), 67–85.

Dill, B. T. (1979). The dialectics of black womanhood. *Signs: Journal of Women in Culture and Society, 4*(3), 543–555.

Dill, B. T., & Zambrana, R. E. (2009). *Emerging intersections: Race, class, and gender in theory, policy, and practice.* New Brunswick, NJ: Rutgers University Press.

Ferguson, R. A. (2003). *Aberrations in black: Toward a queer of color critique.* Minneapolis: University of Minnesota Press.

Hancock, A. M. (2007). When multiplication doesn't equal quick addition: Examining intersectionality as a research paradigm. *Perspectives on Politics, 5*(1), 63–79.

Hancock, A. M. (2008). Intersectionality as a normative and empirical paradigm. *Politics & Gender, 3*(2), 248–254.

Harnois, C. E. (2005). Different paths to different feminisms? Bridging multiracial feminist theory and quantitative sociological gender research. *Gender & Society, 19*(6), 809–828.

Harnois, C. E. (2009). Imagining a "feminist revolution": Can multiracial feminism revolutionize quantitative social science research? In M. T. Berger & K. Guidroz (Eds.), *The intersectional approach: Transforming the academy through race, class, and gender* (pp. 157–172). Chapel Hill, NC: UNC Press.

hooks, b. (1984). *Feminist theory: From margin to center.* Cambridge, MA: South End Press.

Johnson, E. P., & Henderson, M. G. (Eds.). (2005). *Black queer studies: A critical anthology.* Durham, NC: Duke University Press.

Ken, Ivy. (2007). Race-class-gender theory: An image(ry) problem. *Gender Issues, 24*, 1–20.

Ken, Ivy. (2008). Beyond the intersection: A new culinary metaphor for race-class-gender studies. *Sociological Theory, 26*(2), 152–172.

King, D. (1988). Multiple jeopardy, multiple consciousness: The context of a black feminist ideology. *Signs: Journal of Women in Culture and Society, 14*(1), 42–72.

Knapp, G. A. (2005). Race, class, gender: Reclaiming baggage in fast-travelling theories. *European Journal of Women's Studies, 12*(3), 249–265.

Kohlman, M. H. (2006). Intersection theory: A more elucidating paradigm of quantitative analysis. *Race, Gender & Class, 13*, 42–59.

Kohlman, M. H. (2010). Race, rank and gender: The determinants of sexual harassment for men and women of color in the military. In V. Demos & M. Segal (Vol. Eds.), *Advances in gender research: Vol. 14. Interactions and intersections of gendered bodies at work, at home, and at play* (pp. 65–94). Boston: Elsevier.

Landry, Bart. (2000). *Black working wives: Pioneers of the American family revolution.* Berkeley: University of California Press.

Lorde, A. (1984). *Sister outsider.* Freedom, CA: The Crossing Press.

MacKinnon, C. (2010, March 11). *Panelist remarks on "Rounding intersectionality: Critical foundations and contested trajectories."* Paper at the 4th Annual Critical Race Studies Symposium—Intersectionality: Challenging Theory, Reframing Politics, Transforming Movements, UCLA School of Law, Los Angeles, CA.

McCall, L. (2001). *Complex inequality: Gender, class, and race in the new economy.* New York: Routledge.

McCall, L. (2005). The complexity of intersectionality. *Signs: Journal of Women in Culture and Society, 30*(3), 1771–1800.

Mohanty, C. T. (1988). Under western eyes: Feminist scholarship and colonial discourses. *Feminist Review, 30,* 61–88.

Mohanty, C. T. (2003). *Feminism without borders.* Durham, NC: Duke University Press.

Moraga, C. (1983). *Loving in the war years.* Boston: South End Press.

Organista, C. K. (2007). *Solving Latino psychosocial and health problems: Theory, practice, and populations.* Hoboken, NJ: John Wiley & Sons, Inc.

Sandoval, C. (1991). U.S. third world feminism: The theory and method of oppositional consciousness in the postmodern world. *Genders, 10,* 1–24.

Simien, E. (2007). Doing intersectionality research: From conceptual issues to practical examples. *Politics and Gender, 3*(2), 264–271.

Valentine, G. (2007). Theorizing and researching intersectionality: A challenge for feminist geography. *Professional Geographer, 59,* 10–21.

Weber, Lynn. (2009). *Understanding race, class, gender, and sexuality: An intersectional framework* (2nd ed.). New York: Oxford.

Yuval-Davis, N. (2006). Intersectionality and feminist politics. *The European Journal of Women's Studies, 13*(3), 193–210.

Introduction to Reading 8

In this piece, Nikki Jones points to the need to combine an intersectional analysis when studying "doing gender." This piece was published as part of a symposium, 20 years after the original article on "doing gender" by Candace West and Donald Zimmerman. During those 20 years, many changes occurred in the approaches to studying gender, including development of the literature on intersectional analysis, as Bonnie Thornton Dill and Marla H. Kohlman described in the previous reading. In this article, Jones uses research from her recent study of Black girls and inner-city violence to provide an in-depth look at the need to combine intersectional analysis with the "doing gender" theoretical framework. As you read through this article, consider why it is so important to use an intersectional approach when studying "doing gender."

1. What does this article mean by "categorical identity"?

2. What does intersectional analysis add to our understanding of "doing gender"?

3. Give an example of how Kiara was "doing gender," and explain how that used interactional analysis.

"I Was Aggressive for the Streets, Pretty for the Pictures"

Gender, Difference, and the Inner-City Girl

Nikki Jones

It is a late June afternoon and I am standing outside of a café on Fillmore Street in San Francisco. I am holding flyers for Kiara[1], a young woman I met a few hours earlier. Kiara is 22 years old with a light brown complexion and long, wavy hair that suggests a multiracial heritage. Her style of dress is 1980s-retro. She wears a purple lace glove with the finger cut off on her right hand, a short-sleeved jacket over a yellow and green Brazil fútbol jersey, and tight denim jeans that ride low, causing her belly to peek out sometimes between her jeans and her jersey. Two large star-shaped earrings dangle from her ears and a small white flower is tucked into her hair. She was born and raised in the Fillmore, a once-vibrant Black neighborhood that is now quickly gentrifying after decades of blight and neglect. I have conducted field research here since 2005 and just finished interviewing Kiara inside the café. Kiara's grandmother, like many older Black Fillmore residents, migrated from the South. She owned the house in which she raised Kiara after Kiara's mother was killed by her father, who, Kiara tells me, was a big-time drug dealer in the neighborhood before he was sent to prison. Kiara remembers how her father's tough reputation influenced how others interacted with her in the neighborhood; even though she was a child she garnered a level of respect. She learned early on how to manage her interactions with others differently in different situations: "[as a child] I had the street element, and I was aggressive for the streets, pretty for the pictures."

Kiara is helping to collect signatures for an antiredevelopment campaign in Hunter's Point-Bayview, a larger and even more distressed Black neighborhood in San Francisco. Kiara offers to give me a tour of the Fillmore and I follow along as she walks with clipboard in hand. Kiara's play on mainstream and local expectations of race, gender, class, sexuality, and power is on full display during her brief interactions with strangers. She confidently, assertively, even aggressively approaches men on the street to sign her petition and then draws on normative expectations of manhood and femininity to encourage them to add their names to the list: Babies and women are in danger, she tells them, letting the implication that real men would sign up to protect babies and women hang in the air. She switches from aggressive to demure just long enough to flirt with a man passing by on the street and then to defiant when she passes the police station on the corner. "They don't give a fuck!" she declares loudly. A few moments later we stop to observe the RIPs scratched into the concrete sidewalk of a neighborhood block "where a lot of the trouble happens." Kiara calls these scratches that mark the murders of young Black men "modern-day hieroglyphics." She gets silent and still, but just for a moment. She has work to do so she keeps on moving.

Twenty years after the publication of West and Zimmerman's "Doing Gender" (1987) critical and feminist scholars have the analytical tools to observe and represent Kiara's interactions on this

From Jones, Nikki. 2009."" I Was Aggressive for the Streets, Pretty for Pictures'"": Gender, Difference and the Inner-City Girl." *Gender & Society* (1): 89–93.

city block in ways that illuminate how gender, race, and class are accomplished during situated interaction. An interactional analysis of Kiara's walk through the Fillmore reveals moments where the accomplishment of gender, race, or class emerges as most significant. Such an analysis is also likely to reveal moments when Kiara violates or manipulates the normative expectations associated with categorical identity, and the consequences of her doing so. Yet, as Patricia Hill Collins writes in her critical response to "Doing Difference" (1995), such an analysis, on its own, is not likely to reveal how the social contexts in which these interactions take place are shaped by the "messy" intersection of various systems of oppression (1995, 491–94). Kiara and other neighborhood residents describe these oppressive forces as "Redevelopment," referring to the urban redevelopment agency that many longtime Fillmore residents hold responsible for decades of neighborhood underdevelopment and exploitation. Another oppressive force that has shaped life for young people in the neighborhood—boys and girls—is the local police force, including the city's gang task force, which has grown stronger in the nation's never-ending War on Drugs.

If we focus only on interactional accomplishments of categorical identity we can miss the chance to illuminate the recursive relationship *between* Kiara's interactions with others, her identity (or identities), and these larger oppressive forces, which are shaped by various overlapping and intersecting -isms. To be fair, I do not think such an omission is a necessary or desired outcome of the theoretical frameworks of "doing gender" or "doing difference" (West and Fenstermaker 1995). However, the ubiquitous use (or misuse) of the respective frameworks can sometimes leave the impression that a scholar's most important objective is to "test" the respective theoretical approaches—spotting gender or difference here, there, and everywhere—not, instead, to use these frameworks to illuminate the complicated and sometimes contradictory ways in which situated interaction is linked to structural circumstances.

My recent ethnographic work on Black girls and inner-city violence does not set out to test either framework. My analysis is deeply and *simultaneously* informed by the interactional concerns of West, Zimmerman, and Fenstermaker *and* the theoretical and political concerns of Patricia Hill Collins, Howard Winant, and other critical race and feminist scholars. After the sometimes contentious but important debates on how to conceptualize intersecting identities and oppressions, I find that drawing on both approaches helps me to more accurately represent the lives of young women like Kiara. Drawing on both interactional analysis and Black feminist thought encourages us to situate Black women's and girl's experiences, *including their interactional experiences,* at the center of our empirical investigations. Such an integrative approach challenges us to develop better explanations for how interaction, identity, and various structural -isms are linked. Additionally, such an approach pushes social scientists to consider Black women and girls not simply as problems to be solved or explained (e.g., single mothers or "violent" girls) but rather draws attention to the dilemmas and contradictions that Black women and girls encounter and in some measure reconcile in their everyday lives. This is Black feminist interactional studies, perhaps.

At the same time that she is "doing gender" or "doing difference" with others, for example, Kiara is also deeply invested in a struggle for survival. "It's about being a survivor," she responds when I ask her how she developed the strong sense of independence that she revealed during our interview, "and we have to survive." This overarching concern for survival was also revealed during my field research amongst African American inner-city girls in Philadelphia (Jones 2004 & 2008). In a recent article, for example, I describe how inner-city girls work the "code of the street," (Jones 2008) which is described by urban ethnographer and race scholar Elijah Anderson (1999) as a *system of accountability* that governs formal and informal interactions in distressed urban areas, especially interpersonal violence. At the heart of "the code" is a battle for respect and *manhood*. In *Black Sexual Politics* (2004), Patricia Hill Collins writes that as Black men embrace "the code," they embrace a hegemonic masculinity that is based on the *coupling* of strength with dominance—white men with wealth and power are able to demonstrate such masculinity through economic or military dominance (in addition to physical dominance). Poor Black men in distressed urban areas must rely primarily on physical domination, which makes them and others in their community more vulnerable to violent victimization.

African American inner-city girls may have no manhood to defend, yet the shared circumstances of inner-city life engender a shared concern for physical safety and survival. Over time, girls coming of age in distressed urban areas come to realize too how respect, reputation, and retaliation—the three R's at the heart of the code—organize their social worlds. Much like Kiara, the girls I met knew quite well the situations in which presenting oneself as "aggressive," "good," or "pretty" paid off. Listening to the stories of these girls, it is difficult to imagine them as held hostage to accountability. Instead, they strategically choose from a variety of gender, race, and class displays depending on the situation, the public identity they are invested in crafting, *and* in service of a survival project that has historically defined the lives of poor, Black women and girls in the United States—a project with especially high stakes in neighborhoods like the one in which Kiara has grown up.

These stories complicate our understandings of "doing gender" and "doing difference" in ways that take account the complexities of structure and its intersections with race, class and gender. . . .

NOTE

1. Kiara is a pseudonym.

REFERENCES

Anderson, E. 1999. *Code of the street: Decency, violence, and the moral life of the inner city.* New York: W.W. Norton Press.

Collins, Patricia Hill. 1995. Symposium: On West and Fenstermaker's "Doing difference." *Gender & Society* 9:491–94.

———. 2004. *Black sexual politics: African Americans, gender; and the new racism.* New York and London: Routledge.

Jones, N. 2004. "It's not where you live, it's how you live": How young women negotiate conflict and violence in the inner city. *Annals of the American Academy of Political and Social Science* 595:49–62.

———. 2008. Working "the code": On girls, gender, and inner-city violence. Special issue: Current approaches to understanding female offending. *Australia and New Zealand Journal of Criminology* 4:63–83.

West, Candace, and Sarah Fenstermaker. 1995. Doing difference. *Gender & Society* 9:8–37.

West, Candace, and D. H. Zimmerman. 1987. Doing gender. *Gender & Society* 1:125–51.

Introduction to Reading 9

In this article, Karen D. Pyke and Denise L. Johnson use both the social construction of gender and intersectional analysis to examine the experiences of second-generation Asian American women. They interviewed 100 daughters of Korean American (KA) and Vietnamese American (VA) immigrants to better understand how gender, ethnicity, and culture influenced the meaning respondents gave to their experiences. By living in two worlds, the Asian American women were acutely aware of the social construction of gender within culture, as they had to move between two cultural constructions of femininity. Thus, ethnicity and gender interact in ways that made the women conscious of their decision to "do gender" based on the culturally defined, situational expectations for femininity.

1. Using this article as an example, explain what it means to "do gender."

2. Why don't these women just be "who they are" across situations?

3. How do these women's struggles between cultural definitions of femininity reinforce, and make dominant, White femininity?

—— ASIAN AMERICAN WOMEN AND RACIALIZED FEMININITIES ——

"DOING" GENDER ACROSS CULTURAL WORLDS

Karen D. Pyke and Denise L. Johnson

The study of gender in recent years has been largely guided by two orienting approaches: (1) a social constructionist emphasis on the day-to-day production or doing of gender (Coltrane 1989; West and Zimmerman 1987), and (2) attention to the interlocking systems of race, class, and gender (Espiritu 1997; Hill Collins 2000). Despite the prominence of these approaches, little empirical work has been done that integrates the doing of gender with the study of race. A contributing factor is the more expansive incorporation of social constructionism in the study of gender than in race scholarship where biological markers are still given importance despite widespread acknowledgment that racial oppression is rooted in social arrangements and not biology (Glenn 1999). In addition, attempts to theoretically integrate the doing of gender, race, and class around the concept of "doing difference" (West and Fenstermaker 1995) tended to downplay historical macrostructures of power and domination and to privilege gender over race and class (Hill Collins et al. 1995). Work is still needed that integrates systems of oppression in a social constructionist framework without granting primacy to any one form of inequality or ignoring larger structures of domination.

The integration of gender and race within a social constructionist approach directs attention to issues that have been overlooked. Little research has examined how racially and ethnically subordinated women, especially Asian American women, mediate cross-pressures in the production of femininity as they move between mainstream and ethnic arenas, such as family, work, and school, and whether distinct and even contradictory gender displays and strategies are enacted across different arenas. Many, if not most, individuals move in social worlds that do not require dramatic inversions of their gender performances, thereby enabling them to maintain stable and seemingly unified gender strategies. However, members of communities that are racially and ethnically marginalized and who regularly traverse interactional arenas with conflicting gender expectations might engage different gender performances depending on the local context in which they are interacting. Examining the ways that such individuals mediate conflicting expectations would address several unanswered questions. Do marginalized women shift their gender performances across mainstream and subcultural settings in response to different gender norms? If so, how do they experience and negotiate such transitions? What meaning do they assign to the different forms of femininities that they engage across settings? Do racially subordinated women experience their production of femininity as inferior to those forms engaged by privileged white women and glorified in the dominant culture?

We address these issues by examining how second-generation Asian American women experience and think about the shifting dynamics involved in the doing of femininity in Asian ethnic and mainstream cultural worlds. We look specifically at their assumptions about gender dynamics in the Euro-centric mainstream and Asian ethnic social settings, the way they think about their gendered selves, and their strategies in doing gender. Our analysis draws on and elaborates the theoretical literature concerning the construction of femininities across race, paying particular attention to how controlling images and ideologies shape the subjective experiences of women of color. This is the first study to our knowledge that examines how intersecting racial and gender hierarchies affect the everyday construction of gender among Asian American women.

CONSTRUCTING FEMININITIES

Current theorizing emphasizes gender as a socially constructed phenomenon rather than an innate and stable attribute (Lorber 1994; Lucal 1999; West and Zimmerman 1987). Informed by symbolic interactionism and ethnomethodology, gender is regarded as something people do in social interaction. Gender is manufactured out of the fabric of culture and social structure and has little, if any, causal relationship to biology (Kessler and McKenna 1978; Lorber 1994). Gender displays are "culturally established sets of behaviors, appearances, mannerisms, and other cues that we have learned to associate with members of a particular gender" (Lucal 1999, 784). These displays "cast particular pursuits as expressions of masculine and feminine 'natures'" (West and Zimmerman 1987, 126). The doing of gender involves its display as a seemingly innate component of an individual.

The social construction of gender provides a theoretical backdrop for notions of multiple masculinities put forth in the masculinities literature (Coltrane 1994; Connell 1987, 1995; Pyke 1996). We draw on this notion in conceptualizing a plurality of femininities in the social production of women. According to this work, gender is not a unitary process. Rather, it is splintered by overlapping layers of inequality into multiple forms of masculinities (and femininities) that are both internally and externally relational and hierarchical. The concepts of hegemonic and subordinated masculinities are a major contribution of this literature. . . .

The concept of femininities has served mostly as a placeholder in the theory of masculinities where it remains undertheorized and unexamined. Connell (1987, 1995) has written extensively about hegemonic masculinity but offers only a fleeting discussion of the role of femininities. He suggested that the traits of femininity in a patriarchal society are tremendously diverse, with no one form emerging as hegemonic. Hegemonic masculinity is centered on men's global domination of women, and because there is no configuration of femininity organized around women's domination of men, Connell (1987, 183) suggested the notion of a hegemonic femininity is inappropriate. He further argued that women have few opportunities for institutionalized power relations over other women. However, this discounts how other axes of domination, such as race, class, sexuality, and age, mold a hegemonic femininity that is venerated and extolled in the dominant culture, and that emphasizes the superiority of some women over others, thereby privileging white upper-class women. To conceptualize forms of femininities that are subordinated as "problematic" and "abnormal," it is necessary to refer to an oppositional category of femininity that is dominant, ascendant, and "normal" (Glenn 1999, 10). We use the notion of hegemonic and subordinated femininities in framing our analysis.

Ideas of hegemonic and subordinated femininities resonate in the work of feminist scholars of color who emphasize the multiplicity of women's experiences. Much of this research has focused on racial and class variations in the material and (re)productive conditions of women's lives. More recently, scholarship that draws on cultural studies, race and ethnic studies, and women's studies centers the cultural as well as material processes by which gender and race are constructed, although this work has been mostly theoretical (Espiritu 1997; Hill Collins 2000; St. Jean and Feagin 1998). Hill Collins (2000) discussed "controlling images" that denigrate and objectify women of color and justify their racial and gender subordination. Controlling images are part of the process of "othering," whereby a dominant group defines into existence a subordinate group through the creation of categories and ideas that mark the group as inferior (Schwalbe et al. 2000, 422). Controlling images reaffirm whiteness as normal and privilege white women by casting them as superior.

White society uses the image of the Black matriarch to objectify Black women as overly aggressive, domineering, and unfeminine. This imagery serves to blame Black women for the emasculation of Black men, low marriage rates, and poverty and to control their social behavior by undermining their assertiveness (Hill Collins 2000). While Black women are masculinized as aggressive and overpowering, Asian women are rendered hyperfeminine: passive, weak, quiet, excessively submissive, slavishly dutiful, sexually exotic, and available for white men (Espiritu 1997; Tajima 1989). This Lotus Blossom imagery obscures the internal variation of Asian American

femininity and sexuality, making it difficult, for example, for others to "see" Asian lesbians and bisexuals (Lee 1996). Controlling images of Asian women also make them especially vulnerable to mistreatment from men who view them as easy targets. By casting Black women as not feminine enough and Asian women as too feminine, white forms of gender are racialized as normal and superior. In this way, white women are accorded racial privilege.

The dominant culture's dissemination of controlling imagery that derogates nonwhite forms of femininity (and masculinity) is part of a complex ideological system of "psychosocial dominance" (Baker 1983, 37) that imposes elite definitions of subordinates, denying them the power of self-identification. In this way, subordinates internalize "commonsense" notions of their inferiority to whites (Espiritu 1997; Hill Collins 2000). Once internalized, controlling images provide the template by which subordinates make meaning of their everyday lives (Pyke 2000), develop a sense of self, form racial and gender identities, and organize social relations (Osajima 1993; Pyke and Dang in press). For example, Chen (1998) found that Asian American women who joined predominately white sororities often did so to distance themselves from images of Asian femininity.

In contrast, those who joined Asian sororities were often surprised to find their ideas of Asian women as passive and childlike challenged by the assertive, independent women they met. By internalizing the racial and gendered myth making that circumscribes their social existence, subordinates do not pose a threat to the dominant order. As Audre Lorde (1984, 123) described, "the true focus of revolutionary change is never merely the oppressive situations which we seek to escape, but that piece of the oppressor which is planted deep within us."

Hegemonies are rarely without sites of resistance (Espiritu 2001; Gramsci 1971; Hill Collins 2000). Espiritu (1997) described Asian American writers and filmmakers whose portraits of Asians defy the gender caricatures disseminated in the white-dominated society. However, such images are often forged around the contours of the one-dimensional stereotypes against which the struggle emerges. Thus, controlling images penetrate all aspects of the experience of subordinates, whether in a relationship of compliance or in one of resistance (Osajima 1993; Pyke and Dang in press).

The work concerning the effects of controlling images and the relational construction of subordinated and hegemonic femininities has mostly been theoretical. The little research that has examined how Asian American women do gender in the context of racialized images and ideologies that construct their gender as "naturally" inferior to white femininity provides only a brief look at these issues (Chen 1998; Lee 1996). Many of the Asian American women whom we study here do not construct their gender in one cultural field but are constantly moving between sites that are guided by ethnic immigrant cultural norms and those of the Eurocentric mainstream. A comparison of how gender is enacted and understood across such sites brings the construction of racialized gender and the dynamics of hegemonic and subordinated femininities into bold relief. We examine how respondents employ cultural symbols, controlling images, and gender and racial ideologies in giving meanings to their experiences.

GENDER IN ETHNIC AND MAINSTREAM CULTURAL WORLDS

We study Korean and Vietnamese Americans, who form two of the largest Asian ethnic groups in southern California, the site of this research. We focus on the daughters of immigrants as they are more involved in both ethnic and mainstream cultures than are members of the first generation. . . . The second generation, who are still mostly children and young adults, must juggle the cross-pressures of ethnic and mainstream cultures without the groundwork that a long-standing ethnic enclave might provide. This is not easy. Disparities between ethnic and mainstream worlds can generate substantial conflict for children of immigrants, including conflict around issues of gender (Kibria 1993; Zhou and Bankston 1998).

Respondents dichotomized the interactional settings they occupy as ethnic, involving their immigrant family and other coethnics, and mainstream, involving non-Asian Americans in peer groups and at work and school. They grew up juggling different cultural expectations as they moved from home to school and often felt a pressure to behave differently when among Asian Americans and non-Asian Americans. Although there is no set of monolithic, stable norms in either setting, there are certain pressures, expectations, and structural arrangements that can affect different gender displays (Lee 1996). Definitions of gender and the constraints that patriarchy imposes on women's gender production can vary from culture to culture. The Confucian moral code, which accords male superiority, authority, and power over women in family and social relations, has influenced the patriarchal systems of Korea and Vietnam (Kibria 1993; Min 1998). Women are granted little decision-making power and are not accorded an individual identity apart from their family role, which emphasizes their service to male members. A woman who violates her role brings shame to herself and her family. Despite Western observers' tendency to regard Asian families as uniformly and rigidly patriarchal, variations exist (Ishii-Kuntz 2000). Women's resistance strategies, like the exchange of information in informal social groups, provide pockets of power (Kibria 1990). Women's growing educational and economic opportunities and the rise of women's rights groups in Korea and Vietnam challenge gender inequality (Palley 1994). Thus, actual gender dynamics are not in strict compliance with the prescribed moral code.

As they immigrate to the United States, Koreans and Vietnamese experience a shift in gender arrangements centering on men's loss of economic power and increased dependency on their wives' wages (Kibria 1993; Lim 1997; Min 1998). Immigrant women find their labor in demand by employers who regard them as a cheap labor source. With their employment, immigrant women experience more decision-making power, autonomy, and assistance with domestic chores from their husbands. However, such shifts are not total, and male dominance remains a common feature of family life (Kibria 1993; Min 1998). Furthermore, immigrant women tend to stay committed to the ethnic patriarchal structure as it provides resources for maintaining their parental authority and resisting the economic insecurities, racism, and cultural impositions of the new society (Kibria 1990, 1993; Lim 1997). The gender hierarchy is evident in parenting practices. Daughters are typically required to be home and performing household chores when not in school, while sons are given greater freedom.

Native-born American women, on the other hand, are perceived as having more equality, power, and independence than women in Asian societies, reflecting differences in gender attitudes. A recent study of Korean and American women found that 82 percent of Korean women agreed that "women should have only a family-oriented life, devoted to bringing up the children and looking after the husband," compared to 19 percent of U.S. women (Kim 1994). However, the fit between egalitarian gender attitudes and actual behavior in the United States is rather poor. Patriarchal arrangements that accord higher status to men at home and work are still the norm, with women experiencing lower job status and pay, greater responsibility for family work even when employed, and high rates of male violence. Indeed, the belief that gender equality is the norm in U.S. society obscures the day-to-day materiality of American patriarchy. Despite cultural differences in the ideological justification of patriarchy, gender inequality is the reality in both Asian and mainstream cultural worlds.

* * *

GENDER ACROSS CULTURAL TERRAINS: "I'M LIKE A CHAMELEON. I CHANGE MY PERSONALITY"

The 44 respondents who were aware of modifying their gender displays or being treated differently across cultural settings framed their accounts in terms of an oppressive ethnic world and an egalitarian mainstream. They reaffirmed the ideological constructions of the white-dominated society by casting ethnic and mainstream worlds as monolithic opposites, with internal variations largely ignored. Controlling images that denigrate Asian femininity and glorify white femininity were reiterated in many of the narratives. Women's behavior in ethnic realms was described as submissive and controlled, and that in white-dominated settings as freer and more self-expressive.

Some respondents suggested they made complete personality reversals as they moved across realms. They used the behavior of the mainstream as the standard by which they judged their behavior in ethnic settings. As Elizabeth (19, VA) said,

> I feel like when I'm amongst other Asians . . . I'm much more reserved and I hold back what I think. . . . But when I'm among other people like at school, I'm much more outspoken. I'll say whatever's on my mind. It's like a diametric character altogether. . . . I feel like when I'm with other Asians that I'm the *typical* passive [Asian] person and I feel like that's what's expected of me and if I do say something and if I'm the *normal* person that I am, I'd stick out like a sore thumb. So I just blend in with the situation. (emphasis added)

Elizabeth juxtaposes the "typical passive [Asian] person" and the "normal," outspoken person of the mainstream culture, whom she claims to be. In so doing, she reaffirms the stereotypical image of Asians as passive while glorifying Americanized behavior, such as verbal expressiveness, as "normal." This implies that Asian ethnic behavior is aberrant and inferior compared to white behavior, which is rendered normal. This juxtaposition was a recurring theme in these data (Pyke 2000). It contributed to respondents' attempts to distance themselves from racialized notions of the typical Asian woman who is hyperfeminine and submissive by claiming to possess those traits associated with white femininity, such as assertiveness, self-possession, confidence, and independence. Respondents often described a pressure to blend in and conform with the form of gender that they felt was expected in ethnic settings and that conflicted with the white standard of femininity. Thus, they often described such behavior with disgust and self-loathing. For example, Min-Jung (24, KA) said she feels "like an idiot" when talking with Korean adults:

> With Korean adults, I act more shy and more timid. I don't talk until spoken to and just act shy. I kind of speak in a higher tone of voice than I usually do. But then when I'm with white people and white adults, I joke around, I laugh, I talk, and I communicate about how I feel. And then my voice gets stronger. But then when I'm with Korean adults, my voice gets really high. . . . I just sound like an idiot and sometimes when I catch myself I'm like, "Why can't you just make conversation like you normally do?"

Many respondents distanced themselves from the compliant femininity associated with their Asianness by casting their behavior in ethnic realms as a mere act not reflective of their true nature. Repeatedly, they said they cannot be who they really are in ethnic settings and the enactment of an authentic self takes place only in mainstream settings. . . .

Wilma (21, VA) states, "Like some Asian guys expect me to be passive and let them decide on everything. Non-Asians don't expect anything from me. They just expect me *to be me*" (emphasis added). Gendered behavior engaged in Asian ethnic settings was largely described as performative, fake, and unnatural, while that in white-dominated settings was cast as a reflection of one's true self. The femininity of the white mainstream is glorified as authentic, natural, and normal, and Asian ethnic femininity is denigrated as coerced, contrived, and artificial. The "white is right" mantra is reiterated in this view of white femininity as the right way of doing gender.

The glorification of white femininity and controlling images of Asian women can lead Asian American women to believe that freedom and equity can be acquired only in the white-dominated world. For not only is white behavior glorified as superior and more authentic, but

gender relations among whites are constructed as more egalitarian. . . .

Controlling images of Asian men as hypermasculine further feed presumptions that whites are more egalitarian. Asian males were often cast as uniformly domineering in these accounts. Racialized images and the construction of hegemonic (white) and subordinated (Asian) forms of gender set up a situation where Asian American women feel they must choose between white worlds of gender equity and Asian worlds of gender oppression. Such images encourage them to reject their ethnic culture and Asian men and embrace the white world and white men so as to enhance their power (Espiritu 1997). . . .

In these accounts, we can see the construction of ethnic and mainstream cultural worlds—and Asians and whites—as diametrically opposed. The perception that whites are more egalitarian than Asian-origin individuals and thus preferred partners in social interaction further reinforces anti-Asian racism and white superiority. The cultural dominance of whiteness is reaffirmed through the co-construction of race and gender in these narratives. The perception that the production of gender in the mainstream is more authentic and superior to that in Asian ethnic arenas further reinforces the racialized categories of gender that define white forms of femininity as ascendant. In the next section, we describe variations in gender performances within ethnic and mainstream settings that respondents typically overlooked or discounted as atypical.

Gender Variations Within Cultural Worlds

Several respondents described variations in gender dynamics within mainstream and ethnic settings that challenge notions of Asian and American worlds as monolithic opposites. Some talked of mothers who make all the decisions or fathers who do the cooking. These accounts were framed as exceptions to Asian male dominance.

For example, after Vietnamese women were described in a group interview as confined to domesticity, Ngâ (22, VA), who immigrated at 14 and spoke in Vietnamese-accented English, defined her family as gender egalitarian. She related,

> I guess I grow[sic] up in a *different* family. All my sisters don't have to cook, her husbands[sic] cooking all the time. Even my oldest sister. Even my mom—my dad is cooking. . . . My sisters and brothers are all very strong. (emphasis added)

Ngâ does not try to challenge stereotypical notions of Vietnamese families but rather reinforces such notions by suggesting that her family is different. Similarly, Heidi (21, KA) said, "Our family was kind of *different* because . . . my dad cooks and cleans and does dishes. He cleans house" (emphasis added). Respondents often framed accounts of gender egalitarianism in their families by stating they do not belong to the typical Asian family, with "typical" understood to mean male dominated. This variation in gender dynamics within the ethnic community was largely unconsidered in these accounts.

Other respondents described how they enacted widely disparate forms of gender across sites within ethnic realms, suggesting that gender behavior is more variable than generally framed. Take, for example, the case of Gin (29, KA), a law student married to a Korean American from a more traditional family than her own. When she is with her husband's kin, Gin assumes the traditional obligations of a daughter-in-law and does all the cooking, cleaning, and serving. The role exhausts her and she resents having to perform it. When Gin and her husband return home, the gender hierarchy is reversed. . . .

Controlling images of Asian men as hyperdomineering in their relations with women obscures how they can be called on to compensate for the subservience exacted from their female partners in some settings. Although respondents typically offered such stories as evidence of the patriarchy of ethnic arenas, these examples reveal that ethnic worlds are far more variable than generally described. Viewing Asian ethnic worlds through a lens of racialized gender stereotypes renders such variation invisible or, when acknowledged, atypical.

Gender expectations in the white-dominated mainstream also varied, with respondents sometimes expected to assume a subservient stance as Asian women. These examples reveal that the mainstream is not a site of unwavering gender equality as often depicted in these accounts and made less so for Asian American women by racial images that construct them as compliant. Many respondents described encounters with non-Asians, usually whites, who expected them to be passive, quiet, and yielding. Several described non-Asian (mostly white) men who brought such expectations to their dating relationships. Indeed, the servile Lotus Blossom image bolsters white men's preference for Asian women (Espiritu 1997). As Thanh (22, VA) recounted,

> Like the white guy that I dated, he expected me to be the submissive one—the one that was dependent on the guy. Kind of like the "Asian persuasion," that's what he'd call it when he was dating me. And when he found out that I had a spirit, kind of a wild side to me, he didn't like it at all. Period. And when I spoke up—my opinions—he got kind of scared.

So racialized images can cause Asian American women to believe they will find greater gender equality with white men and can cause white men to believe they will find greater subservience with Asian women. This dynamic promotes Asian American women's availability to white men and makes them particularly vulnerable to mistreatment.

There were other sites in the mainstream, besides dating relationships, where Asian American women encountered racialized gender expectations. Several described white employers and coworkers who expected them to be more passive and deferential than other employees and were surprised when they spoke up and resisted unfair treatment. Some described similar assumptions among non-Asian teachers and professors. Diane (26, KA) related,

> At first one of my teachers told me it was okay if I didn't want to talk in front of the class. I think she thought I was quiet or shy because I'm Asian. . . . [Laughing.] I am very outspoken, but that semester I just kept my mouth shut. I figured she won't make me talk anyway, so why try. I kind of went along with her.

Diane's example illustrates how racialized expectations can exert a pressure to display stereotyped behavior in mainstream interactions. Such expectations can subtly coerce behavioral displays that confirm the stereotypes, suggesting a kind of self-fulfilling prophecy. Furthermore, as submissiveness and passivity are denigrated traits in the mainstream, and often judged to be indicators of incompetence, compliance with such expectations can deny Asian American women personal opportunities and success. Not only is passivity unrewarded in the mainstream; it is also subordinated. The association of extreme passivity with Asian women serves to emphasize their otherness. Some respondents resist this subordination by enacting a more assertive femininity associated with whiteness. Lisa (18, KA) described being quiet with her relatives out of respect, but in mainstream scenes, she consciously resists the stereotype of Asian women as passive by adjusting her behavior. . . .

To act Asian by being reserved and quiet would be to "stand out in a negative way" and to be regarded as "not cool." It means one will be denigrated and cast aside. Katie consciously engages loud and gregarious behavior to prove she is not the typical Asian and to be welcomed by white friends. Whereas many respondents describe their behavior in mainstream settings as an authentic reflection of their personality, these examples suggest otherwise. Racial expectations exert pressure on these women's gender performances among whites. Some go to great lengths to defy racial assumptions and be accepted into white-dominated social groups by engaging a white standard of femininity. As they are forced to work against racial stereotypes, they must exert extra effort at being outspoken and socially gregarious. Contrary to the claim of respondents, gender production in the mainstream is also coerced and contrived. The failure of some respondents to recognize variations in gender behavior within mainstream and ethnic settings probably has much to do with the essentialization of gender and race. That is, as we discuss next, the racialization of gender renders variations in behavior within racial groups invisible.

THE RACIALIZATION OF GENDER: BELIEVING IS SEEING

In this section, we discuss how respondents differentiated femininity by race rather than shifting situational contexts, even when they were consciously aware of altering their own gender performance to conform with shifting expectations. Racialized gender was discursively constructed as natural and essential. Gender and race were essentialized as interrelated biological facts that determine social behavior.

Among our 100 respondents, there was a tendency to rely on binary categories of American (code for white) and Asian femininity in describing a wide range of topics, including gender identities, personality traits, and orientations toward domesticity or career. Racialized gender categories were deployed as an interpretive template in giving meaning to experiences and organizing a worldview. Internal variation was again ignored, downplayed, or regarded as exceptional. White femininity, which was glorified in accounts of gender behavior across cultural settings, was also accorded superiority in the more general discussions of gender.

Respondents' narratives were structured by assumptions about Asian women as submissive, quiet, and diffident and of American women as independent, self-assured, outspoken, and powerful. That is, specific behaviors and traits were racialized. As Ha (19, VA) explained, "sometimes I'm quiet and passive and shy. That's a

Vietnamese part of me." Similarly, domesticity was linked with Asian femininity and domestic incompetence or disinterest, along with success in the work world, with American femininity. Several women framed their internal struggles between career and domesticity in racialized terms. Min-Jung said,

> I kind of think my Korean side wants to stay home and do the cooking and cleaning and take care of the kids whereas my American side would want to go out and make a difference and become a strong woman and become head of companies and stuff like that.

This racialized dichotomy was central to respondents' self-identities. Amy (21, VA) said, "I'm not Vietnamese in the way I act. I'm American because I'm not a good cook and I'm not totally ladylike." In fact, one's ethnic identity could be challenged if one did not comply with notions of racialized gender. In a group interview, Kimberly (21, VA) described "joking around" with coethnic dates who asked if she cooked by responding that she did not. . . .

Similarly, coethnic friends tell Hien (21, VA), "You should be able to cook, you are Vietnamese, you are a girl." To be submissive and oriented toward family and domesticity marks Asian ethnicity. Conformity to stereotypes of Asian femininity serves to symbolically construct and affirm an Asian ethnic identity. Herein lies the pressure that some respondents feel to comply with racialized expectations in ethnic settings, as Lisa (18, KA) illustrates in explaining why she would feel uncomfortable speaking up in a class that has a lot of Asians:

> I think they would think that I'm not really Asian. Like I'm whitewashed . . . like I'm forgetting my race. I'm going against my roots and adapting to the American way. And I'm just neglecting my race.

American (white) women and Asian American women are constructed as diametric opposites. Although many respondents were aware that they contradicted racialized notions of gender in their day-to-day lives, they nonetheless view gender as an essential component of race. Variation is ignored or recategorized so that an Asian American woman who does not comply is no longer Asian. This was also evident among respondents who regard themselves as egalitarian or engage the behavioral traits associated with white femininity. There was the presumption that one cannot be Asian and have gender-egalitarian attitudes. Asian American women can engage those traits associated with ascendant femininity to enhance their status in the mainstream, but this requires a rejection of their racial/ethnic identity. This is evident by the use of words such as "American," "whitewashed," or "white"—but not Asian—to describe such women. Star (22, KA) explained, "I look Korean but I don't act Korean. I'm whitewashed. [Interviewer asks, 'How do you mean you don't act Korean?'] I'm loud. I'm not quiet and reserved."

As a result, struggles about gender identity and women's work/family trajectories become superimposed over racial/ethnic identity. The question is not simply whether Asian American women like Min-Jung want to be outspoken and career oriented or quiet and family oriented but whether they want to be American (whitewashed) or Asian. Those who do not conform to racialized expectations risk challenges to their racial identity and charges that they are not really Asian, as occurs with Lisa when she interacts with her non-Asian peers. She said,

> They think I'm really different from other Asian girls because I'm so outgoing. They feel that Asian girls have to be the shy type who is very passive and sometimes I'm not like that so they think, "Lisa, are you Asian?"

These data illustrate how the line drawn in the struggle for gender equality is superimposed over the cultural and racial boundaries dividing whites and Asians. At play is the presumption that the only path to gender equality and assertive womanhood is via assimilation to the white mainstream. This assumption was shared by Asian American research assistants who referred to respondents' gender egalitarian viewpoints as evidence of assimilation. The assumption is that Asian American women can be advocates of gender equality or strong and assertive in their interactions only as a result of assimilation, evident by the display of traits associated with hegemonic femininity, and a rejection of their ethnic culture and identity. This construction obscures gender inequality in mainstream U.S. society and constructs that sphere as the only place where Asian American women can be free. Hence, the diversity of gender arrangements practiced among those of Asian origin, as well as the potential for social change within Asian cultures, is ignored. Indeed, there were no references in these accounts to the rise in recent years of women's movements in Korea and Vietnam. Rather, Asian ethnic worlds are regarded as unchanging sites of male dominance and female submissiveness.

DISCUSSION AND SUMMARY

Our analysis reveals dynamics of internalized oppression and the reproduction of inequality that revolve around the relational construction of hegemonic and subordinated femininities. Respondents' descriptions of gender performances in ethnic settings were marked by self-disgust and referred to as a mere act not reflective of one's true gendered nature. In mainstream settings, on the other hand, respondents often felt a pressure to comply with caricatured notions of Asian femininity or, conversely, to distance one's self from derogatory images of Asian femininity to be accepted. In both cases, the subordination of Asian femininity is reproduced.

In general, respondents depicted women of Asian descent as uniformly engaged in subordinated femininity marked by submissiveness and white women as universally assertive and gender egalitarian. Race, rather than culture, situational dynamics, or individual personalities, emerged as the primary basis by which respondents gave meaning to variations in femininity. That is, despite their own situational variation in doing gender, they treat gender as a racialized feature

of bodies rather than a sociocultural product. Specific gender displays, such as a submissive demeanor, are required to confirm an Asian identity. Several respondents face challenges to their ethnic identity when they behave in ways that do not conform with racialized images. Indeed, some claimed that because they are assertive or career oriented, they are not really Asian. That is, because they do not conform to the racialized stereotypes of Asian women but identify with a hegemonic femininity that is the white standard, they are different from other women of Asian origin. In this way, they manipulate the racialized categories of gender in attempting to craft identities that are empowering. However, this is accomplished by denying their ethnicity and connections to other Asian American women and through the adoption and replication of controlling images of Asian women.

Respondents who claim that they are not really Asian because they do not conform with essentialized notions of Asian femininity suggest similarities to transgendered individuals who feel that underneath, they really belong to the gender category that is opposite from the one to which they are assigned. The notion that deep down they are really white implies a kind of transracialized gender identity. In claiming that they are not innately Asian, they reaffirm racialized categories of gender just as transgendered individuals reaffirm the gender dichotomy (Kessler and McKenna 1978; Lorber 1994).

However, there are limitations to notions of a transracialized identity as racial barriers do not permit these women to socially pass into the white world, even though they might feel themselves to be more white than Asian. Due to such barriers, they use terms that are suggestive of a racial crossover, such as "whitewashed" or "American" rather than "white" in describing themselves. Such terms are frequently used among Asian Americans to describe those who are regarded as assimilated to the white world and no longer ethnic, further underscoring how racial categories are essentialized (Pyke and Dang in press). Blocked from a white identity, these terms capture a marginalized space that is neither truly white nor Asian. As racial categories are dynamic, it remains to be seen whether these marginalized identities are the site for new identities marked by hybridity (Lowe 1991) or whether Asian Americans will eventually be incorporated into whiteness. This process may be hastened by outmarriage to whites and high rates of biracial Asian Americans who can more easily pass into the white world, thereby leading the way for other Asian Americans. While we cannot ascertain the direction of such changes, our data highlight the contradictions that strain the existing racial and gender order as it applies to second-generation Asian American women.

While respondents construct a world in which Asian American women can experience a kind of transracial gender identity, they do not consider the same possibility for women of other races. A white woman who is submissive does not become Asian. In fact, there was no reference in these accounts to submissive white women who are rendered invisible by racialized categories of gender. Instead, white women are constructed as monolithically self-confident, independent, assertive, and successful—characteristics of white hegemonic femininity. That these are the same ruling traits associated with hegemonic masculinity, albeit in a less exaggerated, feminine form, underscores the imitative structure of hegemonic femininity. That is, the supremacy of white femininity over Asian femininity mimics hegemonic masculinity. We are not arguing that hegemonic femininity and masculinity are equivalent structures. They are not. Whereas hegemonic masculinity is a superstructure of domination, hegemonic femininity is confined to power relations among women. However, the two structures are interrelated with hegemonic femininity constructed to serve hegemonic masculinity, from which it is granted legitimacy.

Our findings illustrate the powerful interplay of controlling images and hegemonic femininity in promoting internalized oppression. Respondents draw on racial images and assumptions in their narrative construction of Asian cultures as innately oppressive of women and fully resistant to change against which the white-dominated mainstream is framed as a paradigm of gender equality. This serves a proassimilation function by suggesting that Asian American women will find gender equality in exchange for rejecting their ethnicity and adopting white standards of gender. The construction of a hegemonic femininity not only (re)creates a hierarchy that privileges white women over Asian American women but also makes Asian American women available for white men. In this way, hegemonic femininity serves as a handmaiden to hegemonic masculinity.

By constructing ethnic culture as impervious to social change and as a site where resistance to gender oppression is impossible, our respondents accommodate and reinforce rather than resist the gender hierarchal arrangements of such locales. This can contribute to a self-fulfilling prophecy as Asian American women who hold gender egalitarian views feel compelled to retreat from interactions in ethnic settings, thus (re)creating Asian ethnic cultures as strongholds of patriarchy and reinforcing the maintenance of a rigid gender hierarchy as a primary mechanism by which ethnicity and ethnic identity are constructed. This marking of ethnic culture as a symbolic repository of patriarchy obscures variations in ethnic gender practices as well as the gender inequality in the mainstream. Thus, compliance with the dominant order is secured.

Our study attempts to bring a racialized examination of gender to a constructionist framework without decentering either race or gender. By examining the racialized meaning systems that inform the construction of gender, our findings illustrate how the resistance of gender oppression among our respondents draws ideologically on the denigration and rejection of ethnic Asian culture, thereby reinforcing white dominance. Conversely, we found that mechanisms used to construct ethnic identity in resistance to the pro-assimilation forces of the white-dominated mainstream rest on narrow definitions of Asian women that emphasize gender subordination. These findings underscore the crosscutting ways that gender and racial oppression operates such that strategies and ideologies focused on the resistance of one form of domination can reproduce another form. A social constructionist approach that examines the simultaneous production of gender and race within the matrix of oppression, and considers the relational construction of hegemonic and subordinated femininities, holds much promise in uncovering the micro-level structures and complicated features of oppression, including the processes by which oppression infiltrates the meanings individuals give to their experiences.

REFERENCES

Baker, Donald G. 1983. *Race, ethnicity and power.* Boston: Routledge Kegan Paul.

Chen, Edith Wen-Chu. 1998. The continuing significance of race: A case study of Asian American women in white, Asian American, and African American sororities. Ph.D. diss., University of California, Los Angeles.

Collins, Patricia Hill. 2000. *Black feminist thought.* New York: Routledge.

Collins, Patricia Hill, Lionel A. Maldonado, Dana Y. Takagi, Barrie Thorne, Lynn Weber, and Howard Winant. 1995. Symposium: On West and Fenstermaker's "Doing difference." *Gender & Society* 9:491–513.

Coltrane, Scott. 1989. Household labor and the routine production of gender. *Social Problems* 36:473–90.

———. 1994. Theorizing masculinities in contemporary social science. In *Theorizing masculinities,* edited by Harry Brod and Michael Kaufman. Thousand Oaks, CA: Sage.

Connell, R. W. 1987. *Gender and power.* Stanford, CA: Stanford University Press.

———. 1995. *Masculinities.* Los Angeles: University of California Press.

Espiritu, Yen L. 1997. *Asian American women and men.* Thousand Oaks, CA: Sage.

———. 2001. "We don't sleep around like white girls do": Family, culture, and gender in Filipina American life. *Signs: Journal of Women in Culture and Society* 26:415–40.

Glenn, Evelyn Nakano. 1999. The social construction and institutionalization of gender and race. In *Revisioning gender,* edited by Myra Marx Ferree, Judith Lorber, and Beth B. Hess. Thousand Oaks, CA: Sage.

Gramsci, Antonio. 1971. *Selections from the prison notebooks of Antonio Gramsci,* edited and translated by Quintin Hoare and Geoffrey Nowell Smith. New York: International.

Ishii-Kuntz, Masako. 2000. Diversity within Asian American families. In *Handbook of family diversity,*

edited by David H. Demo, Katherine Allen, and Mark A. Fine. New York: Oxford University Press.

Kessler, Suzanne, and Wendy McKenna. 1978. *Gender: An ethnomethodological approach.* Chicago: University of Chicago Press.

Kibria, Nazli. 1990. Power, patriarchy, and gender conflict in the Vietnamese immigrant community. *Gender & Society* 4:9–24.

———. 1993. *Family tightrope: The changing lives of Vietnamese Americans.* Princeton, NJ: Princeton University Press.

Kim, Byong-suh. 1994. Value orientations and sex-gender role attitudes on the comparability of Koreans and Americans. In *Gender division of labor in Korea,* edited by Hyong Cho and Oil-wha Chang. Seoul, Korea: Ewha Women's University Press.

Lee, Jee Yeun. 1996. Why Suzie Wong is not a lesbian: Asian and Asian American lesbian and bisexual women and femme/butch/gender identities. In *Queer studies,* edited by Brett Beemyn and Mickey Eliason. New York: New York University Press.

Lim, In-Sook. 1997. Korean immigrant women's challenge to gender inequality at home: The interplay of economic resources, gender, and family. *Gender & Society* 11:31–51.

Lorber, Judith. 1994. *Paradoxes of gender:* New Haven, CT: Yale University Press.

Lorde, Audre. 1984. *Sister outsider.* Trumansberg, NY: Crossing Press.

Lowe, Lisa. 1991. Heterogeneity, hybridity, multiplicity: Marking Asian American differences. *Diaspora* 1:24–44.

Lucal, Betsy. 1999. What it means to be gendered me: Life on the boundaries of a dichotomous gender system. *Gender & Society* 13:781–97.

Min, Pyong Gap. 1998. *Changes and conflicts.* Boston: Allyn & Bacon.

Osajima, Keith. 1993. The hidden injuries of race. In *Bearing dreams, shaping visions: Asian Pacific American perspectives,* edited by Linda Revilla, Gail Nomura, Shawn Wong, and Shirley Hune. Pullman: Washington State University Press.

Palley, Marian Lief. 1994. Feminism in a Confucian society: The women's movement in Korea. In *Women of Japan and Korea,* edited by Joyce Gelb and Marian Lieff. Philadelphia: Temple University Press.

Pyke, Karen. 1996. Class-based masculinities: The interdependence of gender, class, and interpersonal power. *Gender & Society* 10:527–49.

———. 2000. "The normal American family" as an interpretive structure of family life among grown children of Korean and Vietnamese immigrants. *Journal of Marriage and the Family* 62:240–55.

Pyke, Karen, and Tran Dang. In press. "FOB" and "whitewashed": Intra-ethnic identities and internalized oppression among second generation Asian Americans. *Qualitative Sociology.*

St. Jean, Yanick, and Joe R. Feagin. 1998. *Double burden: Black women and everyday racism.* Armonk, NY: M. E. Sharpe.

Schwalbe, Michael, Sandra Godwin, Daphne Holden, Douglas Schrock, Shealy Thompson, and Michele Wolkomir. 2000. Generic processes in the reproduction of inequality: An interactionist analysis. *Social Forces* 79:419–52.

Tajima, Renee E. 1989. Lotus blossoms don't bleed: Images of Asian women. In *Making waves,* edited by Asian Women United of California. Boston: Beacon.

West, Candace, and Sarah Fenstermaker. 1995. Doing difference. *Gender & Society* 9:8–37.

West, Candace, and Don H. Zimmerman. 1987. Doing gender. *Gender & Society* 1:125–51.

Zhou, Min, and Carl L. Bankston III. 1998. *Growing up American.* New York: Russell Sage.

Introduction to Reading 10

One of the most recent applications of intersectionality is in global/transnational research, as mentioned by Bonnie Thornton Dill and Marla H. Kohlman in the first reading in this chapter. In this article, Bandana Purkayastha develops the meaning of intersectionality using a transnational framework. As Nikki Jones did in her analysis of inner-city girls, Purkayastha also considers race in this context. As you will see from this piece, scholars are still struggling with what intersectional analysis means, but the process of doing so is exciting. This article gives good examples of how we could and should study the intersections of multiple identities while also considering a transglobal context.

1. What is meant by "transnational spaces"?

2. How does Purkayastha recommend doing an intersectional analysis in transnational spaces?

3. What does she mean by "axes of domination"? What other ones can you name in addition to race?

INTERSECTIONALITY IN A TRANSNATIONAL WORLD

Bandana Purkayastha

As a late entrant into the world of sociology, I read Patricia Hill Collins's *Black Feminist Thought: Knowledge, Consciousness, and the Politics of Empowerment* (1990) in a graduate seminar on gender. . . . Over the years, insights of many other scholars have helped me to understand intersectionality. As Hae Yeon Choo and Myra Marx Ferree (2010) have recently pointed out, these diverse works on intersectionality have highlighted the importance

From Purkayastha, Bandana. 2012. "Intersectionality in a Transnational World." *Gender & Society* (1): 55–66.

of "including the perspectives of multiply marginalized people, especially women of color; an analytic shift from addition of multiple independent strands of inequality toward a multiplication and thus transformation of their main effects into interactions; and a focus on seeing multiple institutions as overlapping in their co-determination of inequalities to produce complex configurations" (2010, 4). Nonetheless, I remain grateful to Professor Hill Collins for moving the conversation on intersectionality, in the early 1990s, to a more visible level.

Professor Hill Collins's work has remained dynamic, expanding far beyond the original idea of power relations organized through intersecting axes of race/class/gender (Collins 1990) to her recent articulation of the "intersecting power relations of race, class, gender, ethnicity, sexuality, age, ability, nation" (Collins 2010, 8). In this brief essay, I touch upon two related aspects of intersectionality that require additional clarification as we study social lives in the twenty-first century. My observations are focused on the ways in which we understand "race" even as our lives expand onto transnational—including virtual—social spaces. . . .

SOCIAL LIVES IN TRANSNATIONAL SPACES

Over the past decade, a rapidly growing literature has described how individuals and groups maintain connections across countries so that social lives are constructed, not only in single countries, but in transnational spaces. Transnational spaces are composed of tangible geographic spaces that exist across multiple nation-states *and* virtual spaces. With improvements in personal and media communication and travel technology, the ability to move money easily across the globe, and the marketing and ease of consuming "cultural" products—including fashions, cosmetics, music, foods, and art—have made it easier for many groups to create lives that extend far beyond the boundaries of single nation-states. We now know about first-generation immigrant "transnational villagers"

who build lives in more than one country by traveling back and forth regularly, organizing family lives across countries, and remitting and investing money, as well as engaging in politics in "homelands" (e.g., Guevarra 2009; Hondagneu-Sotelo and Avila 1997; Levitt 2001; Purkayastha 2009). We also know about post-immigrant generations who actively maintain links with their parents' homelands (e.g., Purkayastha 2005); cyber migrants who work for Northern employers but are geographically based in the South (e.g., Abraham 2010); and participants in web-based communities, some of whom seek community, while others try on less essentialist, choice-driven, multiple, fragmented, and hybrid identities on the web and thus dilute the consequences of gendering, racialization, class, and other social hierarchies to which they are subjected in their tangible lives (e.g., Diamandaki 2003; Ignacio 2006; Lee 2003; Mitra 1997; Mitra and Gajjala 2008; Narayan and Purkayastha 2011). Other scholars have analyzed web-based transnational linkages that enable geographically dispersed groups to form close-knit political networks (e.g., Earl 2006; Narayan, Purkayastha, and Banerji, forthcoming; Pudrovska and Ferree 2004). As a rapidly growing number of people are tied to transnational spaces—that is, they build lives that combine intersecting local, regional, national, and transnational spaces—single nation-states no longer wholly contain their lives.

At the same time, nation-states have responded in a variety of ways to control social lives in transnational spaces. For instance, the literature on immigration shows how nation-states are creating gendered categories of "overseas citizens" in order to attract remittances from migrants (e.g., Guevarra 2009) or to draw on the expertise or lobbying power of people settled in other countries (Purkayastha 2009). Equally important, nation-states have attempted to expand their ability to control people across transnational spaces; ideologies, interactions, and institutions that have sustained raced/gendered/classed and other hierarchies *within nations* have expanded in new ways across nations.[1] For most of the twentieth century, nation-states maintained separate apparatus for controlling groups within nations (e.g., police, prisons) from the apparatus used to dominate and control groups/states outside nations (e.g., the military, foreign intelligence agencies, facilities to house prisoners of wars). Now, these tools of control are increasingly blurred within nations; for instance, policies such as the PATRIOT Act and organizations such as Homeland Security have blurred the distinction between foreign surveillance and national surveillance in the United States. Security agreements *across* nations have created transnational security regions, where profiles developed in one powerful country are likely to be rapidly disseminated and acted on in other countries within the transnational security regime (Purkayastha 2009; Vertovec 2001). A *suspect* in a terrorism case in Scotland or Spain can, almost immediately, be arrested in Australia or the United States.[2] The profile of a "turbaned terrorist" or the suspicions against "Muslim-looking" people have generated contemporary racial profiles so that Sikh men—who wear turbans to comply with their religious tenets—and a range of people of Middle Eastern and South Asian origin are profiled as potential security threats. They are searched more stringently at airports, subject to extra questioning at national borders, subject to surveillance for communicating with people in "enemy countries," frequently visiting these countries, or sending money to "suspect" organizations through institutional arrangements as they travel through security regime (see Iwata and Purkayastha 2011; Purkayastha 2009). These new global security arrangements intersect with other processes for controlling racially marked populations within nations.

Overall, then, transnational spaces are composed of tangible and virtual social spaces that exist through and beyond single nation-states. Individuals, groups, corporations, and nation-states continue to expand their purview into such spaces.[3] At the same time, those who cannot access transnational spaces—for a variety of reasons, including the digital divide and stringent government control over travel and internet access—are marginalized in new ways within this expanded context. Contemporary discussions of marginalization and privilege have to take these new developments into account.

INTERSECTIONALITY IN TRANSNATIONAL SPACES

While her earlier work on Black feminist thought was focused on the United States, in her recent writings Professor Hill Collins recognizes the expansion of social life beyond the nation-state (e.g., Collins 2010). She discusses the dispersion and consumption of cultural products, such as hip-hop, around the globe and the cultural familiarity this engenders among consumers, and the possibilities for "creat(ing) shifting patterns of face-to-face and mediated interactions . . . (as) new technologies create organizational opportunities for new sorts of political communities" (2010, 18). She discusses the ways in which people imagine local and far-flung political communities using new technologies, and the ways in which these multiple communities somewhat dilute concentrated power of the privileged. Despite this recognition of other worlds of experience, Professor Hill Collins has not, as far as I am aware, discussed the structures of domination and control in transnational spaces. As a result, it is not clear how our current conceptualization of intersectionality—including the expanded version of race/class/gender/age/ability/sexuality/ethnicity/nation—might change if we incorporate social life in transnational space.

Professor Hill Collins has offered a powerful critique of the "race-neutral" scholarship on gender, and her discussions of racism (and the ways this racism interacts with other axes of domination) led to the visibility of concepts such as "controlling images" and "women of color." Her references to Black women and other people of color in the United States continue to serve as a reminder of their continuing marginalization and open up some space to include their experiences in developing theory. But she does not discuss the deviations from Euro-American organization of racial hierarchies in different countries around the globe, which coexist with global-level Euro-American racialization processes. As a result, it is not always clear when and how we are to conceptualize "race" within the intersectionality matrix if we study transnational social lives.

I will begin with a simple example that focuses on women of color. A Ugandan Black immigrant and a Ugandan Indian immigrant—whose family lived for many generations in Uganda before being forcibly evicted by Idi Amin—are both racially marginalized, though in different ways, in the United States. While both share the effects of gendered/racialized migration policies that would prohibit or slow the process through which they might form families in the United States, their experiences differ in other ways. The Ugandan Black migrant is likely to experience the gamut of racisms experienced by African Americans, while the Indian Ugandan is likely to experience the racisms faced by Muslims and "Muslim-looking" people in the United States, and they may share other structural discriminations experienced by Asian Americans (Narayan and Purkayastha 2009). These similarities and differences are consistent with racist ideologies, interactions, and institutional arrangements in the United States. But if both return to their home country Uganda, they would encounter a different set of privileges and marginalization in this Black-majority country; the Black Ugandan migrant is advantaged here (though the other intersecting factors would together shape her exact social location). If both visit or temporarily live in India, the Indian-origin Uganda-born person may experience the privileges associated with the dominant group in the country. However, if she is a Muslim or a low-caste Hindu, she might experience a different set of social hierarchies. Similarly, Japanese-origin people from Brazil who returned to Japan, or Japanese-origin Americans who were forced to return to Japan, encountered different sets of social hierarchies. A broadly similar argument could be made about the relative position of Blacks and Indians under the different historical circumstances, for instance, during the apartheid regime and after apartheid in South Africa (see Govinden 2008).

There are variations of who is part of the privileged majority versus the marginalized minority *within* a country, and these hierarchies do not always fit the white-yellow/brown-Black hierarchy extant in Western Europe and North America. Thus concepts such as "women of color"—which act as an effective framework for indicating the social location of these women in Western Europe and North America, and continuing global hierarchies *between* countries in the global North and South—do not work as well if we wish to track the array of the axes of power and domination within countries *along with* existing global-level hierarchies. Yet considering these multiple levels is important if intersectionality is to retain its explanatory power in an increasingly transnational world where within-country *and* between-country structures shape people's experiences.

The possibility of forming community on virtual spaces and using the web to maintain meaningful connections with people in other countries also emphasizes the need to consider transnational spaces. A South African Black female immigrant in the United States who is able to maintain active connections with her friends, family, and political networks in her home country (via phone, email, and a variety of web-based media) may be able to minimize some of the toll of racism she experiences by making her South African relationships most salient in her life. The Indian-origin post-immigrant-generation American who regularly participates in a religio-social Hindu online community and visits India regularly is also able to position herself as a member of the majority group in India (and the Indian diaspora) even as she experiences the deleterious effects of structural racism in the United States. In other words, people who can access transnational social spaces attempt to balance their lack of privilege in one country (their raced/classed/gendered/ability/sexual/age/nationality status in one nation-state) by actively seeking out privilege and power in another place and/or in virtual spaces.

While many of the axes Professor Hill Collins identified—race, gender, class, sexuality, age, ability, and nation—remain relevant, they may not work in the same way as "women of color" constructs suggest. Being able to build transnational lives—the ability of groups to live within and beyond single nation-states—suggests that it is quite possible for groups to be part of *the racial majority and minority simultaneously* (Purkayastha 2010). Indeed, in places where caste and religious or ethnic hierarchies—with their own set of ideologies, interactions, and institutional structures—are more salient, we should consider the relative importance of these axes of domination within those countries (and the extent to which these structure transnational social lives) as we use intersectional frameworks.

I do not intend to suggest that we stop considering racial hierarchies. Along with variations in who makes up the racial majority or minority *within* different countries, hierarchies among nation-states continue to promote Western hierarchies of race and whiteness, yellowness, and Blackness across the world in ways that are broadly similar to the period of colonialism (see, e.g., Gilroy 1989; Kim 2008; Kim-Puri 2007; Nandy 2006; Sardar et al. 1993). Such racial hierarchies are maintained through ideologies, actions, and institutional arrangements associated with political and economic control. As Evelyn Nakano Glenn and her colleagues have documented, color-based hierarchies continue to structure people's lives in many countries around the globe, especially as "fairness as beauty" is marketed to places where the majority of the people are nonwhite (Glenn 2008).

Since Professor Collins's discussions focus on the United States and minority groups within the boundaries of this nation-state, the ideas about race she discusses are built upon the structures that are particularly relevant to the United States and Western Europe. While intersectionality remains an important framework, we need to encapsulate marginalization

structures that are salient in other locales and the ways in which these hierarchies play out in transnational spaces.

* * *

Last Remarks

As a scholar who continues to use intersectionality as my primary theoretical framework, I can enumerate many ways in which the work of Professor Hill Collins and others who have developed this framework have improved our ability to study social lives. The framework remains important, but we have to pay attention to and elucidate the complexities of using this framework beyond Euro-American societies. Understanding and attending to the complexities of transnationalism—composed of structures within, between, and across nation-states, and virtual spaces—alerts us to look for other axes of domination and the limits of using "women of color" concepts, as we use them now, to look across *and* within nation-states to understand the impact of transnationalism. My examples here were focused on those who can access transnational spaces. A focus on transnational intersectionality should alert us to the position of those who are unable to afford access to technology to build virtual communities, to participate in a medium because they are not proficient in English, which has become the dominant language in virtual spaces, or to build transnational social lives because of active government surveillance and control of their lives or because they are too poor and isolated to access transnational tangible and virtual spaces.

While I focused on "race" in this brief essay, the other axes of domination are likely to show some variations if we analyze multiple and simultaneous social locations to develop a better understanding of intersectionality. The organization of power and processes of marginalization has continued to change in this century. We need to further elucidate the theoretical implications and methodologies for adequately capturing different mechanisms of domination and how these meld with the ones with which we are most familiar within Euro-American scholarship.

NOTES

1. The existence of global matrices of domination are not new phenomena—colonialism sustained the power and privilege of white Euro-America over Africa, Asia, and Latin America for centuries—but the contemporary organization of economic/social/political power, privilege, and marginalization reflect the development of transnational social spaces.

2. I deliberately picked Scotland and Spain because an Indian doctor in Australia was charged with complicity in the Glasgow bombings, while an American lawyer was charged with the Spanish bombings. Both were proven innocent (see Armaline, Glasberg, and Purkayastha 2011 for further details).

3. Individuals and groups need not participate in two or more countries (or virtual communities) equally. Indeed, their node of experience is often their country of residence. Other countries or virtual communities are often part of a larger field of experience, and the salience of these other spaces is likely to vary. My point here is that we need to seriously consider the node *and* the field, as these contribute to the experiences of privilege and marginalization that shape our lives in more complex ways than the model of intersectionality, based on single nations, suggests.

REFERENCES

Abraham, Margaret. 2010. Globalization, work and citizenship: The call centre industry in India. In *Contours of citizenship: Women, diversity and practices of citizenship*, edited by Margaret Abraham, Esther Ngan-ling Chow, Laura Maratou-Alipranti, and Evangelia Tastsoglou. Aldershot, UK: Ashgate.

Choo, Hae Yeon, and Myra Marx Ferree. 2010. Practicing intersectionality in sociological research: A critical analysis of inclusions, interactions, and institutions in the study of inequalities. *Sociological Theory* 28:129–49.

Collins, Patricia Hill. 1990. *Black feminist thought: Knowledge, consciousness, and the politics of empowerment*. Boston: UnwinHyman.

Collins, Patricia Hill. 2010. The new politics of community. *American Sociological Review* 75:7–30.

Diamandaki, K. 2003. Virtual ethnicity and digital diasporas: Identity construction in cyber-space. *Global Media Journal*. http://lass.calumet.purdue.edu/cca/gmj/sp03/graduatesp03/gmj-sp03grad-diamandaki.htm (accessed June 15, 2010).

Earl, Jennifer. 2006. Pursuing social change online: The use of four protest tactics on the Internet. *Social Science Computer Review* 24:362–77.

Gilroy, Paul. 1989. *There ain't no Black in the Union Jack*. Chicago: University of Chicago Press.

Glenn, Evelyn Nakano. 2008. *Shades of citizenship*. Stanford, CA: Stanford University Press.

Govinden, Devarakhsnam. 2008. *Sister outsiders: The representation of identity and difference in selected writings by South African Indian women*. Pretoria: University of South Africa Press.

Guevarra, Anna. 2009. *Marketing dreams, manufacturing heroes: The transnational labor brokering of Filipino workers*. New Brunswick, NJ: Rutgers University Press.

Hondagneu-Sotelo, Pierette, and Ernestine Avila. 1997. I'm here, but I'm there: The meanings of Latina transnational motherhood. *Gender & Society* 11:548–71.

Ignacio, Emily. 2006. *Building diaspora: Filipino community formation on the Internet*. New Brunswick, NJ: Rutgers University Press.

Iwata, Miho, and Bandana Purkayastha. 2011. Cultural human rights. In *Human rights in our own backyard: Social justice and resistance in the U.S.*, edited by William Armaline, Davita Glasberg, and Bandana Purkayastha. Philadelphia: University of Pennsylvania Press.

Kim, Nadia. 2008. *Imperial citizens: Koreans and race from Seoul to LA*. Stanford, CA: Stanford University Press.

Kim-Puri, H.-J. 2007. Conceptualizing gender/sexuality/state/nation: An introduction. *Gender & Society* 19:137–59.

Lee, Rachel. 2003. *Asian America.net: Ethnicity, nationalism, and cyberspace*. New York: Routledge.

Levitt, Peggy. 2001. *The transnational villagers*. Berkeley: University of California Press.

Mitra, Ananda. 1997. Virtual commonality: Looking for India on the Internet. In *Virtual culture: Identity and communication in cyber-society*, edited by S. Jones. Thousand Oaks, CA: Sage.

Mitra, Rahul, and Radhika Gajjala. 2008. Queer blogging in Indian digital diasporas: A dialogic encounter. *Journal of Communication Inquiry*, originally published online July 16, 2008.

Nandy, Ashis. 2006. *The intimate enemy: Loss and recovery of self under colonialism.* New Delhi, India: Oxford University Press.

Narayan, Anjana, and Bandana Purkayastha. 2009. *Living our religions: South Asian Hindu and Muslim women narrate their experiences.* Stirling, VA: Kumarian Press.

Narayan, Anjana, and Bandana Purkayastha. 2011. Talking gender superiority in virtual spaces. *Journal of South Asian Diasporas* 3:53–69.

Narayan, Anjana, Bandana Purkayastha, and Sudipto Banerji. Forthcoming. Constructing virtual, transnational identities on the web: The case of Hindu student groups in the U.S. and UK. Special Issue on Virtual Ethnicities. *Journal of Intercultural Studies.*

Pudrovska, T., and M. M. Ferree. 2004. Global activism in "virtual space": The European women's lobby in the network of transnational women's NGOs on the web. *Social Politics: International Studies in Gender State and Society* 11:117–43.

Purkayastha, Bandana. 2005. *Negotiating ethnicity: Second-generation South Asian Americans traverse a transnational world.* New Brunswick, NJ: Rutgers University Press.

Purkayastha Bandana. 2009. Another word of experience? South Asian diasporic groups and the transnational context. *Journal of South Asian Diasporas* 1:85–99.

Purkayastha, Bandana. 2010. Interrogating intersectionality: Contemporary globalization and racialized gendering in the lives of highly educated South Asian Americans and their children. *Journal of Intercultural Studies* 31:29–47.

Sardar, Ziauddin, Ashis Nandy, Merryl Wyn Davies, and Claude Alvares. 1993. *The blinded eye: 500 years of Christopher Columbus.* New York: Apex Press; Goa, India: The Other India Press.

Vertovec, Steven. 2001. Transnational challenges to the "new" multiculturalism. www.transcomm.ox.ac.uk/working papers.

❧ Topics for Further Examination ❧

- Using an academic database, look up the work of Patricia Hill Collins, Bonnie Thornton Dill, Maxinne Baca Zinn, Raewyn Connell (formerly R. W. Connell), or others mentioned in the Introduction to Chapter 2 to find out what is currently being done on intersectionality. (Use parentheses around their names and ask for referred journals only.)
- Do a Web search using "feminist theory" and another category of difference and inequality (i.e., "feminist theory" and "race").
- Using the Web, locate information on those cited in the Introduction to Chapter 2: Audre Lorde, bell hooks, Angela Davis, Gloria Anzaldua, or Sojourner Truth. When doing so, try to find the names of others who challenged the whiteness of the women's movement.

3

GENDER AND THE PRISM OF CULTURE

Now that we have introduced you to the ways the contemporary U.S. gender system interacts with, and is modified by, a complex set of categories of difference and inequality, we turn to an exploration of the ways the prism of culture interacts with gender definitions and arrangements. Generations of researchers in the social sciences have opened our eyes to the array of "gender-scapes" around the globe. When we look through our kaleidoscope at the interaction between the prisms of gender and culture, we see different patterns that blur, blend, and are cast into a variety of culturally gendered configurations (Baker, 1999).

WHAT IS CULTURE?

Culture consists of the "implicit and explicit patterns of representations, actions, and artifacts" that are created and shared by people in their networks of interaction and social environments (DiMaggio & Markus, 2010, p. 348). The social scientific view of culture makes it clear that, without culture, human experience would have little, if any, shape or meaning (Schwalbe, 2005). That is, culture provides people with the assumptions and expectations on which their social interactions are built and in which their identities, behaviors, feelings, and thoughts are forged.

Two concepts that are useful for thinking about gender in the contemporary United States, as well as about the cultural contexts discussed in the chapter readings, are *cultural frames* and *cultural tool kits* (DiMaggio & Markus, 2010). The term *frame* refers to socially created, shared schemas by which people organize their social relations and coordinate behavior in the contexts in which they interact (Ridgeway, 2009). In particular, cultural frames rely on beliefs that cast people into categories or types, such as age-based categories (e.g., children and adults) and gender-based categories (e.g., women and men) (Ridgeway, 2009).

In the modern United States, the dominant gender frame defines people as belonging to one of two, and only two, sex/gender/sexuality categories, as discussed in Chapter 1. This frame is the lens through which many, if not most, Americans perceive and label others and themselves. Central to the frame are sex/gender/sexuality stereotypes of women and men as opposite types of people, and of men, in general, as having a higher status than women (Ridgeway, 2009). As you move through the readings in this chapter, compare and contrast gender frames. For example, the articles by Christine Helliwell and Maria Alexandra Lepowsky examine cultural worlds in which people's beliefs about sex and gender—and thus their representations, identities, and institutions—depart dramatically from American beliefs.

Ann Swidler (1986) forwarded the concept of culture as a "tool kit," or repertoire of "habits, skills, and styles from which people construct 'strategies of action'" (p. 273). From the vantage point of culture as tool kit, people solve life problems—individually and collectively—by drawing on various items in their cultural repertoire (e.g., beliefs, language, skills, images, and clothing; p. 273). As you consider the readings in this chapter, think about the gender "items" in the cultural tool kits employed by the people whose worlds are the focus of research. For example, what sensibilities, styles, and skills (p. 277) are in the cultural tool kits of the "Russian" women in the reading by Martina Cvajner, and how do those sensibilities, styles, and skills influence their actions?

To repeat, cultures are created by people in the different social worlds in which they live, day-to-day and over time. Consequently, cultures can be strikingly different (DiMaggio & Markus, 2010, p. 349), as expressed in the extraordinary sex/gender/sexuality variation found within and across networks and groups. For example, in some cultures, such as the Sambia of New Guinea, people do not perceive or categorize people as homosexual, and yet members of such cultures may regularly engage in same-gender sex (Herdt, 1997).

Not only do different groups of people produce different cultures, but the cultures they produce are dynamic. That is, people continually generate and alter culture both as individuals and as members of particular networks and groups; as a result, all cultures undergo change as their members evaluate, resist, and challenge beliefs and practices (DiMaggio & Markus, 2010; Stone & McKee, 1999). To illustrate, in the United States

today, racial stereotypes are eroding, in part because scientists and social scientists have demonstrated that race is a social fiction rather than a biological fact and in part because the ongoing civil rights movement has been successful in dismantling much of the racist infrastructure of American society.

The prisms of gender and culture are inextricably intertwined. That is, people construct specific gender beliefs and practices in relation to particular cultural traditions and societal conditions. Cultures are gendered in distinctive ways, and gender systems, in turn, shape both material and symbolic cultural products (see, e.g., Chapter 5). As you will discover, the cross-cultural analyses of gender presented in this chapter provide critical support for the social constructionist argument that gender is a situated, negotiated, contested, and changing set of practices and understandings.

Let's begin with a set of observations about gender in different cultures. Do you know there are cultures in which individuals can move from one gender category to another without being stigmatized? If you traveled from country to country around the world, you would find cultures in which men are gentle, soft-spoken, and modest, and cultures in which women are viewed as strong and take on roles labeled masculine in the United States. Although we hear news about extreme forms of oppression of women in some places in the world (e.g., bride burning in parts of India), there are other places where women and men live in relative harmony and equality. Also, there are cultures in which the social prisms of difference and inequality that operate in the United States (e.g., social class, race, sexual orientation) are minimal, inconsequential, or nonexistent (see the chapter reading by Helliwell).

THE PROBLEM OF ETHNOCENTRISM IN CROSS-CULTURAL RESEARCH

If you find any of these observations unsettling or even shocking, then you have probably tapped into the problem of bias in cross-cultural studies.

One of the great challenges of cross-cultural research is learning to transcend one's own cultural assumptions to be able to value and understand cultural differences. It takes practice, conscious commitment, and self-awareness to get outside one's own cultural frame. After all, seeing what our culture wants us to see is precisely what socialization is about. Not only do cultural blinders make it difficult for us to see what gender is and how it is configured and reconfigured by various social prisms within our own culture, but they can make it even more challenging to grasp the profoundly different ways people in other cultures think about and organize human relations.

We tend to "see what we believe," which means we are likely to deny gender patterns that vary from our own cultural experience and/or to misinterpret patterns that are different from our own. For example, the Europeans who first explored and colonized Africa were horrified by the ways African forms of gender and sexuality diverged from their own. They had no framework in which to understand warrior women, such as Nzinga of the Ndongo kingdom of the Mbundu (Murray & Roscoe, 1998). Nzinga was king of her people, dressed as a man, and was surrounded by a harem of young men who dressed as women and were her "wives" (Murray & Roscoe, 1998). However, her behavior made sense in the context of her culture, one in which people defined gender as situational and symbolic, thus allowing for alternative genders (Murray & Roscoe, 1998). In this chapter, Cvajner directly addresses the struggle she experienced with her negative stereotypes of the "Russian" women at the center of her ethnographic research. She had to transcend her negative stereotypes to understand why the "Russians" acted as they did in the context of "Alpinetown."

It is a challenge to resist the tendency toward ethnocentrism (i.e., the belief that the ideas and practices of one's own culture are the standard and that divergent cultures are substandard or inferior). However, the rewards for bracketing the ethnocentric attitude are extremely valuable because one is then able to understand how and why gender operates in cultures that are different from one's own experience and, thus, from one's cultural frame. Thanks to the wide-ranging research of sociologists and anthropologists, we are increasingly able to grasp the peculiarities of our gender system and understand more deeply lifeways, including genderscapes, in other places in the world.

The readings in this chapter will introduce you to some of the variety in gender beliefs and practices across cultures and illustrate three of the most important findings of cross-cultural research on gender: (1) There is no universal definition or experience of gender; indeed, gender is not constituted as oppositional and binary in all societies. (2) Gender inequality, specifically the dominance of men over women, is not the rule everywhere in the world. (3) Gender arrangements, whatever they may be, are socially constructed and, thus, ever evolving.

THERE IS NO UNIVERSAL DEFINITION OR EXPERIENCE OF GENDER

Although people in many contemporary cultures perceive at least some differences between women and men, and assign different tasks and responsibilities to people based on gender categories, these differences vary both from culture to culture and within cultures. There is no unified ideal or definition of masculinity or femininity across cultures. In some cultures, such as the Ju/'hoansi of Namibia and Botswana, women and men alike can become powerful and respected healers, while in others, such as the United States today, powerful healing roles are dominated by men (Bonvillain, 2001). Among the seminomadic, pastoral Tuareg of the Sahara and the Sahel, women have considerable economic independence as livestock owners, herders, gardeners, and leathersmiths, while in other cultural groups, such as the Taliban of Afghanistan, women are restricted to household labor and economic dependence on men (Rasmussen, 2001).

The readings in this chapter highlight some of the extraordinary cross-cultural differences in beliefs about men and women and in the tasks and rights assigned to them. They offer insights into how gender is shaped across cultures by a number of factors, including ideology, participation in economic production, and control over sexuality and reproduction. For example, in the chapter reading with the titillating title "It's Only a Penis," Helliwell provides an account of the Gerai of Borneo, a cultural group in which rape does not exist. Helliwell argues that the Gerai belief in the biological sameness of women and men is a key to understanding their rape-free society. Her research offers an important account of how assumptions about human biology, in this case femaleness and maleness, are culturally shaped.

In addition, the two-sex (male or female), two-gender (feminine or masculine), and two-sexual-orientation (homosexual or heterosexual) system of Western culture is not a universal mode of categorization and organization. As you know from reading Serena Nanda's article on gender variants in Native North America (Chapter 1), the two-spirit role was widespread and accepted in many American Indian tribes. Gilbert Herdt (1997), an expert on the anthropology of sexual orientation and gender, points out that the two-spirit role reached a high point in its cultural elaboration among the Mojave Indians, who "sanctioned both male (alyha) and female (hwame) two-spirit roles, each of which had its own distinctive social positions and worldviews" (p. 92).

GENDER INEQUALITY IS NOT THE RULE EVERYWHERE

Gender and power go together but not in only one way. The relationship of power to gender in human groups varies from extreme male dominance to relative equality between women and men. Most societies in the contemporary world and many in the past have been organized so that men, in general, have greater access to and control over valued resources such as wealth, authority, and prestige. At the extreme are intensely patriarchal societies, such as traditional China and India, in which women were dominated by men in multiple contexts and relationships. In traditional China, for example, sons were preferred, female infanticide was common, divorce could be initiated only by husbands, restrictions on girls and women were embodied in the mutilating practice of foot binding, and the suicide rate among young wives—who typically endured extreme isolation and hardship—was higher than in any other age and gender category (Bonvillain, 2001).

The United States also has a history of gender relations in which White men as a group have had power over women as a group (and over men of color). For many decades, men's power was overt and legal. For example, in the 19th century, husbands were legally empowered to beat their wives, women did not have voting rights, and women were legally excluded from many occupations (Stone & McKee, 1999). Today, gender inequality takes more covert and subtle forms. For example, women earn less, on average, than do men of equal educational and occupational level; women are far more likely to be sexually objectified; and women are more likely to shoulder the burden of a double workday inside and outside the home (Coltrane & Adams, 2001; Chapters 7 and 8).

Understanding the relationship between power and gender requires us to use our sharpest sociological radar. To start, it is important to understand that power does not reside in individuals per se. For example, neither presidents nor bosses have power in a vacuum. They require the support of personnel and special resources such as media, weapons, and money. Power is a group phenomenon, and it exists only so long as a powerful group, its ruling principles, and its control over resources are sustained (Kimmel, 2000).

In addition, not all members of an empowered group have the same amount of power. In the United States and similar societies, male power benefits some men more than others. In fact, many individual men do not hold formal positions of power, and many do not feel powerful in their everyday lives (Johnson, 2001; Kimmel, 2000). Yet major institutions and organizations (e.g., government, big business, the military, the mass media) in the United States are gendered masculine, with controlling positions in those arenas dominated by men, but not just any men (Johnson, 2001). Controlling positions are overwhelmingly held by White men who typically come from privileged backgrounds and whose lives appear to conform to a straight and narrow path (Johnson, 2001; Kimmel, 2000). As we learned in Chapter 2, the relationship of gender to power in a nation such as the United States is complicated by interactions among structures of domination and subordination such as race, social class, and sexual orientation. In her chapter reading, Cvajner examines the role domination and subordination play in the construction of hyper-femininity among "Russian" women in the towns of Northern Italy.

Not all societies are as highly and intricately stratified by gender, race, social class, and other social categories of privilege and power as is the United States. Many cultural groups organize relationships in ways that give most or all adults access to similar rights, prestige, decision-making authority, and autonomy in their households and communities. Traditional Agta, Ju/'hoansi, and Iroquois societies are good examples. In other cultural groups, such as the precontact Tlingit and Haida of the Canadian Pacific coastal region, relations among people were based on their position in economic and status hierarchies, yet egalitarian valuation of women and men prevailed (Bonvillain, 2001).

The point is that humans do not inevitably create inequalities out of perceived differences. Thus, even though there is generally some type of division of labor by gender across cultures today, differences in men's and women's work do not inexorably lead to patriarchal relations in which men monopolize high-status positions in important institutions and women are relegated to a restricted world of low-status activities and tasks. To help illustrate, Lepowsky's

ethnography of Vanatinai social relations provides us with a model of a society in which the principles of personal autonomy and freedom of choice prevail. The gender ideology of the Vanatinai is egalitarian, and their belief in equality manifests itself in daily life. For example, women as well as men own and inherit land and other valuables. Women choose their own marriage partners and lovers, and they divorce at will. Any individual on Vanatinai may try to become a leader by demonstrating superior knowledge and skill.

Gender inequality is not the rule everywhere. Male dominance, patriarchy, gender inequality—whatever term one uses—is not the inevitable state of human relations. Additionally, patriarchy itself is not unitary. Patriarchy does not assume a particular shape, and it does not mean that women have no control or influence in their communities. Even in the midst of patriarchy, women and men may create identities and relationships that allow for autonomy and independence. See, for example, Annie George's chapter reading on the emergence of more egalitarian relations between working-class Indian women and men.

GENDER ARRANGEMENTS ARE EVER EVOLVING

The cross-cultural story of gender takes us back to the metaphor of the kaleidoscope. Life is an ongoing process of change from one pattern to another. We can never go back to "the way things were" at some earlier moment in time, nor can we predict exactly how the future will unfold. This is, of course, the story of gender around the world. For example, the chapter reading by George explores the links between changes in the meaning and practice of male honor and the rise of greater autonomy among married women in a working-class neighborhood of Mumbai, India.

Two of the major sources of change in gender meanings and practices across cultures are culture contact and diffusion of beliefs and practices around the globe (Ritzer, 2004; Sorenson,

2000). Among the most well-documented accounts of such change have been those that demonstrate how Western gender systems were imposed on people whose gender beliefs and arrangements varied from Western assumptions and practices. For example, Native American multiple gender systems were actively, and sometimes violently, discouraged by European colonists (Herdt, 1997; see Nanda's reading in Chapter 1). Today, globalization—a complex process of worldwide diffusion of practices, images, and ideas (Ritzer, 2004)—raises the problem of the development of a world order, including a gender order, that may be increasingly dominated by Western cultural values and patterns (Held, McGrew, Goldblatt, & Perraton, 1999; see Chapter 10 for further discussion). Cenk Özbay, in his chapter reading, examines the emergence of exaggerated masculinity among rent boys in Istanbul. As part of his analysis, he offers insights into the process of diffusion as it plays out in the interpenetration of Western gay culture and the gender/sexuality tool kits of the rent boys and gay men of Istanbul.

Culture contact and diffusion via globalization are by no means the only source of changing gender arrangements (see Chapter 10 for detailed discussion of gender change). The forces of change are many and complex, and they have resulted in a mix of tendencies toward rigid, hierarchical gender relations and toward gender flexibility and equality, depending on the specific cultural context and forces of change experienced by particular groups of people. In all this, there is one fact: People are not bound by any set of gender beliefs and practices. Culture change is inevitable, and so is change in the genderscape.

REFERENCES

Baker, C. (1999). *Kaleidoscopes: Wonders of wonder.* Lafayette, CA: C&T.

Bonvillain, N. (2001). *Women and men: Cultural constructs of gender* (3rd ed.). Upper Saddle River, NJ: Prentice Hall.

Coltrane, S., & Adams, M. (2001). Men, women, and housework. In D. Vannoy (Ed.), *Gender mosaics* (pp. 145–154). Los Angeles: Roxbury.

DiMaggio, P., & Markus, H. R. (2010). Culture and social psychology: Converging perspectives. *Social Psychology Quarterly, 73*(4), 347–352.

Held, D., McGrew, A., Goldblatt, D., & Perraton, J. (1999). *Global transformations.* Stanford, CA: Stanford University Press.

Herdt, G. (1997). *Same sex, different cultures.* Boulder, CO: Westview Press.

Johnson, A. G. (2001). *Privilege, power, and difference.* Mountain View, CA: Mayfield.

Kimmel, M. (2000). *The gendered society.* New York: Oxford University Press.

Murray, S. O., & Roscoe, W. (1998). *Boy-wives and female-husbands: Studies of African homosexualities.* New York: St. Martin's Press.

Rasmussen, S. (2001). Pastoral nomadism and gender. In C. B. Brettell & C. F. Sargent (Eds.), *Gender in cross-cultural perspective* (pp. 280–293). Upper Saddle River, NJ: Prentice Hall.

Ridgeway, C. (2009). Framed before we know it: How gender shapes social relations. *Gender & Society, 23*(2), 145–160.

Ritzer, G. (2004). *The globalization of nothing.* Thousand Oaks, CA: Pine Forge Press.

Schwalbe, M. (2005). *The sociologically examined life.* New York: McGraw-Hill.

Sorenson, M. L. S. (2000). *Gender archeology.* Cambridge, UK: Polity Press.

Stone, L., & McKee, N. P. (1999). *Gender and culture in America.* Upper Saddle River, NJ: Prentice Hall.

Swidler, A. (1986). Culture in action: Symbols and strategies. *American Sociological Review, 51*, 273–286.

Introduction to Reading 11

Anthropologist Christine Helliwell provides a challenging account of a cultural group, the Gerai of Indonesia, in which rape does not exist. She links the freedom from rape among the Gerai people to the relatively egalitarian nature of their gender relations. Helliwell's research questions many gender beliefs held by members of Western cultures today.

1. How are men's and women's sexual organs conceptualized among the Gerai, and what are the consequences for Gerai understandings of sexual intercourse?

2. Genitalia do not determine identity in Gerai. What does?

3. What does Helliwell mean when she states that "rape imposes difference as much as it is produced by difference" (2000, p. 812)?

"It's Only a Penis"

Rape, Feminism, and Difference

Christine Helliwell

In 1985 and 1986 I carried out anthropological fieldwork in the Dayak community of Gerai in Indonesian Borneo. One night in September 1985, a man of the village climbed through a window into the freestanding house where a widow lived with her elderly mother, younger (unmarried) sister, and young children. The widow awoke, in darkness, to feel the man inside her mosquito net, gripping her shoulder while he climbed under the blanket that covered her and her youngest child as they slept (her older children slept on mattresses nearby). He was whispering, "be quiet, be quiet!" She responded by sitting up in bed and pushing him violently, so that he stumbled backward, became entangled with her mosquito net, and then, finally free, moved across the floor toward the window. In the meantime, the woman climbed from her bed and pursued him, shouting his name several times as she did so. His hurried exit through the window, with his clothes now in considerable disarray, was accompanied by a stream of abuse from the woman and by excited interrogations from wakened neighbors in adjoining houses.

I awoke the following morning to raucous laughter on the longhouse verandah outside my apartment where a group of elderly women gathered regularly to thresh, winnow, and pound rice. They were recounting this tale loudly, and with enormous enjoyment, to all in the immediate vicinity. As I came out of my door, one was engaged in mimicking the man climbing out the window, sarong falling down, genitals askew. Those others working or lounging near her on the verandah—both men and women—shrieked with laughter.

When told the story, I was shocked and appalled. An unknown man had tried to climb into the bed of a woman in the dead, dark of night? I knew what this was called: attempted rape. The woman had seen the man and recognized him (so had others in the village, wakened by her shouting). I knew what he deserved: the full weight of the law. My own fears about being a single woman alone in a strange place, sleeping in a dwelling that could not be secured at night, bubbled to the surface. My feminist sentiments poured out. "How can you laugh?" I asked my women friends; "this is a very bad thing that he has tried to do." But my outrage simply served to fuel the hilarity. "No, not bad," said one of the old women (a particular friend of mine), "simply stupid."

I felt vindicated in my response when, two hours later, the woman herself came onto the verandah to share betel nut and tobacco and to broadcast the story. Her anger was palpable, and she shouted for all to hear her determination to exact a compensation payment from the man. Thinking to obtain information about local women's responses to rape, I began to question her. Had she been frightened? I asked. Of course she had—Wouldn't I feel frightened if I awoke in the dark to find an unknown person inside my mosquito net? Wouldn't I be angry? Why then, I asked, hadn't she taken the opportunity, while he was entangled in her mosquito net, to kick him hard or to hit him with one of the many wooden implements near at hand? She looked shocked. Why would she do that? she asked—after all, he hadn't hurt her. No, but he had wanted to, I replied. She looked at me with puzzlement. Not able to find a local word for rape in my vocabulary, I scrabbled to explain myself: "He was trying to have sex with you." I said, "although you didn't want to. He was trying to hurt you." She looked at me, more with pity than with puzzlement now, although both were mixed in her expression. "Tin [Christine], it's only a penis" she said. "How can a penis hurt anyone?"

Rape, Feminism, and Difference

A central feature of many feminist writings about rape in the past twenty years is their concern to eschew the view of rape as a natural function of male biology and to stress instead its bases in society and culture. It is curious, then, that so much of this work talks of rape in terms that suggest—either implicitly or explicitly—that it is a universal practice. To take only several examples: Pauline Bart and Patricia O'Brien tell us that "every female from nine months to ninety years is at risk" (1985, 1); Anna Clark argues that "all women know the paralyzing fear of walking down a dark street at night. . . . It seems to be a fact of life that the fear of rape imposes a curfew on our movements" (1987, 1); Catharine MacKinnon claims that "sexuality is central to

women's definition and forced sex is central to sexuality," so "rape is indigenous, not exceptional, to women's social condition" (1989b, 172) and "all women live all the time under the shadow of the threat of sexual abuse" (1989a, 340); Lee Madigan and Nancy Gamble write of "the global terrorism of rape" (1991, 21–2); and Susan Brison asserts that "the fact that all women's lives are restricted by sexual violence is indisputable" (1993, 17). . . . This is particularly puzzling given that Peggy Reeves Sanday, for one, long ago demonstrated that while rape occurs widely throughout the world, it is by no means a human universal: some societies can indeed be classified as rape free (1981).

There are two general reasons for this universalization of rape among Western feminists. The first of these has to do with the understanding of the practice as horrific by most women in Western societies. In these settings, rape is seen as "a fate worse than, or tantamount to, death" (S. Marcus 1992, 387): a shattering of identity that, for instance, left one North American survivor feeling "not quite sure whether I had died and the world went on without me, or whether I was alive in a totally alien world" (Brison 1993, 10). . . .

A second, equally deep-seated reason for the feminist tendency to universalize rape stems from Western feminism's emphasis on difference between men and women and from its consequent linking of rape and difference. Two types of difference are involved here. The first of these is difference in social status and power; thus rape is linked quite explicitly, in contemporary feminist accounts, to patriarchal social forms. Indeed, this focus on rape as stemming from difference in social position is what distinguishes feminist from other kinds of accounts of rape (see Ellis 1989, 10). In this view, inequality between men and women is linked to men's desire to possess, subjugate, and control women, with rape constituting a central means by which the freedom of women is limited and their continued submission to men ensured. Since many feminists continue to believe that patriarchy is universal—or, at the very least, to feel deeply ambivalent on this point—there is a tendency among us to believe that rape, too, is universal.[1]

However, the view of women as everywhere oppressed by men has been extensively critiqued within the anthropological literature. A number of anthropologists have argued that in some societies, while men and women may perform different roles and occupy different spaces, they are nevertheless equal in value, status, and power.[2] . . .

But there is a second type of difference between men and women that also, albeit largely implicitly, underlies the assumption that rape is universal, and it is the linkage between this type of difference and the treatment of rape in feminist accounts with which I am largely concerned in this article. I refer to the assumption by most Western feminists writing on rape that men and women have different bodies and, more specifically, different genitalia: that they are, in other words differently sexed. Furthermore, it is taken for granted in most feminist accounts that these differences render the former biologically, or "naturally," capable of penetrating and therefore brutalizing the latter and render the latter "naturally" able to be brutalized. . . . Rape of women by men is thus assumed to be universal because the same "biological" bodily differences between men and women are believed to exist everywhere.

Unfortunately, the assumption that preexisting bodily difference between men and women underlies rape has blinded feminists writing on the subject to the ways the practice of rape itself creates and inscribes such difference. This seems particularly true in contemporary Western societies where the relationship between rape and bodily/genital dimorphism appears to be an extremely intimate one. Judith Butler (1990, 1993) has argued (following Foucault 1978) that the Western emphasis on sexual difference is a product of the heterosexualization of desire within Western societies over the past few centuries, which "requires and institutes the production of discrete and asymmetrical oppositions between 'feminine' and 'masculine' where these are understood as expressive attributes of 'male' and 'female'" (1990, 17).[3] The practice of rape in

Western contexts can only properly be understood with reference to this heterosexual matrix, to the division of humankind into two distinct—and in many respects opposed—types of body (and hence types of person).[4] While it is certainly the case that rape is linked in contemporary Western societies to disparities of power and status between men and women, it is the particular discursive form that those disparities take—their elaboration in terms of the discourse of sex—that gives rape its particular meaning and power in these contexts.

Sharon Marcus has already argued convincingly that the act of rape "feminizes" women in Western settings, so that "the entire female body comes to be symbolized by the vagina, itself conceived of as a delicate, perhaps inevitably damaged and pained inner space" (1992, 398). I would argue further that the practice of rape in these settings—both its possibility and its actualization—not only feminizes women but masculinizes men as well.[5] This masculinizing character of rape is very clear in, for instance, Sanday's ethnography of fraternity gang rape in North American universities (1990b) and, in particular, in material on rape among male prison inmates. In the eyes of these rapists the act of rape marks them as "real men" and marks their victims as not men, that is, as feminine.[6] In this iconography, the "masculine" body (along with the "masculine" psyche), is viewed as hard, penetrative, and aggressive, in contrast to the soft, vulnerable, and violable "feminine" sexuality and psyche. Rape both reproduces and marks the pronounced sexual polarity found in these societies.

Western understandings of gender difference have almost invariably started from the presumption of a presocial bodily difference between men and women ("male" and "female") that is then somehow acted on by society to produce gender. In particular, the possession of either male genitals or female genitals is understood by most Westerners to be not only the primary marker of gender identity but, indeed, the underlying cause of that identity. . . .

I seek to do two things in this article. First, in providing an account of a community in which rape does not occur, I aim to give the lie to the widespread assumption that rape is universal and thus to invite Western feminists to interrogate the basis of our own tendency to take its universality for granted.[7] The fundamental question is this: Why does a woman of Gerai see a penis as lacking the power to harm her, while I, a white Australian/New Zealand woman, am so ready to see it as having the capacity to defile, to humiliate, to subjugate and, ultimately, to destroy me?

Second, by exploring understandings of sex and gender in a community that stresses identity, rather than difference, between men and women (including men's and women's bodies), I aim to demonstrate that Western beliefs in the "sexed" character of bodies are not "natural" in basis but, rather, are a component of specifically Western gendering and sexual regimes. And since the practice of rape in Western societies is profoundly linked to these beliefs, I will suggest that it is an inseparable part of such regimes. This is not to say that the practice of rape is always linked to the kind of heterosexual regime found in the West; even the most cursory glance at any list of societies in which the practice occurs indicates that this is not so.[8] But it is to point out that we will be able to understand rape only ever in a purely localized sense, in the context of the local discourses and practices that are both constitutive of and constituted by it. In drawing out the implications of the Gerai stress on identity between men and women for Gerai gender and sexual relations, I hope to point out some of the possible implications of the Western emphasis on gender difference for Western gender and sexual relations—including the practice of rape.

GENDER, SEX, AND PROCREATION IN GERAI

Gerai is a Dayak community of some seven hundred people in the Indonesian province of Kalimantan Barat (West Borneo).[9] In the twenty months I spent in the community, I heard of no cases of either sexual assault or attempted sexual assault (and since this is a community in which privacy as we understand it in the West is almost nonexistent—in which surveillance by neighbors is at a very high level [see Helliwell 1996]—I would certainly have heard of any such cases had they occurred). In addition, when I questioned men and women about sexual assault, responses ranged from puzzlement to outright incredulity to horror.

While relations between men and women in Gerai can be classified as relatively egalitarian in many respects, both men and women nevertheless say that men are "higher" than women (Helliwell 1995, 364). This greater status and authority does not, however, find expression in the practice of rape, as many feminist writings on the subject seem to suggest that it should. This is because the Gerai view of men as "higher" than women, although equated with certain kinds of increased potency vis-à-vis the world at large, does not translate into a conception of that potency as attached to and manifest through the penis—of men's genitals as able to brutalize women's genitals.

Shelly Errington has pointed out that a feature of many of the societies of insular Southeast Asia is a stress on sameness, even identity, between men and women (1990, 35, 39), in contrast to the Western stress on difference between the passive "feminine" object and the active, aggressive "masculine" subject.[10] Gerai understandings of gender fit Errington's model very well. In Gerai, men and women are not understood as fundamentally different types of persons: there is no sense of a dichotomized masculinity and femininity. Rather, men and women are seen to have the same kinds of capacities and proclivities, but with respect to some, men are seen as "more so" and with respect to others, women are seen as "more so." Men are said to be braver and more knowledgeable about local law (adat), while women are said to be more persistent and more enduring. All of these qualities are valued. Crucially, in terms of the central quality of nurturance (perhaps the most valued quality in Gerai), which is very strongly marked as feminine among Westerners, Gerai people see no difference between men and women. As one (female) member of the community put it to me: "We all must nurture because we all need."[11] The capacity both to nurture and to need, particularly as expressed through the cultivation of rice as a member of a rice group, is central to Gerai conceptions of personhood: rice is the source of life, and its (shared) production humanizes and socializes individuals (Helliwell, forthcoming). Women and men have identical claims to personhood based on their equal contributions to rice production (there is no notion that women are somehow diminished as persons even though they may be seen as less "high"). As in Strathern's account of Hagen (1988), the perceived mutuality of rice-field work in Gerai renders inoperable any notion of either men or women as autonomous individual subjects.

It is also important to note that while men's bravery is linked to a notion of their greater physical strength, it is not equated with aggression—aggression is not valued in most Gerai contexts.[12] As a Gerai man put it to me, the wise man is the one "who fights when he has to, and runs away when he can"; such avoidance of violence does not mark a man as lacking in bravery. . . . While it is recognized that a man will sometimes need to fight—and skill and courage in fighting are valued—aggression and hotheadedness are ridiculed as the hallmarks of a lazy and incompetent man. In fact, physical violence between adults is uncommon in Gerai, and all of the cases that I did witness or hear about were extremely mild.[13] Doubtless the absence of rape in the community is linked to this devaluing of aggression in general. However, unlike a range of other forms of violence (slapping, beating with a fist, beating with an implement, knifing, premeditated killing, etc.), rape is not named as an offense and accorded a set punishment under traditional Gerai law. In addition, unlike these other forms of violence, rape is something that people in the community find almost impossible to comprehend ("How would he be able to do such a thing?" one woman asked when I struggled to explain the concept of a man attempting to put his penis into her against her will). Clearly, then, more is involved in the absence of rape in Gerai than a simple absence of violence in general.

Central to all of the narratives that Gerai people tell about themselves and their community is the notion of a "comfortable life": the achievement of this kind of life marks the person and the household as being of value and constitutes the norm to which all Gerai people aspire. Significantly, the content of such a life is seen as identical for both men and women: it is marked by the production of bountiful rice harvests each year and the successful raising of a number of healthy children to maturity. The core values and aspirations of men and women are thus identical; of the many life histories that I collected while in the community—all of which are organized around this central image—it is virtually impossible to tell those of men from those of women. Two points are significant in this respect. First, a "comfortable life" is predicated on the notion of a partnership between a man and a woman (a conjugal pair). This is because while men and women are seen to have the same basic skills and capacities, men are seen to be "better" at certain kinds of work and women to be "better" at other kinds. Second, and closely related to this, the Gerai notion of men's and women's work does not constitute a rigid division of labor: both men and women say that theoretically women can perform all of the work routinely carried out by men, and men can perform all of the work routinely carried out by women. However, men are much better at men's work, and women are much better at women's work. Again, what we have here is a stress on identity between men and women at the expense of radical difference.

This stress on identity extends into Gerai bodily and sexual discourses. A number of people (both men and women) assured me that men sometimes menstruate; in addition, menstrual blood is not understood to be polluting, in contrast to how it is seen in many societies that stress more strongly the difference between men and women. While pregnancy and childbirth are spoken of as "women's work," many Gerai people claim that under certain circumstances men are also able to carry out this work—but, they say, women are "better" at it and so normally undertake it. In line with this claim, I collected a Gerai myth concerning a lazy woman who was reluctant to take on the work of pregnancy and childbirth. Her husband instead made for himself a lidded container out of bark, wood, and rattan ("like a betel nut container"), which he attached around his waist beneath his loincloth and in which he carried the growing fetus until it was ready to be born. On one occasion when I was watching a group of Gerai men cut up a boar, one, remembering an earlier conversation about the capacity of men to give birth, pointed to a growth in the boar's body cavity and said with much disapproving shaking of the head: "Look at this. He wants to carry his child. He's stupid." In addition, several times I saw fathers push their nipples into the mouths of young children to quiet them; while none of these fathers claimed to be able to produce milk, people nevertheless claimed that some men in the community were able to lactate, a phenomenon also attested to in myth. Men and women are thought to produce the same genital fluid, and this is linked in complex ways to the capacity of both to menstruate. All of these examples demonstrate the community's stress on bodily identity between men and women.

Furthermore, in Gerai, men's and women's sexual organs are explicitly conceptualized as the same. This sexual identity became particularly clear when I asked several people who had been to school (and hence were used to putting pencil to paper) to draw men's and women's respective organs for me: in all cases, the basic structure and form of each were the same. One informant, endeavoring to convince me of this sameness, likened both to wooden and bark containers for holding valuables (these vary in size but have the same basic conical shape, narrower at the base and wider at the top). In all of these discussions, it was reiterated that the major difference between men's and women's organs is their location: inside the body (women) and outside the body (men).[14] In fact, when I pressed people on this point, they invariably explained

that it makes no sense to distinguish between men's and women's genitalia themselves; rather, it is location that distinguishes between penis and vulva.[15]

Heterosexuality constitutes the normative sexual activity in the community and, indeed, I was unable to obtain any information about homosexual practices during my time there. In line with the stress on sameness, sexual intercourse between a man and a woman in Gerai is understood as an equal coming together of fluids, pleasures, and life forces. The same stress also underlies beliefs about conception. Gerai people believe that repeated acts of intercourse between the same two people are necessary for conception, since this "prepares" the womb for pregnancy. The fetus is deemed to be created through the mingling of equal quantities of fluids and forces from both partners. Again, what is seen as important here is not the fusion of two different types of bodies (male and female) as in Western understandings; rather, Gerai people say, it is the similarity of the two bodies that allows procreation to occur. As someone put it to me bluntly: "If they were not the same, how could the fluids blend? It's like coconut oil and water: they can't mix!"

What needs to be stressed here is that both sexual intercourse and conception are viewed as involving a mingling of similar bodily fluids, forces, and so on, rather than as the penetration of one body by another with a parallel propulsion of substances from one (male) body only into the other, very different (female) one. What Gerai accounts of both sexual intercourse and conception stress are tropes of identity, mingling, balance, and reciprocity. In this context it is worth noting that many Gerai people were puzzled by the idea of gender-specific "medicine" to prevent contraception—such as the injectable or oral contraceptives promoted by state-run health clinics in the area. Many believed that, because both partners play the same role in conception, it should not matter whether husband or wife received such medicine (and indeed, I knew of cases where husbands had taken oral contraceptives meant for their wives). This suggests that such contraceptive regimes also serve (like the practice of rape) to reinscribe sex difference between men and women (see also Tsing 1993, 104–20). . . .

While Gerai people stress sameness over difference between men and women, they do, nevertheless, see them as being different in one important respect: their life forces are, they say, oriented differently ("they face different ways," it was explained to me). This different orientation means that women are "better" at certain kinds of work and men are "better" at other kinds of work—particularly with respect to rice-field work. Gerai people conceive of the work of clearing large trees for a new rice field as the definitive man's work and regard the work of selecting and storing the rice seed for the following year's planting—which is correlated in fundamental ways with the process of giving birth—as the definitive woman's work. Because women are perceived to lack appropriate skills with respect to the first, and men are perceived to lack appropriate skills with respect to the second, Gerai people say that to be viable a household must contain both adult males and adult females. And since a "comfortable life" is marked by success in production not only of rice but also of children, the truly viable household must contain at least one conjugal pair. The work of both husband and wife is seen as necessary for the adequate nurturance of the child and successful rearing to adulthood (both of which depend on the successful cultivation of rice). Two women or two men would not be able to produce adequately for a child since they would not be able to produce consistently successful rice harvests; while such a household might be able to select seed, clear a rice field, and so grow rice in some rudimentary fashion, its lack of expertise at one of these tasks would render it perennially poor and its children perennially unhealthy, Gerai people say. . . .

Gender difference in Gerai, then, is not predicated on the character of one's body, and especially of one's genitalia as in many Western contexts. Rather, it is understood as constituted in the differential capacity to perform certain kinds of work, a capacity assigned long before one's bodily being takes shape.[16] In this respect it is important to note that Gerai ontology rests on a belief in predestination, in things being as they should (see Helliwell 1995). In this understanding, any individual's semongan is linked in multifarious and unknowable ways to the cosmic order, to the "life" of the universe as a whole. Thus the new fetus is predestined to become someone "fitted" to carry out either men's work or women's work as part of the maintenance of a universal balance. Bodies with the appropriate characteristics—internal or external genitalia, presence or absence of breasts, and so on—then develop in line with this prior destiny. At first sight this may not seem enormously different from Western conceptions of gender, but the difference is in fact profound. While, for Westerners, genitalia, as significant of one's role in the procreative process, are absolutely fundamental in determining ones identity, in Gerai the work that one performs is seen as fundamental, and genitalia along with other bodily characteristics, are relegated to a kind of secondary, derivative function.

Gerai understandings of gender were made quite clear through circumstances surrounding my own gender classification while in the community. Gerai people remained very uncertain about my gender for some time after I arrived in the community because (as they later told me) "I did not . . . walk like a woman, with arms held out from the body and hips slightly swaying; I was 'brave' trekking from village to village through the jungle on my own; I had bony kneecaps; I did not know how to tie a sarong in the appropriate way for women; I could not distinguish different varieties of rice from one another; I did not wear earrings; I had short hair; I was tall" (Helliwell 1993, 260). This was despite the fact that people in the community knew from my first few days with them both that I had breasts (this was obvious when the sarong that I wore clung to my body while I bathed in the river) and that I had a vulva rather than a penis and testicles (this was obvious from my trips to defecate or urinate in the small stream used for that purpose, when literally dozens of people would line the banks to observe whether I performed these functions differently from them). As someone said to me at a later point, "Yes, I saw that you had a vulva, but I thought that Western men might be different." My eventual, more definitive classification as a woman occurred . . . (a)s I learned to distinguish types of rice and their uses, I became more and more of a woman (as I realized later), since this knowledge—including the magic that goes with it—is understood by Gerai people as foundational to femininity. . . .

Gerai people talk of two kinds of work as defining a woman: the selection and storage of rice seed and the bearing of children.[17] But the first of these is viewed as prior, logically as well as chronologically. People are quite clear that in the womb either "someone who can cut down the large trees for a ricefield is made, or someone who can select and store rice." When I asked if it was not more important whether or not someone could bear a child, it was pointed out to me that many women do not bear children (there is a high rate of infertility in the community), but all women have the knowledge to select and store rice seed. In fact, at the level of the rice group the two activities of "growing" rice and "growing" children are inseparable: a rice group produces rice in order to raise healthy children, and it produces children so that they can in turn produce the rice that will sustain the group once their parents are old and frail (Helliwell, forthcoming). For this reason, any Gerai couple unable to give birth to a child of their own will adopt one, usually from a group related by kinship. The two activities of growing rice and growing children are constantly talked about together, and the same imagery is used to describe the development of a woman's pregnancy and the development of rice grains on the plant. . . .

Gerai, then, lacks the stress on bodily—and especially genital—dimorphism that most feminist accounts of rape assume. Indeed, the reproductive organs themselves are not seen as "sexed." In a sense it is problematic even to use the English categories woman and man when

writing of this community, since these terms are saturated with assumptions concerning the priority of biological (read, bodily) difference. In the Gerai context, it would be more accurate to deal with the categories of, on the one hand, "those responsible for rice selection and storage" and, on the other, "those responsible for cutting down the large trees to make a ricefield." There is no discursive space in Gerai for the distinction between an active, aggressive, penetrating male sexual organ (and sexuality) and a passive, vulnerable, female one. Indeed, sexual intercourse in Gerai is understood by both men and women to stem from mutual "need" on the part of the two partners; without such need, people say, sexual intercourse cannot occur, because the requisite balance is lacking. . . . the sexual act is understood as preeminently mutual in its character, including in its initiation. The idea of having sex with someone who does not need you to have sex with them—and so the idea of coercing someone into sex—is thus almost unthinkable to Gerai people. In addition, informants asserted that any such action would destroy the individual's spiritual balance and that of his or her rice group and bring calamity to the group as a whole.[18]

In this context, a Gerai man's astonished and horrified question "How can a penis be taken into a vagina if a woman doesn't want it?" has a meaning very different from that of the same statement uttered by a man in the West. In the West, notions of radical difference between men and women—incorporating representations of normative male sexuality as active and aggressive, normative female sexuality as passive and vulnerable, and human relationships (including acts of sexual intercourse) as occurring between independent, potentially hostile, agents—would render such a statement at best naive, at worst misogynist. In Gerai, however, the stress on identity between men and women and on the sexual act as predicated on mutuality validates such a statement as one of straightforward incomprehension (and it should be noted that I heard similar statements from women). In the

Gerai context, the penis, or male genitalia in general, is not admired, feared, or envied. . . . In fact, Gerai people see men's sexual organs as more vulnerable than women's for the simple reason that they are outside the body, while women's are inside. This reflects Gerai understandings of "inside" as representing safety and belonging, while "outside" is a place of strangers and danger, and it is linked to the notion of men as braver than women.[19] In addition, Gerai people say, because the penis is "taken into" another body, it is theoretically at greater risk during the sexual act than the vagina. This contrasts, again, quite markedly with Western understandings, where women's sexual organs are constantly depicted as more vulnerable during the sexual act—as liable to be hurt, despoiled, and so on (some men's anxieties about vagina dentata not withstanding). In Gerai a penis is "only a penis": neither a marker of dimorphism between men and women in general nor, in its essence, any different from a vagina.

Conclusions

With this background, I return now to the case with which I began this article—and, particularly, to the great differences between my response to this case and that of the Gerai woman concerned. On the basis of my own cultural assumptions concerning the differences—and particularly the different sexual characters—of men and women, I am inclined (as this case showed me) to read any attempt by a man to climb into a woman's bed in the night without her explicit consent as necessarily carrying the threat of sexual coercion and brutalization. The Gerai woman, in contrast, has no fear of coerced sexual intercourse when awakened in the dark by a man. She has no such fear because in the Gerai context . . . women's sexuality and bodies are no less aggressive and no more vulnerable than men's.

In fact, in the case in question, the intruding man did expect to have intercourse with the woman.[20] He claimed that the woman had already

agreed to this through her acceptance of his initiatory gifts of soap.[21] The woman, however, while privately agreeing that she had accepted such gifts, claimed that no formal agreement had yet been reached. Her anger, then, did not stem from any belief that the man had attempted to sexually coerce her ("How would he be able to do such a thing?"). Because the term "to be quiet" is often used as a euphemism for sexual intercourse in Gerai, she saw the man's exhortation that she "be quiet" as simply an invitation to engage in sex with him, rather than the implicit threat that I read it to be.[22] Instead, her anger stemmed from her conviction that the correct protocols had not been followed, that the man ought to have spoken with her rather than taking her acceptance of the soap as an unequivocal expression of assent. She was, as she put it, letting him know that "you have sexual relations together when you talk together. Sexual relations cannot be quiet."[23]

Yet, this should not be taken to mean that the practice of rape is simply a product of discourse: that brutality toward women is restricted to societies containing particular, dimorphic representations of male and female sexuality and that we simply need to change the discourse in order to eradicate such practices.[24] Nor is it to suggest that a society in which rape is unthinkable is for that reason to be preferred to Western societies. To adopt such a position would be still to view the entire world through a sexualized Western lens.

In order to understand the practice of rape in countries like Australia and the United States, then—and so to work effectively for its eradication there—feminists in these countries must begin to relinquish some of our most ingrained presumptions concerning difference between men and women and, particularly, concerning men's genitalia and sexuality as inherently brutalizing and penetrative and women's genitalia and sexuality as inherently vulnerable and subject to brutalization. Instead, we must begin to explore the ways rape itself produces such experiences of masculinity and femininity and so inscribes sexual difference onto our bodies.

NOTES

1. Among "radical" feminists such as Andrea Dworkin and Catharine MacKinnon this belief reaches its most extreme version, in which all sexual intercourse between a man and a woman is viewed as akin to rape (Dworkin 1987; MacKinnon 1989a, 1989b).

2. Leacock 1978 and Bell 1983 are well-known examples. Sanday 1990a and Marcus 1992 are more recent examples, on Minangkabau and Turkish society, respectively.

3. See Laqueur 1990 for a historical account of this process.

4. On the equation of body and person within Western (especially feminist) thought, see Moore 1994.

5. See Plaza 1980: "[Rape] is very sexual in the sense that [it] is frequently a sexual activity, but especially in the sense that it opposes men and women: it is social sexing which is latent in rape. . . . Rape is sexual essentially because it rests on the very social difference between the sexes" (31).

6. The material on male prison inmates is particularly revealing in this respect. As an article by Stephen Donaldson, a former prisoner and the president of the U.S. advocacy group Stop Prisoner Rape, makes clear, "hooking up" with another prisoner is the best way for a prisoner to avoid sexual assaults, particularly gang rapes. Hooking up involves entering a sexual liaison with a senior partner ("jocker," "man," "pitcher," "daddy") in exchange for protection. In this arrangement, the rules are clear: the junior partner gives up his autonomy and comes under the authority of the senior partner; he is often expected by the senior partner to be as feminine in appearance and behavior as possible, including shaving his legs, growing long hair, using a feminine nickname, and performing work perceived as feminine (laundry, cell cleaning, giving backrubs, etc.) (Donaldson 1996, 17, 20). See also the extract from Jack Abbott's prison letters in Halperin 1993 (424–25).

7. While I am primarily concerned here with the feminist literature (believing that it contains by far the most useful and insightful work on rape), it needs to be noted that many other (nonfeminist) writers also believe rape to be universal. See, e.g., Ellis 1989; Palmer 1989.

8. For listings of "rape-prone" societies, see Minturn, Grosse, and Haider 1969; Sanday 1981.

9. I carried out anthropological fieldwork in Gerai from March 1985 to February 1986 and from June 1986 to January 1987. The fieldwork was funded by an Australian National University Ph.D. scholarship and carried out under the sponsorship of Lembaga Ilmu Pengetahuan Indonesia. At the time that I was conducting my research a number of phenomena were beginning to have an impact on the community—these had the potential to effect massive changes in the areas of life discussed in this article. These phenomena included the arrival of a Malaysian timber company in the Gerai region and the increasing frequency of visits by Malay, Bugis, Chinese, and Batak timber workers to the community; the arrival of two American fundamentalist Protestant missionary families to live and proselytize in the community; and the establishment of a Catholic primary school in Gerai, resulting in a growing tendency among parents to send their children (both male and female) to attend Catholic secondary school in a large coastal town several days' journey away.

10. The Wana, as described by Jane Atkinson (1990), provide an excellent example of a society that emphasizes sameness. Emily Martin points out that the explicit Western opposition between the "natures" of men and women is assumed to occur even at the level of the cell, with biologists commonly speaking of the egg as passive and immobile and the sperm as active and aggressive even though recent research indicates that these descriptions are erroneous and that they have led biologists to misunderstand the fertilization process (1991). See also Lloyd 1984 for an excellent account of how (often latent) conceptions of men and women as having opposed characteristics are entrenched in the history of Western philosophical thought.

11. The nurture-need dynamic (that I elsewhere refer to as the "need-share dynamic") is central to Gerai sociality. Need for others is expressed through nurturing them; such expression is the primary mark of a "good" as opposed to a "bad" person. See Helliwell (forthcoming) for a detailed discussion.

12. In this respect, Gerai is very different from, e.g., Australia or the United States, where, as Michelle Rosaldo has pointed out, aggression is linked to success, and women's constitution as lacking aggression is thus an important element of their subordination (1980, 416; see also Myers 1988, 600).

13. See Helliwell 1996, 142–43, for an example of a "violent" altercation between husband and wife.

14. I have noted elsewhere that the inside-outside distinction is a central one within this culture (Helliwell 1996).

15. While the Gerai stress on the sameness of men's and women's sexual organs seems, on the face of it, to be very similar to the situation in Renaissance Europe as described by Laqueur 1990, it is profoundly different in at least one respect: in Gerai, women's organs are not seen as emasculated versions of men's—"female penises"—as they were in Renaissance Europe. This is clearly linked to the fact that, in Gerai, as we have already seen, people is not synonymous with men, and

women are not relegated to positions of emasculation or abjection, as was the case in Renaissance Europe.

16. In this respect Gerai is similar to a number of other peoples in this region (e.g., Wana, Ilongot), for whom difference between men and women is also seen as primarily a matter of the different kinds of work that each performs.

17. In Gerai, pregnancy and birth are seen not as semimystical "natural" processes, as they are for many Westerners, but simply as forms of work, linked very closely to the work of rice production.

18. Sanday 1986 makes a similar point about the absence of rape among the Minangkabau. See Helliwell (forthcoming) for a discussion of the different kinds of bad fate that can afflict a group through the actions of its individual members.

19. In Gerai, as in nearby Minangkabau (Sanday 1986), vulnerability is respected and valued rather than despised.

20. The man left the community on the night that this event occurred and went to stay for several months at a nearby timber camp. Community consensus—including the view of the woman concerned—was that he left because he was ashamed and distressed, not only as a result of having been sexually rejected by someone with whom he thought he had established a relationship but also because his adulterous behavior had become public, and he wished to avoid an airing of the details in a community moot. Consequently, I was unable to speak to him about the case. However, I did speak to several of his close male kin (including his married son), who put his point of view to me.

21. The woman in this particular case was considerably younger than the man (in fact, a member of the next generation). In such cases of considerable age disparity between sexual partners, the older partner (whether male or female) is expected to pay a fine in the form of small gifts to the younger partner, both to initiate the liaison and to enable its continuance. Such a fine rectifies any spiritual imbalance that may result from the age imbalance and hence makes it safe for the relationship to proceed. Contrary to standard Western assumptions, older women appear to pay such fines to younger men as often as older men pay them to younger women (although it was very difficult to obtain reliable data on this question, since most such liaisons are adulterous and therefore highly secretive). While not significant in terms of value (women usually receive such things as soap and shampoo, while men receive tobacco or cigarettes), these gifts are crucial in their role of "rebalancing" the relationship. It would be entirely erroneous to subsume this practice under the rubric of "prostitution."

22. Because Gerai adults usually sleep surrounded by their children, and with other adults less than a meter or two away (although the latter are usually inside different mosquito nets), sexual intercourse is almost always carried out very quietly.

23. In claiming that "sexual relations cannot be quiet," the woman was playing on the expression "be quiet" (meaning to have sexual intercourse) to make the point that while adulterous sex may need to be even "quieter" than legitimate sex, it should not be so "quiet" as to preclude dialogue between the two partners. Implicit here is the notion that in the absence of such dialogue, sex will lack the requisite mutuality.

24. Foucault, e.g., once suggested (in a debate in French reprinted in La Folie Encerclee [see Plaza 1980]) that an effective way to deal with rape would be to decriminalize it in order to "desexualize" it. For feminist critiques of his suggestion, see Plaza 1980; de Lauretis 1987; Woodhull 1988.

REFERENCES

Atkinson, Jane Monnig. 1990. "How Gender Makes a Difference in Wana Society" In *Power and Difference: Gender in Island Southeast Asia,* ed. Jane Monnig Atkinson and Shelly Errington, 59–93. Stanford, Calif.: Stanford University Press.

Bart, Pauline B., and Patricia H. O'Brien. 1985. *Stopping Rape: Successful Survival Strategies.* New York: Pergamon.

Bell, Diane. 1983. *Daughters of the Dreaming.* Melbourne: McPhee Gribble.

Brison, Susan J. 1993. "Surviving Sexual Violence: A Philosophical Perspective." *Journal of Social Philosophy 24*(1): 5–22.

Butler, Judith. 1990. *Gender Trouble: Feminism and the Subversion of Identity.* New York and London: Routledge.

———. 1993. *Bodies That Matter: On the Discursive Limits of "Sex."* New York and London: Routledge.

Clark, Anna. 1987. *Women's Silence, Men's Violence: Sexual Assault in England, 1770–1845.* London and New York: Pandora.

de Lauretis, Teresa. 1987. "The Violence of Rhetoric: Considerations on Representation and Gender." In her *Technologies of Gender: Essays on Theory, Film and Fiction,* 31–50. Bloomington and Indianapolis: Indiana University Press.

Donaldson, Stephen. 1996. "The Deal behind Bars" *Harper's* (August): 17–20.

Dworkin, Andrea. 1987. *Intercourse*. London: Secker & Warburg.

Ellis, Lee. 1989. *Theories of Rape: Inquiries into the Causes of Sexual Aggression*. New York: Hemisphere.

Errington, Shelly. 1990. "Recasting Sex, Gender, and Power: A Theoretical and Regional Overview" In *Power and Difference: Gender in Island Southeast Asia*, ed. Jane Monnig Atkinson and Shelly Errington, 1–58. Stanford, Calif.: Stanford University Press.

Foucault, Michel. 1978. *The History of Sexuality*. Vol. 1, *An Introduction*. Harmondsworth: Penguin.

Halperin, David M. 1993. "Is There a History of Sexuality?" In *The Lesbian and Gay Studies Reader*, ed. Henry Abelove, Michele Barale, and David M. Halperin, 416–31. New York and London: Routledge.

Helliwell, Christine 1993. "Women in Asia: Anthropology and the Study of Women." In *Asia's Culture Mosaic*, ed. Grant Evans, 260–86. Singapore: Prentice Hall.

———. 1995. "Autonomy as Natural Equality: Inequality in 'Egalitarian' Societies." *Journal of the Royal Anthropological Institute* 1(2): 359–75.

———. 1996. "Space and Sociality in a Dayak Longhouse." In *Things as They Are: New Directions in Phenomenological Anthropology*, ed. Michael Jackson, 128–48. Bloomington and Indianapolis: Indiana University Press.

———. Forthcoming. *"Never Stand Alone": A Study of Borneo Sociality*. Williamsburg: Borneo Research Council.

Laqueur, Thomas. 1990. *Making Sex: Body and Gender from the Greeks to Freud*. Cambridge, Mass., and London: Harvard University Press.

Leacock, Eleanor. 1978. "Women's Status in Egalitarian Society: Implications for Social Evolution." *Current Anthropology* 19(2): 247–75.

Lloyd, Genevieve. 1984. *The Man of Reason: "Male" and "Female" in Western Philosophy*. London: Methuen.

MacKinnon, Catharine A. 1989a. "Sexuality, Pornography, and Method: 'Pleasure under Patriarchy.'" *Ethics* 99:314–46.

———. 1989b. *Toward a Feminist Theory of the State*. Cambridge, Mass., and London: Harvard University Press.

Madigan, Lee, and Nancy C. Gamble. 1991. *The Second Rape: Society's Continued Betrayal of the Victim*. New York: Lexington.

Marcus, Julie. 1992. *A World of Difference: Islam and Gender Hierarchy in Turkey*. Sydney: Allen & Unwin.

Marcus, Sharon. 1992. "Fighting Bodies, Fighting Words: A Theory and Politics of Rape Prevention." In *Feminists Theorize the Political*, ed. Judith Butler and Joan W. Scott, 385–403. New York and London: Routledge.

Martin, Emily 1991. "The Egg and the Sperm: How Science Has Constructed a Romance Based on Stereotypical Male-Female Roles." *Signs: Journal of Women in Culture and Society* 16(3): 485–501.

Minturn, Leigh, Martin Grosse, and Santoah Haider. 1969. "Cultural Patterning of Sexual Beliefs and Behaviour." *Ethnology* 8(3): 301–18.

Moore, Henrietta L. 1994. *A Passion for Difference: Essays in Anthropology and Gender*. Cambridge and Oxford: Polity.

Myers, Fred R. 1988. "The Logic and Meaning of Anger among Pintupi Aborigines." *Man* 23(4): 589–610.

Palmer, Craig. 1989. "Is Rape a Cultural Universal? A Re-Examination of the Ethnographic Data." *Ethnology* 28(1): 1–16.

Plaza, Monique. 1980. "Our Costs and Their Benefits." *m/f* 4: 28–39.

Rosaldo, Michelle Z. 1980. "The Use and Abuse of Anthropology: Reflections on Feminism and Cross-cultural Understanding." *Signs* 5(3): 389–417.

Sanday, Peggy Reeves. 1981. "The Socio-Cultural Context of Rape: A Cross-Cultural Study." *Journal of Social Issues* 37(4): 5–27.

———. 1986. "Rape and the Silencing of the Feminine." In *Rape*, ed. Sylvana Tomaselli and Roy Porter, 84–101. Oxford: Blackwell.

———. 1990a. "Androcentric and Matrifocal Gender Representations in Minangkabau Ideology." In *Beyond the Second Sex: New Directions in the Anthropology of Gender*, ed. Peggy Reeves Sanday and Ruth Gallagher Goodenough, 141–68. Philadelphia: University of Pennsylvania Press.

———. 1990b. *Fraternity Gang Rape: Sex, Brotherhood, and Privilege on Campus*. New York and London: New York University Press.

Strathern, Marilyn. 1988. *The Gender of the Gift: Problems With Women and Problems With Society in Melanesia*. Berkeley: University of California Press.

Tsing, Anna Lowenhaupt. 1993. *In the Realm of the Diamond Queen: Marginality in an Out-of-the-Way Place*. Princeton, N.J.: Princeton University Press.

Woodhull, Winifred. 1988. "Sexuality, Power, and the Question of Rape." In *Feminism and Foucault: Reflections on Resistance*, ed. Irene Diamond and Lee Quinby, 167–76. Boston: Northeastern University Press.

Introduction to Reading 12

Martina Cvajner is a sociologist who lives and works in Italy. This reading reflects her interest in ethnographic research on gender, sexuality, social class, and emigration. Cvajner draws the reader into her research experience with mature women who have emigrated from the former USSR to work as caregivers in the homes of wealthy Italians by exploring her personal struggle to overcome her negative stereotypes of the physical appearance and sexuality of these women. Her stereotypes, as she states, are rooted in the cultural biases of the Italians of Alpinetown and similar Italian towns. Cvajner's entrée into the worlds of the "Russian" women was facilitated by her ability to speak "Russian" and her willingness to forge close relationships with the women, even accompanying several back to the Ukraine to spend time with their children, other relatives, and friends. The focal concept of the study, hyper-femininity, is examined in detail as a strategy employed by the "Russians" to differentiate themselves from Italian women and to establish claims to decency, respect, and social worth.

1. What are the negative stereotypes of "Russian" emigrant women held by the natives of Alpinetown? Why, according to Cvajner, do the emigrant women defiantly perform a type of hyper-femininity that seems to confirm the stereotypes? And why does Cvajner refer to the Italians as "natives"?

2. Discuss "beauty-as-effort" by using examples from the reading, and then compare and contrast with your observations of women "doing hyper-femininity" in the United States.

3. What are the "cherished roles" of the emigrant women in their home countries, such as Ukraine, and how/why are those roles degraded and marginalized by the natives of Alpinetown?

HYPER-FEMININITY AS DECENCY

BEAUTY, WOMANHOOD, AND RESPECT IN EMIGRATION

Martina Cvajner

In the last decade or so, strolling in the public squares of the small Italian city of Alpinetown, one is increasingly witness to a most curious performance, one that often raises eyebrows, perplexity and occasionally annoyance among the natives. These days, passers-by frequently include groups of mature platinum blondes. Wearing heavy make-up and stiletto heels, scantily clad in . . . bright colors. They are commonly described by locals as being loud, defiant, 'excessive'.

Cvajner, Martina. 2011. "Hyper-femininity as Decency: Beauty, Womanhood, and Respect in Emigration." *Ethnography 12*(3), p. 356.

The shock is even greater when the same performance is carried into the mountain parks, where loud talk, extravagant clothing and strangely prepared barbecues challenge radically the natives' definition of the surrounding peaks as a place of silence, physical effort and ascetic attire. When I was among the locals, wearing my . . . understated academic clothes, I could easily eavesdrop and experience the reactions generated by these promenades: their performance was perceived as utterly inappropriate, as a challenge—a pushy, overbearing use of 'their' public space. The disapproval towards this heroically displayed hyper-femininity was palpable. The strolling women were clearly and unambiguously identified as members of a specific group, the 'Russians' or 'Slavs', the women emigrating from Eastern Europe to work as live-in maids or careworkers for Italian households. Their performance was also taken as self-explanatory, as an epiphany of their actual intentions: to seduce some old, simple-minded Italian or 'steal some husband' in order to exploit them economically.

The stereotypes I listened to were hardly new. The hyper-feminine, unruly, mature woman from Eastern Europe willing to go through a great deal to secure a Western wealthy partner has developed into a specific character within the European social imaginary, represented increasingly in novels, films and news media reportage (Hornby, 2007; Lewycka, 2005; Sabuschko, 2006). . . . It has even triggered, as in the Italian town of Montecatini in 2007, waves of moral panic. In that usually sleepy city, a cluster of local committees was created to lobby the police and the local administration to protect the 'Italian family' against the temptations induced by the seductresses camouflaged as careworkers. Such protest quickly reverberated across the national news media, was the subject of the most popular primetime talk shows and is still very much present in the Italian blogosphere—with Google returning more than 142,000 references to a query using the keywords 'Montecatini' and 'russe' ('Russian'). These stereotypes are not without consequences for the life chances of these women. During my fieldwork, the women I met were conscious that

being identified as 'Slavs', given this reputation, would frequently imply reduced job opportunities, more suspicious attitudes by the families they worked for, colder reception in the philanthropic agencies most of them had to rely upon for emergencies, as well as a multitude of small degradation ceremonies in urban contexts such as shops, public gardens and even churches. Still, during the years of my fieldwork, I did not observe any reduction in this kind of public performance; they actually became more frequent and sophisticated.

My goal in this article is to explore and make sense of the meanings of the public performances by the groups of migrant women I spent time with in Alpinetown. Why did they adopt such a hyper-feminine, yet defiant, mode of marking their presence in the public space? Why did they react to the stigma imposed upon them through an essentializing objectification? Why did they adopt a public display of their 'Selves' that they know . . . is stigmatized by a great many natives? Why did they cherish so much a way of presenting themselves so radically at odds with the message of traditional values, modesty and humility prescribed by the traditional image of the foreign careworker?

These specific questions are strongly related to those that lie at the core of this urban ethnography project. The overarching task is to understand why members of a marginalized group, acting to protect their own moral worth, engage in behaviors that are highly consistent with the stigmatizing expectations of the majority, thus providing elements that may be used to structure or legitimize forms of discrimination. These questions resonate also with a central concern of gender studies, from Simone de Beauvoir (1949) to Susan Bordo (1993): the attempt to explain why, as a way to protect their own agency, women willingly comply with a structure of expectation centered on a male-defined notion of beauty and seductiveness.

In this article, I focus on the growing body of recent literature dealing with hyper-femininity, defined as 'a particularly exaggerated, emphasized and ideal performance of femininity'

(Praechter, 2006) or, more simply, as the attempt by women to present themselves as 'sassy, sexy and successful' (Allan, 2009: 145). For scholars of hyper-femininity, the main question is how and why significant segments of the young generation of Western women, in neo-liberal and post-feminist times, are not outraged by the re-sexualization and re-commodification of women's bodies in popular culture but actually perceive it as a channel for the construction of new femininities organized around an ideology of irony, sexual confidence and autonomy (Gill, 2003, 2008). The phenomenon of hyper-femininity has been recently . . . studied in a variety of settings, mostly concerned with youth cultures. A key achievement of this body of literature has been going beyond the idea that such phenomena could be explained only as instances of women's 'false consciousness' or as delusions induced by the media industry (McRobbie, 2009).

In this article, I wish to expand such research in three ways. First, I will analyze the meaning of hyper-feminine public performances in reference to a low-status group of (mature) women, moving beyond the focus on middle-class youth subcultures. I hope in this way to explore the fruitfulness of the concept beyond the areas where it was originally developed, highlighting the need to pay more attention to the intersectionality of gender, class and ethnicity. Second, I will reconstruct how hyper-femininity may actually come to constitute an important resource for some groups of migrant women, as a way to compensate for the damages that emigration has caused to their sense of decency and moral worth. Third, while much of the current literature on hyper-femininity is concerned primarily with working out the affinities of these phenomena with neoliberal ideologies and conditions—thus paying great attention to the macro-role of media and advertising—I will focus here mostly on how such performances operate within interactions in specific settings, from the ground up, as elements of a possible strategy for the presentation of the Self in Goffman's sense (1956). I hope in this way to contribute to the strengthening of the still neglected intellectual interchange between feminist scholarship and symbolic interactionism (see also Crossley, 2001; Jackson and Scott, 2010; West and Zimmerman, 1987).

DISCOVERING THE SIGNIFICANCE OF HYPER-FEMININITY

To answer these questions, I utilize data collected during a three-year period of ethnographic research in a northern Italian town that I will call Alpinetown. From 2005 to 2007, I observed a group of women that migrated from countries formerly part of the USSR, primarily from Ukraine and Moldova. . . . Most of them had migrated alone, outside any established migratory chains. A majority had entered Italy with a tourist visa and had subsequently overstayed, finding employment as live-in maids or careworkers. To be sure, these flows represent a reaction to the breakdown of the former Soviet empire but, much more noticeably, they escalated with the economic crisis that hit some of the former USSR republics in the second half of the 1990s. Such crises lowered living standards, closed down the traditional circular migration systems of seasonal work and shuttle trade and implied for many the total loss of security, such as permanent employment and savings.

In the personal narratives of many of the women I interviewed and chatted with, such crises were also linked with the collapse of their conjugal relationships. . . . Emigration became in many areas not only a survival strategy for the household but also an exit strategy from unappealing or broken marriages. . . . Nearly all the women were 'pioneers', emigrating alone, with little migratory socialization and without reliable social networks in the receiving countries. Their migration process had been risky, as it had to rely at many crucial points upon the goodwill of mere acquaintances or even sheer luck. . . . Lacking contacts and economic resources, most of the women had to enter the labor market through the least appealing sector: live-in carework with around-the-clock responsibility for older persons or, more rarely, small children (Catanzaro and Colombo, 2009). . . .

When I started my ethnographic project, I had only a few personal contacts with some of these women. As a Russian speaker, in a city where their language was a rarity, it was often easy to start conversations through random encounters in the streets. . . . In the first months of my fieldwork, I was mostly concerned with my position in the group and with the ways in which I could introduce my research project to them. In both cases, my initial expectations and fears turned out to be vastly exaggerated. I quickly realized that my position was liminal, right in between outsider and insider. My personal background was Yugoslav, not Soviet; I was speaking their language but it was not my mother tongue; I had been an emigrant, but I had arrived much earlier; I had been a careworker myself, but I was (at the time I met them) employed in a white-collar job. I initially feared these two latter features could be interpreted as placing me above them. In reality, the assessment I received was quite different. As I was younger than most of them, still single and with no children, all my 'professional achievements' could not compensate for the assumption that I did not know how to live and I was badly in need of help and advice. I gratefully embraced the status of novice, and it helped me a lot—giving me ample room to ask . . . questions and to participate as an observer to a variety of endeavors. . . . I was helped by the fact that the group was recent and participation in it highly variable: at certain times we were more than 40, at others just four or five. Many . . . entered the group for a few months, and then a change of job—a very frequent event given the occupation—could easily imply a change of residence and a weakening of participation. After a while, I was just someone who was there.

Given their working conditions, and the fact that most of the women lived with their employers, many of my observations were conducted in the few hours during the day when these women joined their compatriots in the main hall of the railway station, at the bus station, on the city's main street, in a church, in public gardens and, very seldom, in private houses. As an acknowledged 'junior' member, I participated in a variety

of roles: I sold Avon and AmWay goods (mainly cosmetics and underwear), helped organize a course in Italian cooking, traveled back to the homeland with some of them, walked for hours, participated in barbecues in the mountain parks, attended church functions and disco nights out, brokered medical appointments and provided ad hoc legal counsel, visited dime-stores and discount supermarkets, participated in the informal Eastern European open-air market supplied by regular minivan traders, hosted women in my flat and was hosted by the few that actually had a place to receive guests. Apart from the (many) hours they worked, my participation in their lives was . . . pervasive. We became friends—and with some, very close friends—granting each other over time the honored title of '*sestre* [sisters]' (and with it, the confidence to have a few very sisterly fights!).

Very early in my fieldwork, I was introduced to the unexpected importance of hyper-feminine performances through a kind of pedagogic exercise meant to celebrate both my membership in the group and my initiation to their wisdom. I recorded the event in my fieldnotes in the following way:

> On an evenly Saturday afternoon we were having our usual 'look-at-us' stroll. We go up and down the Main Street in Alpinetown. Most of us wear glossy make-up, stiletto heels, miniskirts, dressed heavy-belly-in-the-wind. The colors of the clothes fight one another, and mini-layers desperately try to cover the uncoverable. '*Martushka, move! We have to make a woman out of you!*' My metamorphosis has become the main event of the day: I was to become eventually (and ultimately!) what every 'normal' female human being *deeply* desires: *a real woman*. Up to the very moment, I was just me: *femininely insignificant.* Everything changes when our boisterous crew enters the inexpensive Chinese shop loaded with cheap, shiny goods. The sales assistants shyly approach us, obviously fearing we might try to steal one of their fake furs, while the rest of the shop pays close attention to the show. '*Martushka! I found some stuff that really seems "you",*' Tatyana yelled. I felt trapped in the Chinese shop. All five friends were intimately committed to my feminine resurrection. They quickly chose a

white fake fur with a golden metal belt similar to the one encircling the already selected, white, shiny high-heeled thigh-high boots. Underneath the fake fur, diaphanous, purple and green, gossamer-thin, short dress left little to the imagination. I felt embarrassed—they were legitimately happy and proud. They were generously sharing their knowledge with a naïve, 'young' and obviously ignorant woman who badly needed advice for discovering her real feminine self. They knew better. The clothes they selected were meant for all my public appearances, including the workplace: '*Martushka, how can you imagine that a professor wants to talk to you if he doesn't even understand if you are a man or a woman! That is why you are alone and you have no kids! Who wants a woman that is not a woman!*' cried Natasha. The Chinese women assisting us were rather impressed by what the 'real females' had achieved. I was desperately hoping that none of my Italian friends would pass by. (Author fieldnotes, 46/2005)

This experience made me think for the first time about the meaning of this way of dressing and presenting one's self for a group of women who had very little money and a vested interest— as most were at the time irregular migrants—in *not* drawing attention to themselves. My curiosity grew as I started tallying up the frequency of such performances and the effort and resources put into them. I also found interesting that the meanings of the hyper-feminine performances in public spaces, which I so frequently observed and sometimes enacted, were usually presented as 'natural' by my informants. In responding to my myriad queries, they presented these elements matter-of-factly, as 'just the way a real woman should dress and behave', and rarely, as 'the way we do it in Ukraine' (or Moldova). At the same time, while performing, they were ready to stress in a variety of ways that 'it was great not to be a foreign domestic worker for a while', to compare systematically their flamboyant attire to the Italian 'half-women' that crossed our path, to insist that, no matter what they whispered to each other, men admired them. The performance, besides being fun, was definitely a statement.

When I travelled with them to Ukraine, I also noticed that, although many elements of their aesthetic presentation were similar or identical, the meanings were . . . different in at least two ways: socially, performing a hyper-feminine role was something reserved for audiences of relatives and friends, while the interactions with strangers or acquaintances were largely dominated by considerations of differential ownership of goods, education and successful offspring; in terms of their own accounts, moreover, such attire in the homeland was justified nearly exclusively as a duty to one's man or to the family social standing. As Tanya once told me— repeating what many other women had told me—when she was married in Ukraine, *she had to wear make-up even when she went to throw out the garbage*. Not to do so would have been a lack of respect for her husband. In Alpinetown, with no husbands and no relatives, they accounted for the pleasures of these performances in terms of authenticity, independence and social recognition. . . .

I consequently started to think of the hyper-feminine performances not as a legacy of their pre-emigration past but as a transformative process born out of the experience of migration itself (Dedirdirek and Whitehead, 2004). They represented a ritual that allowed for a sharp detachment of the migrant woman's 'real' Self from the degrading dimension of being a newly arrived careworker. And this ritual process is a reminder, to oneself perhaps more than to others, that the 'real' life, the life where an adequate amount of recognition and respect is granted, has been only temporarily suspended. Even at the cost of being considered wild and possibly immoral, such a presentation of the Self challenged all the expectations attached to being an immigrant domestic worker. It codified symbolically an element of radical . . . competition with Italian women, who were usually their direct bosses, the members of the household who gave orders and complained about the quality of the work done. Additionally, and importantly, these performances reproduced an ambiguous, but not polluted, reference to their places of origin as mythical spaces inhabited by 'real women' and 'real men'. In doing so, the women developed a convincing, and quite sophisticated, performative conception of gender, defining their triumphant womanhood as a hard won achievement that should command an adequate degree of moral worth and social respect.

THE MORALITY OF HYPER-FEMININITY: "DOING GENDER" IN EMIGRATION

Most of my informants accounted for the pleasure of their hyper-feminine performances in essentialist terms, as the outcome either of natural or cultural legacies. But the more I participated in their lives, and the more attention I paid to such elements of our time together, the more I came to realize that such performances were actually lived as a conscious achievement, as something that had to be carefully planned, reflectively managed and morally assessed.

The primary requirement for these performances had to do with the stage props (Goffman, 1956), the ritualistic apparatus—posture, clothes, make-up, hairstyle—centered on the exaltation of femininity and based upon a claim of full womanhood that represents a sharp and clear-cut distinction from whatever may appear mannish or androgynous. In their view, full competence in the use of such elements, as well as not being shy in employing the most flamboyant ones, was both a moral quality and an open challenge to Italian women, considered unworthy because they were sloppy, stressed out and too individualistic, in short, mannish. Many of the techniques and the props for these performances were drawn from a homeland repertoire. But their meaning was radically different: in the home country, such performances took place in a homogeneous environment in which others shared the same conceptions of femininity. It was a performance assessed in terms of more or less femininity.

In Italy, the very same practice takes place independently of, in fact against, the native conceptions of femininity and beauty. It becomes a performance of similarity versus difference. While we were strolling around, for example, a main topic of conversation was the bad taste,

taken as indicia of bad character, of the Italian women, with their dominant use of shades of black or grays, their limited use of bright colors, the restricted use of make-up and the choice of 'modest' haircuts. In their view, these were not real 'women'. Such critique was not only aesthetic: it was moral. It was frequently linked to claims about how bossy and unreasonable their employers were and legitimating a broad claim that whatever those women were enjoying in terms of wealth, household stability or marital fidelity was just a matter of sheer luck—or even unfair advantage. Tetyana, for example, often framed her complaints about her 'mean' employer with references to her underwear, which she considered *a grandmother's underpants.* Nadya, in the same way, often expressed her anger for being tightly controlled—and often criticized—in her work by a woman that *should have rather asked her how to choose an appropriate dress.* It was as if the performances were the means to claim the right—in the name of higher and more intense femininity—to be considered something different from a 'foreign domestic worker' and to be recognized as a potential, and indeed desirable, woman and *thus* an individual to be respected and taken into consideration.

At the core of these attitudes was the taken for granted vision that being a woman was not a biographical condition but rather an achievement that required lots of *effort.* To understand this point took me a great deal of time and several puzzling experiences. One of the things that always struck me during my research was the frequent clash between the physical characteristics of the women I met—often looking older than their actual age, heavily overweight, tired and worn out—and their outspoken interest in using whatever little was left of their very low salaries (after bills had been paid and remittances sent) for cosmetics, underwear and girdles. Similarly, I was often struck by the tendency of some women to systematically favor flashy clothes that seemed to me entirely inappropriate for flattering their physical features and shape. . . . Another element that struck me was the apparent indifference to the performance context: at almost every occasion in my early fieldwork, the initial impression I held was that these women were constantly dressing inappropriately and behaving as if they had no special interest in ever doing otherwise.

To understand it, I had to change some taken-for-granted assumptions on what it meant to take care of one's body and public appearance. Previously . . . taking care of my body involved eating healthy food, jogging, being dressed comfortably and pursuing a style that made me feel at ease. Entering the field led to a radical revision of this view of self-appreciation. I came to realize that their very different view of 'taking care of the body' was the consequence of a symbolic logic that identifies being a woman not with the physical aspect as such, but with the radicalism of the effort required to do so. For my informants . . . beauty was something to be constructed. The body, in other words, is a canvas that counts—to define if and whether a person is a woman—not for its intrinsic qualities but for the degree of effort and creativity of what is being painted on it. If you take care of yourself, you are a woman. The key element of such a vision is that, while the level of physical beauty is largely entrusted to luck, being a 'woman' is largely the result of will and competence, the ability to groom one's appearance with the necessary intensity and skill (and, of course, resources). In this sense, the status of a 'woman who looks nice' is a status to which every woman should aspire, but most importantly, it is a status that cannot be denied to anyone: any of us could be beautiful if we commit ourselves to creating our own beauty. There is little reason to doubt their commitment to such an ideal: I had witnessed their ability to endure tremendous sacrifices—from tight girdles to fasting—in maintaining and reproducing these ideals even under the extremely difficult conditions of full-time carework. This notion of beauty-as-effort implies several consequences.

The first is the broad significance of beauty for all kinds of social interactions. Such beauty-as-effort is not only meaningful in sexual terms, but it has a broad range of relational meanings.

Beauty certifies the strength of character of the woman and thus strengthens her trustworthy standing. This was the rationale by which the perceived sloppiness of their female employers could easily be used as proof of their lack of moral character, and this was the reason why all the women were constantly policing themselves—and me in particular—for any sign of assimilation to the Italian ways. When conflict within the group arose, the battle cry for establishing alliances was always centered on the accusation that the 'enemy' was becoming sloppy, relaxed and, implicitly, 'Italianish'.

Second, such effort has an important collective dimension. Appearance is not the surface of an inner Self, but rather a publicly verifiable effort, certified and co-signed by friends and by males. Beauty must be validated by the male gaze . . . and the women were quite outspoken in looking for this kind of recognition. During my fieldwork, I was repeatedly shocked by the ways in which the very same women that preached to me on the key importance of being a devoted wife and mother (and blaming me for not being so yet) were also—and often at the same time—engaging in foul-mouthed and naturalistic representations of their capacity to trigger men's sexual attractions in an indiscriminate way. During our performances, all indicia of male desire among the public . . . were at once satirized, appreciated and praised. I learned quickly, however, that the male gaze is only one form of recognition, and not necessarily the most accurate one. An equally important source of recognition for one's womanhood derives from the membership in a community of women sharing the same ideal. This generative mechanism of beauty—a synonym for care—becomes also a crucial element of solidarity among the women. Every woman can be beautiful if she relies on the expertise of her friends, and the more impartial, and thus important, judgment of your beauty is the opinion of the other women who understand your efforts. In the end, this network is sometimes more important for the validation of the women's beauty than that of men who, as many women disconsolately said, 'are just interested in what you have between your legs'.

A third important consequence of beauty-as-effort is that taking care of one's body has little to do with the physical features of the body or with personal preferences in matters of aesthetic judgment. Contrary to my original understanding of beauty as being at ease with myself, the women I was living with were adamant in stressing that effort toward a specific ideal was the key to womanhood. One day I was invited by some women to attend an AmWay event in the rooms of an organization closely linked to the local Greek Catholic church. As I had been invited by the women who had a stronger religious identification, and that were often critical of the . . . sexual morals of their compatriots, I was expecting a different way of understanding and practicing womanhood. The event, however, provided further fascinating details on the shared nature of the hyper-feminine ideal. The event was organized to celebrate the visit of Lyuba, a Ukrainian careworker and AmWay salesperson who, after a spell in Alpinetown, was now living (and working) in another Mediterranean country. Nadya, a main actor in the local church, was fond of her: she was high up in the pyramidal AmWay system—she 'knew her job well and was a beautiful woman'. The women greeted her with reverence after which, in a firm tone of voice, she ordered them to sit around the table and take out a pen and paper for making notes.

The women looked at her with adoration when she began to talk about her life before the magical AmWay products saved her both physically and psychologically. She explained that before the AmWay diet she was fat and ugly. She disliked her body and felt as if she was 'half a woman'. Lyuba was a huge woman wearing a pink shirt tied up in front and a pair of tight jeans. Her quite generous form was proudly exhibited. She wore red blush on the cheeks, pink lipstick, bluette eyelashes, and her eyebrows were thin and partially redesigned with a black pencil. The haircut was . . . reminiscent of the 1980s. She acted professionally and almost in an authoritarian way: her goal was to teach the women how to appear at their best. She had come to Alpinetown for a teaching session: she was looking for a woman who needed physical restoration and I was the chosen one. Before starting the work on me, she asked all the women to touch my skin and feel how old it felt (I was the youngest one there). They all nodded. First, Lyuba applied a purifying mask, remarking, 'Her skin is really dirty.' Again, they all nodded. After the purifying mask, I was ordered to wash my face and return in order to have the make-up applied. I tried to explain to her that make-up looked really bad on me and she replied that this was because I did not know how to properly use it. She said that since my skin was too light, pale in fact, she should apply a darker foundation that made my skin copper-like. I said it was better not to because the neck was white, and the two things together would be quite jarring. My opinion did not matter: olive-like foundation, red blush, greenish eyeliner with eye shadow, a lot of mascara (for a 'cat-like' look, according to Lyuba) and bright red lips. I looked absolutely awful, but the way I felt was . . . not a significant element in the picture. The other women of course adored it and they defined it as the way in which any woman, regardless of her physical body, should look. For all the participants, the educational content of the seminar was not learning more about the goods they were hoping to sell in the future, but rather to understand better how a woman should appear. The tricks she taught needed to emphasize the femininity of a woman wearing make-up. This essentially meant completely covering the skin with an artificial layer that . . . explicitly called attention to its artificial (and intentionally so) . . . character.

This notion of beauty-as-effort was, however, flexible enough to include new understandings of beauty. As for many Eastern European women, to be slim was not initially considered particularly important (Frederick et al., 2008). In Italy, however, to be slim is a dominant criterion. After a while, many women started complaining of being heavy, and my fellow Avon sellers were quick to seize the demand and started to offer slimming creams and girdles. The sales, like the others, took place in a public space—the waiting room of the bus station—where there were lots of random, usually Italian, bystanders. Most of them witnessed the performance of the women—who reacted to the novelty testing and exhibiting the slimming girdles with loud comments—with some visible signs of uneasiness. Exhibitionism in this case was a way of having fun, even more so if the casual bystanders look puzzled and even slightly uneasy. But it was also enacted on the premise that—taking care of their bodies—they were doing exactly the right thing. . . .

The willingness to spend a lot of effort and to undergo heavy sacrifices to pursue this ideal of womanhood was the key element in their collective resistance to the widely held stereotype of themselves as 'stealers of husbands'. For them, the question was not if many of them had romantic relations . . . with Italian men. They were actually more than willing to recognize that this was so. The frequency of romantic relationships with Italian males was not explained, however, by the predatory attitudes of the 'Slavs' but rather by the pettiness and sloppiness of Italian women. It was often acknowledged that the Italian women were wealthier, had more free time and were often younger and in better physical shape. But precisely for these reasons their refusal to adhere to an ideal of effort-based beauty was morally reproachable. As one woman once complained about her employer, she dressed in 'unsexy garments, sleeps in ugly underwear, behaves as if she was not interested to keep a man! While they need to be sexy even when going to bed.' On the contrary, the same woman—as she told me in another chat—wore sexy lingerie—specifically, a thong—all the time while working. She explained to me that wearing thongs while working . . . was her way to deal with the threat to her womanhood posed by emigration and carework. The thong, she continued, was a way to remind oneself that she was a real woman, only temporarily forced to work 'as a slave' for a household. Such use of sexy underwear as

symbolic protection may well not be idiosyncratic. In the days I spent in the waiting room of the bus station selling Avon products, I . . . ended up specializing in underwear. The thong was among the best sellers, and both buyers and other sellers often stressed how wearing a certain type of underwear—being invisible—was a perfect way of not shocking the employers while at the same time maintaining one's dignity. This opposition between the careworker—who is a woman who takes care of her body and makes every effort to be a woman—and the Italian female employer—who is wealthy yet sloppy—was the basis for the women's resistance to their stereotyping. It was not that they were instrumental seductresses willing to cheat on naïve men; it was rather that Italian men were able to recognize in their efforts and sacrifices to be women (despite the hardship) the presence of highly cherished moral qualities. From their point of view, the effort and sacrifices involved in their hyper-feminine performances were not radically alternative to their being prospective good partners, devoted wives and good mothers. On the contrary, the qualities that made hyper-femininity possible were the best proof of their moral standing, thus making them perfect candidates for such roles.

THE SIGNIFICANCE OF HYPER-FEMININITY IN EMIGRATION

. . . Many of the migrant women in Alpinetown came from the same quite large Ukrainian Oblast (region), and I realized it would also be quite important to observe them back home. . . . I was able . . . to travel to Ukraine with the few women who had succeeded in acquiring legal documents.

The most striking observation I made during these travels was the loss of significance of the hyper-feminine rituals during the time we spent there. Most of the things that were presented to me as absolutely essential in Alpinetown in terms of dress code, make-up and public appearance became less important. The importance of womanhood, of course, did not disappear. In fact, a main activity during these return trips for all the women with daughters was to go shopping, a process through which they tried to restore a channel of mother–daughter transmission of the correct womanhood. Dresses, cosmetics and underwear were also among the most common gifts to (female) relatives and friends. Moreover, most of these return trips had some kind of public event—usually a night out—where all the tricks and tools I learned in Alpinetown were strictly enforced and expected. . . . On these occasions, however, the emphasis was not controversial but rather celebratory: as in many other instances of Ukrainian public life, hyper-femininity was a way to mark the distance from the prudishness and grayness of the Soviet past (Romanets, 2010). Still, the women I was travelling with were much less concerned with their performance of womanhood and less systematic in their policing of other women. In many cases, they were also willing to accept a more complex and pluralistic vision of what the womanhood ideal should be, wearing, for example, more discreet colors or endorsing items of Italian fashion previously despised.

In the beginning, I thought these changes could be explained as consequences of the social control operating in their sending areas. . . . However I slowly came to think that the reasons for such a change were not to be found in the features of the local context that repressed certain ways of acting, but rather in the features of it that allowed them a larger and more complex panel of choices. In short, during the liminal time of the trip back home they could perform in public a larger variety of cherished social roles, and the emphasis on hyper-femininity could become weaker and less intense, relegating it as one element in a larger repertoire. . . .

First, nearly all the women were mothers. And they found a great deal of satisfaction in this role. Although most of them did not have partners/husbands before emigration, and many of the remaining others had lost them during the years of isolation in Italy, nearly all of them had children and, in a few cases, grandchildren. The need to provide for their children had actually been a main factor in their decision to emigrate. Natalia, for example, told me about her migration decision with a single, powerful, memory: her son begging the other boys in the neighborhood to use a bicycle, as he did not have one. And a large part of their remittances goes toward securing a decent living standard and an advanced education for their children. To be a long-distance mother implied heavy emotional strain and, not infrequently, difficult relationship dynamics with the children (Tolstokorova, 2010). Still, during their return trips, they could and actually did perform motherhood in the public space with relative ease. They could go shopping with their kids, as well as visiting schoolteachers and public institutions. And they often tried to match the timing of their return trips with some event concerning their children: graduation, a theater performance or more simply a birthday. In all these instances, their motherhood was acknowledged and celebrated, as when Tanya started proudly crying during a school ceremony, when her son openly thanked her for having emigrated in order to help him.

As for motherhood, the difference from their situation in Alpinetown was staggering. . . . Most of them felt that in Alpinetown being a mother was a liability. They often perceived that the Italians with whom they discussed their children were dubious about their being at the same time 'women emigrants' and 'good mothers'. Moreover, they felt that talking too much about their children and how much they missed them was often taken by their employers as an attempt to cash in on their sympathy to gain some privilege. Alina once told me how hurt she had been by the fact that—after having talked to her employers about the coming birthday of her daughter—she had not received any monetary gratuity that would have allowed her to send some extra money for the occasion. She had not asked openly for it, but she had taken for granted that the employer, knowing how poor she was, would have spontaneously supported her in trying to be a caring mother. For their employers, on the contrary, their motherhood was just a detail or an organizational nuisance. . . .

Another role they could effectively perform in their hometowns was that of the respectable member of a household. The women were clearly, through their remittances, the main breadwinners of their households, and the shopping sprees that accompanied their return home, as well as the variety of gifts they brought with them, provided public recognition of this fact (Mansoo and Quillin, 2007). Their important role was acknowledged in many ways, from small family parties to the . . . liberty to reproach some family members for not having spent the remittances in adequate ways. The quality and quantity of the maintenance work for the house—or for the building of a new one—were often discussed in detail at large gatherings, with the emigrant women in a clear position of control. This often engendered quite a few conflicts, with the women often feeling their relatives were taking advantage of their hard-earned money. But it still provided them with a strong feeling of membership and a strong legitimation for their emigration. . . .

A final difference between their experiences during the return trips and their lives in emigration was in their role as consumers. During their return trips, as I have already described, the women were big spenders, enjoying in the local context a kind of superior economic citizenship. They were highly looked after customers, as it was expected they would order only expensive goods and services. The difficulties and humiliation of their working life were far away and well hidden, while the level of consumption they could guarantee to their families was highly visible and provided a strong source of recognition. In contrast, in Alpinetown, they felt marginalized and despised on at least two counts: first, they had to work hard in a kind of trade that they themselves, even more than their employers, regarded

as degrading. Carework, with its strict dependence on a person or a family, rather than an abstract and removed employer, appeared, in their own words, as a form of slavery, and they felt polluted by it. Being careworkers, moreover, was not only a fact but also a matter of expectations. The few women who had succeeded in finding another occupation regularly complained that they were still assumed to be careworkers. Second, the salary they would get from such work could sustain an adequate level of remittances but little else. As consumers in the local market of Alpinetown, they were the least desirable of all customers, the kind for which a difference of a few cents would still make the difference. They rarely felt welcomed in bars and shops.

In short, the differences I noted between the two contexts made me think of the salience of hyper-femininity not in isolation, but in the context of the other ways in which the women could perform in the public space and stake a legitimate claim to social worth. Rather than looking at hyper-femininity in isolation, I realized that it should be understood through looking at the set of possible Selves these women may utilize as scripts and regulative ideals for their public presence. Some of these Selves may be unavoidable but despised (the undocumented migrant, the careworker and, to some degree, the mistress). Others may be highly cherished but difficult to perform, owing to the lack of adequate props for the public stage, the absence of a sympathetic audience or a deficiency of plausible scripts (the mother, the responsible member of a family, the sophisticated consumer). Womanhood may consequently become one of the very few scripts available that make it possible to detach oneself from a degrading condition and claim one's right to social worth. . . . The emphasis on such a hyper-feminine code, as I was often told, was useful (and pleasurable) as a way to remind themselves, as well as others, that they *worked* as domestic workers, but they *were not* domestic workers. Through the celebrations of womanhood on their own terms, they were able to articulate and reproduce a distinctive identity that detached them from the roles they felt coerced to participate in as well as to enact their notion of a decent life, which they wished to attain but were unable to gain.

The Wider Uses of Gender Symbolism

The primary focus of this article has been to make sense of the emphasis—in their public presentations—of these migrant women on a highly charged, hyper-feminine, notion of womanhood, despite the fact that such performances are highly stigmatized and play a role in strengthening heavily exclusionary stereotypes. The meaning of these hyper-feminine presentations of the Self for the actors involved is rooted in a detailed and sophisticated performative notion of beauty, seen not as a consequence of certain physical attributes but rather as the outcome of a moral and character-strengthening effort. Hyper-feminine performances are used by these women to draw a boundary between them and the Italian women and to advance a claim to dignity and social worth. . . . Using comparatively the results of ethnographic observations in Italy and Ukraine, I have stressed how the significance of hyper-femininity is neither a constant nor a mere reproduction of traditional homeland culture. I argue, on the contrary, that the strong significance of hyper-femininity during emigration is contingent upon a symbolic economy aimed at preserving their feeling of personal dignity. Hyper-femininity—far from being the outcome of 'backwards' attitudes—becomes a way to claim their right to a decent life and a modicum of social recognition. A main implication of my findings is that the notion of hyper-femininity may be usefully generalized beyond the Western middle-class contexts to which it was originally applied, to address the various ways in which women of different backgrounds make use of gender symbolism to establish a claim to social worth and respect. The fact that this search for respect ultimately determines a strategy that, in many cases, further essentializes and stigmatizes these women is a tragic paradox worth further consideration.

References

Allan AJ (2009) The importance of being a 'lady': Hyper-femininity and heterosexuality in the private, single-sex primary school. *Gender and Education* 21(2): 145–158.

Bordo S (1993) *Unbearable Weight: Feminism, Western Culture and the Body.* Berkeley: University of California Press.

Catanzaro R and Colombo A (eds) (2009) *Badanti e Co. Il lavoro domestico straniero in Italia.* Bologna: Il Mulino.

Dedirdirek H and Whitehead J (2004) Sexual encounters, migration and desire in post-socialist contexts. *Focaal—European Journal of Anthropology* 43: 3–13.

Frederick DA, Forbes GB, et al. (2008) Female body dissatisfaction and perceptions of the attractive female body in Ghana, the Ukraine, and the United States. *Psychological Topics* 18(2): 203–219.

Gill R (2003) From sexual objectification to sexual subjectification: The resexualisation of women's bodies in the media. *Feminist Studies* 3(1): 100–106.

Gill R (2008) Culture and subjectivity in neoliberal and postfeminist times. *Subjectivity* 25: 432–445.

Goffman E (1956) *The Presentation of Self in Everyday Life.* Harmondsworth: Penguin.

Jackson S and Scott S (2010) Rehabilitating interactionism for a feminist sociology of sexuality. *Sociology* 44: 811–826.

Lewycka M (2005) *A Short History of Tractors in Ukrainian.* London: Penguin.

Mansoo A and Quillin B (2007) *Migration and Remittances: Eastern Europe and the former Soviet Union.* Washington, DC: The World Bank.

McRobbie A (2009) *The Aftermath of Feminism: Gender, Culture and Social Change.* London: SAGE.

Praechter C (2006) Masculine femininities/feminine masculinities: Power, identities and gender. *Gender and Education* 18(3): 253–263.

Romanets M (2010) Postcolonial on/scenity: The sexualization of political space in post-independence Ukraine. *Canadian-American Slavic Studies* 44(1): 178–199.

Sabuschko O (2006) *Feldstudienen Uber Ukrainischen Sex.* Wien: Droschl.

Tolstokorova AV (2010) Where have all the mothers gone? The gendered effect of labour migration and transnationalism on the institution of parenthood in Ukraine. *Anthropology of East Europe Review* 28(1): 184–210.

West C and Zimmerman DH (1987) Doing gender. *Gender and Society* 1(2): 125–151.

Introduction to Reading 13

Sociologist Cenk Özbay used participant observation and interviews to understand the world of "rent boys" in contemporary Istanbul, Turkey. Özbay speaks Turkish and created a "careful ethnographic plan" to move with relative ease in the bars where he observed interactions among rent boys, gay men, and transvestites. Rent boys come from poor neighborhoods in the outlying areas of Istanbul, neighborhoods called *varoş*. Ranging in age from 16 to 25, rent boys are heterosexually identified and engage in compensated sex with gay men. The key concept in this reading is "exaggerated masculinity." Özbay examines the ways rent boys perform exaggerated masculinity as a strategy for dealing with their sexual interactions with gay men. Be sure to read the footnotes at the end of this article, because they provide valuable details about rent boys.

1. What are the tactics used by rent boys to maintain their masculine identities vis-à-vis gay men? How does *varoş* play a role in these tactics?

2. Discuss the risks faced by rent boys in their construction and maintenance of exaggerated masculinity.

3. Compare and contrast Özbay's concept of "exaggerated masculinity" with Cvajner's concept of hyper-femininity (in the previous reading).

NOCTURNAL QUEERS

RENT BOYS' MASCULINITY IN ISTANBUL

Cenk Özbay

Recently, 'rent boys'[1] have become increasingly visible in the queer social spaces of Istanbul. Rent boys engage in different forms of compensated sex (Agustin, 2005) with other men. They construct their masculine identities through their clandestine homoerotic involvements. They invent and practice an embodied style that I call 'exaggerated masculinity'[2] in order to mark their manly stance and deal with the risks that same-sex sexual activities pose for the reproduction of their masculine selves. In this article, I examine how these heterosexually identified rent boys assemble and perform exaggerated masculinity in order to negotiate the tensions between their local socially excluded environments and a burgeoning western-style gay culture[3] while they conduct their 'risky' sexual interactions with other men.

Male prostitution takes place in different social settings around the world across a wide diversity of class, racial, cultural, and organizational arrangements (see, for example, Aggleton, 1999; Dorais, 2005; Fernández-Dávila et al., 2008; Hall, 2007; Jackson and Sullivan, 1999; McNamara, 1994;

Özbay, Cenk, "Nocturnal Queers: Rent Boys' Masculinity in Istanbul." 2010. *Sexualities 13*(5), p. 645.

Minichiello et al., 2001; Mujtaba, 1997; Schifter, 1998; West, 1993). . . . By studying male prostitution we can gain insight into the social dynamics behind how dissident sexualities are experienced and interpreted in the margins of hegemonic masculinities. In this article, I aim to make a contribution to the gap in the field of compensated sex between men of different social classes who embody distinct masculinities in . . . non-western sexual geographies by using the Istanbul case in which a number of southern sexual cultures such as the Mediterranean, East European and Islamic meet and interface (Bereket and Adam, 2008; Tapinc, 1992). . . .

Rent boys come from lower-class neighborhoods in the outskirts of the Istanbul metropolitan region called *varoş*—a term . . . similar to the Brazilian 'favela' (Goldstein, 2003) and the French 'banlieue' (Wacquant, 2008). Rent boys (aged between 16 and 25) are mostly sons of the recently migrated large families that have coped with dislocation, poverty, and cultural exclusion. They speak Turkish with different regional accents, which show their symbolic marginalization and lack of cultural capital. Rent boys self-fashion their masculinity to produce a niche for themselves within a highly stratified, increasingly hegemonic gay culture in Istanbul. This self-fashioning via the embodied, stylized, continuously refined exaggerated masculinity operates through an 'outsider within' (Collins, 1986) position amongst self-identified gay men in Istanbul.

Varoş boys narrate a story . . . of their 'real' selves while they strive to become rent boys, which they claim is a temporary and transitory position. Exaggerated masculinity is a critical part of this construction in the context of male prostitution. *Varoş* boys transform themselves to achieve the rent boy identity through a discursive process, in which they reiterate the rules and characteristics of being a rent boy, and through a bodily process in which they learn and do exaggerated masculinity. . . .

In . . . Istanbul . . . *varoş* is a highly marginalized social identity regarding the mainstream culture of the middle classes. When they attempt to enter the spaces of the western-style gay venues in Istanbul *varoş* boys are discriminated against and rejected in terms of their alterity to the . . . modern, urban, and liberal lifestyles that middle classes have long adopted.

'Rent boy' emerges in the liminal space between the *varoş* identity and the local reflection of the global gay culture: A rent boy neither becomes gay nor stays as *varoş*. Rent boys animate a dynamic process of cultural hybridization and theatrical displays of exaggerated masculinity as a response to double marginalization. While they strategically use their *varoş* backgrounds to underline their masculinity and consolidate their authenticity in order to attract gay men who are supposed to have a fantasy of having sex with heterosexual men, they concomitantly take advantage of their encounters with middle-class gay men and empower themselves in their *varoş* environments. In this sense, the agility of the identity of rent boy permits its subjects to be enriched and strengthened in the symbolic hierarchies that they face in both *varoş* and gay cultures. Masculine embodiment and its deliberate and nuanced uses become crucial in rent boys' symbolic and material culture. . . .

VAROŞ AS CULTURE AND IDENTITY

After the 1980 military coup, neoliberal reforms in Turkey transformed both Istanbul's position within the country as well as its own socio-spatial organization. The population in Istanbul has multiplied almost four times and recently approached 12 million people. Urban segregation and social fragmentation escalated and reshaped Istanbul as a space of contestation in which previously silenced social groups including Islamists, Kurds, and queers claimed legitimacy and public visibility (Kandiyoti, 2002; Keyder, 1999, 2005).

Varoş was one of the names given by the middle-class . . . citizens of Istanbul . . . to the illegal squatter settlement neighborhoods around the city and to the migrant people who built houses and worked in the temporary jobs in the informal sector (White, 2004). . . . *Varoş* became synonymous with a regressive, 'pre-modern' subjectivity that is abject and disenfranchised.

In the 1990s, the term *varoş* started to designate urban poverty instead of backwardness and rurality while people living in *varoş* areas were increasingly identified as the 'threatening Other' (Demirtas and Sen, 2007; Erman, 2004). *Varoş* was constructed as a space where fundamental Islamism, Kurdish separatism, illegality, criminality, and violence met. Through media representations, *varoş* was otherized in terms of culture, economy, ethnicity, and politics. . . . At the same time, inhabitants of *varoş* reclaimed and appropriated the word as a way to identify their own cultural position distinctly from the Istanbulite. . . .

Rent boys are the children of *varoş*. They tactically constitute their identities as *varoş* to underline their differences from their gay clients not only in terms of sexuality but also in terms of class position. In this sense, being *varoş* refers to an embodied cultural difference as well as certain gendered meanings regarding masculinity. Rent boys repetitively state that they are 'real' men because they are coming from *varoş*. In this way, *varoş* is naturalized and linked to an inherent masculinity that gay men do not (and cannot) have. In other words, *varoş* becomes a sign of an uncontaminated, natural, physical, and authentic masculinity, while gay stands for feminine values and norms such as culture, refinement, and cleanness. In a symbolic order of masculinity, *varoş* boys turn to be 'naturally' and unchangeably masculine while gay men's bodies represent a modern, inauthentic, and imperfect masculinity.

TACTICS OF MASCULINITY

In addition to the symbolic significance of *varoş* in creating a 'naturally' virile character, rent boys also employ tactics to maintain their masculine identities vis-à-vis gay men. The most important strategy is being 'top only'. Thus, rent boys claim that they engage sexually with other men only when they play the top (active) role.[4]

Protecting their bodies from penetration and becoming sexually available only as tops allow rent boys to reclaim their incontestably masculine identities. The gender of their sexual partner does not make a real difference either for their sexual repertoire or for their erotic subjectivities (for a similar situation among Brazilian male prostitutes, see Parker, 1998).

Another way that rent boys secure their masculinity is their heterosexualizing discourse. When they talk, rent boys position themselves in relation to an imagined girlfriend, fiancé, or long-term lover to-be-married with whom they have ongoing emotional and sexual affairs. When challenged, this discursive heterosexuality enables rent boys to prove their 'real' heterosexual identities. In order to distinguish themselves from gay men and to buttress their masculinity, rent boys also humiliate and denigrate gay men. It is important to note that rent boys' homophobia is, in most cases, a performative 'utterance' (Butler, 1993) to help maintain their masculine identities. It does not really prevent them from mingling, negotiating, and having sex with gay men in other situations.

Masculinity has always been a contested subject in the construction of queer sexualities in Turkey (Bereket and Adam, 2006; Hocaoglu, 2002; Özbay and Soydan, 2003; Tapinc, 1992; Yuzgun, 1986). However, rent boys' 'top only' positions and homophobic utterances are only one aspect of the exaggerated performances of masculinity. Different than the archetypical macho sexual pose of Latin America (Lancaster, 1994) rent boys do not brag about their sexual escapades with gay men. Instead, they have an evasive manner about their queer sexual practices. In addition to homophobia, the silence of rent boys about their homosexual involvements coincides with the tradition of the strict separation of intimate affairs from public sphere in some Muslim societies as Murray calls it 'the will not to know' (Murray, 1997). . . .

Within the framework of interpenetrating western gay culture and local constellations of gender and sexuality, masculinity matters for rent boys and gay men on another level: the appeal of passing and acting straight (Clarkson, 2006). Gay men in Istanbul have an increasing obsession with the 'straight-acting' and 'straight-looking' self-presentation, which demands a certain degree of heterosexual masculinity for erotic engagement. This fetishism for the 'more masculine' attributes and bodily gestures contributes to a hierarchy in which feminine qualities, as in effeminate men, are deemed inferior and unwanted, while masculine traits are presented as rare, desired, and superior. The negative attitude towards effeminacy and the desire for more masculine attributes contribute to an exaggerated masculinity to prevail as the 'most masculine', and thus craved, in the gay culture in Istanbul. Rent boys take advantage of this erotic climate and relocate themselves in the eyes of their potential clients. Put in other words, rent boys convert their erotic and sexual positionalities into social and economic capital through their use of the encounter and desire between different masculinities.

THE INTERPLAY OF MULTIPLE MASCULINITIES

Since gender is conceptualized as a continual 'doing' rather than as a natural 'being' (Butler, 1999: 25; West and Zimmerman, 1987) gendered subjectivities are constituted through 'the repeated stylization of the body, a set of repeated acts within a highly rigid regulatory frame that congeal over time to produce the appearance of substance, of a natural sort of being' (Butler, 1999: 33). Gendered subjectivity comes into being via the constellation of bodily performances within the 'regulatory frame' of the heterosexual matrix. Rent boys subvert their regular and 'normal' heterosexual script with male prostitution while they simultaneously try to re-stabilize it by enacting exaggerated masculinity—a style that requires well-defined gendered performances before different audiences. The omnipresent sense of risk inaugurates the possibility for the exaggeratedly masculine identity to be questioned and imperiled. In this sense, the rent

boy's masculinity is a[n] . . . insecure subject position that needs to be repetitively asserted and proven while it continuously introduces new risks to be contemplated by rent boys in order to achieve their heterosexual and masculine status.

In her seminal works, Raewyn Connell (1987, 1995) demonstrated that multiple masculinities coexist and interact in a society at any given time. The encounter and dialogue between a *varoş* boy and a middle-aged upper-class gay man might be seen as a manifestation of what Connell terms the relations between divergent masculinities. These relations ought to be seen through the prism of power. In this sense, the culturally exalted hegemonic masculinity brings complicity, subordination, intimidation, and exploitation into relations between different masculinities. The exclusion of same-sex desire is critical for the constitution of hegemonic masculinity (Connell, 2000: 83). As a model, an ideal, or a reference point, hegemonic masculinity—in relation to the heterosexual matrix—affects all other ways of being a man including its imitations (as in rent boys) as well as the resistant or alternative versions (as in queer masculinity).

In the eastern Mediterranean region, configurations of masculinities take shape between the westernizing influences of modernity and the history of Islamic culture and tradition (Bereket and Adam, 2008; Ghoussoub and Sinclair-Webb, 2000; Ouzgane, 2006). The case of rent boys in Istanbul is not an exception . . . .

LOCATING RENT BOYS

Place: Taksim Square.
Time: Any evening, especially after 10 p.m.

The crowded Istiklal Street, which is a major promenade connected to . . . Taksim Square, is full of intermeshing people from all classes, ages, genders, ethnicities, religions, sexualities, and cultures representing Istanbul's social diversity. Among the carnivalesque crowd an attentive eye can notice some young men walking or leaning against walls, checking the passerby. It is obvious for these attentive eyes that these young men, who carefully prepared themselves for the peak hours, reciprocate with curious gazes that can speak the same language of the looker. Around midnight these young men suddenly disappear from the street. Now, it is . . . bar time.

After paying the entry fee (around $10) I enter Bientot, the most famous and much frequented club of rent boys in Istanbul. Bientot is very close to the vivid Istiklal Street, near a well-known transgender dance club and the only gay bathhouse of the city. Bientot, like two other similar bars, is a 'limitative and disciplining' (Hammers, 2008) space in the sense that types of people (i.e. rent boys, transvestites, clients) are set, their roles are prescribed (i.e. who dances, who looks, who buys drinks), and interactions between visitors are stabilized (i.e. negotiations, flirting, cruising, kissing). . . . Gay men (whether clients of rent boys or not) told me that they do not 'have fun' in Bientot as they do in other gay bars and they come here just to see or talk to the *varoş* boys only in the predefined ways that are available to them.

Bientot is full of its . . . frequenters: Several single gay men from all ages, some mixed friend groups, several transvestites, and more than 70 rent boys. In general, everyone seems to know each other. Everybody except rent boys drinks and rests on the walls surrounding the dance floor enjoying music (popular Turkish pop songs of the day) while most of the rent boys dance in a unique style without drinking unless a client is generous enough to buy them one. . . .

Here is a quotation from my field notes immediately after arriving home from Bientot:

> A shocking place . . . High volume of music, really bad ventilation, the smell of alcohol, the smell of sweat, the smell of cologne, the smoke from cigarettes . . . You can't escape from the piercing looks into your eyes. These looks are masculine, you can tell, but they are also very inviting and flirtatious, which contradicts . . . the assertive masculinity. The dancing bodies are very close to each other. They are very straight looking like the ordinary boys at the street; but, on the other hand, the male-to-male intimacy of the dance destroys

the desired heterosexual ambiance. It seems like they are straight boys in a gay club, dancing together passionately. . . .

PLAYING WITH FIRE: ELEMENTS OF RENT BOYS' STYLE

A weekly TV show filmed the gay bathhouse near Bientot with hidden cameras in early 2005. After recording each possible 'proof' of male prostitution (including negotiations for prices and actions) the programmers tried to talk with the manager of the bathhouse about the organization . . . while he kept refuting that he hired rent boys. During the interview the camera focuses on a young rent boy, half naked in his towel, arguing angrily with another one about the recruitment of new rent boys that they already knew. He said 'I told you don't bring everyone here from your neighborhood. Look at me. I only bring my brother. You may have a fight with one of them in the future and he can go and tell people, including your father, what you do here. You are playing with fire. I told you this before. Don't play with fire.'

. . . This warning against 'playing with fire' is neither unique to this rent boy nor restricted within the walls of the bathhouse. It offers a useful framework to better comprehend a rent boy's unceasing physical and social negotiations with other rent boys, gay men, and transvestites. Rent boy is a conditional and fragile identity. It surfaces between the contradictory discursive and sexual practices, which subvert the line between homo and heterosexuality. It is a contingent performance that links the *varoş* culture of Istanbul and the ostensibly global gay life-style. It is an interplay of competing working- and upper-middle class meanings and signifiers. Through the incessant play of risk taking, a rent boy invests his heterosexuality as well his social position and kinship networks which are likely to be harmed by an undesired disclosure, as the rent boy quoted earlier fears.

Here, I follow Agustin's (2005: 619) proposition to define and study prostitution, sex work, and compensated sex as a 'culture' to expose the previously under-researched links with systems of inequality and the production of social meaning. Wright (2005: 243) also highlights the 'percolation of queer theoretical concerns' and 'an array of cultural studies interventions' into the sociology of masculinities in order to pose new questions on masculine performances, cultural practices, and 'engenderment' processes that men undertake through the routes of non-hegemonic masculinities in diverse settings. Hence, I frame exaggerated masculinity as a product of the culture of rent boys in Istanbul. Rent boys learn, practice, and transform exaggerated masculinity through the mechanisms of social control and self-governance. The process of the construction and reconstruction of exaggerated masculinity is constantly under risk of disappointment and failure.

. . . Risk appears three-fold in animating exaggerated masculinity by rent boys. First and foremost, rent boys' involvement with male prostitution should not be revealed to their friends, family, and extended relatives. Otherwise, they cannot sustain their ordinary lives as young, decent, and respected members of their community On the other hand, while the rent boy reproduces *varoş* culture as corroboration to his 'natural' masculinity, he should also play with and transmute it symbolically in order to have a subject position within gay culture instead of being abjected. So, the second risk is . . . a nuanced middle space between the two unwanted identities that a rent boy must navigate carefully: staying as an unmodified *varoş* or becoming (too) gay. While connecting closely with gay men, rent boys' third risk is about protecting their heterosexuality. Although rent boys have sex with gay men, they are not supposed to have a gay identity. In sum, a rent boy has to control meticulously and manage risk regarding his bodily acts, behaviors, and relations with other people in order not to be exposed while balancing between the discrepant meanings of *varoş* and gay positions. In this framework, I will now outline the elements of how rent boys sustain exaggerated masculinity through their risk-taking activities and their entanglements with different segments of the culture of male sex work in Istanbul.

The Body

The first point of risk that rent boys take into consideration focuses on their bodies. Almost all rent boys have athletic or skinny bodies. . . . They think that their gay clients like their bodies as skinny, fatless, and 'toned' and not over-muscular and 'hung'. They also believe that they look younger this way. . . . Hakan (aged 22) says, 'body is everything we have in this job, of course we need to take care of it'. Rent boys have a certain tension around their bodies in order to keep them in good condition, to seem young(er), and not to lose their virility through developing an over-muscled look.

Appearance

Another significant issue in the material culture of rent boys is about what they wear and how they look. Most rent boys wear denim jeans. They almost never wear shorts even when it is unbearably hot and humid in Istanbul. Burak (aged 18) states that 'real men never wear shorts, jeans are the best'. For their upper parts they commonly opt for white. 'White is better because it looks more attractive when you are tanned. Also, it shines in the dark bar and makes you more visible', says Arda (aged 23). Black tops are also very popular for their taste because it is deemed to be more masculine and mature. They also wear some bright and lively colors like red and yellow to be seen in the bar. . . .

Rent boys do not wear earrings as Okan (aged 18) told me, 'Earrings would harm masculinity.' They are more tolerant towards wristbands, chains, and rings, but earrings are identified with gays and/or foreigners. . . . Rent boys in Istanbul insist on wearing sports shoes and sneakers even on snowy days. . . .

Perfume

Perfumes and colognes are significant manifestations of rent boys' risky relations with their gay clientele. It is always good for a rent boy to have the fragrance of a charming perfume because it increases his attractiveness when his client has to whisper into his ear in the noisy bar. Perfumes are very expensive for rent boys' budgets but sometimes they receive perfumes after satisfying a client with their sexual performance. . . . As Burak told me, 'if you smell [of] perfume, it shows that you recently got some work done'.

The risky point is . . . the gendered quality of the fragrance. The fragrance must smell masculine because otherwise it cannot contribute to the exaggerated masculinity of the rent boy. . . . On the other hand, a client who uses a very masculine perfume for himself endangers a rent boy's masculinity because it implies that the gay client was not a feminine man and he could turn active in sexual penetration. . . .

Most of the rent boys that I talked to said that they were against stealing or any other kind of criminal activity. On the other hand, they also revealed that they were not against asking for or even stealing perfumes from gays' houses after they have sex. Perfumes clearly are the exception for rent boys' moral stance against stealing. Hasan (aged 24) says 'when I see a nice perfume I ask for it. Honestly, if he does not want to give it to me I will try to take it anyway. I don't think this is stealing.' Hakan also noted that 'I am not interested in anything else, but if he has a nice perfume I will take it . . . He can buy another bottle easily and I will smell nice. Good deal.' Murat (aged 23) states that 'perfume is a connection between the Rich's life and mine. I can take it, I can use it and when I smell it I remember what I did and I enjoy about it. It makes my life more beautiful.'

Dance

Dance is another risky subject in the context of male prostitution in Istanbul. Rent boys have to dance in the bar in order to be seen by clients. The particular motions and gyrations of the boys' dancing give the impression that they are carrying out a predefined script of performing a task, but not reflecting pleasure by moving in a relaxed manner with the music and the rhythm. In other words, when rent boys dance, they perform another requirement of their work. Their dance is never visibly homoerotic although their bodies are pretty close and sometimes touch each other. It has its own sense of humor: If a rent boy puts himself at the back of another, the one in the front bounces in sudden panic—in an anxiety to save his back (his bottom). It manifests a rigid top-bottom code concerning the control and defense of your own back and a constant search to attack the others' backs.

If a rent boy oversteps the boundary of touching another's back or exhibits signs of pleasure, other rent boys explicitly disapprove the act and call him 'pervert', *ergo*, humorous pleasure that comes from sodomizing others should be limited to activity with gays and not with other rent boys. In the bar, this is the main reason behind physical fights amongst rent boys. Thus, bodily humor is dangerous to play with, although avoiding it brings social exclusion because a rent boy ought to dance. He needs to 'show' in order to charm his audience. A motionless rent boy renders himself invisible, which seriously reduces his chances of finding a client. Anil (aged 20) says, 'dancing is the moment where we get the gays. We attract them when we dance. They love to watch us.'

Most importantly, a rent boy has to dance without looking feminine. Okan says, 'it is better not to do it [dance] if you do it like a girl'. Riza (aged 24) told me 'you should not shake your ass like a belly dancer. Arms and legs must be straight. Gaze is also important.' There are strict performative codes that most rent boys obey to protect the masculine image during the dance: The body should not be curved or shaken too much and it must repeat the same rough movements without flexibility. It must show strength. Shoulders and arms should be kept wide open, the waist should move only back and forth, imitating the sexual act of penetration. Dance is controlled and regulated by the surveillance of other rent boys. As long as they can perform it according to the unwritten rules of exaggerated masculinity, dance guarantees rent boys' masculine identities and makes them the center of attraction before potential clients.

Friends

As I recounted earlier . . . taking part in male prostitution or being seen while cruising is very risky. . . . Concealment paralyzes friendship mechanisms amongst rent boys. Most of the time, they come to the bars or other cruising places alone or at most in the company of one other rent boy, who is supposed to be trustworthy (mostly one's kin, for example a cousin). They usually know other rent boys personally and they have an intimate network of gossip and information exchange. They also spend time together chatting and dancing in the bars, but they always wind up alone while working or cruising. The solitude of rent boys might be seen as a tactic to increase their chance of negotiation for higher prices or as a part of the tradition of mendacity about what they do for how much. It actually protects them from unwanted rumors and from the dangers of unexpected disclosure. Can (aged 21) elaborates that 'I know some people in the bar, some other 'rents' but I never see them out of the bar. Nobody knows that I am coming here in my neighborhood. I must be very careful. When my regular friends ask I tell them I will hang out with my cousins.' Mert (aged 24) adds, 'If you go out together he [a friend] can say that Mert let the guy fuck him, Mert turned bottom, etc. If he won't say it today, he will say it tomorrow. This is how it works. So, it is better to be alone instead of dealing with gossip and lies.'

Another point that poses a risk to the exaggerated masculinity is about emotions and sexual attraction between rent boys. In order to sustain fraternal heterosexuality, homoeroticism must be tamed and eliminated (Connell, 2000; Sedgwick,

1986). In male prostitution, who is feminine (gay) and who is masculine (rent boy) is rigidly defined. For rent boys, intimate relations are allowed only between these distinct gendered groups and not within them. Therefore, the possibility or manifestation of any kind of affect, eroticism, or sexuality between rent boys subverts their masculine positions as well as their 'natural' heterosexuality. Just like the uneasiness when they dance together, the risk of emotional and bodily intimacy as well as the ways it might be talked about create a certain tension and prevent rent boys from becoming further attached to each other.

Drinks and Drugs

. . . Drinking alcoholic beverages in the bar is a vital chance to look like an adult and demonstrate toughness. Soft drinks and soda are not preferred because they look juvenile and gentle. Beer is the drink that rent boys consume mostly because it is the cheapest and the most masculine beverage. . . . Beer is easy to drink while dancing, and more importantly, it does not make one drunk easily. Alcohol is a very risky issue just like drugs. Mixing different beverages, drinking tequila shots fast, or taking drugs can make a rent boy dizzy—sometimes almost unconscious. Emre (aged 25) notes 'gays try to make you drunk by buying you many drinks. They want to use you when you are drunk. If you are new here they can easily entrap you. You can have sex for no money, or worse things can happen'. These 'worse things' that Emre notes may lead to losing the masculine pose and roughness, which was carefully constructed. . . .

Transvestites

My framing of risk for rent boys' exaggerated masculinity includes their multifaceted relations with transvestite sex workers. Almost all the rent boys that I talked with have had sexual experiences with transvestites. A rent boy and a transvestite can become friends, sexual partners, and even lovers. The stories told about rent boys and transvestites range from scandals such as a drunken rent boy who was raped by a transvestite to some poignant love stories. Despite the fact that they are in two different sides of sex work neither rent boys nor transvestites pay to have sex with each other. As Aykut (aged 25) says 'we are free for them, they are free for us. For all the rest, only money talks.'

While transvestites enjoy the young virility and 'real' masculinity of rent boys, the latter are happy to show how masculine and sexually active they are by having sex with the 'girls'. In most cases, a transvestite mentors an inexperienced rent boy and she teaches him how to have good sex. Although it seems a mutually satisfying relationship, these escapades with transvestites are indeed very risky for rent boys. Transvestites can easily ridicule a rent boy for not having a sufficiently large penis or for not achieving a fulfilling sexual performance. Emir (aged 20) said, 'I saw many guys like this. Everybody knows that they ejaculate really fast or it [the penis] is really small because one of the girls talked about it. They can still convince some clients, especially tourists, but it is more difficult to find a client for them.' Such a public display of physical or sexual insufficiency would permanently destroy a rent boy's sources of masculine respectability and reputation.

Safe Sex

The last component of what I conceptualize as risk for rent boys' construction of the exaggerated masculinity, is about 'sexual risk' (Fernández-Dávila et al., 2008) and bodily health. All the rent boys that I conducted interviews with had knowledge about STDs, HIV, condoms and how to use them. Nevertheless, my conversations with both rent boys and their clients testify that rent boys have a certain disinclination and resistance to concede their vulnerability and to use a condom during sexual intercourse. They prefer to have *doğal* (natural) or *çiplak* (naked, without a condom) sex especially when the client asks for or pays more. Ilker (aged 19) told me 'I use it

[a condom] sometimes. It does not really bother me. I prefer cleaner gays so it is not a big threat for me. I know many rents do it without condoms with tourists because they pay more. It is crazy because there is a higher chance for a foreigner to be sick.' Their negative attitude might originate from the practical difficulty to use condoms, or as more likely, the construction of their masculine self-identities rejects expressions of fear and protection while it promotes courage and adventure. Rent boys interpret the sexual encounter as an opportunity to challenge and prove their manhood as Ozgur (aged 22) says, 'little boys might get scared of it, but for me, it is not the case. I know how to fuck a guy without a condom in a safe way. It is not necessary for me to put one on. I can protect myself.' Also, some clients opt for unprotected sex with younger rent boys whom they believe do not have a long sexual history and are thus 'cleaner'. On the other hand, Burak mentioned, 'Probably because I am younger they ask my age and how many times I did it [having sex]. Then, they say "it is OK with you, you are clean" and I don't put a condom on. That's what they want.' Therefore, rent boys' desire to demonstrate their courage and fearlessness operates along with some clients' demands for unprotected sex and produces a risky and dangerous encounter for both sides.

CONCLUDING REMARKS

In this article, I have explained how rent boys in Istanbul have developed cultural, bodily, symbolic, and material strategies both to challenge tacitly and to negotiate inventively with the social norms of hegemonic male sexuality (Plummer, 2005) and hegemonic masculinity (Connell, 1995). The 'top only' sexual positions whereby they make themselves sexually available, the protection of their bodies from penetration, and the distance they place between themselves and feminine connotations by the way they dance, smell, or dress, can be seen as attempts to save the penis-and-penetration-centered hegemonic virile sexuality. On the other hand, the enactment of exaggerated masculinity and the production of a story of authentic manhood via *varoş* culture are manifestations of their complicity in the hegemonic forms of masculinity in Istanbul despite their dissident sexual practices that contradict these narratives.

Is it acceptable for the embodiments of hegemonic masculinity, or its imitations, to operate alongside queer sex? Is it possible for one to reclaim his privileged heterosexual status while he engages in compensated sex with other men? Gary W. Dowsett and his colleagues note that the definitions and conceptualizations in which masculinities have been theorized are in need of reconsideration and recalibration since 'the prevailing formulation of masculinity represents a failure to engage with the creative meanings and embodied experiences evident in non-hegemonic sexual cultures, and with the effects these meanings and experiences may generate beyond their boundaries' (2008:124). In this sense, rent boys and their ambivalent sexual acts and identifications provide an excellent case for such inquiries regarding their involvement with the active meaning-making process of sexuality and masculinity. As a response to the possible inquiries and challenges towards their heterosexual and masculine self-identities, they use exaggerated masculinity in order to be able to continue their everyday lives as heterosexual members of their families and kinship networks. In other words, exaggerated masculinity repairs and masks the subverting effects of compensated sex for rent boys' heterosexuality and makes them closer to the hegemonic ideal of masculinity. They perform an assiduous self-governance through symbols and implicit meanings vis-à-vis different and contradictory class positions, gender identities, and sexual acts.

Rent boys constitute exaggerated masculinity relationally and strategically at the nexus of contradictory contexts of the local *varoş* culture and the impact of the global gay culture. Risk is central in understanding the mechanisms of exaggerated masculinity since it is a fragile, insecure, playful combination of various bodily acts, gestures, and symbols. . . .

NOTES

1. Rent boy (as in English) is the term my informants use for defining themselves. They say '*ben bir rent bovum*' (1 am a rent boy) or just '*rentim*' (I am rent). Sometimes they prefer to say, '*parayla veya ücretli çikiyorum*' (1 am going for money). I never encountered any other terms, either in the English versions or in Turkish translations, such as *erkek fahişe (male prostitute)*, *seks işçisi (sex worker)* or *jigolo (gigolo)* used by my informants, their clients, or in the mass media. The subject of this article, rent boys, who are from the *varoş* segments of the city, is the only group of men who engage in compensated sex (receiving money or gifts) in the gay scene in Istanbul (Hocaoglu, 2002).

2. I prefer to describe the rent boys' stylized embodiment as 'exaggerated masculinity' in order to underline its theatrical, playful, performative, and decontexualizing characteristics. It is a constellation of learnt, imitated, calculated, and socially regulated displays of doing masculinity. There are other similar terms for such excessive masculine performances like hypermasculinity (Healey, 1996) or machismo (Gutmann, 1996) that are conceptualized in different webs of relations.

3. With the western-style gay culture, I basically mean the emergence of men who call themselves gay (as in English) or sometimes *gey* in Turkish (Bereket and Adam, 2006) because they engage in sexual, erotic, and emotional relations with other men. There are many components of this culture including enclosed spaces called gay bars or gay clubs, and access to foreign or local websites with gay content for various purposes such as online dating. Before the emergence of the modern gay identity in Turkey there were various sorts of same-sex sexual relations going on under different identifications and social organizations (Tapinc, 1992; Yuzgun, 1986).

4. Rent boys claim that they are 'top only' in order to insist they do not let their clients penetrate their bodies, while they can insert their penises into their clients' bodies through oral and anal sex. Rent boys also claim that they never touch their client's penises and they never let their clients caress their bodies. In addition to the 'top only' rule, some of the rent boys I talked to stated that they never kiss their clients from their mouths and some told me that they do not 'make out' with clients and delimit their sexual activities with oral and anal penetration (Özbay, 2005).

REFERENCES

Aggleton P (ed.) (1999) *Men Who Sell Sex: International Perspectives on Male Prostitution and HIV/AIDS.* Philadelphia, PA: Temple University Press.

Agustin LM (2005) The cultural study of commercial sex. *Sexualities* 8(5): 618–631.

Bereket T and Adam BD (2006) The emergence of gay identities in Turkey. *Sexualities* 9(2): 131–151.

Bereket T and Adam BD (2008) Navigating Islam and same-sex liaisons among men in Turkey. *Journal of Homosexuality* 55(2): 204–222.

Butler J (1993) *Bodies That Matter: On the Discursive Limits of 'Sex'.* New York: Routledge.

Butler J (1999) *Gender Trouble: Feminism and the Subversion of Identity.* New York: Routledge.

Clarkson J (2006) 'Everyday Joe' versus 'pissy, bitchy, queens': Gay masculinity on straight acting.com *The Journal of Men's Studies* 14(2): 191–207.

Collins PH (1986) Learning from the outsider within. *Social Problems* 33(6): 14–32.

Connell RW (1987) *Gender and Power: Society, the Person and Sexual Politics.* Stanford, CA: Stanford University Press.

Connell RW (1995) *Masculinities.* Berkeley: University of California Press.

Connell RW (2000) *The Men and the Boys.* Berkeley: University of California Press.

Demirtas N and Sen S (2007) Varoş Identity: The Redefinition of Low Income Settlements in Turkey. *Middle Eastern Studies* 43(1): 87–106.

Dorais M (2005) *Rent Boys: The World of Male Sex Workers.* Montreal: McGill-Queen's University Press.

Dowsett GW, Williams H, Ventuneac A, et al. (2008) Taking it like a man: Masculinity and barebacking online. *Sexualities* 11(1/2): 121–141.

Erman T (2004) Gecekondu Çalişmalarinda 'Öteki' Olarak Gecekondulu Kurgulari. *European Journal of Turkish Studies* 1. URL (accessed 15 June 2010): http://www.ejts.org/document85.html.

Ghoussoub M and Sinclair-Webb E (eds) (2000) *Imagined Masculinities: Male Identity and Culture in the Modern Middle East.* London: Saqi.

Goldstein DM (2003) *Laughter Out of Place: Race, Class, Violence, and Sexuality in a Rio Shantytown.* Berkeley: University of California Press.

Gutmann MC (1996) *The Meanings of Macho: Being a Man in Mexico City.* Berkeley: University of California Press.

Hall T (2007) Rent-boys, barflies, and kept men: Men involved in sex with men for compensation in Prague. *Sexualities* 10(4): 457–472.

Hammers CJ (2008) Making space for an agentic sexuality? The examination of a lesbian/queer bathhouse. *Sexualities* 11(5): 547–572.

Healey M (1996) *Gay Skins: Class, Masculinity, and Queer Appropriation.* London: Cassell.

Hocaoglu M (2002) *Escinsel Erkekler.* Istanbul: Metis.

Jackson P and Sullivan G (eds) (1999) *Lady Boys, Tom Boys, Rent Boys: Male and Female Homosexualities in Contemporary Thailand.* New York: Haworth.

Kandiyoti D (2002) Introduction: Reading the fragments. In: Kandiyoti D and Saktanber A (eds) *Fragments of Culture: The Everyday of Modern Turkey.* London: IB: Tauris, 1–21.

Keyder C (ed.) (1999) *Istanbul: Between the Global and the Local.* Boston. MA: Rowman & Littlefield Publishers.

Keyder C (2005) Globalization and social exclusion in Istanbul. *International Journal of Urban and Regional Research* 29(1): 124–134.

Lancaster R (1994) *Life is Hard: Machismo, Danger, and the Intimacy of Power in Nicaragua.* Berkeley: University of California Press.

McNamara RP (1994) *The Times Square Hustler: Male Prostitution in New York City.* New York: Praeger.

Minichiello V, Mariño R, Browne J, et al. (2001) Male sex workers in three Australian cities: Sociodemographic and sex work characteristics. *Journal of Homosexuality* 42(1): 29–51.

Mujtaba H (1997) The other side of midnight: Pakistani male prostitutes. In: Murray S and Roscoe W (eds) *Islamic Homosexualities: Culture, History, and Literature.* New York: New York University Press, 267–274.

Murray S (1997) The will not to know: Islamic accommodations of male homosexuality. In: Murray S and Roscoe W (eds) *Islamic Homosexualities: Culture, History, and Literature.* New York: New York University Press, 14–54.

Ouzgane L (ed.) (2006) *Islamic Masculinities.* London: Zed.

Özbay C (2005) Virilities for rent: Navigating masculinity, sexuality and class in Istanbul. Unpublished MA thesis, Bogazici University.

Özbay C and Soydan S (2003) *Escinsel Kadinlar.* Istanbul: Metis.

Parker R (1998) *Beneath the Equator: Cultures of Desire, Male Homosexuality, and Emerging Gay Communities in Brazil*. New York: Routledge.

Plummer K (2005) Male sexualities. In: Kimmel M, Hearn J and Connell RW (eds) *Handbook of Studies On Men and Masculinities*. Thousand Oaks, CA: SAGE, 178–195.

Schifter J (1998) *Lila's House: Male Prostitution in Latin America*. New York: Haworth Press.

Sedgwick EK (1986) *Between Men: English Literature and Male Homosexual Desire*. New York: Columbia University Press.

Tapinc H (1992) Masculinity, femininity, and Turkish male homosexuality. In: Plummer K (ed.) *Modern Homosexualities: Fragments of Lesbian and Gay Experience*. London: Routledge, 39–50.

Wacquant L (2008) *Urban Outcasts: A Comparative Sociology of Advanced Marginality*. Cambridge: Polity.

West C and Zimmerman D (1987) Doing gender. *Gender & Society* 1(2): 125–151.

Wright L (2005) Introduction to 'queer' masculinities. *Men & Masculinities* 7(3): 243–247.

Yuzgun A (1986) *Escinsellik*. Istanbul: Huryuz.

Introduction to Reading 14

This article offers a wonderful analysis of the relational nature of masculinities and femininities in the context of the changing lives of working-class married people in a suburban community in Mumbai, India. Sociologist Annie George discusses the ways women's "discourses" on men's actions provoke men to assume a new honorable masculinity that is softer and more accepting of women's autonomy.

1. Describe the research approach employed by George for this study.

2. Discuss the role of sexual self-control in the idea of honorable masculinity.

3. How did women's "discourses" contribute to the reshaping of definitions of (honorable) masculinity?

REINVENTING HONORABLE MASCULINITY

DISCOURSES FROM A WORKING-CLASS INDIAN COMMUNITY

Annie George

Maintenance of personal and family honor and avoidance of shame are central concerns of Indian communities. Honor in Indian contexts is typically viewed as engendered and embodied. Yet notions of honor and gendered identities—masculinities and femininities—have ambiguous and contradictory meanings that shift in relation to contexts and histories over time. In this article, I provide an interpretive account of honor and masculinities that operates among a group of working-class men and women of Mumbai, India,[1] through analyses of two related discourses: men's accounts of sexual self-control and women's accounts of "understanding" men. For a section of working-class men of Mumbai, sexual self-control forms a central constituent of a gendered, embodied notion of honorable masculinity. For working-class women, however, economic provisioning and absence of physical and sexual violence are critical markers of honorable masculinity. The linkage of these conditions is surprising because Indian discourses on honor hold that women's bodies and actions, and not those of men, are the primary markers of personal and family honor (Dube 1986; Gold 1994; Jefferey, Jeffrey, and Lyon 1989; Kumar 1994; Ram 1991; Sharma and Vanjare 1993).

Men's claims about sexual control within marriage—when a popular interpretation of marriage is men's social license to have relatively unregulated sexual access, the so-called male right in marriage—destabilize received ideas of both honor and masculinities in Indian literature and are my starting point to explore emerging forms of honorable masculinities in particular Indian communities. I make two related arguments about emerging masculinities and honor. First, men's actions and women's discourses on men's actions critically shape men's honor. Second, the masculinities men seek must be considered contemporaneously with the femininities[2] that are emerging around them. Traditional avenues for men to gain honor were that of providing adequately for their families and exercising control over their wives and children. Men controlled their wives' sexuality, movements outside the house, and access to and control over productive resources. However, consequent to social and economic changes in their everyday lives and increased participation of women in economic activities outside the house, men and women are redefining hegemonic ideas about gendered identities and creating new, even contradictory, discourses on gendered honorability.

STUDY LOCALE AND METHODS

This study was conducted for a period of twelve months from November 1995 in Kaamgar Nagar (a pseudonym), a community of approximately three hundred thousand people in suburban Mumbai. Kaamgar Nagar comprised a government-recognized shantytown surrounded by people living "illegally" on land that was not designated for slum settlements. Some residents were born in Kaamgar Nagar; others migrated to the city from all over India. We gained access to potential participants through nongovernment organizations that worked in Kaamgar Nagar introducing us to the people of the area.[3] We contacted thirty-seven currently married men, of whom twenty-three agreed to participate in the study.[4] All men had middle school education, were married more than five years, and had at least one live child.

Although all men participants were employed, they had a hard time supporting their families, which typically had three adults and three children. Ten men were self-employed in skilled and unskilled trades as plumber, electrician, flower seller, newspaper vendor, and so on. Seven had permanent jobs in the private and public sector. Of the remaining, three were contract labor, and the others were daily wage earners. The range of monthly income in this group varied from one thousand to five thousand rupees.[5] Only one man owned the 10×12 feet tenement that was their home.

We also conducted repeated in-depth interviews with sixty-five married women residents of Kaamgar Nagar, similar in social class to the men participants. We gathered information from separate focus-group discussions with married men and women and observations and interviews with other residents and regulars of the study site. But data were primarily obtained through repeated in-depth interviews because this method has been used successfully to elicit sensitive information (Balmer et al. 1995; Hammersley and Atkinson 1995; Helitzer-Allen, Makhambera, and Wangel 1994). Each participant was interviewed two to three times, and interviews lasted between half an hour and two hours. They were interviewed at their homes; in local teashops; their work sites, if self-employed and eventually, because of the lack of privacy and frequent interruptions, in a local school classroom after school hours. Areas of discussion included sexual experiences, negotiation and decision making within marriage, sexual experiences outside marriage, perceptions of sexual risk, and the use of risk-reduction practices. Discussions, conducted in Hindi and Marathi, were audiotaped, transcribed, translated into English, sorted, and coded by categories that were generated through the data themselves. An in-depth content analysis was then conducted on the data in relation to the category of *sexual control* to provide insights into men's and women's ideas of marital sex and ideal gendered masculinity.

Sexual Control in Marriage

Men used the English word *control* to refer to three distinct sets of activities: periodic sexual abstinence with one's wife, avoidance of sexual relations outside marriage, and the practice of withdrawal as a form of contraception.[6] In this article, I focus on the first two uses of this concept.

Men's narratives indicated that they sought to observe normative expectations for sex within marriage. These rules of action related to frequency of sex at various stages in life, times and places for sex, and permissible sex acts and partners. During the early years of marriage, couples were expected to have frequent sex for physical pleasure and procreation. After fathering a number of children, however, men were expected to focus attentions as well on their families and the world around and gradually to decrease their interest in sex. Men considered their sexuality to be unruly by nature and in need of control. They believed that, in contrast to women's sexual interests and needs, which declined sharply after having several children, men's sexual urges did not decrease even after many years of marriage and being sexually active. Thus, most men said they were unable to practice the expectation of

decreasing sexual activity even when they had achieved their desired family size. They desired sex more often than their wives did, leading them to conclude that their desire was "in excess." Men reported practicing sexual control by not having *jyada* (excessive) relations with their wives. Sambhaji,[7] thirty-three-years-old and married thirteen years, discussed this dynamic of sexual control as follows:

> After two children usually a woman's urge decreases whereas in the case of a man it remains the same even till fifty years of age. Even if I try to have sexual intercourse with my wife she does not get involved in it. I want it every day whereas she does not. At this age what is the use of a strong sex urge? We have three children. In young age we were too enthusiastic about sex, we enjoyed as much as we could. Now we have to "control."

Here, Sambhaji's notions about appropriate activities for a man of his age and marital status guided his practice of sexual self-control. Men who reported being in a position similar to Sambhaji's made similar remarks about having to struggle with their sexuality. These views suggest that men considered honor to be embodied through self-control. Married men had social permission to have sexual access to their wives; yet some married men reportedly chose self-control.

Women's narratives corroborated these views, and most women appreciated monogamous, understanding[8] men who moderated their demands for marital sex. Gauri, married twelve years, described her husband as follows:

> He is understanding (samajdhar). He does not want [sex] everyday, just once in fifteen days, once in a month. . . . If I tell my husband that today I don't have the mood he says, "That's okay, let's forget it." People in our family and even other people say your husband is very understanding.

Here, the woman, her family, and people in her daily life evaluate as honorable her husband's refusal to engage in coercive marital sex. In contrast, dishonorable husbands were reported to coerce wives to have sexual relations. Many women we interviewed reported regular experience of coercive sex, and some mentioned that their husbands also engaged in sex outside marriage.[9] One such woman was Zeenat, who, when seeking treatment from a local doctor for symptoms of a sexually transmitted infection she contracted from her husband, noted that the doctor evaluated her husband negatively. When the doctor learned that Zeenat's husband was a taxi driver she said, "[Sexually transmitted infections] are a specialty among wives of drivers. Drivers are greedy for sex. One woman is just not enough for them. They go to outside women and come to their wives for sex without a care that this [sexual ill health] happens."

Through her narrative Zeenat sought to convey that it was not only she but also others such as medical doctors who perceived her husband as dishonorable because of his actions: first of having sex outside marriage, and then of coercing his wife to have sexual relations and face the consequences of his lack of sexual control.

HONOR AT HOME, DISHONOR OUTSIDE

Sex outside marriage was the foil against which married men spoke of marital sex, sexual self-control, and, by extension, honorable masculinity. Since marriage is the only culturally sanctioned means by which a person could have sexual relations, men talked about their wives as being "women of the house" and "proper women." In contrast, they described sex outside marriage as "wrong, bad work" *(galat kaam)* that men did with "wrong, bad women" *(galat aurat)*. These cultural rules on marital sexuality contextualize Khalil's answer to a question about whether he ever had a sexual relationship outside marriage. He said, "When we have everything in the house, why should we walk on the wrong path?" This quotation, which is typical of other men's views, foregrounds the notion that sex outside marriage with an "outside woman" outside the house was a loss of sexual control. Men knew that sexual illnesses

could be prevented through monogamy,[10] and sexual control was a means of preventing sexual illness—the bodily marker of dishonor and the absence of self-control.[11]

A study (Verma, Rangaiyan, and Narkhede n.d.) conducted in Kaamgar Nagar of practitioners providing treatment for male sexual problems supports this interpretation. Verma et al. found that medical practitioners causally linked sexual illness to absence of sexual control. The practitioners attributed perceived causes of various male sexual problems like boils and sores in the genital area, white discharge, thinning of semen, wet dreams and lack of erection to an excess of unsatisfied sexual desire, masturbation, and sexual intercourse. Oral and anal sex and sex with "cheap" women are also considered important reasons for *garmi,* a serious illness. Participants in our study shared these beliefs. Thus, Vinayak's answer that his "nature was clean" in response to a question on whether he thought he was susceptible to a sexually transmitted disease shows the connections he made between sexual control and its trade-offs, such as the avoidance of stigmatizing illness and the consolidation of personal honor.

Our discussions with men did not specifically include the type of sexual act they practiced with their wives. We learned about cultural expectations of permissible sex acts when men talked about its transgression. Many men described their current married sex life as "boring." Only Bhimrao said that he had extramarital sex because he was "fed up of doing the same thing again and again" with his wife. He went to sex workers after marriage because they did things that "one could not do with the wife." From local constructions of honorable masculinity, this man was doubly out of control in this instance: he had sex outside marriage, and engaged in sexual acts that were outside the realm of marital sex.

Vasant, who had watched pornographic films after marriage, spoke elliptically about sexual acts permitted in marriage. He opined that any man would feel like doing some of the things he saw being done in these films, but a man "will not do such a thing with his own wife, maybe with an outside woman." Because he considered his desire as reasonable, he claimed that control was even harder. Few Indian studies on sexual behavior list the type of sex acts performed by sex workers. One study of Calcutta sex workers (Jana and Chakroborty 1994) reported that while the "usual mode" of sexual intercourse was vaginal, the majority of sex workers also practiced oral sex, and one-quarter practiced group sex.[12] Sex outside marriage could provide men with alternative sexual practices, which they considered more interesting than marital sex. Yet this analysis of men's narratives suggests that men sought honor through claims of resisting nonnormative sex.

SEX OUTSIDE MARRIAGE: LOSS OF CONTROL AND HONOR

Male respondents frequently mentioned controlling one's desire to have sex with a woman other than one's wife as a form of sexual control. I did not get the impression that all male respondents, if given social sanction, would have sex outside marriage. Rather, men spoke of the nonavailability of extramarital sex as a kind of loss. Societal double standards ensured that men who had extramarital sexual relations were censured less than their female partners were; yet the existence of censures helped men maintain control. Several men spoke of wanting to avoid the dishonor of having wives and kin discover their extramarital relationships. Gopal said that men would not admit having sexual relations outside marriage because of "shame."

> Articulating a widespread local belief that regular provisioning was a fundamental mark of a responsible man, Ramesh said he did not want to "lower his head with the shame of being known as one who did not provide for his family." Some men juxtaposed sex outside marriage and economic provisioning. Men reportedly avoided sex outside marriage, even when sex at home was boring, because they were uneasy paying for transient pleasures with scarce money that could be spent on

the family. Even a one-time extramarital episode was expensive, and men weighed the benefit against other ways the family could use the money.

. . . (M)en viewed the desire for sex outside marriage as their unreasonable craving for sexual pleasure which, putatively, was already available to them through marriage. Also related was the notion of the issues to which responsible men should give primacy, namely, family provision and stability and sexual control.

COMPETING MASCULINITIES, COMPETING CLAIMS

Control was seen as a necessary practice to further a family's social advancement. Men who practiced sexual control made statements similar to the following, which was Bashir's rationale for sexual control:

> One does feel sexual desire, but we have to keep control over ourselves because we want to move ahead in life. So, even if we have the desire in the mind, the body should avoid it.

Honorable men were those who, from the perspective of their families, neighbors, and communities, had moved ahead in their lives. In the congested living environment of slum characterized by one-room houses with porous walls, the boundaries between private and public life were slippery. Family life spilled onto the streets; neighbors saw, heard, and talked about the goings-on in each other's houses. A man's wife and the community around empathized with men who tried to advance in life through the performance of honorable masculinity and were critical of men who did not. Men who did not adhere to local notions of honorable masculinity, particularly economic provisioning, were labeled "weak" or a "mouth to feed." Mahmood expressed this belief as follows: "My wife doesn't work. When I am working, where is the need for her to work?" In reality, women in Kaamgar Nagar worked to support their families and reportedly persuaded husbands to put aside concerns about male honor in favor of economic stability through women's wage work. Lakshmi's narrative elaborates this point.

> The children are growing up and expenses are increasing. I wanted to work, but he would say, "No, don't work. The woman of the house should not go out." Now that I am on this job, he feels ashamed. He says that in our family, no woman before me went out to earn money. People talk. They say, "Is this man so weak that he is sending his wife to work?" That's why he told me that if I am going to work, it is on my own responsibility. Nobody should accuse him that he sent his wife to work, that he is weak. There should be no talk like this.

Men's concerns about personal honor constrained customary ideas about gendered divisions of labor and marital power relations. Like Lakshmi, two of every three women we interviewed worked to complement the man's earnings, and one in three women was the main wage earner of the family. In contrast, all the men we interviewed claimed to be regular providers with stay-at-home wives, have no addictions, and control their wives without excessive use of force.[13] Ten male respondents went further and claimed to practice sexual control. In sharp contrast to men's claims—and some women's claims for their men—we learned of dishonorable masculinities from female respondents. In such narratives, men were portrayed as being unreliable or nonproviders who were addicted to gambling or alcohol, having extramarital sexual relations, and being "excessively" physically violent toward the wife and or children.[14] I present segments of three women's narratives, each of which highlights women's perspectives on (dis) honor and masculinity.

Farida highlighted the reversal of traditional gendered division of labor when she described her husband as follows: "Today he is not feeding me. I am feeding him." Farida's husband worked irregularly, although he was a skilled mechanic who, she claimed, could find work easily. She worked as a construction laborer to make ends meet. As their financial situation deteriorated, Farida removed her two older children from school and put them to work with her. Additionally, she herself started working night shifts at an export factory.

However, after some time, he stopped working and at the time we interviewed her, Farida was working her day job and night shifts at the export factory, and she reported that she and her husband were . . . objects of neighborhood talk. This vignette reveals the engendered nature of honorability where the man's "dishonorable" actions were as severely censured by his neighbors as the necessary wage-earning, yet allegedly honor-damaging, actions of his wife.

Girija recounted the story of her neighbors' reactions to her husband's extramarital activities.

> My husband was going behind one woman in our area. That woman's brother saw him with me. He asked, "Who is she, what is she to you?" My husband said, "My wife." Then that woman's brother said, "Despite having a wife, why are you behind my sister?" He slapped my husband a few times. Now [that man] meets me in the bazaar sometimes and asks me whether my husband behaves properly.

This vignette indicates that neighbors differentiated among actions of the individuals in a marital dyad and awarded respect accordingly. It also indicates that cultural expectations and public surveillance constrain men to control their actions. Similar to the case of Farida above and that of Sheila to follow, Girija's narrative shows the workings of public evaluation of individual actions of men and women to accord personal and family honor.

Sheila noted that word had spread in their community that her husband's family was "not good." She observed,

> Marriages do not take place in their family. They are unreliable providers, alcoholics, wife beaters. Only [her husband] is married. His older brother is single. The one older than him, he married a woman but would not work and feed the family.

She left him and married somebody else. And there is yet another one older than him. He tricked a girl to marry him saying that things are good at our place. But when the girl came here and saw the situation, she left within three months. When he went to bring her back, her parents beat him and sent him away. Now, marriages do not take place in their family.

This narrative shows that, contrary to received ideas about women's actions shaping family honor, it was the cumulative effect of actions of individual men of a family and public talk about these actions that damaged their personal and family honor.

Women's narratives, like the ones just presented, indicate that individual (in)actions were consequential for personal and family honor and that men lost honor through public knowledge of and women's discourses on men's actions. Instead of being tied to women's actions alone, personal and family honor in this framework are also defined by men's actions. Women's discourses suggest that urban residents differentiate between family and individual honor and the personal honor of individuals in marital dyads. This explains why women can claim personal honor while being married to men who dishonor families through their actions.

EMERGING HONORABLE MASCULINITIES

The question still remains, however, what do men gain through claims to practice sexual control, a private action, when they can gain honor through public actions such as providing for their families and being moderate in other activities? This analysis of honorable and dishonorable masculinities in a working-class community of Mumbai suggests that masculinities and men's personal honor are co-constituted through men's own actions, private and public,[15] sexual and otherwise, and women's discourses about men's actions. Contemporaneously, emerging masculinities are shaped by, and in turn shape, emerging femininities.

Mature, responsible men in the *grihastha*—householder—stage were expected to maintain a balance among public actions of pursuing economic advancement and social and religious commitments and private actions of pursuing sexual pleasure. Working-class men of Mumbai found it hard to provide regularly and/or adequately for their families; often, they resorted to borrowing large sums of money to meet family needs. When men did not make regular economic provisions for the family, their wives had to seek wage work. Women became de facto heads of families and acted in ways that could be perceived by their husbands and communities as being out of the bounds of male control, although women and families also acknowledged the circumstances and the necessity of women taking on these responsibilities. Women worked outside the house for wages and made independent decisions relating to family concerns, children, and expenditure of money; some assertive women resisted coercive marital sex. Thus, autonomous wives challenged men's efforts to forge traditional, honorable masculinities.

In situations of fluid gender roles and authority, men sought honor to command influence and renegotiate power relations between themselves and their wives. . . . Working-class men in contemporary Mumbai sought to reestablish a dominant position in their families through the accrual of personal honor, at least in the sexual arena, which then would legitimate their claim to power and position as head of family. Alter's (1994, 55) point . . . that men in positions of power, when confronted by what they perceive to be an almost apocalyptic transformation of society, are forced to see the extreme contingency and the fictional basis of their gendered position. As a result, they critically deconstruct elements of that ideology in search of a more primary, natural truth about themselves and claim to practice celibacy to embody their gender. By locating a "truth" of their gendered identities in sexual self-control, some contemporary working-class Mumbai men translate an ideology of domination into an insidious form of biological determinism and as a means to claim moral piety and personal honor.

Women and men worked to create positive evaluations for their responses to changing social realities such as autonomous wives and men who "allowed" the existence of such wives. Discursively, men constructed themselves as honorable by presenting themselves as moderate and in control. The concepts of *moderation* and *excess* show the linkages between sexual control and honor. The shared belief of the local people was that men who practiced moderation in observable activities such as earning money, consuming alcohol, and controlling their wives were also assumed to be moderate in their private actions. Men's primary gain through sexual control is the honor of being perceived by their wives, families, and neighbors as honorable men. Some men reportedly sought honor through the practice of moderation in their sexual and familial lives, while others indulged in excesses and continued to be unreliable providers. Therefore, men who claimed to practice sexual control, despite their difficult economic situation, increasingly autonomous wives, and social sanction to enjoy conjugal rights, could claim personal honor. This is a source of their view of themselves as honorable, in sharp contrast to men in similar circumstances who lost control of themselves and resorted to "unmanly" behavior.

Women, in contrast to men, used the concept of *understanding* husbands to seek positive valuation and honor for an emerging form of masculinity that allowed women to work for wages, assume greater responsibility and decision-making power in the home, and assume greater control of marital sexual experiences and that did not readily resort to violence to exert authority over women. Normalizing this new masculinity serves to normalize a newly emerging autonomous femininity. Formerly, gendered identities and honor were based on men's ideas of women's actions, thereby allowing men to define idealized gendered identities and relations of domination and resistance between men and women. By reversing this pattern and constructing honor also through women's ideas of men's actions, urban working-class women are recasting and stretching the contours of honorable

masculinities and femininities and gender relations. When women discursively construct male honor as related to men's actions in the area of provisioning, (absence of) violence against women, and sexual control, they provoke men to assume responsibility for their personal and family honor. . . . Women's discourses on men's actions also facilitate the emergence and acceptability of a "softer" masculinity in contrast to other masculinities that are characterized by consumption (Anandhi, Jeyaranjan, and Krishnan 2002; Osella and Osella 2000), violence (Butalia 2000; Menon and Bhasin 1998) or sexual dominance of women (George 1998; Khan et al. 1996). Through discourse, women seek to normalize an assertive, autonomous femininity that exists alongside this emerging masculinity.

NOTES

1. Formerly known as Bombay, Mumbai lies on India's west coast and is India's commercial capital.
2. And other emerging social realities. For an account of emerging Dalit (formerly untouchable) masculinity in the context of changing caste relations in a rural Indian context, see Anandhi, Jeyaranjan, and Krishnan (2002).
3. The author conceptualized the study of which these data form one part. She interviewed female respondents and participated in focus-group discussions and observations. A male researcher assistant, under the supervision of the author, conducted interviews with male respondents.
4. The men who refused to participate probably differed from those who did; they were, however, demographically similar to the participants. The participants came from Hindu, Muslim, and Buddhist communities, mainly from Maharashtra State (of which Mumbai is the capital), with a few from other Indian states. However, there were no major differences along community lines with respect to data described in this article.
5. In 1995, the exchange rate for the U.S. dollar was approximately thirty-eight rupees for one dollar.
6. It is interesting to note that none of the men mentioned masturbation in their discussion of sexual control. However, for a discussion of masturbation as a sexual illness that resulted from "excess" and, hence,

implicitly, from lack of self-control, see Verma, Rangaiyan, and Narkhede (n.d.). I thank Adele Clarke for bringing this point to my attention.

7. All names used are pseudonyms.

8. For a discussion of urban middle-class Indian women's constructions of "understanding" husbands, see Puri (1999, 141–43).

9. Thirty-one of sixty-five female respondents reported the experience of sexual coercion by husbands, and fifteen reported that husbands had extramarital relationships.

10. Condom use was rare among this group of men. Less than 1 percent of them reported regular use of condoms.

11. The deep sense of shame involved when a man contracts a sexually transmitted infection has been reported by HIV-positive men; see Bharat (1997).

12. Recent unpublished studies of male sexual activities from various rural and urban locations in India indicate that men who practice extramarital sex reported a variety of sexual acts: vaginal, oral, and anal sex practiced individually with a woman partner and also in groups of men with one or more women (Bert Pelto, pers. comm., March 9, 2004).

13. This is no doubt an artifact of self-selection, as we only formally interviewed those men and women who volunteered to do so.

14. Of the sixty-five we interviewed formally, thirty-four claimed they could not rely on their husbands for regular economic support, thirty-two reported experiences of physical violence from the husband, thirty-five reported to have husbands who abused alcohol, fifteen reported that husbands had extramarital relations and/or "second wives," and thirty-one reported to experience of sexual coercion by the husband. These statistics also are an artifact of self-selection. It appears that the majority of men and women who participated considered themselves to embody local ideas of honorable gender identity.

15. Indeed, characterization of actions as private or public are erroneous, as such distinctions blur in real-life situations.

References

Alter, J. S. 1994. Celibacy, sexuality, and the transformation of gender into nationalism in north India. *Journal of Asian Studies* 53:45–66.

Anandhi, S., J. Jeyaranjan, and R. Krishnan. 2002. Work, caste and competing masculinities: Notes from a Tamil village. *Economic and Political Weekly* 26 (October): 1–16.

Balmer, D. H., E. Gikundi, M. Kanyotu, and R. Waithaka. 1995. The negotiating strategies determining coitus in stable heterosexual relationships. *Health Transition Review* 5:85–95.

Bharat, S. 1997. Household and community responses to HIV/AIDS: Executive summary of a study in Mumbai. *Indian Journal of Social Work* 58:90–98.

Butalia, U. 2000. *The other side of silence: Voices from the partition of India.* Durham, NC: Duke University Press.

Dube, L. 1986. On the construction of gender. Hindu girls in patriarchal India. *Economic and Political Weekly* 30 (April): WS11–19.

George, A. 1998. Differential perspectives of men and women in Mumbai, India, on sexual relations and negotiations within marriage. *Reproductive Health Matters* 6:87–96.

Gold, A. G. 1994. Gender, violence and power: Rajasthani stories of shakti. In *Women as subjects: South Asian histories,* edited by N. Kumar, 68–90. New Delhi, India: Stree.

Hammersley, M., and P. Atkinson. 1995. *Ethnography principles in practice.* New York: Routledge.

Helitzer-Allen, D., M. Makhambera, and A. M Wangel. 1994. Obtaining sensitive information: The need for more than focus groups. *Reproductive Health Matters* 3:75–81

Jana, S., and A. K. Chakroborty. 1994. Community based survey of STD/HIV infection among commercial sex workers in Calcutta, India. Part II. Sexual behavior, knowledge and attitude towards STD. *Journal of Communicable Diseases* 26:168–71.

Jefferey, P., R. Jeffrey, and A. Lyon. 1989. *Labour pains and labour powers: Women and childbearing in India.* London: Zed Books.

Khan, M. E., R. Townsend, R. Sinha, and S. Lakhanpal. 1996. Sexual violence within marriage. *Seminar,* no. 447:32–35.

Kumar, N. 1994. *Women as subjects: South Asian histories.* New Delhi, India: Stree.

Menon, R., and K. Bhasin. 1998. *Borders & boundaries: Women in India's partition.* New Brunswick, NJ: Rutgers University Press.

Osella, F., and C. Osella. 2000. Migration, money and masculinity in Kerala. *Journal of the Royal Anthropological Institute* 6:117–33.

Puri, J. 1999. *Women, body, desire in post-colonial India: Narratives of gender and sexuality.* New York: Routledge.

Ram, K. 1991. *Mukkuvar women: Gender, hegemony and capitalist transformation in a south Indian fishing community.* London: Zed Press.

Sharma, M., and U. Vanjare. 1993. The political economy of reproductive activities in a Rajasthan village. In *Explorations of South Asian systems,* edited by A. W. Clarke, 24–65. New Delhi, India: Oxford University Press.

Verma, R. K., G. Rangaiyan, and S. Narkhede. n.d. Cultural perceptions and categorization of male sexual health problems by practitioners and men in a Mumbai slum population. Unpublished report.

Introduction to Reading 15

Maria Alexandra Lepowsky is an anthropologist who lived among the Melanesian people of Vanatinai, a small, remote island near New Guinea, from 1977 to 1979, for 2 months in 1981, and again for 3 months in 1987. She chose Vanatinai, which literally means "motherland," because she wanted to do research in a place where "the status of women" is high. The egalitarianism of the Vanatinai challenges the Western belief in the universality of male dominance and female subordination.

1. What is the foundation of women's high status and gender equality among the people of Vanatinai?

2. What does gender equality mean on Vanatinai? Does it mean that women and men split everything fifty-fifty? Are men and women interchangeable?

3. What are the similarities and differences between the egalitarianism of the Gerai people (depicted in Christine Helliwell's article in this chapter) and that of the people of Vanatinai?

GENDER AND POWER

Maria Alexandra Lepowsky

Vanatinai customs are generally egalitarian in both philosophy and practice. Women and men have equivalent rights to and control of the means of production, the products of their own labor, and the products of others. Both sexes have access to the symbolic capital of prestige, most visibly through participation in ceremonial exchange and mortuary ritual. Ideologies of male superiority or right of authority over women are notably absent, and ideologies of gender equivalence are clearly articulated. Multiple levels of gender ideologies are largely, but not entirely, congruent. Ideologies in turn are largely congruent with practice and individual actions in expressing gender equivalence, complementarity, and overlap.

There are nevertheless significant differences in social influence and prestige among persons. These are mutable, and they fluctuate over the lifetime of the individual. But Vanatinai social relations are egalitarian overall, and sexually egalitarian in particular, in that at each stage in the life cycle all persons, female and male, have equivalent autonomy and control over their own actions, opportunity to achieve both publicly and privately acknowledged influence and power over the actions of others, and access to valued goods, wealth, and prestige. The quality of generosity, highly valued in both sexes, is explicitly modeled after parental nurture. Women are not viewed as polluting or dangerous to themselves or others in their persons, bodily fluids, or sexuality.

Vanatinai sociality is organized around the principle of personal autonomy. There are no chiefs, and nobody has the right to tell another adult what to do. This philosophy also results in some extremely permissive childrearing and a strong degree of tolerance for the idiosyncrasies of other people's behavior. While working together, sharing, and generosity are admirable, they are strictly voluntary. The selfish and antisocial person might be ostracized, and others will not give to him or her. If kinfolk, in-laws, or neighbors disagree, even with a powerful and influential big man or big woman, they have the option, frequently taken, of moving to another hamlet where they have ties and can expect access to land for gardening and foraging. Land is communally held by matrilineages, but each person has multiple rights to request and be given space to make a garden on land held by others, such as the mother's father's matrilineage. Respect and tolerance for the will and idiosyncrasies of individuals is reinforced by fear of their potential knowledge of witchcraft or sorcery.

Anthropological discussions of women, men, and society over the last one hundred years have been framed largely in terms of "the status of women," presumably unvarying and shared by all women in all social situations. Male dominance and female subordination have thus until recently been perceived as easily identified and often as human universals. If women are indeed universally subordinate, this implies a universal primary cause: hence the search for a single underlying reason for male dominance and female subordination, either material or ideological.

More recent writings in feminist anthropology have stressed multiple and contested gender statuses and ideologies and the impacts of historical forces, variable and changing social contexts, and conflicting gender ideologies. Ambiguity and contradiction, both within and between levels of ideology and social practice, give both women and men room to assert their value and exercise power. Unlike in many cultures where men stress women's innate inferiority, gender relations on Vanatinai are not contested, or antagonistic: there are no male versus female ideologies which vary markedly or directly contradict each other. Vanatinai mythological motifs, beliefs about supernatural power, cultural ideals of the sexual division of labor and of the qualities inherent to men and women, and the customary freedoms and restrictions upon each sex at different points in the life course all provide ideological underpinnings of sexual equality.

Since the 1970s writings on the anthropology of women, in evaluating degrees of female power and influence, have frequently focused on the disparity between the "ideal" sex role pattern of a culture, often based on an ideology of male dominance, publicly proclaimed or enacted by men, and often by women as well, and the "real" one, manifested by the actual behavior of individuals. This approach seeks to uncover female social participation, overt or covert, official or unofficial, in key events and decisions and to learn how women negotiate their social positions. The focus on social and individual "action" or "practice" is prominent more generally in cultural anthropological theory of recent years. Feminist analyses of contradictions between gender ideologies of female inferiority and the realities of women's and men's daily lives—the actual balance of power in household and community—have helped to make this focus on the actual behavior of individuals a wider theoretical concern.[1]

In the Vanatinai case gender ideologies in their multiple levels and contexts emphasize the value of women and provide a mythological charter for the degree of personal autonomy and freedom of choice manifested in real women's lives. Gender ideologies are remarkably similar (though not completely, as I discuss below) as they are manifested situationally, in philosophical statements by women and men, in the ideal pattern of the sexual division of labor, in taboos and proscriptions, myth, cosmology, magic, ritual, the supernatural balance of power, and in the codifications of custom. Women are not characterized as weak or inferior. Women and men are valorized for the same qualities of strength, wisdom, and generosity. If possessed of these qualities an individual woman or man will act in ways which bring prestige not only to the actor but to the kin and residence groups to which she or he belongs.

Nevertheless, there is no single relationship between the sexes on Vanatinai. Power relations and relative influence vary with the individuals, sets of roles, situations, and historical moments involved. Gender ideologies embodied in myths, beliefs, prescriptions for role-appropriate behavior, and personal statements sometimes contradict each other or are contradicted by the behavior of individuals.

* * *

Material and Ideological Bases of Equality

Does equality or inequality, including between men and women, result from material or ideological causes? We cannot say whether an idea preceded or followed specific economic and social circumstances. Does the idea give rise to the act, or does the act generate an ideology that justifies it or mystifies it?

If they are congruent ideology and practice reinforce one another. And if multiple levels of ideology are in accord social forms are more likely to remain unchallenged and fundamentally unchanged. Where levels of ideology, or ideology and practice, are at odds, the circumstances of social life are more likely to be challenged by those who seek a reordering of social privileges justified according to an alternative interpretation of ideology. When social life embodies these kinds of contradictions, the categories of people in power—aristocrats, the rich, men—spend a great deal of energy maintaining their power. They protect their material resources, subdue the disenfranchised with public or private violence, coercion, and repression, and try to control public and private expressions of ideologies of political and religious power.

On Vanatinai, where there is no ideology of male dominance, the material conditions for gender equality are present. Women—and their brothers—control the means of production. Women own land, and they inherit land, pigs, and valuables from their mothers, their mothers' brothers, and sometimes from their fathers equally with men. They have the ultimate decision-making power over the distribution of staple foods that belong jointly to their kinsmen and that their kinsmen or husbands have helped labor to grow. They are integrated into the prestige economy, the ritualized exchanges of ceremonial valuables. Ideological expressions, such as the common saying that the woman is the owner of the garden, or the well-known myth of the first exchange between two female beings, validate material conditions.

I do not believe it would be possible to have a gender egalitarian society, where prevailing expressions of gender ideology were egalitarian or valorized both sexes to the same degree, without material control by women of land, means of subsistence, or wealth equivalent to that of men. This control would encompass anything from foraging rights, skills, tools, and practical and sacred knowledge to access to high-paying, prestigious jobs and the knowledge and connections it takes to get them. Equal control of the means of production, then, is one necessary precondition of gender equality. Vanatinai women's major disadvantage is their lack of access to a key tool instrumental in gaining power and prestige, the spear. Control of the means of production is potentially greater in a matrilineal society.

* * *

GENDER IDEOLOGIES AND PRACTICE IN DAILY LIFE

In Melanesian societies the power of knowing is privately owned and transmitted, often through ties of kinship, to heirs or younger supporters. It comes not simply from acquiring skills or the experience and the wisdom of mature years but is fundamentally a spiritual power that derives from ancestors and other spirit forces.

In gender-segregated societies, such as those that characterize most of Melanesia, this spiritual knowledge power is segregated as well into a male domain through male initiations or the institutions of men's houses or male religious cults. Most esoteric knowledge—and the power over others that derives from it—is available to Vanatinai women if they can find a kinsperson or someone else willing to teach it to them. There are neither exclusively male nor female collectivities on Vanatinai nor characteristically male versus female domains or patterns of sociality (cf. Strathern 1987:76).

Decisions taken collectively by Vanatinai women and men within one household, hamlet, or lineage are political ones that reverberate well beyond the local group, sometimes literally hundreds of miles beyond. A hundred years ago they included decisions of war and peace. Today they include the ritualized work of kinship, more particularly of the matrilineage, in mortuary ritual. Mortuary feasts, and the interisland and inter-hamlet exchanges of ceremonial valuables that support them, memorialize the marriages that tied three matrilineages together, that of the deceased, the deceased's father, and the widowed spouse. Honoring these ties of alliance, contracted by individuals but supported by their kin, and threatened by the dissolution of death, is the major work of island politics. . . .

The small scale, fluidity (cf. Collier and Rosaldo 1981), and mobility of social life on Vanatinai, especially in combination with matriliny, are conducive of egalitarian social relations between men and women and old and young. They promote an ethic of respect for the individual, which must be integrated with the ethic of cooperation essential for survival in a subsistence economy. People must work out conflict through face to face negotiation, or existing social ties will be broken by migration, divorce, or death through sorcery or witchcraft.

Women on Vanatinai are physically mobile, traveling with their families to live with their own kin and then the kin of their spouse, making journeys in quest of valuables, and attending mortuary feasts. They are said to have traveled for these reasons even in precolonial times when the threat of attack was a constant danger. The generally greater physical mobility of men in human societies is a significant factor in sexual asymmetries of power, as it is men who generally negotiate and regulate relationships with outside groups (cf. Ardener 1975:6).

Vanatinai women's mobility is not restricted by ideology or by taboo, and women build their own far-ranging personal networks of social relationships. Links in these networks may be activated as needed by the woman to the benefit of her kin or hamlet group. Women are confined little by taboos or community pressures. They travel, choose their own marriage partners or lovers, divorce at will, or develop reputations as wealthy and generous individuals active in exchange.

BIG MEN, BIG WOMEN, AND CHIEFS

Vanatinai giagia, male and female, match Sahlins's (1989) classic description of the Melanesian big man, except that the role of gia is gender-blind. There has been renewed interest among anthropologists in recent years in the big man form of political authority.[2] The Vanatinai case of the female and male giagia offers an intriguing perspective. . . .

Any individual on Vanatinai, male or female, may try to become known as a gia by choosing to exert the extra effort to go beyond the minimum contributions to the mortuary feasts expected of every adult. He or she accumulates ceremonial valuables and other goods both in order to give them away in acts of public generosity and to honor obligations to exchange partners from the local area as well as distant islands. There may be more than one gia in a particular hamlet, or even household, or there may be none. A woman may have considerably more prestige and influence than her husband because of her reputation for acquiring and redistributing valuables. While there are more men than women who are extremely active in exchange, there are some women who are far more active than the majority of men.

Giagia of either sex are only leaders in temporary circumstances and if others wish to follow, as when they host a feast, lead an exchange expedition, or organize the planting of a communal yam garden. Decisions are made by consensus, and the giagia of both sexes influence others through their powers of persuasion, their reputations for ability, and their knowledge, both of beneficial magic and ritual and of sorcery or witchcraft. . . .

On Vanatinai power and influence over the actions of others are gained by achievement and demonstrated superior knowledge and skill, whether in the realm of gardening, exchange, healing, or sorcery. Those who accumulate a surplus of resources are expected to be generous and share with their neighbors or face the threat of the sorcery or witchcraft of the envious. Both women and men are free to build their careers through exchange. On the other hand both women and men are free not to strive toward renown as giagia but to work for their own families or simply to mind their own business. They can also achieve the respect of their peers, if they seek it at all, as loving parents, responsible and hardworking lineage mates and affines, good gardeners, hunters, or fishers, or skilled healers, carvers, or weavers.

Mead (1935) observes that societies vary in the degree to which "temperament types" or "approved social personalities" considered suitable for each sex or a particular age category differ from each other. On Vanatinai there is wide variation in temperament and behavior among islanders of the same sex and age. The large amount of overlap between the roles of men and women on Vanatinai leads to a great deal of role flexibility, allowing both individual men and women the freedom to specialize in the activities they personally enjoy, value, are good at performing, or feel like doing at a particular time. There is considerable freedom of choice in shaping individual lifestyles.

An ethic of personal autonomy, one not restricted to the powerful, is a key precondition of social equality. Every individual on Vanatinai from the smallest child to an aged man or woman possesses a large degree of autonomy. Idiosyncrasies of personality and character are generally tolerated and respected. When you ask why someone does or does not do something, your friends will say, emphatically and expressively, "We [inclusive we: you and I both] don't know," "It is something of theirs" [their way], or, "She doesn't want to."

Islanders say that it is not possible to know why a person behaves a certain way or what thoughts generate an action. Persisting in a demand to "know" publicly the thoughts of others is dangerous, threatening, and invasive. Vanatinai people share, in part, the perspectives identified with postmodern discussions of the limits of ethnographic representation: it is impossible to know another person's thoughts or feelings. If you try they are likely to deceive you to protect their own privacy or their own interests. Your knowing is unique to you. It is your private property that you transmit only at your own volition, as when you teach magical spells to a daughter or sister's son.[3]

The prevailing social sanction is also individualistic: the threat of somebody else's sorcery or witchcraft if you do not do what they want or if you arouse envy or jealousy. But Vanatinai cultural ideologies stress the strength of individual will in the face of the coercive pressures of custom, threat of sorcery, and demands to share.

This leads to a Melanesian paradox: the ethic of personal autonomy is in direct conflict to the ethic of giving and sharing so highly valued on Vanatinai, as in most Melanesian cultures. Nobody can make you share, short of stealing from you or killing you if you refuse them. You have to want to give: your nurture, your labor, your valuables, and your person. This is where persuasion comes in. It comes from the pressure of other people, the force of shame, and magical seduction made potent by supernatural agency. Vanatinai custom supplies a final, persuasive argument to resolve this paradox: by giving, you not only strengthen your lineage and build its good name, you make yourself richer and more powerful by placing others in your debt.

What can people in other parts of the world learn from the principles of sexual equality in Vanatinai custom and philosophy? Small scale facilitates Vanatinai people's emphasis on face-to-face negotiations of interpersonal conflicts without the delegation of political authority to a small group of middle-aged male elites. It also leaves room for an ethic of respect for the will of the individual regardless of age or sex. A culture that is egalitarian and nonhierarchical overall is more likely to have egalitarian relations between men and women.

Males and females on Vanatinai have equivalent autonomy at each life cycle stage. As adults they have similar opportunities to influence the actions of others. There is a large amount of overlap between the roles and activities of women and men, with women occupying public, prestige-generating roles. Women share control of the production and the distribution of valued goods, and they inherit property. Women as well as men participate in the exchange of valuables, they organize feasts, they officiate at important rituals such as those for yam planting or healing, they counsel their kinfolk, they speak out and are listened to in public meetings, they possess valuable magical knowledge, and they work side by side in most subsistence activities. Women's role as nurturing parent is highly valued and is the dominant metaphor for the generous men and women who gain renown and influence over others by accumulating and then giving away valuable goods.

But these same characteristics of respect for individual autonomy, role overlap, and public participation of women in key subsistence and prestige domains of social life are also possible in large-scale industrial and agricultural societies. The Vanatinai example suggests that sexual equality is facilitated by an overall ethic of respect for and equal treatment of all categories of individuals, the decentralization of political power, and inclusion of all categories of persons (for example, women and ethnic minorities) in public positions of authority and influence. It requires greater role overlap through increased integration of the workforce, increased control by women and minorities of valued goods—property, income, and educational credentials—and increased recognition of the social value of parental care. The example of Vanatinai shows that the subjugation of women by men is not a human universal, and it is not inevitable. Sex role patterns and gender ideologies are closely related to overall social systems of power and prestige. Where these systems stress personal autonomy and egalitarian social relations among all adults, minimizing the formal authority of one person over another, gender equality is possible.

Notes

1. See, for example, Rogers (1975) and Collier and Rosaldo (1981) on ideal versus real gender relations. Ortner (1984) summarizes approaches to practice; cf. Bourdieu (1977).

2. The appropriateness of using the big man institution to define Melanesia versus a Polynesia characterized by chiefdoms, the relationship of big men to social equality, rank, and stratification, and the interactions of this form of leadership with colonialism and modernization are central issues in recent anthropological writings on big men (e.g., Brown 1987, Godelier 1986, Sahlins 1989, Strathern 1987, Thomas 1989, Lederman 1991). I discuss the implications of the Vanatinai case of the giagia at greater length in Lepowsky (1990).

3. See, for example, Clifford (1983), Clifford and Marcus (1986), and Marcus and Fischer (1986) on representations. In this book I have followed my own cultural premises and not those of Vanatinai by publicly attributing thoughts, motives, and feelings to others and by trying to find the shapes in a mass of chaotic and sometimes contradictory statements and actions. But my Vanatinai friends say, characteristically, that my writing is "something of mine"—my business.

REFERENCES

Ardener, Edwin. 1975. "Belief and the Problem of Women." In Shirley Ardener, ed., *Perceiving Women*. London: Malaby.

Bourdieu, Pierre. 1977. *Outline of a Theory of Practice*. T. R. Nice. Cambridge: Cambridge University Press.

Brown, Paula. 1987. "New Men and Big Men: Emerging Social Stratification in the Third World, A Case Study from the New Guinea Highlands." *Ethnology* 26:87–106.

Clifford, James. 1983. "On Ethnographic Authority." *Representations* 1:118–146.

Clifford, James, and George Marcus, eds. 1986. *Writing Culture: The Poetics and Politics of Ethnography*. Berkeley: University of California Press.

Collier, Jane, and Michelle Rosaldo. 1981. "Politics and Gender in Simple Societies." In Sherry Ortner and Harriet Whitehead, eds., *Sexual Meanings: The Cultural Construction of Gender and Sexuality*. Cambridge: Cambridge University Press.

Godelier, Maurice. 1986. *The Making of Great Men: Male Domination and Power Among the New Guinea Baruya*. Cambridge: Cambridge University Press.

Lederman, Rena. 1991. "'Interests' in Exchange: Increment, Equivalence, and the Limits of Bigmanship." In Maurice Godelier and Marilyn Strathern, eds., *Big Men and Great Men: Personifications of Power in Melanesia*. Cambridge: Cambridge University Press.

Lepowsky, Maria. 1990. "Big Men, Big Women, and Cultural Autonomy." *Ethnology* 29(10): 35–50.

Marcus, George, and Michael Fischer, eds. 1986. *Anthropology as Cultural Critique: An Experimental Moment in the Human Sciences*. Chicago: University of Chicago Press.

Mead, Margaret. 1935. *Sex and the Temperament in Three Primitive Societies*. New York: William Morrow.

Ortner, Sherry. 1984. "Theory in Anthropology Since the Sixties." *Comparative Studies in Society and History* 26(1): 126–166.

Rogers, Susan Carol. 1975. "Female Forms of Power and the Myth of Male Dominance: A Model of Female/Male Interaction in Peasant Society." *American Ethnologist* 2:727–756.

Sahlins, Marshall. 1989. "Comment: The Force of Ethnology: Origins and Significance of the Melanesia/Polynesia Division." *Current Anthropology* 30:36–37.

Strathern, Marilyn. 1987. "Introduction." In Marilyn Strathern, ed., *Dealing with Inequality: Analysing Gender Relations in Melanesia and Beyond*. Cambridge: Cambridge University Press.

Thomas, Nicholas. 1989. "The Force of Ethnology: Origins and Significance of the Melanesia/Polynesia Division." *Current Anthropology* 30:27–34.

❦ Topics for Further Examination ❧

- Locate and read scholarly research on the Hijras of India, the Fa'afafines of Samoa, and the Kathoey of Thailand.
- Look up scholarly studies that discuss the special history of the egalitarian gender system of the Iroquois Confederacy.
- Challenge ethnocentrism by exploring scholarly and journalistic accounts of the ways in which Middle Eastern women, including women who wear the hijab, have played key roles in the uprisings in Egypt, Tunisia, Bahrain, and elsewhere in that area of the world.

PART II

PATTERNS

4

LEARNING AND DOING GENDER

We began this book by discussing the shaping of gender in Western and non-Western cultures. Part II expands on the idea of prisms by examining the *patterns* of gendered experiences that emerge from the practices of daily life and the interaction of gender with other socially constructed prisms. Patterns of individuals' lives are influenced by gender and other social prisms, just as multiple patterns are created by the refraction of light as it travels through a kaleidoscope containing prisms.

GENDERED PATTERNS

Social patterns are at the center of social scientists' work. Schwalbe (1998), a sociologist, defines social patterns as "a regularity in the way the world works" (p. 101). For example, driving down the "right" side of the street is a regularity American people appreciate. You will read about different gendered patterns in Part II, many of which are regularities you will find problematic because they deny the individuality of women and men. Clearly, there are exceptions to social patterns; however, these exceptions are in the details, not in the regularity of social behavior itself (Schwalbe, 1998). Patterns in society are not simple and are even contradicted by other patterns. We have rigid gender expectations for things such as which colors are appropriate for children, teens, and even adults. At the same time, we practice resistance to these patterns and fluidity in the way gender is displayed in daily life. For example, an upper-class man might feel comfortable wearing a pink polo shirt to a golf tournament but not so comfortable putting a pink shirt on his 2-year old son.

A deeper understanding of how and why particular social patterns and practices exist helps us interpret our own behavior and the world around us. Gender, as we discussed in Part I, is not a singular pattern of masculinity or femininity that carries from one situation to another. Instead, it is complex, multifaceted, and ever changing, depending on the social context, whom we are with, and where we are. Gender is also interpreted differently based on the community or group we associate with. That is, African American women are much less likely to adhere to idealized forms of gender or, as Karen D. Pyke and Denise L. Johnson labeled it in Chapter 2, hegemonic femininity—White, middle-class femininity. Our behavior in almost all situations is framed within our knowledge of idealized gender—hegemonic masculinity and emphasized femininity. Whether we resist or ridicule gender practices, we are almost always aware of them.

Keep the concepts of hegemonic masculinity and emphasized femininity in mind as we examine social patterns of gender. To illustrate this, let's return to the stereotype discussed in the introduction to this book—that women talk more than men. We know from research that the real social pattern in mixed-gender groups is that men talk more, interrupt more, and change the topic more often than do women (Anderson & Leaper, 1998; Brescoli, 2011; Wood, 1999). The stereotype, while trivializing women's talk and ignoring the dominance of men in mixed-gender groups, maintains the patterns of dominance and subordination associated with hegemonic masculinity and emphasized femininity, influencing women's as well as men's behaviors. Girls—particularly White, middle-class girls—are encouraged to use a pleasant voice and not talk too much. Later, as they grow older and join mixed-gender groups at work or in play, women's voices are often ignored and they are subordinated as they monitor what they say and how often they talk, checking to make sure they are not dominating the conversation. And since gender is relational, others learn that girls talk too much and should either shut up or speak in a "nice voice." Gender is an ever-present force in defining daily behavior and is used in marketing to entice us to "buy into" gender as we purchase all kinds of products (Chapter 5). By examining how these idealized versions of masculinity and femininity pattern daily practices and idealized images of masculinity and femininity, we can better understand the patterns and meanings of our behavior and the behaviors of others.

Gendered patterns of belief and behavior influence us throughout our lives, from birth until old age, in almost every activity in which we engage. Readings in Part II examine the process and consequences of learning to do gender (Chapter 4) and then describe gendered patterns

in work (Chapter 7) and in daily intimate relationships with family and friends (Chapter 8). We also explore how gendered patterns affect our bodies, sexualities, and emotions (Chapter 6), and how patterns of dominance, control, and violence enforce gender patterns (Chapter 9).

The patterns that emerge from the gender kaleidoscope are not unique experiences in individual lives; they are regularities that occur in many people's lives. They are not static patterns that remain the same across lifetimes or history, nor are they singular patterns with one and only one way of doing gender. Gendered patterns are many and fluid across time and space. If you don't pay attention, gendered patterns may seem as though they are individual choices. Institutions and groups enforce gendered patterns and practices in the home, workplace, and daily life, as described in the readings throughout Part II. These patterns overlap and reinforce gender differences and inequalities. For example, gender discrimination in wages affects families' decisions about parenting roles and relationships. Since most men still earn more than most women, the choices of families who wish to break away from idealized gender patterns and practices are limited (see Chapters 7 and 8).

LEARNING AND DOING GENDER

We begin this part of the book by examining the processes by which we acquire self-perceptions and behaviors and learn our culture's expectations for idealized patterns of masculinities and femininities (Chapters 4 and 5). The readings in this chapter emphasize that, regardless of our inability or unwillingness to attain idealized femininity and masculinity, almost everyone in a culture learns what idealized gender is and organizes their lives around those expectations, even if in resistance to them. Of course, the genderscape is complex. While some people resist idealized gender and others try to ignore these signals, some communities develop alternatives to idealized gender, such as that in Irene Padavic and Jonniann Butterfield's article on lesbian co-parenting in Chapter 8. The term sociologists use to describe how we learn gender is *gender socialization*, and sociologists approach it from a variety of different perspectives (Coltrane, 1998).

Socialization is the process of teaching members of a society the values, expectations, and practices of the larger culture. Socialization takes place in all interactions and situations, with families and schools typically having primary responsibility for socializing infants and children in Western societies. Early attempts to explain gender socialization gave little attention to the response of individuals to agents of socialization such as parents, peers, and teachers and to the influence of mass media and a consumer culture. There was an underlying assumption in this early perspective that individuals were blank tablets (tabulae rasae) on which the cultural definitions of idealized gender and other appropriate behaviors were written. This perspective assumed that, as individuals developed, they took on a gender identity appropriate to their biological sex category (Howard & Alamilla, 2001).

Social scientists now realize that individuals are not blank tablets; gender socialization is not just something that is "done" to us. Theorists now describe socialization into gender as a series of complex and dynamic processes. Individuals create, as well as respond to, social stimuli in their environments (Carlton-Ford & Houston, 2001; Howard & Alamilla, 2001). Moreover, socialization doesn't simply end after childhood. Socialization is a process that lasts across one's lifetime, from birth to death (Lutfey & Mortimer, 2003), and occurs continually with everyone we interact with—friends, peers, coworkers, and acquaintances—as well as the environment around us, including mass media. Furthermore, changes in gender ideology occur across the life course as well as across race–gender categories (Vespa, 2009). For example, beauty means something different for a young child, teenager, or older person. Throughout our lives, we assess cues around us and behave as situations dictate. All socialization is, of course, reinforced by societal institutions, as Barbara J. Risman discussed

in her article in Chapter 1. Thus, whether we want it or not, idealized gender is a key factor in determining what is appropriate throughout our lives—even though few of us actually attain an idealized form of gender.

SOCIALIZING CHILDREN

There are many explanations for why children gravitate toward idealized gender-appropriate behavior. Family members are not the only ones who teach children to behave as "good boys" or "good girls." Almost every person a child comes into contact with and virtually all aspects of a child's material world (e.g., toys, books, clothing) reinforce gender. Stories repeated across many generations portray idealized gender in books, as described in the reading by Janice McCabe, Emily Fairchild, Liz Grauerholz, Bernice A. Pescosolido, and Daniel Tope in this chapter. It is not long, then, before most children come to understand that they should be "boys" or "girls" and segregate themselves accordingly. Adults play a major role in teaching gender, as the readings by Emily W. Kane in this chapter and Adie Nelson in Chapter 5 find. Not just parents but also teachers teach gender. When teachers separate children into gender-segregated spaces in lunch lines or playground areas, they reinforce gender differences (Sadker & Sadker, 1994; Thorne, 1993).

Most children quickly understand the idealized gender-appropriate message directed toward them and try to behave accordingly. Although not all boys are dominant and not all girls are subordinate, studies in a variety of areas find that most White boys tend toward active and aggressive behaviors, while most White girls tend to be quieter and more focused on relationships. The patterning for African American boys is similar, where boys who do not act in gender-appropriate ways are seen as "soft" or feminine (Carter, 2005). The article by Richard Mora in this chapter illustrates how Latino boys experience puberty individually and collectively as they struggle to construct "hard" masculine identities. These patterns have been documented in school and in play (e.g., Sadker & Sadker, 1994; Thorne, 1993).

The consequences for gender-appropriate behavior are considerable. Gender-appropriate behavior is related to lower self-confidence and self-esteem for girls (e.g., Eder, 1995; Orenstein, 1994; Spade, 2001), whereas boys are taught to "mask" their feelings and compete with everyone for control, thus isolating themselves and ignoring their own feelings (e.g., Connell, 2000; Messner, 1992; Pollack, 2000).

The dominant pattern of gender expectations, the "pink and blue syndrome" described in Chapter 1 (Paoletti, 2012), begins at birth. As Sharon E. Preves notes in her article in Chapter 1, once external genital identification takes place, immediate expectations for masculine and feminine behavior follow. Exclamations of "He's going to be a great baseball (or football or soccer) player" and "She's so cute" are accompanied by gifts of little sleepers in pink or blue with gender-appropriate decorations. Try as we might, it is very difficult to find gender-neutral clothing for children (see Nelson's article in Chapter 5). These expectations, and the way we treat young children, reinforce idealized gender constructions of dominance and subordination and illustrate how dominant the role of marketing and consumer culture is in defining idealized gender.

SOCIAL INSTITUTIONS AND SOCIALIZATION

Many of our social institutions segregate children and adults by gender as well as playing a major role in creating gendered identities. One very obvious example of institutions separating gender and socializing children differently is the Boy Scouts and Girl Scouts. These are two prominent social institutions organized to socialize children. A controversy occurred in 2012 as to whether to allow a transgendered boy who identified as a girl into the Girl Scouts, challenging formerly rigid gender categorizations used to group children. Despite the absurdity of trying to

separate genders in a world with more gender fluidity, the Girl Scout and Boy Scout organizations still socialize children in gender-specific ways. Boy Scouts are more likely to offer science-based activities and less likely to offer art activities than are the Girl Scouts (Denny, 2011). While the Girl Scouts promote what Denny calls an image of the "up-to-date traditional woman" for young girls, with an emphasis on communal activities, Boy Scout badges are given for activities, with a general focus on ability and assertiveness. By creating these separate spaces with very different expectations for boys and girls, we are socializing our children in gender difference and inequality.

Schools also reinforce separate and unequal spheres for boys and girls (Orenstein, 1994; Sadker & Sadker, 1994; Thorne, 1993). Considerable research by the American Association of University Women (1992, 1998, 1999) documents how schools "shortchange" girls. Schools are social institutions that maintain patterns of power and dominance. Indeed, we teach dominance in schools in patterns of teacher/student interactions such as respecting the responses of boys while encouraging girls to be helpers in the classroom (Grant, 1985; Sadker & Sadker, 1994). A recent study, using data collected from individuals during their high school years (2002, 2004, and 2006) finds that gender socialization in schools varies based on the race of the student. For example, math teachers tend to hold a biased perception of girls' abilities, particularly when comparing the abilities of White girls with those of White boys (Riegle-Crumb & Humphries, 2012). The reading by Maria Charles in this chapter describes how schools reinforce choices related to science, technology, engineering, and mathematics (STEM), eventually solidifying the gender segregation of STEM careers. Unfortunately, gender socialization and expectations continue well into the STEM careers, with some women scientists enforcing gender norms and expectations by distancing themselves from femininity and "typical feminine practices" as other women fight gender discrimination (Rhoton, 2011). Thus, according to Rhoton, women scientists prefer to associate with females who act the role of "scientist" rather than with females who practice femininity, further reinforcing the perception of appropriate gender in science. And, unfortunately, a climate of gender difference and inequality continues, as you will read about in the article by Christine L. Williams, Chandra Muller, and Kristine Kilanski in Chapter 7.

In effect, children are taught that males and females are different and that they are expected to behave accordingly. In Chapter 5, you will read more about how capitalist societies reinforce and maintain gender difference and inequality for children and adults. Television, music, books, clothing, and toys differentiate and prescribe idealized gender behavior for girls and boys. For example, studies of children's books find some distinctive patterns that reinforce idealized forms of gender. As McCabe et al. discuss in their reading in this chapter, boys outnumber girls in books published across the 20th century. Although books continue to depict traditional gender patterns, on the plus side, researchers find that girls and women are more likely to be portrayed in gender-atypical roles in many recent children's books (Gooden & Gooden, 2001).

However, not all boys and men are allowed to be dominant across settings (Eder, 1995), and few girls come close to achieving idealized femininity. Ann Arnett Ferguson (2000) describes how schools discourage African American boys from claiming their Blackness and masculinity. Although White boys may be allowed to be "rambunctious" and disrespectful, African American boys are punished more severely than their White peers when they "act out," and there is less tolerance for African American boys who try to dominate. Girls also exist within a hierarchy of relationships (Eder, 1995). Girls from racial, ethnic, economically disadvantaged, or other subordinated groups must fight even harder to succeed under multiple systems of domination and inequality in schools. To help illustrate this, Bettie (2002) compared the paths to success for upwardly mobile White and Mexican American high school girls and found

some similarities in gender experiences at home and school, such as participation in sports, that facilitated mobility for both groups of girls. There were also differences in their experiences because race was always salient and a barrier for the Mexican American girls. However, Bettie believes that achieving upward mobility may have been easier for these Mexican American girls than for their brothers because it is easier for girls to transgress gender boundaries. Their brothers, on the other hand, felt pressure to "engage in the rituals of proving masculinity" even though this behavior was rejected by those in control at school (p. 419).

Bettie's (2002) study emphasizes the fact that multiple social prisms of difference and inequality create an array of patterns, which would not be possible if gender socialization practices were universal. Individuals' lives are constructed around many factors, including gender. Cultural values and expectations influence, and frequently contradict, the maintenance of hegemonic masculinity and emphasized femininity in Western societies. Pyke and Johnson's reading in Chapter 2 and Mora's article in this chapter illustrate how the practice of gender is strongly influenced by culture. The process of gender socialization is rooted in the principle that women and men are not equal and that the socially constructed categories of difference and inequality (gender, race, ethnicity, class, religion, age, culture, etc.) are legitimate.

Sports, particularly organized sports, provide other examples of how institutionalized activities reinforce the gender identities children learn. Boys learn the meaning of competition and success, including the idea that winning is everything (e.g., Messner, 1992). Girls, on the other hand, are more often found on the edges of the playing field, or on the sides of the playground, watching the boys (Thorne, 1993). And, as you will read in Chapter 9, moms are typically relegated to the sidelines as well, while men coach. Even though more girls are playing sports, Matthew B. Ezzell in his article in this chapter describes a climate in which females are still expected to maintain some level of femininity during athletic competitions. Yet not all children play in the same ways. Goodwin (1990) finds that children from urban, lower-class, high-density neighborhoods—where households are closer together—are more likely to play in mixed-gender and mixed-age groups. In suburban, middle-class households, which are farther apart than urban households, parents are more likely to drive their children to sporting activities or houses to play with same-sex/gender, same-age peers. The consequences of social class and place of residence are that lower-class children are more comfortable with their sexuality as they enter preadolescence and are less likely to gender segregate in school (Goodwin, 1990).

Sports and play continue to segregate us and define gender throughout our lives. Although the formal rules for women's and men's rugby are the same, the reading by Ezzell in this chapter illustrates how adult women pressure themselves and other women to perform emphasized femininity, even when playing by the same game rules as do men. Although women are increasingly participating in traditionally "male" sports activities, the gendered nature of these sports remains in the institutions supporting the activities (Buysse & Embser-Herbert, 2004), the game rules, and the minds of the participants, even in traditionally "male" sports such as basketball (Berlage, 2004), ice hockey (Theberge, 2000), and body building (Wesely, 2001). Socialization into gender does not stop at any particular age but occurs throughout our lifetimes and throughout our activities.

Gender Transgressions

Children learn to display idealized gender behaviors; however, they at times step out of gender-appropriate zones. As noted earlier, girls and women are more likely to transgress and do masculine things than boys and men are to participate in feminine activities. McGuffey and Rich (1999) find that girls who transgress into the "boys' zone" may eventually be respected by their male playmates if they are good at conventionally male activities, such as playing baseball. Boys, however, are harassed and teased when they try to participate in any activity associated with girls (McGuffey & Rich, 1999). By denying boys access to girls' activities, the dominance of masculinity is reinforced when boys are ridiculed because they are not sufficiently dominant or because they "throw like a girl." And, as Mora shows in his reading in this chapter, boys reinforce and maintain masculinity in one another. They goad one another to perform what Schrock and Schwalbe (2009) call "manhood acts."

As you can see, learning gender is complicated. Clearly, gender is something that we "do" as much as learn, and in doing gender, we are responding to structured expectations from institutions in society as well as interpersonal cues from those we are interacting with. Throughout our lives, every time we enter a new social situation, we look around for cues and guides to determine how to behave in an appropriate manner. In some situations, we might interpret gender cues as calling for a high degree of idealized gender difference and inequality, while in other situations, the clues allow us to be more flexible. We create gender as well as respond to expectations for it. And we change gender when we resist it!

Doing Masculinity and Femininity Throughout Our Lives

Most men have learned to "do" the behaviors that maintain hegemonic masculinity, while at the same time suppressing feelings and behaviors that might make them seem feminine (Connell, 1987). As a result, being a "man" or a "woman" requires an awareness of and responses to the other gender. Our cues and behaviors change whether we are responding to someone we identify as being of the same gender or of a different gender. That is, masculinities or femininities are enacted based on how those we are interacting with are displaying femininities or masculinities (Connell & Messerschmidt, 2005).

As argued, hegemonic masculinity is maintained in a hierarchy in which only a few men achieve close-to-idealized masculinity, with everyone else subordinated to them—women, poor White men, men of color, gay men, and men from devalued ethnic and religious groups. Furthermore, this domination is not always one-on-one but, rather, can be institutionalized in the structure of the situation. As you read the articles in this chapter, you will see that gender is not something we learn once in one setting, such as a shot for rabies. Instead, we learn to do gender over time in virtually everything we undertake. And, although we do gender throughout our lives, we rarely achieve idealized gender; yet, by doing gender, we continue to maintain a system of gender difference and inequality.

Also, remember that learning to do gender is complicated by the other prisms that interact in our lives. Recall the lessons from Chapter 2 and remember that gender does not stand alone but, rather, is reflected in other social identities.

It is not easy to separate the learning and doing of gender from other patterns. As you read selections in other chapters in Part II of this book, you will see the influence of social processes and institutions on how we learn and do gender across all aspects of our lives. Before you start to read, ask yourself how you learned gender and how well you do it. Not succeeding at doing gender is normal. That is, if we all felt comfortable with ourselves, no one would be striving for idealized forms of gender—hegemonic masculinity or emphasized femininity. Imagine a world in which we all feel comfortable just the way we are! As you read through the rest of this book, ask yourself why that world doesn't exist.

REFERENCES

American Association of University Women. (1992). *How schools shortchange girls.* Washington, DC: American Association of University Women Educational Foundation.

American Association of University Women. (1998). *Gender gaps: Where schools still fail our children.* Washington, DC: American Association of University Women Educational Foundation.

American Association of University Women. (1999). *Voices of a generation: Teenage girls on sex, school, and self.* Washington, DC: American Association of University Women Educational Foundation.

Anderson, K. J., & Leaper, C. (1998). Meta-analysis of gender effects on conversational interruption: Who, what, when, where, and how. *Sex Roles, 39*(3–4), 225–252.

Berlage, G. I. (2004). Marketing and the publicity images of women's professional basketball players from 1997 to 2001. In J. Z. Spade & C. G. Valentine (Eds.), *The kaleidoscope of gender: Prisms, patterns, and possibilities* (pp. 377–386). Belmont, CA: Wadsworth.

Bettie, J. (2002). Exceptions to the rule: Upwardly mobile White and Mexican American high school girls. *Gender & Society, 16*(3), 403–422.

Brescoli, V. (2011). Who takes the floor and why: Gender, power, and volubility in organizations. *Administrative Science Quarterly, 56*(4), 622–641.

Buysse, J. M., & Embser-Herbert, M. S. (2004). Constructions of gender in sport: An analysis of intercollegiate media guide cover photographs. *Gender & Society, 18*(1), 66–81.

Carlton-Ford, S., & Houston, P. V. (2001). Children's experience of gender: Habitus and field. In D. Vannoy (Ed.), *Gender mosaics: Societal perspectives* (pp. 65–74). Los Angeles: Roxbury.

Carter, P. L. (2005). *Keepin' it real: School success beyond Black and White.* New York: Oxford University Press.

Coltrane, S. (1998). *Gender and families.* Thousand Oaks, CA: Pine Forge Press.

Connell, R. W. (1987). *Gender and power: Society, the person, and sexual politics.* Stanford, CA: Stanford University Press.

Connell, R. W. (2000). *The men and the boys.* Berkeley: University of California Press.

Connell, R. W., & Messerschmidt, J. W. (2005). Hegemonic masculinity: Rethinking the concept. *Gender & Society, 19*(6), 829–859.

Denny, K. E. (2011). Gender in context, content, and approach: Comparing gender messages in Girl Scout and Boy Scout handbooks. *Gender & Society, 25*(1), 27–47.

Eder, D. (1995). *School talk: Gender and adolescent culture.* New Brunswick, NJ: Rutgers University Press.

Ferguson, A. A. (2000). *Bad boys: Public schools in the making of Black masculinity.* Ann Arbor: University of Michigan Press.

Gooden, A. M., & Gooden, M. A. (2001). Gender representation in notable children's picture books: 1995–1999. *Sex Roles, 45*(1–2), 89–101.

Goodwin, M. H. (1990). *He-said-she-said: Talk as social organization among Black children.* Bloomington: Indiana University Press.

Grant, L. (1985). Race-gender status, system attachment, and children's socialization in desegregated classrooms. In L. C. Wilkinson & C. Bagley Marret (Eds.), *Gender influences in classroom interaction* (pp. 57–77). New York: Academic Press.

Howard, J. A., & Alamilla, R. M. (2001). Gender and identity. In D. Vannoy (Ed.), *Gender mosaics: Societal perspectives* (pp. 54–64). Los Angeles: Roxbury.

Lutfey, K., & Mortimer, J. C. (2003). Development and socialization through the adult life course. In J. Delamater (Ed.), *Handbook of social psychology* (pp. 183–204). New York: Kluwer/Plenum.

McGuffey, C. S., & Rich, L. B. (1999). Playing in the gender transgression zone. *Gender & Society, 13*(5), 608–627.

Messner, M. A. (1992). *Power at play: Sports and masculinity.* Boston: Beacon Press.

Orenstein, P. (1994). *School girls: Young women, self-esteem, and the confidence gap.* New York: Anchor Books.

Paoletti, J. B. (2012). *Pink and blue: Telling the boys from the girls in America.* Bloomington: Indiana University Press.

Pollack, W. S. (2000). *Real boys' voices.* New York: Penguin Putnam.

Rhoton, L. A. (2011). Distancing as a gendered barrier: Understanding women scientists' gender practices. *Gender & Society, 25*(6), 696–716.

Riegle-Crumb, C., & Humphries, M. (2012). Exploring bias in math teachers' perceptions of students' ability by gender and race/ethnicity. *Gender & Society, 26*(2), 290–322.

Sadker, D., & Sadker, M. (1994). *Failing at fairness: How our schools cheat girls.* New York: Simon & Schuster.

Schrock, D., & Schwalbe, M. (2009). Men, masculinity, and manhood acts. *Annual Review of Sociology, 35,* 277–295.

Schwalbe, M. (1998). *The sociologically examined life: Pieces of the conversation.* Mountain View, CA: Mayfield.

Spade, J. Z. (2001). Gender and education in the United States. In D. Vannoy (Ed.), *Gender mosaics: Societal perspectives* (pp. 85–93). Los Angeles: Roxbury.

Theberge, N. (2000). *Higher goals: Women's ice hockey and the politics of gender.* Albany: State University of New York Press.

Thorne, B. (1993). *Gender play: Girls and boys in school.* New Brunswick, NJ: Rutgers University Press.

Vespa, J. (2009). Gender ideology construction: A life course and intersectional approach. *Gender & Society, 23*(3), 363–387.

Wesely, J. K. (2001). Negotiating gender: Bodybuilding and the natural/unnatural continuum. *Sociology of Sport Journal, 18,* 162–180.

Wood, J. T. (1999). *Gendered lives: Communication, gender, and culture* (3rd ed.). Belmont, CA: Wadsworth.

Introduction to Reading 16

Many people erroneously believe that the reason women do not pursue careers in STEM (science, technology, engineering, and mathematics) fields is because of innate differences between females and males. This article takes a different direction in trying to understand why these fields are so sex segregated. Maria Charles pursues cultural, economic, social, and institutional explanations for sex segregation in these areas. She compares gender across culture to give a deeper explanation for why there are fewer women than men in STEM careers in the United States.

1. Are interests in STEM subjects in school innate? Why or why not?

2. As you read this article, consider three arguments you could make for why more women do not pursue STEM careers in the United States.

3. What does Charles mean when she says "believing in difference can actually produce difference"? How does this fit with a socialization explanation?

WHAT GENDER IS SCIENCE?

Maria Charles

Gender equality crops up in surprising places. This is nowhere more evident than in science, technology, engineering, and mathematics (STEM) fields. The United States should be a world leader in the integration of prestigious male-dominated occupations and fields of study. After all, laws prohibiting discrimination on the basis of sex have been in place for more than half a century, and the idea that men and women should have equal rights and opportunities is practically uncontested (at least in public) in the U.S. today.

This egalitarian legal and cultural context has coincided with a longstanding shortage of STEM workers that has spurred countless initiatives by government agencies, activists, and industry to attract women into these fields. But far from leading the world, American universities and firms lag considerably behind those in many other countries with respect to women among STEM students and workers. Moreover, the countries where women are best represented in these fields aren't those typically viewed as modern or "gender-progressive." Far from it.

Sex segregation describes the uneven distributions of women and men across occupations, industries, or fields of study. While other types of gender inequality have declined dramatically since the 1960s (for example, in legal rights, labor force participation rates, and educational attainment), some forms of sex segregation are remarkably resilient in the industrial world.

In labor markets, one well-known cause of sex segregation is discrimination, which can occur openly and directly or through more subtle, systemic processes. Not so long ago, American employers' job advertisements and recruitment efforts were targeted explicitly toward either men or women depending on the job. Although these gender-specific ads were prohibited under Title VII of the 1964 Civil Rights Act, less blatant forms of discrimination persist. Even if employers base hiring and promotion solely on performance-based criteria, their taken-for-granted beliefs about average gender differences may bias their judgments of qualification and performance. (See Chapter 7 for a fuller discussion of sex segregation and discrimination in the labor force.)

Discrimination isn't the whole story. It's well-established that girls and young women often avoid mathematically-intensive fields in favor of pursuits regarded as more human-centered. Analyses of gender-differentiated choices are controversial among scholars because this line of inquiry seems to divert attention away from structural and cultural causes of inequalities in pay and status. Acknowledging gender-differentiated educational and career preferences, though, doesn't "blame the victim" unless preferences and choices are considered in isolation from the social contexts in which they emerge. A sociological analysis of sex segregation considers how the economic, social, and cultural environments influence preferences, choices, and outcomes. Among other things, we may ask what types of social context are associated with larger or smaller gender differences in aspirations. Viewed through this lens, preferences become much more than just individuals' intrinsic qualities.

An excellent way to assess contextual effects is by investigating how career aspirations and patterns of sex segregation vary across countries. Recent studies show international differences in the gender composition of STEM fields, in beliefs about the masculinity of STEM, and in girls' and women's reported affinity for STEM-related activities. These differences follow unexpected patterns.

STEM AROUND THE WORLD

Many might assume women in more economically and culturally modern societies enjoy greater equality on all measures, since countries generally "evolve" in an egalitarian direction as they modernize. This isn't the case for scientific and technical fields, though.

Statistics on male and female college graduates and their fields of study are available from the United Nations Educational, Scientific, and Cultural Organization (UNESCO) for 84 countries covering the period between 2005 and 2008. Sixty-five of those countries have educational systems large enough to offer a full range of majors and programs (at least 10,000 graduates per year).

One way of ranking countries on the sex segregation of science education is to compare the (female-to-male) gender ratio among science graduates to the gender ratio among graduates in all other fields. By this measure, the rich and highly industrialized U.S. falls in about the middle of the distribution (in close proximity to Ecuador, Mongolia, Germany, and Ireland—a heterogeneous group on most conventional measures of "women's status"). Female representation in science programs is weakest in the Netherlands and strongest in Iran, Uzbekistan, Azerbaijan, Saudi Arabia, and Oman, where science is disproportionately female. Although the Netherlands has long been considered a gender-traditional society in the European context, most people would still be intrigued to learn that women's representation among science graduates is nearly 50 percentage points lower there than in many Muslim countries. . . . The most gender-integrated science programs are found in Malaysia, where women's 57-percent share of science degree recipients precisely matches their share of all college and university graduates.

"Science" is a big, heterogeneous category, and life science, physical science, mathematics, and computing are fields with very different gender compositions. For example, women made up 60 percent of American biology graduates, but only about 19 percent of computing graduates, in 2008, according to the National Center for Educational Statistics.

But even when fields are defined more precisely, countries differ in some unexpected ways. A case in point is computer science in Malaysia and the U.S. While American computer scientists are depicted as male hackers and geeks, computer science in Malaysia is deemed well-suited for women because it's seen as theoretical (not physical) and it takes place almost exclusively in offices (thought to be woman-friendly spaces). In interviews with sociologist Vivian Lagesen, female computer science students in Malaysia reported taking up computing because they like computers and because they and their parents think the field has good job prospects. The students also referenced government efforts to promote economic development by training workers, both male and female, for the expanding information technology field. About half of Malaysian computer science degrees go to women.

Engineering is the most strongly and consistently male-typed field of study worldwide, but its gender composition still varies widely across countries. Female representation is generally weaker in advanced industrial societies than in developing ones. In our 2009 article in the *American Journal of Sociology*, Karen Bradley and I found this pattern using international data from the mid-1990s; it was confirmed by more recent statistics assembled by UNESCO. Between 2005 and 2008, countries with the most male-dominated engineering programs include the world's leading industrial democracies (Japan, Switzerland, Germany, and the U.S.) along with some of the same oil-rich Middle Eastern countries in which women are so well-represented among science graduates (Saudi Arabia, Jordan, and the United Arab Emirates). Although women do not reach the fifty-percent mark in any country, they come very close in Indonesia, where 48 percent of engineering graduates are female (compared to a 49 percent share of all Indonesian college and university graduates). Women comprise about a third of recent engineering graduates in a diverse group of countries including Mongolia, Greece, Serbia, Panama, Denmark, Bulgaria, and Malaysia.

While engineering is uniformly male-typed in the West, Lagesen's interviews suggest Malaysians draw gender distinctions among engineering *subfields*. One female student reported, ". . . In chemical engineering, most of the time you work in labs. . . . So I think it's quite suitable for females also. But for civil engineering . . . we have to go to the site and check out the constructions."

GIRL GEEKS IN AMERICA

Women's relatively weak presence in STEM fields in the U.S. is partly attributable to some economic, institutional, and cultural features that are common to affluent Western democracies. One such feature is a great diversity of educational and occupational pathways. As school systems grew and democratized in the industrial West, educators, policymakers, and nongovernmental activists sought to accommodate women's purportedly "human-centered" nature by developing educational programs that were seen to align functionally and culturally with female domestic and social roles. Among other things, this involved expansion of liberal arts programs and development of vocationally-oriented programs in home economics, nursing, and early-childhood education. Subsequent efforts to incorporate women, *as women,* into higher education have contributed to expansion in humanities programs, and, more recently, the creation of new fields like women's studies and human development. These initiatives have been supported by a rapid expansion of service-sector jobs in these societies.

In countries with developing and transitional economies, though, policies have been driven more by concerns about advancing economic development than by interests in accommodating women's presumed affinities. Acute shortages of educated workers prompted early efforts by governments and development agencies to increase the supply of STEM workers. These efforts often commenced during these fields' initial growth periods— arguably before they had acquired strong masculine images in the local context.

Another reason for stronger sex segregation of STEM in affluent countries may be that more people (girls and women in particular) can afford to indulge tastes for less lucrative care and social service work in these contexts. Because personal economic security and national development are such central concerns to young people and their parents in developing societies, there is less latitude and support for the realization of gender-specific preferences.

Again, the argument that women's preferences and choices are partly responsible for sex segregation doesn't require that preferences are innate. Career aspirations are influenced by beliefs about ourselves (What am I good at and what will I enjoy doing?), beliefs about others (What will they think of me and how will they respond to my choices?), and beliefs about the purpose of educational and occupational activities (How do I decide what field to pursue?).

And these beliefs are part of our cultural heritage. Sex segregation is an especially resilient form of inequality because people so ardently believe in, enact, and celebrate cultural stereotypes about gender difference.

Believing Stereotypes

Relationship counselor John Gray has produced a wildly successful series of self-help products in which he depicts men and women as so fundamentally different that they might as well come from different planets. While the vast majority of Americans today believe women should have equal social and legal rights, they also believe men and women are very different, and they believe innate differences cause them to *freely choose* distinctly masculine or feminine life paths. For instance, women and men are expected to choose careers that allow them to utilize their hard-wired interests in working with people and things, respectively.

Believing in difference can actually produce difference. Recent sociological research provides strong evidence that cultural stereotypes about gender difference shape individuals' beliefs about their own competencies ("self-assessments") and influence behavior in stereotype-consistent directions. Ubiquitous cultural depictions of STEM as intrinsically male reduce girls' interest in technical fields by defining related tasks as beyond most women's competency and as generally unenjoyable for them. STEM avoidance is a likely outcome.

Shelley Correll's social psychological experiment demonstrates the self-fulfilling effects of gender beliefs on self-assessments and career preferences. Correll administered questions purported to test "contrast sensitivity" to undergraduates. Although the test had no objectively right or wrong answers, all participants were given identical personal "scores" of approximately 60 percent correct. Before the test, subjects were exposed to one of two beliefs: that men on average do better, or that men and women perform equally well. In the first group, male students rated their performance more

highly than did female students, and male students were more likely to report aspiring to work in a job that requires contrast sensitivity. No gender differences were observed among subjects in the second group. Correll's findings suggest that *beliefs about difference* can produce gender gaps in mathematical self-confidence even in the absence of actual differences in ability or performance. If these beliefs lead girls to avoid math courses, a stereotype-confirming performance deficit may emerge. . . .

Enacting Stereotypes

Whatever one believes about innate gender difference, it's difficult to deny that men and women often behave differently and make different choices. Partly, this reflects inculcation of gender-typed preferences and abilities during early childhood. This "gender socialization" occurs through direct observation of same-sex role models, through repeated positive or negative sanctioning of gender-conforming or nonconforming behavior, and through assimilation of diffuse cultural messages about what males and females like and are good at. During much of the 20th century, math was one thing that girls have purportedly not liked or been good at. Even Barbie said so. Feminists and educators have long voiced concerns about the potentially damaging effects of such messages on the minds of impressionable young girls.

But even girls who don't believe STEM activities are inherently masculine realize others do. It's likely to influence their everyday interactions and may affect their life choices. For example, some may seek to affirm their femininity by avoiding math and science classes or by avowing a dislike for related activities. Sociologists who study the operation of gender in social interactions have argued that people expect to be judged according to prevailing standards of masculinity or femininity. This expectation often leads them to engage in behavior that reproduces the gender order. This "doing gender" framework goes beyond socialization because it doesn't require that gender-conforming dispositions are internalized at an early age, just that people know others will likely hold them accountable to conventional beliefs about hard-wired gender differences.

The male-labeling of math and science in the industrial West means that girls and women may expect to incur social sanctions for pursuing these fields. Effects can be cumulative: taking fewer math classes will negatively affect achievement in math and attitudes toward math, creating a powerful positive feedback system.

Celebrating Stereotypes

Aspirations are also influenced by general societal beliefs about the nature and purpose of educational and occupational pursuits. Modern education does more than bestow knowledge; it's seen as a vehicle for individual self-expression and self-realization. Parents and educators exhort young people, perhaps girls in particular, to "follow their passions" and realize their "true selves." Because gender is such a central axis of individual identity, American girls who aim to "study what they love" are unlikely to consider male-labeled science, engineering, or technical fields, despite the material security provided by such degrees.

Although the so-called "postmaterialist" values of individualism and self-expression are spreading globally, they are most prominent in affluent late-modern societies. Curricular and career choices become more than practical economic decisions in these contexts; they also represent acts of identity construction and self-affirmation. Modern systems of higher education make the incursion of gender stereotypes even easier, by allowing wide latitude in course choices.

The ideological discordance between female gender identities and STEM pursuits may even generate attitudinal aversion among girls. Preferences can evolve to align with the gender composition of fields, rather than vice versa. Consistent with these arguments is new evidence showing that career-related aspirations are more gender-differentiated in advanced industrial than in developing and transitional

societies. . . . [T]he gender gap in eighth-graders' affinity for math, confidence in math abilities, and interest in a math-related career is significantly smaller in less affluent countries than in rich ("postmaterialist") ones. Clearly, there is more going on than intrinsic male and female preferences.

QUESTIONING STEM's MASCULINITY

Playing on stereotypes of science as the domain of socially awkward male geniuses, CBS's hit comedy "The Big Bang Theory" stars four nerdy male physicists and one sexy but academically challenged waitress. (Female physicists, when they do show up, are mostly caricatured as gender deviants: sexually unattractive and lacking basic competence in human interaction.) This depiction resonates with popular Western understandings of scientific and technical pursuits as intrinsically masculine.

But representations of scientific and technical fields as *by nature* masculine aren't well-supported by international data. They're also difficult to reconcile with historical evidence pointing to long-term historical shifts in the gender-labeling of some STEM fields. In *The Science Education of American Girls*, Kim Tolley reports that it was *girls* who were overrepresented among students of physics, astronomy, chemistry, and natural science in 19th century American schools. Middle-class boys dominated the higher-status classical humanities programs thought to require top rational powers and required for university admission. Science education was regarded as excellent preparation for motherhood, social work, and teaching. Sociologist Katharine Donato tells a similar story about the dawn of American computer programming. Considered functionally analogous to clerical work, it was performed mostly by college-educated women with science or math backgrounds. This changed starting in the 1950s, when the occupation became attractive to men as a growing, intellectually demanding, and potentially lucrative field. The sex segregation of

American STEM fields—especially engineering, computer science, and the physical sciences—has shown remarkable stability since about 1980.

The gender (and racial) composition of fields is strongly influenced by the economic and social circumstances that prevail at the time of their initial emergence or expansion. But subsequent transformative events, such as acute labor shortages, changing work conditions, and educational restructuring can effect significant shifts in fields' demographic profiles. Tolley, for example, links men's growing dominance of science education in the late 19th and early 20th century to changing university admissions requirements, the rapid growth and professionalization of science and technology occupations, and recurrent ideological backlashes against female employment.

A field's designation as either "male" or "female" is often naturalized through cultural accounts that reference selected gender-conforming aspects of the work. Just as sex segregation across engineering subfields is attributed to physical location in Malaysia (inside work for women, outside work for men), American women's overrepresentation among typists and sewers has been attributed to these occupations' "feminine" task profiles, specifically their requirements for manual dexterity and attention to detail. While the same skills might be construed as essential to the work of surgeons and electricians, explanations for men's dominance of these fields are easily generated with reference to other job requirements that are culturally masculine (technical and spatial skills, for example). Difference-based explanations for sex segregation are readily available because most jobs require diverse skills and aptitudes, some equated with masculinity, some with femininity.

LOOKING FORWARD

What then might be done to increase women's presence in STEM fields? One plausible strategy involves changes to the structure of secondary education. Some evidence suggests more girls and women complete degrees in math and science in educational systems where curricular choice is restricted or delayed; *all* students might take mathematics and science throughout their high-school years or the school might use performance-based tracking and course placement. Although such policies are at odds with Western ideals of individual choice and self-expression, they may weaken penetration of gender stereotypes during the impressionable adolescent years.

Of course, the most obvious means of achieving greater integration of STEM is to avoid reinforcing stereotypes about what girls and boys like and what they are good at. Cultural shifts of this sort occur only gradually, but some change can be seen on the horizon. The rise of "geek chic" may be one sign. Aiming to liberate teen-aged girls from the girls-can't-do-math and male-math-nerd stereotypes, television star and self-proclaimed math geek Danica McKellar has written three how-to math books, most recently *Hot X: Algebra Exposed*, presenting math as both feminine and fun. Even Barbie has been updated. In contrast to her math-fearing Teen Talk sister of the early 1990s, the new Computer Engineer Barbie, released in December 2010, comes decked out in a tight t-shirt printed in binary code and equipped with a smart phone and a pink laptop. Of course, one potential pitfall of this math-is-feminine strategy is that it risks swapping one set of stereotypes for another.

So, what gender is science? In short, it depends. When occupations or fields are segregated by sex, most people suspect it reflects fields' inherently masculine or feminine task content. But this presumption is belied by substantial cross-national variability in the gender composition of fields, STEM in particular. Moreover, this variability follows surprising patterns. Whereas most people would expect to find many more female engineers in the U.S. and Sweden than in Columbia and Bulgaria, new data suggest that precisely the opposite is true.

Ironically, the freedom of choice that's so celebrated in affluent Western democracies seems to help construct and give agency to stereotypically gendered "selves." Self-segregation of careers may occur because some believe they're naturally good at gender-conforming activities (attempting to build on their strengths), because they believe that certain fields will be seen as appropriate for people like them ("doing" gender), or because they believe they'll enjoy gender-conforming fields more than gender-nonconforming ones (realizing their "true selves"). It's just that, by encouraging individual self-expression in post-materialist societies, we may also effectively promote the development and expression of culturally gendered selves.

RECOMMENDED RESOURCES

Shelley J. Correll, "Constraints into Preferences: Gender, Status, and Emerging Career Aspirations." *American Sociological Review* (2004), 69:93–113. Presents evidence from experiments on how beliefs about gender influence beliefs about our own competence and constrain career aspirations.

Paula England, "The Gender Revolution: Uneven and Stalled." *Gender & Society* (2010), 24:149–166. Offers reasons for the persistence of some forms of gender inequality in the United States.

Wendy Faulkner, "Dualisms, Hierarchies and Gender in Engineering." *Social Studies of Science* (2000), 30:759–92. Explores the cultural linkage of masculinity and technology within the engineering profession.

Sarah Fenstermaker and Candace West (eds.), *Doing Gender, Doing Difference: Inequality, Power, and Institutional Change* (Routledge, 2002). Explores how and why people reproduce gender (and race and class) stereotypes in everyday interactions.

Cecilia L. Ridgeway, *Framed by Gender: How Gender Inequality Persists in the Modern World* (Oxford University Press, 2011). Describes how cultural gender beliefs bias behavior and cognition in gendered directions and how this influence may vary by context.

Yu Xie and Kimberlee A. Shauman, *Women in Science: Career Processes and Outcomes* (Harvard University Press, 2003). Uses data from middle school to mid-career to study the forces that lead fewer American women than men into science and engineering fields.

Introduction to Reading 17

The following reading by sociologist Emily W. Kane helps us understand the role of parents in enforcing gender, particularly when children prefer not to conform to normative gender patterns. She describes her findings from interviews with 42 New England parents, primarily from southern and central Maine. These 24 mothers and 18 fathers reflect a diverse group across race, social class, and sexual orientations. Although the parents typically had more than one child, the interviews focused on preschool children—22 sons and 20 daughters. Hearing how parents respond to gender-atypical behavior provides deeper meaning to the process of gender socialization.

1. Why are girls not challenged more by parents when they do not conform to gender expectations?

2. At what point do parents stop preschoolers who are not conforming to gender, particularly boys?

3. How do mothers and fathers see their roles differently in the gender socialization process?

"No Way My Boys Are Going to Be Like That!"

Parents' Responses to Children's Gender Nonconformity

Emily W. Kane

Parents begin gendering their children from their very first awareness of those children, whether in pregnancy or while awaiting adoption. Children themselves become active participants in this gendering process by the time they are conscious of the social relevance of gender, typically before the age of two. I address one aspect of this process of parents doing gender, both for and with their children, by exploring how parents respond to gender nonconformity among preschool-aged children. As West and Zimmerman (1987, 136) note, "to 'do' gender is not always to live up to normative conceptions of femininity or masculinity; it is to engage in behavior *at the risk of gender assessment*." I argue that many parents make efforts to stray from and thus expand normative conceptions of gender. But for their sons in particular, they balance this effort with conscious attention to producing a masculinity approximating hegemonic ideals. This balancing act is evident across many parents I interviewed regardless of gender, race/ethnicity, social class, sexual orientation, and partnership status. But I also argue that within that broader pattern are notable variations. Heterosexual fathers play a particularly central role in accomplishing their sons' masculinity and, in the process, reinforce their own as well. Their expressed motivations for that accomplishment work often involve personal endorsement of hegemonic masculinity. Heterosexual mothers and gay parents, on the other hand, are more likely to report motivations that invoke accountability to others for

crafting their sons' masculinity in accordance with hegemonic ideals.

* * *

Responses to Gender Nonconformity

Mothers and fathers, across a variety of social locations, often celebrated what they perceived as gender nonconformity on the part of their young daughters. They reported enjoying dressing their daughters in sports-themed clothing, as well as buying them toy cars, trucks, trains, and building toys. Some described their efforts to encourage, and pleased reactions to, what they considered traditionally male activities such as t-ball, football, fishing, and learning to use tools. Several noted that they make an effort to encourage their young daughters to aspire to traditionally male occupations and commented favorably on their daughters as "tomboyish," "rough and tumble," and "competitive athletically." These positive responses were combined with very little in the way of any negative response. The coding of each interviewee for the combination of positive/neutral and negative responses summarizes this pattern clearly: Among parents commenting about daughter(s), the typical combination was to express only positive responses. For example, a white, middle-class, heterosexual mother noted approvingly that her five-year-old daughter "does a lot of things that a boy would do, and we encourage that," while a white, upper-middle-class, lesbian mother reported that she and her partner intentionally "do [a lot] of stuff that's not stereotypically female" with their daughter. Similarly, a white, upper-middle-class, heterosexual father indicated with relief that his daughter is turning out to be somewhat "boyish": "I never wanted a girl who was a little princess, who was so fragile. . . . I want her to take on more masculine characteristics." An African American, working-class, heterosexual father also noted this kind of preference: "I don't want her just to color and play with dolls, I want her to be athletic."

A few parents combined these positive responses with vague and general negative responses. But these were rare and expressed with little sense of concern, as in the case of an African American, low-income, heterosexual mother who offered positive responses but also noted limits regarding her daughter: "I wouldn't want her to be too boyish, because she's a girl." In addition, no parents expressed only negative responses. These various patterns suggest that parents made little effort to accomplish their daughters' gender in accordance with any particular conception of femininity, nor did they express any notable sense of accountability to such a conception. Instead, parental responses may suggest a different kind of gendered phenomenon closely linked to the pattern evident in responses toward sons: a devaluing of traditionally feminine pursuits and qualities. Although many parents of daughters reported positive responses to what they consider typical interests and behaviors for a girl, most also celebrated the addition of atypical pursuits to their daughters' lives, and very few noted any negative response to such additions.

It is clear in the literature that there are substantial gendered constraints placed on young girls, and any devaluation of the feminine is potentially such a constraint. But the particular constraint of negative responses by parents to perceived gender nonconformity was not evident in my interview results. It is possible that negative response from parents to perceived departures from traditional femininity would be more notable as girls reach adolescence. Pipher (1998, 286) argues that parents of young girls resist gender stereotypes for their daughters but that "the time to really worry is early adolescence. That's when the gender roles get set in cement, and that's when girls need tremendous support in resisting cultural definitions of femininity." Thorne (1994, 170) invokes a similar possibility, claiming that girls are given more gender leeway than boys in earlier childhood, "but the leeway begins to tighten as girls approach adolescence and move into the heterosexualized gender system of teens and adults." The question of whether negative parental responses might be less gender differentiated in adolescence cannot be addressed with my interview data and remains instead an intriguing question for future research.

In stark contrast to the lack of negative response for daughters, 23 of 31 parents of sons expressed at least some negative responses, and 6 of these offered only negative responses regarding what they perceived as gender nonconformity. Of 31 parents, 25 did indicate positive responses as well, but unlike references to their daughters, they tended to balance those positive feelings and actions about sons with negative ones as well. The most common combination was to indicate both positive and negative responses.

Domestic Skills, Nurturance, and Empathy

Parents accepted, and often even celebrated, their sons' acquisition of domestic abilities and an orientation toward nurturance and empathy. Of the 25 parents of sons who offered positive/neutral responses, 21 did so in reference to domestic skills, nurturance, and/or empathy. For example, they reported allowing or encouraging traditionally girl toys such as dolls, doll houses, kitchen centers, and tea sets, with that response often revolving around a desire to encourage domestic competence, nurturance, emotional openness, empathy, and nonviolence as attributes they considered nontraditional but positive for boys. These parents were reporting actions and sentiments oriented toward accomplishing gender in what they considered a less conventional manner. One white, low-income, heterosexual mother taught her son to cook, asserting that "I want my son to know how to do more than boil water, I want him to know how to take care of himself." Another mother, this one a white, working-class, heterosexual parent, noted that she makes a point of talking to her sons about emotions: "I try to instill a sense of empathy in my sons and try to get them to see how other people would feel." And a white, middle-class, heterosexual father emphasized domestic competence when he noted that it does not bother him for his son to play with dolls at his cousin's house: "How then are they going to learn to take care of their children if they don't?" This positive response to domestic activities is consistent with recent literature on parental coding of toys as masculine, feminine, or neutral, which indicates that parents are increasingly coding kitchens and in some cases dolls as neutral rather than exclusively feminine (Wood, Desmarais, and Gugula 2002).

In my study, mothers and fathers expressed these kinds of efforts to accomplish gender differently for their sons with similar frequency, but mothers tended to express them with greater certainty, while fathers were less enthusiastic and more likely to include caveats. For example, this mother described her purchase of a variety of domestic toys for her three-year-old son without ambivalence: "One of the first big toys [I got him] was the kitchen center. . . . We cook, he has an apron he wears. . . . He's got his dirt devil vacuum and he's got his baby [doll]. And he's got all the stuff to feed her and a highchair" (white, low-income, heterosexual mother).

Some mothers reported allowing domestic toys but with less enthusiasm, such as a white, low-income, heterosexual mother who said, regarding her three-year-old son, "He had been curious about dolls and I just said, you know, usually girls play with dolls, but it's okay for you to do it too." But this kind of caution or lack of enthusiasm, even in a response coded as positive or neutral due to its allowance of gender-atypical behavior, was more evident among fathers, as the following quote illustrates: "Occasionally, if he's

not doing something, I'll encourage him to maybe play with his tea cups, you know, occasionally. But I like playing with his blocks better anyway" (white, middle-class, heterosexual father).

Thus, evident among both mothers and fathers, but with greater conviction for mothers, was widespread support among parents for working to "undo" gender at the level of some of their sons' skills and values. However, this acceptance was tempered for many parents by negative responses to any interest in what I will refer to as iconic feminine items, attributes, or activities, as well as parental concern about homosexuality.

Icons of Femininity

A range of activities and attributes considered atypical for boys were met with negative responses, and for a few parents (3 of 31 parents of sons) this even included the kind of domestic toys and nurturance noted above. But more common were negative responses to items, activities, or attributes that could be considered icons of femininity. This was strikingly consistent with Kimmel's (1994, 119) previously noted claim that the "notion of anti-femininity lies at the heart of contemporary and historical constructions of manhood," and it bears highlighting that this was evident among parents of very young children. Parents of sons reported negative responses to their sons' wearing pink or frilly clothing; wearing skirts, dresses, or tights; and playing dress up in any kind of feminine attire. Nail polish elicited concern from a number of parents too, as they reported young sons wanting to have their fingernails or toenails polished. Dance, especially ballet, and Barbie dolls were also among the traditionally female activities often noted negatively by parents of sons. Of the 31 parents of sons, 23 mentioned negative reactions to at least one of these icons.

Playing with nail polish and makeup, although tolerated by some parents, more often evoked negative responses like this one, from a white, upper-middle-class, gay father, speaking about his four-year-old son's use of nail polish: "He put nail polish on himself one time, and I said 'No, you can't do that, little girls put nail polish on, little boys don't.'"

Barbie dolls are an especially interesting example in that many parents reported positive responses to baby dolls, viewing these as encouraging nurturance and helping to prepare sons for fatherhood. Barbie, on the other hand, an icon of femininity, struck many parents of sons as more problematic. Barbie was often mentioned when parents were asked whether their child had ever requested an item or activity more commonly associated with the other gender. Four parents—three mothers and one father—indicated that they had purchased a Barbie at their son's request, but more often parents of sons noted that they would avoid letting their son have or play with Barbie dolls. Sometimes this negative response was categorical, as [when] a mother of a three-year-old son noted that "there's not many toys I wouldn't get him, except Barbie." A father offers a similar negative reaction to Barbie in relation to his two young sons: "If they asked for a Barbie doll, I would probably say no, you don't want [that], girls play with [that], boys play with trucks" (white, middle-class, heterosexual father).

Along with material markers of femininity, many parents expressed concern about excessive emotionality (especially frequent crying) and passivity in their sons. For example, a white, upper-middle-class, heterosexual father, concerned about public crying, said about his five-year-old son, "I don't want him to be a sissy. . . . I want to see him strong, proud, not crying like a sissy." Another father expressed his frustration with his four-year-old son's crying over what the father views as minor injuries and indicated action to discourage those tears: "Sometimes I get so annoyed, you know, he comes [crying], and I say, 'you're not hurt, you don't even know what hurt is yet,' and I'm like 'geez, sometimes you are such a little wean?'" you know?" (white, middle-class, heterosexual father).

Passivity was also raised as a concern, primarily by fathers. For example, one white, middle-class, heterosexual father of a five-year-old

noted that he has told his son to "stop crying like a girl," and also reported encouraging that son to fight for what he wants: "You just go in the corner and cry like a baby. I don't want that. If you decide you want [some] thing, you are going to fight for it, not crying and acting like a baby and hoping that they're going to feel guilty and give it to you."

A mother who commented negatively about passivity even more directly connected her concern to how her son might be treated: "I do have concerns. . . . He's passive, not aggressive. . . . He's not the rough and tumble kid, and I do worry about him being an easy target" (white, working-class, heterosexual mother).

Taken together, these various examples indicate clearly the work many parents are doing to accomplish gender with and for their sons in a manner that distances those sons from any association with femininity. This work was not evident among all parents of sons. But for most parents, across racial, class, and sexual orientation categories, it was indeed evident.

Homosexuality

Along with these icons of feminine gender performance, and arguably directly linked to them, is the other clear theme evident among some parents' negative responses to perceived gender nonconformity on the part of their sons: fear that a son either would be or would be perceived as gay. Spontaneous connections of gender nonconformity and sexual orientation were not evident in parents' comments about daughters, nor among gay and lesbian parents, but arose for 7 of the 27 heterosexual parents who were discussing sons.

The fact that the connection between gender performance and sexual orientation was not raised for daughters, and that fear of homosexuality was not spontaneously mentioned by parents of daughters whether in connection to gender performance or not, suggests how closely gender conformity and heterosexuality are linked within hegemonic constructions of masculinity. Such connections might arise more by adolescence in relation to daughters, as I noted previously regarding other aspects of parental responses to gender nonconformity. But for sons, even among parents of very young children, heteronormativity appears to play a role in shaping parental responses to gender nonconformity, a connection that literature on older children and adults indicates is made more for males than females (Antill 1987; Hill 1999; Kite and Deaux 1987; Sandnabba and Ahlberg 1999). Martin's (2005) recent analysis also documents the importance of heteronormativity in the advice offered to parents by experts. She concludes that expert authors of child-rearing books and Web sites are increasingly supportive of gender-neutral child rearing. But especially for sons, that expert support is limited by implicit and even explicit invocations of homosexuality as a risk to be managed. As McCreary (1994, 526) argues on the basis of experimental work on responses to older children and adults, "the asymmetry in people's responses to male and female gender role deviations is motivated, in part, by the implicit assumption that male transgressions are symptomatic of a homosexual orientation." This implicit assumption appears to motivate at least some parental gender performance management among heterosexual parents, even for children as young as preschool age. Given the connections between male heterosexuality and the rejection of femininity noted previously as evident in theories of hegemonic masculinity, the tendency for parents to associate gender performance and sexual orientation for sons more than daughters may also reflect a more general devaluation of femininity.

Mothers Versus Fathers in the Accomplishment of Masculinity

. . . Although both mothers and fathers were equally likely to express a combination of positive and negative responses to their sons' perceived gender nonconformity, with domestic skills and empathy accepted and icons of femininity rejected, the acceptance was more pointed for mothers, and the rejection was more pointed for fathers. More fathers (11 of 14) than mothers (12 of 17) of sons indicated negative reactions to at least one of the icons discussed. Fathers also indicated more categorically negative responses: 7 of the 14 fathers but only 2 of the 17 mothers reported simply saying "no" to requests for things such as Barbie dolls, tea sets, nail polish, or ballet lessons, whether actual requests or hypothetical ones. Although fewer parents referred to excessive emotionality and passivity as concerns, the 6 parents of sons who did so included 4 fathers and 2 mothers, and here too, the quotes indicate a more categorical rejection by fathers.

Another indication of more careful policing of icons of femininity by fathers is evident in comments that placed age limitations on the acceptability of such icons. Four fathers (but no mothers) commented with acceptance on activities or interests that they consider atypical for boys but went on to note that these would bother them if they continued well past the preschool age range. The following quote from a father is typical of these responses. After noting that his four-year-old son sometimes asks for toys he thinks of as "girl toys," he went on to say, "I don't think it will ruin his life at this age but . . . if he was 12 and asking for it, you know, My Little Pony or Barbies, then I think I'd really worry" (white, middle-class, heterosexual father). While comments like this one were not coded as negative responses, since they involved acceptance, I mention them here as they are consistent with the tendency for fathers to express particular concern about their sons' involvement with icons of femininity.

Three of 15 heterosexual mothers and 4 of 12 heterosexual fathers of sons responded negatively to the possibility of their son's being, or being perceived as, gay. These numbers are too small to make conclusive claims comparing mothers and fathers. But this pattern is suggestive of another arena in which fathers—especially heterosexual fathers—may stand out, especially taken together with another pattern. Implicit in the quotes offered above related to homosexuality is a suggestion that heterosexual fathers may feel particularly responsible for crafting their sons' heterosexual orientation. In addition, in comparison to mothers, their comments are less likely to refer to fears for how their son might be treated by others if he were gay and more likely to refer to the personal disappointment they anticipate in this hypothetical scenario. I return to consideration of these patterns in my discussion of accountability below.

Parental Motivations for the Accomplishment of Masculinity

The analysis I have offered thus far documents that parents are aware of their role in accomplishing gender with and for their sons. Although some parents did speak of their sons as entirely "boyish" and "born that way," many reported efforts to craft a hegemonic masculinity. Most parents expressed a very conscious awareness of normative conceptions of masculinity (whether explicitly or implicitly). Many, especially heterosexual mothers and gay parents, expressed a sense that they felt accountable to others in terms of whether their sons live up to those conceptions. In numerous ways, these parents indicated their awareness that their sons' behavior was at risk of gender assessment, an awareness rarely noted with regard to daughters. Parents varied in terms of their expressed motivations for crafting their sons' masculinity, ranging from a sense of measuring their sons against their own preferences for normative masculinity (more common among heterosexual fathers) to concerns about accountability to gender assessment by peers, other adults, and society in general (more common among heterosexual mothers and gay parents, whether mothers or fathers).

* * *

Conclusion

The interviews analyzed here, with New England parents of preschool-aged children from a diverse array of backgrounds, indicate a considerable endorsement by parents of what they perceive as gender nonconformity among both their sons and their daughters. This pattern at first appears encouraging in terms of the prospects for a world less constrained by gendered expectations for children. Many parents respond positively to the idea of their children's experiencing a greater range of opportunities, emotions, and interests than those narrowly defined by gendered stereotypes, with mothers especially likely to do so. However, for sons, this positive response is primarily limited to a few attributes and abilities, namely, domestic skills, nurturance, and empathy. And it is constrained by a clear recognition of normative conceptions of masculinity (Connell 1987, 1995). Most parents made efforts to accomplish, and either endorsed or felt accountable to, an ideal of masculinity that was defined by limited emotionality, activity rather than passivity, and rejection of material markers of femininity. Work to accomplish this type of masculinity was reported especially often by heterosexual fathers; accountability to approximate hegemonic masculinity was reported especially often by heterosexual mothers, lesbian mothers, and gay fathers. Some heterosexual parents also invoked sexual orientation as part of this conception of masculinity, commenting with concern on the possibility that their son might be gay or might be perceived as such. No similar pattern of well-defined normative expectations or accountability animated responses regarding daughters, although positive responses to pursuits parents viewed as more typically masculine may well reflect the same underlying devaluation of femininity evident in negative responses to gender nonconformity among sons.

In the broader study from which this particular analysis was drawn, many parents invoked biology in explaining their children's gendered tendencies. Clearly, the role of biological explanations in parents' thinking about gender merits additional investigation. But one of the things that was most striking to me in the analyses presented here is how frequently parents indicated that they took action to craft an appropriate gender performance with and for their preschool-aged sons, viewing masculinity as something they needed to work on to accomplish. These tendencies are in contrast to what Messner (2000) summarizes eloquently in his essay on a gender-segregated preschool sports program. He observes a highly gender-differentiated performance offered by the boys' and girls' teams during the opening ceremony of the new soccer season, with one of the girls' teams dubbing themselves the Barbie Girls, while one of the boys' teams called themselves the Sea Monsters. He notes that parents tended to view the starkly different approaches taken by the boys and girls as evidence of natural gender differences. "The parents do not seem to read the children's performances of gender as social constructions of gender. Instead, they interpret them as the inevitable unfolding of natural, internal differences between the sexes" (Messner 2000, 770).

I agree with Messner (2000) that this tendency is evident among parents, and I heard it articulated in some parts of the broader project from which the present analysis is drawn. I began this project expecting that parents accept with little question ideologies that naturalize gender difference. Instead, the results I have presented here demonstrate that parents are often consciously aware of gender as something that they must shape and construct, at least for their sons. This argument extends the literature on the routine accomplishment of gender in childhood by introducing evidence of conscious effort and awareness by parents as part of that accomplishment. This awareness also has implications for efforts to reduce gendered constraints on children. Recognition that parents are sometimes consciously crafting their children's gender suggests the possibility that they could be encouraged to shift that conscious effort in less gendered directions.

In addition to documenting this parental awareness, I am also able to extend the literature by documenting the content toward which parents' accomplishment work is oriented. The version of hegemonic masculinity I have argued underlies parents' responses is one that includes both change and stability. Parental openness to

domestic skills, nurturance, and empathy as desirable qualities in their sons likely represents social change, and the kind of agency in the accomplishment of gender to which Fenstermaker and West (2002) refer. As Connell (1995) notes, hegemonic masculinity is historically variable in its specific content, and the evidence presented in this article suggests that some broadening of that content is occurring. But the clear limits evident within that broadening suggest the stability and power of hegemonic conceptions of masculinity. The parental boundary maintenance work evident for sons represents a crucial obstacle limiting boys' options, separating boys from girls, devaluing activities marked as feminine for both boys and girls, and thus bolstering gender inequality and heteronormativity.

Finally, along with documenting conscious awareness by parents and the content toward which their accomplishment work is oriented, my analysis also contributes to the literature by illuminating the process motivating parental gender accomplishment. The heterosexual world in general, and heterosexual fathers in particular, play a central role in that process. This is evident in the direct endorsement of hegemonic masculinity many heterosexual fathers expressed and in the accountability to others (presumably heterosexual others) many heterosexual mothers, lesbian mothers, and gay fathers expressed. Scholarly investigations of the routine production of gender in childhood, therefore, need to pay careful attention to the role of heterosexual fathers as enforcers of gender boundaries and to the role of accountability in the process of accomplishing gender. At the same time, practical efforts to loosen gendered constraints on young children by expanding their parents' normative conceptions of gender need to be aimed at parents in general and especially need to reach heterosexual fathers in particular. The concern and even fear many parents—especially heterosexual mothers, lesbian mothers, and gay fathers—expressed about how their young sons might be treated if they fail to live up to hegemonic conceptions of masculinity represent a motivation for the traditional accomplishment of gender. But those reactions could also serve as a motivation to broaden normative conceptions of masculinity and challenge the devaluation of femininity, an effort that will require participation by heterosexual fathers to succeed.

REFERENCES

Antill, John K. 1987. Parents' beliefs and values about sex roles, sex differences, and sexuality. *Review of Personality and Social Psychology* 7:294–328.

Connell, R. W. 1987. *Gender and power.* Stanford, CA: Stanford University Press.

———. 1995. *Masculinities.* Berkeley: University of California Press.

Fenstermaker, Sarah, and Candace West, eds. 2002. *Doing gender, doing difference.* New York: Routledge.

Hill, Shirley A. 1999. *African American children.* Thousand Oaks, CA: Sage.

Kimmel, Michael S. 1994. Masculinity as homophobia. In *Theorizing masculinities,* edited by Harry Brod. Thousand Oaks, CA: Sage.

Kite, Mary E., and Kay Deaux. 1987. Gender belief systems: Homosexuality and the implicit inversion theory. *Psychology of Women Quarterly* 11:83–96.

Martin, Karin A. 2005. William wants a doll, can he have one? Feminists, child care advisors, and gender-neutral child rearing. *Gender & Society* 20:1–24.

McCreary, Donald R. 1994. The male role and avoiding femininity. *Sex Roles* 31:517–31.

Messner, Michael. 2000. Barbie girls versus sea monsters: Children constructing gender. *Gender & Society* 14:765–84.

Pipher, Mary. 1998. *Reviving Ophelia.* New York: Ballantine Books.

Sandnabba, N. Kenneth, and Christian Ahlberg. 1999. Parents' attitudes and expectations about children's cross-gender behavior. *Sex Roles* 40:249–63.

Thorne, Barrie. 1994. *Gender play.* New Brunswick, NJ: Rutgers University Press.

West, Candace, and Don Zimmerman. 1987. Doing gender. *Gender & Society* 1:124–51.

Wood, Eileen, Serge Desmarais, and Sara Gugula. 2002. The impact of parenting experience on gender stereotyped toy play of children. *Sex Roles* 47:39–49.

Introduction to Reading 18

In this piece, Janice McCabe, Emily Fairchild, Liz Grauerholz, Bernice A. Pescosolido, and Daniel Tope conducted a quantitative analysis of Little Golden Books (1942–1993), Caldecott award winners (1938–2000), and *Children's Catalog* (1900–2000). This sample covers a wide range of children's books: Little Golden Books are relatively inexpensive and available widely, including in grocery stores; the Caldecott award is given annually by the Association for Library Service to Children for "the most distinguished picture book for children" (books receiving honorable mention were also included in the sample); and *Children's Catalog* is an extensive listing of all books for children. McCabe et al. coded gender information from titles and main characters—including animals if they were the subject of the story—for 5,618 books. Their findings of the distribution of female and male characters in children's books throughout the 20th century might surprise you.

1. Were males or females more likely to be included in the titles of books and as main characters?

2. In which type of book were the differences in gender representation more extreme?

3. Why does it matter that both sexes are not equally represented in the books studied?

Gender in Twentieth-Century Children's Books

Patterns of Disparity in Titles and Central Characters

Janice McCabe, Emily Fairchild, Liz Grauerholz, Bernice A. Pescosolido, and Daniel Tope

Research on gender representation in children's literature has revealed persistent patterns of gender inequality, despite some signs of improvement since Weitzman et al.'s (1972) classic study more than 35 years ago. Recent studies continue to show a relative absence of women and girls in titles and as central characters (e.g., Clark, Lennon, and Morris 1993; Hamilton et al. 2006), findings that mirror those from other sources of children's media, including cartoons and coloring books (e.g., Fitzpatrick and McPherson 2010; Klein and Shiffman 2009). Theoretically, this absence reflects a "symbolic annihilation" because it denies existence to women and girls by ignoring or underrepresenting them in cultural products (Tuchman 1978). As such, children's books reinforce, legitimate, and reproduce a patriarchal gender system.

Because children's literature provides valuable insights into popular culture, children's worlds, stratification, and socialization, gender representation in children's literature has been researched extensively. Yet most studies provide snapshots of a small set of books during a particular time period while making sweeping claims about change (or lack thereof) and generalizing to all other books. . . . While examining particular books during limited time periods may reveal important insights about these periods and books, we know little about representation of males and females in the broad range of books available to children throughout the twentieth century. . . .

Children's Understandings of Gender: Schemas, Reader Response, and Symbolic Annihilation

No medium has been more extensively studied than children's literature. This is no doubt due, in part, to the cultural importance of children's books as a powerful means through which children learn their cultural heritage (Bettelheim 1977). Children's books provide messages about right and wrong, the beautiful and the hideous, what is attainable and what is out of bounds—in sum, a society's ideals and directions. Simply put, children's books are a celebration, reaffirmation, and dominant blueprint of shared cultural values, meanings, and expectations.

Childhood is central to the development of gender identity and schemas. By preschool, children have learned to categorize themselves and others into one of two gender identity categories, and parents, teachers, and peers behave toward children based on these categories. The development of a gender identity and understandings of the expectations associated with it continue throughout childhood. Along with parents, teachers, and peers, books contribute to how children understand what is expected of women and men and shape how they think of their place in the social structure: Through stories, "children learn to constitute them selves [sic] as bipolar males or females with the appropriate patterns of power and desire" (Davies 2003, 49). Books are one piece of a socialization and identity formation

McCabe, Janice, Emily Fairchild, Liz Grauerholz, Bernice A. Pescosolido, and Daniel Tope. 2011. "Gender in Twentieth Century Children's Books: Patterns of Disparity in Titles and Central Characters." *Gender & Society* 25(2): 197–226.

process that is colored by children's prior understandings of gender, or gender schemas. Because schemas are broad cognitive structures that organize and guide perception, they are often reinforced and difficult to change. It takes consistent effort to combat dominant cultural messages (Bem 1983), including those sent by the majority of books.

The extensive body of research (often referred to as "reader response") examining the role of the reader in constructing meanings of literature (e.g., Applebee 1978; Cullingford 1998) comes to a similar conclusion. We interpret stories through the filter of our prior knowledge about other stories and everyday experiences; in other words, schemas shape our interpretations. Reading egalitarian books to children over a sustained period of time shapes children's gender attitudes and beliefs (e.g., Barclay 1974; Trepanier-Street and Romatowski 1999). However, one book is unlikely to drastically change a child's gender schema.

The effects of gender schemas can be seen in children's preferences for male characters. Boys and, to a lesser extent, girls prefer stories about boys and men (e.g., Bleakley, Westerberg, and Hopkins 1988; Connor and Serbin 1978). This research suggests that children see girls and women as less important and interesting. Even seeming exceptions to the pattern of male preference support the underlying premise: When boys identify with a girl as a central character, they redefine her as a secondary character (Segel 1986) and they identify male secondary characters as central characters when retelling stories (Davies 2003). Patterns of gender representation in children's books, therefore, work with children's existing schemas and beliefs about their own gender identity. A consistently unequal pattern of males and females in children's books thus contributes to and reinforces children's gender schemas and identities.

While representation in the media conveys social existence, exclusion (or underrepresentation) signifies nonexistence or "symbolic annihilation" (Tuchman 1978). Not showing a particular group or showing them less frequently than their proportion in the population conveys that the group is not socially valued. This phenomenon has been documented in a range of outlets—from television (Tuchman 1978) to introductory sociology textbooks (Ferree and Hall 1990) to animated cartoons (Klein and Shiffman 2009). Yet, research on "symbolic annihilation" has neglected children's books and failed to tie representations to broader historical changes.

HISTORICAL CHANGE: GENDER THROUGHOUT THE TWENTIETH CENTURY

Inequitable gender representations may have diminished over time in the United States, corresponding with women gaining rights throughout the century (e.g., voting and reproductive rights) and entrance into the public sphere via the workplace, politics, and media. However, it seems more likely that there will be periods of greater disparity and periods of greater parity, corresponding with upsurges in feminist activism and backlash against progressive gender reforms. For instance, Cancian and Ross (1981) identified a curvilinear pattern in newspapers and magazines' coverage of women, finding that coverage peaked during the first wave of feminist activism (1908–1920) and dipped until the second wave was well underway in 1970, when it began to rise again.

Thus, we have reason to believe that representations during midcentury—after the 19th Amendment gave women the right to vote but before the second-wave women's movement—may differ from other parts of the century. Historians have identified the 1930s as a time of backlash against the changes in gender expectations and sexual freedom of the 1920s (Cott 1987; Scharf 1980). While resistance to these changes existed in the first two decades of the century (Kimmel 1987), the tide shifted with the Great Depression. Women were scorned for taking "male jobs" (Evans 1997; Scharf 1980), the increase in the number of women in the professions "came to a halt" (Scharf 1980, 85), and the media asked "Is Feminism Dead?" in 1935

(Scharf 1980, 110). Even when women's employment skyrocketed during WWII, traditional notions of gender persisted through the valuation of the "domestic ideology" (Evans 1997; Friedan 1963; Rupp and Taylor 1987) and women were "criticized for failing to raise their sons properly" (Evans 1997, 234). This gender traditionalism and antifeminism persisted into the 1960s, although feminist challenges to gender expectations began to swell again with President Kennedy's Commission on the Status of Women, the Equal Pay Act, the publication of *The Feminine Mystique*, and the founding of the National Organization for Women (Rupp and Taylor 1987). The cumulative effects of these events were apparent in the 1970s as feminism rapidly expanded in a second wave of activism (Cancian and Ross 1981; Evans 1997). Although there was some resistance to feminism during the 1980s (Evans 1997; Faludi 1991), this latter part of the century saw a more consistent presence of activism; by the mid-1990s, feminist solidarity was growing among younger women (Evans 1997) identified as feminism's "third wave."

Based on these patterns of feminist activism and backlash, we expect representation of women and girls to be closer to parity during activist periods (1900–1929 and 1970–2000) and more absent during greater gender traditionalism (1930–1969). We link the theoretical concept of symbolic annihilation to gender representation throughout the century.

* * *

FINDINGS

Twentieth-Century Representations

We first provide general yearly trends of the percentage of books featuring males and females in titles, as well as among central characters. Here, the unit of analysis is year rather than book. With all book series combined, there are 101 cases (representing 5,618 books across 101 years).

Because we are interested primarily in (dis)parity between representations of male and female characters, we focus on the *presence* of males or females. However, it is noteworthy that male or female characters are not present in many titles: 55 to 57 percent of Caldecott award winners and *Children's Catalog*; 43 percent in Little Golden Books. There were also some instances in which it was not possible to determine whether a character was male or female: 4 percent of Goldens, 8 percent of Caldecotts, and 19 percent of *Catalogs* had at least one such character.

[There are] three interesting patterns in representations. First, there is a clear disparity across all measures: Males are represented more frequently than females in titles and as central characters. For instance, on average, 36.5 percent of books each year include a male in the title compared to 17.5 percent that include a female. By no measure are females present more frequently than males. In fact, the mode for males in titles is 33, meaning that the most common distribution is that one-third of the books published that year include a male in the title, whereas the mode for females is 0, meaning that the most common distribution is that no book titles include females. Similarly, the mode for male central characters (overall) is 50, but 0 for females. . . . For instance, 13 years had no male animal characters while 24 years had no female animals. Examining each variable's range shows that males are present in up to 100 percent of the books, but females never exceed 75 percent. More striking, no more than 33 percent of books published in a year contain central characters who are adult women or female animals, whereas adult men and male animals appear in up to 100 percent.

Second, [there are] important variations by type of character. The greatest parity exists for child central characters; the greatest disparity exists for animal characters. Boys appear as central characters in 26.4 percent of books and girls in 19 percent, but male animals are central characters in 23.2 percent of books while female animals are in only 7.5 percent. The data show one instance of a higher range of books including female characters than male: that for children, where up to 75 percent of books in a year contain girl central characters while a maximum of 50 percent contain boys. It should be noted, however, that only one year has 75 percent girls and that most years have higher ranges for boys than for girls.

Third, there are differences across book series, but—as with variations by type of character—these differences are by degree, not direction. Regardless of book series, males are always represented more often than females in titles and as central characters; however, the *extent* of the disparities differs. Golden Books tend to have the most unbalanced representations; Goldens have the highest mean and mode of males in the titles of any of the book types and the highest mean value of male central characters, followed by Caldecotts and the *Catalog*. The greatest disparity—animal characters—and the smallest—child characters—are also consistent across book types.

...All of the male to female comparisons...are statistically significant; in other words, for each variable in each book series, males are present in significantly more books than are females. When all books are combined, we find 1,857 (out of 5,618) books where males appear in the titles, compared to 966 books with females; a ratio of 1.9:1. For central characters, 3,418 books featured any male and 2,098 featured any female (1.6:1). Once again, the greatest disparity is for animal characters (2.6:1) and the least for child characters (1.3:1). . . .

A closer look at the types of characters with the greatest disparity reveals that only one Caldecott winner has a female animal as a central character without any male central characters. The 1985 Honor book *Have You Seen My Duckling?* . . . follows Mother Duck asking other pond animals this question as she searches for a missing duckling. One other Caldecott has a female animal without a male animal also in a central role; however, in *Officer Buckle and Gloria*, the female dog is present alongside a male police officer. Although female animal characters do exist, books with male animals, such as *Barkley* . . . and *The Poky Little Puppy* . . . were more than two-and-a-half times more common across the century than those with female animals.

The greatest disparity in titles and overall characters occurs among the Little Golden Books and Caldecott award winners and the least disparity in the *Catalog* books. . . . Regardless of type of character (i.e., child or adult, human or animal), books in the *Catalog* are significantly more equal than the Goldens. . . .

Trends by Historical Period

Data presented thus far provide a general picture of disparity in children's books. However, we expect historical and social factors to affect representation. . . . Books published during the 1930s–1960s are more likely than earlier or later decades to feature males in the titles and, with one exception (1900s), as central characters. Books in early and later years are more likely to feature females, such as Harriet and Mirette while midcentury books, like *The Poky Little Puppy* feature more males. In rare cases, there are actually more females than males in both the early and later parts of the twentieth century. . . . The most equitable category is child central characters. In contrast, animal characters are the least equitable. Although the most recently published books come quite close to parity for human characters (ratios of 0.9:1 [children] to 1.2:1 [adults] for the 1990s), a significant disparity remains for animals (1.9:1). All of [our analyses] show a nonlinear pattern, with greatest inequality midcentury.

* * *

Discussion

Gender is a social creation; cultural representation, including that in children's literature, is a key source in reproducing and legitimating gender systems and gender inequality. The messages conveyed through representation of males and females in books contribute to children's ideas of what it means to be a boy, girl, man, or woman.

The disparities we find point to the symbolic annihilation of women and girls, and particularly female animals, in twentieth-century children's literature, suggesting to children that these characters are less important than their male counterparts.

We provide a comprehensive picture of children's books and demonstrate disparities on multiple measures. Still, there may be reason to believe that our findings are conservative regarding the unequal representation children actually experience. This is due in part to how gender schemas and developing gender ideologies are compounded. Reader response research suggests that as children read books with male characters, their preferences for male characters are reinforced, and they will continue reaching for books that feature boys, men, and male animals. Children's exposure, moreover, is likely narrower than the range of books we studied.

Adults also play important roles as they select books for their own children and make purchasing decisions for schools and libraries. Because boys prefer male central characters while girls' preferences are less strong, textbooks in the 1980s advised: "the ratio of 'boy books' should be about two to one in the classroom library collection" (Segel 1986, 180). Given this advice, disparities in actual libraries and classrooms could be even larger than what we found. Although feminist stories have circulated since at least the 1970s, "neither feminist versions of old stories nor new feminist stories are readily available in bookshops and libraries, and schools show almost no sign of this development" (Davies 2003, 49). Therefore, combating the patterns we found with "feminist stories" requires parents' conscious efforts. While some parents do this, most do not. A study of parents' reasons for selecting books finds most choices are based on parents' personal childhood favorites—indicating the continued impact of books from generations ago—and rarely on concern for stereotypes, particularly gender stereotypes (Peterson and Lach 1990).

Our historical lens allowed us to see change over time, but not consistent improvement. Rather, our findings support what other studies of media have shown: that coverage of social groups corresponds to changes in access to political influence (Burstein 1979; Cancian and Ross 1981). We found that the period of greatest disparity between males and females in children's books was the 1930s–1960s—precisely the period following the first-wave women's movement. Historians have noted, "No question, feminism came under heavy scrutiny—and fire—by the end of the 1920s" (Cott 1987, 271), coinciding with the beginning of this midcentury period. And, "'women's lib' was on everyone's lips" by 1970 (Evans 1997, 287), coinciding with the end of this period. Certainly, shifts in gender politics affect representation. . . .

Why is there a persistence of inequality among animal characters? There is some indication that publishers, under pressure to publish books that are more balanced regarding gender, used animal characters in an attempt to avoid the problem of gender representation. . . . As one book editor in Turow's (1978) study of children's book publishing remarked about the predominant use of animal central characters: "It's easier. You don't have to determine if it's a girl or boy—right? That's such a problem today. And if it's a girl, God forbid you put her in a pink dress" (p. 89). However, our findings show that most animal characters are sexed and that inequality among animals is greater—not less—than that among humans. The tendency of readers to interpret even gender-neutral animal characters as male exaggerates the pattern of female underrepresentation. For example, mothers (even those scoring high on the Sex Role Egalitarianism Questionnaire) frequently label gender-neutral animal characters as male when reading or discussing books with their children (DeLoache, Cassidy, and Carpenter 1987) and children assign gender to gender-neutral animal characters (Arthur and White 1996). Together with research on reader interpretations, our findings regarding imbalanced representations among animal characters suggest that these characters could be particularly powerful, and potentially overlooked, conduits for gendered messages. The persistent pattern of disparity among animal characters may reveal a subtle kind of symbolic annihilation of women disguised through animal imagery—a strategy noted by others (Adams 2004; Irvine 2007; Grauerholz 2007).

Although children's books have provided a steady stream of characters privileging boys and men over girls and women, examining representation across the long range illuminates areas where such messages are being challenged. Clearly, children's book publishing has been responsive to social change, and girls are more likely to see characters and books about individuals like themselves today than midcentury. Feminist activism during the 1970s specifically targeted children's books. For example, the publication of Weitzman et al.'s (1972) study appears to have influenced the publishing industry in important ways. Weitzman received funding from the NOW Legal Defense and Education Fund to reproduce children's book illustrations for a slide show to parents, educators, and publishers. This presentation made its way around the world in an effort to promote social change (Tobias 1997). Some argue that Weitzman et al.'s study profoundly shaped the children's book industry as a "rallying point for feminist activism," including the creation of "nonsexist" book lists and feminist publishing companies and the "raising of consciousness among more conventional publishers, award committees, authors, parents, and teachers" (Clark, Kulkin, and Clancy 1999, 71). The linear change we found since 1970 for most measures suggests this second-wave push for gender equity in children's books may have had a lasting impact.

Nonetheless, disparities remain in recent years, and our findings suggest ways that children's books are less amenable to change, especially in the case of animals. Although we do not know the complete impact of unequal representation on children, these data, in conjunction with previous research on the development and maintenance of gender schemas and gender identities, reinforce the importance of continued attention to symbolic annihilation in children's books. While children do not always interpret messages in books in ways adults intend (see, e.g., Davies 2003), the messages from the disparities we find are reinforced by similar—or even more unequal—ones among characters in G-rated films (Smith et al. 2010), cartoons (Klein and Shiffman 2009), video games (Downs and Smith 2010), and even coloring books (Fitzpatrick and McPherson 2010). This widespread pattern of underrepresentation of females may contribute to a sense of unimportance among girls and privilege among boys. Gender is a structure deeply embedded in our society, including in children's literature. This research highlights patterns that give us hope for the success of feminist attention to issues of disparity and remind us that continued disparities have important effects on our understandings of gender and ourselves.

REFERENCES

Adams, Carol. 2004. *The sexual politics of meat*. New York: Continuum.

Applebee, Arthur. 1978. *The child's concept of a story*. Chicago: University of Chicago Press.

Arthur, April G., and Hedy White. 1996. Children's assignment of gender to animal characters in pictures. *The Journal of Genetic Psychology* 157:297–301.

Barclay, Lisa K. 1974. The emergence of vocational expectations in preschool children. *Journal of Vocational Behavior* 4:1–14.

Bem, Sandra Lipsitz. 1983. Gender schema theory and its implications for child development: Raising gender-aschematic children in a gender-schematic society. *Signs* 8:598–616.

Bettelheim, Bruno. 1977. *Uses of enchantment*. New York: Vintage.

Bleakley, Mary Ellen, Virginia Westerberg, and Kenneth D. Hopkins. 1988. The effect of character sex on story interest and comprehension in children. *American Education Research Journal* 25:145–55.

Burstein, Paul. 1979. Public opinion, demonstrations, and the passage of anti-discrimination legislation. *Public Opinion Quarterly* 43:157–72.

Cancian, Francesca M., and Bonnie L. Ross. 1981. Mass media and the women's movement: 1900–1977. *The Journal of Applied Behavioral Science* 17:9–26.

Clark, Roger, Heidi Kulkin, and Liam Clancy. 1999. The liberal bias in feminist social science research on children's books. In *Girls, boys, books, toys: Gender in children's literature and culture*, edited by B. L. Clark and M. R. Higonnet. Baltimore: Johns Hopkins University Press.

Clark, Roger, Rachel Lennon, and Leanna Morris. 1993. Of Caldecotts and Kings: Gendered images in recent American children's books by black and non-black illustrators. *Gender & Society* 7:227–45.

Connor, Jane Marantz, and Lisa A. Serbin. 1978. Children's responses to stories with male and female characters. *Sex Roles* 4:637–45.

Cott, Nancy F. 1987. *The grounding of modern feminism*. New Haven, CT: Yale University Press.

Cullingford, Cedric. 1998. Children's literature and its effects: The formative years. London: Continuum.

Davies, Bronwyn. 2003. Frogs and snails and feminist tales: Preschool children and gender. Rev. ed. Cresskill, NY: Hampton Press.

DeLoache, Judy S., Deborah J. Cassidy, and C. Jan Carpenter. 1987. The three bears are all boys: Mothers' gender labeling of neutral picture book characters. *Sex Roles* 17:163–78.

Downs, Edward, and Stacy L. Smith. 2010. Keeping abreast of hypersexuality: A video game character content analysis. *Sex Roles* 62:721–33.

Evans, Sara. M. 1997. Born for liberty: A history of women in America. New York: Free Press.

Faludi, Susan. 1991. Backlash: The undeclared war against American women. New York: Doubleday.

Ferree, Myra Marx, and Elaine J. Hall. 1990. Visual images of American society: Gender and race in introductory sociology textbooks. *Gender & Society* 4:500–33.

Fitzpatrick, Maureen L., and Barbara J. McPherson. 2010. Coloring within the lines: Gender stereotypes in contemporary coloring books. *Sex Roles* 62:127–37.

Friedan, Betty. 1963. *The feminine mystique*. New York: W. W. Norton.

Grauerholz, Liz. 2007. Cute enough to eat: The transformation of animals into meat for human consumption in commercialized images. *Humanity & Society* 31:334–54.

Hamilton, Mykol C., David Anderson, Michelle Broaddus, and Kate Young. 2006. Gender stereotyping and under-representation of female characters in 200 popular children's picture books: A twenty-first century update. *Sex Roles* 55:757–65.

Irvine, Leslie. 2007. Introduction: Social justice and the animal question. *Humanity & Society* 31:299–304.

Kimmel, Michael. 1987. Men's responses to feminism at the turn of the century. *Gender & Society* 1:261–83.

Klein, Hugh, and Kenneth S. Shiffman. 2009. Underrepresentation and symbolic annihilation of socially disenfranchised groups ("out groups") in animated cartoons. *Howard Journal of Communications* 20:55–72

Peterson, Sharyl Bender, and Mary Alyce Lach. 1990. Gender stereotypes in children's books: Their prevalence and impact on cognitive and affective development. *Gender & Education* 2:185–97.

Rupp, Leila J., and Verta Taylor. 1987. *Survival in the doldrums: The American women's rights movement, 1945 to the 1960s*. New York: Oxford University Press.

Scharf, Lois. 1980. *To work and to wed: Female employment, feminism, and the Great Depression*. Westport, CT: Greenwood Press.

Segel, Elizabeth. 1986. "As the twig is bent . . .": Gender and childhood reading. In *Gender and reading: Essays on readers, texts, and contexts*, edited by E. A. Flynn and P. P. Schweickart. Baltimore: The Johns Hopkins University Press.

Smith, Stacy L., Katherine M. Pieper, Amy Granados, and Marc Choueiti. 2010. Assessing gender-related portrayals in top-grossing G-rated films. *Sex Roles* 62:774–86.

Tobias, Shelia. 1997. *Faces of feminism: An activist's reflections on the women's movement*. Boulder, CO: Westview.

Trepanier-Street, Clary A., and Kimberly Wright Romatowski. 1999. The influence of children's literature on gender role perceptions: A reexamination. *Early Childhood Education Journal* 26:155–59.

Tuchman, Gaye. 1978. The symbolic annihilation of women by the mass media. In *Hearth and home: Images of women in the mass media*, edited by G. Tuchman, A. K. Daniels, and J. Benét. New York: Oxford University Press.

Turow, Joseph. 1978. Getting books to children: An exploration of publisher-market relations. Chicago: American Library Association.

Weitzman, Lenore, Deborah Eifler, Elizabeth Hokada, and Catherine Ross. 1972. Sex-role socialization in picture books for preschool children. *American Journal of Sociology* 77:1125–150.

Introduction to Reading 19

While puberty is a time of biological changes, adolescence brings its own set of social changes, particularly in a larger culture that is ambivalent, at best, to the emergent sexuality of teens. In this article, Richard Mora examines how 10 sixth-grade, second-generation, immigrant Puerto Rican and Dominican boys experience puberty. He conducted a 2-year ethnographic study of sixth-graders at their school in a Northeastern urban area. In this article, he focuses on the experiences of these 10 working-class Latino boys whom he observed both in school and out of school, as they invited him to join them in other activities. Mora describes how these boys experienced and interpreted their changing bodies during puberty and the following year. It is interesting to see how the boys used this biological change, such as the growth of pubic hair, to reinforce toughness and masculinity.

1. After reading this article, how would you explain how gender socialization occurs? Who socializes teen boys, and how does socialization happen?

2. Why was it so important to these boys to prove their masculinity to themselves and others during puberty, and why were these issues different in the seventh grade? Are they learning the "basics" of hegemonic masculinity?

3. What parts of these boys' experiences might be generalized beyond the Latino population Mora studied?

"Do It for All Your Pubic Hairs!"

Latino Boys, Masculinity, and Puberty

Richard Mora

Introduction

Pubescence brings about the most noticeable changes to the male body, second only to neonatal development (Martin 1996). The social meanings ascribed to these physical changes, and puberty itself, are locally situated (Janssen 2006). Hence, understanding how boys make sense of puberty, as well as how they interpret and socially construct their bodies during pubescence, may illuminate how boys' bodies figure into gender identities, given that doing gender involves bodies (Butler 1993; West and Zimmerman 1987) and that masculinity is a life-long project involving the changing physical body (Connell 2005). Yet the literature lacks thorough and sustained in situ examinations of how diverse boys employ their bodies to

Mora, Richard. 2012, forthcoming."'Do It for All Your Pubic Hairs!': Latino boys, Masculinity, and Puberty." *Gender & Society.*

construct masculine identities during pubescence across a range of sociocultural contexts.

The present article seeks to contribute to the literature on masculinity by examining the gender construction of Latino boys, an understudied segment of the U.S. population. More to the point, it addresses the following research question: How do 10 sixth-grade, second-generation, immigrant Dominican and Puerto Rican boys, who publicly acknowledge that they are experiencing puberty, construct their masculine identities and employ their bodies at school? The question emerged early on in a two-and-a-half-year ethnographic study, when review of daily field notes suggested that both gender identity and puberty held social meanings within their group. Given that masculinity is defined by peers and is constructed collectively (Swain 2003) via social interactions (West and Zimmerman 1987), peer relations were closely examined. Not assuming a priori that puberty mattered to the boys allowed for emic understandings of how the peer group influenced boys' views of their bodies and pubescence.

The data suggest that among the boys puberty was a social accomplishment connected to masculine enactments informed by the dominant gendered expectations of peers at school and in their neighborhoods, the hegemonic masculine practices espoused by commercial hip hop rappers, and the dominant gender orders in the United States and both Dominican and Puerto Rican societies. . . .

The Body and Masculinity

Research shows that boys pay attention to their physical appearance for both functional and aesthetic purposes (Grogan and Richards 2002). Masculine power is ascribed to muscular male physiques. Aware that their bodies are interpreted and gendered by others, boys and men from distinct socioeconomic and racial backgrounds work on their bodies with the intent of achieving the ideal male physique attributed to high masculine status (McCabe and Ricciardelli 2004; Pope, Phillips, and Olivardia 2000). Consequently,

boys and men consider a "flabby body" less manly (Lilleaas 2007, 42). British research suggests that men and boys of varying age associate fat with lack of control and weakness (Grogan and Richards 2002). While there is some evidence that Latino men may also disapprove of flabbiness (Pope, Phillips, and Olivardia 2000, 206), little research examines Latino boys' view of their bodies and masculinity.

In schools, boys of distinct ages, races, and social classes negotiate their masculine identities and social standing by demonstrating their physical dexterity, strength, and athleticism (Davison 2000; Eder, Evans, and Parker 1995; Hasbrook and Harris 1999; Walker 1988). On school campuses, sports usually provide a venue for successful gender performances (Connell 2005). Those who use their bodies successfully during sporting activities can amass "physical capital" and gain masculine status (Swain 2000, 2003). What is more, for many low-income African American and Dominican boys (Dance 2002; Ferguson 2001; Lopez 2003), doing gender at school might involve using their bodies to fight, in spite of school rules. It is likely that physical development influences how boys use their bodies.

Boys enter puberty approximately two and a half years earlier than their counterparts did at the beginning of the twentieth century (Frankel 2003). Presently, the age range for the onset of puberty in boys is nine to 14 years (compared to 8 to 13 years in girls) (Katz and Misra 2011). The mean age of initial growth spurts for boys is approximately 11 years, approximately 2 years later than for girls (Abbassi 1998; Katz and Misra 2011). As a result, sixth-grade classrooms may have boys who have yet to experience pubescence and girls who look like young adult women (Eccles 1999, 38).

Boys take pride in displaying both their growing bodies and their bodily control (Davison 2000; Prendergast and Forrest 1997, 1998; Vaccaro 2011). Still, some boys experience anxiety around physiological changes, particularly those whose changes come later (Martin 1996). Boys who experience puberty later than their peers do tend to be less popular. Retrospective data based on interviews with a group of mostly white working- and middle-class high school students suggest that, compared to girls, boys tend to experience puberty alone and hardly discuss such matters with peers (Martin 1996). . . .

Masculinity at School and Boy Peer Groups

Research indicates that in schools, boys' masculinity typically involves performing dominant heterosexual identities (Kehily 2001; Mac an Ghaill 1994; Martino and Pallotta-Chiarolli 2003; Renold 2005; Walker 1988), with peers regularly policing male heterosexuality (Chambers, Tincknell, and Loon 2004; Eder, Evans, and Parker 1995; Epstein, O'Flynn, and Telford 2000; Nayak and Kehily 2001). More often than not, high-status boys dictate the hegemonic masculinities that regulate and maintain the gender order (Gardiner 2000; Lopez 2003; Mac an Ghaill 1994; Martino 1999, 2000; Martino and Pallotta-Chiarolli 2003; McGuffey and Rich 1999; Pascoe 2007; Swain 2000, 2003). Though boys typically try on and test masculine identities in the presence of friends (Ferguson 2001), they nonetheless often construct their masculinities by regulating gender boundaries (Ferguson 2001; Kehily 2001; Renold 2001, 2005; Swain 2003; Witt 2000). In addition, they typically promote "compulsory heterosexuality" within their peer groups (Epstein, 2001; Epstein and Johnson 1998; Korobov 2005; Redman et al. 2002; Martino 2000).

The "panopticonic regimes of surveillance" present in peer groups normalize heterosexuality (Martino and Pallotta-Chiarolli 2003). Peers accuse those who do not live up to heteronormative expectations of being homosexuals (Dalley-Trim 2007; Eliasson, Isaksson, and Laflamme 2007; Mac an Ghaill 1994; Pascoe 2007; Renold 2003), emphasizing the importance of heterosexuality (Schrock and Schwalbe 2009). In many male peer groups, to be a boy means not being a sissy or girl (Thorne 1993), as masculinity involves the rejection of femininity and homosexuality. Hence,

boys across racial and class groups typically define their gender identities against "the dual Others," namely girls and boys deemed feminine (Epstein 2001, 106; Gilbert and Gilbert 1998; Haywood and Mac an Ghaill 2001; Nilan 2000). As research makes clear, students are active agents in the making of masculinities (Connell 2000), and the ongoing gender policing within peer groups demands that boys must be vigilant about abiding by gender expectations and putting forth context-appropriate masculine performances. The consequences of not abiding by heteronormative expectations may vary in different contexts. The present study documents some of the consequences for Latino boys at an urban middle school.

Schools themselves influence gender construction among students. School staff members regularly promulgate heteronormativity with gendered school policies and activities (Connell 2005; Eder, Evans, and Parker 1995; Martino and Pallotta-Chiarolli 2003; Renold 2001, 2003, 2005; Swain 2000, 2003). Teachers and school officials, for example, influence the gender identities of Black and Latino students by ascribing deviant labels to them (Ferguson 2001; Lopez 2003). In a study examining the social mobility of Caribbean youth residing in New York City, Lopez (2003) finds that Dominican young men divested in school largely because they were singled out for more scrutiny by high school officials and security guards, and so invested in constructing their masculine identities on the streets by hanging out, dating, and making money.

Ethnoracial Identity, Class, and Masculinity

Youth from varied racial and class backgrounds construct their masculinities in different manners. For second-generation Caribbean youth, for example, proving masculinity is an experience that involves racial stigma (Lopez 2003). Furthermore, some young men of color in the United States, especially those who are working-class or poor, adopt coping mechanisms, such as the "cool pose" used by African

American males (Majors and Billson 1993) and the "masculine protest behaviors" of urban youth, including Puerto Ricans (De La Cancela 1993, 34), to deal with their marginalized position in society. Male youths from low-income neighborhoods may enact masculinities that include the use of stoic personas—"tough fronts" by Black youth (Dance 2002) and "cara de palo" (wooden club-face) by U.S.-based Puerto Ricans (Thomas 1987)—and the use of their bodies as weapons to gain status and ward off potential assailants (Majors and Billson 1993). Such presentations of self by urban youth are oftentimes part of a "code of the streets," a set of cultural ideas that dictate social expectations and conduct in urban localities, particularly those where neighborhood violence is a common occurrence (Anderson 2000).

Studies of masculine practices among U.S. Latinos and Latin American men tend to focus on machismo, or the cult of manliness (Arciniega et al. 2008; Casas et al. 1994; De La Cancela 1993; Falicov 2010; Gutmann 1996; Mirandé 1997; Torres, Solberg, and Carlstrom 2002). Early research equated machismo with behaviors attributed to working-class men and peasants from Latin America (Ramirez 1999), including male dominance, assertiveness, aggressiveness, and the valuing of physical strength and courage (Mosher 1991). However, Latin American women and individuals from various non-Latin American cultures and countries also display characteristics associated with machismo (Doyle 1995). In addition, the term carries different emic meanings in different Latin American countries (De La Cancela 1993), and some emic variants are not rooted in the dominance of women (Doyle 1995). As a result, many scholars have moved away from an overly simplified understanding of machismo (Casas et al. 1994; De La Cancela 1991; Gutmann 1996; Mirandé 1997; Torres 1998; Torres, Solberg, and Carlstrom 2002). As Torres, Solberg, and Carlstrom (2002) explain, the rearticulation of machismo has given rise to "*the dialectical perspective* . . . [which] depicts machismo as both progressive and reactionary patterns of

behaviors intimately related to the socioeconomic and historical elements of society" (167). Nonetheless, scholars and journalists still often equate the term with negative male attitudes and behaviors (Gutmann 1996).

. . . Neither the boys nor the girls that I observed used [the term *machismo*] to describe masculine behavior. That is, the term was not emic. Furthermore, the negative connotations associated with machismo would racially bias the interpretation of the data. As a result, machismo is an inadequate descriptor. In addition, the fact that a wide range of characteristics are associated with "the cult of manliness" limits its explanatory power.

* * *

FINDINGS

"Puberty Is Now": Changing Bodies

While in the sixth grade, the boys were experiencing their sexual maturation—a fact they declared publicly. During a science class discussion on physical development, for example, a boy loudly interjected, "Puberty is now." In addition, the boys' exchanges regularly included references to puberty and the biological changes that come with it. When a boy appeared exceedingly "wild" (i.e., hyperactive), the other boys attributed it to hormonal changes brought on by puberty and, using language introduced by one of them, jokingly rebuked him with statements such as, "Control your hormones!" and "Let your hormones relax, c'mon. Your hormones are gonna get tired." Such commentary highlights the importance of control over one's body, an ability associated with maturity, masculinity, and adolescence, and not boyhood.

Like other boys (Dixon 1997; Martino and Pallotta-Chiarolli 2003), the boys at Romero viewed penises as appendages that distinguish boys from girls and are associated with males' manhood and dominance. They frequently brought up male genitalia to playfully disparage one another's masculine identities. One afternoon, banter about a banana resulted in the charge that Rudy, the shortest boy, had an undersized penis. . . .

Here, Steven and Cesar used Rudy to demarcate the low masculine status attributed to smaller male bodies. As the only boy frequently referred to as "shrimp," "small fry," or "enano [midget]," Rudy was not perceived as physically dominant, which led to the accusation that he has a small penis. The data highlight the interplay between the body and the construction of gendered identities (Butler 1993; Connell 2005).

The boys also referenced puberty to emphasize the relative nature of masculine status within their peer group's gender order. An exchange about male genitalia, for example, led Brandon to ask Steven whether he had experienced his first menstruation. . . .

Brandon's depiction of Steven as a girl who is yet to experience menstruation called both Steven's gender and pubescent development into question. Here menarche, as a signifier of femininity, undermines the possibility of masculinity.

In all, I counted 43 references to secondary sex characteristics, of which nearly two dozen were during public acts of verbal one-upmanship. Participating in banter and verbal one-upmanship was a cultural, gendered expectation the boys willingly met at Romero as well as with male cousins and friends they visited in the Dominican Republic or Puerto Rico. Like other working-class Dominican (De Moya 2004) and Puerto Rican youth (Ramírez 1999), the boys constructed their masculine identities and dominance with their verbal exchanges. Contrary to the retrospective accounts of high school students (Martin 1996), the boys at Romero experienced puberty within their homosocial group, rather than alone.

The boys mentioned penises much more during the sixth grade than at any comparable period thereafter, and stopped publicly referencing puberty after the sixth grade. The stark difference from one academic year to the next likely reflects how much more willing the boys were to discuss the initial phases of their pubescence at a time when they wanted their bodies to communicate their physical development, which is not to say that they did not consider subsequent pubescent changes significant.

Bodies in Transition

The boys compared the size of their flexed biceps and the firmness of their abdomens on almost a daily basis, and by doing so assessed their bodies. With comments like, "I'm stronger," they frequently vied to carry boxes and crates for teachers. Through these verbal interactions, the boys enacted a social hierarchy based on the gender status attributed to muscular development, which was proof of a boy's physical transition beyond boyhood and of his willingness to control and transform his physique.

The boys openly shared their desire to possess the "sociocultural ideal male physique—strong, lean, muscular, and fit "(McCabe and Ricciardelli 2004). A telling example of how much they yearned for muscular bodies worthy of admiration is a portrait one of them drew of himself and his four closest friends in the class. The drawing, which according to the illustrator depicted his friends and him "in five or six years," was of five stoic young men, each wearing a tank top and baggy pants, with extremely muscular arms and chests, relatively small waists, and a weapon—either a knife, a gun, or a crowbar—in his hand. The figures are exaggerated versions of the males whose physiological aesthetic and style the boys were interested in replicating—namely, the muscular rappers they favored, the older youth at Romero, and the Black and Latino young men in the boys' neighborhoods, most of whom valued strong bodies and who, per the local "code of the street," were willing to use their bodies as weapons in a fight. Both broad and localized cultural expectations associated with masculinity and male bodies informed the boys' imaginings of future male selves during puberty.

For the boys, gladiators and other warrior types, including professional wrestlers and video game characters, also served as evidence that superior male physiques were an accomplishment, the result of physical training. Consider

Michael's reference to gladiators in a fantasy replete with his aspiration to have a sculpted body and to use it in a notable manner:

> As students worked independently on an assignment on ancient Rome, Michael says to me, "Richard, I'm going to build a time machine and go back [to ancient Rome]. I'm going to work out so when I go I'm strong. I'm going to get a scar." He moves a finger along his right cheek. "I'm going to fight like the gladiators."

For both cultural and practical reasons, Michael and the rest of the boys valued tough, strong bodies skilled at fighting. Culturally, among Dominican and Puerto Rican youth at and around Romero, like among many of their peers in the Caribbean (De Moya 2004; Ramírez 1999), there was the expectation that men defend themselves. Practically, Michael and the boys were cognizant that in their neighborhoods physical fights between adolescent boys were a reality. Additionally, like marginalized, urban, African American boys (Dance 2002) and youth (Majors and Billson 1993), the Latino boys at Romero were willing to use their bodies as weapons in order to protect their physical well-being or masculine status.

Since the boys prized muscular definition, they were quite preoccupied with the amount of fat (or "flubber") on their bodies. Like other boys (James 2000), they too held fatness in low regard, equating it with a lack of bodily control. A telling incident is what transpired after the nurse had summoned the entire class for a yearly basic health examination. Rudy returned, came over to me and said, "Richard, I was nervous." I asked Rudy why he was nervous and he replied, "I don't know. My flubber. My Jell-O rolls." Then, both Pedro and Rodrigo came into the room smiling and in a celebratory tone simultaneously yelled, "I don't have no flubber!"

Aware that others scrutinized their bodies, many of the boys with flubber masked their concerns with self-deprecating humor. Michael, for example, occasionally lifted his shirt, exposing his stomach, and asked peers, "Do you think I'm fat?" Additionally, the handful of boys who had

flubber sought to communicate that they nonetheless possessed physical strength. For example, while discussing his physical appearance with a thinner, taller female classmate, a boy stated, "I don't care if I don't have a six-pack [defined abdominal muscles]. I got muscles. That's why you couldn't take the ball away from me [during a basketball game]." . . .

Some bodies are valued differently depending in part on the social context (Butler 1993; Connell 2005). In the boys' social world, a muscular male body was a physical representation of manliness and evidence of the physiological shift from boyhood and childhood toward male adulthood and manliness. Among their peers and the Black, Dominican, and Puerto Rican youths in their neighborhoods, muscular physiques signaled bodily control, an important trait in an urban, low-income context where the use of male bodies as weapons was common. . . .

Physical Strength, Toughness, and Masculine Status

At Romero, there were no school-sanctioned sports teams. Thus, unlike the boys in other studies (Eder, Evans, and Parker 1995; Martin 1996; Stein and Reiser 1994; Swain 2000, 2003), the boys at Romero lacked the opportunity to acquire masculine status by displaying their physical toughness and might on the field or court. That may explain why the boys opted to bring their masculinity "into action" through a wide array of physical activities, particularly arm wrestling matches, bloody knuckles, and slap hands, all of which the school banned to curtail verbal and physical confrontations (Swain 2003, 311). With these localized and ritualized physical enactments, the boys sought to initiate themselves into manhood, and thus punished their bodies while defining, exploring, and patrolling the boundaries of their collective masculine practices. They did this mostly in the lunch area, where it was easier to evade teachers' surveillance.

The boys eagerly engaged in various tests of strength replete with masculine performativity. For example, when Alberto refused to lend Jorge a colored pencil, their interaction turned into a physical challenge, after which Albert declared himself a man, in effect questioning Jorge's manhood. . . .

The boys made such public declarations of manliness whenever they successfully used their bodies to best others. On average, there were six brash comments, like "I'm a man" or "I'm *the* man," per day of observation.

The boys' loud proclamations drew the attention of teachers, one of whom assured me that the boys "don't think of themselves as boys, they think of themselves as men." However, in time, I learned that when they referred to themselves as men they were simply voicing their masculine aspirations. In one another's presence, the boys readily admitted to being preadolescent boys or, as they put it, "pre-teenagers." Thus, it seems that with their declarations, the boys were attempting to make sense of their ongoing and impending physical development while also attempting to construct tough masculine identities worthy of praise in their social worlds.

The most notable manner by which the boys publicly asserted their masculine identities was through arm wrestling matches. On average, I observed approximately a dozen arm wrestling matches per site visit. The boys used the outcomes of these challenges to rank themselves and to compare their relative physiological development. . . .

The boys also sought out opportunities to arm wrestle older boys with bigger, more developed physiques. Most of the seventh- and eighth-grade boys accepted challenges only after the younger boys playfully took on a tough persona and accused them of being "scared." The older boys won every one of these matches handily. However, interactions with older, male schoolmates provided the boys opportunities to try on the stoic "cara de palo" that was central to the presentation of self embodied by many rappers and urban youth, including Dominicans and Puerto Ricans that resided around Romero (Thomas 1987). Additionally, by arm wrestling seventh- and eighth-graders, the sixth-grade boys displayed their bravado to older boys who

put forth the confident, tough, masculine personas the sixth-grade boys attempted to emulate both at Romero and outside of school, where being assaulted by adolescent youths was a real possibility.

Like the older boys, the sixth-grade girls also greatly influenced how the boys viewed their physicality and masculinity. Over the course of the second semester, the boys were challenged approximately two dozen times by both the girls in their class peer group and those in the other sixth-grade class. The boys rebuffed these challenges because many of their female peers were physically stronger, a fact the boys acknowledged only among themselves. For the boys to arm wrestle girls and lose would have been humiliating since they publicly claimed that males are physically stronger than females.

Their homosocial peer group offered the boys not just a refuge, but also "a performative space where heterosexuality and masculinity can be fused and displayed" (Kehily 2001, 179). The banter that punctuated arm wrestling matches was a performativity that reified their heteronormative masculine narrative. Along with grunts and laughter, all the boys regularly lobbed joking accusations of homosexuality and unmanliness at one another, for a tally of over 50 individual instances. Here is a case in point:

Ignacio asks Albert, "You're the son of a fag?"

Albert smiles and screams, "Do it [arm wrestle] for all your pubic hairs!"

With a homophobic slur commonly used in the boys' social worlds to stress the heteronormativity underpinning gender practices, Ignacio implied that Albert's poor performance was evidence of his father's homosexuality. Like his peers, Ignacio coupled heterosexual masculinity and physical strength—a perspective in line with the hegemonic masculinities in the boys' neighborhoods, in their respective countries of origin (De Moya 2004; Ramírez 1999), and in the United States (Connell 2000, 2005; Kimmel and Messner 1998). Albert, for his part, then associated boys' corporeal might with pubic hairs, a key signifier of puberty.

To highlight corporeal might and other masculine traits exalted in their homosocial peer group, the boys belittled any boy that did not adequately display the traits by calling him "a girl" or "a woman"—a finding echoed in Thorne (1993) and Fine (1987). . . .

Perhaps because they craved external validation, the boys were quick to praise one another for exhibiting grit during physical activities. Such public praise was sometimes a form of gender policing that reinforced the notion that manhood required the withstanding of pain in "sporting situations" (Vaccaro 2011, 71). . . .

Aware that their masculine status was dependent on how they utilized their bodies, the boys regularly tried to convince each other to engage in public physical challenges. For example, one afternoon, Raul held out his right clenched fist and invited another boy to play bloody knuckles with him: "C'mon, punch my knuckles. It's like a massage. It doesn't hurt me. It's like a massage. C'mon, give me a massage." When rebuffed, boys usually tried to goad their prospective competitors with statements such as "Don't be a sissy" and "Don't be a girl." More often than not, boys who declined a challenge were also met with ridicule from other peers. All this pressure and gender policing rarely failed. . . .

Little Boys, No More

Though the boys and girls were the same age, the girls were generally taller and appeared older than their actual age. As a result, the girls interpreted their own bodies as closer to adulthood and maturity than the boys' bodies. Consider what a girl asserted during a discussion in health class:

> Angelica: "The girls are growing up. They are thinking ahead. They are getting mature and the boys are not." A number of boys yell out in protest, "What?!"

The girls' reaction bothered the boys because it differed from the flirtatious interactions the girls had with many seventh-grade boys, whom the girls described as "tall" and "fine" (i.e., attractive). Throughout the observations, the girls made 26 statements in which they referred to the boys as "little boys" because of what they deemed their "childish" behavior, such as punching lockers, arm wrestling during class, and play fighting. Similarly, eighth-grade girls regularly called some of the boys "cute" and ruffled their hair, which the boys found condescending. In doing so, the girls at Romero voiced physical expectations for adolescent manliness and influenced the boys' construction of masculine identities. The data are in accordance with previous findings that girls look upon boys whose bodies demonstrate no visible signs of development as children (Dixon 1997).

Teachers also influenced the boys' perceptions of their own physical development. Their teachers mostly infantilized them with regular, public chastisements for acting "like babies" when they "whined" about one another's behavior. Less often, teachers pointed out how particular boys were physically "changing.". . .

The boys wanted recognition for their physical development, and did not want to hear how much they physically resembled younger boys. Consequently, partly to avoid derision, the boys maintained their homosocial peer group during the sixth grade, but their female peers and teachers nonetheless influenced their masculine identities.

After the summer between the sixth and seventh grade, the boys returned to school physically transformed. All of them were taller, and most of them had shed much of the "flubber" that had occupied their minds just months earlier. Most of the boys were now taller than their female classmates. At the beginning of the seventh grade, their teachers and female peers complimented them on their physiological development, which may explain why many of them walked with more of a swagger and projected greater confidence than they had three months prior. Furthermore, from the seventh grade on, the boys rarely engaged in the physical games and challenges of "little boys." That is, they hardly made a public show of their physical strength or their ability to endure physical pain.

Instead, they turned much of their attention to public displays of acceptable heteronormative masculinity, namely flirting with and trying to woo teenage girls. The boys and girls spent a lot of time and energy flirting with one another during the seventh and eighth grade. The boys' hegemonic masculinity dictated that they had to learn to flirt in order to woo teenage girls and women. The most common form of flirting involved *piropos*, or "'amorous compliments,' often undesired by the females at whom they are directed" (Bailey 2000, 562). I documented 51 *piropos*. Among the various *piropos* used by the boys were statements used in Spanish songs as well as by older peers and relatives on the streets of their neighborhoods and of their countries of origin. For example, some of the boys regularly said something like, "¡Oh, mami! Tu sí 'tas Buena. (Oh, baby! You *are* fine.)" The boys delivered most of their *piropos* in the presence of male peers, who acknowledged particularly clever compliments.

Into the flirtatious exchanges, the boys and girls often incorporated sexual innuendos that called attention to their own developed bodies and to those of the individuals they desired. These sorts of interactions allowed the boys and girls to express their physical attraction to one another and to explore the personal and physical boundaries of potential boyfriends and girlfriends. . . .

During these suggestive exchanges, boys displayed their compliance with compulsory heterosexuality and augmented their masculine status in the eyes of both their male and female peers by effectively flirting. Since wooing teenage girls could enhance a boy's masculine status, many of the boys claimed to have also flirted with and successfully wooed girls during their visits to Puerto Rico and/or the Dominican Republic—a claim that could not be ascertained, nor dismissed.

These findings suggest that once their physical development was apparent to others, the boys no longer felt such a pressing need to do masculinity by engaging in excessively competitive physical activities, and instead focused on enacting the heteronormative masculinity expected of males by peers at school and in their neighborhoods, as well as at home. By turning their energies toward wooing girls, the Dominican boys in the group behaved much like some of their peers in the Dominican Republic, who were expected to "show a vivid and visible erotic interest in all females that come close" by the age of 12 or 13, after the onset of puberty (De Moya 2004, 74).

CONCLUSION

By showing how Dominican and Puerto Rican boys collectively construct masculinity during pubescence, this article provides important insights into how diverse boys viewed their bodies and how multiple cultures inform the intersection of masculinity, ethnicity, and gender. The boys wanted height and physical musculature so that others, particularly their female peers and teachers, would no longer read them as "little boys." They yearned for muscular bodies that approximated the "sociocultural ideal male physique" highly valued by many males, including the young Dominican and Puerto Rican men in their urban neighborhoods, and their favorite rappers and wrestlers (McCabe and Ricciardelli 2004). Thus, with their declarations, banter, and physical activities, each of the boys sought to communicate that he was on his way beyond childhood and was preparing his body for a social world wherein physical confrontations between males were commonplace. Ironically, female classmates, many of whom were taller and physically stronger, associated the boys' enactments of masculinity not with manliness but rather with childishness. Still, the boys enacted gender hierarchies based on, and espoused the male dominance of, their models of masculinity—rappers and older boys at Romero, and in their neighborhoods. They professed that male bodies were naturally strong, and considered their female classmates' greater physical strength and height a temporary fact. Together, the cultural influences to which the boys were exposed reiterated the appropriateness of both hegemonic masculinities and of those masculine practices that provided status and some level of protection in their social worlds.

. . . Overall, the findings discussed earlier suggest that pubescence is a social process as much as a biological transformation, a social process that is interactional, collective, embodied, and situated in classed, gendered, and ethnoracialized contexts. In addition, the data contribute to the study of gender and masculinities by explicating how the boys, as U.S.-born Dominicans and Puerto Ricans residing in low-income neighborhoods, constructed their masculine identities while seeking to abide by the dominant gender expectations in localized social worlds and the norms from their countries of origin. . . .

REFERENCES

Abbassi, V. 1998. Growth and normal puberty. *Pediatrics* 102:507–11.

Anderson, E. 2000. *Code of the streets: Decency, violence and the moral life of the inner city*. New York: Norton.

Arciniega, G. M., T. C. Anderson, Z. G. Tovar-Blank, and T. J. G. Tracey. 2008. Toward a fuller conception of machismo: Development of a traditional machismo and caballerismo scale. *Journal of Counseling Psychology* 55:19–33.

Butler, J. 1993. *Bodies that matter: On the discursive limits of "sex."* New York: Routledge.

Casas, J. M., B. R. Wagenheim, R. Banchero, and J. Mendoza-Romero. 1994. Hispanic masculinity: Myth or psychological schema meriting clinical considerations. *Hispanic Journal of Behavioral Sciences* 16:315–31.

Chambers, D., E. Tincknell, and J. V. Loon. 2004. Peer regulation of teenage sexual identities. *Gender and Education* 16:297–315.

Connell, R. W. 2000. *The men and the boys*. Berkeley: University of California Press.

Connell, R. W. 2005. *Masculinities*. 2nd ed. Berkeley: University of California Press.

Dalley-Trim, L. 2007. "The boys" present . . . Hegemonic masculinity: A performance of multiple acts. *Gender and Education* 19:199–217.

Dance, L. J. 2002. *Tough fronts*. New York: Routledge Falmer.

Davison, K. G. 2000. Boys' bodies in school: Physical education. *Journal of Men's Studies* 8:255–66.

De La Cancela, V. 1991. Working affirmatively with Puerto Rican men: Professional and personal reflections. In *Feminist approaches for men in family therapy*, edited by M. Bograd. Binghamton, NY: Harrington Park Press.

De La Cancela, V. 1993. "Coolin": The psychosocial communication of African and Latino men. *Urban League Review* 16:33–44.

De Moya, A. 2004. Power games and totalitarian masculinity in the Dominican Republic. In *Interrogating Caribbean masculinities: Theoretical and empirical analyses*, edited by R. E. Reddock. Kingston: University of West Indies Press.

Dixon, C. 1997. Pete's tool: Identity and sex-play in the design and technology classroom. *Gender and Education* 9:89–104.

Doyle, J. A. 1995. *The male experience*. 3rd ed. Madison, WI: Brown & Benchmark.

Eccles, J. S. 1999, The development of children ages 6 to 14. *Future of Children* 9:30–44.

Eder, D., C. C. Evans, and S. Parker. 1995. *School talk: Gender and adolescent culture*. New Brunswick: Rutgers University Press.

Eliasson, M. A., K. Isaksson, and L. Laflamme. 2007. Verbal abuse in school: Constructions of gender among 14- to 15-year-olds. *Gender and Education* 19:587–605.

Epstein, D. 2001. Boyz' own stories: Masculinities and sexualities in schools. In *What about the boys?: Issues of masculinity in schools,* edited by W. Martino and B. Meyenn. Philadelphia: Open University Press.

Epstein, D., and R. Johnson. 1998. *Schooling sexualities*. Buckingham, UK: Open University Press.

Epstein, D., S. O'Flynn, and D. Telford. 2000. "Othering" education: Sexualities, silences, and schooling. *Review of Research in Education* 25:127–79.

Falicov, C. J. 2010. Changing constructions of machismo for Latino men in therapy: "The devil never sleeps." *Family Process* 49:309–29.

Ferguson, A. A. 2001. *Bad boys: Public schools in the making of black masculinity*. Ann Arbor: University of Michigan Press.

Fine, G. A. 1987. *With the boys: Little league baseball and preadolescent culture*. Chicago: University of Chicago Press.

Frankel, L. 2003. Puberty. In *Men and masculinities: A social, cultural, and historical encyclopedia,* edited by M. Kimmel and A. Aronson. Vol. II: K-Z. Santa Barbara: ABC-CLIO.

Gardiner, J. K. 2000. Masculinity, the teening of America, and empathic targeting. *Signs* 25:1257–61.

Gilbert, R., and P. Gilbert. 1998. *Masculinity goes to school.* New York: Routledge.

Grogan, S., and H. Richards. 2002. Body image: Focus groups with boys and men. *Men and Masculinities* 4:219–32.

Gutmann, M. C. 1996. *The meanings of macho: Being a man in Mexico City.* Berkeley: University of California Press.

Hasbrook, C. A., and O. Harris. 1999. Wrestling with gender: Physicality and masculinities among inner-city first and second graders. *Men and Masculinities* 1:302–18.

Haywood, C., and M. Mac an Ghaill. 2001. The significance of teaching English boys: Exploring social change, modern schooling and the making of masculinities. In *What about the boys?: Issues of masculinity in schools,* edited by W. Martino and B. Meyenn. Philadelphia: Open University Press.

James, A. 2000. Embodied being(s): Understanding the self and the body in childhood. In *The body, childhood, and society,* edited by A. Prout. Houndmills: Macmillan.

Janssen, D. F. 2006. "Become big, and I'll give you something to eat": Thoughts and notes on boyhood sexual health. *International Journal of Men's Health* 5:19–35.

Katz, M., and M. Misra. 2011. Delayed puberty, short stature, and tall stature. In *The Mass General Hospital for Children adolescent medicine handbook,* edited by Mark A. Goldstein. New York: Springer.

Kehily, M. 2001. Bodies in school: Young men, embodiment, and heterosexual masculinities. *Men and Masculinities* 4:173–85.

Kimmel, M., and M. Messner, eds. 1998. *Men's lives.* 4th ed. Boston: Allyn & Bacon.

Korobov, N. 2005. Ironizing masculinity: How adolescent boys negotiate heteronormative dilemmas in conversational interaction. *Journal of Men's Studies* 13:225–46.

Lilleaas, U. 2007. Masculinities, sport, and emotions. *Men and Masculinities* 10:39–53.

Lopez, Nancy. 2003. *Hopeful girls, troubled boys: Race and gender disparity in urban education.* New York: Routledge.

Mac an Ghaill, M. 1994. *The making of men: Masculinities, sexualities and schooling.* Buckingham: Open University Press.

Majors, R., and J. M. Billson. 1993. *Cool pose: The dilemmas of black manhood in America.* New York: Touchstone.

Martin, K. A. 1996. *Puberty, sexuality and the self: Boys and girls at adolescence.* New York: Routledge.

Martino, W. 1999. "Cool boys," "party animals," "squids," and "poofters": Interrogating the dynamics and politics of adolescent masculinities in school. *British Journal of the Sociology of Education* 20:239–63.

Martino, W. 2000. Policing masculinities: Investigating the role of homophobia and heteronormativity in the lives of adolescent schoolboys. *Journal of Men's studies* 8:213–36.

Martino, W., and M. Pallotta-Chiarolli. 2003. *So what's a boy?: Addressing issues of masculinity and schooling.* Berkshire, UK: Open University Press.

McCabe, M. P., and L. A. Ricciardelli. 2004. A longitudinal study of pubertal timing and extreme body change behaviors among adolescent boys and girls. *Adolescence* 39:145–66.

McGuffey, C. S., and B. L. Rich. 1999. Playing in the gender transgression zone. *Gender & Society* 13:608–27.

Mirandé, A. 1997. *Hombres y machos: Masculinity and Latino culture.* Boulder, CO: Westview Press.

Mosher, D.L. 1991. Macho men, machismo, and sexuality. *Annual Review of Sex Research* 2:199–247.

Nayak, A., and M.J. Kehily. 2001. "Learning to laugh": A study of schoolboy humour in the English secondary school. In *What about the boys?: Issues of masculinity in schools,* edited by W. Martino and B. Meyenn. Philadelphia: Open University Press.

Nilan, P. 2000. "You're hopeless, I swear to God": Shifting masculinities in classroom talk. *Gender and Education* 12:53–68.

Pascoe, C. J. 2007. *Dude, you're a fag: Masculinity and sexuality in high school.* Berkeley: University of California Press.

Pope, H. G., K. A. Phillips, and R. Olivardia. 2000. *The Adonis complex: The secret crisis of male body obsession.* New York: Free Press.

Prendergast, S., and S. Forrest. 1997. Gendered groups and the negotiation of heterosexuality in school. In *New sexual agendas,* edited by L. Segal. London: Macmillan.

Prendergast, S., and S. Forrest. 1998. Shorties, low-lifers, hard nuts and kings: Boys and the transformation of emotions. In *Emotions in social life: Social theories and contemporary issues*, edited by G. Bendelow and S. Williams. London: Routledge.

Ramírez, Rafael L. 1999. *What it means to be a man: Reflections on Puerto Rican masculinity*, translated by Rosa E. Casper. New Brunswick, NJ: Rutgers University Press.

Redman, P., D. Epstein, M. J. Kehily, and M. Mac an Ghaill. 2002. Boys bonding: Same-sex friendship, the unconscious and heterosexual discourse. *Discourse* 23:179–91.

Renold, E. 2001. Learning the "hard" way: Boys, hegemonic masculinity and the negotiation of learner identities in the primary school. *British Journal of Sociology of Education* 22:369–85.

Renold, E. 2003. "If you don't kiss me, you're dumped": Boys, boyfriends and heterosexualised masculinities in the primary school. *Educational Review* 55:179–94.

Renold, E. 2005. *Girls, boys and junior sexualities: Exploring children's gender and sexual relations in the primary school*. London: Routledge Falmer.

Schrock, D., and M. Schwalbe. 2009. Men, masculinity, and manhood acts. *Annual Review of Sociology* 35:277–95.

Stein, J. H., and L. W. Reiser. 1994. A study of white middle-class adolescent boys' responses to "semerache." *Journal of Youth and Adolescence* 23:373–84.

Swain, J. 2000. "The money's good, the fame's good, the girls are good": The role of playground football in the construction of young boys' masculinity in a junior school. *British Journal of Sociology of Education* 21:95–109.

Swain, J. 2003. How young schoolboys become somebody: The role of the body in the construction of masculinity. *British Journal of Sociology of Education* 24:299–314.

Thomas, P. 1987. *Down these mean streets*. New York: Alfred A. Knopf.

Thorne, B. 1993. *Gender play: Girls and boys in school*. New Brunswick: Rutgers University Press.

Torres, J.B. 1998. Masculinity and gender roles among Puerto Rican men: Machismo on the U.S. mainland. *American Journal of Orthopsychiatry* 68:16–26.

Torres, J. B., V. S. H. Solberg, and A. H. Carlstrom. 2002. The myth of sameness among Latino men and their machismo. *American Journal of Orthopsychiatry* 72:163–81.

Vaccaro, C. A. 2011. Male bodies in manhood acts: The role of body-talk and embodied practice in signifying culturally dominant notions of manhood. *Sociology Compass* 5:65–76.

Walker, J. C. 1988. *Louts and legends: Male youth culture in an inner city school*. Sydney: Allen & Unwin.

West, C., and D. H. Zimmerman. 1987. Doing gender. *Gender & Society* 1:125–51.

Witt, S. D. 2000. The influence of peers on children's socialization to gender roles. *Early Child Development and Care* 162:1–7.

Introduction to Reading 20

This reading provides an in-depth and theoretical analysis of ways we "do" gender in everyday activities, thus supporting the gender structure of our collective lives. Matthew B. Ezzell spent 13 months as a participant observer studying a women's rugby team at a large, public university in the southeastern United States. He identified himself as a "white, (pro) feminist man" who recognized his position of privilege in our society. This created both problems and advantages as he carried out his research. The women on this team were very open while, at the same time, testing their performance of emphasized femininity on him—a member of the White, male audience, the target of their displays of gender. Notice the various strategies the women used to enforce appropriate gendered performances for themselves and other players on their team.

1. What is the advantage to these women of "defensive othering"?

2. How does their use of the strategies described in this article support traditional forms of gender?

3. As you read through this article, think about the ways we do gender. Try to come up with other situations in which women may participate in "identifying with the dominants" and thus reinforce traditional patterns of gender.

"Barbie Dolls" on the Pitch

Identity Work, Defensive Othering, and Inequality in Women's Rugby

Matthew B. Ezzell

Identities are the "meanings one attributes to oneself as an object" (Burke and Tully 1977:883). Michael L. Schwalbe and Douglas Mason-Schrock (1996) expound on this understanding by focusing on identity claims as "indexes of the self" (p. 115). By this, they mean that identities are not meanings in and of themselves, but signs that individuals and groups use to *evoke* meanings in the form of responses from others. Identities, then, are signifiers of the self. They are not fixed, as if they were personality traits, but mutable consequences of reflection and interaction (Blumer 1969; McCall and Simmons 1978; Strauss 1959). Accordingly, individuals and groups can *work on* their identities. Identity work is "anything people do, individually or collectively, to give meaning to themselves or others" (Schwalbe and Mason-Schrock 1996:115).

Race, class, and gender, as Candace West and Don H. Zimmerman (1987) and West and Sarah Fenstermaker (1995) have argued, are interlocking systems of oppression; moreover, they are

the social arrangements from which we derive our core identities. This view implies that identity creation and affirmation are parts of the process whereby inequality is reproduced. The study of identity work, thus, has the potential to yield insight into the processes that uphold large-scale inequalities. Conversely, we can learn about social change by studying the dynamics of identity change (see, e.g., Stryker, Owens, and White 2000).

What happens when, as part of their identity work, members of subordinated groups act in ways that challenge dominants' expectations for their groups, yet seek approval from dominants? How do they manage this potential dilemma? I examine these questions through an ethnographic analysis of collegiate female athletes, addressing how they resist and reproduce inequality through interaction. Specifically, I analyze how a group of female rugby players, responding to subordinated status and the stigma that arose from their transgression of conventional gendered norms, managed their identities as women, as athletes, and, for most of them, as heterosexuals. Some of their strategies fall into the category of "defensive othering." This occurs when subordinates "[accept] the legitimacy of a devalued identity imposed by the dominant group, but then [say], in effect, 'There are indeed Others to whom this applies, but it does not apply to me'" (Schwalbe et al. 2000:425). Michael Schwalbe and associates include defensive othering as one of the generic processes in the reproduction of inequality. They note:

> To call these processes "generic" does not imply that they are unaffected by context. It means, rather, that they occur in multiple contexts wherein social actors face similar or analogous problems. The precise form a process takes in any given setting is a matter for empirical determination. (p. 421)

This paper offers such an empirical analysis within a specific context. I expand on the work of Schwalbe and associates by adding two subcategories of defensive othering, offering insights into how inequality is reproduced through face-to-face interaction. In particular, I analyze how the players (a) *identified with dominants* (identifying with the values associated with dominant group members)[1] and (b) engaged in what I call *normative identification* (identifying with the normative values prescribed by dominants for subordinated group members). Also, I discuss how the players deflected stigma through a boundary maintenance process I call *propping up dominants* (reinforcing the idea that dominant group members are, and should be, dominant).

In brief, I offer a situated analysis of the processes of identity management in a sexist and homophobic context. The female "ruggers" at the heart of this study were successful athletes throughout high school, but they did not make it onto varsity collegiate teams in their high school sports. Rugby provided an attractive alternative. A nationally competitive, yet nonvarsity sport at their university, rugby is unique among women's sports in having the same rules and equipment as the men's game. The sport offered identity resources for the women, as athletes, because of its hypermasculine structure and style of play. These same aspects of the game, however, exposed the players, as women, to sexist and homophobic stigma from outsiders. In response to the conditions under which they interacted, the players worked to create a seemingly contradictory (collective) identity that was simultaneously tough, fit, feminine, and heterosexual. It is an identity I call *heterosexy-fit*.[2]

The players' construction and accomplishment of this identity challenged the notion that women are passive and incompetent at a male-defined activity (sports), but also unintentionally reinforced ideas and practices that contribute to women's subordination. In this sense, the identity work of the women at the heart of this study is similar to the "apologetic" model of resistance (when women "apologize" for their gendered transgressions by emphasizing other conventional aspects of gender presentation and performance) found among female athletes (see Broad 2001; Felshin 1974; Griffin 1992, 1998; Messner 2002; and Sabo 1993). Apologetics have also been found among women in other traditionally male-defined and -centered institutions. . . .

I argue that the heterosexy-fit identity of the female ruggers in the current study represents an updated version of "emphasized femininity" (Connell 1987) that combines toughness, assertiveness, and hard-body athleticism along with more conventional feminine qualities.[3] This expands on the "contemporary emphasized femininity" found among female cheerleaders (Adams and Bettis 2003; Grindstaff and West 2006), athletes in a sport in which performed femininity is part of the sport itself. Further, my findings stand in sharp contrast to research on other women's rugby teams, which has largely focused on the sport as a site of transgressive (Chase 2006; Howe 2003; Wheatley 1994) and "unapologetic" queer (Broad 2001) resistance. Throughout the paper, I will highlight the features of the specific context in which my participants interacted that shaped their identity work in ways to mark them as unique within the world of women's rugby.

Finally, this is a case study of a single rugby team, and it is not my intention to generalize my findings to the population of female rugby players, particularly given the uniqueness of this team within the larger rugby culture. Instead, I use the data from this case to cull the strategies of identity work that members of any subordinated group may use when they challenge prescribed norms for their group but still seek the approval of dominants.

* * *

SPORT AND DEFENSIVE OTHERING

Historically, one coping strategy for subordinated group members working within systems of oppression and privilege is the imitation of dominants (Miller 1976). Because these systems are dominated by, identified with, and centered on members of the oppressor class (Johnson 2006), this involves taking on and/or supporting the norms, values, and behaviors of that class (see Gramsci 1971). At times, members of subordinated groups may engage in defensive othering—reinforcing the power of stigmatizing labels by arguing that the label is true for other members of their social category, but not for themselves. . . .

Members of subordinated groups may use defensive othering to specifically deflect resistance to their participation in dominant-identified institutions. One such institution for women in Western societies is sport (Bolin and Granskog 2003; Burstyn 1999; Heywood and Dworkin 2003; Lenskyj 1986; Lorber 1994; Messner 1990). Women's participation in sport challenges the essentialist equation of femininity with physical weakness and passivity. Historically, the institution has been a core site for boys' and men's socialization into and performance of hegemonic masculinity (Connell 1987; Messner 2002). Not surprisingly, female athletes' participation has been met with resistance by many men and some women. Pat Griffin (1992) notes that women who were caught *watching* male

athletes competing in the early Greek Olympics were put to death. Men justified women's exclusion from and restriction within sport (and other core institutions) based on medical and paternalistic arguments about protecting women's health and reproductive functions. Over time, the rhetorics evolved, taking on a heterosexist frame. Men positioned athletic women as dangerous and masculinized lesbians. This was done, Griffin notes, as a means of social control to keep women in the roles of wife and mother. It also worked to reinscribe a belief in "natural" differences between men and women that legitimate gender inequalities. . . .

Female athletes have responded to sexist and heterosexist stigma in a variety of ways. Griffin highlights strategies female athletes use to confront the stigma—for example, education campaigns, lesbian/queer visibility, and heterosexual/homosexual solidarity—and strategies they use to reproduce or accommodate the stigma—for example, silence, denial, and attacks on lesbians in sport. An additional strategy of accommodation is apology, when female athletes "compensate" for their sport participation by emphasizing traditional notions of white, middle class femininity and heterosexuality (see Broad 2001; Felshin 1974; Griffin 1992, 1998; Messner 2002; Sabo 1993). Apologetics are institutionalized in athletic practices like cheerleading (see Adams and Bettis 2003; Grindstaff and West 2006), in which female participants are encouraged or required to wear short skirts, don makeup, and smile while performing athletic and acrobatic movements that require stamina and technical skill. As Laura Grindstaff and Emily West (2006) argue, this represents a contemporary version of emphasized femininity that combines athleticism with a (hetero)sexualized performance of normative femininity (see also Heywood and Dworkin 2003). As the current study demonstrates, in addition to being performed through gender display, apologetics can be enacted through defensive othering: Those other female athletes may be "mannish lesbians," but not me.

Research on female athletes in a range of sports reveals resistance to conventional gendered and sexual norms and expectations alongside the adoption of apologetics. This represents the athletes' active and tense negotiations of masculinity and femininity, resistance, and reproduction (see, notably, Cahn 1994; Griffin 1998). Yet researchers have found a different process in studies of women's rugby. P. David Howe (2003), Elizabeth E. Wheatley (1994), and Laura Frances Chase (2006) found the sport, a traditionally male-defined and -identified practice, to be a site of transgressive resistance for female athletes. They argued that their participants challenged sport's status as a "male domain" (Howe 2003:242), created a vision of "sport in general (and of rugby, specifically) that provides an alternative to male-centered, -defined, -controlled, and -practiced sport" (Wheatley 1994:207), and resisted "dominant discourses of normative femininity" (Chase 2006:232). Additionally, K. L. Broad (2001) found her participants to adopt a queer "unapologetic" resistance comprised of "transgressing gender, destabilizing the heterosexual/homosexual binary, and 'in your face' confrontations of stigma" (p. 182). Rugby, it would seem, offers fertile ground for resistance.

I found, however, a more complicated engagement with strategies of resistance and reproduction on the Comp U Women's Rugby Football Club. In the following sections, I show how the Comp U ruggers, subordinated by men as women and as female athletes, engaged in defensive othering by identifying with dominants *and* dis-identifying with women outside of their team. The players *identified with dominants* by positioning themselves as closer to men and men's style of play within the institution of sport relative to nonathletic women generally and to female athletes outside of rugby specifically. They engaged in *normative identification* by positioning themselves as closer to conventional notions of femininity and heterosexuality than other female ruggers. Finally, the players *propped up dominants* by reasserting the superiority of men as athletes and as the standard for athletic play. These strategies emerged when the players ran head-on into stereotypes about female athletes—particularly female rugby players—both on and off of campus.

IDENTIFYING WITH DOMINANTS

Given the historical association between (white, middle class) women and physical weakness and passivity, many women have interpreted their sport practice as an act of resistance (see, e.g., Heywood and Dworkin 2003). The female ruggers at Comp U, however, did not do this. Even as their success on the pitch (the rugby playing field) shattered the belief that all women are passive, the players used their athleticism to suggest that only *they*, and not women *as a class*, were tough and aggressive. Further, they used their status as ruggers to position themselves above women in general, whom they dismissed as weak. In doing so the players identified with dominants, claiming a heightened status relative to other members of their subordinated group (women) through closer identification with the behavior and traits associated with members of the dominant class (men).

To contest the image of themselves, as women, as being weak, the female ruggers distinguished themselves from women in (white) sororities. Frequently, the Comp U players referred to these women as "sorostitutes." This term—combining "sorority" and "prostitute"—implied promiscuity on the part of sorority women. Yet, the Comp U players commonly engaged in bantering, joking, and bragging about drunken sexual escapades. They did not believe, moreover, that the women in sororities literally sold sex acts. In fact, it was the ruggers themselves who held an eroticized mud wrestling fundraiser annually, selling access to the sexual display of their bodies as the most lucrative fundraiser of the year. Why, then, did the Comp U ruggers sexually libel women in sororities?

The players' reasons for setting up "sorostitutes" as a foil became clearer when they created a t-shirt listing the "Top Ten Reasons to Play on the Comp U Women's Rugby Football Club." One reason was: "You just laugh when people ask what sorority you're in." I asked Frankie, a vet player, what this meant and she explained that (white) "sorority girls in general are stereotyped to be, you know, like, pansy girly-girls, makeup all the time, and that kind of stuff." Yet most, if not all, of the Comp U players wore makeup (for some, even during games) and were invested in the same conventionally feminine appearance that sorority women projected. Moreover, women on the rugby team spoke glowingly about how rugby offered the same benefits for which sororities are often celebrated (see Robbins 2004): a sense of community and belonging, social outlets in the forms of parties and dances, and social networks that could offer payoffs in the future. Also, both groups were predominantly white and middle to upper middle class. These similarities with nonathletic ("girly-girl") sorority women potentially threatened the Comp U players' identities as tough and aggressive. In response, they asserted that despite similarities in their gender presentation, they were different from—and superior to—women in sororities because they were not "pansies" (weak). The Comp U players, then, claimed a closer association to the dominant (masculine) persona.

* * *

The players put forward the identity of "rugger," and its attendant toughness, as an expression of their true athletic self. They did this by creating a life narrative in which their previous sport participation, though extensive and positive, was lacking. In this way, they projected a consistent self in the face of not making it onto collegiate varsity teams in their previous sports. As they spoke, the players cast themselves as too competitive for the less (physically) demanding sports they had played in high school. Many noted that they were "always angry" as children, were "too aggressive" for other sports, or "always wanted to hit people.". . .

When I asked in interviews about what made a good rugby player, the women responded: "an aggressive personality," "an anger management problem to work out," "someone really intense," "a competitive personality," "it's just in their genes," or someone "with that little bit of craziness in 'em." The players thus justified their claim to the rugger identity by naturalizing

aggression and competition: This is who I am. Female rugby players, in this account, are not just different from other female athletes; they are *better*. Carter, one of the coaches, echoed these sentiments in an interview: "You get girls who play soccer and play basketball and you get them to come out here and stand on the sidelines and watch this and you tell me how many of them will raise their hands and say they want to try it: Not very many."

Were the players tough? By many measures of successful rugby play (see Schacht 1996), they were. They valorized hard tackles and played through pain and injury, sometimes incurring permanent damage to their bodies. They policed dirty play by opponents with targeted hits and other forms of retribution that sometimes left opposing players unconscious or sent them to the hospital. And, they taunted their defeated opponents. Tammie, who refused treatment for torn shoulder ligaments for over a year in order to continue playing, famously tackled a player who had been "talking trash" during the game, then stood over her and yelled, "Get up, bitch; I'm not done with you yet!" Words like "bitch" are used in traditionally male sports to denigrate boys and men who show a lack of aggression or masculinity (Messner 2002). Some women attempt to claim the word as a sign of toughness, or to undermine its stigmatizing power by "choosing" it (see Miya-Jervis and Zeisler 2007). By using this word to subordinate her opponent, however, Tammie adopted and reinforced this sexist theme of the larger institution of sport and positioned the Comp U team, and Comp U players, as masculine (tough) in relation to their feminine (weak) opponents. . . .

NORMATIVE IDENTIFICATION

Marilyn Frye (1983) notes that the socially constructed lines dividing dominant and subordinated groups are vigilantly policed, often by members of both groups. When members of subordinated groups cross these lines, they may experience backlash and social sanction. She notes that homophobia is used as a policing resource to maintain sex inequality. Faced with such threats, women (or members of other subordinated groups) may engage in *normative identification*, aligning themselves with the norms and values prescribed by dominants for a subordinated group.

To the extent that the Comp U players made successful claims to an essential toughness in comparison to women in general as well as other female athletes, they created a dilemma for themselves. Historically, athletic women have been stereotyped as masculine lesbians (Blinde and Taub 1992; Griffin 1992). The very things that made rugby attractive as a resource for the players' identity work—its pervasive physicality and its similarity to the men's game—made the Comp U players vulnerable to such labeling. The players were keenly aware of this. When I asked them about the dominant view of female ruggers, they said, in matter-of-fact or angry tones: "scary, butch lesbians," "she-males," "he-shes," "lesbian man-beasts," and "butch, big—definitely gay." Many players reported experiencing intense resistance from their parents. One player told me that when she told her mother she was playing rugby her mother responded, "Isn't that a dyke sport?" They also ran into social sanction from friends. Peg, a fourth-year player known on the team for her aggressive play, told me that when one of her male friends heard her talking about playing rugby he said, "Peg, if you turn out to be a lesbian, I'll kill you." He was "joking," but Peg received the message of his sanction loud and clear. Comp U players did not say that these stereotypes were false or try to strip them of their stigmatizing power. They asserted only that the stereotypes did not apply to *them*.

Comp U players positioned themselves as the exception to the rule by emphasizing their conformity to traditional notions of white, middle class, heterosexual femininity—what Griffin (1992) calls "promoting a heterosexy image" (p. 252)—in their style of dress and appearance on and off the pitch. They thus engaged in normative identification. The players essentialized their femininity and heterosexuality, claiming them as natural expressions of their selves.

Additionally, they privileged their smaller physical size—in comparison to female rugby players on other teams—as a mark of their hard work and dedication to the sport, treating their bodies as social projects—objects that are shaped, scrutinized, and negotiated (see Bourdieu 1984; Brumberg 1997; Foucault 1977). They saw themselves as both *essentially* different (heterosexual and feminine) from other female ruggers, as well as relationally superior athletes as a result of their *accomplished* fitness.

Essential Femininity and Heterosexuality

Conventional femininity carries with it compulsory heterosexuality (Frye 1983; Griffin 1992; Rich 1994). One way for women to engage in normative identification as an attempt to please the dominant group (or at least not alienate them) while breaking other gendered norms is to make an appeal to their own "natural" femininity and heterosexuality. More than simply "apologizing" for the transgression by emphasizing other conventional gendered norms, this strategy involves claiming those norms as an essential aspect of the self. The women on the Comp U rugby team, coming up against expressed and internalized sanctions for their tough and aggressive (unfeminine) rugby play, did exactly this.

During interactions at practices and games, the players negotiated and policed acceptable gender and sexual performances for each other and for the team as a whole. For example, at a game early in the season, Doris, a newbie, saw an opposing player whose biological sex she could not clearly identify. She asked Carter, one of the coaches, if there were any coed teams:

> He answered, "No, there are no coed teams. In women's rugby, you'll see a lot of *interesting-looking* women, but they *are* always women." Maeve, a vet player, said "They're all *technically* women." Doris laughed.

* * *

Maeve's qualification that women who were masculine in appearance were only "technically" women. . . . Such comments positioned the Comp U team as the exception and, as the comments came from veteran players, modeled acceptable gender performances for the newbies. A few of the Comp U players self-identified as lesbian or bisexual and two of the players were openly dating one another, but the team, as a collectivity, presented itself as heterosexual.

* * *

[A]s noted earlier, naturalized aggression was the most common account I heard from players when I asked how they came to play rugby. This account worked to validate the athletes' claim to the identity of tough rugby player; but, it also came close to outsiders' beliefs that all lesbians are aggressive, hence all female rugby players are lesbians. Susie dealt with this problem by essentializing the feminine gender performance of *this* team: "we just tend to be effeminate people."

Comp U players often claimed that they were special because, in addition to being tough, they were also heterosexual *and* feminine—closer to normative expectations of (white, middle class) women than other female ruggers. Importantly, the overwhelmingly white status of the team enabled their use of this strategy. Black women are typically stereotyped as more "masculine" than white women (Collins 2004; Kaplan 1987), and may not have been able to draw on this strategy in the same ways. Thus, the players used their racial identities, here and elsewhere, as a buffer in their identity work.

Time and again, in practices and in interviews, players touted the "diversity" on the team and noted how welcoming the club was to anyone who was serious about the sport. Seeing the team as "open" may have been important for the players because it suggested that they were good people. Despite their claims of inclusivity, though, the players were disproportionately "feminine" in appearance, white, and heterosexual. This had not always been the case.

The third- and fourth-year players remembered a time when the team was less heterosexual and feminine identified and fractured along

lines of sexuality (the racial makeup of the team, though, had consistently been white dominated). According to Susie: "there was a big division on the team between the straight girls and the lesbians on the team . . . I mean, they wouldn't stay in the same rooms in the hotels and stuff. It was a big issue."

* * *

[T]here was a conscious decision to move away from a lesbian, or lesbian-*perceived*, collective identity (and lesbian-identified players) in order to attract and please rugby men. Vet players socialized the newbies to adopt this account. When I asked Tina, a newbie, what she had heard about the previous tension, she said, "somebody told me one time the whole reason was because the team used to be composed of all angst-ridden, butch, man-hating lesbians."

Two players, both respected and valued athletes on the team who fit the privileged heterosexy-fit presentation of self, began openly dating during my research. Importantly, they did not self-identify as lesbians. Hannah, one of the women, explained to me, "I'm *not* a lesbian, but I'm dating Wendy . . . That's our major thing. We're like, why do you need the label?"[4] Still, after they went public with their relationship, Frankie, who was Christian identified, told them they were "going to hell." Her intervention was not well-received by the team. Joanne, a respected fourth-year player, said, "That was tough for a while. People were really angry with Frankie because of that. We don't want that."

* * *

The Comp U female ruggers were invested in a collective heterosexual identity. They were not, however, intolerant homophobes allergic to any sign of lesbianism. The problem was the homophobic context that compelled them to publicly distance themselves from the stigma and stereotypes attached to their sport. . . .

Why would the heterosexual-identified players give so much weight to the male players' response? Female athletes—and female rugby players in particular—are stereotyped as butch lesbians, so the heterosexual-identified players said they feared that most men would not be attracted to them. Male rugby players, in this context, became even more important as potential dating partners. Frankie put it simply: "I think that a girl rugby player is intimidating for a lot of guys, *except* for the guy rugby players." The women, then, tried to recruit players who would be deemed attractive to heterosexual men. Eden, a second-year player, said, "It's just like, we've kind of, over the years, weeded them [physically larger, lesbian-identified players] out and kind of replaced them with girls that are more like us and athletic and everything." This highlights the importance of recruitment as a resource for the team's collective identity.

The players' belief in an already reduced dating pool was compounded by the fact that female students were the majority at Comp U. The players reported that "the ratio" created fierce competition for men as dating partners. Mo, a second-year player, told me that a popular men's magazine had described the women at Comp U as "goddesses." Given the players' ages and the undergraduate culture of romance (see Holland and Eisenhart 1990), it makes sense that dating was important to them. Because outsiders stereotype female rugby players as masculine lesbians, and "goddesses" were their competition for dates, it is not surprising that they emphasized feminine and heterosexual signifiers on and off the pitch. Surprising or not, their use of defensive othering relied on and reinforced heteronormative ideals of body presentation and performance.

Accomplishing Fitness

In another example of defensive othering through normative identification, the players positioned themselves as better than other female ruggers because of their smaller physical size and greater commitment to fitness, qualities closer to normative understandings of "femininity." To claim these qualities, players used a contradictory mix of essentialist and social constructionist rhetoric. . . . As described above, the players on the Comp U women's rugby team made use of an essentialist rhetoric in which they were simultaneously tough, feminine, and heterosexual. Yet, they also used a rhetoric of accomplishment that treated the body as a project—an interpreted, governed, and fashioned social object.

Throughout my observations, players repeatedly told me how physically different—that is, smaller and more "fit"—*their* members were compared to other women's rugby teams. The players granted toughness, seemingly by default, to all female ruggers through their assertions of a naturalized aggression as the foundation of rugby play. But being "fit"—a body presentation that often necessitates the middle class privileges of gym memberships, flexible schedules, and access to sports teams and equipment—was an accomplishment reached through hard work. The players' idea of fitness (strong, yet smaller and thin) located them closer to conventional understandings of white, middle class femininity (and, thus, heterosexuality) and reaffirmed their claims of difference from nonathletic (unfit) women in general. . . .

Being "fit" and not "fat" was something for which this team was known. In fact, as many players and both coaches told me with pride, Comp U players were called "The Barbie Dolls" within the national rugby community. Male players from opposing teams applauded the Comp U women during warm-ups before games, calling out: "Let's hear it for the hottest rugby team in the South!" And, male business associates of one of the coaches, after seeing images of the team, remarked: "There's no way those girls play rugby!" Told that the "girls" did just that, the men said, "Tell your girls that the boys from New Jersey say hello."

Players reinforced team norms for body size through their informal interactions. In the middle of the fall semester of 2002, the vet players on the Comp U team held an initiation for the newbies, attended by both the men's and the women's teams. As part of the evening's events, the vets required the newbies to dress up as characters and perform skits. . . .

Not being "fit"—being larger than the "size-zero bod[ies]" on the Comp U team—was regarded with derision and contempt.

In these ways the players used a rhetoric of accomplishment, in addition to their appeals to an essential toughness and heterosexuality, to position themselves as superior to other female ruggers, other female athletes, and nonathletic women—an updated version of emphasized femininity I call heterosexy-fit. . . .

This heterosexy-fit identity emerged out of the contradictions between "tough" and "feminine," the seemingly incompatible identities to which the players made simultaneous claim. It was enabled by the team's whiteness and middle class privileges, and it was a rewarding identity in a variety of ways. Constructing it relied, however, on the devaluation of other female athletes and women in general. The defensive othering of the women ruggers thus helped to maintain women's status as others within the dominant gender order.

PROPPING UP DOMINANTS

In addition to defensive othering, maintaining boundaries between dominant and subordinate groups is an essential component of the reproduction of inequality (Schwalbe et al. 2000). Boundary maintenance allows members of dominant groups to hoard resources, and is thus not usually in the interest of subordinates. But, because the Comp U players saw the rugby men as comprising a small and threatened dating pool, they had an investment in protecting their access to these men. Their identity work as tough athletes challenged the conventional equation of women with physical weakness and passivity, thus pushing them closer to the status of men. This could have been interpreted as unattractive by rugby men, and the Comp U female ruggers worried that it did. To position themselves above other women by virtue of their toughness, but still below men, the players maintained the boundary between men and women by propping up dominants—(re)asserting the superiority of dominant group members.

The female players, in short, put men forward as essentially superior athletes.

As mentioned earlier, the female ruggers at Comp U were proud of the fact that they played by the same rules as the men. However, they did not want to play *against* or *with* the men. Tammie said:

> I'm not this kind of person that thinks, "Oh, girls should be able to play with the boys if they want to." No. Like, I would never step on that field and play full-contact rugby with the boys. They're so much stronger than me I would get killed, you know? . . . 'Cause I mean, yeah, there is that level of difference there and nobody can do anything about it . . . I'm just happy I can play exactly what they play, just on my level.

To the women, the men were the more valued rugby players, and the women sought higher status by approaching, but not surpassing, the men's style of play as the standard. The men's valued status was evident when I asked Tammie why she liked playing by the same rules as the men: "I think it's a big deal because I think men's rugby teams really respect you for it." Joanne said, "Men's games are a lot more fast-paced. I mean, obviously, we're not ever gonna be able to sprint quite as fast." She, like Tammie, reinforced the idea of men's natural athletic prowess.

Not wanting to be tackled by an opponent who is physically larger and stronger is understandable. And male athletes, on average, may be faster than female athletes.[5] But reinforcing the men's superiority in these ways worked as a form of boundary maintenance that lessened the potential threat the women posed to the men, thus increasing the female players' desirability. Yes, the women were tough athletes on the pitch, but they were tough *with other women*, not with men. In addition to maintaining the boundary between women and men, this strategy reasserted the women's specialness by distancing them from other female athletes who believe that women can do anything that men do. Jana derisively described such players as "super unathletic" (unfit) and "definite feminists," in contrast to the "fit" and apolitical ruggers on the Comp U team. . . .

Carter put it simply: "There's a big gap between [men's and women's] playing ability."....

I asked both coaches what accounted for the differences they had noted between the men's and women's games and styles of play. They highlighted a mix of nature and nurture. They said there were inherent differences between men's and women's physical abilities and "drives," but they acknowledged that social conditioning also played a role. Their message to the players, however, was clear: Real ruggers are men and the women's game is derivative and, thus, second class.

... Men's and women's bodies fall along a continuum of human differences; however, there are average differences between them. The most valued sports, in terms of media coverage and funding, are typically organized through rules, strategies, and norms that privilege men's bodies (Messner 2002). This does not mean that men are inherently better athletes. It only means that what is valued in sport reflects the premium put on size, strength, and masculine behavior.

By propping up dominants, Comp U's female players (with help from their coaches) strengthened their claim to a heterosexy-fit identity that did not threaten men or male dominance. They positioned themselves and their sport as exceptional in that they (and it) were tough and aggressive, while they were also feminine, heterosexual, and sexy. They "knew their place" (below men), and thus could be desirable to men.

CONCLUSION

The female rugby players at Comp U were successful athletes in high school, but found themselves unable to compete in their chosen sports at the varsity level at Comp U. So they turned to rugby, an intensely physical yet nonvarsity sport, as an alternative. They stepped onto the pitch and met with success, only to find themselves stigmatized by outsiders as "butch lesbians." Instead of resisting and rejecting the power of such stigma, as others have found female rugby players to do,

the Comp U players turned to defensive othering, casting themselves as the exception to the stereotype, and thereby unintentionally reinforcing the dominant heterosexist ideology. In doing so, they created a unique identity as heterosexy-fit—simultaneously tough, heterosexual, and conventionally attractive.

The women's presentation of the heterosexy-fit identity helped them respond to sexist and homophobic stigma and backlash to women's participation in sport. They wanted to be seen as tough and serious athletes without sacrificing their sexual appeal to men. To some extent they succeeded. For example, the heterosexy-fit identity: insulated them from outsiders' negative beliefs; granted them higher status relative to other women, other athletic women generally, and other female ruggers in particular; and, promoted an individual and collective presentation of self they personally valued and saw as desirable to rugby men. The women did not create the conditions of inequality under which they acted, nor did they create the devalued identities imposed on them. Understandably, they managed their identities in ways that promoted a sense of self-worth and affirmation. However, their solution to the identity dilemmas they faced reinforced the stigmatizing power of the devalued identities they sought to deflect. . . .

NOTES

1. Miller (1976) discusses the tendency for some subordinated group members to imitate dominants in various forms. The process I highlight here is an example of that.

2. Although the players did not use the term heterosexy-fit, it reflects the constellation of meanings they sought to attach to themselves. This identity is similar to the identity constructed and performed by the moderate weightlifters that Shari Dworkin (2001) studied who "actively pressed beyond thinness ideals but also feared masculinization and what might be considered a loss of heterosexual attractiveness" (p. 346).

3. I am indebted to the comments of an anonymous reviewer for emphasizing this point.

4. Some might argue that such a statement is a challenge to essentialist understandings of sexual identity, one that calls into question the heterosexual/homosexual binary. While such an analysis makes sense, my data do not suggest any degree of intentionality on Hannah's part toward such an end, and internalized homophobia within the homophobic context of the team may be a more appropriate reading. In interviews and in team interaction, the players conflated "lesbian" with "feminist," "man-hating," and "butch."

5. As Lorber (1993) notes, these average differences in strength and speed may largely be due to gender socialization and conditioning. For example, in the first twenty years of women's marathon competition, they "reduced their finish times by more than one-and-one-half hours" (p. 570).

References

Adams, Natalie and Pamela Bettis. 2003. "Commanding the Room in Short Skirts: Cheering as the Embodiment of Ideal Girlhood." *Gender Society* 17(1):73–91.

Blinde, Elaine M. and Diane E. Taub. 1992. "Women Athletes as Falsely Accused Deviants: Managing the Lesbian Stigma." *Sociological Quarterly* 33:521–33.

Blumer, Herbert. 1969. *Symbolic Interactionism: Perspective and Method.* Berkeley: University of California Press.

Bolin, Anne and Jane Granskog. 2003. *Athletic Intruders: Ethnographic Research on Women, Culture, and Exercise.* Albany: State University of New York Press.

Bourdieu, Pierre. 1984. *Distinction: A Social Critique of the Judgment of Taste.* London, UK: Routledge.

Broad, K. L. 2001. "The Gendered Unapologetic: Queer Resistance in Women's Sport." *Sociology of Sport* 18:181–204.

Brumberg, Joan Jacobs. 1997. *The Body Project: An Intimate History of American Girls.* New York: Vintage Books.

Burke, Peter J. and Judy C. Tully. 1977. "The Measurement of Role Identity." *Social Forces* 55:881–97.

Burstyn, Varda. 1999. *The Rites of Men: Manhood, Politics, and the Culture of Sport.* Toronto: University of Toronto Press.

Cahn, Susan K. 1994. *Coming on Strong: Gender and Sexuality in Twentieth-Century Women's Sports.* Cambridge, MA: Harvard University Press.

Chase, Laura Frances. 2006. "(Un)Disciplined Bodies: A Foucauldian Analysis of Women's Rugby." *Sociology of Sport Journal* 23:229–47.

Collins, Patricia Hill. 2004. *Black Sexual Politics: African Americans, Gender, and the New Racism.* New York: Routledge.

Connell, R. W. 1987. *Gender and Power.* Stanford, CA: Stanford University Press.

Felshin, Jan. 1974. "The Triple Option . . . for Women in Sport." *Quest* 21:36–40.

Foucault, Michel. 1977. *Discipline and Punish.* London, UK: Allen Lane.

Frye, Marilyn. 1983. *The Politics of Reality: Essays in Feminist Theory.* New York: The Crossing Press.

Gramsci, Antonio. 1971. *Selections from the Prison Notebooks.* New York: International Publishers.

Griffin, Pat. 1992. "Changing the Game: Homophobia, Sexism, and Lesbians in Sport." *Quest* 44: 251–65.

———. 1998. *Strong Women, Deep Closets: Lesbians and Homophobia in Sport.* Champaign, IL: Human Kinetics.

Grindstaff, Laura and Emily West. 2006. "Cheerleading and the Gendered Politics of Sport." *Social Problems* 53:500–18.

Heywood, Leslie and Shari L. Dworkin. 2003. *Built to Win: The Female Athlete as Cultural Icon.* Minneapolis: University of Minnesota Press.

Holland, Dorothy C. and Margaret A. Eisenhart. 1990. *Educated in Romance: Women, Achievement, and College Culture.* Chicago: University of Chicago Press.

Howe, P. David. 2003. "Kicking Stereotypes into Touch: An Ethnographic Account of Women's Rugby." Pp. 227–46 in *Athletic Intruders: Ethnographic Research on Women, Culture, and Exercise,* edited by A. Bolin and J. Granskog. Albany: State University of New York Press.

Johnson, Allan. G. 2006. *Privilege, Power, and Difference.* 2d ed. Boston: McGraw-Hill.

Kaplan, Elaine Bell. 1987. "'I Don't Do No Windows': Competition between the Domestic Worker and the Housewife." Pp. 92–105 in *Competition: A Feminist Taboo?,* edited by V. Miner and H. E. Longino. New York: The Feminist Press.

Lenskyj, Helen. 1986. *Out of Bounds: Women, Sport, and Sexuality.* Toronto, Canada: Women's Press.

Lorber, Judith. 1993. "Believing is Seeing: Biology as Ideology." *Gender and Society* 7:568–81.

————. 1994. *Paradoxes of Gender.* New Haven, CT: Yale University Press.

McCall, George and J. L. Simmons. 1978. *Identities and Interaction.* 2d ed. New York: Free Press.

Messner, Michael A. 1990. "Men Studying Masculinity: Some Epistemological Questions in Sport Sociology." *Sociology of Sport Journal* 7:136–53.

————. 2002. *Taking the Field: Women, Men, and Sports.* Minneapolis: University of Minnesota Press.

Miller, Jean Baker. 1976. *Toward a New Psychology of Women.* Boston: Beacon Press.

Miya-Jervis, Lisa and Andi Zeisler, eds. 2007. "About Bitch." *Bitch: Feminist Response to Pop Culture.* Retrieved June 14, 2007 (www.bitchmagazine .org/about.shtml).

Rich, Adrienne. 1994. *Blood, Bread, and Poetry: Selected Prose (1979–1985).* Reissue ed. New York: W. W. Norton & Company, Inc.

Robbins, Alexandra. 2004. *Pledged: The Secret Life of Sororities.* New York: Hyperion.

Sabo, Don. 1993. "Psychosocial Impacts of Athletic Participation on American Women: Facts and Fables." Pp. 374–87 in *Sport in Contemporary Society, an Anthology,* edited by D. S. Eitzen. New York: St. Martin's Press.

Schacht, Steven. P. 1996. "Misogyny on and off the 'Pitch.'" *Gender and Society* 10:550–65.

Schwalbe, Michael and Douglas Mason-Schrock. 1996. "Identity Work as Group Process." Pp. 115–49 in *Advances in Group Processes* (vol. 13), edited by B. Markovsky, M. Lovaglia and R. Simon. Greenwich, CT: JAI Press.

Schwalbe, Michael, Sandra Godwin, Daphne Holden, Douglas Schrock, Shealy Thompson, and Michele Wolkomir. 2000. "Generic Processes in the Reproduction of Inequality: An Interactionist Analysis." *Social Forces* 79:419–52.

Strauss, Anselm L. 1959. *Mirrors and Masks: The Search for Identity.* Glencoe, IL: Free Press.

Stryker, Sheldon, Timothy J. Owens, and Robert W. White. 2000. *Self, Identity, and Social Movements.* Minneapolis: University of Minnesota Press.

West, Candace and Sarah Fenstermaker. 1995. "Doing Difference." *Gender and Society* 9:8–37.

West, Candace and Don H. Zimmerman. 1987. "Doing Gender." *Gender and Society* 1:125–51.

Wheatley, Elizabeth E. 1994. "Subcultural Subversions: Comparing Discourses on Sexuality in Men's and Women's Rugby Songs." Pp. 193–211 in *Women, Sport, and Culture,* edited by S. Birrell & C. L. Cole. Champaign, IL: HumanKinetics.

❦ Topics for Further Examination ❧

- Go to the main websites for Girl Scouts (http://www.gsusa.org) and Boy Scouts (http://www .scouting.org) and compare the two organizations. Are their programs similar or different? What similarities and differences do you observe in the websites themselves? What effect do these organizations have on gender socialization?
- Go to the U.S. Department of Education website (http://www.ed.gov) and search for differences in men and women in higher education.
- Do a search for the Women's National Rugby Foundation to learn more about the sport and its history in the United States. Also look up another, typically male sport that females now play, such as "women's" basketball or ice hockey.

5

BUYING AND SELLING GENDER

I n the video *Adventures in the Gender Trade* (Marenco, 1993), Kate Bornstein, a transgender performance artist and activist, looks into the camera and says, "Once you buy gender, you'll buy anything to keep it." Her observation goes to the heart of deep connections between economic processes and institutionalized patterns of gender difference, opposition, and inequality in contemporary society. Readings in this chapter examine the ways modern marketplace forces such as commercialization, commodification, and consumerism exploit and construct gender. However, before we explore the buying and selling of gender, we want to review briefly the major elements of contemporary American economic life—elements that embody corporate capitalism—which form the framework for the packaging and delivery of gender to consumers.

DEFINING CORPORATE CAPITALISM

Corporate capitalism is an economic system in which large national and transnational corporations are the dominant forces. The basic goal of corporate capitalism is the same as it was when social scientists such as Karl Marx studied early capitalist economies: converting money into more money (Johnson, 2001). Corporate capitalists invest money in the production of all sorts of goods and services for the purpose of selling at a profit. Capitalism, as Gitlin (2001) observes, requires a consumerist way of life.

In today's society, corporate capitalism affects virtually every aspect of life—most Americans work for a corporate employer, whether a fast-food chain or bank, and virtually everyone buys the products and services of capitalist production (Johnson, 2001; Ritzer, 1999). Those goods and services include things we must have to live (e.g., food and shelter) and, most important for contemporary capitalism's survival and growth, things we have learned to want or desire (e.g., microwave ovens, televisions, cruises, fitness fashions, cosmetic surgery), even though we do not need them to live (Ritzer, 1999).

From an economic viewpoint, we are a nation of consumers—people who buy and use a dizzying array of objects and services conceived, designed, and sold to us by corporations. George Ritzer (1999), a leading analyst of consumerism, observes that consumption plays such a big role in the lives of contemporary Americans that it has, in many respects, come to define our society. In fact, as Ritzer notes, Americans spend most of their available resources on consumer goods and services. Corporate, consumer capitalism depends on luring people into what he calls the "cathedrals of consumption"—such as book superstores, shopping malls, theme parks, fast-food restaurants, and casinos—where we will spend money to buy an array of goods and services.

Our consumption-driven economy counts on customers whose spending habits are relatively unrestrained and who view shopping as pleasurable. Indeed, Americans spend much more today than they did just 40 years ago (Ritzer, 1999). Most of our available resources go to purchasing and consuming "stuff." Americans consume more of everything and more varieties of things than do people in other nations. We are also more likely to go into debt than Americans of earlier generations and people in other nations today. Some social scientists (e.g., Schor, 1998, p. 204) use the term *hyperconsumption* to describe what seems to be a growing American passion for and obsession with consumption.

Ritzer (2011) also argues that the Great Recession, beginning in 2007, was preceded by "the greatest consumer-driven expansion" in U.S. history and resulted in "perhaps the greatest economic setbacks," including high unemployment and foreclosure rates. He and others such as Robert Manning (2011) and Juliet Schor (2010) are persuaded that hyperconsumption and our "business-as-usual" economy (Schor, 2010) are unsustainable, if not outright dysfunctional, and they predict that as these economic patterns move to other economies, such as those in Asia (Ritzer, 2011), we will witness economic setbacks in those nations similar to the Great Recession in the United States. Indeed, Jie Yang's chapter reading discusses some of the excesses in the development of consumer capitalism in China—especially in the beauty economy, which has expanded at a breathtaking rate.

MARKETING GENDER

Gender is a fundamental element of the modern machinery of marketing. It is an obvious resource from which the creators and distributors of goods and services can draw ideas, images, and messages. The imagery of consumer culture thrives on gender difference and asymmetry. For example, consumer emblems of hyperfemininity and hypermasculinity, such as Barbie and GI Joe, stand in stark physical contrast to each other (Schiebinger, 2000). This is not happenstance. Barbie and GI Joe intentionally reinforce belief in the idea of essential differences between women and men. The exaggerated, gendered appearances of Barbie and GI Joe can be purchased by adult consumers who have the financial resources to pay for new cosmetic surgeries, such as breast and calf implants, that literally inscribe beliefs about physical differences between women and men into their flesh (Sullivan, 2001).

As Walters (2001) observes, turning difference into "an object of barter is perhaps the quintessentially American experience" (p. 289). Indeed, virtually every product and service, including the most functional, can be designed and consumed as masculine or feminine (e.g., deodorants, bicycles, greeting cards, wallpaper, cars, and hairstyles). In a recent study of gender differences in prices charged for personal care products and services (i.e., women pay more), Duesterhaus, Grauerholz, Weichsel, and Guittar (2011) underscore the fact that "marketers have successfully convinced women and men that the gendered products they sell [e.g., body lotions and deodorants] are in fact different . . . and consumers have 'bought into' this essentialist-based marketing" (p. 187).

Gender-coding of products and services is a common strategy employed by capitalist organizations to sell their wares. It is also integral to the processes by which gender is constructed, because it frames and structures gender practices. As contemporary anthropologists argue, material culture (e.g., weaponry, musical instruments, cloth and clothing, residential buildings) are a significant "medium through which people come to know and understand themselves" and others (Tilley, 2011, p. 348).

To illustrate how consumer culture participates in the construction of gender through one material form, let's look at the gender coding of clothing. Gender archeologist Sorenson (2000) observes that clothing is an ideal medium for the expression of a culture's gender beliefs because it is an extension of the body and an important element in identity and communication. No wonder corporate capitalists have cashed in on the business of fabricating gender through dress (Sorenson, 2000). Sorenson notes that simple observation of the clothing habits of people reveals a powerful pattern of "dressing gender" (p. 124). Throughout life, she argues, the gender coding of colors, patterns, decorations, fabrics, fastenings, trimmings, and other aspects of dress create and maintain differences between boys and girls and men and women. Even when clothing designers and manufacturers create what appear to be "unisex" fashions (e.g., tuxedos for women), they incorporate just enough gendered elements (e.g., lacy trim or a revealing neckline) to ensure that the culturally created gender categories—feminine and masculine—are not completely erased. Consider the lengths to which the fashion industry has gone to create dress that conveys a "serious yet feminine" business appearance for the increasing number of women in management and executive levels of the corporate world (Kimle & Damhorst, 1997). Contemplate the ferocity of the taboo against boys and men wearing skirts and dresses. Breaking the taboo (except on a few occasions, such as Halloween) typically results in negative sanctions. The reading in this chapter by Adie Nelson examines the extent to which even fantasy dress for children ends up conforming to gender stereotypes.

Gender-coded clothing is one example of corporate exploitation of gender to sell all kinds of goods and services, including gender itself. Have we arrived at a moment in history when identities, including gender identity, are largely shaped within the dynamics of consumerism? Will we,

as Bornstein observed, buy anything to keep up gender appearances? The readings in this chapter help us answer these questions. They illuminate some of the key ways capitalist, consumer culture makes use of cultural definitions and stereotypes of gender to produce and sell goods and services.

In our "consumers' republic" (Cohen, 2003), the mass media (e.g., television and magazines) play a central role in delivering potential consumers to advertisers whose job it is to persuade us to buy particular products and services (Kilbourne, 1999; Ritzer, 1999). The advertising industry devotes itself to creating and keeping consumers in the marketplace, and it is very good at what it does. Today's advertisers use sophisticated strategies for hooking consumers. The strategies work because they link our deepest emotions and most beloved ideals to products and services by persuading us that identity and self-worth can be fashioned out of the things we buy (Featherstone, 1991; Zukin, 2004). Advertisers transform gender into a commodity and convince consumers that we can transform ourselves into more masculine men and more feminine women by buying particular products and services. Men are lured into buying cars that will make them feel like hypermasculine machines, and women are sold a wondrous array of cosmetic products and procedures that are supposed to turn them into drop-dead beauties.

Urla and Swedlund (1995) explore the story that Barbie, a well-advertised and wildly popular toy turned icon, tells about femininity in consumer culture. They note that although Barbie's long, thin body and big breasts are remarkably unnatural, she stands as an ideal that has played itself out in the real body trends of *Playboy* magazine centerfolds and Miss America contestants. The authors provide evidence that between 1959 and 1978, the average weight and hip size for women centerfolds and beauty contestants decreased steadily. A follow-up study for 1979 to 1988 found the acceleration of this trend with "approximately 69 percent of Playboy centerfolds and 60 percent of Miss America contestants weighing in at 15 percent or more below their expected age and height category" (p. 298). One lesson we might glean from this story is that a toy (Barbie) and real women (centerfolds and beauty contestants) are converging in a culture in which the bonds of beauty norms are narrowing and tightening their grip on both products and persons (Sullivan, 2001; see also Erin Hatton and Mary Nell Trautner's reading in Chapter 6). To illustrate the extent of media's influence even further, Kirsten B. Firminger's piece on representations of males in teenage girls' magazines demonstrates the power of print media to guide readers not only toward consumption of gendered products and services but also toward consumption of (stereo)types of people who are packaged much like other gendered products.

Any analysis of the marketing of femininity and masculinity has to take into account the ways the gendering of products and services is tightly linked to prisms of difference and inequality such as sexuality, race, age, and ability/disability. Consumer culture thrives, for example, on heterosexuality, whiteness, and youthfulness. Automobile advertisers market cars made for heterosexual romance and marriage. Liquor ads feature men and women in love (Kilbourne, 1999). Recent research on race and gender imagery in the most popular advertising medium, television, confirms the continuing dominance of images of White, affluent young adults. "Virtually all forms of television marketing perpetuate images of White hegemonic masculinity and White feminine romantic fulfillment" (Coltrane & Messineo, 2000, p. 386). In spite of what is called niche marketing or marketing to special audiences such as Latinos, gay men, and older Americans, commercial television imagery continues to rely on stereotypes of race, gender, age, and the like (Coltrane & Messineo, 2000). Stereotypes sell.

Two readings in this chapter address intersections of prisms of difference and inequality in consumer culture. The first, by Kimberly Hoang, is an intriguing analysis of women sex workers in Ho Chi Minh City, Vietnam, who sell impressions of themselves as dark-skinned, poor women to Western businessmen and budget travelers who not only want to purchase sex and intimacy but also want to see themselves as helping poor, Third World women. The workers Hoang studied "racialized their bodies" by using skin darkeners and wearing either simple clothing or ethnic, Orientalizing dresses to cater to the racialized, sexualized, and gendered stereotypes of Western men. The second reading, by Toni Calasanti and Neal King, offers detailed insight into the mass-marketing of "successful aging" products, services, and activities to older men in the United States. They highlight the fact that marketing that targets older people plays on the stigma of aging in American culture and, specifically, on the often desperate attempts of aging men to hang on to youthful manliness.

CAN YOU BUY IN WITHOUT SELLING OUT?

The tension between creativity, resistance, and rebellion on the one hand, and the lure and power of commercialization on the other is a focus of much research on consumerism and consumer culture (Quart, 2003; Schor, 2004). Can we produce and consume the gendered products and services of corporate capitalism without wanting and trying to be just like Barbie or Madonna, the Marlboro Man or Brad Pitt? Does corporate, commercial culture consume everything and everyone in its path, including the creators of countercultural forms?

The latter question is important. Consider the fact that "grunge," which began as antiestablishment fashion, became a national trend when companies such as Diesel and Urban Outfitters co-opted and commercialized it (O'Brien, 1999). Then contemplate how commercial culture has cleverly exploited the women's movement by associating serious social issues and problems with trivial or dangerous products. "New Freedom" is a maxi pad. "ERA" is a laundry detergent. Cigarette ads often portray smoking as a symbol of women's liberation (Kilbourne, 1999). Commercial culture is quite successful in enticing artists of all sorts to "sell out." For example, Madonna began her career as a rebel who dared to display a rounded belly. But, over time, she has been "normalized," as reflected in the transformation of her body to better fit celebrity appearance norms (Bordo, 1997).

The culture of the commodity is also successful in mainstreaming the unconventional by turning nonconformity into obedience that answers to Madison Avenue (Harris, 2000). Analysts of the commodification of gayness have been especially sensitive to the potential problems posed by advertising's recent creation of a largely fictional identity of gay as "wealthy White man" with a lifestyle defined by hip fashion (Walters, 2001). What will happen if lesbian and gay male styles are increasingly drawn into mass-mediated, consumer culture? Will those modes of rebellion against the dominance of heterosexism lose their political clout? Will they become mere "symbolic forms of resistance, ineffectual strategies of rebellion" (Harris, 2000, p. xxiii)?

THE GLOBAL REACH OF AMERICAN GENDER IMAGES AND IDEALS

The global reach of American culture is yet another concern of consumer culture researchers. Transnational corporations are selling American popular culture and consumerism as a way of life in countries around the world (Kilbourne, 1999; Ritzer, 1999). People across the globe are now regularly exposed to American images, icons, and ideals. For example, *Baywatch,* with its array of perfect (albeit cosmetically enhanced) male and female bodies, was seen by more people in the world than any other television show during the years it aired (Kilbourne, 1999). American popular music and film celebrities dominate the world scene. Everyone knows Marilyn Monroe and James Dean, Tom Cruise and Julia Roberts.

You might ask, and quite legitimately, so what? The answer to that question is not a simple one, in part because cultural import–export relations are intricate. As Gitlin (2001) observes, "the cultural gates . . . swing both ways. For example, American rhythm and blues influenced Jamaican ska, which evolved into reggae, which in turn was imported to the United States via Britain" (p. 188). However, researchers have been able to document some troubling consequences of the global advantage of American commercial, consumer culture for the lifeways of people outside the United States. Thus, social scientists (e.g., Collins, 2009; Connell, 1999; Herdt, 1997) are tracing how American categories of sexual orientation are altering the modes of organization and perception of same-gender relations in some non-Western societies that have traditionally been more fluid and tolerant of sexual diversity than the United States or have constructed different, non-Western performances of gay masculinity.

Scientists are also documenting the impact of American mass media images of femininity and masculinity on consumers in far corners of the world. The island country of Fiji is one such place. Researchers have discovered that as the young women of Fiji consume American television on a regular basis, eating disorders such as anorexia nervosa are being recorded for the first time. The ultra-thin images of girls and women that populate U.S. TV shows and ads have become the measuring stick of femininity in a culture in which an ample, full body was previously the norm for women and men (Goode, 1999). The troubling consequences of the globalization of American consumer culture do not end with these examples. Consider the potential negative impact of idealized images of whiteness in a world in which most people are brown. Or how about the impact of America's negative images of older women and men on the people of cultures in which the elderly are revered?

Although corporate, capitalist economies provide many people with all the creature comforts they need and more, as well as making consumption entertaining and more accessible, there is a price to pay (Ritzer, 1999). This chapter explores one troubling aspect of corporate, consumer culture—the commodification and commercialization of gender.

A few final questions emerge from our analysis of patterns of gender in relationship to consumer capitalism. How can the individual develop an identity and self-worth *not* contingent on and defined by a whirlwind of products and services? How do we avoid devolving into caricatures of stereotyped images of femininity and masculinity whose needs and desires can be met only by gendered commodities? Is Bornstein correct when she states, "Once you buy gender, you'll buy anything to keep it"? Or can we create and preserve alternative ways of life, even those that undermine the oppression of dominant images and representations?

REFERENCES

Bordo, S. (1997). Material girl: The effacements of postmodern culture. In R. Lancaster & M. di Leonardo (Eds.), *The gender/sexuality reader* (pp. 335–358). New York: Routledge.

Cohen, L. (2003). *A consumers' republic: The politics of mass consumption in postwar America.* New York: Vintage Books.

Collins, D. (2009). We're there and queer: Homonormative mobility and lived experience among gay expatriates in Manila. *Gender & Society, 23*(4), 465–493.

Coltrane, S., & Messineo, M. (2000). The perpetuation of subtle prejudice: Race and gender imagery in 1990s television advertising. *Sex Roles, 42,* 363–389.

Connell, R. W. (1999). Making gendered people: Bodies, identities, sexualities. In M. Ferree, J. Lorber, & B. Hess (Eds.), *Revisioning gender* (pp. 449–471). Thousand Oaks, CA: Sage.

Duesterhaus, M., Grauerholz, L., Weichsel, R., & Guittar, N. A. (2011). The cost of doing femininity: Gendered disparities in pricing of personal care products and services. *Gender Issues, 28*(4), 175–191.

Featherstone, M. (1991). The body in consumer culture. In M. Featherstone, M. Hepworth, & B. S. Turner (Eds.), *The body: Social process and cultural theory* (pp. 170–196). London: Sage.

Gitlin, T. (2001). *Media unlimited: How the torrent of images and sounds overwhelms our lives.* New York: Henry Holt.

Goode, E. (1999, May 20). Study finds TV alters Fiji girls' view of body. *New York Times,* A17.

Harris, D. (2000). *Cute, quaint, hungry and romantic: The aesthetics of consumerism.* Cambridge, MA: Da Capo Press.

Herdt, G. (1997). *Same sex, different cultures.* Boulder, CO: Westview.

Johnson, A. (2001). *Privilege, power, and difference.* Mountain View, CA: Mayfield.

Kilbourne, J. (1999). *Can't buy my love.* New York: Simon & Schuster.

Kimle, P. A., & Damhorst, M. L. (1997). A grounded theory model of the ideal business image for women. *Symbolic Interaction, 20*(1), 45–68.

Manning, R. D. (2011). Crisis in consumption OR American capitalism: A sociological perspective on the consumer-led recession. *Consumers, Commodities & Consumption, 13*(1). Retrieved December 12, 2011, from http://csrn.camden.rutgers.edu/newsletters/13-1/manning.htm

Marenco, S. (with Bornstein, K.). (1993). *Adventures in the gender trade: A case for diversity* [Motion picture]. New York: Filmakers Library.

O'Brien, J. (1999). *Social prisms.* Thousand Oaks, CA: Pine Forge Press.

Quart, A. (2003). *Branded: The buying and selling of teenagers.* New York: Basic Books.

Ritzer, G. (1999). *Enchanting a disenchanted world.* Thousand Oaks, CA: Pine Forge.

Ritzer, G. (2011). The dinosaurs of consumption. *Consumers, Commodities & Consumption, 13*(1). Retrieved December 12, 2011, from http://csrn.camden.rutgers.edu/newsletters/13-1/ritzer.htm

Schiebinger, L. (2000). Introduction. In L. Schiebinger (Ed.), *Feminism and the body* (pp. 1–21). New York: Oxford University Press.

Schor, J. (1998). *The overspent American.* New York: Basic Books.

Schor, J. (2004). *Born to buy.* New York: Scribner.

Schor, J. (2010). *Welcome to Plenitude.* Retrieved April 12, 2012, from http://www.julietschor.org/2010/05/welcome-to-plenitude/

Sorenson, M. L. S. (2000). *Gender archaeology.* Cambridge, UK: Polity Press.

Sullivan, D. A. (2001). *Cosmetic surgery: The cutting edge of commercial medicine in America.* New Brunswick, NJ: Rutgers University Press.

Tilley, C. (2011). Materializing identities: An introduction. *Journal of Material Culture, 16,* 347–357.

Urla, J., & Swedlund A. C. (1995). The anthropometry of Barbie: Unsettling ideals of the feminine body in popular culture. In J. Terry & J. Urla (Eds.), *Deviant bodies: Critical perspectives on difference in science and popular culture* (pp. 277–313). Bloomington: Indiana University Press.

Walters, S. D. (2001). *All the rage: The story of gay visibility in America.* Chicago: University of Chicago Press.

Zukin, S. (2004). *Point of purchase: How shopping changed American culture.* New York: Routledge.

Introduction to Reading 21

Adie Nelson's article offers a marvelously detailed analysis of one way the modern marketplace reinforces gender stereotypes—the gender coding of children's Halloween costumes. Nelson describes the research process she employed to label costumes as masculine, feminine, or neutral. She provides extensive information about how manufacturers and advertisers use gender markers to steer buyers, in this case parents, toward "gender-appropriate" costume choices for their children. Overall, Nelson's research indicates that gender-neutral costumes, whether ready-to-wear or sewing patterns, are a tiny minority of all the costumes on the market.

1. Many perceive Halloween costumes as encouraging children to engage in fantasy play. How does Nelson's research call this notion into question?

2. Describe some of the key strategies employed by manufacturers to "gender" children's costumes. What strategies do manufacturers use to "gender" adults' costumes? To answer the latter question, look at adult costumes online or in costume shops in malls.

3. How do Halloween costumes help reproduce an active-masculine/passive-feminine dichotomy?

THE PINK DRAGON IS FEMALE

HALLOWEEN COSTUMES AND GENDER MARKERS

Adie Nelson

The celebration of Halloween has become, in contemporary times a socially orchestrated secular event that brings buyers and sellers into the marketplace for the sale and purchase of treats, ornaments, decorations, and fanciful costumes. Within this setting, the wearing of fancy dress costumes has such a prominent role that it is common, especially within large cities, for major department stores and large, specialty toy stores to begin displaying their selection of Halloween costumes by mid-August, if not earlier. It is also evident that the range of masks and costumes available has broadened greatly beyond those identified by McNeill (1970), and that both children and adults may now select from a wide assortment of ready-made costumes depicting, among other things, animals, objects, superheroes, villains, and celebrities. In addition, major suppliers of commercially available sewing patterns, such as Simplicity and McCall's, now routinely include an assortment of Halloween costumes in their fall catalogues. Within such catalogues, a variety of costumes designed for infants, toddlers, children, adults, and, not infrequently, pampered dogs are featured.

From Nelson, Adie. 2000. "The Pink Dragon is Female: Halloween Costumes and Gender Markers." *Psychology of Women Quarterly*, 24.

On the surface, the selection and purchase of Halloween costumes for use by children may simply appear to facilitate their participation in the world of fantasy play. At least in theory, asking children what they wish to wear or what they would like to be for Halloween may be seen to encourage them to use their imagination and to engage in the role-taking stage that Mead (1934) identified as play. Yet, it is clear that the commercial marketplace plays a major role in giving expression to children's imagination in their Halloween costuming. Moreover, although it might be facilely assumed that the occasion of Halloween provides a cultural "time out" in which women and men as well as girls and boys have tacit permission to transcend the gendered rules that mark the donning of apparel in everyday life, the androgyny of Halloween costumes may be more apparent than real. If, as our folk wisdom proclaims, "clothes make the man" (or woman), it would be presumptuous to suppose that commercially available children's Halloween costumes and sewing patterns do not reflect both the gendered nature of dress (Eicher & Roach-Higgins, 1992) and the symbolic world of heroes, villains, and fools (Klapp, 1962, 1964). Indeed, the donning of Halloween costumes may demonstrate a "gender display" (Goffman, 1966, p. 250) that is dependent on decisions made by brokering agents to the extent that it is the aftermath of a series of decisions made by commercial firms that market ready-made costumes and sewing patterns that, in turn, are purchased, rented, or sewn by parents or others. . . .

Building on Barnes and Eicher's (1992, p. 1) observation that "dress is one of the most significant markers of gender identity," an examination of children's Halloween costumes provides a unique opportunity to explore the extent to which gender markers are also evident within the fantasy costumes available for Halloween. To the best of my knowledge, no previous research has attempted to analyze these costumes nor to examine the ways in which the imaginary vistas explored in children's fantasy dress reproduce and reiterate more conventional messages about gender.

In undertaking this research, my expectations were based on certain assumptions about the perspectives of merchandisers of Halloween costumes for children. It was expected that commercially available costumes and costume patterns would reiterate and reinforce traditional gender stereotypes. Attempting to adopt the marketing perspective of merchandisers, it was anticipated that the target audience would be parents concerned with creating memorable childhood experiences for their children, envisioning them dressed up as archetypal fantasy characters. In the case of sewing patterns, it was expected that the target audience would be primarily mothers who possessed what manufacturers might imagine to be the sewing skills of the traditional homemaker. However, these assumptions about merchandisers are not the subject of the present inquiry. Rather, the present study offers an examination of the potential contribution of marketing to the maintenance of gender stereotypes. In this article, the focus is on the costumes available in the marketplace; elsewhere I examine the interactions between children and their parents in the selection, modification, and wearing of Halloween costumes (Nelson, 1999).

METHOD

The present research was based on a content analysis of 469 unique children's Halloween ready-made costumes and sewing patterns examined from August 1996 to November 1997 at craft stores, department stores, specialty toy stores, costume rental stores, and fabric stores containing catalogues of sewing patterns. Within retail stores, racks of children's Halloween costumes typically appeared in August and remained in evidence, albeit in dwindling numbers, until early November each year. In department stores, a subsection of the area generally devoted to toys featured such garments; in craft stores and/or toy stores, children's Halloween costumes were typically positioned on long racks in the center of a section devoted to the commercial paraphernalia now associated with the celebration of Halloween (e.g., cardboard witches, "Spook trees," plastic pumpkin containers). Costumes were not segregated by gender within the stores (i.e., there were no separate aisles or sections for boys' and girls' costumes); however, children's costumes were typically positioned separately from those designed for adults. . . .

All costumes were initially coded as (a) masculine, (b) feminine, or (c) neutral depending on whether boys, girls, or both were featured as the models on the packaging that accompanied a ready-to-wear costume or were used to illustrate the completed costume on the cover of a sewing pattern. . . . The pictures accompanying costumes may act as safekeeping devices, which discourage parents from buying "wrong"-sexed costumes. The process of labeling costumes as masculine, feminine, or neutral was facilitated by the fact that these public pictures (Goffman, 1979) commonly employed recognizable genderisms. For example, a full-body costume of a box of crayons could be identified as feminine by the long curled hair of the model and the black patent leather pumps with ribbons she wore. In like fashion, a photograph depicting the finished version of a sewing pattern for a teapot featured the puckish styling of the model in a variant of what Goffman (1979, p. 45) termed "the bashful knee bend" and augmented this subtle cue by having the model wear white pantyhose and Mary-Jane shoes with rosettes at the base of the toes. Although the sex of the model could have been rendered invisible, such feminine gender markers as pointy-toed footwear, party shoes of white and black patent leather, frilly socks, makeup and nail polish, jewelry, and elaborately curled (and typically long and blonde) hair adorned with bows/barrettes/hairbands facilitated this initial stage of costume placement. By and large, female models used to illustrate Halloween costumes conformed to the ideal image of the "Little Miss" beauty pageant winner; they were almost overwhelmingly White, slim, delicate-boned blondes who did not wear glasses. Although male child models were also overwhelmingly White, they were more heterogeneous in height and weight and were

more likely to wear glasses or to smile out from the photograph in a bucktooth grin. At the same time, however, masculine gender markers were apparent. Male models were almost uniformly shod in either well-worn running shoes or sturdy-looking brogues, while their hair showed little variation from the traditional little boy cut of short back and sides.

The use of gender-specific common and proper nouns to designate costumes (e.g., Medieval Maiden, Majorette, Prairie Girl) or gender-associated adjectives that formed part of the costume title (e.g., Tiny Tikes Beauty, Pretty Witch, Beautiful Babe, Pretty Pumpkin Pie) also served to identify feminine costumes. Similarly, the use of the terms "boy," "man," or "male" in the advertised name of the costume (e.g., Pirate Boy, Native American Boy, Dragon Boy) or the noted inclusion of advertising copy that announced "Cool dudes costumes are for boys in sizes" was used to identify masculine costumes. Costumes designated as neutral were those in which both boys and girls were featured in the illustration or photograph that accompanied the costume or sewing pattern or in which it was impossible to detect the sex of the wearer. By and large, illustrations for gender-neutral ads featured boys and girls identically clad and depicted as a twinned couple or, alternatively, showed a single child wearing a full-length animal costume complete with head and "paws," which, in the style of spats, effectively covered the shoes of the model. In addition, gender-neutral costumes were identified by an absence of gender-specific nouns and stereotypically gendered colors.

Following this initial division into three categories, the contents of each were further coded into a modified version of Klapp's (1964) schema of heroes, villains, and fools. In his work, Klapp suggested that this schema represents three dimensions of human behavior. That is, heroes are praised and set up as role models, whereas villains and fools are negative models, with the former representing evil to be feared and/or hated and the latter representing figures of absurdity inviting ridicule. However, although Klapp's categories were based on people in real life,

I applied them to the realm of make-believe. For the purposes of this study, the labels refer to types of personas that engender or invite the following emotional responses, in a light-hearted way from audiences: heroes invite feelings of awe, admiration, and respect, whereas villains elicit feelings of fear and loathing, and fools evoke feelings of laughter and perceptions of cuteness. All of the feelings, however, are mock emotions based on feelings of amusement, which make my categories quite distinct from Klapp's. For example, although heroes invite awe, we do not truly expect somebody dressed as a hero to be held in awe. . . .

For the purposes of this secondary classification of costumes, the category of hero was broadened to include traditional male or female heroes (e.g., Cowboy, Robin Hood, Cinderella, Cleopatra), superheroes possessing supernatural powers (e.g., Superman, Robocop, Xena, the Warrior Princess) as well as characters with high occupational status (e.g., Emergency Room Doctor, Judge) and characters who are exemplars of prosocial conformity to traditional masculine and feminine roles (e.g., Team USA Cheerleader, Puritan Lady, Pioneer Boy). The category of villain was broadly defined to include symbolic representations of death (e.g., the Grim Reaper, Death, The Devil, Ghost), monsters (e.g., Wolfman, Frankenstein, The Mummy), and antiheroes (e.g., Convict, Pirate, The Wicked Witch of the West, Catwoman). Fool was a hybrid category, distinguished by costumes whose ostensible function was to amuse rather than to alarm.

Within this category, two subcategories were distinguished. The first subcategory, figures of mirth, referred to costumes of clowns, court jesters, and harlequins. The second, nonhuman/inanimate objects, was composed of costumes representing foodstuffs (e.g., Peapod, Pepperoni Pizza, Chocolate Chip Cookie), animals and insects, and inanimate objects (e.g., Alarm Clock, Bar of Soap, Flower Pot). Where a costume appeared to straddle two categories, an attempt was made to assign it to a category based on the dominant emphasis of its pictorial representation. For example, a costume labeled Black Widow Spider could be classified as either an insect or a villain. If the accompanying illustration featured a broadly smiling child in a costume depicting a fuzzy body and multiple appendages, it was classified as an insect and included in the category of nonhuman/inanimate objects; if the costume featured an individual clad in a black gown, long black wig, ghoulish makeup, and a sinister mien, the costume was classified as a villain. Contents were subsequently reanalyzed in terms of their constituent parts and compared across masculine and feminine categories. In all cases, costumes were coded into the two coding schemes on the basis of a detailed written description of each costume. . . .

RESULTS

The initial placement of the 469 children's Halloween costumes into masculine, feminine, or neutral categories yielded 195 masculine costumes, 233 feminine costumes, and 41 gender-neutral costumes. The scarcity of gender-neutral costumes was notable; costumes that featured both boys and girls in their ads or in which the gender of the anticipated wearer remained (deliberately or inadvertently) ambiguous accounted for only 8.7% of those examined. Gender-neutral costumes were more common in sewing patterns than in ready-to-wear costumes and were most common in costumes designed for newborns and very young infants. In this context, gender-neutral infant costumes largely featured a winsome assortment of baby animals (e.g., Li'l Bunny, Beanie the Pig) or foodstuffs (e.g., Littlest Peapod). By and large, few costumes for older children were presented as gender-neutral; the notable exceptions were costumes for scarecrows and emergency room doctors (with male/female models clad identically in olive-green "scrubs"), ready-made plastic costumes for Lost World/Jurassic Park hunters, a single costume labeled Halfman/Halfwoman, and novel sewing patterns depicting such inanimate objects as a sugar cube, laundry hamper, or treasure chest.

Beginning most obviously with costumes designed for toddlers, gender dichotomization was promoted by gender-distinctive marketing devices employed by the manufacturers of both commercially made costumes and sewing patterns. In relation to sewing patterns for children's Halloween costumes, structurally identical costumes featured alterations through the addition or deletion of decorative trim (e.g., a skirt on a costume for an elephant) or the use of specific colors or costume names, which served to distinguish masculine from feminine costumes. For example, although the number and specific pattern pieces required to construct a particular pattern would not vary, View A featured a girl-modeled Egg or Tomato, whereas View B presented a boy-modeled Baseball or Pincushion. Structurally identical costumes modeled by both boys and girls would be distinguished through the use of distinct colors or patterns of material. Thus, for the peanut M & M costumes, the illustration featured girls clad in red or green and boys clad in blue, brown, or yellow. Similarly, female clowns wore costumes of soft pastel colors and dainty polka dots, but male clowns were garbed in bold primary colors and in material featuring large polka dots or stripes. Illustrations for ready-to-wear costumes were also likely to signal the sex of the intended wearer through the advertising copy: models for feminine costumes, for example, had long curled hair, were made up, and wore patent leather shoes. Only in such costumes as Wrinkly Old Woman, Grandma Hag, Killer Granny, and Nun did identifiably male children model female apparel. . . .

[A]lthough hero costumes constituted a large percentage of both masculine and feminine costumes, masculine costumes contained a higher percentage of villain costumes, and feminine costumes included substantially more fool costumes, particularly those of nonhuman/inanimate objects. It may be imagined that the greater total number of feminine costumes would provide young girls with a broader range of costumes to select from than exists for young boys, but in fact the obverse is true. . . . [W]hen finer distinctions were made within the three generic categories, hero costumes for girls were clustered in a narrow range of roles that, although distinguished by specific names, were functionally equivalent in the image they portray. It would seem that, for girls, glory is concentrated in the narrow realm of beauty queens, princesses, brides, or other

exemplars of traditionally passive femininity. The ornate, typically pink, ball-gowned costume of the princess (with or without a synthetic jeweled tiara) was notable, whether the specific costume was labeled Colonial Belle, the Pumpkin Princess, Angel Beauty, Blushing Bride, Georgia Peach, Pretty Mermaid, or Beauty Contest Winner. In contrast, although hero costumes for boys emphasized the warrior theme of masculinity (Doyle, 1989; Rotundo, 1993), with costumes depicting characters associated with battling historical, contemporary, or supernatural Goliaths (e.g., Bronco Rider, Dick Tracy, Sir Lancelot, Hercules, Servo Samurai, Robin the Boy Wonder), these costumes were less singular in the visual images they portrayed and were more likely to depict characters who possessed supernatural powers or skills.

Masculine costumes were also more likely than feminine costumes to depict a wide range of villainous characters (e.g., Captain Hook, Rasputin, Slash), monsters (e.g., Frankenstein, The Wolfman), and, in particular, agents or symbols of death (e.g., Dracula, Executioner, Devil Boy, Grim Reaper). Moreover, costumes for male villains were more likely than those of female villains to be elaborate constructions that were visually repellant; to feature an assortment of scars, mutations, abrasions, and suggested amputations; and to present a wide array of ingenious, macabre, or disturbing visual images. For example, the male-modeled, ready-to-wear Mad Scientist's Experiment costume consisted of a full-body costume of a monkey replete with a half-head mask featuring a gaping incision from which rubber brains dangled. Similarly, costumes for such characters as Jack the Ripper, Serial Killer, Freddy Krueger, or The Midnight Stalker were adorned with the suggestion of bloodstains and embellished with such paraphernalia as plastic knives or slip-on claws.

In marked contrast, the costumes of female villains alternated between relatively simple costumes of witches in pointy hats and capes modeled by young girls, costumes of the few female arch villains drawn from the pages of comic books, and, for older girls, costumes that were variants of the garb donned by the popular TV character

Elvira, Mistress of the Dark (i.e., costumes that consisted of a long black wig and a long flowing black gown cut in an empire-style, which, when decorated with gold brocade or other trim at the top of the ribcage, served to create the suggestion of a bosom). The names of costumes for the female villains appeared to emphasize the erotic side of their villainy (e.g., Enchantra, Midnite Madness, Sexy Devil, Bewitched) or to neutralize the malignancy of the character by employing adjectives that emphasized their winsome rather than wicked qualities (e.g., Cute Cuddly Bewitched, Little Skull Girl, Pretty Little Witch).

Within the category of fools, feminine costumes were more likely than masculine costumes to depict nonhuman/inanimate objects (33.1% of feminine costumes vs. 17.4% of masculine costumes). Feminine costumes were more likely than masculine costumes to feature a wide variety of small animals and insects (e.g., Pretty Butterfly, Baby Cricket, Dalmatian Puppy), as well as flowers, foodstuffs (BLT Sandwich, Ice Cream Cone, Lollipop), and dainty, fragile objects such as Tea Pot. For example, a costume for Vase of Flowers was illustrated with a picture of a young girl wearing a cardboard cylinder from her ribcage to her knees on which flowers were painted, while a profusion of pink, white, and yellow flowers emerged from the top of the vase to form a collar of blossoms around her face. Similarly, a costume for Pea Pod featured a young girl wearing a green cylinder to which four green balloons were attached; on the top of her head, the model wore a hat bedecked with green leaves and tendrils in a corkscrew shape. When costumed as animals, boys were likely to be shown modeling larger, more aggressive animals (e.g., Velociraptor, Lion, T-Rex); masculine costumes were unlikely to be marketed with adjectives emphasizing their adorable, "li'l," cute, or cuddly qualities. In general, boys were rarely cast as objects, but when they were, they were overwhelmingly shown as items associated with masculine expertise. For example, a costume for Computer was modeled by a boy whose face was encased in the computer monitor and who wore, around his midtorso, a keyboard held up by suspenders. Another masculine costume depicted a young boy wearing a costume for Paint Can; the lid of the can was crafted in the style of a chef's hat, and across the cylindrical can worn from midchest to mid-knee was written "Brand X Paint" and, in smaller letters, "Sea Blue." Although rarely depicted as edibles or consumable products, three masculine costumes featured young boys as, variously, Root Beer Mug, Pepperoni Pizza, and Grandma's Pickle Jar.

DISCUSSION

Although the term "fantasy" implies a "play of the mind" or a "queer illusion" (Barnhart, 1967, p. 714), the marketing illustrations for children's Halloween costumes suggest a flight of imagination that remains largely anchored in traditional gender roles, images, and symbols. Indeed, the noninclusive language commonly found in the names of many children's Halloween costumes reverberates throughout many other dimensions of the gendered social life depicted in this fantastical world. For example, the importance of participation in the paid-work world and financial success for men and of physical attractiveness and marriage for women is reinforced through costume names that reference masculine costumes by occupational roles or titles but describe feminine costumes via appearance and/or relationships (e.g., "Policeman" vs. "Beautiful Bride"). Although no adjectives are deemed necessary to describe Policeman, the linguistic prompt contained in Beautiful Bride serves to remind observers that the major achievements for females are getting married and looking lovely. In addition to costume titles that employ such sex-linked common nouns as Flapper, Bobby Soxer, Ballerina, and Pirate Wench, sex-marked suffixes such as the -ess (e.g., Pretty Waitress, Stewardess, Gypsy Princess, Sorceress) and -ette (e.g., Majorette) also set apart male and female fantasy character costumes. Costumes for suffragettes or female-modeled police officers, astronauts, and fire fighters were conspicuous only by their absence.

Gender stereotyping in children's Halloween costumes also reiterates an active-masculine/passive-feminine dichotomization. The ornamental passivity of Beauty Queen stands in stark contrast to the reification of the masculine action figure, whether he is heroic or villainous. In relation to hero figures, the dearth of female superhero costumes in the sample would seem to reflect the comparative absence of such characters in comic books. Although male superheroes have sprung up almost "faster than a speeding bullet" since the 1933 introduction of *Superman,* the comic book life span of women superheroes has typically been abbreviated, "rarely lasting for more than three appearances" (Robbins, 1996, p. 2). Moreover, the applicability of the term "superhero" to describe these female characters seems at least somewhat dubious. Often their role has been that of the male hero's girlfriend or sidekick "whose purpose was to be rescued by the hero" (Robbins, 1996, p. 3).

In 1941 the creation of *Wonder Woman* (initially known as Amazon Princess Diana) represented a purposeful attempt by her creator, psychologist William Marston, to provide female readers with a same-sex superhero.... Nevertheless, over half a decade later, women comic book superheroes remain rare and, when they do appear, are likely to be voluptuous and scantily clad. If, as Robbins (1996, p. 166) argued, the overwhelmingly male comic book audience "expect, in fact demand that any new superheroines exist only as pinup material for their entertainment," it would seem that comic books and their televised versions are unlikely to galvanize the provision of flat-chested female superhero Halloween costumes for prepubescent females in the immediate future.

The relative paucity of feminine villains would also seem to reinforce an active/passive dichotomization on the basis of gender. Although costumes depict male villains as engaged in the commission of a wide assortment of antisocial acts, those for female villains appear more nebulous and are concentrated within the realm of erotic transgressions. Moreover, the depiction of a female villain as a sexual temptress or erotic queen suggests a type of "active passivity" (Salamon, 1983), whereby the act of commission is restricted to wielding her physical attractiveness over (presumably) weak-willed men. The veritable absence of feminine agents or symbols of death may reflect not only the stereotype of women (and girls) as life-giving and nurturing, but also the attendant assumption that femininity and lethal aggressiveness are mutually exclusive.

Building on the Sapir–Whorf hypothesis that the language we speak predisposes us to make particular interpretations of reality (Sapir, 1949; Whorf, 1956) and the assertion that language provides the basis for developing the gender schema identified by Bem (1983), the impact of language and other symbolic representations must be considered consequential. The symbolic representations of gender contained within Halloween costumes may, along with specific costume titles, refurbish stereotypical notions of what women/girls and men/boys are capable of doing even within the realm of their imaginations. Nelson and Robinson (1995) noted that deprecatory terms in the English language often ally women with animals. Whether praised as a "chick," "fox," or "Mother Bear" or condemned as a "bitch," "sow," or an "old nag," the imagery is animal reductionist. They also noted that language likens women to food items (e.g., sugar, tomato, cupcake), with the attendant suggestion that they look "good enough to eat" and are "toothsome morsels." Complementing this, the present study suggests that feminine Halloween costumes also employ images that reduce females to commodities intended for amusement, consumption, and sustenance. A cherry pie, after all, has only a short shelf life before turning stale and unappealing. Although a computer may become obsolete, the image it conveys is that of rationality, of a repository of wisdom, and of scientifically minded wizardry.

In general, the relative absence of gender-neutral costumes is intriguing. Although it must remain speculative, it may be that the manufacturers of ready-to-wear and sewing pattern costumes subscribe to traditional ideas about gender and/or believe that costumes that depart from these ideas are unlikely to find widespread acceptance. Employing a supply–demand logic, it may be that marketing analysis of costume sales confirms their suspicions. Nevertheless, although commercial practices may reflect consumer preferences for gender-specific products rather than biases on the part of merchandisers themselves, packaging that clearly depicts boys or girls—but not both—effectively promotes gendered definitions of products beyond anything that might be culturally inherent in them. This study suggests that gender-aschematic Halloween costumes for children compose only a minority of both ready-to-wear costumes and sewing patterns. It is notable that, when male children were presented modeling female garments, the depicted character was effectively desexed by age (e.g., a wizened, hag-like "grandmother") or by calling (e.g., a nun).

The data for this study speak only to the gender practices of merchandisers marketing costumes and sewing patterns to parents who themselves may be responding to their children's wishes. Beyond this, the findings do not identify precisely whose tastes are represented when these costumes are purchased. It is always possible that, despite the gendered nature of Halloween costumes presented in the illustrations and advertising copy used to market them, parents and children themselves may engage in creative redefinitions of the boundary markers surrounding gender. A child or parent may express and act on a preference for dressing a male in a pink, ready-to-wear butterfly costume or a female as Fred Flintstone and, in so doing, actively defy the symbolic boundaries that gender the Halloween costume. Alternatively, as a strategy of symbolic negotiation, those parents who sew may creatively experiment with recognizable gender markers, deciding, for example, to construct a pink dragon costume for their daughter or a brown butterfly costume for their son. Such amalgams of gender-discordant images may, on the surface, allow both male and female children to experience a broader range of fantastical roles and images. However, like Persian carpets, deliberately flawed to forestall divine wrath, such unorthodox Halloween costumes, in their structure and design, may nevertheless incorporate fibers of traditional gendered images.

REFERENCES

Barnes, R., & Eicher, J. B. (1992). *Dress and gender: Making and meaning in cultural contexts.* New York: Berg.

Barnhart, C. L. (1967). *The world book dictionary: A–K.* Chicago: Field Enterprises Educational Corporation.

Bem, S. L. (1983). Gender schema theory and its implications for child development: Raising gender-aschematic children in a gender-schematic society. *Signs: Journal of Women in Culture and Society, 8,* 598–616.

Doyle, J. A. (1989). *The male experience.* Dubuque, IA: Wm. C. Brown.

Eicher, J. B., & Roach-Higgins, M. E. (1992). Definition and classification of dress: Implications for analysis of gender roles. In R. Barnes & J. B. Eicher (Eds.), *Dress and gender. Making and meaning in cultural contexts* (pp. 8–28). New York: Berg.

Goffman, E. (1966). Gender display. *Philosophical Transactions of the Royal Society of London, 279,* 250.

Goffman, E. (1979). *Gender advertisements.* London: Macmillan.

Klapp, O. (1962). *Heroes, villains and fools.* Englewood Cliffs, NJ: Prentice-Hall.

Klapp, O. (1964). *Symbolic leaders.* Chicago: Aldine.

McNeill, F. M. (1970). *Hallowe'en: Its origins, rites and ceremonies in the Scottish tradition.* Edinburgh: Albyn Press.

Mead, G. H. (1934). *Mind, self and society.* Chicago: University of Chicago Press.

Nelson, E. D. (1999). *Dressing for Halloween, doing gender.* Unpublished manuscript.

Nelson, E. D., & Robinson, B. W. (1995). *Gigolos & Madame's bountiful: Illusions of gender, power and intimacy.* Toronto: University of Toronto Press.

Robbins, T. (1996). *The Great Women Super Heroes.* Northampton, MA: Kitchen Sink Press.

Rotundo, E. A. (1993). *American manhood: Transformations in masculinity from the revolution to the modern era.* New York: Basic Books.

Salamon, E. (1983). *Kept women: Mistress of the '80s.* London: Orbis.

Sapir, E. (1949). *Selected writings of Edward Sapir on language, culture and personality.* Berkeley: University of California Press.

Whorf, B. L. (1956). The relation of habitual thought and behavior to language. In J. B. Carroll (Ed.), *Language, thought, and reality* (pp. 134–159). Cambridge, MA: Technology Press of MIT.

Introduction to Reading 22

Kimberly Hoang, a sociologist and Vietnamese American woman, conducted 22 months of participant observation and ethnography in a variety of roles (e.g., hostess and bartender) in a variety of settings (e.g., bars, cafes, malls, streets) in which sex workers and their clients met in Ho Chi Minh City (HCMC), Vietnam, between 2006 and 2007 and 2009 and 2010. When she began her project she discovered that the women sex workers she studied, all over the age of 18, were not only aware of the conditions of their work but also willing participants in sex work because it offered financial opportunities for themselves and their families that could not be matched by doing factory work or service-sector work. In this article, Hoang focuses on two sex work arenas, one catering to Western budget travelers and the other to Western businessmen. She highlights the complexities of client–worker relationships, in particular the ways sex workers sell impressions of themselves as dark-skinned, poor women to Western men who embrace fantasies of helping poor women living in the third world.

1. Why/how does Hoang challenge the widespread view in Western nations that sex workers in countries such as Vietnam are kidnapped, sold, or forced into sex work?

2. Discuss the ways buying and selling gender, race, and class are incorporated into the sex worker–client relationship in Hoang's study.

3. How do you feel about the ways sex workers "dupe" clients and, in turn, clients play into the "game" as described in this article?

───────────── PERFORMING THIRD WORLD POVERTY ─────────────

RACIALIZED FEMININITIES IN SEX WORK

Kimberly Hoang

Over the last two decades, the issue of human trafficking has captivated governments, NGOs, researchers, and activists around the world. Images of women in handcuffs and chains circulate through print, television, and online news outlets, perpetuating a view of trafficked women as victims of Third World poverty who are kidnapped, sold, or forced into sex work. As governments, corporations, religious organizations, and celebrities devote millions of dollars to save trafficked women, they neglect to conduct systematic research on the ground to assess this problem.

This article advances the scholarship on sex trafficking by providing a different lens through which to examine the sex industry. Rather than viewing women as victims of global poverty who are kidnapped, forced, or duped into the sex industry, I follow the work of Brennan (2004),

Hoang, Kimberly. 2013. "Performing Third World Poverty: Racialized Femininities in Sex Work."

Mahdavi (2011), and Parreñas (2011) to analyze the complex social structures that shape the *range of choices* available to women in their relationships with clients, club owners, and brokers. I show how sex workers in Ho Chi Minh City [HCMC], Vietnam capitalized on media images and NGO narratives that portray sex workers as victims to advance their lives. By *performing Third World poverty*, sex workers who freely entered the sex industry portrayed themselves as victims to procure large remittances from their male clients.

In this article, I raise two primary questions. First, how do sex workers capitalize on global economic restructuring to improve not only their lives but also the lives of their extended families? Second, how do male clients make sense of and respond to sex workers' performances of Third World poverty? To answer these questions, I turn to my ethnographic research in HCMC's sex industry conducted over a total of 22 months in two phases between 2006–2007 and 2009–2010 as well as in-depth interviews with 71 sex workers and 55 clients in two niche markets that catered to Western budget travelers/tourists and Western businessmen who were part of a transnational circuit.[1] I show that just as organizations in the developed world pull on the heartstrings of their donors in the "fight" to end human trafficking, sex workers capitalize on globally circulating narratives to dupe male clients for money and visas by engaging in strategic and racialized performances of third world poverty. This article also looks at how male clients respond, react to, and make meaning out of sex workers' performances as they open their wallets to "save" women from a lifetime of poverty or entrapment in sex work. As such, this article also fills a gap in the literature by paying attention to both sides of client and sex-worker relationships.

GLOBAL SEX WORK

In recent years, sex work abolitionists examined the lives of women forced into the sex trade (Bales and Soodalter 2009; Bolkovac and Lynn 2011; Siddharth 2009). Their work fueled a worldwide explosion of representations of Third World women as victims routinely bought and sold to fulfill male sexual desires. These efforts sensationalized poor Third World women as victims while making heroes of those who studied them and worked to save them. These efforts also prompted serious policy changes regarding the sex industry.

Sex work abolitionists sensationalize this "multibillion dollar industry" and the "millions of women" kidnapped and forced into sex work without engaging in systematic, in-depth research of the women involved.

In addition, abolitionists assert that in order to end human trafficking, we need to eliminate the demand side of the equation. These researchers depict male sex patrons as predators who brutalize poor Third World women. However, very few studies engage in any kind of systematic research on the men who patronize these establishments. As I have shown elsewhere (Hoang 2011), male patrons of sex work vary a great deal in their behaviors, motivations, and desires. These men are involved in complex, and sometimes intimate relationships with sex workers, that involve much more than one-time direct sex-for-money exchanges as sex workers engage in a variety of emotional labors that involve a complex intermingling of money and intimacy (Bernstein 2007; Hoang 2010).

A parallel body of research emerged in recent years from sociologists and anthropologists who conducted in-depth ethnographies inside the bars and brothels where sex workers work. These researchers engaged in systematic research, spending a significant amount of time building rapport with sex workers (Brennan 2005), working alongside them (Parreñas 2011; Zheng 2009), and providing complex analyses of the *choices* women made as they entered into sex work. These studies show that, contrary to popular belief, women often knowingly and willingly entered into complex arrangements with brokers, club owners, and entertainment establishments in what Parreñas (2011) refers to as a process of *indentured mobility*.

This article builds on these studies by illustrating how sex workers in HCMC, Vietnam *perform Third World poverty* to procure large sums of money from Western male clients and how they strategically darkened their skin to embody what I term *racialized femininities*. This article not only points to women's *range* of choices in entering sex work but also highlights how workers strategically capitalize on global economic restructuring to enhance their socioeconomic trajectories. More importantly, I illustrate two sides of the client-worker relationship.

SEX TRAFFICKING: DUPED VICTIMS OR HUSTLERS?

In 2006, when I first began preliminary research for this project, I went to Vietnam equipped with information on local NGOs who "helped" the women I thought I would find. I visited a small but growing number of organizations looking to save victims of sex trafficking. However, I was shocked to find that few of the sex workers I met had been duped or sold into the sex trade. Many workers migrated to HCMC from villages to work in factories or the service sector before entering into sex work. During a tour of a local NGO, I was surprised to find that the organization had set up a private business exporting garments made by local sex workers to be sold abroad with "fair trade" stickers and pamphlets with images of women in handcuffs or trapped behind barbed wire fences.

Naively, I approached the workers and asked them how they ended up in this small clothing factory. At first, the women were quiet and refused to acknowledge my presence. After a long moment of awkward silence, Ai-Nhi, a 19 year-old worker, said to me, "I got caught on the street and had to spend several months in the rehabilitation center. This organization came to get me, so I am here now, but I would rather be in the bars." Dumbfounded, I asked her why she would rather be there and she responded:

I used to work in a factory making $70 US a month. I did that for many years but I was not making enough money to send to my family, so I quit and went to work on the streets . . . One day, I got caught and was sent into the center, and then this woman told me that I could get out early if I went with this organization that would teach me how to sew clothes. I agreed so that I could get out of the center . . . I am here now doing the same thing I was trying to escape. . . . They say they want to help us, but they are only helping themselves. I get paid $30 million VND [$200 US] a month to work here . . . [but] I know that they sell these clothes for a lot more money abroad. . . .

When I asked the women if they were happier in this shop sewing clothes than engaging in sex work, Ha, a 23 year-old worker, told me that she could make a lot more money in the bars where she also had more control over her time. She told me to go to the backpackers' area (*khu tay ba lo*) where I would meet several women who went right back into the bars after leaving the rehabilitation center. She wrote down the name of a bar in that area and told me to talk to the women working there. This was my first introduction to sex work in the backpackers' area, where I would eventually meet several women and their clients who were Western men traveling on a budget.

PERFORMING THIRD WORLD POVERTY

Racialized Bodies

In 2006, both budget travelers and transnational businessmen spent time in the backpackers' area of HCMC. However, by 2009, the area was run down by transient tourists looking to explore Vietnam as cheaply as possible and Western businessmen had carved out a distinct niche in the sex industry. In the backpackers' area, clients could walk into bars where women would immediately greet them, serve them drinks, wipe their faces with wet towels, and provide them with shoulder massages. Men would receive all of these services just by ordering a $2 US beer. The women in this bar engaged in a variety of practices to make their bodies desirable to their male clients. For example, all of the workers darkened their skin with bronzers and skin creams. When I asked the workers why they did so, Xuong, a 26 year-old worker, said to me:

> The men here like darker skin and women who just came up from the village. Girls who just come up from the villages get the most clients because they look fresh. Men like women with dark skin. They will always touch you and say, 'Wow, your skin is so dark and soft.'

Altering their skin color was the most notable strategy these women adopted to racialize their bodies to look like poor women in a Third World country. Those who were darker often received more attention, particularly from white men traveling on a budget.

Sex workers in the backpackers' area also wore very plain clothing consisting of jean skirts or shorts and a plain tank top because they wanted to convey to their clients that they were poor workers. One afternoon while helping Thu, a 22 year-old worker, pack for a trip home, I rummaged through her clothes and noticed that she had a lot of beautiful dresses. When I asked her why she never wore them to work, she explained:

> I have two sets of clothes—one for work and one for the village. I don't wear nice clothes to work because I don't want the men to think that I have money. If they think that I have money, they will not give me any money. I have to make sure that I look like a poor village girl.

Thu was not the only one who strategically dressed down in the bars. All of the sex workers did the same because it allowed them to convey an image that they were poor workers who could not even afford food, let alone nice things. They saved their nicer clothing for their visits to the village because these displays of wealth at home de-stigmatized their work in the bars.

Sex workers who catered to Western businessmen also played into their clients' racialized desires by strategically darkening their skin. However, rather than wearing simple clothing, these workers wore low-cut versions of the traditional Vietnamese *Ao dai*. Women who catered to Western businessmen dressed in ethnic dresses that made them look exotic while allowing workers to appear more expensive than the women in the poor backpackers' area. Lilly, the owner of the bar I studied in this district, reminded her workers on a daily basis that the clients in her bar were respectable businessmen, not cheap backpackers. The women who catered to this higher-paying clientele should therefore dress accordingly. She commissioned a tailor to come to her shop to measure all of her workers and sew their uniforms. Each dress was cut a little differently so that each woman would have a unique look. However, all of the dresses were made of the same faux silk Chinese fabric that closed in around the neck but had an opening that exposed women's cleavage and slits along the skirt to expose the workers' full thigh and bottom.

By darkening their skin and dressing in either plain clothing or exotic, Orientalizing garments, sex workers racialized their bodies to make themselves desirable to their clients. Their outward appearance was crucial to attracting men into the bars. However, workers also had to engage in a variety of emotional and bodily labors (Hoang 2010) to maintain ties with their clients and procure small and large sums of money from them. The next section examines how women enacted *Third World poverty* in ways that extended beyond simple self-presentation in order to attract long-term remittances from their clients.

PERFORMANCES OF POVERTY

Regardless of whether women catered to Western men traveling on a budget or Western businessmen, all of the women engaged in various performances of gender (West and Zimmerman 1987) through their embodied practices and through relational work (Zelizer 2005) with their clients. I learned of women's strategies to *perform Third World poverty* through the English lessons that I provided them in the afternoons. I visited *Naughty Girls*, the bar in the backpackers' area, at 2:00 pm, three to four days a week for four months between 2009–2010 to provide the women with free English lessons. Many of the women were excited about the opportunity to work with someone who would help them translate fabricated stories without judging them for lying or duping their clients. During these days, I helped women translate a series of emails, text messages, and key phrases that they wanted to have in their back pockets. They asked me to help them translate phrases like "My motorbike broke down. I have to walk to work. Can you help me buy new motorbike?" and "My father very sick and no one in my family help so I have to work. I am from An Giang village. You go to village before?"

During these lessons, I often asked the women why they lied to their clients and why they were careful not to display too much wealth in front of them. Xuan, a 19 year-old worker, said to me:

> A lot of the men here think that Vietnam is still a poor country. They want to hear that your family is poor and that you have no options so you came here to work. If you make them feel sorry for you as a poor Vietnamese village girl, they will give you a lot more money. We lie to them because it works ... We tell them that Vietnam is changing and growing so fast and that the price of food and gas has gone up and people from poor rural areas cannot afford to live off of the rice fields anymore.

The act of creating fictive stories about their "rural lives" enabled many women to procure large sums of money from clients through remittances. Xuan's strategic move allowed her to capitalize on Vietnam's changing position in the global economy and the widening inequalities between local rich and local poor. The women I studied were certainly much more financially secure than their family members who worked in the rice fields, textile or manufacturing industries, or even as service workers in HCMC. In an informal interview with Vy, a 22 year-old worker, she said to me:

> Western men in America hear about girls who are sold and forced to sell their bodies, but no one here is forced to do anything. I come to the bar to work and if I want to have sex with a client, I have sex with him. If I don't, then I won't. No one forces me to do anything I don't want to do. People come here trying to give us condoms or save us, but how can they help me when I make more than them?

In that same conversation Chau, a 23 year-old worker interjected and said:

> There are some men who come to Vietnam often and they know what bar life is like ... There are other men who are new to Vietnam—it is their first trip. Sometimes after sex, I will cry in the room and tell them how hard my life is and how mean the bar owner is. I will tell him that I want to get out and that I need $5000 US to pay for my debt to get out. So they help us.

Sex workers like Vy and Chau were aware of images that circulated across the globe of Asian sex workers as victims forced into a trade that involved horrific forms of violence. Their lives did not match these representations, but they capitalized on the images to procure large sums of money from their clients. Several men willingly provided the $5000 US the workers requested or some portion of that amount to "save" them from their life as a bargirl. In this way, sex workers also helped men feel like superior Western men from strong nations who were engaged in charity projects by helping poor women desperately looking to change their lives in a developing nation.

In their quest to see an authentic Vietnam, from a local's perspective, male clients often asked women if they would take them on tours of their villages and hometowns. Sex workers whose families were based in the city sometimes relied on their connections in the bar to take clients on tours of the Mekong Delta to visit with fake families. For example, in a conversation that I had with Thuy-Linh, she said:

> I am going to Kien Giang tomorrow with one of the guys here because he wants to see my village, but most of my family lives in Saigon now. We moved here about 10 years ago ... I am taking him to stay with Vi's family so that he will think that I am really poor and maybe give me money to rebuild the house or help my family out.

Several clients expressed a desire to visit villages where they could walk through rice fields, ride bicycles, and bargain for produce in street markets. Therefore, the women in the bars organized tours to visit fake families in nearby villages. In my conversations with the workers about these tours, I was struck by their awareness of their clients' desire to see Vietnam as a developing Third World country. They organized tours that would portray an "authentic" Vietnam removed from signs of global change, modernization, and capitalism. More often than not, sex workers were happy to play into their clients' desires because doing so enabled them to ask for larger sums of money.

In conversations with the clients upon their return from visiting the Mekong Delta, many expressed a sense of deep sadness for the conditions of poverty that the women portrayed to them. For example, after spending three days in with Nhi's family in their village, John, a man in his late 50s to early 60s, said to me:

> There are so many things that we in the West take for granted. Roofs over our heads, hot water, shoes . . . When I was with Nhi, I had to shower with buckets of cold water. It was so disgusting because I was brushing my teeth and I didn't realize that the bucket had a bunch of maggots in there. I felt these tiny worms swimming around in my mouth and I had to spit it out. I asked them how much it would cost to put in a proper shower and they said $500 US, so I gave it to them. They were such gracious hosts to me that I wanted to give something back.

While workers certainly employed strategies to embody Third World poverty, they also engaged in performances that highlighted their poverty in relation to the economic situations of their clients. John sympathized with Nhi's life and her conditions of poverty, and he genuinely wanted to help provide her family with a new faucet. Regardless of whether they were to women's true families, these visits to the village allowed workers to capitalize on their client's genuine concern, compassion, and empathy. Men provided women with money to help them escape poverty and transition from a basic standard of living to a comfortable standard of living.

By allowing men to believe that they were fulfilling the provider role, workers performed a femininity that was linked to financial dependence. Clients displayed a class-based masculinity in relation to these women. Several of the men I spoke with expressed a desire to have a traditional marriage where men were the economic providers and women took care of the home. However, because they could not maintain these roles in the US, many hoped to develop these relationships across transnational spaces in less-developed nations. In a long conversation with Jason, a man in his mid-sixties from Montana, he told me:

> Men like me probably make women like you very uncomfortable. We come here and get hooked to younger women . . . I grew up at a time in America when women stayed home and took care of the family while men worked. My wife and I were happily married for many years. When she died two years ago, my world fell apart. I didn't know how to cook, or clean, or take care of myself. I was depressed. I needed a wife . . . [or] someone to take care of me. In Asia . . . some women still hold on to those traditional values, and I can afford to take care of a woman on my retirement fund.

It was clear in Jason's mind that while he could not be an economic provider for a woman in the US, he could successfully assert his masculinity across transnational borders because of Vietnam's status as a Third World country. The act of creating fictive stories about their "rural lives" enabled many women to procure large sums of money from clients like Jason through remittances. These scripts enabled men to act as the economic provider and in effect preserve a sense of masculinity lost back at home.

CLIENTS' SCRIPTED PERFORMANCES

Not all men were as easily duped for their money. By 2009, stories had circulated among male clients of workers lying to them for their money. I sat in the bars listening day after day as men warned each other of the various ways that they might be tricked. However, I was surprised to find that several of the men I spoke with actually preferred to be unaware of workers' desires to consume luxury goods like nicer clothing, expensive cellular phones, and electronics because those items symbolized access to global capital, mobility, status, and most importantly, dignity in their work. For example, Edward, a 38 year-old man from the US said to me:

> We're not as naive as you think we are. We know better. But here is the thing. When you walk into a bar, everyone plays a role. The girls pretend to act excited to see us and flirt with us. We flirt back. They tell us about their poor families and we give them money here and there to help them. We may never know their real stories, but that is not the point. The point is that they make us feel like strong men who can provide for them and they get paid for it.

Some clients developed long-term relationships or friendships with a few workers; those relationships also involved a certain level of duplicity. Howard, a 39 year-old expatriate from Sweden, told me about his experience with duplicitous games:

> I have known this one worker for three years now and I still do not know very much about her. I feel comfortable there. It is predictable. I go in and have the same conversation with her every night. Someone could write a short story about this because it is the same script every single night. I come in and tell her I missed her, that I think she looks beautiful. She tells me about her family and money problems and I pretend to care. Sometimes we have sex, and that is it.

Relationships between clients and sex workers were bound by a set of predictable scripts that allowed clients to feel comfortable. As Howard described, when he walked into a bar, he also engaged in an emotional performance by telling a woman he saw on a regular basis that he missed her, thought she was beautiful, and was concerned about her financial situation.

These games became particularly apparent when new clients came in with friends who were regulars. Often, I listened in as men coached each other on what were appropriate and inappropriate behaviors within the bar. For example, one night while I was working in *Secrets*, a bar that catered to Western expatriates, I listened as Kevin, a regular client, explained the workings of the bar to his friend, Joseph. Kevin said:

> The girls in this bar are really nice. They are very low-key. You can talk and flirt with them with no pressure. If you like them, *you* ask them to meet you afterwards for about $100 US. It is a game. They play it and you play it.

Indeed, clients paid for a service from sex workers who worked as bartenders and hostesses. However, the clients also performed their own scripts in relation to the workers. They informed each other of the unspoken set of norms that guided interactions between workers and clients in the bar. Male clients did not always believe that the workers were truthful, but that was beside the point, because both men and women played a particular role inside the bars. Regardless of their truth, scripted interactions enabled men to maintain a comfortable and predictable relationship with workers based on a fantasy that they were heroic saviors helping women in need.

CONCLUSION

The issue of human trafficking has become a topic of great interest around the world. Celebrities like Demi Moore, Lucy Liu, and Ricky Martin and fashion designers such as Calvin Klein, Donna Karan, and Diane Von Furstenberg have committed resources to raise awareness around the issue of sex trafficking. Presidents George W. Bush and Barack Obama both agree that the US should commit resources to save women from the horrors of forced sexual labors internationally. Through in-depth ethnography, this article explores beneath the surface of this issue to examine the lives of men and women deeply embedded in the sex industry. None of the women I describe in this article were kidnapped, forced, or duped into sex work. Rather, they made conscious choices to sell sex because they saw factory work and service work as more exploitative forms of labor.

This is not to say that trafficking does not occur, or that women are not subject to forms of *indentured mobility* (Parreñas 2011). Rather, I suggest that the story involves greater complexity than the representations of NGOs might suggest. Indeed, women capitalize on images of victimized women and on Vietnam's rapid economic restructuring by *performing Third World poverty* to get money from their clients. Some clients played into these stories because it allowed them to preserve a sense of masculinity lost back at home. While nearly all of the men that I met in 2006 believed the sex workers' lies, by 2009, enough men had been duped that stories of women procuring large sums of money by lying began to circulate among Western clients. Even with this knowledge, clients and sex workers both engaged in scripted practices and discourses related to Third World poverty and women's victimhood. These scripts not only allowed "men to be men," as Nhi put it, but to enable men to be Western men from developed nations by maintaining a fantasy that they are helping poor women living in the Third World. Beyond images of barbed wire and handcuffs are actual men and women engaged in complex relationships. As governments and activists intervene in women's lives, aid efforts must move beyond the sex industry and into other locations such as factories to address the multiple and interconnected sources of women's "exploitation."

NOTE

1. I have used pseudonyms for all individuals and bars in this paper to protect the anonymity of my research participants.

REFERENCES

Bales, Kevin and Ron Soodalter. 2009. *The Slave Next Door: Human Trafficking and Slavery in New America Today.* Berkeley: University of California Press.

Bernstein, Elizabeth. 2007. *Temporarily Yours: Intimacy, Authenticity, and the Commerce of Sex.* Chicago: University of Chicago Press.

Bolkovac, Kathryn and Cari Lynn. 2011. *The Whistleblower: Sex Trafficking, Military Contractors, and One Woman's Fight for Justice.* New York: Palgrave Macmillan.

Brennan, Denise. 2004. *What's Love Got to Do with It? Transnational Desires and Sex Tourism in the Dominican Republic.* Durham: Duke University Press.

———. 2005. "Methodological Challenges in Research with Trafficked Persons: Tales from the Field." *International Migration* 43:35–54.

Hoang, Kimberly. 2010. "Economies of Emotion, Familiarity, Fantasy and Desire: Emotional Labor in Ho Chi Minh City's Sex Industry." *Sexualities* 13:255–272.

———. 2011. "'She's Not a Low Class Dirty Girl': Sex Work in Ho Chi Minh City, Vietnam." *Journal of Contemporary Ethnography* 40:367–396.

Mahdavi, Pardis. 2011. *Gridlock: Labor, Migration, and Human Trafficking in Dubai.* Palo Alto: Stanford University Press.

Parreñas, Rhacel. 2011. *Illicit Flirtations.* Palo Alto: Stanford University Press.

West, Candace and Don Zimmerman. 1987. "Doing Gender." *Gender and Society* 1:125–151.

Zelizer, Viviana. 2005. *The Purchase of Intimacy.* Princeton: Princeton University Press.

Introduction to Reading 23

This reading is a good example of the application of intersectional analysis, employing categories of gender, age, and social class. The authors studied a mass-marketed program of so-called "successful aging" that targets old men in an effort to persuade them to spend their money on products and activities that will supposedly make them look and feel youthfully and heterosexually virile and successful. Toni Calasanti and Neal King analyze the ageism of "successful aging" consumer campaigns and their implications for old men's "physical health, unequal access to wealth, heterosexual dominance, and fears of impotence" (from abstract).

1. How does ageism permeate "successful aging" consumer campaigns?

2. Why is it important to examine age relations and their intersections with other inequalities?

3. Discuss the "dirty"/"impotent" double bind and its link to the rise of "successful aging" consumer programs.

FIRMING THE FLOPPY PENIS

AGE, CLASS, AND GENDER RELATIONS IN THE LIVES OF OLD MEN

Toni Calasanti and Neal King

The rise of a consumer market that targets old people and their desire to remain young brings into sharp relief the problems that old age poses to manhood. This article proposes an expansion of research approaches to the lives of old men so that they may enrich our understandings of masculinities at a time when scientific breakthroughs and high-priced regimens sell visions of manhood renewed. We begin with a brief review of the (relative lack of) research on old men, continue with a look at the mass marketing of "successful aging," and conclude with an overview of the potential rewards that sustained scholarship on the old, and a theorizing of age relations as a dimension of inequality, can offer the studies of men and masculinities.

(YOUNG) MEN'S STUDIES

Studies of old men are common in the gerontological literature, but those that theorize masculinity remain rare. As in many academic endeavors, men's experiences have formed the basis for much research, but this androcentric foundation goes largely unexplored because manhood has served as invisible norm rather than as explicit focus of theory. Men's lives have formed the standard for scholarship on retirement, for example, to such an extent that even the *Retirement History Study,* a longitudinal study conducted by the Social Security Administration, excluded married women as primary respondents (Calasanti 1993). In recent years, feminist gerontologists have urged that scholars examine not only women but gender relations as well, and a handful of scholars such as Woodward (1999), Cruikshank (2003), and Davidson (2001) have done so. Despite the proliferation of feminist theorizing, however, most mainstream gerontological studies of women still ignore gender (Hooyman 1999), and research on men lags further. Few studies examine old men *as men* or attend to masculinity as a research topic.

At the same time, profeminist studies of masculinity have studied neither old men nor the age relations that subordinate them. Ageism, often inadvertent, permeates this research, stemming

---

from failures to study the lives of old men, to base questions on old men's accounts of their lives, or to theorize age the way we have theorized relations of gender, race, and class. Mentions of age inequality arise as afterthoughts, usually at the ends of lists of oppressions, but they remain unexamined. As a result, our understanding and concepts of manhood fall short because they assume, as standards of normalcy, men of middle age or younger. Aging scholars' inattention to old *men,* combined with men's studies' lack of concern with *old* men, not only renders old men virtually invisible but also reproduces our own present and future oppression. This article examines a range of popular representations of old men in the context of research about their lives to outline some ways in which the vital work on men and masculinity might benefit by taking age relations into account as a form of inequality that intersects with gender, race, sexuality, and class.

Denial of Aging

Our ageism—both our exclusion of the old and our ignorance of age relations as an inequality affecting us all—surfaces not only in our choices of what (not) to study but also in how we theorize men and masculinities. Listening to the old and theorizing the inequality that subordinates them require that we begin with elementary observations. People treat signs of old age as stigma and avoid notice of them in both personal and professional lives. For instance, we often write or say "older" rather than "old," usually in our attempts to avoid negative labels. But rather than accept this stigma attached to the old and help people to pass as younger than that, we should ask what seems so wrong with that stage of life. In a more aggregate version of this ageism, one theorizes old age as social construction and then suggests that people do not automatically become old at a particular age. One continues to treat "old age" as demeaning and merely seeks to eradicate recognition of it by granting reprieves from inclusion in the group. As well intended as such a theoretical move may be, it

exacts a high price. It maintains the stigma rather than examining or removing it. As Andrews (1999) observed, all life cycle stages are social constructions, but "there is not much serious discussion about eliminating infancy, adolescence, or adulthood from the developmental landscape. It is only old age which comes under the scalpel" (302). Emphasis on the socially constructed status of this age category does nothing to eliminate its real-world consequences.

Old age has material dimensions, the consequences of actors both social and biological: bodies *do* age, even if at variable rates, just as groups categorize and apportion resources accordingly. Emphasizing their subjective nature makes age categories no less real. Bodies matter; and the old are not, in fact, just like the middle-aged but only older. They are different, even though cultures and people within them define the differences in divergent ways. We need to consider the social construction of old age in conjunction with the aging of bodies (which, in a vexing irony, we understand only through social constructions).

Successful Aging

A more refined form of ageism attempts to portray old age in a positive light but retains the use of middle age as an implicit standard of goodness and health, in contrast to which the old remain deviant. One may see this ageism in the popular notion that men should "age successfully." From this "anti-aging" perspective, some of the changes that occur with age might seem acceptable—gray hair and even, on occasion, wrinkles—but other age-related changes do not, such as losses of libido, income, or mobility. Aging successfully requires that the old maintain the activities popular among the middle-aged. Successful aging, in effect, requires well-funded resistance to culturally designated markers of old age, including relaxation. Within this paradigm, those signs of seniority remain thoroughly stigmatized.

To be sure, a research focus on men who have aged "successfully" flows from good intentions. Study of successful agers helps us negate stereotypes of the old as "useless," unhappy, and the like. Nevertheless, a theory of the age relations underlying this movement must recognize their interrelations with class, sexual, and racial inequalities. The relevant standards for health and happy lifestyles have been based on leisure activities accessible only to the more well-to-do and middle-aged: tennis, traveling, sipping wine in front of sunsets, and strolls on the beaches of tony resorts that appear in the advertising campaigns for such lifestyles.

The dictate to age successfully by remaining active is both ageist and ignorant of the lives of the working classes. Spurred by the new anti-aging industry, the promotional images of the "active elder" are bound by gender, race, class, and sexuality. The sort of consumption and lifestyles implicated in ads for posh retirement communities with their depiction of "'imagineered' landscapes of consumptions marked by 'compulsively tidy lawns' and populated by 'tanned golfers'" (McHugh 2000, 110) assumes a sort of "active" lifestyle available only to a select group: men whose race and class make them most likely to be able to afford it, and their spouses.

Regimens of successful aging also encourage consumers to define any old person in terms of "what she or he is no longer: a mature productive adult" (McHugh 2000, 104). One strives to remain active to show that one is not really old. In this sense, successful aging means not aging and not being old because our constructions of old age contain no positive content. Signs of old age continue to operate as stigma, even in this currently popular model with its many academic adherents. The successful aging movement disapproves implicitly of much about the lives of the old, pressuring those whose bodies are changing to work hard to preserve their "youth" so that they will not be seen as old. As a result, the old and their bodies have become subject to a kind of disciplinary *activity*. This emphasis on productive activity means that those who are chronically impaired, or who prefer to be contemplative, become "problem" old people, far too comfortable just being "old" (Katz 2000; Holstein 1999).

This underlying bias concerning successful aging and "agelessness" is analogous to what many white feminists have had to learn about race relations, or indeed many men have had to learn about gender relations. Many whites began with the notion that nonwhites were doing fine as long as they acted like whites (just as women in many workplaces were deemed OK to the extent that they acted like men). That actual diversity would benefit our society was news to many, its recognition hard-won by activists of color who championed an awareness of the structuring effects of race relations. Only when we can acknowledge and validate these constructed differences do we join the fights against racism and sexism. The same is true of age relations and the old. We must see the old as legitimately different from the middle-aged, separated by a systematic inequality—built on some set of biological factors—that affects all of our lives. To theorize this complex and ever-changing construction is to understand age relations.

The experience of ageism itself varies by gender and other social inequalities (just as the experience of manhood varies by age and the like). Others have already pointed to the double standard of aging whereby women are seen to be old sooner than men (Calasanti and Slevin 2001). But the experience of ageism varies among different social hierarchies. Women with the appropriate class background, for instance, can afford to use various technologies to "hide" signs of aging bodies (such as gray hair and wrinkles) that will postpone their experiences of ageism. Some women of color, such as African Americans, accept more readily the superficial bodily signs of aging that might bother middle-class white women. Within their communities, signs of aging may confer a status not affirmed in the wider culture (Slevin and Wingrove 1998). By failing to reflect on our own ageism and its sources, we have left age relations and its intersections with such other inequalities unquestioned and misunderstood. We have given lip service to age relations by placing it on a list of oppressions, but we have only begun to theorize them. And so we have left unexplored one of the most important systems shaping manhood.

Examining age relations and its intersections with other inequalities will allow us to address ageism in its deepest form and address the structural inequities that deny power to subgroups of the old. It involves breaking the ethical hold that successful, active aging has on our views of aging. Just as feminists have argued for women's emancipation from stigmatizing pressure to avoid the paths that they might like to take, so too must the old be free to choose ways to be old that suit them without having to feel like slackards or sick people. Old age should include acceptance of inactivity as well as activity, contemplation as well as exertion, and sexual assertiveness as well as a well-earned break. Old people will have achieved greater equality with the young when they feel free not to try to be young, when they need not be "exceptional," and when they can be frail, or flabby, or have "age spots" without feeling ugly. *Old* will have positive content and not be defined mainly by disease, mortality, or the absence of economic value.

OLD MEN IN POPULAR CULTURE

The study of masculinity benefits from a look at mass-produced images of old men, because they suggest much about the changing definitions of their problems and the solutions offered. Viewed in context of the experiences of diverse old men as well as the structural constraints on various groups, these popular images illustrate the pressures to be masculine and ways in which men respond to accomplish old manhood. On one hand, the goal of consumer images is to convince others to buy products that will help them better their lives. What is instructive about such images is what they reveal about how people—in this case, aging men—should go about improving their lives (i.e., what it is that they should strive for). On the other hand, images of powerful older men—such as CEOs and politicians—periodically appear in the news media, demonstrating what old men should be striving for in the consumer ads: money, power, and the like. We use mass-produced images of old men, then, to explore the

ways that men and masculinities intersect with other systems of inequality—including age relations—to influence various experiences of manhood.

Current Images: New Manhood in Old Age

The recent demographic shift toward an aged population has inspired consumer marketers to address the old with promises of "positive" or successful aging. A massive ad campaign sells anti-aging—the belief that one should deny or defy the signs and even the fact of aging, and treat the looks and recreation of middle-aged as the appropriate standards for beauty, health, and all around success. As Katz (2001–2002) recently put it, "The ideals of positive aging and anti-ageism have come to be used to promote a widespread anti-aging culture, one that translates their radical appeal into commercial capital" (27). These ads present a paradox for old men, whom ads depict as masculine but unable by virtue of infirmity and retirement to achieve the hegemonic ideals rooted in the lives of the young. Thus, old masculinity is always wanting, ever in need of strenuous affirmation. Even when blessed with the privileges of money and whiteness, old men lack two of hegemonic masculinity's fundamentals: hard-charging careers and robust physical strength. The most current ads promise successful aging with interesting implications for these forms of male privilege.

"Playing Hard"

The first image in this "new masculinity" shows men "playing hard," which differs from previous ads in important ways. It emphasizes activities modeled after the experiences of middle-aged, white, middle-class men. Men pursue leisure but not in terms of grandparenting, reading, or other familial and relaxing pastimes. Instead, they propel themselves into hard play as consumers of expensive sports and travel. Having maintained achievement orientations during their paid-work years, they now intensify their involvement in the expanding consumerist realm, trading production or administration for activity-based consumption. They compete not against other men for salaries and promotions but against their own and nature's incursions into their health as they defy old age to hobble them.

Katz (2001–2002) noted that many ads portray the "older person as an independent, healthy, flexi-retired 'citizen'; who bridges middle age and old age without suffering the time-related constraints of either. In this model . . . 'retirement is not old age'" (29). For instance, McHugh observed that the marketing of sunbelt retirement communities includes the admonition to seniors to busy themselves in the consumption of leisure, to "rush about as if their very lives depended upon it" (McHugh 2000, 112). Similarly, Aetna advertisements selling retirement financial planning show pictures of retired men in exotic places, engaging in such activities as surfing or communing with penguins. Captions offer such invitations as

> Who decided that at the age of 65 it was time to hit the brakes, start acting your age, and smile sweetly as the world spins by? . . . [W]hen you turn 65, the concept of retirement will be the only thing that's old and tired. (*Newsweek* January 5, 1998, 9)

This active consumer image reinforces a construction of old age that benefits elite men in two ways. First, it favors the young in that the old men pictured do nothing that would entitle them to pay. Instead, they purchase expensive forms of leisure. Readers can infer that old men neither need money nor deserve it. Retired, their roles center around spending their money (implicitly transferring it to the younger generations who do need and deserve it). Such ads affirm younger men's right to a cushion from competition with senior men for salaried positions, power, and status. Second, this active consumer image favors the monied classes by avoiding any mention of old men's financial struggles or (varied) dependence on the state. Indeed, age relations work to heighten economic inequalities, such that the greatest differences in income and wealth appear among the old (Calasanti and

Slevin 2001). This polarization of income and wealth creates a demographic situation in which only the most privileged men—white, middle-class or better, and physically similar to middle-aged men—can engage in the recreation marketed.

There, we see an additional benefit to the young of such images of men—the emphasis on the physical abilities that the young are more likely to have. Featherstone and Hepworth (1995) noted that the consumer images of "positive aging" found in publications for those of retirement age or planning retirement ultimately have "serious shortcomings" because they do not counter the ageist meanings that adhere to "other" images of the old, that is, "decay and dependency." In other words, we look more kindly on those old persons engaged in "an extended plateau of active middle age typified in the imagery of positive aging as a period of youthfulness and active consumer lifestyles" (46). In this sense, the new, "positive," and consumer-based view of the old is one steeped in middle-aged, middle-class views and resources. The wide variety of retirement and other magazines—and, more recently, a large and expanding number of Web sites—convey the idea that the body can be "serviced and repaired, and . . . cultivate the hope that the period of active life can be extended and controlled" through the use of a wide range of advertised products (44). This image does not recognize or impute value to those more often viewed to be physically dependent, for example. As a result, those men who are able to achieve this masculine version of "successful aging" appear acceptable within this paradigm, but this new form of acceptance does not mitigate the ways in which we view the old. It denies the physical realities of aging and is thus doomed to failure. Not only are the majority of old men left out of this image of new masculinity for old men, but also the depiction is in itself illusory and transitory. Note the gender inequality in these depictions of aging denied through consumption. Most women participate in the lifestyles of the well-to-do as parts of married couples, dependent on men. Old men may lose status relative to younger men but still maintain privilege in relation to old women.

However hollow such promises of expensive recreation might be for most men, the study of men's physical aggression and self-care suggests that illusions drive many indeed and that men will often sacrifice health and even their lives to accomplish this exaggerated sense of physical superiority to women and resistance to the forces of nature. Researchers of health, violence, and manhood have already documented the harms that men do to themselves. Whether disenfranchised men of color in neighborhoods of concentrated poverty (Franklin 1987; Lee 2000; Staples 1995), athletes desperate to perform as champions (Dworkin and Messner 1999; Klein 1995; White, Young, and McTeer 1995), or ordinary men expressing rage through violence (Harris 2000) and refusing to consult physicians when ill (Courtenay 2000), all manner of men undercut themselves and endanger their lives in the pursuit of their ideals. Harris (2000, 782), for instance, referred to the violence as part of the "doing" of manhood, in line with the sociological theory of gender as accomplishment (Fenstermaker and West 2002). Injury in the pursuit of masculinity extends to social networks, which men more often than women neglect to the point of near isolation and desolation (Courtenay 2000). For those not killed outright, the accumulated damage results in debilitating injury and chronic disease leading to depression (White, Young, and McTeer 1995; Charmaz 1995), fatal heart disease (Helgeson 1995), and high rates of suicide born of lonely despair (Stack 2000). The effect of all of this on old manhood is tremendous, with men experiencing higher death rates than women at every age except after age ninety-five (Federal Interagency Forum on Aging-Related Statistics 2000), at which point few men remain alive.

More important to this discussion, however, than the results of such self-abuse on old age are the effects of age relations on this doing of manhood. To be sure, criminal combat and bone-crunching sports decline with age (much earlier in life, actually) such that old men commit few assaults and play little rugby. The increasing fragility of their bodies leads to relatively sedate lifestyles. Nevertheless, the recent anti-aging boom sells the implicit notion that relaxation equals death or at least defeat and that, once he retires, only high-priced recreation keeps a man a man. Age and gender ideals to which any man can be held accountable shift from careerism to consumption, from sport to milder recreation, but maintain notions of performance all the while.

The theoretical gain here lies in recognizing the historical (and very recent) shift to old manhood as a social problem solved through the consumption of market goods. Men throughout history and across the globe appear always to feel defensive about manhood, in danger of losing or being stripped of it (Solomon-Godeau 1995). This theme takes different forms in different periods, however, and in our own appears as the notion that old men lose their hardness if they relax but can buy it back from leisure companies and medical experts.

"Staying Hard"

Given the importance of heterosexuality to hegemonic masculinity, we should consider the ways in which age and gender interact with sexuality, so often equated for men with "the erect phall[us]" (Marsiglio and Greer 1994, 126). Although graceful acceptance by men of their declining sexual desire had previously served as a hallmark of proper aging (Marshall and Katz 2002), current depictions of old men's masculinity focus on virility as expressed in a (hetero) sexuality enabled by medical products. "Staying hard" goes hand-in-hand with playing hard in the construction of age-appropriate gender ideals in this consumer economy.

Examples of the link among continued sexual functioning, manhood, and resistance to aging, in a context of individual responsibility and control, appear throughout the anti-aging industry, which has been growing as a part of our popular culture through the proliferation of Web sites, direct-mail brochures, journal and magazine advertisements, blurbs in academic newsletters, appearances on talk shows and infomercials, self-help paperbacks, and pricey seminars designed to empower the weakening old. For instance, a few passages from *Newsweek* (Cowley 1996) on the movement toward the use of human growth hormone (HGH) and testosterone draw connections among virility, aging, masculinity, individual control, and consumerism.

> Five years ago, on the eve of his 50th birthday, Ron Fortner realized that time was catching up with him. . . . His belly was soft, his energy and libido were lagging and his coronary arteries were ominously clogged up. After his advancing heart disease forced him into a quintuple bypass operation, Fortner decided he wasn't ready to get old. He . . . embarked on a hormone-based regimen designed to restore his youthful vigor. . . . [H]e started injecting himself with human growth hormone. . . . He claims the results were "almost instantaneous." First came a general sense of wellbeing. Then within weeks, his skin grew more supple, his hair more lustrous and his upper body leaner and more chiseled. . . . Awash in all these juices, he says he discovered new reserves of patience and energy, and became a sexual iron man. "My wife would like a word with you," he kids his guru during on-air interviews, "and that word is stop." (Cowley 1996, 68, 70)

Significantly, a yearlong supply of HGH in 1996 ran between $10,000 and $15,000, making it most accessible to elite men.

Another "success story" from the article concerns

> Robert, a 56-year-old consultant who wore a scrotal patch [for testosterone] for two and a half years. . . . Since raising his testosterone level from the bottom to the top of the normal range, Robert has seen his beard thicken, his body odor worsen and his libido explode. "Whether it's mental or physical, you start feeling older when you can't do physical things like you could," he says. "Sexually, I'm more comfortable because I know I'm dependable." His only complaint is that he's always covered with little rings of glue that won't come off without a heavy-duty astringent. (Cowley 1996, 71–72)

Finally, the story concludes by noting that

> as the population of aging males grows, the virility preservation movement is sure to grow with it. "Basically, it's a marketing issue," says epidemiologist John McKinley, director of the New England Research Institute. . . . "The pharmaceutical industry is going to ride this curve all the way to the bank." (Cowley 1996, 75)

Scientific discourse and practice equate, especially for men, sex with "not aging," and propose technology to retain and restore sexual "functionality" (Katz and Marshall 2003). Indeed, as anti-aging guru Dr. Karlis Ullis, author of *Age Right* and *Super T* (for testosterone), proclaims on his Web site, "Good, ethical sex is the best anti-aging medicine we have" (2003). The appearance of such chemical interventions as sildenafil (Viagra) and the widespread advertising campaigns to promote them have also helped to reconstruct old manhood. A recent ad shows an old, white, finely dressed couple dancing a tango, with the man above and the woman leaning back over his leg. The strenuous dance combines with the caption to convey his virility: "Viagra: Let the dance begin" (*Good Housekeeping* April 1999, 79). Here is a man who likes to be on top and has the (newly enhanced) strength to prove it. Still another ad affirms the role of phallic sex in marital bliss. The bold letters next to a black man with visibly graying hair state, "With Viagra, she and I have a lot of catching up to do." And, at the bottom: "Love life again" (*Black Enterprise* March 2000, 24–5).

Such ideals of virility appear in age-defying ads for active leisure—such as one for Martex towels, which features the caption, "Never, ever throw in the towel." Below this line, three old men stand, towels around their waists, in front of three surfboards that stand erect, stuck in the beach sand. Beneath, one reads that the towels are "for body and soul" (*Oprah* April 2001, 118). An Aetna financial planning ad shows an old white man paddling in the surf, his erect board standing upward between his legs. The caption reads, "A Rocking Chair Is a Piece of Furniture.

Not a State of Mind" (*Newsweek* October 27, 1997, 15). In the ideal world of these ads, age is a state of mind, one to be conquered through public displays of a phallic, physical prowess. One accomplishes old manhood, then, by at least appearing to try to live up to some of the ideals pictured in these magazines. The resulting widespread doing of old manhood as consumption of the right products and maintenance of the right activities serves in turn to render natural the ideals toward which men strive.

Masculinity and sexual functioning have long been linked to aging in our popular culture, but the nature of his relationship has shifted as age relations have transformed and come under medical authority. Contemporary drug marketers build on an ancient quest but market it in new ways.

By the 1960s, therapists blamed psychological factors for male impotence and suggested that "to cease having sex would hasten aging itself" (Katz and Marshall 2003, 7). They later redefined male impotence as a physiological event—"erectile dysfunction"—to be addressed through such technologies as penile injections and sildenafil (Viagra)—and declared intercourse vital to successful aging (Marshall and Katz 2002; Potts 2000). More recently, advertisers have catered to a popular notion of "male menopause"—an umbrella label for the consequences of the fears of loss that expectations of high performance, in the context of women's rising status, can engender (Featherstone and Hepworth 1985). Marketers have built their depictions of old manhood on these links among sex, success, and masculinity. Sexual functioning now serves as a vehicle for reconstructions of manhood as "ageless," symbolizing the continued physical vigor and attractiveness derived from the experiences of younger men. To the extent that men can demonstrate their virility, they can still be men and stave off old age and the loss of status that accrues to that label.

To be sure, this shift in advertising imagery toward the phallic can work to the benefit of old men, convincing people to take them seriously as men full of potency as well as consumer power. To stop our analysis there, however, leaves unquestioned the ageism on which these assertions rest, the fact that we root these ideals of activity and virility in the experiences of the younger men. The ads avoid sexuality based on attributes other than hard penises and experiences other than heterosexual intercourse, and these are hegemonic sexual symbols of the young. The little research available suggests that orgasm and intercourse recede in importance for some old men, who turn to oral sex and other expressions of love (Wiley and Bortz 1996). But these phallic ads value men only to the extent that they act like younger, heterosexual (and wealthy) men. Their emphases on both playing and staying hard reveal some of the ways in which gender and other inequalities shape old age. Old men are disadvantaged in relation to younger men, no matter how elite they may be.

The renewed emphasis on sexual intercourse among old men also reinforces the gender inequalities embedded in phallic depictions of bodies and sexuality. Historically, women's bodies and sexualities have been of only peripheral interest in part because they did not fit the "scientific" models based on men's physiologies. For example, rejuvenators were uncomfortable touting sex gland surgery for women (one variation promoted grafting the ovaries of chimpanzees to those of female patients) partly because they knew that they could not restore fertility in women. Thus, when they did speak of women, they tended to focus instead on the "mental" fertility that might result. Part of the problem was that women's "losses" in terms of sexuality (i.e., menopause) occurred much earlier in life. Those women were often "young," which confounded the equation of "loss of sexuality" with "old" (Hirshbein 2000).

People continue to define old women's sexuality in relation to old men's, assessing it in terms of penile-vaginal penetration. An old woman, in such popular imagery, remains passive and dependent on her man's continued erection for any pleasure of her own. Research on old women's accounts of their experiences, however, makes clear that these models represent little of what they want from their sex lives.

These popular definitions also ignore that many old women have no partners at all. Even if old women "accept" and try to live up to the burden of being sexual and "not old" in male-defined terms, there are not enough old men for them to be partnered (and our age-based norms do not allow them to date younger men).

Finally, the ageism implicit in the demand to emulate the young is self-defeating and ignores the reality that even with technology and unlimited resources, bodies still change. Ultimately, individuals cannot control this; it is a "battle" one cannot win.

THEORIZING AGE, CLASS, AND GENDER RELATIONS

The rewards for the inclusion of a marginalized group into research extend beyond the satisfaction of listening to oft-ignored voices. The study of old manhood stands to enrich our theories of masculinity as social problem, as disciplinary consumer object, as the accomplishment of heterosexuality, and as the "crisis"-torn struggle to achieve or resist the hegemonic ideals spread through our popular culture.

Studying age relations can render insights into ways that we theorize gender. For instance, Judith Kegan Gardiner (2002) suggested that we clarify gender relations by making an analogy to age relations. This would help reconstruct thinking about gender in our popular culture, she argued, because many people already recognize *continuity* in age categories while they still see gender as dichotomous. People already see themselves as *performing* age-appropriate behavior ("acting their ages") while continuing to take for granted the doing of gender (Fenstermaker and West 2002). And popular culture more fully recognizes enduring group *conflicts* (over divisions of resources) between generations than between sexes. Gardiner (2002) suggested that a fuller theorizing of age relations has much to offer the study of men, that scholars may move beyond their polarization of biological and social construction, and that our popular culture

may more fully appreciate the power struggles that govern gender relations.

We recommend just this view—of age and gender, race and class, and other dimensions of inequality—as accomplished by social as well as biological actors; as accountable to ever-changing ideals of age- and sex-appropriate behavior; as constructed in the context of a popular culture shaped by consumer marketing and technological change; and as imposing disciplinary regimens in the names of good health, empowerment, beauty, and success.

Taken together, the mass media reviewed above posit ideals of old manhood to which most if not all men find themselves held accountable. To the men fortunate enough to have been wealthy or well paid for their careerism, corporations (often with the support of those gerontologists who implicitly treat old age as a social problem) sell regimens through which those old men may live full lives, working, playing, and staying hard. If careerism kept the attention of these men from their families and leisure lives, constricting their social networks and degrading their physical health, then this high-priced old age serves as a promised payoff. Once retired, those few wealthy enough to do it can enjoy a reward: high-energy time with a spouse and some friends, enjoyment of tourism, surfing, and sex. Men sacrificed much, even their lives, in their pursuits of hegemonic masculine status. Those who survive face a rougher time with old age as a result: few sources of social support and bodies weakened by self-abuse. Thus, the accomplishment of manhood comes to require some response to the invitation to strain toward middle-age activities. Some men reach with all of their strength for the lifestyle ideals broadcast so loudly, whereas many give up for lack of means to compete, and still others deliberately resist. In a cruel irony, the ideals move all the further out of reach of the men who pursued them with such costly vigor in younger years and damaged their health beyond repair. The final push for hegemonic masculinity involves spending money and enjoying health that many old men do not have to pursue the recreation and phallic sex that the ads tell them they need.

Certainly, the study of old men offers striking views of a popular struggle over heterosexuality (although the study of old gay men will surely be as transforming, the near total lack of research on them prevents us from speculating how). Widely held views of old men's sexuality suggest dominance over women as a form of virility. But, as bodies change, outright predation recedes as an issue and impotency moves to the center of concern. A popular (consumer) culture that figures old manhood in terms of *loss* hardly departs from any trend in images of masculinity. Men have always felt that they were losing their manhood, their pride, and their virility, whether because their penises actually softened or because women gained status and so frightened them. But the study of this transition—from the feelings of invincibility that drive the destructiveness of youth to the growing expectation of vulnerability—throws old masculinity into a valuable relief. For instance, theories that center on violence and predation capture little of the realities of old men's lives, just as scholarly emphasis on coercion and harassment of women excludes most of the experiences of old women. For old women, the more important sexual theme may be that of being *cast aside* (Calasanti and Slevin 2001, 195). For old men, *impotence* in its most general sense, leading to many responses ranging from suicidal depression to more graceful acceptance, may be a more productive theme. It serves as both positive and negative ideal in a classic double-bind: old men should, so as not to intrude on the rights of younger men, retreat from the paid labor market; but they should also, so as to age successfully, never stop consuming opportunities to be active. They should, so as not to be "dirty," stop becoming erect; but they should also, so as to age successfully, never lose that erection. Old men fear impotence to the point that many suffer it who otherwise would not. Anxieties drain them at just the moment when expectations of aggressive consumption, of proving themselves younger than they are, reach their heights.

The notion that men accomplish age just as they do gender has much to offer, with its sensitivity to relations of inequality, its moment-to-moment accountability to unreachable but hegemonic ideals, and the perpetually changing nature of such accomplishments. Never have erections been so easily discussed in public, and never has this "dirty"/"impotent" double bind been tighter, than since the rise of this consumer regimen. Nor have old men, before now, lived under such pressure to remain active further into their lengthening life spans. The ideals of manhood that tempted so many to cripple themselves in younger years now loom large enough to shame those who cannot play tennis or waltz the ballrooms of fancy resorts. The study of manhood should take careful notice of the ways in which men do old manhood under such tight constraints. The popular images that we have reviewed provide ideals of old manhood, but they do not necessarily describe the lives of very many old men. Given how little we know of the ways in which old men respond to such ideals, the research task before us seems clear.

CONCLUSION

Scholars tend to ignore age relations in part because of our own ageism. Most are not yet old, and even if we are, we often deny it (Minichiello, Browne, and Kendig 2000). Most people know little about the old because we seldom talk to them. Family and occupational segregation by age leave the old outside the purview of the work that most young people do.

Resulting in part from such segregation, the study of men, although no more than any other social science and humanist scholarship, has focused on the work, problems, sexuality, and consumption patterns of the young. This neglect of the old results in theories of masculinity that underplay the lengths to which men go to play and stay hard, the long-term effects of their strenuous accomplishment of manhood, and the variety of ways in which men remain masculine once their appetites for self-destruction begin to wane. Research on the old can reveal much about the desperate struggle for hegemonic masculinity and the varied ways in which men begin to redefine manhood. At the same time, it also uncovers the young and middle-aged biases that inhere in typical notions of masculinity that tend to center on accomplishments and power in the productive sphere, for instance. Few researchers have considered the reality of masculinities not directly tied to the fact of or potential for paid labor.

To leave age relations unexplored reinforces the inequality that subordinates the old, an inequality that we unwittingly reproduce for ourselves. Unlike other forms of oppression, in which the privileged rarely become the oppressed, we will all face ageism if we live long enough. As feminists, scientists, and people growing old, we can better develop our sense of interlocking inequalities and the ways in which they shape us, young and old. Our theories and concepts have too often assumed rather than theorized these age relations. The study of men and masculinity and the scholarship on age relations are just beginning to inform each other.

References

Andrews, M. 1999. The seductiveness of agelessness. *Ageing and Society 19*(3): 301–18.

Calasanti, T. M. 1993. Bringing in diversity: Toward an inclusive theory of retirement. *Journal of Aging Studies 7*(2): 133–50.

Calasanti, T. M., and K. F. Slevin. 2001. *Gender, social inequalities, and aging.* Walnut Creek, CA: Alta Mira.

Charmaz, K. 1995. Identity dilemmas of chronically ill men. In *Men's health and illness: Gender, power, and the body,* edited by D. Sabo and D. F. Gordon, 266–91. Thousand Oaks, CA: Sage.

Courtenay, W. H. 2000. Behavioral factors associated with disease, injury, and death among men: Evidence and implications for prevention. *Journal of Men's Studies 9*(1): 81–142.

Cowley, Geoffrey. 1996. Attention: Aging Men. *Newsweek,* September 16, 68–75.

Cruikshank, M. 2003. *Learning to be old: Gender, culture, and aging.* Lanham, MD: Rowman & Littlefield.

Davidson, K. 2001. Later life widowhood, selfishness, and new partnership choices: A gendered perspective. *Ageing and Society* 21:297–317.

Dworkin, S. L., and M. A. Messner. 1999. Just do . . . what? Sport, bodies, gender. In *Revisioning gender,* edited by M. M. Ferree, J. Lorber, and B. B. Hess, 341–61. Thousand Oaks. CA: Sage.

Featherstone, M., and M. Hepworth. 1985. The male menopause: Lifestyle and sexuality. *Maturitas* 7:235–46.

———. 1995. Images of positive aging: A case study of Retirement Choice magazine. In *Images of aging: Cultural representations of later life,* edited by M. Featherstone and A. Wernick, 29–47. London: Routledge.

Federal Interagency Forum on Aging-Related Statistics. 2000. *Older Americans 2000: Key indicators of well-being.* http://www.agingstats.gov.

Fenstermaker, S., and C. West, eds. 2002. *Doing gender, doing difference: Inequality, power, and institutional change.* New York: Routledge.

Franklin, C. 1987. Surviving the institutional decimation of black males: Causes, consequences, and intervention. In *The making of masculinities: The new men's studies,* edited by H. Brod, 155–69. Winchester, MA: Allen and Unwin.

Gardiner, J. K. 2002. Theorizing age and gender: Bly's boys, feminism, and maturity masculinity. In *Masculinity studies & feminist theory: New directions,* edited by J. K. Gardiner, 90–118. New York: University of Columbia Press.

Harris, A. P. 2000. Gender, violence, and criminal justice. *Stanford Law Review* 52:777–807.

Helgeson, V. S. 1995. Masculinity, men's roles, and coronary heart disease. In *Men's health and illness: Gender, power and the body,* edited by D. Sabo and D. F. Gordon, 68–104. Thousand Oaks, CA: Sage.

Hirshbein, L. D. 2000. The glandular solution: Sex, masculinity and aging in the 1920s. *Journal of the History of Sexuality 9*(3): 27–304.

Holstein, Martha. 1999. Women and productive aging: Troubling implications. In *Critical gerontology: Perspectives from political and moral economy,* edited by Meredith Minkler and Carroll L. Estes, 359–73. Amityville, NY: Baywood.

Hooyman, N. R. 1999. Research on older women: Where is feminism? *The Gerontologist* 39:115–18.

Katz, S. 2000. Busy bodies: Activity, aging, and the management of everyday life. *Journal of Aging Studies 14*(2): 135–52.

———. 2001–2002. Growing older without aging? Positive aging, anti-ageism, and anti-aging. *Generations 25*(4): 27–32.

Katz, S., and B. Marshall. 2003. New sex for old: Lifestyle, consumerism, and the ethics of aging well. *Journal of Aging Studies 17*(1): 3–16.

Klein, A. M. 1995. Life's too short to die small: Steroid use among male bodybuilders. In *Men's health and illness: Gender power and the body,* edited by D. Sabo and D. F. Gordon, 105–21. Thousand Oaks, CA: Sage.

Lee, M. R. 2000. Concentrated poverty, race, and homicide. *Sociological Quarterly 41*(2): 189–206.

Marshall, B., and S. Katz. 2002. Forever functional: Sexual fitness and the ageing male body. *Body & Society 8*(4): 43–70.

Marsiglio, William, and Richard A. Greer. 1994. A gender analysis of older men's sexuality. In *Older men's lives,* edited by Edward H. Thompson, Jr., 122–40. Thousand Oaks, CA: Sage.

McHugh, K. 2000. The "ageless self"? Emplacement of identities in sun belt retirement communities. *Journal of Aging Studies 14*(1): 103–15.

Minichiello, V., J. Browne, and H. Kendig. 2000. Perceptions and consequences of ageism: Views of older people. *Ageing and Society 20*(3): 253–78.

Potts, A. 2000. The essence of the "hard on": Hegemonic masculinity and the cultural construction of "erectile dysfunction." *Men and Masculinities 3*(1): 85–103.

Slevin, K. F., and C. R. Wingrove. 1998. *From stumbling blocks to stepping stones: The life experiences of fifty professional African American women.* New York: New York University Press.

Solomon-Godeau, A. 1995. Male trouble. In *Constructing masculinities,* edited by M. Berger, B. Wallis, and S. Watson, 69–76. New York: Routledge.

Stack, S. 2000. Suicide: A 15-year review of the sociological literature. *Suicide & Life-Threatening Behavior 30*(2): 145–76.

Staples, R. 1995. Health among Afro-American males. In *Men's health and illness: Gender, power, and the body,* edited by D. Sabo and D.F. Gordon, 121–38. Thousand Oaks, CA: Sage.

Ullis, Karlis. 2003. *Agingprevent.com.* http://www.agingprevent.com/flash/index.html.

White, P. G., K. Young, and W. G. McTeer. 1995. Sport, masculinity, and the injured body. In *Men's health and illness: Gender, power, and the body,* edited by D. Sabo and D. F. Gordon, 158–82. Thousand Oaks, CA: Sage.

Wiley, D., and W. M. Bortz. 1996. Sexuality and aging—usual and successful. *Journal of Gerontology 51A*(3): M142–M146.

Woodward, K., ed. 1999. *Figuring age: Women, bodies, generations.* Bloomington: Indiana University Press.

Introduction to Reading 24

Anthropologist Jie Yang analyzes the role of the female body, beauty, and youth in the emergence of consumer capitalism in China. Yang emphasizes that bodies, beauty, and youth are widely employed in selling products and training women to become consumers. This reading discusses the significant shift in China from the gender egalitarian ideology of the Mao era to the contemporary, post-Mao ideology that emphasizes gender difference and has paved the way for exploitation of women's labor. Yang's focus on beauty salons as sites of gender oppression and her detailed examination of the discourse of *nennu* and *shunu* are particularly helpful in understanding the centrality of gender in the vast economic restructuring of China.

1. What are *nennu* and *shunu*? Describe parallel concepts in the "beauty economy" of the United States.

2. Discuss the major differences between the gender ideologies and practices of the Mao and post-Mao eras in China.

3. How are women exploited in the "beauty economy" of China, and how does this exploitation go beyond women's physical labor? Is women's labor sold and exploited in similar ways in the United States?

NENNU AND SHUNU

GENDER, BODY POLITICS, AND THE BEAUTY ECONOMY IN CHINA

Jie Yang

At the beauty salon in Beijing where I interviewed people during the summers of 2007 and 2008, a woman who had already undergone plastic surgery to smooth out most of the wrinkles on her face was trying acupuncture to suppress her appetite and lose weight.[1] This woman, now in her midfifties, told me that when they were young, she and other women of her generation were called upon to focus only on work and socialist construction (*shehui zhuyi jianshe*) without paying much attention to their appearance or personal life.[2] But now she wanted to make up for her lost youth by taking advantage of new cosmetics and technologies to make herself look young and beautiful. Looking younger and more attractive was also a form of revenge for her, because her husband had had a series of affairs with younger women. Much to her disappointment, not only did her husband not appreciate her efforts, but he also ridiculed her as an "old, yellow cucumber wearing green paints, pretending to be young" (*lao huanggua shua luqi, zhuang nen*). But this did not stop her. Rather, she tried harder to find all possible ways to look younger and be more competitive. A former party secretary of a factory in Beijing, she dramatically shifted her outlook regarding her body and her way of managing her body in the post-Mao era. Although she expressed her frustration about a culture that values appearance and youth more than personality and encourages men to forsake their wives for young mistresses, she said she would try harder to keep her husband.

This woman is one of the millions of Chinese women who visit beauty salons nearly every week, and her commitment to beautification and self-transformation is part of a popular discourse in recent years on *nennu* and *shunu*, two gendered representations of consumer subjects based on their cosmetics, fashion, and consumption patterns. *Nennu* literally means "tender" younger women and feminine youth, and *shunu* refers to "ripe" older women and feminine maturity. The two terms appear in advertisements, fashion magazines, television shopping channels, beauty and health care services, and everyday discourse. This discourse constitutes and legitimates China's so-called beauty economy (*meinu jingji*), referring to everything from beauty pageants and modeling competitions to advertisements, cosmetics, plastic surgery, beauty and health care services, and television and cinema, which link women's beauty with the economy (Xu and Feiner 2007). The beauty economy was ranked fifth in China's consumer goods industry, following the real estate, automobile, tourism, and telecommunications industries (*China Daily* 2004a).

Offering various ways for ripe women to transform themselves into tender women as its main plotline, the discourse of *nennu* and *shunu* serves to increase people's awareness of beauty and health and ensures the continued growth of China's beauty economy.[3] Also, the terms *nen* and *shu* in Chinese refer to the degree of edibility of food or fruits, pointing to an eating or tasting male subject and appealing to eroticism and sexuality to enhance people's desire for consumption. Highlighting the fact that the female body sells products, beauty sells products, and eroticism and sexuality sell products (Brownell

From Jie Yang. 2011. "*Nennu and Shunu*: Gender, Body Politics, and the Beauty Economy in China." *Signs 36*(2).

2001; Schein 2001), the discourse reinforces the essential role of the female body, feminine beauty, and feminine youth in developing consumer capitalism in China. The two gendered representations constitute not only a key site for constructing ideal consumer subjects (Croll 2006a, 2006b) but also a biopolitical strategy to govern people's bodies and lives and develop consumerism. These two gendered representations resemble the two female images that dominated Chinese television advertising in 1992–93 and were identified by Beth Notar as the "sexy young thing" and the "Good Wife, Wise Mother," which constituted advertising strategies to bring together two gender ideologies representing "Western modernity" and "Confucian tradition," respectively (1994, 29–30). While the maternal images trained women to pursue a commodity-assisted form of domesticity, the sexy images constructed women as consuming and desiring individuals and were deployed as vehicles for sale (Schein 2001). Since young women in their twenties could fulfill both gender roles, they were considered most appealing to consumers (Notar 1994, 31). Therefore, tender women (*nennu*) symbolize ideal consumer subjects.

This discourse of *nennu* and *shunu* also signifies the shift of gender ideology from the Maoist position, which erased gender differences between men and women to maximize the use of female labor, to the post-Mao position, which naturalizes and even essentializes biological differences between men and women in order to meet the demands of labor reduction for a market economy (Young 1989; Rofel 1999; Yang 1999).[4] With the rampant development of consumerism, the post-Mao official gender ideology celebrates femininity as increasingly associated with beauty, youth, and sexuality. While in Mao's era beauty and fashion were frowned upon as frivolous and decadent, China now has the world's eighth-largest and Asia's second-largest cosmetics market (Godfrey 2004). Indeed, scholars have identified such ideological shifts in cosmetic surgery and body politics.[5] They have also noted the rise of sexualized and commodified female bodies in the post-Mao era.[6]

The two gender representations of *nennu* and *shunu* seem to see the body and its functions as symbols or products of discourses rather than as pragmatic individual or social activities of production and appropriation. Instead of fulfilling productive and reproductive imperatives, the post-Mao (female) body and its erotic-aesthetic functions are celebrated to enhance consumption. Reducing material, bodily activities to merely erotic-aesthetic functions suppresses the collective, plural, and social aspects of embodiment in favor of its private, individualistic features (T. Turner 1994, 44). It is a consumerist body, an ideological representation of consumer capitalism. As Mike Featherstone suggests, with the development of consumerism, images of youth and beauty become loosely associated with the desire for mass consumption of goods (1982, 27–28). The body is both a vehicle of pleasure and a new expression of self. It becomes a possession used for social and professional advancement: appearance, display, and impression management are the capital goods of the consumer economy. Bodily qualities such as youth, beauty, fitness, and slimness have acquired new importance as tokens of class and status distinctions (Bourdieu 1984). The discourse of *nennu* and *shunu* thus provides a compelling site to examine "how intimately the body is involved in the goals of production as (economic) support, as principle of the managed (psychological) integration of the individual and as (political) strategy of social control" (Baudrillard 1998, 136) and how the female body, female beauty, and sexuality are mobilized to develop China's beauty economy. This essay demonstrates the centrality of the body in explaining women's oppression and in explaining the gendered social in post-Mao China. However, the emphasis on such corporeality as feminine beauty, youth, and sexuality in this discourse of *nennu* and *shunu* exhausts women's overall utility, defines women through their beauty and sexuality, and even downplays the contributions of rural migrant women and laid-off female workers who are the main beauty and health care providers and cosmetics manufacturing laborers (see the section "Gender exploitation in the beauty economy" below).

This discourse of *nennu* and *shunu* is promoted by a complex combination of forces, both national and transnational. In the post-Mao era, the state appears to retreat from direct involvement in many domains of activity that relate to the market economy, but a state mode of production and investment continues to operate alongside foreign companies, private enterprises, and transnational joint ventures (Yang 1999, 10).[7] Therefore, people's (especially women's) actual perspectives and involvement in the beauty economy are multifaceted, often consisting of competing or contradictory discourses and practices. . . . This essay thus offers a nuanced depiction of (women's) voices and experiences of the beauty economy to counteract the reductive discourse of *nennu* and *shunu*, which, by highlighting the erotic or aesthetic function of the female body in the beauty economy, downplays women's diverse, concrete contributions to the beauty industry. It focuses on the social, economic, and political implications of the ideological emphasis on the transformation from ripe women to tender women as a driving force for the beauty industry in China.

The research began with my interest in beauty salons as gendered reemployment programs promoted by China's Women's Federation for laid-off female workers. I then expanded it to research on the broader beauty economy.

LABOR, THE BODY, AND BIOPOLITICS

The discourse of *nennu* and *shunu* not only signifies the transition of the source of (gender) identity formation from the labor process to the post-Mao market but also seems to indicate that gender is less grounded in labor than in the body in post-Mao China: women are in decline in the public sphere of labor and are being sexualized by a masculine business and entertainment culture (Yang 1999, 11). . . .

. . . The focus on the body is part of China's shift in governing from Mao's emphasis on the

public and politics to the post-Mao emphasis on the individual and the body as a way to prove to the capitalist world that China has overcome the ideological excesses of Maoist socialism in order to stake out a position in the global market (Wang 1998). Indeed, in the post-1989 context, the rise of consumerist culture is not merely an economic event but also a political event, because the penetration of such culture into people's daily lives is carrying out the task of reproducing hegemonic ideology (Wang 1998, 29). . . .

The discourse of *nennu* and *shunu* seems to derive from China's domestic imperative to transform its political economy from Mao's planned economy to a market economy. This discourse began with the familiar topic of women's liberation. But the post-Mao liberation of women is opposite of Mao's program of women's liberation. For Mao, women's liberation meant women's participation in the public sphere of labor. This appeared to resonate with certain types of Western feminism, but Mao maximized the use of women's labor for nation building. Since the early 1980s, the liberation of women's bodies has been perceived as a form of therapy to redress women's exhaustion as a result of their participation in the labor process in Mao's planned economy. Liberating women's bodies from labor leaves the body available to be freely adorned and exploited and then to be used as a commodity to sell (to be sold or to sell other products); the body needs to be viewed narcissistically rather than merely functionally for its owner to adorn it with objects and to consume goods, services, and technologies (Baudrillard 1998). When viewed through the discourse of *nennu* and *shunu*, the gendered layoffs at state-owned enterprises since the mid-1990s and the development of consumerism become legitimate; women's bodies, and therefore women, are being liberated.

BEAUTY AND AESTHETIC GOVERNANCE

The images constructed through the discourse of *nennu* and *shunu* are ideal body images. Emphasizing the significance of constructed beauty in consumerism promotes both ideal aesthetic judgment and the consumption of beauty products and services. Medical technology has made possible the construction of the body as a personal project through cosmetic surgery, organ transplant, and transsexual surgery. Women's bodies then become testing grounds for both innovative technologies and new consumption patterns. For example, idolizing feminine beauty through the two gendered representations of *nennu* and *shunu* has contributed to a surging demand for cosmetic surgery in China.

In December 2004, China hosted its first Miss Plastic Surgery Pageant in Beijing, sponsored by both cosmetic surgery hospitals and private beauty clinics. Nineteen finalists aged 17–62 vied to become the country's best "artificial beauty" (*renzao meinu*). One qualification for participation was to present certificates from medical professionals to prove that the participant was cosmetically altered. Reflecting the pillars of consumerism—personal liberty and freedom of choice—the Miss Plastic Surgery Pageant celebrates the freedom, right, and "natural" desire to pursue beauty through any possible means. The oldest contestant, sixty-two-year-old Liu Yulan, said that she cherished the chance to show off her wrinkle-free face and wanted to send a message to society that the love of beauty is not limited by age. The second-oldest, Long Yan, forty-seven, said the surgery that smoothed out her facial wrinkles and removed excess fat all over her body had improved her life greatly.[8] Feeling much younger and more confident, Long said, "Becoming beautiful is everyone's right. It's a very natural desire" (*China Daily* 2004b).

Celebrating the freedom to consume and to invest in one's body aesthetically is key to the discourse of *nennu* and *shunu*. An organizer of this beauty contest said that the purpose of the contest was to allow society to understand and accept those women who choose to transform their looks with cosmetic surgery; everybody should have the right to pursue beauty, for pretty women have more opportunities and are more successful than others (*China Daily* 2004b).

Brownell also notes that unlike Mao's era, when cosmetic surgery was attacked and denounced as bourgeois, the post-Mao era celebrates it as an expression of freedom, individuality, and human nature (2005, 142). Indeed, such emphasis on freedom and individuality both develops consumerism and acts as a neoliberal technology to promote the kind of individualism and lifestyles typical of a market economy. As a woman who helped market beauty salon products on a Beijing street in July 2007 (and who persuaded me to buy her cosmetic products) said, "Good looks boost your ego and your mood, and enhance your market competitiveness and your success in life."[9]

. . . In what follows, I will discuss the role of state feminism in the expansion of the beauty industry and show how beauty and beauty salons constitute key sites for both economic growth and new subject formation.

STATE FEMINISM AND THE BEAUTY ECONOMY

According to a survey article on China's beauty industry (*China Daily* 2004a), this industry consisted of approximately 1.54 million beauty and spa salons, 3,750 cosmetics enterprises, and 673 related professional training institutes. It registered double-digit growth, with an annual production value of 168 billion yuan (US$20.5 billion) in 2003, which was largely attributed to women seeking to upgrade their appearances. Take the cosmetics sector as an example. The sales volume of China's cosmetics industry was 200 million yuan ($24.1 million) in 1982 and surged to 52 billion yuan ($6.27 billion) in 2003. This sector stimulates social demand, attracts private investment, and eases job pressure: it created 7.3 million jobs, and other relevant sectors (i.e., hairdressing, beauty product manufacturing, training, and advertising) offered 14 million jobs in 2004.

The sector of the beauty economy that essentializes gender most is beauty pageants and modeling competitions (Cohen, Wilk, and Stoeltje 1996). In 2003, China endorsed Miss China and broadcast the Miss Universe Pageant. In 2004, six major international beauty competitions and numerous regional beauty pageants took place in China. Lu Junqing, in his Chinese bestseller ***Meili liandan zhang dami*** [Beautiful faces grow rice], estimates that every dollar spent on beauty pageants generates four additional dollars of income (2004, 28). Lu's book celebrates women's beauty as a way of gaining access to all that is important, and it is, as claimed by its author, a groundbreaking book for China's beauty economy. Since beauty has increasingly become the defining feature of femininity, gender is thus used to multiply economic growth. Indeed, the beauty economy links gender, culture, and economy in ways that change both individual consciousness and shared ideologies to make them amenable to the goals of the neoliberal economy (Xu and Feiner 2007, 308).

For example, the 2003 Miss Universe Pageant not only delivered $3.6 billion to the local economy (Lu 2004, 42) but also made Sanya a city of world-class beauty and a paradise for tourists: its 2004 total tourism earnings were predicted to grow by 26 percent to 3.7 billion yuan ($446 million; *China Daily* 2005). Beauty contests reflect people's eagerness for instant success and quick profits by taking advantage of physical beauty or gender identity. For example, there is a popular belief among female university students that good looks outweigh good academic performance as a means of securing a bright future. . . .

The development of the beauty economy capitalizes on the erotic-aesthetic functions of the female body and also relies on women's labor and the use value of their bodies. Indeed, the rapid expansion of the beauty economy is driven not only by China's aspiration for economic growth and global preeminence but also by its paramount concern for social stability in the wake of the massive layoffs. Since the mid-1990s, layoffs from former state-owned enterprises have posed potential threats for post-Mao governance, and such layoffs are gendered: statistical evidence shows women as apparent targets.[10] Under these circumstances, in April 1995

a national reemployment project was established. Beauty salons, characterized by labor-intensive, flexible operations and massive market potential, are lauded by the ACWF (All-China Women's Federation) as an efficient way to reemploy laid-off women.[11] During the peak of gendered layoffs, between 1998 and 2003, women's organizations at different levels even used beauty salons as business incubators to train laid-off women and support them in establishing their own beauty and hair salons (Yang 2007).

A famous example is Li Yanwen, a former laid-off woman worker who succeeded in transforming her hair salon into a business incubator for other laid-off women to acquire hairdressing skills (Zhao 2003, 14). Her wholehearted embrace of the beauty economy was broadcast on China's Central Television program *Famous Entrepreneurs* (*Shang jie ming jia*) in 2002, and thus she became a role model for other women. In effect, as an entrepreneur and a capitalist, Li recruited laid-off women in the exploitive capacity of apprentices: in exchange for their free labor, she gave them free training. It is common for salons to employ one or two technicians with beauty and hairdressing experience and then hire a number of people as apprentices, who are then trained by the technicians. Such apprenticeships constitute a technically legal and efficient way of making profit, as apprenticeships involve long work hours and little or no payment. The next section provides more details about the form and degree of exploitation at beauty salons.

GENDER EXPLOITATION IN THE BEAUTY ECONOMY

In China, the role of feminine beauty and feminine youth in developing consumerism is emphasized, and the value of women's actual physical, aesthetic, and emotional labor at beauty salons or wellness centers is downplayed. Private ownership predominates, and there is a lack of efficient government supervision with the result that exploitation in the beauty industry has been prevalent, including, for example, low wages, health risks, no job security, irregular work schedules, sexual harassment, and unpaid aesthetic and emotional labor. Beauty salons are a doubly gendered space, employing mostly women and frequented mainly by women. As is common in female-dominated occupations, women are paid far less than in male-dominated industries. For example, women working at a beauty salon in suburban Beijing were reportedly paid 600–1,000 yuan a month (approximately $100–$160) while the 2004 average salary in Beijing was about 1,900 yuan (approximately $300). Women working at salons have no job security. To keep their jobs, women will often work obediently even while facing physical, emotional, or sexual abuse from their bosses or clients.[12] Some women are reluctant to resist clients' unwanted sexual advances for fear of losing their jobs, since there is a huge pool of laid-off female workers and rural migrant women. A woman in her early twenties told me about the physical abuses at a beauty salon in Beijing: "Clients are our God. We have to be available at any time when there is a client. Meals are delayed. Breaks are cancelled. Without efficient supervision from the government, it's okay to work you like slaves. . . . In order to start my own salon earlier, I have to put up with this and learn things."

The same woman told me that she had developed stomach problems as a result of such irregular meal times. But she was willing to endure such suffering because she saw her current work as an empowering process to prepare her for future entrepreneurial projects. Another woman told me that she had developed bladder and bowel infections as a result of not being allowed to leave a client waiting when appointments were booked one after another; there was no time for meal or toilet breaks. Indeed, with the evident withdrawal of the state from the direct involvement in the market and the private sector, extreme forms of labor exploitation have emerged in recent years.

But this exploitation goes further than that of women's physical labor; their aesthetic and emotional labor is also exploited. Anne Witz, Chris Warhurst, and Dennis Nickson define aesthetic labor as the mobilization, development, and commodification of embodied dispositions (2003, 37). Aesthetic labor has become fundamental to the contemporary service industries. Workers enter the labor market with capacities and skills that are seen as part of the raw material that is molded and commodified by industries in pursuit of profit and the promotion of the company image. The molding of the physicality of workers is required as the material signifier of the aesthetics and ethos of an organization like a beauty salon. It is often managed through gendered techniques of corporeal management, demanding skills and labor that are often naturalized as inherent to women and therefore not remunerated (Black 2004). For example, one laid-off female worker who was reemployed at a beauty salon said that, for her, the biggest challenge of her work at the salon was that she was required to always wear a heavy layer of delicately applied makeup to match the ethos of her new workplace. She did not want to cover her face with layers of cosmetics, which she believed could be potentially toxic and could cause her harm in the long run. Also, the time and effort for applying the makeup are not rewarded, and the skills required are considered intuitively feminine rather than learned skills and therefore are not rewarded either. Indeed, beauty salons require their workers to use and advocate for their salons and their beauty products. In contrast to many of their previous employment situations, such as alongside men in factories, in the gender-based beauty industry women are often expected to become living advertisements for the beauty salons and for their products and services. These women's bodies or physicalities become not only the software of the salon but also part of its hardware. They are the living embodiment of the ethos and aesthetics of the workplace (Witz, Warhurst, and Nickson 2003).

Beauty salons are regarded not only as sites of beauty or physical therapy but also as sites of emotional therapy. In order to build up their own clientele, care workers have to learn how to manage their own emotions and their clients' emotions in order to construct intimate, meaningful relationships with their clients. A nineteen-year-old woman told me that she found it most challenging to be always nice and patient with clients: "You are not only working on their faces and bodies, but also become a container for their anger and frustration [*chu qi tong*]. I often feel drained and impatient, but I have to control myself and make them feel comfortable, feel good, so they'll come again. When I leave and have my own salon, they may follow me."

Such emotional management is similar to what Arlie Hochschild describes as the emotional labor of flight attendants: to "induce or suppress feeling in order to sustain the outward countenance that produces the proper state of mind" (1983, 7). To balance between staged and authentic feelings is inherently alienating and causes estrangement of parts of the private self. It is also emotional labor that is unacknowledged and unpaid. This young woman justified her own exploitation by co-opting such unpaid emotional labor as a step to building up clientele for her own future salon.

Indeed, many beauty therapists know how to strategically use the salon and their bodies as resources to establish themselves and launch their careers. At a salon in Jinan where I did my fieldwork in summer 2007, one of my informants was a woman in her early twenties who came to befriend a steady male client, eventually becoming his lover. She managed to turn the exploitation of her body into what she considered the success of the opening of a small boutique in the city. Zhang Zhen (2000) uses the notion of the "rice bowl of youth" to depict women who have the ability to transform their youth and beauty into potentially lucrative employment opportunities and to maximize the use of their body capital to achieve various goals in life.[13]

CONCLUSION

In his best-selling book *The New Wellness Revolution: How to Make a Fortune in the Next Trillion Dollar Industry* (2007), Paul Zane Pilzer suggests that health food, beauty products, and fitness centers will soon constitute a trillion-dollar wellness industry, springing from people's desire to feel good and look good. China's beauty industry seems a perfect example of what Pilzer predicts. What Pilzer does not adequately address, and what is the concern of this essay, is the fundamental role gender plays in the wellness revolution and regime of consumption. China's rampant development of the beauty economy and consumer capitalism largely capitalizes on femininity and female labor. Women as consumers, laborers, and the consumed have proven to be flexible and instrumental resources for the consumerist regime.

China's new consumer culture, upgraded with economic growth, has embraced the beauty industry as a booming market, largely based on the production and consumption of feminine beauty, feminine youth, and female bodies. It has both offered women the means to consume by opening a part of the labor market to them and offered them up as commodities for their own consumption. . . .

The increasing commodification of all aspects of corporeality in China is driven by the rampant development of consumer capitalism. In the discourse of *nennu* and *shunu*, the emphasis on the (female) body and the (feminine) self . . . plays a key role in the depoliticizing and individualizing move in which power and oppression are dislocated from those in positions of power onto the individual (consumer) subject.

Somewhere behind this discourse, women motivated by the male-dominated power hierarchy cultivate men's pleasure and taste. Although I have not fully developed this aspect in this essay because of space limitations, the two gendered representations of *nennu* and *shunu* reassert the cultural dominance of a masculine gaze and a male body politic and highlight how diffuse masculine domination is (Wolf 1992; Bourdieu 2001). . . . But the aspect of individual agency must also be considered. The beauty economy constitutes an enabling process for women to assume an active subject position in their consumption and to strategically use their beauty and youth to achieve their own goals and interests. The balance and manipulation of this agency, and resistance to it, are key to both women's empowerment and feminist activisms.

NOTES

1. The data used in this essay are drawn from my interviews with about thirty-two beauty care workers, twenty-five beauty salon clients, and fourteen managers in Changping, Beijing, and Jinan during the summers of 2003, 2007, and 2008, as well as from analysis of media reports from 2003 to 2008. To protect the privacy of my informants, I have either purposefully not named them or used fictional names. All translations are mine.

2. This is part of the gender ideology of Maoist socialism (Young 1989; Rofel 1999; Yang 1999; Hanser 2008). The post-Mao shift of gender ideology entails the displacement of the look, voice, and subjectivity of women from the labor process to the market. Such ideological transformation generates new desires and new narratives.

3. Although the main plotline of this discourse is the transformation of ripe women into tender women, this does not mean that the transformation cannot go the other way. In a public debate (*Dushi Nubao 2007*), ripe women were defined as those who have a rich life experience, economic independence, and a successful career. But contradictorily, a conclusion of the debate was that the secret behind tender women growing and maturing was packaging themselves in more elegant and mature ways. Appearance and packaging were still vital in the conversion from tender women to ripe women.

4. Since the mid-1990s, the slogan "men stay at work; women go home" has constituted the rationale behind the massive gendered layoffs at former state-owned enterprises. The post-Mao era celebrates gender polarity, and assumed biological differences between the sexes have been given primacy in discussions of women's work and position in society.

5. See Notar (1994), Brownell (1998, 2001, 2005), Yang (1999), and Brownell and Wasserstrom (2002). Susan Brownell (2005), by demonstrating its social meanings in relation to Chinese nationalism and transnationalism, provides a history of cosmetic surgery in China from being considered a dangerous bourgeois deviation to a post-Mao source of national pride.

6. See Notar (1994), Brownell (1998, 2001), Yang (1999), Schein (2000, 2001), Zhang (2000), and Hanser (2008).

7. Take advertising as an example. Advertising expanded from fewer than ten state-run agencies in 1980 to almost seven thousand mostly nonstate agencies in 1987 (Schein 2001, 300). Such a gigantic advertising industry is mainly promoted by transnational capital, but as Wang Hui (1998) suggests, state ideologies imbue this industry.

8. The beauty criteria are increasingly influenced by Western standards of beauty. The model of beauty is white: contestants typically preferred surgery for bigger busts, thicker lips, more defined eyes, and other stereotypical features of Western beauty standards.

9. This discourse suggests that packaging oneself by wearing youthful clothes, going to beauty or physical therapy, etc., could relieve psychological stress as a result of intensive market competition and make people feel young. The gap for women between their actual age and their apparent age after being packaged is claimed to be ten to fifteen years. By contrast, relief from psychological stress is used especially as a lure to recruit men to beauty salons or fitness centers.

10. The State Statistical Bureau's 1997 survey of 15,600 households in seventy-one cities across the country reveals that women constitute 62.8 percent of laid-off workers, while they account for less than 39 percent of the total urban workforce (Wang 2003).

11. Within this framework, 30,000 training centers and 4,000 employment agencies have been set up in the country since the late 1990s.

12. Many salons openly advertise in local newspapers soliciting single, beautiful young women between the ages of eighteen and twenty-two in order to attract male clients.

13. The fetishism of the female body is also related to the changing value of youth from signifying Maoist revolution to signifying consuming pleasure in the market economy in Chinese society (Zhang 2000, 106).

REFERENCES

All-China Women's Federation. 2003. "Zhang Xiaomei: Economist in the Beauty Industry." May 8. http://www.womenofchina.cn/Profiles/ Businesswomen/200358.jsp.

Baudrillard, Jean. 1998. *The Consumer Society: Myths and Structures*. Trans. Chris Turner. London: Sage.

Black, Paula. 2004. *The Beauty Industry: Gender, Culture, Pleasure*. London: Routledge.

Bourdieu, Pierre. 2001. *Masculine Domination*. Trans. Richard Nice. Oxford: Polity.

Brownell, Susan. 2001. "Making Dream Bodies in Beijing: Athletes, Fashion Models, and Urban Mystique in China." In *China Urban: Ethnographies of Contemporary Culture*, ed. Nancy N. Chen, Constance D. Clark, Suzanne Z. Gottschang, and Lyn Jeffrey, 123–42. Durham, NC: Duke University Press.

———. 2005. "China Reconstructs: Cosmetic Surgery and Nationalism in the Reform Era." In *Asian Medicine and Globalization*, ed. Joseph S. Alter, 132–50. Philadelphia: University of Pennsylvania Press.

Brownell, Susan, and Jeffrey N. Wasserstrom, eds. 2002. *Chinese Femininities, Chinese Masculinities: A Reader*. Berkeley: University of California Press.

China Daily. 2004a. "Beauty Treatment Heading Up." *China Daily*, November 4. http://www.chinadaily.com.cn/engfish/doc/2004-11/04/content_388479.htm.

———. 2004b. "China Braces for First Miss Plastic Surgery." *China Daily*, December 17. http://www.chinadaily.com.cn/english/doc/2004-12/17/content_401180.htm.

———. 2005. "Beauty Economy' Questioned at NPC Session." '*China Daily*, March 14. http://www.chinadaily.com.cn/english/doc/2005-03/14/content_424582.htm.

Cohen, Colleen Ballerino, Richard Wilk, and Beverly Stoeltje. 1996. *Beauty Queens on the Global Stage: Gender, Contests, and Power*. New York: Routledge.

Croll, Elisabeth J. 2006a. *China's New Consumers: Social Development and Domestic Demand*. New York: Routledge.

———. 2006b. "Conjuring Goods, Identities and Cultures." In *Consuming China: Approaches to Cultural Change in Contemporary China*, ed. Kevin Latham, Stuart Thompson, and Jakob Klein, 22–41. London: Routledge.

Dushi Nubao [Urban women newspaper]. 2007. "Nennu shunu zhuangbai" [The packaging of tender women and ripe women]. *Dushi Nubao*, August 3, 17.

Godfrey, Mark. 2004. "World 'Beauty Markers' Knocking China Door." *China Daily*, April 16.

http://www2.chinadaily.com.cn/english/doc/2004-04/06/content_321064.htm.

Hanser, Amy. 2008. *Service Encounters: Class, Gender, and the Market for Social Distinction in Urban China*. Stanford, CA: Stanford University Press.

Hochschild, Arlie Russell. 1983. *The Managed Heart: Commercialization of Human Feeling*. Berkeley: University of California Press.

Lu Junqing. 2004. *Meili liandan zhang dami* [Beautiful faces grow rice]. Shanghai: Dangdai shijie chubanshe.

Notar, Beth. 1994. "Of Labor and Liberation: Images of Women in Current Chinese Television Advertising." *Visual Anthropology Review* 10(2): 29–44.

Pilzer, Paul Zane. 2007. *The New Wellness Revolution: How to Make a Fortune in the Next Trillion Dollar Industry*. 2nd ed. Hoboken, NJ: Wiley.

Rofel, Lisa. 1999. *Other Modernities: Gendered Yearnings in China after Socialism*. Berkeley: University of California Press.

Schein, Louisa. 2000. *Minority Rules: The Miao and the Feminine in China's Cultural Politics*. Durham, NC: Duke University Press.

———. 2001. "Chinese Consumerism and the Politics of Envy: Cargo in the 1990s." In *Whither China: Intellectual Politics in Contemporary China*, ed. Zhang Xudong, 285–314. Durham, NC: Duke University Press.

Turner, Terence. 1994. "Bodies and Anti-bodies: Flesh and Fetish in Contemporary Social Theory." In *Embodiment and Experience: The Existential Ground of Culture and Self*, ed. Thomas J. Csordas, 27–47. New York: Cambridge University Press.

Wang Hui. 1998. "Contemporary Chinese Thought and the Question of Modernity." Trans. Rebecca E. Karl. *Social Text 55* 16(2): 9–44.

Witz, Anne, Chris Warhurst, and Dennis Nickson. 2003. "The Labor of Aesthetics and the Aesthetics of Organization." *Organization* 10(1): 33–54.

Wolf, Naomi. 1992. *The Beauty Myth: How Images of Beauty Are Used against Women*. New York: Anchor.

Xu, Gary, and Susan Feiner. 2007. "*Meinü Jingji*/China's Beauty Economy: Buying Looks, Shifting Value, and Changing Place." *Feminist Economics* 13(3–4): 307–23.

Yang, Jie. 2007. "'Re-employment Stars': Language, Gender and Neoliberal Restructuring in China." In *Words, Worlds and Material Girls Language,*

Gender and Global Economies, ed. Bonnie McElhinny, 72–103. Berlin: Mouton de Gruyter.

Yang, Mayfair Meihui. 1999. *Spaces of Their Own: Women's Public Sphere in Transnational China*. Minneapolis: University of Minnesota Press.

Zhang Zhen. 2000. "Mediating Time: The 'Rice Bowl of Youth' in Fin de Siècle Urban China." *Public Culture* 12(1): 93–113.

Zhao Xinzheng. 2003. Editorial. *Beijing Laodong wubao* [Beijing labor noon newspaper], April 23, 14.

Introduction to Reading 25

Kirsten B. Firminger's research on representations of males in five different popular teenage girls' magazines reveals that girls are encouraged to become informed consumers of boys, who are presented as shallow, highly sexual, emotionally inexpressive, and insecure, but also as potential sources of romance, intimacy, and love. Boys appear as products, much like other products and services being sold to girls. Girls are represented as responsible for good shopping, including selecting the right guy.

1. How do teenage girls' magazines function as a guide to selecting boys?

2. What are the links between girls' beauty and fashion products and the presentation of boys as products?

3. Discuss the implications of the author's final sentences: "Bottom line: look at dating as a way to sample the menu before picking your entrée. In the end, you'll be much happier with the choice you make! Yum!"

Is He Boyfriend Material?

Representation of Males in Teenage Girls' Magazines

Kirsten B. Firminger

In the pages of popular teenage girls' magazines, boys are presented (in)congruently as the providers of potential love, romance, and excitement and as highly sexual, attracted to the superficial, and emotionally inexpressive. The magazines guide female readers toward avoiding the "bad" male and male behavior (locking up their feelings tighter than Fort Knox) and obtaining the "good" male and male behavior (setting you apart from other girls). Within girls' magazines, success in life and (heterosexual) love is girls' responsibility, tied to their ability to self-regulate, make good

Firminger, Kirsten B. 2006. "Is He Boyfriend Material? Representation of Males in Teenage Girls' Magazines." *Men and Masculinities, 8*(3), p. 298. Reprinted with permission of Sage Publications, Inc.

choices, and present themselves in the "right" way. The only barriers are girls' own lack of self-esteem or limited effort (Harris 2004). While the "girl power" language of the feminist movement is used, its politics and questioning of patriarchal gender norms are not discussed. Instead, the magazines advocate relentless surveillance of self, boys, and peers. Embarrassing and confessional tales, quizzes, and opportunities to rate and judge boys and girls on the basis of their photos and profiles encourage young women to "fashion" identities through clothes, cosmetics, beauty items, and consumerism.

Popular teenage girls' magazines. In the United States, teenage girls' magazines are read by more than 75 percent of teenage girls (Market profile: Teenagers 2000). The magazines play an important role in shaping the norms and expectations during a crucial stage of identity and relationship development. Currie (1999) found that some readers consider the magazines' content to be more compelling than their own personal experiences and knowledge. Magazines are in the business of both selling themselves to their audience and selling their audience to advertisers (Kilborne 1999). Teenage girls are advertised as more loyal to their favorite magazines than to their favorite television programs, with magazines touted as "a sister and a friend rolled into one" (Market profile: Teenagers 2000). Magazines attract and keep advertisers by providing the right audience for their products and services, suppressing information that might offend the advertiser, and including editorial content saturated in advertiser-friendly advice (Kilborne 1999).

In this textual environment, consumerist and individualist attitudes and values are promoted to the exclusion of alternative perspectives. Across magazines, one relentless message is clear: "the road to happiness is attracting males for successful heterosexual life by way of physical beautification" (Evan et al. 1991; see also Carpenter 1998, Currie 1999, Signorelli 1997). Given the clarity of this message, little work has been done focusing on the portrayal of males that the girls are supposed to attract. I began my

research examining this question: how are males and male behavior portrayed in popular teenage girls' magazines?

METHOD

To explore these questions, I designed a discursive analysis of a cross-section of adolescent girls' magazines, sampling a variety of magazines and analyzing across them for common portrayals of males. *Seventeen* and *YM* are long-running adolescent girls' magazines. *Seventeen* has a base circulation of 2.4 million while *YM* has a circulation of 2.2 million *(Advertising Age* 74: 21). As a result of the potential of the market, the magazines that are directed at adolescent girls have expanded to include the new *CosmoGirl* (launched in 1999) and *ELLEgirl* (in 2001). Very successful, *CosmoGirl* has a base circulation of 1 million. *ELLEgirl* reports a smaller circulation of 450,000 *(Advertising Age* 74: 21). Chosen as an alternative to the other adolescent girls' magazines, *Girls' Life* is directed at a younger female audience and is the winner of the 2000, 1999, and 1996 Parents' Choice Awards Medal and of the 2000 and 1998 Parents' Guide to Children's Media Association Award of Excellence. The magazine reports it is the number one magazine for girls ages 10 to 15, with a circulation of 3 million (http://www.girlslife.com/infopage .php, retrieved May 23, 2004).

I coded two issues each of *Seventeen, YM, CosmoGirl, ELLEgirl,* and *Girls' Life,* for a total of ten issues. Magazines build loyalty with their readers by presenting the same kinds of material, in a similar form, month after month (Duke 2002). To take into account seasonal differences in content, I purchased the magazines six months apart, once during December 2002 and once during July 2003. While the magazines range in their dates of publication (for instance, Holiday issue, December issue, January issue, etc.), all the magazines were together at the same newsstand at the singular time of purchase.

RESULTS

Within the pages of the magazines, articles and photo layouts focus primarily on beauty, fashion, and celebrities and entertainment, boys and love, health and sex, and self-development. The magazines specialize, with emphasis more or less on one of these topics over the other: *ElleGirl* presents itself as more fashion focused, while self-development is the emphasis for *Girls' Life*'s younger audience. Within the self-development sections, one can find articles focusing on topics such as activities, school, career aspirations, volunteering, sports, and politics. However, even in these articles, focus is on the social, interpersonal aspects of relationships and on consumption instead of the actual doing and mastery of activities.

Advertising permeates the magazines, accounting for 20.8 percent to 44.8 percent of the pages. Additionally, many of the editorial articles, presumably noncommercial, are written in ways that endorse specific products and services (see Currie 1999, for more information on "advertorials"). For instance, one advice column responded to a reader's inquiry about a first kiss by recommending ". . . [having] the following supplies [handy] for when the magical moment finally arrives: Sugarless mints, yummy flavored lip gloss (I dig Bonne Bell Lip Smackers). . . ."

Male-focused content. On average, 19.7 percent of the pages focused on males,[1] ranging from a minimum of 13.6 percent in *ELLEGirl* to a maximum 26.6 percent in *Seventeen.* Articles on boys delve into boys' culture, points of view, opinions, interests, and hobbies, while articles on girls' activities focus more pointedly on the pursuit of boys. Girls learn "Where the boys are," since the "next boyfriend could be right under your nose." They are told,

> Where to go: Minor-league ballparks. Why: Cute guys! . . . Who'll be there: The players are just for gazing at; your targets are the cuties in the stands. And don't forget the muscular types lugging soda trays up and down the aisles. What to say: Ask him

what he thinks about designated hitters (they're paid just to bat). He'll be totally impressed that you even brought up the subject.

Males are offered up to readers in several different formats. First we read profiles, then we meet "examples," we are allowed question and answer, we are quizzed, and then we are asked to judge the males. Celebrity features contain in-depth interviews with male celebrities, while personal short profiles of celebrities or "regular" guys include a photo, biographical information, hobbies, interests, and inquiries such as his "three big requirements for a girlfriend" and "his perfect date." In question-and-answer articles, regular columnists answer selected questions that the readers have submitted.[2] Some columns consistently focus on boys, such as "GL Guys by Bill and Dave" and *YM's* "Love Q and A," while others focus on a variety of questions, for instance *ELLEgirl's* "Ask Jennifur." Profiles of noncelebrity males are presented and judged in rating articles. The magazines publish their criteria for rating boys, via rhetorical devices such as "the magazine staffs' opinions" or the opinion polls of other teenage girls.

Ratings include categories such as "his style," "dateable?," and "style factor." For example, in *CosmoGirl's* Boy-a-Meter article, "Dateable?: I usually go for dark hair, olive skin, and thick eyebrows. But his eyes make me feel like I could confide in him," or *ELLEgirl's* The Rating Game, "He's cute, but I don't dig the emo-look and the hair in the face. It's girlie." Readers can then assess their opinions in relation to those of other girls and the magazine staff.

Romantic stories and quotes enable readers to witness "real" romance and love and compare their "personal experiences" to those presented in the magazines. For instance, "Then one day I found a note tucked in my locker that said, 'You are different than everyone else. But that is why you are beautiful.' At the bottom of the note it said, 'From Matt—I'm in your science class.' We started dating the next day." These can also be rated, as the magazine staff then responded, "Grade: A. He sounds like a very smart boy."

Finally, the readers can then test their knowledge and experiences through the quizzes in the magazines, such as *Seventeen*'s quiz, "Can your summer love last?" with questions and multiple-choice answers:

> As he's leaving for a weeklong road trip with the guys, he: A) tells you at least 10 times how much he's going to miss you. B) promises to call you when he gets a chance. C) can't stop talking about how much fun it will be to "get away" with just his buddies for seven whole days.

Over the pages, boys as a "product" begin to merge with the [other] products and services being sold to girls in "training" as informed consumers, learning to feel "empowered" and make good "choices." While a good boy is a commodity of value, the young women readers learn that relationships with boys should be considered disposable and interchangeable like the other products being sold, "Remember, BFs come and go, but best friends are forever! Is he worth it? Didn't think so."

Embarrassing and confessional stories. Short embarrassing or confessional stories submitted by the readers for publication provide another textual window through which young women can view gender politics; one issue of *YM* included a special pull-out book focused exclusively on confessionals.[3] Kaplan and Cole (2003) found in their four focus groups that the girls enjoy the embarrassing and confessional stories because they reveal "what it is like to be a teenage girl."

On average, two-thirds of the confessional/embarrassing stories were male focused; in 42–100 percent of the stories males were the viewing audience for, or participant in, a girl's embarrassing/confessional moment. Often these stories involve a "cute boy," "my boyfriend," or "my crush." For example:

> My friends and I noticed these cute guys at the ice cream parlor. As we were leaving with our cones, the guys offered to walk with us.

> I was wearing my chunky-heeled shoes and feeling pretty awesome . . . until I tripped. My double scoop flew in the air and hit one of the guys. Oops.

Teenage girls within these stories are embarrassed about things that have happened, often accidentally, with males typically as the audience. While this may allow the female readers to see that they are not the only ones who have experienced embarrassing moments, it also reinforces the notion of self-surveillance as well as socializes girls to think of boys as the audience and judges of their behavior (Currie 1999).

Representations of males. To assess how males are represented, I coded content across male-focused feature articles and "question and answer" columns.[4] These articles contained the most general statements about boys and their behaviors, motivations, and characteristics (for example, "Guys are a few steps behind girls when it comes to maturity level"[5]).

A dominant tension in the representations of boys involves males' splitting of intimacy from sexuality. The magazine advises girls as they negotiate these different behaviors and situations, trying to choose the "right" guy (who will develop an intimate relationship with a girl), reject the "bad" guy (who is focused only on sex), or if possible, change the "bad" guy into the "good" guy (through a girl's decisions and interactions with the male).

> My boyfriend and I were together for 10 months when he said he wanted to take a break—he wasn't sure he was ready for such a commitment. The thought of him seeing other people tore me apart. So every day while we were broken up, I gave him something as a sign of my feelings for him: love sayings cut out from magazines, or cute comics from the paper. Eventually he confessed that he had just been confused and that he loved me more than ever.

As girls are represented as responsible for good shopping, they are represented also as responsible for selecting/changing/shaping male behavior. If girls learn to make the right choices, they can have the right relationship with the right guy, or convert a "bad"/confused boy into a good catch.

The tension is most evident in stories about males' high sex drive, attraction to superficial appearances, emotional inexpressiveness, and fear of rejection and contrasted with those males who are "keepers": who keep their sex drive in check, value more than just girls' appearances, and are able to open up. The articles and advice columns blend the traditional and the feminist; encompassing both new and old meanings and definitions of what it means to be female and male within today's culture (Harris 2004).

The males' sex drive. The "naturally" high sex drive of males rises as the most predominant theme across the magazines. Viewed as normal and unavoidable in teenage boys, girls write to ask for an explanation and advice, and they are told:

> You invited a guy you kind of like up to your room (just to talk!) and he got the wrong idea. This was not your fault. Guys—especially unchaperoned guys on school trips—will interpret any move by a girl as an invitation to get heavy. And I mean any move. You could have sat down next to him at a lab table and he would have taken that as a sign from God that you wanted his body.

When it comes to the topic of sexuality, traditional notions surround "appropriate behavior" for young women and men. Girls learn that males respect and date girls who are able to keep males' sex drive in check and who take time building a relationship. Girls were rarely shown as being highly sexual or interested only in sexual relationship with a boy. Girls are supposed to avoid potentially dangerous situations (such as being alone with a boy) and draw the line (since the males frequently are unable to do so). If they don't, they can be labeled sluts.

> Don't even make out with someone until you're sure things are exclusive. When you hook up with him too early, you're giving him the message that you are something less than a goddess (because, as you know, a goddess is guarded in a temple, and it's not easy to get to her). Take it from me when I tell you that guys want to be with girls they consider goddesses. So treat your body as a temple—don't let just anyone in.

Valuing superficial appearances. Driven by sex, males were shown as judging and valuing girls based on their appearance.

> That's bad, but it's scarier when combined with another sad male truth: They're a lot more into looks than we are.
>
> Okay, I'm the first to admit that guys can be shallow and insipid and *Baywatch* brainwashed to the point where the sight of two balloons on a string will turn them on.

Since males are thought to be interested in the superficial, girls sought advice on how to be most superficially appealing, asking what do guys prefer, including the size of a girl's breasts, hair color, eye color, height, and weight. Girls are portrayed as wanting to know how to present themselves to attract boys, demonstrating an interaction between girls' ideas and understanding of what males want and girls' own choices and behaviors.

Boys are emotionally inexpressive. Across features, readers learn about boys' inability or unwillingness to open up and share their feelings. However, the articles suggest also that if a girl is able to negotiate the relationship correctly, she could get a guy to trust her.

> Let's say you go to the pet store and see a really cute puppy you'd like to pet but, every time you try, he pulls away because he was treated badly in the past. People aren't much different. Move very slowly, and build up trust bit by bit. Show this guy you're into him for real, and he'll warm up to you. Puppy love is worth the wait.

Girls are responsible for doing the emotional work and maintenance and for being change agents in relationships, not allowing room for or even expecting males to take on any of these tasks (see also Chang 2000).

Boys' insecurity and fear of rejection. Boys are displayed as afraid of rejection. Reflecting the neoliberal ideology of "girl power," girls were urged by the magazines to take the initiative in seeking out and approaching boys. This way they are in control of and responsible for their fate, with only lack of confidence, self-esteem, and effort holding them back from finding romance and love.

> So in the next week (why waste more time?), write him a note, pull him aside at a party, or call him up with your best friend by your side for support. Hey, he could be psyched that you took the initiative.
>
> So I think you may have to do the work. If there's a certain guy you're feelin' and you think he's intimidated by you, make the first move. Say something to relax him, like, "What's up? My name is Chelsea." After that, he'll probably start completing sentences.

Males' potential—the "keepers." "Consider every guy to be on a level playing field—they all have potential." Boys were shown to have "potential" and girls were advised to search out the "right" guys.

> He does indeed sound dreamy. He also sounds like a total gentleman, considering he hasn't attempted to jump your bones yet, so the consensus is: He's a keeper.
>
> Most guys are actually smarter than you think and are attracted to all sorts of things about the female species. Yes, big boobs definitely have their dedicated fan base, but so do musical taste, brains, a cute laugh, style and the ability to throw a spiral football (to name just a few). What's a turn-on or dealbreaker for one guy is a nonevent for another.

These boys become the center of the romantic stories and quotes about love and relationships. Resulting from and sustained by girls' self-regulation, personal responsibility, effort, and good choices (as guided by the tools and advice provided by the magazines), these boys are for keeps.

DISCUSSION

Within the magazines, girls are invited to explore boys as shallow, highly sexual, emotionally inexpressive, and insecure and boys who are potential boyfriends, providing romance, intimacy, and love. Males' high sex drive and interest in superficial appearances are naturalized and left unquestioned in the content of the magazines; within a "girl power" version of compulsory heterosexuality, girls should learn the right way to approach a boy in order to get what they want—"the road to happiness is attracting males for successful heterosexual life by way of physical beautification" (Evans et al. 1991). Girls walk the fine line of taking advantage of males' interest in sex and appearance, without crossing over into being labeled a slut. Socialized to be purchasers of beauty and fashion products that promise to make them attractive to boys, girls are "in charge" of themselves and the boys they "choose." It's a competitive market so they better have the right understanding of boys, as well as the right body and outfit to go with it.

The magazines' portrayals, values, and opinions are shaped by their need to create an advertiser-friendly environment while attracting and appealing to the magazines' audience of teenage girls. Skewing the portrayal of males and females to their target audience, magazine editors, writers, and, though I have not highlighted it here—advertisers take advantage of gender-specific fantasies, myths, and fears (Craig 1993). Boys become another product, status symbol, and identity choice. If girls' happiness requires finding romance and love, girls should learn to be informed consumers of boys. By purchasing the magazines, they have a guide to this process, guaranteed to help them understand "What his mixed signals really mean." In addition, if boys are concerned with superficial appearances, it is to the benefit of girls to buy the advertised products and learn "The best swimsuit for [their] bod[ies]."

As girls survey and judge themselves and others, possessions and consumption become the metric for assessing status (Rohlinger 2002; Salamon 2003), the cultural capital for teenagers in place of work, community, and other activities (Harris 2004). The feminist "girl empowerment" becomes personal, appropriated to sell products. The choice and purchase of products and services sold in the magazines promise recreation and transformation, of not only one's outward appearance but also of one's inner self, leading to happiness, satisfaction, and success (Kilborne 1999). Money is the underlying driving force in magazine content. However, while the magazines focus on doing good business, girls are being socialized by the magazines' norms and expectations.

"Bottom line: look at dating as a way to sample the menu before picking your entrée. In the end, you'll be much happier with the choice you make! Yum!"

NOTES

1. Percentage of male-focused pages was taken out of total editorial pages, not including advertising pages. Confessional/embarrassing stories did not count toward the total number of pages because of inconsistencies in unit of analysis, with the confessional stories having a variable number of male-focused stories. I analyzed those separately. Feature articles (unique, nonregular) counted if the article focused on or if males significantly contributed to the narrative in the article (for instance, "Out of bounds: A cheerleader tells the story of how the coach she trusted attacked her"). If the feature was equally balanced with focused sections on both boys and girls (for example, if the article is sectioned into different topics or interviews), only pages that focused on males were counted.

Because of the limited nature of the study, I chose to focus purely on the content that was decided upon by the editorial/writing (called "editorial content" within this article) staff of the magazines, since they establish the mission and tone of the content across all of the issues of the magazine. While I acknowledge the influential presence of advertising, I did no analysis of the content of the advertising pages or photographs. The analysis consists only of the written content of the magazines.

2. The magazines report that the question-and-answer columns and embarrassing/confessional tales are "submitted by readers." However, they do not report how they choose the questions and stories that are published, or whether the magazine staff edits this content.

3. *ELLEgirl* did not contain embarrassing or confessional stories.

4. The unit of analysis was the smallest number of sentences that contained a complete thought, experience, or response, ranging from one sentence to a paragraph. For example, "The fact is you can't change other people. He has to change himself—but perhaps your concern will convince him to make some changes." I took this approach so that the meaning and context of a statement was not lost in the coding. Whole paragraphs could not always be used because they sometimes contained contrasting or multiple themes.

5. The other articles that were not included in the coding focused predominantly on a specific boy or a celebrity male and his interests/activities, or on stories including a boy, or activities to do with a boy, rather than making broad statements about how all boys act (for example, "When he was in kindergarten, his mom enrolled Elijah [Wood] in a local modeling and talent school" or "One time, my boyfriend dared me to sneak out of the house in the middle of the night while my parents were sleeping and meet him at a park.").

REFERENCES

Carpenter, L. M. 1998. From girls into women: Scripts for sexuality and romance in *Seventeen* Magazine, 1974–1994. *The Journal of Sex Research* 35: 158–168.

Chang, J. 2000. Agony-resolution pathways: How women perceive American men in *Cosmopolitan*'s agony (advice) column. *The Journal of Men's Studies* 8: 285–308.

Craig, S. 1993. Selling masculinities, selling femininities: Multiple genders and the economics of television. *The Mid-Atlantic Almanack* 2: 15–27.

Currie, D. H. 1999. *Girl talk: Adolescent magazines and their readers*. Toronto: University of Toronto Press.

Duke, L. 2002. Get real!: Cultural relevance and resistance to the mediated feminine ideal. *Psychology and Marketing* 19: 211–233.

Evans, E., J. Rutberg, and C. Sather. 1991. Content analysis of contemporary teen magazines for adolescent females. *Youth and Society* 23: 99–120.

Girls' Life magazine: About us. Retrieved May 23, 2004 from http://www.girlslife.com/infopage.php.

Kaplan, E. B. and L. Cole. 2003. "I want to read stuff on boys": White, Latina, and Black girls reading *Seventeen* magazine and encountering adolescence. *Adolescence* 38:141–159.

Market profile: Teenagers. 2000. Magazine Publishers of America.

Rohlinger, D. 2002. Eroticizing men: Cultural influences on advertising and male objectification. *Sex Roles: A Journal of Research* 46: 61–74.

Salamon, S. 2003. From hometown to nontown: Rural community effects of suburbanization. *Rural Sociology* 68: 1–24.

Signorelli, N. 1997. *A content analysis: Reflections of girls in the media, a study of television shows and commercials, movies, music videos, and teen magazine articles and ads*. Children Now and Kaiser Family Foundation Publication.

❧ Topics for Further Examination ❧

- Find articles and websites that offer critiques of gender stereotypes in the mass media, popular culture, and consumer culture. For intriguing insights into sexism in "art," visit www.guerrilla girls.com.
- Google automobile ads. Compare and contrast the gendered "marketing" strategies within and across manufacturers. Select other products and compare, contrast, and critique.
- Check out song lyrics by artists who criticize hegemonic masculinity and emphasized femininity. For example, Google Pink's lyrics for the tune titled "Stupid Girls."

6

TRACING GENDER'S MARK ON BODIES, SEXUALITIES, AND EMOTIONS

This chapter explores the ways gender patterns weave themselves into three of the most intimate aspects of the self: body, sexuality, and emotion. The readings we have selected make the general sociological argument that there is no body, sexuality, or emotional experience independent of culture. That is, all cultures sculpt bodies, shape sexualities, and produce emotions. One of the most powerful ways a gendered society creates and maintains gender difference and inequality is through its "direct grip" on these intimate domains of our lives (Schiebinger, 2000, p. 2). Gender ideals and norms require work to be done in, and on, the body to make it appropriately feminine or masculine. The same ideals and norms regulate sexual desire and expression, and require different emotional skills and behaviors of women and men.

At first glance, it may seem odd to think about body, sexuality, and emotion as cultural and gendered products. But consider the following questions: Do you diet, lift weights, dehair your legs or face, or use makeup? In public places, do you feel more comfortable sitting with legs splayed or legs crossed at the ankles? Are you conscious of how you feel and move your body through city streets when you are alone at night? How you answer these questions offers insight into the types of gendered body work you do. Now think about the gendering of sexuality in the United States. The mark of gender on sexual desire and expression is clear and deep, tied to gendered body ideals and norms. Whose breasts are eroticized and why? Are women who have many sexual partners viewed in the same way as men who have many sexual partners? Why are many heterosexually identified men afraid of being perceived as homosexual? Why do women shoulder the major responsibility for contraceptive control? Like sexuality, emotions are embodied modes of being. And like sexuality and body, emotions are socially regulated and constructed. They are deeply gendered.

Consider these questions: Do you associate emotionality with women or men? Is an angry woman taken as seriously as an angry man? Why do we expect women's body language (e.g., their touch and other gestures) to be more affectionate and gentle than men's? What is your reaction to these word pairs—tough woman/soft man? The readings in this chapter explore the complex and contradictory ways bodies, sexualities, and emotions are brought into line with society's gender scheme. Two themes unite the readings. First, they demonstrate how the marking of bodily appearance, sexual desire and behavior, and emotional expression as masculine or feminine reinforces Western, U.S. culture's insistence on an oppositional gender binary pattern. Second, the readings show how patterns of gender inequality become etched into bodies, sexualities, and emotions.

GENDERED BODIES

All societies require body work of their members (Black & Sharma, 2004; Lorber & Moore, 2007). But not all societies insist on the molding of men's and women's bodies into visibly oppositional and asymmetrical types—for example, strong male bodies and fragile female bodies. Only societies constructed around the belief and practice of gender dualism and hierarchy require the enactment of gender inequality in body work. To illustrate, consider the fact that the height ideal and norm for heterosexual couples in America consists of a man who is taller and more robust than his mate (Gieske, 2000). This is not a universal cultural imperative. As Sabine Gieske states, the tall man/short woman pattern was unimportant in 18th century Europe. In fact, the ideal was created in the Victorian era under the influence of physicians and educators who defined men as naturally bigger and stronger than women. The expectation that men be taller than their female partners persists today, even though the average height gap between men and women is closing (Schiebinger, 2000). The differential height norm is so strong that many contemporary Americans react to the pairing of a short man and a tall woman with the kind of shock and disapproval typically directed at interracial couples (Schiebinger, 2000).

How are bodies made feminine and masculine as defined by U.S. culture? It takes work, and lots of it. Well into the 20th century, American gender ideology led men and women alike to perceive women as frail in body and mind. Boys and men were strongly exhorted to develop size, muscle power, physical skills, and the "courage" to beat each other on the playing field and the

battlefield, while girls and women were deeply socialized into a world of distorted body image, dangerous dieting, and physical incompetence (Dowling, 2000). Throwing, running, and hitting "like a girl" was a common cultural theme that we now understand to be a consequence of the cultural taboo against girls developing athletic stature and skills. As Collette Dowling notes, "There is no inherent biological reason for girls not to throw as far, as fast, or as hard as boys do" (p. 64). But there is a cultural reason: the embodiment of the belief in gender difference and inequality. We literally translate the "man is strong, woman is weak" dictum into our bodies. This dictum is so powerful that many people will practice distressed and unhealthy body routines and regimens to try to emulate the images of perfect male and female bodies. The mere threat of seeming masculine or mannish has kept a lot of girls and women from developing their own strength, and the specter of seeming effeminate or sissy has propelled many boys and men into worlds in which their bodies are both weapons and targets of violence (Dowling, 2000).

The reading by Orna Sasson-Levy examines the often harsh, even violent, individualized bodily and emotional practices that transform Israeli men into combat soldiers who will serve the interests of the state, as well as reinforcing a strong link between hegemonic masculinity and Israeli militarism.

American men, especially young men, are expected to express stereotyped masculinity through their bodies by the way they move, sit, gesture, eat, and so forth. However, men's bodies are not held to equally severe ideals of attractiveness and expectations of body work as women's bodies. Gender inequality is etched into women's flesh in more debilitating and painful ways.

American cultural definitions of femininity equate attractiveness with a youthful, slim, fit body that, in its most ideal form, has no visible "flaws"—no hair, pores, discolorations, perspiration marks, body odors, or trace of real bodily functions. In fact, for many women, the body they inhabit must be constantly monitored and managed—dehaired, deodorized, denied food—so that it doesn't offend. At the extreme, girls and women turn their own bodies into fetish objects to which they devote extraordinary amounts of time and money. What are the models of feminine bodily perfection against which girls and women measure themselves and are evaluated by others? The images and representations are all around us in magazine ads, TV commercials and programs, music videos, and toy stores.

Although much media and scholarly attention has been paid to topics such as anorexia and "fear of fat" among thin women, Janna Fikkan and Esther Rothblum (2011) bring together wide-ranging data on what may be a far more troubling issue, "the disproportionate degree of bias experienced by fat women" in the United States (p. 576). Fikkan and Rothblum use the term *fat* because it is descriptive while, as they point out, the term *overweight* implies "unfavorable comparison" to a socially constructed standard and, similarly, the term *obese* is problematic, created by medical practitioners through a biased medical–economic lens (p. 576; see also Kwan, 2010, p. 147). They emphasize two aspects of the oppression of women by impossible ideals of thinness: (1) "The ever thinner cultural ideal means that practically every woman will feel badly about her body," and (2) "because of the pervasiveness and gendered nature of weight-based stigma, a majority of women stand to *suffer significant discrimination*" because they do not and cannot conform to a near-impossible bodily ideal intended to enforce gender inequality (Fikkan & Rothblum, 2011, p. 590). "Weight bias" against women has far-reaching and significant harmful consequences in almost every aspect of women's lives—including, for example, discrimination in hiring, wages, and promotion in the workplace; barriers to good health care; and degrading representation in the mass media (pp. 578–585).

In sharp contrast, the evidence is clear that men pay few if any penalties in any realm of life (e.g., employment and romantic relationships) for being robust and large-bodied (Fikkan & Rothblum, 2011). Samantha Kwan's (2010) study of fat women and men reinforces the findings of Fikkan and Rothblum. As she states, the men in her research sample experienced "very little body consciousness" and rarely spoke of concerns about body management (Kwan, 2010, p. 153). For example, they viewed dining out in pleasurable terms and had no qualms about eating with gusto. Just think of ads for man-sized meals and foods and consider the glaring fact that a comparable "feminine" concept (e.g., woman-sized meal) is either unimaginable or would have the opposite meaning.

Kwan's (2010) study provides us with a useful framework for understanding what scholars such as Joan Chrisler (2011) argue is the threat, even hatred, of women's bodies in patriarchies. Kwan theorizes that a "Western cultural body-hierarchy" has created what she calls body privilege, "an invisible package of unearned assets that thin or normal-sized individuals can take for granted" in everyday life (p. 147). This body-hierarchy is complicated and mediated by prisms such as race and sexual orientation. It appears from as-yet-limited research that lesbians and African American women are more likely to experience greater body satisfaction and protection (via family and community support) from the oppressive ideal of thinness compared with White, heterosexual women (Fikkan & Rothblum, 2011; Kwan, 2010).

The embodiment of women's subordination in gender-stratified societies takes some extreme forms. For example, in highly restrictive patriarchies, women's bodies may be systematically deformed, decimated, and restricted. Foot binding in traditional China is one of the most dramatic examples of an intentionally crippling gender practice. Although foot binding may seem to have no parallels in Western societies, in her reading in this chapter, sociologist Fatema Mernissi challenges the ethnocentric tendency to dismiss practices such as foot binding in China—and the veiling of women in some nations today—as alien or primitive. She does so by revealing the symbolic violence hammered directly on the Western female body by fashion codes and cosmetic industries that place Western women in a state of constant anxiety and insecurity. Mernissi's work suggests the usefulness of comparing practices such as foot binding in China to cosmetic surgery, extreme dieting, and body sculpting among contemporary Western girls and women. Consider the following questions: What do these seemingly different forms of body work have in common? Do they serve similar functions? How do they replicate gender inequality?

The story of the gendering of bodies in the United States is not only about oppositional and asymmetrical masculinity and femininity. Prisms of difference and inequality come into play. Let's consider one prism—race—to illustrate this point. What's the answer to the question, "Mirror, mirror on the wall, who's the fairest of them all?" (Gillespie, 1998). You know what it is. The beauty standard is White, blonde, and blue-eyed. It is not Asian American, African American, Latin American, or Native American. In other words, there is a hierarchy of physical attractiveness, and the Marilyn Monroes and Madonnas of the world are at the top. Yes, there are African and Asian American models and celebrities. But they almost always conform to White appearance norms. When they don't, they tend to be exoticized as the "Other." Just consider the fact that eyelid surgery, nasal implants, and nasal tip refinement procedures are the most common cosmetic surgery procedures undergone by Asian American patients, largely women (Kaw, 1998). The facial features that Asian American women seek to alter, including small, narrow eyes and a flat nose, are those that define them as racially different from White norms (Kaw, 1998). Racial and gender ideologies come together to reinforce an ethnocentric and racist beauty standard that devalues the "given" features of minority women. The medical system has cashed in on it by promoting a beauty standard that requires the surgical alteration of features that don't fit the ideal.

GENDERED SEXUALITIES

Like the body, sexuality is shaped by culture. The sexualization process in a gendered society such as the United States is tightly bound to cultural ideas of masculinity and femininity. In dominant Western culture, a real man and a real woman are assumed to be opposite human types, as expressed in the notion of the "opposite sex." In addition, both are assumed to be heterosexual as captured in the notion that "opposites attract." Conformity to this gendered sexual dichotomy is strictly enforced.

The term *compulsory heterosexuality* refers to the dominance of heterosexual values and the fact that the meanings and practices of nonhetero(sexuality) as well as hetero(sexuality) are shaped by the dominant heterosexual script. For example, "real sex" is generally conceived of as coitus or penile–vaginal intercourse. This "coital imperative," as Nicola Gavey, Kathryn McPhillips, and Marion Doherty call it in their reading in this chapter, limits the control individuals have in determining what counts as sexual activity. The coital imperative frames women's sexuality as passive/receptive and men's as active/penetrative. That is, this imperative defines sex as something men "do" to women. Gavey and her coauthors also analyze the negative impact that privileging of men's sexual needs above women's has on the capacity for men and women to have truly reciprocal, safe sexual relations. Katz and Tirone (2009) document a similar pattern of sexual compliance among many undergraduate women students in heterosexual dating relationships and the negative effects of women's compliant behavior on their own well-being.

Importantly, the Western obsession with the homosexual/heterosexual distinction is relatively new. Created in the 19th century, it became a mechanism by which masculinity and femininity could be further polarized and policed (Connell, 1999). Gay masculinity and lesbian femininity came to be defined as abnormal and threatening to the "natural gender order." Consequently, for many Westerners, the fear of being thought of as homosexual has a powerful impact on presentation of self. Men and boys routinely police each other's behavior and mete out punishment for any suggestion of "effeminacy" (Connell, 1999; Plante, 2006), while women and girls who engage in masculinized activities such as military service and elite sports risk being labeled lesbians.

Contemporary Western gender and sexuality beliefs have spawned stereotypes of lesbians as "manly" women and gay men as "effeminate." The reality is otherwise. For example, research shows that many gay men and lesbians are gender conformists in their expression of sexuality (Kimmel, 2000). Gay men's sexual behavior patterns tend to be masculine—oriented toward pleasure, orgasm, experimentation, and many partners—while lesbian sexuality is quite womanly in a Western sense, emphasizing sexual intimacy within romantic relationships. However, this account of nonheterosexuality is incomplete. Recent research suggests that compared with heterosexuals, nonheterosexuals have more opportunities to reflect on and experiment with ways of being sexual. Although the meanings attached to sexuality in society at large shape their erotic encounters, they are also freer to challenge the dominant sexual scripts (Weeks, Heaphy, & Donovan, 2001).

The imposition of gender difference and inequality on sexuality in societies such as the United States is also reflected in the sexual double standard. The double standard, which emphasizes and normalizes male pleasure and female restraint, is a widespread product and practice of patriarchy. Although Western sexual attitudes and behaviors have moved away from a strict double standard, the sexual lives of women remain more constrained than those of men. For example, girls and women are still under the control of the good-girl/bad-girl dichotomy, a cultural distinction that serves to pit women against each other and to produce sexual relations between women and men that can be confusing and dissatisfying. Men grow up with expectations to embrace a sexual script by which they gain status from sexual experience (Kimmel, 2000). Women grow up with expectations to believe that to be sexually active is to compromise their value—but, at the same time, to be flirtatious and sexy. Doesn't this seem confusing? Imagine the relationship misunderstandings and disappointments that can emerge out of the meeting of these "opposite-sex" sexual scripts.

In their chapter reading, Erin Hatton and Mary Nell Trautner offer persuasive evidence that the sexual double standard persists and has intensified in new negative ways for girls and women. They studied more than 40 years of covers of *Rolling Stone* magazine and found that although sexualized images of both men and women have increased, women are more frequently sexualized than men and, most significantly, women are "increasingly likely to be 'hypersexualized,'" but men are not (p. 256). Hatton and Trautner conclude that the dramatic increase in hypersexualized representations of women signifies a dangerous trend toward a narrowing of culturally acceptable ways to do femininity, including the diminishment of other aspects of "emphasized femininity" such as sociability and nurturance (p. 274).

The prisms of difference and inequality alter the experience and expression of gendered sexuality in significant ways in the United States. For example, Trautner (2005) found that social class differences are scripted and represented as sexual differences in exotic dance clubs catering to clientele who come from either the middle class or the working class. Dancers in working-class clubs are more likely to perform stereotypes of bad-girl sexuality, while those who dance in middle-class clubs enact good-girl sexuality. Rebecca Plante (2006), an expert on the sociology of sexuality, analyzes the intersection of race and sexuality in the United States and argues that African Americans "do not enter the discourse and debate about sexualities from the same place where white, middle-class people enter" (p. 231). Black sexuality was historically stereotyped as perverted and predatory, a theme that continues today in pornographic and other representations of African American men in particular. In a recent study of Black women who work in the pornography industry, Mireille Miller-Young (2010) confirms Plante's observations about the interactions among gender, race, and sexuality. Miller-Young found that Black women are "devalued as hyperaccessible and superdisposable in an industry that simultaneously invests in and ghettoizes fantasies about black sexuality" (p. 219).

Gendered Emotions

Masculinity and femininity are defined as emotionally opposed in Western culture (Bendelow & Williams, 1998). This opposition expresses itself in both obvious and subtle ways. The obvious opposition is that the emotions that can be expressed—for example, anger and love—and how they are expressed are tied to gender. Boys and men must appear "hard" by hiding or shutting down feelings of vulnerability, such as fear, while girls and women are encouraged to be "soft"—that is, emotionally in touch, vulnerable, and expressive. Consider the impact of learning and enacting different, even oppositional, emotional scripts and feeling rules on intimate relationships. If men are not supposed to be vulnerable, then how can they forge satisfying affectionate bonds with women and other men? Additionally, men who embrace the gender–emotion stereotype of hard masculinity may pay a price in well-being by concealing their own pain, either physical or psychological (Real, 2001; Shields, Garner, Di Leone, & Hadley, 2006; Vaccaro, Schrock, & McCabe, 2011). Also, it is important to recognize the negative consequences of gendered emotionality for girls and women. Although girls and women receive cultural encouragement to be "in touch with" themselves and others emotionally, this has strong associations with weakness and irrationality. Thus, Shields et al. (2006) observe that the strong cultural association between emotionality and femininity has emphasized "the comparatively ineffectual nature of women's emotion" (p. 63). When women express emotion according to cultural rules, they run the risk of being labeled hypersensitive, temperamental, and irrational. The stereotype of the emotionally erratic and unstable woman has been widely used in efforts to undermine the advancement of women in politics, higher education, the professions, business, and other realms of public life. You know how it goes: "We can't risk having a moody, irritable, irrational woman at the helm."

How do the prisms of difference and inequality interact with gendered emotions? Looking through a number of prisms simultaneously, we can see that the dominant definition of hard, stiff-upper-lip masculinity is White, heterosexual, and European (Seidler, 1998). Hegemonic masculinity assigns rationality and reason to privileged adult men. All other people, including women,

minorities, and children, are assumed to be more susceptible to influence by their bodies and emotions and, as a consequence, less capable of mature, reasoned decision making (Seidler, 1998). The chapter reading by Aaronette M. White and Tal Peretz employs an intersectional analysis of Black masculinities and emotions to show how men can challenge hegemonic masculinity and its related negative emotional patterns by applying feminism in their daily lives and participating in antisexist organizations. White and Peretz offer a useful framework, based on case studies, for thinking about how men in the context of feminist and profeminist organizations can transform their feelings, identities, and relationships in ways that contribute to the dismantling of patriarchy (see R. W. Connell's reading in Chapter 10).

We'd like to conclude this chapter introduction by asking you to think about individual and collective strategies to reject conformity to patterns of gendered body work, sexual expression, and emotionality that demean, disempower, and prove dangerous to women and men. What would body work, emotional life, and sexual desire and experience be like if they were not embedded in and shaped by structures of inequality? How would personal growth, self-expression, and communication with others change if we were not under the sway of compulsory attractiveness, compulsory heterosexuality, the sexual double standard, and gendered emotional requirements? How would your life change? What can we do, as individuals and collectively, to resist and reject the pressure to bring our bodies, sexual experience, and emotional life in line with oppressive and dangerous ideals and norms?

REFERENCES

Bendelow, G., & Williams, S. J. (1998). Introduction: Emotions in social life. In G. Bendelow & S. Bendelow (Eds.), *Emotions in social life* (pp. xv–xxx). London: Routledge.

Black, P., & Sharma, U. (2004). Men are real, women are "made up." In J. Spade & C. Valentine (Eds.), *The kaleidoscope of gender* (pp. 286–296). Belmont, CA: Wadsworth.

Chrisler, J. C. (2011). Leaks, lumps, and lines: Stigma and women's bodies. *Psychology of Women Quarterly, 35*(2), 202–214.

Connell, R. W. (1999). Making gendered people. In M. Feree, J. Lorber, & B. Hess (Eds.), *Revisioning gender* (pp. 449–471). Thousand Oaks, CA: Sage.

Dowling, C. (2000). *The frailty myth.* New York: Random House.

Fikkan, J. L., & Rothblum, E. D. (2011). Is fat a feminist issue? Exploring the gendered nature of weight bias. *Sex Roles, 66,* 575–592.

Gieske, S. (2000). The ideal couple: A question of size? In L. Schiebinger (Ed.), *Feminism and the body* (pp. 375–394). New York: Oxford University Press.

Gillespie, M. A. (1998). Mirror mirror. In R. Weitz (Ed.), *The politics of women's bodies* (pp. 184–188). New York: Oxford University Press.

Katz, J., & Tirone, V. (2009). Women's sexual compliance with male dating partners: Associations with investment in ideal womanhood and romantic well-being. *Sex Roles, 60,* 347–356.

Kaw, E. (1998). Medicalization of racial features: Asian-American women and cosmetic surgery. In R. Weitz (Ed.), *The politics of women's bodies* (pp. 167–183). New York: Oxford University Press.

Kimmel, M. (2000). *The gendered society.* New York: Oxford University Press.

Kwan, S. (2010). Navigating public spaces: Gender, race, and body privilege in everyday life. *Feminist Formations, 22*(2), 144–166.

Lorber, J., & Moore, L. J. (2007). *Gendered bodies: Feminist perspectives.* Los Angeles: Roxbury.

Miller-Young, M. (2010). Putting hypersexuality to work: Black women and illicit eroticism in pornography. *Sexualities, 13*(2), 219–235.

Plante, R. (2006). *Sexualities in context.* Cambridge, MA: Westview Press.

Real, T. (2001). Men's hidden depression. In T. Cohen (Ed.), *Men and masculinity* (pp. 361–368). Belmont, CA: Wadsworth.

Schiebinger, L. (2000). Introduction. In L. Schiebinger (Ed.), *Feminism and the body* (pp. 1–21). New York: Oxford University Press.

Seidler, V. J. (1998). Masculinity, violence and emotional life. In G. Bendelow & S. Williams (Eds.), *Emotions in social life* (pp. 193–210). London: Routledge.

Shields, S., Garner, D., Di Leone, B., & Hadley, A. (2006). Gender and emotion. In J. Stets & J. Turner (Eds.), *Handbook of the sociology of emotions* (pp. 63–83). New York: Springer.

Trautner, M. N. (2005). Doing gender, doing class: The performance of sexuality in exotic dance clubs. *Gender & Society, 19*(6), 771–778.

Vaccaro, C. A., Schrock, D. P., & McCabe, J. M. (2011). Managing emotional manhood: Fighting and fostering fear in mixed marital arts. *Social Psychology Quarterly, 74*(4), 414–437.

Weeks, J., Heaphy, B., & Donovan, C. (2001). *Same sex intimacies: Families of choice and other life experiments.* New York: Routledge.

Introduction to Reading 26

Fatema Mernissi is a well-known Moroccan sociologist and Islamic scholar. She has done research in a number of countries, including the United States. This article is a chapter from her book titled *Scheherazade Goes West.* Mernissi challenges Westerners to think about the ways their feminine beauty images and practices can be as hurtful and humiliating to women as the enforced veiling of women in nations such as Iran and Saudi Arabia. In fact, she argues that the "size 6" ideal is a more violent restriction than the Muslim veil.

1. How do definitions of feminine beauty differ in Morocco compared with the United States?

2. What does Mernissi mean when she states the Western man establishes male domination by manipulating time and light?

3. Read the final paragraph of this article carefully. Why does Mernissi end on this note?

Size 6

The Western Woman's Harem

Fatema Mernissi

It was during my unsuccessful attempt to buy a cotton skirt in an American department store that I was told my hips were too large to fit into a size 6. That distressing experience made me realize how the image of beauty in the West can hurt and humiliate a woman as much as the veil does when enforced by the state police in extremist nations such as Iran, Afghanistan, or Saudi Arabia. Yes, that day I stumbled onto one of the keys to the enigma of passive beauty in Western harem fantasies. The elegant saleslady in the American store looked at me without moving from her desk and said that she had no skirt my size. "In this whole big store, there is no skirt for me?" I said. "You are joking." I felt very suspicious and thought that she just might be too tired to help me. I could understand that. But then the saleswoman added a condescending judgment, which sounded to me like an Imam's fatwa. It left no room for discussion:

"You are too big!" she said.

"I am too big compared to what?" I asked, looking at her intently, because I realized that I was facing a critical cultural gap here.

"Compared to a size 6," came the saleslady's reply.

Her voice had a clear-cut edge to it that is typical of those who enforce religious laws. "Size 4 and 6 are the norm," she went on, encouraged by my bewildered look. "Deviant sizes such as the one you need can be bought in special stores."

That was the first time that I had ever heard such nonsense about my size. In the Moroccan streets, men's flattering comments regarding my particularly generous hips have for decades led me to believe that the entire planet shared their convictions. It is true that with advancing age, I have been hearing fewer and fewer flattering comments when walking in the medina, and sometimes the silence around me in the bazaars is deafening. But since my face has never met with the local beauty standards, and I have often had to defend myself against remarks such as zirafa (giraffe), because of my long neck, I learned long ago not to rely too much on the outside world for my sense of self-worth. In fact, paradoxically, as I discovered when I went to Rabat as a student, it was the self-reliance that I had developed to protect myself against "beauty blackmail" that made me attractive to others. My male fellow students could not believe that I did not give a damn about what they thought about my body. "You know, my dear," I would say in response to one of them, "all I need to survive is bread, olives, and sardines. That you think my neck is too long is your problem, not mine."

In any case, when it comes to beauty and compliments, nothing is too serious or definite in the medina, where everything can be negotiated. But things seemed to be different in that American department store. In fact, I have to confess that I lost my usual self-confidence in that New York environment. Not that I am always sure of myself, but I don't walk around the Moroccan streets or down the university corridors wondering what people are thinking about me. Of course, when I hear a compliment, my ego expands like a cheese soufflé, but on the whole, I don't expect to hear much from others. Some mornings, I feel ugly because I am sick or tired; others, I feel wonderful because it is sunny out or I have written a good paragraph. But suddenly, in that peaceful American store that I had entered so triumphantly, as a sovereign consumer ready to spend money, I felt savagely attacked. My hips, until then the sign of a relaxed and uninhibited maturity, were suddenly being condemned as a deformity.

"And who decides the norm?" I asked the saleslady, in an attempt to regain some self-confidence by challenging the established rules. I never let others evaluate me, if only because I remember my childhood too well. In ancient Fez, which valued round-faced plump adolescents, I was repeatedly told that I was too tall, too skinny, my cheekbones were too high, my eyes were too slanted. My mother often complained that I would never find a husband and urged me to study and learn all that I could, from storytelling to embroidery, in order to survive. But I often retorted that since "Allah had created me the way I am, how could he be so wrong, Mother?" That would silence the poor woman for a while, because if she contradicted me, she would be attacking God himself. And this tactic of glorifying my strange looks as a divine gift not only helped me to survive in my stuffy city, but also caused me to start believing the story myself. I became almost self-confident. I say almost, because I realized early on that self-confidence is not a tangible and stable thing like a silver bracelet that never changes over the years. Self-confidence is like a tiny fragile light, which goes off and on. You have to replenish it constantly. "And who says that everyone must be a size 6?" I joked to the saleslady that day, deliberately neglecting to mention size 4, which is the size of my skinny twelve-year-old niece.

At that point, the saleslady suddenly gave me an anxious look. "The norm is everywhere, my dear," she said. "It's all over, in the magazines, on television, in the ads. You can't escape it. There is Calvin Klein, Ralph Lauren, Gianni Versace, Giorgio Armani, Mario Valentino, Salvatore Ferragamo, Christian Dior, Yves Saint-Laurent, Christian Lacroix, and Jean-Paul Gaultier. Big department stores go by the norm."

She paused and then concluded, "If they sold size 14 or 16, which is probably what you need, they would go bankrupt." She stopped for a minute and then stared at me, intrigued. "Where on earth do you come from? I am sorry I can't help you. Really, I am." And she looked it too. She seemed, all of a sudden, interested, and brushed off another woman who was seeking her attention with a cutting, "Get someone else to help you, I'm busy." Only then did I notice that she was probably my age, in her late fifties. But unlike me, she had the thin body of an adolescent girl. Her knee length, navy blue, Chanel dress had a white silk collar reminiscent of the subdued elegance of aristocratic French Catholic schoolgirls at the turn of the century. A pearl-studded belt emphasized the slimness of her waist. With her meticulously styled short hair and sophisticated makeup, she looked half my age at first glance.

"I come from a country where there is no size for women's clothes," I told her. "I buy my own material and the neighborhood seamstress or craftsman makes me the silk or leather skirt I want. They just take my measurements each time I see them. Neither the seamstress nor I know exactly what size my new skirt is. We discover it together in the making. No one cares about my size in Morocco as long as I pay taxes on time. Actually, I don't know what my size is, to tell you the truth." The saleswoman laughed merrily and said that I should advertise my country as a paradise for stressed working women. "You mean you don't watch your weight?" she inquired, with a tinge of disbelief in her voice. And then, after a brief moment of silence, she added in a lower register, as if talking to herself: "Many women working in highly paid fashion-related jobs could lose their positions if they didn't keep to a strict diet." Her words sounded so simple, but the threat they implied was so cruel that I realized for the first time that maybe "size 6" is a more violent restriction imposed on women than is the Muslim veil. Quickly I said good-bye so as not to make any more demands on the saleslady's time or involve her in any more unwelcome, confidential exchanges about age-discriminating salary cuts. A surveillance camera was probably watching us both. Yes, I thought as I wandered off, I have finally found the answer to my harem enigma. Unlike the Muslim man, who uses space to establish male domination by excluding women from the public arena, the Western man manipulates time and light. He declares that in order to be beautiful, a woman must look fourteen years old. If she dares to look fifty, or worse, sixty, she is beyond the pale. By putting the spotlight on the female child and framing her as the ideal of beauty, he condemns the mature woman to invisibility. In fact, the modern Western man enforces Immanuel Kant's nineteenth-century theories: To be beautiful, women have to appear childish and brainless. When a woman looks mature and self-assertive, or allows her hips to expand, she is condemned as ugly. Thus, the wars of the European harem separate youthful beauty from ugly maturity.

These Western attitudes, I thought, are even more dangerous and cunning than the Muslim ones because the weapon used against women is time. Time is less visible, more fluid than space. The Western man uses images and spotlights to freeze female beauty within an idealized childhood, and forces women to perceive aging—that normal unfolding of the years—as a shameful devaluation. "Here I am, transformed into a dinosaur," I caught myself saying aloud as I went up and down the rows of skirts in the store, hoping to prove the saleslady wrong—to no avail. This Western time-defined veil is even crazier than the space-defined one enforced by the Ayatollahs.

The violence embodied in the Western harem is less visible than in the Eastern harem because aging is not attacked directly, but rather masked as an aesthetic choice. Yes, I suddenly felt not only very ugly but also quite useless in that store, where, if you had big hips, you were simply out of the picture. You drifted into the fringes of nothingness. By putting the spotlight on the prepubescent female, the Western man veils the older, more mature woman, wrapping her in shrouds of ugliness. This idea gives me

the chills because it tattoos the invisible harem directly onto a woman's skin. Chinese footbinding worked the same way: Men declared beautiful only those women who had small, childlike feet. Chinese men did not force women to bandage their feet to keep them from developing normally—all they did was to define the beauty ideal. In feudal China, a beautiful woman was the one who voluntarily sacrificed her right to unhindered physical movement by mutilating her own feet, and thereby proving that her main goal in life was to please men. Similarly, in the Western world, I was expected to shrink my hips into a size 6 if I wanted to find a decent skirt tailored for a beautiful woman. We Muslim women have only one month of fasting, Ramadan, but the poor Western woman who diets has to fast twelve months out of the year. *"Quelle horreur,"* I kept repeating to myself, while looking around at the American women shopping. All those my age looked like youthful teenagers.

According to the writer Naomi Wolf, the ideal size for American models decreased sharply in the 1990s. "A generation ago, the average model weighed 8 percent less than the average American woman, whereas today she weighs 23 percent less. . . . The weight of Miss America plummeted, and the average weight of Playboy Playmates dropped from 11 percent below the national average in 1970 to 17 percent below it in eight years."[1] The shrinking of the ideal size, according to Wolf, is one of the primary reasons for anorexia and other health-related problems: "Eating disorders rose exponentially, and a mass of neurosis was promoted that used food and weight to strip women of . . . a sense of control."[2] Now, at last, the, mystery of my Western harem made sense. Framing youth as beauty and condemning maturity is the weapon used against women in the West just as limiting access to public space is the weapon used in the East. The objective remains identical in both cultures: to make women feel unwelcome, inadequate, and ugly. The power of the Western man resides in dictating what women should wear and how they should look. He controls the whole fashion industry, from cosmetics to underwear. The West, I realized, was the only part of the world where women's fashion is a man's business. In places like Morocco, where you design your own clothes and discuss them with craftsmen and women, fashion is your own business. Not so in the West. As Naomi Wolf explains in *The Beauty Myth,* men have engineered a prodigious amount of fetishlike, fashion-related paraphernalia: "Powerful industries—the $33-billion-a-year diet industry, the $20-billion cosmetic industry, the $300-million cosmetic surgery industry, and the $7-billion pornography industry—have arisen from the capital made out of unconscious anxieties, and are in turn able, through their influence on mass culture, to use, stimulate, and reinforce the hallucination in a rising economic spiral."[3]

But how does the system function? I wondered. Why do women accept it? Of all the possible explanations, I like that of the French sociologist, Pierre Bourdieu, the best. In his latest book, *La Domination Masculine,* he proposes something he calls *"la violence symbolique":* "Symbolic violence is a form of power which is hammered directly on the body, and as if by magic, without any apparent physical constraint. But this magic operates only because it activates the codes pounded in the deepest layers of the body."[4] Reading Bourdieu, I had the impression that I finally understood Western man's psyche better. The cosmetic and fashion industries are only the tip of the iceberg, he states, which is why women are so ready to adhere to their dictates. Something else is going on on a far deeper level. Otherwise, why would women belittle themselves spontaneously? Why, argues Bourdieu, would women make their lives more difficult, for example, by preferring men who are taller or older than they are? "The majority of French women wish to have a husband who is older and also, which seems consistent, bigger as far as size is concerned," writes Bourdieu.[5]

Caught in the enchanted submission characteristic of the symbolic violence inscribed in the mysterious layers of the flesh, women relinquish what he calls "les signes ordinaires de la hiérarchie sexuelle," the ordinary signs of sexual hierarchy, such as old age and a larger body. By so doing, explains Bourdieu, women spontaneously accept the subservient position. It is this spontaneity Bourdieu describes as magic enchantment.[6] Once I understood how this magic submission worked, I became very happy that the conservative Ayatollahs do not know about it yet. If they did, they would readily switch to its sophisticated methods, because they are so much more effective. To deprive me of food is definitely the best way to paralyze my thinking capabilities.

Both Naomi Wolf and Pierre Bourdieu come to the conclusion that insidious "body codes" paralyze Western women's abilities to compete for power, even though access to education and professional opportunities seem wide open, because the rules of the game are so different according to gender. Women enter the power game with so much of their energy deflected to their physical appearance that one hesitates to say the playing field is level. "A cultural fixation on female thinness is not an obsession about female beauty," explains Wolf. It is "an obsession about female obedience. Dieting is the most potent political sedative in women's history; a quietly mad population is a tractable one."[7] Research, she contends, "confirmed what most women know too well—that concern with weight leads to a 'virtual collapse of self-esteem and sense of effectiveness' and that . . . 'prolonged and periodic caloric restriction' resulted in a distinctive personality whose traits are passivity, anxiety, and emotionality."[8]

Similarly, Bourdieu, who focuses more on how this myth hammers its inscriptions onto the flesh itself, recognizes that constantly reminding women of their physical appearance destabilizes them emotionally because it reduces them to exhibited objects. "By confining women to the status of symbolical objects to be seen and perceived by the other, masculine domination . . . puts women in a state of constant physical insecurity. . . . They have to strive ceaselessly to be engaging, attractive, and available."[9] Being frozen into the passive position of an object whose very existence depends on the eye of its beholder turns the educated modern Western woman into a harem slave. "I thank you, Allah, for sparing me the tyranny of the 'size 6 harem,'" I repeatedly said to myself while seated on the Paris-Casablanca flight, on my way back home at last. "I am so happy that the conservative male elite does not know about it. Imagine the fundamentalists switching from the veil to forcing women to fit size 6."

How can you stage a credible political demonstration and shout in the streets that your human rights have been violated when you cannot find the right skirt?

NOTES

1. Naomi Wolf, *The Beauty Myth: How Images of Beauty Are Used Against Women* (New York Anchor Books, Doubleday, 1992), p. 185.

2. Ibid., p. 11.

3. Ibid., p. 17.

4. Pierre Bourdieu: "La force symbolique est une forme de pouvoir qui s' exerce sur les corps, directement, et comme par magie, en dehors de toute contrainte physique, mais cette magie n'opère qu'en s'appuyant sur des dispositions déposées, tel des ressorts, au plus profond des corps." In *La Domination Masculine* (Paris: Editions du Seuil, 1998), Ibid. p. 44. Here I would like to thank my French editor, Claire Delannoy, who kept me informed of the latest debates on women's issues in Paris by sending me Bourdieu's book and many others. Delannoy has been reading this manuscript since its inception in 1996 (a first version was published in Casablanca by Edition Le Fennec in 1998 as "Êtes-Vous Vacciné Contre le Harem").

5. *La Domination Masculine*, Ibid. p. 41.

6. Bourdieu, Ibid. p. 42.

7. Wolf, Ibid. p. 187.

8. Wolf, quoting research carried out by S. C. Woolly and O. W. Woolly, Ibid. pp. 187–188.

9. Bourdieu, *La Domination Masculine*. p. 73.

Introduction to Reading 27

Orna Sasson-Levy, a sociologist at Bar-Ilan University in Israel, is a specialist in gender and ethnic aspects of military and militarism. She is the author of *Identities in Uniform: Masculinities and Femininities in the Israeli Military* (2006, Israel: The Magnes Press). In this article, she offers extensive analysis of the transformative bodily and emotional practices that have become key to framing male combat service in Israel as an individualistic enterprise in which the soldier perceives his military activities as "masculine self-actualization." Sasson-Levy argues that young men in Israel are willing to kill and be killed not only for the good of the collective but also in the name of individualized hegemonic masculinity. The author's exploration of links between sexist views and nationalist views in Israel has resulted in both praise and condemnation.

1. How does the soldier's body provide the "material infrastructure" of the connection between military service and the state?

2. Discuss the role of self-control and thrill as sources of the soldier's "status of exclusivity and its justification."

3. How does gendering of the soldier's body act as a control mechanism that encourages young men to go to war and risk their lives?

——— Individual Bodies, Collective State Interests ———

The Case of Israeli Combat Soldiers

Orna Sasson-Levy

This article seeks to advance a new understanding of the ways in which hegemonic institutions are embodied and reproduced through the construction of extreme masculinities. In particular, I focus on the management of the body and emotions among Israeli combat soldiers as an interface between state and military constructions and individual experience.

Until recently, most writing on the military and gender focused on the problematic of women's military service, while taking men's service for granted. However, Kovitz suggests that research should "shift from problematizing women's service to problematizing that of men" (Kovitz 2003, 1). For Kovitz, the main question is why men agree to go to war and not why women are excluded from it. More specifically, she asks how democratic societies, whose liberal values would seem to contradict the coercive values found in the military, succeed in persuading men that they want to enlist in the army and participate in warfare.

The primary question this article raises, then, concerns how states convince young men to go to war. This is not a new question, and it has been answered before in different ways. First and foremost, states generate nationalist feelings in their subjects by constructing collective identities based on (real or invented) traditions and a common origin, and develop militarized patterns of socialization that prepare their youth to join the military forces (Furman 1999). At the same time, they produce (or maintain) a perception of

existential threat, which can be very real or utterly constructed. In both cases, men enlist into the army in response to the call of the state.

The state's call to sign up for military service is supplemented by a promise for equal citizenship. In the West, military service and war have been integral to the definition of citizenship (Janowitz 1994; Tilly 1996). Thus, minority groups sought to perform military service to demonstrate their political loyalty and worthiness as citizens and to enhance their civic standing (Burk 1995; Gill 1997).

These appeals to men to risk their lives for the good of the collective are always gendered. Militaries have been identified as masculine institutions not only because they are populated with men but also because they constitute a major arena for the construction of masculine identities and play a primary role in shaping images of masculinity in society at large (Barrett 1996; Connell 1995; Morgan 1994). Nagel (1998) shows that terms like *honor, cowardice, bravery, heroism, duty,* and *adventure* are hard to distinguish as either nationalistic or masculine. Thus, despite far-reaching political, social, and technological changes, the warrior is still a key symbol of masculinity (Morgan 1994, 165), and militaries are often described as "the last bastion of masculinity" (Addelston and Stirratt 1996). The chance to "become a man" is therefore another important enticement into military life.

Another reason for mobilization is economic: when the military in many Western states shifted from mandatory conscription to all-volunteer forces, it was often those in dire economic situations who enlisted. In the United States, for example, military service is perceived as a path for social mobility, and most soldiers sign up for economic reasons (Moskos 1993, 86; Enloe 1980). And, finally, in some countries, though not as many as in the past, men enlist because of coercive state laws requiring mandatory conscription, which is the case in Israel.

Most of these reasons for enlistment are related to the formation of the modern nation state and are thus relevant to Israel as well. However, with the impact of globalization, the configuration of the modern nation-state is rapidly changing (Comaroff 1996), and the link between citizen and state is taking on a new character, a consequence of which is changing mobilization rates. In Israel, the impact of globalization has been a gradual shift from a collective orientation toward a more individualistic one (Horowitz and Lissak 1989; Ram 1999).[1] The roots of this social shift are usually traced to the end of the 1970s, with Israel's signing of a peace accord with Egypt, the growth of the capitalist free market, and the influence of globalizing developments that accelerated processes of privatization. These processes stimulated the decline of communal public spiritedness and the rise of an individualistic orientation that emphasizes self-fulfillment and human and civic rights (Shafir and Peled 1998).

One might expect that the decline of Israeli collectivism would result in the devaluing of the militaristic ethos in general and the status of the warrior in particular. Moreover, the current armed conflict is not perceived as posing an existential threat to Israel's security and does not demand total mobilization. In such a situation of a protracted "low-intensity" conflict, the state may well encounter difficulties in maintaining the dominance of a republican discourse, which exalts the self-sacrifice of the masculine combat soldier.

However, in spite of social and ideological changes, Israel's Jewish community perceives the military as the emblem of pure patriotism and as one of the major symbols of the collective (Kimmerling 1993). In this militaristic culture, the (Jewish) combat soldier has achieved the status of hegemonic masculinity and is identified with good citizenship.

There seems to be a gap, then, between the individualistic trends and the tenacity of the status of the combat soldier. How can we explain the persistence of the warrior's hegemonic status, despite the changes in the relationship between the individual and the collective, the citizen and the nation-state? In this ambivalent social context, how can the state create and maintain "armed masculinity" (Snyder 1999) as a normative social ideal? My aim in this article is to propose other, more subtle ways through which men are lured into fighting at a time when the link between the individual and the state is being transformed.

In the past few years, there has been a growing interest in militarized masculine bodies (Armitage 2003). The research in this field explores how the masculine civilian body is adapted to military use and demonstrates how, with the inculcation of military principles, the body is classified, transformed, and reshaped to meet military and state goals (Ben-Ari 1998; Higate 2003; Peniston-Bird 2003). I suggest that we should look at the connection between these transformative body techniques and the motivation or persuasion question posed by Kovitz, to analyze how specific constructions of militarized bodies lure men into fighting and thus serve the interests of the state. Based on in-depth interviews with combat soldiers, I argue that the construction of the Israeli combat soldier involves two seemingly opposing themes: on one hand, self-control, and on the other, thrill (in Hebrew, *rigush*). While the theme of self-control is characterized by introversion, self-restraint, and self-repression, the theme of thrill accentuates the outward expression of wild, unrestrained feelings, stemming from life-endangering events, adventurous activities, and unique opportunities the military offers for intimacy among men. These interdependent themes accentuate a growing sense of agency and self-actualization, thus allowing, and even promoting, their interpretation through an individualistic frame. The individualistic framing of bodily and emotional practices enables an ambivalent and nonpolitical interpretation of military actions, as it disguises the coercive nature of military service and obscures the collective state interests that are served by the individual male body.

THEORETICAL OVERVIEW: GENDERED BODY AND EMOTION MANAGEMENT

Social theories have shifted in the past two decades from emphasizing the cognitive dimension of identity construction to exploring the embodiment of identities (Shilling 1993, 3). The growing interest in the sociology of the body derives both from feminist thought, which highlighted women's bodies as the major political site of patriarchal domination (Bordo 1993), and from Foucault's (1975, 1978, 1980) writings, which enabled research on the "history of the body" and provided the outline for it.

Foucault's innovation lies in analyzing the body as produced by and existing in the discourses and social institutions that govern it. For Foucault (1975), the body is an object of power and a direct locus of social control. His ultimate example of the external construction of the body is the soldier, who, by the late eighteenth century, had "become something that can be made; out of formless clay, an inept body, the machine required can be constructed" (p. 135). The soldier's docile body serves to exemplify the link between daily practices on one hand and the large-scale organization of power on the other (Dreyfus and Rabinow 1982).

While Foucault's writings portrayed the body as a surface to be written on, other sociologists argue that one does not have to accept naturalistic or sociobiological views to acknowledge the body's materiality and corporeality, which always limit its range of possibilities. Frank, for example, proposes to analyze the body as constituted in the intersection of an equilateral triangle, the points of which are institutions, discourses,

and corporeality (Frank 1991, 48–49). Similarly, Shilling (1993, 12) conceptualizes the body as "an unfinished biological and social phenomena, which is transformed, within certain limits, as a result of its entry into and participation in society." Foucault himself, in his later writings, attributed more agency to the individual, suggesting that a theory of domination must start with the body dominating itself (Foucault 1978). Social analysis has thus expanded from studying the body as an object of social control and discipline "in order to legitimate different regimes of domination" (Bordo 1993; Foucault 1980) to perceiving the body as participating in its own shaping, as it creates meaning and performs social action (Davis 1997).

As a signifier of social identity, the body participates in the constitution of social inequalities. This is clear when we look at men's and women's bodies. Connell (1987) argued that by neglecting biological similarities and exaggerating biological differences, gendered practices create corporeal differences between men and women where none existed previously. These differences are then used to justify and legitimize the original hierarchal social categories.

Frank (1991) points to two types of bodies that can characterize the combat soldier: the disciplined body (pp. 54–61) and the dominating body (pp. 69–79). When the disciplined body, which "makes itself predictable through its regimentation" (p. 55), directs practices of discipline and control upon others, this body turns into the second type, the dominating body, which is, according to Frank, exclusively male. A prime example of the dominating body can be found in *Male Fantasies*, Theweleit's (1987–1989) rich description and analysis of masculinities constructed in the German Freikorps, an army unit that was formed at the end of World War I (soldiers in this unit later served in the SA and SS). For the German fascist, Theweleit argues, there existed only two types of bodies; the first was the erect, steel-hard, "organized machine" body of the German master. This controlled and emotionally bereft male warrior ideal reacts with revulsion and fear to the second body, the flaccid and fluid female body of the negative Other, lurking inside the male body.

As is obvious from this analysis, bodies and embodiment cannot be discussed in isolation from emotions, which are experienced through the body and shape the way we experience it (Csordas 1993). Similarly to the body, emotions "are treated as material things" (Lutz and White 1986, 407), as a universal aspect of human experience that is least subjected to social construction (Abu-Lughod and Lutz 1990, 1). However, the historical and cultural variability of emotions suggests that "subjective experiences and emotional beliefs are both socially acquired and socially structured" (Thoits 1989, 319; Rosaldo 1984). Emotions can thus be understood as *discursive practices*, which are "created in, rather than shaped by, speech" (Abu-Lughod and Lutz 1990, 10, 12).

As socially constructed *ideological practices*, emotions are always "involved in negotiation over the meaning of events, over rights and morality, over control of resources" (Lutz 1988, 5). Power relations determine what must, can, or cannot be said about the self and emotions; what is believed to be true or false about them; and what can only be said about them by certain individuals and not others. These "feeling rules" (Hochschild 1983) are always gendered; since women are believed to be "more emotional than men," any discourse on emotion is also a discourse on gender (Lutz 1988, 69). The masculine imperative for emotional self-control, which is especially pertinent to combat soldiers, confers men with prestige and locates them in a superior position to women. Emotional norms are thus produced by dominant institutional arrangements and function to sustain them (Thoits 1989, 328). This is particularly accurate when one examines "extreme" gender identities that are constituted by and for the state, identities such as warrior masculinity.

COMBAT MASCULINITY AND THE STATE

Military service, and especially warfare, is one of the primary means by which Western states established their power within societies (Tilly 1985; Giddens 1985). The link between war and state building is expressed in the republican ethos, which defines the subject's citizenship according to his (but not her) contribution to the state. In militaristic societies, the most significant contribution to the state is participating in the armed forces. This connection between military service and the state is based upon the glorification of militarized masculinity, with the soldier's body providing its material infrastructure.

Following the transition to voluntary professional armies in Western nation-states, the military lost some of its power to shape the meaning of citizenship. In Israel, however, the link between citizenship, military service, and masculinity carries a special meaning (Kimmerling 1993). War and routine conflict management have played a central role in shaping Israel's Jewish community of citizens, a community in which civic virtue is often constructed in terms of military virtue (Helman 1997). In this social context, the Jewish combat soldier has achieved the status of hegemonic masculinity,[2] which has become synonymous with good citizenship (Lomsky-Feder and Ben Ari 1999; Sasson-Levy 2003a). Although combat soldiers make up only 20 percent of the total complement (Cohen 1997, 86), the ideal of warrior masculinity is consensual, transcending ethnic, religious, and class boundaries (though not national ones).

War and military service are represented as enabling the male subject to "become a man" (Morgan 1994; Mosse 1996; Peniston-Bird 2003). Although the military should not be seen as constructing a single embodied masculinity (Barrett 1996; Enloe 1988; Higate 2003; Morgan 1994; Theweleit 1987–1989), theoretical literature on the combat soldier's identity tends to emphasize the single aspect of physical and emotional self-control (Arkin and Dubrofsky 1978; Ben-Ari 1998). War provides the opportunity to nurture the individual's ability to endure pain and even mutilation and to control emotion. Any sign of weakness, vulnerability, or even sensitivity can be interpreted in the military as a sign of homosexuality and, hence, of "failed masculinity" (Petersen 1998, 53).

The Israeli militarized body is fashioned according to a utopian collectivist and gendered ideology, emphasizing the "chosen body" of the healthy, strong, and active Jewish male (Weiss 2002). This "perfect" body, which in reality was the lot of only a select few, was seen as an ideal type, and comparisons with it generated a hierarchy of bodies, defining the boundaries of the collective and its internal stratification (see also Peniston-Bird 2003). The combat soldier—who possesses the perfect body—proves his masculinity through emotional self-control that is attained to cope with stress, anxiety, chaos, and confusion, all of which characterize the battlefield (Ben-Ari 1998, 42–46). As the schema of the battle is also a schema for achieving and reaffirming Jewish Israeli manhood (Ben-Ari 1998, 112), controlling one's emotions is perceived as successfully passing the test of masculinity.

My argument is that alongside the discourse of self-control and discipline, an additional discourse of thrill and excitement enacts and shapes the body and emotions of the warrior in different ways. The discourse of thrill is of critical importance, as it is emphasized by soldiers as a major force in mobilizing their motivation and willingness to go to war. Thrill plays an important role both in the discourse the army uses to lure men into soldiering and in the narratives of soldiers themselves. It appears, then, that even within the military cultural arena, which has been presented as the epitome of hegemonic top-down construction, there are signs of agency, where soldiers actively seek bodily and emotional experiences with which to constitute and assert themselves.

METHOD

This article is based on interviews with twenty male combat soldiers within one year of their release from army service: one artillery man, three infantry soldiers, three parachutists, four from the engineering corps, three from reconnaissance units, one from the navy, four from the armored forces, and one former combat intelligence officer.

Body practices and emotional management were not the main focus of the interviews. However, these issues were raised by the soldiers so often that I was forced to recognize their centrality in the military experience of the combat soldier. In comparison, noncombat soldiers whom I also interviewed (see Sasson-Levy 2003b) did not talk about body practices in the interviews at all.

It is important to note right from the start that there is no unified and universal version of "Israeli combat masculinity." The masculine model of the pilot, for example, is quite different from that of men in the armored forces, the navy, or the infantry brigades. Moreover, there are even differences between one infantry brigade and another. For instance, the masculinity of the paratroopers' unit in Israel emphasizes rationality, self-control, and self-discipline, while the men of the Golani infantry brigade accentuate resistance to discipline and rebelliousness along with physical capabilities and courage. These different masculine identities indicate that the act of fighting itself does not require one specific gendered ideology and that there is nothing "natural" or essential about the warrior's identity that derives from the act of fighting itself. Due to space limitations, this article cannot show the different nuances of armed masculinity in Israel and can only delineate its general contours.

BODILY AND EMOTIONAL SELF-CONTROL

Soldiering the Body

According to military belief, "masculinity is determined primarily by a healthy body, not a healthy mind" (Arkin and Dobrofsky 1978, 156). Having a masculine body that is healthy, strong, and sturdy is a prerequisite to becoming a combat soldier. However, having the right body is insufficient; one must also be willing to shape and discipline it so that it meets military objectives. Therefore, the tests for combat units (held a few months before enlistment) examine both the physical abilities of adolescent boys and their willingness to stretch these capacities to the limits. Yonatan, who served in the prestigious air force rescue unit, explained, "In basic training, you receive all your credit through physical activity alone. The minute you're physically inactive [if you're injured], you're a leper, you're a leech, you're a parasite, and you're good for nothing."[3]

In other interviews, soldiers repeatedly emphasized the theme of self-control over their bodies. To be more precise, the men did not talk about self-control as much as they described their struggles to achieve control over their bodies. Eldad, a tank commander, explained,

> During long marches, the strain would push people into screaming at each other, really cursing one another; their legs would hurt and they'd feel that this is the end, that they'd reached their limit, and then they would see that they could stretch that limit a little further. This exercise teaches them that the limit is not where they thought it was but always a little further.

Basic training is devoted to forging and strengthening the male body, to taking it to new extremes. At the same time, it inscribes on the body the signs of one's specific combat role. Through the specific body management of each unit, the soldiers shape a new military identity. Simple daily activities such as walking, eating, and sitting assume a new form and meaning. Guy, an infantry soldier in an elite unit, vividly described the unique bodily dimensions of each unit, even during supposedly "passive" activities such as platoon talks:

> We would see the other platoons, sitting relaxed and talking to their commanders. But in my unit, we would have to sit absolutely straight, our gun upright and hands stretched straight in front of the body. The talk could last forty-five minutes, or an hour, but if a fly zooms by your eyes and you take your hand off your rifle to shoo the fly away, you pay. You start running, and running, and running.

Guy's description of his unit's specific style demonstrates how military thinking and culture are transmitted through the body and imprinted on it (Foucault 1975). His quote alludes to the central role of the body in military punishment. As one of the main mechanisms for discipline, punishment is often inflicted directly on the body, through recurring "stretcher hikes," carrying heavy loads, crawling on thorns, doing dozens of push-ups or hundreds of sit-ups, and more. Physical punishment inscribes on the soldier's body the fear of military discipline and the dread of authority, until he internalizes military principles and they become a part of who he is. Thus, formal homogenization processes, such as uniforms and haircuts, are accompanied by violent mechanisms that aim at creating a standardized combatant male body.

Foucault (1975, 138) argued that "the military apparatus explores and studies the soldier's body in order to break it down and rearrange it according to its needs." Indeed, at the end of basic training, if the soldier completes it "in one piece" (and not all do), he has a body capable of things it was not capable of before; he has built the "body of a soldier." Dudi, an officer in the combat engineering corps, said,

> I never understood how it works, but after you're in the army for about a year, all these problems vanish. I don't know why, but I guess the body adjusts somehow. As a commander, I would carry things much heavier than during basic training, and I would say to myself that this is it, you just get used to it. I guess that just as the soles of your feet are getting rough, the skin on your back also gets rough at a certain stage.

The thick skin that Dudi develops "should not be understood metaphorically" (Theweleit 1987–1989, 144). The physical transformation bears institutional implications: as the soldier ceases to experience his body's pain or hunger as his own (Frank 1991, 56), soldiering becomes easier and more tolerable. Now, the soldier can better meet the needs of the state.

Bodily Masculinity Rites

The transformation of a body into a "soldier's body" has an unmistakable gendered meaning. Through the soldiering "body project" (Connell 1995, 50), men's bodies become visibly different from those of women. In this sense, the soldier's embodiment plays a central role in the social construction of polarized gender identities and hierarchal gender regimes (Connell 1987). While intense physical strain prepares soldiers for combat conditions, it also serves as a selection mechanism and a rite of passage into Israeli hegemonic masculinity.

Service in the Israeli military is seen as the primary rite of passage that initiates adolescent boys into full membership in the masculine Zionist civil religion (Aronoff 1999; Mazali 1993; Levy-Schreiber and Ben-Ari 2000). Reuven's description of crucial moments during basic training indicates that the body is the main arena for these militarized rites of passage:

> The procedure is you get into the shooting position; you have to remain firm so that nothing moves you. We would get into shooting position, stand in line, and the officer . . . the bastard . . . he would come and kick us in the knees, the chest, the muscles of the legs, and we're supposed to stand firm, not to move, the muscles all tight . . . all your strength is invested in holding the weapon so that when he kicks you again it won't move you and won't make you shoot off-target.
>
> If I moved . . . did you notice my eye's reflex action? If that would have happened to me then it would have been a sign that I was frightened and that would have meant I was finished. He would have grabbed me by the shoulders and kneed me in the gut. He would beat me to a pulp.

Recall Spencer's (1965, 103) description of rites of passage through public circumcision by the Samburu: "Each youth, placed on view before his male relatives and prospective in-laws, must remain motionless and silent during the cutting. Even an involuntary twitch would be interpreted as a sign of fear." The similarities between the two descriptions of rites of passage—one in an African culture, the other in a seemingly modern western culture—are self-evident. In the same way, parachuting in the Israeli army is viewed as "a test which allows those who pass it to join an exclusive club, to be initiated into an elite group" (Aran 1974, 150).

Soldiers who go through military hardships intuitively understand that those who withstand them will achieve elite status. As hardship becomes the mark of masculinity, soldiers not only expect to suffer in basic training but are also proud of it and reiterate this in the interviews, as if to validate their hegemonic status (see also Gill 1997). Moreover, most combat soldiers complete basic training with various physical afflictions, some of which will never disappear. Military casualties are often the most dramatic claim to centrality in Israeli society (Aronoff 1999, 42). Therefore, the soldiers are proud of their wounds and scars, which serve as evidence of their willingness to sacrifice their bodies for the good of the collective.

The combat body project not only creates hierarchal gender differences, however, but also stratifies male bodies. The "chosen body" (Weiss 2002) of the combat soldier depends on the existence of the wrong body, the body that fails to become a combat soldier. The literature often specifies female or homosexual bodies as representative of the "wrong" military body. However, the soldiers I talked to did not compare themselves to women or homosexuals but mostly to other male heterosexual soldiers who had failed to endure the physical training—that is, the fat soldier, the lazy soldier, the "crybaby," or the soldier who is too small. As Robert Connell (1995, 75) notes, masculinity is a relational identity that is often constructed in relation to other masculinities. Michael Kimmel quotes the playwright David Mamet, saying, "Women have, in men's minds, such a low place on the social ladder . . . that it's useless to define yourself in terms of a woman. What man needs is men's approval" (Kimmel 1996, 7).

This self-comparison among men is, for Connell (1995), the reason behind most acts of violence. Most episodes of major violence are transactions among men, used as a means of drawing boundaries and making exclusions (Connell 1995, 83). Violence can become a way of claiming or asserting masculinity in struggles between groups. This is obvious in the attitudes of combat soldiers to those of their peers who do not meet the hegemonic model of masculinity.

Among those who fail the tests, the fat soldier is especially prone to abuse. The overweight soldier represents the opposite of "everything military." Omer, the tank driver, told the following story, which demonstrates the moral threat embodied in the fat soldier's body:

> We wouldn't let soldiers weep during punishments. We had this fat soldier, Danny. He would cry as a matter of principle, whether or not it was difficult. I remember that fatso starting to put on a show as if he was throwing up. I told him, "Hey, watch it, I'm warning you. Shut up," I told him, "You're crying like a little girl."

Danny, the antihero of this story, is doubly wrong—he is fat and cries. The other soldiers are angry with him because they see him as a spoiled, childish liar—all the characteristics that represent for them the opposite of manhood— but also because they worry that his behavior will reflect negatively on them. "It projects on all of us," Omer said. "We wanted to be seen as good guys, the best team." Those who have the wrong body present a threat to the masculinity of the whole group, a threat to social solidarity, and therefore, they constitute a legitimate target for ostracism, ridicule, and abuse. Thus, militarized initiation rites may produce group bonding, solidarity, and coherence (Winslow 1999), but they also create and maintain hierarchical differences among men.

Emotional Control

The perception of emotional control as a signifier of masculinity and hence of higher status (Lutz 1988) is not unique to the Israeli context. Emotional control has been associated with masculinity in Western culture from the early writings of the Greek philosophers through Kant, Descartes, and Hegel (Ortner 1974; Lloyd 1986). In their writings, men's emotional self-control (in other words, the emphasis on reason) signifies superiority (Seidler 1989) and is used to arrange and justify gendered hierarchies. Militarized masculinities seem particularly "obsessed" with emotional control. The Israeli combat soldier refers to emotional control or composure (in Hebrew, *kor ruach*—literally, "coolness of spirit"; Ben-Ari 1998, 45) as a personal and professional masculine achievement, an ideal that should be adopted by all soldiers. Kor ruach, which refers to the ability to act with confidence, poise, and composure under trying circumstances (Ben-Ari 1998, 45), is perceived as a key element of effective performance in day-to-day situations and especially in times of crisis. Alon, a tank commander, said, "Eventually, I became a better commander, more professional, and more understanding. I mean, I became better at commanding with composure: they shoot at us and I remain composed, a soldier tries to commit suicide and I remain composed." Alon describes a process by which he gradually achieves composure. This is important because he equates composure with successfully performing as an officer and considers it a criterion for evaluating competence. Similarly to Alon, other soldiers I talked to also did not perceive emotional self-control as a given masculine characteristic. Rather, they described it as an attribute that one learns, acquires, and perfects as one develops into a more professional soldier (and by extension, "more of a man"). Rami, a combat medic, described how the military creates this composure during the medics' course. Note how he links emotional composure to hypermasculinity:

> [In the medics course,] you come in, play with the dog, it wags its tail and all that, and a minute later, you see him in pieces like in a butcher's shop. It's this kind of act, which says, "I'm macho. I'm not afraid of blood." They want to get you to a certain threshold, so they show you pictures of horrible things. Victims of accidents, smashed limbs, smashed people. They show this to you so that you get accustomed to all this kind of stuff.

While the military applauds emotional self-control and develops mechanisms for teaching and even enforcing it, it would not be accurate to say that the army forbids all emotional expression. Rather, there seems to be an unwritten social and spatial "emotional mapping," similar to Hochschild's (1983, 18) "emotional rules," that dictates which emotions are allowed, when, where, and for what audience. Soldiers are encouraged, for example, to feel motivation and ambition; they can express happiness and pride on the day they complete basic training or more advanced courses; they are allowed to feel homesick (but only to a limited degree); and they are expected to feel desire for women. Most of all, they are supposed to feel affection and camaraderie toward other soldiers in the unit, an emotion that the army creates and exploits (and to which I will return later).

However, the demand for emotional self-control is often loaded with internal contradictions and paradoxical effects. First, acquiring emotional self-control facilitates the soldier's "automatic docility" (Foucault 1975), as it ensures that the soldier will not rebel or be paralyzed by fear in combat. By guaranteeing a high level of obedience and passivity, the imperative of emotional self-discipline provides a solid base for the constitution of the conformist citizen. However, paradoxically, the docility of the "good citizen" is experienced by the soldier as increased self-control and heightened masculinity. Thus, compulsory military service contributes to the disciplining of the citizen and reproduces the association between rational and restrained masculinity (Seidler 1989) and the interests of the state.

The second paradox relates to the fact that although power and control are perceived as central to the definition of *combat masculinity*, in reality, the combat soldier has only a limited degree of autonomy. To become a combat soldier, one must surrender one's autonomy and obey one's commanders for the major part of everyday life. Amos, a paratrooper, expressed this paradox when he explained how he survived basic training: "You simply have to say O.K., you, the army, can do whatever you want with me. I . . . in the end, I will make it. Even if I'm the last one, I will get there and succeed." When Amos says, "You can do whatever you want with me," we learn that the power and control of the combat soldier are paradoxically achieved by surrendering control over the self. Moreover, giving up autonomy is

not a passive project. On the contrary, the soldier needs to mobilize all his willpower to get through his seemingly endless training and to gain control over his body and emotions. Obedience is associated here with strenuous effort, hard physical work, and a strong will. Stiehm observed that "patriarchy promises power and benefits to the young men who ultimately prove themselves. But is that proof one of talent, of merit or of morality? No. It is, in fact, proof of submission. It is evidence of obedience. It is a demonstration of compliance and of willingness to risk and sometimes sacrifice" (Stiehm 1989, 227). As a reward for their strenuous efforts to attain physical and emotional self-control, soldiers are given the opportunity to experience physical and emotional thrill, which is regarded as an exclusive experience of combat soldiers.

THRILL

While most of the literature focuses on the theme of self-control, a second, and apparently contradictory, theme of thrill (in Hebrew, *rigush*—or "rush" in American slang) appeared time and again in the soldiers' narratives. Rigush implies intense feelings, both emotional and physical, that derive from extraordinary experiences that are perceived as inaccessible in everyday life. While militarized masculinity demands emotional control, military life nonetheless provides unique opportunities for experiencing the extraordinarily deep feeling of rigush.

The major source of rigush is the risk to one's life involved in being a combat soldier. Israeli culture imparts the heroic notion of self-sacrifice to Israeli males from early childhood. Even at this age, children are exposed to themes of persecution, heroism, and war, which recur throughout the year. Aronoff, for instance, claims that the memorialization of the dead soldier is so central in Israeli culture that it has evolved into a "national cult of the dead" (Aronoff 1999, 43). Although the ethos of self-sacrifice has been modified in the past twenty years (Zerubavel 1995), it still constitutes a major part of the combat soldiers' narratives. Dudi, a platoon commander in the combat engineering corps, explained,

> Do I think the army makes a man out of the boy? Look, it all depends on where you serve. The army turns a child into a man only if he serves in a combat unit. There you have to deal with issues of life and death, you get a sense of proportion concerning what life is all about, and you understand what is real in life. But I don't think the army makes men out of everybody. If you were in the units where I served, or in the infantry, or even in the armored corps or artillery [then it does], but the rest of the units—I can't guarantee it.

For Dudi, masculinity is directly associated with confronting issues of life and death and is achieved through facing the biggest test of all: the willingness to sacrifice one's life for one's country. Self-sacrifice is the sign of the hero, he who has the courage to rise above his basic instinct for life and fight for the good of his imagined community. Serving as a combat soldier provides one of the very few chances in life to receive recognition for heroism, which is a source of honor and thrill in itself. Endangering one's life is seen by soldiers as the ultimate actualization of both masculinity and nationality, and thus, it serves as a criterion in social and military stratification systems (Weiss 2002; E. Levy 1998; Lomsky-Feder 1998). Soldiers perceive life-threatening events as rewards in and of themselves, a source of gratifying rigush. This is what Alon, the tank commander, said about it:

> When we were in Lebanon, they shot at me lots of times. It gives you a feeling of gratification. To my mom, it sounded dumb, but I felt gratified. Because when they shoot at you, you feel the best in the world. Whether you returned fire or not, it doesn't matter. The minute they shoot at you, you already feel satisfaction. Why? Because your life was at risk. . . . It's a special feeling, reserved only for combat soldiers.

The Lebanon war (1982–2000) was perceived by many Israelis as a war of choice rather than a war of self-defense, and it was therefore a bone

of contention in Israeli society, a cause for demonstrations and political strife. Alon and his friends, however, interpreted their combat experience in Lebanon as an adventurous and thrilling way to actualize their masculinity and seldom talked about the political meanings and ramifications of their service.

Somewhat different voices were heard when the soldiers talked about serving in the occupied territories, where they were primarily fighting against civilians. There, the soldiers were more aware of the political meanings of their military service and expressed moral doubts. Yet only a tiny minority of soldiers refused to serve in the territories, an act which had the potential to modify the link between masculinity and self-sacrifice in Israel (Helman 1997).

Only three of the combat soldiers whom I interviewed spoke out explicitly against the collective ethos of risking one's life. Eli, from the Nachal infantry brigade, said,

> Look, most of the soldiers that were killed were from *Giva'ati* [another infantry brigade]. In my brigade, people didn't like getting killed. We liked the good life, we liked doing things wisely. If you ask people honestly if they want to fight, without the pretence of the other guys, they'll say no.

Yoram, a soldier in the prestigious bomb squad unit, reached the same conclusion but only during a long trip abroad after his release from the army. Apparently, his long stay outside of Israel enabled his estrangement, lending a new perspective to his role as combat soldier:

> When I was in South America, I became very, very antimilitaristic. I had thoughts I never had before. . . . I asked myself: Do I really want to die for my country? Am I really prepared to die for my country? No way. What kind of twisted thinking is that? I've only got one life, what good will it do if I . . . what good will it do me?

Yoram and Eli represent an alternative perspective. They do not see life-endangering events as exciting and prestigious goals in their own right. By disclaiming the ethos of self-sacrifice, they abrogate the connection between masculinity and risking one's life. However, they reflect the opinions of only a small minority of combat soldiers; furthermore, they continue to serve as combat soldiers when called to reserve duty.[4]

A second source of militarized thrill lies in having control over weapons and technology. Sally Hacker (1989) has pointed out that basic pleasure is gained from the ability to operate complicated technological instruments. This widespread masculine fascination with technology (Morgan 1994, 173) seems to increase when it involves weaponry, which is linked to control, hierarchy, prestige, and power over others.

Rami, a combat medic in the armored corps, described an officer giving the command to open fire:

> You see the armored regiment commander waging a war with his words. . . . It's a crazy male act, wacko machoism. He utters these few phrases, and then he lets them go, as if letting go of their reins, or as if he's lifting the gate at the horse race, and you see forty tanks fire at once. . . . You cannot but be impressed.

Rami associates the enjoyment of warfare technologies with domination and hypermasculinity. Note the sexual undercurrent in his choice of metaphor of "letting go of the horses at the race." Hacker (1989) has pointed out illuminating parallels between technology and eroticism: both inscribe feelings on the body through kinesthetic experience, the pleasure in both is shaped by domination and control, and both are defined predominantly by men and are stratified by gender. When the soldiers express the "near orgasmic excitement of nighttime explosions" (Morgan 1994, 173), technologies of destruction become erotic in and of themselves (Hacker 1989, 46–55). Indeed, describing weapons in terms of sexual metaphors is by now utterly clichéd, but soldiers do it often, especially when talking about the actual act of shooting. Eli, an infantry soldier who was earlier quoted expressing his rejection of the ethos of sacrifice and military values, admitted that he enjoys shooting:

> Why do I like shooting? I don't know, I can't even explain to myself what I love about it. But it's both something physical, and something you can see. It's real, it moves. And there are very close and immediate measures of success. And maybe it's also the feeling, of, ha . . . [sexual] relief.

This "peculiar masculine eroticism of technology" (Hacker 1989, 46) was reiterated by many soldiers when referring to rifles, tanks, or hand grenades, again turning a blind eye to the violent and destructive effects of the technologies of war.

A third source of excitement was the unique feeling of youthful adventure that characterizes combat life. "If you like action, you'll love [military] service in the territories," said Guy.[5] In a similar way, Alon only saw "fun" in the occupied city of Hebron, where forty-two thousand Palestinians are bullied and intimidated by five hundred extremist rightwing Jewish settlers:

> In Hebron, we would go wherever we felt like. We'd raise hell. They'd throw stones, shoot at you, and throw things at you. What a mess. It's just paradise for those who like this kind of thing. It was the most action you could get.

Ofer, an officer from the engineering corps, said explicitly, "I love action. Action itself. Once, I didn't sleep for three days because I couldn't bear the thought that something would happen and I wouldn't be there."

The excitement of dangerous situations is felt in the body itself, in the tone of the muscles, the heartbeat, and the bloodstream. Parachuting, for example, which involves both exhilaration and fear, "brings men into a state of trance, a sort of ecstasy" (Aran 1974, 125, 131). This is a unique emotional "perk" that the military offers to combat soldiers. They feel that they are "alive," their bodies, emotions, and senses all exposed and active. "I was willing to die for the thrill," said a soldier in an interview with a daily newspaper (Alon 1998, 22).

> True, in bungee jumping or car racing, one can also experience an emotional and physiological rush associated with achieving and proving hypermasculinity. But the differences between bungee

jumping and combat are not trivial. First, combat is more dangerous as it is connected to real risks to one's life, and second, one does not enter it out of choice—it is always linked to the interests of the state. Its significance, then, is always beyond the individual.

The last source of excitement, albeit an unspoken one, is military homosociality (Sedgwick 1985). Military service provides rare legitimacy for physical and emotional intimacy among men, including homoerotic sensations, without the stigma of homosexuality. Yoram, from the bomb squad, explained,

> It was in the army that all the barriers about physical contact between men came down. In the army, there is always touching. You walk together, shower together, you touch, you live, everything together. I think most people in the army touch each other. I really can't explain it. Maybe it's because it's so tough in the army, so you slap each other and it helps; it feels good.

The soldiers' narratives on men's bonding in the military reveal the contradictions inherent within combat masculinity. While hegemonic masculinity does not allow for emotional expressiveness, it does create specific areas in which physical and emotional intimacy among men is allowed and even encouraged. This intimacy, known as "camaraderie in arms," is a significant motif in Israel's heroic epics and is conveyed to Israeli youth long before they enlist into the army. Camaraderie in arms is described in Israeli culture (through popular songs, canonical prose and poetry, and Memorial Day rituals, for instance) as a lifelong relationship that flourishes despite social or political differences. Research among eighteen-year-old boys found that they rank camaraderie in arms as one of the main motivating factors for enlisting to combat units (E. Levy 1998, 263). The perception of camaraderie as a significant reward for military service (Lieblich 1989) is reflected in the words of Oren Abman, an infantry lieutenant colonel, who was quoted in the newspaper as saying, "The amazing intimacy that is created among men after combat, the affection they express for each other, it may sound strange to you, but it doesn't exist even in sex" (Becker 2000). Abman creates a hierarchy whereby the bond between warriors is superior to any relationship with a woman. Ofer, from the engineering corps, added,

> [It's] freezing cold, everybody is hugging and huddling under the covers with each other. No problem. These are the fun parts of the army that you remember later, and you miss them. It's all so natural, there's nothing sexual in these relationships. Even today, I don't hug everyone I bump into on the street, but if he's an army buddy, then yes, I'll hug him.
> The fraternity I told you about—hugging an army buddy but not another guy—it couldn't happen with women.

Ofer proclaims an exclusive link between male intimacy and combat life, but he hastens to reject any homoerotic interpretation of this relationship, thus reinforcing the centrality of heterosexuality in the construction of hegemonic masculinity. Apparently, the social license for male intimacy is only awarded to combat soldiers (and football players), probably because they have already proven their masculinity beyond any doubt (Chapkis 1988). Noncombat soldiers, on the other hand, often talk with envy about warriors' camaraderie, which they missed out on by not serving in combat units.

By marking the uniqueness of the combat soldier, camaraderie in arms creates an exclusive, imagined community of warriors, a community that embodies "the essence of Israeliness" (Helman 1997). This masculine community is based on inner unity and homogeneity and connects the individual with the state. At the same time, the mutual commitment among men serves to draw hierarchal boundaries between those who are entitled to belong to dominant groups and those who will never be able to, namely, women, Palestinian citizens of Israel, and lower class noncombat soldiers.

DISCUSSION: THE INDIVIDUAL BODY AND THE COLLECTIVE STATE

As we have seen, the management of the Israeli combat soldier's body and emotions merges two seemingly contradictory themes: self-control and thrill. This combination creates someone who ostensibly has the agency to take charge of his destiny—a man who can control his body and emotions—and dares to take risks and enjoys them. Thus, the combination of self-control and thrill accentuates values of autonomy and self-actualization, which call for an individualistic frame of interpretation.

The individualization of military practices leads soldiers to interpret their military experience in ambivalent and nonpolitical terms. For example, in the interviews, soldiers often framed their growing obedience to military discipline as increasing physical and emotional self-control, which created a strong sense of agency and empowerment. As we saw in the soldiers' quotations, life-endangering events were perceived as unique and rewarding opportunities for self-actualization. The strict surveillance typical of military life was interpreted as their own choice and sometimes even as a privilege, a sign of the intensity of their specific combative "trials of manhood" (Ben-Ari 1998). The authoritarian principles and practices of the military are thus disguised as belonging to, and even as promoting, an individualistic discourse.

The individualization of the soldier's body can be seen as an expression of the effects of globalization on Israeli society. One primary effect of globalization in the cultural sphere is the permeation of consumerist values, which present self-fulfillment as a prime social virtue (Shafir and Peled 1998; Ram 1999). In a consumerist society, with its focus on the individual, cultivation of the masculine body is seen, for the first time in Israeli history, as no less legitimate than the cultivation of the feminine body. Military bodily transformation, which involves strenuous efforts, can be framed in this context as a personal choice that brings prestige. Thus, the

soldier's identity is not that of the Spartan, who is willing to sacrifice himself for the good of the collective. Rather, it can be seen as an individual effort to improve oneself, a masculine personal achievement of self-actualization.

When military combat service is framed in an individualistic discourse, it turns out to have a dual, ambivalent nature. This duality in the perception of the military blurs the boundaries between choice and compulsion, and the coercive nature of military service becomes obscured. This dual nature of military experience enables mandatory conscription to be perceived as voluntary and fulfilling (Y. Levy 1993). In fact, only volunteers can serve in the most prestigious, dangerous, and secretive units. Thus, voluntarism becomes a status symbol in itself. At the same time, voluntarism conceals the military disciplining of Israel's body of citizens.

Likewise, the "individual" nexus of self-control and thrill masks the price entailed by combat masculinity and conceals its repressive nature. Current research has pointed at some of the mental and physical injuries suffered by combat soldiers, but since I interviewed only soldiers who served their full terms of three years as combat soldiers, I could not expose the more brutal damages of combat military service, such as physical and emotional disability. Most soldiers who encounter serious emotional difficulties do not stay in combat courses, and at times, they are exempt from service altogether. Thus, the voices of the soldiers who did not conform to the norm are missing, as are the voices of the mentally impaired or those suffering posttraumatic symptoms. It is these injured and distressed soldiers who pay the high price for the image of the ideal of combat masculinity in Israel.

Furthermore, as noted earlier, when soldiers perceive their militaristic activities as masculine self-actualization, they can ignore their moral and political consequences. The individualistic interpretation of military endeavors enables the soldier to overlook the evils that are often carried out in the name of combat masculinity. Thus, the individualistic framing allows for the perpetuation of

Israel's militant aggressive policies, in particular the nearly forty-year-long occupation of the West Bank and (until recently) the Gaza Strip.

Therefore, the individualized body and emotion management of the combat soldier serves the symbolic and pragmatic interests of the state, as it reinforces and reproduces the cooperation between hegemonic masculinity and Israeli militarism: young men are still willing to kill and be killed for the good of their country but now in the name of individualized dominant masculinity. It is the individual body that functions as the instrument of the militaristic state. The gendering of the soldier's body turns out to be a control mechanism that encourages young men to go to war and risk their lives.

Individualism here is harnessed for the good of the collective and is hence an instrument that creates, in a roundabout way, collectivism and obedience to the state. The soldier's autonomy and individualism are a kind of illusion, a facade, because as the body of the soldier is transformed, he becomes part of the state. His body is the material superstructure that links the (male) individual to the state.

I claim that the combat soldier is "marked" as an idealized figure that others cannot emulate. Levy-Schreiber and Ben-Ari (2000), for example, follow Connell (1987, 85) in claiming that through military body practices, state power becomes naturalized, as if it belongs to the order of nature. I argue to the contrary: through military body practices, the soldier's power becomes unique and visible; the body belongs to the order of nation, signifying the link between manhood and nationhood. Through specific gendered body practices, and their relation with the nation-state, particular male bodies become more significant than others (Petersen 1998, 42). When the body of the adolescent boy turns into the muscular and brave body of the combat soldier, this transformation marks him with an air of heroism and masculinity, the signs of devotion and contribution to the state. His uniform, posture, walk, muscle tone, facial expression, and manner of speech, all signal both self-control and anticipation of the rare thrill of combat. This body provides the combat soldier with a physical presence that many Israelis claim they can identify even from afar. The soldier's body becomes a focus for public identification, a source of national pride, and a locus of sympathy and support. The signs of the nation are inscribed on the body, and the soldier's body becomes the symbol of the nation. This national symbol provides a common, consensual symbol around which a Jewish Israeli imagined community gathers—a symbol that is both masculine and militarized. Nationality, that unseen, imagined quality, receives a public visual expression in the body of the soldier. Thus, the body of the combat soldier is signified by the mark of the nation and serves as a signifier of the gendered nation-state.

NOTES

1. Others modify this statement, arguing that the collective ethos has been replaced by two contesting ideologies that crystallized as the major alternatives for future development. The first ideology is a neo-Zionist ethnonationalism (Ram 1999, Shafir and Peled 1998), which characterizes the lower classes and the religious groups. This ideology elevates the exclusionary Jewish collectivity and its motherland, rather than the Israeli state, as a political community defined by common citizenship (Ram 1999, 333–35). The second, competing ideology is a liberal-individual-oriented post-Zionist one (Ram 1999; Shafir and Peled 1998). Held by the secular, mostly Ashkenazi middle class and the Israeli Palestinians, this sensibility values individual rights more highly than collective glory. In sharp contrast to neo-Zionism, it is less national, considering the collectivity as a tool for the welfare of the individual (Ram 1999, 333).

2. Evidence of the soldier's dominant status is found in various studies that indicate that young men (and most women) rank the combat soldier at the top of social and military hierarchies (E. Levy 1998; Sasson-Levy 2000). Applications for various prestigious combat units exceed available places by a ratio of eight to one (Cohen 1997, 107). Combat soldiers receive higher salaries during military service and enjoy a range of privileges after their release. For example, they are entitled to academic scholarships

and grants that are not available to noncombat soldiers. In the economic and political realms, Israeli ex-colonels still enjoy immense power, as is clear from their growing presence in Israeli governments. In the cultural sphere, the consensual esteem for the combat soldier is reflected in the many commercials that use his image to sell anything from cell phones and medical insurance to laundry detergent and cream cheese. Noncombat soldiers, on the other hand, do not feature in commercials and are rarely represented in the media at all (E. Levy 1998).

3. All names have been changed to protect the soldiers' privacy.

4. Real resistance, however, is not to be found among combat soldiers. Young Israeli men who resist the warrior ethos either make a special effort not to serve in combat roles or refuse to serve in the army altogether, for ideological or personal reasons. In refusing to serve, they express dissension over the essence of the warrior ethos and rejection of the militarized nature of hegemonic Jewish Israeli masculinity. The majority, however, still strongly support compulsory military service in general and the warrior ethos in particular (Lomsky-Feder and Ben-Ari 1999; Cohen 1997).

5. All the soldiers interviewed used the English word action in their Hebrew speech.

REFERENCES

Abu-Lughod, L., and C. A. Lutz. 1990. Introduction: Emotion, discourse, and the politics of everyday life, In *Language and the politics of emotion*, edited by C. A. Lutz and L. Abu-Lughod, 1–23. Cambridge, UK: Cambridge University Press.

Addelston, J., and M. Stirratt. 1996. The last bastion of masculinity. In *Masculinities in organizations*, edited by C. Cheng, 54–76. Thousand Oaks, CA: Sage.

Alon, M. 1998. Perhaps the I.D.F. prefers its heroes dead? [Hebrew] *Yediot Aharonot*, November 27.

Aran, G. 1974. Parachuting. *American Journal of Sociology* 80(1): 124–53.

Arkin, W., and L. R. Dubrofsky. 1978. Military socialization and masculinity. *Journal of Social Issues* 34(1): 151–69.

Armitage, J. 2003. Militarized bodies: An introduction. *Body and Society* 9(4): 1–12.

Aronoff, M. 1999. Wars as catalysts of political and cultural change. In *The military and militarism in Israeli society*, edited by E. Lomsky-Feder and E. Ben-Ari, 37–57. Albany: State University of New York Press.

Barrett, F. 1996. The organizational construction of hegemonic masculinity: The case of the U.S. navy. *Gender, Work and Organization* 3(3): 129–42.

Becker, A. 2000. The last ones on the ridge [Hebrew]. *Ha'aretz weekend supplement*, June 16, pp. 76–80.

Ben-Ari, E. 1998. *Mastering soldiers*. New York: Berghan.

Bordo, S. 1993. *Unbearable weight*. Berkeley: University of California Press.

Burk, J. 1995. Citizenship status and military service: The quest for inclusion by minorities and conscientious objectors. *Armed Forces and Society* 21(4): 503–29.

Chapkis, W. 1988. Sexuality and militarism. In *Women and the military system*, edited by E. Isaksson, 106–13. New York: St. Martin's.

Cohen, S. 1997. Towards a new portrait of the (new) Israeli soldier. *Israeli Affairs* 3(3/4): 77–117.

Comaroff, J. L. 1996. Ethnicity, nationalism, and the politics of difference in an age of revolution. In *The politics of difference: Ethnic premises in a world of power*, edited by E. N. Wilmsen and P. McAllister. Chicago: University of Chicago Press.

Connell, R. W. 1987. *Gender and power: Society, the person and sexual politics*. Stanford, CA: Stanford University Press.

———. 1995. *Masculinities*. Berkeley: University of California Press.

Csordas, J. T. 1993. Somatic modes of attention. *Cultural Anthropology* 8(2): 135–56.

Davis, K. 1997. Embodying theory: Beyond modernist and postmodernist reading of the body. In *Embodied practices: Feminist perspectives on the body*, edited by K. Davis, 1–23. London: Sage.

Dreyfus, H., and P. Rabinow. 1982. *Michel Foucault: Beyond structuralism and hermeneutics*. Sussex, UK: Harvester.

Enloe, C. 1980. *Ethnic soldiers: State security in divided society*. Athens: University of Georgia Press.

———. 1988. *Does khaki become you?* London: Pandora.

Foucault, M. 1975. *Discipline and punishment: The birth of the prison*. New York: Vintage.

———. 1978. *The history of sexuality*. New York: Vintage.

———. 1980. *Power/knowledge*. New York: Pantheon.

Frank, A. W. 1991. For sociology of the body: An analytical review. In *The body*, edited by M. Featherstone, M. Hepworth, and B. S. Turner, 36–102. London: Sage.

Furman, M. 1999. Army and war: Collective narratives of early childhood in contemporary Israel. In *The military and militarism in Israeli society*, edited by E. Lomski-Feder and E. Ben-Ari, 141–69. New York: State University of New York Press.

Giddens, A. 1985. *The nation-state and violence*. Berkeley: University of California Press.

Gill, L. 1997. Creating citizens, making men: The military and masculinity in Bolivia. *Cultural Anthropology* 12(4): 527–50.

Hacker, S. 1989. *Pleasure, power and technology: Some tales of gender, engineering and the cooperative workplace*. Boston, MA: Unwin Hyman.

Helman, S. 1997. Militarism and the construction of community. *Journal of Political and Military Sociology* 25:305–32.

Higate, P. 2003. *Military masculinities: Identity and the state*. Westport, CT: Praeger.

Hochschild, A. 1983. *The managed heart: The commercialization of human feeling*. Berkeley: University of California Press.

Horowitz, D., and M. Lissak. 1989. *Troubles in utopia: The overburdened polity of Israel*. Albany: State University of New York Press.

Janowitz, M. 1994. Military institutions and citizenship in Western societies. In *Citizenship*, edited by B. Turner and P. Hamilton. London: Routledge.

Kimmel, M. 1996. *Manhood in America*. New York: Free Press.

Kimmerling, B. 1993. Patterns of militarism in Israel. *European Journal of Sociology* 34:196–223.

Kovitz, M. 2003. The roots of military masculinity. In *Military masculinities: Identities and state*, edited by P. Higate, 1–14. Westport, CT: Praeger.

Levy, E. 1998. Heroes and helpmates: Militarism, gender and national belonging in Israel. PhD diss., University of California, Irvine.

Levy, Y. 1993. The role of the military sphere in constructing the social-political order in Israel [Hebrew]. PhD diss., Tel Aviv University.

Levy-Schreiber, E., and E. Ben-Ari. 2000. Body building, character building and nation-building: Gender and military service in Israel. *Studies in Contemporary Judaism* 16:171–90.

Lieblich, A. 1989. *Transition to adulthood during military service: The Israeli case*. Albany: State University of New York Press.

Lloyd, G. 1986. Selfhood, war and masculinity. In *Feminist challenges: Social and political theory*, edited by C. Pateman and E. Gross, 63–76. Boston: Northeastern University Press.

Lomsky-Feder, E. 1998. *As if there was no war: The perception of war in the life stories of Israeli men* [Hebrew]. Jerusalem: Magnes.

Lomsky-Feder, E., and E. Ben-Ari, eds. 1999. *The military and militarism in Israeli society*. Albany: State University of New York Press.

Lutz, C. 1988. *Unnatural emotions*. Chicago: Chicago University Press.

Lutz, C., and G. White. 1986. The anthropology of emotions. *Annual Review of Anthropology* 15:405–36.

Mazali, R. 1993. Military service as initiation rite. *Challenge* IV(4): 36–7.

Morgan, D. H. J. 1994. Theatre of war: Combat, the military and masculinities. In *Theorizing masculinities*, edited by H. Brod and M. Kaufman, 165–83. London: Sage.

Moskos, C. 1993. From citizens' army to social laboratory. *Wilson Quarterly* 17:83–94.

Mosse, G. L. 1996. *The image of man: The creation of modern masculinity*. Oxford, UK: Oxford University Press.

Nagel, J. 1998. Masculinity and nationalism: Gender and sexuality in the making of nations. *Ethnic and Racial Studies* 21(2): 242–70.

Ortner, S. 1974. Is female to male as nature is to culture. In *Women culture and society*, edited by M. Rosaldo and L. Lamphere. Stanford, CA: Stanford University Press.

Peniston-Bird, C. 2003. Classifying the body in the Second World War: British men in and out of uniform. *Body & Society* 9(4): 31–48.

Petersen, A. 1998. *Unmasking the masculine: "Men" and "Identity" in a skeptical age*. London: Sage.

Ram, U. 1999. The state and the nation: Contemporary challenges to Zionism in Israel. *Constellations* 6(3): 325–39.

Rosaldo, M. 1984. Toward an anthropology of self and feeling. In *Cultural theory essays on mind, self and emotion*, edited by R. Shweder and R. Le Vine, 137–57. Cambridge, UK: Cambridge University Press.

Sasson-Levy, O. 2000. Constructions of gender identities within the Israeli army. PhD diss., Hebrew University, Jerusalem.

———. 2003a. Feminism and military gender practices: Israeli women soldiers in "masculine" roles. *The Sociological Inquiry* 73(3): 440–65.

———. 2003b. Military, masculinity and citizenship: Tensions and contradictions in the experience of blue-collar soldiers. *Identities: Global Studies in Culture and Power* 10(3): 319–45.

Sedgwick, E. K. 1985. *Between men—English literature and male homosocial desire*. New York: Columbia University Press.

Seidler, V. 1989. *Rediscovering masculinity*. London: Routledge.

Shafir, G., and Y. Peled. 1998. Citizenship and stratification in an ethnic democracy. *Ethnic and Racial Studies* 21(3): 408–28.

Shilling, C. 1993. *The body and social theory*. London: Sage.

Snyder, C. R. 1999. *Citizen-soldier and manly warriors: Military service and gender in the civic republic tradition*. Lanham, MD: Rowman & Littlefield.

Spencer, P. 1965. *The Samburu: A study of gerontocracy in a nomadic tribe*. Berkeley: University of California Press.

Stiehm, J. H. 1989. *Arms and the enlisted woman*. Philadelphia: Temple University Press.

Theweleit, K. 1987–1989. *Male fantasies*. Minneapolis: University of Minnesota Press.

Thoits, P. 1989. The sociology of emotions. *Annual Review of Sociology* 15:317–42.

Tilly, C. 1985. War making and state making as organized crime. In *Bringing the state back in*, edited by P. Evans, D. Rueschemeyer, and T. Skocpol, 169–91. Cambridge, UK: Cambridge University Press.

———. 1996. The emergence of citizenship in France and elsewhere. *International Review of Social History* 40(3): 223–36.

Weiss, M. 2002. *The chosen body: The politics of the body in Israeli society*. Stanford, CA: Stanford University Press.

Winslow, D. 1999. Rites of passage and group bonding in the Canadian airborne. *Armed Forces and Society* 25(3): 429–57.

Zerubavel, Y. 1995. *Recovered roots: Collective memory and the making of Israeli national tradition*. Chicago: University of Chicago Press.

Introduction to Reading 28

In this reading, Erin Hatton and Mary Nell Trautner employ a longitudinal content analysis of images of women and men on the covers of more than four decades of *Rolling Stone* magazine. Their central finding is that images of women, not men, have become dramatically "hypersexualized." The authors argue that this finding points to a dangerous trend—a shrinking repertoire of culturally acceptable ways of "doing femininity" and, thus, the continuing subordination of women to men.

1. In the realm of popular media images, how does hypersexualization differ from sexualization, and why is the difference important in understanding gender inequality?

2. According to research, what are the negative consequences on real women and girls of hypersexualized images of women?

3. Why did the authors choose to title this reading "Equal Opportunity Objectification"?

4. What is the value of conducting longitudinal research of the type reported on in this reading?

EQUAL OPPORTUNITY OBJECTIFICATION?

THE SEXUALIZATION OF MEN AND WOMEN ON THE COVER OF *ROLLING STONE*

Erin Hatton and Mary Nell Trautner

INTRODUCTION

In recent years, a number of scholars and journalists have argued that American culture has become "sexualized" (APA Task Force 2007; Attwood 2009; Olfman 2009) or even "pornified" (Paul 2005; see also Dines 2010; McRobbie 2004; Paasonen et al. 2007). This widely examined phenomenon has been given a plethora of names, including "the rise of raunch culture" (Levy 2005), "striptease culture" (McNair 2002), "porno chic" (McRobbie 2004; Rush and La Nauze 2006), "rape culture" (Ezzell 2009), the "mainstreaming of prostitution" (Farley 2009), and the "amazing expanding pornosphere" (McNair 2002). "Increasingly *all* representations of women," Gill (2007:81) argues, "are being refracted through sexually objectifying imagery" (emphasis in original). It is not only women who are sexualized in the popular media, scholars argue; men are sexualized as well (Bordo 1999; Pope et al. 2000; Rohlinger 2002). "The erotic male," Rohlinger (2002:70) contends, "is increasingly becoming *the* depiction that dominates mainstream conceptions of masculinity" (emphasis in original).

Researchers find evidence for the increased sexualization of women and men in a spate of cultural artifacts, including the mainstream popularity of adult film actress Jenna Jameson and her memoir, *How to Make Love Like a Porn Star* (e.g., Dines 2010; Levy 2005; Paul 2005); the "skyrocketing" number of undressed men in advertisements (Pope et al. 2000:56); the prevalence of pole-dancing exercise classes for women

(e.g., Farley 2009; Levy 2005); the "blatant sexual fetishization—even idolatry—of the male organ" in TV and movies (Bordo 1999:30); and the success of "Girls Gone Wild," the "reality" television program and website that feature young women being urged to take off their clothes by off-screen cameramen in exchange for a T-shirt with the show's logo (e.g., Dines 2010; Farley 2009; Levy 2005; Paul 2005).

Yet analyzing only sexualized cultural artifacts—and there are certainly many to choose from—does not provide conclusive evidence that American culture has become "pornified." Indeed, it is easy to dismiss such charges unless we know whether sexualized representations of women and men have become more common—or more intensely sexualized—over time. Moreover, although the existence of sexualized images of men might suggest that, today, the popular media is something of an "equal opportunity objectifier" as some observers suggest (e.g., Frette 2009; Taylor and Sharkey 2003), the simple presence of images of sexualized men does not signal equality in media representations of women and men.

In a longitudinal content analysis of more than four decades of *Rolling Stone* magazine covers (1967–2009), we begin to answer such questions. Using a unique analytical framework that allows us to measure both the frequency and intensity of sexualization, we find that representations of women and men have indeed become more sexualized over time, though women continue to be more frequently sexualized than men. Yet our most striking finding is

From Hatton, Erin and Mary Nell Trautner. 2011. "Equal Opportunity Objectification? The Sexualization of Men and Women on the Cover of *Rolling Stone*." *Sexuality & Culture* 15: 256–278.

the change in *how* women—but not men—are sexualized. Women are increasingly likely to be "hypersexualized," while men are not. In our analysis, hypersexualization is the combination of a multitude of sexualized attributes—body position, extent of nudity, textual cues, and more—the cumulative effect of which is to narrow the possible interpretations of the image to just, as de Beauvoir (1949) wrote, "the sex." Our findings thus not only document changes in the sexualization of men and women in popular culture over time, they also point to a narrowing of the culturally acceptable ways for "doing" femininity (West and Fenstermaker 1995; West and Zimmerman 1987) as presented in popular media.

These findings are important because research has shown that sexualized images may legitimize or exacerbate violence against women and girls, sexual harassment, and anti-women attitudes among men (Farley 2009; Kalof 1999; Lanis and Covell 1955; Machia and Lamb 2009; MacKay and Covell 1997; Malamuth and Check 1981; Malamuth et al. 2000; Milburn et al. 2000; Ohbuchi et al. 1994; Ward 2002; Ward et al. 2005), increase rates of body dissatisfaction and/or eating disorders among men, women, and girls (Abramson and Valene 1991; Aubrey and Taylor 2009; Aubrey et al. 2009; Groesz et al. 2002; Hargreaves and Tiggemann 2004; Harrison 2000; Hofschire and Greenberg 2001; Holmstrom 2004; Lucas et al. 1991; Pope et al. 2000; Stice et al. 1994; Tiggeman and Slater 2001; Turner et al. 1997), increase teen sexual activity (Brown at al. 2005; Brown et al. 2006; Pardun et al. 2005; Villani 2001), and decrease women and men's sexual satisfaction (American Psychological Association 2007; Roberts and Gettman 2004; Weaver et al. 1984; Zillmann and Bryant 1988).

Before turning to our findings, we consider research on the sexualization of women and men within the broader literature on gender and the media. We then discuss our data and methods, outlining our analytical framework that measures both the incidence and extent of sexualization. We conclude with a discussion of the implications of our findings.

SEXUALIZATION, GENDER, AND THE MEDIA

In *Gender Advertisements*, Erving Goffman (1979) sought to uncover the covert ways that popular media constructs masculinity and femininity. In a detailed analysis of more than 500 advertisements, Goffman contrasted women's lowered heads with men's straight-on gazes, men's strong grasps versus women's light touches, women's over-the-top emotional displays with men's reserved semblances, and more. The relationship between men and women, Goffman argued, was portrayed as a parent-child relationship, one characterized by male power and female subordination. . . .

Missing from Goffman's analysis, however, was an examination of the sexualization of women (and men) in these images.

Many contemporary studies of gender and sexualization in popular culture take as their starting point Goffman's analysis . . . (e.g., Binns 2006; Johnson 2007; Kang 1997; Krassas et al. 2001, 2003; Lindner 2004; Rohlinger 2002; Umiker-Sebeok 1996). This is somewhat perplexing given that Goffman specifically excluded questions related to sexualization and objectification in his study. But these researchers have attempted to redress this mismatch by adding variables intended to capture sexualization. For example, in an examination of advertisements in women's magazines in 1979 and 1991, Kang (1997) added two new variables to Goffman's coding categories: body display (degree of nudity) and independence (self-assertiveness). Using this expanded empirical framework, Kang finds that while some aspects of gender stereotyping—such as men shown as taller than women—had virtually disappeared by 1991, body displays of women had increased. Interpreting this combination of increases and decreases in gender stereotyping as a kind of balancing scale, Kang concludes that little changed in advertisements' portrayal of women over the 11-year time span. "Twelve years after the Goffman study," Kang writes, "magazine advertisements are still showing the same stereotyped images of women" (988–989). But a closer look at Kang's data, in fact, reveals substantial changes: nude or partially nude images of women increased nearly 30% from 1979 to 1991.

Lindner (2004) further developed Kang's analytical framework in a study of women in advertisements in *Time* and *Vogue* from 1955 to 2002. In addition to Goffman's and Kang's coding schemes, Lindner used three other variables: movement (the ability to move fast and far), location (domestic versus public), and objectification (whether the major function of the model is to "be looked at"). Using these measures, Lindner finds that both magazines rely on gender stereotypes but in different ways, particularly in terms of sexualization. "Stereotyping in *Time* occurs without the use of sexualized images of women," Lindner concludes, "whereas in *Vogue*, these sexualized images are the primary way of portraying women in positions of inferiority and low social power" (419–420). Although her data reveal a clear difference between the two magazines, they do not indicate any change in the sexualization of women over time. . . .

Krassas et al. (2003) also built on Goffman's framework in a study of sexualized representations of women and men in two men's magazines, *Maxim* and *Stuff*, in 2001. In addition to Goffman's categories, the authors added measures of nudity (breast/chest and buttock exposure) and objectification (some concealment of face combined with some level of body exposure). Using these variables, the authors find that—in 2001 at least—women were much more likely than men to have exposed breasts and buttocks, and were three times more likely to be sexually objectified.

These studies have made important steps in empirically examining sexualized representations of women and men in popular media. But they tell only part of the story. For example, Krassas et al. (2003) analyze images of both men and women, but only at a single point in time. Kang (1997) and Lindner (2004) examine change over time, but look only at images of women. This raises the question of whether men too have been increasingly sexualized in popular culture, as some have suggested (e.g., Bordo 1999; Pope et al. 2000;

Rohlinger 2002; Thompson 2000). Additionally, Kang (1997) and Lindner (2004) datasets may not be sufficient to adequately measure change over time. Kang's analysis is based on only 2 years of data (1979 and 1991), and Lindner's analysis is based on just twelve issues of each magazine across five decades.

Furthermore, although each of the studies described uses additional variables in order to measure sexualization, in our assessment they do not yet capture the full range of sexualized attributes. They do not include variables for genital accentuation (but see Krassas et at. 2001), open mouths and/or tongue exposure, sex acts or simulations (but see Reichert and Carpenter 2004; Reichert et al. 1999; Soley and Kurzbard 1986), and sexual referents in the textual description of the images (but see Johnson 2007; Soley and Kurzbard 1986). And, perhaps more importantly, all studies of sexualization measure only the presence or absence of aspects of sexualization in isolation. As a consequence, while they document the incidence of sexualized attributes, they do not measure whether the image as a whole—the woman rather than just her breasts—has become more frequently or more intensely sexualized over time. In the following section, we outline our empirical framework that builds on these studies to provide a more comprehensive measure of sexualization.

Data and Methods

We examine the covers of *Rolling Stone* for two key reasons. First and foremost, *Rolling Stone* is a well-known popular culture magazine in the U.S. Although in the early years the magazine focused almost exclusively on music and music culture, by the 1970s its covers regularly featured an array of pop culture icons not limited to the music world. Today the magazine is well known for its coverage of politics, film, television, current events and, of course, popular music. Its covers generally feature a wide range of celebrities, including comedians, actors, musicians, models, politicians, record producers, military analysts, civil rights activists, journalists, film directors, athletes, and more. As a result, representations of men and women on the cover of *Rolling Stone* resemble popular cultural images broadly, particularly more so than lifestyle magazines which are often explicitly about sex, relationships, or sexuality. Our second reason for choosing *Rolling Stone* is its longevity. Launched in 1967, *Rolling Stone* has published more than one thousand covers across its lifespan. This extensive dataset offers an ideal window into changes in the sexualization of women and men in popular culture over time.

Dataset

There are 1,046 covers of *Rolling Stone,* starting with its first issue in November of 1967 through the end of 2009 (including those issues that featured multiple covers). We downloaded all covers from the *Rolling Stone* website in January 2010. We then cross-checked the cover images and their dates with two books that chronicled the history of *Rolling Stone* (Gatten 1993; Rolling Stone 2006), as well as with another website which had compiled all of its covers (Kabouter 2010).

Of the full set of 1,046 covers, we excluded 115 from our analysis for a number of reasons: they did not portray people (e.g., just text or cartoon characters), they showed crowds with no discernable image to code, or they featured collages of covers that had previously been published. Of the remaining 931 covers, 651 featured only men and 205 featured only women (either alone or in groups). In those covers that showed groups of either men or women, we coded the central figure in the image (usually this was literally the person at the center of the image, but at times it was the dominant person in terms of his/her size or action). Another 75 covers featured women and men together. In those cases, the central man and woman were each coded separately. We thus analyzed a total of 1,006 cover images (726 images of men and 280 images of women) across 42 years of *Rolling Stone* magazine.

Coding Scheme

We conceptualize representations of women and men as falling along a continuum of sexualization: images may be not at all sexualized, slightly sexualized, clearly sexualized, or highly sexualized. To capture these differences, we developed a 23-point additive scale consisting of 11 separate variables, the sum of which indicates the degree to which an image is sexualized. We briefly describe each of the variables below, and Table 6.1 shows the frequency distribution for each.

Clothing/Nudity (0–5 points)

A number of studies have found style of clothing and extent of nudity to be important markers of sexualization (e.g., Johnson 2007; Kang 1997; Krassas et al. 2003; Lambiase and Reichert 2006; Nitz et al. 2007; Paek and Nelson 2007; Reichert 2003; Reichert and Carpenter 2004; Reichert et al. 1999; Soley and Kurzbard 1986; Soley and Reid 1988). We developed a six-point scale for this variable, ranging from unrevealing clothing (0 points) to completely naked (5 points). Those images that featured models wearing slightly revealing clothing, such as women wearing shirts with modestly low necklines or exposed arms and shoulders, scored a "1" on this measure. Images that scored a "2" in this category featured models wearing clothing that was somewhat revealing; this included exposed midriffs on both women and men. Images that scored a "3" featured models wearing highly revealing and/or skin-tight clothing. Images that scored "4" in this category featured models wearing swimsuits and lingerie, that is, apparel that is not generally considered "clothing" at all. Images that scored a "5" in this category featured models wearing nothing at all (or only minimal clothing, such as socks and shoes but nothing else).

Touch (0–3 points)

A number of researchers have examined the use of "touch" to suggest sexualization in media images (e.g., Reichert and Carpenter 2004; Reichert et al. 1999; Soley and Kurzbard 1986).

Table 6.1 Frequency Distribution of Coding Categories for Men (M) and Women (W)

	Coded as "0"		Coded as "1"		Coded as "2"	
	M	W	M	W	M	W
Clothing/nudity	n = 554 (77%)	n = 78 (28%)	n = 70 (10%)	n = 44 (16%)	n = 56 (8%)	n = 20 (7%)
Touch	n = 496 (69%)	n = 141 (50%)	n = 206 (28%)	n = 93 (33%)	n = 20 (3%)	n = 39 (14%)
Pose	n = 659 (91%)	n = 149 (53%)	n = 50 (7%)	n = 99 (35%)	n = 15 (2%)	n = 34 (12%)
Mouth	n = 595 (82%)	n = 154 (55%)	n = 116 (16%)	n = 105 (37%)	n = 13 (2%)	n = 23 (8%)
Breasts	n = 653 (90%)	n = 154 (55%)	n = 54 (7%)	n = 59 (21%)	n = 17 (2%)	n = 69 (24%)
Genitals	n = 666 (92%)	n = 213 (76%)	n = 48 (7%)	n = 42 (15%)	n = 10 (1%)	n = 27 (10%)
Buttocks	n = 718 (99%)	n = 254 (90%)	n = 3 (<1%)	n = 16 (6%)	n = 3 (<1%)	n = 12 (4%)
Text	n = 652 (90%)	n = 177 (63%)	n = 52 (7%)	n = 79 (28%)	n = 20 (3%)	n = 26 (9%)
Head vs. body shot	n = 258 (36%)	n = 40 (14%)	n = 466 (64%)	n = 242 (86%)	—	—
Sex act	n = 720 (99%)	n = 277 (98%)	n = 4 (1%)	n = 5 (2%)	—	—
Sexual role play	n = 719 (99%)	n = 259 (92%)	n = 5 (1%)	n = 23 (8%)	—	—

	Coded as "3"		Coded as "4"		Coded as "5"	
	M	W	M	W	M	W
Clothing/nudity	n = 30 (4%)	n = 38 (13%)	n = 7 (1%)	n = 76 (27%)	n = 7 (1%)	n = 26 (9%)
Touch	n = 2 (<1%)	n = 9 (3%)	—	—	—	—
Pose	—	—	—	—	—	—
Mouth	—	—	—	—	—	—
Breasts	—	—	—	—	—	—
Genitals	—	—	—	—	—	—
Buttocks	—	—	—	—	—	—
Text	—	—	—	—	—	—
Head vs. body shot	—	—	—	—	—	—
Sex act	—	—	—	—	—	—
Sexual role play	—	—	—	—	—	—

We analyzed the nature of "touch" for each cover image on a 0–3 scale. Our measure included all forms of touch, including self-touch, touching others, and being touched. Cover models who were neither touching nor being touch scored "0" on this measure. "Casual touching," for example, a model clasping his hands together or resting her arm on someone else's shoulder, scored a "1." Those images that scored a "2" exhibited some kind of provocative touching. These included, for example, Cameron Diaz lifting her shirt and resting her hand on her bare stomach just under her breast (August 22, 1996). The highest score in this category—3 points—was given to those covers that featured explicitly sexual touching (by oneself or someone else). These included, for example, David Spade pinching a woman's nipple (September 16, 1999) and Janet Jackson's breasts being cupped by disembodied male hands (September 16, 1993).

Pose (0–2 points)

Extending Goffman's (1979) analysis of body posture to studies of sexualization, researchers have analyzed an image's pose as a key element of its sexualization (e.g., Johnson 2007; Krassas et al. 2003; Lambiase and Reichert 2006). We created three codes to capture sexualized body postures. Images in which the cover model was not posed in any way related to sexual activity—standing upright, for example—scored "0" in this category. Images scored "1" for a variety of poses that were suggestive or inviting of sexual activity, including lifting one's arms overhead and any kind of leaning or sitting. Images that scored a "2" on this measure were overtly posed for sexual activity; this included lying down or, for women, sitting with their legs spread wide open.

Mouth (0–2 points)

Goffman (1979) found that women were often shown in advertisements to be covering their mouths or sucking on their finger as part of what he called "licensed withdrawal"—a lack of presence and, therefore, power. Although a number of studies have analyzed images in terms of their licensed withdrawal (e.g., Binns 2006; Kang 1997; Lindner 2004), we are not aware of any study that has examined a model's mouth as an element of his or her sexualization. In our study of *Rolling Stone* covers, however, we found mouths to be an important characteristic of sexualization and we developed three scores to measure it. The lowest score (0 points) was for mouths that did not suggest any kind of sexual activity, including closed lips, broad toothy smiles, and active singing, talking, or yelling. One point was given to mouths that were somewhat suggestive of sex; this included images in which the model's lips were parted slightly but not smiling. Images that scored a "2" featured models whose mouths were explicitly suggestive of sexual activity: This included models whose mouths were wide open but passive (not actively singing or yelling but, perhaps, posed for penetration), whose tongue was showing, or who had something (such as a finger) in his or her mouth.

Breasts/Chest; Genitals; Buttocks (0–2 points each)

A small number of studies have examined whether a focal point of the image is the model's breasts/chest, genitals, and/or buttocks (e.g., Krassas et al. 2001, 2003; Rohlinger 2002). We used these as three separate variables, scoring each of them on a 0–2 scale. Those images in which these body parts were either not visible or not a focal point scored a "0" for each of the three variables. If one or more of these body parts were somewhat emphasized—if, for example, a women's breasts were a centerpiece of the image but still mostly concealed by clothing—the image received a "1" in the appropriate category. If one of these body parts was a major focus of the image—if a model's pants were unbuttoned and pulled down, for example—the image received a "2" for that variable.

Text (0–2 points)

Relatively few studies analyze an image's text as part of its sexualization (but see Johnson 2007; Soley and Kurzbard 1986). In our examination of

Rolling Stone cover images, however, we found the text describing an image to be an important element of its sexualization. We coded only the text on the magazine cover that was directly related to the cover image. Most of these "coverlines" were not related to sex or sexuality and scored "0" on this measure. Text that contained some sexual innuendo, such as "Kid Rock Gets Lucky" (October 10, 2007), scored "1" in this category, and coverlines that made explicit references to sex or sexuality, such as "Asia Argento: She Puts the Sex in XXX" (September 5, 2002), scored "2."

Head vs. Body Shot (0–1 point)

A number of studies in this field distinguish between those images which are primarily headshots, featuring only the model's head and perhaps shoulders, and those which feature substantially more of their body (e.g., Baumann 2008; Goffman 1979; Lambiase and Reichert 2006; Johnson 2007; Schwarz and Kurz 1989). On our scale of sexualization, headshots scored "0" and body shots scored "1."

Sex Act (0–1 point)

Perhaps because relatively few popular media images depict models engaging in (or simulating) sex acts, only a few studies measure this variable (e.g., Reichert and Carpenter 2004; Reichert et al. 1999; Soley and Kurzbard 1986). In our analysis of *Rolling Stone* magazine covers, however, a small but hard to ignore number of such images prompted the creation of this new variable. Images in which the cover model was engaged in a sex act (e.g., kissing or embracing someone while lying naked in bed) or simulating a sex act (e.g., affecting fellatio or masturbation) scored "1" in this category.

Sexual Role Play (0–1 point)

Finally, although we found no studies that measured symbols of sexual role playing—such as infantilization (e.g., child-like clothes) or bondage/domination (e.g., leather bustier, leather straps, dog collars, studded bracelets)—in our analysis the infrequent yet conspicuous presence of such symbols led to the creation of this variable. Cover images that suggested sexual role playing scored "1" in this category.

Analytic Strategy

We coded the covers of *Rolling Stone* in several passes. The authors first worked together to establish coding rules for all variables, jointly coding three randomly selected years of covers. The second author then coded the remaining cover images, working closely with the first author to resolve any questions that arose. . . .

After coding was complete, the images' scores on the 23-point scale of sexualization clustered into three distinct groups: nonsexualized images (which scored 0–4 points), sexualized images (5–9 points), and hypersexualized images (10 or more points). We tested for reliability between coders for these three categories as well. In our 10% random sample of covers, there was near-perfect agreement between authors' categorization of images as nonsexualized, sexualized, and hypersexualized: Kappa was found to be .972 ($p < .001$).

Dividing the images into these three categories—nonsexualized, sexualized, and hypersexualized—captures important differences between them. Consider, for example, the two images presented in Figure 6.1. Both covers feature people who are naked and in a kneeling position, yet the impact of the images is quite different. The band members of Blind Melon are clearly sexualized—they are naked and the text asserts that they are "ripe and ready"—but they are not hypersexualized. They are not posed to engage in sexual activity; they do not touch themselves or each other; they are not arching their backs to emphasize their chests, genitals, or buttocks (in fact, their backs are rather slumped); and they gaze somberly into the camera, with their mouths closed. In fact, their nudity and textual description seem at odds with their otherwise nonsexualized characteristics.

In contrast, the cover image of Laetitia Casta is *hypersexualized*. Like the members of Blind Melon, she is both naked and kneeling, but her back is arched to emphasize her breasts and buttocks. Rather than posing on an unremarkable white background, Casta is kneeling on a bed of pink rose petals. Her body faces away from the camera, but her head is tilted back and is turned so that her eyes can meet the viewer's gaze. Her lips are slightly parted. Her arm is raised over her head and touches her hair, which falls down her back. Her skin glistens, as though it has just been oiled. Casta, the text tells us, is the star of *Rolling Stone*'s "hot list."

The difference between these two images is clear, yet measuring nudity alone would not capture it. Our scale of sexualization does. By our measure, the Blind Melon cover scored 9 points, placing it at the top of the sexualized category. The Casta image, by contrast, scored 15 points, placing it well into the hypersexualized category. A gestalt-level analysis confirms this difference; in this paper we offer the tools to measure it. In the following sections, we detail our findings and discuss their implications.

FINDINGS

Before looking at questions of intensity, we first examine changes in the frequency of sexualized images over time. In order to do so, we combine sexualized and hypersexualized images into one category and compare them to nonsexualized images. The data show that sexualized representations of women have increased significantly ($\chi^2 = 6.8$, $p < .01$), and sexualized representations of men have also increased, but not significantly ($\chi^2 = .99$). . . .

These findings speak clearly to debates about the sexualization of men in popular media. While sexualized images of men have increased, men are still dramatically less likely to be sexualized than women. This difference is further highlighted by looking at the numerical frequency of such images: In the 2000s, there were 28 sexualized images of men (17% of male images) but 57 sexualized images of women (83% of female images), and there were 136 nonsexualized

Figure 6.1 Sexualization vs. hypersexualization

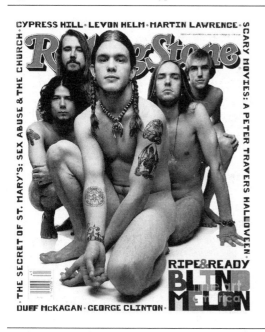 

images of men (83% of male images) but only 12 nonsexualized images of women (17% of female images). Perhaps even more telling is the difference between men and women at the low end of the scale. In the 2000s, there were 35 images of men which scored a "0" on our scale and another 39 images which scored just 1 point, indicating that these images displayed no (or almost no) sexualized attributes. Together they accounted for 45% of all images of men in the 2000s. By contrast, there was not a single image of a woman in the 2000s that scored 0 points, and only 2 images of women scored 1 point on the scale, accounting for less than 3% of images of women in the 2000s.

Intensity of Sexualization

The difference in the sexualization of men and women is even more striking when we examine the intensity of their sexualization. In our analysis, we find a broad range in the degree of sexualization—some images are only somewhat sexualized while others are so intensely sexualized that we have labeled them "hypersexualized." In order to capture such differences, we split the sexualized category into two groups: those that were simply sexualized (such as the Blind Melon image described above) and those that were hypersexualized (such as the Casta image).

Looking first at images of men, we see that the vast majority of them—some 83% of men in the 2000s—fall in the nonsexualized category. This represents a noteworthy, though comparatively small, decrease from the 1960s when 89% of men were not sexualized. Many nonsexualized images of men are close-up head-shots (36% across all years): they do not show the man's body nor do they indicate any level of nudity with bare shoulders or chest. Typically the man's mouth is closed and he is looking directly into the camera, though at times he might be smiling or looking to one side. The text in such images usually does not carry any sexual innuendo. On more than four decades of *Rolling Stone*'s covers, 162 images of men—or 22%—

scored a zero on our scale, displaying no sexualized attributes.

Other images of men in the nonsexualized category are slightly more sexualized. One example of this is a 1997 image of actor Brad Pitt (April 3). On our scale, this image scored 4 points, placing it at the top of the nonsexualized category. The cover shows Pitt's face and part of his torso (1 point). He is wearing a plush white bathrobe (1 point), which is open to reveal part of his chest (1 point). He looks directly into the camera through tousled hair, his lips are very slightly parted (1 point). The text reads, "Leader of the Pack: Brad Pitt Talks Tough."

Although the majority of men on the cover of *Rolling Stone* are not sexualized, a sizeable minority fall into the sexualized (but not hypersexualized) category. In the 1960s, 10.5% of men were sexualized, and in the 1970s their proportion increased slightly to 12%. In the 1980s, sexualized representations of men dropped to just 5%, but in the 1990s sexualized images of men increased to 13.3%. Their numbers continued to increase somewhat, so that in the 2000s 14.6% of images of men were sexualized.

A 2006 cover featuring singer Justin Timberlake (September 21) offers an example of this category of sexualized men. On our scale, Timberlake's image scored 8 points—double that of the Brad Pitt cover described above—and falls squarely within the sexualized category. The image shows Timberlake's body from the thighs up (1 point). He is wearing a white T-shirt and jeans; he is looking directly into the camera and smiling broadly. Timberlake is carrying a guitar over one shoulder as if he were off to a gig, but his white T-shirt is soaking wet (3 points), clinging to his body and revealing his chest (2 points). The text reads, "Justin Timberlake: Wet Dream, The New King of Sex Gets Loose" (2 points).

Although sexualized images of men such as this one have become more common over time, *Rolling Stone* rarely features hypersexualized images of men. In the 1960s, there were no such images and, in the 1970s, there was just one hypersexualized image of a man, representing 1% of male images in that decade. In the 1980s, 2% of men were hypersexualized and, in the 1990s, 3% were. But in the 2000s, hypersexualized images of men dropped again to just over 2%.

The most prominent example of this category is a 2009 cover featuring pop singer Adam Lambert (June 25) (see Fig. 6.2). On our scale, the image scored 13 points, the highest score among men on the cover of *Rolling Stone*. The cover shows Lambert's body from the thighs up (1 point). He is lying on a bed (2 points) with his arms lifted overhead, conveying a sense of sexual passivity or vulnerability. One of his hands touches his hair (2 points). His eyes, which are lined with make-up, gaze into the camera, and his lips are slightly parted (1 point). Lambert is wearing tight black jeans and an unbuttoned black shirt (3 points), revealing part of his chest (1 point). His legs are spread and a bright green snake crawls up his leg, its head remarkably near his genitals (2 points). The text reads, "The Liberation of Adam Lambert: Wild Idol" (1 point). Given that Lambert is openly gay, perhaps it is not surprising that he is the most intensely sexualized man on the cover of *Rolling Stone*, since popular media portrayals of gay men often over-emphasize their sexuality (Gross 2001; Nardi and Bolton 1998). But what *is* perhaps surprising about this image is its comparison to the highest scoring image of women, described below.

Turning to images of women, we see different trends not only in the frequency but also in the intensity of their sexualization. Overall, nonsexualized representations of women have decreased since the start of *Rolling Stone*. In the 1960s, 56% of women on the magazine's cover were nonsexualized. In the 1970s, nonsexualized images of women increased slightly to 58% and then, in the 1980s, dropped to 49%. In the 1990s, nonsexualized images of women took a sharp downturn, falling to 22%. In the 2000s, just 17% of women were nonsexualized.

A 2009 cover featuring country singer Taylor Swift (March 15) offers an example of this

Figure 6.2 Hypersexualized man

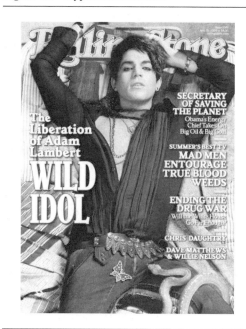

nonsexualized category. On our scale, Swift's image scored 3 points, placing it in the nonsexualized category even though it contains minor elements of sexualization, much like the Brad Pitt cover described above. The image shows Swift's upper body (1 point). She is wearing a white halter top that reveals her shoulders and arms (1 point), though her body is largely covered by her long blonde hair. Swift stares directly into the camera; her lips are closed. She is holding a guitar as though she is just about to play it, her fingers poised over the guitar strings. The text reads, "Taylor Swift: Secrets of a Good Girl" (1 point).

Just as nonsexualized images of women such as this one have become less common, in recent years sexualized (but not hypersexualized) images of women have also become less prevalent, though to a much lesser extent. In the 1960s, 33% of women on the cover of *Rolling Stone* were sexualized. This rate increased somewhat over the next several decades, taking an upturn in the 1990s to 42%. In the 2000s, however, sexualized (but not hypersexualized) images of women decreased by nearly half to 22%. But, as we will see in a moment, an even greater increase in hypersexualized images of women more than made up the difference.

A 2008 portrait of pop star Britney Spears (December 11) is an example of this sexualized category. On our scale, this image scored 6 points, placing it near the bottom of the category's range. The cover shows Spears' body from the hips up (1 point). She is looking away from the camera and smiling widely, as though she were laughing heartily. Her tousled blonde hair falls below her shoulders. She is wearing low-slung jeans and a gray T-shirt, which is rolled up to reveal much of her stomach (3 points). One hand holds her cheek (1 point), conveying a sense of youthful enthusiasm, and her other hand rests in her jeans' belt loop, pulling down her pants slightly (1 point) to reveal a glimpse of a tattoo below. The text reads, "Yes She Can! Britney Returns."

Although sexualized images of women such as this one have become less common in recent years, hypersexualized images of women have increased significantly since the start of *Rolling Stone* magazine. In the 1960s, there was just one hypersexualized image of a woman, representing 11% of images of women at the time. In the 1970s, 6% of women on the magazine's cover were hypersexualized and, in the 1980s, that number more than doubled to 13%. Hypersexualized images of women increased even more in the 1990s and 2000s, reaching 36 and 61% in each decade, respectively. As these data show, in the 2000s women were three and a half times more likely to be hypersexualized than nonsexualized, and nearly five times more likely to be sexualized to any degree (sexualized or hypersexualized) than nonsexualized. . . .

In our analysis, it might seem that the hypersexualized category encompasses a wide range of sexualized images because its scale (10–23) is wider than the other categories. Yet even with such a wide range, the images in this category leave little room for interpretation as being about anything other than sex. To demonstrate this, it is

Figure 6.3 Hypersexualized women

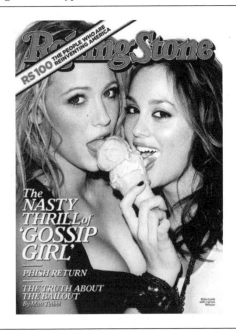

instructive to look at two images of hypersexualized women, one at each end of the category's range (see Fig. 6.3). An example of the lower end of this category is a 2009 image of Blake Lively and Leighton Meester (April 2), two leads of the television show "Gossip Girl." On our scale, this image scored 12 points, one point less than the Adam Lambert cover, the top scorer among men. The image shows the upper bodies of both women (1 point), though Lively's portrait dominates the cover. She is wearing a very low-cut black tank top (3 points) that reveals much of her breasts (2 points). Meester leans in towards Lively; her face is touching Lively's hair (1 point), suggesting that beyond the image their bodies are also pressed together. The focal point of the image is a dripping, double-scoop ice cream cone, a phallus-like object which Lively holds up for both women to lick (1 point). Their mouths are wide open and their protruding tongues (2 points) are covered in ice cream. The text reads, "The Nasty Thrill of 'Gossip Girl'" (2 points).

Compare this image to one at the top end of the hypersexualized category: a 2002 cover featuring pop singer Christina Aguilera (November 14). This image scored 20 points, earning the highest score in our dataset. The picture shows nearly all of Aguilera's body (1 point). She is naked (5 points), except for black fishnet stocking on her lower legs and black motorcycle boots (1 point). She is lying on a bed (2 points), which is covered with a rippling red satin sheet. Her head is tilted downwards, but she is looking into the camera. Her lips are parted (1 point), and her long hair is spread out around her shoulders. Aguilera's left hand holds a guitar, but only decoratively, not giving any indication that it is an instrument she might play. The guitar's neck is strategically placed so that it covers her left nipple. Her right hand clasps her other breast, not to cover it but to push it up provocatively. Her breasts are otherwise uncovered (2 points). Aguilera's body is contorted so that not only are her breasts exposed, but her buttocks (2 points) and, to a lesser degree, her genitals (1 point) are accentuated. The text reads, "Christina Aguilera: Inside the Dirty Mind of a Pop Princess" (2 points).

The new predominance of hypersexualized images of women such as these is illustrated further by examining the numerical frequency of such images. In the 2000s, there were 12 non-sexualized images of women, 15 sexualized images, and 42 hypersexualized images.[1] By contrast, there were 136 nonsexualized images of men, 24 sexualized images, and only 4 hypersexualized images of men in the 2000s. That there are more sexualized images of men than women should not be too surprising. Images of men have long dominated the cover of *Rolling Stone*. (Recall that our dataset is comprised of 726 images of men compared to 280 images of women.) What is surprising, however, is the asymmetry in nonsexualized and hypersexualized representations of men and women. In the 2000s, there were more than 10 times the number of hypersexualized images of women than men, and there were more than 11 times the number of nonsexualized images of men than women.

DISCUSSION AND CONCLUSION

In *The Male Body: A New Look at Men in Public and in Private*, Susan Bordo (1999) describes the different implications for men and women when they are sexualized in the same way. As evidence, she analyzes advertisements in which women and men are shown with their pants around their ankles. Bordo (1999:28) argues that women in such images seem "stripped or exposed," even more than if their pants were off altogether, because they resemble rape or murder victims shown in movies and television. By contrast, Bordo observes, men shown with their pants around their ankles convey "much the same confident, slightly challenging machismo" as they would otherwise.

If similarly sexualized images can suggest victimization for women but confidence for men, consider the implications when women are sexualized at the same rate as men are *not* sexualized, as they were on the covers of *Rolling Stone* in the 2000s. And the vast majority of those sexualized images of women—some

74%—were hypersexualized, meaning that they did not exhibit only one or two signals of sex, but a multitude of them. Often women in these images were shown naked (or nearly so); they were shown with their legs spread wide open or lying down on a bed—in both cases sexually accessible; they were shown pushing up their breasts or pulling down their pants; they were described as having "dirty minds" or giving "nasty thrills"; and, in some cases, they were even shown to be simulating fellatio or other sex acts.

Some researchers argue against using the phrase "sexual objectification" to describe such images because they often depict women as active, confident, and/or sexually desirous (e.g., Bordo 1999; Gill 2003, 2008, 2009). We argue, however, that the intensity of their sexualization suggests that "sexual object" may indeed be the only appropriate label. The accumulation of sexualized attributes in these images leaves little room for observers to interpret them in any way other than as instruments of sexual pleasure and visual possession for a heterosexual male audience. Such images do not show women as sexually agentic musicians and actors; rather, they show female actors and musicians as ready and available for sex.

Yet some scholars have criticized such statements as overly homogenizing because they render invisible differences in this process of sexualization (e.g., Gill 2009).[2] In our view, however, the very problem is one of homogenization. We argue that the dramatic increase in hypersexualized images of women—along with the corresponding decline in nonsexualized images of them—indicates a decisive narrowing or homogenization of media representations of women. In *Female Chauvinist Pigs: Women and the Rise of Raunch Culture*, journalist Ariel Levy (2005:5) describes this trend: "A tawdry, tarty, cartoonlike version of female sexuality has become so ubiquitous, it no longer seems particular. What we once regarded as a *kind* of sexual expression," Levy writes, "we now view *as* sexuality" (emphases in original). In this article we offer empirical evidence for this claim.

Of concern is that this narrowing down of media representations of women to what Levy calls a single "cartoonlike version of female sexuality"—or what we might call "hypersexualized femininity"—suggests a corresponding narrowing of culturally acceptable ways to "do" femininity (West and Fenstermaker 1995; West and Zimmerman 1987). This is not to say that there are no culturally available alternatives for women and girls as they make decisions about how to look and behave, but it does suggest that there may increasingly be fewer competing cultural scripts for ways of doing femininity. Thus, at least in popular media outlets such as *Rolling Stone,* it seems that just one aspect of femininity—sexuality, and *hypersexuality* at that—has overshadowed other aspects of "emphasized femininity" (Connell 1987), such as nurturance, fragility, and sociability. Although such characteristics are themselves problematic, the ascendancy of only one version of femininity (and, at the same time, one version of female sexuality) seems particularly troubling. . . .

NOTES

1. Some might attribute the increase in the hypersexualization of women on the cover of *Rolling Stone* to a change in management: In 2002, *Rolling Stone* hired a new managing editor, Ed Needham, who was the former editor of *FHM*—the rather notorious "lad mag" that regularly features scantily-clad women on its covers. A closer look at our data, however, reveals a strong increase in the hypersexualization of women on the cover of *Rolling Stone* since the 1980s. Moreover, the proportion of hypersexualized images of women actually peaked at 78% in 1999, well before Needham's tenure. Hypersexualized images of women reached their second highest point (75%) in 2002, the first year of Needham's appointment, and then again in 2006, after Needham's 2-year stint at the magazine had ended.

2. Although a number of researchers have found that nonwhites are often sexualized in print media (Collins 1990; Hansen and Hansen 2000; West 2009), our analyses show no discernable difference in the frequency or intensity of sexualization of whites and nonwhites. Overall, 12% of women and 12% of men

on the cover of *Rolling Stone* were nonwhite. They were nonsexualized, sexualized, and hypersexualized at about the same rate as their white counterparts.

REFERENCES

Abramson, E., & Valene, P. (1991). Media use, dietary restraint, bulimia, and attitudes toward obesity: A preliminary study. *British Review of Bulimia and Anorexia Nervosa, 5*, 73–76.

American Psychological Association (APA) Task Force. (2007). *Report of the APA task force on the sexualization of girls*. Washington, DC: American Psychological Association. Retrieved 10 March 2010 from http://www.apa.org/pi/women/pro grams/girls/report-full.pdf.

Attwood, F. (2009). *Mainstreaming sex: The sexualization of western culture*. London: I.B. Tauris.

Aubrey, J., Stevens, J., Henson, K., Hopper, M., & Smith, S. (2009). A picture is worth twenty words (about the self): Testing the priming influence of visual sexual objectification on women's self-objectification. *Communication Research Reports, 26*, 271–284.

Aubrey, J. S., & Taylor, L. (2009). The role of lad magazines in priming men's chronic and temporary appearance-related schemata: An investigation of longitudinal and experimental findings. *Human Communication Research, 35*, 28–58.

Baumann, S. (2008). The moral underpinnings of beauty: A meaning-based explanation for light and dark complexions in advertising. *Poetics, 36*, 2–23.

Binns, R. K. (2006) 'On the cover of a *Rolling Stone*': A content analysis of gender representation in popular culture between 1967–2004. M.A. Thesis, Wichita State University, Wichita, KS.

Bordo, S. (1999). *The male body: A new look at men in public and in private*. New York: Farrar, Straus, and Giroux.

Brown, J., Halpern, C. T., & L'Engle, K. L. (2005). Mass media as a sexual super peer for early maturing girls. *Journal of Adolescent Health, 36*, 420–427.

Brown, J., L'Engle, K. L., Pardun. C., Guo, G., Kenneavy, K., & Jackson, C. (2006). Sexy media matter: Exposure to sexual content in music, movies, and magazines predicts black and white adolescents' sexual behavior. *Pediatrics, 117*, 1018–1027.

Collins, P. H. (1990). *Black feminist thought: Knowledge, consciousness, and the politics of empowerment*. New York: Routledge.

Connell, R. W. (1987). *Gender & power: Society, the person, and sexual politics*. Palo Alto, CA: Stanford University Press.

de Beauvoir, S. (1949, 1972). *The second sex*. New York: Penguin.

Dines, G. (2010). *Pornland: How porn has hijacked our sexuality*. Boston, MA: Beacon Press.

Ezzell, M. (2009). Pornography, lad mags, video games, and boys: Reviving the canary in the cultural coal mine. In S. Olfman (Ed.), *The sexualization of childhood*. Westport, CT: Praeger.

Farley, M. (2009). Prostitution and the sexualization of children. In S. Olfman (Ed.), *The sexualization of childhood*. Westport, CT: Praeger.

Frette, J. (2009). Men are altered and objectified too: Ryan Reynolds graces the cover of *Entertainment Weekly*. Retrieved 20 December 2010 http://www.examiner.com/women-s-issues-in-national/men-are-altered-and-objectified-too-ryan-reyn olds-graces-the-cover-of-entertainment-weekly.

Gatten, J. (1993). *The* Rolling Stone *index: Twenty-five years of popular culture, 1967–1991*. Ann Arbor, MI: Popular Culture, Ink.

Gill, R. (2003). From sexual objectification to sexual subjectification: The resexualisation of women's bodies in the media. *Feminist Media Studies, 3*, 100–106.

Gill. R. (2007). *Gender and the media*. Cambridge, UK: Polity Press.

Gill, R. (2008). Empowerment/sexism: Figuring female sexual agency in contemporary advertising. *Feminism & Psychology, 18*, 35–60.

Gill, R. (2009). Beyond the "sexualization of culture" thesis: An intersectional analysis of "sixpacks," "midriffs" and "hot lesbians" in advertising. *Sexualities, 12*, 137–160.

Goffman, E. (1979). *Gender advertisements*. Cambridge, MA: Harvard University Press.

Groesz, L., Levine, M., & Mumen, S. (2002). The effect of experimental presentation of thin media images on body satisfaction: A meta-analytic review. *International Journal of Eating Disorders, 31*, 1–16.

Gross, L. (2001). *Up from invisibility: Lesbians, gay men, and the media in America*. New York: Columbia University Press.

Hansen, C., & Hansen, R. (2000). Music and music videos. In D. Zillmann & P. Vorderer (Eds.), *Media* entertainment: The psychology of its appeal. Mahwah, NJ: Erlbaum.

Hargreaves, D., & Tiggemann, M. (2004). Idealized media images and adolescent bodyimage: "Comparing" boys and girls. Body Image, 1, 351–361.

Harrison, K. (2000). The body electric: Thin-ideal media and eating disorders in adolescents. Journal of Communication. 50, 119–143.

Hofschire, L., & Greenberg, B. (2001). Media's impact on adolescents' body dissatisfaction. In J. Brown & J. R. Steele (Eds.), Sexual teens, sexual media. Mahwah, NJ: Erlbaum

Holmstrom, A. (2004). The effects of the media on body image: A meta-analysis. Journal of Broadcasting & Electronic Media, 48, 196–217.

Johnson, S. (2007). Promoting easy sex without genuine intimacy: Maxim and Cosmopolitan cover lines and cover images. In M.-L. Galician & D. L. Merskin (Eds.), Critical thinking about sex, love, romance in the mass media: Media literacy applications. Mahwah, NJ: Erlbaum.

Kabouter. (2010). Rolling Stone magazine cover gallery. Retrieved 1 April 2010. http://rateyourmusic.com/list/kabouter/rolling_stone_magazine_cover-gallery.

Kalof, L. (1999). The effects of gender and music video imagery on sexual attitudes. Journal of Social Psychology, 139, 378–385.

Kang, M.-E. (1997). The portrayal of women's images in magazine advertisements: Goffman's gender analysis revisited. Sex Roles, 37, 979–996.

Krassas, N., Blauwkamp, J., & Wesselink, P. (2001). Boxing Helena and corseting Eunice: Sexual rhetoric in Cosmopolitan and Playboy magazines. Sex Roles, 44, 751–771.

Krassas, N., Blauwkamp, J., & Wesselink, P. (2003). "Master your johnson": Sexual rhetoric in Maxim and Stuff magazines. Sexuality and Culture, 7, 98–119.

Lambiase, J., & Reichert, T. (2006). Sex and the marketing of contemporary consumer magazines: How men's magazines sexualized their covers to compete with Maxim. In T. Reichert & J. Lambiase (Eds.), Sex in consumer culture: The erotic content of media, marketing. Mahwah, NJ: Erlbaum.

Lanis, K., & Covell, K. (1995). Images of women in advertisements: Effects on attitudes related to sexual aggression. Sex Roles, 32, 639–649.

Levy, A. (2005). Female chauvinist pigs: Women and the rise of raunch culture. New York: Free Press.

Lindner, K. (2004). Images of women in general interest and fashion magazine advertisements from 1955 to 2002. Sex Roles, 51, 409–421.

Lucas, A., Beard, C. M., O'Fallon, W. M., & Kurland, L. (1991). 50-year trends in the incidence of anorexia nervosa in Rochester, Minn.: A population-based study. American Journal of Psychiatry, 148, 917–922.

Machia, M., & Lamb, S. (2009). Sexualized innocence: Effects of magazine ads portraying adult women as sexy little girls. Journal of Media Psychology, 21, 15–24.

MacKay, N., & Covell, K. (1997). The impact of women in advertisements on attitudes toward women. Sex Roles, 36, 573–583.

Malamuth, N., Addison, T., & Koss, M. (2000). Pornography and sexual aggression: Are there reliable effects and can we understand them? Annual Review of Sex Research, 11, 26–91.

Malamuth, N., & Check, J. (1981). The effects of mass media exposure on acceptance of violence against women: A field experiment. Journal of Research in Personality, 15, 436–446.

McNair. B. (2002). Striptease culture: Sex, media and the democratization of desire. London, New York: Routledge.

McRobbie, A. (2004). The rise and rise of porn chic. Times Higher Education Supplement. Retrieved 1 June 2010. http://timeshighereducation.co.uk/story.asp?sectioncode=26&storycode=182087.

Milburn, M., Mather, R., & Conrad, S. (2000). The effects of viewing R-rated movie scenes that objectify women on perceptions of date rape. Sex Roles, 43, 645–664.

Nardi, P., & Bolton, R. (1998). Gay bashing: Violence and aggression against gay men and lesbians. In P. M. Nardi & B. E. Schneider (Eds.), Social perspectives in lesbian, gay studies: A reader. London: Routledge.

Nitz, M., Reichert, T., Aune, A. S., & Velde, A. V. (2007). All the news that's fit to see? The sexualization of television news journalists as a promotional strategy. In T. Reichert (Ed). Investigating the use of sex in media promotion, advertising. Binghamton, NY: Best Business Books.

Ohbuchi, K.-I., Ikeda, T., & Takeuchi, G. (1994). Effects of violent pornography upon viewers' rape myth beliefs: A study of Japanese males. Psychology, Crime, and the Law, 1, 71–81.

Olfman, S. (Ed.). (2009). The sexualization of childhood. Westport, CT: Praeger.

Paasonen. S., Nikunen, K., & Saarenmaa, L. (Eds.). (2007). *Pornification: Sex and sexuality in media culture.* Oxford: Berg.

Paek, H.-J., & Nelson, M. (2007). A cross-cultural and cross-media comparison of female nudity in advertising. In T. Reichert (Ed.), *Investigating the use of sex in media promotion, advertising.* Binghamton, NY: Best Business Books.

Pardun, C., L'Engle, K. L., & Brown, J. (2005). Linking exposure to outcomes: Early adolescents' consumption of sexual content in six media. *Mass Communication and Society, 8,* 75–91.

Paul, P. (2005). *Pornified: How pornography is transforming our lives, our relationships, and families.* New York: Times Books.

Pope, H. Jr., Phillips, K., & Olivardia, R. (2000). *The Adonis complex: The secret crisis of male body obsession.* New York: Free Press.

Reichert, T. (2003). *The erotic history of advertising.* Amherst, NY: Prometheus.

Reichert, T., & Carpenter, C. (2004). An update on sex in magazine advertising: 1983 to 2003. *Journalism & Mass Communications Quarterly, 81,* 823–837.

Reichert, T., Lambiase, J., Morgan, S., Carstarphen, M., & Zavoina, S. (1999).Cheesecake and beefcake: No matter how you slice it, sexual explicitness in advertising continues to increase. *Journalism & Mass Communication Quarterly, 76,* 7–20.

Roberts, T.-A., & Gettman, J. (2004). Mere exposure: Gender differences in the negative effects of priming a state of self-objectification. *Sex Roles, 51,* 17–27.

Rohlinger, D. (2002). Eroticizing men: Cultural influences on advertising and male objectification. *Sex Roles, 46,* 61–74.

Rolling Stone. (2006). *1,000 covers: A history of the most influential magazine in pop culture.* New York: Abrams.

Rush, E., & La Nauze, A. (2006). *Corporate paedophilia: Sexualisation of children in Australia.* Canberra: The Australia Institute.

Schwarz, N., & Kurz, E. (1989). What's in a picture? The impact of face-ism on trait attribution. *European Journal of Social Psychology, 19,* 311–316.

Soley, L., & Kurzbard. G. (1986). Sex in advertising: A comparison of 1964 and 1984 magazine advertisements. *Journal of Advertising, 15,* 46–64.

Soley, L., & Reid, L. (1988). Taking it off: Are models in magazine ads wearing less? *Journalism Quarterly, 65,* 960–966.

Stice, E., Schupak-Neuberg, E., Shaw, H., & Stein, R. (1994). Relation of media exposure to eating disorder symptomatology: An examination of mediating mechanisms. *Journal of Abnormal Psychology, 103,* 836–840.

Taylor, E., & Sharkey, L. (2003). Em & Lo's sex myths: Women's bodies are sexier. *The Guardian* (22 March). Retrieved 20 December 2010. http://www.guardian.co.uk/lifeandstyle/2003/mar/22/weekend.emmataylor.

Thompson, M. (2000). Gender in magazine advertising: Skin sells best. *Clothing and Textiles Research Journal, 18,* 178–181.

Tiggeman, M., & Slater, A. (2001). A test of objectification theory in former dancers and non-dancers. *Psychology of Women Quarterly, 2,* 57–64.

Turner, S., Hamilton, H., Jacobs, M., Angood, L., & Dwyer, D. H. (1997). The influence of fashion magazines on the body image satisfaction of college women: An exploratory analysis. *Adolescence, 32,* 603–614.

Umiker-Sebeok, J. (1996). Power and construction of gendered spaces. *International Review of Sociology, 6,* 389–404.

Villani, S. (2001). Impact of media on children and adolescents: A 10-year review of the research. *Journal of the American Academy of Child and Adolescent Psychiatry, 40,* 392–401.

Ward, L. M. (2002). Does television exposure affect emerging adults' attitudes and assumptions about sexual relationships? Correlational and experimental confirmation. *Journal of Youth & Adolescence, 31,* 1–15.

Ward, L., Monique, E., & Hansbrough, E. W. (2005). Contributions of music video exposure to black adolescents' gender and sexual schemas. *Journal of Adolescent Research, 20,* 143–166.

Weaver, J., Masland, J., & Zillmann, D. (1984). Effect of erotica on young men's aesthetic perception of their female sexual partners. *Perceptual and Motor Skills, 58,* 929–930.

West, C. (2009). Still on the auction block: The sexploitation of black adolescent girls in rape music and hip-hop culture. In S. Olfman (Ed.), *The sexualization of childhood.* Westport, CT: Praeger.

West, C., & Fenstermaker, S. (1995). Doing difference. *Gender & Society, 9,* 8–37.

West, C., & Zimmerman, D. (1987). Doing gender. *Gender & Society, 1,* 125–151.

Zillmann, D., & Bryant, J. (1988). Pornography's impact on sexual satisfaction. *Journal of Applied Social Psychology, 18,* 438–453.

Introduction to Reading 29

Nicola Gavey, Kathryn McPhillips, and Marion Doherty conducted in-depth interviews with 14 New Zealand women, ages 27 to 37, who came from diverse work experiences and educational backgrounds. The authors questioned the women about their past and current experiences with condoms, their heterosexual relationships and practices, their personal views of condoms, and how they thought others viewed condoms. The authors focused on the conflict between public health campaigns, which encourage women to demand condom use by male partners, and dominant heterosexual scripts that limit the ways women may control the course and outcomes of heterosexual encounters.

1. What are the two main "discursive arenas" or organizing principles of heterosexual sex that constrain women's sexual pleasure and activity?

2. Why do the authors believe that advice to women that encourages them to be assertive in sexual relationships with men is problematic?

3. Why did many of the women in this study have experiences of engaging in unwanted sex with men? How is this study's analysis of engaging in unwanted sex helpful to understanding the phenomenon of date rape?

"If It's Not On, It's Not On"—or Is It?

Nicola Gavey, Kathryn McPhillips, and Marion Doherty

If it's not on, it's not on!" Slogans such as these exhort women not to have sexual intercourse with a man unless a condom is used. Health campaigns targeting heterosexuals with this approach imply that it is women who should act assertively to control the course of their sexual encounters to prevent the spread of HIV/AIDS and other sexually transmitted infections (STIs). Researchers and commentators, too, have sometimes explicitly concluded that it is women in particular who should be targeted for condom promotions on the basis of assumptions such as "the disadvantages of condom use are fewer for girls" (Barling and Moore 1990). . . .

Aside from the obvious question of whether women should be expected to take greater responsibility for sexual safety, this approach relies on various assumptions that deserve critical attention. For example, what constraints on women's abilities to unilaterally control condom use are overlooked in these messages? What assumptions about women's sexuality are embedded in the claim that the disadvantages of condoms are fewer for women? That is, is safer sex simply a matter of women deciding to use

From Gavey, Nicola, Kathryn McPhillips, and Marion Doherty. 2001. "'If It's Not On, It's Not On' —or Is It." *Gender & Society* 15(6), p. 917. Copyright © 2001. Published by Sage Publications on behalf of Sociologists for Women in Society.

condoms at all times and assertively making this happen, or do the discursive parameters of heterosex work to subtly constrain and contravene this message? Moreover, are condoms as unproblematic for women's experiences of sex as the logic offered for targeting women implies? These questions demand further investigation given that research has repeatedly shown the reluctance of heterosexuals to consistently use condoms despite clear health messages about their importance. There is now a strong body of feminist research suggesting that condom promotion in Western societies must compete against cultural significations of condom*less* sexual intercourse as associated with commitment, trust, and "true love" in relationships (e.g., Holland et al. 1991; Kippax et al. 1990; Willig 1995; Worth 1989; see also Hollway 1989). Here, we contribute to this body of work, which collectively highlights how women's condom use needs to be understood in relation to some of the complex gender dynamics that saturate heterosexual encounters. In particular, we critically examine (1) the concept of women's control over condom use that is tacitly assumed in campaigns designed to promote safer sex and condoms to women and (2) the foundational assumption of such campaigns that condoms are relatively unproblematic for women's sexual experiences. . . .

We suggest there are two main discursive arenas that need to be considered in critically evaluating strategies that assume women's ability to control condom use and the appropriateness of targeting women in particular for messages of (hetero)sexual responsibility. These are (1) a male sex drive discourse (Hollway 1984, 1989) and the corresponding scarcity of discourse around female desire (Fine 1988), and (2) the constraints of a "coital imperative" on how much control women (or men) have in determining what sexual activity counts as "real sex." We suggest that there are two important points where these kinds of discursive influences converge for women in ways that mediate the possibilities for condom use, that is, the sites of identity and pleasure.

ASSERTION, IDENTITY, AND CONTROL

* * *

Public sexual health education fervently promotes the rights of women to demand condom use by male partners. Against a backdrop of implied male aversion to condoms, both the Planned Parenthood Federation of America (1998–2001) and the Family Planning Association (2000) in New Zealand offer mock scripts that despite an air of gender neutrality suggest ways women can assert their right to insist on a condom being used for sexual intercourse. In this section, we consider what these kinds of hard-line "calls to assertiveness" might look like in practice. The excerpt below is taken from the interview with Rose, a young woman in her early 20s. At the very beginning of the interview, in response to a question about her "current situation, in terms of your relationships," she said, "My last experience was fairly unpleasant and so I thought I'll really try and um devote myself to singledom for a while before I rush into anything." In this one-night stand, approximately three weeks prior to the interview, Rose did manage to successfully insist that her partner use a condom. Her account of this experience is particularly interesting for the ways in which it graphically demonstrates the kinds of interactional barriers that a woman might have to overcome to be assertive about using a condom; moreover, it demonstrates how even embodiments of the male sex drive discourse that are not perceived to be coercive can act out levels of sexual urgency that provide a momentum that is difficult to stop. Although the following quote is unusually long, we prefer to present it intact to convey more about the flavor of the interaction she describes. We will refer back to it throughout this article and want to keep the story intact.

Nicola: So were condoms involved at all in that—

Rose: Yeah um, actually that's quite an interesting one because we were both very drunk, but I still had enough sense to make it a priority, you know, and I started to realize that things were getting to the point where he seemed to be going ahead with it, without a condom, and I was—had to really push him off at one point and—'cause I kept saying sort of under my breath, are you going to get a condom now, and—and he didn't seem to be taking much notice, and um—

Nicola: So you were actually saying that?

Rose: Yeah. I was—

Nicola: In a way that was audible for him to—

Rose: Yeah. (NICOLA: Yeah) And um—at least I think so. (NICOLA: Yeah) And—and it got to the point where [laughing] I had to push him off, and I think I actually called him an arsehole and—I just said, look fuck, you know, and—and so he did get one then but it seemed—

Nicola: He had some of his own that he got?

Rose: Yeah. (NICOLA: Yeah) Yeah it was at his flat and he had them. In fact that was something I'd never asked beforehand. I presumed he would have some. And um he did get one and then you know—and that was okay, but it was sort of like you know if I hadn't demanded it, he might've gone ahead without it. And I am fairly sure that he's pretty, um—you know he has had a pretty dubious past, and so that worried me a bit. I know he was very drunk and out of control and, um—otherwise the whole situation would never have occurred I'm sure, but still I had it together enough, thank God, to demand it.

Nicola: And you actually had to push him off?

Rose: Yeah, I think—I'm pretty sure that I did, you know it's—it's all quite in a bit of a haze, [laughing] (NICOLA: laughing) but um, it wasn't that pleasant, the whole experience. It was—he was pretty selfish about the whole thing. And um—yeah.

Nicola: How much old—how—You said that he was a bit older than you.

Rose: Ohh, he's only twenty-eight or nine, but that's quite a big difference for me. I usually see people that are very much in my own age-group. Mmm.

Nicola: And um, you said that it was kind of disappointing sexually and otherwise and he was quite selfish, (ROSE: laughter) like at the point where you know you were saying, do you want to get—are you going to get a condom, at that point were you actually wanting to have sexual intercourse?

Rose: Um, mmm, that's a good question. I can't remember the whole thing that clearly. And I seem to remember that I was getting um—I was just getting sick of it, or—[laughing] or—I might have been, but my general impression was that it was quite a sort of fumble bumbled thing, and—and it was quite—he just didn't—he didn't have it together. He wasn't—he possibly would've been better if he was less drunk, but he was just sort of all over the place and um—and I was just thinking, you know, I want to get this over and done with. Which is not the [laughing] best way to go into—into that sort of thing and um—yeah I—I remember at points—just at points getting into it and then at other points it just being a real mess. Like he couldn't—he wasn't being very stimulating, he was trying to be and bungling it 'cause he was drunk. And being too rough and just too brutish, just yeah. And um—

Nicola: When you say he was trying to [laughing] be, what do you—

Rose: Ohh, he was just like you know, trying to use his hands and stuff and just it—it was just like a big fumble in the dark (NICOLA: Right) type thing. I mean I'm sure h—I hope he's not usually that bad it was just like—I was in—sometimes—most of the time in fact I was just saying, look don't even bother. [laughing] You obviously haven't got it together to make it pleasurable. So in some ways—

Nicola: You—you said you were thinking that or you said that?

Rose: I just sort of—I did push his hand away and just say, look don't bother. Because—and I thought at that point that probably penetration would be, um, more pleasurable, yeah. But—and then—yeah. And I think I was actually wanting to just go to sleep and

I kept—I think I um mentioned that to him as well and said, you know why don't we— we're we're not that capable at the moment, why don't we leave it. But he wasn't keen on [laughing] that idea.

Nicola: What did he—is that from what he said, or just the fact that he didn't—

Rose: I think he just said, ohh no, no, no we can't do that. It was kind of like we had to put on this big passionate spurt but um it just seemed quite farcical, considering the state we were both in. And um, so I—yeah I thought if—yeah I thought it would probably be the best idea to [laughing] just get into it and like as I—as I presumed—ohh, actually I don't know what I expected, but he didn't last very long at all, which was quite a relief and he was quite—he was sort of a bit apologetic and like ohh you know, I shouldn't have come so soon. And I was just thinking, oh, now I can go to sleep. [laughter] Yes, so I just um—since then I've just been thinking, um one-night stands ahh don't seem to be the way to go. They don't seem to be much fun and [laughing] I'm not that keen on the idea of a relationship either at the moment. So I don't know. Who—I— it's hard to predict what's going to happen but—mmmm.

This unflattering picture of male heterosexual practice painted by Rose's account classically illustrates two of the dominant organizing principles of heterosexual sex—a male sex drive discourse and a coital imperative. The male sex drive discourse (see Hollway 1984, 1989) holds that men are perpetually interested in sex and that once they are sexually stimulated, they need to be satisfied by orgasm. Within the terms of this discourse, it would thus not be right or fair for a woman to stop sex before male orgasm (normatively through intercourse). This discursive construction of male sexuality thus privileges men's sexual needs above women's; the absence of a corresponding discourse of female desire (see Fine 1988) or drive serves to indirectly reinforce these dominant perceptions of male sexuality.

The extent to which male behavior, as patterned by the male sex drive discourse, can constrain a woman's attempts to insist on condom use are graphically demonstrated in Rose's account. The man she was with behaved with such a sense of sexual urgency and unstoppability that although she was able to successfully ensure a condom was used, it was only as a result of particularly determined and persistent efforts. He was unresponsive to her verbal requests and did not stop proceeding with intercourse until Rose became more directly confrontational— calling him "an arsehole" and physically pushing him off. At this point, he eventually did agree to wear a condom and did not use his physical strength to resist and overcome her actions to retain or take control of the situation. We will come back to analysis of Rose's account later in the article. . . .

PLEASING A MAN

The male sex drive discourse constructs masculinity in ways that directly affect women's heterosexual experiences as evidenced in the above description . . . of Rose['s] . . . experience. However, as we alluded to above, this discursive framework can also constitute women's sexual subjectivity in complex and more indirect ways. For example, for some women situated within this discursive framework, their ability to "please a man" may be a positive aspect of their identity. In this sense, a woman can be recruited into anticipating and meeting a man's "sexual needs" (as they are constituted in this discursive framework) as part of her ongoing construction of a particular kind of identity as a woman.

Sarah reported not liking condoms. She said she did not like the taste of them; she did not like the "hassle" of putting them on, taking them off, and disposing of them; and that they interfered with her sexual pleasure. However, it seemed that her reluctance to use them was also related to her sexual identity and her taken-for-granted assumptions about men's needs, desires, and expectations of her during sex. Sarah traced some of her attitudes toward sex to her upbringing and her mother's attitudes in which the male sex drive discourse was strongly ingrained.[1] She directly connected the fact that "when I've started, I never stop" to her difficulty in imagining asking a man to use a condom. As she said in an ironic tone, "If a man gets a hard-on you've gotta take care of it because he gets sick. You know these are the mores I was brought up with. So you can't upset his little precious little ego by asking to use a condom, or telling if he's not a good lover."

Sarah explained her own ambivalence toward this male sex drive discourse by drawing on a psychoanalytic distinction between the conscious and unconscious mind:

I mean I've hopefully done enough therapy to have moved away from that, but it's still in your bones. You know there's my conscious mind can say, that's a load of bullshit, but my unconscious mind is still powerful enough to drive me in some of these moments, I would imagine.

Thus, despite having a rational position from which she rejected the male sex drive discourse, Sarah found that when faced with a man who wanted to have sex with her, her embodied response would be to acquiesce irrespective of her own desire for sex. Her reference to this tendency being "in [her] bones" graphically illustrates how she regarded this as a fundamental influence. It is evocative of Judith Butler's suggestion "that discourses do actually live in bodies. They lodge in bodies, bodies in fact carry discourses as part of their own lifeblood" (Meijer and Prins 1998, 282). Sarah recalled an incident where her own desire for sex ceased immediately on seeing the man she was with undress, but she explained that she would not be prepared to stop things there:

Sarah: He's the hairiest guy I ever came across. I mean—but no way I would stop. I mean, as soon as he took his shirt off I just kind of about puked [laughing], but I ain't gonna say—I mean having gone to all these convolutions to get this thing to happen there's no way I'm gonna back down at that stage.

Nicola: So when he takes his shirt off he's just about the most hairiest guy you've ever met, which you find really unappealing.

Sarah: Terribly.

Nicola: Um, but you'd rather go through with it?

Sarah: Well I wouldn't say rather, but I do it.

Sarah also described another occasion where she met a man at a party who said, "do you want to get together? and I said, well, you know, I just want to cuddle, and he said, well, that's fine, okay." She explained that it was very important to her to make her position clear before doing anything. However, they ended up having sexual intercourse, because as she said,

Sarah: I was the one. I mean we cuddled, and then I was the one that carried it further.

Nicola: And what was the reason for that?

Sarah: As I said, partly 'cause I want to and partly 'cause if ohh he's got a hard-on you have to.

For women like Sarah, it seemed that an important part of their identity involved being a "good lover." This required having sexual intercourse to please a man whenever he wanted it and, in Sarah's case, to the point of anticipating this desire on the basis of an erect penis.... Given these expectations, and her belief that most men do not like condoms, it is not surprising that she had developed an almost fatalistic attitude toward her own risk of contracting HIV, such that she could say, "There's a part of me that also says, as long as I'm clear and not passing it on, I'm not gonna worry. You know, and if I get it, hey, it was meant to be."

For understanding the actions of Sarah and women like her, the assertiveness model is not at all helpful. In these kinds of sexual encounters, Sarah's lack or possession of assertiveness skills is beyond the point. What stops her from acting assertively to avoid undesired sex are deeply inscribed features of her own identity—characteristics that are not related to fear of assertion so much as the production of a particular kind of self. Well before she gets to the point of acting or not acting assertively, she is motivated by other (not sexual) desires, about what kind of woman she wants to *be*.

In a similar way to Sarah, an important part of Sally's identity was having "integrity about sexuality." She explained her position in relation to not "leading somebody on" in terms of a desire for honesty:

> And so—and I—that really was clinched somehow that you didn't lead somebody on and so that's part of—that's one of the sort of ways in which I understand that contract notion, really. And so maybe that had something to do with how I see myself about being a person with a reasonable—with integrity about sexuality. I won't go into something with false promises kind of thing.

Prior to these comments, Sally talked about the origins of her beliefs about this kind of contractual notion where it was not possible to be physically intimate with someone unless you were prepared to have intercourse. She remembered feeling awful about touching a man's penis when she was younger:

> I had been unfair because of the—I suppose the feeling of sort of cultural value of—of the belief that men somehow you know it's tormenting to them to leave a cock unappeased (N:[laughter]) [laughing] basically or something like that.

Like Sarah, Sally too reflected on her experiences in a way that highlights the limitations of attempting to influence sexual behavior based on understandings of people as unitary rational actors. Sally discussed a six-month relationship with a past lover in which she had not used condoms. She said that she had made the decision not to use condoms because she already had an intrauterine device (IUD) and because they were seen to connote a more temporary rather than long-lasting relationship (a view ironically reinforced by the advice of a nurse at the Family Planning Clinic):

Sally: It's like condoms are about more casual kinds of encounters or I mean—I mean, I'm kind of—um they are kind of anti-intimacy at some level.

Nicola: And so if you'd used condoms with him, that would've meant—

Sally: Maybe it would have underscored its temporariness or its—yeah, its lack of permanence. I don't understand that. What I've just said really particularly. It doesn't [seem] very rational to me. [laughter]

Nicola: [laughter] No it wasn't very rational and I—

Sally: [indistinguishable] it seems to be coming out of you know, somewhere quite deeper about um—I think it goes back to that business about ideals stuff. And I think that's one of the things about not saying no, you know. And that the ideal woman and lover—the ideal woman is a good lover and doesn't say no. Something like that. And it is incredibly counterproductive [softly] at my present time in life. [sigh/laugh]

Sally's reference to the ideal woman who is a good lover (because) she does not say no implicitly recognizes the strength of male sex drive discourse and its effect on her sexual experiences. In a construction that is similar to Sarah's, Sally refers to this kind of influence as "deeper" than her "rational" views. She presents an appreciation of this kind of cultural ideal as internalized in some way that is capable of having some control over her behavior despite her assessment of this as "counterproductive."

Engaging in Unwanted Sex

Many of the women in this study recounted experiences of having sex with men when they did not really want to, for a variety of reasons. This now common finding (e.g., Gavey 1992) underscores the extent to which women's control of sex with men is limited by various discursive constraints in addition to direct male pressure, force, or violence. As Bronwyn said, it is part of "the job":

Nicola: You said that you enjoy intercourse up to a point. Um, beyond that point, um, what are your reasons for continuing, given that you're not enjoying it?

Bronwyn: Ohh I just think it's part of my function if you like [laughter] that sounds terribly cold-blooded, but it is, [laughing] you know, it's part of the job.

Nicola: The job of—

Bronwyn: Being a wife. A partner or whatever.

Rose's account of her confrontational one-night stand, discussed previously, can be seen to be influenced in complex and subtle ways by the discursive construction of normative heterosexuality in which male sexuality and desire are supreme. She described the encounter as being quite unpleasant and disappointing, both sexually and in the way that he treated her—with respect to condoms and more generally throughout the experience. She described his actions during the encounter as clumsy and not the least bit sexually arousing ("He wasn't being very stimulating, he was trying to be and bungling it because he was drunk. And being too rough and just too brutish") and at one stage she suggested that they give up and go to sleep but he rejected this idea very strongly. Despite the extremely unsatisfactory nature of the sexual interaction and despite Rose's demonstrated skills of acting assertively, she did continue with the encounter until this man had had an orgasm through vaginal intercourse. It is difficult to understand why she would have done this without appreciating the power of the male sex drive discourse and the coital imperative in determining the nature of heterosexual encounters.

Although she did not define herself as a victim of the experience, Rose's account also makes clear that somehow she did not feel it was an option to end sex unless he gave the okay:

> It was sort of like—and I guess in that case he didn't have my utmost respect by that point. But it was sort of like, um, you know, he'd—he seemed to be just going for it, and I really really—I was drunk and sort of dishevelled and—and pretty resigned to having a bit of loose un—and unsatisfactory time which I didn't have a lot of control over.

She partially attributed this lack of control over the situation to the fact that the encounter took place at his flat, but this seems to be reinforced by underlying assumptions about sexuality and the primacy of his desires:

> Um, but it was kind of like he had his idea of what was going to happen and um I sort of realized after a while that he was so intent on it and the best thing to do was to just comply I guess, and make it as pleasurable as possible. Try and get into the same frame of mind that he was in. And—and yeah. Mmm, get it over with. It sounds really horrible in retrospect, it wasn't that bad it was just lousy, you know. It was just sort of a poor display of [laughing] everything. I suppose. Of intelligence and—and good manners. [laughter]

Part of the reason for the ambivalent nature of her account (swinging from describing what happened in very negative terms to playing down the experience as a poor display of manners) can be argued to originate from her positioning within a kind of liberal feminist discourse about sex. She had made a point of saying that she did not think things went in stages and defining herself in opposition to a model of female sexuality as fragile and in need of protection. The result of the connection between this liberal discourse of sexuality and that of the male sex drive is that she is left with no middle ground from which to negotiate within a situation of this kind. The absence of an alternative discourse of active female sexuality leaves her in a position of no return once she has consented to heterosexual relations and when certain minimal conditions are fulfilled (for her, this was the use of condoms). If heterosexuality were instead discursively constructed in such a way that women's sexual pleasure was central rather than optional, it makes sense that Rose may have felt able to call an end to this sex—which was, after all, so unpleasant that it led to her resolve to "devote [herself] to singledom for a while."

THE QUESTION OF PLEASURE

"I'm probably atypical from what I read of women in the fact that I personally don't like condoms." Sarah made this comment in the first minutes of the interview, and then much later she shared her assumption about how men regard using condoms: "Most men hate it. I've never asked them, but . . . that's the feeling I have from what I've read or heard." Sarah's generalized views about how women and men regard condoms echo dominant commonsense stories in Western culture. That is, most men do not like using condoms—a view shared by 80.5 percent of women in one large U.S. sample (Valdiserri et al. 1989), while women do not mind them. To explain her own dislike of condoms, Sarah was forced to regard herself as atypical. In the following section, we will discuss evidence that challenges the tacit assumption that condoms are relatively unproblematic for women.

Enforcers of the Coital Imperative: Condoms as Prescriptions for Penetration

Research on how men and women define what constitutes "real sex" has repeatedly found that a coital imperative exists that places penis-vagina intercourse at the center of (hetero)sex (Gavey, McPhillips, and Braun 1999; Holland et al. 1998; McPhillips, Braun, and Gavey 2001). The strength of this imperative was also reflected in the current research—as one woman explained, "I don't think I worked out a model of being with someone like naked intimate touching which doesn't have sex at the end of it" (Sally defined sex as penis-vagina intercourse during the interview). Although this coital imperative could be viewed as forming part of the male sex drive discourse examined above, it is addressed separately here as it has particular consequences for safer sex possibilities.

Condoms seem to reinforce the coital imperative in two interconnected ways, both in terms of their symbolic reinforcement of the discursive construction of sex as *coitus* and through their material characteristics that contribute at a more practical level to rendering sex as finished after coitus. In the analyses that follow, we will be attending to the material characteristics of condoms as women describe them.

As discussed earlier, we adopt a realist reading of women's accounts here. What the women told us about the ways in which condoms help to structure the material practice of heterosex casts a shadow over the assumption that condoms are unproblematic for women's sexual experience. These accounts illuminate how the male sexual drive discourse can shape not only the ways people speak about and experience heterosex, but also the ways in which a research lens is focused on heterosexual practice to produce particular ways of seeing that perpetuate commonsense priorities and silences (which, in this case, privilege men's pleasure above women's). That is, the ways in which condoms can interfere with a woman's sexual pleasure are relatively invisible in the literature, which tends, at least implicitly, to equate "loss of sexual pleasure" with reduced sensation in the penis, or disruption of desire and pleasure caused by the act of putting a condom on. As the following excerpts show, the material qualities of condoms have other particular effects on the course of sex. These effects are especially relevant both to the question of a woman's pleasure and to the way in which the coital imperative remains unchallenged as the definitive aspect of heterosex.

While many of the women said they like (sometimes or always) and/or expect sexual intercourse (i.e., penis-vagina penetration) when having sex with a man, many of the women noted how condoms operated to enforce intercourse as the finale of sex. Several women found this to be a disadvantage of condoms, in that they tend to limit what is possible sexually, making sex more predictable, less spontaneous, playful, and varied. That is, once the condom is on, it is there for a reason and one reason only—penile penetration. It signals the beginning of "the end." Women who identified this disadvantage tended to be using condoms for contraceptive purposes and so were comparing sex that involved condoms unfavorably to intercourse with some less obtrusive form of contraception such as the pill or an IUD, or with no contraception during a "safe" time of the month.

For example, Julie found that condoms prescribed penetration at a point where she could be more flexible if no condom was involved:

> That's what I mean about the condom thing. It's like this is *the act* you know, and you have to go through the whole thing. Whereas if you don't use condoms, you know, like he could put it in me and then we could stop and then put it in again, you know, you can just be a bit more flexible about the whole thing.

The interconnection between the material characteristics of condoms (its semen-containing properties require "proper use") and the discursive construction of the encounter (coitus is spoken about as "*the act*") has the effect of constraining a woman's sexual choices and leaving this generally unspoken coital imperative unchallenged. The discursive centrality of coitus within heterosex is materially reinforced by the practical difficulties associated with condoms, as Deborah said,

> Once you've put on the condom . . . that limits you. Once you've got to the stage in sex that you put a condom on, you then—it's not that you can't change plans, but it's a hassle if you then decided that you might like to move to do um—you might like to introduce oral sex at this stage, as opposed to that stage, then you have to take it off, or you don't, or—

* * *

Thus, condoms not only signaled when penetration would take place, but their use served to reinforce the taken-for-granted axiom of heterosexual practice, that coitus is the main sexual act. Furthermore, one woman (Sally) described how the need for a man to withdraw his penis soon after ejaculation when using a condom disrupted the postcoital "close feeling" she enjoyed. These excerpts can be seen to represent a form of resistance to the teleological assumptions of the coital imperative; women's accounts of desiring different forms of sexual pleasure (including, but by no means limited to, emotional pleasures) may provide rich ground for exploring safer sex options. This potentially productive area has yet to be fully exploited by traditional health campaigns, which perhaps reflects the lack of acknowledgment given to discourses of female sexual desire and pleasure in Western culture in general (see also Fine 1988).

Some women also talked about the effect using condoms had on their sexual pleasure by using the language of interruption and "passion killing" more commonly associated with men. Sarah, who rarely used condoms, said that "it breaks the flow":

> I have a lot of trouble reaching an orgasm anyway, and it's probably one of the reasons I don't like something that's interrupting, because I do go off the boil very quickly. Um, once it's on and it's sort of decided that penetration tends to be what happens. I don't suppose it's a gold rule, but it seems to be the way it is. So you know there's no more warm-up.

Unlike health campaigns directed at the gay community, which have emphasized the range of possible sex acts carrying far less risk of HIV infection than penile penetration, campaigns aimed at heterosexuals have done little to challenge the dominant coital imperative.[2] Health campaigns that promote condoms as the only route to safer sex implicitly reinforce this constitution of heterosexuality and the dominance of the male sex drive discourse. As the responses of the women in this study demonstrate, this reluctance to explore other safer sex possibilities may be a missed opportunity for increasing erotic possibilities for women at the same time as increasing opportunities for safer sex. The fact that all of these women spent some time talking about the ways in which condoms can operate to enforce the coital imperative or reduce their desire indicates the importance of taking women's pleasure into account when designing effective safer sex programs. That is, it may simply not be valid to assume that "the disadvantages of condom use are fewer for girls" (Barling and Moore 1990) if we expect women's sexual desires and pleasures to be taken as seriously as men's. Special effort may be required to ask different questions to understand women's experiences in a way that doesn't uncritically accept a vision of heterosex as inherently constrained through the lens of the coital imperative and male sex drive discourses.

DISCUSSION

* * *

Holland et al. (1998) have argued that heterosexual relations as they stand are premised on a construction of femininity that endangers women. Evidence for this position can be drawn from the current study as the interaction of discourses determining normative heterosexuality produces situations in which women are unable to always ensure their safety during sexual encounters. Holland et al. (1998) have argued that a refiguring of femininity is needed to ensure that women have a greater chance of safer heterosexual encounters. One of the prerequisites for change of this kind would be acknowledgment of the discourses of active female desire, which have traditionally been repressed (Fine 1988). Indeed, our research here suggests that the claim that condoms are "relatively unproblematic" for women is based on a continued relegation of the importance of women's sexual pleasure, relative to men's. Without challenging the gendered nature of dominant representations of desire, and more critically examining the coital imperative, condom promotion to women is likely to remain a double-edged practice. As both a manifestation and a reinforcement of normative forms of heterosex, it may be of limited efficacy in promoting safer heterosex.

NOTES

1. It should be emphasized that Sarah's mother's attitudes would have been in line with contemporary thought at the time. Take, for example, the advice of "A Famous Doctor's Frank, New, Step-by-Step Guide

to Sexual Joy and Fulfillment for Married Couples" (on front cover of Eichenlaub 1961, 36), published when Sarah was nearly an adolescent: Availability: If you want good sex adjustment as a couple, you must have sexual relations approximately as often as the man requires. This does not mean that you have to jump into bed if he gets the urge in the middle of supper or when you are dressing for a big party. But it does mean that a woman should never turn down her husband on appropriate occasions simply because she has no yearning of her own for sex or because she is tired or sleepy, or indeed for any reason short of a genuine disability. (Eichenlaub 1961, 36)

2. While some sexuality education directed at teenagers might be more likely to encourage alternatives to coital sex, and hence broader definitions of safer sex (e.g., Family Planning Association 1998; see Burns 2000), this is still less evident in material designed for the "mature sexuality" of heterosexual adults.

REFERENCES

Barling, N. R., and S. A. Moore. 1990. Adolescents' attitudes towards AIDS precautions and intention to use condoms. *Psychological Reports* 67:883–90.

Burns, M. 2000. "What's the word?" A feminist, post-structuralist reading of the NZ Family Planning Association's sexuality education booklet. *Women's Studies* 16:115–41.

Eichenlaub, J. E. 1961. *The marriage art.* London: Mayflower.

Family Planning Association. 1998. *The word—On sex, life & relationships* [Booklet]. Auckland, New Zealand: Family Planning Association. [ISBN 0–9583304–8-4]

———. 2000. *Condoms* [Pamphlet]. Auckland, New Zealand: Family Planning Association. (Written and produced in 1999. Updated 2000).

Fine, M. 1988. Sexuality, schooling, and adolescent families: The missing discourse of desire. *Harvard Educational Review* 58:29–53.

Gavey, N. 1992. Technologies and effects of heterosexual coercion. *Feminism & Psychology* 2:325–51.

Gavey, N., K. McPhillips, and V. Braun. 1999. Interruptus coitus: Heterosexuals accounting for intercourse. *Sexualities* 2:37–71.

Holland, J., C. Ramazonaglu, S. Scott, S. Sharpe, and R. Thomson. 1991. Between embarrassment and trust: Young women and the diversity of condom use. In *AIDS: Responses, interventions, and care,* edited by P. Aggleton, G. Hart, and P. Davies. London: Falmer.

Holland, J., C. Ramazonaglu, S. Sharpe, and R. Thomson. 1998. *The male in the head: Young people, heterosexuality and power.* London: The Tufnell.

Hollway, W. 1984. Gender difference and the production of subjectivity. In *Changing the subject: Psychology, social regulation and subjectivity,* edited by J. Henriques, W. Hollway, C. Urwin, and V. Walkerdine. London: Methuen.

———. 1989. *Subjectivity and method in psychology: Gender, meaning, and science.* London: Sage.

Kippax, S., J. Crawford, C. Waldby, and P. Benton. 1990. Women negotiating heterosex: Implications for AIDS prevention. *Women's Studies International Forum* 13:533–42.

McPhillips, K., V. Braun, and N. Gavey. 2001. Defining heterosex: How imperative is the "coital imperative"? *Women's Studies International Forum* 24:229–40.

Meijer, I. C., and B. Prins. 1998. How bodies come to matter: An interview with Judith Butler. *Signs: Journal of Women in Culture and Society* 23:275–86.

Planned Parenthood Federation of America, Inc. 1998–2001. *Condoms.* Retrieved 18 June 2001 from the World Wide Web: http://www.planned parenthood.org

Valdiserri, R. O., V. C. Arena, D. Proctor, and F. A. Bonati. 1989. The relationship between women's attitudes about condoms and their use: Implications for condom promotion programs. *American Journal of Public Health* 79:499–501.

Willig, C. 1995. "I wouldn't have married the guy if I'd have to do that." Heterosexual adults' accounts of condom use and their implications for sexual practice. *Journal of Community and Applied Social Psychology* 5:75–87.

Worth, D. 1989. Sexual decision-making and AIDS: Why condom promotion among vulnerable women is likely to fail. *Studies in Family Planning* 20:297–307.

Introduction to Reading 30

Aaronette M. White and Tal Peretz explore the ways gendered and raced emotions play a key role in deep changes in the perceptions and practices of masculinity of two African American men who have extensive involvement in the profeminist men's movement. They do so through analysis of the men's "narratives" of becoming aware and becoming active in the feminist movement. Although two case studies cannot be fully representative of profeminist African American men, they contribute to the ethnographic research tradition that has produced the richest, most detailed understanding of the complexities of masculinities.

1. What is the relationship between emotions and gender inequality in the contemporary United States? How do men benefit from this inequality?

2. Discuss the processes by which the two African American men transformed negative into positive emotions and how that transformation motivated them to act on behalf of gender equality.

3. How did the men in this reading transcend both street and middle-class representations of Black masculinity?

EMOTIONS AND REDEFINING BLACK MASCULINITY

MOVEMENT NARRATIVES OF TWO PROFEMINIST ORGANIZERS

Aaronette M. White and Tal Peretz

An emerging group of profeminist[1] African American men have participated in feminist collective action and founded organizations congruent with the mission and objectives of the profeminist men's movement (Brothers Absolutely Against Sexual Assault and Domestic Violence 1992; Atlanta Committee for Black Liberation 1996; Black Men for the Eradication of Sexism 2001; Men Acting Against Rape 2001; White 2001). The African American members of these organizations, particularly the founding members, have been understudied by masculinities study scholars and social movement researchers. Therefore, this study investigated the role of emotions in the narratives of 2 African American founding members of profeminist men's organizations, particularly the way emotions transformed their perceptions of masculinity and practices of masculinity. Their narratives serve as a model for future research on the role of emotions and the importance of a race-gendered intersectional analysis of emotion norms in the development of profeminist masculinities.

EMOTIONS, COGNITIONS, AND MASCULINITY

By viewing constructions of masculinities and emotions as socially situated political processes, we can investigate cognitive and emotional patterns that serve patriarchal ideology and how founders of profeminist men's organizations attempt to counter such patterns. Cognitions and emotions together shape profeminist masculinities; also, emotions serve rational and strategic purposes that are necessary to challenge unequal power relations (Taylor 2000; Whittier 2001; Taylor and Rupp 2002; Holmes 2004; Reger 2004). Yet, social scientists have focused on the more cognitive aspects of identity (e.g., schemata and discourses) rather than the emotions that underlie identity shifts and transformations (Goodwin, Jasper, and Polletta 2001). Moreover, social movement scholars who have conducted recent work on emotions, gendered identities, and political action have neglected the interconnected roles of race and gender in the construction of emotion norms (Britt and Heise 2000; Taylor 2000; Reger 2004).

As other scholars have noted, it is difficult to study strongly held identities without noticing people's feelings about the specific beliefs that underlie personally important identities (Hercus 1999; Taylor 2000; Goodwin, Jasper, and Polletta 2001). Thus, the cultural and intersectional approach to the emotions that underlie various masculinities presented in this exploratory study recognizes how culture shapes gendered expressions of emotions depending on the man's racial background.

The profeminist men's movement and its men's groups legitimize new emotional norms and practices through conceptions of masculinity that help men to redefine manhood, as well as alter unequal power relations between men and women and each other.[2] They emphasize (a) that masculinity, men's roles, and sexism are

From White, Aaronette M. 2010. "Emotions and Redefining Black Masculinity: Movement Narratives of Two Profeminist Organizers." *Men and Masculinities 12*(4), p. 403.

inseparable from the social and economic conditions and power relations that oppress women and men; (b) the importance of men applying feminism to their daily lives; and (c) men's participation in organized antisexist action (Goldrick-Jones 2002, 164). In contrast, other men's groups prioritize men's social, emotional, or sexual lives in ways that often substitute the personal for the political instead of forging a link between the two (Robinson 2000; Goldrick-Jones 2002; Newton 2005). Profeminist men's organizations teach men to share emotions in subversive ways that challenge how society defines masculinity thereby shaping potentially new masculinities. The activities these men engage in to create, present, and sustain the appropriate expression of feelings for men are referred to as "emotion work" (Hochschild 1990, 118). In the following section, we explain how emotion work is a gendered process. Then, we expand our understanding of this process by demonstrating how race is also an important, yet previously neglected, sociocultural component of emotion work using case studies of 2 Black cofounders of profeminist men's organizations.

Emotion Work in Feminist Social Movements

An important insight from sociology is that emotions and emotional displays are governed by gendered norms referred to as "feeling rules" (Hochschild 1990). Certain feelings and emotional displays are considered "masculine" whereas others are considered "feminine." The emotional behavior in which people engage can thus be considered gender appropriate or inappropriate, conforming or deviant. For example, because of women's lesser power and status in patriarchal societies, women, more than men, are required to suppress anger; when women express anger they are viewed as "unladylike," "inappropriate," and "emotionally deviant" and are often reprimanded (Hercus 1999, 37). Men experience the same range of emotions as women do. However, they are pressured to repress, suppress,

and express them according to rules prescribing what is "manly" or appropriate for men (Robinson 2000; Shields 2002).

Polarizing gender norms construct male superiority and "manliness" as the ability to suppress feelings of vulnerability by not showing or talking about them. Men are allowed to express stereotypically "tough" or "hard" emotions such as anger and resentment and "soft" emotions (e.g., tears of joy or sadness) only under extreme conditions, such as winning the Super Bowl or losing property and loved ones during a natural disaster (Shields 2002). To counter these patriarchal "feeling rules" or emotion norms, feminist organizations challenge socially constructed gender differences in expression as part of their efforts to eradicate larger gender inequities (Hercus 1999; Taylor and Rupp 2002; Holmes 2004; Reger 2004). Furthermore, feminists develop their own feeling rules or "feminist emotion cultures" (Taylor 1995, 229).

In general, feminist organizations encourage women to transform destructive emotions such as shame, fear, and depression into anger or righteous indignation toward the unjust social and cultural practices of patriarchy (Hercus 1999; Taylor 2000; Holmes 2004; Reger 2004). For instance, in the movement against sexual assault, shared feelings of shame, grief, and fear are discussed and turned into pride, anger, and joy (White 2001; Simmons 2003; Garfield 2005). In gay men, lesbian, bisexual and transgendered movements, self-destructive emotions that detract from one's self-esteem are countered through slogans, rituals, and other movement activities that transform self-conceptions in positive ways (e.g., Britt and Heise 2000; Gould 2002).

Profeminist men's organizations encourage men to trade guilt, shame, feelings of inadequacy, and anger associated with trying to live up to unrealistic standards of manhood, for empathy, compassion, and pride through feminist collective action (Goldrick-Jones 2002; Katz 2006). Feminist organizations use certain emotional strategies and activities to encourage collective action as well as to increase the salience of a personal feminist identity, whether the organization includes only women, men, or both (Hercus 1999; Goldrick-Jones 2002; Reger 2004). Movement members often experience emotional boosts from participating in events that reinforce this new identity. . . .

Thus, emotions and cognitions are invariably linked in feminist organizations and are shaped by the activities of these organizations. However, even though profeminist men's organizations are influenced by broader feminist emotion norms, these groups face different challenges and emotional processes than those founded by women. Specifically, social institutions enforce a pattern of practices that valorize and police men while excluding and discrediting women, through what gender theorists refer to as "hegemonic masculinity" (Connell 1995). Moreover, hegemonic masculinity affects Black men's emotion work processes and conceptions of masculinity in ways that require an intersectional cultural analysis that includes race and gender.

AFRICAN AMERICAN MEN, EMOTIONS AND HEGEMONIC MASCULINITY

Although multiple representations of masculinity exist within and across various cultures, hegemonic masculinity represents the dominant ideal, whereas the other representations are considered subordinate approximations (Connell and Messerschmidt 2005). Men who most closely conform to the hegemonic or dominant ideal in a particular context (e.g., White, heterosexual, wealthy, and able-bodied) accrue more opportunities to dominate not only women but also other men (Connell 1995). . . . This creates an ongoing pressure among men to "prove one's manhood," so that even marginalized men (e.g., gay men, poor men of color, and disabled men) conform to the hegemonic ideal. Why? Because they benefit from a "patriarchal dividend," that is, the advantage men in general gain from the subordination of women within their subgroup (Connell 1995).

Specifically, homophobic and heterosexist notions about what is "manly" pressure men to conform to hegemonic, patriarchal rules about

feelings. Thus, "real" men are expected to exercise control over their emotions as well as their control over women and men lower in status. Through teasing and bullying of boys in school for "sissiness" and describing a boy or man as "girly," "too soft," or a "wuss," the association with anything that seems "feminine" is repressed as boys and men distance themselves from any behavior that may indicate homosexuality or vulnerability (Connell and Messerschmidt 2005; Katz 2006). Therefore, most boys and men conform to such rules to avoid the negative emotions (embarrassment and shame) and consequences (being bullied or ostracized by male peers) that arise when their masculinity is questioned (Shields 2002; Katz 2006). This policing of the emotional dimensions of social relationships reflects inequalities of power. Thus, profeminist men's organizations teach that men have a stake in dismantling patriarchy and the hegemonic masculinity norms associated with it. These feeling rules, however, may play out differently among Black men because ideas about normalcy and deviancy regarding masculinity draw heavily on ideas about gender, but also race, class, and sexuality (Collins 2004, 44).

On one hand, Black men seeking to redefine how they think and feel about masculinity issues are pressured by hegemonic masculinity norms to be just like White men (73). On the other hand, Black men's attempts to prove themselves strong without being threatening, while maintaining a healthy self-concept about their manhood create inevitable tensions between "middle-class normative concepts of Black respectability and working-class or street-oriented concepts of Black authenticity" (81). Patricia Hill Collins (2004) explains:

> The cluster of representations for Black working-class men deems them less manly than White men and therefore weaker. Because these men do not participate appropriately in society (absent fathers, criminals, etc.), they weaken it. They are also deemed less capable of undertaking the tasks of strong men, for example, exhibiting the self-discipline to study hard in school, work in low-paying jobs, save their money, and support their children.

Their strength lies in their violence and sexual prowess. . . . In contrast to this site of weakness, representations of middle-class Black men who may be doing well but who pose little threat to White society present another dimension of weakness. Because they fail to confront the new racism . . . [they] represent emasculated and feminized versions of Black masculinity. (179)

. . . The class-specific representations of Black masculinity within African American communities position certain Black masculinities as strong or weak whereas between (racial)-group representations define any Black masculinity as the opposite of normal (White) hegemonic masculinity: "Whiteness" is at the center of the hegemonic description of manhood itself (Collins 2004, 178, 193). How do African American organizers of profeminist men's groups reconcile these multiple aspects (or subordinate approximations) of hegemonic masculinity?

Building on previous studies, our findings suggest that through a positively defined Black masculinity, African American profeminist men organizers highlight the favorable aspects of feminist practices and encourage yet another deviant form of masculinity—albeit a feminist one. In what follows, we analyze how 2 African American founders of profeminist men's organizations negotiated specific profeminist feeling rules and Black masculinities using movement literature and organizational activities. Gender issues certainly matter to these African American men; however, their profeminist masculinities, activist practices, and the emotion norms they promote within their organizations are simultaneously shaped by race and the power that these factors confer in our society.

METHODOLOGICAL AND PROCEDURAL CONSIDERATIONS

Following a 1996 conference sponsored by Black Men for the Eradication of Sexism (BMES) entitled "To Be Black, Male, and Feminist/ Womanist," and over a 7-year period thereafter, the first author established informal networks that resulted in a nationwide study of Black women and men who self-identify as "feminist," "profeminist," or "antisexist" (White 2006). That survey identified 2 African American men who had cofounded feminist men's organizations as students.

Each man came from a traditional working-class household and was in his early 20s when the group began. Albert Bryant,[3] a self-identified heterosexual African American man originally from California, cofounded Men Acting Against Rape (MAAR) with 1 Latino man and 2 White men in 2002 at a public, predominantly White coed university in California. Carlos Ramirez, a self-identified heterosexual Black Latino originally from New York, cofounded BMES in 1994 at a private Black men's college in Georgia with African American men. Both groups explicitly used feminist ideology in their mission statements.

In-depth, face-to-face, semistructured interviews of the 2 African American founders collected in 2004 served as the primary sources for our study. The open-ended interview lasted 4–5 hr for each man and targeted 25 topics including the oral history of the respective organizations, family relationships, childhood and adult friendships, work-related experiences, exposure to leftist politics, educational experiences, and attitudes and experiences concerning gender roles, sexuality, race and ethnicity issues, and feminist activism.

. . . Two common themes emerged from each founder's interview when narrative data regarding the founding of their respective organizations were interpreted from the transcripts by the author. Similar, in part, to Hunt and Bedford's (1994) findings among peace activists, each man's movement narrative included a process of (a) "becoming aware" of an injustice to a woman that resulted in negative emotions, and (b) "becoming active" in the feminist movement in ways that allowed him to transfer negative emotions into positive ones. The findings are additionally contextualized by including information from each group's Web site.

CULTIVATING PROFEMINIST MASCULINITIES

Both Albert and Carlos used organizational activities such as discussing profeminist men's literature and public demonstrations to counter hegemonic masculinity feeling rules and displays and to cultivate profeminist Black feminist masculinities. The profeminist writers whose texts they read helped each man reconstruct his personal story and masculinity as profeminist, emphasizing an ethic of responsibility. Thus, through the reframing of their narratives using a profeminist lens, their negative individual emotions became politicized and motivated them to act.

Becoming Aware

Albert of MAAR. Since 2002, Albert's multiracial organization, MAAR, has emphasized how rape affects men through the women they know and might come to know. MAAR's literature asserts, "even though the pain that men feel in no way compares to the pain and oppression that women experience who are raped, men are also profoundly, personally and politically, affected by rape and need to articulate the ways rape has affected them" (Funk 1993, 20). MAAR's Web site posts members' narratives and narratives from antirape literature, acknowledging that rape is an extremely intense and emotional topic and warning that feelings of vulnerability, fear, anger and disgust are common reactions to rape (http://www.ucdmaar .org). Thus, through its literature, the frequent updating of its Web site, an ongoing editorial writing campaign in the student newspaper, and various on-campus men's discussion groups, the organization attempts to teach men new ways to describe their feelings to each other; transform feelings of powerlessness into feelings of hope; and act in ways that prevent the rape of women. MAAR's literature warns men who engage in antirape activism that they must recognize and acknowledge the feelings that arise from ongoing deep and honest discussions about sexual violence and its impact on women and men (Funk 1993). Albert describes on

MAAR's Web site and in his interview how his aunt's rape "traumatized" him, made him "feel really bad," and "really powerless":

> I was affected by rape at a very early age, I believe six or seven years old. My aunt was raped over twenty years ago by a stranger. The man was eventually caught and served time in jail. When I was seven, my aunt, sister, other family friends, and I went to a restaurant and my aunt saw the man who raped her standing in line. When she saw him she lost all control. . . . I was traumatized by seeing my aunt so upset. . . . My aunt still has major issues with sex and intimacy with men because of her rape. I have felt compelled to do whatever I can to see that no other women have to go through what she deals with on a daily basis. . . . I felt really bad that happened to her. . . . My ex-girlfriend was also raped by her ex-boyfriend before we met. That made me feel really powerless because I was in love with her. I wish I could have helped her more in some way . . . but I felt that I wasn't in the position to do some of the things she needed.

Albert's feelings attest to what MAAR's reading materials state: "listening to a friend, lover, colleague, or family member describe how they've been sexually victimized can be incredibly painful. . . . The pain can be so great that men become paralyzed, full of guilt, and incredibly ashamed" (Funk 1993, 18, 148). Albert's testimony suggests feelings of helplessness and sadness. As a mobilizing strategy, MAAR's Web site and literature emphasize that working to stop rape can quell men's feelings of guilt, shame, and helplessness. Exchanging these negative, debilitating emotions for feeling "response-able" suggests that men "have the ability to respond to the situation in a proactive way that improves it" (Funk 1993, 91). Therefore, MAAR's message is that profeminist antirape activism can lead to feelings of hope and empowerment.

Albert Bryant's "becoming aware" narrative continued years after learning about his aunt's rape:

> My freshman year in college I took the Intro to Women's Studies course recommended by my girlfriend. Then, I became really interested in Women's Studies, took more classes, and made it

my minor. I also started doing some independent reading of feminist literature, particularly on the internet, then I started referring to myself as "profeminist."

The previous passage demonstrates how the course helped Albert reframe how he thought about rape prevention and the following passage demonstrates how he felt about his role as a man. His frustration leads him to ask new questions about rape.

In the Intro to Women's Studies class, we got on the topic of sexual assault and risk-reduction methods that focused on what women could do. . . . I talked about why men aren't more active and how risk reduction is not the same as violence prevention. . . . [T]he instructor mentioned how she thought men should be more involved in violence prevention and that maybe I could do something about this problem. . . . I really didn't have the wherewithal to do it at the time because I was a first-year student, I wasn't very well-versed in campus politics, and I didn't know who to turn to.

Albert's "becoming aware" narrative and feelings of frustration transition into "becoming active" and a hopefulness about how the efforts of men could prevent rape:

Luckily, in the spring of 2002, two fraternity members on campus who also knew loved ones or family members who had been raped, launched a call for interested men to come to an organizational meeting. When I saw the announcement, I liked everything they had to say and was already on board because I had wanted to start something like this group when I was a freshman . . . So, I showed up at the meeting and another guy showed up and we all became the four founding members.

Although MAAR's Web site does not mention race- or ethnicity-specific information, Albert noted in his interview that "being an African American profeminist" man allows him to "challenge the stereotype that all men, particularly that Black men, are rapists." BMES's Web site and literature, however, directly address racial issues as it redefines feeling rules for Black men,

and Carlos explicitly addresses how race interconnects with his profeminist identity.

Carlos of BMES. Between 1994 and 1997—the height of BMES's organization's activities—BMES used personal testimony to link Black men's feelings about their cultural reality to structural inequalities and feminist collective action. In addition to feelings of guilt, shame, pain, and disgust about the sexist injustices Black women encounter, many African American men experience anger and defensive feelings stemming from the ongoing plight of the endangered Black men (Dyson 2001; Collins 2004). Although the "endangered Black male" discourse rightly documents disproportionately high homicide, illiteracy, imprisonment, and unemployment rates for Black men, that discourse inadvertently minimizes the ways in which African American men benefit from patriarchy (Collins 2004; White 2008). BMES teaches Black men to feel differently about "Eurocentric (read as 'hegemonic') notions of manhood," acknowledge the plight of Black women, and act in new ways that create a "holistic interpretation of manhood" (Black Men for the Eradication of Sexism [BMES] 2001). Movement narratives describing members' feelings about their role as Black men in a sexist society appeared in newsletter editorials, spoken-word performances (also referred to in their literature as "poetry slams") on campus, and conference materials.

In the following passage, Carlos makes clear that he resisted the patriarchal ideas that were pervasive on his college campus and that the practice of such ideas left him feeling frustrated about how men treated women on campus:

During my first year at college, a group of sisters from the Black women's college down the street came to my dormitory room to hang out with me, but I wasn't there. A guy in the dormitory started harassing one of the women. She wanted him to leave her alone, but he wouldn't stop. None of the other guys on the floor did anything or said anything to help her. She was really afraid that he was going to hurt her because he had pushed her up against the wall, and the dude was big! Some of the other women helped her get away from the guy. They told me about it the next day. So, I wrote a note and posted it on the dormitory floor. I don't remember exactly what it said, but it was something like "ALL OF YOU SHOULD KNOW BETTER AND SHOULDN'T BE DISRESPECTING A SISTER. IF YOU HAVE A PROBLEM, MY NAME IS CARLOS AND I LIVE ON THE SECOND FLOOR IN ROOM 224." That night about five brothers came to my room and said "Do you know who wrote that note?" and I said "Yeah, I did." They confronted me for about 10 min. I think I did most of the talking, even though I was nervous and didn't know whether they came to talk or fight. They eventually left and denied any wrongdoing, but guilt was written all over their faces.

Carlos was clearly upset about what happened to his friends during their visit to his dormitory, and he was also nervous or afraid when confronting the men who had intimidated his friends. Both Carlos and Albert's movement narratives provide concrete illustrations of hegemonic masculinity as a pattern that can be oppressive to women and harmful to men. When men like Carlos and Albert admit to being pained by the effects of men's violence toward women they know, the women's stories appeared to become their own stories, allowing them to empathize with women and identify with feminist solutions. These men place their negative experiences and emotions in a feminist framework that links patriarchy to both women and men's suffering.

In his interview, Carlos Ramirez also described being introduced to reevaluation counseling (see http://www.rc.org for an introduction and overview of cocounseling) and the cocounseling community by an African American feminist woman. That experience helped him connect the ideological underpinnings of his past and his current activism in African American organizations to an emotional context. Within this emotional context, according to Carlos's interview, he was able to deal with how various racial stereotypes and other injustices affect his feelings about being a Black man.

Re-evaluation counseling is a process [in which] people learn to free themselves from the effects of past painful experiences. The process teaches you how to emotionally express your pain and then move beyond it. By learning to express yourself emotionally, you become more effective in looking out for your interests and the interests of others. Plus, you learn to act more successfully against injustices because you are not emotionally blocked. So, I participated in men's groups where they would ask you "What do you like about being a man?" "What don't you like about being a man?" I took some of the material discussed in re-evaluation counseling and adapted it for use in the antisexist men's discussion groups. I used to just think of social justice issues as being only political and as something that was outside of my personal life. I didn't question how I felt inside about such issues. Re-evaluation counseling sessions helped me see how political issues and unjust stereotypes had affected me emotionally. As a result, I developed an interest in changing how I felt as well as changing the external political conditions. I also came to realize that there were things that I did to other people that perpetuated the system I was organizing against! So, I started to make these connections that summer, thanks to my friendship with this particular Black feminist woman.

Although Carlos does not specify particular emotions in the previous passage, he stressed how reevaluation counseling helped him "get in touch with various emotions." In contrast with other therapeutic practices, reevaluation counseling is grounded in an explicitly political framework whereby people—most of whom are activists across various social movements—aim to liberate themselves (and each other) from the emotional ties that bind them to the oppressive values within a society (see Itzen 1985; King 2005). The cocounseling relationship is a reciprocal one in which people take turns at being the "listener" and "listened to" as a means of overcoming the emotional and rational dimensions of oppression (Jackins 1994). As feminist sociologist Debra King states: "In order to maintain their oppositional stance on issues, activists must constantly negate the hegemonic messages and norms that permeate society. Sustaining their identities as activists therefore entails perpetual vigilance and attention to this aspect of their identity work. It is not, however, just the dissonance of ideas that activists need to attend to, but also the dissonance of emotions" (2005, 152–153). Later in the interview, Carlos describes how he incorporated practices from cocounseling in his organization's discussion groups by asking members, "What do you like about being a Black man, and what is difficult to like about being a Black man?"

Movement narratives allow profeminist men to disclose intimate details of their personal lives to each other, to public audiences, and through various campus events as a strategy that reinforces new profeminist cognitive and emotional norms. This feminist reframing of their ideas about manhood and their feelings about gender relations motivates, empowers, and sustains them in healthy ways as they demand societal change as well as change within themselves. . . .

BECOMING ACTIVE

Both men made their developing masculinities public by writing about them on Web sites, sharing them through speeches, campus presentations, and discussion groups. These activities transformed the private experiences of each man's reactions to injustice against women into public events that "normalized" emotions usually considered weak and effeminate when expressed by Black men.

Albert of MAAR. Albert retells his story in the organization's internal men's discussion groups and in MAAR sessions open to the public. In addition, MAAR publicizes men's testimonies about how rape has affected them and those they love to garner attention on campus as part of an annual event. MAAR members print and enlarge these stories on huge poster boards, display them on a frame in the center of campus, and post excerpts on their Web site (http://ucdmaar.org). Their literature and activities emphasize how reactions to rape are not necessarily masculine or feminine, but human. Furthermore, accepting responsibility for preventing rape is another way of demonstrating strength as their mission statement asserts: "We intend to help males realize

that their strength is not for hurting;" thus, MAAR frames antirape activism as an act of "manly strength."

Carlos of BMES. After certain "becoming aware" experiences, Carlos Ramirez too was encouraged by his romantic partner to take his first Women's Studies course. His narrative continues with an organization that predated BMES:

> I co-founded a student group that organized a lot of campus and grassroots political activities for African American empowerment. My roommate and I co-founded the group during a bus trip to Washington, D.C. for a political rally after the Rodney King verdict. He believed that all men were sexist because we live in a sexist culture and reap the benefits of male privilege associated with the culture. So, we addressed sexism in our Black empowerment group and stated these grand visions in our group's platform . . . [O]ver time, sexism became a big problem in our group. At first we would always make sure that both a man and a woman were featured during public programs in order to avoid promoting men solely. But, over time more men joined the organized because we started thinking, "Let's bring back the Black Panthers!" We started emphasizing self-defense training, and men started to take on a more dominant role in public events. Many of our women members sort of drifted away, including the woman I was dating. [She] was known as the feminist voice of reason in the group, so, when she left the group, things really got bad.

Being tough and having street smarts are important components of Black masculinity, particularly urban versions of Black masculinity, and the Black Power Movement during the late 60s ushered in a new politicized version of this toughness (see Newton 2005). Because of mass media marketing, the commodification of Black nationalist symbols from the 60s, and the glamorization of the thug life via rap and hip-hop culture in the 80s and 90s, Carlos's organization experienced the tensions and contradictions of their generation. Using artist Tupac Shakur's life and death as an example of a child of a Black Panther who straddled the ideals of revolutionary politics and the macho materialistic aspects of hip-hop culture, Black feminist scholar and cultural critic Michael Eric Dyson describes Tupac's contradictory "revolutionary ambition and thug passion" accordingly, "thug ambition is unapologetically predatory, circumventing the *fellow feeling* [our emphasis] and group solidarity demanded of revolutionaries" (Dyson 2001, 64).[4] In a similar vein, Carlos's romantic partner confronted him about how narrowly Black nationalist and rigidly sexist the group had become. Male members' initial compassion and empathy for Black women had been replaced by patriarchal-induced resentment in an effort to retain Black working-class sensibilities. Carlos initially felt hurt and became defensive.

> My partner accused me of being antisexist around her privately, but trying to look cool around other guys instead of checking them on their sexism when I was in public. She asked me, "How are you going to confront the sexism of other guys in addition to being antisexist around me?" She suggested that a Black men's group against sexism would be a good idea and that I should organize it. . . . It took a while for the idea to take root. . . . It was inevitable that my growing awareness of sexism and patriarchy would collide directly with the sexist dynamics within the Black empowerment student organization. . . . I started confronting members of the group about their sexist language. . . . Some of the men in the group made me aware that I was "getting on their nerves." I started feeling ostracized the way some of the women had felt before they resigned from the group. At first, a few men in the group . . . started to refer to me as "some really weird guy" and tried to put me down by saying I must be "pussy-whipped" by the woman I was dating. Shortly after these confrontations, I . . . resigned from the group.

Carlos's narrative suggests feelings of frustration, alienation, and disappointment leading to his resignation. Heterosexist put-downs and having his masculinity challenged also played a role. . . . By calling Carlos "pussy-whipped," his peers openly questioned his ability to assert a Black male heterosexuality that is synonymous with strong (particularly, working-class or

street-oriented) Black manhood (Collins 2004; Payne 2006). His attempt to counter racialized and gendered feeling rules for Black men that pressure them to engage in self-censorship and denial about how they exploit Black women in their attempts to mimic the patriarchal power of White men resulted in his peers defining him as weak. Thus, in addition to race and class, we see how sexuality, particularly "hyperheterosexism" is connected to feeling rules that underlie . . . Black masculinities. Nonetheless, Carlos's narrative transitions into his growing activity in the profeminist movement, positive feelings surface and his perceived "weakness" in one setting is perceived as strength in the other setting.

Excitement about reading Black feminist literature, meeting African American feminists, and learning that Black men could be feminists were all integral to his "becoming aware" and "becoming active" narratives. This excitement exemplifies the pleasures of social movement participation (see Goodwin, Jasper, and Polletta 2001) and how some men regain their self-respect and happiness as a result of feminist support. Behavior that was previously deemed weak became the norm in a feminist setting.

> My girlfriend used to talk about a Black male professor who she described as a feminist. So, one day I said, "Well, why is he a feminist?" She gave me her reasons. Then, I said, "Why can't I be a feminist, I can be that." She pretty much said, "Then be it." Shortly thereafter, I took a feminist class, at the Black women's college, that she recommended. I loved that class. . . . My consciousness just skyrocketed! The professor always had her class organize some feminist activity at the end of the course. . . . My class decided to organize a speak-out on Freaknic, the Black College Spring Break weekend where nudity and the lewdest, "freakiest" behavior [are] encouraged. It is also a weekend where many women are raped, sexually harassed, and generally disrespected by the male participants. I decided to announce the starting of an antisexist men's group at the speak-out.

Carlos's positive interactions with the instructor and other women in the course heightened his consciousness and thoughts about gender issues, while increasing his feelings of pride, compassion, and acceptance. The emotional boosts he obtained in class for his burgeoning profeminist identity restored his dignity and countered derogatory challenges to his masculinity by his male peers. His girlfriend affirmed that Black men could be feminists and his class reinforced the idea that he was, indeed, becoming one. At this point, Carlos's "becoming active" narrative reflects hope and feelings of responsibility:

> I waited until the end of the speak-out, got up, said some things about Freaknic, then told the brothers present that we need to organize a group that would help us correct our sexist behavior and put in check the sexist behavior of others. . . . We sat in a circle and planned our first meeting. That was how our Black men's antisexist group got started.

Similar to Albert, Carlos recounts his story in the organization's internal men's discussion groups and in BMES's sessions open to the public. Movement narratives of BMES members are also routinely shared during antisexist training workshops with community youth. Although self-concept changes resulting from movement participation do not occur quickly, constantly retelling their movement narratives during antisexist events (even the retelling of their stories in the research interview) nourish their budding feminist masculinities and new profeminist emotion norms. Moreover, becoming aware and becoming active appear to represent continuous cycles throughout each man's profeminist development.

CONCLUSION

Both Albert and Carlos's movement narratives connect their frustrations about manhood and the difficulty expressing themselves emotionally to the price men pay for patriarchal power and an illusion of superiority. However, both men's narratives avoided a singular focus on men's emotional health, relying on information gathered from feminist literature to place hegemonic

masculinity feeling rules in an historical and political context. By critiquing the male privilege hidden behind situation-specific male inexpressivity, both men uncovered the myth of male strength perpetuated by patriarchal feeling rules (e.g., real men do not cry, do not feel pain, are not soft, and are not afraid) and the price men pay for maintaining that myth. Feelings of inadequacy and anger are attributed to patriarchy, rather than to their mothers, feminist women, or even their fathers.

Rather than forcing themselves to choose between street representations of Black masculinity . . . and middle-class representations of Black masculinity . . . both cofounders shared how they learned to express their rage through feminist activism and in the safety of group activities. . . . Each man's narrative also revealed how he used his organization to practice expressing emotions previously considered taboo. Public speeches and other group activities provided ample opportunities for both men to practice experiencing and expressing emotions traditionally described as feminine (e.g., compassion, empathy, tenderness, and concern) and others that suggest human vulnerability and sensitivity (e.g., love, fear, pain, anguish, and deep sorrow). Their personal narratives redefined "manly strength" and how to use emotions to fight injustice.

Feminist readings by men and women were often cited in their interviews to frame their narratives. For example, profeminist literature equipped the men with the language and logic to say "the system and its norms are bad," rather than "I am male and therefore bad" leading to pride and countering shame. Thus, organizational activities provided opportunities that allowed each man to address the public and how to write, speak, and feel—in fact, how to live—as profeminist men.

These narratives described how they became aware of an injustice to a woman that made them feel bad emotionally, and how they became active in the profeminist men's movement in ways that helped transform negative feelings into positive ones. The effective use of personal movement narratives in discussion groups, public speeches, and annual poster presentations cultivated counter-hegemonic feeling rules and displays and encouraged a redefinition of Black masculinity emphasizing an ethic of responsibility. This profeminist masculine identity encouraged the men to think and feel differently about masculinity.

In fact, the effect of storytelling on identity is cumulative, according to some theorists, such that what a person chooses to share in a group, a speech, or even a written testimony becomes increasingly important to that person's identity (Wuthnow 1994; Polletta 1998; Kiecolt 2000). If the person receives affirmative feedback, the aspect of identity presented in the story is reinforced and legitimated. Thus, being affirmed as profeminist among a group of men in and of itself can have a significant impact on the way an individual man feels about himself. When these men share their movement narratives, they experience themselves as different from traditional men. Nonetheless, they are also somewhere on the continuum of sexism by virtue of being socialized in a sexist society (Funk 1993). As MAAR's literature states, " . . . all of us do some good things and some not-so-good-things . . . the point is that we as men can confront our own behaviors" (Funk 1993, 93). For both Carlos Ramirez and Albert Bryant, their profeminist organizations provided an environment where feminist social change was being practiced and discussed. Furthermore, consistent with previous findings, their personal movement narratives suggest that personal and social change are interrelated and take place across various interactions (Kiecolt 2000).

For each founder, creating these organizations was an extension of his interactions with and affective ties to other, like-minded people. Both men became more aware and active through feminist partners who encouraged them to take their first Women's Studies course. Interactions with the professor and students in those courses also had a profound impact on their beliefs about social justice and gender issues. However, emotions were attached to those new beliefs such that each cognitive shift they experienced about gender issues was accompanied by an emotional one.

Anxieties, disappointments, and shame about men's violence against women were traded for hope, enthusiasm, and the pleasures of participating in feminist classes, public events, and discussion groups. For these 2 men, in particular, their emotions were strong enough to lead them to cofound profeminist men's organizations. However, despite these similarities, the narratives evidenced noticeable differences that merit special attention. The cultural settings of each campus and the specific historical periods during which each organization was founded created some major differences in their profeminist masculinities.

BMES, founded on a predominantly Black men's college campus, is more vocal about racism than MAAR because the preexisting political identification of its members included participation in Black nationalist politics with an anticapitalist stance. The civil rights movement, particularly the Black Power movement, provided a sharper focus on injustice from which to interpret feminism, along with hip-hop culture. Furthermore, the presence of a predominantly Black female college down the street and the location of both colleges in African American urban communities shaped BMES's interactions with Black feminist women and its outreach activities with Black male youth. Finally, BMES was founded shortly after the police beating of Rodney King and student uprisings in Atlanta in response to the verdict acquitting the officers involved. Racial issues between Blacks and Whites had become polarized, and historically Black student campuses experienced a resurgence of radical Black politics. Thus, BMES's profeminist collective identity and agenda appear broader than MAAR's given its intersectional analyses and influences.

MAAR was founded 7 years later in a predominantly White northern California suburb where racial issues are not as polarized, and on a predominantly White but racially diverse campus with appreciable numbers of Latinos, Asian Americans, and African Americans. Because of that diversity, also reflected in the founders, and because an interracial rape case (Kobe Bryant), not an interracial police brutality case (Rodney King), was being publicized, MAAR may have chosen strategically to emphasize profeminism across racial differences despite Albert's infusion of race issues in his personal profeminist identity. The predominantly White and interracial composition of MAAR were also contributing factors. Although both founders might be lumped together under the press-generated category "Generation X," this political cohort exhibited considerable variation based on regional politics (the South vs. the West Coast) and historical events, thereby indicating diversity among profeminist men in ways that resemble diversity among feminist women (Whittier 1995; Henry 2004).

Limitations

Our selection of the 2 men from this larger sample was driven by theoretical concerns about developing an intersectional analysis of Black masculinity and emotion work, and as an exploratory study, was not intended to be representative of founders of profeminist men's organizations or even Black profeminist men. Rather, our interest was in the degree to which individual narratives would reveal underlying raced-gendered emotion work processes and themes for future research. Despite this emphasis, the lack of generalizability of our findings is a limitation of the study. . . .

Despite such limitations, the men's narratives suggest that positive, alternative Black masculinities and identities can be conceived and enacted through profeminist men's organizations and that emotions occur in contexts that are gendered and racialized. Most important, certain emotions (e.g., empathy, grief, guilt, fear, and anger as well as pride and hope) appear to be pivotal in this process given the effects of hegemonic masculinity and the stereotypes about Black heterosexual masculinity on Black men. Profeminist Black men must grapple with culture-specific, class-based masculinity representations that define a weak masculinity as one that is not authentically Black. Thus, many African American men may be particularly reluctant to join predominantly White male–led profeminist organizations because of their unwillingness to submit to what they may perceive as weak "White male authority" on matters regarding their manhood—even when joining or forming coalitions with organizations might be congruent with their social justice interests.[5]

On one hand, organizational autonomy (e.g., Carlos's experiences in BMES) allows Black men the ability to challenge predominantly White political and economic leadership arrangements that heretofore have required their deferential compliance. On the other hand, Black men who are members of predominantly White profeminist organizations may address this power imbalance by assuming leadership positions and primary organizing roles as Albert did in MAAR. By providing examples of 2 African American men who served in leadership positions in 2 profeminist organizations in which one was predominantly Black and the other predominantly White, we provide a vision for the different ways Black men can be recruited to the profeminist men's movement.[6]

Notes

1. The terms "antisexist," "profeminist," and "feminist" are used interchangeably.

2. The profeminist men's movement in the United States has operated mainly through local communities in decentralized ways. Many profeminist men's collectives advocate for the prevention of violence against women through community education via training workshops, men's support groups, protest rallies, antiviolence parades, mass media campaigns, and fund-raising programs for women's shelters. In addition to these networks, the profeminist men's movement in the United States is associated with a nationally recognized organization, the National Organization for Men Against Sexism (see Goldrick-Jones 2002).

3. Pseudonyms have been used for study participants.

4. See Payne (2006) for an opposing point of view regarding street-life oriented masculinity.

5. Recently, an indeterminate number of profeminist Black men participate in a network of left-wing predominantly African American social movement organizations loosely affiliated with an umbrella organization called the Black Radical Congress and its Black Feminist Caucus.

6. Profeminist men's groups must organize men in ways that create a positive profeminist emotion culture while challenging negative rules for men that serve patriarchy and detract from their overall self-esteem. Striking this balance can be emotionally difficult, and feelings of frustration, disappointment, and burnout are common, because of unrealistic expectations of immediate social change. Black Men for the Eradication of Sexism (BMES) is no longer active, and while Men Acting Against Rape (MAAR) is still active, it has downsized its Web site and intense writing campaigns (personal communication, Carlos Ramirez, 2007; personal communication, Albert Bryant, 2007).

REFERENCES

Atlanta Committee for Black Liberation. 1996. A call to end the oppression of women and to advance the black liberation movement: A position paper on the million man march. In *Fertile ground: Memories and visions*, eds. Kalamu ya Salaam, and Kysha N. Brown, 267–83. New Orleans, LA: Runagate.

Black Men for the Eradication of Sexism. 2001. Mission statement of black men for the eradication of sexism: Morehouse college, 1994. In *Traps: African American men on gender and sexuality*, eds. Rudolph Byrd, and Beverly Guy-Sheftall, 200–204. Bloomington, IN: Indiana Univ. Press.

Britt, Lory, and David Heise. 2000. From shame to pride in identity politics. In *Self, identity, and social movements*, eds. Sheldon Stryker, Timothy Owens, and Robert W. White, 252–70. Minneapolis, MN: Univ of Minnesota Press.

Collins, Patricia Hill. 2004. *Black sexual politics: African Americans, gender, and the new racism.* New York: Routledge.

Connell, Robert, W. 1995. *Masculinities.* Berkeley, CA: Univ of California Press.

Connell, Robert W, and James W. Messerschmidt. 2005. Hegemonic masculinity: Rethinking the concept. *Gender and Society* 19:829–859.

Dyson, Michael Eric. 2001. *Holler if you hear me: Searching for Tupac Shakur.* New York: Basic Books.

Funk, Rus Ervin. 1993. *Stopping rape: A challenge for men.* Philadelphia, PA: New Society.

Garfield, Gail. 2005. *Knowing what we know: African American women's experiences of violence and violation.* New Brunswick, NJ: Rutgers Univ. Press.

Goldrick-Jones, Amanda. 2002. *Men who believe in feminism.* Westport, CT: Praeger.

Gould, Deborah B. 2002. Life during wartime: Emotions and the development of ACT UP. *Mobilization: An International Journal* 7:177–200.

Henry, Astrid. 2004. *Not my mother's sister: Generational conflict and third-wave feminism.* Bloomington, IN: Indiana Univ Press.

Hercus, Cheryl. 1999. Identity, emotion and feminist collective action. *Gender and Society* 13:34–55.

Hochschild, Arlie, R. 1990. Ideology and emotion management: A perspective and path for future research. In *Research agendas in the sociology of emotions,* ed. Theodore D. Kemper, 117–42. Albany, NY: State Univ of New York Press.

Holmes, Mary. 2004. Feeling beyond rules: Politicizing the sociology of emotion and anger in feminist politics. *European Journal of Social Theory* 7:209–27.

Hunt, Scott, and Robert Benford. 1994. Identity talk in the peace and justice movement. *Journal of Contemporary Ethnography* 22:488–517.

Itzen, Catherine. 1985. Margaret Thatcher is my sister: Counselling on divisions between women. *Women's Studies International Forum* 8:73–83.

Jackins, Harvey. 1994. *The Human side of human beings: The theory of re-evaluation counseling.* Seattle, WA: Rational Island Publishers.

Katz, Jackson. 2006. *The Macho Paradox: Why some men hurt women and how all men can help.* Naperville, IL: Sourcebooks.

Kiecolt, Jill K. 2000. Self-change in social movements. In *Self, identity, and social movements,* eds. Sheldon Stryker, Timothy Owens, and Robert W. White, 110–31. Minneapolis, MN: Univ of Minnesota Press.

King, Debra. 2005. Sustaining activism through emotional reflexivity. In *Emotions and social movements,* eds. Helena Flam, and Debra King, 150–69. New York: Routledge.

Newton, Judith. 2005. Reenchanting white masculinity: The profeminist heritage of men's liberation. In *From panthers to promise keepers: Rethinking the men's movement,* 107–36. Lanham, MD: Rowman and Littlefield.

Payne, Yasser. 2006. "A gangster and a gentleman": How street life-oriented, U.S.-born African men negotiate issues of survival in relation to their masculinity. *Men and Masculinities* 8:288–297.

Polletta, Francesca. 1998. Contending stories: Narrative in social movements. *Qualitative Sociology* 21:419–46.

Reger, Jo. 2004. Organizational emotion work through consciousness-raising: An analysis of a feminist organization. *Qualitative Sociology* 27:205–22.

Robinson, Sally. 2000. *Marked men: White masculinity in crisis.* New York: Columbia Univ Press.

Shields, Stephanie. 2002. *Speaking from the heart: Gender and the social meaning of emotion.* New York: Cambridge Univ Press.

Simmons, Aishah S. 2003. Using celluloid to break the silence about sexual violence in the black community. In *Violence in the lives of black women: Battered, black, and blue,* ed. Carolyn M. West, 179–86. Binghamton, NY: Haworth.

Taylor, Verta. 1995. Watching for vibes: Bringing emotions into the study of feminist organizations. In *Feminist organization: Harvest of the new women's movement,* eds. Myra Marx Ferree, and Patricia Yancey Martin, 223–33. Philadelphia, PA: Temple Univ Press.

Taylor, Verta. 2000. Emotions and identity in women's self-help movements. In *Self, identity, and social movements,* eds. Sheldon Stryker, Timothy Owens, and Robert W. White, 271–99. Minneapolis, MN: Univ of Minnesota Press.

Taylor, Verta, and Rupp Leila J. 2002. Loving internationalism: The emotion culture of transnational women's organizations, 1888–1945. *Mobilization: An International Journal* 7:141–58.

White, Aaronette M. 2001. I am because we are: Combined race and gender political consciousness among African American women and men anti-rape activists. *Women's Studies International Forum* 24:11–24.

White, Aaronette M. 2006. Racial and gender attitudes as predictors of feminist activism among self-identified African American feminists. *Journal of Black Psychology* 32:1–24.

Whittier, Nancy. 1995. *Feminist generations: The persistence of radical women's movements.* Philadelphia, PA: Temple Univ Press.

Whittier, Nancy. 2001. Emotional strategies: The collective reconstruction and display of oppositional emotions in the movement against child sexual abuse. In *Passionate politics: Emotions and social movements,* eds. J. Goodwin, J. Jasper, and F. Polletta, 233–55. Chicago: Univ of Chicago Press.

Wuthnow, Robert. 1994. *Sharing the journey: Support groups and America's new quest for community.* New York: Free Press.

❦ Topics for Further Examination ❧

- Look up research and websites on patterns of eating disorders and cosmetic surgery procedures among women and men in the United States today. Discuss the gender and racial politics of procedures such as skin bleaching, brachioplasty, and labiaplasty.
- Conduct research on LGBT (lesbian, gay, bisexual, transgender) hate crimes. Analyze the central role that heteronormativity and heterosexism play in those hate crimes.
- Compare and contrast the messages about gendered emotions in ads, articles, columns, and other features in popular women's and men's magazines.

7

GENDER AT WORK

Throughout this book, we emphasize the social construction of gender, a dominant prism in people's lives. This chapter explores some of the ways the social and economic structures within capitalist societies create gendered opportunities and experiences at work, and how work and gender affect life choices, particularly as they relate to family and parenting. The gendered patterns of work that emerge in capitalist systems are complex, like those of a kaleidoscope. These patterns reflect the interaction of gender with other social prisms such as race, sexuality, and social class. Readings in this chapter support points made throughout the book. First, women's presence, interests, orientations, and needs tend to be diminished or marginalized within occupational spheres. Second, one can use several of the concepts we have been studying to understand the relationships of men and women at work, including hegemonic masculinity, "doing gender," the commodification of gender, and the idea of separate spaces for men and women.

In this chapter, we explore the construction and maintenance of gender within both paid and unpaid work in the United States, including two articles that consider gender in the global workplace. We begin with a discussion of work and gender inequality. The history of gender discrimination in the paid labor market is a long one (Reskin & Padavic, 1999), with considerable social science research that documents gendered practices in workplace organizations. The first reading, by Joan Acker, discusses what she calls "inequality regimes," or the ways work organizations create and maintain inequality across the intersections of gender, race, and social class. In this piece, she looks beneath the surface to almost invisible institutional practices that maintain unequal opportunities within organizations (see also Acker, 1999). In this chapter, a reading by Christine L. Williams, Chandra Muller, and Kristine Kilanski uses Acker's paradigm to examine the characteristics of gendered organizations that women geoscientists face in the global oil and gas industry.

Consider the various ways the workforce in the United States is gendered. Think about different jobs (e.g., nurse, engineer, teacher, mechanic, domestic worker) and ask yourself if you consider them to be "male" or "female" jobs. Now take a look at Table 7.1, which lists job categories used by the Bureau of Labor Statistics (2012b). You will note that jobs tend to be gender typed; that is, men and women are segregated into particular jobs. The consequences for men and women workers of this continuing occupational gender segregation are significant in the maintenance of gendered identities. Included in Table 7.1 are jobs predominantly held by men (management, architecture and engineering,

Table 7.1 2006 Median Weekly Salary and Percentages of Men and Women in Selected Occupational Categories by Gender and Race/Ethnic Group[1]

Occupational Category	Total Number Employed in Category (16 years and older) (all numbers in thousands)	White Women	% in Category	White Men	% in Category	Black Women	% in Category	Black Men	% in Category	Hispanic[2] Women	% in Category	Hispanic[2] Men	% in Category
				Median Weekly Wages									
All occupations	$756 100,457	$703	34.8%	$856	46.1%	$595	6.1%	$653	5.4%	$518	5.7%	$571	9.4%
Management, professional, and related occupations													
Management occupations	$1,237 10,891	$1,032	33.3%	$1,447	52.1%	$916	3.9%	$1,136	3.2%	$880	3.3%	$1,022	4.7%
Business and financial operations occupations	$1,038 5,170	$937	44.7%	$1,240	35.8%	$854	7.1%	$990	3.6%	$819	4.7%	$1,127	3.2%
Computer and mathematical occupations	$1,305 3,296	$1,121	16.9%	$1,362	56.8%	$1,002	2.8%	$861	4.3%	$858[3]	1.1%	$1,190	4.6%
Architecture and engineering occupations	$1,315 2,494	$1,114	10.1%	$1,350	73.7%	$1,136[3]	0.9%	$1,047	5.0%	$1,071[3]	0.8%	$1,111	5.8%
Life, physical, and social science occupations	$1,108 1,043	$1,078	36.1%	$1,151	54.2%	$772[3]	3.8%	$1,104[3]	4.0%	$1,170[3]	2.3%	$904[3]	3.5%
Community and social services occupations	$813 1,931	$769	45.5%	$939	28.4%	$668	13.0%	$760	6.9%	$704	7.0%	$893	3.8%
Legal occupations	$1,277 1,259	$1,017	44.1%	$1,791	40.4%	$919	6.1%	$1,427[3]	2.3%	$847	4.0%	$1,294[3]	1.8%

Occupational Category	Total Number Employed in Category (16 years and older) (all numbers in this table are in thousands)	White Women	% in Category	White Men	% in Category	Black Women	% in Category	Black Men	% in Category	Hispanic² Women	% in Category	Hispanic² Men	% in Category
		Median Weekly Wages											
Education, training, and library occupations	$919	$881		$1,129		$785		$915		$772		$981	
	6,518		61.9%		22.9%		8.4%		2.2%		6.4%		1.9%
Arts, design, entertainment, sports, and media occupations	$929	$857		$989		$775[3]		$967		$727		$897	
	1,464		37.3%		49.7%		2.5%		4.6%		4.3%		5.7%
Health care practitioner and technical occupations	$995	$977		$1,162		$777		$775		$869		$963	
	5,725		59.0%		19.3%		9.3%		2.3%		5.3%		2.3%
Service occupations													
Health care support occupations	$487	$490		$537		$362		$492		$479		$563	
	2,190		56.4%		8.2%		24.2%		3.9%		13.8%		2.2%
Protective service occupations	$757	$631		$840		$583		$632		$729		$725	
	2,798		11.5%		65.2%		5.8%		12.7%		2.4%		10.6%
Food preparation and serving related occupations	$409	$393		$424		$363		$413		$367		$402	
	3,930		36.4%		38.2%		7.8%		6.8%		9.7%		17.5%
Building and grounds cleaning and maintenance occupations	$465	$399		$504		$420		$489		$382		$416	
	3,339		24.3%		52.7%		6.7%		9.4%		13.8%		23.5%
Personal care and service occupations	$453	$422		$575		$423		$509		$390		$557	
	2,121		50.8%		18.7%		12.6%		4.2%		12.3%		4.6%
Sales and office occupations													
Sales and related occupations	$670	$578		$839		$442		$603		$437		$619	
	9,294		35.1%		48.4%		5.5%		4.4%		5.7%		6.7%

(Continued)

Occupational Category	Total Number Employed in Category (16 years and older) (all numbers in this table are in thousands)	White Women	White Men	Black Women	Black Men	Hispanic² Women	Hispanic² Men
		% in Category	% in Category	% in Category	% in Category	% in Category	% in Category
		Median Weekly Wages					
Office and administrative support occupations	$623 / 13,695	$618 / 58.1%	$679 / 21.6%	$590 / 9.7%	$579 / 3.9%	$576 / 9.3%	$583 / 5.0%
Natural resources, construction, and maintenance occupations							
Farming, fishing, and forestry occupations	$430 / 775	$366 / 16.5%	$444 / 75.0%	$432³ / 1.7%	$496³ / 2.9%	$348 / 9.3%	$410 / 42.6%²
Construction and extraction	$717 / 5,031	$585 / 1.7%	$726 / 88.2%	$669³ / 0.2%	$625 / 5.9%	$487³ / 0.4%	$524 / 30.4%
Installation, maintenance, and repair occupations	$806 / 4,159	$770 / 2.7%	$814 / 84.0%	$664³ / 0.4%	$718 / 7.3%	$607³ / 0.5%	$676 / 14.8%
Production, transportation, and material moving occupations							
Production occupations	$605 / 7,058	$488 / 18.9%	$685 / 61.8%	$473 / 4.0%	$556 / 7.2%	$416 / 6.9%	$522 / 15.6%
Transportation and material moving occupations	$614 / 6,275	$478 / 9.4%	$643 / 68.5%	$517 / 2.4%	$619 / 14.2%	$377 / 2.8%	$531 / 19.1%

[1] Data for this table were taken from the *Current Population Survey*, Table A2: Usual Weekly Earnings of Employed Full-Time Wage and Salary Workers by Intermediate Occupation, Sex, Race, and Hispanic or Latino Ethnicity and Non-Hispanic Ethnicity, Annual Averages 2011 (Bureau of Labor Statistics, 2012a).

[2] Categories of race and ethnicity are overlapping in this table, as Hispanic is a non-exclusive category. Therefore, an individual can identify as both Hispanic and White or Black. This overlap is particularly apparent for the category "farming, fishing, and forestry occupations."

[3] These estimates do not meet BLS standard for statistical reliability (50,000 cases); therefore, they must be used cautiously.

and construction) and those predominantly held by women (education, health care support, and office and administrative support).

Gender segregation of jobs is linked with pay inequity in the labor force. In 2010, full-time women workers earned, on average, 81.8% of what men earned, or median weekly earnings of $669 compared with $884 for men (Bureau of Labor Statistics, 2011). As you look through Table 7.1, locate those jobs that are the highest paid and determine whether they employ more men or more women. Also, compare women's to men's salaries across occupational categories. Clearly, a "gender wage gap" is evident in Table 7.1. Even in those job categories predominantly filled by women, men earn more than women. For example, going beyond the data in Table 7.1 and looking specifically at elementary and middle school teachers—a traditionally female job in which women outnumber men 4.26 to 1—the 2011 median weekly earnings for men, regardless of race or ethnicity, is $1,022 compared with $933 for women (an $89/week or $4,628/year average difference; Bureau of Labor Statistics, 2011). The article by Adia Harvey Wingfield in this chapter discusses the "glass escalator" effect, where men in predominately female jobs earn more and get promoted more easily. But, as she discusses in her article, the glass escalator effect does not have a similar impact for African American men, as shown in Table 7.1. And there is no glass escalator effect for women in traditionally male jobs. For example, looking at the specific occupation of lawyer, men still outnumbered women 1.91 to 1 in 2011 and also out-earned women $1,884 to $1,631 (a $253/week or $13,156/year difference on average; Bureau of Labor Statistics, 2011).

The pattern you see does not deny that *some* women are CEOs of corporations, and today we see women workers everywhere, including on construction crews. However, although a few women crack what is often called "the glass ceiling," getting into the top executive or hypermasculine jobs is not easy for women and minority group members. The glass ceiling refers to the point at which women and others, including racial minorities, reach a position in their organizations beyond which they cannot continue on an upward trajectory (Purcell, MacArthur, & Samblanet, 2010; see also the articles by Acker, and Williams, Muller, and Kilanski in this chapter). Informal networks generally maintain the impermeability of glass ceilings, with executive women often isolated and left out of "old boys' networks," finding themselves "outsiders on the inside" (Davies-Netzley, 1998, p. 347). Similar internal mechanisms within union and trade-related organizations also keep women and minority group members out, because "knowing" someone often helps get a job in the higher paid, blue-collar occupations.

GENDER, RACE, AND SOCIAL CLASS AT WORK

When we incorporate the prism of race, segregation in the workforce and pay inequality become more complex, as illustrated in the Wingfield article in this chapter. Another look at Table 7.1 indicates that individuals who identify as Hispanic or Latino and African American earn less than White, non-Hispanic men and women, although minority men earn more than White women in some occupational categories. In addition, Hispanic and African American women and men are much less likely to be found in the job categories with higher salaries than their percentages in the labor force would suggest. The continuing discrimination against African Americans, Hispanics, and other ethnic minority groups (as indicated in Table 7.1) shows patterns similar to the discrimination against women, both in the segregation of certain job categories and in the wage gap that exists within the same job category. These processes operate to keep African American, Hispanic, and other marginalized groups "contained" within a limited number of occupational categories in the labor force.

The inequities of the workplace carry over into retirement (Calasanti & Slevin, 2001). Women and other marginalized groups are at a disadvantage when they retire, because their salaries are lower during their paid work years. Calasanti and Slevin find considerable inequalities in retirement income, which indicate that the inequalities in the labor force have a long-term effect for women and racial/ethnic minorities. They argue that only a small group of the workforce—privileged White men—are able to enjoy their "golden years," and the reasons for this situation are monetary.

Efforts to change inequality in the workplace by combating wage and job discrimination through legislation have included both gender and race. In 1963, Congress passed the Equal Pay Act, prohibiting employment discrimination by sex but not by race. Men and women in the same job, with similar credentials and seniority, could no longer receive different salaries. Although this legislation was an important step, Blankenship (1993) cites two weaknesses in it. First, by focusing solely on pay equity, this legislation did not address gender segregation or gender discrimination in the workplace. Thus, it was illegal to discriminate by paying a woman less than a man who held the same job, but gender segregation of the workforce and differential pay across jobs was legal. As Blankenship notes, this legislation saved "men's jobs from women" (p. 220) because employers could continue to segregate their labor force into jobs that were held by men and those held by women and then pay the jobs held by men at a higher rate. Second, this legislation did little to help minority women, as a considerable majority of employed women of color were in occupations such as domestic workers in private households or employees of hotels/motels or restaurants that were not covered by the act (Blankenship, 1993).

In 1964, Congress passed Title VII of the Civil Rights Act. They drafted this legislation to address racial discrimination in the labor force. This act prohibited discrimination in "hiring, firing, compensation, classification, promotion, and other conditions of employment on the basis of race, sex, color, religion, or national origin" (Blankenship, 1993, p. 204). Sex-based discrimination was not originally part of this legislation but was added at the last minute, an addition that some argue was to ensure the bill would not pass Congress. However, the Civil Rights Act did pass Congress and women were protected along with the other groups. Unfortunately, the enforcement of gender discrimination legislation was much less enthusiastic than that for race discrimination (Blankenship, 1993).

Blankenship (1993) argues that the end result of these two pieces of legislation to overcome gender and race discrimination was to "protect white men's interests and power in the family" (p. 221), with little concern about practices that kept women and men of color out of higher paying jobs. Sadly, these attempts seem to have had little impact on race and gender discrimination (Sturm & Guinier, 1996). In this chapter, articles by Acker, and Williams, Muller, and Kilanski describe the more subtle ways wage discrimination can take place in a high-paying occupational field. Take another look at Table 7.1 and think about the ways the different allocations of jobs and wages affect women's and men's lives across race and social class—their ability to be partners in relationships and their ability to provide for themselves and their families.

As you think about the differences that remain in wage inequality, consider what still needs to be accomplished. Pay equity may seem like a simple task to accomplish. After all, now we have laws that should be enforced. However, the process by which most companies determine salaries is quite complex. They rank individual job categories based on the degree of skill needed to complete job-related tasks. Ronnie Steinberg (1990), a sociologist who has studied comparable worth of jobs for more than 30 years, portrays a three-part process for determining wages for individual jobs. First, jobs are evaluated based on certain job characteristics, such as "skill, effort, responsibility, and working conditions" (p. 457). Second, job complexity is determined by applying a "value to different levels of job complexity" (p. 457). Finally, the values determined in the second step help set wage rates for the job. However, care work and other types of work typically performed by women are undervalued in this wage-setting process (England, 2005; Steinberg, 1990).

On the surface, this system of determining salaries seems consistent and "compatible with meritocratic values," where each person receives pay based on the value of what he or she actually does on the job (Steinberg, 1987, p. 467). What is recognized as "skill," however, is a matter of debate and is typically decided by organizational leaders who are predominately White, upper-class men. The gender and racial bias in the system of determining skills is shocking. Steinberg (1990, p. 456) gives an example from the State of Washington in 1972 in which two job categories, legal secretary and heavy equipment operator, were evaluated as "equivalent in job complexity," but the heavy equipment operator was paid $400 more per month than the legal secretary. Although it appears that all wages are determined in the same way based on the types of tasks they do at work, Steinberg (1987, 1990, 1992) and others (including Acker in this chapter) argue that the processes used to set salaries are highly politicized and biased.

GENDER DISCRIMINATION AT WORK

One way of interpreting why these gendered differences continue in the workforce is to examine workplaces as gendered institutions, as discussed in the introduction to this book. Acker, and Williams, Muller, and Kilanski—in the first two readings in this chapter—and other researchers examine work as a gendered institution (Acker, 1999). For example, Martin (1996) studied managerial styles and evaluations of men and women in two different organizations: universities and a multinational corporation. She found that when promotions were at stake, male managers mobilized hegemonic masculinity to benefit themselves, thus excluding women. Understanding the processes and patterns by which hegemonic masculinity is considered "normal" within organizations is one avenue to understanding how organizations work to maintain sex segregation and pay inequity. These "inequality regimes" disadvantage all but a few, and, as Acker notes in this chapter, things are likely to get worse rather than better.

Gender discrimination at work is much more than an outcome of cultural or socialization differences in women's and men's behaviors in the workplace. Corporations have vested interests in exploiting gender labor. The exploitation of labor is a key element in the global as well as the U.S. economy, particularly as companies seek to reduce labor costs. Women in particular are likely targets for large, multinational corporations. In developing nations, companies exploit poor women's desires for freedom for themselves and responsibility to their families. The reading by Steven C. McKay illustrates these points as he describes local factories in the Philippines owned by three multinational corporations based in three different countries and three different cultures. The gendered assumptions, policies, and practices these corporations bring to their factories in the Philippines reflect the cultures of their home countries and illustrate the various ways "inequality regimes" are created in the workplace. As you read McKay's description of how corporations structure their employees' work experiences, ask yourself how other structures and patterns within the workplace reinforce gender difference and inequality in men's and women's identities, relationships, and opportunities.

Looking at some of the top-wage jobs in the United States, Williams, Muller, and Kilanski in this chapter describe some of the subtle and not-so-subtle mechanisms of discrimination for geoscientists in the global gas and oil industry. The "inequality regimes" surrounding career trajectories and compensation patterns make meritocracy a myth and discourage women from trying because it is clear that they are on an uneven playing field. As you read the articles in this chapter, consider those mechanisms and others where gender segregates workplaces and keeps women from advancing into particular jobs.

THE EFFECT OF WORK ON OUR LIVES

The work we do shapes our identities, affecting our expectations for ourselves and others (Kohn, Slomczynski, & Schoenbach, 1986) and our emotions. It is not just paid work that affects our orientations toward self and others (Spade, 1991) but also work done in the home. In Western societies, work also defines leisure, with leisure related to modernization and the definition of work being "done at specific times, at workplaces, and under work-specific authority" (Roberts, 1999, p. 2). Although the separation of leisure from work is much more likely to be found in developed societies, work is not always detached from leisure, as evidenced by the professionals who carry home a briefcase at the end of the day or the beepers that summon individuals to call their workplaces (see the article by Carla Shows and Naomi Gerstel in Chapter 8).

WOMEN'S WORK

Care work is one gendered pattern that restricts women's leisure more so than men's (England, 2005). Women's leisure is often less an escape from work and more a transition to another form of work—domestic work. In an international study using time budgets collected from almost 47,000 people in 10 industrialized countries, Bittman and Wajcman (2000) found that men and women have a similar amount of free time; however, women's free time tends to be more fragmented by demands of housework and caregiving. Another study using time budgets found that women spent 30.9 hours on average performing various different family care tasks such as cooking, cleaning, repairs, yard work, and shopping, while men spent 15.9 hours per week performing such tasks (Robinson & Godbey, 1997, p. 101). Women also reported more stress in the Bittman and Wajcman (2000) study, which the authors attributed to the fact that "fragmented leisure, snatched between work and self-care activities, is less relaxing than unbroken leisure" (p. 185).

Domestic work, while almost invisible and generally devalued, cannot be left out of a discussion of work and leisure (Gerstel, 2000). Care work is devalued—particularly unpaid care work, which rests largely on women's shoulders. Gerstel refers to the contribution of women to care work as "the third shift." As a result, domestic labor and caregiving, being unpaid, are done by people least valued in the paid market, and the undervaluation of care work carries over to the paid market as well. Look again at Table 7.1 and identify those job categories that encompass care work, such as health support workers and personal care and service workers. Now compare salaries and percentages of men and women in these caregiving jobs. As you start to consider these issues, ask why we undervalue care work—the unpaid care work in the home as well as care work in the workplace. Why are men encouraged not to participate in care work, and why are women the default caregivers? How is it that the work of the home is undervalued, and how is this pattern related to the workplace and the amount of leisure time available to men and women?

WORK, FAMILY, AND PARENTING

With care work perceived as a "feminine" activity, it is not surprising that women's lives are more likely to be focused around, or expected to be focused around, care work activities. As Kathleen Gerson discusses in her reading in this chapter, couples have started to modify expectations for marriage and marital responsibilities in response to changes in educational attainment and workforce participation of women. Gerson describes the dilemmas faced and strategies tried by young people as they attempt to balance commitment to a relationship and autonomy in their lives. Caregiving and parenting have been transformed, and both men and women must respond to the constraints on their time as they balance what they want in their lives with idealized gender roles and the relationships of their own parents.

Decisions about caregiving and parenting are much more difficult for young couples, however, when society and work organizations assume they are a private (read "woman's") responsibility. Contrast the work/family policies of other industrialized nations to that of the United States as described in the article by Gwen Moore in this chapter. She looks at the lives of elite men and women in a comparative analysis of how these leaders of industrialized nations balance their work lives and family lives. Unfortunately, considerable gender differences remain, but other countries provide a much broader support network for dual-worker families, as will be discussed in the next chapter. What work/family policies would you like to see the United States adopt?

We can illustrate only a few patterns of work in this chapter. The rest you can explore on your own as you take the examples from the readings and apply them to your own life. When you read through the articles in this chapter, consider the consequences of maintaining gendered patterns at work for yourself and your future. While you are at it, consider why these patterns still exist and what these patterns of inequality look like in your life.

References

Acker, J. (1999). Gender and organizations. In J. S. Chafetz (Ed.), *The handbook of the sociology of gender* (pp. 171–194). New York: Kluwer Academic/Plenum.

Bittman, M., & Wajcman, J. (2000). The rush hour: The character of leisure time and gender equity. *Social Forces, 79*(1), 165–189.

Blankenship, K. M. (1993). Bringing gender and race in: U.S. employment discrimination policy. *Gender & Society, 7*(2), 204–226.

Bureau of Labor Statistics. (2011). Table 18: Median usual weekly earnings of full-time wage and salary workers by detailed occupation and sex, 2010 annual averages. In *Women in the labor force: A databook.* Retrieved July 2, 2012, from http://www.bls.gov/cps/wlf-databook2011.htm

Bureau of Labor Statistics. (2012a). Table A-2: Usual weekly earnings of employed full-time wage and salary workers by intermediate occupation, sex, race, and Hispanic or Latino ethnicity and non-Hispanic ethnicity, annual averages 2011 [Unpublished data]. In *Current Population Survey.*

Bureau of Labor Statistics. (2012b). Table A-26: Usual weekly earnings of employed full-time wage and salary workers by detailed occupation and sex [Unpublished data]. In *Current Population Survey.*

Calasanti, M., & Slevin, K. F. (2001). *Gender, social inequalities, and aging.* Walnut Creek, CA: AltaMira Press.

Davies-Netzley, S. A. (1998). Women above the glass ceiling: Perceptions on corporate mobility and strategies for success. *Gender & Society, 12*(3), 339–355.

England, P. (2005). Emerging theories of care work. *Annual Review of Sociology, 31*(1), 381–399.

Gerstel, N. (2000). The third shift: Gender and care work outside the home. *Qualitative Sociology, 23*(4), 467–483.

Kohn, M. L., Slomczynski, K. M., & Schoenbach, C. (1986). Social stratification and the transmission of values in the family: A cross-national assessment. *Sociological Forum, 1,* 73–102.

Martin, P. Y. (1996). Gendering and evaluating dynamics: Men, masculinities, and managements. In D. Collinson & J. Hearn (Eds.), *Men as managers, managers as men* (pp. 186–209). Thousand Oaks, CA: Sage.

Purcell, D., MacArthur, K. R., & Samblanet, S. (2010). Gender and the glass ceiling at work. *Sociology Compass, 4*(9), 705–717.

Reskin, B. F., & Padavic, I. (1999). Sex, race, and ethnic inequality in United States workplaces. In J. S. Chafetz (Ed.), *Handbook of the sociology of gender* (pp. 343–374). New York: Kluwer Academic/Plenum.

Roberts, K. (1999). *Leisure in contemporary society.* Oxon, UK: CABI.

Robinson, J. P., & Godbey, G. (1997). *Time for life: The surprising ways Americans use their time.* University Park: Pennsylvania State University Press.

Spade, J. Z. (1991). Occupational structure and men's and women's parental values. *Journal of Family Issues, 12*(3), 343–360.

Steinberg, R. J. (1987). Radical changes in a liberal world: The mixed success of comparable worth. *Gender & Society, 1*(4), 446–475.

Steinberg, R. J. (1990). Social construction of skill: Gender, power, and comparable worth. *Work and Occupations, 17*(4), 449–482.

Steinberg, R. J. (1992). Gendered instructions: Cultural lag and gender bias in the Hay System of job evaluation. *Work and Occupations, 19*(4), 387–423.

Sturm, S., & Guinier, L. (1996). Race-based remedies: Rethinking the process of classification and evaluation: The future of Affirmative Action. *California Law Review.*

Introduction to Reading 31

Joan Acker draws from her vast research on gender, class, work, and organizations to describe the structure of organizations that maintain gender, class, and race disparities in wages and power in organizations. She also explores why inequalities in organizational structures and practices are not likely to change. She describes "inequality regimes," or practices and policies embedded in the organization itself, and shows how they work to create and maintain inequality across gender, race, and class. In this article, Acker provides detailed examples of how organizations maintain the gender inequalities in wages described in Table 7.1 and also why individuals seem powerless to overcome these gender inequalities.

1. Using your own life, think about whether you can identify any "inequality regimes" in the organizations you have worked in.

2. How does her description of inequality regimes explain the data in Table 7.1?

3. Look for examples in this reading of how inequality regimes influence the decisions individuals make relative to autonomy and commitment, as discussed in the last reading in this chapter, by Kathleen Gerson.

INEQUALITY REGIMES

GENDER, CLASS, AND RACE IN ORGANIZATIONS

Joan Acker

All organizations have inequality regimes, defined as loosely interrelated practices, processes, actions, and meanings that result in and maintain class, gender, and racial inequalities within particular organizations. The ubiquity of inequality is obvious: Managers, executives, leaders, and department heads have much more power and higher pay than secretaries, production workers, students, or even professors. Even organizations that have explicit egalitarian goals develop inequality regimes over time, as considerable research on egalitarian feminist organizations has shown (Ferree and Martin 1995; Scott 2000).

I define inequality in organizations as systematic disparities between participants in power and control over goals, resources, and outcomes; workplace decisions such as how to organize work; opportunities for promotion and interesting work; security in employment and benefits; pay and other monetary rewards; respect; and pleasures in work and work relations. Organizations vary in the degree to which these disparities are present and in how severe they are. Equality rarely exists in control over goals and resources, while pay and other monetary rewards are usually unequal. Other disparities may be less evident, or a high degree of equality might exist in

From Acker, Joan. 2006. "Inequality Regimes: Gender, Class, and Race in Organizations," *Gender & Society,* 20(4): 441–464. Copyright © 2006. Published by Sage Publications on behalf of Sociologists for Women in Society.

particular areas, such as employment security and benefits.

Inequality regimes are highly various in other ways; they also tend to be fluid and changing. These regimes are linked to inequality in the surrounding society, its politics, history, and culture. Particular practices and interpretations develop in different organizations and subunits. One example is from my study of Swedish banks in the late 1980s (Acker 1994). My Swedish colleague and I looked at gender and work processes in six local bank branches. We were investigating the degree to which the branches had adopted a reorganization plan and a more equitable distribution of work tasks and decision-making responsibilities that had been agreed to by both management and the union. We found differences on some dimensions of inequality. One office had almost all women employees and few status and power differences. Most tasks were rotated or shared, and the supervision by the male manager was seen by all working in the branch as supportive and benign. The other offices had clear gender segregation, with men handling the lucrative business accounts and women handling the everyday, private customers. In these offices, very little power and decision making were shared, although there were differences in the degrees to which the employees saw their workplaces as undemocratic. The one branch office that was most successful in redistributing tasks and decision making was the one with women employees and a preexisting participatory ethos.

* * *

WHAT VARIES? THE COMPONENTS OF INEQUALITY REGIMES

Shape and Degree of Inequality

The steepness of hierarchy is one dimension of variation in the shape and degree of inequality. The steepest hierarchies are found in traditional bureaucracies in contrast to the idealized flat organizations with team structures, in which most, or at least some, responsibilities and decision-making authority are distributed among participants. Between these polar types are organizations with varying degrees of hierarchy and shared decision making. Hierarchies are usually gendered and racialized, especially at the top. Top hierarchical class positions are almost always occupied by white men in the United States and European countries. This is particularly true in large and influential organizations. The image of the successful organization and the image of the successful leader share many of the same characteristics, such as strength, aggressiveness, and competitiveness. Some research shows that flat team structures provide professional women more equality and opportunity than hierarchical bureaucracies, but only if the women function like men. One study of engineers in Norway (Kvande and Rasmussen 1994) found that women in a small, collegial engineering firm gained recognition and advancement more easily than in an engineering department in a big bureaucracy. However, the women in the small firm were expected to put in the same long hours as their male colleagues and to put their work first, before family responsibilities. Masculine-stereotyped patterns of on-the-job behavior in team-organized work may mean that women must make adaptations to expectations that interfere with family responsibilities and with which they are uncomfortable. In a study of high-level professional women in a computer development firm, Joanne Martin and Debra Meyerson (1998) found that the women saw the culture of their work group as highly masculine, aggressive, competitive, and self-promoting. The women had invented ways to cope with this work culture, but they felt that they were partly outsiders who did not belong.

Other research (Barker 1993) suggests that team-organized work may not reduce gender inequality. Racial inequality may also be maintained as teams are introduced in the workplace (Vallas 2003). While the organization of teams is often accompanied by drastic reductions of supervisors' roles, the power of higher managerial levels is usually not changed: Class inequalities are only slightly reduced (Morgen, Acker, and Weigt n.d.).

The degree and pattern of segregation by race and gender is another aspect of inequality that varies considerably between organizations. Gender and race segregation of jobs is complex because segregation is hierarchical across jobs at different class levels of an organization, across jobs at the same level, and within jobs (Charles and Grusky 2004). Occupations should be distinguished from jobs: An occupation is a type of work; a job is a particular cluster of tasks in a particular work organization. For example, emergency room nurse is an occupation; an emergency room nurse at San Francisco General Hospital is a job. More statistical data are available about occupations than about jobs, although "job" is the relevant unit for examining segregation in organizations. We know that within the broad level of professional and managerial occupations, there is less gender segregation than 30 years ago, as I have already noted. Desegregation has not progressed so far in other occupations. However, research indicates that "sex segregation at the job level is more extensive than sex segregation at the level of occupations" (Wharton 2005, 97). In addition, even when women and men "are members of the same occupation, they are likely to work in different jobs and firms" (Wharton 2005, 97). Racial segregation also persists, is also complex, and varies by gender.

Jobs and occupations may be internally segregated by both gender and race: What appears to be a reduction in segregation may only be its reconfiguration. Reconfiguration and differentiation have occurred as women have entered previously male-dominated occupations. For example, women doctors are likely to specialize in pediatrics, not surgery, which is still largely a male domain. I found a particularly striking example of the internal gender segregation of a job category in my research on Swedish banks (Acker 1991). Swedish banks all had a single job classification for beginning bank workers: They were called "aspiranter," or those aspiring to a career in banking. This job classification had one description; it was used in banking industry statistics to indicate that this was one job that was not gender segregated. However, in bank branches,

young women aspiranters had different tasks than young men. Men's tasks were varied and brought them into contact with different aspects of the business. Men were groomed for managerial jobs. The women worked as tellers or answered telephone inquiries. They had contact only with their immediate supervisors and coworkers in the branch. They were not being groomed for promotion. This was one job with two realities based on gender.

The size of wage differences in organizations also varies. Wage differences often vary with the height of the hierarchy: It is the CEOs of the largest corporations whose salaries far outstrip those of everyone else. In the United States in 2003, the average CEO earned 185 times the earnings of the average worker; the average earnings of CEOs of big corporations were more than 300 times the earnings of the average worker (Mishel, Bernstein, and Boushey 2003). White men tend to earn more than any other gender/race category, although even for white men, the wages of the bottom 60 percent are stagnant. Within most service-sector organizations, both white women and women of color are at the bottom of the wage hierarchy.

The severity of power differences varies. Power differences are fundamental to class, of course, and are linked to hierarchy. Labor unions and professional associations can act to reduce power differences across class hierarchies. However, these organizations have historically been dominated by white men with the consequence that white women and people of color have not had increases in organizational power equal to those of white men. Gender and race are important in determining power differences within organizational class levels. For example, managers are not always equal. In some organizations, women managers work quietly to do the organizational housekeeping, to keep things running, while men managers rise to heroic heights to solve spectacular problems (Ely and Meyerson 2000). In other organizations, women and men manage in the same ways (Wajcman 1998). Women managers and professionals often face gendered contradictions when they attempt to use organizational power in actions similar to those of men. Women enacting power violate conventions of relative subordination to men, risking the label of "witches" or "bitches."

Organizing Processes That Produce Inequality

Organizations vary in the practices and processes that are used to achieve their goals; these practices and processes also produce class, gender, and racial inequalities. Considerable research exists exploring how class or gender inequalities are produced, both formally and informally, as work processes are carried out (Acker 1989, 1990; Burawoy 1979; Cockburn 1985; Willis 1977). Some research also examines the processes that result in continuing racial inequalities. These practices are often guided by textual materials supplied by consultants or developed by managers influenced by information and/or demands from outside the organization. To understand exactly how inequalities are reproduced, it is necessary to examine the details of these textually informed practices.

Organizing the general requirements of work. The general requirements of work in organizations vary among organizations and among organizational levels. In general, work is organized on the image of a white man who is totally dedicated to the work and who has no responsibilities for children or family demands other than earning a living. Eight hours of continuous work away from the living space, arrival on time, total attention to the work, and long hours if requested are all expectations that incorporate the image of the unencumbered worker. Flexibility to bend these expectations is more available to high-level managers, predominantly men, than to lower-level managers (Jacobs and Gerson 2004). Some professionals, such as college professors, seem to have considerable flexibility, although they also work long hours. Lower-level jobs have, on the whole, little flexibility. Some work is organized as part-time, which may help women to combine work and family obligations, but in the

United States, such work usually has no benefits such as health care and often has lower pay than full-time work (Mishel, Bernstein, and Boushey 2003). Because women have more obligations outside of work than do men, this gendered organization of work is important in maintaining gender inequality in organizations and, thus, the unequal distribution of women and men in organizational class hierarchies. Thus, gender, race, and class inequalities are simultaneously created in the fundamental construction of the working day and of work obligations.

Organizing class hierarchies. Techniques also vary for organizing class hierarchies inside work organizations. Bureaucratic, textual techniques for ordering positions and people are constructed to reproduce existing class, gender, and racial inequalities (Acker 1989). I have been unable to find much research on these techniques, but I do have my own observations of such techniques in one large job classification system from my study of comparable worth (Acker 1989). Job classification systems describe job tasks and responsibilities and rank jobs hierarchically. Jobs are then assigned to wage categories with jobs of similar rank in the same wage category. Our study found that the bulk of sex-typed women's jobs, which were in the clerical/secretarial area and included thousands of women workers, were described less clearly and with less specificity than the bulk of sex-typed men's jobs, which were spread over a wide range of areas and levels in the organization. The women's jobs were grouped into four large categories at the bottom of the ranking, assigned to the lowest wage ranges; the men's jobs were in many more categories extending over a much wider range of wage levels. Our new evaluation of the clerical/secretarial categories showed that many different jobs with different tasks and responsibilities, some highly skilled and responsible, had been lumped together. The result was, we argued, an unjustified gender wage gap: Although women's wages were in general lower than those of men, women's skilled jobs were paid much less than men's skilled jobs, reducing even further the average pay for women when compared with the average pay for men. Another component in the reproduction of hierarchy was revealed in discussions with representatives of Hay Associates, the large consulting firm that provided the job evaluation system we used in the comparable worth study. These representatives would not let the job evaluation committees alter the system to compare the responsibilities of managers' jobs with the responsibilities of the jobs of their secretarial assistants. Often, we observed, managers were credited with responsibility for tasks done by their assistants. The assistants did not get credit for these tasks in the job evaluation system, and this contributed to their relatively low wages. But if managers' and assistants' jobs could never be compared, no adjustments for inequities could ever be made. The hierarchy was inviolate in this system.

In the past 30 years, many organizations have removed some layers of middle management and relocated some decision making to lower organizational levels. These changes have been described as getting rid of the inefficiencies of old bureaucracies, reducing hierarchy and inequality, and empowering lower-level employees. This happened in two of the organizations I have studied—Swedish banks in the late 1980s (Acker 1991), discussed above, and the Oregon Department of Adult and Family Services, responsible for administration of Temporary Assistance to Needy Families and welfare reform (Morgen, Acker, and Weigt n.d.). In both cases, the decision-making responsibilities of frontline workers were greatly increased, and their jobs became more demanding and more interesting. In the welfare agency, ordinary workers had increased participation in decisions about their local operations. But the larger hierarchy did not change in either case. The frontline employees were still on the bottom; they had more responsibility, but not higher salaries. And they had no increased control over their job security. In both cases, the workers liked the changes in the content of their jobs, but the hierarchy was still inviolate.

In sum, class hierarchies in organizations, with their embedded gender and racial patterns, are constantly created and renewed through organizing practices. Gender and sometimes race, in the form of restricted opportunities and particular expectations for behavior, are reproduced as different degrees of organizational class hierarchy and are also reproduced in everyday interactions and bureaucratic decision making.

Recruitment and hiring. Recruitment and hiring is a process of finding the worker most suited for a particular position. From the perspectives of employers, the gender and race of existing jobholders at least partially define who is suitable, although prospective coworkers may also do such defining (Enarson 1984). Images of appropriate gendered and racialized bodies influence perceptions and hiring. White bodies are often preferred, as a great deal of research shows (Royster 2003). Female bodies are appropriate for some jobs; male bodies for other jobs.

A distinction should be made between the gendered organization of work and the gender and racial characteristics of the ideal worker. Although work is organized on the model of the unencumbered (white) man, and both women and men are expected to perform according to this model, men are not necessarily the ideal workers for all jobs. The ideal worker for many jobs is a woman, particularly a woman who, employers believe, is compliant, who will accept orders and low wages (Salzinger 2003). This is often a woman of color; immigrant women are sometimes even more desirable (Hossfeld 1994).

Hiring through social networks is one of the ways in which gender and racial inequalities are maintained in organizations. Affirmative action programs altered hiring practices in many organizations, requiring open advertising for positions and selection based on gender- and race-neutral criteria of competence, rather than selection based on an old boy (white) network.

These changes in hiring practices contributed to the increasing proportions of white women and people of color in a variety of occupations. However, criteria of competence do not automatically translate into gender- and race-neutral selection decisions. "Competence" involves judgment: The race and gender of both the applicant and the decision makers can affect that judgment, resulting in decisions that white males are the more competent, more suited to the job than are others. Thus, gender and race as a basis for hiring or a basis for exclusion have not been eliminated in many organizations, as continuing patterns of segregation attest.

Wage setting and supervisory practices. Wage setting and supervision are class practices. They determine the division of surplus between workers and management and control the work process and workers. Gender and race affect assumptions about skill, responsibility, and a fair wage for jobs and workers, helping to produce wage differences (Figart, Mutari, and Power 2002).

Wage setting is often a bureaucratic organizational process, integrated into the processes of creating hierarchy, as I described above. Many different wage-setting systems exist, many of them producing gender and race differences in pay. Differential gender-based evaluations may be embedded in even the most egalitarian-appearing systems. For example, in my study of Swedish banks in the 1980s, a pay gap between women and men was increasing within job categories in spite of gender equality in wage agreements between the union and employers (Acker 1991). Our research revealed that the gap was increasing because the wage agreement allowed a small proportion of negotiated increases to be allocated by local managers to reward particularly high-performing workers. These small increments went primarily to men; over time, the increases produced a growing gender gap. In interviews we learned that male employees were more visible to male managers than were female employees. I suspected that the male managers also felt that a fair wage for men was actually higher than a fair wage for women. I drew two implications from these findings: first, that individualized wage-setting produces inequality, and second, that to understand wage inequality it is necessary to delve into the details of wage-setting systems.

Supervisory practices also vary across organizations. Supervisory relations may be affected by the gender and race of both supervisor and subordinate, in some cases preserving or reproducing gender or race inequalities. For example, above I described how women and men in the same aspiranter job classification in Swedish banks were assigned to different duties by their supervisors. Supervisors probably shape their behaviors with subordinates in terms of race and gender in many other work situations, influencing in subtle ways the existing patterns of inequality. Much of this can be observed in the informal interactions of workplaces.

Informal interactions while "doing the work." A large literature exists on the reproduction of gender in interactions in organizations (Reskin 1998; Ridgeway 1997). The production of racial inequalities in workplace interactions has not been studied so frequently (Vallas 2003), while the reproduction of class relations in the daily life of organizations has been studied in the labor process tradition, as I noted above. The informal interactions and practices in which class, race, and gender inequalities are created in mutually reinforcing processes have not so often been documented, although class processes are usually implicit in studies of gendered or racialized inequalities.

As women and men go about their everyday work, they routinely use gender-, race-, and class-based assumptions about those with whom they interact, as I briefly noted above in regard to wage setting. Body differences provide clues to the appropriate assumptions, followed by appropriate behaviors. What is appropriate varies, of course, in relation to the situation, the organizational culture and history, and the standpoints of the people judging appropriateness. For example, managers may expect a certain class deference or respect for authority that varies with the race and gender of the subordinate; subordinates may assume that their positions require deference and respect but also find these demands demeaning or oppressive. Jennifer Pierce (1995), in a study of two law firms, showed how both gendered and racialized interactions shaped the organizations' class relations: Women paralegals were put in the role of supportive, mothering aides, while men paralegals were cast as junior partners in the firms' business. African American employees, primarily women in secretarial positions, were acutely aware of the ways in which they were routinely categorized and subordinated in interactions with both paralegals and attorneys. The interaction practices that re-create gender and racial inequalities are often subtle and unspoken, thus difficult to document. White men may devalue and exclude white women and people of color by not listening to them in meetings, by not inviting them to join a group going out for a drink after work, by not seeking their opinions on workplace problems. Other practices, such as sexual harassment, are open and obvious to the victim, but not so obvious to others. In some organizations, such as those in the travel and hospitality industry, assumptions about good job performance may be sexualized: Women employees may be expected to behave and dress as sexually attractive women, particularly with male customers (Adkins 1995).

The Visibility of Inequalities

Visibility of inequality, defined as the degree of awareness of inequalities, varies in different organizations. Lack of awareness may be intentional or unintentional. Managers may intentionally hide some forms of inequality, as in the Swedish banks I studied (Acker 1991). Bank workers said that they had been told not to discuss their wages with their coworkers. Most seem to have complied, partly because they had strong feelings that their pay was part of their identity, reflecting their essential worth. Some said they would rather talk about the details of their sex lives than talk about their pay.

Visibility varies with the position of the beholder: "One privilege of the privileged is not to see their privilege." Men tend not to see their gender privilege; whites tend not to see their race privilege; ruling class members tend not to see their class privilege (McIntosh 1995). People in dominant groups generally see inequality as existing somewhere else, not where they are. However, patterns of invisibility/visibility in organizations

vary with the basis for the inequality. Gender and gender inequality tend to disappear in organizations or are seen as something that is beside the point of the organization. Researchers examining gender inequality have sometimes experienced this disappearance as they have discussed with managers and workers the ways that organizing practices are gendered (Ely and Meyerson 2000; Korvajärvi 2003). Other research suggests that practices that generate gender inequality are sometimes so fleeting or so minor that they are difficult to see.

Class also tends to be invisible. It is hidden by talk of management, leadership, or supervision among managers and those who write and teach about organizations from a management perspective. Workers in lower-level, nonmanagement positions may be very conscious of inequalities, although they might not identify these inequities as related to class. Race is usually evident, visible, but segregated, denied, and avoided. In two of my organization studies, we have asked questions about race issues in the workplace (Morgen, Acker, and Weigt n.d.). In both of these studies, white workers on the whole could see no problems with race or racism, while workers of color had very different views. The one exception was in an office with a very diverse workforce, located in an area with many minority residents and high poverty rates. Here, jobs were segregated by race, tensions were high, and both white and Black workers were well aware of racial incidents. Another basis of inequality, sexuality, is almost always invisible to the majority who are heterosexual. Heterosexuality is simply assumed, not questioned.

The Legitimacy of Inequalities

The legitimacy of inequalities also varies between organizations. Some organizations, such as cooperatives, professional organizations, or voluntary organizations with democratic goals, may find inequality illegitimate and try to minimize it. In other organizations, such as rigid bureaucracies, inequalities are highly legitimate. Legitimacy of inequality also varies with political and economic conditions. For example, in the United States in the 1960s and 1970s, the civil rights and the women's movements challenged the legitimacy of racial and gender inequalities, sometimes also challenging class inequality. These challenges spurred legislation and social programs to reduce inequality, stimulating a decline in the legitimacy of inequality in many aspects of U.S. life, including work organizations. Organizations became vulnerable to lawsuits for discrimination and took defensive measures that included changes in hiring procedures and education about the illegitimacy of inequality. Inequality remained legitimate in many ways, but that entrenched legitimacy was shaken, I believe, during this period.

Both differences and similarities exist among class, race, and gender processes and among the ways in which they are legitimized. Class is fundamentally about economic inequality. Both gender and race are also defined by inequalities of various kinds, but I believe that gender and racial differences could still conceivably exist without inequality. This is, of course, a debatable question. Class is highly legitimate in U.S. organizations, as class practices, such as paying wages and maintaining supervisory oversight, are basic to organizing work in capitalist economies. Class may be seen as legitimate because it is seen as inevitable at the present time. This has not always been the case for all people in the United States; there have been periods, such as during the depression of the 1930s and during the social movements of the 1960s, when large numbers of people questioned the legitimacy of class subordination.

Gender and race inequality are less legitimate than class. Antidiscrimination and civil rights laws limiting certain gender and race discriminatory practices have existed since the 1950s. Organizations claim to be following those laws in hiring, promotion, and pay. Many organizations have diversity initiatives to attract workforces that reflect their customer publics. No such laws or voluntary measures exist to question the basic legitimacy of class practices, although measures such as the Fair Labor Standards Act could be interpreted as mitigating the most severe damages from those practices. In spite of antidiscrimination and affirmative action laws, gender and race inequalities continue in work organizations. These inequalities are often legitimated through arguments that naturalize the inequality (Glenn 2002). For example, some employers still see women as more suited to child care and less suited to demanding careers than men. Beliefs in biological differences between genders and between racial/ethnic groups, in racial inferiority, and in the superiority of certain masculine traits all legitimate inequality. Belief in market competition and the natural superiority of those who succeed in the contest also naturalizes inequality.

Gender and race processes are more legitimate when embedded in legitimate class processes. For example, the low pay and low status of clerical work is historically and currently produced as both a class and a gender inequality. Most people take this for granted as just part of the way in which work is organized. Legitimacy, along with visibility, may vary with the situation of the observer: Some clerical workers do not see the status and pay of their jobs as fair, while their bosses would find such an assessment bizarre. The advantaged often think their advantage is richly deserved. They see visible inequalities as perfectly legitimate.

High visibility and low legitimacy of inequalities may enhance the possibilities for change. Social movements may contribute to both high visibility and low legitimacy while agitating for change toward greater equality, as I argued above. Labor unions may also be more successful when visibility is high and legitimacy of inequalities is low.

Control and Compliance

Organizational controls are, in the first instance, class controls, directed at maintaining the power of managers, ensuring that employees act to further the organization's goals, and getting workers to accept the system of inequality. Gendered and racialized assumptions and expectations are embedded in the form and content of controls and in the ways in which they are implemented.

Controls are made possible by hierarchical organizational power, but they also draw on power derived from hierarchical gender and race relations. They are diverse and complex, and they impede changes in inequality regimes.

Mechanisms for exerting control and achieving compliance with inequality vary. Organization theorists have identified many types of control, including direct controls, unobtrusive or indirect controls, and internalized controls. Direct controls include bureaucratic rules and various punishments for breaking the rules. Rewards are also direct controls. Wages, because they are essential for survival in completely monetized economies, are a powerful form of control (Perrow 2002). Coercion and physical and verbal violence are also direct controls often used in organizations (Hearn and Parkin 2001). Unobtrusive and indirect controls include control through technologies, such as monitoring telephone calls or time spent online or restricting information flows. Selective recruitment of relatively powerless workers can be a form of control (Acker and Van Houten 1974). Recruitment of illegal immigrants who are vulnerable to discovery and deportation and recruitment of women of color who have few employment opportunities and thus will accept low wages are examples of this kind of control, which preserves inequality.

Internalized controls include belief in the legitimacy of bureaucratic structures and rules as well as belief in the legitimacy of male and white privilege. Organizing relations, such as those between a manager and subordinates, may be legitimate, taken for granted as the way things naturally and normally are. Similarly, a belief that there is no point in challenging the fundamental gender, race, and class nature of things is a form of control. These are internalized, often invisible controls. Pleasure in the work is another internalized control, as are fear and self-interest. Interests can be categorized as economic, status, and identity interests, all of which may be produced as organizing takes place. Identities, constituted through gendered and racialized images and experiences, are mutually reproduced along with differences in status and economic advantage.

Those with the most powerful and affluent combination of interests are apt to be able to control others with the aim of preserving these interests. But their self-interest becomes a control on their own behavior.

* * *

GLOBALIZATION, RESTRUCTURING, AND CHANGE IN INEQUALITY REGIMES

Organizational restructuring of the past 30 years has contributed to increasing variation in inequality regimes. Restructuring, new technology, and the globalization of production contribute to rising competitive pressures in private-sector organizations and budget woes in public-sector organizations, making challenges to inequality regimes less likely to be undertaken than during the 1960s to the 1980s. The following are some of the ways in which variations in U.S. inequality regimes seem to have increased. These are speculations because, in my view, there is not yet sufficient evidence as to how general or how lasting these changes might be.

The shape and degree of inequality seem to have become more varied. Old, traditional bureaucracies with career ladders still exist. Relatively new organizations, such as Wal-Mart, also have such hierarchical structures. At the same time, in many organizations, certain inequalities are externalized in new segmented organizing forms as both production and services are carried out in other, low-wage countries, often in organizations that are in a formal, legal sense separate organizations. If these production units are seen as part of the core organizations, earnings inequalities are increasing rapidly in many different organizations. But wage inequalities are also increasing within core U.S.-based sectors of organizations.

White working- and middle-class men, as well as white women and all people of color, have been affected by restructuring, downsizing, and the export of jobs to low-wage countries. White men's advantage seems threatened by these changes, but at least one study shows that white men find new employment after layoffs and downsizing more rapidly than people in other gender/race categories and that they find better jobs (Spalter-Roth and Deitch 1999). And a substantial wage gap still exists between women and men. Moreover, white men still dominate local and global organizations. In other words, inequality regimes still seem to place white men in advantaged positions in spite of the erosion of advantages for middle- and lower-level men workers.

Inequalities of power within organizations, particularly in the United States, also seem to be increasing with the present dominance of global corporations and their free market ideology, the decline in the size and influence of labor unions, and the increase in job insecurity as downsizing and reorganization continue. The increase in contingent and temporary workers who have less participation in decisions and less security than regular workers also increases power inequality. Unions still exercise some power, but they exist in only a very small minority of private-sector organizations and a somewhat larger minority of public-sector unions.

Organizing processes that create and re-create inequalities may have become more subtle, but in some cases, they have become more difficult to challenge. For example, the unencumbered male worker as the model for the organization of daily work and the model of the excellent employee seems to have been strengthened. Professionals and managers, in particular, work long hours and often are evaluated on their "face time" at work and their willingness to put work and the organization before family and friends (Hochschild 1997; Jacobs and Gerson 2004). New technology makes it possible to do some jobs anywhere and to be in touch with colleagues and managers at all hours of day and night. Other workers lower in organizational hierarchies are expected to work as the employer demands, overtime or at odd hours. Such often excessive or unpredictable demands are easier to meet for those without daily family responsibilities. Other gendered aspects of organizing processes may be

less obvious than before sex and racial discrimination emerged as legal issues. For example, employers can no longer legally exclude young women on the grounds that they may have babies and leave the job, nor can they openly exclude consideration of people of color. But informal exclusion and unspoken denigration are still widespread and still difficult to document and to confront.

The visibility of inequality to those in positions of power does not seem to have changed. However, the legitimacy of inequality in the eyes of those with money and power does seem to have changed: Inequality is more legitimate. In a culture that glorifies individual material success and applauds extreme competitive behavior in pursuit of success, inequality becomes a sign of success for those who win.

Controls that ensure compliance with inequality regimes have also become more effective and perhaps more various. With threats of downsizing and off-shoring, decreasing availability of well-paying jobs for clerical, service, and manual workers, and undermining of union strength and welfare state supports, protections against the loss of a living wage are eroded and employees become more vulnerable to the control of the wage system itself. That is, fear of loss of livelihood controls those who might challenge inequality.

Conclusion

* * *

Greater equality inside organizations is difficult to achieve during a period, such as the early years of the twenty-first century, in which employers are pushing for more inequality in pay, medical care, and retirement benefits and are using various tactics, such as downsizing and outsourcing, to reduce labor costs. Another major impediment to change within inequality regimes is the absence of broad social movements outside organizations agitating for such changes. In spite of all these difficulties, efforts at reducing inequality continue. Government regulatory agencies, the Equal Employment Opportunity Commission in particular, are still enforcing antidiscrimination laws that prohibit discrimination against specific individuals (see www .eeoc.gov/stats/). Resolutions of complaints through the courts may mandate some organizational policy changes, but these seem to be minimal. Campaigns to alter some inequality regimes are under way. For example, a class action lawsuit on behalf of Wal-Mart's 1.3 million women workers is making its way through the courts (Featherstone 2004). The visibility of inequality seems to be increasing, and its legitimacy decreasing. Perhaps this is the opening move in a much larger, energetic attack on inequality regimes.

REFERENCES

Acker, Joan. 1989. *Doing comparable worth: Gender, class and pay equity.* Philadelphia: Temple University Press.

———. 1990. Hierarchies, jobs, and bodies: A theory of gendered organizations. *Gender & Society* 4:139–58.

———. 1991. Thinking about wages: The gendered wage gap in Swedish banks. *Gender & Society* 5:390–407.

———. 1994. The gender regime of Swedish banks. *Scandinavian Journal of Management* 10:117–30.

Acker, Joan, and Donald Van Houten. 1974. Differential recruitment and control: The sex structuring of organizations. *Administrative Science Quarterly* 19:152–63.

Adkins, Lisa 1995. *Gendered work.* Buckingham, UK: Open University Press.

Barker, James R. 1993. Tightening the iron cage: Concertive control in self-managing teams. *Administrative Science Quarterly* 38:408–37.

Burawoy, Michael 1979. *Manufacturing consent.* Chicago: University of Chicago Press.

Charles, Maria, and David B. Grusky. 2004. *Occupational ghettos: The worldwide segregation of women and men.* Stanford, CA: Stanford University Press.

Cockburn, Cynthia. 1985. *Machinery of dominance.* London: Pluto.

Ely, Robin J., and Debra E. Meyerson. 2000. Advancing gender equity in organizations: The challenge and importance of maintaining a gender narrative. *Organization* 7:589–608.

Enarson, Elaine. 1984. *Woods-working women: Sexual integration in the U.S. Forest Service.* Tuscaloosa, AL: University of Alabama Press.

Featherstone, Lisa. 2004. *Selling women short: The landmark battle for workers' rights at Wal-Mart.* New York: Basic Books.

Ferree, Myra Max, and Patricia Yancey Martin, eds. 1995. *Feminist organizations.* Philadelphia: Temple University Press.

Figart, D. M., E. Mutari, and M. Power. 2002. *Living wages, equal wages.* London: Routledge.

Glenn, Evelyn Nakano. 2002. *Unequal freedom: How race and gender shaped American citizenship and labor.* Cambridge, MA: Harvard University Press.

Hearn, Jeff, and Wendy Parkin. 2001. *Gender, sexuality and violence in organizations.* London: Sage.

Hochschild, Arlie Russell. 1997. *The time bind: When work becomes home & home becomes work.* New York: Metropolitan Books.

Hossfeld, Karen J. 1994. Hiring immigrant women: Silicon Valley's "simple formula." In *Women of color in U.S. society,* edited by M. B. Zinn and B. T. Dill. Philadelphia: Temple University Press.

Jacobs, Jerry A., and Kathleen Gerson, 2004. *The time divide: Work, family, and gender inequality.* Cambridge, MA: Harvard University Press.

Korvajärvi, Päivi. 2003. "Doing gender"—Theoretical and methodological considerations. In *Where have all the structures gone? Doing gender in organizations, examples from Finland, Norway and Sweden,* edited by E. Gunnarsson, S. Andersson, A. V. Rosell, A. Lehto, and M. Salminen-Karlsson. Stockholm, Sweden: Center for Women's Studies, Stockholm University.

Kvande, Elin, and Bente Rasmussen. 1994. Men in male-dominated organizations and their encounter with women intruders. *Scandinavian Journal of Management* 10:163–74.

Martin, Joanne, and Debra, Meyerson. 1998. Women and power: Conformity, resistance, and disorganized coaction. In *Power and influence in organizations,* edited by R. Kramer and M. Neale. Thousand Oaks. CA: Sage.

McIntosh, Peggy. 1995. White privilege and male privilege: A personal account of coming to see correspondences through work in women's studies.

In *Race, class, and gender: An anthology,* 2nd ed., edited by M. L. Andersen and P. H. Collins. Belmont, CA: Wadsworth.

Mishel, L., J. Bernstein, and H. Boushey. 2003. *The state of working America 2002/2003.* Ithaca, NY: Cornell University Press.

Morgen, S., J. Acker, and J. Weigt. n.d. *Neo-Liberalism on the ground: Practising welfare reform.*

Perrow, Charles. 2002. *Organizing America.* Princeton, NJ: Princeton University Press.

Pierce, Jennifer L. 1995. *Gender trials: Emotional lives in contemporary law firms.* Berkeley: University of California Press.

Reskin, Barbara. 1998. *The realities of affirmative action in employment.* Washington, DC: American Sociological Association.

Ridgeway, Cecilia. 1997. Interaction and the conservation of gender inequality. *American Sociological Review* 62:218–35.

Royster, Dierdre A. 2003. *Race and the invisible hand: How white networks exclude Black men from bluecollar jobs.* Berkeley: University of California Press.

Salzinger, Leslie. 2003. *Genders in production: Making workers in Mexico's global factories.* Berkeley: University of California Press.

Scott, Ellen. 2000. Everyone against racism: Agency and the production of meaning in the anti racism practices of two feminist organizations. *Theory and Society* 29:785–819.

Spalter-Roth, Roberta, and Cynthia Deitch. 1999. I don't feel right-sized; I feel out-of-work sized. *Work and Occupations* 26:446–82.

Vallas, Steven P. 2003. Why teamwork fails: Obstacles to workplace change in four manufacturing plants. *American Sociological Review* 68: 223–50.

Wajcman, Judy. 1998. *Managing like a man.* Cambridge, UK: Polity.

Wharton, Amy S. 2005. *The Sociology of gender.* Oxford, UK: Blackwell.

Willis, Paul. 1977. *Learning to labor.* Farmborough, UK: Saxon House.

Introduction to Reading 32

In this article, Christine L. Williams, Chandra Muller, and Kristine Kilanski use Joan Acker's theory (from the previous reading) to examine the work experiences of women geoscientists in oil and gas companies. The 30 women they interviewed are highly educated (22 had master's degrees, and 8 had PhDs), ranged in age from 30 to 52 (average age 38), and worked in 14 different companies, including large global corporations such as Exxon-Mobil, BP, and Shell. They used snowball sampling to locate the women they interviewed by asking women at professional meetings they attended to refer them to other women who held similar jobs. Through this process, they were also able to include three women who had left the industry. In-depth interviews with these women ranged from 1 to 2 hours. They also did observations at three professional meetings and interviewed three men supervisors. Their findings give us an inside look at the job experiences of women in STEM (science, technology, engineering, and mathematics; see also the article by Maria Charles in Chapter 4) fields and help us understand why women leave these fields.

1. Do men and women "do gender" in these professional fields, thus maintaining a system of inequality?

2. How does the "looser" style of "new management" practices in these powerful global corporations advantage or disadvantage women?

3. Using the findings from this study, explain why women engineers earn less than men.

GENDERED ORGANIZATIONS IN THE NEW ECONOMY

Christine L. Williams, Chandra Muller, and Kristine Kilanski

After making spectacular strides toward gender equality in the twentieth century, women's progress in the workplace shows definite signs of slowing (England 2010). Although women have entered occupations previously closed to them, many jobs remain as gender segregated today as they were in 1950. At both the top and the bottom of the employment pyramid, women continue to lag behind men in terms of pay and authority, despite closing gender gaps in educational attainment and workplace seniority. What accounts for these persistent gender disparities?

To explain gender inequality at work, many sociologists draw on Joan Acker's (1990) theory of gendered organizations. Acker argued that gender inequality is tenacious because it is built into the structure of work organizations. Even the very definition of a "job" contains an implicit preference for male workers (Acker 1990). Employers prefer to hire people with few distractions outside of work who can loyally devote themselves to the organization. This preference excludes many women, given the likelihood that they hold primary care responsibilities for family members. Consequently, for many employers the "ideal worker" is a man (see also Williams 2001).

Acker (1990) further identified five processes that reproduce gender in organizations: the division of labor, cultural symbols, workplace interactions, individual identities, and organizational logic. The latter process—organizational logic—was at the center of Acker's original critique of gendered organizations (Acker 1990) and is the focus of this article. The concept of organizational logic draws attention to how hierarchies are rationalized and legitimized in organizations. It encompasses the logical systems of work rules, job descriptions, pay scales, and job evaluations that govern bureaucratic organizations. Acker describes organizational logic as the taken-for-granted policies and principles that managers use to exercise legitimate control over the workplace. Workers comply because they view these policies and principles as "natural" or normal business practices.

While others had previously identified organizational logic as key to the reproduction of class inequality, Acker's breakthrough identified it as a source of gender inequality as well, even though it appears gender neutral on the surface. . . .

For example, organizations supposedly use logical principles to develop job descriptions and determine pay rates. But Acker argues that managers often draw on gender stereotypes when undertaking these tasks, privileging qualities associated with men and masculinity that then become reified in organizational hierarchies. Through organizational logic, therefore, gender discourses are embedded in organizations, and gender inequality at work results.

A great deal of research supports Acker's theoretical claims (for a review, see Britton and Logan 2008). But in the decades since the article was published, the social organization of work has changed considerably. Starting in the 1970s, organizations began to experience downsizing, restructuring, computerization, and globalization (DiMaggio 2001; Kalleberg 2000; Vallas 2011). Referred to as "work transformation," this general and vast process of change is affecting the structure of work in the United States and around the world. Whereas in the past, many workers looked forward to a lifetime of loyal service to a single employer, workers in the so-called new economy

From Williams, Christine, Chandra Muller, and Kristine Kilanski. 2012 (forthcoming). "Gendered Organizations in the New Economy." *Gender & Society*.

expect to change employers frequently in search of better opportunities and in response to lay-offs, mergers, and downsizing. Organizational logic is changing, too. Under the former system, workers carried out narrow and specific tasks identified by their job descriptions and were evaluated and compensated by managers who controlled the labor process. Today, as corporations shed layers of management, work is increasingly organized into teams composed of workers with diverse skills who work with considerable discretion on time-bounded projects and are judged on results and outcomes, often by peers. Furthermore, in the new economy, standardized career "ladders"—with clearly demarcated rungs that lead to higher-paying and more responsible positions—are being eliminated or replaced by career maps, or "I-deals," which are individualized programs of career development. Networking has become a principal means through which workers identify opportunities for advancement both inside and outside their firms (Babcock and Laschever 2003; DiMaggio 2001; Osnowitz 2010; Powell 2001; Rousseau 2005; Vallas 2011).[1]

In this study, we seek to extend Acker's (1990) analysis and critique of gendered organizations by investigating how gender is embedded in the organizational logic of the new economy. Acker's theory explains how gender is embedded in traditional organizations that value and reward worker loyalty and that are characterized by standardized job descriptions, career ladders, and manager-controlled evaluations—features that do not characterize jobs in the new economy. We investigate how organizational logic is gendered when work is precarious, teams instead of managers control the labor process, career maps replace career ladders, and future opportunities are identified primarily through networking.

GEOSCIENTISTS IN THE OIL AND GAS INDUSTRY

To investigate gendered organizations in the new economy, we draw upon our research on women geoscientists in the oil and gas industry. Women geoscientists have increased their numbers radically in recent decades, currently constituting about 45 percent of graduates with master's degrees in geology, the entry-level credential in the field (AGI 2011). Also, according to anecdotal data, women geoscientists are entering professional careers in industry in almost equal numbers as men. Despite these encouraging advances, there is a strong perception that women stall out in mid-career and eventually leave their jobs at the major companies (AAPG 2009). This pattern is not uncommon among women scientists in general (Preston 2004). The glass ceiling is firmly in place in the oil and gas industry, with very few women represented at the executive levels and on boards of directors (*Catalyst* 2011).

The oil and gas industry is an ideal setting to study gendered organizations in the new economy for several reasons. First, it is arguably the most powerful, global, essential, and lucrative industry in the world. In 2007, the largest oil and gas companies made roughly two trillion dollars (U.S.) in combined revenue and 150 billion dollars in profit (Pirog 2008). Despite its critical importance, few sociologists have examined the gender dynamics in this industry (see Miller 2004 for an exception). Second, the industry has a high demand for so-called knowledge workers (scientists and engineers), which is a defining feature of the new economy; one solution to the perceived shortage of these workers has been to increase the numbers of women in these fields (National Academy of Sciences 2010). Third, and most importantly for our analysis, the industry has been in the forefront of implementing the new organizational logic (McKee, Mauthner, and Maclean 2000). Throughout the 80s and 90s, the industry experienced numerous mergers, leading to reorganization and downsizing that exacerbated the vulnerability of its workforce. Consistent with the general process of work transformation, the major corporations have altered the career structure for their professional workforce by institutionalizing career maps and teamwork. The expectation of frequent career moves has enhanced the importance of networking for professional success. These innovations make the oil and gas industry a paradigmatic case for investigating gendered organizations in the twenty-first century.

* * *

FINDINGS

Organizational changes associated with the new economy are reflected in the careers of geoscientists in the oil and gas industry. Gone is the expectation of a lifelong career spent in loyal service to a single employer. Oil and gas companies frequently expand and contract their workforce in response to economic cycles and mergers (Yergin 1993). . . .

Job insecurity is described by [one] respondent as both a constant and a "very scary" feature of the oil and gas industry.

The constant threat of layoffs no doubt causes high levels of stress and performance pressures for geoscientists. But how is performance measured? In periods of downsizing and merging, how do individuals survive the periodic cuts and even succeed in the industry?

Given the work geoscientists are hired to do, it would seem that whoever finds the most oil and gas would receive the most rewards. Indeed, after a respondent drilled a successful well, headhunters tried to lure her away from her current company, offering incentives such as stock options. But corporations have good reason to be wary of using this particular metric of productivity, since it may incentivize geologists to overstate their claims, a risky and costly prospect for companies. To protect themselves from this lone wolf phenomenon and insure greater reliability, companies instituted the team structure. This geologist, who experienced both individual- and team-based work, explains the economic stakes:

> When I first started in the mid-80s, I was working an exploration play in northern Louisiana, and the engineer who was going to drill a well for me was based in Corpus Christi. I never met him. I would do my maps and put them in the mail because we didn't have electronic submission. We might have a few conference calls before we drilled a million dollar well. That

was when it cost $50,000 a day to drill a well. Now a well in the Gulf of Mexico is a million dollars a day. And so, [changing to the team structure] was part of that. You had to be able to get people face-to-face. There was too much on the line from a risk standpoint, and from a financial standpoint.

In the experience of this geologist, teams produce more reliable results than do individuals working alone. With more people involved, she believes that companies get better advice on where to drill and also where not to drill, lessening their economic risks.

Teams are now a standard organizational form for scientists working in industry (Connelly and Middleton 1996). The Bureau of Labor Statistics (2009) identifies the ability to work on teams as an important feature of geoscientists' careers. The women we talked to worked on teams ranging in size from five to 20. Some teams were interdisciplinary, while others were composed of members with a single specialty, all of whom were investigating a particular "play" or geographical area for potential drilling. Individuals' team assignments typically last from three to five years, and many require relocation to a different city, oil field, and/or country. Each team is headed by a supervisor, typically a professional peer working alongside the rest of the team. Supervisors also move around to different teams every few years. The result is a work organization in perpetual flux, with teams forming and disbanding, and team members and supervisors constantly circulating around the country and, indeed, all over the globe.

Even though work is team based and essentially collaborative, careers are still individual. Raises, promotions, and opportunities are allocated to individuals, not to teams (although team members can receive additional bonuses if their collective results contribute to a company's profits). Out of this particular context, oil and gas companies replaced career ladders and standardized job descriptions with career maps—individualized programs for career development. A career map establishes goals and sets expectations that are then used to monitor a worker's productivity and evaluate his or her performance. The supervisor plays a central role in crafting workers' career maps and making sure that they have the tools to achieve their goals. As the primary channel to management, the supervisor identifies high performers on the team, recommends raises and bonuses, and determines the quality of future placements. Thus, individual workers must gain the support of their supervisors in order to further their careers in the industry.

A second major pathway to success in the oil and gas industry is through networking. In many of the large corporations, professionals are assigned mentors for their first three to five years, but by mid-career, we were told, they are basically left on their own to find support and encouragement as well as opportunities for career growth. Networking is viewed by respondents as the principal means to this end. Networks can be internal or external, formal or informal. Through these networks professionals gain exposure for lateral moves (after layoffs) and for leadership opportunities.

The new organizational logic appears gender neutral on the surface. Some have argued that because the new system of teams, career maps, and networking is less rigid than the older system of standardized career ladders and job descriptions, it may be more compatible with women's careers (e.g., Hewlett 2007). In fact, the transition to the new economy has taken place at the same time that major corporations have embraced gender and racial/ethnic diversity (Eisenstein 2009). The giant oil and gas companies tout their efforts to recruit women and minority men. Both Chevron and BP, for example, feature women scientists in recent publicity campaigns. Nevertheless, as we explain in the remainder of this article, these new forms may explain persistent patterns of gender inequality. . . .

Teamwork

In some recent studies, the team structure has been found to attenuate gender inequality in organizations (Kalev 2009; Plankey Videla 2006; Reskin 2002; Smith-Doerr 2004). However, we found that women may be disadvantaged on male-dominated teams. By the very nature of teamwork, the individual's contribution to the final product is obscured. Yet because careers are still individual, members of the team must engage in self-promotion to receive credit and rewards for their personal effort. Our study suggests that women encounter difficulties when promoting their accomplishments and gaining the credibility of their supervisors and other team members. This finding is consistent with experimental studies showing that, in general, women are given disproportionately less credit than men for the success they achieve when they work on teams in male-dominated environments (Heilman and Haynes 2005).

Because female workers are not given the benefit of the doubt in assessments of their work efforts by others, it is especially important that they are willing and able to tout their contributions to team accomplishments. Many of the women we interviewed are conscious of the importance of self-promotion, though they are not always secure in their ability to do it effectively. One geoscientist shared her misgivings about her own presentation skills, as well as her hunch that presentation skills may be more important than scientific ability to get ahead in industry:

> I don't know especially if you have to be as good, or if you have to be just as loud and belligerent as the other people. You definitely/the personality here is, to prove your point, you have to bang the table sometimes. I think women are more reluctant to do that. It's not me to do that.

This woman attributes her reluctance to "bang the table" to her personality, which she suggests is a reflection of an essential gender difference. But the following quote, from the only woman geoscientist in her entire division, indicates that women may be regarded negatively when they promote themselves:

> It's kind of interesting that I feel that I have to fight more to keep promoting what my expertise is. And it keeps getting kind of pushed back. The other people with less expertise in structural geology,

they seem to get a little more recognition. Now, they've been working for the company for years. But still, I'm the one that has the expertise in that area. I just don't know how to do it. You don't want to be the one that yells and screams all the time. It's a delicate balance to keep promoting yourself.

Virtually everyone we interviewed talked about the fine line, or "delicate balance," between being assertive and being a "bitch." This perennial dilemma faced by women in the workplace is exacerbated in a team structure that requires workers to engage in assertive self-promotion in order to achieve recognition.

One woman reflected on her experience speaking at a partner meeting, at which she was the only woman, and youngest person, in attendance:

I had to stand up and tell why I thought the well location should be somewhere and I could absolutely tell that no one was taking me seriously. They didn't care what I had to say—it was very obvious. Part of that I'm sure is being young, part of it was being the first time I had to stand up and tell them that. Because now, after eleven years, I can stand up and I can talk [laughs], but you have to get to that point. You have to know your stuff. I know that I have to cross every "t" and dot every "i," because if I don't, someone is going to pick it apart. There will be some man in the audience that wants to heckle you because he can—and I know that.

As this observation suggests, the difficulties that women encounter with self-promotion may be compounded by age. The following quote also indicates that younger women may face additional hurdles when attempting to bring attention to their accomplishments:

I think automatically that anything I say is questioned. My supervisor, in my first go-round through the performance, told me I had to speak up—I have to believe what I'm saying, and I can't let them railroad me . . . which, I think he feels is more of an age thing. You get some credibility with age. I'm sure some people think you get more credibility being a guy. [I've got] kind of the short stick on both of those.

Her supervisor admonished her for not being assertive enough. But she perceived that, even when she did speak up, her views were constantly challenged because she was the only woman and the youngest member of the team.

At the professional meetings we attended, we observed that age is often treated as a status group in the industry. For example, when executives discussed "diversity" goals at their companies, they included age as well as gender and race/ethnicity. Layoffs that occurred in the 1980s and late 1990s were reported to have contributed to a large age gap among industry geoscientists (with a virtual absence of workers aged 35–45). Some of the geoscientists that we interviewed believed the age gap contributed to tension within teams. Young geoscientists do not always receive the recognition they seek from the older generation nearing retirement.

However, youth tends to operate differently based on gender and race. Youth can convey certain advantages to men, who may become the protégés of senior men (Roper 1994). In contrast, young women struggle to get noticed in positive ways. Some young women described feeling sexualized by men in their work teams. Others told us that they succeeded only because they fell into the "daughter" role with senior male mentors. Both roles are constraining in the quest for professional credibility. As Ollilainen and Calasanti (2007) have argued, family metaphors can disadvantage women who work on teams by encouraging a gendered division of labor and compelling women to engage in uncompensated emotional labor. Furthermore, in white male-dominated teams, metaphorical family roles may be available only to white women (Bell and Nkomo 2001).

Minority women may be disadvantaged compared to white men and women in additional ways, according to one Asian American woman we interviewed:

It's all sorts of behaviors and soft skills that they look at for leadership potential. And a lot of the Asian people don't do well in those because we're culturally expected to be modest and we're culturally expected to not stand out. It's OK for us to be introverted or quiet. You actually get respected for being quiet, a man of few words. But at [my oil and gas company], that is not how you get success.

This statement suggests that self-promotion may have different meanings for racial/ethnic minority men and women. Furthermore, other research suggests that those who engage in it may be viewed negatively by white colleagues and supervisors (Harvey Wingfield 2010).

Interestingly, we observed that women who worked in gender-balanced teams (absent in some companies) felt like they received greater recognition and respect for their contributions. If correct, this observation would confirm theories of tokenism that predict less bias in numerically balanced work groups (Kanter 1977). But how do teams achieve this numerical balance? Supervisors play a key role in determining the composition of the work group. However, as we suggest in the next section, supervisor's discretionary power is not necessarily exercised in the interest of gender equality.

In sum, in order to achieve recognition and rewards for their contributions, individuals working on teams must be willing and able to stand out from the group and advertise their accomplishments. Our findings suggest that this apparently gender neutral requirement can discriminate against women. As other researchers have found (Babcock and Laschever 2003; Bowles, Babcock, and Lai 2007; Broadbridge 2004), self-promotion can have negative meanings and consequences for women in male-dominated environments. When work is organized on the teamwork model, gender inequality is the likely result.

Career Maps

In many companies, career maps have replaced standardized career ladders for highly valued professionals. The purpose of a career map is to chart an individualized course of professional development that incorporates both the company's needs and the personal aspirations of the worker. Sometimes called "I-deals" (Rousseau 2005),

these idiosyncratic arrangements often include employees' plans for reduced or flexible hours (e.g., to accommodate family needs) in addition to their career ambitions. Career maps are normally negotiated with supervisors, and they evolve over time.

Respondents were mostly positive about career maps because of the perception that they allow workers to manage their own careers. This was preferable to having, in the words of one geologist, "big brother" determine their futures with a one-size-fits-all set of career expectations (see also Hewlett 2007). However, in practice, the geoscientists we interviewed experienced several problems with career maps, stemming from the perceived ineptitude or gender bias of their supervisors. First, difficulties can arise if the criteria drawn are too vague or subjective. A woman with a PhD in geophysics explained that some workers, and especially new employees, struggled to figure out their job responsibilities. Supervisors sometimes assigned work without explaining the steps necessary or directing new employees to the resources needed to complete their assigned tasks. In fact, it wasn't until right before she left the industry that [one] particular woman felt she understood the "work flow." . . .

Without standardized job descriptions, workers can experience confusion about their job duties. Developing excellent communication skills becomes mandatory in this new context. One geologist attributed her success in the industry to the fact that she has "effectively communicated my career plan to the right people." She said, "Not everyone is so fortunate. . . . I do know of some people who haven't had as much influence on where they have gone. But when I've spoken with them, I really feel like they have not effectively communicated what they wanted to do." From her perspective, it is up to individual workers—not the corporation—to ensure that careers stay on the right track.

A second problem with career maps is that decisions about raises, promotions, and other rewards based on this system can appear arbitrary. This woman shared her confusion and frustration that her husband—who had started his job around the same time she did—had been promoted "a lot faster" than she had:

> And I've seen that, just on the side, watching. . . . I'm like, "OK, what are you doing differently that I need to do to get this going?" He said, "Nothing. I haven't done anything." He is a quiet guy by nature. So he didn't know why he was getting promoted himself. And I thought that was very interesting.

The lack of common job descriptions and career ladders contributes to uncertainty about why some individuals receive recognition and others do not. Because career maps are tailored to the individual—and because most companies prohibit employees from sharing salary information—it is difficult for workers to compare their career progress with others.[2]

Third, geoscientists perceive problems with career maps when supervisors do not actively advocate for them. A 35-year-old geologist working at a major described the importance of supervisors in obtaining good project assignments. . . .

This worker was grateful when a supervisor several levels above her recommended her for a job opening. Even though she didn't end up receiving that job, she felt "fortunate" to have been considered. She wondered aloud, "How do I get that to happen again?"

When opportunities are experienced as a windfall, workers are unsure how to advance themselves. At the same time, workers felt pressured to take any opportunities presented by a supervisor. Turning down more than one assignment was believed to foreclose them from receiving any in the future.

Without a supportive supervisor, careers can flounder. One geologist found herself in a precarious position when her supervisor left the company and another group subsumed her team. The manager of this group was an engineer rather than a geologist, which this respondent saw as a disadvantage. Not only did the person in charge of assigning and judging her work not understand it, he was already responsible for the careers of a large number of people. Without a supervisor advocating for her, this geologist said

she felt "unnerved" and stressed out because she didn't know what her next assignment or career move would be.

While all of these issues with supervisors' discretion over career maps can impact both men and women equally, women may be especially disadvantage if their supervisors harbor gender biases. As we know from previous research, supervisors who harbor biases against women (or in favor of men) can easily derail women's careers, even in the sciences (DiTomaso et al. 2007). Virtually every woman we interviewed encountered an individual supervisor at some point in her career who stymied her advancement. One geoscientist felt her career at a midsize company was progressing well until she was assigned a new supervisor. The new supervisor would accept her work only if she had it preapproved by a male employee on her team. . . .

Gender bias is also expressed in supervisors' decisions about whom to hire into their teams. Studies suggest that managers favor people who are like themselves, a process known as "homosocial reproduction" (Elliott and Smith 2004; Kanter 1977). Gender differences emerge because women are rarely in a position to make personnel decisions. Even when women are in a supervisory position, their hiring decisions may be scrutinized. One female supervisor hired a woman to her team. When asked if it was controversial to pick a woman, she said that she "got that comment" but was able to defend herself because she had offered the job to a man first. She said, "I wasn't out looking for a female. It turns out we got a female in the group. In this particular case, she is the best fit." Thus, she was put on the defensive for a practice that is common among male supervisors. When gender bias appears to favor women, it is noticed and controversial (a topic we return to in the next section).

Part of developing a career map involves planning for maternity leave and flexible schedules, including part-time. Supervisors often have a great deal of control over these arrangements. One woman said the human resources (HR) department at the major company where she worked "purposefully wrote the rules [regarding flex time] kind of in a gray zone," leaving them open to the interpretation of supervisors. Smaller companies, which often lack formal HR departments, may give supervisors even more discretion than the larger companies do. However, a number of women working at majors gave examples of how supervisory discretion could impact workers' knowledge and ability to take advantage of flexible working options. . . .

This situation captures a paradox at the heart of career maps. On the one hand, they enable greater flexibility in career development, which some argue is in women's best interests (Hewlett 2007). As this geologist attests, "everybody" is unlikely to "want the same thing." On the other hand, if designing a career map that accommodates motherhood depends on having a sympathetic supervisor, potential gender bias is built into the organization. The lack of a "consistent, accepted solution" is frustrating and anxiety producing. . . .

Those we interviewed who had experience working in European offices experienced standardized maternity leave policies that were part of their host country's social welfare system. However, those who worked for European companies in the U.S. faced similarly limited options as those working in U.S. companies, with only supervisor-approved accommodations for maternity leave and part-time schedules available to them.

Because this study was motivated in part to understand women's attrition from the industry, we asked respondents their opinions about why women leave. Many speculated that it was because women tend to "opt out" of the labor force to bear and raise children, which they considered a deeply personal choice. Interestingly, few could cite specific examples. And the three women we talked to who left the industry did not regard children or family as their primary reason for leaving. Nevertheless, we contend that the institution of career maps, which grants supervisors the ability to negotiate family accommodations on a case-by-case basis, may leave mothers without viable and meaningful alternatives. Furthermore, in an industry characterized by

constant mergers and downsizing, we suspect that some women may use the framework of "opting out" as a face-saving way to explain a decision to leave prior to an impending layoff. Unfortunately, this framing reinforces the stereotype that women naturally prioritize family over careers and absolves organizations of the responsibility for structuring the workplace in more equitable ways.

In sum, career maps give supervisors a great deal of discretion over individuals' career development. In the absence of accountability or an effective affirmative action program, supervisory discretion can be a breeding ground for gender bias (Reskin and McBrier 2000). Given the difficulty of comparing career progression in this context, patterns of gender and racial disparities may be obscured. Nevertheless, the logic of career maps encourages workers to blame themselves, not the organization, when their careers are stymied.

Networking

Virtually everyone we talked to said that networks are fundamental to achieving professional success. In an industry where lay-offs are common and anticipated, workers must rely on their formal and informal networks to survive periodic cuts and to identify new opportunities. Yet, as we know from numerous research studies, networks are highly gendered and racialized (Burt 1998; Loscocco et al. 2009; McGuire 2002; Smith 2007). A geophysicist who worked for several large companies and who now owns her own consulting business explained that many people, and women especially, "work hard as opposed to work smart." Networking, rather than simply doing one's job well, was, she believed, the key to success in the industry. She reflected on the importance of this knowledge to boosting one's career: "If I had known then what I know now, I would be CEO of a company."

In the male-dominated oil and gas industry, not surprisingly, the most powerful networks are almost exclusively male. Often these are organized around golf or hunting (Morgan and

Martin 2006). The women we interviewed provided classic accounts of exclusion from these groups.

> The men at upper management were quite comfortable making seat-of-the-pants decisions with each other, and they trusted each other. They had lunch together, they played golf together, they trusted each other. If somebody is going to make a seat-of-the-pants decision, the other guy's going to say "fine." A woman comes in and tries to make a seat-of-the-pants decision, same process, same gut kind of thing, you're not going to be trusted, you're not going to be believed.

Some women perceive that men's networks, sustained through company-sponsored sports and hunting/fishing trips, are not considered networks at all, even though in these spaces men are likely to develop strong relationships of mutual trust (see also DiTomaso et al. 2007). In one egregious case, a woman described how female strippers were positioned at each putting green at an annual company-sponsored golf tournament. While some women have no interest in attending these networking events, others try to fit in because of their critical importance to success in the industry. One independent producer told us that although she doesn't play golf, she makes it a point to "ride in the cart." Another woman tried to join her male colleagues' fantasy football league. Although they were resistant to letting a woman join, she was finally allowed when one man agreed to be her partner (to the others' chagrin).

In response to this exclusion, and in acknowledgment of the importance of networking for career development, some corporations have formed official women's networks. However, these networks have dubious status in corporations and joining may not be in women's best interest. For instance, DiTomaso and colleagues argue that "special mentoring programs for women set up by companies may be a disadvantage for those who use them" (DiTomaso et al. 2007, 198). The women we interviewed concurred, viewing women's corporate-sponsored networks as neither powerful nor especially useful. . . .

One problem [mentioned] was that the company brought together all women from the company, rather than just geoscientists. While she saw value in allowing women to network from across the company, she thought the other women came from "a little bit of a different perspective." Moreover, this type of networking is unlikely to result in future opportunities for a geologist.

At some companies, the women's network is not limited to women, the rationale being that in the interests of "equal opportunity," women should not receive "special treatment." Consequently, when women's groups are formed, they rarely address issues concerning discrimination or inequality. Topics like work-family balance are sometimes addressed, but in a way that does not challenge the structure or policies of the organization. For example, a few years after joining the major at which she works, one respondent and her colleagues started an online "family support network" in order to provide employees with children a chance to connect and give them a place to ask questions and receive advice. This "grass-roots network" received immense support from top managers and has since become institutionalized. . . .

Importantly, this network requires no resources from the employer, nor does it challenge the company's limited support for new parents. Yet the existence of the network makes the company appear to be doing something to promote gender equity.

Furthermore, while some women appreciate this focus on work-family balance, others find it alienating because they do not have children, and feel oppressed by the assumption that they do. For example, one woman spoke of receiving an invitation to a "women in science" session at a local seismic conference. She explained that she was originally excited to hear the experiences of "wicked smart" women scientists talking about how to thrive in a male-dominated environment. Instead she was disappointed that the group focus would be on motherhood. She added, "I don't tend to seek out female-dominated groups because you inadvertently end up sitting next to someone talking about their kids—which is fine. I can hear about your kids for a while. But I don't want to have kids."

On the other hand, some convey more than a hint of cynicism about corporate-sponsored events that highlight the accomplishments of senior women. One woman expressed frustration that corporate diversity events seemed to feature the same senior women retelling their success stories. She explained, "Marilyn is [the company's] poster child. But for every Marilyn there are fifteen women who are not getting what Marilyn gets"—referring to the same opportunities, exposure, and access to powerful networks.

Given the perceived limitations of official women's networks, some women turn to informal networks instead. Unfortunately, these also occupy a highly dubious space in the corporate world. They may be perceived as mere outlets for complaining, venting, or "bitching." A woman who organized a weekend retreat for a group of senior executive women was criticized by detractors for arranging a "ladies' boondoggle," an accusation she felt was "outrageous" because men do equivalent outings all the time.

Not surprisingly, some women are reluctant to disclose their interest in forming or joining a women's group. One woman talked about returning from an AAPG [American Association of Petroleum Geologists] event with the idea of starting a women's mentoring group to mimic those in the larger companies. She and a small group of women had started to organize, but had decided it was in their best interest to keep their intentions secret. This woman expressed palpable fear that if found out, the women involved would suffer negative repercussions since company policy strictly forbids any discussion of salary or contracts among employees. These women knew they were taking a chance by organizing a women's group, so they were planning to hold their meeting 200 miles away in order to avoid detection.

Networking has always been important for professional development. In the new economy, strong networks are needed not only to thrive but to survive periodic downsizing and layoffs. The heightened importance of networking places women geoscientists in a paradoxical position: They are often excluded from powerful men's networks, yet women's formal networks, when they exist, are not powerful and may actually have negative consequences for women's career development. Women's informal networks may be forced to operate under the radar. Because of the centrality of networking, the resulting gender inequality is thus embedded in the organizational logic of the new economy.

CONCLUSION

The traditional career model, in which a worker spends his or her entire career with one employer, in some, cases climbing a defined career ladder, is on the decline (Vallas 2011). Workers today expect to switch jobs and employers frequently throughout their careers. While some moves are in response to better opportunities, in many cases they are the result of corporate practices, common to some industries, that make workers vulnerable to job loss.

The new career model, created by corporations to reduce their economic risk and responsibility for workers, has several defining features. Under this new model, employees are evaluated based on individualized standards developed in conjunction with their direct supervisors, rather than by a standardized assessment tool. Although workers are evaluated on an individual basis, work is typically performed by self-managed teams. As it is difficult to determine individuals' level of effort, supervisors have a great deal of discretionary power in rewarding employees for a job well done (i.e., giving employees good team placements). The proliferation of career maps may obscure inequality in the pace of career progress. Given the level of job insecurity, the ability to maintain large networks to identify job opportunities inside and outside of the organization becomes critically important for successful careers.

We examined the careers of geoscientists in the oil and gas industry—an industry at the forefront of implementing these organizational changes—to explore the gendered consequences of these job features. Our research suggests that teams, career maps, and networking reflect gendered organizational logics. To excel at teamwork, individuals must be able to engage in self-promotion, which can be difficult for women in male-dominated environments—even though they are the ones who may need to do it the most. In contexts where supervisors have discretion over careers, gender bias can play a significant role in the allocation of rewards. And networking is gendered in ways that disadvantage women.

These features of work organization are not new, and, in fact, previous research has shown that all three of these elements can be problematic for women (Bowles, Babcock, and Lai 2007; Broadbridge 2004; Burt 1998; Loscocco et al. 2009; McGuire 2002; Ollilainen and Calasanti 2007). This article's contribution has been to connect them to work transformation. Previously, gender inequality has been institutionalized (in part) through the mechanisms of career ladders, job descriptions, and formal evaluations (Acker 1990). In the new economy, these elements of organizational logic have been replaced by teams, career maps, and networking. These have become principal mechanisms through which gender inequality is reproduced in the new economy. . . .

Our findings suggest that addressing workplace gender inequality in the twenty-first century will require focused attention on transforming these job features, or altering their consequences for women. For example standard options for organizing career maps should be made available to workers. In the interest of gender equity, workers should be informed of the I-deals and salaries of their peers. In addition, supervisors should be made accountable to diversity goals, and incentivized to encourage workers to use company flexibility options. While companies should encourage networking activities, all corporate-sponsored events must include women and minority men, and informal male-only social events must somehow be made culturally taboo. These are the sorts of changes that we believe will enhance the careers of women scientists in the new economy.

When Joan Acker (1990) first articulated the organizational logic underlying gendered organizations, she was operating under the assumptions of the traditional career model. Those assumptions no longer apply in many organizations. Organizations are still gendered, but the mechanisms for reproducing gender disparities are different than those in the traditional career path. By exploring women's experiences

of work in the new economy, we add an essential but previously missing dimension to the critique of work transformation. By paying close attention to the new organizational logic, we hope that effective policies can be devised to enhance gender equality in the twenty-first century workplace.

NOTES

1. These descriptions of "old" and "new" forms of work organizations refer to trends that in actual practice can overlap considerably, so they should be treated as "ideal types" in the Weberian sense.

2. The proliferation of career maps may also make it difficult for human resource departments to detect patterns (and potential disparities) in men's and women's career development.

REFERENCES

AAPG (American Association of Petroleum Geologists). 2009. Results from the American Association of Petroleum Geologists (AAPG) Professional Women in the Earth Sciences (PROWESS) Survey. American Association of Petroleum Geologists. June 7, 2011, http://www.aapg.org/committees/prowess/AAPG_Jun3.final.pdf.

Acker, Joan. 1990. Hierarchies, jobs, bodies: A theory of gendered organizations. *Gender & Society* 4:139–58.

AGI (American Geological Institute). 2011. Currents 30–35: Minorities, temporary residents, and gender parity in the geosciences. June 27, 2011, http://www.agiweb.org/workforce/webinar-videos/video_currents30–35.html.

Babcock, L., and S. Laschever. 2003. *Women don't ask: Negotiation and the gender divide.* Princeton, NJ: Princeton University Press.

Bell, E. E., and S. Nkomo. 2001. *Our separate ways: Black and white women and the struggle for professional identity.* Boston: Harvard Business School Press.

Bowles, H. R., Babcock, L., and L Lai. 2007. Social incentives for gender differences in the propensity to initiate negotiations: Sometimes it does hurt to ask. *Organizational Behavior and Human Decision Processes* 103:84–103.

Britton, D., and L. Logan. 2008. Gendered organizations: Progress and prospects. *Sociology Compass* 2:107–21.

Broadbridge, A. 2004. It's not what you know, it's who you know. *Journal of Management Development* 23:551–62.

Bureau of Labor Statistics. 2009. Geoscientists and hydrologists. December 13, 2011, http://www.bls.gov/oco/ocos312.htm.

Burt, Ronald S. 1998. The gender of social capital. *Rationality and Society* 10:5–46.

Catalyst. 2011. Women in U.S. mining, quarrying, and oil and gas extraction. September 12, 2011, http://www.catalyst.org/publication/503/women-in-us-mining-quarrying-and-oil-gas-extraction.

Connelly, J. D., and J. C. Middleton. 1996. Personal and professional skills for engineers: One industry's perspective. *Engineering Science and Education Journal* 5:139–42.

DiMaggio, Paul. 2001. *The twenty-first century firm.* Princeton, NJ: Princeton University press.

DiTomaso, N., C. Post, R. Smith, G. Farris, and R. Cordero. 2007. The effects of structural position on allocation and evaluation decisions for scientists and engineers in industrial R&D. *Administrative Science Quarterly* 52:175–207.

Elliott, J., and R. Smith. 2004. Race, gender, and workplace power. *American Sociological Review* 69:365–86.

England, Paula. 2010. The gender revolution: Uneven and stalled. *Gender & Society* 24:149–66.

Harvey Wingfield, Adia. 2010. Are some emotions marked "whites only"? Racialized feeling rules in professional workplaces. *Social Problems* 57:251–68.

Heilman, M.E., and M.C. Haynes. 2005. No credit where credit is due: Attributional rationalization of women's success in male-female teams. *Journal of Applied Psychology* 90:905–16.

Hewlett, Sylvia A. 2007. *Off-ramps and on-ramps: Keeping talented women on the road to success.* Boston, MA: Harvard Business School Publishing.

Kalev, Alexandra. 2009. Cracking the glass cages? Restructuring and ascriptive inequality at work. *American Journal of Sociology* 114:1591–1643.

Kalleberg, Arne. 2000. Nonstandard employment relations. *Annual Review of Sociology* 26:341–65.

Kanter, Rosabeth Moss. 1977. *Men and women of the corporation.* New York: Basic.

Loscocco, K., S. M. Monnat, G. Moore, and K. B. Lauber. 2009. Enterprising women: A comparison of women's and men's small business networks. *Gender & Society* 23:388–411.

McGuire, G. M. 2002. Gender, race, and the shadow structure: A study of informal networks and inequality in a work organization. *Gender & Society* 16:303–22.

McKee, L., N. Mauthner, and C. Maclean. 2000. Family friendly policies and practices in the oil and gas industry: Employer's perspectives. *Work, Employment and Society* 14:557–71.

Miller, Gloria E. 2004. Frontier masculinity in the oil industry: The experience of women engineers. *Gender; Work and Organization* 11:47–73.

Morgan, L., and K. Martin. 2006. Taking women professionals out of the office: The case of women in sales. *Gender & Society* 20:108–28.

National Academy of Sciences. 2010. *Rising above the gathering storm, revisited: Rapidly approaching category 5.* Washington, DC: National Academies Press.

Ollilainen, M., and T. Calasanti. 2007. Metaphors at work: Maintaining the salience of gender in self-managing teams. *Gender & Society* 21:5–27.

Osnowitz, Debra. 2010. *Freelancing expertise: Contract professionals in the new economy.* Ithaca, NY: ILR Press.

Pirog, Robert. 2008. *Oil industry profit review 2007.* Washington, DC: Congressional Research Service. September 1, 2011, assets.opencrs.com/rpts/RL34437_20080404.pdf.

Plankey Videla, Nancy. 2006. Gendered contradictions: Managers and women workers in self-managed teams. *Research in the Sociology of Work* 16:85–116.

Powell, Walter W. 2001. The capitalist firm in the 21st century: Emerging patterns in western enterprise. In *The twenty-first century firm,* edited by Paul DiMaggio. Princeton, NJ: Princeton University Press.

Preston, Anne E. 2004. *Leaving science. Occupational exit from science careers.* New York: Russell Sage Foundation.

Reskin, Barbara. 2002. Rethinking employment discrimination and its remedies. In *The new economic sociology: Developments in an emerging field,* edited by M. F. Guillen, R. Collins, P. England, and M. Meyer. New York: Russell Sage.

Reskin, B., and D. McBrier. 2000. Why not ascription? Organizations' employment of male and female managers. *American Sociological Review* 65:210–33.

Roper, Michael. 1994. *Masculinity and the British organization man since 1945*. Oxford: Oxford University Press.

Rousseau, Denise. 2005. *I-deals: Idiosyncratic deals employees bargain for themselves*. Armonk, NY: M. E. Sharpe.

Smith, Sandra. 2007. *Lone pursuit: Distrust and defensive individualism among the Black poor*. New York: Russell Sage.

Smith-Doerr, Laurel. 2004. *Women's work: Gender equality versus hierarchy in the life sciences*. Boulder, CO: Lynne Rienner.

Vallas, Steven. 2011. *Work: A critique*. Boston: Polity Books.

Williams, Joan. 2001. *Unbending gender: Why family and work conflict and what to do about it*. New York: Oxford University Press.

Yergin, Daniel. 1993. *The prize: The epic quest for oil, money, and power*. New York: Free Press.

Introduction to Reading 33

Sociologists and others use the term *glass ceiling* to describe the barriers to promotion and advancement that women face in the world of work. At the same time, however, it is argued that men have a glass escalator, particularly men employed in what are traditionally women's jobs. In this article, Adia Harvey Wingfield describes the glass escalator and gives an overview of the research on men in traditionally female occupations. While men make up 8% of all nurses, the percentage of nurses who are Black men is unknown. Therefore, this study helps us understand the intersections of race and class and how the experiences of Black men differ from those of White men in previous studies. Wingfield's study gives insight into the various ways race and gender intersect to discriminate against Black men in the workplace.

1. How are the experiences of the Black men she studied different from the results of previous studies of White men?

2. Do Black male nurses do masculinity differently than White male nurses? Why or why not?

3. What forms of discrimination are described in this article? What would you recommend to eradicate such discrimination?

RACIALIZING THE GLASS ESCALATOR

RECONSIDERING MEN'S EXPERIENCES WITH WOMEN'S WORK

Adia Harvey Wingfield

Sociologists who study work have long noted that jobs are sex segregated and that this segregation creates different occupational experiences for men and women (Charles and Grusky 2004). Jobs predominantly filled by women often require "feminine" traits such as

Wingfield, Adia Harvey. 2009. "Racializing the Glass Escalator: Reconsidering Men's Experiences With Women's Work." *Gender & Society* 23(1): 5–26. Published by Sage Publications on behalf of Sociologists for Women in Society.

nurturing, caring, and empathy, a fact that means men confront perceptions that they are unsuited for the requirements of these jobs. Rather than having an adverse effect on their occupational experiences, however, these assumptions facilitate men's entry into better paying, higher status positions, creating what Williams (1995) labels a "glass escalator" effect.

The glass escalator model has been an influential paradigm in understanding the experiences of men who do women's work. Researchers have identified this process among men nurses, social workers, paralegals, and librarians and have cited its pervasiveness as evidence of men's consistent advantage in the workplace, such that even in jobs where men are numerical minorities they are likely to enjoy higher wages and faster promotions (Floge and Merrill 1986; Heikes 1991; Pierce 1995; Williams 1989, 1995). Most of these studies implicitly assume a racial homogenization of men workers in women's professions, but this supposition is problematic for several reasons. For one, minority men are not only present but are actually overrepresented in certain areas of reproductive work that have historically been dominated by white women (Duffy 2007). Thus, research that focuses primarily on white men in women's professions ignores a key segment of men who perform this type of labor. Second, and perhaps more important, conclusions based on the experiences of white men tend to overlook the ways that intersections of race and gender create different experiences for different men. While extensive work has documented the fact that white men in women's professions encounter a glass escalator effect that aids their occupational mobility (for an exception, see Snyder and Green 2008), few studies, if any, have considered how this effect is a function not only of gendered advantage but of racial privilege as well.

In this article, I examine the implications of race–gender intersections for minority men employed in a female-dominated, feminized occupation, specifically focusing on Black men in nursing. Their experiences doing "women's work" demonstrate that the glass escalator is a racialized as well as gendered concept.

THEORETICAL FRAMEWORK

In her classic study *Men and Women of the Corporation*, Kanter (1977) offers a ground-breaking analysis of group interactions. Focusing on high-ranking women executives who work mostly with men, Kanter argues that those in the extreme numerical minority are tokens who are socially isolated, highly visible, and adversely stereotyped. Tokens have difficulty forming relationships with colleagues and often are excluded from social networks that provide mobility. Because of their low numbers, they are also highly visible as people who are different from the majority, even though they often feel invisible when they are ignored or overlooked in social settings. Tokens are also stereotyped by those in the majority group and frequently face pressure to behave in ways that challenge and undermine these stereotypes. Ultimately, Kanter argues that it is harder for them to blend into the organization and to work effectively and productively, and that they face serious barriers to upward mobility.

Kanter's (1977) arguments have been analyzed and retested in various settings and among many populations. Many studies, particularly of women in male-dominated corporate settings, have supported her findings. Other work has reversed these conclusions, examining the extent to which her conclusions hold when men were the tokens and women the majority group. These studies fundamentally challenged the gender neutrality of the token, finding that men in the minority fare much better than do similarly situated women. In particular, this research suggests that factors such as heightened visibility and polarization do not necessarily disadvantage men who are in the minority. While women tokens find that their visibility hinders their ability to blend in and work productively, men tokens find that their conspicuousness can lead to greater opportunities for leadership and choice assignments (Floge and Merrill 1986; Heikes 1991). Studies in this vein are important because they emphasize organizations—and occupations—as gendered institutions that subsequently create dissimilar experiences for men and women tokens (see Acker 1990).

In her groundbreaking study of men employed in various women's professions, Williams (1995) further develops this analysis of how power relationships shape the ways men tokens experience work in women's professions. Specifically, she introduces the concept of the glass escalator to explain men's experiences as tokens in these areas. Like Floge and Merrill (1986) and Heikes (1991), Williams finds that men tokens do not experience the isolation, visibility, blocked access to social networks, and stereotypes in the same ways that women tokens do. In contrast, Williams argues that even though they are in the minority, processes are in place that actually facilitate their opportunity and advancement. Even in culturally feminized occupations, then, men's advantage is built into the very structure and everyday interactions of these jobs so that men find themselves actually struggling to remain in place. For these men, "despite their intentions, they face invisible pressures to move up in their professions. Like being on a moving escalator, they have to work to stay in place" (Williams 1995, 87).

The glass escalator term thus refers to the "subtle mechanisms in place that enhance [men's] positions in [women's] professions" (Williams 1995, 108). These mechanisms include certain behaviors, attitudes, and beliefs men bring to these professions as well as the types of interactions that often occur between these men and their colleagues, supervisors, and customers. Consequently, even in occupations composed mostly of women, gendered perceptions about men's roles, abilities, and skills privilege them and facilitate their advancement. The glass escalator serves as a conduit that channels men in women's professions into the uppermost levels of the occupational hierarchy. Ultimately, the glass escalator effect suggests that men retain consistent occupational advantages over women, even when women are numerically in the majority (Budig 2002; Williams 1995).

Though this process has now been fairly well established in the literature, there are reasons to question its generalizability to all men. In an early critique of the supposed general neutrality

of the token, Zimmer (1988) notes that much research on race comes to precisely the opposite of Kanter's conclusions, finding that as the numbers of minority group members increase (e.g., as they become less likely to be "tokens"), so too do tensions between the majority and minority groups. . . . Reinforcing, while at the same time tempering, the findings of research on men in female-dominated occupations, Zimmer (1988, 71) argues that relationships between tokens and the majority depend on understanding the underlying power relationships between these groups and "the status and power differentials between them." Hence, just as men who are tokens fare better than women, it also follows that the experiences of Blacks and whites as tokens should differ in ways that reflect their positions in hierarchies of status and power. . . .

Relationships With Colleagues and Supervisors

One key aspect of riding the glass escalator involves the warm, collegial welcome men workers often receive from their women colleagues. Often, this reaction is a response to the fact that professions dominated by women are frequently low in salary and status and that greater numbers of men help improve prestige and pay (Heikes 1991). Though some women workers resent the apparent ease with which men enter and advance in women's professions, the generally warm welcome men receive stands in stark contrast to the cold reception, difficulties with mentorship, and blocked access to social networks that women often encounter when they do men's work (Roth 2006; Williams 1992). In addition, unlike women in men's professions, men who do women's work frequently have supervisors of the same sex. Men workers can thus enjoy a gendered bond with their supervisor in the context of a collegial work environment. These factors often converge, facilitating men's access to higher-status positions and producing the glass escalator effect.

The congenial relationship with colleagues and gendered bonds with supervisors are crucial to riding the glass escalator. Women colleagues often take a primary role in casting these men into leadership or supervisory positions. In their study of men and women tokens in a hospital setting, Floge and Merrill (1986) cite cases where women nurses promoted men colleagues to the position of charge nurse, even when the job had already been assigned to a woman. In addition to these close ties with women colleagues, men are also able to capitalize on gendered bonds with (mostly men) supervisors in ways that engender upward mobility. Many men supervisors informally socialize with men workers in women's jobs and are thus able to trade on their personal friendships for upward mobility. Williams (1995) describes a case where a nurse with mediocre performance reviews received a promotion to a more prestigious specialty area because of his friendship with the (male) doctor in charge. According to the literature, building strong relationships with colleagues and supervisors often happens relatively easily for men in women's professions and pays off in their occupational advancement.

For Black men in nursing, however, gendered racism may limit the extent to which they establish bonds with their colleagues and supervisors. The concept of gendered racism suggests that racial stereotypes, images, and beliefs are grounded in gendered ideals (Collins 1990, 2004; Espiritu 2000; Essed 1991; Harvey Wingfield 2007). Gendered racist stereotypes of Black men in particular emphasize the dangerous, threatening attributes associated with Black men and Black masculinity, framing Black men as threats to white women, prone to criminal behavior, and especially violent. Collins (2004) argues that these stereotypes serve to legitimize Black men's treatment in the criminal justice system through methods such as racial profiling and incarceration, but they may also hinder Black men's attempts to enter and advance in various occupational fields.

For Black men nurses, gendered racist images may have particular consequences for their relationships with women colleagues, who may view Black men nurses through the lens of controlling images and gendered racist stereotypes that emphasize the danger they pose to women. This may take on a heightened significance for white

women nurses, given stereotypes that suggest that Black men are especially predisposed to raping white women. Rather than experiencing the congenial bonds with colleagues that white men nurses describe, Black men nurses may find themselves facing a much cooler reception from their women coworkers.

Gendered racism may also play into the encounters Black men nurses have with supervisors. In cases where supervisors are white men, Black men nurses may still find that higher-ups treat them in ways that reflect prevailing stereotypes about threatening Black masculinity. Supervisors may feel uneasy about forming close relationships with Black men or may encourage their separation from white women nurses. In addition, broader, less gender-specific racial stereotypes could also shape the experiences Black men nurses have with white men bosses. Whites often perceive Blacks, regardless of gender, as less intelligent, hardworking, ethical, and moral than other racial groups (Feagin 2006). Black men nurses may find that in addition to being influenced by gendered racist stereotypes, supervisors also view them as less capable and qualified for promotion, thus negating or minimizing the glass escalator effect.

Suitability for Nursing and Higher-Status Work

The perception that men are not really suited to do women's work also contributes to the glass escalator effect. In encounters with patients, doctors, and other staff, men nurses frequently confront others who do not expect to see them doing "a woman's job." Sometimes this perception means that patients mistake men nurses for doctors; ultimately, the sense that men do not really belong in nursing contributes to a push "*out of the most feminine-identified areas and up to those regarded as more legitimate for men*" (Williams 1995, 104). The sense that men are better suited for more masculine jobs means that men workers are often assumed to be more able and skilled than their women counterparts. As Williams writes (1995, 106), "Masculinity is often associated with competence and mastery," and this implicit definition stays with men even when they work in feminized fields. Thus, part of the perception that men do not belong in these jobs is rooted in the sense that, as men, they are more capable and accomplished than women and thus belong in jobs that reflect this. Consequently, men nurses are mistaken for doctors and are granted more authority and responsibility than their women counterparts, reflecting the idea that, as men, they are inherently more competent (Heikes 1991; Williams 1995).

Black men nurses, however, may not face the presumptions of expertise or the resulting assumption that they belong in higher-status jobs. Black professionals, both men and women, are often assumed to be less capable and less qualified than their white counterparts. In some cases, these negative stereotypes hold even when Black workers outperform white colleagues (Feagin and Sikes 1994). The belief that Blacks are inherently less competent than whites means that, despite advanced education, training, and skill, Black professionals often confront the lingering perception that they are better suited for lower-level service work (Feagin and Sikes 1994). Black men in fact often fare better than white women in blue-collar jobs such as policing and corrections work (Britton 1995), and this may be, in part, because they are viewed as more appropriately suited for these types of positions. . . .

As minority women address issues of both race and gender to negotiate a sense of belonging in masculine settings (Ong 2005), minority men may also face a comparable challenge in feminized fields. They may have to address the unspoken racialization implicit in the assumption that masculinity equals competence. Simultaneously, they may find that the racial stereotype that Blackness equals lower qualifications, standards, and competence clouds the sense that men are inherently more capable and adept in any field, including the feminized ones.

Establishing Distance From Femininity

An additional mechanism of the glass escalator involves establishing distance from women

and the femininity associated with their occupations. Because men nurses are employed in a culturally feminized occupation, they develop strategies to disassociate themselves from the femininity associated with their work and retain some of the privilege associated with masculinity. Thus, when men nurses gravitate toward hospital emergency wards rather than obstetrics or pediatrics, or emphasize that they are only in nursing to get into hospital administration, they distance themselves from the femininity of their profession and thereby preserve their status as men despite the fact that they do "women's work." Perhaps more important, these strategies also place men in a prime position to experience the glass escalator effect, as they situate themselves to move upward into higher-status areas in the field.

Creating distance from femininity also helps these men achieve aspects of hegemonic masculinity, which Connell (1989) describes as the predominant and most valued form of masculinity at a given time. Contemporary hegemonic masculine ideals emphasize toughness, strength, aggressiveness, heterosexuality, and, perhaps most important, a clear sense of femininity as different from and subordinate to masculinity (Kimmel 2001; Williams 1995). Thus, when men distance themselves from the feminized aspects of their jobs, they uphold the idea that masculinity and femininity are distinct, separate, and mutually exclusive. When these men seek masculinity by aiming for the better paying or most technological fields, they not only position themselves to move upward into the more acceptable arenas but also reinforce the greater social value placed on masculinity. Establishing distance from femininity therefore allows men to retain the privileges and status of masculinity while simultaneously enabling them to ride the glass escalator.

For Black men, the desire to reject femininity may be compounded by racial inequality. Theorists have argued that as institutional racism blocks access to traditional markers of masculinity such as occupational status and economic stability, Black men may repudiate femininity as a way of accessing the masculinity—and its attendant status—that is denied through other routes (hooks 2004; Neal 2005). Rejecting femininity is a key strategy men use to assert masculinity, and it remains available to Black men even when other means of achieving masculinity are unattainable. Black men nurses may be more likely to distance themselves from their women colleagues and to reject the femininity associated with nursing, particularly if they feel that they experience racial discrimination that renders occupational advancement inaccessible. Yet if they encounter strained relationships with women colleagues and men supervisors because of gendered racism or racialized stereotypes, the efforts to distance themselves from femininity still may not result in the glass escalator effect.

On the other hand, some theorists suggest that minority men may challenge racism by rejecting hegemonic masculine ideals. . . . The results of these studies suggest that Black men nurses may embrace the femininity associated with nursing if it offers a way to combat racism. In these cases, Black men nurses may turn to pediatrics as a way of demonstrating sensitivity and therefore combating stereotypes of Black masculinity, or they may proudly identify as nurses to challenge perceptions that Black men are unsuited for professional, white-collar positions.

Taken together, all of this research suggests that Black men may not enjoy the advantages experienced by their white men colleagues, who ride a glass escalator to success. In this article, I focus on the experiences of Black men nurses to argue that the glass escalator is a racialized as well as a gendered concept that does not offer Black men the same privileges as their white men counterparts. . . .

Findings Reception From Colleagues and Supervisors

When women welcome men into "their" professions, they often push men into leadership roles that ease their advancement into upper-level positions. Thus, a positive reaction from colleagues is critical to riding the glass escalator. Unlike white men nurses, however, Black men do not describe encountering a warm reception from women colleagues (Heikes 1991). Instead, the men I interviewed find that they often have unpleasant interactions with women coworkers who treat them rather coldly and attempt to keep them at bay. Chris is a 51-year-old oncology nurse who describes one white nurse's attempt to isolate him from other white women nurses as he attempted to get his instructions for that day's shift:

> She turned and ushered me to the door, and said for me to wait out here, a nurse will come out and give you your report. I stared at her hand on my arm, and then at her, and said, "Why? Where do you go to get your reports?" She said, "I get them in there." I said, "Right. Unhand me." I went right back in there, sat down, and started writing down my reports.

Kenny, a 47-year-old nurse with 23 years of nursing experience, describes a similarly and particularly painful experience he had in a previous job where he was the only Black person on staff:

> [The staff] had nothing to do with me, and they didn't even want me to sit at the same area where they were charting in to take a break. They wanted me to sit somewhere else. . . . They wouldn't even sit at a table with me! When I came and sat down, everybody got up and left.

These experiences with colleagues are starkly different from those described by white men in professions dominated by women (see Pierce 1995; Williams 1989). Though the men in these studies sometimes chose to segregate themselves, women never systematically excluded them. Though I have no way of knowing why the women nurses in Chris's and Kenny's workplaces physically segregated themselves, the pervasiveness of gendered racist images that emphasize white women's vulnerability to dangerous Black men may play an important role. For these nurses, their masculinity is not a guarantee that they will be welcomed, much less pushed into leadership roles. As Ryan, a 37-year-old intensive care nurse says, "[Black men] have to go further to prove ourselves. This involves proving our capabilities, *proving to colleagues that you can lead*, be on the forefront" (emphasis added). The warm welcome and subsequent opportunities for leadership cannot be taken for granted. In contrast, these men describe great challenges in forming congenial relationships with coworkers who, they believe, do not truly want them there.

In addition, these men often describe tense, if not blatantly discriminatory, relationships with supervisors. While Williams (1995) suggests that men supervisors can be allies for men in women's professions by facilitating promotions and upward mobility, Black men nurses describe incidents of being overlooked by supervisors when it comes time for promotions. Ryan, who has worked at his current job for 11 years, believes that these barriers block upward mobility within the profession:

> The hardest part is dealing with people who don't understand minority nurses. People with their biases, who don't identify you as ripe for promotion. I know the policy and procedure, I'm familiar with past history. So you can't tell me I can't move forward if others did. [How did you deal with this?] By knowing the chain of command, who my supervisors were. Things were subtle. I just had to be better. I got this mostly from other nurses and supervisors. I was paid to deal with patients, so I could deal with [racism] from them. I'm not paid to deal with this from colleagues.

Kenny offers a similar example. Employed as an orthopedic nurse in a predominantly white environment, he describes great difficulty getting promoted, which he primarily attributes to racial biases:

> It's almost like you have to, um, take your ideas and give them to somebody else and then let them present them for you and you get no credit for it. I've applied for several promotions there and, you know, I didn't get them. . . . When you look around to the, um, the percentage of African Americans who are actually in executive leadership is almost zero percent. Because it's less than one percent of the total population of people that are in leadership, and it's almost like they'll go outside of the system just to try to find a Caucasian to fill a position. Not that I'm not qualified, because I've been master's prepared for 12 years and I'm working on my doctorate.

According to Ryan and Kenny, supervisors' racial biases mean limited opportunities for promotion and upward mobility. This interpretation is consistent with research that suggests that even with stellar performance and solid work histories, Black workers may receive mediocre evaluations from white supervisors that limit their advancement (Feagin 2006; Feagin and Sikes 1994). For Black men nurses, their race may signal to supervisors that they are unworthy of promotion and thus create a different experience with the glass escalator.

Strong relationships with colleagues and supervisors are a key mechanism of the glass escalator effect. For Black men nurses, however, these relationships are experienced differently from those described by their white men colleagues. Black men nurses do not speak of warm and congenial relationships with women nurses or see these relationships as facilitating a move into leadership roles. Nor do they suggest that they share gendered bonds with men supervisors that serve to ease their mobility into higher-status administrative jobs. In contrast, they sense that racial bias makes it difficult to develop ties with coworkers and makes superiors unwilling to promote them. Black men nurses thus experience this aspect of the glass escalator differently from their white men colleagues. They find that relationships with colleagues and supervisors stifle, rather than facilitate, their upward mobility.

Perceptions of Suitability

Like their white counterparts, Black men nurses also experience challenges from clients who are unaccustomed to seeing men in fields typically dominated by women. As with white men nurses, Black men encounter this in surprised or quizzical reactions from patients who seem to expect to be treated by white women nurses. . . .

Yet while patients rarely expect to be treated by men nurses of any race, white men encounter statements and behaviors that suggest patients expect them to be doctors, supervisors, or other higher-status, more masculine positions (Williams 1989, 1995). In part, this expectation accelerates their ride on the glass escalator, helping to push them into the positions for which they are seen as more appropriately suited.

(White) men, by virtue of their masculinity, are assumed to be more competent and capable and thus better situated in (nonfeminized) jobs that are perceived to require greater skill and proficiency. Black men, in contrast, rarely encounter patients (or colleagues and supervisors) who immediately expect that they are doctors or administrators. Instead, many respondents find that even after displaying their credentials, sharing their nursing experience, and, in one case, dispensing care, they are still mistaken for janitors or service workers. Ray's experience is typical:

> I've even given patients their medicines, explained their care to them, and then they'll say to me, "Well, can you send the nurse in?"

Chris describes a somewhat similar encounter of being misidentified by a white woman patient:

> I come [to work] in my white uniform, that's what I wear—being a Black man, I know they won't look at me the same, so I dress the part—I said good evening, my name's Chris, and I'm going to be your nurse. She says to me, "Are you from housekeeping?" . . . I've had other cases. I've walked in and had a lady look at me and ask if I'm the janitor. . . .

These negative stereotypes can affect Black men nurses' efforts to treat patients as well. The men I interviewed find that masculinity does not automatically endow them with an aura of competency. In fact, they often describe interactions with white women patients that suggest that their race minimizes whatever assumptions of capability might accompany

being men. They describe several cases in which white women patients completely refused treatment. Ray says,

> With older white women, it's tricky sometimes because they will come right out and tell you they don't want you to treat them, or can they see someone else.

Ray frames this as an issue specifically with older white women, though other nurses in the sample described similar issues with white women of all ages. Cyril, a 40-year-old nurse with 17 years of nursing experience, describes a slightly different twist on this story:

> I had a white lady that I had to give a shot, and she was fine with it and I was fine with it. But her husband, when she told him, he said to me, I don't have any problem with you as a Black man, but I don't want you giving her a shot.

While white men nurses report some apprehension about treating women patients, in all likelihood this experience is compounded for Black men (Williams 1989). Historically, interactions between Black men and white women have been fraught with complexity and tension, as Black men have been represented in the cultural imagination as potential rapists and threats to white women's security and safety—and, implicitly, as a threat to white patriarchal stability (Davis 1981; Giddings 1984). In Cyril's case, it may be particularly significant that the Black man is charged with giving a shot and therefore literally penetrating the white wife's body, a fact that may heighten the husband's desire to shield his wife from this interaction. White men nurses may describe hesitation or awkwardness that accompanies treating women patients, but their experiences are not shaped by a pervasive racial imagery that suggests that they are potential threats to their women patients' safety.

This dynamic, described primarily among white women patients and their families, presents a picture of how Black men's interactions with clients are shaped in specifically raced and gendered ways that suggest they are less rather than more capable. These interactions do not send the message that Black men, because they are men, are too competent for nursing and really belong in higher-status jobs. Instead, these men face patients who mistake them for lower-status service workers and encounter white women patients (and their husbands) who simply refuse treatment or are visibly uncomfortable with the prospect. These interactions do not situate Black men nurses in a prime position for upward mobility. Rather, they suggest that the experience of Black men nurses with this particular mechanism of the glass escalator is the manifestation of the expectation that they should be in lower-status positions more appropriate to their race and gender.

Refusal to Reject Femininity

Finally, Black men nurses have a different experience with establishing distance from women and the feminized aspects of their work. Most research shows that as men nurses employ strategies that distance them from femininity (e.g., by emphasizing nursing as a route to higher-status, more masculine jobs), they place themselves in a position for upward mobility and the glass escalator effect (Williams 1992). For Black men nurses, however, this process looks different. Instead of distancing themselves from the femininity associated with nursing, Black men actually embrace some of the more feminized attributes linked to nursing. In particular, they emphasize how much they value and enjoy the way their jobs allow them to be caring and nurturing. Rather than conceptualizing caring as anathema or feminine (and therefore undesirable), Black men nurses speak openly of caring as something positive and enjoyable.

This is consistent with the context of nursing that defines caring as integral to the profession. As nurses, Black men in this line of work experience professional socialization that emphasizes and values caring, and this is reflected in their statements about their work. Significantly, however, rather than repudiating this feminized component of their jobs, they embrace it. Tobias, a 44-year-old oncology nurse with 25 years of experience, asserts,

> The best part about nursing is helping other people, the flexibility of work hours, and the commitment to vulnerable populations, people who are ill.

Simon, a 36-year-old oncology nurse, also talks about the joy he gets from caring for others. He contrasts his experiences to those of white men nurses he knows who prefer specialties that involve less patient care:

> They were going to work with the insurance industries, they were going to work in the ER where it's a touch and go, you're a number literally. I don't get to know your name, I don't get to know that you have four grandkids, I don't get to know that you really want to get out of the hospital by next week because the following week is your birthday, your 80th birthday and it's so important for you. I don't get to know that your cat's name is Sprinkles, and you're concerned about who's feeding the cat now, and if they remembered to turn the TV on during the day so that the cat can watch *The Price is Right.* They don't get into all that kind of stuff. OK, I actually need to remember the name of your cat so that tomorrow morning when I come, I can ask you about Sprinkles and that will make a world of difference. I'll see light coming to your eyes and the medicines will actually work because your perspective is different.

Like Tobias, Simon speaks with a marked lack of self-consciousness about the joys of adding a personal touch and connecting that personal care to a patient's improvement. For him, caring is important, necessary, and valued, even though others might consider it a feminine trait.

For many of these nurses, willingness to embrace caring is also shaped by issues of race and racism. In their position as nurses, concern for others is connected to fighting the effects of racial inequality. Specifically, caring motivates them to use their role as nurses to address racial health disparities, especially those that disproportionately affect Black men. Chris describes his efforts to minimize health issues among Black men:

> With Black male patients, I have their history, and if they're 50 or over I ask about the prostate exam and a colonoscopy. Prostate and colorectal death is so high that that's my personal crusade.

Ryan also speaks to the importance of using his position to address racial imbalances:

> I really take advantage of the opportunities to give back to communities, especially to change the disparities in the African American community. I'm more than just a nurse. As a faculty member at a major university, I have to do community hours, services. Doing health fairs, in-services on research, this makes an impact in some disparities in the African American community. [People in the community] may not have the opportunity to do this otherwise.

As Lamont (2000) indicates in her discussion of the "caring self," concern for others helps Chris and Ryan to use their knowledge and position as nurses to combat racial inequalities in health. Though caring is generally considered a "feminine" attribute, in this context it is connected to challenging racial health disparities. Unlike their white men colleagues, these nurses accept and even embrace certain aspects of femininity rather than rejecting them. They thus reveal yet another aspect of the glass escalator process that differs for Black men. As Black men nurses embrace this "feminine" trait and the avenues it provides for challenging racial inequalities, they may become more comfortable in nursing and embrace the opportunities it offers.

Conclusions

Existing research on the glass escalator cannot explain these men's experiences. As men who do women's work, they should be channeled into positions as charge nurses or nursing administrators and should find themselves virtually pushed into the upper ranks of the nursing profession. But without exception, this is not the experience these Black men nurses describe. Instead of benefiting from the basic mechanisms of the glass escalator, they face tense relationships with colleagues, supervisors' biases in achieving promotion, patient stereotypes that inhibit caregiving, and a sense of comfort with some of the feminized aspects of their jobs. These "glass barriers" suggest that the glass escalator is a racialized concept as well as a gendered one. The main contribution of this study is the finding that race and gender intersect to determine which men will ride the glass escalator. The proposition that men who do women's work encounter undue opportunities and advantages appears to be unequivocally true only if the men in question are white.

* * *

References

Acker, Joan. 1990. Hierarchies, jobs, bodies: A theory of gendered organizations. *Gender & Society* 4:139–58.

Britton, Dana. 1995. *At work in the iron cage.* New York: New York University Press.

Budig, Michelle. 2002. Male advantage and the gender composition of jobs: Who rides the glass escalator? *Social Forces* 49(2): 258–77.

Charles, Maria, and David Grusky. 2004. *Occupational ghettos: The worldwide segregation of women and men.* Palo Alto, CA: Stanford University Press.

Collins, Patricia Hill. 1990. *Black feminist thought.* New York: Routledge.

———. 2004. *Black sexual politics.* New York: Routledge.

Connell, R. W. 1989. *Gender and power.* Sydney, Australia: Allen and Unwin.

Davis, Angela. 1981. *Women, race, and class.* New York: Vintage.

Duffy, Mignon. 2007. Doing the dirty work: Gender, race, and reproductive labor in historical perspective. *Gender & Society* 21:313–36.

Espiritu, Yen Le. 2000. *Asian American women and men: Labor, laws, and love.* Walnut Creek, CA: AltaMira.

Essed, Philomena. 1991. *Understanding everyday racism.* New York: Russell Sage.

Feagin, Joe. 2006. *Systemic racism.* New York: Routledge.

Feagin, Joe, and Melvin Sikes. 1994. *Living with racism.* Boston: Beacon Hill Press.

Floge, Liliane, and Deborah M. Merrill. 1986. Tokenism reconsidered: Male nurses and female physicians in a hospital setting. *Social Forces* 64:925–47.

Giddings, Paula. 1984. *When and where I enter: The impact of Black women on race and sex in America.* New York: HarperCollins.

Harvey Wingfield, Adia. 2007. The modern mammy and the angry Black man: African American professionals' experiences with gendered racism in the workplace. *Race, Gender, and Class* 14(2): 196–212.

Heikes, E. Joel. 1991. When men are the minority: The case of men in nursing. *Sociological Quarterly* 32:389–401.

hooks, bell. 2004. *We real cool.* New York: Routledge.

Kanter, Rosabeth Moss. 1977. *Men and women of the corporation.* New York: Basic Books.

Kimmel, Michael. 2001. Masculinity as homophobia. In *Men and masculinity,* edited by Theodore F. Cohen. Belmont, CA: Wadsworth.

Lamont, Michelle. 2000. *The dignity of working men.* New York: Russell Sage.

Neal, Mark Anthony. 2005. *New Black man.* New York: Routledge.

Ong, Maria. 2005. Body projects of young women of color in physics: Intersections of race, gender, and science. *Social Problems* 52(4): 593–617.

Pierce, Jennifer. 1995. *Gender trials: Emotional lives in contemporary law firms.* Berkeley: University of California Press.

Roth, Louise. 2006. *Selling women short: Gender and money on Wall Street.* Princeton, NJ: Princeton University Press.

Snyder, Karrie Ann, and Adam Isaiah Green. 2008. Revisiting the glass escalator: The case of gender segregation in a female dominated occupation. *Social Problems* 55(2): 271–99.

Williams, Christine. 1989. *Gender differences at work: Women and men in non-traditional occupations.* Berkeley: University of California Press.

———. 1992. The glass escalator: Hidden advantages for men in the "female" professions. *Social Problems* 39(3): 253–67.

———. 1995. *Still a man's world: Men who do women's work.* Berkeley: University of California Press.

Zimmer, Lynn. 1988. Tokenism and women in the workplace: The limits of gender neutral theory. *Social Problems* 35(1): 64–77.

Introduction to Reading 34

With the globalization of the economy, it is interesting to read Steven C. McKay's examination of the workplace policies and practices of three different high-tech companies in the Philippines. These factories are owned by three different multinational companies from America, Europe, and Japan. Each multinational corporation brings its own culture, but it also brings gendered assumptions to its factory in the Philippines. While the basic needs of workers for decent wages, reasonable hours, and safe working conditions are the same around the world, these companies used gendered assumptions to attract and maintain their workforce, not always to the benefit of the women and men working for them.

1. Which of the three factories has the most female-friendly practices?

2. What workplace practices and gender-based assumptions about work disadvantage women in these factories?

3. Why was it so difficult for women to be promoted from "operators" of machines to technical positions?

Hard Drives and Glass Ceilings

Gender Stratification in High-Tech Production

Steven C. McKay

Rapid industrialization and foreign direct investment in developing countries since the 1960s touched off what has become a three-decades-old debate about the impact of technology and "the global assembly line" on women and the division of labor (see Mills 2003). Recent trends in globalization, technological change, and flexible work reorganization have reawakened the debate (Acker 2004; Kelkar and Nathan 2002). In the electronics industry, where women have dominated production work, technological upgrading has been held up as a potential avenue for increased women's employment, empowerment, and socioeconomic mobility (Kuruvilla 1996; Yun 1995). Yet others argue that globalization and more flexible work organization may only intensify the exploitation of women workers and exacerbate occupational gender segmentation (Fox 2002; Joekes and Weston 1994).

While many recent studies document global restructuring, they—like earlier studies of women workers—tend to frame their analysis in terms of whether employment in advanced electronics represents either empowerment or exploitation. Thus, Chhachhi (1999) poses but cannot possibly answer the question of whether women electronic workers in India represent "dormant volcanoes," with a new, structural potential to explode, or "fresh green vegetables," that remain naïve, docile, and dominated by global capital.

However, focusing on either empowerment or exploitation becomes an analytical cul-de-sac, particularly given the wide variations in how

firms organize high-tech production, how workers struggle over and make sense of their own employment, and the gendered meanings that emerge from these intersecting processes within a specific sociopolitical context. In this article, I concentrate on the myriad ways gender and inequality are constituted—even within a single industry and in a single national context—analyzing at multiple levels the links between gender ascription and the division of labor (Mills 2003). At the workplace level, I focus on management's structuring of the shop floor and key sources of variation that influence how advanced technologies and flexible work are organized, stratified, and gendered (Salzinger 2003). Equally important, I also examine the extra-organizational contexts—particularly the role of the state and persistent gender ideologies—that shape firm-level decision making as well as workers' assessments and action. Finally, to better assess the meaning of flexible production for women workers, I analyze high-tech work in terms of its impact on a range of issues concerning the gender division of labor. Specifically, I focus on the degree to which the three firms' gender and flexibility strategies address women's more "practical" everyday responsibilities and individual survival needs within the existing gendered division of labor versus their impact on the more "strategic" gender interest of women in "extending the conditions for choices to be made about the gender division of labor" (Chhachhi and Pittin 1998, 71, emphasis added; Molyneux 1985). In this sense, I hope to gauge to what extent changes

From McKay, S. C. "Hard Drives and Glass Ceilings: Gender Stratification in High-Tech Production," *Gender & Society* 20: 207–235. Published by Sage Publications on behalf of Sociologists for Women in Society.

in the organization of high-tech work directly challenge deeper gender inequality or "the structural roots of unequal access to resources and control" (Chow and Lyter 2002, 41). . . .

Data and analysis are based on 11 months of interview and observation-based field research conducted in the Philippines in 1999 and follow-up research conducted during several weeks in 2003. Following interviews with human resource managers or staff at 20 firms, I selected three cases, representing the three dominant types of electronics products produced in the Philippines—disk drives, discrete semiconductors, and integrated chips—and the diverse nationalities of the home corporation.

* * *

The State, the Electronics Industry, and Gender

The Philippines has been a site of low-cost electronics assembly since the early 1970s, in large part because it offers—and the Philippine state has helped guarantee—an investment context favored by foreign high-tech manufacturers: political and economic stability; inexpensive, educated, and disciplined labor; good infrastructure; few operational restrictions; and investment/tax incentives tailored to the electronics industry (Austria 1999; Ernst 2002). State-led labor control has gone hand in hand with foreign investment policies at least since the early 1970s, when then-president Ferdinand Marcos launched an export-oriented industrialization program while also declaring martial law, rewriting the labor code, banning all strikes in export manufacturing, and cracking down on militant labor (Bello, Kinley, and Elinson 1982). The debt crisis of the 1980s only increased the Philippines's dependence on foreign investment, as structural adjustment packages attached to International Monetary Fund loans forced the Philippines to further open its economy and compete directly with other developing countries—particularly Malaysia, Thailand, and Indonesia—for mobile

investment capital (Bello et al. 2004). By the 1990s, the Philippines had fully embraced a neoliberal economic growth model, centered on courting foreign investment through reregulating employment and production conditions, especially in its booming export-processing zones (World Bank 1997). . . .

As it has since the 1970s, the electronics industry continues to hire primarily women for factory operator positions largely because women can be paid less and are viewed as more patient, docile, and detail oriented (Chant and McIlwaine 1995). Management's desire to develop such a "cheapened" labor force is directly connected to the intensity of the labor process: production workers still make up 82 percent of the electronics workforce. Overall, 74 percent of the electronics industry workers are women and 78 percent younger than 30. But the workforce is increasingly well educated: More than 60 percent of the workers are high school graduates, and 37 percent have college degrees (Bureau of Labor Relations 1999).

Although women have made strides through their electronics employment, they still face a host of challenges, particularly given prevailing gender ideologies and complex gender relations in the Philippines. Women in the Philippines are sometimes viewed as having relatively more power than women in other Asian countries since women in the Philippines traditionally control domestic budgets and make most household decisions (Eviota 1992). And the preference for women in two key industries, electronics and garments, has contributed to overall employment and wage gains made by women in recent decades. While women's labor force participation rates have remained stable since 1975 at about 47 percent, women make up nearly 70 percent of the export industry workforce, women's unemployment rate (9.9 percent) is slightly below the men's rate (10.3 percent), and the wage differential between women and men, at 87 percent, is one of the lowest for a developing country (National Statistical Coordination Board 2001; Seguino 2000).

Despite these gains, employers' preference for female labor both taps into and reproduces gender ideologies and gendered labor market segmentation that systematically undervalues the labor of young educated women (Chant and McIlwaine 1995). As Parrenas (2001) points out, although women dominate the workforces of the two largest foreign exchange earning sectors—overseas contract labor and electronics—women are nevertheless constructed through Philippine families, churches, and the state as "secondary earners," whose proper roles of "mother," "daughter," and/or caregiver tie them primarily to the home, particularly after marriage (Eviota 1992). Thus, although many women have secured formal waged work through electronics assembly jobs, they nevertheless still confront a rigid gender division of labor, gendered labor control strategies, and gendered associations with technology. These issues, which only intensify as firms upgrade production technologies, will be discussed in each of the cases below.

Storage Ltd.

Storage Ltd., a subsidiary of a leading Japanese hard disk drive producer, demonstrates that while new flexibilities do lead to different labor practices than those documented in earlier studies of transnational assembly, such restructuring may also sharpen gendered labor control regimes. The firm's $124 million plant, operational since 1996, assembles and tests high-end hard disk drives for computer servers, requiring expensive semi-automated machinery, sophisticated quality control systems, and enormous startup costs. To meet these demands, Storage Ltd. has chosen a labor process and control regime that diverge somewhat from past practices in electronics and other export industries. For example, the firm does not subcontract out its labor-intensive assembly nor rely on temporary workers to boost its external flexibility (Standing 1999). Instead, to meet quality standards and enhance internal flexibility, the firm develops multi-skilled workers, trained to operate from one to three machines or work stations. Such training can take up to three months and considerable firm investment, so the firm tries hard to keep turnover down, making all employees permanent after six months and providing some positive incentives. For example, although base pay is only minimum wage, the company does pay more for overtime, pushing take-home pay up to 300 pesos per day (about US$6) or 50 percent more than the legal minimum. The company also provides transportation, free uniforms, subsidized meals, emergency medical insurance, and 12 days of sick and vacation leave a year—benefits relatively high by local standards.

Yet in other ways, the demanding character of disk drive production coupled with cut-throat cost competition has led the firm to develop more sophisticated forms of gendered labor control focused on stability, cost saving, and "disciplinary management." First, the actual production process remains quite labor intensive: The plant employs more than 9,000 workers, 87 percent of whom are shop floor operators, who churn out more than 1.5 million disk drives per month. To maintain such high productivity, the firm uses both high-tech strategies and more traditional direct control. On the technical side, the firm relies on a computerized assembly line that automatically gathers data for statistical process control, providing managers and customers with real-time productivity and quality data down to the individual workstation. On the social side, there is strict enforcement of company rules. As one human resources staff member admitted, "For most operators, they have no control. They are treated like robots; told what to do, when, where and how. Every movement is controlled. . . . They are told where to go, when to eat. And everything is timed, even going to the bathroom." While officially, there are three 8-hour shifts, in practice, there are only two 12-hour shifts with 4 hours of daily forced overtime. The workweek is six and often seven days a week. The long hours clearly take a toll on workers. Irma, a production operator noted, "The overtime is just too much. I only sleep five hours a day. I get home (from the night shift) at nine a.m., I'm asleep by ten. Then, I get up again at three or four p.m. just so I can do my laundry and clean up before I go in again."

In addition to such in-plant intensity, the firm utilizes and helps construct gender stereotypes to dampen its labor costs and extend its labor control far beyond the factory. The process begins in hiring. The company selectively recruits rural women, assuming—to some degree correctly—that they have fewer labor market options and will thus be cheaper, more dependent on the firm, and willing to put up with the demanding labor process. The profile of the company's 9,000 workers is remarkably uniform: 88 percent are women; 83 percent between 16 and 22, with an average age of 21; and 97 percent single. Fifty-one percent have some college or vocational training, and the rest are high school graduates. The reasons given for this rigid hiring profile follow and reinforce the gender stereotypes and "public narratives" about the nature of women's work that have become the norm in export factories around the world (Mills 2003). Managers say they prefer women because the work requires "patience, dexterity, and attention to detail," while men are viewed as lazy, sloppy, impatient, and generally magulo or disruptive. The company also wants intelligent, English-speaking workers, but ones without high job, pay, or promotion expectations. For this reason, management again prefers women—stereotyped as loyal but not ambitious—and does not hire anyone at the operator level with more than two years of college. This gendered hiring and job allocation essentially cuts women operators off from promotions to the more lucrative technical jobs, since these positions require a three-year technical or four-year college degree. Women operators can thus aspire only to a horizontal move to office clerk or to a climb up a short job ladder to line leader or quality control inspector. Technicians and engineers in the plant are almost all men.

Finally, Storage Ltd. also tries to localize its labor control, tapping into gender subordination at the family and community level. For example, when screening potential workers, recruiters ask extensively about an applicant's family and her role in the household. While seemingly innocent, the line of questioning aims to judge an applicant's level of dependence and reflects another of the firm's gendered strategies: to hire oldest daughters. Since the eldest are usually responsible for aiding parents and younger siblings, they are considered less likely to quit. The firm also maintains a Background Investigation Unit to scrutinize both workers and their families and make links with village-level officials to head off potential unionizing efforts. Before workers are made permanent following six months' probationary employment, the Background Investigation Unit conducts a home visit to interview workers' parents, inspect their residence, and contact the lowest-level officials. Primary targets for investigations are those reported to have gotten married since being hired and who may be hiding families back home.

The firm's sophisticated labor control strategies have important implications for both women's practical needs and strategic gender interests. In a practical sense, employment at Storage Ltd. does benefit women workers by providing permanent work paying above-minimum wages in a high-status industry. Ironically, because the firm can legally and explicitly target women with little experience and few labor market options, it has created a workforce that is grateful for its jobs despite the demanding working conditions, yet one with little collective or individual bargaining power to directly confront the hierarchical divisions of labor. Although workers complained of the overtime and lack of rest days, they also referred to the work as "clean" and "light," particularly in contrast to the physically demanding and low-status agricultural- or informal-sector work in their rural hometowns. For many, the job also gave them their first experience of living away from parents, increased status, control over income, and a means to fulfill independently their basic survival needs. As one operator noted, "This is my first job and I'm satisfied with the pay and benefits. . . . Working for 12 hours is not so bad. The work's pretty light . . . my parents treat me better now that I already have my own job." . . .

Integrated Production

Integrated Production, a subsidiary of an American semiconductor firm producing advanced integrated circuits, shows a different gendered strategy to promote labor stability, as well as the possible—but unrealized—potential of high-tech flexible production for women. Production at the firm's $200 million plant opened in late 1996 is less standardized, less labor intensive, and more automated than at Storage Ltd. At the core of the labor process are engineers and technicians, who make up more than 20 percent of the workforce and are crucial for ramping up production, programming in flexibility, and keeping the lines running. Due to the high level of automation, only 55 percent of the 1,373 permanent employees are production workers. These operators play only a minor role in flexible production: They work under strict supervision and are told to simply check the computer readouts from the quality control programs and report any problems to engineers.

Yet the automated machinery is extremely expensive and critical to production, so Integrated Production, like the other firms in the study, wants to minimize turnover or production disruption and thus provides training and employs only permanent workers. However, unlike Storage Ltd., Integrated Production combines its "hard" engineering-intensive labor process with a "soft" strategic labor relations approach—modeled after a Silicon Valley variant of the American human resources model—that stresses positive incentives, loyalty, and "empowerment" through ritual participation (Katz and Darbishire 2000). First, although take-home pay is actually less than at the other two firms, production operators are monthly-paid salaried employees, considered a notch up in status from daily-paid laborers. In addition, workers receive other benefits such as stock options, education reimbursement, and a free computer after two years. The firm also provides an assortment of morale-boosting activities, such as outings, sports fests, and pizza parties. The employee relations manager boasted, "It is really like an American company [in America]—there's really toilet paper in the bathroom, really free coffee all the time." Finally, the company "empowers" individual workers through an employee suggestion program and open intercompany communication.

Yet the firm also studiously avoids—and actively disrupts—any collective worker action through anti-union trainings and surveillance.

The organization of work and labor relations is also gendered, in ways both similar to and different from that at Storage Ltd. Overall, the firm has one of the most balanced gender ratios of the companies visited: 38 percent men and only 63 percent women. But when broken down by position, the gender segregation typical of the industry becomes clearer: All nine directors and 90 percent of the engineers and technicians are men, while 85 percent of shop floor workers are women. As we will see below, this strict gender division of labor makes upward mobility for current women operators into new technical positions extremely difficult.

Nevertheless, gender strategies differ. First, unlike Storage Ltd., the firm is less concerned with trying to maximize women's multiple labor market vulnerabilities by recruiting only from rural areas and screening out experienced or married workers. The human resources manager complained that local rural residents are poorly educated. . . . Rather, the firm puts a premium on educated workers, requiring a minimum of two years of college or technical training and preferring college graduates. Its emphasis on education has led to a frontline workforce dominated by women yet demographically distinct from other plants: Only 60 percent of workers are younger than 24 years of age, and only 70 percent are single. Operators are more likely from urban areas, 95 percent have finished at least two-year technical degrees, and a large portion are college graduates.

However, the firm's gendered strategy to hire educated women but to maintain a strict gender division of labor has also created problems. In part because these women are well educated, they also have higher career aspirations, more labor market options, and more individual bargaining power. Thus, the firm must rely more on positive rather than negative incentives to reduce turnover. In fact, some women took jobs in production in the hopes that they could eventually move up in the company. . . . In terms of internal promotion, the technical job ladder has far better prospects for earning and security but requires increasingly specific qualifications and is thus generally blocked to nontechnically trained (if formally educated) operators. . . . The mismatch between women's high education and blocked mobility has led to a turnover rate of more than 9 percent, the highest among the three companies. . . .

As the plant moves toward full automation, the new technical operators, who are slated to replace other shop floor workers, will still handle basic production but also take on responsibilities of current technicians, performing all minor maintenance and repairs. These enhanced operator positions would then have a direct promotional ladder leading to full technicians and possibly engineers—an avenue previously closed to operators. If women operators were to gain access to these jobs, their increased skills and mobility could provide more decision-making power over the division of labor and help break down gendered notions associated with technology and technical positions that have helped keep women out of technical work.

Unfortunately, such potential remains unrealized. First, the firm requires these new technical operators to have at least two years' training from an accredited electronics training school. In fact, managers, operating under gendered assumptions about women's technical (in)capacities, do not fill these new positions by training current operators. Rather, the firm recruits directly from engineering or technical schools, where almost all the trainees, and thus all the new technical operators, are men.

In other ways, technological upgrading may already be shifting management's gendered notions about electronics assembly, effectively masculinizing the work and the workforce. The human resources manager explained that, in the early days, women dominated semiconductor assembly in the Philippines because "everyone followed the dictum that women work better with small things." But with the increase in the number of technicians and technical operators, he noted, "Guys are beginning to gain ground."

Specifically, men have been gaining ground by masculinizing the new machines and processes.

For example, the manager noted that the new automated machines are not as "gender specific" as old machines and that production has become "less dependent on the fine skills of women. . . . The machines have large screens instead of microscopes, so [operators] don't need 20/20 vision or the patience to sit at a scope." Thus, there is a regendering process as managers and skilled male workers try to capture a new technology or area of production and revalue previously feminized assembly labor. The human resources manager went on to explain why women do not make "ideal workers": "Women get sick, they need maternity leave, have monthly periods." Men, on the other hand, were seen as "stronger" and able to work longer shifts. Here, the manager referred to the 12-hour day as an important reason for the shifting gender balance. According to the manager, "with the long shifts, we need more stamina and not agility. . . . Guys are strong and can work for 24 hours. With the right pay, they will do anything." Thus, the demands of an essentially still-standardized labor process become regendered: from the stereotyped call for feminized patience into a new demand for masculine stamina. In such cases, where the gendering of technology is widening the divide between male technical workers and female shop floor operators, women operators facing mass layoffs and blocked paths to promotion ladders may find that upgrading serves neither their practical survival needs nor their strategic gender interests.

Discrete Manufacturing

Discrete Manufacturing, a branch of a leading European electronics multinational that produces discrete semiconductors, refutes arguments that electronics work is necessarily exploitative of women workers, particularly if workers act collectively. Yet the introduction of new technologies may threaten the hard-fought gains won through unionization. The $110 million plant, opened in 1994, employs nearly 3,500 permanent employees, 85 percent of whom are factory workers and almost half of whom transferred from an older assembly plant. Relocation allowed management to reorganize production with more automated equipment, new line layouts, increased multiskilling, and the introduction of teamwork. But the firm was constrained from taking full advantage of an otherwise greenfield investment since workers at Discrete Manufacturing are unionized and have been able to check management's ability to introduce flexibility in the same manner as at the other two firms.

Discrete Manufacturing also differs in how its gendered employment practices have played out over time. Ironically, Discrete Manufacturing— like other foreign electronics firms—originally recruited women with only high school educations because it too sought "cheap assembly hands" for its labor-intensive plant. However, workers at the older plant successfully unionized during the height of the Philippine labor movement's organizing surge in the turbulent 1980s. When production and the workforce shifted to the new plant, management initially hired a human resources director to bust the union. But when the union successfully resisted these attempts, the firm shifted to a more cooperative stance. This crucial development helped women workers, who traditionally have little bargaining power, to collectively shape an agenda for fulfilling both their practical needs and, to some extent, their strategic gender interests.

The most immediate areas in which unionization has made a difference are in pay and benefits. Although new workers' base pay is similar to that at other firms, experienced production workers earn nearly three and a half times the starting rate. The high pay is a big reason so many women have stayed with the company. Thus, while the firm's overall gender balance is similar to other electronics firms—75 percent of the factory workers are women—the workforce is quite a bit older. Among factory workers, 77 percent are 26 years old or older, with an average age of 29, and less than 1 percent are younger than 20. In part a reflection of their older age, 35 percent of operators are married. Interestingly, 72 percent of married women had spouses who were unemployed, meaning that a large percentage of women workers, 26 percent, were sole breadwinners for their families. It is also interesting to note that the older women remain largely unmarried.

While managers joked that there are "a lot of *sultera* [old maids] in this company," this pattern may also reflect women's ability to delay marriage, since earning a decent wage has allowed them some measure of independence (Chant and McIlwaine 1995; Wolf 1992).

The breadth of benefits—which are negotiated rather than simply defined by management—also reflects workers' own priorities as both workers and women. First, all union members enjoy general provisions such as seniority-based pay, family health insurance, and protection against layoffs and subcontracting. Second, workers have negotiated gender-sensitive benefits not found in most other companies. For example, maternity leave and childbirth subsidies take into account the kind of delivery (caesarian, normal, or miscarriage). Since women in the Philippines are usually responsible for attending to sick family members or emergencies, workers have negotiated benefits such as bereavement assistance and a total of 26 days of leave a year. Women are also often responsible for family finances, so they have bargained for an array of low-interest loans and subsidies for housing, education, and emergencies to finance expenses.

With the unionized status and negotiated benefits, many workers recognize their jobs as some of the best in the industry and are committed to staying with the firm. Carmen, a production operator, stated, "The work is hard. . . . Two machines I have to watch over and I'm standing the whole shift," but, "I'm not planning to look for anything else. I figure I'll be here at Discrete Manufacturing for the next 10 years. There's a CBA [collective bargaining agreement]. My projection . . . is that it's really lifetime employment." Indeed, the average tenure of the 24 operators interviewed was 4.75 years, and the overall yearly turnover rate was between just 3 and 5 percent. That these women remain in the workforce and consider themselves "lifetime" employees is again in contrast to other studies that have focused on the temporary nature of women's factory work.

But despite wide gains by the union, workers now face a dual challenge: technological upgrading and a restive management trying to reassert its command over the labor process. Like Integrated

Production, Discrete Manufacturing is also experimenting with a new, fully automated assembly line run by new technical operators. And also like Integrated Production, the technical operator positions have the potential for increasing upward mobility. Previously, when new equipment was introduced, the union had been able to negotiate technical training for its frontline workers, ensuring gradual upgrading of skills. Initially, when the new technical operator positions were developed, union officers tried to get these positions filled by senior workers, who are primarily women. However, management has taken this opportunity of more radical redesign to enhance its control over workers. Invoking their claim to "management prerogative" over production issues, managers have refused to promote existing operators into the technical operator positions. Thus, the firm, like Integrated Production, is not filling these positions with its women employees but with new "fresh graduates" of four-year engineering or two-year electronics training programs, who all happen to be men. Thus, it is clear that while women workers have made many gains through their employment and collective bargaining, the industry is also changing in ways that may not bode well for the future.

* * *

CONCLUSIONS: REALIZING PRACTICAL AND STRATEGIC GENDER INTERESTS

The three case studies demonstrate that the impact of high-tech employment and technological upgrading on women workers varies: It is impossible to speak of exploitation or empowerment. But how then to assess the variation and what it might mean for the gendering of high-tech production in the future? To conclude, it will be useful to return to the issue of practical needs versus strategic gender interests.

Focusing first on the practical material needs of women, the cases confirm what other studies have also pointed out: that multinational electronics firms tend to pay higher wages and provide higher job security and better working conditions than local factories or the informal sector (Elson 1999; Mills 2003). In this sense, work in the electronics sector does seem to help meet women's daily needs and improve their lives. Workers themselves often have positive assessments of their jobs, as waged work helps increase their mobility, independence, and control over income. Equally important for interviewees has been the higher status that their "clean" and "modern" employment in the electronics industry provides. As others have argued, these gains from formal-sector jobs are significant and may help women workers renegotiate power and gender relations within their families, particularly regarding child care and household spending decisions (Chant and McIlwaine 1995). Nevertheless, these "practical" gains are made within existing gender divisions of labor—both in the firms and in wider Philippine society—which still slot women into lower-level, secondary positions (Eviota 1992; Parrenas 2001). Workers' positive views of seemingly punishing factory work are also relative to the limited options these women face in the informal economy or service sector due to the persistence of gender-stratified labor markets. Thus, while women workers do benefit from their factory jobs, such labor is embedded in and subjected to persistent gender ideologies that employers have long used to feminize and cheapen assembly work. Therefore, work in the electronics sector, in and of itself, is unlikely to lead to a transformation of traditional gender divisions of labor.

The dialectics of gendered work organization are most extreme in the case of Storage Ltd. While the firm may serve its women employees' survival needs by hiring them, it also has by far the most exploitative gendered labor control strategy. By consciously leveraging wider gender inequalities in the labor market, the firm creates a kind of asymmetrical agency, which allows a sense of individual worker autonomy and empowerment yet only within the confines of existing organizational and gender hierarchies that help (re)produce rather than challenge management's authority in production and broader gendered social relations.

Nevertheless, the variation across the three firms in terms of individual versus collective bargaining power suggests that the most potent vehicle for maximizing the benefits of industrial work is through collective organization (Elson 1999; Hutchinson and Brown 2001). At Discrete Manufacturing, a group of initially marginal women workers—selected along stereotypical lines for their cheapness and docility—have in fact increased their income security, class mobility, and autonomy by negotiating a gender-income sensitive contract that addresses worker-defined needs. This is similar to Fernandez's (2001) findings that although technological upgrading can lead to greater wage inequality, an active union can at least help mitigate the most polarizing gender and racial effects. Unfortunately, the conditions at Discrete Manufacturing are not widely shared: Despite similar structural conditions of permanent employment across most of the industry, fewer than 10 percent of electronics firms in the Philippines are unionized.

But more important, even impressive collective bargaining agreements such as the one at Discrete Manufacturing do not directly address strategic gender interests, as they focus primarily on improving wages and benefits and not on challenging the gender division of labor. Thus, the development in the industry that has the most potential for transforming workplace gender hierarchies and expanding women's choices about the gender division of labor is the emergence of the technical operator. As shown most vividly at Integrated Production—but also at Discrete Manufacturing—the new technical operator positions fuse the jobs, responsibilities, and promotional ladders of production workers (traditionally women) and technicians (traditionally men). These positions, which are likely to dominate high-end production facilities not only in the Philippines but across the global industry could allow current women operators to breach both the glass ceiling for women that has predominated in high-tech production work and the gendered associations with technology that have helped reproduce and sustain it. Yet despite the real potential that technological upgrading holds for realizing strategic gender interests, management at both firms chose to extend—rather than challenge—traditional associations

between masculinity and technology, demonstrating the power and durability of gendered ideologies and frameworks.

Thus, while the gendering of work is always an ongoing, contested, and negotiated process, the ongoing trope of productive femininity, low unionization rates, and the complicity of the Philippine government means that there are few checks on management's power to implement and gender the new technology in ways it sees fit. And given the polarizing character of high-tech production and the current trends in the global industry toward automation, downsizing, and the masculinization of production, women electronics workers may witness—but have little access to—more skilled high-tech manufacturing jobs that the industry is finally producing.

REFERENCES

Acker, Joan. 2004. Gender, capitalism and globalization. *Critical Sociology 30*(1): 17–41.

Austria, Myrna S. 1999. *Assessing the competitiveness of the Philippine IT industry.* PIDS discussion paper. Makati: Philippine Institute for Development Studies.

Bello, Walden, David Kinley, and Elaine Elinson. 1982. *Development debacle: The World Bank in the Philippines.* San Francisco: Institute for Food and Development Policy.

Bureau of Labor Relations. 1999. *Labor management schemes and workers' benefits in the electronics industry.* Unpublished draft. Manila, Philippines: Bureau of Labor Relations.

Chant, Sylvia, and Cathy McIlwaine. 1995. *Women of a lesser cost: Female labor, foreign exchange and Philippine development.* London: Pluto.

Chhachhi, Amrita. 1999. *Gender, flexibility, skill and industrial restructuring: The electronics industry in India.* Working paper series no. 296. The Hague, the Netherlands: Institute of Social Studies.

Chhachhi, A., and R. Pittin. 1998. Multiple identities, multiple strategies: Confronting state, capital and patriarchy. In *Labor worldwide in the era of globalization,* edited by P. Waterman and R. Munck. London: Macmillan.

Chow, E. N., and D. M. Lyter. 2002. Studying development with gender perspectives: From mainstream theories to alternative frameworks. In *Transforming gender and development in East Asia,* edited by E. N. Chow. New York: Routledge.

Elson, Diane. 1999. Labor markets as gendered institutions: Equality, efficiency and empowerment issues. *World Development 27*(3): 611–27.

Ernst, Dieter. 2002. *Digital information systems and global flagship networks: How mobile is knowledge in the global network economy?* East West Center working papers, economics series no. 48. Honolulu, HI: East West Center.

Eviota, Elizabeth U. 1992. *The political economy of gender: Women and the sexual division of labor in the Philippines.* London: Zed Books.

Fernandez, Roberto. 2001. Skill-biased technological change and wage inequality: Evidence from a plant retooling. *American Journal of Sociology, 107*(2): 273–320.

Fox, J. 2002. Women's work and resistance in the global economy. In *Labor and capital in the age of globalization,* edited by B. Berberoglu. Lanham, MD: Rowan and Littlefield.

Hutchinson, Jane, and Andrew Brown, eds. 2001. *Organizing labour in globalizing Asia.* London: Routledge.

Joekes, Susan, and Ann Weston. 1994. *Women and the new trade agenda.* New York: UNIFEM.

Katz, Harry C., and Owen Darbishire. 2000. *Converging divergences.* Ithaca, NY: Cornell University Press.

Kelkar, G., and D. Nathan. 2002. Gender relations and technological change in Asia. *Current Sociology 50*(3): 427–41.

Kuruvilla, Sarosh. 1996. Linkages between industrialization strategies and industrial relations/human resource policies: Singapore, Malaysia, the Philippines and India. *Industrial & Labor Relations Review 49*(4): 635–58.

Mills, Mary Beth. 2003. Gender and inequality in the global labor force. *Annual Review of Anthropology 32*:41–62.

Molyneux, Maxine. 1985. Mobilization without emancipation? Women's interests, the state and revolution in Nicaragua. *Feminist Studies 11*:225–54.

National Statistical Coordination Board. 2001. *Various years. Statistics on men and women in the Philippines.* Government of the Philippines. Available from http://www.nscb.gov.ph/stats/wmfact.htm.

Parrenas, R. S. 2001. *Breaking the code: Women, migration, and the 1987 family code of the Republic of the Philippines.* Paper presented at the Workshop on Globalization and the Asian "Migrant" Family, National University of Singapore, 16 April.

Salzinger, Leslie. 2003. *Gender in production: Making workers in Mexico's global factories.* Berkeley: University of California Press.

Seguino, Stephanie. 2000. Accounting for gender in Asian economic growth. *Feminist Economics 6*(3): 27–58.

Standing, Guy. 1999. Global feminization through flexible labor: A theme revisited. *World Development 27*(3): 583–602.

Wolf, Diane L. 1992. *Factory daughters: Gender, household dynamics, and rural industrialization in Java.* Berkeley: University of California Press.

World Bank. 1997. *Philippines: Managing global integration.* Vol. 2, report no. 17024-PH. Poverty Reduction & Economic Management Sector, East Asia and the Pacific Office. Washington, DC: World Bank.

Yun, Hing Ai. 1995. Automation and new work patterns: Cases from Singapore's electronics industry. *Work, Employment & Society 9*(2): 309–27.

Introduction to Reading 35

Sociologist Gwen Moore is known for her research on men and women elites in the most prestigious and visible careers in industrialized countries. This article compares the experiences of men and women elites in 27 industrialized nations on their orientations toward careers and families, and reports on the various social support structures available. She explores interpersonal dynamics in the family—who does the unpaid work of the household, including child care—and the social systems that support work and family in these countries.

1. How is the work experience of women elites different from men's?

2. What social support systems made the work lives of these elite workers easier?

3. Is it easier for men to "have it all" in terms of elite jobs and families?

MOMMIES AND DADDIES ON
THE FAST TRACK IN OTHER WEALTHY NATIONS

Gwen Moore

Social and cultural contexts, as well as public policies, shape the experiences of women and men in demanding occupations. Women's employment in influential positions in the public and private sectors varies cross-nationally. Taking politics as an example, in the 2003 Swedish election, more than 45 percent of the parliamentarians who were elected are women. This contrasts sharply with the United States, where women hold just 14 percent of congressional seats, a smaller proportion than in fifty-nine other nations (InterParliamentary Union Web site, www.ipu.org, accessed January 16, 2004). Still, men hold nearly all top economic posts in all countries throughout the world (Adler and Izraeli 1994; Wirth 2001). These variations across countries and sectors demonstrate the importance of placing the topic of work and family in an international perspective.

In this comment, I will compare some work-family themes to research outside of the United States, especially to the findings of a mid-1990s survey of approximately twelve hundred women and men who held the highest positions in elected politics and private business in twenty-seven capitalist industrial nations, including twenty-one European nations, Australia, New Zealand, and others in North America and Asia (Vianello and Moore 2000). This collaborative project—the Comparative Leadership Study—gathered information on the leaders' backgrounds and careers, experiences in office, and gender and career attitudes as well as current family characteristics (Vianello and Moore 2000).

Consistent with findings on lawyers, professors, scientists, and finance managers, the majority of the women and men in the Comparative Leadership Study were or had been married or cohabiting. Marriage was more common for the men leaders than for their women counterparts, as has been found in previous research. Eighteen percent of the women and 8 percent of the men had never married. Virtually all of the men (94 percent) and most (75 percent) of the women leaders were currently married or cohabiting (Neale 2000, 158–59).

Most leaders of both sexes in the international study were also parents. Just over one-fourth of the women and less than 10 percent of the men had no children (Kuusipalo, Kauppinen, and Nuutinen 2000, Table 15.1). Among parents, women more often had just one child (Neale 2000, 158–59). The vast majority of men (88 percent) and three-fifths of women were living with both a partner and at least one child at the time of the survey (Kuusipalo, Kauppinen, and Nuutinen 2000, Table 15.1).

Most top business and political leaders in the comparative study, as well as those in professional and managerial positions in the United States, marry and have at least one child. These leaders face the dilemma of combining a demanding career and family life.

How do they manage this work-family conflict? Rarely by cutting back on working time. Even in countries with relatively shorter workweeks and longer vacations than the United States, the national leaders in our study reported far longer working hours than the general workforce in their country (Woodward and Lyon 2000; also see Jacobs and Winslow 2004). Politicians average more than sixty-five hours per week and business leaders about ten hours fewer, with little gender difference (Woodward and Lyon 2000, Table 8.1). In addition, few female leaders and almost none of their male colleagues had worked part-time or interrupted their careers for care work (Neale 2000; also see Epstein et al. 1998). Especially among managerial elites, the typical career proceeds without interruption from its beginning (Blair-Loy 2003).

In dual-career families, both partners work hard and long in paid employment. Taking time from paid work for child care or household labor is difficult. Some leaders—mostly men—have spouses who were not in paid employment, worked part-time, or had less demanding occupations. Dual-career families—with both partners in senior positions in the labor force—were far more common for the women leaders in our study than for the men (see Boulis 2004 for similar patterns among physicians). More than 70 percent of the men—and just more than one-third of the women—had partners who were not in paid employment or who worked in nonprofessional jobs with no supervisory responsibilities (Kuusipalo, Kauppinen, and Nuutinen 2000, Table 15.2; see Stone and Lovejoy 2004).

Most leaders earn high enough salaries to pay others to perform some of the household labor and child care. Yet most women in our research did some of these tasks themselves in spite of their long workweeks. The amounts done differ considerably between men and women. Well more than half of the men and none of the women reported that their spouse had cared for their children when they were preschoolers (Kuusipalo, Kauppinen, and Nuutinen 2000, Table 15.4). Likewise, one in five women (nearly all politicians) and no men had cared for their preschool children themselves (Neale 2000, Tables 13.1 and 13.2; Kuusipalo, Kauppinen, and Nuutinen 2000, Table 15.4). Child care responsibilities clearly fell disproportionately on women, even for those holding top economic and political positions.

In response to a question about the division of household labor, few women (9 percent) and about a quarter of the men reported doing none (Kuusipalo, Kauppinen, and Nuutinen 2000, Table 15.2). Nearly a third of the women business and political leaders said they did more than half of the household labor themselves, including 13 percent of the women business leaders who reported doing all the housework (Neale 2000, 164–65; Kuusipalo, Kauppinen, and Nuutinen 2000, Table 15.2; Esseveld and Andersson 2000, Table 16.2).

Family responsibilities, including care of young children and completion of household labor, fall disproportionately on women, even among those in top leadership positions in the professions, management, and politics. Marriage and, even more, parenthood impinge on women's careers to a far larger extent than they do on similarly situated men's. Compared to women, fast-track men are more frequently married and parents. And men also more often have wives who are not in a demanding career and are thus more available for child care, housework, and involvement in building his career (see Stone and Lovejoy 2004). Women are frequently married to highly placed men who have as many time constraints as they do and thus are less available for sharing family labor and focusing on advancing the woman's career.

Research beyond the United States generally paints a similar picture to that portrayed. . . . But this broad picture obscures variations in patterns within regions or countries. When one looks more closely at work-family conflicts in

European and other industrialized countries variations appear. National cultural norms and social policies provide contexts for the employment and family lives of workers in demanding occupations (see Wax 2004).

The Nordic countries stand out as models of (relatively) woman- and family-friendly societies. Gender equality norms and government policies support women's equal participation in public life, and women's rates of paid employment are high. According to Kuusipalo, Kauppinen, and Nuutinen (2000), the Nordic countries have replaced the male breadwinner model with the dual-earner model. They wrote, "Parental leave, flexible working hours and state childcare support women's right to work and men's right to fatherhood" (p. 178). Data from the Nordic countries in the Comparative Leadership Study (Denmark, Finland, Norway, and Sweden) do show fewer gender differences in family status and duties than are seen in other areas of Europe, North America, Asia, Australia and New Zealand (Vianello and Moore 2000, pt. III).

Public child care is available in the Nordic countries, and about 30 percent of leaders placed their preschool children in it. Nordic male leaders were more involved in household labor than men in the other regions: 20 percent reported doing at least half of the housework themselves. Nordic men's higher rate of household labor may be partly due to Nordic norms against employing private household workers.

Despite men's greater participation in family care in the Nordic countries, women do even more. Twice as many women leaders reported caring for their preschool children (26 percent of women vs. 14 percent of men), and nearly two-thirds of women reported doing at least half of the housework (Esseveld and Andersson 2000). Primarily mothers, not fathers, apparently use the generous parental leave policies available in the Nordic countries.

Career pathways and occupational settings also affect work-family conflicts. . . . Careers in management and science, for instance, require an early and steady commitment from aspirants, often beginning in high school. Dropping in and out or beginning a career later in life is hardly an option for these fields. In the Comparative Leadership Study, businesswomen had the lowest rates of marriage and childbearing (Vianello and Moore 2000). By contrast, some top careers are more flexible and more easily entered at an older age. Elected politicians, for example, often enter politics in their late twenties or even thirties. Politics, then, is not closed to women who have reared children or begun in other careers. Some strategies to improve the work-family balance for women and men in demanding careers seem unrealistic for those in senior leadership positions. Jerry Jacobs (forthcoming) has called for institutions to clearly state that tenure-track faculty are expected to work no more than fifty hours per week to create a "family-compatible workstyle." Reduced working hours for national leaders in politics, business, or voluntary associations is not a workable solution. Top leaders in key institutions are expected to show total devotion to their work (e.g., Kanter 1977; Blair-Loy 2003). Possibly more feasible is Phyllis Moen's (2004) advocacy of social expectations that careers include "second acts" and "time-outs" allowing men and women to develop integrated career and family lives. For those aspiring to national elite positions, a time-out early in their career to have and rear children—as taken by many women politicians—could facilitate a more compatible career and family life.

An international perspective on the work-family conflicts helps to show in what ways the United States is similar to and different from other countries. In many ways, the United States differs little, as I have shown above. Yet the Nordic countries appear more successful in lessening work-family conflicts, even for women and men in top positions. These countries have made extraordinary progress in opening political decision-making positions to women. Women are prominent among prime ministers, cabinet members, and members of parliament in Denmark, Finland, Norway, and Sweden. Women constitute a critical mass in their parliaments, erasing their token status and normalizing the image of politics as a woman's game as well as a man's game (Kanter 1977; Epstein 1988). Scholars and policy makers would benefit from a closer examination of these models promoting gender equality.

REFERENCES

Adler, Nancy J., and Dafna N. Izraeli, eds. 1994. *Competitive frontiers: Women managers in a global economy.* Cambridge, MA: Blackwell.

Blair-Loy, Mary. 2003. *Competing devotions: Career and family among women executives.* Cambridge, MA: Harvard University Press.

Boulis, Ann. 2004. The evolution of gender and motherhood in contemporary medicine. *Annals of the American Academy of Political and Social Science* 596:172–206.

Epstein, Cynthia Fuchs. 1988. *Deceptive distinctions: Sex, gender, and the social order.* New Haven, CT: Yale University Press.

Epstein, Cynthia Fuchs, Carroll Seron, Bonnie Oglensky, and Robert Saute. 1998. *The part-time paradox: Time norms, professional lives, family, and gender.* New York: Routledge.

Esseveld, Johanna, and Gunnar Andersson. 2000. Career life-forms. In *Gendering elites: Economic and political leadership in 27 industrialised societies,* edited by M. Vianello and G. Moore, 189–204. London: Macmillan.

Jacobs, Jerry A., and Sarah E. Winslow. 2004. Overworked faculty: Job stresses and family demands. *Annals of the American Academy of Political and Social Sciences* 596:104–129.

Jacobs, Jerry A. Forthcoming. The faculty time divide. *Sociological Forum.*

Kanter, Rosabeth. 1977. *Men and women of the corporation.* New York: Basic Books.

Kuusipalo, Jaana, Kaisa Kauppinen, and Iira Nuutinen. 2000. Life and career in north and south Europe. In *Gendering elites: Economic and political leadership in 27 industrialised societies,* edited by M. Vianello and G. Moore, 177–88. London: Macmillan.

Moen, Phyllis. 2004. Integrative careers: Time in, time out, and second acts. Presidential Address, Eastern Sociological Society meetings, February 20.

Neale, Jenny. 2000. Family characteristics. In *Gendering elites: Economic and political leadership in 27 industrialised societies,* ed. M. Vianello and G. Moore, 157–68. London: Macmillan.

Stone, Pamela, and Meg Lovejoy. 2004. Fast-track women and the "choice" to stay home. *Annals of the American Academy of Political and Social Science* 596:62–83.

Vianello, Mino, and Gwen Moore, eds. 2000. *Gendering elites: Economic and political leadership in 27 industrialised societies.* London: Macmillan.

Wax, Amy L. 2004. Family-friendly workplace reform: Prospects for change. *Annals of the American Academy of Political and Social Science* 596:36–61.

Wirth, Linda. 2001. *Breaking through the glass ceiling: Women in management.* Geneva, Switzerland: International Labour Office.

Woodward, Alison, and Dawn Lyon. 2000. Gendered time and women's access to power. In *Gendering elites: Economic and political leadership in 27 industrialised societies,* edited by M. Vianello and G. Moore, 91–103. London: Macmillan.

Introduction to Reading 36

Sociologist Kathleen Gerson has studied work and family patterns for some time. Her first book examining women's and men's roles in families, published in 1985, examined the decisions women make about work, career, and motherhood. This book was aptly titled *Hard Choices.* In this reading, she considers what she has learned from studying men's and women's choices about work and family, exploring the moral dilemmas that she has observed and considering those that young people face as they negotiate familial relationships and work responsibilities. This article uses more recent data she collected from life history interviews with 120 men and women from ages 18 to 32. These individuals lived in New York City and surrounding areas and represent a diverse group of young people, both in race and social class.

1. What does Gerson mean by "the tension between autonomy and commitment"?

2. What changes does she observe in heterosexual relationships?

3. What is neotraditionalism, and how does it affect men and women in heterosexual relationships?

MORAL DILEMMAS, MORAL STRATEGIES, AND THE TRANSFORMATION OF GENDER

LESSONS FROM TWO GENERATIONS OF WORK AND FAMILY CHANGE

Kathleen Gerson

Choosing between self-interest and caring for others is one of the most fundamental dilemmas facing all of us. To reconcile this dilemma, modern societies in general—and American society in particular—have tried to divide women and men into different moral categories. Since the rise of industrialism, the social organization of moral responsibility has expected women to seek personal development by caring for others and men to care for others by sharing the rewards of independent achievement.

Although labeled "traditional," this gendered division of moral labor represents a social form and cultural mandate that rose to prominence in the mid-twentieth century but reached an impasse as the postindustrial era opened new avenues for work and family life. . . . At the outset of the twenty-first century, women and men face rising conflicts over how to resolve the basic tensions between family and work, public and private, autonomy and commitment. They are searching for new strategies for reconciling an "independent self" with commitment to others.

While the long-term trajectory of change remains unclear, new social conditions have severely undermined the link between gender and moral obligation. The young women and men who have come of age amid this changing social landscape face risks and dangers, but they also inherit an unprecedented opportunity to forge new, more egalitarian ways to balance self-development with commitment to others. To enable them to do so, however, we must reshape work and family institutions in ways that overcome beliefs and practices that presume gender differences in moral responsibility. . . .

While it is important to assert that it is just as valuable to pursue emotional connection and provide care as it is to create an independent self or provide economically for a family, it is also critical to question the premise that women and men can be separated into distinct, opposed, or unchanging moral categories. As Epstein argues, any vision of dichotomous gender distinctions is not only inaccurate; it is also an ideological construct that justifies and reinforces inequality. Connell points out that "masculinities" and "femininities" vary across historical time and space. Lorber and Risman, among others, question the concept of gender itself, pointing to the

From Gerson, Kathleen. 2002. "Moral Dilemmas, Moral Strategies, and the Transformation of Gender: Lessons From Two Generations of Work and Family Change," *Gender & Society,* 16(1): 8–28. Copyright © 2002. Published by Sage Publications on behalf of Sociologists for Women in Society.

social paradoxes and cultural contradictions to which all human actors must respond in constructing their public and private selves. These theorists recognize that gender is a social institution, not an inherent trait, and that it shapes organizations and opportunity structures as well as personal experiences (Connell 1987, 1995; Epstein 1988; Lorber 1994; Risman 1998).

There are good analytic and empirical reasons to reject the use of gender to resolve the knotty moral conflicts between public and private, work and family, self and other. It is difficult to avoid the conclusion that using gender in this way is more prescriptive than descriptive. Such approaches may depict how women and men should behave, but they do not provide an accurate description or explanation of how women and men actually do behave or how they would behave if alternative options were available. Certainly, the proportion who have conformed to gendered injunctions about appropriate moral choices has varied substantially across societies, subcultures, and historical periods. Countless women and men have been labeled "deviant" for their reluctance or inability to uphold idealized conceptions of gender. A framework of gendered moralities helps justify inequalities and stigmatize those who do not conform.

* * *

NEW DILEMMAS, AMBIGUOUS STRATEGIES

How does this generation view its moral choices? As adult partnerships have become more fluid and voluntary, they are grappling with how to form relationships that balance commitment with autonomy and self-sufficiency. As their mothers have become essential and often sole breadwinners for their households, they are searching for new ways to define care that do not force them to choose between spending time with their children and earning an income. And in the face of rising work-family conflicts, they are looking for definitions of personal identity that do not pit their own development against

creating committed ties to others. As young women and men wrestle with these dilemmas, they are questioning a division of moral responsibility that poses a conflict between personal development and caring for others.

Seeking Autonomy, Establishing Commitment

The decline of permanent marriage has raised new and perplexing questions about how to weigh the need and desire for self-sufficiency against the hope of creating an enduring partnership. In wrestling with this quandary, young women and men draw on lessons learned in their families and personal relationships. Yet, they also recognize that past experiences and encounters can provide, at best, a partial and uncertain blueprint for the future.

Few of the women and men who were interviewed reacted in a rigidly moralistic way to their parents' choices. Among those whose parents chose to divorce (or never marry), about 45 percent viewed the breakup as a prelude to growing difficulty, but the other 55 percent supported the separation and felt relief in its aftermath. Danisha, a 21-year-old African American, concluded that conflict would have emerged had her parents stayed together. . . .

And at 26, Erica, who grew up in a white middle-class suburb, supported her parents' decision to separate and received more support from each of them in its aftermath:

> I knew my parents were going to get divorced, because I could tell they weren't getting along. They were acting out roles rather than being involved. They were really drifting apart, so it was something perfectly natural to me. In the new situation, I spent more valuable time with my parents as individuals. So time with my father and mother was more meaningful to me and more productive.

Among those whose parents stayed together, almost 60 percent were pleased and, indeed, inspired by, their parents' lifelong commitment, but about 40 percent concluded that a breakup would have been better than the persistently unhappy, conflict-ridden relationship they watched unfold. Amy, a 24-year-old Asian American, explains:

> I always felt my parents would have divorced if they didn't have kids and didn't feel it was so morally wrong. They didn't really stick together because they were in love. I know all couples go through fights and stuff, but growing up, it seemed like they fought a lot, and each of them has made passing comments—like, "Oh, I would have divorced your mom by now" or "I would have left your dad a thousand times." [So] I wouldn't have broken down or been emotionally stressed if my parents divorced. I didn't want to hear the shouting, and I didn't want to see my mom cry anymore. And I was also afraid of my dad, because he would never lay a hand on my mom, but he's scary. He could be violent.

Whether their parents stayed together or parted, most concluded that neither steadfast commitment nor choosing to leave has moral meaning in the abstract. The value of enduring commitment depends on the quality of the relationship it embodies.

When considering their own aspirations, almost everyone hopes to establish a committed, lasting relationship with one partner. Yet, they also hold high standards for what a relationship should provide and anticipate risks in sustaining such a commitment. Across the divides of gender, race, and class, most agree that a satisfying and worthwhile relationship should offer a balance between autonomy and sharing, sacrifice and support. . . .

Amy imagines a partnership that is equal and fluid, capable of adapting to circumstances without relinquishing equity:

> I want a fifty-fifty relationship, where we both have the potential of doing everything. Both of us working, and in dealing with kids, it would be a matter of who has more flexibility with regard to their career. And if neither does, then one of us will have to sacrifice for one period, and the other for another.

Most acknowledge, however, that finding a lasting and satisfying relationship represents an ideal that is hard to reach. If it proves unattainable, they agree that being alone is better than remaining in an unhappy or destructive union. Building a full life thus means developing the self in multiple ways. . . . Across the range of personal family experiences, most also agree that children suffer more from an unhappy home than from separated parents. . . .

Women and men both wonder if it is possible to establish relationships that strike a good balance between self-affirmation and commitment, providing and receiving support. Having observed their parents and others struggle with varying degrees of success against the strictures of traditional gender categories, they are hopeful but guarded about the possibilities for resolving the tension between autonomy and commitment in their own lives. . . .

Care as Time, Care as Money

If the rise of fluid adult partnerships has heightened the strains between commitment and autonomy, then the rise of employed mothers and the decline of sole male breadwinners have made the meaning of care ambiguous. Now that most children—whether living in single-parent or two-parent households—depend on the earnings of their mothers, parents face conflicts in balancing the need to provide economic support with the need to devote time and attention.

Rigid notions of gendered caring do not fit well with most family experiences, and the majority express support for parents who transgressed traditional gender categories. Among those who grew up in two-earner households, four out of five support such an arrangement, most with enthusiasm. Across race, class, and gender groups, they believe that two incomes provided the family with increased economic resources, more flexibility against the buffeting of economic winds, and greater financial security. . . .

Of course, this means they see a mother's employment as largely beneficial. Whether in a two-parent or single-parent home, women and men agree that an independent base enhanced a mother's sense of self, contributed to greater parental equality, and provided an uplifting model. Rachel, 24 and from a white, working-class background, explains, "I don't think that I missed out on anything. I think it served as a more realistic model. . . ."

Kevin, 25 and from a middle-class, white family, agrees:

> For quite a while, my mom was the main bread-winner. She was the one who was the driving force in earning money. My mother's persona was really hard working, and that's something I've strived to be with in and to emulate. I didn't think it was wrong in any way. I actually feel it's a very positive thing. Whatever my relationships, I always want and appreciate people who work, and I'm talking about female involvement. It's part of who I am, and it makes me very optimistic knowing that hard work can get you somewhere.

They also deemed highly involved fathers, whether in two-earner or single-parent households, as worthy examples. Daniel, now 23, describes his Irish father's atypical working hours and parental involvement:

> My father was always around. He's a fire fighter, so he had a lot of free time. When he was home, he was usually coaching me and my brother or cooking dinner or taking us wherever we wanted to go. He was the only cook up until me and my brother started doing it. So I want to make sure that, if I get married and have kids, I'm there for my kids.

In contrast, those who grew up in a largely traditional household expressed more ambivalence. Although half felt fortunate to have had a mother devoted primarily to their care, the other half would have preferred for their mothers to pursue a more independent life. At 21, Justin, who grew up in a white, largely middle-class suburb, looks back on his mother's domestic focus with a strong conviction that it took its toll on the whole household. . . .

Breadwinning fathers may also elicit mixed reactions. Their economic contributions are appreciated but not necessarily deemed sufficient. A good father, most concluded, takes time and offers emotional support as well. At 29, Nick, who grew up in a white working-class neighborhood and remembers feeling frustrated by his own father's distance, is seeking joint custody of his own young daughter:

> I have seen a lot of guys who have kids and have never changed a diaper, have never done anything for this child. Don't call yourself daddy. Even when she was saying, "Oh, she might not be yours," it didn't matter to me. This child is counting on me.

In this context, care becomes a slippery concept. Across family circumstances, these young adults judge an ideal parent—whether mother or father—to be one who supports her or his children both economically and emotionally. . . .

If fathers should resemble traditional conceptions of mothers, then mothers should resemble fathers when it comes to work outside the home.

Gabriel, a white 25-year-old who was raised by his father after his parents divorced when he was in grade school, explains,

> In terms of splitting parental stuff, it should be even. Kids need a mother and a father. And I'm really not high on the woman giving up her job. I have never wanted to have a wife who didn't make a salary. But not for the sake of leeching off of her, but so that she was independent. . . .

If such an ideal proves beyond reach, as many expect it will be, women and men agree that families should apportion moral labor however best fits their circumstances—whether or not this means conforming to classic notions of gender difference. Mothers can and often do demonstrate care through paid work and fathers through involvement. Now 26 and raising a child on her own, Crystal, an African American, rejects a natural basis for mothering:

> I don't really believe in the mother instinct. I don't believe that's natural. Some people really connect with their children, and some people just don't. I think it should be whoever is really going to be able to be there for that child.

In the end, the material and emotional support a child receives matters more than the type of household arrangement in which it is provided. . . .

Identity Through Love, Identity Through Work

In a world where partnerships are fragile and domesticity is devalued, young women and men are confronting basic questions about identity and self-interest. Do they base their personal wellbeing and sense of self on public pursuits or be struck between them?

In pondering their parents' lives, most could find no simple way to define or measure self-interest. While a minority uphold traditional gendered identities, most do not find such resolutions viable. Women are especially likely to conclude that it is perilous to look to the home as the sole source of satisfaction or survival. Reflecting on the many examples of mothers and other women who languished at home, who were bereft when marriages broke up, or who found esteem in the world of paid work, 9 out of 10 express the hope that their lives will include strong ties to the workplace and public pursuits. . . .

On the other side of the gender divide, many men have also become skeptical of work-centered definitions of masculine identity. As traditional jobs have given way to unpredictable shifts in work prospects, they are generally guarded about the prospect of achieving stable work careers. Having observed fathers and friends who found work either dissatisfying or too demanding, two-thirds of the men concluded that, while important, work alone could not provide their lives with meaning. These young men hope to balance paid work and personal attachments without having to sacrifice the self for a job or paycheck. Traditional views persist, but they increasingly compete with perspectives that define identity in more fluid ways. Widely shared by those who grew up in different types of families, these outlooks also transcend class and race differences. They cast doubt on some post-feminist assertions that a "new traditionalism" predominates among young women and men (Crittenden 1999). . . .

Yet, beyond the apparent similarities, a gender divide emerges. With one-third of men—but far fewer women—preferring traditional arrangements over all others, women are more likely to uphold flexible views of gender for themselves and their partners. More important, women and men both distinguish between their ideals and their chances of achieving them. If most hope to integrate family and work—and to find partners with whom to share the rewards and burdens of both—far fewer believe they can achieve this lofty aspiration. It is difficult to imagine integrating private with public obligations when most workplaces continue to make it difficult to balance family and job. And it is risky to build a life dependent on another adult when relationships are unpredictable. . . .

AN EMERGING GENDER DIVIDE: AUTONOMY AND NEOTRADITIONALISM AS FALLBACK POSITIONS

The ideal of a balanced self continues to collide with an intransigent social world. New generations must thus develop contingent strategies for less than ideal circumstances. If egalitarian aspirations cannot be reached, what options remain? Here, women and men tend to diverge. Indeed, even as they are developing similar ideals, they are preparing for different outcomes. If an egalitarian commitment proves unworkable, most men would prefer a form of "modified traditionalism" in which they remain the primary if not sole family breadwinner and look to a partner to provide the lion's share of domestic care. Women, in contrast, tend to look toward autonomy as preferable to any form of traditionalism that would leave them and their children economically dependent on someone else.

As young women and men consider the difficulties of building balanced, integrated lives, they move from ideals to consider the fallback positions that would help them avert worst-case scenarios. Here, as we see below, the gender gap widens. Women, in hoping to avoid economic and social dependence, look toward autonomy, while men, in hoping to retain some traditional privileges, look toward modified forms of traditional arrangements. Yet, both groups hope to resolve these conflicts as they construct their lives over time.

Women and Autonomy

Among the women, 9 out of 10 hope to share family and work in a committed, mutually supportive, and egalitarian way. Yet, most are skeptical that they can find a partner or a work situation that will allow them to achieve this ideal. Integrating caretaking with committed work remains an uphill struggle, and it seems risky to count on a partner to sustain a shared vision in the long run. Even a modified version of traditionalism appears fraught with danger, for it creates economic vulnerability and constricted options in the event that a relationship sours or a partner decides to leave. Four out of five women thus prefer autonomy to a traditional marriage, concluding that going it alone is better than being trapped in an unhappy relationship or being abandoned by an unreliable partner. . . .

Autonomy for women means, at its core, economic self-sufficiency. A life that is firmly rooted in the world of paid work provides the best safeguard against being stuck in a destructive relationship or being left without the means to support a family. Healthy relationships, they reason, are based on a form of economic individualism in which they do not place their economic fate in the hands of another. Rachel declares,

> I'm not afraid of being alone, but I am afraid of being with somebody who's a jerk. I can spend the rest of my life alone, and as long as I have my sisters and my friends, I'm okay. I want to get married and have children, but I'm not willing to just do it. It has to be under the right circumstances with the right person.

Men and Neotraditionalism

Young men express more ambivalence about the choice between autonomy and traditionalism. If a committed, egalitarian ideal proves out of reach, about 40 percent would opt for independence, preferring to stress the autonomous self so long associated with manhood and now increasingly affirmed by women as well. But six out of 10 men would prefer a modified traditionalism in which two earners need not mean complete equality. This split among men reflects the mix of options they confront. Work remains central to constructing a masculine identity, but it is difficult to find work that offers either economic security or good opportunities for family involvement. Without these supports, men are torn between avoiding family commitments and trying to retain some core advantages provided by traditional arrangements.

From men's perspective, opting for the autonomy conferred by remaining unmarried, unattached, or childless relieves them of the economic burden of earning a family wage in an uncertain economy, but it also risks cutting them off from close, committed, and lasting intimate connections. A neotraditional arrangement, in contrast, offers the chance to create a family built around shared breadwinning but less than equal caretaking. In this scenario, men may envision a dual-earner arrangement but still expect their partner to place family first and weave work around it. Josh, a white 27-year-old who was raised by his father after his mother was diagnosed with severe mental illness, asserts,

> All things being equal, it should be shared. It may sound sexist, but if somebody's gonna be the breadwinner, it's going to be me. First of all, I make a better salary. If she made a much better salary, then I would stay home, but I always feel the need to work, even if it's in the evenings or something. And I just think the child really needs the mother more than the father at a young age.

Modified traditionalism provides a way for men to cope with economic uncertainties and women's shifting status without surrendering some valued privileges. It collides, however, with women's growing desire for equality and rising need for economic self-sufficiency.

Resolving Moral Dilemmas Over Time

In the absence of institutional supports, postponing ultimate decisions becomes a key strategy for resolving the conflicts between commitment and self-development. For women as much as men, the general refrain is, "You can't take care of others if you don't take care of yourself." Michael wants to be certain his girlfriend has created a base for herself at the workplace before they marry, hoping to increase the chances the marriage will succeed and to create a safety net if it fails:

> There are a lot of problems when two people are not compatible socially, economically. When Kim gets these goals under her belt, and I have my goals established, it'll be a great marriage. You have to nurture the kind of marriage you want. You have to draw it out before you can go into it.

For Jennifer, 19 and white, autonomy also comes first. Commitment may follow, but only when she knows there is an escape route if the relationship deteriorates:

> I will have to have a job and some kind of stability before considering marriage. Too many of my mother's friends went for that—let him provide everything—and they're stuck in a relationship they're not happy with because they can't provide for themselves or the children they now have. The man is not providing for them the way they need, or he's just not a good person. Most of them have husbands who make a lot more money, or they don't even work at all, and they're very unhappy, but they can't leave. So it's either welfare or putting up with somebody else's crap.

Establishing an independent base becomes an essential step on the road to other goals, and autonomy becomes a prerequisite for commitment. This developmental view rejects the idea that individualism and commitment are in conflict by defining the search for independence as a necessary part of the process of becoming able to care for others. To do that, women as well as men tend to look to work, and its promise of autonomy, to complete the self. For those with children as well as those who are childless, lifelong commitments can be established when "you feel good enough about yourself to create a good relationship." . . .

These strategies are deeply felt and intensely private responses to social and personal conflicts that seem intractable. More fundamental solutions await the creation of systematic supports for balancing work and family and for providing women and men with equal opportunities at the workplace and in the home. Without these supports, new generations must cope as best they can, remaining both flexible and guarded. . . .

CONCLUSION: TOWARD A NEW MORAL ORDER?

Deeply rooted social and cultural changes have created new moral dilemmas while undermining a traditional gendered division of moral labor. The widespread and interconnected nature of these changes suggests that a fundamental, irreversible realignment is under way. Less clear is whether it will produce a more gender-equal moral order or will, instead, create new forms of inequality. The long-term implications are necessarily cloudy, but this ambiguity has created some new opportunities along with new risks.

While large-scale social forces are propelling change in a general direction, the specific forms it takes will depend on how women and men respond, individually and collectively, to the dilemmas they face. Those who have come of age during this period are adopting a growing diversity of moral orientations that defies dichotomous gender categories. Their experiences point to a growing desire for a social order in which women and men alike are afforded the opportunity to integrate the essential life tasks of achieving autonomy and caring for others.

Yet, persistent inequalities continue to pose dilemmas, especially for those who aspire to integrate home and work in a balanced, egalitarian way. To understand these processes, we need to focus on the social conditions that create such dilemmas and can transform, and potentially dissolve, the link between gender and moral responsibility. Of course, eradicating this link might only mean that women are allowed to adopt the moral strategies once reserved for men. We also need to discover how to enable everyone, regardless of gender, class, or family situation, to balance care of others with care of self.

The possibilities have never been greater for creating humanistic, rather than gendered, conceptions of moral obligation. New moral dilemmas have prompted women and men to develop innovative strategies, but the long-term resolution of these dilemmas depends on reorganizing our social institutions to foster gender equality and a better balance between family and work. Freud once commented that a healthy person is able "to love and to work." Achieving this vision depends on creating a healthy society, where all citizens are able to combine love and work in the ways they deem best.

REFERENCES

Connell, R. W. 1987. *Gender and power.* Stanford, CA: Stanford University Press.

———. 1995. *Masculinities.* Berkeley and Los Angeles: University of California Press.

Crittenden, Danielle. 1999. *What our mothers didn't tell us: Why happiness eludes the modern woman.* New York: Simon & Schuster.

Epstein, Cynthia F. 1988. *Deceptive distinctions: Sex, gender and the social order.* New Haven, CT: Yale University Press.

Lorber, Judith. 1994. *Paradoxes of gender.* New Haven, CT: Yale University Press.

Risman, Barbara J. 1998. *Gender vertigo: American families in transition.* New Haven, CT: Yale University Press.

❦ Topics for Further Examination ❧

- Check out the most recent research on women and work done by the Institute for Women's Policy Research (http://www.iwpr.org) and the current activism under way at 9 to 5 National Association of Working Women (http://www.9to5.org/).
- Using the web, find a list of the top executives in a sample of the largest firms in this country and calculate a gender ratio of women to men (Hint: Fortune 500 is one such list).
- Find information on work/family policies in different countries. You should be able to find articles in an academic database or just by searching the web. We suggest comparing across countries, checking to see how the policies in the United States compare with those in other countries.

8

GENDER IN INTIMATE RELATIONSHIPS

Although social institutions and organized activities such as work, religion, education, and leisure provide frameworks for our lives, it is the relationships within these activities that hold our lives together. What surprises many people is that these everyday relationships are patterned. We don't mean "the daily routine" kind of patterns; we are referring to patterns across individuals and relationships related to gender. For example, sociologists consider "the family" to be more than just a personal relationship; they view it as a social institution, with relatively fixed roles and responsibilities that meet some basic needs in society such as caring for dependent members and providing emotional support for its members. As you read through this chapter, you will come to realize how social norms influence all gendered relationships, including intimate relationships. This introduction and the readings in this chapter illustrate two key points. First, gendered intimate relationships always evolve, often in response to social changes unrelated to the relationships themselves. Second, gender is embedded in an idealized version of intimacy—the traditional family—that is not the reality in the United States and most parts of the world today, as illustrated in readings in Chapters 1 and 3.

Before going on about these details of intimacy, let's stop for a moment and look at relationships in general. The word *relationship* takes on many different meanings in our lives. We can have a relationship with the server at our favorite restaurant because he or she is usually there when we dine out. We have relationships with our friends; some we may have known most of our lives, others we have met more recently. And we have relationships with our family and with people who are like family. Some of these relationships surround us with love, economic support, intimacy, and/or almost constant engagement. All these relationships are shaped by gender. You have already read about relationships at work in Chapter 7; in this chapter, you will read about how gender shapes more intimate relationships—from friendships to partnering to parenting.

GENDERED RELATIONSHIPS

Consider the impact of gender on our relationships. We can have many friends, with whom we share affection. In the past, researchers often argued that friendships varied by gender in predictable and somewhat stereotypical ways. That is, they described women's friendships as more intimate, or focused on sharing feelings and private matters, while describing men's friendships as more instrumental or focused around doing things, such as golfing or fishing. To illustrate, Cancian (1990) argued that men were more instrumental or task oriented in their love relationships, whereas women expected emotional ties. For example, in Cancian's study, when one man was asked how he expressed his love to his wife, he told the interviewer that he washed her car.

While Cancian's study is revealing, it is important to remember that other social prisms influence the gendering of our relationships, putting social constraints and expectations on even our most intimate times. For example, Walker (1994) found that while both men and women hold stereotypical views of gendered behavior in friendships, actual friendship patterns were more complex and related to the social class of the individual. Even though working-class men recognized what was gender-appropriate behavior for friendships, they tended to describe their friendships in ways that would be defined as more stereotypically female (disclosure and emotional intimacy), while professional women tended to describe more masculine friendship patterns with other women. These exceptions to stereotypical views of gendered friendships, however, are also patterned; that is, they appear to vary by social class and reflect the constraints of work lives. Readings in this chapter contribute to our understanding of how prisms of class and race influence gendered patterns in relationships.

GENDER AND CHANGING LIVING ARRANGEMENTS

One of the strongest gendered influences on relationships is the expectation that only men and women will fall in love and marry. As we have emphasized throughout this book, American culture assumes idealized intimate relationships to be heterosexual, accompanied by appropriate gendered behaviors and, of course, based in nuclear families. You will notice that we did not include the word *family* in the title of this chapter. We did this because the stereotypical vision of family— mom, dad, two kids, and a dog, all living in a house behind a white picket fence—is only a small percentage of households today and never was the predominant form of family relationships.

As we explore relationships in this chapter, it is important to begin by examining how households actually are patterned. In Table 8.1, we list the various household configurations and the percentage in each category by race and ethnicity in the United States today. These data may surprise you. Relationships in the United States are changing, as indicated by the diversity noted in Table 8.1. Only 49.3% of all Americans age 15 or older were married and living with a spouse in 2011, with more than half of individuals over 15 in the United States living in another situation (U.S. Census Bureau, 2012a). These percentages differ for racial and ethnic groups. For example, 29.2% of Black people are married with a partner present, and 74% of Black women and 67.1% of Black men are not in a marital relationship with a spouse present (see Table 8.1). Clearly, race and ethnicity influence the patterns of intimate relationships of men and women.

The increase in single and nonfamily households reflects both a trend toward postponing marriage and a longer life expectancy. A White boy born in 2010 can expect to live 76.5 years on average, and a White girl, 81.3 years (U.S. Census Bureau, 2012c). These life expectancies are shaped by other social factors such as race and social class as well as gender. For example, the average life expectancy for a Black boy born in 2010 is 70.2 years and for a Black girl, 77.2 years (U.S. Census Bureau, 2012c).

Increased life expectancy means we have more "time," therefore postponing first marriage makes sense. The median age at first marriage has risen for both men and women. In 1980, the median age at first marriage for women was 22 and for men 25 (24.7); however, by 2010, the estimated median age at first marriage increased to 26 (26.1) for women and 28 (28.2) for men (U.S. Census Bureau, 2011). Also, because we

Table 8.1   Marital Status of People 15 Years and Over in the United States, 2011

	Percentage			
	White Non-Hispanic	*Black*	*Hispanic*	*Asian*
Married				
Spouse Present	54.0	29.2	42.4	57.5
Spouse Absent	0.9	2.2	2.9	3.0
Widowed	6.4	5.7	3.5	4.6
Divorced	10.7	11.2	7.4	4.5
Separated	1.6	4.3	3.7	1.3
Never Married	26.2	47.4	40.0	29.0
Women Only				
	White Non-Hispanic	*Black*	*Hispanic*	*Asian*
Married				
Spouse Present	52.7	26.0	44.2	57.4
Spouse Absent	1.0	2.3	2.2	2.9
Widowed	10.0	8.5	5.6	7.4
Divorced	11.5	12.5	8.8	5.5
Separated	1.7	4.8	4.4	1.7
Never Married	23.1	45.9	34.9	25.1
Men Only				
	White Non-Hispanic	*Black*	*Hispanic*	*Asian*
Married				
Spouse Present	55.5	33.0	40.8	57.7
Spouse Absent	0.9	2.0	3.6	3.1
Widowed	2.7	2.4	1.7	1.5
Divorced	9.9	9.6	6.0	3.4
Separated	1.6	3.9	3.1	0.9
Never Married	29.5	49.2	44.9	33.4

Source: U.S. Census Bureau (2012a).

live longer, we may be less inclined to stay in a bad relationship, since it could last for a very long time. The distributions in Table 8.1, are influenced by multiple "prisms" beyond race and ethnicity in the patterning of relationships across groups in the United States.

THE "IDEALIZED" FAMILY

The growing diversity of household and family configurations in the United States has reshaped and challenged the rigid gender roles that pattern the ways we enter, confirm, maintain, and envision long-term intimate relationships. Not surprisingly, the rigid gender roles associated with that mythical little home behind the white picket fence, with mom staying at home to care for children and dad heading off to work, is not the reality for households in the United States. Instead, we have many different household patterns, with some households headed by a single person, same-sex households, and others unrelated by blood or family bonds living together. Some new household patterns include more single-person households. Others, such as grandparents raising grandchildren or single parents (typically mothers) raising children alone, often arise out of divorce and/or poverty. Whatever the reasons, the idealized, traditional family with its traditional gendered relationships never really was the norm (Coontz, 2000) and certainly is not the norm in American households today.

To illustrate how rare that idealized family is, only 22.7% of all parent family groups with their own children under 15 years of age in 2010 had a stay-at-home mother; another 154,000 married-couple family groups, or 0.7%, had stay-at-home fathers (U.S. Census Bureau, 2012b). And in 2011, more than half (60.6%) of all mothers with children under the age of 3 were in the labor force, with 37.6% working full-time (Bureau of Labor Statistics, 2012). And when you look only at mothers who are married with children under the age of 3 with spouses present, 40.0% are working full-time (Bureau of Labor Statistics, 2012). Considering that well over half of women with very young children are employed, it is easy to see that only a small percentage of households fit the "Ozzie and Harriet" model for families, with mom at home taking care of the children while dad is off at work. Like gender, "the family" is a culturally constructed concept that often bears little resemblance to reality. The idealized, traditional family with separate and distinct gender roles does not exist in most people's lives.

Historically, families changed considerably in terms of how they are formed and how they function. While enduring relationships typically involve affection, economic support, and concern for others, marriage vows of commitment are constructed around love in the United States today. In previous generations, most marriage vows promised commitment and love "until death do us part." However, marriages in the 1800s, even when rooted in love, often were based on economic realities. These 19th century marriages were likely to evolve into fixed roles for men and women linked to the economy of the time, roles that reinforced gender difference but not necessarily gender inequality. For example, farm families developed patterns that included different, but not always unequal, roles for men and women, with both earning money from different tasks on the farm (Smith, 1987). In the latter half of the 19th century and into the early 1900s, families—particularly immigrant families—worked together to earn enough for survival. Women often worked in the home, doing laundry and/or taking in boarders, and many children worked in the factories (Bose, 2001; Smith, 1987).

What changed and how did the current idealized roles of men and women within the stereotypical traditional family come to be? Martha May (1982) argues that the father as primary wage earner was a product of early industrialization in the United States. She notes that unions introduced the idea of a family wage in the 1830s to try to give men enough income so their wives and children were not forced to work. In the early 1900s, Henry Ford expanded this idea and developed a plan to pay his male workers $5.00 per day if their wives did not work for money (May, 1982). The Ford Motor Company then hired sociologists to go into workers' homes to make sure that the wives were not working for pay either outside or inside the home (i.e., taking boarders or doing laundry) before paying this family wage to male workers (May, 1982). In fact, very few men actually were paid the higher wage (May, 1982). You might ask, why was Ford Motor Company so interested in supporting the family with an adequate wage? At that time, factories faced high turnover because work on these first assembly lines was demanding, paid very little, and the job was much more rigid and unpleasant than the farm work that most workers were accustomed to. Ford enacted this policy to reduce this turnover and lessen the threat of unionization. Thus, one reason behind the social construction of the "ideal family" was capitalist motivation to tie men to their jobs for increased profits, not individual men wanting to control their families (May, 1982).

These historical and structural changes in the family affect our interpersonal relationships both inside and outside of marriage. A key factor in relationships is power, as Veronica Jaris Tichenor discusses in this chapter. She examines different explanations for the gendered distribution of power in relationships and proposes a new way to think about power.

SAME-SEX/GENDER COUPLES

A change that is hidden in Table 8.1 is the growing number of same-sex/gender couples. Beginning with the 2000 Census, the category "unmarried partner" was added to the questionnaire, allowing an estimated count of same-sex/gender couples. In 2010, the Census Bureau estimated that 0.6% of households described themselves as partners of same sex/gender (Lofquist, Lugaila, O'Connell, & Feliz, 2012). It is important to note that the identification of same-sex/gender relationships is complicated by the use of terms to define these relationships, all of which are imprecise—*sex*, *gender*, and *sexuality*. Each of these terms refers to a false dichotomy (Lucal, 2008; also see the introduction to Chapter 1), with the expectation that there are two and only two categories in each. However, social relationships and individuals are much more complicated than male/female, man/woman, and heterosexual/homosexual. As Rust (2000) notes, *same-sex* may be appropriate in some instances and *same-gender* in others as we describe one social context versus another. For example, *same-sex* may be appropriate for describing sexual interactions between men in prisons. Many male prisoners in the United States define themselves as heterosexual and maintain that identity in sexual relationships with other incarcerated men by having sexual interactions in which they are the penetrators, thus feminizing their male partners. Given the inadequacy of these categories to describe the complexity of sex, gender, and sexual identities and the shifting terminology used to do so, we use *same-sex/gender* in our text throughout this book. However, we honor authors' use of their terminology in readings selected for this book.

The legal parameters for same-sex/gender couples are rapidly changing, although there is still considerable resistance to same-sex/gender marriage. Massachusetts was the first state to allow same-sex/gender marriages in 2004, with other states in the United States following, especially more recently. Politicians in the United States run for or against same-sex/gender marriage as they attempt to draw votes their way. The Netherlands, Norway, and Canada were among the first nations to allow same-sex/gender marriages, with gender-neutral marriage laws that transcend the problematic terms *same-sex* and *opposite-sex* and instead extend marriage rights to any two adults. However, many other countries legally recognize same-sex/gender couples, giving them some of the rights of married couples. Same-sex/gender couples also create families and, in doing so, redefine gender, parenthood, and family, as Irene Padavic and Jonniann Butterfield describe in their article in this chapter. Padavic and Butterfield help us understand the constraints on parenting children within lesbian families as the reactions of others constrain their mothering behaviors. Indeed, parenting relationships, while continuously changing, are clearly socially constructed, and expectations for motherhood and fatherhood have strong impacts on gendered behavior across societies (Christopher, 2012; Gregory and Milner, 2011).

FEMINIZATION AND JUVENILIZATION OF POVERTY

Another reality of today's families that differs from the idealized, traditional family is the number of children living in poverty, with only a broken picket fence, if that. Using data from the

U.S. Census Bureau, the Children's Defense Fund (2011) reported that in 2010, more than 16.4 million children (under the age of 18) were living in poverty (or $1,860 per month for a family of four) and 10% of those children lived in extreme poverty or on an annual income that was less than half of the poverty level (less than $930/month). More than half (60.7%) of children living in poverty are in single-parent families, and the majority of those (46.9%) are in single-mother families. The youngest children are the most vulnerable, with one in four children under 5 living in poverty in 2010 (Children's Defense Fund, 2011). This change in household composition challenges idealized gendered relationships expected in families but also relates to social class inequalities tied to gender. The increase in the number of households headed by poor women raising children has been called the feminization or juvenilization of poverty (Bianchi, 1999; McLanahan & Kelly, 1999). Diana Pearce coined the term *the feminization of poverty* in 1978 (Bianchi, 1999, p. 308), at a time when the number of poor, women-headed families rapidly increased. The rate of women's poverty relative to men's fluctuates over time and is 50% to 60% higher than for men (p. 311), a reflection of the inequality in wages for men and women discussed in Chapter 7. These rates also reflect racial and ethnic inequalities, with 25.3% of Black children under the age of 5 and 17.3% of Hispanic children under the age of 5 living in extreme poverty, while the rates for White non-Hispanic and Asian children are 6.0% and 6.5%, respectively (Children's Defense Fund, 2011).

The juvenilization of poverty refers to an increase in the poverty rates for children that began in the early 1980s, whether in single- or two-parent families (Bianchi, 1999). Unfortunately, the juvenilization of poverty is now at its highest rate since 1993, when it was at a high of 22.7% (Children's Defense Fund, 2011). The feminization and juvenilization of poverty are serious problems, and both are gender as well as race and social class issues. The article by Jennifer Utrata about single mothers in Russia shows how these mothers and their mothers use extended household support networks to rear children and illustrates how social context influences choices single women have as they raise their children.

GOVERNMENT POLICIES AND FAMILY RELATIONSHIPS

Governmental policies play a role in shaping families in the form of tax laws, health and safety rules, and other legislation. These policies have real gender implications, as discussed in the article by Berit Brandth and Elin Kvande about the attempts to incorporate fathers into family/work leave policies in Norway. A multitude of policies frame parents' decisions to have children, structure how much time parents have with their children, and shape how children are expected to act in societies, with varying impact across social class (Williams, 2010). Early in the 20th century in the United States, health and safety laws increased the age of employment for factory workers (Bose, 2001) and are still in effect in terms of dictating what age a child can begin to work for pay. These laws related to the creation of adolescence, with the expectation that children would remain in school throughout high school. Another act of legislation, the dependent deduction on tax returns, was first intended to encourage families to have more children at a time when politicians worried about the declining birth rate in this country. At the same time and for the same reason, Canada instituted a policy that is still in place in which women are given a payment each month for every child under the age of 18. The government makes this payment directly to the mother, based on the assumption that, in a two-parent family, the mother assumes responsibility for the children. The forms, however, allow for the payment to go to the father if written documentation is submitted to indicate that he is the primary caregiver. While only a nominal sum, it was distributed across social classes as an incentive to bear and raise children. In 2007, Canada also instituted the Universal Child Care Benefit, which provides $100 per month for child care for each child under age 6.

Work-family policies vary across nations, as Brandth and Kvande illustrate in this chapter, and can enforce or challenge gendered assumptions about roles at work and home. Williams (2010) describes U.S. policies as "family-hostile." Policies and laws affect all relationships because they often idealize the woman's role in two-parent families and reinforce hegemonic masculinity and emphasized femininity, while ignoring other choices and life situations, such as same-sex/gender couples. The impact of policies and practices on relationships in poor families is also considerable, making it difficult to "do" idealized gender because living, in and of itself, is challenging.

CHANGING RELATIONSHIPS

Marital and parenting relationships have changed considerably over time, as has the way sociologists study the family (Ferree, 2010). In addition to government regulations, the feminization of the workforce has affected men's and women's roles in marriages (Blackwelder, 1997). The fact that most families now have two workers has changed relationships in the home. Kathleen Gerson, in the previous chapter, described how young people imagine their commitments to marriage and family, balancing that against the autonomy they believe is necessary to succeed in the world of work. This is not an unrealistic assessment. Carla Shows and Naomi Gerstel in their reading in this chapter study emergency medical technicians and physicians to examine how men's work lives impact their relationships with their children and spouses. They describe how the structure of work, embedded in a social class hierarchy, has a strong influence on the possibilities for fathering behaviors and the subsequent parenting relationships with one's spouse. The constraints of social class may surprise you as you read about how work affects fathering and as you compare the options these fathers have with those in place for fathers in Norway, as discussed in Brandth and Kvande's article in this chapter. Race is another prism that influences families and parenting and should also be

considered as it relates to social class and gender differences in salaries, discussed in Chapter 7.

Gender difference and inequality continue to permeate and frame ever-evolving relationships even though fathers are more involved in household labor, particularly caring for children (Bianchi, Robinson, & Milkie, 2006). However, while there may be more equal distribution of household labor today, mothers continue to feel the pressure of caring for children and the household (Bianchi et al., 2006). Thus, the idealized, traditional gendered responsibility for women in the United States to care for children and the household remains, even though most women work outside the home. Jacobs and Gerson (2001) argue that the changes in family composition and gender relations have created situations in which members of families, particularly women and most particularly single women, are overworked, with little free time left for themselves or their families. They describe the situation as particularly acute for those couples whose work weeks are 100 hours or more and who tend to be highly educated men and women with prestigious jobs. Shows and Gerstel and other readings in this chapter help us understand how patterns at work can influence patterns at home and lead to the moral dilemma between commitment and autonomy that Gerson discussed in the previous chapter. It is important to keep in mind that many social factors, including public policy as well as social class position, influence the decisions people make in terms of work hours outside and inside the home (Craig, 2011; Hook, 2010).

The readings in this chapter provide a fuller understanding of how our most intimate relationships are socially constructed around gender. As friends, lovers, parents, and siblings, we are defined in many ways by our gender. Compare, for instance, the dilemmas young people face in Gerson's reading in the previous chapter with the realities of the couples in the selections by Tichenor, Shows and Gerstel, and Padavic and Butterfield, and of single mothers in Russia in the reading by Utrata. Ask yourself what choices you have made or wish to make as you consider how gender influences what you expect in your intimate relationships. It is important to keep in mind that many social factors, including public policy as well as social class position, influence the decisions people make in terms of work hours outside and inside the home (Craig, 2011; Hook 2010).

REFERENCES

Bianchi, S. M. (1999). Feminization and juvenilization of poverty: Trends, relative risks, causes, and consequences. *Annual Review of Sociology, 25,* 307–333.

Bianchi, S. M., Robinson, J. P., & Milkie, M. A. (2006). *Changing rhythms of American family life.* New York: Russell Sage Foundation.

Blackwelder, J. K. (1997). *Now hiring: The feminization of work in the United States, 1900–1995.* College Station: Texas A&M University Press.

Bose, C. E. (2001). *Women in 1900: Gateway to the political economy of the 20th century.* Philadelphia: Temple University Press.

Bureau of Labor Statistics. (2012). Table 6: Employment status of mothers with own children under 3 years old by single year of age of youngest child and marital status, 2010–2011 annual averages. In *Women in the labor force: A data book.* Retrieved February 6, 2013, from http://www.bls.gov/news.release/famee.t06.htm/

Cancian, F. M. (1990). The feminization of love. In C. Carlson (Ed.), *Perspectives on the family: History, class and feminism* (pp. 171–185). Belmont, CA: Wadsworth.

Children's Defense Fund. (2011). *Child poverty in America fact sheet.* Washington, DC: Author. Retrieved July 30, 2011, from http://www.childrensdefense.org/policy-priorities/ending-child-poverty/

Christopher, K. (2012). Extensive mothering: Employed mothers' constructions of the good mother. *Gender & Society, 26*(1), 73–96.

Coontz, S. (2000). *The way we never were: American families and the nostalgia trap.* New York: Basic Books.

Craig, L. (2011). How mothers and fathers share childcare: A cross-national time-use comparison. *American Sociological Review, 76*(6), 834–861.

Ferree, M. M. (2010). Filling the glass: Gender perspectives on families. *Journal of Marriage and Family, 72*(3), 420–439.

Gregory, A., & Milner, S. (2011). What is "new" about fatherhood: The social construction of fatherhood in France and the UK. *Men and Masculinities, 14*(5), 588–606.

Hook, J. L. (2010). Gender inequality in the welfare state: Sex segregation in housework, 1965–2003. *American Journal of Sociology, 115*(5), 1480–1523.

Jacobs, J. A., & Gerson, K. (2001). Overworked individuals or overworked families? Explaining trends in work, leisure, and family time. *Work and Occupations, 28*(1), 40–63.

Lofquist, D., Lugaila, T., O'Connell, M., & Feliz, S. (2012, April). Table 3: Household type by race and Hispanic origin. In *Households and Families: 2010* (p. 8). Washington, DC: U.S. Census Bureau. Retrieved from http://www.census.gov/prod/cen2010/briefs/c2010br-14.pdf

Lucal, B. (2008). Building boxes and policing boundaries: (De)constructing intersexuality, transgender, and bisexuality. *Sociology Compass, 2*(2), 519–536.

May, M. (1982). The historical problem of the family wage: The Ford Motor Company and the five dollar day. *Feminist Studies, 8*(2), 399–424.

McLanahan, S. S., & Kelly, E. L. (1999). The feminization of poverty: Past and future. In J. S. Chafetz (Ed.), *Handbook of the sociology of gender* (pp. 127–145). New York: Kluwer Academic/Plenum.

Rust, P. C. R. (2000). *Bisexuality in the United States: A social science reader.* New York: Columbia University Press.

Smith, D. (1987). Women's inequality and the family. In N. Gerstel & H. E. Gross (Eds.), *Families and work* (pp. 23–54). Philadelphia: Temple University Press.

U.S. Census Bureau. (2011, November). Table MS-2: Estimated median age at first marriage, by sex: 1890 to present. In *Current Population Survey.* Retrieved July 27, 2012, from www.census.gov/population/socdemo/hh-fam/ms2.xls

U.S. Census Bureau. (2012a). *America's families and living arrangements: 2011.* Retrieved July 26, 2012, from http://www.census.gov/hhes/families/data/cps2011.html

U.S. Census Bureau. (2012b). Table 68: Parents and children in stay at home parent family groups, 1995 to 2010. In *America's families and living arrangements.* Retrieved July 30, 2012, from http://www.census.gov/population/www/socdemo/hh-fam/cps2010.html

U.S. Census Bureau. (2012c). Table 104: Expectation of life at birth and projections. In *The 2012 statistical abstract: The national data book.* Retrieved

February 5, 2013, from http://www.census.gov/compendia/statab/2012/tables/12s0104.pdf

Walker, K. (1994). Men, women, and friendship: What they say and what they do. *Gender & Society, 8*(2), 246–265.

Williams, J. C. (2010). The odd disconnect: Our family-hostile public policy. In K. Christensen & B. Schneider (Eds.), *Workplace flexibility: Realigning 20th-century jobs for a 21st century workforce* (pp. 23–54). Ithaca, NY: ILR Press.

Introduction to Reading 37

In this selection, sociologist Veronica Jaris Tichenor develops a theoretical critique of previous explanations for power distributions in marriage. She uses this critique to argue for the development of a new conceptualization of power and a different way of explaining why power is gendered in heterosexual marriages. The gendered distribution of power in relationships can shape virtually every aspect of our daily lives. This reading makes us think about where power in relationships comes from and how power is used in relationships that are supposed to be based on love. So, as you read this article, think about the theories explaining power discussed herein and ask why men and women might accept gendered power in our relationships and why such relationships are so difficult to change.

1. Compare some of the explanations Tichenor gives for gender and power in marriage to the theories discussed in the introduction to this book.

2. If you accept Tichenor's explanation of gendered power as hidden power, what would we have to change to create equality in heterosexual relationships?

3. Think about people you know. What does a gendered power relationship look like? What does an equal power relationship look like?

THINKING ABOUT GENDER AND POWER IN MARRIAGE

Veronica Jaris Tichenor

The balance of power in most marriages reflects the ideology of separate spheres in the conventional marital contract. Of course, this contract is not a written document; it consists of cultural understandings of the reciprocal rights and obligations that each spouse has within the institution of marriage. According to this unwritten contract, these rights and obligations are divided along gender lines, which construct men as breadwinners and women as mothers and homemakers. The man's main responsibilities are to provide for the family economically and to represent the family to the community or the world at large. The woman's main responsibility is to care for the home, husband, and children. If spouses hold up their end of the bargain, this exchange is considered both reasonable and fair.

While this model may seem overstated and outdated, Joan Williams (2000) argues that the basic assumptions of this contract persist. This complementary organization of market work and family life exists as a system that Williams calls "domesticity." Under this system, men are entitled and encouraged to perform as "ideal workers" in the marketplace, unencumbered by the demands of family life. Women, whether engaged in paid labor or not, are marginalized in the workplace by their domestic responsibilities. They continue to be seen and treated by employers as mothers or potential mothers, which limits their options and opportunities at work. That women maintain responsibility for domestic labor and child care hampers their ability to engage in paid labor as ideal workers (i.e., men). So while the assumption that women will be engaged only in domestic labor has changed in recent years, the underlying contract that delegates breadwinning responsibility to men and domestic responsibility to women remains largely unchallenged.

The conventional marital contract does not simply divide responsibilities between spouses; it also reinforces men's power within marriage. This is because the responsibilities and tasks of husbands and wives are valued differently. Within most U.S. families, the income that the husband earns is the most highly valued asset. It confers a higher status on the husband, both within and outside the relationship, and has been used to justify men's greater power in marriage, especially in terms of decision-making practices and control over the family's financial resources. Historically, men have wielded power based on their greater incomes, and wives were expected to defer to their husbands' authority. By contrast, women's caring work at home has not been accorded the same status as breadwinning. That it is unpaid work signifies its lesser value, and the ability to refuse to do such work is one of the privileges men typically enjoy in marriage (Hochschild 1989). The conventional marital contract, then, underscores the greater value of the man's contributions (income), while devaluing those of the woman (domestic services). In short, the bargain implied by the conventional marital contract is the key to continued gender inequality in marriage (Williams 2000).

Admittedly, life has changed dramatically for married couples, especially in the last several decades. This model of husband as sole breadwinner and wife as homemaker describes the reality of only 25 percent of married couples in the United States today (Raley et al. 2003). Transformations in the economy have made it impossible for all but a comparative handful of families to enjoy a moderate standard of living on only one income. This makes it tempting to think of the man-as-breadwinner/woman-as-homemaker model of married life as outdated and irrelevant.

However, marriages are still constructed against the backdrop of the conventional marital contract. Culturally, we still hold men accountable for breadwinning and women for mothering, regardless of whatever additional responsibilities they may take on. In most circles, men are still revered and respected based on the kind of work they perform and the standard of living their families are able to enjoy because of it. Remember that most of the men with higher-earning wives profiled in recent news articles felt like outcasts or failures for not being the major earners. Women are still expected to keep neat homes and present clean, well-adjusted, and well-mannered children to the outside world. Poorly behaved children might still be asked, "Didn't your mother teach you any better than that?"

This means that men and women get more "credit," both inside and outside the marital relationship, for engaging in activities that are consistent with conventional gender identities. While a wife's income may be important to the family, her employment lacks the social legitimacy accorded her husband's work. Women's paid work is typically seen as an option, rather than a duty. Since social convention does not obligate a woman to provide for her family, she is not protected from housework or other domestic intrusions on her breadwinning activities as a man would be.

Women typically retain responsibility for the household and simply add the role of worker onto those of mother and homemaker (Hochschild 1989; Rubin 1994). Women also receive less social approval than do men for engaging in paid work and may even face condemnation for "neglecting" domestic duties (Popenoe 1989). Similarly, while men may help out with the workload at home, and in middle- to upper-middle-class circles might receive a great deal of social approval for doing so, their domestic labor is not a substitute for breadwinning; even the most involved father rarely opts out of providing altogether (Coltrane 1996; Deutsch 1999). In short, the meanings attached to paid work and domestic labor are fundamentally different for men and women, and tend to reinforce the identities of breadwinner and mother/homemaker embedded in the conventional marital contract.

The continued distinction between mothering and breadwinning as gendered activities means that we can think of these identities enduring "gender boundaries"—ways to mark the difference between women and men (Connell 1987; Potuchek 1997). While women may work outside the home, men still have the responsibility to provide that makes them breadwinners. Though men may help with housework or child care, it is still a woman's duty to provide the level of attention and care associated with mothering. The lines dividing these gendered responsibilities are still clearly drawn (Williams 2000).

If it is true that breadwinning is the central identity for men, and mothering is the central identity for women, this could be problematic for dual-earner couples. If wives are also providing an income, what distinguishes them from their husbands? In most dual-earner couples, men still outearn their wives, often by a large margin (Raley et al. 2003). Couples typically respond to this shift in behavior by thinking of husbands as the primary breadwinners, with wives as secondary earners simply "helping out" (Potuchek 1997; Willinger 1993). Similarly, couples see women's mothering and domestic responsibilities as primary, and their work commitments are often organized around the needs

of the family (Hochschild 1989; Williams 2000). In this way, men can see themselves as still meeting the masculine imperative of providing for their families, and wives can see themselves as good mothers, despite being employed outside the home (Coltrane 1996).

Of course, having both spouses in the workforce could represent an opportunity to change the gendered expectations and meanings surrounding breadwinning by rejecting the idea of separate spheres embedded in the conventional marital contract. Husbands and wives could think of themselves as co-providers with a joint responsibility to meet the financial obligations of the family. They could then share the responsibilities for maintaining a clean, orderly home and raising healthy children. Sharing all family work (both paid and unpaid) more equally could break down these rigid gender boundaries.

We know that some couples have worked successfully to erode these boundaries (Coltrane 1996; Deutsch 1999; Risman and Johnson-Sumerford 1998; Schwartz 1994). These couples consciously share the work of providing and caring for a family in ways that begin to undermine the breadwinner/mother identities, as well as the power imbalance associated with them. However, even some of these partnerships contain rumblings of gender unease. For example, men and women in these relationships often collaborate to maintain some gender specialization; women want to guard part of the domestic domain as their own (Hertz 1989) or want to feel like "I'm still the mom" (Coltrane 1996; Deutsch 1999), and men still think of providing as their own responsibility (Wilkie 1993). Such expectations are so strong that even couples with higher-earning wives continue to cling to them (Brennan, Barnett, and Gareis 2001). These results suggest that spouses are often more comfortable with a certain level of conventional gender asymmetry in their relationships.

Williams (2000) describes this pull toward the conventional as being caught in a "gender force field." While conventional gender expectations do not determine behavior, they can exert a strong pull that can be difficult to resist and can wear people down over time. For example, after couples have their first child, the call of traditional roles and expectations can be particularly loud. With a new life depending on them, men often feel a greater need to be a good provider, and even women who had planned to continue working after their child's birth can feel unexpectedly drawn toward staying at home (Cowan and Cowan 1992; Rexroat and Shehan 1987).

In other words, even though spouses' behavior is changing, as women continue to be a strong presence in the workforce and some men become more engaged in domestic labor, it may be too threatening to give up all their conventional gender expectations—it does not feel right. This means that as men and women are engaged in similar activities, such as providing for the family, the breadwinning and mothering boundaries can take on great importance; that is, these boundaries become a crucial way for husbands and wives to create and maintain a sense of gender difference (Potuchek 1997).

So even though the conventional marital contract no longer describes the reality of most U.S. couples, by maintaining the gender boundaries of mothering and breadwinning, dual-earner couples reinforce the bargain implied by the old contract (Brennan et al. 2001; Coltrane 1996; Potuchek 1997; Wilkie 1993). This finding is significant because of the power dynamics embedded in the contract. As we have seen, the activities associated with mothering and breadwinning are differentially valued, with breadwinning generally conferring more privileges than does mothering. If employed women are not defined as breadwinners, they may lose access to these privileges. In other words, by maintaining the gender boundaries written into the conventional marital contract, spouses may undercut women's power within marriage.

However, all of this assumes that men's power within marriage is truly rooted in their greater economic resources. While this assumption has driven much of the research on marital power, the accumulating evidence suggests that it is flawed. If money is the key to the power dynamics within marriage, we would expect the balance of power to shift as women have begun to share breadwinning with their husbands. In fact, earning an income has done little to increase women's power, which undermines the fair exchange of income earned by male breadwinners for the domestic services of their wives implied by the conventional marital contract. This means that we need to rethink the money/power link within marriage.

MARITAL POWER AS THE EXCHANGE OF RESOURCES

Early attempts to talk about the balance of power within marriages rested on the assumptions embedded in the conventional marital contract. This research (beginning with Blood and Wolfe 1960) was driven by resource and exchange theories that link the balance of power in marriages to the relative contributions, or resources, of spouses. Resources are anything of value, tangible or intangible, that partners bring to a relationship. They include money, occupational or social status, education, love and affection, physical attractiveness, special knowledge or expertise, services (such as performing domestic labor or giving back rubs), and so on. Under the conventional marital contract, men contribute their incomes, as well as the status attached to their occupations, in exchange for domestic labor and child-care services from their wives.

The resource/exchange model views power as the ability to prevail in a variety of household decisions, ranging from how much to spend each week on groceries to when and if the family should move. Since men and women both reported that husbands had more control over most decisions, Blood and Wolfe concluded that husbands had more power in their marriages. They also concluded that this power came, not from the influence of patriarchal ideology, but from husbands' contributing the more socially valued resources (income and status) to the marriage. Thus, resources such as income and status represent the potential for exercising power. And while both spouses have access to some resources, men have more power in marriages because they contribute the more important resources to the relationship.

This logic is compelling and has held sway both inside and outside the academy: The more you give, the more you should receive in return. However, if this conceptualization of power within marriage were accurate, we would expect to see a shift in the balance of power between spouses over the last several decades as women have moved into the paid labor force in great numbers. According to resource and exchange theory assumptions, women who contribute economically to the relationship should be able to exercise greater control over finances and decision making, and buy a certain amount of relief from domestic labor and childrearing responsibilities.

However, the marital power literature over the past few decades demonstrates that this is not happening (see, for example, Bianchi et al. 2000; Blumberg 1984; Blumstein and Schwartz 1983, 1991; Hochschild 1989; Perry-Jenkins and Folk 1994; Pleck 1985; Wright et al. 1992). Women may gain a greater measure of control over finances or household decisions, but few couples report patterns that could be characterized as egalitarian. Husbands continue to exercise greater control in financial matters and decision making.

Similarly, women's employment has done little to alter the division of domestic labor. Husbands may help a little more with household chores and child care, but much of the research argues that these changes reflect shifts in the proportion of work being done by each spouse. In other words, it looks like men are doing more because women, who are now further crunched for time, are doing less. . . . It is clear that merely earning a wage does not significantly enhance a woman's power in most marriages.

As we have said, one reason for this continued imbalance of power may be that men typically outearn their wives, often by a large margin. This income advantage continues to lend legitimacy to the husband's authority within the marriage. He may not be earning all the money,

but he is still earning most of it. This circumstance may allow spouses to continue to think of their economic assets as largely his and to justify his continued control over them. However, this is only a partial explanation for the enduring imbalance of power within marriage. If women's income buys them so little, then power is not about money—or at least, not entirely about money. Gender is also a factor.

Two examples from studies of marital power suggest that this is the case. The first example comes from Blood and Wolfe's (1960) work. One of their most interesting findings, given their reliance on resource and exchange theory, is that the wives in their sample who worked outside the home full time got the least amount of help with domestic labor from their husbands. It is not just that these wives could not exchange their income for more help with domestic labor from their husbands, but that they got the worst deal overall of any group of wives when they were contributing the most (in terms of paid and domestic labor) to their relationships. The second example comes from Arlie Hochschild's *The Second Shift* (1989). Hochschild reported that, while substantial sharing of domestic duties was not common in her sample of dual-earner couples, among couples where women earned more than their husbands, none of the men shared the housework and child-care duties. These results directly challenge the exchange of resources implied by the conventional marital contract, since these wives got no credit for the substantial incomes they contributed.

More recent quantitative research has produced results similar to Hochschild's and demonstrates that there is a curvilinear relationship between income contributed and the amount of housework each spouse performs (Brines 1994; Greenstein 2000; Bittman et al. 2003). Husbands who are sole (or major) breadwinners successfully trade their income for domestic labor, but wives who are the major breadwinners in their families are unable to negotiate a similar deal. That is, wives who earn all a family's income perform about the same amount of housework as wives who earn no income at all. Their husbands seem to receive domestic services, rather than to compensate for their wives' unusually high earnings by taking on more household labor. Their wives' earnings disrupt a balance of power that feels culturally right, and either these men attempt to restore that balance by asserting their right as men to their wives' domestic labor, or wives take on more household work voluntarily to avoid further assaulting their husbands' masculinity. Couples engage in "gender display" (Brines) or "deviance neutralization" (Greenstein) to restore a sense that spouses are meeting their conventional obligations. However, the exact dynamic by which gender overrides the money-equals-power equation among these couples is unclear.

That higher-earning wives cannot trade their income for a reduction in their domestic labor burden undermines the theoretical assumptions of the bulk of research on power in marriages. These results demonstrate that men's power in marriage does not come from their income or their role as (primary) breadwinner—or at least, it does not come from these resources alone. Husbands in dual-earner families retain and enjoy some rights or privileges as men. Thus, it makes sense to talk about gender as exerting an influence on marital power dynamics that is independent of income earned by spouses. We can then think of gender as a separate structure that shapes the balance of power within marriage.

GENDER AS STRUCTURE

Because gender so thoroughly pervades social life, it is often conceptualized as a cultural dynamic that is "woven into" other institutions, meaning that beliefs about gender and gender differences are used to maintain and justify other social practices. However, gender also exists as a separate entity (Lorber 1994). That is, while gender is indeed embedded in and shapes the practices of other social institutions, it also exerts an influence that is separable from all other institutions.

In the case of marital power, men's ability to retain their control and privileges, even in the absence of the economic dominance that has legitimated this power advantage, suggests that gender exerts an influence on marital power dynamics that is distinct from men's successful enactment of breadwinner responsibilities. In short, that men retain their power advantages in these circumstances points to gender as both a separate and a stable entity.

This means that we can talk about gender as structure (Risman 1998). This structure exists and operates on multiple levels within social life: institutional, interactional, and individual. At the institutional level, gender exists as beliefs about what men and women are or should be and as organizational practices that serve to reinforce these beliefs. The typing of women and men into particular occupations, the gap in wages between men and women, and the glass ceiling in organizations are all examples of gendered organizational practices. But gender at the institutional level also exists as ideology. Beliefs that men should be stronger and rational and women weaker and emotional are part of conventional gender ideology. The conventional marital contract, with the expectation that men are breadwinners and women are mothers and homemakers, is also part of gendered ideology. These institutional-level beliefs and practices organize the behavior of men and women at the interactional and individual levels.

At the interactional level, gender shapes face-to-face communication. That is, we interact with others as men and women, drawing on the cultural expectations for behavior that exist at the institutional level. Perhaps our best conceptualization of how the gender structure operates at the interactional level comes from West and Zimmerman (1987). They argue that men and women "do gender" as they interact with others in ordinary settings. Within a given context, individuals must clearly demonstrate to others that they are appropriately masculine or feminine. Men and women are aware of the gendered expectations for dress, speech, and behavior that exist at the institutional level, and they manage their conduct in light of the possibility that they may be held accountable to these standards by others.

For example, aside from cassocks or ceremonial kilts, men in Western societies do not wear skirts, but not because of any inherent property of the garment. Skirts are actually quite practical in terms of allowing freedom of movement and can be more comfortable than pants, particularly in warm weather when they generate their own breeze. However, since skirts have been successfully typed as women's clothing, no self-respecting (conventional) male would be caught dead in one. Those rare males who choose to adopt this style of dress risk social sanctions ranging from disapproval to ridicule to physical violence. They also risk being labeled inappropriately feminine and, therefore, not men. This example demonstrates that although conventional gender expectations may not completely determine behavior, even the smallest rules can be quite compelling. So while men and women do not always conform to the expectations for their sex categories, all know that deviations may come at a cost.

While "doing gender" encompasses a wide range of behaviors, the primary activities for men and women are the doing of dominance and submission (Berk 1985; West and Zimmerman 1987). This means that gender differences are not neutral but tied to larger power structures. At the institutional level, men enjoy greater economic and political power. At the interactional level, men assert their authority and women defer to this authority. This gender imperative is particularly salient in the context of heterosexual love relationships and marriage. Cultural notions of a man as "head of the household" or "king of his castle" continue to resonate, even if more subtly than in the past. Correspondingly, being a wife has typically entailed a certain level of service to one's husband. All spouses have to negotiate their relationships against the backdrop of these expectations, whether in congruence with or in opposition to them. That is, while spouses

may choose to challenge conventional expectations or practices, others may still hold spouses accountable to conventional standards. These conventional assumptions regarding gender continue to shape the interactions of spouses and remain a central part of how men and women think about themselves as husbands and wives.

Gender is also a fundamental component of identity construction; it is impossible to think of ourselves separately from our identity as a man or woman. At the individual level, the gender structure constrains men and women as they attempt to construct meaningful identities. That is, doing gender is an internal process as well (Acker 1992). Individuals often hold themselves accountable to conventional conceptions of gender-appropriate behavior, regardless of the standards imposed by those around them. That is, it is important to feel that one is behaving in a way consistent with one's identity as a man or woman.

The research reviewed thus far suggests that, within marriage, the gendered identities of breadwinner and mother may still resonate for spouses and represent an important touchstone for constructing individual identities. Still, for husbands and wives, this identity construction occurs in the context of the couple; doing gender is a team performance. One spouse's failure to engage his or her part appropriately may reflect negatively on the partner. For example, having a wife who makes substantially more money may represent a significant threat to a man's gender identity, given that breadwinning is such a fundamental component of masculinity in U.S. culture, and the couple must find a way to manage this tension. Spouses must construct gender identities in tandem to find a balance that feels right to them, both as a couple and as individuals.

Although we can conceptualize these three levels of the gender structure as distinct from one another, they operate simultaneously and reinforce each other. While institutional practices and ideologies shape microlevel behavior, behavior on the interactional and individual levels has an impact on gender at the institutional level, for it is through microlevel dynamics that the larger gender structure is either challenged or reproduced. For example, at the microlevel, couples with higher-earning wives could represent a potential site of gender change. They could challenge the conventional link between breadwinning and power by sharing domestic labor, decision-making power, and the responsibility to provide equally. They could rewrite the gender scripts of the conventional marital contract and expand the possibilities for both men and women in marriage.

In spite of this opportunity, it seems that women's incomes have bought them little in their marriages because the gender structure assures men certain privileges within the marital relationship. As we have seen, the gender structure seems to have accommodated women's paid labor by constructing men as primary breadwinners, and therefore still due the privileges attached to this activity. However, couples with higher-earning wives present a more serious challenge to the gender structure. These couples disrupt the cultural link between gender, money, and power more profoundly and create new tensions for spouses to manage. These couples' efforts to preserve men's authority and interpersonal dominance despite women's economic advantage highlight the difficulty of rewriting conventional gender scripts and demonstrate the resilience of the gender structure in the face of potential challenges to it.

Conceptual Issues in Analyzing Power

Love: What's Power Got to Do With It?

Conducting research on marital power raises some sticky questions, because we are not used to thinking that power operates in our most intimate relationships. In U.S. culture, marriage is supposed to be based on romantic love. This notion requires that our relationships be ruled by our hearts and emotions, as in "I'm so crazy about her" or "He just swept me off my feet." This overpowering emotion often puts us beyond the reach of reason. We do not rationally calculate whether we should be in love with someone; we act largely on the basis of feelings. In fact, thinking rationally about a relationship, or weighing its pros and cons, opens us up to the charge that we are not really in love.

Being involved in a romantic relationship also means being focused on the other. That is, love requires a certain degree of altruism. One's personal desires cannot always be primary. Romantic love often requires putting the needs of one's partner first to make her or him happy or even to preserve the relationship. This selfless giving is often the standard used to assess the nature of our feelings. Only when we can place the interests of the other before our own is our caring and commitment seen as genuine.

This emphasis on affection and altruism leaves little room for power considerations in a love relationship. In fact, Western culture sets up love and power as opposites. If love means a denial of self for the sake of the other, power implies a calculation of one's rational self-interest above the interests of the other. Power means forcing another to do something she or he would prefer not to do, or even taking advantage of another for personal gain. Power considerations, then, seem anathema to the kind of blissful relationship idealized by our cultural emphasis on romantic love.

It is the equation of power with this kind of domination that makes us reluctant to admit that power plays a role in our love relationships. Few people want to think of having power over (or being subordinate to) their beloved. However, power is not simply domination; power also refers to autonomy—the ability to act according to one's wishes and desires. Using this conceptualization of power, the need for love and the need for power are no longer mutually exclusive dynamics in a love relationship but are intimately connected. Great acts of love depend on a free and autonomous self capable of both feeling and action. In this way, love and power are both fundamental dynamics in any healthy relationship (Nyberg 1981).

Even if we think of power as autonomy rather than domination, we can see how power and love exist in tension with one another in any relationship. Fulfilling one's own desires can sometimes mean thwarting those of one's partner, raising important questions, such as, How much should I give up to make my partner happy? and What do I have a right to expect from my partner in return? Conflicting desires or needs between spouses mean that at some point one person's autonomy will be sacrificed to meet the desires of the other. Often these issues exist on an unconscious level and surface in a relationship only in the context of "fairness," as in, Why do I have to do all the cleaning? or Why do you always get your way? Despite the clear power implications of these issues, they are rarely framed as evidence of differential power between spouses.

Conceptualizing and Measuring Power Within Marriage

The widespread cultural denial of the presence of power in love relationships makes it difficult to conceptualize and measure power within marriage. Most obviously, one spouse's exerting his or her will over the other (overt power) gives us a concrete way to examine the balance of power in a relationship, and much of the work on marital power has taken this factor as its starting point. Spouses have been asked to report on how much "say" each spouse has in a wide range of decisions commonly made by married couples. One's ability to influence or control decision making is a fundamental indicator of one's power within the relationship.

However, power dynamics, particularly within marriage, can be much more nuanced and subtle, and decision-making outcomes tell only part of the story. The process of making decisions, including the various ways in which partners can influence negotiations, also reveals

much about who exerts more control within the relationship. For example, while one spouse may be making what appear to be important decisions, it is possible that these are merely tasks delegated by the other partner. Paying the bills could put one spouse in a position of power by allowing her or him to closely monitor the family's finances and make at least some monetary decisions unilaterally. However, in other circumstances, paying the bills may be a task dumped on a spouse by a partner who considers this job menial and stressful. Therefore, knowing how couples come to decisions can be a more important indicator of the balance of power between spouses than the actual outcome of the decision-making process.

The ability to suppress issues, or "non-decision making," is also an important indicator of power. This kind of power would show up in the successful resolution of conflict or resistance in the past in ways that keep similar conflicts from reemerging (latent power). In this case, the partner who "lost" the first round on a particular issue might fear open confrontation if she or he attempts to renegotiate the outcome, and therefore lives with the past decision rather than actively pursuing her or his desires. Power then lies with the partner who is able to avoid discussion or conflict over an issue once it has been settled to her or his satisfaction.

Considering overt and latent power, as well as power processes, gives us a number of ways to assess the balance of power in a relationship. But even these approaches do not examine all the possible avenues for exercising power. Steven Lukes (1974, 1986) has conceptualized power in a way that allows us to explore power dynamics that are embedded in larger cultural assumptions or ideologies. He advocates what he calls a three-dimensional view of power, which examines overt and latent power but also attempts to uncover power that is "hidden." Lukes argues that the ability to keep particular issues from entering the arena of conflict is a more thorough-going exercise of power than any overt struggle for dominance. The most effective exercise of power draws on prevailing ideological constructions, so that an individual's or group's domination seems beneficial, reasonable, or natural. In this way, the most adept uses of power are largely hidden.

Hidden power can be exercised in a variety of ways: through individual decisions, institutional procedures, or by dominant values that shape interaction (e.g., conventional gender expectations). Consensus may seem to exist, as ideology masks the contradictions in lived experience; but uncovering these contradictions reveals the exercise of power. We can easily see the distinction between the various conceptualizations of power by looking at the issue of domestic labor. If a husband and wife struggle over domestic labor, and the husband successfully resists his wife's request for him to do more around the house, he has exercised overt power. If his wife then accepts the situation and avoids raising the issue again out of fear of renewed conflict, he has exercised latent power. But even if this issue is never raised between the two spouses because the wife accepts it as her duty to bear the domestic labor burden—even when she is employed outside the home—her husband has benefited from the hidden power in prevailing gendered practices and ideology.

Aafke Komter (1989) adapted Lukes's framework to her examination of the hidden power in Dutch marriages. She found that husbands benefit from the implicit hierarchy of cultural worth that values men over women, and that couples rely on conventional gender expectations to explain inequities in their relationships. For example, men explained that their wives perform more housework because they were "better at it" or "enjoyed it more." These explanations reinforce conventional gender expectations and obscure men's power advantage in these relationships.

This conceptualization of hidden power . . . allows us to assess how cultural expectations regarding gender at the institutional level affect both the interactions between spouses and their attempts to construct meaningful identities. Attention to hidden power can sensitize us to the subtle ways in which gender expectations shape the power dynamics within marriage.

While this conceptualization of power moves us forward theoretically, it represents only half the battle. Measuring power can be equally challenging because power cannot generally be measured in any direct way. Rather, theoretically driven indications of power are measured. Within the context of a marriage, the ability to prevail in the face of conflict is an obvious reflection of one's power. The relative level of control spouses exercise over financial and other family decisions has also been seen as indicative of the relative power of each spouse. More recently, especially as women have moved into the workforce, the division of domestic labor has been used to reflect the balance of power between spouses. The assumption here is that performing such labor is onerous and undesirable, and that a spouse will avoid this labor if she or he has the power to do so. And men's strong resistance to performing household chores, despite women's labor-force participation (as well as their continued efforts to get men to help), has been viewed as a successful expression of men's power or privilege (Hochschild 1989).

REFERENCES

Acker, Joan. 1992. "Gendered Institutions: From Sex Roles to Gendered Institutions." *Contemporary Sociology* 21:565–569.

Berk, Sarah Fenstermaker. 1985. *The Gender Factory: The Apportionment of Work in American Households*. New York: Plenum Press.

Bianchi, Susan, Melissa Milkie, Liana Sayer, and John Robinson. 2000. "Is Anyone Doing the Housework? Trends in the Gender Division of Household Labor." *Social Forces* 79:191–228.

Bittman, Michael, Paula England, Liana Sayer, Nancy Folbre, and George Matheson. 2003. "When Does Gender Trump Money? Bargaining and Time in Household Work." *American Journal of Sociology* 109:186–214.

Blood, Robert O., and Donald M. Wolfe. 1960. *Husbands and Wives*. Glencoe, Ill.: Free Press.

Blumberg, Rae Lesser, 1984. "A General Theory of Gender Stratification." In *Sociological Theory 1984,* edited by R. Collins. San Francisco: Jossey-Bass.

Blumstein, Philip, and Pepper Schwartz. 1983. *American Couples: Money, Work, Sex.* New York: Morrow.

———. 1991. "Money and Ideology: Their Impact on Power and the Division of Household Labor." In *Gender, Family, and Economy,* edited by R. L. Blumberg. Newbury Park, Calif.: Sage.

Brennan, Robert, Rosalind C. Barnett, and Karen Gareis. 2001. "When She Earns More Than He Does: A Longitudinal Study of Dual Earner Couples." *Journal of Marriage and the Family* 63:168–182.

Brines, Julie. 1994. "Economic Dependency, Gender, and the Division of Labor at Home." *American Journal of Sociology* 100:652–688.

Coltrane, Scott. 1996. *Family Man: Fatherhood, Housework, and Gender Equity.* New York: Oxford University Press.

Connell. R. W. 1987. *Gender and Power: Society, the Person, and Sexual Politics.* Stanford, Calif.: Stanford University Press.

Cowan, Carolyn Pape, and Philip A. Cowan. 1992. *When Partners Become Parents: The Big Life Change for Couples.* New York: Basic Books.

Deutsch, Francine. 1999. *Halving It All: How Equally Shared Parenting Works.* Cambridge: Harvard University Press.

Greenstein, Theodore. 2000. "Economic Dependence, Gender, and the Division of Labor at Home: A Replication and Extension." *Journal of Marriage and the Family* 62:322–335.

Hertz, Rosanna. 1989. "Dual Career Corporate Couples: Shaping Marriages through Work." In *Gender in Intimate Relationships: A Microstructural Approach,* edited by B. Risman and P. Schwartz. Belmont, Calif.: Wadsworth.

Hochschild, Arlie. 1989. *The Second Shift.* New York: Viking.

Komter, Aafke. 1989. "Hidden Power in Marriage." *Gender & Society* 3:187–216.

Lorber, Judith. 1994. *Paradoxes of Gender.* New Haven: Yale University Press.

Lukes, Steven. 1974. *Power: A Radical View.* London: Macmillan.

———. 1986. *Power.* Oxford: Basil Blackwell.

Nyberg, David. 1981. *Power over Power.* Ithaca, N.Y.: Cornell University Press.

Perry-Jenkins, Maureen, and Karen Folk. 1994. "Class, Couples, and Conflict: Effects of the Division of Labor on Assessments of Marriage in Dual-Earner Families." *Journal of Marriage and the Family* 56:165–180.

Pleck, Robert. 1985. *Working Wives, Working Husbands.* Beverly Hills: Sage.

Popenoe, David. 1989. *Disturbing the Nest: Family Change and Decline in Modern Society.* New York: Aldine de Gruyter.

Potuchek, Jean. 1997. *Who Supports the Family? Gender and Breadwinning in Dual-Earner Families.* Stanford, Calif.: Stanford University Press.

Raley, Sara, Marybeth Mattingly, Suzanne Bianchi, and Erum Ikramullah. 2003. "How Dual Are Dual-Income Couples? Documenting Change from 1970–2001." Presented at the annual meeting of the American Sociological Association, Atlanta, Georgia, August.

Rexroat, Cynthia, and Constance Shehan. 1987. "The Family Life Cycle and Spouses' Time in Housework." *Journal of Marriage and the Family* 49:737–750.

Risman, Barbara. 1998. *Gender Vertigo: American Families in Transition.* New Haven: Yale University Press.

Risman, Barbara, and Danielle Johnson-Sumerford. 1998. "Doing It Fairly: A Study of Post-Gender Marriages." *Journal of Marriage and Family* 60:23–40.

Rubin, Lillian Breslow. 1994. *Families on the Faultline.* New York: Harper-Collins.

Schwartz, Pepper. 1994. *Love between Equals: How Peer Marriage Really Works.* New York: Free Press.

West, Candace, and Donald Zimmerman. 1987. "Doing Gender." *Gender & Society* 1:125–151.

Wilkie, Jane Riblett. 1993. "Changes in U.S. Men's Attitudes toward the Family Provider Role." *Gender & Society* 7:261–279.

Williams, Joan. 2000. *Unbending Gender: Why Family & Work Conflict and What to Do about It.* New York: Oxford University Press.

Willinger, Beth. 1993. "Resistance and Change: College Men's Attitudes toward Family and Work in the 1980's." In *Men, Work, and Family,* edited by Jane Hood. New York: Sage.

Wright, Eric Olin, Karen Shire, Shu-Ling Hwang, Maureen Dolan, and Janeen Baxter. 1992. "The Non-Effects of Class on the Gender Division of Labor in the Home: A Comparative Study of Sweden and the U.S." *Gender & Society* 6:252–281.

Introduction to Reading 38

As we emphasize throughout this book, gender is not a static state. This piece by Jennifer Utrata helps us understand how gender intersects with age for women across the aging process. Using data gathered from both participant observation and in-depth interviews with 90 single mothers and 30 grandmothers in a midsized Russian city, Utrata provides an in-depth look at how care work is delegated among adult daughters and their mothers. This delegation of care work is based on youth privilege, in which younger women have more opportunities in the workforce and their mothers are expected to fill in the gaps raising the grandchildren while their daughters pursue jobs. She also points out how institutional changes, such as changes in Russian child-care policies, capitalism, and history—in this piece, the influence of World War II—can alter gendered expectations for family members. This piece helps us look at the intersection of age and gender in families through the social prism of culture.

1. What is the role of the *babushka* in Russian society? Is it valued? Why or why not?

2. How do the expectations for single mothers and grandmothers in Russian families compare with the expectations for them in your community?

3. What elements of social structure and institutional change influenced the position of *babushki* and single mothers in Russian society? In your community?

YOUTH PRIVILEGE

DOING AGE AND GENDER IN RUSSIA'S SINGLE-MOTHER FAMILIES

Jennifer Utrata

Feminists have long quipped that—in the absence of husbands taking on an equal share of housework and child care—what a working mother really needs is a wife. This old refrain is given a new twist in Russia, where grandmothers frequently help to raise their grandchildren and assist their adult daughters with household work. In Russian households, women are held responsible for the bulk of the "second shift" (Hochschild 1989; Zdravomyslova 2010), but the domestic division of labor depends heavily on arrangements worked out between adult daughters and their mothers (Temkina 2010, 94). In Russia's single-mother families, the absence of a male breadwinner magnifies the importance of these negotiations for support between mothers and grandmothers.

Many Russian single mothers do not raise their children alone. Instead they rely on the support of their own mothers—their children's grandmothers, affectionately called *babushki* in Russian (*babushka* in the singular)—to manage

From Utrata, Jennifer. 2011. "Youth Privilege: Doing Age and Gender in Russia's Single-Mother Families." *Gender & Society* 25(5): 616–641. Published by Sage Publications on behalf of Sociologists for Women in Society.

the triple burden of paid work, child rearing, and housework. Women turn to one another out of mutual need, sharing financial resources, produce from the family's *dacha* (country land plot), child care, housework, and emotional support. Given the reduction in state supports for mothers during the post-Soviet transition to market capitalism (Teplova 2007), this inter-generational support system is more important than ever before for families of all kinds. For single mothers, a babushka's contributions are critical, especially in the first few years after a divorce or breakup.

Yet the support exchanged between grand-mothers and single-mother adult daughters is neither automatic nor unproblematic. Instead, support is negotiated, with unequal power rela-tions shaping these negotiations. [S]ingle moth-ers frequently characterize a grandmother's contributions of child care, housework, and income in terms of a lack of choice. Single mothers also naturalize a grandmother's sup-port as an expression of love. Grandmothers, however, do not take the support of adult daughters for granted in the same way or to nearly the same extent. Age and gender rela-tions intersect, producing different sets of opportunities and constraints for single mothers and grandmothers. Single mothers and grand-mothers benefit from mutual support and often have close emotional bonds, but we need age and gender relations perspectives to understand both the complexity of women's negotiations in families and the contours of Russia's gendered transition to capitalism.

In this article, drawing on ethnographic and in-depth interview data, I explore how single mothers and grandmothers are held accountable for doing gendered age differently. I ask whether the changing post-Soviet context, where "gender relations are in flux and old certainties have dis-solved" (Tartakovskaya 2000, 128), further influences these intergenerational negotiations. Although I focus on the interactional level, I also make linkages to institutional aspects of Russia's labor and marriage markets (Risman 2004) that systematically shape women's "choices.". . .

THEORIZING THE INTERSECTIONALITY OF AGE AND GENDER RELATIONS

On the one hand, although there is a considerable amount of research on aging women (Calasanti and Slevin 2006; McMullin 1995), social geron-tologists tend to "add on" gender without a deeper analysis of how gender relations structure social life as people get older (Allen and Walker 2006; Connidis and Walker 2009; Ginn and Arber 1995). Focusing in large part on the com-parative disadvantages that women face as they age, scholarship reinforces an oversimplified "double jeopardy" perspective that foregrounds "misery" (Krekula 2007, 163). Theories of doing gender as a routine accomplishment have only partially been incorporated into the social geron-tology literature (Connidis and Walker 2009) and have been "profoundly marginalized" in family studies (Ferree 2010, 422).

On the other hand, feminist scholars tend to privilege race, class, and gender as the primary forms of inequality worthy of serious attention (West and Fenstermaker 1995), neglecting age. Ethnicity, nation, and sexual orientation are sometimes included as other major forms, but age is frequently either missing or relegated to the periphery (Calasanti and Slevin 2001, 2006; Connidis and Walker 2009; King 2006; McMullin 2000). Age is one of several primary cultural identities through which people routinely cate-gorize each other (Ridgeway and Correll 2004, 522), but age relations remain undertheorized.

Yet people also "do age." This process of doing age (or doing gendered age; Moore 2001) is similar to what Krekula (2009, 10) recently termed "age coding." Doing age is a practice, directing our attention to *"action, activities, and processes"* at the individual and institutional levels. There are tensions surrounding the desig-nation of age, but awareness is increasing that age "has a flexible and interactional nature" (Moore 2001, 836). Taking age relations seri-ously requires that we see age as a primary organizing principle of power. Age is similar to other axes of inequality, but unique in that group membership changes over time. All of us will experience the advantages and disadvantages of age relations, assuming we live long enough (Calasanti 2006). Age groups "gain *identities and power* in relation to one another" (Calasanti, Slevin, and King 2006, 17) and intersect with other forms of power relations. We need to theorize when and how age relations become important in specific contexts.

It is not merely chronological age that makes someone young or old. In the Russian case, one's family status as a single mother or grandmother also shapes age identities and performances. Just as the lynchpin of the "doing gender" approach is accountability to sex category membership, the process of doing age requires accountability to age category (i.e., socially perceived age). Age is not inherently oppressive but, like gender, can become so because of "the inferences from and the consequences of those differences" (West and Zimmerman 2009, 117). Women who are perceived as being of a certain age, and are seen as grandmothers, are constrained to do gender differently from single-mother daughters, with social institutions holding women accountable. Particular configurations of age relations, or ways of doing age, produce youth privilege while making it seem "natural."

Youth privilege is typically invisible to those who have it. Therefore, I highlight how much single-mother families rely on the labor of older women (DeVault 1991), illuminating the privilege that relative youth grants single mothers. Yet this is no simple story of oppression. Age relations are increasingly contested within families. Some grandmothers in Russia, especially those from more middle-class backgrounds (Zdravomyslova 2010), are beginning to resist the assumption that they are 24/7 backup caregivers, drawing on newer discourses of femininity that value leisure and development of the self. Nevertheless, considering the added pressures accompanying the transition to capitalism, and the retrenchment of state supports that older women experience acutely, many grandmothers end up resigning themselves to their "lack of choice" in doing whatever they can to help single-mother daughters.

AGE AND GENDER RELATIONS IN FAMILIES: THE POST-SOVIET TRANSITION TO MARKET CAPITALISM

Russian families have been in the throes of a "quiet revolution" (Zakharov 2008) since the early 1990s. Premature male mortality and declining population rates have captured the lion's share of scholarly attention, but new attitudes about family, marriage, and gender are also emerging. The Soviet Union had one of the highest divorce rates in the world by the late 1970s (Moskoff 1983), but now in addition to a still-high divorce rate (4.9 per 1,000 in 2009) close to one-third of all births are nonmarital (Demographic Yearbook of Russia 2010). Marriage and remarriage rates are down, cohabitation is growing, fertility has declined, and single-mother households have increased dramatically (Afontsev et al. 2008).

In spite of these changes, the gender order established during the Soviet period is mostly intact. However, there are much weaker institutional supports for it. Russian women have long worked outside the home, but the Soviet state institutionalized a gender contract whereby men were expected to be first and foremost successful workers, the leaders and builders of communism. Women were supported by the state as "worker-mothers," second-order breadwinners with primarily responsibility for home and family (Ashwin 2000; Ashwin and Lytkina 2004). Women's double burden was naturalized as the status quo.

There is a long history of grandmothers' extensive contributions to Russian family life. Grandmothers contribute to heterosexual married households as well, but have probably done even more for single-mother households. After Russia experienced a catastrophic loss of men during the Second World War, several generations of men and women were raised without fathers present. Soviet families resembled African American families in that mothers often became responsible for primary breadwinning while grandmothers took over responsibility for housework and child care (Gurko 2003). Even when fathers were present, everyday life was supported by extended mothering (Afontsev et al. 2008; Rotkirch 2000; Teplova 2007).

Post-Soviet men are still expected to concentrate on primary breadwinning. Many men are connected to the household mainly through their income contributions (Ashwin and Lytkina 2004; Rotkirch 2000), remaining somewhat on the margins of family life. Women continue to be responsible, with the support of grandmothers, for child care, housework, and paid work (Zdravomyslova 2010), as well as for ensuring the household's very survival (Burawoy, Krotov, and Lytkina 2000; Clarke 2002).

New market pressures make getting and keeping a job more complicated than during the Soviet period. At the same time, the institutions that once supported women as mothers and workers no longer function adequately (Zdravomyslova 2010). Women have fared relatively well in comparison to men's many difficulties in adapting to market capitalism (Ashwin and Lytkina 2004; Burawoy, Krotov, and Lytkina 2000; Kiblitskaya 2000; Rotkirch 2000; Utrata 2008b), but women have nonetheless suffered serious setbacks. Discriminatory labor markets supporting "unencumbered" workers without caregiving responsibilities have weakened women's job prospects (Teplova 2007) and put mothers at a significant disadvantage. State supports for mothers have dwindled, including dramatic cuts in state-sponsored child care facilities (Klugman and Motivans 2001; Teplova 2007). The enforcement of child support has declined (Gurko 2008), and social connections and close kin remain critical (Caldwell 2004; Höjdestrand 2009).

Changes in post-Soviet family leave laws, later incorporated into Article 256 of the 2001 Russian Labor Code, give some recognition to grandmothers' provision of child care. However, the Russian state and scholarship is still relatively silent about the grandmothers who are central figures in family life (Rotkirch, Temkina, and Zdravomyslova 2007). The number of mothers living with children and grandparents increased during the 1990s (Lokshin, Harris, and Popkin 2000), with one-third of children in single-mother

households living with at least one grandparent (Kanji 2010). Irrespective of where grandparents reside, relying on parents is the primary survival strategy for single mothers (Clarke 2002). Grandparents care for nearly 50 percent of Russia's preschool-aged children (Teplova 2007) and provide more pragmatic help to their adult children than vice-versa (Kanji 2009; Tchernina and Tchernin 2002, 552).

Single mothers are expected to provide well for their children through achieving some success in the "masculine" endeavor (Ashwin and Lytkina 2004) of primary breadwinning. In practice, this means that mothers must find child care at all costs (Zdravomyslova 2010). Grandmothers typically contribute most to families. Russia has the largest gender gap in life expectancy in the world, with men's life expectancy now 62 years and women's 74, so there are more women than men pensioners. Women retire earlier than men, at age 55 (age 60 for men), and nearly one-fifth of all pensioners work after retirement, often contributing earnings and a pension to their children (Tchernina and Tchernin 2002). Fathers die earlier, there is little paternal involvement after divorce (Utrata 2008a), and "unlimited self-sacrifice primarily is conceived of as a female and motherly quality" (Höjdestrand 2009, 125).

There may be a "crisis of the grandmother's role in the family" (Zdravomyslova 2010, 204), but further research is needed to illuminate how grandmothers negotiate family life (Clarke 2002, 207–8; Utrata 2008b). The gendered work of survival binds women together, but also creates "grounds for tensions and conflicts" (Shevchenko 2009, 93). Even in the Soviet period, older women had begun associating retirement with leisure rather than babysitting and housework. Responsibilities were often foisted on grandmothers because of inadequate child care facilities and minimal assistance from men with chores (Sternheimer 1985). These conditions have continued, and market pressures make grandmothers feel more dependent than before on adult children. However, older people increasingly argue that limits should be set on what adult children receive, especially in middle-class families (Caldwell 2004, 86). More women are coming to value autonomy and self-fulfillment, with fewer embracing the traditional babushka's self-sacrificial duties (Zdravomyslova 2010).

Considering the centrality of the grandmother-adult daughter relationship in Russian families, age relations are an essential part of gender relations. . . . I demonstrate how the intersection of age and gender relations pressures grandmothers into doing care work on behalf of adult daughters. In spite of significant conflict, youth privilege, structured by institutions, is produced—and sometimes challenged—at the interactional level.

* * *

FINDINGS AND DISCUSSION

For single mothers, doing gendered age means providing for one's family well, while still caring for children. Single mothers are in no way generally privileged in Russia's gender-segregated labor markets. Still, in relation to grandmothers (and in relation to those mothers lacking babushka support), single mothers with babushka support are encouraged to fulfill ideal-worker norms on the job and to keep their options open concerning marriage. Regardless of their desires and options, grandmothers feel pressured to do gendered age by performing unpaid care work on behalf of adult daughters.

Single Mothers: Privileged in Labor and Marriage Markets

Grandmothers may enjoy their work, but it is hard for older women to find good jobs. Most employers prefer younger workers, especially in the private sector (McMullin and Berger 2006; Teplova 2007). Discrimination against mothers is open, widespread, and unchecked (Teplova 2007). Natasha clarified aspects of this gender and age bias in employment: "In Russia we don't exactly have equality between women and men.

Let's just say that 'equality' is a somewhat relative term. All the same, employers prefer men. . . . And if a woman is over 40, well, she's no longer needed." Nearly every woman interviewed commented on employers refusing to hire mothers of young children and preferring women under 40. Private employers do not want to pay for sick or maternity leave, so women feel pressured to demand nothing and advance quickly. Even when child care is available, employers do not trust that women will not take sick leave when children are too ill for group care.

The major way to circumvent aspects of the discrimination against mothers is to have someone else, typically babushka, available to care for children. Many single mothers cannot work unless grandmothers provide child care (Kanji 2010). Single mothers with babushka support are able to better approximate ideal-worker norms (Williams 2000). Women argue that the early career-building years should be prioritized for single mothers regardless of grandmothers' desires. As Vika explained: "Sure, my mom wants to keep working. But she can take time off and not have it hurt her in the same way that calling in sick would hurt me. Mostly she has agreed to take a sick day if Anya wakes up sick. There's no other way." Although the "mostly" here suggests some ambiguity concerning negotiations, Vika is secure enough in her own job and class position to assert her youth privilege relative to her mother's job. Institutional arrangements favoring younger workers naturalize Vika's views that her own job matters more.

Single mothers report feeling "like a man" in the single mother-grandmother relationship, working more hours and doing less care work at home. Olga reflected: "Employers will take the worker who doesn't have any problems with kids. Luckily my mom can cover for me." Single mothers described feeling freer to concentrate on their careers with a babushka's support at home, buffered against potential disruptions. Masha reflected: "I suppose I haven't experienced discrimination because I have someone with whom I can leave my child—my mom. . . . I trust in her 100 percent and she'll look after my son even better than I can at times. And we get along very well. She never hindered my professional growth or job searches.". . .

Most grandmothers, however, continue to work after retirement (Kanji 2009). Even when babushki work for pay, they provide daughters with support. Grandmothers take sick leave to help daughters and face less societal pressure to be economically successful in their jobs. Single mothers are expected to work on becoming better primary breadwinners and are seen as more autonomous because of their relative youth (Shevchenko 2009). Thus, social expectations concerning age category, family status, and gender prioritize the careers of single mothers, making it difficult for grandmothers to challenge these norms.

Mothers in the private sector were more likely to argue that it is impossible to succeed at work without babushka support. But mothers in the lower-paid state sector also saw a babushka's support as essential. Yuliya reflected on whether she would face discrimination if she had to suddenly look for work:

> No, I wouldn't. . . . If I didn't have her [babushka's] support, then yes, I'd face discrimination. . . . Therefore I'm a little bit protected. And I can let myself work more in general. . . . This is a big advantage. . . . I have an entire detachment at home—my grandma, great-grandma, and my sister!

Yuliya, who earns more money in her freelance evening job writing term papers than she does as a librarian, still feels that a babushka offers protection, and allows her to devote additional time to supplementary breadwinning.

Single mothers with babushka support also have more time for friends, leisure, and other consumption activities. Grandmothers help married mothers as well (Utrata 2008b), but married mothers face additional gender constraints as wives serving husbands in heterosexual households. Like single mothers elsewhere who experience the gendered character of household work as less constraining (DeVault 199 1, 105) mothers experience a major reduction in household work and gendered rituals of deference,

amplified further when grandmothers take over much of the second shift work. Sonya has an apartment one block away from her mother's, but she still prefers to live with her mother most days: "My mother has many household problems on her hands. That is, she buys groceries, makes dinner, cleans the house. And so for me things are simpler. I have a child who is fed and looked after, but for many women it is a matter of coming home, making dinner, and all of that." Women seldom seriously consider that a man partner might help significantly with household work or child care.

Some women initially presented themselves as equal partners on a team, but after further probing it became clear that youth privilege shaped intergenerational negotiations. Grandmothers were often responsible for more repetitive and time-consuming work. A "family myth" of egalitarianism (Hochschild 1989) is common in heterosexual families, but in Russia a similar "leisure gap" emerged based on age and gender. Grandmothers did gendered age by spending more time in the kitchen and with grandkids (or felt they should), whereas single mothers had more opportunities to visit with friends, exercise, or take care of themselves.

In part because grandmothers experienced more state supports when raising their own children, they feel more dependent on their daughters today. This feeling of dependence is somewhat diminished for those grandmothers with more class resources or income on which to rely. But generally babushki are concerned about daughters who must cope with state cutbacks, reduced enforcement of child support, and new market pressures. Lusya observed: "Vera works all the time. I mean I worked hard all my life too, but at least I got child support every month and I knew I'd have something to eat. She's got it worse."

Galina and her mother Polina, for instance, expressed satisfaction with unequal arrangements. Galina reflected: "If I lived alone, then things would be difficult. But my mom and I have a common household where I handle all of the child care—my mom doesn't really help me much with Ana—but she does all of the laundry, cooks, and handles everything else." Showing me her manicured nails and the family photos she spent many evenings editing, she proclaimed: "My friends wonder how I find the time to do it all. But my mom makes it possible!" Polina also worked full-time, but she knew her health would eventually decline, leaving her with only her daughter to depend upon. It was not that Galina's income gave her power. Instead Galina's perceived *potential* for higher income, due to her relative youth, shaped women's negotiations.

Most women feel they cannot rely on the state, nor on any man. Besides her daughter's income potential, Polina confided that Galina was young enough to have a chance of meeting a decent man, with access to a man's salary that the women could use. Thus, Polina ceded authority to Galina in child rearing, but she still watched Ana often so that Galina could attend social functions. Polina reflected, "What choice do I have? I worked my whole life for nothing, I have not even a penny to show for it. And what if I get sick? I cannot expect anything from the state. I can only count on my daughter." Polina laughed when I asked about her free time. Gesturing toward the stovetop, she said: "That's my free time. I'm done with men." The state's retreat from supporting women as worker-mothers has left a vacuum that grandmothers feel obliged to fill, both for their daughter's well-being and their own. Working-class grandmothers feel this obligatory duty more acutely, but given the uncertainty that is part of daily life in Russia, many middle-class grandmothers feel similarly dependent on their children.

Marriage markets place a premium on relative youth, and single mothers, especially those under 40, feel entitled to pursue more social outlets than older women. Grandmothers are expected to facilitate these possibilities for daughters through providing child care. Some babushki also have boyfriends, but these men are typically married and the relationship rarely involves much practical support. One grandmother reflected, "Ksenia still has time to get her private life in order . . . for me the chances are probably slim." The younger generation of women directly benefits, in terms of leisure,

by this invisibility of older women as "sexual cast-offs" (Calasanti 2003, 213).

Even when grandmothers want to relax, daughters' social calendars are prioritized. Toward the end of fieldwork I invited Tatyana, a middle-class, 59-year-old working grandmother, to a local concert. Planning just one night off proved rather complicated. We enjoyed an evening out, but she felt stressed about "clearing the date" with her daughter more than I had anticipated. This was so even though Tatyana cooks for her daughter's family (while living separately) and watches her granddaughter most evenings so that Olga can study or spend time with her boyfriend Mikhail. Mikhail occasionally helped out at the dacha, so Tatyana felt the family might benefit further from his continued support. Because of family status and age, older women are expected to sacrifice more for the family's well-being.

Grandmothers: The Reserve Army of Feminine Self-Sacrifice

While it is certainly possible for a grandmother's unpaid work to be considered the equivalent of market work, this rarely occurs. Earning money has increased in importance during Russia's transition, so single mothers who fail to give much credit to babushka's efforts reflect broader societal values that relegate unpaid care work to grandmothers based on age and gender. In married heterosexual households, mothers are expected to do gender by taking on more of this devalued care work. Unwittingly perhaps, many single mothers accept the value of primary bread-winning over care work, leaving much of the latter to their children's grandmothers and obscuring the significance of grandmothers' contributions.

With few exceptions, single mothers assume that a grandmother's unpaid work is a natural result of feeling sorry for daughters as they struggle to make ends meet. Women speak of a grandmother's "love" and "lack of choice" in the same breath. Vera, for instance, said little about her mother's extensive support until I probed further:

No one helps me.

But your mother . . . ?

Well, my mother helps in that she gets around 30 U.S. dollars a month after working for 47 years. But I get double that from my salary.

Does your mom ever help with dinner or around the apartment?

Of course, yes. She does, and she watches Kostya for me. Sometimes I don't manage to get the cooking or washing done in time. . . . In principle I could do everything myself but my mom loves me and she feels sorry for me. *[laughter]* She always helps me, she never refuses.

Many mothers presented themselves as able to "do everything" singlehandedly, when in practice a babushka made this supermom strategy possible. Freedom is conceived of as more limited for older women, especially grandmothers. Grandmothers may want to care because they are valued primarily for it, constrained to perform unpaid work based on their age and family status, and fearful about future implications of the state's retrenchment of support.

The transition to capitalism in Russia is gendered (Gal and Kligman 2000). "Masculine" values of autonomy and independence are prioritized among women as well as men. Single mothers must earn money. But they also distance themselves from the self-sacrifice associated with femininity in Russia. Values of feminine self-sacrifice and selfless caregiving are mapped onto the bodies of older women. Older women are pressured to offer their unpaid labor to their families because of their age and age-related assumptions about family status. Single mothers do perform care work, value their children, and spend time with them. Yet at the same time single mothers are keenly aware that their social value and worth as *single* mothers under market capitalism comes from economic success in what is often described by them as a "man's world" of work.

Women without babushka support offer additional insights into this dominant pattern of taking babushki for granted. Mothers without support speak poignantly about their child's lack of love. Besides practical support, a babushka's support is also about love, care, and sacrifice, qualities assumed to emanate more naturally from older women. Ludmila, a hairdresser whose mother passed away, is doing quite well with additional financial support of a brother in New York. Still she believes that her daughter is unlucky:

> My daughter needs a babushka. She doesn't need a papa. . . . But she doesn't have enough of me. . . . I am always out there making money in order to support her well so that she won't need for anything. . . . She has no babushki to spend time with her. Because of this I worry. I feel sorry for her when she goes to bed alone . . . she doesn't have enough kindness.

Single mothers may be loving, but labor market demands on primary breadwinners are such that grandmothers are upheld as the best sources of care because of age and family status. This is the flip side of the devaluation of grandmother's care work that occurs even more frequently. Grandmothers are expected to have a reduced commitment to outside work, and they are held accountable for doing gendered age accordingly.

A babushka's support represents a kind of unsullied-by-the-market, idealized form of care. Babushki are expected to both satisfy children's emotional needs for love while providing practical support to ease the burdens of working mothers. A grandmother's own desires are rather invisible. A gathering with a few working-class friends one night further drove home this idea of babushki as boundless sources of support. Renata, a childless woman whose mother had passed away, confided that she had greatly feared raising a child alone: "In this country, as long as you have your mother, you're fine. A mother is the closest person a woman can have."

Cross-Generational Conflicts: Navigating Unequal Power Relations

Age and gender relations are shaped by other axes of inequality, especially class. Most grandmothers express a desire to take more time for themselves, but working-class grandmothers feel less entitled. Even so, the transition to capitalism diminishes some of these class effects since so many families consider the post-Soviet future unstable and unpredictable (Shevchenko 2009). Rather than constituting distinct groups of grandmothers, older women vacillate between new discourses of femininity emphasizing self-fulfillment and older discourses foisting unpaid work on willing grandmothers. Grandmothers try to set limits on their support, but it is quite a struggle. Zhenya described this process of negotiation:

> Let's assume she says, "Mama, take Seriozha today," but I say "I can't." Of course this happens at times. I can't say that I'm such an ideal babushka, that I do everything. No. But I can see for myself how she is doing, and if it's really needed, then naturally I help. But if she simply wants to rest, well then . . . no, I raised you, enough, you raise your own kids yourself. But generally we don't ever resent each other. . . .

Babushki sometimes differentiate between grandmothers who sacrifice themselves for the sake of adult children versus those who care for themselves. Luba underscored the necessity of boundaries: "When my granddaughter was born, I clearly said to myself, yes, I'm a babushka. But not constantly. . . . I also have my own plans!" . . .

Luba aligns herself with a growing number of babushki who help adult daughters but take care of themselves, insisting that their support be treated as a gift rather than taken for granted.

Nevertheless, grandmothers speak of enforcing limits more often than they do it. Cultural discourses often change faster than practices (Hochschild 1989). In the United States, for instance, "divorce culture"—where marriage is optional and contingent and divorce is a gateway (Hackstaff 1999)—has given women some negotiating power vis-à-vis husbands. But in Russia, no culture of divorce exists between grandmothers and single mothers.

Most conflicts occur when daughters fail to prioritize breadwinning sufficiently and take their youth-related privileges too far. Grandmothers complain about daughters spending insufficient time with children or too much time with boyfriends. Even though she lives separately, Katya has the support of her own mother, Marina, as well as her grandmother. She receives constant financial and practical support. Lacking a higher education, Katya feels her best shot at success lies in developing her photography skills, but her mother disagrees and wants Katya to take any kind of paying job. Katya knows she must earn money, but she feels entitled to develop her talents in a way her own mother does not. . . .

Katya accepts her need to earn money, but, unlike her mother and grandmother, she will not work at any low-paying job. Even without a job, she spends less time with Ilyousha than her "parents." Her grandmother cares for Ilyousha while her mother Marina works all day at a factory job. Marina buys Ilyousha's pampers, walking 35 minutes to work each way to save on bus fare. Katya realizes that without babushka support she would have to work at "awful" jobs rather than pursuing her dreams. She added, tellingly: "Parents give you power."

Katya has no income, so her power in relation to her "parents" is due to her relative youth and family status. As a younger woman, she feels entitled to have fun and pursue her dreams. This privilege was evident one evening when Marina had invited me for dinner. After waiting nearly an hour, we began eating without Katya. Marina and Valentina explained that Katya gave them "nothing to boast about" since she refused to hold down a regular job and instead wanted to rely on their sacrifices. Two hours later, Katya burst into the room proclaiming "I'm famished!" and began digging in to the dishes warming on the stovetop. Katya spoke about the challenges of starting a photography business and finding time for her boyfriend, but the family's daily survival depended on both babushki. Marina wished her daughter would not spend her last ruble on a taxi ride or coffee drink. Yet because she cannot count on the state, Marina feels vulnerable because of her age and class standing. She cannot indulge in a café drink. Katya, economically dependent on her mother, still has substantial bargaining power. Marina earns little, hoping for her daughter's potential success. She hopes Katya will meet a new man, or get lucky as a freelancer, so she stifles her complaints and supports her daughter.

Greater amounts of feminine self-sacrifice are demanded from older women, but babushki feel upset when daughters take their gendered youth privilege too far. The amount of care work women are expected to perform varies by age, but single mothers were criticized at times for unduly burdening babushki. Svetlana praised her mother Nina as a woman who can "do everything" but felt her own job entitled her to more leisure. . . .

Youth privilege, re-created daily in the process of doing gendered age, is real, strengthened by dominant cultural beliefs and institutional arrangements. However, relative youth is not always experienced as privilege at the individual level, especially for lower-class women lacking higher education. In a few cases, babushki became breadwinners while single-mother daughters managed the second shift. This division of labor was defined as temporary and aberrational. Rita felt guilty about not being able to earn more money as a filter operator; her inability to do age appropriately made her uncomfortable. She cannot imagine finding better-paid work without a higher education and without a babushka on constant call.

Although better off economically, Aleftina, too, was unusual in that her ex-husband, a wealthy New Russian, paid for her apartment and gave her a monthly "allowance." Yet she felt like a failed mother because she did not have a successful career as others expected based on her age and family status. Doing gendered age for single mothers means doing well in the market economy. Aleftina was struggling. She wrote children's books, but it earned her very little and her mother didn't consider it a "real job." Femininity for younger women requires more than self-sacrifice. Without a man, women must make it on their own. Aleftina's sons do not respect her, she confided, wanting only to be "rich like Daddy." Aleftina has some support from her mother, but Zoya supports her less than most because she has her own father, a senior-level war veteran, to care for at home. Single mothers are generally privileged by their youth relative to grandmothers. Yet at the same time some younger women,

finding success elusive, hardly feel privileged by the pressure to be superwomen.

* * *

[Y]outh privilege is implicit in many families, part of processes that maintain gender inequality, particularly when buttressed by institutional practices and cultural beliefs about who is entitled to leisure or career fulfillment. Unpacking these age and gender relations should yield additional rich theoretical insights. While it is possible for single mothers and grandmothers to begin to value the equal sharing of paid work and care work, and to undo strictly gendered notions of who does what, structural factors in gendered labor markets often discourage change. The Russian state has withdrawn many supports for families, and while there is some evidence that political leaders recognize women's burdens, the state does little to ease them, leaving families to manage (Rotkirch, Temkina, and Zdravomyslova 2007). In the West, too, many good jobs are built around a masculine ideal worker who is available around the clock with no domestic responsibilities. Even when women can afford child care, the devaluation of care work and lack of societal and state support for it continues. Attention to age relations, and older women, should be part of remedying the devaluation of care work.

England (2010) recently described this stalled gender revolution, emphasizing the persistent cultural devaluation of the feminine as a major theme. In addition to institutions that favor unencumbered male workers, my research suggests that women themselves accept these devaluations, unwittingly perpetuating age and gender hierarchies about what counts as "work," where status lies, and who should handle the bulk of the work at home. Yet even when women want to change the status quo, to argue for their right to leisure or growth, without changes in policies or markets, it is difficult to change gender and age arrangements that devalue "feminine" unpaid care work. It may also be difficult to revalue care work without more men doing it.

I am convinced that part of undoing gender (Risman 2004, 445) involves more explicit attention to the intersectionality of gender and other axes of power, including neglected forms such as age. Although making the unpaid labor of older women visible is worthwhile, the Russian case also reinforces the idea that care work must be recognized and revalued at the institutional level. Otherwise older women are fighting an uphill battle and single mothers are complicit in validating paid work to the detriment of "feminine" care work. Youth, after all, is by definition short-lived, its privileges precarious. Many single mothers are left to make do without any babushka support. And even "luckier" single mothers will eventually find themselves accountable for doing gendered age differently, faced with the bottomless expectations and more marginalized status of Russia's older women.

REFERENCES

Afontsev, S., G. Kessler, A. Markevich, V. Tyazhelnikova, and T. Valetov. 2008. The urban household in Russia and the Soviet Union, 1900–2000: Patterns of family formation in a turbulent century. *The History of the Family* 13:178–194.

Allen, K. R., and A. J. Walker. 2006. Aging and gender in families: A very grand opening. In *Age matters: Realigning feminist thinking*, edited by T.M. Calasanti and K.F. Slevin. New York: Routledge.

Ashwin, S., ed. 2000. *Gender, state and society in Soviet and Post-Soviet Russia.* London: Routledge.

Ashwin, S., and T. Lytkina. 2004. Men in crisis in Russia: The role of domestic marginalization. *Gender & Society* 18:189–206.

Burawoy, M., P. Krotov, and T. Lytkina. 2000. Involution and destitution in capitalist Russia: Russia's gendered transition to capitalism. *Ethnography* 1(1): 43–65.

Calasanti, T. 2003. Theorizing age relations. In *The need for theory: Critical approaches to social gerontology*, edited by S. Biggs, A. Lowenstein, and J. Hendricks. Amityville, NY: Baywood.

Calasanti, T. M., and K. F. Slevin. 2001. *Gender, social inequalities, and aging.* Walnut Creek, CA: AltaMira Press.

Calasanti, T. M., and K. F. Slevin, eds. 2006. *Age matters: Re-aligning feminist thinking.* New York: Routledge.

Calasanti, T., K. F. Slevin, and Neal King. 2006. Ageism and feminism: From "et cetera" to center. *NWSA Journal* 18(1): 13–30.

Caldwell, M. L. 2004. *Not by bread alone: Social support in the New Russia.* Berkeley: University of California Press.

Clarke, S. 2002. *Making ends meet in contemporary Russia: Secondary employment, subsidiary agriculture and social networks.* Cheltenham, UK: Edward Elgar.

Connidis, I. A., and A. J. Walker. 2009. (Re)visioning gender, age, and aging in families. In *Handbook of feminist studies*, edited by S. A. Lloyd, A. L. Few, and K. R. Allen. Thousand Oaks, CA: Sage.

Demographic Yearbook of Russia. 2010. *Statistical Handbook/Federal State Statistics Service (Rosstat).* Moscow: Information and Publishing Centre, Statistics of Russia.

DeVault, M. L. 1991. *Feeding the family: The social organization of caring as gendered work.* Chicago: University of Chicago Press.

England, P. 2010. The gender revolution: Uneven and stalled. *Gender & Society* 24:149–66.

Ferree, M. M. 2010. Filling the glass: Gender perspectives on families. *Journal of Marriage and Family* 72:420–39.

Gal, S., and G. Kligman. 2000. *The politics of gender after socialism: A comparative-historical essay.* Princeton, NJ: Princeton University Press.

Ginn, J., and S. Arber. 1995. "Only connect": Gender relations and ageing. In *Connecting gender and ageing: A sociological approach*, edited by S. Arber and J. Ginn. Buckingham: Open University Press.

Gurko, T. A. 2003. *Roditel'stvo: Sotsiologicheskie aspekty* [Parenthood: Sociological Aspects]. Moscow: Tsentr obshchechelovecheskikh tsennostei.

Gurko, T. A. 2008. Faktor kachestvennogo i kolichestvennogo vosproizvodstva naseleniia [Alimonies: A factor for qualitative and quantitative population reproduction]. *Sotsiologicheskie Issledovaniya* 34:110–20.

Hackstaff, K. B. 1999. *Marriage in a culture of divorce.* Philadelphia: Temple University Press.

Hochschild, A. R., with A. Machung. 1989. *The second shift.* New York: Avon.

Höjdestrand, T. 2009. *Needed by nobody: Homelessness and humanness in Post-socialist Russia.* Culture and society after socialism series, edited by B. Grant and N. Ries. Ithaca: Cornell University Press.

Kanji, S. 2009. Age group conflict or cooperation? Children and pensioners in Russia in crisis. *International Journal of Sociology and Social Policy* 29:372–87.

Kanji, S. 2010. Labor force participation, regional location, and economic well-being of single mothers in Russia. *Journal of Family and Economic Issues*. Published online, April 27.

Kiblitskaya, M. 2000. Once we were kings: Male experiences of loss of status at work in post-communist Russia. In *Gender, state and society in Soviet and post-Soviet Russia*, edited by S. Ashwin. London: Routledge.

King, N. 2006. The lengthening list of oppressions: Age relations and the feminist study of inequality. In *Age matters: Realigning feminist thinking*, edited by T. M. Calasanti and K. F. Slevin. New York: Routledge.

Klugman, J., and A. Motivans, eds. 2001. *Single parents and child welfare in the New Russia. UNICEF*. New York: Palgrave.

Krekula, C. 2007. The intersection of age and gender: Reworking gender theory and social gerontology. *Current Sociology* 55:155–71.

Krekula, C. 2009. Age coding—On age-based practices of distinction. *International Journal of Ageing and Later Life* 4(2): 7–31.

Labor Code of the Russian Federation, 2001. Federal Law No. 197-FZ. http://www.ilo.org/dyn/natlex/docs/WEBTEXT/60535/65252/E01RUS01.htm#chap 19

Lokshin, M., K. M. Harris, and B. M. Popkin. 2000. Single mothers in Russia: Household strategies for coping with poverty. *World Development* 28:2183–98.

McMullin, J. A. 1995. Theorizing age and gender relations. In *Connecting gender and ageing: A sociological approach*, edited by S. Arber and J. Ginn. Buckingham: Open University Press.

McMullin, J. A. 2000. Diversity and the state of sociological aging theory. *The Gerontologist* 40:517–530.

McMullin, J. A., and E. D. Berger. 2006. Gendered ageism/age(ed) sexism: The case of unemployed older workers. In *Age matters: Realigning feminist thinking*, edited by T. M. Calasanti and K. F. Slevin. New York: Routledge.

Moore, V.A. 2001. "Doing" racialized and gendered age to organize peer relations: Observing kids in summer camp. *Gender and Society* 15:835–58.

Moskoff, W. 1983. Divorce in the USSR. *Journal of Marriage and the Family* 45:419–25.

Ridgeway, C. L., and S. J. Correll. 2004. Unpacking the gender system: A theoretical perspective on gender beliefs and social relations. *Gender & Society* 18:510–31.

Risman, B. J. 2004. Gender as a social structure: Theory wrestling with activism. *Gender & Society* 18:429–50.

Rotkirch, A. 2000. *The man question: Loves and lives in late 20th century Russia*. Helsinki: Department of Social Policy.

Rotkirch, A., A. Temkina, and E. Zdravomyslova. 2007. Who helps the degraded housewife? Comments on Vladimir Putin's demographic speech. *European Journal of Women's Studies* 14:349–57.

Shevchenko, O. 2009. *Crisis and the everyday in Postsocialist Moscow*. Bloomington, IN: Indiana University Press.

Sternheimer, S. 1985. The vanishing babushka: A roleless role for older soviet women? *Current Perspectives on Aging and the Life Cycle* 1:315–33.

Tartakovskaya, I. 2000. The changing representation of gender roles in the Soviet and post-Soviet press. In *Gender, state and society in Soviet and post-Soviet Russia*, edited by S. Ashwin. London: Routledge.

Tchernina, N. V., and E. A. Tchernin. 2002. Older people in Russia's transitional society: Multiple deprivation and coping responses. *Ageing and Society* 22:543–62.

Temkina, A. 2010. Childbearing and work-family balance among contemporary Russian women. *Finnish Yearbook of Population Research* XLV:83–101.

Teplova, T. 2007. Welfare state transformation, childcare, and women's work in Russia. *Social Politics* 14:284–322.

Utrata, J. 2008a. Keeping the bar low: Why Russia's nonresident fathers accept narrow fatherhood ideals. *Journal of Marriage and Family* 70:1297–1310.

Utrata, J. 2008b. Counting on motherhood, not men: Single mothers and social change in the New Russia. PhD diss., University of California, Berkeley.

West, C., and S. Fenstermaker. 1995. Doing difference. *Gender & Society* 9:8–37.

West, C., and D. H. Zimmerman. 2009. Accounting for doing gender. *Gender & Society* 23:112–22.

Williams, J. 2000. *Unbending gender: Why family and work conflict and what to do about it*. New York: Oxford University Press.

Zakharov, S. 2008. Russian federation: From the first to second demographic transition. *Demographic Research* 19:907–72.

Zdravomyslova, E. 2010. Working mothers and nannies: Commercialization of childcare and modifications in the gender contract (a sociological essay). *Anthropology of East Europe Review* 28:200–225.

Introduction to Reading 39

The social construction of gender is embedded in institutions as well as interactions between individuals, as Irene Padavic and Jonniann Butterfield show in this article. They interviewed 17 women who were nonbiological and nonlegal co-parents of children in lesbian families. These women, from an area near a medium-sized city in Florida, were identified using a snowball sampling method in which individuals interviewed were asked for names of other women in a similar situation. Motherhood and the expectations surrounding it, particularly the expectation that a biological birth was part of the mothering identity, proved to be a major barrier for the nonbiological co-parents they interviewed. These co-parents struggled with "undoing" the social construction of familial expectations, which links gender and biology to mothering, as they attempted to co-parent their children. The obstacles they faced were not just legal but also social, as individuals these women came in contact with during parenting refused to believe that they were their children's "real" mothers who could make daily decisions for their children. Their findings tell us a great deal about how gendered and fixed the identity of "mother" is.

1. What were the obstacles that stood in the way of co-parenting for these women?

2. What were the differences between lesbian co-parents who identified themselves as "mothers," "fathers," and "mathers"?

3. How does the new category some of these women created, "mathers," allow for a less gendered vision of parenting? What stands in the way of a less gendered vision of parenting without a heterosexual, gendered parenting dichotomy?

MOTHERS, FATHERS, AND "MATHERS"

NEGOTIATING A LESBIAN CO-PARENTAL IDENTITY

Irene Padavic and Jonniann Butterfield

In a society marked by binary categorizations and an ideological preference for a "one mother–one father" family model, lesbian co-parents muddy the waters. Previous research on the identity struggles of lesbian co-parents has focused on their experiences as mothers, but in doing so scholars themselves may have inadvertently reinscribed the heteronormative relationships that many lesbian families seek to dismantle. The assumption that women engaged in parenting want to be "mothers," with all the behavioral prescriptions the role entails, precludes an understanding of how the existence of lesbian families can help unhinge sex from gender. This article argues that to gain a more complete understanding of lesbian families, we must

Padavic, Irene and Jonniann Butterfield. 2011. "Mothers, Fathers, and 'Mathers': Negotiating a Lesbian Co-parental Identity." *Gender & Society* 25(2): 176–196. Published by Sage Publications on behalf of Sociologists for Women in Society.

consider how co-parents negotiate a *parental* identity, rather than presuming that women parents want to *mother*. This article asks how a nonbiological woman parent determines a parental identity in a system constrained by language that offers only two options (mother or father) and in which the dominant motherhood ideology disqualifies her from achieving the status of good mother. Moreover, it asks how these personal and interpersonal dynamics play out in an institutional context that refuses to legally recognize them as parents.

We employ a social constructionist approach to identity and to gender, which suggests that identities are variable and actively created through interactions (Schwalbe and Mason-Schrock 1996) and that because gender is dynamic, it can be "undone" as well as "done" (Deutsch 2007; West and Zimmerman 1987). As a result of this dynamism, "gender can be openly challenged by non-gendered practices in ordinary interaction, in families, childrearing, language, and organization of space" (Lorber 2000,88). Lesbian parents have the unique opportunity to experience parenthood and raise children outside the gendered heterosexual context, and by doing so, they can destabilize gendered arrangements (Dalton and Bielby 2000; Weston 1991).

The possibility of undoing gender via such innovative family arrangements is one thing; emotionally creating such "brave new families" (Stacey 1998) is another, and previous research indicates that doing so is not a simple matter, particularly for a nonbiological lesbian parent, who "is denied access to any socially sanctioned parental category" (Gabb 2005,594). When the state fails to legally recognize the legitimacy of both parents in such families—as is the case in most of the United States (notwithstanding huge civil rights gains in some jurisdictions)—the task of securing a parental identity is especially difficult. Understanding how women parents lacking a legal entitlement to parenthood struggle to forge a parental identity is important because identifying the pitfalls such women face and the successful strategies they devise

may provide hope for others seeking to create a society in which gender and sexuality cease to exist as categories that privilege some groups over others.

BARRIERS TO IDENTITY CREATION: THE MOTHERHOOD HIERARCHY, LANGUAGE, AND THE LEGAL SYSTEM

Social expectations present lesbian co-parents with at least three barriers to smoothly constructing a sense of themselves as parents. First, all women become parents in a society that promotes a motherhood ideology validating the identity claims only of mothers who meet certain criteria (Chase and Rogers 2001; Hequembourg and Farrell 1999). Family law, social policies, and cultural representations endorse the married, middle-class, white, heterosexual family as the ideal (Abramovitz 1996; Fineman 1995; Roberts 1997; Thorne 1993), and a "motherhood hierarchy" rewards those who most closely conform to it. The most honored mother is "a heterosexual woman, of legal age, married in a traditional nuclear family, fertile, pregnant by intercourse with her husband, and wants to bear children" (DiLapi 1989, 110). Moreover, much societal and legal reluctance to accept lesbians as good mothers derives from fear that their children will be psychologically harmed or more likely to identify as homosexual (Thompson 2002), despite considerable research evidence to the contrary (Stacey and Biblarz 2001). Media pundits and politicians have also pathologized lesbian parents, portraying them as egocentric and immoral and their relationships as unstable (Hequembourg 2007; Richey 2010). Women who fail to mother in ways congruent with motherhood ideals are subject to "deviance discourses" (Miall and March 2006, 46) and to being labeled as unfit or bad (Arendell 2000). Thus, lesbian parents face a continual struggle to have their parental identity legitimized in a social context that renders it tenuous.

A second barrier is that the language used to identify parents relies on the norm of "one mother–one father," which provides no descriptively accurate label for women who lack a biological or legal tie to the child. Naming is a central—and fraught—component of identity for many lesbian parents. As Gabb (2005, 594) noted, the "materiality of language" is crucial because people come into being only via the power of discourse. Research (Aizley 2006; Sullivan 2004) indicates that co-parents often feel caught in an identity limbo since they neither fit neatly into the "mother" category (because they did not give birth) nor (because they are not men) fit into the only other possibility offered in a binary system, that of "father." While some appreciate this limbo and devise terms such as *lesbian dad, dyke daddy, high-femme dad, mamma II,* and the Hebrew word for mother, *ima* (Aizley 2006), most describe facing difficulty being validated by the outside world and having to continuously justify their family structure, including to people in the gay community (Dunne 2000). Outsiders hold a cultural attachment to the notion that there can be only one mother and that fathers are men, and reactions to the presence of two women parents can run from confusion to discomfort to outright rejection. As one co-parent in Dunne's (2000, 24) study put it, "Well if you're not the biological mother, then what the hell are you?"

The third barrier to creating a parental identity is that co-parents often must surmount a formidable hurdle: the legal system. In many jurisdictions, when lesbian couples create families through artificial insemination, only the birth parent has a legal tie to the child; the other parent has no legally recognized standing. Second-parent adoption is a solution for couples residing in a state permitting it (assuming they have the funds to do this), but 82 percent of states do not explicitly allow this (Human Rights Campaign 2010).

Our analysis seeks to answer the question of how lesbian co-parents, who cannot conform to societal definitions of good mothering because of both their lesbianism and their nonbiological relationship to their child, contend with the problem of creating a parental—not necessarily a maternal—identity. What factors facilitate and impede their search for a parental identity? How might other lesbian parents and social change agents benefit from an understanding of these factors?

* * *

Results

Co-parents in our study reported that developing a parental identity entailed an emotional struggle made worse by legally sanctioned discrimination and interpersonal discrimination. For virtually all, grappling with what it means to be a "mother" in a dichotomous "either mother or father" social order was the starting point. Most co-parents engaged in behaviors to align their sense of themselves as parents with the categories available—mother or father—but a third group created a new, hybrid category that stretched the limits of heteronormative categorizations.

Threats to Parental Identity Stemming From Social and From Legal Discrimination

Most of the women we interviewed described how their sense of themselves as legitimate parents was undermined by forays into the public sphere, and virtually all said that this discomfiture was compounded enormously by their lack of legal rights. Of the 17 co-parents, 10 gave examples of interactions in public that required them to field questions about their relationship to their child and the structure of their household. Outsiders, including doctors, teachers, and other parents, challenged co-parents' claims, and thus their identities, by not understanding or accepting them as parents. Ruth explained,

> Other people are really attached to the idea that there can only be one mom. Every Saturday Margaret and I take Cameron to Play Center, and

there are lots of other parents there. Even though we know a lot of the parents there now because it's a thing for us to go and so we have explained our situation, I feel like most of them don't take me seriously. Just last week, one of the mothers said that her kid was having a birthday party and Cameron was invited and said she would see if it was okay with Margaret. I said, "You don't need to ask her. Cameron can go. We don't have any other plans." She told me point-blank that she really thought that she should ask Margaret since she was Cam's mother. I had to walk away.

Gretchen said,

We started seeing a new doctor, who one of my gay friends told me was gay-friendly. I took our daughter for a vaccination and one of the questions on the form asked what my relationship to the patient was and I put "mather" [a combination of the words *mother* and *father*] and then in parentheses I wrote "parent." When we got in front of the doctor, he asked what a mather was. I told him that I am her parent, but don't consider myself a mother or father. Then he asked me if the child was biologically mine and of course I said no, but I was getting defensive. He refused to give my daughter the vaccination because I was not a legal parent or guardian. He then asked to speak to me alone. He actually told me that in his medical opinion, referring to myself as a mather was harmful to our daughter. This put me into a tailspin about whether I was messing up our daughter.

Stories like these were commonplace. Such troubling interactions are similar to those reported by step-parents, whose lack of biological relationship can also provide grounds for challenge from institutions (Mason et al. 2002). Yet the barely muted hostility in the above excerpts (flatly denying a motherhood claim in the one case and making accusations of bad parenting in the other) raises the possibility of anti-lesbian-family sentiment. Although step-parents facing a question about parental status can usually assume benign intent, lesbian co-parents cannot, which may explain reactions of "having to walk away" and going into a "tailspin."

More destructive to the co-parents' sense of identity, however, was the lack of a legal right to their children. Unlike the public interactions that give rise to social discrimination, which they could choose to ignore, the state's position that women co-parents are not legally allowed to act in the role of parent has more encompassing psychological and social ramifications. Almost all (16 of 17) co-parents indicated they struggled with their parental identities because they were not legally recognized parents, which influenced how they thought about themselves as parents and how they felt others perceived them. For many, legal discrimination was a greater hindrance than the lack of biological relatedness for developing a parental identity. . . .

Karen said,

I knew it would be rough at the beginning to see my partner breastfeed and not have that biological connection, but that can be somewhat compensated by being a legal parent. When you can't establish a legal connection, though, it is really hard to feel like a good parent. Right now, I feel like a nanny or mommy's sidekick.

Thus, the state's lack of acknowledgment undermined their sense of parental identity and compounded any insecurity stemming from the absence of a biological tie. The women felt the lack of a legally recognized status not only in an abstract sense; the feeling was reinforced by institutional structures and policies. The school system was a key site where their lack of rights was brought home to them. Karen continued,

And I think that's how my son's teachers view me. I can't sign any of the official paperwork at school. She has to do the official important stuff. I get delegated to bring in cupcakes or whatever. Apparently, they will allow us non-moms to do that. . . .

The lack of legal rights makes the whole outside world, not just the school system or doctor's office, an arena of potential danger. As their status can always be challenged, many co-parents felt the need to arm themselves with documentation to bolster their claims as legitimate parents. Even so, in a state that allows co-parents no real legal parental status, officials may simply ignore these documents, leaving them vulnerable. . . .

The lack of legal recognition coupled with the lack of institutional acknowledgment, even in matters as trivial as signing report cards, undermined these women's sense of themselves as parents. They found it difficult to feel like parents in the face of the institutional cold shoulder, and they also perceived that their lack of a legal relationship delegitimized their parental status to outsiders. In sum, these women's sense of themselves as parents was undermined by contact with people who distrusted them and a legal system that disenfranchised them.

Parental Identity Construction

A question on the interview guide asked about the word the woman used to describe herself as a parent, but it turned out that naming was a centerpiece of women's stories that required little prompting. One group referred to themselves as mothers, another group rejected that label as not fitting their sense of themselves as masculine and identified as fathers, and a third group collectively coined the term *mather* to denote the amalgam of mother and father characteristics with which they identified.

Mothers. Of the 17 co-parents, 6 were committed to adopting a mother identity despite their lack of biological or legal links to their child. These women said they felt maternal, had longed to be mothers, and wanted to be called mom or mamma, but they encountered many obstacles that undermined their ability to pull this off. One obstacle was that the language they constantly heard was at odds with their identity claims. According to Ruth,

> I'm not the "mother." I'm the "non-legal parent," the "non-birth parent," the "non-adoptive parent." There are so many things I'm *not* in relation to my child that it feels like a battle to be a parent at all. It's exhausting.

Being defined by what they are not loosens the link to motherhood. Seeing a hyphen or hearing an adjective before the mother word, as frequently happened, made clear their tenuous claim to the status and also underlines the power of language in identity construction.

The mothers expressed feelings of futility, being second best, and not succeeding at being a mother, all of which caused them to question their self-worth and sense of themselves as mothers. These negative feelings were brought on by challenges from many quarters. Karen described her feeling of futility stemming from various reminders of her ambiguous status as a mother:

> I have always wanted a baby. I was the quintessential little girl who wanted to be a mom when she grew up. Well, when I realized I was gay I knew it wasn't going to be easy, but I still wanted a baby. Now I have the baby, but I didn't *have* the baby. Before she was born, I kept saying, "It won't bother me. I know I'm her mother. I don't need a law to say so." Well, I was wrong. I feel like a mother, I do, but not *the* mother. It's like I am always getting slapped in the face. "Oh, you can't breastfeed. Oh, you can't sign this paper. Oh, you have to be related to do that." It's exhausting. . . .

Such reminders, whether intentional or not, police the boundaries of who can be accepted in the motherhood ranks and take an emotional toll.

Samantha considered herself a mother but felt second best because she did not give birth to her child and felt pressured to justify her relationship to him:

> When I was in grad school, I would say something about Evan and people would start with the questions. Like, how do you have a kid? You were never pregnant. Did you adopt? And then I would do this whole explanation thing, like, well, my partner actually birthed him, but he's my kid too. This always made me feel really bad, like I wasn't a real parent you know? One day my [academic] advisor said, "Why don't you just say 'Yes, I'm his mother'? Stop explaining and apologizing." And after that I did. But it took me a long time to get to that place.

As these experiences indicate, the extent of society's commitment to the norm of blood relationships defining the link between parents and children is difficult to overestimate (Katz Rothman 2006; Miall and March 2006). In a study of lesbian families in the United Kingdom, Gabb (2005) also found a pervasive sense of second-class citizenship among nonbiological mothers.

The notion that mothers should be feminine and not masculine is another norm that society readily enforces. A woman who used the mother label despite considering herself masculine faced social pressure to fit into a binary schema of feminine mother and masculine father:

> I look butch. So when my partner and I are together, people assume I must be the "dad" because everyone assumes there is a mom and a dad, even in a lesbian couple. I feel people look us over, like, "Okay, who is the butch here?" Even though I am masculine, I still think of myself as a mother. A second-class mother, but still a mother. I guess I don't buy that mothers have to be feminine and dads have to be masculine. But, it's hard because everyone else thinks like that. Sometimes I have doubts about myself as a mother, but I know I am *not* a father.

Despite people's reaction to her masculine identity, she insisted on the mother label and was willing to stand up to social pressure urging her to reconsider. Since motherhood and femininity go hand in glove in the popular consciousness (Chodorow 1989; Glenn 1994), her decision forced beholders to question automatic associations between motherhood and femininity, thus raising an alternative to the given order of things. Yet maintaining that stance was an ongoing, lonely, "hard" struggle.

Norms about who may and may not be a mother can also penetrate interactions in the intimate realm, and some co-parents felt expendable even in the privacy of their homes. Yolanda explained,

> I think of myself as a mom, but I don't know that anyone else does, even my partner sometimes. I am not identified anywhere as a parent. It goes as far as photographs. I am always the one taking the photograph. So I am not even in very many pictures. It is always "take a picture of us." Like they are the real family.

Taylor similarly felt that her claim of being a mother was contested in the private sphere:

> I even feel like my partner doesn't consider me an equal mother. We had been debating whether or not to get a certain vaccination. One day she came home and told me that she decided to get the vaccination done. I was floored. I couldn't believe that she made that kind of executive decision without me. And this was right after she had read me the riot act because I got Shaun a buzz cut without consulting her. I felt so irrelevant.

For the one-third of interviewees who wanted to think of themselves as mothers, the challenge did not lie in knowing the parental term they desired; as one said, "I know in my heart I'm [a] mom." Rather, the challenge lay in surmounting stumbling blocks in the form of marginalization by norms linking femininity and motherhood, by outsiders, by the legal institution, by other children, and even by their partners, which left their mother identity in question. Women in this category struggled to validate their mother identity in the face of social forces that positioned them as inferior, including a language that positioned them as *non*-birth mothers, *second* mothers, *other* mothers, and so on, diminishing their ability to embrace the mother label as strongly as they wanted and creating a void that is not merely social ("What name should I respond to?") but also personal ("Who am I as a parent?"). Despite challenges and personal doubts, these women nevertheless were living evidence of an alternative family form. As they went about their daily public business—a family headed by two mothers—they transgressed the deeply held belief that families contain one and only one mother and by doing so weakened it.

Fathers. About one-third of the women we interviewed also honored the gender binary, but they did so by inverting it; for example, "I don't look like a mother and I don't feel like a mother, so I must be a father." Women in this sample who identified as fathers all described themselves as masculine or "butch." They had strong and clear ideas about how mothers looked and acted and felt they failed to embody these ideas, leading them to reject the mother label and adopt the alternative. According to one,

> I am butch. How could I possibly be a mom? It's laughable, really! I would rather ride bikes and play ball with the boys, which is something I think fathers typically do. I do some things moms do, I guess, but I don't feel like a mom. I guess it's more a mental thing. And maybe it's a gender thing. I don't want to be a man, but I guess I kind of feel like a guy.

According to another,

> I struggle with it because I know I'm a woman, but I don't look like a mom. I wear work boots and flannels. I drive a truck, not a SUV. And I sure don't act like the moms I knew growing up or the moms I know now. I don't bake cookies. I'm not nurturing in that way. I mean, I am in my own way, but more like a dad, I guess. I don't feel comfortable being called mom, because I don't feel like one. It just doesn't fit me. It makes it difficult, though, because it is really hard for other people to understand that I'm a woman but I feel more like dad. It's confusing.

For these women, a gender identity as masculine precluded using the mother label; indeed, the thought of doing so was "laughable." None tried to keep the mother label and change the meaning of motherhood to include "riding bikes and playing ball" to better fit their personal attributes. Instead, motherhood remained the domain of people like "the moms I knew growing up or the moms I know now." The only other option they saw, and the one they acted on, was to declare themselves fathers.

It was not a perfect fit. A key source of unease was the negative associations many had with heterosexual fathers' behavior, which one described as "not involved with the kid, not affectionate, and a disciplinarian." Mallory had a similar disaffection for the fathering with which she was familiar:

I chose father, because I am just not a mother. But, it still bugs me. Maybe it's because I am very woman-identified, a lesbian, and I don't like stuff men do, but I don't like how fathers act. I see some at the park when their kid cries, and they do that "toughen up" macho shit. I don't want to be a father like that.

Since their experiences of fathering are based on observations of men, they, as women, had an understandably hard time defining what fathering consists of when done by someone who is not a man. They did not want to practice the fathering style with which they were familiar, nor did they want to be genderless parents (also see Sullivan 2004). As one woman said, "Even though I think of myself as a dad, I am still a woman and a lesbian." Lacking guidance from existing practice about how to father as women, they tried to invent it. One woman chose a new term for "father" partly to facilitate a new practice of fathering:

> My family is Italian, so Kevin calls me Babbo, which is father in Italian. Calling myself Babbo lets me get a little bit away from the actual dad term, because I don't want to be that 1950s dad. I want to be a lesbian dad, a Babbo. I hope I can figure it out as I go along. I'm not girly at all, but I would like to be a girly father, whatever that means.

She chose a term that allowed her freedom from "acting like the fathers I know," but like the other fathers she struggled with the lack of models. None felt they had a clear sense of how to father in a new way, and variations of her "whatever that means" statement were common.

While most assumed the father label or a close variant on their own volition, this was not the case for all. Some felt pressured by their families and friends to conform to the one mother–one father model. Mallory described how her son pushed her to assume the role of his father:

> I am an androgynous person, and once I picked up Jack at the park and heard him say to his friend, "That's my dad." He had never referred to me as

that before; he always called me by my name. Another time he said, "When we go into the store, can you lower your voice?" I think it comes from the social idea that you have a mom and a dad. It made me realize that it was kind of selfish not to be mom or dad for his sake. Jack seemed to think of me as dad, and I sure didn't think of myself as mom—he has one of those—so here I am. A dad.

Krista described the tension with her partner that similarly pushed her to call herself a father:

To be fair, I am not the mother type, but my partner insisted, very firmly, that I was to take the role of the father. For example, she wants to pick out his clothes because she thinks that's something mothers do. One day I tried to dress him and she freaked out. She felt like I was invading her territory. Oh, another example is our baby shower. She referred to it as *her* baby shower and didn't even want me to come, but I kind of crashed it. One of the presents was a baby book. She told me that since she was the mother I wouldn't be the one putting stuff in the book, so I went out and bought my own. She flew off the handle. She wants to be the mother and wants me to be a father, so clearly that's what I am. Now I just have to figure out what that means exactly.

Important people in their lives did not permit Mallory and Krista the option of choosing non-alignment with the "father" pole of the gender binary, although for one the pressure was gentle and for the other more coercive. In a final example, Veronica also chose the father label under pressure, although her attempt to adapt to the binary choice was more agonized than for others we interviewed:

People would hold the baby and then pass her back to me and say, "Okay, go back to your Mommy." I think I turned red every time someone said that. The first time I tried to refer to myself as "Mom," I practically had to choke it out. . . . My friends and my girlfriend said, "Just go by 'Daddy.'" But I wasn't down with that either. There is stuff out there like "dyke daddy," but can you imagine the kid calling you that? I can just imagine her telling her teacher, "Yeah, my dyke daddy is picking me up today." Nope. Doesn't work. Poor kid!

She continued,

My friends and girlfriend said things like, "Well you have to come up with *something*. The baby needs to understand who you are." I felt accountable, and I couldn't come up with a way to make it right for everyone.

She ended up referring to herself as a father but having the child use her first name, although she was dissatisfied with this solution. As her story makes clear, having a child was a key moment precipitating an upswing in gender coercion and self-policing. Her close companions pressed her—for the sake of the child—to put aside personal discomfort and choose a label, and an imagined internalized teacher forced her to consider the cost to the child of adopting the gender-radical "dyke daddy" label. As she said, unknowingly echoing West and Zimmerman (1987), when it came to parenting, she felt "accountable" to traditional practices and ideology.

These co-parents identified as fathers because their sense of themselves as masculine precluded using the mother label; for some, pressure from people they were close to also entered into the decision. With no language for the category of "not-mother-and-not-quite-father-either," they used the only other option language afforded: father. Their fit with the label was far from perfect, and all admitted to not knowing how to enact the fatherhood role with their children. Despite these problems, by adopting the father label, these women disrupt the prescription that "fathers are men," and thus their very presence in society as fathers helps deconstruct the edifice of the gender binary.

Mathers. Of 17 co-parents, six labeled themselves *mathers*. The term was born of an informal support group that had met for about a year before coining it. The group had begun with gatherings of a few friends meeting biweekly as a lesbian co-parent support group, and in short order acquaintances and friends joined. At the suggestion of one member, they advertised the group at a local LGBT center and on a LGBT Internet forum, and over the course of six months the group grew to about 15 people from across the region.

Interviewees clearly articulated the central problem discussed at these support group meetings: they felt like neither mothers nor fathers and lamented the lack of any other categorization. They sought a label mainly to assuage their pervasive worry about what their children would call them (see also Gabb 2005). Many had experimented with "mother" and "father" and were dissatisfied. Much meeting time was devoted to discussion of the various parental labels popular among lesbian parents, but the consensus was that none fit the bill. They sought a label their children could use publicly and privately and that the co-parents themselves felt good about. After a year of what they described as agonizing discussions, a group member suggested the *mather* term as a gender-bending, gender-blending hybridization of mother and father. . . .

Respondents saw the term as a flexible, dynamic word that captured a larger idea about parenting outside the rigid, gendered mother–father dichotomy, and each co-parent could mold the term as she saw fit.

The common experience seemed to be that once they had established a label, they could now more clearly flesh out their familial roles. Jan explained,

> I don't even know if there is anything a mather does that is really that different from what a mother or father does. Being a mather is more a way of thinking, like a way of dealing with feeling uncertain about what you are. . . . As a mather, I can tell my kid, "Hey, families don't have to have moms and dads. They can be whatever." And I don't have to just do "mom things" or "dad things." We do everything together. We talk, paint, wrestle, whatever. When you think of yourself as mom or dad, there are lots of things that go along with that. Like if you're mom then you do certain things, and dads do certain things. Being a mather, I feel like I can cross those lines

without penalties. Like I can play ball with my kid and wear my hat backwards, but I can also let myself be vulnerable.

Jan and others invoked fun (talk, paint, wrestle, play ball, wear backward caps, play, laugh) and conveyed a light heartedness that contrasts starkly to the anxiety pervading the group discussions that preceded the term's invention.

The term had a decidedly serious side as well: women who used it were adamant about deploying the term to promote social change. They wanted their children to call them mather, they introduced themselves as their child's mather, and they considered themselves pioneering agents of social change. . . .

Addison relished how using the term made her feel like a change agent:

> Being a mather feels like activism. I see lots of my gay friends feel like they have to choose. But my options are mom *or* dad, so "Hmm, which do I feel more like?" I get to bust out of those categories. I get to introduce myself to my daughter's teachers and say, "I'm Addison, Jillian's mather." Inevitably, after they get over their shock, they ask me what that means and I get to educate them! I feel like I will make it easier for other parents down the road who don't want to have to be mom or dad. Man, it's about social change.

All the co-parents, not just mathers, promoted social change by bucking strongly held norms, yet it is far easier and more fulfilling to do so with group backing. The contrast is sharp between the angst Lorraine and Addison attribute to their nonmather friends and the sense of empowerment they themselves felt. Some others described how the mather mentality transcended the parental role to affect their sense of self. According to Jan,

> Since I started thinking of myself as a mather, I have changed in lots of ways. I feel more free to express myself without thinking about gender. I stopped thinking about gender when I parent,

so I guess it makes sense it would happen in other areas of my life. For example, sometimes now I wear a tie and men's dress shoes to work. which I never would have done before. It's not because I want to be a man; it's because I have always liked the look and now I feel free to do it.

The mathers' stories compared to those of the other groups illustrate the power of language, social support, and a collective identity. The fathers and mothers faced the same challenge as the mathers—feeling like neither a mother nor father—but unlike them lacked a language to redefine themselves and their role. Having a language carved out an ideological space for mathers to redefine their family role, and the realization that they could exist outside the binary reduced their stress significantly. Mathers were the only group that sought validation from significant others outside the privatized home sphere, and by their accounts, the collective act of defiantly creating a new identity and seeking opportunities to educate others about it was empowering. Even so, it was no panacea, as evidenced by the mather sent into a "tailspin" by her doctor's accusation that her choice of label was harming the child. As for effecting social change, like the mothers and fathers, their presence is testimony to the possibility of alternatives to the heteronormative family, and the proliferation of such possibilities increases the likelihood of more appearing.

Discussion and Conclusion

An approach that assumes that because co-parents are women they seek to identify as mothers conceals the complexity of parental identity development for lesbian co-parents. Previous research on the identity struggles of women who parent in the face of a lack of biological ties to their children has focused on their experiences of becoming and being mothers and described such women as members of

"dual-mother families," or as "comothers," who negotiate "mothering experiences." This assumption of a link between female sex and mother identity has precluded asking how co-parents negotiate womanhood, intimate relationships, and social expectations to construct a *parental* identity that may be at variance with the mother identity.

These women faced both external and internal assaults on their sense of themselves as parents. The institutions and people they regularly encountered—play groups, schools, doctors, children's friends, and, perhaps most importantly, the law—explicitly challenged their parental identity claims. Most women faced anguished identity struggles because of these external assaults and because they felt like their lesbian parenting fit neither into the biologically inflected "mother" category nor into the father category, the only other possibility the language offers in a binary gender system. Mathers seemed to have had the most successful resolution of the internal dilemma, but they too paid an emotional toll from facing the constant external challenges from people and institutions unwilling to recognize their consciously blended roles and identities.

What do these results imply for the goal of destabilizing gendered arrangements (Lorber 2005)? On one hand, they confirm the continuing hold on the public and private imagination exerted by the "motherhood institution" (Bernard 1974; Rich 1977). As an institution, motherhood still grants and withholds the material, institutional, and cultural supports that make child rearing easy or difficult (Bernard 1974; Chase and Rogers 2001; Rich 1977). It still shapes what mothers do and how they feel about it, and it privileges women who fit cultural notions about appropriate characteristics of mothers and disfranchises those who do not. As long as rigid prescriptions for gendered behavior are inscribed in the institution—especially when they are backed by law—members of excluded groups will remain in identity limbo. Thus, while planned lesbian families have the potential to help decenter the gender- and power-laden heterosexual nuclear family (e.g., Dalton and Bielby 2000; Weston 1991), this study illustrates that the task is not easy. On the other hand, there is a positive conclusion to be drawn as well. Social change is propelled forward by people, like these lesbian parents, who refuse to live lives consonant with the given order. The mothers were transgressive by embodying a two-mother family, the fathers disrupted the prescription that "fathers are men," and the mathers generated a new family role and included education about it as part of their mission. These women's transgression of the gender binary makes further transgressions more likely and makes a utopian vision of a non-heteronormative family less distant.

The findings point to the necessity of continuing the civil rights struggle, and lesbian parents need not stand alone in the larger struggle to break down parenting ideology and laws. They have common cause with other groups who also suffer from the exclusivity of the good mother category and thus have a stake in degendering the mothering institution. . . .

REFERENCES

Abramovitz, Mimi. 1996. *Regulating the lives of women: Social welfare policy from colonial times to present*. Boston: South End.

Aizley, Harlyn. 2006. *Confessions of the other mother: Non-biological mothers tell all*. Boston: Beacon.

Arendell, Terry. 2000. Conceiving and investigating motherhood: The decade's scholarship. *Journal of Marriage and Family* 62:1192–1207.

Bernard, Jessie. 1974. *The future of motherhood*. New York: Dial Press.

Chase, Susan E., and Mary F. Rogers. 2001. *Mothers and children: Feminist analyses and personal narratives*. New Brunswick, NJ: Rutgers University Press.

Chodorow, Nancy. 1989. *Feminism and psychoanalytic theory*. New Haven, CT: Yale University Press.

Dalton, S., and D. Bielby. 2000. That's our kind of constellation: Lesbian mothers negotiate institutionalized understandings of gender within the family. *Gender & Society* 14:36–61.

Deutsch, Francine M. 2007. Undoing gender. *Gender & Society* 21:106–27.

DiLapi, E. M. 1989. Lesbian mothers and the motherhood hierarchy. *Journal of Homosexuality* 18:101–21.

Dunne, Gillian. 2000. Opting into motherhood: Lesbians blurring the boundaries and transforming the meanings of parenthood and kinship. *Gender & Society* 14:11–35.

Fineman, Martha. 1995. *The neutered mother, the sexual family, and other twentieth century tragedies*. New York: Routledge.

Gabb, Jacqui. 2005. Lesbian motherhood: Strategies of familial-linguistic management in lesbian parent families. *Sociology* 39:385–603.

Glenn, Evelyn N. 1994. Social constructions of mothering: A thematic overview. In *Mothering: Ideology experience, agency*, edited by E. N. Glenn, G. Chang, and L. R. Forcey. New York: Routledge.

Hequembourg, A. 2007. *Lesbian motherhood: Stories of becoming*. Binghamton. NY: Hawthorne Press.

Hequembourg, A., and M. Farrell. 1999. Lesbian motherhood: Negotiating marginal-mainstream identities. *Gender & Society* 13:540–57.

Human Rights Campaign. 2010. Parenting laws: Second-Parent Adoption. http://www.hrc.org/documents/parenting_laws_maps.pdf (accessed 19 December 2010).

Katz Rothman, B. 2006. Adoption and the culture of genetic determinism. In *Adoptive families in a diverse society*, edited by K. Wegar. New Brunswick, NJ: Rutgers University Press.

Lewin, Ellen. 1993. *Lesbian mothers*. Ithaca, NY: Cornell University Press.

Lorber, Judith. 2000. Using gender to undo gender. *Feminist Theory* 1:75–95.

Lorber, Judith. 2005. *Breaking the bowls: Degendering and feminist change*. New York: Norton.

Mason, M. A., S. Hanison-Jay, G. M. Svare, and N. H. Wolfinger. 2002. Stepparents: De-facto parents or legal strangers? *Journal of Family Issues* 23:507–22.

Miall, C. E., and K. March. 2006. Adoption and public opinion: Implications for social policy and practice in adoption. In *Adoptive families in a diverse society*, edited by K. Wegar New Brunswick, NJ: Rutgers University Press.

Rich, Adrienne. 1977. *Of woman born: Motherhood as experience and institution*. New York: Bantam.

Richey, Warren. 2010. Florida ban on gay adoption unconstitutional, court declares, *Christian Science Monitor*, 23 September. www.csmonitor .com/USA/Justice/2010/0923/Florida-ban-on-gay-adoption-unconstitutional-court-rules (accessed 8 January 2011).

Roberts, Dorothy. 1997. *Killing the Black body: Race, reproduction and the meaning of liberty*. New York: Pantheon.

Schwalbe, Michael L., and Douglas Mason-Schrock. 1996. Identity work as group process. *Advances in Group Processes* 13:113–47.

Stacey, Judith. 1998. *Brave new families: Stories of domestic upheaval in late twentieth century America*. Berkeley: University of California Press.

Stacey, Judith, and Timothy J. Biblarz. 2001. (How) does the sexual orientation of parents matter? *American Sociological Review* 66:159–83.

Sullivan, Maureen. 2004. *The family of woman*. Berkeley: University of California Press.

Thompson, Julie. 2002. *Mommy queerest*. Amherst: University of Massachusetts Press.

Thorne, Barrie. 1993. Feminism and the family: Two decades of thought. In *Rethinking the family: Some feminist questions*, 2nd ed., edited by B. Thorne and M. Yalom. New York: Longman.

West, Candace, and Don H. Zimmerman. 1987. Doing gender. *Gender & Society* 1:121–51.

Weston, Kath. 1991. *Families we choose: Lesbians, gays, kinship*. New York: Columbia University Press.

Introduction to Reading 40

In this reading, Carla Shows and Naomi Gerstel suggest that social contexts and the conditions of work as they are linked to social class can have a powerful impact on the choices men make in parenting. The authors compare the "public fatherhood" of physicians to the more "private fatherhood" of EMTs, examining how work conditions and work culture impact these men's choices for fatherhood. The data they use in this reading are from a larger study (Study of Work Hours and Schedules), which includes surveys, observations at nine work sites, and intensive interviews with 13 physicians and 18 EMTs (emergency medical technicians) in the northeastern part of the United States. This research helps explain the results of other studies, which find that working-class fathers are much more involved in their children's lives than professional fathers, and helps us understand how social class shapes gendered relationships in families.

1. What do the authors mean by "public" and "private" fatherhood?

2. What social factors are related to their finding that fathers in working-class homes are more involved parents? How do these factors challenge traditional gendered expectations for men and women and facilitate gender change?

3. What could workplaces do to encourage more involved parenting for all workers?

FATHERING, CLASS, AND GENDER

A COMPARISON OF PHYSICIANS AND EMERGENCY MEDICAL TECHNICIANS

Carla Shows and Naomi Gerstel

A large and growing literature documents recent changes and growing variation in the relationship of gender, paid work, and parenting. Although most of this research focuses on the range of women's experiences, some suggests that most men still emphasize employment as central to their practice of fatherhood (Lamb 1995; Orloff and Monson 2002; Townsend 2002), leaving far more of the parenting and daily caregiving to mothers (Casper and Bianchi 2002; Craig 2006). Few studies, however, focus on the varied experiences of men to examine how employment shapes fatherhood (Astone et al. forthcoming), fewer explore how parenting shapes men's employment (Lundberg and Rose 2000), and almost none compare fathers in different class positions.

This article examines the relationship between class and fatherhood. We compare two groups of fathers, one in a professional occupation and the other in a nonprofessional occupation; we argue that these map broadly onto two class locations— one upper middle class (physicians) and the other working class (emergency medical technicians, or EMTs). We first compare these men's class-linked practices of fatherhood and, second, argue that their ways of doing fatherhood entail enactments of distinctive masculinities, based in the dynamics of their occupational and familial relations, which have consequences for doing (or undoing) gender.

To address the first issue, we argue that these two groups of men practice different types of fathering—with physicians emphasizing "public fatherhood" and EMTs performing not only public fatherhood but also participating in the daily routines of "private fatherhood." Second, we suggest these different fathering practices can be explained by the contrasting employment conditions of each group and the gendered character of their families, especially their wives' involvement in the labor market and parenting. . . .

FATHERHOOD, MASCULINITY, AND CLASS

Much recent work on the relationship of masculinity to the practice of paid work and domestic life (Coltrane and Adams 2001; Cooper 2000; Townsend 2002) draws on the now classic theoretical formulation of Connell (1992, 1995). Developing the concept of "hegemonic masculinity," she argues that much older literature used a categorical model of gender that treated men as an undifferentiated group, but contemporary research documents a considerable range of masculinities. While prior scholarship tended to conflate sex and gender, Connell offers a counterview; she suggests diverse masculinities can be traced to the "social dynamics generated within gender relations" (1992, 735) and through other structures that vary across social locations. In fact, class is a social location Connell emphasizes, although she criticizes work on masculinity for being "class-bound" (1992, 735). Further, Connell and others (e.g., Brines 1994; Griswold 1993; Kimmel 2000, 2006) suggest that men's involvement in gender relations at

From Shows, Carla and Gerstel, Naomi, "Fathering, Class, and Gender: A Comparison of Physicians and Emergency Medical Technicians," *Gender & Society,* 23(2), pp. 161–187. Copyright © 2009. Published by SAGE Publications on behalf of Sociologists for Women in Society.

home, especially parenting, provide an important locus of institutionalized inequality and significant site for the (re)construction and expression of various masculinities.

Researchers suggest that the way men combine family and paid work now entails two models of masculinity: (1) the still dominant "neotraditional model of masculinity" (Gerson 2007) in which men put their job prospects (or breadwinning) first but rely on their partners for daily care of children; and (2) an alternate, more egalitarian, model of a "newly constituted masculinity" (Cooper 2002), which entails substantial sharing in the daily care of children in addition to market work (see also Dowd 2000; Townsend 2002).

Some research looks at the relationship of social class to the two models of masculinity. Much quantitative research, especially time-use studies, examines the number of hours men spend with their children; summarizing this literature, Pleck and Masciadrelli (2004, 238) conclude there is "no consistent relationship between paternal involvement and socioeconomic variables." Recent qualitative work on fathering, however, finds some differences by class.

For working-class men, some studies suggest the priority of the breadwinner model, showing that working-class men feel that their masculinity is threatened when they cannot enact the primary breadwinner model of fatherhood (Gerson 1993). Williams (2000), however, indicates that a disjuncture exists between this ideology and the practice of fatherhood, especially for working-class men whose ability to fulfill the primary breadwinner role is waning. Indeed, Pyke (1996) finds that some working-class men emphasize a hypermasculine provider role while sharing in family work. Using longitudinal English data, Sullivan (2006) shows that men assumed more responsibility for family work if they were employed in working-class (manual or clerical) jobs. Deutsch (1999) similarly finds that, among the alternative-shift working-class couples she studied, men did much of the work of parenting even while insisting that their wives were the primary parents.

Research on middle-class fathers finds a contrasting pattern. A number of qualitative studies suggest that such fathers, especially professionals or the "educational elite," espouse some version of egalitarian parenthood (Cooper 2000; Deutsch 1999; LaRossa 1997; Risman 1998). Yet researchers suggest that middle-class fathers do not enact these ideals (Griswold 1993; LaRossa 1997) due to employment constraints as well as the culture of masculinity in which they believe (Coltrane 2004; Cooper 2000; Pyke 1996). Coltrane (2004) argues that whereas managerial and professional couples were the most likely to share family work in the 1970s and 1980s, by the 1990s and 2000s most sharing occurred in the working-class.

Not only does the level of paternal involvement vary by class, but the type of engagement varies as well. Coltrane and Adams (2001) find that if men participate in "enrichment" or leisure activities with children, they are less likely to do daily chores such as cooking and cleaning. Lareau (2002, 749) ties this variation in type of engagement to class. She shows that middle-class parents were much more likely to participate in organized leisure activities with their children than working-class families, who tend to have "more free time and deeper, richer ties with their extended families." As this quotation suggests, one important aspect of Lareau's (2003) work is that she does not simply focus on the nuclear family but widens her lens to include extended kin. Her work suggests that there is class variation in these ties—with working-class parents significantly more likely than those in the middle-class to rely on relatives for help with children (for review, see Gerstel and Sarkisian 2008). These ties shape the demands on both fathers and mothers. Although these studies provide important leads for comparing working-class to middle-class fathers, few have made these explicit comparisons.

WORK HOURS, SCHEDULES, AND FAMILIES

The total hours of household employment have climbed because of women's increased work hours (Jacobs and Gerson 2004). This is particularly true for parents: Paid working time has increased dramatically for mothers since 1970 (Bluestone and Rose 2000), and the sum of estimated annual hours worked by U.S. mothers and fathers is higher than those of parents in any other country (Bianchi, Robinson, and Milkie 2006). Gender is essential to understanding these hours. On one hand, some research suggests that men do more routine child care when they are employed fewer hours (Coltrane 2000). On the other, while mothers tend to cut back their hours of employment, research suggests that fathers increase their work hours after the birth of a child (e.g., Jacobs and Gerson 2004; for exception, see Astone et al. 2010). Importantly, class influences hours and schedules, with professionals working longer workweeks than other occupational groups (Jacobs and Gerson 2004) and the working-class more likely to alternate shifts (Presser 2003). Although longer workweeks decrease fathers' participation in family work, alternative schedules increase it (Barnett and Gareis 2002; Deutsch 1999; Presser 2003). This suggests a bifurcation of job hours and schedules by class.

GENDER WITHIN FAMILIES: FATHERING AND MOTHERING

As Connell (1992, 1995) argues, the organization of gender relations is central to the practice of masculinity. When employed, wives challenge the neotraditional model of masculinity, or as Griswold (1993, 220) puts it, "Women's [paid] work, in short, has destroyed the old assumptions about fatherhood and required new negotiations of gender relations." Research has shown that fathers are likely to be somewhat more involved in parenting when their wives are employed. Moreover, fathers' child care and work time correlates with the employment schedules of mothers (Bianchi, Robinson, and Milkie 2006; Brayfield 1995). Coltrane (2000) argues that the employment schedules of wives and husbands are perhaps the most consistent and important predictors of domestic sharing that researchers have documented. Furthermore, researchers find

that when wives have higher relative earnings, or when the gap between husbands' and wives' earnings is lower, the gendered gap in the division of domestic labor is reduced (Cooke 2007).

Although we might expect the influence of mothers on fathers to vary by class, little literature examines this connection. In one important study of equal parenting, Deutsch (1999) finds that mothers influence fathers' participation by either fighting for more equal participation (especially in the middle class) or by using alternate schedules (especially in the working class). Other research shows that among the affluent, wives not only develop an ideology of intensive mothering but also sometimes make the decision to withdraw from the labor force to concentrate on mothering; this frees fathers to focus on breadwinning (e.g., see Blair-Loy 2003). For working-class wives, it is much more difficult to "opt out" (Boushey 2005; Kuperberg and Stone 2008). Indeed, as Stone (2007) argues, opting out is often dependent on the earnings of highly paid husbands. Extending these findings, one of the arguments we make in this article is that wives influence fathers' involvement in parenting but do so in ways that vary dramatically by class.

* * *

PHYSICIANS AND PUBLIC FATHERING: "BEING THERE"

Physicians tended to highlight participation in or presence at their children's public events as the way they were involved in their children's lives. Even with their long hours or hectic schedules, physicians emphasized their concerted attempts to attend those activities. Sometimes this kind of paternal involvement required creativity in scheduling:

> I coached [my son's] soccer, and the way I coached his soccer was I would book two hours in my afternoon and I would not have patients there, and I would go to [town] and coach his practice and do the work, bring him home and then go back to work, and then work 'til 9:00.

As this father's comment suggests, doctors let their children influence their schedules because they can; when they choose to do so, they exert significant control over their schedules. Physicians engage in other public activities with their children as well. When we were observing in his office, a surgeon showed us—with pride—his phone's screen with a photo of his daughter dressed for Halloween, saying she was going trick-or-treating with him. But during our interview with this physician, he barely mentioned his daughter, suggesting her daily care was his wife's domain.

"Being there" for public events was important to these physicians. Yet even when they were able to leave the office to attend their children's events, work sometimes followed. One physician had a $3,000 car phone installed so that he could return phone calls while watching his children. . . .

Though able to be physically present at the game, his attention was divided between his family and his work. Yet to him, being at the game was what mattered. He is demonstrating, possibly to himself, his child, and the community, that he cares as a father. In some sense, the very difficulty of his being there makes this demonstration all the more dramatic.

Through their participation in these activities, the doctors are publicly "doing fatherhood." This performance of gender and fatherhood entails signs of "*paternal* visibility" (Coltrane 1996; West and Zimmerman 1987) to their children and the wider community. Moreover, like the men Townsend (2002) studied, a large part of what it means to them to be a father is to be a provider. Many of these physicians adopted a neotraditional model of masculinity (Gerson 2007)—one suggesting that what it means to be a good father is to be a good breadwinner and provide financially. This is reinforced by the income associated with class position: Participation in public activities often requires a significant financial outlay. How do we explain such public fathering? To answer that question, we first look at the physicians' jobs and then turn to their family lives.

THE DEMANDS OF PHYSICIANS' PAID WORK

In the survey, physicians reported working an average of 50 hours per week. However, these hours are underestimates. As became clear in the intensive interviews, many physicians did not include nondirect patient care or off-hours work in response to survey questions asking how many hours they work. They did not report activities such as checking work-related e-mail, participating in hospital committees, staying current in medical literature (often required for recertification), or being on-call; including these activities often led to estimates of 60 or more hours per week.

While much work entailed direct patient care, paperwork—documenting patients' visits and illnesses, preparing material for insurance companies, making referrals—kept physicians at their desks in the evenings, well after their patients went home. Most said that paperwork could easily take an extra two or three hours per day. We observed a number of them eating lunch on the run, coming in early and staying until 7:00 or 8:00 p.m., even if they finished patient care by 5:00. Sitting at their desks, they completed necessary documentation for patient records, referrals, and "most of all for insurance companies." Several said that since their office had "gone electronic," they would often go to their home computers in the evening to enter patient data they "just had not gotten to during the day." These were hours when their families were likely available or in need of routine care.

Being available to patients was important to many physicians and often meant being on-call. While physicians could sometimes rotate their on-call status with their colleagues, their turn often interrupted their home lives. One hospital physician described being on-call in this way: "I mean, you can't do anything; you're basically . . . it's like a full day of work." Or as another doctor put it, "You're always aware your beeper is there and could go off at any time; you can't just relax." Importantly, much of this work occurred before or after shifts or during weekends—that is, at key moments when family members are likely to be home.

To explain their long hours, physicians talked about a number of causes. They emphasized the hours and schedules of medical school and residency that helped socialize them to their current long hours. . . . Many years in school, long hours studying and in residency, and hundreds of thousands of dollars for training push physicians toward intense career commitment. As one physician succinctly said, "There was just no time for anything else."

* * *

[D]octors learn that respect—especially as men physicians—is related to extremely long hours on the job, which means fewer hours at home. Later in the interview, [one doctor] commented that he felt sad that he could not spend more time at home having dinner with his family or putting his children to bed. But his version of fatherhood and masculinity, which he learned in part from the "hazing" in medical school and from the hierarchy in medicine, requires long hours on the job rather than a schedule with fewer hours and more direct family involvement.

Physicians also talked about a sense of obligation to be available to their patients. A private practice physician explained, "I mean, if you take care of people it's really . . . you're at their mercy and not yours. People don't choose when they get sick, and you have to take care of them when they're sick." Although they sometimes tried, physicians found it difficult to "hand off" patients to others—either because of patient insistence and "loyalty" to them or because of a special skill and relationship with that particular patient. . . .

Money—to pay back medical school debt, to maintain a particular style of life and consumption—also kept them on the job. Earning income was essential to understanding themselves as physicians, men, and fathers. Indeed, public fatherhood required a significant income. One physician said, "If I wanted to see less patients I would see less patients. The problem is your income takes a hit. And there's so many things taking a hit on your income anyway."

One doctor who worked 60 hours a week reported, "We don't have an extravagant lifestyle by any means, but I am afraid we have gotten used to a particular way of living. I have to work the hours I do to get what we now think we need." At a meeting in which emergency room doctors were arranging shifts for November and December, one doctor said he did not want to work on Christmas. The ER director reminded this younger doctor that he and his wife wanted a new kitchen and, with a smile, indicated it was the young doctor's obligation to provide the domestic accoutrements they desired. The young doctor agreed to come Christmas day. Overall, then, training, paperwork, obligation to patients, the medical hierarchy, desire for respect as men, and the particular style of life that their breadwinning could provide kept these doctors on the job and away from the daily routines of their families.

THE DEMANDS OF FAMILY: THE ROLE OF PHYSICIANS' WIVES

The ways doctors organized gender relations at home made it possible to work the long hours they did. As the survey showed, physician fathers were likely to have either stay-at-home wives or part-time employed wives (43 percent of physicians had employed wives compared to 86 percent of EMTs; physicians' employed wives also worked far fewer hours: an average of 13 hours compared to 30 for the employed EMT wives). With an occasional exception, the physicians' wives chose jobs that were less demanding or allowed them to work part-time so they could be available for their families; these choices also allowed their husbands to spend long hours on the job. Some doctors said that they sometimes relied on "nannies" or "au pairs" to help with child care and that this allowed their wives to pursue their own careers. Yet even with such paid child care, many physicians relied primarily on their wives to provide daily and routine parenting. One physician's wife, a physician herself, worked part-time so their children could have a parent who was "more available."

Though this father perceives himself to be equally involved, he admitted,

> Quite honestly, on a day-to-day basis, kids need mom more than they need dad, and I honestly think that's true. . . . I don't know whether . . . it's not meant to be a sexist statement or anything like that, but we both share in the house . . . I mean I'll do stuff for the kids just as much as she will, just not as frequently.

This physician's comment entails seemingly contradictory assertions. He views his participation as "just as much" as his wife but "just not as frequent." Thus, the unequal practices entailed in public fathering were sometimes invisible to the physicians. Struggling with an involved father ideology in the context of their demanding work, they often feel unable to reduce job demands to participate in routine daily child care. In doing so, they reinforce the gender order rather than contest it.

Physicians often seemed at a loss when asked whether they took off time to care for their sick children. When asked if he ever stayed home with his kids when they were sick, a doctor explained why his wife typically stayed home with them. . . .

[T]his physician felt very pressed by his obligation to care for his patients, an obligation that took precedence over staying home with his children when they were sick. The structure of his job and family life led him to organize his time so that he took care of patients and his wife took care of their kids.

Leaving most of the care of the children to their wives was not an easy bargain for the physicians. While a minority of EMTs (about one-third) had a family member who wanted them to reduce their hours, more than half of the physician fathers reported the same ($\chi^2 = 9.42$; $p < .05$). Occasionally a doctor would emphasize the loss and pain that this sort of parenting entailed. Tears rolled down the cheek of one doctor as he described his need to be in the hospital while his wife was bathing and putting their children to bed.

Even among the doctors, there was some heterogeneity: A very small minority reported reducing hours or shifts in response to their wives' pleas. One doctor who divided his time between patients and research told us he shortened his workday at his wife's insistence: "My wife said I needed to [come home], essentially, and I agreed with her. I didn't have the insight to see the impact of what not being home was having on people." The chief physician at a large medical center said that he tried to come home "by 7:00" at the request of his wife. He told us about their conversations, centering on her telling him to restrict work and "to come home at a certain hour." Gesturing toward the piles of paper on his desk, he remarked that it was often difficult to get home for dinner, especially with the paperwork that piled up by the end of the day. But he tried. Among the male physicians, however, these two were exceptional.

EMTs are very different from physicians. Their fathering routinely emphasized private fathering and more intensive involvement in caregiving. This difference can be explained by the structure of their paid work as well as gendered relations at home.

EMTs AND PRIVATE FATHERING: "STEALING TIME"

While the physician fathers were likely to do what they could to attend public events with their children, EMT fathers were much more likely to participate in the daily care of their kids. The EMTs emphasized private fathering in ways that the physicians did not. They talked about routine involvement in the lives of their children—picking them up from day care or school, feeding them dinner, or staying home with them when they got sick. One stated,

> My son's out of school at 2:30 in the afternoon. That means that I have to leave here about 2:15 to make sure I'm at the school to pick him up.

Another remarked,

Last year I took three out of my five sick days to stay home when one of the smaller ones was sick. So I'll use them more for that than for anything else.

One went further and put it succinctly:

I will totally refuse the overtime. Family comes first for me.

To explain their fathering, we turn first to their jobs and then to their homes.

THE DEMANDS OF EMTs' PAID WORK

In the survey, EMT fathers reported working an average of 45 hours per week, but EMTs worked closer to 60 hours when including the hours devoted to second jobs. More than two-thirds of the EMT fathers reported having a second job; only 9 percent of the doctors did. In their second jobs, however, many EMTs worked per diem, which allowed them to choose if and when to work. Moreover, when the EMTs went home, they left their jobs behind: They did not have paperwork, nor were they on call. Thus, it is not primarily the number of hours that explains the differences in parenting. Although they resembled the physicians in long, often exhausting hours, the boundaries between work and family were much clearer for EMTs.

Even more than the number of hours, the shifts they work are consequential for their family lives. Many of the EMT fathers in our study work rotating shifts, nights, weekend, and holidays, and in some sense, they had little control over these schedules. At the beginning of each year, management handed them a booklet with their shifts for the next 12 months. Compared to physicians, EMTs were much more likely to report working two or more weekends in the previous 30 days (almost all of the EMT fathers compared to only half of the physicians). But EMTs were able to leave at the conclusion of their shifts, while physicians stayed after their shifts ended. Moreover, unlike physicians who were often unavailable to their families during key hours of their days, EMTs often worked during the hours that their families were sleeping.

In addition to the structure of shifts, relations with coworkers were important in shaping the way these two groups of men organized fatherhood. In contrast to the physicians, EMTs used swaps to create flexibility in their seemingly inflexible, nonstandard schedules. Often with the support of management, EMTs would switch shifts with another EMT or cover for each other for a few hours. Swaps were a useful means of acquiring "off" time without using their limited vacation or sick days. These exchanges were used in response to family needs; the EMTs in some sense "stole" time to be available for family. One EMT often asked someone to cover for him for a few hours at the end or beginning of his shifts so that he could attend his teenage sons' sporting events. Swaps were not just used to attend athletic events. Others would swap when they had to take their kids to medical appointments or pick them up from school. Some of the older or childless EMT men covered for those with younger children. As EMTs highlighted, reciprocity—utilized over the short as well as the long term—was key to swapping, even for a few hours. One EMT had often been on the receiving end of swaps; now that his daughter is older, he happily returns the favor, saying his daughter "is just older and it's nice to have that flexibility to give back to other people that was given to you, to be able to do things like that. I don't mind doing it."

While both occupations offer round-the-clock services, the doctors have to be personally available because one doctor is often not a suitable substitute for another (due to specialized skills or a special relationship with a patient). In contrast, EMTs' skill levels, work requirements, and relationships to patients were more similar to one another; because they were interchangeable, they could practice such "swaps," collectively making possible more daily sharing of fatherhood.

Income played an important role as well, but one that depended on the father's orientation to consumption as well as family demands.

In contrast to physicians, overtime (with time-and-a-half pay) is financially important for EMTs. Due to their small staff, overtime was a significant part of the fire department's ability to function; they relied on a callback system to remain fully staffed at all times. Thus, EMTs were "called back" to the station when the ambulance went out to answer a call. Returning to work could generate a lot of overtime pay for those who answered callbacks, but it was voluntary, and the EMT fathers consciously limited their overtime. The key to this decision was often their sense that they needed to participate in the labor of the home. . . .

While physicians considered the time-money trade-off very carefully, and a few said they would give up some time and reduce their incomes, EMTs—who made considerably less money—routinely turned down overtime in exchange for time with their families. This is not to say that the EMT fathers were always happy to give up the overtime. Many refused it because they were solely responsible for their children at the time they received the call to come in for overtime. In these decisions, EMTs discussed both their worries about pay and their guilt in having to "choose" between spending time with their families and going to work. For one EMT father, the guilt he feels results from wanting or needing to go in for financial reasons but also believing his daughters are "only this age once" and "entitled to their father." . . .

In the interviews, differences between physicians and EMTs in the importance of training also became clear. While the latter were dedicated to patient care, they were not trained in a schema that routinely prioritized work over all other areas of life.

Demands of Family: The Role of Wives and Extended Kin

Differences in their wives' employment and responses to their husbands' employment were critical to understanding the different styles of fathering. According to the survey data, a large majority (86 percent) of EMT wives were employed, whereas fewer than half of the physicians' wives had jobs. Moreover, EMT wives contributed much more to the family income: The gap between mothers' and fathers' mean income was significantly smaller in the EMT families ($32,000) than in the physicians' families ($177,000) ($t = 4.69$, $p < .00$). EMTs' wives who worked for pay, worked substantially more hours than the physicians' wives. Thus, the wives' work hours in concert with explicit demands on their husbands' schedules shaped how much time the men devoted to work and how much they devoted to family.

Like other working-class men, many of the EMT fathers alternated shifts with their wives. But the difference did not simply reside in the structure of jobs. After their children were born, EMTs' wives often insisted that their husbands alternate shifts as well as reduce their paid work hours so they could contribute to daily family care. Their wives had, and used, their power in the relationships. Wives played a key role in callback responses because of their own work schedules and because they wanted (and often insisted) their husbands to be home. An EMT father of two young girls reported that he loves working on the ambulance and would like to answer more callbacks but has learned to accept his wife's signals about accepting overtime. . . .

The wives' influence ranged from subtle signals to outright demands. One EMT kept his pager off and his cell phone on silent at night because his wife told him that callbacks interrupt her sleep and she did not like him going in at night. In another exchange, while eating lunch in the fire station, one EMT responded to the question, "Do your families ever ask you to not come in?" by laughing and saying, "No, they tell you: You're not going in." The other EMTs sitting around joined in the laughter and nodded in agreement.

To be sure, given the demands of two jobs in these families, the EMTs and their wives often had to rely on other people to help take care of their children. Unlike the physicians, however, they often relied on extended family rather than paid child care. One EMT said that he had "definitely roped in" his mother or brother with last-minute child care dilemmas. When another EMT was unable to pick up his son from school on his two daytime shifts, his mother would be there. They relied on kin care because they trusted their relatives and found such help less expensive and more flexible than hired help.

Importantly, EMT fathers did not manipulate their schedules begrudgingly. Like many of the working-class fathers in Francine Deutsch's (1999) study, many of the EMTs seemed happy with their schedules because they allowed the EMTs to participate in childcare. While most of the fathers reported being happy with their current schedules (91 percent) on the survey, it was in the interviews that the EMTs discussed their families as a key reason for that happiness. As one remarked, "I love the fact that I can be home with my kids a lot, because it's long hours at times, but honestly, I get four days off in a row with my kids. How many people get that much?" These working-class men exhibit a model of masculinity—based both at home and on the job—that provides valued involvement in their children's daily lives.

CONCLUSION: PUBLIC AND PRIVATE FATHERS

Much has been written about the way gender shapes participation in family and work, but much of that literature focuses on women. In contrast, we focus on men and the ways that their class location shapes gender, family, and work. We argue that class shapes the gendered relations and processes rooted in jobs and the domestic division of labor, which in turn shape the ways men behave as fathers. Illustrating that masculinity is neither unitary nor homogeneous, our findings emphasize the "multiple masculinities—some subordinate, some dominant—which are created by differences in . . . class and occupation" (Cooper 2000, 7). Class locations are major contributors to the construction of masculinities because of their role in shaping fatherhood.

Class location sometimes sustains but sometimes refashions the gender order (and the social relations constituting it). Our data accords with the few qualitative pieces that suggest that fathers who are least likely to ideologically endorse gender equality (the working-class) are the most likely to engage in equitable actions (e.g., Deutsch 1999; Pyke 1996; Williams 2000). . . .

By comparing these two groups of men, we can specify the particular class-based strategies and conditions found in both jobs and families that contribute to variations in masculinity, the gender order, and fatherhood. Numerous aspects of their jobs were important in shaping the way EMTs practiced fatherhood. While physicians spent long hours on one job, EMTs often worked more than one job and used alternative schedules (a difference found by others in comparisons of the working and middle class; for example, see Presser 2003). In addition, as Acker (2006, 449) suggests in her discussion of class, lower-level jobs tend to have less scheduling flexibility than professionals, but she also notes that these differences are "created and renewed through organizational practices . . . and are also reproduced in everyday interactions." Indeed, in some sense, while the doctors could exert a fair amount of control over their schedules, the EMTs had little control over their rigid schedules, which they received from management a year in advance. But the EMTs could alter these obligations by relying on their relationships with other men at work: These fathers could turn to coworkers for swaps because of the skill similarity and the tight bonds they formed on the job. This helped them create flexibility in their job schedules. Despite the fact that many workplaces tend to be unresponsive to family demands, and though emergency medical services has typically been seen as a hypermasculine culture (Chetkovich 1997), the EMTs in our study managed to create workplaces responsive to the responsibilities associated with working-class fatherhood.

Not just their jobs were important; their gender relations at home—also similar in a number of ways to other working-class men—mattered as well. They did not only rely on extended kin for help in fathering; EMTs were responsive to their wives' and their children's needs when accepting or declining overtime. Some of them turned down promotions or found new jobs in response to their families. They struggled with these decisions and were often strongly influenced by their wives. Their wives' employment—their hours, shifts, pay—typically shaped the involvement of the EMT fathers as they were more likely to swap alternative schedules with their wives. And as Deutsch (1999) reports as characteristic of other working-class men, their wives' agency also affected their fatherhood: EMT wives often insisted their husbands be available. Although subject to the power and control of others both on the job and at home, many of these fathers appreciated their jobs and families because they allowed daily involvement with their children. Most EMT fathers not only related the requirements but also the pleasures of private fathering. We did not hear protests from them about threats to their masculinity. Perhaps this is because they work in highly masculine jobs and do not need to use family relations to shore up their identity as men. Whatever the cause, these working-class men are "undoing gender" in their interactions at home. These analyses respond to Deutsch's (2007, 127) clarion call to examine when and how interactions become less gendered, for, as she writes, "Gendered institutions can be changed, and the social interactions that support them can be undone."

Physicians, on the other hand, participated less in the daily care of their children. Without much resistance from physicians, their organizations continued to practice as "inequality regimes" (Acker 2006), less responsive to the daily needs of these men's families. With gendered subjectivities, most physicians were silent in the face of conflicts between work and parenting. Though they had some control over their hours, the physicians talked of time constraints. They could change an appointment (as they sometimes did to attend a child's game) or trade money for more time with their children (as a few did). But for a variety of reasons ranging from the identities they formed in residency to

intense patient demands to consumption patterns, most did not do so. In addition, physicians earn significantly more money than EMTs; this made it easier to pay for the kind of public activities entailed in "concerted cultivation" that Lareau (2003) finds at the center of parenting in middle-class families. But it was not just the characteristics of jobs and organizations that made such inequalities in parenting possible: The physicians' wives rarely insisted that they share more fully in the daily hands-on care of their children. Whether because of their own ideological attachment to the importance of their husbands' career or the pleasure gained in the lifestyle it allowed or for a combination of these and other reasons, the physicians' wives were much less likely to make demands on their husbands' time. Moreover, when the wives had jobs, these families paid for child care. Their bargain entails exchange: relatively high income (and perhaps prestige) garnered by the fathers in exchange for the mothers' (and "her" helpers') family care. Because of the conditions and relations located both in paid work and families, the physicians can perform public fathering.

Public fathering demands less time than private fathering, but it is more visible. Garey (1999) argues that nurses often choose night shifts so that their mothering, which occurs during the day, is visible to the community. In a similar vein, these doctors choose a kind of fathering that gives them visibility and likely garnishes praise from community members (whose support their medical practices are dependent upon; Fowlkes 1980).

There is another implication of this paternal visibility: As Hochschild (1989/2003) argued, when families see other families sharing housework, that may help revise the gendered norms of domestic life. This creates a paradox: At the same time as this type of fathering sustains gender inequality within families, its visibility may contribute to the appearance of norms of gender equality to outsiders who observe them.

We have argued here that for these two groups of men, class shapes fathering. We do not, however, mean to argue that physicians represent all middle-class professionals or that EMTs represent all working-class men. There is too much variation across class to make such an argument. In some sense, the findings we report here are most clearly occupational and organizational differences—important components of class but not the only ones. Given the size and character of our sample, we cannot specify the effects of these particular occupational differences, nor can we generalize to other professional groups (like lawyers or academics) or other working-class groups (like factory workers or janitors). In addition, the limits of our sample restrict our ability to generalize to different types of families that may occur even within each of these two groups.

REFERENCES

Acker, Joan. 2006. Inequality regimes: Gender, class and race in organizations. *Gender & Society* 20:441–64.

Astone, Nan Marie, Jacinda Dariotis, Freya Sonenstein, Joseph Pleck, and Kathryn Hynes. 2010. 31: 3–13. How do men's work lives change after fatherhood? *Journal of Family and Economic Issues*.

Barnett, Rosalind Chait, and Karen C. Gareis. 2002. Full time and reduced hours work schedules and marital quality: A study of female physicians with young children. *Work & Occupations* 29:364–79.

Bianchi, Suzanne M., John P. Robinson, and Melissa A. Milkie. 2006. *Changing rhythms of American life*. New York: Russell Sage Foundation.

Blair-Loy, Mary 2003. *Competing devotions*. Cambridge, MA: Harvard University Press.

Bluestone, Barry, and Stephen Rose. 2000. The enigma of working time trends. In *Working time: International trends, theory, and policy perspectives*, edited by L. Golden and D. M. Figart. New York: Routledge.

Boushey, Heather. 2005. Are women opting out? Debunking the myth. Briefing Paper, Center for Economic and Policy Research, Washington DC.

Brayfield, April. 1995. Juggling jobs and kids: The impact of employment schedules on fathers' caring for children. *Journal of Marriage and the Family* 57:321–32.

Brines, Julie. 1994. Economic dependency, gender, and the division of labor at home. *American Journal of Sociology* 100:652–88.

Casper, Lynne, and Suzanne Bianchi. 2002. *Continuity and change in the American family*. Thousand Oaks, CA: Sage.

Chetkovich, Carol A. 1997. *Real heat: Gender and race in the urban fire service*. New Brunswick, NJ: Rutgers University Press.

Coltrane, Scott. 1996. *Family man: Fatherhood, housework and gender equity*. New York: Oxford University Press.

———. 2000. Research on household labor. *Journal of Marriage and the Family* 62:1209–33.

———. 2004. Elite careers and family commitment: It's (still) about gender. *Annals of the American Academy of Political and Social Science* 596:214–20.

Coltrane, Scott, and M. Adams. 2001. Men's family work: Child-centered fathering and the sharing of domestic labor. In *Working families*, edited by Rosanna Hertz and Nancy Marshall. Berkeley: University of California Press.

Connell, R. W. 1992. A very straight guy: Masculinity, homosexual experience, and the dynamics of gender. *American Sociological Review* 57:735–51.

———. 1995. *Masculinities*. Berkeley: University of California Press.

Cooke, Lynn Prince. 2007. Policy pathways to gender power: State-level effects on the US division of housework. *Journal of Social Policy* 36:239–60.

Cooper, Marianne. 2000. Being the "go-to guy": Fatherhood and masculinity and the organization of work in Silicon Valley. *Qualitative Sociology* 23:379–405.

Craig, Lyn. 2006. Does father care mean fathers share? *Gender & Society* 20:259–81.

Deutsch, Francine. 1999. *Halving it all: How equally shared parenting works*. Cambridge, MA: Harvard University Press.

———. 2007. Undoing gender. *Gender & Society* 21:106–27.

Dowd, Nancy E. 2000. *Redefining fatherhood*. New York: New York University Press.

Fowlkes, Martha. 1980. *Behind every successful man: Wives of medicine and academe*. New York: Columbia University Press.

Garey, Anita Ilta. 1999. *Weaving work and motherhood*. Philadelphia: Temple University Press.

Gerson, Kathleen. 1993. *No man's land: Men's changing commitments to family and work*. New York: Basic Books.

———. 2007. What do women and men want? *American Prospect* [online], February 19.

Gerstel, Naomi, and Natalia Sarkisian. 2008. The color of family ties: Race, class, gender, and extended family involvement. In *It's American families: A multicultural reader*, edited by Stephanie Coontz, Maya Parson, and Gabrielle Rayley. New York: Routledge.

Griswold, Robert E. 1993. *Fatherhood in America: A history*. New York: Basic Books.

Hochschild, Arlie Russell. 1989/2003. *The second shift*. New York: Penguin.

Jacobs, Jerry A., and Kathleen Gerson. 2004. *The time divide: Work, family and gender inequality*. Cambridge, MA: Harvard University Press.

Kimmel, Michael. 2000. *The gendered society*. New York: Oxford University Press.

———. 2006. *Manhood in America*. 2nd ed. New York: Oxford University Press.

Kuperberg, Arielle, and Pamela Stone. 2008. The media depiction of women who opt out. *Gender & Society* 22:497–517.

Lamb, Michael E. 1995. The changing roles of fathers. In *Becoming a father*, edited by J. L. Shapiro, M. J. Diamond, and M. Greenberg. New York: Springer.

Lareau, Annette. 2002. Invisible inequality: Social class and childrearing in Black families and white families. *American Sociological Review* 67:747–76.

———. 2003. *Unequal childhoods*. Berkeley: University of California Press.

LaRossa, Ralph. 1997. *The modernization of fatherhood: A social and political history*. Chicago: University of Chicago Press.

Lundberg, Shelly, and Elaina Rose. 2000. Parenthood and the earnings of married men and women. *Labour Economics* 7:689–710.

Orloff, Ann, and Renne Monson. 2002. Citizens, workers, or fathers? Men in the history of U.S. social policy. In *Making men into fathers: Men masculinities and the social policy of fatherhood*, edited by B. Hobson. New York: Cambridge University Press.

Pleck, J. H., and B. Masciadrelli. 2004. Parental involvement of U.S. residential fathers: Levels, sources, and consequences. In *The role of the father in child development*, 4th ed., edited by M. Lamb. New York: Wiley.

Presser, Harriet. 2003. *Working in a 24/7 economy: Challenges for American families*. New York: Russell Sage Foundation.

Pyke, Karen D. 1996. Class-based masculinities: The interdependence of gender, class, and interpersonal power. *Gender & Society* 10:527–49.

Risman, Barbara. 1998. *Gender vertigo*. New Haven, CT: Yale University Press.

Stone, Pamela. 2007. *Opting out? Why women really quit careers and head home*. Berkeley: University of California Press.

Sullivan, Oriel. 2006. *Changing gender relations, changing families: Tracing the pace of change over time*. Lanham, MD: Rowman & Littlefield.

Townsend, Nicholas. 2002. *The package deal: Marriage, work, and fatherhood in men's lives*. Philadelphia: Temple University Press.

West, Candice, and Don H. Zimmerman. 1987. Doing gender. *Gender & Society* 1:125–51.

Williams, Joan 2000. *Unbending gender: Why family and work conflict and what to do about it*. New York: Oxford University Press.

Introduction to Reading 41

Nordic countries have some of the best work–family policies in the world. In this article, Berit Brandth and Elin Kvande examine the impact of Norwegian policies on fathers. They describe two different sets of child-care policies. One set of policies is gendered, or specifying mother or father in terms of eligibility for benefits—that is, each parent has a fixed quota or number of weeks that can be taken off for paid child-care leave. The second set of policies, which they identify as cash-for-care, they define as gender neutral because the parents can "choose" who will use the paid child-care leave benefits. In addition to spelling out what gendered and gender-neutral care policies look like, they also assess the effects of these policies on fathers' use of the leave benefits. Their research uses findings from two sets of data—one that interviewed 31 working parents with small children in the cash-for-care program and another that studied parental leave. Their article provides an important glimpse of how gender inequality can be reinforced or diminished by governmental policies and laws (the "institutions" Barbara J. Risman talked about in the first reading in this book).

1. In 2009, Norway was far ahead of many countries in developing work–family programs. What basic values motivated the development of these policies?

2. What makes a government program gendered? Gender neutral?

3. Look up the current work–family policies in Norway and in your own country. How do the policies compare in terms of breadth of coverage and inclusion of fathers?

GENDERED OR GENDER-NEUTRAL CARE POLITICS FOR FATHERS?

Berit Brandth and Elin Kvande

In this article, we focus on fathers when examining in what ways the two Norwegian family measures contribute to more democratic family practices. The analysis is based on interview data from two studies, one on parental leave and one on cash-for-care. It is concerned with the potential of the two types of policies to include fathers in child care and thus how they function in the development of the welfare state's goal of increased equality and democracy. Much research has been concerned with how and why politics matters. That welfare policies influence individual behavior is evident, but the understanding of the causes or mechanisms at work is much less obvious.

THE DOUBLE TRACK IN NORWEGIAN FAMILY POLICY

The Scandinavian welfare state model builds on universalism and egalitarianism as core values in policy making (Esping-Andersen 2002). A central aim for work/family policy in Norway, as in most other Nordic countries, has been to encourage gender equality. Norway has a high percentage of working mothers (80 percent) combined with a high fertility rate (1.8). This combination has often been seen as an indication of the impact of parenthood policies, facilitating the reconciliation of work and child care for both mothers and fathers.

A Social Democratic government introduced the fathers' quota into the parental leave system. Until the end of the 1990s, it represented a strong gender equality model in Norwegian family policies, by promoting the sharing of both paid and unpaid care work. Parental leave and day care services encouraged the dual-earner and dual-career family.

In 1998, a conservative coalition government came into power. It introduced the cash-for-care system, where parents of toddlers receive a cash payment if they do not use publicly funded child care services. Before its introduction, Norway

Brandth, Berit and Elin Kvande. 2009. "Gendered or Gender-Neutral Care Politics for Fathers?" *The ANNALS of the American Academy of Political and Social Science.* Vol. 629: 177–188.Copyright © American Academy of Political and Social Science.

experienced a very heated and polarized debate. Indeed, the 1998 election has been called the "cash-for-care election." The cash-for-care system was said to guarantee parents "freedom of choice" between using publicly funded day care or staying at home and receiving a cash benefit. Besides the neoliberal idea of choice, it was also motivated by the idea that children ought to spend more time at home together with one of the parents than the parental leave period made possible.

Thus, we can observe a *dualism* in Norwegian family policy (Ellingsæter and Leira 2006). This political dualism has been recognized as a *double track* or a *paradox* in the feminist welfare state literature (Leira 1992; Ellingsæter 2003; Sainsbury 2001) and made Norway an interesting case compared to the other Nordic countries. On the one side, the policy labeled the "work line" involves earnings-related social insurance programs. Benefits are based on the precondition that parents "earn" the right to services from society through participation in working life. Generally speaking, the work line has been a basic principle for the Norwegian welfare state since the early 1990s, and it represents a type of policy that is meant to encourage people to choose employment rather than social security benefits. In this way, family policies are closely connected to employment policies.

To qualify for the parental leave system, which includes the fathers' quota, one has to have been in the workforce for six of the last ten months prior to birth. This is a typical example of how the work line rewards labor achievement, since the amount of parental money is based to some extent on whether one holds a full-time position. The policy represents a strong encouragement for both parents to establish themselves in the labor market before having a baby as it is through paid work that parents earn the right to take paid leave without losing their jobs. This type of policy encourages both parents to combine work and family obligations, and it is built on the model where both mothers and fathers should be employed. The idea of this policy is to result in a democratic and equal relationship.

The other track in Norwegian family policy has been advocating policies that are not dependent on the parents' participation in working life. The underlying idea is to strengthen the family as a caring unit through cash payments. It thus valorizes unpaid work and care and is in opposition to employment policies. The cash-for-care scheme, which was introduced in 1998, is based on this idea to strengthen the family as a care producer by providing cash benefits irrespective of the parents' work activities. It is constructed as a gender-neutral measure. This track has come to support a traditional division of work in the family, with father as the provider and mother as the caregiver, which could be labeled a traditional family model or the male breadwinner family model. More freedom of choice has been a crucial argument for cash measures in general, and the policy tends to refer to cash given particularly to facilitate one of the parents staying home. This policy may be seen as democratic in the sense that mothers and fathers in principle are given equal chances to choose to be home to care for the children. In this article, we ask how the gender-neutral cash-for-care and the gendered fathers' quota are perceived and used among fathers.

Gendered Care Policies

Parental leave has had a changing focus over the years. During the early days of leave schemes, motherhood was the focus. Typically, the leave schemes were called "maternity leave" or "postnatal leave." The idea was to protect working mothers from the demands of work to serve their interests as well as the interests of their children. Thus, the nature of the earliest leave schemes was to provide special health protection for women.

In the 1970s, the desire for equality between mothers and fathers was the underlying motivation for the expansion of the leave scheme. Mothers were to be ensured the opportunity to combine participation in the labor market with giving birth to a child and providing care. What was entirely new with the leave reform in this period was that some of the leave could be shared between the parents, which meant abandoning the idea that leave was only an individual right for women. By granting fathers the right to leave, legislation in the 1970s signaled a new political view on men's responsibilities and participation in child care. Both parents were given rights and obligations in relation to their home and their workplace.

In the 1980s and early 1990s, leave schemes were extended gradually. The idea of equal rights was a strong rationale for developing parental leave. However, the parental leave that could be shared did not noticeably influence the fathers' use of leave, and thus the vision of equal parenthood did not get a boost. To further stimulate fathers to take leave, the fathers' quota was introduced. The fathers' quota represents a break with the women-oriented equality politics. Earlier gender equality politics had attempted to make women equal to men and not vice versa.

As mentioned, the fathers' quota is an individual right given to fathers and not to the family as a caregiving entity. With the fathers' quota, an additional rationale emerged—the *child's need for a caring father*. The purpose of a special

Table 8.2 The Norwegian Parental Leave System

Maternity leave	Paid leave reserved for the mother: 3 weeks before parturition; 6 weeks after
"Daddy days"	Welfare leave for father in connection with birth; negotiated pay: 2 weeks
Fathers' quota	Paid leave reserved for father: 6 weeks[a]
Parental leave	Paid leave that may be shared by the parents: either 29 weeks with 100 percent or 39 weeks with 80 percent parental money

Note: Parental leave is paid by national insurance and covers 100 or 80 percent of wages depending on what length of the leave the family chooses. It is most common to choose 80 percent wage compensation and longer leave. There is a ceiling for what is compensated by national insurance of approximately EUR 50,000 (2008).

[a] [In] 2009, fathers' quota [was] extended to 10 weeks.

fathers' quota was that the child would have better contact with the father. Thus, the aim was not only to bolster equal rights but also to strengthen fatherhood. This has been called a development toward a *father-friendly welfare state* (Brandth and Kvande 2003). The schemes are now aimed not only at promoting equality but also fatherhood. Norwegian leave schemes have thus from the beginning been *gendered,* as first mothers and then fathers received individual rights. Individual rights mean that the parents themselves are not allowed to decide which of them is to stay home and mind the child.

From its inception, parental leave has been a *gendered* scheme, as first the mothers and then also the fathers were granted special rights. The reason for introducing the fathers' quota, and later its extension by two weeks in 2005 and 2006, was first an explicit political aim to strengthen the father-child relation but also to change the gendered work division with respect to caring for small children. To accomplish this aim, the principle of special rights for fathers was chosen. Hence, with the fathers' quota, the decision of who would take leave was moved out of the family and onto the structural level to apply to all fathers. It is a right that has been negotiated for men as employed fathers. It is thus not up to each individual father or parental couple to choose who stays at home with the baby.

The Norwegian parental leave scheme is complex and consists of several elements. As seen from Table 8.2, both mothers and fathers have their individual rights (maternity leave and fathers' quota) in addition to joint rights (parental leave). The "daddy days" are two additional weeks of welfare leave for fathers that are not paid for by national insurance and are not included in the total length of the leave. The total parental leave length is fifty-four weeks with 80 percent pay; nine weeks are for mothers and six weeks for fathers [changed to ten weeks in 2009], with thirty-nine weeks to be optionally shared.[1] These thirty-nine weeks are flexible also because they can be taken on a part-time basis.

Gender-Neutral Care Policies

Cash-for-care was introduced in Norway in the autumn of 1998 and, in brief, means that parents with children from one to three years of age may receive public benefits amounting to a cash payment of around EUR 400 a month, provided they do not use a full-time place in a public day care center. This payment is far below earnings from even a low-paid job. The cash-for-care scheme is not dependent on whether parents are working. It is not considered to be wages and thus does not constitute the basis for earning other social and/or welfare benefits.

Cash-for-care can be considered one of the welfare state schemes intended to balance family and work. Cash-for-care aims to encourage parents to spend more time with their children and to use less public care. Therefore, we can say that an intention behind this scheme is to lead to a reassignment of priorities for parental time, from working for a wage to providing care for one's own children. The policy is also promoted as a means of increasing parental choice with respect to child care. Cash-for-care is optional in the sense that it is designed to be *gender neutral*. It leaves it up to the family to choose whether the mother or father, or either of them at all, should stay home with the child. As it follows after the end of the parental leave period when the child has gotten older, it was expected that it would be of interest to fathers. The number of families receiving cash-for-care has gone down as public day care facilities have developed greatly over the past years.

The expectation, controversial in nature, of this reform was that it would lead to a reduction in mothers' working hours. However, research evaluating the reform in the years after (Baklien, Ellingsæter, and Gulbrandsen 2001) has shown that although many parents of one- and two-year-old children receive the payment, mothers have reduced their employment only to a very limited extent, while there has been no impact on fathers' employment or working hours (Baklien, Ellingsæter, and Gulbrandsen 2001; Sletvold 2000).

To summarize, there are a number of important differences between the fathers' quota and cash-for-care as care schemes. The fathers' quota is an *individual right* based on *activity in working life*. This genders it from the very start and makes choice very limited. Cash-for-care has been defined as a payment given to the *family*. It strongly emphasizes *choice* with respect to child care and which of the parents should stay home. Its design is thus *gender neutral*. In this article, we are interested in what ways these dimensions of the schemes influence their take-up or non-take-up by fathers.

* * *

RESULTS

A Special Right Reserved for Fathers

The introduction of the fathers' quota may be designated as a success story in Norwegian care policy when it comes to getting more fathers to spend more time with their children. Our study was interested in how to explain this phenomenon. Our point of departure is the development of fathers' use of the quota. A study from the end of the 1980s found that less than 1 percent of fathers shared the parental leave with the mother (Brandth and Kvande 1989). As long as the leave was relatively short and based on mother and father being free to share the leave between them, the proportion of fathers using it increased modestly from 1 to 4 percent. The fathers' quota was introduced in April 1993, after which there was a dramatic increase in the proportion of fathers who took leave the following years, from 4 percent in 1993 to 85 percent in 2000. During the four years after its introduction, taking leave changed from a minority practice to a majority practice among the fathers. After the extension of the quota to five and then six weeks in 2005 and 2006, the use of it has continued to stay high, with 75 percent of eligible fathers taking five weeks and more in 2007.

When we thus compare the use before and after the fathers' quota, we see that the *special quota* for fathers must have had great effect. The high number of eligible fathers who take leave suggest the importance of a right that is earmarked for them. During the time when it was up to the parents to negotiate whether and how a relatively short leave period would be shared, the mother used all the leave in the vast majority of cases. The use of the gender-neutral leave scheme, which in principle was and is *optional* with respect to who takes the leave, is influenced by the encounter with the gendered society and reflects the prevailing gender patterns. Particularly in a field such as care for young children, which is so strong divided along gender lines, gender-neutral and optional schemes will lead the majority of parents to choose the traditional models (Brandth and Kvande 2005).

The common assumption was that the expansion of the leave time, which happened predominantly during the late 1980s and early 1990s, would lead more fathers to share the optional—and gender-neutral—leave with the mothers. However, this change has only occurred to a very small degree. We may therefore assume that giving fathers a quota (a special right) is the way to create a comprehensive and rapid change in this field.

A Collective Right for Fathers as Employees

An important point with the fathers' quota is that it is a right men are granted as employees and fathers. For many fathers, the fathers' quota has functioned as that extra nudge necessary to get them to take leave at all. One of the fathers we interviewed, who was a warehouse employee and took leave under the fathers' quota when his second son was born, says the following about using the fathers' quota:

> Nor was there anything at my place of work that made it difficult. If they are notified in advance it is quite simple to take leave. I thought perhaps it would be more difficult to obtain the leave than it turned out to be. They were very accommodating, then.

His was one of the workplaces where having the right to leave was considered a natural part of the employment contract the employer had to provide. The right to leave may be compared to the right to cut down on extra working hours. Complying with the rules and norms of working life is part of the cultural context. The main principle in this workplace was normal working hours, and the reward and career structure was tied to a standardized working-hour culture where the formal work contract regulated working hours. Standardized working hours means working regular hours with a clear line drawn between work and leisure.

The "gentle force" function that characterizes the fathers' quota is seen when those who do not see the point of a fathers' quota end up taking leave, albeit reluctantly. A printing press employee we interviewed actually found it unnecessary that he take the fathers' quota. He would rather have worked, also because the mother wanted to be home after the leave period was over. He tried to have the quota transferred to her, but when this was impossible, he took the leave himself. He says, "There was a lot to do at work . . . [but] I'm stubborn enough to take what is mine."

We also find this motivation in the questionnaire study, where 67 percent of the fathers respond that a special right was important and that it should be used accordingly (Brandth and Kvande 2003). These respondents see the fathers' quota as a right the state has given them, virtually as a gift they cannot decline. Most fathers would not have taken leave if the fathers' quota scheme had not been in place. Therefore, many of these men accept the offer from the state with surprise or even some reluctance at the beginning. Nevertheless, the fathers' quota is a right they have been given that they therefore think they must use. The fathers' quota has existed for fifteen years now, and studies show that it has become a norm and is treated as a matter of fact (Svee 2005).

When it is an earmarked right for fathers as employees, the leave also contributes to setting a boundary in relation to the working-life requirements placed on fathers. This is particularly important for fathers working in so-called limitless jobs. Such jobs are found in, for example, the knowledge professions. A typical representative of those who use the fathers' quota to set limits against their job requirements might be a researcher in technological fields. In the type of company where this professional group is working, employees have a large degree of independence and responsibility in their work. It is possible to work at home and juggle working hours. Many of the employees work beyond normal working hours; unregistered overtime is common. They become deeply involved in their vocation, feeling an obligation to their work efforts and their colleagues. It might be difficult to avoid getting carried away by interesting work tasks and to control one's use of time. If an employee is unable to do so, the result is that she or he has to work long hours without compensation.

The high take-up rate of the quota shows the positive consequences of basing its eligibility in employment. Connecting care policy to employment means that it builds on the same thinking as many other welfare benefits and schemes regulating conditions in working life in Norway that are defined as a part of the work contract. Thus, male employees who have become fathers do not have to negotiate individually with their employers about using the right to the fathers' quota, although such negotiations may be possible in some workplaces, notably in the so-called new working life. Having a right that applies to male employees as a group provides a clear benefit; it makes it easier to avoid the stress and strain of being in the minority, or being the only one to take leave to provide care for children. Precisely because the fathers' quota functions as an employee right, it appears to fit into men's and fathers' norms with respect to what are acceptable reasons for absence from work. This fact has probably contributed to its development as a majority practice in the course of a few years.

Gender Neutrality Is Perceived as Gendered

By representing an individual right for fathers, the fathers' quota breaks with the dominating gender scheme in the area of child care and is understood as a masculine gendered right. This approach is different in principle from the optional and gender-neutral thinking that is the basis of the cash-for-care scheme and that has proved not to have the same power to change. The policy does not challenge existing gender structure but allows family life to be marked by gender inequality and the demands of work. In spite of its gender-neutral design, cash-for-care is also understood as gendered, but since in practice it involves part-time work (it is mostly used to reduce working hours), it is gendered as feminine. The freedom to choose makes cash-for-care a scheme for mothers. While its intention of providing the freedom to choose was expected to make cash-for-care gender neutral, the result is nonetheless gendered because it is filtered through the dominating gender scheme. Particularly in a field such as caring for children, which is strongly divided by gender, gender-neutral and optional schemes will lead the majority of the parental couples to adapt to the traditional models.

This illustrates how the general gender structures of society are important contexts when new care policies are introduced. In spite of substantial changes in the past ten years in Norwegian society, the prevalent gender division of work continues to be the familiar pattern where most women have the main responsibility for child care and also spend most time with the children (Kitterød 2002). One of the results is that a large proportion of today's Norwegian women are working part-time. Even if two-provider families have become most common, men spend the most time in working life, which also can be seen as working overtime while the children are small (Kitterød and Kjelstad 2003). Although most of today's Norwegian mothers of young children are employed outside their homes, significant structural forces influence how the policy schemes are understood and used by fathers.

On the individual level, it may also be claimed that work is important for men's construction of their masculine identity and thus for their time priorities (Morgan 1992). Being successful in working life is a cultural ideal. Connell (1987) uses the term *hegemonic masculinity* for the dominating cultural ideals of men. Dominating and subordinate masculinity practices are in competition. Since hegemonic masculine identity for the most part is constructed in relation to participation in working life, it may conflict with being a participating father (Brandth and Kvande 2003). Caregiving related to children continues to be a field where masculinity is put to the test because it is gendered as feminine. The cash-for-care system has not been able to challenge the dominant masculine construction.

While part-time work generally is difficult for men, using the cash-for-care scheme to reduce working hours is also difficult for additional reasons. The men in our research studies never work part-time, which suggests that such part-time work is understood as a female phenomenon. Part-time work is gendered; it is "something women do." "Primarily," one of the men said when asked about the cash-for-care, "we have wanted to spend more time at home with the children. Mostly it is my wife who has been home." Part-time is how women reconcile work and family, and it is often connected to low pay and marginal connections to working life. Therefore, part-time work is not considered relevant for [men]. One of the mothers, a nurse, explained, "I don't think staying at home on cash-for-care is a choice for him in real terms, neither economically nor what it would mean for him to be away from work. "Part-time would increase the risk for stigmatization and not be compatible with a masculine work orientation. The cash-for-care scheme appears to be "infected" by the same gendering and understood as something some women might use.

Even though cash-for-care is designed as a gender-neutral scheme, it is understood and practiced as a gendered one because it is situated in a gendered context. If one of the parents is to stay home, it is generally taken for granted that it is the mother. We find this traditional division of work between women and men not only with couples where the mother and father have different incomes and status in working life but also with couples where the parents generally have equal incomes. If the parents of small children have chosen to use the cash to reduce their working hours, it is the mothers who have done so.

NOTE

1. [On] July 1, 2009 the fathers' [increased] from six to 10 weeks. As a consequence the total parental leave length [is] 56 weeks with 80 percent pay; 37 weeks can be optionally shared.

REFERENCES

Baklien, Bergljot, Anne Lise Ellingsæter, and Lars Gulbrandsen. 2001. *Evaluering av kontantstøtteordningen.* [Evaluation of the cash-for-care measure]. Oslo, Norway: Norges Forskningsråd.

Brandth, Berit, and Elin Kvande. 1989. Like barn deler best. (Equal couples are the best sharers). *Nytt om kvinneforskning.* 13(3): 8–17.

———. 2003. *Fleksible fedre* [Flexible fathers]. Oslo, Norway: Universitetsforlaget.

———. 2005. Fedres valgfrihet og arbeidslivets tidskulturer [Fathers' free choice and working-life's time cultures]. *Tidsskrift for samfunnsforskning* 46(1): 35–54.

Connell, Robert W. 1987. *Gender and power.* Cambridge, UK: Polity.

Ellingsæter, Anne Lise. 2003. The complexity of family policy reform. The case of Norway. *European Societies* 5(4): 419–43.

Ellingsæter, Anne Lise, and Arnlaug Leira, eds. 2006. *Politicising parenthood in Scandinavia. Gender relations in welfare states.* Bristol, UK: Policy Press.

Esping-Andersen, Gösta. 2002. *Why we need a new welfare state.* With D. Gallie, A. Hemerijck, and J. Myles. Oxford: Oxford University Press.

Kitterød, Ragni H. 2002. Store endringer i småbarnsforeldres dagligliv [Major changes in the day-to-day lives of parents with small children]. *Samfunnsspeilet* 16(4–5): 14–22.

Kitterød, Ragni H., and Randi Kjeldstad. 2003. A new father's role? Employment patterns among Norwegian fathers 1991–2001. *Economic Survey* 1:39–51.

Leira, Arnlaug. 1992. *Welfare States and Working Mothers*: *The Scandinavian Experience.* Cambridge: Cambridge University Press.

Morgan, David H. J. 1992. *Discovering men.* London: Routledge.

Sainsbury, Diane. 2001. Gender and the making of welfare states: Norway and Sweden. *Social Politics* 8:113–43.

Sletvold, Lars. 2000. *Kontantstøtteordningens konsekvenser for yrkesaktivitet og likestilling* [The consequences of cash-for-care for employment and equality]. Report 15/00. Oslo, Norway: NOVA.

Svee, Even. 2005. Fedres omsorgspermisjon [Fathers' care leave]. Master's thesis, NTNU, Trondheim, Norway.

❦ Topics for Further Examination ❧

- Search the web for "healthy relationships" and examine the first 20 or so results to see the focus for each website and who is sponsoring it. What does this data collection exercise tell you about how we are to view relationships in our society?
- Check out the most recent research on gender and relationships using an academic database. How does this research differ from that which you found on the web?
- Examine marriage and engagement announcements in your local paper. What race, gender, and sexuality patterns do you find in these short announcements? Do the same thing with a listing of personal ads from a local paper. What does this tell us about expectations for relationships?

9

ENFORCING GENDER

Throughout Part II, we have discussed patterns of learning, selling, and doing gender at work and in intimate relationships. In this final chapter of our section on patterns, we look at patterns surrounding the enforcement of gender. Enforcing gender is about more than just *doing* gender; it is about assault, coercion, and constraints on people's behaviors, as well as more subtle and tacit constraints on identities that are used to enforce gender conformity. Enforcing gender involves a range of social control strategies, such as physical abuse and rape, harassment, gossip and name calling, as well as formal and informal laws and rules created by governments, work organizations, and religions to coerce people to conform to gender norms they might not otherwise wish to obey. Many readings throughout this book are about the enforcement of gender, particularly those in Chapter 4. This chapter extends that prior discussion, explicitly focusing on the different forms of social control used to enforce gender.

The enforcement of gender can have profound effects on women's and men's choices, self-esteem, relationships, and abilities to care for themselves. We argue two main points in this chapter. First, doing gender is not something that we freely choose; rather, there are many times that we are forced to do gender, whether we would wish to do it or not. Second, there are many occasions whereby the very act of maintaining a gendered identity hurts ourselves and others, either physically, emotionally, or both.

SOCIAL CONTROL

Enforcing gender is about the physical and emotional control of everyone. Berger (1963) describes the processes by which we learn to conform to the norms of society as "a set of concentric rings, each representing a system of social control" (p. 73). At the middle of the concentric rings, Berger places the individual. Social control mechanisms, including family and friends, are in the next ring, and the legal and political system of a society are in the outer ring. He argues that most social control of behavior occurs in the inner rings, which he described as "broad coercive systems that every individual shares with a vast number of fellow controlees" (p. 75). As such, most gendered behavior is enforced in those center rings, with the forms of social control differing slightly by gender. For example, homophobia is a control mechanism that is often used to enforce gender patterns for men. Friends or peers who call a boy a "fag" or "sissy" can make him uncomfortable and force him to display hegemonic masculinity. The commodification of gender most often enforces emphasized femininity, with young girls comparing themselves to the idealized images of the media, which is described in Chapter 5.

GENDER VIOLENCE

Although most of the enforcement of gender happens as part of normal interaction, some forms of social control are more coercive, including physical assault, rape, sexual harassment, and even murder. We begin by discussing the harm done when violence is used to enforce gender. We hope you have never experienced physical violence, but many individuals have. The actual incidence of gender violence is not clear. Most intimate partner violence is not reported to the authorities (Centers for Disease Control and Prevention, 2012a; Rennison, 2002), making the incidence of intimate partner violence higher than the statistics suggest. Furthermore, gender violence is often normalized, both in relationships and how we define violence. The reading by Kristin L. Anderson and Debra Umberson in this chapter describes how some men dismiss their acts of violence against female partners as trivial, thus enforcing the idea that men can and should control women. Men are also victims of acts of violence by women, but this violence is likely to be less physically harmful and men may be less likely to talk about it, especially sexual assault (Weiss, 2010), since to claim to be physically harmed by a woman clearly violates gendered expectations.

Women victims of violence often do not report acts of violence because of fear for themselves and their children, based on threats of additional physical violence or the withdrawal of economic support and/or the outcome of emotional abuse, which leads them to believe they "asked for it." Abusers exert "coercive control"

over their victims, making victims fearful for their lives and the lives of loved ones. As such, victims, particularly women, often become psychologically battered and emotionally dependent on their perpetrators (Mahoney, Williams, & West, 2001). Not only does domestic violence lower the victim's self-esteem, but it also impedes the victim's ability to leave an abusive situation because abusers often control the victim's freedom of movement and finances (even for individuals who work for pay outside the home). Abusers also prevent victims from getting the psychological support they need to leave the abusive situation (Mahoney et al., 2001).

Even given concerns about the accuracy and underreporting of the data, statistics detailing incidences of gender violence should give us pause. For 2010, the U.S. Department of Justice (Truman, 2011) reported 135,760 cases of rape and sexual assault by nonstrangers (intimate, other relative, or friend/acquaintance), of which 91.4% were female victims, and another 43,170 cases of rape and sexual assault by strangers, of which 97.2% were female victims (another 5,460 cases were reported in which the relationship to the victim was unknown, and 62.1% of these were female victims). The Centers for Disease Control and Prevention (2012a) define four types of intimate partner violence: physical, sexual, threats of physical or sexual abuse, and emotional abuse. The Centers for Disease Control and Prevention argue that intimate partner violence causes many unreported health-related injuries from physical and emotional abuse, costing an estimated $8.3 billion (in 2003 U.S. dollars). These statistics reflect and reinforce the system of hegemonic masculinity and differential power and control in relationships, as women are more likely than men to be victims of intimate violence.

Gender violence is a form of intimate abuse more likely to affect women. Using data from 1976 to 2005, the U.S. Department of Justice (Fox & Zawitz, 2010) reports that female homicide victims were 6 times more likely to be killed by an intimate acquaintance than were male homicide victims and that 63.6% of homicides were committed by nonstrangers, including 18.3% by spouses and 10.4% by boyfriends or girlfriends (terminology used by the Department of Justice). Even more alarming is that this pattern of abuse begins early in life. The Centers for Disease Control and Prevention (2012b) report that 1 in 11 adolescents reported being a victim of physical dating violence, and studies find that about one in four college women have been raped or were the victims of attempted rape (Bachar & Koss, 2001; Fisher, Cullen, & Turner, 2000).

Unfortunately, this situation of date rape evolves in a culture that encourages and justifies rape and enforces a gender system in which men control women (Boswell & Spade, 1996). The literature provides us with an understanding of the prevalence of rape but has not reduced the likelihood of rape. The reading by Laura Hamilton and Elizabeth A. Armstrong in this chapter examines changing gender norms and sexual mores for young women in college today, illustrating the complex intersections of gender, sexuality, and social class on women's orientation to relationships. Their findings suggest that changing views of sexuality may alter the role of intimate violence in enforcing gender while still enforcing gender (Ronen, 2010).

In fact, researchers have identified a number of rape myths that perpetuate gender differences and maintain a system of male dominance. These myths include the belief that wives cannot be raped by their husbands, that women want to be raped and enjoy rape, that women lie about being raped (Edwards, Turchik, Dardis, Reynolds, & Gidycz, 2011), that rapists are different from other men, and that men cannot stop themselves once they are sexually aroused (Ryan, 2011; the latter myth is also discussed in Chapter 6 in the article by Nicola Gavey, Kathryn McPhillips, and Marion Doherty). Rape myths abound, supported by religious, legal, media, and other institutions (Edwards et al., 2011), and we could even add the one stating that men cannot be raped, particularly by women (Weiss, 2010). This rape myth is substantiated by the fact that rape laws in many states excluded men as victims until the 1980s, and it wasn't until 2012 that the FBI Uniform Crime Code was revised in a way that included males as well as females as victims.

It is important, however, to remember that males are also victims of sexual assault and intimate violence, including being raped by females. Weiss's (2010) comparison of men's and women's reports of sexual victimization in the National Crime Victimization Survey found only a small number of differences between men's and women's reports of victimization. Women were more likely to be victims of rape or attempted rape, with men reporting sexual assaults more often. In addition, while 99% of women reported being victimized by men, 46% of men reported being victimized by women, defying some assumptions about rape and gender. Weiss's findings show that even when men are victimized, their reports of the victimization often enforce gender and masculinity. For example, men are more likely to say that they were too drunk to control the situation or, particularly when victimized by other men, to include descriptions of fighting back. Needless to say, while men as well as women are victimized, gendered expectations influence their experiences.

We argue that the underlying reasons for intimate violence and sexual abuse are complicated and relate to the maintenance of hegemonic masculinity. Hegemonic masculinity depends on the sexual, physical, and emotional degradation of women. Gender is relational. Culturally, males often find that "becoming" a man requires that one show disdain for women. As Beth A. Quinn suggests in her reading in this chapter, many men are expected to disrespect women, and other men congratulate them when they do so. The same patterns and practices we have been discussing throughout this book also explain how men learn to instigate and justify the physical and emotional abuse of women, as described in Anderson and Umberson's reading in this chapter. These patterns also illustrate what encourages men to be violent. Although there have been some changes in the way police and courts handle intimate violence, a long-standing attitude is that the "victims ask for it" (Mahoney et al., 2001)—a pattern that may escalate as women become more sexually active, as described in Hamilton and Armstrong's reading and by others (e.g., Ronen, 2010).

INSTITUTIONALIZED ENFORCEMENT OF GENDER

Although the enforcement of gender mainly occurs in daily activities, as Berger (1963) notes, institutionalized settings also sometimes enforce gender. Organizations either participate in or simply ignore more subtle forms of gender enforcement, such as "girl watching" in office settings, described in Quinn's reading in this chapter. These patterns can be found in schools (e.g., fraternities and school sports teams), the workplace, and men's sports teams (Schact, 1996). Unfortunately, these patterns can even be found in the division of labor among parents who assist with youth sports teams, as Michael A. Messner and Suzel Bozada-Deas describe in their reading in this chapter. In patriarchal societies worldwide, men make the rules (and laws) and write the informal scripts that prescribe behaviors for themselves, other men, and women. These rules, which assume men are the "bosses" and women are the assistants, regardless of individual abilities, become institutionalized in daily patterns of life.

Religion is one institution that often enforces gender difference and inequality. Many religions enforce rules that exclude or segregate women within the practice of that religion. For example, women are excluded from the priesthood in the Catholic Church and marginalized in many other Christian churches (Nesbitt, Baust, & Bailey, 2001). Some Jewish congregations segregate women physically and do not allow women to study the Torah with the same seriousness as men (Rose, 2001). Some Islamic communities also apply rules of gender, such as enforced veiling of women, which women negotiate in a variety of ways (Gerami & Lehnerer, 2001). Religion also defines dichotomous and hierarchical gendered connections in other social institutions, such as the family. Edgell and Docka (2007) conducted ethnographic studies in three churches,

chosen because these churches were serving nontraditional families. They found that churches reinforced a variety of models of families in their programming and preaching, all of which had considerable consequences for the gendered expectations of their parishioners.

In addition, many institutional rules subtly maintain the gendered expectation of the domination of women—including the sexual violation of women by men. Politicians, police, and traffickers construct and maintain the rules supporting human trafficking of women for the sex trade (Kempadoo & Doezema, 1998). These rules allow girls and women to enter countries under dubious documentation and fail to provide the help that trafficked girls and women need to escape lives of prostitution and abuse (Kempadoo & Doezema, 1998). The women sold into virtual sexual slavery, and the men and women who take advantage of vulnerable girls and women, are part of a brutal pattern of gender enforcement. For example, one study of trafficking of women for sex/prostitution estimates that Indonesian women are most likely to go to Japan, Malaysia, and probably Singapore. They are lured to these places by the possibility of jobs in karaoke bars as singers or, in Japan, as cultural ambassadors (American Center for International Labor Solidarity, 2005). Unfortunately, they are forced into and kept in the sex trade by withholding of salary or immigration documents, or by the need to pay off the "debt" they incurred to get to the country. Other women face similar situations as they are forced into domestic labor. The trafficking of women in both contexts helps maintain the sexual domination of women.

Sexual Harassment

In her reading in this chapter, Quinn describes situations that are considered to be sexual harassment. The definition of sexual harassment includes two different types of behaviors (Welsh, 1999). Quid pro quo harassment is that which involves the use of sexual threats or bribery to make employment decisions. Supervisors who threaten to withhold a promotion to someone they supervise unless that person has sex with them engage in quid pro quo harassment. The second form of sexual harassment is termed "hostile environment" harassment, which the U.S. Equal Employment Opportunity Commission defines as consisting of behavior that creates an "intimidating, hostile, or offensive working environment" (Welsh, 1999, p. 170). A hostile environment occurs when a company allows situations that interfere with an individual's job performance.

Unfortunately, we do not know exactly how prevalent sexual harassment is. Reports of the incidence of sexual harassment are not consistent, primarily due to the various ways sexual harassment is measured across studies (Welsh, 1999). Although various studies report that anywhere from 16% to 90% of women experience sexual harassment at their workplace, an attempt to summarize 18 different surveys estimated the prevalence rate at 44% (Welsh, 1999). Any incidence of sexual harassment, however, creates an uncomfortable workplace for the target and perpetuates gender inequality.

Sexual harassment begins early in school settings, even among young schoolchildren (Hand & Sanchez, 2000; National Coalition for Women and Girls in Education [NCWGE], 2012). Although the experience of harassment is greater for girls, with more than half of the girls and 40% of the boys in a 2010 to 2011 survey reporting being sexually harassed (NCWGE, 2012), girls also endure the more demeaning forms of harassment and at a higher rate than do boys (Hand & Sanchez, 2000). Lesbian, gay, bisexual, and transgender youths also experience high levels of sexual harassment, with 85% of those responding to the 2010 to 2011 survey indicating that they had experienced sexual harassment and 19% indicating physical attack.

Unfortunately, sexual harassment continues long beyond high school, as noted by Quinn in this chapter, and helps enforce gender and heterosexuality. Although it is subtler than sexual assault, sexual harassment has serious consequences for the harassed and the harasser. In her reading, Quinn helps us understand how sexual harassment enforces gender for men and women by making women objects of men's masculinity and enforcing the view that men should treat women as objects. The "girl watching" that Quinn describes creates a wall between men and women that makes it impossible for them to relate on an equal basis.

Sometimes we see gender enforcement only when we look at someone else's life circumstances, such as the roles of mothers and fathers in supporting youth sports in Messner and Bozada-Deas's article, the reports of men's use of intimate partner violence in Anderson and Umberson's article, or Quinn's descriptions of "girl watching." Think about your life as you read this chapter and consider the ways conformity to gender is enforced among the people you know and observe, including yourself.

REFERENCES

American Center for International Labor Solidarity. (2005). *When they were sold: Trafficking of women and girls in 15 provinces of Indonesia.* Retrieved from http://www.solidaritycenter.org/files/when_they_were_sold_frontmatter.pdf

Bachar, K., & Koss, M. P. (2001). From prevalence to prevention: Closing the gap between what we know about rape and what we do. In C. M. Renzetti, J. L. Edleson, & R. K. Bergen (Eds.), *Sourcebook on violence against women* (pp. 117–142). Thousand Oaks, CA: Sage.

Berger, P. L. (1963). *An invitation to sociology: A humanistic perspective.* Garden City, NY: Anchor Books.

Boswell, A., & Spade, J. Z. (1996). Fraternities and rape culture: Why are some fraternities more dangerous places for women? *Gender & Society, 10*(2), 133–147.

Centers for Disease Control and Prevention. (2012a). *Understanding intimate partner violence: Fact sheet.* Retrieved from http://www.cdc.gov/violenceprevention/pdf/ipv_factsheet-a.pdf

Centers for Disease Control and Prevention. (2012b). *Understanding teen dating violence: Fact sheet.* Retrieved from http://www.cdc.gov/ViolencePrevention/pdf/TeenDatingViolence2012-a.pdf

Edgell, P., & Docka, D. (2007). Beyond the nuclear family: Familialism and gender ideology in diverse religious communities. *Sociological Forum, 22*(1), 25–50.

Edwards, K. M., Turchik, J. A., Dardis, C. M., Reynolds, N., & Gidycz, C. A. (2011). Rape myths: History, individual and institutional-level presence, and implications for change. *Sex Roles, 65*, 761–773.

Fisher, B. S., Cullen, F. T., & Turner, M. G. (2000). *The sexual victimization of college women.* Washington, DC: Bureau of Justice Statistics. Retrieved from https://www.ncjrs.gov/pdffiles1/nij/182369.pdf

Fox, J. A., & Zawitz, M. W. (2010). *Homicide trends in the United States.* Washington, DC: Bureau of Justice Statistics. Retrieved from http://bjs.ojp.usdoj.gov/content/pub/pdf/htius.pdf

Gerami, S., & Lehnerer, M. (2001). Women's agency and household diplomacy: Negotiating fundamentalism. *Gender & Society, 15*(4), 556–573.

Hand, J. Z., & Sanchez, L. (2000). Badgering or bantering? Gender differences in experience of, and reactions to, sexual harassment among U.S. high school students. *Gender & Society, 14*(6), 718–746.

Kempadoo, K., & Doezema, J. (1998). *Global sex workers: Rights, resistance, and redefinition.* New York: Routledge.

Mahoney, P., Williams, L. M., & West, C. M. (2001). Violence against women by intimate relationship partners. In C. M. Renzetti, J. L. Edleson, & R. K. Bergen (Eds.), *Sourcebook on violence against women* (pp. 143–178). Thousand Oaks, CA: Sage.

National Coalition for Women and Girls in Education. (2012). *Title IX at 40: Working to ensure gender equality in education.* Washington, DC: Author.

Nesbitt, P., Baust, J., & Bailey, E. (2001). Women's status in the Christian church. In D. Vannoy (Ed.), *Gender mosaics: Societal perspectives* (pp. 386–396). Los Angeles: Roxbury.

Rennison, C. M. (2002). *Rape and sexual assault: Reporting to police and medical attention, 1992–2000.* Retrieved from http://bjs.ojp.usdoj.gov/content/pub/pdf/rsarp00.pdf

Ronen, S. (2010). Grinding on the dance floor: Gendered scripts and sexualized dancing at college parties. *Gender & Society, 24*(3), 355–377.

Rose, D. R. (2001). Gender and Judaism. In D. Vannoy (Ed.), *Gender mosaics: Societal perspectives* (pp. 415–424). Los Angeles: Roxbury.

Ryan, K. M. (2011). The relationship between rape myths and sexual scripts: The social construction of rape. *Sex Roles, 65*, 774–782.

Schact, S. P. (1996). Misogyny on and off the "pitch": The gendered world of male rugby players. *Gender & Society, 10*(5), 550–565.

Truman, J. L. (2011, September). *National Crime Victimization Survey: Criminal victimization, 2010.* Washington, DC: U.S. Department of Justice. Retrieved from http://bjs.ojp.usdoj.gov/content/pub/pdf/cv10.pdf

Weiss, K. G. (2010). Male sexual victimization: Examining men's experiences of rape and sexual assault. *Men and Masculinities, 12*(3), 275–298.

Welsh, S. (1999). Gender and sexual harassment. *Annual Review of Sociology, 25*, 169–190.

Introduction to Reading 42

Norms that define women as essentially sexually passive were challenged as *Sex and the City* hit television screens. However, did that television program actually change the way the expression of sexuality is used to enforce gender inequality? This article would suggest that although things have changed, sexuality is still gendered. In this reading, Laura Hamilton and Elizabeth A. Armstrong report their findings from a 4-year ethnographic and interview study of women at a midwestern university. The study began in 2004, when the authors, along with seven other researchers, "occupied" a room on a dormitory floor in what students identified as a "party dorm." In addition to observing and hanging out with the women, they also conducted interviews with 41 of the 53 women who lived on this floor during the first year. This particular paper summarizes the women's reports about hooking up and relationships and how both changed over the course of their study. Their focus on social interaction is particularly valuable in understanding how gender is understood and enforced within the inner circles of Berger's concentric rings of social control, by ourselves and those closest to us, as described in the introduction to this chapter. In addition, the authors provide an intersectional analysis, examining how interaction and meaning of these college relationships varies across social class for the young women they studied. Their findings help us think about how gender continues to influence the expression of sexuality in a world where permanent relationships are delayed and "sex" is the theme for young women as well as men. They also help us understand that gender enforcement, while not consistent, is patterned within intersections of different prisms, such as gender and social class in this piece.

1. How do the women in this study describe "hooking up," and what factors influence their orientation to this expression of sexuality?

2. How did gender influence the expression of sexuality differently for women from different social classes in this study?

3. Do you think heterosexuality will be less important in the future in enforcing gender difference and inequality than it has been in the past? Why or why not?

GENDERED SEXUALITY IN YOUNG ADULTHOOD

Double Binds and Flawed Options

Laura Hamilton and Elizabeth A. Armstrong

As traditional dating has declined on college campuses, hookups—casual sexual encounters often initiated at alcohol-fueled, dance-oriented social events—have become a primary form of intimate heterosexual interaction (England, Shafer, and Fogarty 2007; Paul, McManus, and Hayes 2000). Hookups have attracted attention among social scientists and journalists (Bogle 2008; Glenn and Marquardt 2001; Stepp 2007). To date, however, limitations of both data and theory have obscured the implications for women and the gender system. Most studies examine only the quality of hookups at one point during college and rely, if implicitly, on an individualist, gender-only approach. In contrast, we follow a group of women as they move through college—assessing all of their sexual experiences. We use an interactionist approach and attend to how both gender and class shape college sexuality. . . .

GENDER THEORY AND COLLEGE SEXUALITY

Research on Hooking Up

Paul, McManus, and Hayes (2000) and Glenn and Marquardt (2001) were the first to draw attention to the hookup as a distinct social form. As Glenn and Marquardt (2001, 13) explain, most

From Hamilton, Laura and Elizabeth A. Armstrong. 2009. "Gendered sexuality in young adulthood: Double binds and flawed options." *Gender & Society* 23(5): 259–616. Published by Sage Publications on behalf of Sociologists for Women in Society.

students agree that "a hook up is anything 'ranging from kissing to having sex,' and that it takes place outside the context of commitment." Others have similarly found that *hooking up* refers to a broad range of sexual activity and that this ambiguity is part of the appeal of the term (Bogle 2008). Hookups differ from dates in that individuals typically do not plan to do something together prior to sexual activity. Rather, two people hanging out at a party, bar, or place of residence will begin talking, flirting, and/or dancing. Typically, they have been drinking. At some point, they move to a more private location, where sexual activity occurs (England, Shafer, and Fogarty 2007). While strangers sometimes hook up, more often hookups occur among those who know each other at least slightly (Manning, Giordano, and Longmore 2006).

England has surveyed more than 14,000 students from 19 universities and colleges about their hookup, dating, and relationship experiences. Her Online College Social Life Survey (OCSLS) asks students to report on their recent hookups using "whatever definition of a hookup you and your friends use." Seventy-two percent of both men and women participating in the OCSLS reported at least one hookup by their senior year in college. Of these, roughly 40 percent engaged in three or fewer hookups, 40 percent between four and nine hookups, and 20 percent 10 or more hookups. Only about one-third engaged in intercourse in their most recent hookups, although—among the 80 percent of students who had intercourse by the end of college—67 percent had done so outside of a relationship.

Ongoing sexual relationships without commitment were common and were labeled "repeat," "regular," or "continuing" hookups and sometimes "friends with benefits" (Armstrong, England, and Fogarty 2009; Bogle 2008; Glenn and Marquardt 2001). Ongoing hookups sometimes became committed relationships and vice versa; generally, the distinction revolved around the level of exclusivity and a willingness to refer to each other as "girlfriend/boyfriend" (Armstrong, England, and Fogarty 2009). Thus, hooking up does not imply

interest in a relationship, but it does not preclude such interest. Relationships are also common among students. By their senior year, 69 percent of heterosexual students had been in a college relationship of at least six months.

To date, however, scholars have paid more attention to women's experiences with hooking up than relationships and focused primarily on ways that hookups may be less enjoyable for women than for men. Glenn and Marquardt (2001, 20) indicate that "hooking up is an activity that women sometimes find rewarding but more often find confusing, hurtful, and awkward." Others similarly suggest that more women than men find hooking up to be a negative experience (Bogle 2008, 173; Owen et al. 2008) and focus on ways that hookups may be harmful to women (Eshbaugh and Gute 2008; Grello, Welsh, and Harper 2006).

This work assumes distinct and durable gender differences at the individual level. Authors draw, if implicitly, from evolutionary psychology, socialization, and psychoanalytic approaches to gender—depicting women as more relationally oriented and men as more sexually adventurous (see Wharton 2005 for a review). For example, despite only asking about hookup experiences, Bogle (2008, 173) describes a "battle of the sexes" in which women want hookups to "evolve into some semblance of a relationship," while men prefer to "hook up with no strings attached" (also see Glenn and Marquardt 2001; Stepp 2007).

The battle of the sexes view implies that if women could simply extract commitment from men rather than participating in hookups, gender inequalities in college sexuality would be alleviated. Yet this research—which often fails to examine relationships—ignores the possibility that women might be the losers in both hookups and relationships. Research suggests that young heterosexual women often suffer the most damage from those with whom they are most intimate: Physical battery, emotional abuse, sexual assault, and stalking occur at high rates in youthful heterosexual relationships (Campbell et al. 2007; Dunn 1999). This suggests that gender inequality in college sexuality is systemic, existing across social forms.

Current research also tends to see hooking up as solely about gender, without fully considering the significance of other dimensions of inequality. Some scholars highlight the importance of the college environment and traditional college students' position in the life course (Bogle 2008; Glenn and Marquardt 2001). However, college is treated primarily as a context for individual sexual behavior rather than as a key location for class reproduction. Analyzing the role of social class in sex and relationships may help to illuminate the appeal of hookups for both college women and men.

Gender Beliefs and Social Interaction

Contemporary gender theory provides us with resources to think about gender inequality in college sexuality differently. Gender scholars have developed and refined the notion of gender as a social structure reproduced at multiple levels of society: Gender is embedded not only in individual selves but also in interaction and organizational arrangements (Connell 1987; Glenn 1999; Risman 2004). This paper focuses on the interactional level, attending to the power of public gender beliefs in organizing college sexual and romantic relations.

Drawing on Sewell's (1992) theory of structure, Ridgeway and Correll (2004, 511) define gender beliefs as the "cultural rules or instructions for enacting the social structure of difference and inequality that we understand to be gender." By believing in gender differences, individuals "see" them in interaction and hold others accountable to this perception. Thus, even if individuals do not internalize gender beliefs, they must still confront them (Ridgeway 2009).

Ridgeway and coauthors (Ridgeway 2000; Ridgeway and Correll 2004) assert that interaction is particularly important to the reproduction of gender inequality because of how frequently men and women interact. They focus on the workplace but suggest that gendered interaction in private life may be intensifying in importance

as beliefs about gender difference in workplace competency diminish (Correll, Benard, and Paik 2007; Ridgeway 2000; Ridgeway and Correll 2004). We extend their insights to sexual interaction, as it is in sexuality and reproduction that men and women are believed to be most different. The significance of gender beliefs in sexual interaction may be magnified earlier in the life course, given the amount of time spent in interaction with peers and the greater malleability of selves (Eder, Evans, and Parker 1995). Consequently, the university provides an ideal site for this investigation.

The notion that men and women have distinct sexual interests and needs generates a powerful set of public gender beliefs about women's sexuality. A belief about what women should not do underlies a *sexual double standard:* While men are expected to desire and pursue sexual opportunities regardless of context, women are expected to avoid casual sex—having sex only when in relationships and in love (Crawford and Popp 2003; Risman and Schwartz 2002). Much research on the sexuality of young men focuses on male endorsement of this belief and its consequences (e.g., Bogle 2008; Kimmel 2008; Martin and Hummer 1989). There is an accompanying and equally powerful belief that normal women should always want love, romance, relationships, and marriage—what we refer to as the *relational imperative* (also see Holland and Eisenhart 1990; Martin 1996; Simon, Eder, and Evans 1992). We argue that these twin beliefs are implicated in the (re)production of gender inequality in college sexuality and are at the heart of women's sexual dilemmas with both hookups and relationships.

An Intersectional Approach

Gender theory has also moved toward an intersectional approach (Collins 1990; Glenn 1999). Most of this work focuses on the lived experiences of marginalized individuals who are situated at the intersection of several systems of oppression (McCall 2005). More recently, scholars have begun to theorize the ways in which systems of inequality are themselves linked

(Beisel and Kay 2004; Glenn 1999; McCall 2005). Beisel and Kay (2004) apply Sewell's (1992) theory of structure to intersectionality, arguing that structures intersect when they share resources or guidelines for action (of which gender beliefs would be one example). Using a similar logic, we argue that gender and class intersect in the sexual arena, as these structures both rely on beliefs about how and with whom individuals should be intimate.

Like gender, class structures beliefs about appropriate sexual and romantic conduct. Privileged young Americans, both men and women, are now expected to defer family formation until the mid-twenties or even early-thirties to focus on education and career investment—what we call the *self-development imperative* (Arnett 2004; Rosenfeld 2007). This imperative makes committed relationships less feasible as the sole contexts for premarital sexuality. Like marriage, relationships can be "greedy," siphoning time and energy away from self-development (Gerstel and Sarkisian 2006; Glenn and Marquardt 2001). In contrast, hookups offer sexual pleasure without derailing investment in human capital and are increasingly viewed as part of life-stage appropriate sexual experimentation. Self-protection—both physical and emotional—is central to this logic, suggesting the rise of a strategic approach to sex and relationships (Brooks 2002; Illouz 2005). This approach is reflected in the development of erotic marketplaces offering short-term sexual partners, particularly on college campuses (Collins 2004).

In this case, gender and class behavioral rules are in conflict. Gender beliefs suggest that young women should avoid nonromantic sex and, if possible, be in a committed relationship. Class beliefs suggest that women should delay relationships while pursuing educational goals. Hookups are often less threatening to self-development projects, offering sexual activity in a way that better meshes with the demands of college. We see this as a case wherein structures intersect, but in a contradictory way (Friedland and Alford 1991; Martin 2004; Sewell 1992). This structural contradiction has experiential consequences: Privileged women find themselves caught between contradictory expectations, while less privileged women confront a foreign sexual culture when they enter college.

* * *

THE POWER OF GENDER BELIEFS

The "Slut" Stigma

Women did not find hookups to be unproblematic. They complained about a pervasive sexual double standard. As one explained, "Guys can have sex with all the girls and *it makes them more of a man,* but if a girl does then all of a sudden she's a ho, and she's not as quality of a person" (10-1, emphasis added). Another complained, "Guys, they can go around and have sex with a number of girls and they're not called anything" (6-1). Women noted that it was "easy to get a reputation" (11-1) from "hooking up with a bunch of different guys" (8-1) or "being wild and drinking too much" (14-3). Their experiences of being judged were often painful; one woman told us about being called a "slut" two years after the incident because it was so humiliating (42-3).

Fear of stigma constrained women's sexual behavior and perhaps even shaped their preferences. For example, several indicated that they probably would "make out with more guys" but did not because "I don't want to be a slut" (27-2). Others wanted to have intercourse on hookups but instead waited until they had boyfriends. A couple hid their sexual activity until the liaison was "official." One said, "I would not spend the night there [at the fraternity] because that does not look good, but now everyone knows we're boyfriend/girlfriend, so it's like my home now" (15-1). Another woman, who initially seemed to have a deep aversion to hooking up, explained, "I would rather be a virgin for as much as I can than go out and do God knows who." She later revealed a fear of social stigma, noting that when women engage in nonromantic sex, they "get a bad reputation. I know that I wouldn't want that reputation" (11-1). Her comments highlight the feedback between social judgment and internalized preference.

Gender beliefs were also at the root of women's other chief complaint about hookups—the disrespect of women in the hookup scene. The notion that hooking up is okay for men but not for women was embedded in the organization of the Greek system, where most parties occurred: Sorority rules prohibited hosting parties or overnight male visitors, reflecting notions about proper feminine behavior. In contrast, fraternities collected social fees to pay for alcohol and viewed hosting parties as a central activity. This disparity gave fraternity men almost complete control over the most desirable parties on campus—particularly for the underage crowd (Boswell and Spade 1996; Martin and Hummer 1989).

Women reported that fraternity men dictated party transportation, the admittance of guests, party themes such as "CEO and secretary ho," the flow of alcohol, and the movement of guests within the party (Armstrong, Hamilton, and Sweeney 2006). Women often indicated that they engaged in strategies such as "travel[ing] in hordes" (21-1) and not "tak[ing] a drink if I don't know where it came from" (15-1) to feel safer at fraternity parties. Even when open to hooking up, women were not comfortable doing so if they sensed that men were trying to undermine their control of sexual activity (e.g., by pushing them to drink too heavily, barring their exit from private rooms, or refusing them rides home). Women typically opted not to return to party venues they perceived as unsafe. As one noted, "I wouldn't go to [that house] because I heard they do bad things to girls" (14-1). Even those interested in the erotic competition of party scenes tired of it as they realized that the game was rigged.

The sexual double standard also justified the negative treatment of women in the party scene—regardless of whether they chose to hook up. Women explained that men at parties showed a lack of respect for their feelings or interests—treating them solely as "sex objects" (32-1). This disregard extended to hookups. One told us, "The guy gets off and then it's done and that's all he cares about" (12-4). Another complained of

her efforts to get a recent hookup to call: "That wasn't me implying I wanted a relationship—that was me implying I wanted respect" (42-2). In her view, casual sex did not mean forgoing all interactional niceties. A third explained, "If you're talking to a boy, you're either going to get into this huge relationship or you are nothing to them" (24-3). This either-or situation often frustrated women who wanted men to treat them well regardless of the level of commitment.

The Relationship Imperative

Women also encountered problematic gender beliefs about men's and women's different levels of interest in relationships. As one noted, women fight the "dumb girl idea"—the notion "that every girl wants a boy to sweep her off her feet and fall in love" (42-2). The expectation that women should want to be in relationships was so pervasive that many found it necessary to justify their single status to us. For example, when asked if she had a boyfriend, one woman with no shortage of admirers apologetically explained, "I know this sounds really pathetic and you probably think I am lying, but there are so many other things going on right now that it's really not something high up on my list. . . . I know that's such a lame-ass excuse, but it's true" (9-3). Another noted that already having a boyfriend was the only "actual, legitimate excuse" to reject men who expressed interest in a relationship (34-3).

Certainly, many women wanted relationships and sought them out. However, women's interest in relationships varied, and almost all experienced periods during which they wanted to be single. Nonetheless, women reported pressure to be in relationships all the time. We found that women, rather than struggling to get into relationships, had to work to avoid them.

The relational imperative was supported by the belief that women's relational opportunities were scarce and should not be wasted. Women described themselves as "lucky" to find a man willing to commit, as "there's not many guys like that in college" (15-1). This belief persisted despite the fact that most women were in relationships most of the time. As one woman noted, "I don't think anyone really wants to be in a serious relationship, but most, well actually all of us, have boyfriends" (13-1). Belief in the myth of scarcity also led women to stay in relationships when they were no longer happy. A woman who was "sick of" her conflict-ridden relationship explained why she could not end it: "I feel like I have to meet somebody else. . . . I go out and they're all these asshole frat guys. . . . That's what stops me. . . . Boys are not datable right now because . . . all they're looking for is freshman girls to hook up with. . . . [So] I'm just stuck. I need to do something about it, but I don't know what" (30-3). It took her another year to extract herself from this relationship. Despite her fears, when she decided she was ready for another relationship, she quickly found a boyfriend.

Women also confronted the belief that all women are relationally insatiable. They often told stories of men who acted entitled to relationships, expected their relational overtures to be accepted, and became angry when rebuffed— sometimes stalking the rejecting woman. As one explained about a friend, "Abby was having issues with this guy who likes her. He was like, 'You have to like me. . . . I'm not gonna take no for an answer. I'm gonna do whatever it takes to date you'" (24-3). Another noted that "last semester, this guy really wanted to date me, and I did not want to date him at all. He flipped out and was like, 'This is ridiculous, I don't deserve this'" (12-3). A third eventually gave in when a man continually rejected her refusals: "I was like, if I go [out with him] . . . maybe he'll stop. Because he wouldn't stop." She planned to act "extremely conservative" as a way to convince him that he did not want to be with her (39-4).

Gender beliefs may also limit women's control over the terms of interaction within relationships. If women are made to feel lucky to have boyfriends, men are placed in a position of power, as presumably women should be grateful when they commit. Women's reports suggest that men attempted to use this power to regulate their participation in college life. One noted, "When I got here my first semester

freshman year, I wanted to go out to the parties . . . and he got pissed off about it. . . . He's like, 'Why do you need to do that? Why can't you just stay with me?'" (4-2). Boyfriends sometimes tried to limit the time women spent with their friends and the activities in which they participated. As a woman explained, "There are times when I feel like Steve can get . . . possessive. He'll be like . . . 'I feel like you're always with your friends over me.' He wanted to go out to lunch after our class, and I was like, 'No, I have to come have this interview.' And he got so upset about it" (42-3). Men's control even extended to women's attire. Another told us about her boyfriend, "He is a very controlling person. . . . He's like, 'What are you wearing tonight?' . . . It's like a joke but serious at the same time" (32-4).

Women also became jealous; however, rather than trying to control their boyfriends, they often tried to change themselves. One noted that she would "do anything to make this relationship work." She elaborated, "I was so nervous being with Dan because I knew he had cheated on his [prior] girlfriend . . . [but] I'm getting over it. When I go [to visit him] now . . . I let him go to the bar, whatever. I stayed in his apartment because there was nothing else to do" (39-3). Other women changed the way they dressed, their friends, and where they went in the attempt to keep boyfriends.

When women attempted to end relationships, they often reported that men's efforts to control them escalated. We heard 10 accounts of men using abuse to keep women in relationships. One woman spent months dealing with a boyfriend who accused her of cheating on him. When she tried to break up, he cut his wrist in her apartment (9-2). Another tried to end a relationship but was forced to flee the state when her car windows were broken and her safety was threatened (6-4). Men often drew on romantic repertoires to coerce interaction after relationships had ended. One woman told us that her ex-boyfriend stalked her for months—even showing up at her workplace, showering her with flowers and gifts, and blocking her entry into work until the police arrived (25-2).

Intersectionality: Contradictions Between Class and Gender

Existing research about college sexuality focuses almost exclusively on its gendered nature. We contend that sexuality is shaped simultaneously by multiple intersecting structures. In this section, we examine the sexual and romantic implications of class beliefs about how ambitious young people should conduct themselves during college. Although all of our participants contended with class beliefs that contradicted those of gender, experiences of this structural intersection varied by class location. More privileged women struggled to meet gender and class guidelines for sexual behavior, introducing a difficult set of double binds. Because these class beliefs reflected a privileged path to adulthood, less privileged women found them foreign to their own sexual and romantic logics.

More Privileged Women and the Experience of Double Binds

The Self-Development Imperative and the Relational Double Bind

The four-year university is a classed structural location. One of the primary reasons to attend college is to preserve or enhance economic position. The university culture is thus characterized by the self-development imperative, or the notion that individual achievement and personal growth are paramount. There are also accompanying rules for sex and relationships: Students are expected to postpone marriage and parenthood until after completing an education and establishing a career.

For more privileged women, personal expectations and those of the university culture meshed. Even those who enjoyed relationships experienced phases in college where they preferred to remain single. Almost all privileged women (94 percent) told us at one point that they did not want a boyfriend. One noted, "All my friends here . . . they're like, 'I don't want to deal with [a boyfriend] right now. I want to be on my

own'" (37-1). Another eloquently remarked, "I've always looked at college as the only time in your life when you should be a hundred percent selfish. . . . I have the rest of my life to devote to a husband or kids or my job . . . but right now, it's my time" (21-2).

The notion that independence is critical during college reflected class beliefs about the appropriate role for romance that opposed those of gender. During college, relational commitments were supposed to take a backseat to self-development. As an upper-middle-class woman noted, "College is the only time that you don't have obligations to anyone but yourself. . . . I want to get settled down and figure out what I'm doing with my life before [I] dedicate myself to something or someone else" (14-4). Another emphasized the value of investment in human capital: "I've always been someone who wants to have my own money, have my own career so that, you know, 50 percent of marriages fail. . . . If I want to maintain the lifestyle that I've grown up with . . . I have to work. I just don't see myself being someone who marries young and lives off of some boy's money" (42-4). To become self-supporting, many privileged women indicated they needed to postpone marriage. One told us, "I don't want to think about that [marriage]. I want to get secure in a city and in a job. . . . I'm not in any hurry at all. As long as I'm married by 30, I'm good" (13-4). Even those who wanted to be supported by husbands did not expect to find them in college, instead setting their sights on the more accomplished men they expected to meet in urban centers after college.

More privileged women often found committed relationships to be greedy—demanding of time and energy. As one stated, "When it comes to a serious relationship, it's a lot for me to give into that. [What do you feel like you are giving up?] Like my everything. . . . There's just a lot involved in it" (35-3). These women feared that they would be devoured by relationships and sometimes struggled to keep their self-development projects going when they did get involved. As an upper-class woman told us, "It's hard to have a boyfriend and be really excited about it and still not let it consume you" (42-2). This situation was exacerbated by the gender beliefs discussed earlier, as women experienced pressure to fully devote themselves to relationships.

Privileged women reported that committed relationships detracted from what they saw as the main tasks of college. They complained, for example, that relationships made it difficult to meet people. As an upper-middle-class woman who had just ended a relationship described, "I'm happy that I'm able to go out and meet new people. . . . I feel like I'm doing what a college student should be doing. I don't need to be tied down to my high school boyfriend for two years when this is the time to be meeting people" (14-3). A middle-class woman similarly noted that her relationship with her boyfriend made it impossible to make friends on the floor her first year. She explained, "We were together every day. . . . It was the critical time of making friends and meeting people, [and] I wasn't there" (21-2).

Many also complained that committed relationships competed with schoolwork (also see Holland and Eisenhart 1990). An upper-middle-class woman remarked, "[My boyfriend] doesn't understand why I can't pick up and go see him all the time. But I have school. . . . I just want to be a college kid" (18-3). Another told us that her major was not compatible with the demands of a boyfriend. She said, "I wouldn't mind having a boyfriend again, but it's a lot of work. Right now with [my major] and everything . . . I wouldn't have time even to see him" (30-4). She did not plan to consider a relationship until her workload lessened.

With marriage far in the future, more privileged women often worried about college relationships getting too serious too fast. All planned to marry—ideally to men with greater earnings—but were clear about the importance of temporary independence. Consequently, some worked to slow the progression of relationships. One told us, "I won't let myself think that [I love him]. I definitely don't say that. . . . The person he loves is the person he is going to marry. . . . At the age we are at now, I feel like I don't want anything to be

more serious than it has to be until it is" (34-3). Eight privileged women even dated men they deemed unsuitable for marriage to ensure autonomy. One noted, "He fits my needs now because I don't want to get married now. I don't want anyone else to influence what I do after I graduate" (33-3). Others planned to end relationships when boyfriends were not on the same page. An upper-middle-class woman explained, "[He] wants to have two kids by the time he's thirty. I'm like, I guess we're not getting married. . . . I'd rather make money and travel first" (43-3).

For more privileged women, contradictory cultural rules created what we call the *relational double bind*. The relational imperative pushed them to participate in committed relationships; however, relationships did not mesh well with the demands of college, as they inhibited classed self-development strategies. Privileged women struggled to be both "good girls" who limited their sexual activity to relationships and "good students" who did not allow relational commitments to derail their educational and career development.

The Appeal of Hookups and the Sexual Double Bind

In contrast, hookups fit well with the self-development imperative of college. They allowed women to be sexual without the demands of relationships. For example, one upper-class woman described hooking up as "fun and non-threatening." She noted, "So many of us girls, we complain that these guys just want to hook up all the time. I'm going, these guys that I'm attracted to . . . get kind of serious." She saw her last hookup as ideal because "we were physical, and that was it. I never wanted it to go anywhere" (34-2). Many privileged women understood, if implicitly, that hooking up was a delay tactic, allowing sex without participation in serious relationships.

As a sexual solution for the demands of college, hooking up became incorporated into notions of what the college experience should be.

When asked which kinds of people hook up the most, one woman noted, "All. . . . The people who came to college to have a good time and party" (14-1). With the help of media, alcohol, and spring break industries, hooking up was so institutionalized that many took it for granted. One upper-middle-class woman said, "It just happens. It's natural" (15-1). They told us that learning about sexuality was something they were supposed to be doing in college. Another described, "I'm glad that I've had my one-night stands and my being in love and having sex. . . . Now I know what it's supposed to feel like when I'm with someone that I want to be with. I feel bad for some of my friends. . . . They're still virgins" (29-1).

High rates of hooking up suggest genuine interest in the activity rather than simply accommodation to men's interests. Particularly early in college, privileged women actively sought hookups. One noted, "You see a lot of people who are like, 'I just want to hook up with someone tonight.' . . . It's always the girls that try to get the guys" (41-1). Data from the OCSLS also suggest that college women like hooking up almost as much as men and are not always searching for something more. Nearly as many women as men (85 percent and 89 percent, respectively) report enjoying the sexual activity of their last hookup "very much" or "somewhat," and less than half of women report interest in a relationship with their most recent hookup.

In private, several privileged women even used the classed logic of hooking up to challenge stereotyped portrayals of gender differences in sexuality. As one noted, "There are girls that want things as much as guys do. There are girls that want things more, and they're like, 'Oh it's been a while [since I had sex].' The girls are no more innocent than the guys. . . . People think girls are jealous of relationships, but they're like, 'What? I want to be single'" (34-1). When asked about the notion that guys want sex and girls want relationships another responded, "I think that is the absolute epitome of bullshit. I know so many girls who honestly go out on a Friday night and they're like, 'I hope I get some

ass tonight.' They don't wanna have a boyfriend! They just wanna hook up with someone. And I know boys who want relationships. I think it goes both ways" (42-2). These women drew on gender-neutral understandings of sexuality characteristic of university culture to contradict the notion of women's sexuality as inevitably and naturally relational.

For more privileged women, enjoyment of hookups was tightly linked to the atmosphere in which they occurred. Most were initiated at college parties where alcohol, music, attractive people, sexy outfits, and flirting combined to generate a collective erotic energy. As one woman enthusiastically noted, "Everyone was so excited. It was a big fun party" (15-1). Privileged women often "loved" it when they had an "excuse to just let loose" and "grind" on the dance floor. They reported turning on their "make-out radar" (18-1), explaining that "it's fun to know that a guy's attracted to you and is willing to kiss you" (16-1). The party scene gave them a chance to play with adult sexualities and interact for purely sexual purposes—an experience that one middle-class woman claimed "empowered" her (17-1).

Hookups enabled more privileged women to conduct themselves in accordance with class expectations, but as we demonstrated earlier, the enforcement of gender beliefs placed them at risk of sanction. This conflict gets to the heart of a *sexual double bind:* While hookups protected privileged women from relationships that could derail their ambitions, the double standard gave men greater control over the terms of hooking up, justified the disrespectful treatment of women, supported sexual stigma, and produced feelings of shame.

Less Privileged Women and the Experience of Foreign Sexual Culture

Women's comfort with delaying commitment and participating in the hookup culture was shaped by class location. College culture reflects the beliefs of the more privileged classes. Less privileged women arrived at college with their own orientation to sex and romance, characterized by a faster transition into adulthood. They often attempted to build both relationships and career at the same time. As a result, the third of the participants from less privileged backgrounds often experienced the hookup culture as foreign in ways that made it difficult to persist at the university.

Less privileged women had less exposure to the notion that the college years should be set aside solely for educational and career development. Many did not see serious relationships as incompatible with college life. Four were married or engaged before graduating—a step that others would not take until later. One reminisced, "I thought I'd get married in college. . . . When I was still in high school, I figured by my senior year, I'd be engaged or married or something. . . . I wanted to have kids before I was 25" (25-4). Another spoke of her plans to marry her high school sweetheart: "I'll be 21 and I know he's the one I want to spend the rest of my life with. . . . Really, I don't want to date anybody else" (6-1).

Plans to move into adult roles relatively quickly made less privileged women outsiders among their more privileged peers. One working-class woman saw her friendships dissolve as she revealed her desire to marry and have children in the near future. As one of her former friends described,

> She would always talk about how she couldn't wait to get married and have babies. . . . It was just like, Whoa. I'm 18. . . . Slow down, you know? Then she just crazy dropped out of school and wouldn't contact any of us. . . . The way I see it is that she's from a really small town, and that's what everyone in her town does . . . get married and have babies. That's all she ever wanted to do maybe? . . . I don't know if she was homesick or didn't fit in. (24-4)

This account glosses over the extent to which the working-class woman was pushed out of the university—ostracized by her peers for not acclimating to the self-development imperative and, as noted below, to the campus sexual climate. In fact, 40 percent of less privileged women left the university, compared to 5 percent of more privileged women. In all cases, mismatch between the sexual culture of women's hometowns and that of college was a factor in the decision to leave.

Most of the less privileged women found the hookup culture to be not only foreign but hostile. As the working-class woman described above told us,

> I tried so hard to fit in with what everybody else was doing here. . . . I think one morning I just woke up and realized that this isn't me at all; I don't like the way I am right now. . . . I didn't feel like I was growing up. I felt like I was actually getting younger the way I was trying to act. Growing up to me isn't going out and getting smashed and sleeping around. . . . That to me is immature. (28-1)

She emphasized the value of "growing up" in college. Without the desire to postpone adulthood, less privileged women often could not understand the appeal of hooking up. As a lower-middle-class woman noted, "Who would be interested in just meeting somebody and then doing something that night? And then never talking to them again? . . . I'm supposed to do this; I'm supposed to get drunk every weekend. I'm supposed to go to parties every weekend . . . and I'm supposed to enjoy it like everyone else. But it just doesn't appeal to me" (5-1). She reveals the extent to which hooking up was a normalized part of college life: For those who were not interested in this, college life could be experienced as mystifying, uncomfortable, and alienating.

The self-development imperative was a resource women could use in resisting the gendered pull of relationships. Less privileged women did not have as much access to this resource and were invested in settling down. Thus, they found it hard to resist the pull back home of local boyfriends, who—unlike the college men they had met—seemed interested in marrying and having children soon. One woman noted after transferring to a branch campus, "I think if I hadn't been connected with [my fiancé], I think I would have been more strongly connected to [the college town], and I think I probably would have stayed" (2-4). Another described her hometown boyfriend: "He'll be like, 'I want to see you. Come home.'... The stress he was putting me under and me being here my first year. I could not take it" (7-2). The following year, she moved back home. A third explained about her husband, "He wants me at home.... He wants to have control over me and ... to feel like he's the dominant one in the relationship.... The fact that I'm going to school and he knows I'm smart and he knows that I'm capable of doing anything that I want ... it scares him" (6-4). While she eventually ended this relationship, it cost her an additional semester of school.

Women were also pulled back home by the slut stigma, as people there—perhaps out of frustration or jealousy—judged college women for any association with campus sexual culture. For instance, one woman became distraught when a virulent sexual rumor about her circulated around her hometown, especially when it reached her parents. Going home was a way of putting sexual rumors to rest and reaffirming ties that were strained by leaving.

Thus, less privileged women were often caught between two sexual cultures. Staying at the university meant abandoning a familiar logic and adopting a privileged one—investing in human capital while delaying the transition to adulthood. As one explained, attending college led her to revise her "whole plan": "Now I'm like, I don't even need to be getting married yet [or] have kids.... All of [my brother's] friends, 17- to 20-year-old girls, have their ... babies, and I'm like, Oh my God.... Now I'll be able to do something else for a couple years before I settle down ... before I worry about kids" (25-3). These changes in agendas required them to end relationships with men whose life plans diverged from theirs. For some, this also meant cutting ties with hometown friends. One resolute woman, whose friends back home had turned on her, noted, "I'm just sick of it. There's nothing there for me anymore. There's absolutely nothing there" (22-4).

Discussion

The Strengths of an Interactional Approach

Public gender beliefs are a key source of gender inequality in college heterosexual interaction. They undergird a sexual double standard and a relational imperative that justify the disrespect of women who hook up and the disempowerment of women in relationships—reinforcing male dominance across social forms. Most of the women we studied cycled back and forth between hookups and relationships, in part because they found both to be problematic. These findings indicate that an individualist, battle of the sexes explanation not only is inadequate but may contribute to gender inequality by naturalizing problematic notions of gender difference.

We are not, however, claiming that gender differences in stated preferences do not exist. Analysis of the OCSLS finds a small but significant difference between men and women in preferences for relationships as compared to hookups: After the most recent hookup, 47 percent of women compared to 37 percent of men expressed some interest in a relationship. These differences in preferences are consistent with a multilevel perspective that views the internalization of gender as an aspect of gender structure (Risman 2004). As we have shown, the pressure to internalize gender-appropriate preferences is considerable, and the line between personal preferences and the desire to avoid social stigma is fuzzy. However, we believe that widely shared beliefs about gender difference contribute more to gender inequality in college heterosexuality than the substantively small differences in actual preferences.

The Strengths of an Intersectional Approach

An intersectional approach sheds light on the ambivalent and contradictory nature of many college women's sexual desires. Class beliefs associated with the appropriate timing of marriage clash with resilient gender beliefs—creating difficult double binds for the more privileged women who strive to meet both. In the case of the relational double bind, relationships fit with gender beliefs but pose problems for the classed self-development imperative. As for the sexual double bind, hookups provide sexual activity with little cost to career development, but a double standard penalizes women for participating. Less privileged women face an even more complex situation: Much of the appeal of hookups derives from their utility as a delay strategy. Women who do not believe that it is desirable to delay marriage may experience the hookup culture as puzzling and immature.

An intersectional approach also suggests that the way young heterosexuals make decisions about sexuality and relationships underlies the reproduction of social class. These choices are part of women's efforts to, as one privileged participant so eloquently put it, "maintain the lifestyle that I've grown up with." Our participants were not well versed in research demonstrating that college-educated women benefit from their own human capital investments, are more likely to marry than less educated women, and are more likely to have a similarly well-credentialed spouse (DiPrete and Buchmann 2006). Nonetheless, most were aware that completing college and delaying marriage until the mid-to-late twenties made economic sense. Nearly all took access to marriage for granted, instead focusing their attention on when and whom they would marry.

The two-pronged strategy of career investment and delay of family formation has so quickly become naturalized that its historical novelty is now invisible. It is based on the consolidation of class, along with heterosexual, privilege: Heterosexual men and women attempt to maximize their own earning power and that of their spouse—a pattern that is reflected in increased levels of educational homogamy (Schwatz and Mare 2005; Sweeney 2002). Consolidation of privilege is made possible by women's greater parity with men in education and the workforce. In this new marital marketplace, a woman's educational credentials and earning potential are more relevant than her premarital sexual activity, assuming she avoids having a child before marriage.

Relationship commitments that block educational and career investments, particularly if they foreclose future opportunities to meet men with elite credentials, are a threat to a woman's upward mobility.

The gender implications of the consolidation of privilege are most visible when contrasted with gender specialization—a marital strategy once assumed to be universal. Marriage was thought to be a system of complementary interdependence in which the man specialized in the market and the woman in domesticity (Becker 1991). Men maximized earning power while women accessed these benefits by marrying those with greater educational or career credentials. Gender specialization does not logically demand chastity of women; however, historically it has often been offered for trade in the marital marketplace. When this occurs, women's sexual reputation and economic welfare are linked. Although this connection has long been attenuated in the United States, it still exists. For example, the term "classy" refers simultaneously to wealth and sexual modesty.

As marriage in the United States has become less guided by gender specialization and more by the consolidation of privilege, gender inequality—at least within the marriages of the privileged—may have decreased. At the same time, class inequality may have intensified. The consolidation of privilege increases economic gaps between the affluent who are married to each other, the less affluent who are also married to each other and the poor, who are excluded from marriage altogether (also see Edin and Kefalas 2005; England 2004; Schwartz and Mare 2005; Sweeney 2002). The hookup culture may contribute in a small way to the intensification of class inequality by facilitating the delay necessary for the consolidation of privilege. . . .

REFERENCES

Armstrong, Elizabeth A., Paula England, and Alison C. K. Fogarty. 2009. Orgasm in college hookups and relationships. In *Families as they really are*, edited by B. Risman. New York: Norton.

Armstrong, Elizabeth A., Laura Hamilton, and Brian Sweeney. 2006. Sexual assault on campus: A multilevel, integrative approach to party rape. *Social Problems* 53:483–99.

Arnett, Jeffrey Jensen. 2004. Emerging adulthood: The winding road from the late teens through the twenties. New York: Oxford.

Becker, Gary S. 1991. *A treatise on the family.* Cambridge, MA: Harvard University Press.

Beisel, Nicola, and Tamara Kay. 2004. Abortion, race, and gender in nineteenth century America. *American Sociological Review* 69:498–518.

Bogle, Kathleen A. 2008. *Hooking up: Sex, dating, and relationships on campus.* New York: New York University Press.

Boswell, A. Ayres, and Joan Z. Spade. 1996. Fraternities and collegiate rape culture: Why are some fraternities more dangerous places for women? *Gender & Society* 10:133–47.

Brooks, David. 2002. Making it: Love and success at America's finest universities. *The Weekly, Standard,* December 23.

Campbell, Jacquelyn C., Nancy Glass, Phyllis W. Sharps, Kathryn Laughon, and Tina Bloom. 2007. Intimate partner homicide. *Trauma, Violence & Abuse* 8:246–69.

Collins, Patricia Hill. 1990. *Black feminist thought: Knowledge, consciousness and the politics of empowerment.* Boston: Unwin Hyman.

Collins, Randall. 2004. *Interaction ritual chains.* Princeton, NJ: Princeton University Press.

Connell, R. W. 1987. *Gender and power: Society, the person, and sexual politics.* Stanford, CA: Stanford University Press.

Correll, Shelley J., Stephen Benard, and In Paik. 2007. Getting a job: Is there a motherhood penalty? *American Journal of Sociology* 112:1297–1338.

Crawford, Mary, and Danielle Popp. 2003. Sexual double standards: A review and methodological critique of two decades of research. *Journal of Sex Research* 40:13–26.

DiPrete, Thomas A., and Claudia Buchmann. 2006. Gender-specific trends in the value of education and the emerging gender gap in college completion. *Demography* 43:1–24.

Dunn, Jennifer L. 1999. What love has to do with it: The cultural construction of emotion and sorority women's responses to forcible interaction. *Social Problems* 46:440–59.

Eder, Donna, Catherine Colleen Evans, and Stephen Parker. 1995. *School talk: Gender and adolescent culture.* New Brunswick, NJ: Rutgers University Press.

Edin, Kathryn, and Maria Kefalas. 2005. *Promises I can keep: Why poor women put motherhood before marriage.* Berkeley: University of California Press.

England, Paula. 2004. More mercenary mate selection? Comment on Sweeney and Cancian (2004) and Press (2004). *Journal of Marriage and the Family* 66:1034–37.

England, Paula, Emily Fitzgibbons Shafer, and Alison C. K. Fogarty. 2007. Hooking up and forming romantic relationships on today's college campuses. In *The gendered society reader,* edited by M. Kimmel. New York: Oxford University Press.

Eshbaugh, Elaine M., and Gary Gute. 2008. Hookups and sexual regret among college women. *Journal of Social Psychology* 148:77–89.

Friedland, Roger, and Robert R. Alford. 1991. Bringing society back in: Symbols. practices, and institutional contradictions. In *The new institutionalism in organizational analysis*, edited by W. W. Powell and P. J. DiMaggio, 232–63. Chicago: University of Chicago Press.

Gerstel, Naomi, and Natalia Sarkisian. 2006. Marriage: The good, the bad, and the greedy. *Contexts* 5:16–21.

Glenn, Evelyn Nakano. 1999. The social construction and institutionalization of gender and race: An integrative framework. In *Revisioning gender,* edited by M. M. Ferree, J. Lorber, and B. B. Hess, 3–43. Thousand Oaks, CA: Sage.

Glenn, Norval, and Elizabeth Marquardt. 2001. *Hooking up, hanging out, and hoping for Mr. Right: College women on mating and dating today.* New York: Institute for American Values.

Grello, Catherine M., Deborah P. Welsh, and Melinda M. Harper. 2006. No strings attached: The nature of casual sex in college students. *Journal of Sex Research* 43:255–67.

Holland, Dorothy C., and Margaret A. Eisenhart. 1990. *Educated in romance: Women, achievement, and college culture.* Chicago: University of Chicago Press.

Illouz, Eva. 2005. *Cold intimacies: The making of emotional capitalism.* Cambridge, UK: Polity.

Kimmel, Michael. 2008. *Guyland: The perilous world where boys become men.* New York: Harper Collins.

Manning, Wendy D., Peggy C. Giordano, and Monica A. Longmore. 2006. Hooking up: The relationship contexts of "nonrelationship" sex. *Journal of Adolescent Research* 21:459–83.

Martin, Karin. 1996. *Puberty, sexuality, and the self: Boys and girls at adolescence.* New York: Routledge.

Martin, Patricia Yancey. 2004. Gender as a social institution. *Social Forces* 82:1249–73.

Martin, Patricia Yancey, and Robert A. Hummer. 1989. Fraternities and rape on campus. *Gender & Society* 3:457–73.

McCall, Leslie. 2005. The complexity of intersectionality. *Signs: Journal of Women in Culture and Society* 30:1771–1800.

Owen, Jesse J., Galena K. Rhoades, Scott M. Stanley, and Frank D. Finchaln 2008. "Hooking up" among college students: Demographic and psychosocial correlates. *Archives of Sexual Behavior,* http://www.sprigerlink.com/content/44j645v7v38013u4/fulltext.html.

Paul, Elizabeth L., Brian McManus and, Allison Hayes. 2000. "Hookups": Characteristics and correlates of college students' spontaneous and anonymous sexual experiences. *Journal of Sex Research* 37:76–88.

Ridgeway, Cecilia L. 2000. Limiting inequality through interaction: The end(s) of gender. *Contemporary Sociology* 29:110–20.

Ridgeway, Cecilia L. 2009. Framed before we know it: How gender shapes social relations. *Gender & Society* 23:145–60.

Ridgeway, Cecilia L., and Shelley J. Correll. 2004. Unpacking the gender system: A theoretical perspective on gender beliefs and social relations. *Gender & Society* 18:510–31.

Risman, Barbara, and Pepper Schwartz. 2002. After the sexual revolution: Gender politics in teen dating. *Contexts* 1:16–24.

Risman, Barbara J. 2004. Gender as a social structure: Theory wrestling with activism. *Gender & Society* 18:429–50.

Rosenfeld, Michael J. 2007. *The age of independence: Interracial unions, same sex unions and the changing American family.* Cambridge, MA: Harvard University Press.

Schwartz, Christine R., and Robert D. Mare. 2005. Trends in educational assortative marriage from 1940 to 2003. *Demography* 42:621–46.

Sewell, William H. 1992. A theory of structure: Duality, agency, and transformation. *American Journal of Sociology* 98:1–29.

Simon, Robin W., Donna Eder, and Cathy Evans. 1992. The development of feeling norms underlying romantic love among adolescent females. *Social Psychology Quarterly* 55:29–46.

Stepp, Laura Sessions. 2007. *Unhooked: How young women pursue sex, delay love, and lose at both.* New York: Riverhead.

Sweeney, Megan M. 2002. Two decades of family change: The shifting economic foundations of marriage. *American Sociological Review* 67:132–47.

Wharton, Amy S. 2005. *The sociology of gender: An introduction to theory and research.* Malden, MA: Blackwell.

Introduction to Reading 43

Enforcing gender happens everywhere in all sorts of institutions. This reading about the division of volunteer labor of parents on youth baseball and soccer teams illustrates how all institutions in our daily lives operate to enforce and maintain traditional and unequal gender categories. The first author spent many years participating in and observing these youth sports in his community. Both authors conducted field observations at practices and games and also participated in clinics for coaches and referees, and did 50 in-depth interviews with both women and men volunteers from the baseball and soccer teams in this community. They present a picture of how gender is seen as natural or essential, despite very clear interactions and expectations that place men and women in roles similar to those in "traditional" families. Unfortunately, this enforcement of gender does not always recognize talents of individual men and women.

1. What do the authors mean by "soft essentialism," and how is it used to enforce a traditional gender division of labor? Find examples of soft essentialism in the reading.

2. What are the ways men and women are sorted into traditional and unequal roles on these teams based on gender?

3. Compare the use of language in this reading to language used in other institutional arenas. We now have "flight attendants" rather than "stewardesses" on airplanes; however, can you think of other instances where we still use language to enforce gender?

SEPARATING THE MEN FROM THE MOMS

THE MAKING OF ADULT GENDER SEGREGATION IN YOUTH SPORTS

Michael A. Messner and Suzel Bozada-Deas

In volunteer work, just as in many families and workplaces, gender divisions are pervasive and persistent. Women are often expected to do the work of caring for others' emotions and daily needs. Women's volunteer labor is routinely devalued in much the same ways that housework and childcare are devalued in the home and women's clerical and other support work is devalued in the professions (Hook 2004). Similarly, men tend to do the instrumental work of public leadership, just as they do in the family and the workplace, and their informal work is valued accordingly.

This article examines the social construction of adult gender divisions of labor in a community volunteer activity, youth sports. A few scholars have examined women's invisible labor in sports (Boyle & McKay, 1995). In her study of a Little League Baseball league, Grasmuck (2005) estimates that the 111 league administrators, head coaches, and assistant coaches (mostly men) contribute a total of 33,330 hours of volunteer labor in a season—an average of about 300 hours per person. Much of the work women do in youth sports is behind-the-scenes support that is less visible than coaching (Thompson 1999). In a study of Little League Baseball in Texas, Chafetz and Kotarba (1999, 48–49) observed that "team mothers" in this "upper middle class, 'Yuppie' Texas community" do gender in ways that result in "the re-creation and strengthening of the community's collective identity as a place where, among other things, women are primarily mothers to their sons." As yet, no study has focused on how this gender divide among adults in youth sports happens. How do most men become coaches, while most women become "team moms"? How do adult gender divisions of labor in youth sports connect with commonsense notions about divisions between women and men in families and workplaces? This is important: Millions of children play community-based youth sports every year, and these athletic activities are a key part of the daily lives of many families. It is also important for scholars of gender—studying segregation in this context can reveal much about how gender divisions are created and sustained in the course of everyday life.

COACHES AND "TEAM MOMS"

In 1995, when we (the first author, Mike, and his family) arrived at our six-year-old son's first soccer practice, we were delighted to learn that his coach was a woman. Coach Karen, a mother in her mid-30s, had grown up playing lots of sports. She was tall, confident, and athletic, and the kids responded well to her leadership. It seemed to be a new and different world than the one we grew up in. But during the next decade, as our two sons played a few more seasons of soccer, two years of youth basketball, and more than a decade of baseball, they never had another woman head coach. It is not that women were not contributing to the kids' teams. All of the "team parents" (often called "team moms")—parent volunteers who did the behind-the-scenes work of phone-calling, organizing weekly snack schedules and team parties, collecting money for gifts for the coaches, and so on—were women. And occasionally, a team had a woman assistant coach. But women head coaches were few and far between.

In 1999, we started keeping track of the numbers of women and men head coaches in Roseville's[1] annual American Youth Soccer Organization (AYSO) and Little League Baseball/ Softball (LLB/S) yearbooks we received at the end of each season. The yearbooks revealed that from 1999 to 2007, only 13.4 percent of 1,490 AYSO teams had women head coaches. The numbers were even lower for Little League Baseball and Softball; only 5.9 percent of 538 teams were managed by women. In both AYSO and LLB/S, women coaches were clustered in the younger kids' teams (ages five to eight) and in coaching girls. Boys—and especially boys older than age 10—almost never had women coaches. These low numbers are surprising for several reasons. First, unlike during the 1950s and 1960s, when there were almost no opportunities for girls to play sports, today, millions of girls participate in organized soccer, baseball, softball, basketball, and other sports. With this demographic shift in youth sports, we expected that the gender division of labor among parents would have shifted

as well. Second, today's mothers in the United States came of age during and after the 1972 institution of Title IX and are part of the generation that ignited the booming growth of female athletic participation. We wondered how it happened that these women did not make a neat transition from their own active sports participation into coaching their own kids. Third, women in Roseville outnumber men significantly in every volunteer activity having to do with kids, such as the Parent and Teacher Association (PTA), Scouts, and school special events. Coaching youth sports is the great exception to this rule. Sport has changed over the past 30 years, from a world set up almost exclusively by and for boys and men to one that is moving substantially (although incompletely) toward gender equity (Messner 2002). Yet, men dominate the very public on-field volunteer leadership positions in community youth sports.

This article is part of a larger study of gender in adult volunteering in two youth sports programs in a small independent suburb of Los Angeles that we call Roseville. Both of the sports leagues are local affiliates of massive national and international organizations. LLB/S and AYSO offer an interesting contrast in youth sports organizations, especially with respect to gender. Little League Baseball began in 1938 and for its first 36 years was an organization set up exclusively for boys. When forced against its will by a court decision in 1974 to include girls, Little League responded by creating a separate softball league into which girls continue to be tracked. Today, LLB/S is an organization that boasts 2.7 million child participants worldwide, 2.1 million of them in the United States. There are 176,786 teams in the program, 153,422 of them in baseball and 23,364 in softball. Little League stays afloat through the labor of approximately 1 million volunteers.

When AYSO started in 1964, it was exclusively for boys, but by 1971, girls' teams had been introduced. Thus, over the years, the vast majority of people who have participated in AYSO have experienced it as an organization set up for boys and girls. AYSO remains today mostly a U.S. organization, with more than 650,000 players on more than 50,000 teams. The national AYSO office employs 50 paid staff members, but like LLB/S, AYSO is an organization largely driven by the labor of volunteers, with roughly 250,000 volunteer coaches, team parents, and referees.

The differently gendered history of these two organizations offers hints as to the origins of the differences we see; there are more women head coaches in soccer than in baseball. Connell (1987) argues that every social institution—including the economy, the military, schools, families, or sport—has a "gender regime," which is defined as the current state of play of gender relations in the institution. We can begin to understand an institution's gender regime by measuring and analyzing the gender divisions of labor and power in the organization (i.e., what kinds of jobs are done by women and men, who has the authority, etc.). The idea that a gender regime is characterized by a "state of play" is a way to get beyond static measurements that result from a quick snapshot of an organizational pyramid and understanding instead that organizations are always being created by people's actions and discourse (Britton 2000). These actions often result in an organizational inertia that reproduces gender divisions and hierarchies; however, organizations are also subject to gradual—or occasionally even rapid—change.

Institutional gender regimes are connected with other gender regimes. Put another way, people in their daily lives routinely move in, out, and across different gender regimes—families, workplaces, schools, places of worship, and community activities such as youth sports. Their actions within a particular gender regime—for instance, the choice to volunteer to coach a youth soccer team—and the meanings they construct around these actions are constrained and enabled by their positions, responsibilities, and experiences in other institutional contexts. We will show how individual decisions to coach or to serve as team parents occur largely through non-reflexive, patterned interactions that are infused with an ascendant gender ideology that we call

"soft essentialism." These interactions occur at the nexus of the three gender regimes of community youth sports, families, and workplaces.

RESEARCH METHODS

The low numbers of women coaches in Roseville AYSO and LLB/S and the fact that nearly all of the team parents are women gave us a statistical picture of persistent gender segregation. But simply trotting out these numbers couldn't tell us how this picture is drawn. We wanted to understand the current state of play of the adult gender regime of youth sports, so we developed a study based on the following question: What are the social processes that sustain this gender segregation? And by extension, we wanted to explore another question: What is happening that might serve to destabilize and possibly change this gender segregation? In other words, are there ways to see and understand the internal mechanisms—the face-to-face interactions as well as the meaning-making processes—that constitute the "state of play" of the gender regime of community youth sports?

* * *

THE COACHES' STORIES

When we asked a longtime Little League Softball manager why he thinks most head coaches are men while nearly all team parents are women, he said with a shrug, "They give opportunities to everybody to manage or coach and it just so happens that no women volunteer, you know?" This man's statement was typical of head coaches and league officials who generally offered up explanations grounded in individual choice: Faced with equal opportunities to volunteer, men just choose to be coaches, while women choose to be team parents.

But our research shows that the gendered division of labor among men and women volunteers in youth coaching results not simply from an accumulation of individual choices; rather, it is produced through a profoundly social process. We will first draw from our interviews with head coaches to illustrate how gender divisions of labor among adult volunteers in youth sports are shaped by gendered language and belief systems and are seen by many coaches as natural extensions of gendered divisions of labor in families and workplaces. We next draw observations from our field notes to illustrate how everyday interactions within the gendered organizational context of youth sports shapes peoples' choices about men's and women's roles as coaches or team parents. Our main focus here will be on reproductive agency—the patterns of action that reproduce the gender division of labor. But we will also discuss moments of resistance and disruption that create possibilities for change.

Gendered Pipelines

When we asked coaches to describe how they had decided to become coaches, most spoke of having first served as assistant coaches—sometimes for just one season, sometimes for several seasons—before moving into head coaching positions. Drawing from language used by those who study gender in occupations, we can describe the assistant coach position as an essential part of the "pipeline" to the head coach position (England 2006). One of the reasons for this is obvious: many parents—women and men—believe that as a head coach, they will be under tremendous critical scrutiny by other parents in the community. Without previous youth coaching experience, many lack the confidence that they feel they need to take on such a public leadership task. A year or two of assistant coaching affords one the experience and builds the confidence that can lead to the conclusion that "I can do that" and the decision to take on the responsibility of a head coaching position.

But the pipeline from assistant coaches to head coaches does not operate in a purely individual voluntarist manner. A male longtime Little League manager and a member of the

league's governing board gave us a glimpse of how the pipeline works when there is a shortage of volunteers:

> One time we had 10 teams and only like six or seven applicants that wanted to be strictly manager. So you kinda eyeball the yearbook from the year before, maybe a couple of years [before], and see if the same dad is still listed as a[n assistant] coach, and maybe now it's time he wants his own team. So you make a lot of phone calls. You might make 20 phone calls and hopefully you are going to get two or three guys that say, "Yes, I'll be a manager."

. . . To understand how it is that most head coaches are men, we need to understand how the pipeline operates—how it is that, at the entry level, women's and men's choices to become assistant coaches and/or team parents are constrained or enabled by the social context.

Recruiting Dads and Moms to Help

There is a lot of work involved in organizing a successful youth soccer, baseball, or softball season. A head coach needs help from two, three, even four other parents who will serve as assistant coaches during practices and games. Parents also have to take responsibility for numerous support tasks like organizing snacks, making team banners, working in the snack bar during games, collecting donations for year-end gifts for the coaches, and organizing team events and year-end parties. In AYSO, parents also serve as volunteer referees. When we asked head coaches how they determined who would help them with these assistant coaching and other support tasks, a very common storyline developed: the coach would call a beginning-of-the-season team meeting, sometimes preceded by a letter or e-mail to parents, and ask for volunteers. Nearly always, they ended up with dads volunteering to help as assistant coaches and moms volunteering to be team parents. . . .

[T]he assistant coach and team parent positions are sometimes informally set up even before the first team meeting and how a coach's assumption that the team parent will be a "team mom" might make it more likely that women end up in these positions. But even coaches—such as the woman soccer coach quoted below—who try to emphasize that team parent is not necessarily a woman's job find that only women end up volunteering:

> Before the season started, we had a team meeting and I let the parents know that I would need a team parent and I strongly stressed parent, because I don't think it should always be a mother. But we did end up with the mom doing it and she assigns snacks and stuff like that.

None of the head coaches we interviewed said that they currently had a man as the team parent. Four coaches recalled that they had once had a man as a team parent (although one of these four coaches said, "Now that I think about it, that guy actually volunteered his wife do it"). When we asked if they had ever had a team parent who was a man, nearly all of the coaches said never. Many of them laughed at the very thought. A woman soccer coach exclaimed with a chuckle, "I just can't imagine! I wonder if they've ever had a 'team mom' who's a dad. I don't know [laughs]." A man soccer coach stammered his way through his response, punctuating his words with sarcastic laughter: "Ha! In fact, that whole concept—I don't think I've ever heard of a team dad [laughs]. Uh—there is no team dad, I've never heard of a team dad. But I don't know why that would be." A few coaches, such as the following woman softball coach, resorted to family metaphors to explain why they think there are few if any men volunteering to be team parents: "Oh, it's always a mom [laughs]. 'Team mom.' That's why it's called 'team mom.' You know, the coach is a male. And the mom—I mean, that's the housekeeping—you know: Assign the snack."

There are gendered assumptions in the language commonly linked to certain professions, so much so that often, when the person holding the position is in the statistical minority, people attach a modifier, such as male nurse, male secretary, woman judge, woman doctor.

Or woman head coach. Over and over, in interviews with coaches, during team meetings, and in interactions during games, practices, and team parties, we noticed this gendered language. Most obvious was the frequent slippage from official term team parent to commonly used term "team mom." But we also noticed that a man coach was normally just called a coach, while a woman coach was often gender marked as a woman coach. As feminist linguists have shown, language is a powerful element of social life—it not only reflects social realities such as gender divisions of labor, it also helps to construct our notions of what is normal and what is an aberration (Thorne, Kramarae, and Henley 1983). One statement from a woman soccer coach, "I wonder if they've ever had a 'team mom' who's a dad," illustrates how gendered language makes the idea of a man team parent seem incongruous, even laughable. In youth sports, this gendered language supports the notion that a team is structured very much like a "traditional" heterosexual family: The head coach—nearly always a man—is the leader and the public face of the team; the team parent—nearly always a woman—is working behind the scenes, doing support work; assistant coaches—mostly men, but including the occasional woman—help the coach on the field during practices and games.

Teams are even talked about sometimes as "families," and while we never heard a head coach referred to as a team's "dad," we did often and consistently hear the team parent referred to as the "team mom." This gendered language, drawn from family relations, gives us some good initial hints as to how coach and team parent roles remain so gender segregated. In their study of self-managing teams, which was intended to break down gender divisions in workplaces, Ollilainen and Calasanti (2007) show how team members' use of family metaphors serves to maintain the salience of gender, and thus, helps to reproduce a gendered division of labor. Similarly, in youth sports contexts, gendered language structures people's conversations in ways that shape and constrain their actions. Is a man who volunteers to be a team parent now a "team mom"?

Gender Ideology and Work/Family Analogies

When we asked the coaches to consider why it is nearly always women who volunteer to be the team parent, many seemed never to have considered this question before. Some of the men coaches seemed especially befuddled and appeared to assume that women's team-parenting work is a result of an almost "natural" decision on the part of the woman. Some men, such as the following soccer coach, made sense of this volunteer division of labor by referring to the ways that it reflected divisions of labor in men's own families and in their community: "In this area we have a lot of stay-at-home moms, so it seems to kind of fall to them to take over those roles." Similarly, a man baseball coach whose wife served as the team parent explained, "I think it's because they probably do it at home. You know, I mean my wife—even though she can't really commit the time to coach, I don't think she would want to coach—uh, she's very good with that [team parent] stuff." . . .

Another man baseball coach broadened the explanation, drawing connections to divisions of labor in his workplace:

> It's kinda like in business. I work in real estate, and most of your deal makers that are out there on the front lines, so to speak, making the deals, doing the shuckin' and jivin', doing the selling, are men. It's a very Good Ol' Boys network on the real estate brokerage side. There are a ton a females who are on the property management side, because it's housekeeping, it's managing, it's like running the household, it's behind the scenes, it's like cooking in the kitchen—[laughs]—I mean, I hate to say that, but it's that kind of role that's secondary. Coach is out in the front leading the squad, mom sitting behind making sure that the snacks are in order and all that. You know—just the way it is. . . .

When explaining why it is that team parents are almost exclusively women, a small number of women coaches also seemed to see it in essentialist terms—like most of the men coaches saw it.

Many women coaches, however, saw the gendering of the team parent position as a problem and made sense of its persistence, as did many of the men, by referring to the ways that it reflects family- and work-related divisions of labor. But several of the women coaches added an additional dimension to their explanations by focusing on why they think the men don't or won't consider doing team parent work. A woman soccer coach said, "I think it's because the dads want to be involved with the action. And they are not interested in doing paperwork and collecting money for photos or whatever it is. They are not interested in doing that sort of stuff." Another woman soccer coach extended this point: "I think it's probably, well, identity, which is probably why not many men do it. You know, they think that is a woman's job, like secretary or nurse or, you know." In short, many of the women coaches were cognizant of the ways that the team parent job was viewed by men, like all "women's work," as nonmasculine and thus undesirable. A woman Little League coach found it ironically funny that her husband, in fact, does most of the cooking and housework at home but will not take on the role of team parent for his daughter's team. When asked if changing the name to "team dad" might get more men to volunteer, she replied with a sigh,

> I don't know. I wish my husband would be a team dad because he's just very much more domesticated than I am [laughs]. You know, "Bring all the snacks, honey, hook us up," you know. I think there's a lot of men out there, but they don't want to be perceived as being domesticated.

This coach's comment illustrates how—even for a man who does a substantial amount of the family labor at home—publicly taking on a job that is defined as "feminine" threatens to saddle him with a "domesticated" public image that would be embarrassing or even humiliating. In sum, most coaches—both women and men—believe that men become coaches and women become team parents largely because these public roles fit with their domestic proclivities and skills. But the women add an important dimension to this explanation: women do the team parent work because it has to be done . . . and because they know that the men will not do it.

FINDING A "TEAM MOM"

The interview data give us a window into how people make sense of decisions that they have made as youth sports volunteers and provide insights into how gendered language and beliefs about men's and women's work and family roles help to shape these decisions. Yet, asking people to explain how (and especially why) things such as gendered divisions of labor persist is not by itself the most reliable basis for building an explanation. Rather, watching how things happen gives us a deeper understanding of the social construction of gender (Thorne 1993). Our observations from team meetings and early season practices reveal deeper social processes at work—processes that shaped people's apparently individual decisions to volunteer for assistant coach or team parent positions. . . .

We observed two occasions when a woman who did not volunteer was drafted by the head coach to be the "team mom." In one case, the reluctant volunteer was clearly more oriented toward assistant coaching, as the following composite story from field notes from the beginning of the season of a seven-year-old boys' baseball team illustrates:

At the first practice, Coach George takes charge, asks for volunteers. I tell him that I am happy to help out at practice and games and that he should just let me know what he'd like me to do. He appoints me Assistant Coach. This happens with another dad, too. We get team hats. Elena, a mother, offers to help out in any way she can. She's appointed "co-team mom" (the coach's wife is the other "team mom"). She shrugs and says okay, fine. Unlike most "team moms," Elena continues to attend all practices. At the fifth practice, Coach George is pitching batting practice to the kids; I'm assigned to first base, the other dad is working with the catcher. Elena (the "team mom")

is standing alone on the sidelines, idly tossing a ball up in the air to herself. Coach George's son suddenly has to pee, so as George hustles the boy off to the bathroom, Elena jumps in and starts pitching. She's good, it turns out, and can groove the pitch right where the kids want it. (By contrast, George has recently been plunking the kids with wild pitches.) Things move along well. At one point, when Coach George has returned from the bathroom, with Elena still pitching to the kids, a boy picks up a ball near second base and doesn't know what to do with it. Coach George yells at the kid: "Throw it! Throw it to the 'team mom!'" The kid, confused, says, "Where is she?" I say, "The pitcher, throw it to the pitcher." Coach George says, "Yeah, the 'team mom.'"

A couple of years later, we interviewed Elena and asked her how it was that she became a team parent and continued in that capacity for five straight years. Her response illuminated the informal constraints that channel many women away from coaching and toward being team parents:

The first year, when [my son] was in kindergarten, he was on a T-ball team, and I volunteered to be manager, and of course the league didn't choose me, but they did allow me to be assistant coach. And I was so excited, and [laughs] of course I showed up in heels for the first practice, because it was right after work, and the coach looked at me, and I informed him that "I'm your new assistant." And he looked at me—and I don't know if distraught is the correct word, but he seemed slightly disappointed, and he went out of his way to ask the parents who were there watching their children if there was anyone who wanted to volunteer, even though I was there. So there was this male who did kind of rise to the occasion, and so that was the end. He demoted me without informing me of his decision [laughs]—I was really enthused, because [my son] was in kindergarten, so I really wanted to be coach—or assistant coach at least—and it didn't happen. So after that I didn't feel comfortable to volunteer to coach. I just thought, okay, then I can do "team mom."

As this story illustrates, women who have the background, skills, and desire to work as on-field assistant coaches are sometimes assigned by head coaches to be "team moms." Some baseball teams even have a niche for such moms: a "dugout coach" (or "dugout mom") is usually a mom who may help out with on-field instruction during practices, but on game days, she is assigned the "indoors" space of the dugout, where it is her responsibility to keep track of the line-up and to be sure that the boy who is on-deck (next up to bat) is ready with his batting gloves and helmet on. The dugout coach also—especially with younger kids' teams—might be assigned to keep kids focused on the game, to keep equipment orderly, to help with occasional first aid, and to help see that the dugout is cleaned of empty water bottles and snack containers after the game is over. In short, the baseball, softball, and soccer fields on which the children play are gendered spaces (Dworkin 2001; Montez de Oca 2005). The playing field is the public space where the (usually male) coach exerts his authority and command. The dugout is like the home—a place of domestic safety from which one emerges to do one's job. Work happens in the indoor space of the dugout, but it is like family labor, behind-the-scenes, supporting the "real" work of leadership that is done on the field.

CHALLENGES AND RESISTANCE

The head coach's common assumption that fathers will volunteer to be assistant coaches and mothers to be "team moms" creates a context that powerfully channels men and women in these directions. Backed by these commonsense understandings of gendered divisions of labor, most men and women just "go with the flow" of this channeling process. Their choices and actions help to reproduce the existing gendered patterns of the organization. But some do not; some choose to swim against the tide. A mother who had several seasons of experience as a head soccer coach described the first team meeting for her youngest child's team:

> At our first team meeting, the coach announced, "I'm looking for a couple of you to help me out as assistant coaches," and he looked directly at the

men, and only at the men. None of them volunteered. And it was really amazing because he didn't even look at me or at any of the other women. So after the meeting, I went up to him and said, "Hey, I've coached soccer for like 10 seasons; I can help you out, okay?" And he agreed, so I'm the assistant coach for him.

This first team meeting is an example of a normal gendered interaction that, if it had gone unchallenged, would have reproduced the usual gender divisions of labor on the team. It is likely that many women in these situations notice the ways that men are, to adopt Martin's (2001) term, informally (and probably unconsciously) "mobilizing masculinities" in ways that reproduce men's positions of centrality. But this woman's 10 years of coaching experience gave her the confidence and the athletic "capital" that allowed her not only to see and understand but also to challenge the very gendered selection process that was taking place at this meeting. Most mothers do not have this background, and when faced with this sort of moment, they go with the flow.

On another occasion, as the following composite story from field notes describes, Mike observed a highly athletic and coaching-inclined woman assertively use her abilities in a way that initially seemed to transcend the gender segregation process, only to be relegated symbolically at season's end to the position of "team mom":

> A new baseball season, the first team meeting of the year; a slew of dads volunteer to be assistant coaches. Coach George combs the women for a "team mom" and gets some resistance; at first, nobody will do it, but then he finds a volunteer. At the first few practices, few assistant coaches actually show up. Isabel, a mom, clearly is into baseball, very knowledgeable and athletic, and takes the field. She pitches to the kids, gives them good advice. On the day when George is passing out forms for assistant coaches to sign, he hands her one too. She accepts it, in a matter-of-fact way. Isabel continues to attend practices, working with the kids on the field.
>
> Though few dads show up for many of the practices, there never seems to be a shortage of dads to serve as assistant coaches at the games. At one game, Coach George invites Isabel to coach third

base, but beyond that, she is never included in an on-field coaching role during a game.

End of season, team party. Coach George hands out awards to all the kids. He hands out gift certificates to all the assistant coaches but does not include Isabel. Then he hands out gift certificates to the "team moms," and includes Isabel, even though I don't recall her doing any team parent tasks. She had clearly been acting as an assistant coach all season long.

This story illustrates how, on one hand, a woman volunteer can informally circumvent the sorting process that pushes her toward the "team mom" role by persistently showing up to practices and assertively doing the work of a coach. As Thorne (1993, 133) points out, individual incidences of gender crossing are often handled informally in ways that affirm, rather than challenge, gender boundaries: An individual girl who joins the boys' game gets defined "as a token, a kind of 'fictive boy,' not unlike many women tokens in predominantly men settings, whose presence does little to challenge the existing arrangements." Similarly, Isabel's successful "crossing" led to her becoming accepted as an assistant coach during practices but rarely recognized as a "real" coach during games. She was a kind of "token" or "fictive" coach whose gender transgression was probably unknown to the many adults who never attended practices. So, in the final moment of the season, when adults and children alike were being publicly recognized for their contributions to the team, she was labeled and rewarded for being a "team mom," reaffirming gender boundaries.

A few coaches whom we interviewed consciously attempted to resist or change this gendered sorting system. Some of the women coaches, especially, saw it as a problem that the team parent job was always done by a woman. A woman softball coach was concerned that the "team mom" amounted to negative role-modeling for kids and fed into the disrespect that women coaches experienced:

The kids think that the moms should just be "team moms." Which means that they don't take the mothers seriously, and I think that's a bad thing.

I mean it's a bad thing. I think that's a lack of respect to women, to mothers.

Another woman Little League coach said that most team parents are women because too many people assume

that's all the women are good for. I think that's what the mentality is. I made it very clear to our parents that it did not have to be a mother, that it could be a father and that I encourage any dad out there that had time to do what team parents are supposed to do, to sign up and do it. But it didn't happen.

Such coaches find that simply degendering the language by calling this role team parent and even stressing that this is not a gendered job is unlikely to yield men volunteers. So what some women coaches do is simply refuse to have a team parent. A woman soccer coach said, "I do it all. I don't have a team parent." Another said, "I think in general, compared to the men who coach, I do more of that [team parent work]." This resistance by women coaches is understandable, especially from those who see the phenomenon of "team mom" as contributing to a climate of disrespect for women coaches. However, this form of resistance ends up creating extra work for women coaches—work that most men coaches relegate to a "team mom."

The very few occasions when a father does volunteer—or is recruited by the coach—to be the team parent are moments of gender "crossing" that hold the potential to disrupt the normal operation of the gender-category sorting process. But ironically, a team parent who is a man can also reinforce gender stereotypes. One man soccer coach told me that the previous season, a father had volunteered to be the team parent, but that

he was a disaster [laughs]. He didn't do anything, you know, and what little he did it was late; it was ineffective assistance. He didn't come, he didn't make phone calls, I mean he was just like a black hole. And so that—that was an unfortunate disaster. This year it's a woman again.

The idea that a man volunteered—and then failed miserably to do the team parent job—may serve ultimately to reinforce the taken-for-granted assumption that women are naturally better suited to do this kind of work.

THE DEVALUATION OF WOMEN'S INVISIBLE LABOR

The Roseville "team moms" we observed were similar to those studied by Chafetz and Kotarba (1999) in terms of their education, professional-class status, and family structure. The Texasville and Roseville "team moms" are doing the same kinds of activities, simultaneously contributing to the "concerted cultivation" of their own children (Lareau 2003) while helping to enhance the social cohesion of the team, the league, and the community.

Despite the importance of the work team parents are doing, it is not often recognized as equivalent to the work done by coaches. Of course, the team parent typically puts in far fewer hours of labor than does the head coach. However, in some cases, the team parents put in more time than some assistant coaches (dads, for instance, whose work schedules don't allow them to get to many practices but who can be seen on the field during a Saturday game, coaching third base). Yet, the team parent's work remains largely invisible, and coaches sometimes talk about team parents' contributions as trivial or unimportant. Several coaches, when asked about the team parent job, disparaged it as "not very hard to do," "an easy job." But our interviews suggest that the women team parents are often doing this job as one of many community volunteer jobs, while most of the men who coach are engaged in this and only this volunteer activity.

* * *

SORTING AND SOFT ESSENTIALISM

In this article, we have revealed the workings of a gender-category sorting process that reflects the interactional "doing" of gender discussed by West and Zimmerman (1987). Through this sorting process, the vast majority of women volunteers are channeled into a team parent position, and the vast majority of men volunteers become coaches. To say that people are "sorted" is not to deny their active agency in this process. Rather, it is to underline that organizations are characterized by self-perpetuating "inequality regimes" (Acker 2006). What people often think of as "free individual choices" are actually choices that are shaped by social contexts. We have shown how women's choices to become team parents are constrained by the fact that few, if any, men will volunteer to do this less visible and less honored job. Women's choices are enabled by their being actively recruited—"volunteered"—by head coaches or by other parents to become the "team mom." Moreover, men's choices to volunteer as assistant coaches and not as team parents are shaped by the gendered assumptions of head coaches, enacted through active recruiting and informal interactions at the initial team meeting.

This gender-category sorting system is at the heart of the current state of play of the gender regime of adult volunteer work in youth sports in Roseville. There are several ways we can see the sorting system at work. First, our research points to the role of gendered language and meanings in this process. The term coach and the term "team mom" are saturated with gendered assumptions that are consistent with most people's universe of meanings. These gendered meanings mesh with—and mutually reinforce—the conventional gendered divisions of labor and power in the organization in ways that make decisions to "go with the flow" appear natural. Second, we have shown how having women do the background support work while men do the visible leadership work on the team is also made to appear natural to the extent that it reiterates the gender divisions of labor that many parents experience in their families and in their workplaces. . . .

In the past, sport tended to construct a categorical "hard" essentialism—boys and men, it was believed, were naturally suited to the aggressive, competitive world of sport, while girls and women were not. Today, with girls' and women's massive influx into sport, these kinds of categorical assumptions of natural difference can no longer stand up to even the most cursory examination. Soft essentialism, as an ascendant professional-class gender ideology, frames sport as a realm in which girls are empowered to exercise individual choice (rehearsing choices they will later face in straddling the demands of careers and family labor), while continuing to view boys as naturally "hard wired" to play sports (and ultimately, to have public careers). Girls are viewed as flexibly facing a future of choices; boys as inflexible, facing a linear path toward public careers. Soft essentialism, in short, initiates kids into an adult world that has been only partially transformed by feminism, where many of the burdens of bridging and balancing work and family strains are still primarily on women's shoulders. Men coaches and "team moms" symbolize and exemplify these tensions.

Time after time, we heard leaders of leagues and some women coaches say that the league leadership works hard to recruit more women coaches but just cannot get them to volunteer. The formal agency here is to "recruit more women coaches." But what Martin (2001) calls the informal practicing of gender (revealed most clearly in our field-note vignettes) amounts to a collective and (mostly) nonreflexive sorting system that, at the entry level, puts most women and men on separate paths. Martin's work has been foundational in showing how gender works in organizations in informal, nonreflexive ways that rely on peoples' "tacit knowledge" about gender. In particular, she points out "how and why well-intentioned, 'good people' practice gender in ways that do harm" (Martin 2006, 255).

Our study shows a similar lack of "bad guys" engaged in overt acts of sexism and discrimination. Instead, we see a systemic reproduction of gender categorization, created nonreflexively by "well intentioned, good people." The mechanisms of this nonreflexive informal practicing of gender are made to seem normal through their congruence with the "tacit knowledge" of soft essentialism that is itself embedded in hegemonic professional-class family and workplace gender divisions of labor. The fact that soft essentialism

emerges from the intersections of these different social contexts means that any attempt to move toward greater equality for women and men in youth sports presupposes simultaneous movements toward equality in workplaces and families.

NOTE

1. Roseville is a pseudonym for the town we studied, and all names of people interviewed or observed for this study are also pseudonyms.

REFERENCES

Acker, Joan. 2006. Inequality regimes: Gender, class and race in organizations. *Gender & Society* 20:441-64.

Boyle, Maree, and Jim McKay. 1995. You leave your troubles at the gate: A case study of the exploitation of older women's labor and "leisure" in sport. *Gender & Society* 9:556–76.

Britton, Dana. 2000. The epistemology of the gendered organization. *Gender & Society* 14:418–34.

Chafetz, Janet Saltzman, and Joseph A. Kotarba. 1999. Little League mothers and the reproduction of gender. In *Inside sports*, edited by Jay Coakley and Peter Donnelly. London and New York: Routledge.

Connell, R. W. 1987. *Gender and power.* Stanford, CA: Stanford University Press.

Dworkin, Shari L. 2001. Holding back: Negotiating a glass ceiling on women's muscular strength. *Sociological Perspectives* 44:333–50.

England, Paula. 2006. Toward gender equality: Progress and bottlenecks. In *The declining significance of gender?* edited by Francine D. Blau, Mary C. Brinton, and David B. Grusky. New York: Russell Sage.

Grasmuck, Sherri. 2005. *Protecting home: Class, race, and masculinity in boys' baseball.* Piscataway, NJ: Rutgers University Press.

Hook, Jennifer L. 2004. Reconsidering the division of household labor: Incorporating volunteer work and informal support. *Journal of Marriage and Family* 66:101–17.

Lareau, Annette. 2003. *Unequal childhoods: Class, race, and family life.* Berkeley: University of California Press.

Martin, Patricia Yancy. 2001. Mobilizing masculinities: Women's experiences of men at work. *Organization* 8:587–618.

———. 2006. Practicing gender at work: Further thoughts on reflexivity. *Gender, Work and Organization* 13:254–76.

Messner, Michael A. 2002. *Taking the field: Women, men, and sports.* Minneapolis: University of Minnesota Press.

Montez de Oca, Jeffrey. 2005. As our muscles get softer, our missile race becomes harder: Cultural citizenship and the "muscle gap." *Journal of Historical Sociology* 18:145–71.

Ollilainen, Marjukka, and Toni Calasanti. 2007. Metaphors at work: Maintaining the salience of gender in self-managing teams. *Gender & Society* 21:5–27.

Thompson, Shona. 1999. The game begins at home: Women's labor in the service of sport. In *Inside sports*, edited by Jay Coakley and Peter Donnelly. London and New York: Routledge.

Thorne, Barrie. 1993. *Gender play: Girls and boys in school.* New Brunswick, NJ: Rutgers University Press.

Thorne, Barrie, Cheris Kramarae, and Nancy Henley. 1983. *Language, gender and society.* Rowley, MA: Newbury House.

West, Candace, and Don Zimmerman. 1987. Doing gender. *Gender & Society* 1:125–51.

Introduction to Reading 44

In this selection, the authors examine domestic violence from the perspective of men. They argue that domestic violence is gendered and the enactment of domestic violence maintains gender. To illustrate these points, Kristin L. Anderson and Debra Umberson conducted interviews with 33 men who were in an educational domestic violence program (Family Violence Diversion Network), using men's own voices to explain their role in violence against women. The men are diverse in terms of social class (mean number of years of education is 13, and mean income is $30,463), age (mean 32), and race and ethnicity (58% European American, 18% African American, and 21% Hispanic). Of the men interviewed, 82% were mandated by the courts to attend this program.

1. What do the authors mean when they say that, through violence, the men "naturalized a binary and hierarchical gender system"?

2. Why don't these men feel remorse over their use of domestic violence?

3. Do you think educational programs, such as the one described in this article, can be effective in reducing domestic violence?

GENDERING VIOLENCE

MASCULINITY AND POWER IN MEN'S ACCOUNTS OF DOMESTIC VIOLENCE

Kristin L. Anderson and Debra Umberson

In the 1970s, feminist activists and scholars brought wife abuse to the forefront of public consciousness. Published in the academic and popular press, the words and images of survivors made one aspect of patriarchy visible: Male dominance was displayed on women's

From Anderson, K. L., & Umberson, D., "Gendering Violence: Masculinity and Power in Men's Accounts of Domestic Violence," in *Gender & Society*, 15(3), 2001: 358–380. Published by Sage Publications on behalf of Sociologists for Women in Society.

bruised and battered bodies (Dobash and Dobash 1979; Martin 1976). Early research contributed to feminist analyses of battery as part of a larger pattern of male domination and control of women (Pence and Paymar 1993; Yllö 1993). Research in the 1980s and 1990s has expanded theoretical understandings of men's violence against women through emphases on women's agency and resistance to male control (Bowker 1983; Kirkwood 1993); the intersection of physical, structural, and emotional forces that sustain men's control over female partners (Kirkwood 1993; Pence and Paymar 1993); and the different constraints faced by women and men of diverse nations, racial ethnic identities, and sexualities who experience violence at the hands of intimate partners (Eaton 1994; Island and Letellier 1991; Jang, Lee, and Morello-Frosch 1998; Renzetti 1992). This work demonstrates ways in which the gender order facilitates victimization of disenfranchised groups.

Comparatively less work has examined the ways in which gender influences male perpetrators' experiences of domestic violence (Yllö 1993). However, a growing body of qualitative research critically examines batterers' descriptions of violence within their relationships. Dobash and Dobash (1998), Hearn (1998), and Ptacek (1990) focus on the excuses, justifications, and rationalizations that batterers use to account for their violence. These authors suggest that batterers' accounts of violence are texts through which they attempt to deny responsibility for violence and to present nonviolent self-identities.

Dobash and Dobash (1998) identify ways in which gender, as a system that structures the authority and responsibilities assigned to women and men within intimate relationships, supports battery. They find that men use violence to punish female partners who fail to meet their unspoken physical, sexual, or emotional needs. Lundgren (1998) examines batterers' use of gendered religious ideologies to justify their violence against female partners. Hearn (1998, 37) proposes that violence is a "resource for demonstrating and showing a person is a man." These studies find that masculine identities are constructed through acts of violence and through batterers' ability to control partners as a result of their violence.

This article examines the construction of gender within men's accounts of domestic violence. Guided by theoretical work that characterizes gender as performance (Butler 1990, 1993; West and Fenstermaker 1995), we contend that batterers attempt to construct masculine identities through the practice of violence and the discourse about violence that they provide. We examine these performances of gender as "routine, methodical, and ongoing accomplishment[s]" that create and sustain notions of natural differences between women and men (West and Fenstermaker 1995, 9). Butler's concept of performativity extends this idea by suggesting that it is through performance that gendered subjectivities are constructed: "Gender proves to be performative—that is, constituting the identity it is purported to be. In this sense, gender is always a doing, though not a doing by a subject who may be said to preexist the deed" (1990, 25). For Butler, gender performances demonstrate the instability of masculine subjectivity; a "masculine identity" exists only as the actions of individuals who stylize their bodies and their actions in accordance with a normative binary framework of gender.

In addition, the performance of gender makes male power and privilege appear natural and normal rather than socially produced and structured. Butler (1990) argues that gender is part of a system of relations that sustains heterosexual male privilege through the denigration or erasure of alternative (feminine/gay/lesbian/bisexual) identities. West and Fenstermaker (1995) contend that cultural beliefs about underlying and essential differences between women and men, and social structures that constitute and are constituted by these beliefs, are reproduced by the accomplishment of gender. In examining the accounts offered by domestically violent men, we focus on identifying ways in which the practice of domestic violence helps men to accomplish gender. We also focus on the contradictions within these accounts to explore the instability of masculine subjectivities and challenges to the performance of gender.

* * *

FINDINGS

How do batterers talk about the violence in their relationships? They excuse, rationalize, justify, and minimize their violence against female partners. Like the batterers studied by previous researchers, the men in this study constructed their violence as a rational response to extreme provocation, a loss of control, or a minor incident that was blown out of proportion. Through such accounts, batterers deny responsibility for their violence and save face when recounting behavior that has elicited social sanctions (Dobash and Dobash 1998; Ptacek 1990).

However, these accounts are also about the performance of gender. That is, through their speech acts, respondents presented themselves as rational, competent, masculine actors. We examine several ways in which domestic violence is gendered in these accounts. First, according to respondents' reports, violence is gendered in its practice. Although it was in their interests to minimize and deny their violence, participants reported engaging in more serious, frequent, and injurious violence than that committed by their female partners. Second, respondents gendered violence through their depictions and interpretations of violence. They talked about women's violence in a qualitatively different fashion than they talked about their own violence, and their language reflected hegemonic notions of femininity and masculinity. Third, the research participants constructed gender by interpreting the violent conflicts in ways that suggested that their female partners were responsible for the participants' behavior. Finally, respondents gendered violence by claiming that they are victimized by a criminal justice system that constructs all men as villains and all women as victims.

Gendered Practice

Men perpetrate the majority of violence against women and against other men in the United States (Bachman and Saltzman 1995). Although some scholars argue that women perpetrate domestic violence at rates similar to men (Straus 1993),

feminist scholars have pointed out that research findings of "sexual symmetry" in domestic violence are based on survey questions that fail to account for sex differences in physical strength and size and in motivations for violence (Dobash et al. 1992; Straton 1994). Moreover, recent evidence from a large national survey suggests that women experience higher rates of victimization at the hands of partners than men and that African American and Latina women experience higher rates of victimization than European American women (Bachman and Saltzman 1995).

Although the majority of respondents described scenarios in which both they and their partners perpetrated violent acts, they reported that their violence was more frequent and severe than the violence perpetrated by their female partners. Eleven respondents (33 percent) described attacking a partner who did not physically resist, and only two respondents (6 percent) reported that they were victimized by their partners but did not themselves perpetrate violence. The twenty cases (61 percent) in which the participants reported "mutual" violence support feminist critiques of "sexual symmetry":

> We started pushing each other. And the thing is that I threw her on the floor. I told her that I'm going to leave. She took my car keys, and I wanted my car keys so I went and grabbed her arm, pulled it, and took the car keys away from her. She—she comes back and tries to kick me in the back. So I just pushed her back and threw her on the floor again. (Juan)

Moreover, the respondents did not describe scenarios in which they perceived themselves to be at risk from their partners' violence. The worst injury reportedly sustained was a split lip, and only five men (15 percent) reported sustaining any injury. Female partners reportedly sustained injuries in 14 cases (42 percent). Although the majority of the injuries reportedly inflicted on female partners consisted of bruises and scratches, a few women were hospitalized, and two women sustained broken ribs. These findings corroborate previous studies showing that women suffer more injuries from domestic violence than men

(Langhinrichsen-Rohling, Neidig, and Thorn 1995). Moreover, because past studies suggest that male batterers underreport their perpetration of violence (Dobash and Dobash 1998), it is likely that respondents engaged in more violence than they described in these in-depth interviews.

Domestic violence is gendered through social and cultural practices that advantage men in violent conflicts with women. Young men often learn to view themselves as capable perpetrators of violence through rough play and contact sports, to exhibit fearlessness in the face of physical confrontations, and to accept the harm and injury associated with violence as "natural" (Dobash and Dobash 1998; Messner 1992). Men are further advantaged by cultural norms suggesting that women should pair with men who are larger and stronger than themselves (Goffman 1977). Women's less pervasive and less effective use of violence reflects fewer social opportunities to learn violent techniques, a lack of encouragement for female violence within society, and women's size disadvantage in relation to male partners (Fagot et al. 1985; McCaughey 1998). In a culture that defines aggression as unfeminine, few women learn to use violence effectively.

Gendered Depictions and Interpretations

Participants reported that they engaged in more frequent and serious violence than their partners, but they also reported that their violence was different from that of their partners. They depicted their violence as rational, effective, and explosive, whereas women's violence was represented as hysterical, trivial, and ineffectual. Of the 22 participants who described violence perpetrated by their partners, twelve (55 percent) suggested that their partner's violence was ridiculous or ineffectual. These respondents minimized their partners' violence by explaining that it was of little concern to them:

> I came out of the kitchen, and then I got in her face, and I shoved her. She shoved, she tried to push me a little bit, but it didn't matter much. (Adam)

I was seeing this girl, and then a friend of mine saw me with this girl and he went back and told my wife, and when I got home that night, that's when she tried to hit me, to fight me. I just pushed her out of the way and left. (Shad)

This minimizing discourse also characterizes descriptions of cases in which female partners successfully made contact and injured the respondent, as in the following account:

> I was on my way to go to the restroom. And she was just cussing and swearing and she wouldn't let me pass. So, I nudged her. I didn't push her or shove her, I just kind of, you know, just made my way to the restroom. And, when I done that she hit me, and she drew blood. She hit me in the lip, and she drew blood. . . . I go in the bathroom and I started laughing, you know. And I was still half lit that morning, you know. And I was laughing because I think it maybe shocked me more than anything that she had done this, you know. (Ed) . . .

Even in the case of extreme danger, such as when threatened with a weapon, respondents denied the possibility that their partners' violence was a threat. During a fight described by Steve, his partner locked herself in the bathroom with his gun:

> We were battering each other at that point, and that's when she was in the bathroom. This is—it's like 45 minutes into this whole argument now. She's in the bathroom, messing with my [gun]. And I had no idea. So I kicked the door in—in the bathroom, and she's sitting there trying to load this thing, trying to get this clip in, and luckily she couldn't figure it out. Why, I don't—you know, well, because she was drunk. So, luckily she didn't. The situation could have been a whole lot worse, you know, it could have been a whole lot worse than it was. I thank God that she didn't figure it out. When I think about it, you know, she was lucky to come out of it with just a cut in her head. You know, she could have blown her brains out or done something really stupid.

This account contains interesting contradictions. Steve stated that he had "no idea" that his partner had a gun, but he responded by kicking down the door to reach her. He then suggested that he was concerned about his partner's safety and that he kicked in the door to save her from doing "something really stupid" to herself. . . .

[The men] described their partners' acts as irrational and hysterical. Such depictions helped respondents to justify their own violence and to present themselves as calm, cool, rational men. Phil described his own behavior of throwing his partner down as a nonviolent, controlled response to his partner's outrageous behavior. Moreover, he suggests that he used this incident to demonstrate his sense of superior rationality to his partner. Phil later reported that a doctor became "very upset" about the marks on his wife's neck two days after this incident, suggesting that he was not the rational actor represented in his account.

In eight other cases (36 percent), respondents did not depict their partner's violence as trivial or ineffectual. Rather, they described their partners' behavior in matter-of-fact terms:

> Then she starts jumping at me or hitting me, or tell me "leave the house, I don't want you, I don't love you" and stuff like that. And I say, "don't touch me, don't touch me." And I just push her back. She keeps coming and hit me, hit me. I keep pushing back, she starts to scratch me, so I push hard to stop her from hurting me. (Mario)

Other respondents depicted their partner's violence in factual terms but emphasized that they perceived their own violence as the greater danger. Ray took his partner seriously when he stated that "she was willing to fight, to defend herself," yet he also mentioned his fears that his own violence would be lethal: "The worst time is when she threw an iron at me. And I'm gonna tell you, I think that was the worst time because, in defense, in retaliation, I pulled her hair, and I thought maybe I broke her neck." Only two respondents—Alan and Jim—consistently identified as victims:

> One of the worst times was realizing that she was drunk and belligerent. I realized that I needed to take her home in her car and she was not capable of driving. And she was physically abusive the whole way home. And before I could get out of the door or get out of the way, she came at me with a knife. And stupidly, I defended myself—kicked her hand to get the knife out. And I bruised her hand enough to where she felt justified enough to call the police with stories that I was horribly abusing. (Jim)

Jim reported that his partner has hit him, stabbed him, and thrown things at him. However, he also noted that he was arrested following several of these incidents, suggesting that his accounts tell us only part of the story. . . .

In contrast to their reported fearlessness when confronted by women wielding weapons, respondents constructed their own capacity for violence as something that should engender fear. These interpretations are consistent with cultural constructions of male violence as volcanic—natural, lethal, and impossible to stop until it has run its course.

Respondents' interpretations of ineffectual female violence and lethal male violence reflect actual violent practices in a culture that grants men more access to violence, but they also gender violence. By denying a threat from women's violence, participants performed masculinity and reinforced notions of gender difference. Women were constructed as incompetent in the practice of violence, and their successes were trivialized. For example, it is unlikely that Ed would have responded with laughter had his lip been split by the punch of another man (Dobash and Dobash 1998). Moreover, respondents ignored their partners' motivations for violence and their active efforts to exert change within their relationships.

The binary representation of ineffectual, hysterical female behavior and rational, lethal male violence within these accounts erases the feminine; violence perpetrated by women and female subjectivity are effaced in order that the respondents can construct masculinities. These representations mask the power relations that determine what acts will qualify as "violence" and thus naturalize the notion that violence is the exclusive province of men.

Gendering Blame

The research participants also gendered violence by suggesting that their female partners were responsible for the violence within their relationships. Some respondents did this by claiming that they did not hit women with whom they were involved in the past:

> I've never hit another woman in my life besides the one that I'm with. She just has a knack for bringing out the worst in me. (Tom) . . .

Respondents also shifted blame onto female partners by detailing faults in their partners' behaviors and personalities. They criticized their partners' parenting styles, interaction styles, and choices. However, the most typically reported criticism was that female partners were controlling. Ten of the 33 respondents (30 percent) characterized their partners as controlling, demanding, or dominating:

> She's real organized and critiquing about things. She wanna—she has to get it like—she like to have her way all the time, you know. In control of things, even when she's at work in the evenings, she has to have control of everything that's going on in the house. And—but—you know, try to get, to control everything there. You know, what's going on, and me and myself. (Adam) . . .

In a few cases, respondents claimed that they felt emasculated by what they interpreted as their partners' efforts to control them:

> You ask the guy sitting next door to me, the guy that's down the hall. For years they all say, "Bill, man, reach down and grab your eggs. She wears the pants." Or maybe like, "Hey man, we're going to go—Oh, Bill can't go. He's got to ask his boss first." And they were right. (Bill)

These representations of female partners as dominating enabled men to position themselves as victims of masculinized female partners. The relational construction of masculinity is visible in these accounts; women who "wear the pants" disrupt the binary opposition of masculinity/femininity. Bill's account reveals that "one is one's gender to the extent that one is not the other gender" (Butler 1990, 22); he is unable to perform masculinity to the satisfaction of his friends when mirrored by a partner who is perceived as dominating.

Moreover, respondents appeared to feel emasculated by unspecified forces. Unlike female survivors who describe concrete practices that male partners utilize to exert control (Kirkwood 1993; Walker 1984), participants were vague about what they meant by control and the ways in which their partners exerted control. . . . Respondents who claimed that their partners are controlling offered nebulous explanations for these feelings, suggesting that these claims may be indicative of these men's fears about being controlled by a woman rather than the actual practices of their partners.

Finally, respondents gendered violence through their efforts to convince female partners to shoulder at least part of the blame for their violence. . . .

Contemporary constructions of gender hold women responsible for men's aggression (Gray, Palileo, and Johnson 1993). Sexual violence is often blamed on women, who are perceived as tempting men who are powerless in the face of their primal sexual desires (Scully 1990). Although interviewees expressed remorse for their violent behavior, they also implied that it was justified in light of their partners' controlling behavior. Moreover, their violence was rewarded by their partners' feelings of guilt, suggesting that violence is simultaneously a performance of masculinity and a means by which respondents encouraged the performance of femininity by female partners.

"The Law Is for Women": Claiming Gender Bias

Participants sometimes rationalized their violence by claiming that the legal system overreacted to a minor incident. Eight of the 33 interviewees (24 percent) depicted themselves as victims of gender politics or the media attention surrounding the trial of O. J. Simpson:

> I think my punishment was wrong. And it was like my attorney told me—I'm suffering because of O. J. Simpson. Mine was the crime of the year. That is, you know, it's the hot issue of the year because of O. J. Two years ago they would have gone "Don't do that again." (Bill) . . .

These claims of gender bias were sometimes directly contradicted by respondents' descriptions of events following the arrival of the police. Four participants (12 percent) reported that the police wanted to arrest their female partner along with or instead of themselves—stories that challenged their claims of bias in the system. A few of these respondents reported that they lied to the police about the source of their injuries to prevent the arrest of their partners. Ed, the respondent who sustained a split lip from his partner's punch, claimed that he "took the fall" for his partner. . . .

When the police arrived, these respondents were in a double bind. They wanted to deny their own violence to avoid arrest, but they also wanted to deny victimization at the hands of a woman. "Protecting" their female partners from arrest allowed them a way out of this bind. By volunteering to be arrested despite their alleged innocence, they became chivalrous defenders of their partners. They were also, paradoxically, able to claim that "gender bias" led to their arrest and participation in the FVDN [Family Violence Diversion Network] program.

* * *

When batterers "protect" their partners from arrest, their oppressor becomes a powerful criminal justice system rather than a woman. Although even the loser gains status through participation in a fight with another man, a man does not gain prestige from being beaten by a woman (Dobash and Dobash 1998). In addition, respondents who stepped in to prevent their partners from being arrested ensured that their partners remained under their control, as Jim suggested when he described "the thin line between being protected by somebody and possessing somebody." By volunteering to be arrested along with his partner, Jim ensured that she was not "taken into possession" (e.g., taken into custody) by the police. By focusing the interviews on "gender bias" in the system, respondents deflected attention from their own perpetration and victimization. Constructions of a bias gave them an explanation for their arrest that was consistent with their self-presentation as rational, strong, and nonviolent actors. Claims of "reverse mentality" also enabled participants to position themselves as victims of gender politics. Several interviewees made use of men's rights rhetoric or alluded to changes wrought by feminism to suggest that they are increasingly oppressed by a society in which women have achieved greater rights. . . . A number of recent studies have examined the increasingly angry and antifeminist discourse offered by some men who are struggling to construct masculine identities within patriarchies disrupted by feminism and movements for gay/lesbian and civil rights (Fine et al. 1997; Messner 1998; Savran 1998). Some branches of the contemporary "men's movement" have articulated a defensive and antifeminist rhetoric of "men's rights" that suggests that men have become the victims of feminism (Messner 1998; Savran 1998). Although none of our interviewees reported participation in any of the organized men's movements, their allusions to the discourse of victimized manhood suggest that the rhetoric of these movements has become an influential resource for the performance of gender among some men. Like the angry men's rights activists studied by Messner (1998), some respondents positioned themselves as the victims of feminism, which they believe has co-opted the criminal justice system and the media by creating "myths" of male domination. The interviews suggest that respondents feel disempowered and that they identify women—both the women whom they batter and women who lead movements to criminalize domestic violence—as the

"Other" who has "stolen their presumed privilege" (Fine et al. 1997, 54): "Now girls are starting to act like men, or try and be like men. Like if you hit me, I'll call the cops, or if you don't do it, I'll do this, or stuff like that" (Juan). Juan contends that by challenging men's "privilege" to hit their female partners without fear of repercussions, women have become "like men." This suggests that the construction of masculine subjectivities is tied to a position of dominance and that women have threatened the binary and hierarchical gender framework through their resistance to male violence.

DISCUSSION: SOCIAL LOCATIONS AND DISCOURSES OF VIOLENCE

Respondents' descriptions of conflicts with female partners were similar across racial, ethnic, and class locations. Participants of diverse socioeconomic standings and racial ethnic backgrounds minimized the violence perpetrated by their partners, claimed that the criminal justice system is biased against men, and attempted to place responsibility for their violence on female partners. However, we identified some ways in which social class influenced respondents' self-presentations.[1]

Respondents of higher socioeconomic status emphasized their careers and the material items that they provided for their families throughout the interviews:

> We built two houses together and they are nice. You know, we like to see a nice environment for our family to live in. We want to see our children receive a good education. (Ted)

> That woman now sits in a 2,700 square foot house. She drives a Volvo. She has everything. A brand-new refrigerator, a brand-new washer and dryer. (Bill)

Conversely, economically disenfranchised men volunteered stories about their prowess in fights with other men. These interviewees reported

that they engaged in violent conflicts with other men as a means of gaining respect:

> Everybody in my neighborhood respected me a lot, you know. I used to be kind of violent. I used to like to fight and stuff like that, but I'm not like that anymore. She—I don't think she liked me because I liked to fight a lot but she liked me because people respected me because they knew that they would have to fight if they disrespected me. You know I think that's one thing that turned her on about me; I don't let people mess around. (Tony) . . .

The use of violence to achieve respect is a central theme in research on the construction of masculinities among disenfranchised men (Messerschmidt 1993; Messner 1992). Although men of diverse socioeconomic standings valorize fistfights between men (Campbell 1993; Dobash and Dobash 1998), the extent to which they participate in these confrontations varies by social context. Privileged young men are more often able to avoid participation in social situations that require physical violence against other men than are men who reside in poor neighborhoods (Messner 1992).

We find some evidence that cultural differences influence accounts of domestic violence. Two respondents who identified themselves as immigrants from Latin America (Alejandro and Juan) reported that they experienced conflicts with female partners about the shifting meanings of gender in the United States:

> She has a different attitude than mine. She has an attitude that comes from Mexico—be a man like, you have to do it. And it's like me here, it's fifty-fifty, it's another thing, you know, it's like "I don't have to do it." . . . I told her the wrong things she was doing and I told her, "It's not going to be that way because we're not in Mexico, we're in the United States." (Juan)

Juan's story suggests that unstable meanings about what it means to be a woman or a man are a source of conflict within his relationship and that he and his partner draw on divergent gender ideologies to buttress their positions. Although many of the respondents expressed uncertainty about appropriate gender performances in the 1990s, those who migrated to the United States may find these "crisis tendencies of the gender order" (Connell 1992, 736) to be particularly unsettling. Interestingly, Juan depicts his partner as clinging to traditional gender norms, while he embraces the notion of gender egalitarianism. However, we are hesitant to draw conclusions about this finding due to the small number of interviews that we conducted with immigrants.

CONCLUSIONS

Many scholars have suggested that domestic violence is a means by which men construct masculinities (Dobash and Dobash 1998; Gondolf and Hannekin 1987; Hearn 1998). However, few studies have explored the specific practices that domestically violent men use to present themselves as masculine actors. The respondents in this study used diverse and contradictory strategies to gender violence and they shifted their positions as they talked about violence. Respondents sometimes positioned themselves as masculine actors by highlighting their strength, power, and rationality compared with the "irrationality" and vulnerability of female partners. At other times, when describing the criminal justice system or "controlling" female partners, they positioned themselves as vulnerable and powerless. These shifting representations evidence the relational construction of gender and the instability of masculine subjectivities (Butler 1990).

Recently, performativity theories have been criticized for privileging agency, undertheorizing structural and cultural constraints, and facilitating essentialist readings of gender behavior: "Lacking an analysis of structural and cultural context, performances of gender can all too easily be interpreted as free agents' acting out the inevitable surface manifestations of a natural inner sex difference" (Messner 2000, 770).

Findings from our study show that each of these criticisms is not necessarily valid.

First, although the batterers described here demonstrate agency by shifting positions, they do so by calling on cultural discourses (of unstoppable masculine aggression, of feminine weakness, and of men's rights). Their performance is shaped by cultural options.

Second, batterers' performances are also shaped by structural changes in the gender order. Some of the batterers interviewed for this study expressed anger and confusion about a world with "TV for women" and female partners who are "too educated." Their arrest signaled a world askew—a place where "the law is for women" and where men have become the victims of discrimination. Although these accounts are ironic in light of the research documenting the continuing reluctance of the legal system to treat domestic violence as a criminal act (Dobash and Dobash 1979), they demonstrate the ways in which legal and structural reforms in the area of domestic violence influence gender performances. By focusing attention on the "bias" in the system, respondents deflected attention from their own perpetration and victimization and sustained their constructions of rational masculinity. Therefore, theories of gender performativity push us toward analyses of the cultural and structural contexts that form the settings for the acts.

Finally, when viewed through the lens of performativity, our findings challenge the notion that violence is an essential or natural expression of masculinity. Rather, they suggest that violence represents an effort to reconstruct a contested and unstable masculinity. Respondents' references to men's rights movement discourse, their claims of "reverse discrimination," and their complaints that female partners are controlling indicate a disruption in masculine subjectivities. Viewing domestic violence as a gender performance counters the essentialist readings of men's violence against women that dominate U.S. popular culture. What one performs is not necessarily what one "is."

Disturbingly, however, this study suggests that violence is (at least temporarily) an effective means by which batterers reconstruct men as masculine and women as feminine. Participants reported that they were able to control their partners through exertions of physical dominance and through their interpretive efforts to hold partners responsible for the violence in their relationships. By gendering violence, these batterers not only performed masculinity but reproduced gender as dominance. Thus, they naturalized a binary and hierarchical gender system.

NOTE

1. We define high socioeconomic status respondents as those who earn at least $25,000 per year in personal income and who have completed an associate's degree. Seven respondents fit these criteria. We define disenfranchised respondents as those who report personal earnings of less than $15,000 per year and who have not completed a two-year college program. Nine respondents fit these criteria.

REFERENCES

Bachman, R., and L. E. Saltzman. 1995. *Violence against women: Estimates from the redesigned survey August 1995.* NCJ-154348 special report. Washington, DC: Bureau of Justice Statistics.

Bowker, L. H. 1983. *Beating wife-beating.* Lexington, MA: Lexington Books.

Butler, J. 1990. *Gender trouble: Feminism and the subversion of identity.* New York: Routledge.

———. 1993. *Bodies that matter: On the discursive limits of sex.* New York: Routledge.

Campbell, A. 1993. *Men, women and aggression.* New York: Basic Books.

Connell, R. W. 1992. A very straight gay: Masculinity, homosexual experience, and the dynamics of gender. *American Sociological Review* 57:735–51.

Dobash, R. E., and R. P. Dobash. 1979. *Violence against wives: A case against the patriarchy.* New York: Free Press.

———. 1998. Violent men and violent contexts. In *Rethinking violence against women,* edited by R. E. Dobash and R. P. Dobash. Thousand Oaks, CA: Sage.

Dobash, R. P., R. E. Dobash, M. Wilson, and M. Daly. 1992. The myth of sexual symmetry in marital violence. *Social Problems* 39:71–91.

Eaton, M. 1994. Abuse by any other name: Feminism, difference, and intralesbian violence. In *The public nature of private violence: The discovery of domestic abuse,* edited by M. A. Fineman and R. Mykitiuk. New York: Routledge.

Fagot, B., R. Hagan, M. B. Leinbach, and S. Kronsberg. 1985. Differential reactions to assertive and communicative acts of toddler boys and girls. *Child Development* 56:1499–1505.

Fine, M., L. Weis, J. Addelston, and J. Marusza. 1997. (In)secure times: Constructing white working-class masculinities in the late 20th century. *Gender & Society* 11:52–68.

Goffman, E. 1977. The arrangement between the sexes. *Theory and Society* 4(3): 301–31.

Gondolf, Edward W., and James Hannekin. 1987. The gender warrior: Reformed batterers on abuse, treatment, and change. *Journal of Family Violence* 2:177–91.

Gray, N. B., G. J. Palileo, and G. D. Johnson. 1993. Explaining rape victim blame: A test of attribution theory. *Sociological Spectrum* 13:377–92.

Hearn, J. 1998. *The violences of men: How men talk about and how agencies respond to men's violence against women.* Thousand Oaks, CA: Sage.

Island, D., and P. Letellier. 1991. *Men who beat the men who love them: Battered gay men and domestic violence.* New York: Harrington Park.

Jang, D., D. Lee, and R. Morello-Frosch. 1998. Domestic violence in the immigrant and refugee community: Responding to the needs of immigrant women. In *Shifting the center: Understanding contemporary families,* edited by S. J. Ferguson. Mountain View, CA: Mayfield.

Kirkwood, C. 1993. *Leaving abusive partners: From the scars of survival to the wisdom for change.* Newbury Park, CA: Sage.

Langhinrichsen-Rohling, J., P. Neidig, and G. Thorn. 1995. Violent marriages: Gender differences in levels of current violence and past abuse. *Journal of Family Violence* 10:159–76.

Lundgren, E. 1998. The hand that strikes and comforts: Gender construction and the tension between body and symbol. In *Rethinking violence against women,* edited by R. E. Dobash and R. P. Dobash. Thousand Oaks, CA: Sage.

Martin, Del. 1976. *Battered wives.* New York: Pocket Books.

McCaughey, M. 1998. The fighting spirit: Women's self-defense training and the discourse of sexed embodiment. *Gender & Society* 12:277–300.

Messerschmidt, J. 1993. *Masculinities and crime: A critique and reconceptualization of theory.* Lanham, MD: Rowman & Littlefield.

Messner, M. A. 1992. *Power at play: Sports and the problem of masculinity.* Boston: Beacon.

———. 1998. The limits of the "male sex role": An analysis of the men's liberation and men's rights movements' discourse. *Gender & Society* 12(3): 255–76.

———. 2000. Barbie girls versus sea monsters: Children constructing gender. *Gender & Society* 14(6): 765–84.

Pence, E., and M. Paymar. 1993. *Education groups for men who batter: The Duluth model.* New York: Springer.

Ptacek, J. 1990. Why do men batter their wives? In *Feminist perspectives on wife abuse,* edited by K. Yllö and M. Bograd. Newbury Park, CA: Sage.

Renzetti, C. M. 1992. *Violent betrayal: Partner abuse in lesbian relationships.* Newbury Park, CA: Sage.

Savran, D. 1998. *Taking it like a man: White masculinity, masochism, and contemporary American culture.* Princeton, NJ: Princeton University Press.

Scully, D. 1990. *Understanding sexual violence: A study of convicted rapists.* Boston: Unwin Hyman.

Straton, J. C. 1994. The myth of the "battered husband syndrome." *Masculinities* 2:79–82.

Straus, M. A. 1993. Physical assaults by wives: A major social problem. In *Current controversies on family violence,* edited by R. J. Gelles and D. R. Loseke. Newbury Park, CA: Sage.

Walker, L. 1984. *The battered woman syndrome.* New York: Springer.

West, C., and S. Fenstermaker. 1995. Doing difference. *Gender & Society* 9:8–37.

Yllö, K. 1993. Through a feminist lens: Gender, power, and violence. In *Current controversies on family violence,* edited by R. J. Gelles and D. R. Loseke. Newbury Park, CA: Sage.

Introduction to Reading 45

Beth A. Quinn's research explores the accounts men and women give for what, on the surface, is a relatively benign form of sexual harassment—watching and rating women at work. To do so, she conducted 43 interviews with men and women, lasting from 1 to 3 hours, asking about relationships at work. She then randomly sampled more than half the original sample (25) from one organization and recruited the remaining individuals from a nearby community college and university. The accounts men give for sexual harassment indicate that they realize the effects of their girl watching on the women they work with and acknowledge that they would not like being watched this way if they were women. The interviews reveal that sexual harassment is instrumental in bonding men together and separating men from women in the workplace.

1. What is the role of objectification and (dis)empathy in maintaining masculinity?

2. How does sexual harassment work to enforce gender for men in the workplace, and what are the effects of such behavior for women and men?

3. What would have to change if "girl watching" were to disappear from the workplace?

Sexual Harassment and Masculinity

The Power and Meaning of "Girl Watching"

Beth A. Quinn

Confronted with complaints about sexual harassment or accounts in the media, some men claim that women are too sensitive or that they too often misinterpret men's intentions (Bernstein 1994; Buckwald 1993). In contrast, some women note with frustration that men just "don't get it" and lament the seeming inadequacy of sexual harassment policies (Conley 1991; Guccione 1992). Indeed, this ambiguity in defining acts of sexual harassment might be, as Cleveland and Kerst (1993) suggested, the most robust finding in sexual harassment research. . . .

This article focuses on the subjectivities of the perpetrators of a disputable form of sexual harassment, "girl watching." The term refers to the act of men's sexually evaluating women, often in the company of other men. It may take the form of a verbal or gestural message of "check it out," boasts of sexual prowess, or explicit comments about a woman's body or imagined sexual acts. The target may be an individual woman or group of women or simply a photograph or other representation. The woman may be a stranger, coworker, supervisor, employee, or client. For the present analysis, girl watching within the workplace is centered.

The analysis is grounded in the work of masculinity scholars such as Connell (1987, 1995) in that it attempts to explain the subject positions of the interviewed men—not the abstract and genderless subjects of patriarchy but the gendered and privileged subjects embedded in this system. Since I am attempting to delineate the gendered worldviews of the interviewed men, I employ the term "girl watching," a phrase that reflects their language ("they watch girls").

I have chosen to center the analysis on girl watching within the workplace for two reasons. First, it appears to be fairly prevalent. For example, a survey of federal civil employees (U.S. Merit Systems Protection Board 1988) found that in the previous 24 months, 28 percent of the women surveyed had experienced "unwanted sexual looks or gestures," and 35 percent had experienced "unwanted sexual teasing, jokes, remarks, or questions." Second, girl watching is still often normalized and trivialized as only play, or "boys will be boys." A man watching girls—even in his workplace—is frequently accepted as a natural and commonplace activity, especially if he is in the presence of other men.[1] Indeed, it may be required (Hearn 1985). Thus, girl watching sits on the blurry edge between fun and harm, joking and harassment. An understanding of the process of identifying behavior as sexual harassment, or of rejecting this label, may be built on this ambiguity.

Girl watching has various forms and functions, depending on the context and the men involved. For example, it may be used by men as a directed act of power against a particular woman or women. In this, girl watching—at least in the workplace—is most clearly identified as harassing by both men and women. I am most interested, however, in the form where it is characterized as only play. This type is more obliquely motivated and, as I will argue, functions as a game men play to build shared masculine identities and social relations.

From Quinn, B., "Sexual Harassment and Masculinity: The Power and Meaning of 'Girl Watching,'" *Gender & Society,* 16(3): 386–402. Copyright © 2002 by Sage Publications, Inc. Reprinted with permission.

Multiple and contradictory subject positions are also evidenced in girl watching, most notably that between the gazing man and the woman he watches. Drawing on Michael Schwalbe's (1992) analysis of empathy and the formation of masculine identities, I argue that girl watching is premised on the obfuscation of this multiplicity through the objectification of the woman watched and a suppression of empathy for her. In conclusion, the ways these elements operate to produce gender differences in interpreting sexual harassment and the implications for developing effective policies are discussed.

Previous Research

The question of how behavior is or is not labeled as sexual harassment has been primarily studied through experimental vignettes and surveys.[2] In both methods, participants evaluate either hypothetical scenarios or lists of behaviors, considering whether, for example, the behavior constitutes sexual harassment, which party is most at fault, and what consequences the act might engender. Researchers manipulate factors such as the level of "welcomeness" the target exhibits and the relationship of the actors (supervisor-employee, coworker-coworker).

Both methods consistently show that women are willing to define more acts as sexual harassment (Gutek, Morasch, and Cohen 1983; Padgitt and Padgitt 1986; Powell 1986; York 1989; but see Stockdale and Vaux 1993) and are more likely to see situations as coercive (Garcia, Milano, and Quijano 1989). When asked who is more to blame in a particular scenario, men are more likely to blame, and less likely to empathize with, the victim (Jensen and Gutek 1982; Kenig and Ryan 1986). In terms of actual behaviors like girl watching, the U.S. Merit Systems Protection Board (1988) survey found that 81 percent of the women surveyed considered "uninvited sexually suggestive looks or gestures" from a supervisor to be sexual harassment. While the majority of men (68 percent) also defined it as such, significantly more men were willing to dismiss such

behavior. Similarly, while 40 percent of the men would not consider the same behavior from a coworker to be harassing, more than three-quarters of the women would.

The most common explanation offered for these differences is gender role socialization. This conclusion is supported by the consistent finding that the more men and women adhere to traditional gender roles, the more likely they are to deny the harm in sexual harassment and to consider the behavior acceptable or at least normal (Gutek and Koss 1993; Malovich and Stake 1990; Murrell and Dietz-Uhler 1993; Popovich et al. 1992; Pryor 1987; Tagri and Hayes 1997). Men who hold predatory ideas about sexuality, who are more likely to believe rape myths, and who are more likely to self-report that they would rape under certain circumstances are less likely to see behaviors as harassing (Murrell and Dietz-Uhler 1993; Pryor 1987; Reilly et al. 1992).

These findings do not, however, adequately address the between-group differences. The more one is socialized into traditional notions of [gender], the more likely it is for both men and women to view the behaviors as acceptable or at least unchangeable. The processes by which gender roles operate to produce these differences remain underexamined. Some theorists argue that men are more likely to discount the harassing aspects of their behavior because of a culturally conditioned tendency to misperceive women's intentions. For example, Stockdale (1993, 96) argued that "patriarchal norms create a sexually aggressive belief system in some people more than others, and this belief system can lead to the propensity to misperceive." Gender differences in interpreting sexual harassment, then, may be the outcome of the acceptance of normative ideas about women's inscrutability and indirectness and men's role as sexual aggressors. Men see harmless flirtation or sexual interest rather than harassment because they misperceive women's intent and responses.

Stockdale's (1993) theory is promising but limited. First, while it may apply to actions such as repeatedly asking for dates and quid pro quo harassment,[3] it does not effectively explain motivations for more indirect actions, such as displaying pornography and girl watching. Second, it does not explain why some men are more likely to operate from these discourses of sexual aggression contributing to a propensity to misperceive.

* * *

FINDINGS: GIRL WATCHING AS "HOMMOSEXUALITY"

> [They] had a button on the computer that you pushed if there was a girl who came to the front counter. . . . It was a code and it said "BAFC"—Babe at Front Counter. . . . If the guy in the back looked up and saw a cute girl come in the station, he would hit this button for the other dispatcher to [come] see the cute girl.
>
> —*Paula, Police Officer*

In its most serious form, girl watching operates as a targeted tactic of power. The men seem to want everyone—the targeted woman as well as coworkers, clients, and superiors—to know they are looking. The gaze demonstrates their right, as men, to sexually evaluate women. Through the gaze, the targeted woman is reduced to a sexual object, contradicting her other identities, such as that of competent worker or leader. This employment of the discourse of asymmetrical heterosexuality (i.e., the double standard) may trump a woman's formal organizational power, claims to professionalism, and organizational discourses of rationality (Collinson and Collinson 1989; Gardner 1995; Yount 1991).[4] As research on rape has demonstrated (Estrich 1987), calling attention to a woman's gendered sexuality can function to exclude recognition of her competence, rationality, trustworthiness, and even humanity. In contrast, the overt recognition of a man's (hetero)sexuality is normally compatible with other aspects of his identity; indeed, it is often required (Connell 1995; Hearn 1985). Thus, the power of

sexuality is asymmetrical, in part, because being seen as sexual has different consequences for women and men.

But when they ogle, gawk, whistle and point, are men always so directly motivated to disempower their women colleagues? Is the target of the gaze also the intended audience? Consider, for example, this account told by Ed, a white, 29-year-old instrument technician.

> When a group of guys goes to a bar or a nightclub and they try to be manly. . . . A few of us always found [it] funny [when] a woman would walk by and a guy would be like, "I can have her." [pause] "Yeah, OK, we want to see it!" [laugh]

In his account—a fairly common one in men's discussions—the passing woman is simply a visual cue for their play. It seems clear that it is a game played by men for men; the woman's participation and awareness of her role seem fairly unimportant.

As Thorne (1993) reminded us, we should not be too quick to dismiss games as "only play." In her study of gender relations in elementary schools, Thorne found play to be a powerful form of gendered social action. One of its "clusters of meaning" most relevant here is that of "dramatic performance." In this, play functions as both a source of fun and a mechanism by which gendered identities, group boundaries, and power relations are (re)produced.

The metaphor of play was strong in Karl's comments. Karl, a white man in his early thirties who worked in a technical support role in the Acme engineering department, hoped to earn a degree in engineering. His frustration with his slow progress—which he attributed to the burdens of marriage and fatherhood—was evident throughout the interview. Karl saw himself as an undeserved outsider in his department and he seemed to delight in telling on the engineers.

Girl watching came up as Karl considered the gender reversal question. Like many of the men I interviewed, his first reaction was to muse about premenstrual syndrome and clothes. When I inquired about the potential social effects of the transformation (by asking him, Would it "be easier dealing with the engineers or would it be harder?") he haltingly introduced the engineers' "game."

Karl: Some of the engineers here are very [pause] they're not very, how shall we say? [pause] What's the way I want to put this? They're not very, uh [pause] what's the word? Um. It escapes me.

Researcher: Give me a hint?

Karl: They watch women but they're not very careful about getting caught.

Researcher: Oh! Like they ogle?

Karl: Ogle or gaze or [pause] stare even, or [pause] generate a commotion of an unusual nature.

His initial discomfort in discussing the issue (with me, I presume) is evident in his excruciatingly formal and hesitant language. The aspect of play, however, came through clearly when I pushed him to describe what generating a commotion looked like: "'Oh! There goes so-and-so. Come and take a look! She's wearing this great outfit today!' Just like a schoolboy. They'll rush out of their offices and [cranes his neck] and check things out." That this is as a form of play was evident in Karl's boisterous tone and in his reference to schoolboys. This is not a case of an aggressive sexual appraising of a woman coworker but a commotion created for the benefit of other men. . . .

PRODUCING MASCULINITY

I suggest that girl watching in this form functions simultaneously as a form of play and as a potentially powerful site of gendered social action. Its social significance lies in its power to form identities and relationships based on these common practices for, as Cockburn (1983, 123) has noted, "patriarchy is as much about relations between man and man as it is about relations between men and women." Girl watching works similarly

to the sexual joking that Johnson (1988) suggested is a common way for heterosexual men to establish intimacy among themselves.

In particular, girl watching works as a dramatic performance played to other men, a means by which a certain type of masculinity is produced and heterosexual desire displayed. It is a means by which men assert a masculine identity to other men, in an ironic "hommosexual" practice of heterosexuality (Butler 1990).[5] As Connell (1995) and others (Butler 1990; West and Zimmerman 1987) have aptly noted, masculinity is not a static identity but rather one that must constantly be reclaimed. The content of any performance—and there are multiple forms—is influenced by a hegemonic notion of masculinity. When asked what "being a man entailed, many of the men and women I interviewed triangulated toward notions of strength (if not in muscle, then in character and job performance), dominance, and a marked sexuality, overflowing and uncontrollable to some degree and natural to the male "species." Heterosexuality is required, for just as the label "girl" questions a man's claim to masculine power, so does the label "fag" (Hopkins 1992; Pronger 1992). I asked Karl, for example, if he would consider his sons "good men" if they were gay. His response was laced with ambivalence; he noted only that the question was "a tough one."

The practice of girl watching is just that—a practice—one rehearsed and performed in everyday settings. This aspect of rehearsal was evident in my interview with Mike, a self-employed house painter who used to work construction. In locating himself as a born-again Christian, Mike recounted the girl watching of his fellow construction workers with contempt. Mike was particularly disturbed by a man who brought his young son to the job site one day. The boy was explicitly taught to catcall, a practice that included identifying the proper targets: women and effeminate men.

Girl watching, however, can be somewhat tenuous as a masculine practice. In their acknowledgment (to other men) of their supposed desire lies the possibility that in being too interested in women the players will be seen as mere school-boys giggling in the playground. Taken too far, the practice undermines rather than supports a masculine performance. . . . A man must be interested in women, but not too interested; they must show their (hetero)sexual interest, but not overly so, for this would be to admit that women have power over them.

The Role of Objectification and (Dis)Empathy

As a performance of heterosexuality among men, the targeted woman is primarily an object onto which men's homosocial sexuality is projected. The presence of a woman in any form—embodied, pictorial, or as an image conjured from words—is required, but her subjectivity and active participation is not. To be sure, given the ways the discourse of asymmetrical sexuality works, men's actions may result in similarly negative effects on the targeted woman as that of a more direct form of sexualization. The crucial difference is that the men's understanding of their actions differs. This difference is one key to understanding the ambiguity around interpreting harassing behavior.

When asked about the engineers' practice of neck craning, Robert grinned, saying nothing at first. After some initial discussion, I started to ask him if he thought women were aware of their game ("Do you think that the women who are walking by . . . ?").

Robert did not want to admit that women might not enjoy it ("that didn't come out right") but acknowledged that their feelings were irrelevant.

Only subjects, not objects, take pleasure or are annoyed. If a woman did complain, Robert thought "the guys wouldn't know what to say." In her analysis of street harassment, Gardner (1995, 187) found a similar absence, in that "men's interpretations seldom mentioned a woman's reaction, either guessed at or observed."

The centrality of objectification was also apparent in comments made by José, a Hispanic man in his late 40s who worked in manufacturing.

For José, the issue came up when he considered the topic of compliments. He initially claimed that women enjoy compliments more than men do. In reconsidering, he remembered girl watching and the importance of intent.

> There is [pause] a point where [pause] a woman can be admired by [pause] a pair of eyes, but we're talking about "that look." Where, you know, you're admiring her because she's dressed nice, she's got a nice figure, she's got nice legs. But then you also have the other side. You have an animal who just seems to undress you with his eyes and he's just [pause], there's those kind of people out there too.

What is most interesting about this statement is that in making the distinction between merely admiring and an animal look that ravages, José switched subject position. He spoke in the second person when describing both forms of looking, but his consistency in grammar belies a switch in subjectivity: you (as a man) admire, and you (as a woman) are undressed with his eyes. When considering an appropriate, complimentary gaze, José described it from a man's point of view; the subject who experiences the inappropriate, violating look, however, is a woman. Thus, as in Robert's account, José acknowledged that there are potentially different meanings in the act for men and women. In particular, to be admired in a certain way is potentially demeaning for a woman through its objectification. . . .

When asked to envision himself as a woman in his workplace, like many of the individuals I interviewed, Karl believed that he did not "know how to be a woman." Nonetheless, he produced an account that mirrored the stories of some of the women I interviewed. He knew the experience of girl watching could be quite different—in fact, threatening and potentially disempowering—for the woman who is its object. As such, the game was something to be avoided. In imagining themselves as women, the men remembered the practice of girl watching. None, however, were able to comfortably describe the game of girl watching from the perspective of a woman and maintain its (masculine) meaning as play.

In attempting to take up the subject position of a woman, these men are necessarily drawing on knowledge they already hold. If men simply "don't get it"—truly failing to see the harm in girl watching or other more serious acts of sexual harassment—then they should not be able to see this harm when envisioning themselves as women. What the interviews reveal is that many men—most of whom failed to see the harm of many acts that would constitute the hostile work environment form of sexual harassment—did in fact understand the harm of these acts when forced to consider the position of the targeted woman.

I suggest that the gender reversal scenario produced, in some men at least, a moment of empathy. Empathy, Schwalbe (1992) argued, requires two things. First, one must have some knowledge of the other's situation and feelings. Second, one must be motivated to take the position of the other. What the present research suggests is that gender differences in interpreting sexual harassment stem not so much from men's not getting it (a failure of the first element) but from a studied, often compulsory, lack of motivation to identify with women's experiences.

In his analysis of masculinity and empathy, Schwalbe (1992) argued that the requirements of masculinity necessitate a "narrowing of the moral self." Men learn that to effectively perform masculinity and to protect a masculine identity, they must, in many instances, ignore a woman's pain and obscure her viewpoint. Men fail to exhibit empathy with women because masculinity precludes them from taking the position of the feminine other, and men's moral stance vis-à-vis women is attenuated by this lack of empathy.

As a case study, Schwalbe (1992) considered the Thomas-Hill hearings, concluding that the examining senators maintained a masculinist stance that precluded them from giving serious consideration to Professor Hill's claims. A consequence of this masculine moral narrowing is that "charges of sexual harassment . . . are often seen as exaggerated or as fabricated out of misunderstanding or spite" (Schwalbe 1992, 46).

Thus, gender differences in interpreting sexually harassing behaviors may stem more from acts of ignoring than states of ignorance.

THE PROBLEM WITH GETTING CAUGHT

But are women really the untroubled objects that girl watching—viewed through the eyes of men—suggests? Obviously not; the game may be premised on a denial of a woman's subjectivity, but an actual erasure is beyond men's power! It is in this multiplicity of subjectivities, as Butler (1990, ix) noted, where "trouble" lurks, provoked by "the unanticipated agency of a female 'object' who inexplicably returns the glance, reverses the gaze, and contests the place and authority of the masculine position." To face a returned gaze is to get caught, an act that has the power to undermine the logic of girl watching as simply a game among men. Karl, for example, noted that when caught, men are often flustered, a reaction suggesting that the boundaries of usual play have been disturbed.[6]

When a woman looks back, when she asks, "What are you looking at?" she speaks as a subject, and her status as mere object is disturbed. When the game is played as a form of hommosexuality, the confronted man may be baffled by her response. When she catches them looking, when she complains, the targeted woman speaks as a subject. The men, however, understand her primarily as an object, and objects do not object.

The radical potential of sexual harassment law is that it centers women's subjectivity, an aspect prompting Catharine MacKinnon's (1979) unusual hope for the law's potential as a remedy. For men engaged in girl watching, however, this subjectivity may be inconceivable. From their viewpoint, acts such as girl watching are simply games played with objects: women's bodies. Similar to Schwalbe's (1992) insight into the senators' reaction to Professor Hill, the harm of sexual harassment may seem more the result of a woman's complaint (and law's "illegitimate" encroachment into the everyday work world) than men's acts of objectification. For example, in reflecting on the impact of sexual harassment policies in the workplace, José lamented that "back in the '70s, [it was] all peace and love then. Now as things turn around, men can't get away with as much as what they used to." Just whose peace and love are we talking about?

* * *

CONCLUSIONS

In this analysis, I have sought to unravel the social logic of girl watching and its relationship to the question of gender differences in the interpretation of sexual harassment. In the form analyzed here, girl watching functions simultaneously as only play and as a potent site where power is played. Through the objectification on which it is premised and in the nonempathetic masculinity it supports, this form of girl watching simultaneously produces both the harassment and the barriers to men's acknowledgment of its potential harm.

The implications these findings have for antisexual harassment training are profound. If we understand harassment to be the result of a simple lack of knowledge (of ignorance), then straightforward informational sexual harassment training may be effective. The present analysis suggests, however, that the etiology of some harassment lies elsewhere. While they might have quarreled with it, most of the men I interviewed had fairly good abstract understandings of the behaviors their companies' sexual harassment policies prohibited. At the same time, in relating stories of social relations in their workplaces, most failed to identify specific behaviors as sexual harassment when they matched the abstract definition. . . . [T]he source of this contradiction lies not so much in ignorance but in acts of ignoring. Traditional sexual harassment training programs address the former rather than the latter. As such, their effectiveness against sexually harassing behaviors born out of social practices of masculinity like girl watching is questionable.

Ultimately, the project of challenging sexual harassment will be frustrated and our understanding distorted unless we interrogate hegemonic, patriarchal forms of masculinity and the practices by which they are (re)produced. We must continue to research the processes by which sexual harassment is produced and the gendered identities and subjectivities on which it poaches (Wood 1998). My study provides a first step toward a more process-oriented understanding of sexual harassment, the ways the social meanings of harassment are constructed, and ultimately, the potential success of antiharassment training programs.

NOTES

1. For example, Maria, an administrative assistant I interviewed, simultaneously echoed and critiqued this understanding when she complained about her boss's girl watching in her presence: "If he wants to do that in front of other men . . . you know, that's what men do."

2. Recently, more researchers have turned to qualitative studies as a means to understand the process of labeling behavior as harassment. Of note are Collinson and Collinson (1996), Giuffre and Williams (1994), Quinn (2000), and Rogers and Henson (1997).

3. Quid pro quo ("this for that") sexual harassment occurs when a person with organizational power attempts to coerce an individual into sexual behavior by threatening adverse job actions.

4. I prefer the term "asymmetrical heterosexuality" over "double standard" because it directly references the dominance of heterosexuality and more accurately reflects the interconnected but different forms of acceptable sexuality for men and women. As Estrich (1987) argued, it is not simply that we hold men and women to different standards of sexuality but that these standards are (re)productive of women's disempowerment.

5. "Hommo" is a play on the French word for man, *homme*.

6. Men are not always concerned with getting caught, as the behavior of catcalling construction workers amply illustrates; that a woman hears is part of the thrill (Gardner 1995). The difference between the workplace and the street is the level of anonymity

the men have vis-à-vis the woman and the complexity of social rules and the diversity of power sources an individual has at his or her disposal.

REFERENCES

Bernstein, R. 1994. Guilty if charged. *New York Review of Books,* 13 January.

Buckwald, A. 1993. Compliment a woman, go to court. *Los Angeles Times.* 28 October.

Butler, J. 1990. *Gender trouble: Feminism and the subversion of identity.* New York: Routledge.

Cleveland, J. N., and M. E. Kerst. 1993. Sexual harassment and perceptions of power: An under-articulated relationship. *Journal of Vocational Behavior* 42(1): 49–67.

Cockburn, C. 1983. *Brothers: Male dominance and technological change.* London: Pluto Press.

Collinson, D. L., and M. Collinson. 1989. Sexuality in the workplace: The domination of men's sexuality. In *The sexuality of organizations,* edited by J. Hearn and D. L. Sheppard. Newbury Park, CA: Sage.

———. 1996. "It's only Dick": The sexual harassment of women managers in insurance sales. *Work, Employment & Society* 10(1): 29–56.

Conley, F. K. 1991. Why I'm leaving Stanford: I wanted my dignity back. *Los Angeles Times,* 9 June.

Connell, R. W. 1987. *Gender and power.* Stanford, CA: Stanford University Press.

———. 1995. *Masculinities.* Berkeley: University of California Press.

Estrich, S. 1987. *Real Rape.* Cambridge, MA: Harvard University Press.

Garcia, L., L. Milano, and A. Quijano. 1989. Perceptions of coercive sexual behavior by males and females. *Sex Roles* 21(9/10): 569–77.

Gardner, C. B. 1995. *Passing by: Gender and public harassment.* Berkeley: University of California Press.

Giuffre, P., and C. Williams. 1994. Boundary lines: Labeling sexual harassment in restaurants. *Gender & Society* 8:378–401.

Guccione, J. 1992. Women judges still fighting harassment. *Daily Journal,* 13 October, 1.

Gutek, B. A., and M. P. Koss. 1993. Changed women and changed organizations: Consequences of and coping with sexual harassment. *Journal of Vocational Behavior* 42(1): 28–48.

Gutek, B. A., B. Morasch, and A. G. Cohen. 1983. Interpreting social-sexual behavior in a work setting. *Journal of Vocational Behavior* 22(1): 30–48.

Hearn, J. 1985. Men's sexuality at work. In *The sexuality of men,* edited by A. Metcalf and M. Humphries. London: Pluto Press.

Hopkins, P. 1992. Gender treachery: Homophobia, masculinity, and threatened identities. In *Rethinking masculinity: Philosophical explorations in light of feminism,* edited by L. May and R. Strikwerda. Lanham, MD: Littlefield, Adams.

Jensen, I. W., and B. A. Gutek. 1982. Attributions and assignment of responsibility in sexual harassment. *Journal of Social Issues* 38(4): 121–36.

Johnson, M. 1988. *Strong mothers, weak wives.* Berkeley: University of California Press.

Kenig, S., and J. Ryan. 1986. Sex differences in levels of tolerance and attribution of blame for sexual harassment on a university campus. *Sex Roles* 15(9/10): 535–49.

MacKinnon, C. A. 1979. *The sexual harassment of working women.* New Haven, CT: Yale University Press.

Malovich, N. J., and J. E. Stake. 1990. Sexual harassment on campus: Individual differences in attitudes and beliefs. *Psychology of Women Quarterly* 14(1): 63–81.

Murrell, A. J., and B. L. Dietz-Uhler. 1993. Gender identity and adversarial sexual beliefs as predictors of attitudes toward sexual harassment. *Psychology of Women Quarterly* 17(2): 169–75.

Padgitt, S. C., and J. S. Padgitt. 1986. Cognitive structure of sexual harassment: Implications for university policy. *Journal of College Student Personnel* 27:34–39.

Popovich, P. M., D. N. Gehlauf, J. A. Jolton, J. M. Somers, and R. M. Godinho. 1992. Perceptions of sexual harassment as a function of sex of rater and incident form and consequent. *Sex Roles* 27(11/12): 609–25.

Powell, G. N. 1986. Effects of sex-role identity and sex on definitions of sexual harassment. *Sex Roles* 14:9–19.

Pronger, B. 1992. Gay jocks: A phenomenology of gay men in athletics. In *Rethinking masculinity: Philosophical explorations in light of feminism,* edited by L. May and R. Strikwerda. Lanham, MD: Littlefield Adams.

Pryor, J. B. 1987. Sexual harassment proclivities in men. *Sex Roles* 17(5/6): 269–90.

Quinn, B. A. 2000. The paradox of complaining: Law, humor, and harassment in the everyday work world. *Law and Social Inquiry* 25(4): 1151–83.

Reilly, M. E., B. Lott, D. Caldwell, and L. DeLuca. 1992. Tolerance for sexual harassment related to self-reported sexual victimization. *Gender & Society* 6:122–38.

Rogers, J. K., and K. D. Henson. 1997. "Hey, why don't you wear a shorter skirt?" Structural vulnerability and the organization of sexual harassment in temporary clerical employment. *Gender & Society* 11:215–38.

Schwalbe, M. 1992. Male supremacy and the narrowing of the moral self. *Berkeley Journal of Sociology* 37:29–54.

Stockdale, M. S. 1993. The role of sexual misperceptions of women's friendliness in an emerging theory of sexual harassment. *Journal of Vocational Behavior* 42(1): 84–101.

Stockdale, M. S., and A. Vaux. 1993. What sexual harassment experiences lead respondents to acknowledge being sexually harassed? A secondary analysis of a university survey. *Journal of Vocational Behavior* 43(2): 221–34.

Tagri, S., and S. M. Hayes. 1997. Theories of sexual harassment. In *Sexual harassment: Theory, research and treatment,* edited by W. O'Donohue. New York: Allyn & Bacon.

Thorne, B. 1993. *Gender Play: Girls and boys in school.* Buckingham, UK: Open University Press.

U.S. Merit Systems Protection Board. 1988. *Sexual harassment in the federal government: An update.* Washington, DC: Government Printing Office.

West, C., and D. H. Zimmerman. 1987. Doing gender. *Gender & Society* 1:125–51.

Wood, J. T. 1998. Saying makes it so: The discursive construction of sexual harassment. In *Conceptualizing sexual harassment as discursive practice,* edited by S. G. Bingham. Westport, CT: Praeger.

York, K. M. 1989. Defining sexual harassment in workplaces: A policy-capturing approach. *Academy of Management Journal* 32:830–50.

Yount, K. R. 1991. Ladies, flirts, tomboys: Strategies for managing sexual harassment in an underground coal mine. *Journal of Contemporary Ethnography* 19:396–422.

❦ Topics for Further Examination ❧

- Visit http://www.mencanstoprape.org to see what men are doing to stop rape.
- Try to find the latest reports of campus rape for your campus and surrounding campuses. Does this surprise you? Try to find organizations that provide support to women who have been sexually abused on your campus.
- Check out the sexual harassment laws for your state. Are they easily accessible? How are they enforced?

PART III

POSSIBILITIES

10

NOTHING IS FOREVER

The title of this chapter represents the principle that change is inevitable. Like the ever-evolving patterns of the kaleidoscope, change is inherent in all life's patterns. Anything can be changed and everything does change, from the cells in our bodies to global politics. There is no permanent pattern, no one way of experiencing or doing anything that lasts forever. This fact of life can be scary, but it can also be energizing. The mystery of life, like the wonder of the kaleidoscope, rests in not knowing precisely what will come next.

The readings in this chapter address the changing terrain of gender. If one takes only a snapshot of life, it may appear as though current gender arrangements are relatively fixed. However, an expanded view of gender, over time and across cultures, reveals the well-researched fact that gender meanings and practices are as dynamic as any other aspect of life. Patterns of gender continuously undergo change, and they do so at every level of experience, from the individual to the global. Michael Schwalbe (2001) observes that there is both chance and pattern in the lives of individuals and in the bigger arena of social institutions. He makes the point that no matter how many rules there might be and no matter how much we know about a particular person or situation, "social life remains a swirl of contingencies out of which can emerge events that no one expects" (p. 127). As a result, life, including its gendered dimensions, is full of possibilities.

Social constructionist theory is especially helpful in understanding the inevitability of change in the gender order. Recall that social constructionist research reveals the processes by which people create and maintain the institution of gender. It underscores the fact that gender is a human invention, not a biological absolute. Particular gender patterns keep going only as long as people share the same ideas about gender and keep doing masculinity and femininity in a routine, predictable fashion (Johnson, 1997; Schwalbe, 2001). Given that humans create gender, gender patterns can be altered by people who, individually and collectively, choose to invent and negotiate new ways of thinking about and doing gender.

At the micro level of daily interaction, individuals participate in destabilizing the binary, oppositional sex/gender/sexuality order. They do so by choosing to bend conventional gender rules or changing the rules altogether by undoing or redoing gender (Bobel & Kwan, 2011; Deutsch, 2007; Lorber, 1994; West & Zimmerman, 2009). For example, women and men are creating new forms of partnership based on shared care work and housework roles (see Kathleen Gerson's article in Chapter 7). Other individuals purposefully transgress the boundaries of sexual and gender identities by mixing appearance cues via makeup, clothing, hairstyle, and other modes of self-presentation (Bobel & Kwan, 2011; Lorber, 1994). Chris Bobel and Samantha Kwan's (2011) research illustrates a variety of ways people employ their bodies in acts of gender resistance and related forms of resistance such as counter-heteronormativity and counter-homonormativity. For example, within the gay community, big men or "bears" are masculine, fat, hairy gay men who, with their admirers ("chasers"), have formed alternative spaces where they can interact in comfort. In addition, they display their bodies with pride and challenge the appearance norms of dominant gay society and the heterosexual world (Pyle & Klein, 2011). Research on embodied resistance, such as bear culture, points to the powerful social fact that "humans can be at once rule-bound and wonderfully inventive agents of social change. We can enact the mandates—trudging along, submitting and rationalizing—but we can also assert ourselves and break away" (Bobel & Kwan, 2011, p. 2). When we do the latter, we engage our potential to alter toxic social patterns such as gender inequality.

TRENDS

At the macro level of the gender order, change comes about through large-scale forces and processes, both planned and unplanned. Trends are unplanned changes in patterns that are sustained over time. For example, Kivisto (1998) states that the Industrial Revolution is a trend, marking the transition from agricultural to industrial economies. This so-called revolution involves complex economic, technological, and related changes, such as urbanization, that have profoundly altered the fabric of social life over time. Consider the impact of industrialization on gender in work and family life in the United States. Prior to industrialization, women's labor was essential to agricultural life. Women, men, and children worked side by side to grow crops, make

clothing, raise animals, and otherwise contribute to the family economy (Lorber, 2001). That is, work and family were closely intertwined and the distinction between home and workplace did not exist (Wharton, 2005).

As the Industrial Revolution got under way, productive work moved from the home into factories, and work came to be defined as valuable only if it resulted in a paycheck. Although essential work was still done at home, it did not produce income. The negative outcome was that household labor was transformed into an invisible and devalued activity. Work and family came to be seen as distinct, firmly gendered domains of life, especially in the middle class. Women and children were relegated to the home and women were expected to be full-time housewives and mothers, while men were ordained to follow wage work, embrace the breadwinner role, and participate in the political arena (Godwin & Risman, 2001; Wharton, 2005).

The profound changes in gender relations and the organization of work and family wrought by the Industrial Revolution continue to be a source of conflict for many women and men in the United States today. For example, although most married women with children now work outside the home, the doctrine of natural separate spheres—unpaid household work for women and paid work for men—continues to operate as an ideal against which "working women" who have children are often negatively evaluated.

Industrialization continues as a force for social change, one that is amplified by processes of globalization. The term *globalization* refers to the increasing interconnectedness of social, political, and economic activities worldwide (Held, McGrew, Goldblatt, & Perraton, 1999). Transnational forces such as geopolitical conflicts, global markets, transnational firms, transnational media, and the migration of labor now strongly influence what happens in specific countries and locales (Connell, 2000). For example, the international trading system—dominated by nations such as the United States—encompasses almost every country in the world, while films and television programs, especially those produced in the West, circulate the globe (Barber, 2002).

Offering a valuable perspective on the impact of globalization in her reading in this chapter, R. W. Connell (2000) argues that it has created a worldwide gender order. This world gender order has several interacting dimensions: (1) a gender division of labor in a "global factory" in which poor women and children provide cheap labor for transnational corporations owned by businessmen from the major economic powers, (2) the marginalization of women in international politics, and (3) the dominance of Western gender symbolism in transnational media.

However, despite the order Connell posits, globalization is not monolithic. There are countervailing forces challenging the homogenizing and hegemonic aspects of globalization. For example, indigenous cultures interact with global cultures to produce new cultural forms of art and music. In addition, globalization has spawned transnational social movements, such as feminism, the slow-food movement, and environmentalism, which address worldwide problems of Western hegemony, global inequality, and human rights. Connell's reading in this chapter includes analysis of the links between local and global social action involving men in gender change. Her discussion of what she calls "the broad cultural shift toward a historical consciousness about gender" provides insight into the complexities of globalization.

SOCIAL MOVEMENTS

Large-scale change may also come about in a planned fashion. Social movements are prime examples of change that people deliberately and purposefully create. They are conscious, organized, collective efforts to work toward cultural and institutional change and share distinctive features, including organization, consciousness, noninstitutionalized strategies (such as boycotts and protest marches), and prolonged duration (Kuumba, 2001). The United States has a long

history of people joining together in organizations and movements to bring about justice and equality. The labor union movement; socialist movement; civil rights movement; and gay, lesbian, bisexual, transgender, intersex movement have been among the important vehicles for change that might not otherwise have happened.

One of the most durable and flexible social movements is feminism (Ferree & Mueller, 2004). Consider the fact that the feminist movement has already lasted for more than two centuries. At the opening of the 19th century, feminism emerged in the United States and Europe. By the early 20th century, feminist organizations appeared in urban centers around the world. By the turn of the 21st century, feminism had grown into a transnational movement in which groups work at local and global levels to address militarism, global capitalism, racism, poverty, violence against women, economic autonomy for women, and other issues of justice, human rights, and peace (Shaw & Lee, 2001).

Research on transnational feminism has proliferated and drawn attention to the complex nature of a "highly diversified, globalized social movement" (Hewitt, 2011, p. 65). As discussed above, Connell's reading in this chapter offers insight into the issue of men and masculinities in relation to gender equality worldwide and does so by discussing the diversity of men's movements, setting out grounds for optimism as well as pessimism in the struggle to end men's privileges.

Other readings in this chapter address challenges facing transnational feminism in women's movements. Briefly, let's look at two of those challenges. The first is developing ways to work together across differences and inequalities among women rooted in cultural, national, religious, and other intersectionalities (Hewitt, 2011; Ryan, 2001). Simply put, "gender is but one strand of oppression among many," and alliances need to be forged across intramovement differences (Hewitt, 2011; Motta, Flesher Fominaya, Eschie, & Cox, 2011). This problem takes many shapes. Not only is it a matter, for example, of class-privileged women and poor women or White women and women of color forming working alliances, but it is also a matter of being attuned to pitfalls in thinking and organizing across differences and inequalities (Motta et al., 2011).

For example, as American feminists have made progress with respect to addressing third world women's issues, they have become "inadequately accountable to issues of difference and inequality among communities of women" within the United States itself (Chowdhury, 2009, p. 53; see the chapter reading by Andrea Smith). One response to this problem is suggested by Chowdhury (2009), who calls for the intertwining of U.S. "anti-racist/ third world feminisms and third world/transnational feminisms" to build connections across multiple borders, both "intra-national and international" (p. 53). Smith's reading in this chapter is a good example of the value of intranational research in relationship to the challenge of complexities of difference and inequality. She enables the marginalized voices of indigenous women in the United States to speak to the reader via her analysis of the complex and varied relationships between Native American women who identify as feminists and those who do not, as well as the extent to which Native feminists work in coalition with non-Native feminists.

Lynne Phillips and Sally Cole's chapter reading draws attention to a second challenge for global feminism: divisions among feminist groups in their visions, goals, strategies, and orientations to change. To illustrate this problem, Phillips and Cole discuss the contrasts between UN-orbit and another-world feminisms. Using data from the feminist organizations they studied in Ecuador and Brazil, Phillips and Cole state that feminists in the U.N. orbit work within the framework of United Nations agencies and national state organizations and, as such, face constraints imposed on their work by those organizations. These feminists tend to define equality as best achieved within the ideology of a "liberal society" (see discussion of liberal and neoliberal feminism in the introduction to this book). Another-world feminists operate within antiglobalization movements (e.g., the

World March of Women and the World Social Forum) and view women's issues as part of a variety of movements for wide and deep social transformation. They maintain relative independence from national political parties and from institutions such as the United Nations. Together, these two feminisms underscore the heterogeneity and dynamism, as well as the tensions and risks, of doing feminist work in the context of globalization (Motta et al., 2011).

Two other readings in this chapter examine effective strategies for building bridges across intersectionalities and between feminist organizations. Suzy D'Enbeau looks at how globalization has changed the ways "feminist activists organize and connect throughout the world" (p. 537). Her research highlights one positive outcome: transnational feminist networks, or TFNs. D'Enbeau's case study of the Association for Women's Rights in Development demonstrates how that TFN has successfully used the Internet to build a collective identity and manage the "tensions of solidarity-diversity" across borders and divisions (p. 543). Finally, Nina Nijsten's article offers 10 tips or tools for creating feminist movements in the 21st century. She developed these tools by studying the strategies of second-wave feminists (see the introduction to this book) and by drawing on her own experiences working in anarchist and antiglobalist groups, writing for a feminist magazine and blog, and discussing critical issues with other feminists in a variety of organizations.

THE COMPLEXITY OF CHANGE

Not only is social change pervasive at micro and macro levels of life and a function of both planned and unplanned processes, it is also uneven and complex (Ridgeway, 2009). Change doesn't unfold in a linear, predictable fashion, and it may be dramatically visible or may take us by surprise. Consider the passage of the Nineteenth Amendment to the U.S. Constitution in 1920, which guaranteed women the right to vote.

This one historic moment uplifted the public status of women and did so in a visible fashion. But more often, change consists of alterations in the fabric of gender relations that are not immediately visible to us, both in their determinants and their consequences.

For instance, we now know that a complex set of factors facilitated the entry of large numbers of single and married women into the paid workforce and higher education in the second half of the 20th century. Those factors included very broad economic, political, and technological developments that transformed the United States into an urban, industrial capitalist nation (Stone & McKee, 1998). Yet no one predicted the extent of change in gender attitudes and relations that would follow the entry of women into the workforce. It is only "after the fact" that the implications have been identified and assessed. For example, marital relationships in the United States have moved toward greater equity in response to the reality that most married women are no longer wholly dependent on their husbands' earnings. As married women have increasingly embraced paid work, their spouses have increasingly reconceptualized and rearranged their priorities so they can devote more attention to parenthood (Goldscheider & Rogers, 2001).

Finally, it is important for us to recognize that change occurs even under oppressive social conditions. Research has demonstrated how patriarchal traditions in seemingly rigid social institutions can be altered. For example, studies of the "forced" integration of women into previously all-male military academies, such as West Point and the Citadel, show that although women struggled against a powerful wall of male resistance, they have in the end demonstrated that they can "do military masculinity" (Kimmel, 2000).

PRISMS OF GENDER AND CHANGE

Returning briefly to the metaphor of the kaleidoscope, let us recall that the prism of gender interacts with a complex array of social prisms of difference and inequality, such as race and sexual orientation. The prisms produce ever-changing patterns at micro and macro levels of life. Our metaphor points to yet another important principle of dynamic gender arrangements. We can link gender change to alterations in other structural dimensions of society, such as race, class, and age. For example, as Americans have moved toward greater consciousness and enactment of gender equality, they have also come to greater consciousness about the roles that heterosexism (i.e., the institutionalization of heterosexuality as the only legitimate form of sexual expression) and homophobia (i.e., the fear and hatred of homosexuality) play in reinforcing rigid gender stereotypes and relationships (see Chapter 6). It has become clear to many seeking gender justice that the justice sought after cannot be achieved without eliminating homophobia and the heterosexist framework of social institutions such as family and work.

Additionally, gender transformation in the United States is inextricably tied to race. This is true both historically and today. The first wave of feminism was an outgrowth of the antislavery movement, and the politics of racial justice led to the second wave of feminism (Freedman, 2002). Racism, as well as ageism, classism, and other forms of oppression, had to be addressed by feminists, because the struggle to achieve equal worth for women had to include all women and men. Anything less would mean failure.

THE INEVITABILITY OF CHANGE

Collectively, the articles in this chapter invite the reader to ask, "Why should I care about or get involved in promoting change in the gender status quo?" That is a good question. After all, why should one go to the trouble of departing from the standard package of gender practices and relationships? Change requires effort and entails risk. On the other hand, the cost of "going with the flow" can be high. There are no safe places to hide from change. Even if we choose "not to rock the boat" by closing ourselves off to inner and outer awareness, change will find us. There are two reasons for this fact of life. First, we cannot live in society without affecting others and in turn being affected by them. Each individual life intertwines with the lives of many other people, and our words and actions have consequences, both helpful and harmful. Every step we take and every choice we make affect the quality of life for a multitude of people. If we choose to wear blinders to our connections with others, we run the risk of inadvertently diminishing their chances, and our own, of living fulfilling lives (Schwalbe, 2001). For example, when a person tells a demeaning joke about women, he or she may intend no harm; however, the (unintended) consequences are harmful. The joke reinforces negative stereotypes, and telling the joke gives other people permission to be disrespectful to women (Schwalbe, 2001).

Second, we can't escape broad, societal changes in gender relations. By definition, institutional- and societal-level change wraps its arms around us all. Think about the widespread impact of laws such as the Equal Pay Act and Title VII, outlawing discrimination against women and people of color, or consider how sexual harassment legislation has redefined and altered relationships in a wide array of organizational settings. Reflect on the enormous impact of the large numbers of women who have entered the workforce since the latter half of the 20th century. The cumulative effect of the sheer numbers of women in the workforce has been revolutionary in its impact on gender relations in family, work, education, law, and other institutions and societal structures.

Given the inevitability of change in gender practices and relationships, it makes good sense to cultivate awareness of who we are and what our responsibilities to one another are. Without awareness, we cannot exercise control over our actions and their impact on others. Social forces shape us, but those forces change. Every transformation in societal patterns reverberates through our lives. Developing the "social literacy" to make sense of the changing links between our personal experience and the dynamics of social patterns can aid us in making informed, responsible choices (O'Brien, 1999; Schwalbe, 2001).

REFERENCES

Barber, B. R. (2002). Jihad vs. McWorld. In G. Ritzer (Ed.), *McDonaldization: The reader* (pp. 191–198). Thousand Oaks, CA: Pine Forge Press.

Bobel, C., & Kwan, S. (2011). Introduction. In C. Bobel & S. Kwan (Eds.), *Embodied resistance: Challenging the norms, breaking the rules* (pp. 1–10). Nashville, TN: Vanderbilt University Press.

Chowdhury, E. H. (2009). Locating global feminisms elsewhere: Braiding US women of color and transnational feminisms. *Cultural Dynamics, 21*(1), 51–78.

Connell, R. W. (2000). *The men and the boys.* Berkeley: University of California Press.

Deutsch, F. (2007). Undoing gender. *Gender & Society, 21,* 106–127.

Ferree, M., & Mueller, C. (2004). Feminism and the women's movement: A global perspective. In D. Snow, S. Soule, & H. Kriesi (Eds.), *The Blackwell companion to social movements* (pp. 576–607). Malden, MA: Blackwell.

Freedman, E. (2002). *No turning back: The history of feminism and the future of women.* New York: Ballantine Books.

Godwin, F. K., & Risman, B. J. (2001). Twentieth-century changes in economic work and family. In D. Vannoy (Ed.), *Gender mosaics* (pp. 134–144). Los Angeles: Roxbury.

Goldscheider, F. K., & Rogers, M. L. (2001). Gender and demographic reality. In D. Vannoy (Ed.), *Gender mosaics* (pp. 124–133). Los Angeles: Roxbury.

Held, D., McGrew, A., Goldblatt, D., & Perraton, J. (1999). *Global transformations.* Stanford, CA: Stanford University Press.

Hewitt, L. (2011). Framing across differences, building solidarities: Lessons from women's rights activism in transnational spaces. *Interface, 3*(2), 65–99.

Johnson, A. (1997). *The gender knot.* Philadelphia: Temple University Press.

Kimmel, M. (2000). Saving the males: The socio-logical implications of the Virginia Military Institute and the Citadel. *Gender & Society, 14*(4), 494–516.

Kivisto, P. (1998). *Key ideas in sociology.* Thousand Oaks, CA: Pine Forge Press.

Kuumba, M. B. (2001). *Gender and social movements.* Walnut Creek, CA: Altamira Press.

Lorber, J. (1994). *Paradoxes of gender.* New Haven, CT: Yale University Press.

Lorber, J. (2001). *Gender inequality: Feminist theories and politics.* Los Angeles: Roxbury.

Motta, S., Flesher Fominaya, C., Eschie, C., & Cox, L. (2011). Feminism, women's movements and women in movements. *Interface, 3*(2), 1–32.

O'Brien, J. (1999). *Social prisms.* Thousand Oaks, CA: Pine Forge Press.

Pyle, N., & Klein, N. L. (2011). Fat. Hairy. Sexy: Contesting standards of beauty and sexuality in the gay community. In C. Bobel & S. Kwan (Eds.), *Embodied resistance: Challenging the norms, breaking the rules* (pp. 78–87). Nashville, TN: Vanderbilt University Press.

Ridgeway, C. (2009). Framed before we know it: How gender shapes social relations. *Gender & Society, 23*(2), 145–160.

Ryan, B. (2001). *Identity politics in the women's movement.* New York: New York University Press.

Schwalbe, M. (2001). *The sociologically examined life.* Mountain View, CA: Mayfield.

Shaw, S. M., & Lee, J. (2001). *Women's voices, feminist visions.* Mountain View, CA: Mayfield.

Stone, L., & McKee, N. P. (1998). *Gender and culture in America.* Upper Saddle River, NJ: Prentice Hall.

West, C., & Zimmerman, D. (2009). Accounting for undoing gender. *Gender & Society, 23*(1), 112–122.

Wharton, A. S. (2005). *The sociology of gender.* Malden, MA: Blackwell.

Introduction to Reading 46

Lynne Phillips and Sally Cole conducted fieldwork, including interviews, in diverse feminist settings in Ecuador and Brazil in 2007 and 2008. The authors focus on two "translations of feminism" that they term "UN-orbit" and "another-world." UN-orbit feminists operate within global institutions such as UNIFEM (United Nations Development Fund for Women). Another-world feminists operate in groups that are independent of international institutions (e.g., the United Nations) and are embedded in the anti- or alterglobalization movement and alternative social forums such as REMTE (Red Latinoamericana Mujeres Transformando la Economia). Phillips and Cole compare and contrast the different locations, practices, challenges, and visions for the future of UN-orbit and another-world feminisms.

1. What is the future vision of feminists in the another-world movement, and how does it differ from the UN-orbit vision?

2. Why do the authors argue that UN-orbit feminism often fails to build coalitions with local women in countries such as Ecuador and Brazil?

3. Discuss the differences between the risks faced by UN-orbit and another-world feminisms.

4. Which "translation," UN orbit or another world, resonates with your vision for global justice and equality? Why?

FEMINIST FLOWS, FEMINIST FAULT LINES

WOMEN'S MACHINERIES AND WOMEN'S MOVEMENTS IN LATIN AMERICA

Lynne Phillips and Sally Cole

The circulation of feminism as text and practice has emerged as an important literature in the effort to understand the worldwide development of feminisms. Within this literature, the flow of feminism—variously labeled global, international, and/or transnational—is never a direct transplant or top-down superimposition but is understood to be "multidirectional" (Ferree and Tripp 2006, viii). Feminism is always interpreted in situated contexts through a multi-layered process that Susan Gal calls "translation" (2003, 93). As Gal points out, translation takes place in specific sets of social relations that mediate the movement of ideas and define the conditions of possible political action. Feminism circulates, but not unchanged (Thayer 2001; Davis 2007). Feminism in practice is pragmatic, and it is recontextualized as it engages with the conditions and implications of particular issues in particular settings. And feminism has been found to be malleable, applicable, and useful to women in a diversity of social settings and political conditions around the globe. Locating feminism "rearticulates marginality or particularity" (Kaplan 1996, 142–43) and engages feminism in concrete projects for social change. Its constant reinterpretation by heterogeneous actors and its continuing utility in a wide diversity of settings indicate how far feminism has moved from prescriptive content or "unlocatable sisterly solidarity" (Ong 2006, 52).

Translation assumes difference. Tensions produced through the recontextualization of feminism in specific places are inevitable in the current global context, where concepts of difference often mask multiple dimensions of unequal power. Feminism as a "goal for social change" (Ferree 2006, 6) necessarily engages at the fault lines of societies and confronts the dynamics of power embedded in race, class, regional, and rural-urban relations for particular women in particular places and at particular points in time. In the process, feminism is continually transformed and resignified. If there is global feminism, it is multiple and heterogeneous, malleable and dynamic, at once everywhere and in very specific places.

During fieldwork in Ecuador and Brazil in 2007 and 2008, we were struck by the variety of forms that feminism was taking and the variety of contexts within which feminists were working.[1] Feminists in Latin America have long practiced what we, following Anne Phillips (1996), call "a politics of presence." From the lipstick lobby that joined struggles to overthrow military dictatorships and build democratic institutions to the anti-free trade and "another world" activism of twenty-first century social and economic justice movements, feminists have chosen to "be present," working to ensure that projects for social transformation take into account what is at stake for women.[2] In this article we argue that one of the key ways that feminism is located in Ecuador and Brazil is through the participation—the presence—of feminists in multiple spaces, including mainstream institutions and "mixed" social movements.[3]

Phillips argues that, in fragile democracies where structural inequalities result in exclusion based on race, ethnicity, religion, or gender, deliberate measures need to be taken in order to increase political representation (presence) and to diversify the ideas and proposals presented for social transformation. In this article we extend Phillips's notion of a politics of presence beyond the arena of formal politics to describe the political practices of feminists who are choosing to be present in a diversity of mixed spaces in order to advance gender equity goals directly and in concrete ways. We analyze the work of feminists in diverse contexts: in a global institution; in the state ministries, secretariats, and advisory councils—what the United Nations calls women's machineries—that are specifically mandated to bring women's issues to national governments; and in the antiglobalization "movement of movements."[4] It is these spaces of feminist presence that we have taken as our research sites.

We conducted interviews with feminists working in the Latin American offices of UNIFEM in Quito and Brasilia; the national women's machineries, the Consejo National de las Mujeres (CONAMU; National council of women) in Ecuador and the Secretaria Especial de Politicas para as Mulheres (SPM; Special secretariat for policy for women) in Brazil; the Red Latinoamericana Mujeres Transformando la Economia (REMTE; Latin American network of women transforming the economy); and two nongovernmental organizations (NGOs) that work with REMTE: Centro Feminista 8 de Marco (CF8; March 8th feminist center) in northeast Brazil and Mujeres Rurales Organizadas de Canton Santa Elena (MUROCSE; Organization of rural women of Canton Santa Elena) in coastal Ecuador. In this article we locate our interviews in a field of sites we regard as broadly traversed by two translations of feminism that, for heuristic purposes, we call the UN-orbit and the another-world translations.[5] . . .

In the following section, we elaborate the emergence of two translations of feminism—the UN-orbit and another-world translations—in this era of late neoliberalism. While we demarcate these two translations for heuristic purposes, our field research and interviews reveal that Latin American feminists engage these two

translations at different times and for different purposes. Moreover, the campaigns, goals, and contexts in which feminisms are translated also change over the life courses and according to the goals of individuals, groups, and movements. With this kind of fluidity in mind, the following discussion draws attention to how and when these two translations meet and diverge.[6]

Two Translations: Contexts, Practices, and Visions

What we are calling the UN-orbit translation broadly refers to an approach to social transformation for gender equality through a systematic, proposal-based global agenda. Working within present global economic and political parameters, feminists participating in the UN orbit translate feminism by mainstreaming gender issues into the public sphere and by lobbying for the introduction, maintenance, and improvement of gender equity policies in institutions and legislation. The goal here is to effect equal economic opportunities, legal equality, and political participation; the future aspired to is a liberal one, free of gender bias and reminiscent of the world of productive individual citizens that Sally Engle Merry (2006) identifies as the culture of the United Nations.

These feminists practice a politics of presence by participating in global institutions (e.g., UNIFEM) and by renovating the women's machineries—the state ministries, secretariats, and advisory councils that are specifically mandated to bring women's issues to national governments. They take as their reference points the Beijing Declaration and Platform for Action of the Fourth World Conference on Women in 1995 and other UN-inspired programs for change that include the Convention for Elimination of all Forms of Discrimination against Women (CEDAW). As a result, they work with the matrices and multiyear plans of results-based management required by global institutions and donors. The requirement to meet externally set targets and goals often involves contracting gender experts who translate feminism by producing literature (knowledge products), running workshops, and advising on a range of issues from poverty reduction to gender-sensitive budgets. Our interviews indicate that, when feminist work in the UN orbit becomes dominated by issues of accountability and results-based management, the possibilities for imagining long-term feminist alternatives are constrained. Nonetheless, in practicing a politics of presence, these feminists are doing the necessary work of translating women's issues for international and national policy in the emergent but still precarious democracies of Brazil and Ecuador.

The other translation traversing our research sites is what we call another-world feminism, which takes its name from the antiglobalization movement of movements, and from the World Social Forum, with its various spin-off alternative social forums. Another world is a charismatic idea (Tsing 2005) that mobilizes diverse groups seeking to build another world—that is, a world different from the one being created by the economic and geopolitical regimes of neoliberal global governance. Another world is, in Anna Lowenhaupt Tsing's terms, a "collaborative object" that "draws groups into common projects at the same time that [it] allows them to maintain separate agendas" (2005, 246). Even if another world means different things to different people, as a charismatic idea—or a matter of concern, as Bruno Latour (2005) puts it—it brings people together. For those participating in another-world translations of feminism, women's issues are not separate from but part of an alternative vision for the future; feminist goals are linked with projects and movements for wide social transformation.

For the activists we interviewed, another world is a feminist world and gender equality is at its foundation. Feminists participating in another-world translations imagine new forms of economic organization through *economia solidária*, combined with new forms of social organization where gender and diversities are transversal axes. In contrast to the UN orbit, here the process is improvised rather than results-managed. The future is imagined as unpredictable.

As they are accountable to themselves and to the world they want to help build, these feminists do not hire outside experts to do "translation work" and to help them meet externally set standards and measures. They find expertise—knowledge—in diverse places, drawing on a repertoire of sources, including local women's groups and feminist scholarship. And they select and translate their own materials, organize discussion groups among themselves, and set up information tables in everyday spaces—such as supermarkets—frequented by a diverse public. Not working within a matrix of measures, indicators, and results, they view their work as accompaniment.[7] A large part of the work of another-world feminists, like those in REMTE, is popular education; REMTE's greatest resource is the network of women it comprises.

The relative independence of REMTE from national and international institutions and national political parties gives it greater flexibility than organizations working within the UN orbit. Nevertheless, REMTE also chooses to serve on advisory councils to a variety of government agencies—for example, in Brazil REMTE sits on the advisory councils for both SPM and the Ministry for the Solidarity Economy. Links to these state machineries constitute part of REMTE's strategic politics of presence. However, as a social movement, REMTE ensures its presence in less institutionalized spaces, collaborating with a diversity of social movements, such as La Vía Campesina (a transnational network of farmers' organizations), the World March of Women, and the World Social Forum, and participating in the mobilization of numerous campaigns including those related to free trade, minimum wage, and consumer rights.[8] As we indicate later in this article, the goals, practices, and arenas of REMTE's work offer broad possibilities for challenging the late neoliberal context that currently shapes democracy-building in Ecuador and Brazil. Yet, as demonstrated in this section, feminist participation in all of these spaces involves risks, and as long as these democracies remain precarious, neither translation is dispensable.

THE UN-ORBIT TRANSLATION

The United Nations and UNIFEM in Latin America

From our perspective, the practice of feminists working in UN agencies and state machineries is better read as feminist activism within institutionalized settings than as institutionalized feminism.[9] The translations set in motion by UNIFEM, for example, have permitted a greater visibility of women's issues in international and national arenas, have increased discussion and debate around gender equality, and have played a role in developing more democratic publics in Latin America. However, the ways in which work is carried out in UN contexts—and the technologies that govern these spaces—limit the kinds of relationships that can be created and maintained by UNIFEM.

As in the case of our other sites of feminist activism, we find that feminists working within and outside the United Nations have considerable mobility and a critical awareness of the paradoxes of UN participation. Valentine Moghadam (2005) notes that, within the transnational feminist networks she studied (e.g., DAWN [Development Alternatives with Women for a New Era] and WEDO [Women's Environment and Development Organization]), feminists often felt that if they were to make a difference in policies and institutions operating at the global level, there were not many choices other than working with the United Nations. As late as 2000, one year before the first World Social Forum, WEDO board member Rosalind Petchesky asserted: "We need democratic, accountable institutions of global governance in the face of globalization. . . . In this respect, the UN system *is all we have*" (quoted in Moghadam 2005, 129). This statement reminds us how diverse the space for global activism has since become.

Much has been written about the history of the UN world conferences on women and the significance of other UN conferences (on the environment, population, racism, etc.) for women's issues since 1975.[10] Our starting point is the Fourth World Conference on Women, the 1995 Beijing conference, because Latin American feminists became more engaged in the UN orbit at that time. The Beijing conference involved unprecedented preconference mobilization of organizations and movements, and the resulting Platform for Action mobilized spaces for state intervention on gender issues throughout the region.

Accounts of the Beijing conference hint at the existence of an unruly Latin American feminism, which requires some explanation. The Latin American feminist *Encuentros* (encounters), which began in 1981, initially to build a regional feminist agenda to challenge authoritarian regimes within Latin America, played a crucial role in solidifying a distinct Latin American feminism that engaged somewhat uneasily in global venues. Part of this distinction derives from the relationships that developed between popular women's movements and the feminist movement in Latin America (Stephen 1997; Pinto 2007). Ethnographic accounts of popular women's movements have shown that members of these movements were and are concerned with improving living conditions and may not identify themselves as feminist; but in Latin America women in popular women's movements have generally viewed feminism as an ally.[11] They have frequently been "side-by-side" (Pinto 2007, 17) in addressing their concerns about dictatorships, corruption, and democracy building.[12] From the beginning, the *Encuentros* had focused on the importance of class issues, but an appreciation of how multiple diversities productively shape feminism within the region has developed over time with the increasing participation of indigenous and Afrodescendent women, lesbians, and women from other parts of Latin America and the Caribbean.[13]

Feminists in Latin America viewed their engagement with the Beijing conference as doubly strategic: it could ensure not only that a Latin American perspective would be heard in Beijing but that, within the region, the preconference process itself could serve as a lever for change. The Beijing conference also offered the opportunity for UN offices to create more extensive alliances with women's organizations in the region. And women's movements, in turn, have expected that the United Nations would seek out leadership from movement activists. Thus, feminists who work in the regional offices of UNIFEM today juggle the expectations of women's movements in Latin America with the expectations of UNIFEM's head office in New York—not only "the whole dreadful burden of bureaucracy that is New York" (as one interviewee put it) but also the ongoing work of getting gender on the agenda in the larger, masculinist organization (Snyder 2006, 45–46).[14]

The current climate at the United Nations also limits the possibilities for UNIFEM to operate as a "movement agency," as Moghadam (2005, 99) dubs it.[15] Not only are there increased demands for efficiency—and for doing more with fewer resources—but new international projects, such as the Millennium Development Goals, reorient expectations for the region (e.g., with a focus on poverty reduction rather than on social transformation). The regional offices are expected to demonstrate concrete results in order to receive and attract more funding. This has meant, first, becoming a more complex bureaucracy (moving from operating "like a small NGO" to functioning as an organization with a more credible "profile" within the United Nations itself, as an officer at UNIFEM-Brazil put it) and, second, relating differently to women's organizations in the region.[16]

One tool for managing these changes has been the "call for proposals" process. In the past, the regional offices received funding requests from organizations throughout the year. Now they screen requests through a call for proposals, which has specific monitoring, deadline, and profile requirements. In 2006, for the first time, UNIFEM's Quito office, for example, sent out e-mails to all registered organizations working on gender issues in the Andean region. A UNIFEM officer in Quito describes the process:

> [Proposals] had to be concrete, of a certain number of pages, and we established the conditions for NGOs. They [organizations] have to have legal status, experience with the work—all the criteria. . . . In the first step, they have to send two pages, a sort of outline. They send a profile saying what the project is about, how much it costs, how they will run it. . . . From there we selected the twenty best and from there we asked them to develop the proposal. . . . For example [we say], "Look, in terms of the conceptual part we don't see the relationship between this and that. The methodological section is weak. . . . [They need to] show sustainability. That is what we value the most: how it will be when UNIFEM pulls out.[17]

The constant monitoring of these projects ensures that "everything that had to come out of the project" is in fact visible in the final results of the project.[18] This practice of monitoring indicates a very different way of working with women's organizations than in the past, as elaborated by a member of UNIFEM-Ecuador: "When results-based management first came out, in truth, it really affected us in the offices. We were used to working in a way that valued the organizations' dynamism, the people's initiative, the fact that you have a project and, if halfway through, something unexpected emerged and you have to change the project, well, it didn't matter, you changed the project. The fact of having that logical framework, that you have to work this way, affected us because it was something new and it changed the whole work organization."[19]

The UNIFEM office in Brazil described similar impacts:

> The Multiyear Funding Framework is a program that assumes results-based management. It's a requirement of the system. That was imposed. But it's—and this is my opinion—an instrument, an analysis that makes it very difficult to capture reality because it is a numerical measure basically, isn't it? How can you work with numbers? . . . For example, we had a campaign, a central campaign entered into by UNIFEM, the 16 Days of Activism to End Violence against Women, in November, December. And at the end of the year, they [UNIFEM-New York] ordered us to do an evaluation of the impact of the campaign in Brazil. The campaign was mainly through the media. In a

country the size of Brazil, which is enormous in territory and in population . . . evaluation was enormously complicated. How could you evaluate? The first question was: "How many people were affected?" How could we know this? Impossible![20]

While UNIFEM officers fulfill their obligation to produce measurable results and while they understand the process as important for funding accountability, their engagement involves a certain critical awareness of the limitations and advantages of results-based management.[21] Officers in both Brazil and Ecuador describe working within this management model:

You have a monitoring system and, because of it, it's impossible for the project to *end* as a failure. You realize at the beginning or halfway through. You won't get to the end and say, "Damn, I was wrong." It's true that it is a straightjacket [*camisa de fuerza*], but in the end, if you adapt and organize yourself from the beginning and you put conditions on it, it becomes a positive instrument.[22]

I understand the preoccupation of the organization [UNIFEM] to measure impact. I understand this perfectly. But at the same time, impact is not something easy to measure. There are many aspects [*caras*] of impact. It's not all immediately visible. And results-based management includes planning also. And results-based planning has very rigid limits, and requires us to work with these matrices that are an inferno in our life. They're like hell for us![23]

Even so, because of the time and energy required to maintain this system, those working in UNIFEM spaces are increasingly pushed toward an agenda of strategic results, defined by the head office and its funders. As activities become more tightly tied to these results, strategies have been developed to achieve more predictable outcomes. One important strategy has been to bring in experts to train staff in results-based management and to identify obstacles to achieving the intended results for specific programs. For example, in 2001 a group of experts from the Organization of American States advised UNIFEM-Ecuador on

how to implement the Inter-American Convention on the Prevention, Punishment, and Eradication of Violence against Women (CIM 2001), and the UNIFEM-Brazil office recently invited Diane Elson as an outside expert to give a workshop, "Gender, Macroeconomics, and Public Policy." The use of experts is thus one technique through which the UN orbit translates feminism.

While UNIFEM may go some way toward achieving expected results, this occurs at a cost. Since the focus is on proposals that are advocacy based and carried out by organizations able to work with results-based management (including proposal writing, midterm evaluations, and computer-based communication), many women's groups are excluded. Support for local projects gives way to work on more replicable projects, those seen as of strategic national and regional significance. As an officer at UNIFEM-Brazil put it: "If we opened support to local projects we would not be able to do anything else. Because the demand is gigantic [*gigantesca*] . . . local projects could be an activity without end."[24] Thus, working in these UN spaces involves a distancing from the concrete experiences of specific women in favor of more generic, abstract experiences that the (imagined) translocal woman shares. Increasingly, knowledge about the experiences of women in the popular and rural sectors is being mediated for UNIFEM—either translated by others or lost entirely.

Inequalities are sharply felt in Latin America, and networks and coalitions on issues of race, ethnicity, and poverty are of strategic importance for the UNIFEM offices. However, because such alliances are viewed instrumentally (i.e., in terms of obtaining results), the translations of forms of discrimination that affect women's lives are necessarily constrained. The results-based model may be useful for securing funds and may help to provide an international profile for particular women's issues, but because the diversity of women's experience is managed within the parameters of this model, the UN orbit limits exploration of alternatives.[25] Still, because an organization like UNIFEM has the capacity to support gender interests in the process of democracy building and because part of UNIFEM's strength derives from its relationship to women's movements, feminists in Latin America continue to work together, not necessarily easily, for particular projects.

ANOTHER WORLD

The another-world translation of feminism comprises a heterogeneous set of networks, articulations, centers, and groups working to create alternative futures in which the diversity of women is tied to questions of economic justice. In our case studies of REMTE, CF8, and MUROCSE, another-world feminists link their work to advance gender equality to campaigns against neoliberal globalization and to movements for utopian futures, including those built around the solidarity economy, food sovereignty, and environmental movements.

A transnational network that builds on and reinforces previously existing women's organizations at national and local levels (Diaz 2007), REMTE was founded in 1997 at a workshop organized by members of women's organizations in Chile, Colombia, Mexico, Nicaragua, and Peru to discuss the impact of structural adjustment programs on women. By 2008 the REMTE network linked feminist organizations in eleven Latin American countries, including REMTE-Ecuador and REF (Rede Economia e Feminismo; Feminism and Economy Network) in Brazil. Coordination of the network rotates among the participating national organizations and is currently based in São Paulo, Brazil, where REMTE has allied its activities with the much larger transnational World March of Women.

Through participation in mixed spaces, REMTE pursues a politics of presence as part of its politics of transformation, arguing, as one REMTE-Ecuador feminist put it, "if women are not present at the moment of decision, those moments are not going to take on our agenda."[26] Initiating risky alliances, working to find common ground, REMTE feminists translate feminism into the mixed spaces of social movements,

state-civil society joint bodies such as the National Advisory Council on the Solidarity Economy in Brazil, and international contexts such as La Vía Campesina and the World Social Forum. Feminists in REMTE also conduct analyses, write brochures, and organize workshops and actions to expose the retrenching of gender inequality within corporate globalization, evident, for example, in the commoditization of women in the beauty industry, the expansion of sex tourism, and the discursive framing of unregulated employment as women's freedom to participate in the labor force. Always working "with and across difference" (Walby 2002, 541)—rather than managing difference—REMTE works to build a robust feminism into its visions for the future.

Our interviewees in REMTE saw their role as one of making themselves available to women's groups and organizations, not directing the process or the outcome of projects. They described multiple dimensions to their work of accompaniment, including advising, providing analysis and training, assisting the auto-organization (*auto-organização*) of women's groups, and supporting the development of leadership. Through these practices of accompaniment and popular education, REMTE makes its critical feminist economic analysis widely available to women's groups, as became evident in our case studies of CF8 and MUROCSE.

In 1993 CF8 was founded in the northeastern Brazilian state of Rio Grande do Norte; it was initially organized around the issue of violence against women. In response to needs expressed by the rural women with whom it was working, CF8 soon expanded its focus: "We realized we couldn't separate the issue of violence from all the other issues that were concerning women and that required change," CF8's current coordinator told us. In 2008 CF8 defined itself as a hybrid NGO—working both to build the women's movement by accompanying local women's groups and to transform global structures by building alliances with other social movements: "We are always discussing, 'How can we work locally to transform local activities but always keep an eye on broader transformation?' We work with local women's needs but with a global vision and with the goal of transforming society. We have a foot in the local with an eye to the global [*um pé no local más com um olhar sobre uma visao mais global*]."[27]

To develop the transformative potential of their work, CF8 feminists sought alliances with the World March of Women and REMTE, as well as with the Movimento dos Trabalhadores Rurais Sem Terra (MST; Landless people's movement), the Central Única dos Trabalhadores (CUT; Rural workers' union), and the Brazilian Forum on the Solidarity Economy. Recently CF8's goals coalesced in the Million Cisterns Project, an internationally funded initiative to address the water crisis in the drought-ridden northeast of Brazil (CF8 2006). Women's groups in new settlements founded by the MST on the outskirts of Mossoró had requested assistance from CF8 to prepare a proposal for a cistern project to help bring water to their households. Through REMTE workshops CF8 had developed a critical analysis of women's unpaid reproductive work in the rural economy. Additionally, CF8 encouraged the women not only to assume responsibility for local coordination but actually to undertake the necessary training and to build the system of pipes and cisterns themselves. The coordinator of CF8 recalled: "In the cistern project, we combined all of our objectives as an organization: assisting women to develop organizational and leadership skills, meeting women's everyday needs [for water], paid work for women, and overturning the gendered division of labor by moving women out of domestic work into the typically masculine manual labor of construction."[28]

In coastal Ecuador MUROCSE began as a response of rural women to the devastating effects of the country adopting the American dollar as its currency as well as other economic policies of successive neoliberal governments, combined with the severe weather conditions associated with El Niño in 1999. With the support of REMTE, the women met in 2000 to reflect on their specific, but highly diverse, situations.

They identified two axes for their work: to promote rural women's productive activities—which included challenging the sexual division of labor in the region—and to initiate dialogue about rural women's rights. In order to reach women across the region, they started a radio program, *Mujeres Rompiendo el Silencio* (Women breaking the silence), inviting politicians, rural women, and REMTE feminists as speakers. When there were hints that the program might end, MUROCSE was showered with feedback from rural women about the importance of what it was doing, indicating to the organization that it had become "a space that empowered rural women."[29] While MUROCSE has other alliances in Ecuador that are important to its work, REMTE connects MUROCSE to international issues through the World March of Women and provides advice. For MUROCSE, this contribution is essential: "We are talking with the grassroots [*de base*] and we have to know the reality of how to manage the state. . . . If I speak to everyone [on the radio], I can't say just anything, I have to speak with wisdom [*juicio*]."[30]

Thus, REMTE and its allies work on two fronts: participation in mixed social movements to ensure the integration of feminist analysis in planning for broad social transformation, and popular education and accompaniment to build the women's movement in their respective national and local contexts. Both the visions for broad social transformation and the practice of accompaniment stand in contrast to the liberal, results-directed coalition building of UNIFEM, as one REMTE—São Paulo interviewee attests: "Some insist that the goal is to look at the different impacts on women and men, but we insist that it's not about measuring impacts. It's to demonstrate that this model operates this way precisely because there are these relations of gender that are structuring the model. It's not a question of just looking at the impacts and trying to minimize them. It's to deconstruct the pillars."[31]

Maintaining energy for such a diversity of projects and alliances is a challenge. And, while their orientation indicates a greater potential for effecting deeper social transformations, another-world feminists face the risk that their energies will be absorbed, and their practices potentially overtaken, by the dynamics of the mixed spaces in which they participate. One CF8 feminist, for example, lamented how much of their time is devoted to trying to convince the men who dominate the policy-drafting boards of the local solidarity economy and ecology movements to integrate women's interests. She summarized the experience: "Our proposals involve broader social transformations and especially changes in the sexual division of labor. The men think this is unnecessary."[32]

CONCLUSION

Working with the concept of feminist translation has raised new questions for us: Under what conditions do feminist practices best connect with the everyday lives of women? When, why, and for whom do transnational sites provide conceptual spaces for rethinking or claiming feminist practices? If the two translations of feminism we have outlined here are the prevailing ones, how do new feminist futures emerge? In this article we propose that answers to these questions lie in identifying the different locations of feminist translations; conceptualizing the practices, goals, and methods that feminists pursue; and examining how the fault lines of these locations shape the visions feminists have for the future.

In tracking the flows and fault lines of feminism in Latin America, we have found translations at work in multiple sites. For our purposes here, we have identified two translations that we call the UN orbit and another world. Feminists in the UN orbit work within UN agencies and conventions and within the national state machineries for women. Feminists participating in another world work with social movements at transnational, regional, national, and local levels. Feminists in both the UN orbit and another world juggle their responsibilities to translate women's issues and their commitment to keep gender on the agenda in otherwise masculinist institutions and social movements. In this way, both practice a politics of presence that takes them into difficult mixed spaces, from the United Nations to the World Social Forum. Therein lie risks for both—from managing women's issues through the adoption of new accounting measures to draining limited political energy away from other feminist work.

But we have also encountered important differences in the practices and visions of these two translations of feminism. On the one hand, feminists practicing within the UN orbit are constrained by the results-based management and expertise-driven orientation of UN agencies and donors that create new exclusions and transform the relations UNIFEM feminists have with other feminists. UNIFEM feminists' collaborations with SPM in Brazil and with CONAMU in Ecuador subject these state agencies to the UN's results-driven orientation. Yet, feminists working within the state agencies are also tied to women's movements in ways that often challenge and moderate the effects of the UN orbit. Feminists working with another-world translations, on the other hand, seek to develop relations of accompaniment with popular women's groups. Unencumbered by the measures of results-based management, they mobilize feminist knowledge in local and regional contexts to challenge masculinist views about the economy and to propose alternative approaches to women's reproductive and productive work.

The fault lines of poverty and inequality figure in the different visions these feminists have for the future. Feminists in the UN orbit work for gender equality within a liberal society. Embedded in this model is a version of diversity that hinders the kinds of networks and coalitions they can build with local women. As a result, UN-orbit translations of feminism often fail to capture the complex realities of the many forms of discrimination that affect women's lives. Feminists working with another-world translations seek a yet-to-be-discovered future that is both feminist and built on economic, cultural, and other diversities. Rather than working instrumentally toward a particular future, they initiate dialogue in their engagement with risky alliances. Their translation of feminism hinges on a politics of transformation—not a reproduction of liberal society but rather a more inclusive feminist economy.

Locating feminism in Latin America has meant understanding alliances to contain "differences and commonalities simultaneously," as Walby (2002, 547) has suggested. We have argued that a strategic politics of presence in multiple sites is required in fragile democracies, yet it is clear that the two translations of feminism we have outlined here frame the kinds of issues that can be brought forward in each context and the strategies that can be pursued to achieve them. The concept of translation has allowed us to identify the different and similar contexts, practices, and visions that shape feminisms. Feminism travels (Thayer 2000; Gal 2003), but our research shows that its movement is configured and that the paths it moves along may be risky.

NOTES

1. We focus on Brazil and Ecuador because they house the two offices of UNIFEM (United Nations Development Fund for Women) in South America (the Southern Cone office in Brasilia, Brazil, and the Andean region office in Quito, Ecuador) and because of our past research experience in these two countries. While the countries differ in significant ways, both have established women's machineries in fulfillment of CEDAW (Convention on the Elimination of All Forms of Discrimination against Women) obligations, and the current governments of both countries are interested in promoting alternative forms of development.

2. The term "another world" is an abbreviation of the phrase "another world is possible" used by the World Social Forum, an annual meeting (since 2001) of activists who are part of the anti- and alterglobalization movement.

3. This is how Latin American feminists refer to spaces comprising public and movement spaces where the primary mobilization is around objectives other than women and feminism. It includes the mixed-gender spaces of political parties; unions; ecology, economic solidarity, agrarian reform, and anti-free trade movements; and the World Social Forum. The term we are translating as mixed spaces is *espaços micros* in Brazil and *espacios mixtos* in Ecuador.

4. The term "movement of movements" refers to the transnational movement comprising a wide diversity of social movements, each originally mobilized around a specific issue (such as gender equality or environmental protection) but that come together in actions against contemporary globalization.

5. There is much current debate on the implications of globalization for ethnographic methods. While our approach shares aspects of George Marcus's move from single-sited to multisited ethnography (1998), Sally Engle Merry's deterritorialized ethnography that explores translation but in specific locations (2006), and Anna Lowenhaupt Tsing's idea of overlapping as elaborated in her ethnography of global connection (2005), we find that taken alone, none of these accommodates the mobilities and movements across sites that interest us here. Nor do they accommodate the Latin Americanness of the sites we discuss which we view as the product of located translations across sites. Thirty-nine interviews were conducted in either Spanish or Portuguese, digitally recorded, transcribed, and translated by the authors.

6. Other translations of feminism we could discuss include feminism within political parties, within unions, in state-level forums, and within indigenous and Afro-descendant movements. There are also other articulations that warrant discussion as translations of feminism (see Vargas 2003; Conway 2007).

7. The term "accompaniment" in Latin America derives from liberation theology and pastoral practice in Christian Base Communities in Brazil (Warren 2001).

8. The World March of Women, a global movement committed to fighting poverty and violence, began in Montréal in 1998. It held its Sixth International Meeting in Lima in 2006, where fifty-nine delegates from twenty-nine countries and the Native Women's Network of the Americas participated.

9. On institutionalized feminism in Latin America, see Alvarez (1997), Macaulay (2000), Alvarez et al. (2002), Blondet (2002), Francheschet (2005), and Lind (2005).

10. See Antrobus 2004; Jain 2005; Tripp 2006; Pietila 2007.

11. There have been notable exceptions, as Victoria González and Karen Kampwirth (2001) make clear.

12. Distinctions between "strategic" and "practical" feminism (Molyneux 1985) or "feminine" and "feminist" movements (Kaplan 1996) have been shown to be analytically limited given the interweaving of women's everyday lives and politics in the region (see Caldeira 1990; Schirmer 1993; Stephen 1997; Paley 2001).

13. See Miller 1991; Stephen 1997; Alvarez et al. 2002; Moghadam 2005; Caldwell 2007.

14. UNIFEM, interview by the authors, March 5, 2007, Brasilia. For reasons of confidentiality, the names of the people we interviewed are not provided.

15. Noeleen Heyzer, a sociologist, came from DAWN to head UNIFEM from 1994 to 2007. Moghadam argues that, with Heyzer at the helm, transnational feminist networks were strongly supported by UNIFEM. Heyzer's career trajectory is but one of the many examples our field research and interviews revealed of feminists moving between and across UN-orbit and another-world translations over time.

16. UNIFEM, interview by the authors, March 5, 2007, Brasilia.

17. UNIFEM, interview by the authors, February 26, 2007, Quito.

18. Ibid.

19. Ibid.

20. UNIFEM, interview by the authors, March 5, 2007, Brasilia.

21. See, by way of comparison, Annelise Riles's (2001) view that those working in the spaces of women and development fail to see how the information they collect is a function of the devices they use: in our case, in contrast, the matrix is understood to serve some purposes but not others.

22. UNIFEM, interview by the authors, February 26, 2007, Quito. We have retained some Spanish and Portuguese terms in these interviews to show how key or unusual phrases are translated.

23. UNIFEM, interview by the authors, March 5, 2007, Brasilia.

24. Ibid.

25. We find the citizenship literature on the politics of difference useful for our analysis here. For example, Phillips (2003) has noted that when the recognition of different groups is primarily seen as a policy issue, the people within those groups cease to become political actors and are constructed instead as socially disadvantaged and in need of support by more powerful others. Likewise, Charles Hale's (2006) concept of neoliberal multiculturalism explains the persistence of racism when the politics of difference overshadow a politics of equality, as tends to happen when liberal economic policies remain in place.

26. REMTE, interview by the authors, February 27, 2007, Quito.

27. CF8, interview by the authors, April 18, 2008, Mossoró.

28. Ibid.

29. MUROCSE, interview by Lynne Phillips, May 5, 2008, Santa Elena.

30. Ibid.

31. REMTE, interview by the authors, April 16, 2008, São Paulo.

32. CF8, interview by the authors, April 18, 2008, Mossoró.

REFERENCES

Alvarez, Sonia E. 1997. "Contradictions of a 'Women's Space' in a Male-Dominant State: The Political Role of the Commissions on the Status of Women in Post-authoritarian Brazil." In *Women, International Development, and Politics: The Bureaucratic Mire*, expanded ed., ed. Kathleen Staudt, 59–100. Philadelphia: Temple University Press.

Alvarez, Sonia E., Elisabeth Jay Friedman, Ericka Beckman, Maylei Blackwell, Norma Stoltz Chinchilla, Nathalie Lebon, Marysa Navarro, and Marcia Ríos Tobar. 2002. "Encountering Latin American and Caribbean Feminisms." *Signs: Journal of Women in Culture and Society* 28(2): 537–79.

Antrobus, Peggy. 2004. *The Global Women's Movement: Origins, Issues, and Strategies*. London: Zed.

Blondet, Cecilia. 2002. "The 'Devil's Deal': Women's Political Participation and Authoritarianism in Peru." In *Gender Justice, Development, and Rights*, ed. Maxine Molyneux and Shahra Razavi, 277–305. Oxford: Oxford University Press.

Caldeira, Teresa Pires de Rio. 1990. "Women, Daily Life and Politics." In *Women and Social Change in Latin America*, ed. Elizabeth Jelin, trans. J. Ann Zammit and Marilyn Thomson, 47–78. London: Zed.

Caldwell, Kia Lilly. 2007. *Negras in Brazil: Re-envisioning Black Women, Citizenship and the Politics of Identity*. New Brunswick, NJ: Rutgers University Press.

CF8 (Centro Feminista 8 de Março [March 8th feminist center]). 2006. "Construindo cisternas, deconstruindo tabus: Mulheres capacitando mulheres para o acesso à água" [Constructing cisterns, deconstructing taboos: Women empowering women through access to water]. *Folha Feminista* [Feminist Journal] 61:1–2.

CIM (Comisión Interamericana de Mujeres [Inter-American commission of women]). 2001. "Violence in the Americas: A Regional Analysis." Final report of Meeting of Experts of the Andean Subregion: Colombia, Ecuador, Peru, and Venezuela. Quito, June 21–22.

CONAMU (Consejo Nacional de las Mujeres [National women's council]). 2004. *Questionnaire to Governments on Implementation of the Beijing Platform for Action (1995) and the Outcome of the Twenty-third Special Session of the General Assembly (2000)*. Quito: CONAMU.

———. 2005. *Plan de igualdad de oportunidades de las mujeres ecuatorianas* [Equal opportunities plan for Ecuadorian women]. Quito: CONAMU.

Conway, Janet. 2007. "Transnational Feminisms and the World Social Forum: Encounters and Transformations in Anti-globalization Spaces." *Journal of International Women's Studies* 8(3): 49–70.

Davis, Kathy. 2007. *The Making of "Our Bodies, Ourselves": How Feminism Travels across Borders*. Durham, NC: Duke University Press.

Diaz, Carmen A. 2007. "Building Bridges between Feminism and Resistance to Free Trade: The Experience of the Latin American Network of Women Transforming the Economy." Master's thesis, University of Montréal.

Ferree, Myra Marx. 2006. "Globalization and Feminism: Opportunities and Obstacles for Activism in the Global Arena." In *Global Feminism: Transnational Women's Activism, Organizing, and Human Rights*, ed. Myra Marx Ferree and Aili Mari Tripp, 3–23. New York: New York University Press.

Ferree, Myra Marx, and Aili Mari Tripp. 2006. "Preface." In their *Global Feminism: Transnational Women's Activism, Organizing, and Human Rights*, vii–ix. New York: New York University Press.

Franceschet, Susan. 2005. *Women and Politics in Chile*. Boulder, CO: Lynne Rienner.

Gal, Susan. 2003. "Movements of Feminism: The Circulation of Discourses about Women." In *Recognition Struggles and Social Movements: Contested Identities, Agency and Power*, ed. Barbara Hobson, 93–118. Cambridge: Cambridge University Press.

González, Victoria, and Karen Kampwirth. 2001. "Introduction." In their *Radical Women in Latin America: Left and Right*, 1–28. University Park: Pennsylvania State University Press.

Hale, Charles R. 2006. *Más que un Indio = More than an Indian: Racial Ambivalence and Neoliberal Multiculturalism in Guatemala*. Santa Fe, NM: School of American Research Press.

Jain, Devaki. 2005. *Women, Development, and the UN: A Sixty-Year Quest for Equality and Justice*. Bloomington: Indiana University Press.

Kaplan, Caren. 1996. *Questions of Travel: Postmodern Discourses of Displacement*. Durham, NC: Duke University Press.

Latour, Bruno. 2005. "From Realpolitik to Dingpolitik or How to Make Things Public." In *Making Things Public: Atmospheres of Democracy*, ed. Bruno Latour and Peter Weibel, 14–41. Cambridge, MA: MIT Press.

Macaulay, Fiona. 2000. "Getting Gender on the Policy Agenda: A Study of a Brazilian Feminist Lobby Group." In *Hidden Histories of Gender and the State in Latin America*, ed. Elizabeth Dore and Maxine Molyneux, 346–67. Durham, NC: Duke University Press.

Marcus, George E. 1998. *Ethnography through Thick and Thin*. Princeton, NJ: Princeton University Press.

Merry, Sally Engle. 2006. *Human Rights and Gender Violence: Translating International Law into Local Justice*. Chicago: University of Chicago Press.

Miller, Francesca. 1991. *Latin American Women and the Search for Social Justice*. Hanover, NH: University Press of New England.

Moghadam, Valentine M. 2005. *Globalizing Women: Transnational Feminist Networks*. Baltimore: Johns Hopkins University Press.

Molyneux, Maxine. 1985. "Mobilization without Emancipation? Women's Interests, the State, and Revolution in Nicaragua." *Feminist Studies* 11(2): 227–54.

Paley, Julia. 2001. *Marketing Democracy: Power and Social Movements in Post-dictatorship Chile*. Berkeley: University of California Press.

Phillips, Anne. 1996. "Dealing with Difference: A Politics of Ideas, or a Politics of Presence?" In *Democracy and Difference: Contesting the Boundaries of the Political*, ed. Seyla Benhabib, 139–52. Princeton, NJ: Princeton University Press.

———. 2003. "Recognition and the Struggle for Political Voice." In *Recognition Struggles and Social Movements: Contested Identities, Agency and Power*, ed. Barbara Hobson, 263–73. Cambridge: Cambridge University Press.

Pinto, Céli Regina Jardim. 2007. "Brazil's National Conferences: A 'Medium Range' Public?" Paper presented at the Latin American Studies Association (LASA) Conference, Montréal, September 5–8.

Riles, Annelise. 2001. *The Network Inside Out*. Ann Arbor: University of Michigan Press.

Schirmer, Jennifer. 1993. "The Seeking of Truth and the Gendering of Consciousness: The Comadres of El Salvador and the Conavigua Widows of Guatemala." In *"Viva": Women and Popular Protest in Latin America*, ed. Sarah A. Radcliffe and Sallie Westwood, 30–64. London: Routledge.

Snyder, Margaret. 2006. "Unlikely Godmother: The UN and the Global Women's Movement." In *Global Feminism: Transnational Women's Activism, Organizing, and Human Rights*, ed. Myra Marx Ferree and Aili Mari Tripp, 24–50. New York: New York University Press.

SPM. 2004. *I Conferência Nacional de Políticas para as Mulheres: Anais* [First national conference on policy for women: Annals]. Brasília: Secretaria Especial de Políticas para as Mulheres.

———. 2006. *Plano National de Politicas para as Mulheres* [National plan for policy for women]. Brasília: Secretaria Especial de Políticas para as Mulheres.

Stephen, Lynn. 1997. *Women and Social Movements in Latin America: Power from Below*. Austin: University of Texas Press.

Thayer, Millie. 2000. "Traveling Feminisms: From Embodied Women to Gendered Citizenship." In *Global Ethnography: Forces, Connections, and Imaginations in a Postmodern World*, ed. Michael Burawoy Joseph A. Blum, Sheba George, Zsuzsa Gille, Teresa Gowan, Lynne Haney, Maren Klawiter, Steven H. Lopez, Seán Ó Riain, and Millie Thayer, 203–33. Berkeley: University of California Press.

———. 2001. "Transnational Feminism: Reading Joan Scott in the Brazilian *Sertão.*" *Ethnography* 2(2): 243–71.

Tripp, Aili Mari. 2006. "The Evolution of Transnational Feminisms: Consensus, Conflict, and New Dynamics." In *Global Feminism: Transnational Women's Activism, Organizing, and Human Rights*, ed. Myra Marx Ferree and Aili Mari Tripp, 51–75. New York: New York University Press.

Tsing, Anna Lowenhaupt. 2005. *Friction: An Ethnography of Global Connection*. Princeton, NJ: Princeton University Press.

Vargas, Virginia. 2003. "Feminism, Globalization and the Global Justice and Solidarity Movement." *Cultural Studies* 17(6): 905–20.

Walby, Sylvia. 2002. "Feminism in a Global Era." *Economy and Society* 31(4): 533–57.

Warren, Jonathan W. 2001. *Racial Revolutions: Antiracism and Indian Resurgence in Brazil*. Durham, NC: Duke University Press.

Introduction to Reading 47

From 2010 to 2012 the critical role of social media in social movements for change became a significant topic of news media reports and academic research, spurred by the so-called Arab Spring and the Occupy Movement. In this context, Suzy D'Enbeau's reading is timely, as she analyzes the organizational and identity-building uses of the Internet by one transnational feminist network (TFN) called the Association for Women's Rights in Development (AWID). D'Enbeau's case study of AWID web pages generated three themes: diversity, transparency, and identity creation. These themes, she argues, offer a potential framework for understanding how TFNs, in general, use online forums to create a shared identity and to manage organizational tension.

1. Why have diversity issues been very important to AWID, and how has AWID used its website to address those issues?

2. What is transparency, and how has AWID addressed transparency questions?

3. What are the ingredients that go into identity as co-construction?

Transnational Feminist Advocacy Online

Identity (Re)Creation Through Diversity, Transparency, and Co-Construction

Suzy D'Enbeau

The globalization of feminism has contributed to significant changes in how feminist activists organize and connect throughout the world (Conway. 2008). In contrast to emphases on the negative impacts of globalization on women, one positive outcome of globalized feminism is what Moghadam (2005b) labels transnational feminist networks (TFNs). TFNs are global advocacy networks that transcend geographical, political, and cultural borders to draw attention to gender and development (GAD) issues, offering alternative solutions, organizational structures, and forms of resistance.[1] In terms of the global justice movement, Moghadam (2005a) notes that TFNs contribute a "call for gender justice as well as economic justice, and for an alternative macroeconomic framework that takes gender relations seriously as a concept and social fact" (p. 354).

TFNs must manage a variety of competing issues around global feminist advocacy, including balancing collective identity, engagement, and openness with global diversity of organizational members and organizational differentiation from other women's rights organizations. Although these issues are nothing new to feminisms, TFNs must address them in a global environment that is dynamic, spontaneous, and unpredictable. TFNs are constrained by gender mainstreaming policies, lack of funding, diverse stakeholder accountability, and lack of resources, to name a few (Dempsey, 2007; Desai, 2007). Moreover, these environmental constraints can impact organizational identity constructions because of potentially competing objectives (e.g., financial sustainability and feminist advocacy) (Gioia, Schultz, & Corley, 2000).

Feminist activists have suggested that strengthening organizational identity can allow TFNs to advocate for change, enhance global solidarity, *and* maintain financial sustainability via organizational differentiation (Clark, Sprenger, & VeneKlasen, 2005; Ferree, 2007). Furthermore, doing so online allows TFNs to harness technology and combine network organizing structures with new forms of communication to expand women's organizing capabilities (Ferree, 2007). Still, TFNs must navigate two collective identities tensions: enhancing solidarity among global members and enhancing organizational identity to compete with other women's organizations (Clark et al., 2005; Kerr, 2007).

From D'Enbeau, Suzy. 2011. "Transnational Feminist Advocacy Online: Identity (Re)Creation Through Diversity, Transparency, and Co-Construction." *Women's Studies in Communication* 34. Copyright © Routledge (The Organization for Research on Women and Communication).

This case study explores how the Association for Women's Rights in Development (AWID), a TFN, membership, and feminist organization, uses the Internet to discursively (re)create its own online organizational identity(ies).[2] To do this, AWID utilizes diversity, transparency, and co-construction as identity-building strategies that help this organization effectively navigate competing organizational requirements of differentiation and collectivity for global movements building. Although the need of feminist organizations to appeal to multiple parties for survival without diluting their message has been examined, how a feminist organization does so across national borders where the very goals, varieties, and labels of feminism are hotly contested makes identity construction especially contentious. Exploring how AWID manages these goals offers insight into how TFNs construct collective identities online for a global audience. . . .

RESULTS AND INTERPRETATIONS

In response to my research question of how a TFN discursively negotiates online identity construction amid competing goals, three themes emerged: (a) diversity as identity-building strategy, (b) transparency as collective and organizational identity management, and (c) identity creation as co-construction. These themes function as strategic discourses to explain how this organization navigates competing organizational goals of collectivity for feminist global movements building, and differentiation for financial and organizational sustainability, offering a glimpse into online transnational identities processes.

Diversity as Identity-Building Strategy

Identity politics associated with diversity have pervaded the context of TFNs, including AWID. Northern feminist organizations are often met with accusations that question their authenticity and the political implications of representation (Eschle, 2004). Dominant definitions of feminism have been critiqued for promoting as universal the perspective of privileged women from the global North and creating a homogenous view of women from the global South (Eschle, 2004: Mohanty, 1997). These prevailing attitudes have made diversity an imperative for all TFNs. In this case, AWID employs diversity as a strategic discourse to encourage solidarity among diverse members.

Because it was started by U.S. scholars and has only recently made the transition to becoming an international organization, diversity issues have been especially salient to AWID and the Web site documents historical shifts in AWID's approach to diversity. For instance, the online explanation of AWID's historical evolution cites that in the mid-1980s. the AWID Board was faced with increasing criticism that the organization was too White to address the rights of women in the global South (Kerr, 2002). To this end, AWID has employed diversity as a strategic site of connection that strengthens its collective and organizational identity. The Web site lists diversity as an AWID value:

> Women come from all backgrounds, beliefs, abilities, and experiences. As such, openness to diversity must be an integral aspect of advancing women's rights. We believe in working together as feminists and gender equality advocates, in learning from each other's diverse realities, and in creating just societies and healthy environments for every person. (AWID, 2011, "About")

Furthermore, throughout its evolution, AWID has consistently and openly addressed identity issues. Much of this controversial debate has concerned the tension between its North American roots and its global focus, as outlined in AWID's online history. Following the 1995 World Conference on Women in Beijing, AWID online was created to provide information services electronically and solidify the organizational identity as "open and diverse" (Kerr, 2002). AWID describes its staffing as "increasingly diverse and global-minded" (AWID, 2011, "Staff"). The organization consistently emphasizes the importance of inclusive debates, encouraging a multitude of critical perspectives to generate a wider understanding of globalization's impact on lives throughout the world (AWID, 2011, "About"). Last, annual report numbers indicate that individual members come from throughout the world, providing support for AWID's commitment to diversity.[3]

AWID has also included a number of initiatives that invite diverse organizational participation. First, AWID's history describes the development of a "Minority Membership" task force that focused on women of color and women of the global South (Kerr, 2002). In this example, AWID reacted to growing criticisms that the organization was too White. Second, to make AWID more inclusive and accessible to women from the global South, AWID offers free memberships for those making less than US$10,000 per year (AWID, 2011, "Individual Memberships"). In this way, AWID attempts to combat the assumption that many northern feminists generalize their own experiences to others. Third, AWID operates in English, Spanish, French, and Arabic, producing publications in all four languages. Fourth, men are explicitly invited to participate as long as they "share a commitment to feminism and women's human rights" (AWID, 2011, "Frequently Asked Questions"). Last, the Web site labels AWID a feminist organization but also states, "You do not have to specifically identify as feminist or use that terminology to be a member of AWID or to engage with our work in advancing women's rights" (AWID, 2011, "Frequently Asked Questions"). These examples point to the strategic use of AWID's online presence to promote diverse membership as a source of solidarity.

Although AWID uses diversity as a way of connecting organizational members, AWID has also attempted to control this diversity. For example, the Web site indicates that, "Membership with AWID is open to anyone who shares our values" (AWID, 2011, "Frequently Asked Questions"), immediately identifying people who are not invited to be a part of the organization.

Whereas the organization makes it clear in an earlier statement that members do not have to be feminist, sharing AWID values is one way to control the types of individuals the organization attracts. Research has noted that some activists are skeptical of the label *feminist* (Moghadam, 2005b). Giving members the option to not identify as feminist may be one way to address this concern. Nevertheless, the Web site explains, "The principles associated with feminism, as well as a rich body of feminist research, dialogue and practice, inform our values and our work" (AWID, 2011, "Frequently Asked Questions"), thus becoming an organizational member means sharing these values.

AWID also regulates involvement within the organization as a method of controlling diverse perspectives. Members are reminded:

> Due to limited resources and our desire to be as effective as possible in our work, we are not able to consider applications to be a country or regional representative of AWID, nor are we able to consider opening local chapters or offices of AWID. But you don't need to represent AWID in order to become involved in our work. (AWID, 2011, "Frequently Asked Questions")

Citing a lack of funding and resources, the organization is able to maintain control over the official representation of its organizational identity.

Thus, in terms of its own organizational identity. AWID encourages a diverse membership to account for multiple women's experiences while controlling for that membership in some ways. Diversity as connection and control directly informs AWID's organizational identity, and this relationship is documented online. At the same time, AWID warns of potential problems when diversity is not privileged. For instance, the Web site explains that activists from the Middle East and North Africa (MENA) region are "often unrepresented at global events—such as UN conferences—where key decisions are taken that affect women in the region." AWID describes one challenge of doing transnational work: many of the regions that need support for GAD programs are underrepresented at global meetings, including those sponsored by AWID. This lack of diversity inhibits development of global women's movements.

In sum, diversity enacts a two-pronged strategic method in terms of identity-building processes. First. AWID is able to project its own espousal of diversity on its Web site in an effort to attract individual members and organizational linkages. The organizational identity of AWID is one that embraces diversity by representing women from all over the world. In this case, diversity is not simply a politically correct thing to do but a means of instilling an appreciation for a space where individuals from anywhere feel as though they belong. On the other hand, AWID's Web site also talks about the potential problems of diversity and global movements building.

Transparency as Collective and Organizational Identity Management

As a strategic discourse, transparency works in two distinct but interrelated ways relating to AWID's organizational identity. First, transparency offers AWID a strategic discourse to address potential discrepancies between AWID's values and its multiple stakeholders. Presenting a transparent identity online allows AWID to avoid some of the identity issues that traditionally plague feminist organizations, such as consistency between organizational values and organizing principles (Lowenstein. 1995). To manage this tension, AWID employs the value of transparency with the assumption that authenticity appeals will encourage a greater understanding and realistic perspective from current and potential organizational stakeholders as well as encourage collective movement building.

First, AWID advocates transparency when addressing the organization's finances. As a registered 50l(c)3 in the United States, AWID is a public charity that receives funding from institutional and individual memberships. The AWID Web site lists all institutional funders, provides links to their Web sites, and includes AWID's annual reports so that stakeholders can access and explore these sources (AWID, 2011, "Funders"). Making visible this financial information enhances organizational credibility and invites the possibility of debate from members. Moreover, it is important for TFNs to indicate where their funding comes from to avoid a fierce sense of competition with other women's organizations that often results from a perception of scarce funding resources (Kerr, 2007). In revealing funding sources, other women's organizations may become aware of potential donors, and network ties may be strengthened based on this feminist model of cooperation and sharing of resources. In this way, transparency can work to support collective identity building with other women's organizations and combat fragmentation within the movement.

AWID also includes this idea of transparency as a part of the organization's shared values. In terms of the value of "responsibility," AWID strives "for transparency, responsible use of our resources, fairness in our relations, accountability, integrity, and excellence" (AWID, 2011, "About"). Other values include diversity; human rights as indivisible and universal; a woman's right to autonomy in all parts of her life; and cooperation. The inclusion of these values helps the organization to shape external perceptions of AWID, further supporting this strategic transparency and employing a sort of values advocacy used to enhance the organization's image. deflect criticism, and establish value premises to draw upon in later discourses (Bostdorff & Vibbert, 1994). The irony is a transparent image is one that is completely exposed, potentially leaving the organization vulnerable to criticism. However, AWID advantageously uses this transparency to maintain authenticity and privilege its feminist organizing principles. Finally, the AWID Web site documents the organization's 20-year history, authored by Joanna Kerr (2002), as it reflexively and reflectively questioned and adapted its identity. First, over the years, the organization has faced criticism that it lacked minority representation, and that members from the global North were overrepresented. Because it was started in the United States, its membership was predominantly Western, a fact that was problematic to many global South feminists. The organizational history documents this criticism as well as its transition to a more "open and diverse" organization (Kerr, 2002, p. 5). The Web site explains, "AWID was criticized for a lack of ideological diversity on its panels, lack of participatory or interactive sessions, and especially the lack of involvement of low-income women, women of color and women from the Third World" (Kerr, 2002, p. 4). Second, identity questions were faced as the board transitioned from a North American to an international board. Third, AWID grappled "with identifying itself either as a professional women's organization or as a professional organization committed to helping women" (Kerr, 2002, p. 4). Fourth. in 2001, the organization changed its name from the Association for Women in Development to the Association for Women's Rights in Development, a move that emphasized the importance of human rights advocacy.[4] The Web site explains:

> The new name was to signal a shift in thinking and practice in the field. AWID sought to bridge the gap between the fields of women's human rights and gender and development. "Women's rights" provides the powerful language and monitoring system to assert that women's rights are an inherent part of all women's lives and gender and development is an enabling tool for overcoming the social realities that violate those rights.

Finally, around this time, the "Board also repositioned its identity squarely as an international organization," beginning with a rotating secretariat, suggesting that the AWID board has attempted to exert significant control over the construction of this organization's identity.

AWID has consistently been both proactive *and* reactive as it has adapted to a complex environment that has placed demands and expectations on this organization. This focus on identity has presented AWID with the opportunity to define and control its reality (for the use of identity to control reality, see Alvesson, 1990). By laying bare its open struggles with authenticity and representation online, AWID is able to establish an organizational identity that adapts to fluid and dynamic globalized contexts. These documented identity struggles allow AWID to proactively articulate decision-making strategies in which the organization managed diversity issues and criticisms.

Cheney (1991) has noted the anonymous nature of much organizational rhetoric. However, the constructed history of AWID is authored by Joanna Kerr, AWID's former executive director. A disclaimer cautions, "Any errors or omissions are solely the responsibility of the author and do not necessarily represent the views of AWID members" (Kerr, 2002, p. 8). Although published work often includes a disclaimer such as this, an alternative interpretation is that the author is named in a symbolic effort to provide this woman with the opportunity to name the history in which this organization is situated. This interpretation is more in line with the overall feminist ideology that AWID privileges, as well as the value of transparency.

Transparency not only works to articulate AWID's organizational identity but also allows AWID to differentiate its focus on GAD issues from other international NGOs and enables connections with other organizations. For instance, the Web site explains this strategic use of transparency:

> Visibility and clarity of purpose are key ingredients to successful fundraising. The more who know about your good work, and the different ways you are having an impact, the more who will want to form alliances, and the more resources you will attract. (Kerr, 2007, p. 113)

Thus visibility, uniqueness or difference, and alliance formation are suggested as potential outcomes of strategic transparency.

In sum, online transparency operates as a strategic discourse that allows AWID to maintain control over its collective online identity, differentiate itself from other women's organizations, and encourage alliance formation.

Identity Creation as Co-Construction

Identity co-construction is enabled by both individual members and institutional linkages of AWID to strengthen global women's movements. Combined, these efforts at co-construction via individuals and organizations work to strengthen identity and combat the notion that organizational differentiation is antithetical to collectivity building.

First, the Web site is intended to be a virtual forum that encourages online communication and collaboration. For instance, the Web site connects members with other women's organizations, highlights GAD research, provides relevant GAD information, and fosters debate. AWID highlights strategic communications as a priority, exemplified in its current work in the development of online discussions *where members* can discuss and debate themes raised during the international forums (AWID, 2011, "Strategic Communications"). The notion of a virtual forum invites participants to co-construct an organizational identity that privileges community, connectedness, and collaboration. In this way, AWID employs a feminist framework of the organization—public relationship that privileges a sharing and balance of power (Aldoory, 2005). AWID also recently launched the Feminist Tech Exchange (FTX) online, which

> brings together women's rights activists from around the world to share and build knowledge and skills on communication rights and information and communications technologies (ICT), from feminist perspectives. Through skills sharing, information exchange and discussions, the FTX explores feminist practices and politics of technology, and raises awareness on the critical role of communication rights in the struggle to advance women's rights worldwide.

With this initiative, AWID further encourages online and technological collaboration, inviting multiple perspectives and participants from throughout the world.

Second, online co-construction of AWID's identity encourages relationships based on dependencies. Buzzanell (1994) highlights a feminist

understanding of communal organizational development in which dependency is valued and collaboration is both individually and organizationally profitable. AWID's Web site provides individuals and other organizations with an abundance of resources including papers, books, presentations, and job listings. AWID is also well-known for sponsoring international forums that bring together stakeholders to discuss current, provocative GAD issues, some of which takes place online. Finally, AWID articulates the importance of "building individual and organizational capacities of those working for women's empowerment and social justice," recognizing the importance of reciprocity in terms of the relationship between the individual and organization (AWID, 2011, "About"). Individuals contribute to the organization through their financial support, GAD expertise, and experiences.

Third, cooperation is offered as a key organizational value: "We work towards a world and an economic system based on social and economic justice, interdependence, solidarity, and respect rather than competition and exploitation" (AWID, 2011, "About"). Cooperation also influences some of the organizations stated objectives. For example, AWID has declared online an explicit goal to cause policy, individual, and institutional change through debate as an integral part of this notion of co-construction by "bringing marginalized voices and perspectives to the table in the pursuit of human rights for all" (AWID, 2011, "About"). Here AWID is not claiming to have or desire complete control over issues that are deemed relevant, policies and programs that seem the most advantageous, or the best methods to achieve gender and economic global justice. Rather, AWID places value in the expertise and experiences of its members.

Fourth, members' expertise is something that AWID regularly draws upon, and much of this collaboration happens via AWID's Web site. For example, the Web site invites members to contribute papers, articles, and announcements (AWID, 2011, "Announcements"). According to the Web site, AWID also welcomes contributions to its themes programs that frame cutting-edge

GAD research on feminist movements and organizations, gender equality and technology, women's rights and economic change, and young women and leadership. For example, AWID declares, "We need your help!" in collecting useful materials from members on feminist movements and organizations:

> We will try to make as many materials as possible available online on this website, but we also will be setting up a database of useful materials you may consult and use online. So, help us collect this useful information and to make it available to women's groups from different regions. (AWID, 2011, "Feminist Movements and Organizations")

Together, research addressing topics associated with these themes encourages members to contribute to AWID's organizational identity and to valuable GAD research.

As part of AWID's members-as-experts focus, the organization invites members to participate in online surveys such as one on movement building and organizational strengthening (2011, "Feminist Movements and Organizations"). This survey includes open-ended questions asking members how they define movement building and organizational strengthening, their most important organizational needs, the role AWID could play in supporting feminist movement building, and the activities AWID should implement to help with movement building and organizational strengthening (AWID, 2011, "Survey on Movement Building"). Together, these co-constructed identity-building strategies use the Internet to encourage AWID's collective identity.

Co-constructing identities of TFNs also relates to developing connections with other feminist networks. In other words, the collective identity of AWID is not just made up of individuals but also includes links with other organizations. These links help to encourage collaboration over competition and can be developed via AWID's Web site. For instance, the Web site explains that in the case of fund-raising, competition among organizations for limited financial resources is often highlighted and seen as

a "coopting" force. Money has rarely been the subject of open discussion—either for fear of appearing motivated for the wrong reasons, or for fear that sharing too much information will lead to another organization's gain and our loss. (Carrasco, Hopenhaym, & Clark, 2007, p. 5)

However, by linking organizations together through processes of collective identity development, AWID works to dispel the myth that the pursuit of money will contribute to the demise of global women's movements.

In sum, co-construction operates as a strategic discourse through emphases on collaboration, dependencies, cooperation, and member expertise. This co-construction is enabled through AWID's Web site.

DISCUSSION

Transnational feminist networks represent a form of feminist organizing that reflects "the opportunities and challenges feminists face in an increasingly globalized world" (Moghadam, 2005b, p. 82). Indeed TFNs must manage feminist organizing tensions such as diversity, openness, and engagement on a global scale to encourage collective identity building while, at the same time, differentiating themselves from other women's rights organizations. This study explores how AWID uses the Internet to discursively (re)create its own organizational identity(ies) amid these competing organizational goals.

First, AWID harnesses diversity as an identity-building strategy that ironically enables solidarity among diverse members. These microlevel diversity discourses are used to manage feminist organizing tensions of solidarity-diversity. As feminist organizations in a global world, TFNs are faced with competing discourses of the local and the global, as well as the individual and the collective. To accommodate these multiple discourses, AWID makes some fundamental assumptions while also accounting for varied experiences. First, AWID offers its support of organizational diversity as a site of connection among members, privileging diversity as a value and recognizing the importance of every woman's lived experience. Online diversity-as-connection discoursers encourage women from varied backgrounds to organize together around women's rights issues, despite their differences. At the same time, AWID maintains control over diversity through explicit statements that let members know in what specific ways their support is needed as well as where it is not. In this way, AWID controls its identity by controlling for diversity.

At the mesolevel, diversity is an essential attribute for TFNs to differentiate themselves from other GAD organizations. At the same time, diversity can also be a significant challenge to collective identity-building processes. Within and across regions throughout the world, women's circumstances, needs, and experiences are extremely different. It is this diversity that can be problematic for collective identity-building efforts, which work to mask difference and homogenize experiences. By drawing attention to the complicated nature of diversity, AWID is able to differentiate itself from other women's organizations—as a transnational network, advocacy group for GAD issues, and global identity to which individuals can ascribe—as well as draw attention to similarities across women's organizations as a coalition-building strategy.

Second, AWID employs transparency as collective and organizational identity management to maintain authenticity in the eyes of organizational members and the broader GAD community as well as differentiate itself from other GAD organizations. Transparency offers a strategic discourse that exposes the organization while allowing AWID to maintain control over its image. Doing so online is the most efficient and effective way for this organization to enact transparency, as AWID's Web site serves as a hub for its global audience. Moreover, transparency in this context is more than simply feminist openness and clarity of motives (Rabrenovic & Roskos, 2001). This transparency is strategic. Exposing all sources of funding as well as the values, mission, and objectives of the organization online allows AWID to present a transparent image that works to enhance the organization's identity. Members may feel empowered by access to this organizational information. AWID is also able to rely on this transparency for future persuasive efforts, citing the organization as accountable, responsible, and one with integrity because of this transparent representation. In this way, AWID controls its representation, including issue framing and selected alternative discourses. At the same time, this transparency can strengthen collective identity to enable connections with other organizations. These alliances can work to decrease perceptions of competition, fragmentation, and isolation among women's organizations and to, ultimately, enable more women's organizations to garner support for GAD agendas. In this way, AWID balances the competing tensions of differentiation and collectivity through transparency as an identity-management strategy.

Finally, AWID's identity is co-constructed with both individual and institutional members to allow for multiple interpretations, working to shift the balance of power between the organization and its members. Through AWID's online forum, members are invited to contribute their expertise to enhance a GAD agenda as well as the organization's image. While AWID has faced pressure to formalize to keep up with a dynamic and ever-growing organizational membership, this alternative network is still able to maintain its feminist ideals, allowing for a collective identity that values cooperation and collaboration. Indeed, it is important to recognize the difference between carrying out a feminist agenda within an organization that already values those principles and inserting feminism into an organization that is not inherently organized in a feminist manner (Porter, 1999). AWID has become more formalized to meet the growing needs of its members as well as the growing demands of broader global advocacy efforts. However, inviting members to co-construct the organizational identity is one way to balance this shift to a more formalized structure with feminist organizing principles. In this way, AWID shifts the balance of power between the organization and its members, giving members some control over the organizational identity. This shift is enabled via the Internet.

Institutions are also invited to co-construct AWID's organizational identity; these linkages are meant to enhance collective identity, strengthen global women's movements, and combat competition among women's organizations. Through these links, AWID is able to pool and showcase the best GAD resources, strategies, and intelligence to advance and promote GAD agendas. Moreover, through co-construction, AWID provides one example of a TFN bridging the physical virtual activism divide. In addition to its international forums, AWID employs its comprehensive, user-friendly Web site, which requires maintenance by a technologically savvy staff. Both of these outlets work to promote a collective identity and prioritize strategic GAD initiatives.

Combined, these three strategic discourses encourage collective identity-building and networking strategies that serve the greater good of strengthening women's movements rather than just the individual TFN itself. These discourses also allow AWID to navigate feminist organizing tensions around diversity, openness, and engagement. The resulting larger collective identity of the overall movement can work to promote GAD issues, gender equity practices, and policies. This network actively works to create and re-create organizational identities that allow the organization to reconcile feminist ideology within a global environment. Diversity, transparency, and co-construction are attributes that enhance this organization's image, and these values encourage a sort of identity flexibility and fluidity that allow for multiple, dynamic meanings. This instability may actually benefit the organization, allowing it to better adapt to the demands of a changing, global environment (Gioia et al., 2000). At the same time, stability is an attractive means of organizational control. As such, AWID tempers this diversity, transparency, and co-construction with some element of control in an effort to maintain a consistent, coherent organizational identity.

Moreover, studying the identity discourses of AWID allows for an understanding of how this organization manages competing values and programmatic agendas. Indeed, AWID articulates the importance of both collective identity building in terms of external individual and organizational linkages as well as differentiation in securing AWID's organizational identity among women's rights organizations. In this way, this study extends research on TFNs and alternative organizational forms by exploring how TFNs use the Internet to develop collective identity amid competing organizational goals. This study also considers how TFNs address conflicts between their fundamental values and their strategies to implement such values. These organizations must locate ways to project predetermined identities as outlined by the organizations and their stakeholders. At the same time, they must meet their second-order needs, such as financial sustainability. These strategic discourses allow AWID to do this. This study also extends communication research on feminist organizing by examining how TFNs navigate feminist organizing tensions. The implications of diversity situated in a context of globalization are explored, as are the ways in which alternative organizational structures manage identity-related issues while recognizing both ideological and material constraints. Last, in terms of global advocacy this study reveals how the Internet can be a helpful resource to promote social reform, educate through access to information, and present a transparent image of an organization (Akhtar, Kumar Malla, & Gregson, 2000). Solidifying organizational identity online can position the GAD movement in a positive light in terms of public awareness and media representation (Clark et al., 2005).

This study provides an understanding of the online identity discourses of one TFN and an explanatory framework that could be applied toward an understanding of how other TFNs make use of a virtual forum to create a collective identity and manage feminist organizing tensions. Future research should look at how organizations and networks that do not rely so heavily on a virtual forum use other materials to avoid the negative implications of the "digital divide" (Akhtar et al., 2000, p. 126) and consider other materials that speak to organizational identity such as pamphlets, brochures, office manuals, and so forth. In addition, interviews with organizational members may provide helpful points of comparison and contrast to enhance these findings.

Nevertheless, considering AWID's collective identity-building strategies may contribute to the successful strategizing of other TFNs working to advance human rights throughout the world. Organizational communication research on identity creates an exciting opportunity to contribute to an innovative, fundamental effort at globalization from below. As global forms of feminist organizing, TFNs present unique sites of study to contribute to positive organizational efforts in this context of globalization.

NOTES

1. It is difficult to determine an exact number of TFNs because these organizations often do not label themselves feminist despite their focus on women's empowerment and gender equity (Moghadam, 2005b). There is also little consensus concerning TFN criteria (Ferree, 2007). However, based on similar criteria of organizations that meet Moghadam's (2005b) definition of TFNs, research notes similar findings. For instance, in their respective research, Ferree (2007) identified 25 TFNs, and Dempsey, Parker, and Krone (2007) identified 30 TFNs.

2. Moghadam (2005b) identifies AWID as a TFN.

3. The following are the percentages of members by region from the 2008 annual report (total members = 5,078): sub-Saharan Africa, 30; East Asia, 5; Eastern Europe, 4; Western Europe, 12; Latin American and Caribbean, 8; Middle East, 2; North America (Canada and United States), 26; North Africa, 1; Pacific, 2; South Asia, 10.

4. The acronym AWID remains the same despite the official name change to the Association for Women's Rights in Development.

REFERENCES

Akhtar, S., Kumar Malla, M., & Gregson, J. (2000). Transparency, accountability and good governance: Role of new information and communication technologies and the mass media. *The International Journal on Media Management, 2*, 124–132.

Aldoory, L. (2005). A (re)conceived feminist paradigm for public relations: A case for substantial improvement *Journal of Communication, 55*, 668–684.

Alvesson, M. (1990). Organization: From substance to image. *Organization Studies, 11*, 373–394.

Association for Women's Rights in Development (AWID). (2011). Retrieved from http://www.awid.org/

Bostdorff, D., & Vibbert, S. (1994). Values advocacy. Enhancing organizational images, deflecting criticism, and grounding future argument. *Public Relations Review, 20*, 141–158.

Buzzanell, P. M. (1994). Gaining a voice: Feminist organizational communication theorizing. *Management Communication Quarterly, 7*, 339–383.

Carrasco, L., Hopenhaym, K., & Clark, C. (2007). Where is the money for women's rights work on ICI's? A brief look at the funding landscape for women's organizations working on information and communication technologies. Retrieved from http://www.genderit.org/content/where-money-womens-rights-work-ict-brief-look-funding-landscape-women%E2%80%99s-organisations-workin

Cheney, G. (1991). *Rhetoric in an organizational society*. Columbia, SC: University of South Carolina Press.

Clark, C., Sprenger, E., & VeneKlasen, L. (2005). Where is the money for women's right? Assessing resources and the role of donors in the promotion of women's rights and the support of women's rights organizations: An action research project of the Association for Women in Development. Retrieved from http://awid.org/Library/Where-is-the-Money-for-Women-s-Rights

Conway, J. (2008). Geographies of transnational feminisms: The politics of place and scale in the World March of Women. *Social Politics, 15*, 207–231.

Desai, M. (2007). The messy relationship between feminisms and globalizations. *Gender & Society, 21,* 797–803.

Ferree, M. M. (2007). On-line identities and organizational connections: Networks of transnational feminist websites. In I. Lenz, C. Ullrich, & B. Fersch (Eds.), *Gender orders unbound: Globalisation, restructuring, and reciprocity* (pp. 141–165). Opladen, Germany: Barbara Budrich.

Gioia, D., Schultz, M., & Corley, K. (2000). Organizational identity, image, and adaptive instability. *Academy of Management Review, 25*, 63–81.

Kerr, J. (2002). From "WID" to "GAD" to women's rights: The first twenty years of AWID. Retrieved from http://awid.org/Library/From-WID-to-GAD-to-Women-s-Rights-The-First-Twenty-Years-of-AWID

Kerr, J. (2007). The second FundHer report: Financial sustainability for women's movements worldwide. Retrieved from http://awid.org/Library/Where-is-the-money-for-women-s-rights-The-Second-Fundher-Report-Financial-Sustainability-for-Women-s-Movements-Worldwide

Lowenstein, A. (1995). A tale of two feminist businesses: Women and Children First, West End Wax. In L. Edwalds & M. Stocker (Eds.), *The woman-centered economy: Ideals, reality, and the space between* (pp. 189–197). Chicago, IL: Third Side Press.

Moghadam, V. (2005a). Globalization and transnational feminist networks (or how neoliberalism and fundamentalism riled the world's women). In R. Appelbaum & W. Robinson (Eds.), *Critical globalization studies* (pp. 349–358). New York, NY: Routledge.

Moghadam, V. (2005b). *Globalizing women. Transnational feminist networks.* Baltimore, MD: The Johns Hopkins University Press.

Mohanty, C. T. (1997). Under western eyes: Feminist scholarship and colonial discourses. In N. Visvanathan, L Duggan, L. Nisonoff, & N. Wiegersma (Eds.), *The women, gender, and development reader* (pp. 79–86). London. England: Zed Books.

Porter, M. (1999). Introduction: Caught in the web? Feminists doing development. In M. Porter & E. Judd (Eds.), *Feminists doing development* (pp. 1–14). London, England: Zed Books.

Rabrenovic, G., & Roskos, L. (2001). Introduction: Civil society, feminism, and the gendered politics of war and peace. *NWSA Journal, 13*, 40.

Introduction to Reading 48

Nina Nijsten is a feminist activist from Belgium. She belongs to a feminist collective and is a writer and illustrator for a feminist magazine and blog. Inspired by the visions and strategies of do-it-yourself (DIY) methods, radical alternatives, and democratic organizing, Nijsten discusses 10 tools for building a sustainable feminist movement.

1. Discuss the links between Nijsten's feminist viewpoint and the "another-world" feminist translation described in the reading by Lynne Phillips and Sally Cole.

2. Why does Nijsten include "fun and rest" in her list of tools?

3. How did the second wave of feminism shape Nijsten's perspective and activism?

SOME THINGS WE NEED FOR A FEMINIST REVOLUTION

Nina Nijsten

INTRODUCTION

Everything looked so promising in the 1970s, an era of hope for radical feminist changes. Feminist bookstores, consciousness-raising groups, women's healthcare projects, feminist writings and research, feminist media and culture, activist collectives, women's houses, women-run publishing houses, huge protest marches and other projects. Alternatives as well as resistance

From Nijsten, Nina. 2011. "Some Things We Need for a Feminist Revolution." *Interface: A Journal for and about Social Movements 3*(2).

and criticism to move our society towards a more equal and women-positive place. The feminist activism of the so-called second wave is a source of inspiration for me because at that time women gathered in large numbers to take action together, create projects that envisioned their feminist future and think radically and critically about gender, power and oppression.

But somehow it ended, and although some of these radical initiatives are still there, maybe in a somewhat other shape, a lot of it is gone too. Work and knowledge has disappeared (like the magazines and books that were written at the time and are hard to find today) or forgotten (like analyses about sexism and patriarchy and experiences with activism and alternatives). We do have equal opportunities institutions now, women's lobby organisations and official gender studies courses. But is this better? Can they give us everything we long(ed) for? And what about autonomy, participation and accessibility? Do we want an open radical autonomous democratically organised mass movement or a few professional specialists (politicians, university researchers, journalists) who will do the work for us?

I miss and I missed the second wave—I was born too late—but the feminist struggles of those days serve as an example to me. My activism in a radical feminist collective that's influenced by radical left, LGBTQ and anti-racist movements and in a national women's rights organisation that was founded in the early 1970s, as well as my experiences in anarchist and anti-globalist groups, reading about feminism's past, discussing with other feminists, writing for a feminist blog, corresponding with feminist zine writers and attending feminist festivals shaped my views on feminist activism. For me, feminism is about ending sexist oppression, and even though previous generations of feminists have not (yet) succeeded in this mission, I believe they were on the right track.

In the second wave of feminism several do-it-yourself methods, democratic organisation structures and radical alternatives were developed and applied. Some of these are also used in radical left and alterglobalist groups today. This text was inspired by those visions and strategies. It's about the idea that we have to—and we can—do it ourselves, as a feminist movement. I offer a few basic tips for building a movement. . . .

The tips in this text are only a beginning though. There's more needed to reach a feminist utopia and we have to continue discussing and thinking about feminist strategies. I'd like to learn from the experiences of previous generations of feminists to know which strategies work and to avoid the mistakes of the past. We need a feminist movement that is strong enough to resist and survive a conservative backlash, a network that stretches beyond generations and geographical regions. So it's time to (re)organise and co-operate again and build an autonomous feminist movement. No more little waves followed by backlashes: it's time for a flood!

10 Things to Build a Movement

(1) collective activism

(2) non-hierarchical organising

(3) networks

(4) meetings

(5) spaces

(6) means

(7) education

(8) media

(9) protest and alternatives

(10) fun and rest

1. Collective Activism

The previous generations of feminists have struggled to make this world a better place for women and create a more egalitarian non-sexist society. But there remains a lot to be done and if we don't act, nothing will change. Therefore, if we want to end sexist oppression, we have to organise ourselves and take action, together. From the 1960s on, feminists gathered and formed small groups in which they could discuss and plan projects and actions. Such groups combined the forces of individual feminists. Together they could make much more happen than each on their own.

Sexism is a structural issue, not just an individual problem—as we know "the personal is political." So we can't fight sexism on our own, as separate individuals. You can stand up for yourself, speak out, make the people around you aware about feminist issues and engage in certain little projects or solo actions, but this isn't enough to make real change. Together with other people you can do more and achieve more. The resources, woman-power and knowledge will be greater when combined. Actions organised and carried by a larger group appear more powerful and because of this also more effective. More voices making demands and having their say can push harder on the agenda. Besides, collective action gives courage and support for the activists themselves: we can learn from each other and encourage each other. It's much more motivating and pleasant to work together because you'll feel stronger as a group and understood as an individual, as I've noticed in the groups I'm involved in. I didn't feel alone with my feminist concerns and ideas—they didn't seem odd, utopian or extreme and they weren't ridiculed, there was support for not fitting in society's gender norms and for little rebellious acts (not shaving my legs for example) and the enthusiasm to take action together against injustice and gender discrimination (like sexist billboards, street harassment and so on) is always inspiring. So it's vital to organise ourselves in geographic or thematic groups, collectives, platforms and federations.

2. Non-Hierarchical Organising

Feminist organisations nowadays are often hierarchically structured organisations. But if we want to end inequality, shouldn't we be setting an example? In a world that consists of patriarchal institutions and companies in which only a few are in power, tell others what to do and decide over everyone else's faith, feminist organisations should try to investigate alternatives for hierarchical organisational models. Having women in the position of manager, director or coordinator just isn't enough. Feminist groups can be small-scale experiments to practice living and working together as a larger feminist society. So they should be structured and organised in an egalitarian, democratic and non-hierarchical way. Organising in feminist groups should reflect feminist ideals of sisterhood and equality. Our ideals can not be postponed until "after the revolution." If you fight against inequality, then it's only normal that you don't accept unequal decision-making power and hierarchical structures in your own group.

Not only formal hierarchies, but also informal hierarchies which produce invisible elites and power positions should be avoided or removed. The small groups in the 1960s/1970s I mentioned before often suffered from the existence of informal leaders who weren't officially elected, but who still took on more decision-making roles and representational tasks because the unofficial hidden hierarchical structure of the group based on friendships and privileges allowed this to happen (Freeman 2002). The structure of groups should not only be intentionally non-hierarchical but also be consciously structured and open. Non-hierarchy can not be assumed to happen automatically.

There are lots of techniques and roles that have been developed to help organisations work and discuss in a non-hierarchical way and avoid informal leadership as well: clearly defining how decisions are made, agreed division of tasks, rotation of leadership roles (like facilitators for meetings and spokespersons), rounds during meetings, temporarily splitting into smaller groups (when the group becomes too big to discuss and not everyone is able to speak), workshops to unlearn master suppression techniques[1], hand gestures to communicate easier and faster, talking sticks or cards to avoid that some people talk all the time and others don't have the chance to speak, writing down the agenda before the meeting starts, writing down the minutes of the meeting, taking breaks, sharing useful skills and resources, self-criticism and self-evaluation, etc. We can learn a lot from the experiences of second wave feminist groups, radical left collectives and anarcha-feminist activists who both defied sexism in anarchist groups and hierarchical structures in feminist organisations.

3. Networks

One collective isn't going to pull the plug out of patriarchy, but when there are a lot of them working together, we increase our power. . . .

. . . Just like it's better for individual activists to organise themselves collectively, collectives are stronger together than separately. This working relationship should also be structured in a non-hierarchical co-operative manner and local collectives should keep their autonomy. Such networks are useful for sharing information and local news, exchanging ideas, setting up projects or campaigns together, offering support, inspiration and solidarity. Where formal networks don't exist yet, groups can cooperate and network informally, supporting each other's actions, distributing each other's publications and keeping each other informed about plans and activities.

4. Meetings

In a time of faceless internet activism and a lack of visibility of our movement in the media, we might feel alone and disempowered. We can hardly grasp the real size, diversity, creativity and strengths of our movement, if we don't see and meet all those feminists who are out there. The feeling of isolation and being misunderstood by our surroundings can not be solved only be forming feminist facebook groups or discussing on blogs. When we meet in real life, we get a better idea about how big, diverse and powerful the feminist movement is and we'll be motivated to keep on fighting. Meeting each other is important to build a strong network.

Meeting other feminist groups and activists can happen at feminist gatherings and meetings such as feminist action camps, open women's studies conferences, international festivals like Ladyfest, alternative book fairs, brainstorm/skill-sharing weekends, activist meetings, radical summer schools, women's film festivals, international women's day activities and demonstrations. I've always found attending such gatherings inspiring and could bring fresh ideas to my group back home. In the second feminist wave, events like this brought lots of women together and sustained the movement. Today, there exist lots of feminist events and activities and you can organise your own where you invite and meet other feminists. Don't forget to bring your address book!

5. Spaces

Public space is generally not women-friendly. Women are traditionally encouraged to stay at home, on their own. But we need to reclaim public spaces and create some of our own where we feel safe and welcomed. This world has few (public) places where women, lesbians, queers, transpeople and girls feel totally at ease, at home, free and safe. A woman needs a room of her own as a creative workplace, said Virginia Woolf in her book *A Room Of One's Own,* but women and feminists also need free spaces for ourselves as a group and a movement. That's why feminist spaces are needed: collective rooms of our own.

Spaces where we can be ourselves, where we can relax and meet each other, where activities can happen and plans can be made, where we can talk, organise, educate and learn, find and give support, and inspire each other. Examples of such spaces are women's centres, lesbian cafés, anti-sexist squats, women's art galleries, feminist book shops, women's herstory archives and feminist libraries. The existence of feminist collective spaces can have an enormous influence on the growth of our movement. We need meeting spaces, workplaces and "safe havens." I've seen that groups and projects rise when there's for example an activist squat or friendly community house to get together. Whenever such locations are known to be feminist-minded and places where feminists meet, it's a lot easier to find other feminist activists (Enke 2007) and plan actions and projects together.

6. Means

Action groups and non-profit organisations need means: financial means, material and a workplace or meeting space. . . . To fund our campaigns, buy equipment, print publications and so on, we need to look at ways to raise money. This isn't always easy and may involve some ethical discussions about who to accept funding from and where to spend it on.

Government funding or grants are one possible—but not the only—solution. Even though the State is part of patriarchy, the government's money is better spent on feminist projects than on something like the army. So why not try to send an application? The only risk to keep in mind is that your organisation may become dependent and soften its viewpoints and campaigns. Sponsorship of feminist-friendly enterprises and women's funds (such as Mama Cash[2]) is another possibility. Other ideas for collecting financial means are benefit concerts/parties, an art auction, selling merchandise (T-shirts, stickers, benefit CD), garage sales, membership fees and donations. There are also ways to save money: look for someone who can make free copies or maybe there are some old sheets and paint on your attic to make banners and flags.

7. Education

Education is crucial for social/left movements, including the feminist movement. It can erase inequalities based on schooling, teach skills and knowledge that isn't taught in school and raise awareness about feminist and other social justice issues. Traditional education often replicates gender norms and doesn't teach feminist values, theory or herstory. By offering alternative additional forms of education, we can try to counter these gaps and shortcomings. The transmission of skills and knowledge can be organised in for example workshops, lectures, interactive presentations, group discussions, educational walks, alternative media and film screenings.

Consciousness-raising groups and reading groups are two other methods commonly used by feminists which serve the purpose of education and raising awareness very well. In consciousness-raising groups, which were popular mainly in the second wave, women share experiences and personal stories to discover the fact that their personal problems as women are political. Consciousness-raising groups can make women aware of the system of sexism and the necessity of feminist activism. Such gatherings of women can also lead to planning and organising actions to counter the sexism that was discussed. A feminist reading group looks similar to a consciousness-raising group, but it starts from an essay or a book instead of from personal experiences. The conversations can be theoretical, activist/strategic, personal or a combination of those three.

The group discussions in reading groups, consciousness-raising groups and workshops can contribute to making and sharing DIY research and theory about gender, emancipation, politics and society. The production of knowledge should not be left to so-called experts, professionals or observers/outsiders. Because we as feminist activists experience our activism first-hand and have valid opinions that deserve to be heard, we should document and analyse our collective experiences in the patriarchal system and our resistance to it and write down, share and publish our own feminist theories, criticisms, herstory and strategies. This kind of theory production and distribution is accessible and inclusive too, something that's lacking in academic surroundings.

8. Media

Patriarchal propaganda is targeted at us daily in the shape of advertisements, films, TV soaps, magazines, papers, video clips and so on. Through repetition of sexist messages in the mainstream media, sexism is being normalised. The "malestream" media is never neutral nor objective, even though they claim to be. Certain messages, images and speakers are chosen and others are silenced or ignored, and this choice is influenced by cultural norms, hegemonic opinions, economic interests and political ideologies. Feminists criticise the content of mainstream media (gender stereotypes, women's issues being ignored, etc), its representation of women, the working conditions in the media industry and the exclusion of women at decision-making levels.

As feminists we can react to the sexism in the mainstream media in different ways: feminist journalists can try to change the mainstream media from within, activists and pressure groups can analyse and criticise the media industry and feminists can make their own media. Creating our own media means being able to voice and spread our feminist opinions and ideas. It can target the feminist movement itself or a broader audience. Feminist media can be made in any medium—zines, blogs, film, radio, self-published books, etc—and subject-wise it can be very diverse: f.e. sharing experiences and theories about sexism in society, talking about what your ideal feminist world would look like or reporting on actions and projects. Feminist media can also be feminist poetry, posters and street-art, music and theatre. All of them create a forum on which feminist ideas are expressed, spread and discussed.

In the previous decades, magazines such as *Schoppenvrouw* (Belgium) or *Spare Rib* (UK) and riot grrrl zines were an alternative for traditional consumer-oriented women's magazines which focus on beauty, attracting men and housekeeping. They also offered a means of communication among feminists and between feminists and the broader society. Nowadays, digital media such as blogs can reach huge numbers of people craving for feminist literature, but paper media still flourish.

9. Protest and Alternatives

So now we know how to organise ourselves and what we need, but what will we do in our groups and networks? How will we fight patriarchy, misogyny and sexism and create the world we dream of?

When working towards a feminist society we need activism that questions and fights against what's wrong in our current society (i.e. protest) *and* activism that builds something new and creates a better world here and now (i.e. alternatives). We have to be critical of sexism and other forms of oppression and their manifestations. We point to shortcomings and injustices in our society and make visible what has been normalised and naturalised (like gender roles and racist prejudice) in order to change it. It is important to raise awareness about violence, discrimination and oppression and to show that this can and should stop. Some examples of actions that can be used to resist and protest sexism are: blockades, occupations, street theatre, adbusting, protest letters, DIY media, Take Back The Night marches, boycott actions, radical cheerleading, strikes, a noise demo, filing complaints and placing huge banners on buildings or lamp posts.

. . . Instead of "waiting for the revolution," feminist activists and collectives can experiment with, develop and build feminist alternatives that reflect the image of what a feminist world could look like. Whatever is missing, we can do, create or make it happen ourselves, right now. For example: feminists in the second wave have taught courses about women's history or female artists when this wasn't part yet of the curriculum at regular schools, they have founded women's houses and shelters and they've written alternative women's magazines. Other examples are Jane and Women On Waves (who both carried out abortions in places and times where this was/is illegal)[3] and *Our Bodies Ourselves* (a collectively written book that encouraged women to examine their own bodies and demystified healthcare). Creating alternative non-sexist language is relevant too for feminists, such as the word *Ms*—to replace *Miss* and *Mrs* which refer to women's marital status—that was invented by American feminists and has now become a common word in English vocabulary. Gender neutral words like *se*—to replace *she* and *he*—are added by transfeminist activists. All of these alternatives can serve as an inspiring example for others—showing that things can be different.

10. Fun and Rest

For me, feminist activism is a lot of fun. It's exciting, relaxing and empowering. The feminist movement offers an open, warm and safe space where I feel at home and where I can be myself and make friends. It gives me energy and inspiration especially when everyday sexism can be so frustrating and disempowering. I enjoy going out at night with markers and stickers in my pockets, brainstorming and making plans with friends, laughing about each other's anti-sexist jokes, sharing experiences and learning, writing for a feminist publication and receiving feedback from readers, visiting feminist festivals and meeting feminists from other places. . . . I love creative activism: making banners, designing funny stickers, drawing feminist comics, doing craft-street-art actions, painting feminist slogans on T-shirts, watching performances of feminist theatre, playing in a feminist band. . . .

But sometimes activism can make you stressed and exhausted. The road to revolution can be long and hard because of set-backs, backlashes or continuously negative comments. Sometimes you need a break from the action and the constant fight against patriarchy. Sometimes you feel alone, powerless, worn-out. . . . Then it might be time for some rest. It's better to take a break or holiday or go slower than completely burn out and quit activism. This freedom to withdraw as long as necessary to refuel your batteries has to be supported by the movement, because activism shouldn't be self-sacrifice. Feminist activists have the responsibility to look after each other and make sure we don't get discouraged. Sometimes feminist free spaces can be resting places too and going to a women-only/queer party, watching a feminist film or just a hug can already help a lot!

CONCLUSION

. . . Building a sustainable movement by working on the ten "tools" I've outlined is only a beginning. We always have to rethink what we need and what we want. Once we have a network consisting . . . of feminist collectives, organisations and consciousness-raising groups, alternative media, educational projects, sufficient financial means, spaces and events to meet, diverse forms of activism and time to take a break, we can keep going and look to the future. But we have to keep in mind, we can't do without any of them if we want to succeed in ending patriarchy.

NOTES

1. http://hem.bredband.net/b125645/Artemis/Techniques/ (accessed 31.08.2011)
2. http://www.mamacash.org (accessed 31.08.2011)
3. Jane, also known as the Abortion Counselling Service Of Women's Liberation, is a group that was part of the Chicago Women's Liberation Union. Women On Waves are pro-choice activists from the Netherlands who travel with a boat to the coasts of countries where abortion is illegal to perform abortions for women in need. At the same time they criticise the anti-abortion laws.

REFERENCES

Baxandall, Rosalyn and Linda Gordon 2000. *Dear Sisters: Dispatches from the Women's Liberation Movement*. New York: Basic Books.

Byerly, Carolyn M. and Karen Ross 2006, 2008. *Women & Media: A Critical Introduction*. Malden, Oxford, Carlton: Blackwell Publishing.

Crimethinc 2005. *Recipes For Disaster: an Anarchist Cookbook*. Olympia: CrimethInc. Workers' Collective.

Echols, Alice 1989, 2003. *Daring To Be Bad: Radical Feminism in America: 1967–1975*. Minneapolis: University of Minnesota Press.

Embrechts, Evie 2010. "Crisis in Feminism: Time to Refocus" in *Scum Grrrls*, 17.

Enke, Anne 2007. *Finding the Movement: Sexuality, Contested Space, and Feminist Activism*. Durham and London: Duke University Press.

Faludi, Susan 1992. *Backlash: The Undeclared War Against Women*. London: Vintage.

Faulder, Carolyn, Christine Jackson and Mary Lewis 1976. *The Women's Directory.* London: Virago.

Freeman, Jo. 2002. "The Tyranny of Structurelessness." Pp. 54–61 in *Quiet Rumours: an Anarcha-feminist Reader,* edited by Dark Star, Edinburgh, San Francisco: AK Press/Dark Star.

hooks, bell 1984. *Feminist Theory: From Margin to Center.* Cambridge: South End Press.

Levine, Cathy. 2002. "The Tyranny of Tyranny." Pp. 63-66 in *Quiet Rumours: An Anarcha-feminist Reader,* edited by Dark Star, Edinburgh, San Francisco: AK Press/Dark Star.

McQuiston, Liz 1997. *Suffragettes to She-Devils: Women's Liberation and Beyond.* London: Phaidon Press Ltd.

Tieneke and Rymke 1992. *De Tweede Golf Voorbij? Gesprekken met negentien Vrouwen over hun Aktieve Jaren in de Vrouwenbeweging.* Utrecht: Atalanta.

The Trapese Collective 2007. *Do It Yourself: A Handbook for Changing Our World.* London: Ann Arbor: Pluto Press.

Van Mechelen, Renée 1996. *De Meerderheid Een Minderheid: de Vrouwenbeweging in Vlaanderen: feiten, herinneringen en bedenkingen omtrent de tweede golf.* Leuven: Uitgeverij Van Halewyck.

Van Mechelen, Renée 1979. *Uit Eigen Beweging: Balans ven de Vrouwenbeweging in Vlaanderen 1970–1980.* Leuven: Kritak.

Introduction to Reading 49

This reading addresses the complex and varied feminist theories developed by Native American women activists, the struggle against sexism within Native communities and society at large, and the importance of developing coalitions with non-Native feminists. In addition, Andrea Smith analyzes current Native feminist sovereignty projects that address both colonialism and sexism through an intersectional framework. Smith, who is Cherokee, is a longtime antiviolence and Native American activist and scholar. She is a leading expert on violence against women of color.

1. Why is gender justice integral to issues of survival for indigenous people?

2. How does the boarding school project reveal connections between interpersonal gender violence and state violence?

3. How does Native feminist theory and activism contribute to feminist politics at large?

NATIVE AMERICAN FEMINISM, SOVEREIGNTY, AND SOCIAL CHANGE

Andrea Smith

When I worked as a rape crisis counselor, every Native client I saw said to me at one point, "I wish I wasn't Indian." My training in the mainstream antiviolence movement did not prepare me to address what I was seeing—that sexual violence in Native communities was inextricably linked to processes of genocide and colonization. Through my involvement in organizations such as Women of All Red Nations (WARN, Chicago), Incite!

Women of Color against Violence (www.incite-national.org), and various other projects, I have come to see the importance of developing organizing theories and practices that focus on the intersections of state and colonial violence and gender violence. In my ongoing research projects on Native American critical race feminisms, I focus on documenting and analyzing the theories produced by Native women activists that intervene both in sovereignty and feminist struggles.[1] These analyses serve to complicate the generally simplistic manner in which Native women's activism is often articulated within scholarly and activist circles.

NATIVE WOMEN AND FEMINISM

One of the most prominent writings on Native American women and feminism is Annette Jaimes's (Guerrero) early 1990s article, "American Indian Women: At the Center of Indigenous Resistance in North America." Here, she argues that Native women activists, except those who are "assimilated," do not consider themselves feminists. Feminism, according to Jaimes, is an imperial project that assumes the givenness of U.S. colonial stranglehold on indigenous nations. Thus, to support sovereignty Native women activists reject feminist politics:

> Those who have most openly identified themselves [as feminists] have tended to be among the more assimilated of Indian women activists, generally accepting of the colonialist ideology that indigenous nations are now legitimate sub-parts of the U.S. geopolitical corpus rather than separate nations, that Indian people are now a minority with the overall population rather than the citizenry of their own distinct nations. Such Indian women activists are therefore usually more devoted to "civil rights" than to liberation per se. . . . Native American women who are more genuinely sovereigntist in their outlook have proven themselves far more dubious about the potentials offered by feminist politics and alliances.[2] According to Jaimes, the message from Native women is the same, as typified by these quotes from one of the founders of WARN, Lorelei DeCora Means:

> We are American Indian women, in that order. We are oppressed, first and foremost, as American Indians, as peoples colonized by the United States of America, not as women. As Indians, we can never forget that. Our survival, the survival of every one of us—man, woman and child—as Indians depends on it. Decolonization is the agenda, the whole agenda, and until it is accomplished, it is the only agenda that counts for American Indians.

The critique and rejection of the label of feminism made by Jaimes is important and shared by many Native women activists. However, it fails to tell the whole story. Consider, for instance, this quote from Madonna Thunder Hawk, who cofounded WARN with Means:

> Feminism means to me, putting a word on the women's world. It has to be done because of the modern day. Looking at it again, and I can only talk about the reservation society, because that's where I live and that's the only thing I know. I can't talk about the outside. How I relate to that term feminist, I like the word.
>
> When I first heard, I liked it. I related to it right away. But I'm not the average Indian woman; I'm not the average Indian activist woman, because I refuse to limit my world. I don't like that. . . . How could we limit ourselves? "I don't like that term; it's a white term." Pssshhh. Why limit yourself? But that's me.

My point is not to set Thunder Hawk in opposition to Means: both talk of the centrality of land and decolonization in Native women's struggle. Although Thunder Hawk supports many of the positions typically regarded as "feminist," such as abortion rights, she contends that Native struggles for land and survival continue to take precedence over these other issues. Rather, my argument is that Native women activists' theories about feminism, about the struggle against sexism both within Native communities and the society at large, and about the importance of working in coalition with non-Native women are complex and varied. These theories are not monolithic and cannot simply be reduced to the dichotomy of feminist versus nonfeminist. Furthermore, there is not necessarily a relationship between the extent to which Native women call themselves feminists, the extent to which they work in coalition with non-Native feminists or value those coalitions, whether they are urban or reservation-based, and the extent to which they are "genuinely sovereigntist." In addition, the very simplified manner in which Native women's activism is theorized straightjackets Native women from articulating political projects that both address sexism and promote indigenous sovereignty simultaneously.

Central to developing a Native feminist politic around sovereignty is a more critical analysis of Native activist responses to feminism and sexism in Native communities. Many narratives of Native women's organizing mirrors Jaimes's analysis—that sexism is not a primary factor in Native women's organizing. However, Janet McCloud recounts how the sexism in the Native rights movement contributed to the founding of the Indigenous Women's Network in 1985:

> I was down in Boulder, Colorado and Winona LaDuke and Nilak Butler were there and some others. They were telling me about the different kinds of sexism they were meeting up with in the movement with the men, who were really bad, and a lot of these women were really the backbone of everything, doing a lot of the kind of work that the movement needed. I thought they were getting discouraged and getting ready to pull out and I thought, "wow, we can't lose these women because they have a lot to offer." So, we talked about organizing a women's conference to discuss all the different problems. . . . Marsha Gomez and others decided to formally organize. I agreed to stay with them as a kind of a buffer because the men were saying the "Indignant Women's Organization" and blah, blah, blah. They felt kind of threatened by the women organizing.[3]

My interviews with Native women activists also indicate that sexism in Native communities is a central concern:

> Guys think they've got the big one, man. Like when [name of Native woman in the community] had to go over there and she went to these Indians because they thought they were a bunch of swinging dicks

and stuff, and she just let them have it. She just read them out. What else can you do? That's pretty brave. She was nice, she could have laid one of them out. Like you know, [name of Native man in the community], well of course this was more extreme, because I laid him out! He's way bigger than me. He's probably 5'11", I'm five feet tall. When he was younger, and I was younger, I don't even know what he said to me, it was something really awful. I didn't say nothing because he was bigger than me, I just laid him out. Otherwise you could get hurt. So I kicked him right in his little nut, and he fell down on the floor—"I'm going to kill you! You bitch!" But then he said, you're the man! If you be equal on a gut and juice level, on the street, they don't think of you as a woman anymore, and therefore they can be your friend, and they don't hate you. But then they go telling stuff like "You're the man!" And then what I said back to him, was "I've got it swinging!"

And although many Native women do not call themselves feminists for many well-thought-out reasons, including but not limited to the reasons Jaimes outlines, it is important to note that many not only call themselves feminist but also argue that it is important for Native women to call themselves feminists. And many activists argue that feminist, far from being a "white" concept, is actually an indigenous concept white women borrowed from Native women.

(INTERVIEWEE 1)

I think one of the reasons why women don't call themselves feminists is because they don't want to make enemies of men, and I just say, go forth and offend without inhibition. That's generally why I see women hold back, who don't want to be seen as strident. I don't want to be seen as a man-hater, but I think if we have enough man-haters, we might actually have the men change for once. . . . I think men, in this particular case, I think men are very, very good at avoiding responsibility and avoiding accountability and avoiding justice. And not calling yourself a feminist, that's one way they do that. Well, feminism, that's for white women. Oh feminists, they're not Indian. They're counter-revolutionary. They're all man-haters. They're all ball-busters. They've gotten out of order. No, first of all that presumes that Native women weren't active in shaping our identity before white women came along. And that abusive male behavior is somehow traditional, and it's absolutely not. So I reject that. That's a claim against sovereignty. I think that's a claim against Native peoples. I think it's an utter act of racism and white supremacy. And I do think it's important that we say we're feminists without apology.

(INTERVIEWEE 2)

[On Native women rejecting the term "feminist"] I think that's giving that concept to someone else, which I think is ridiculous. It's something that there has to be more discussion about what that means. I always considered, they took that from us, in a way. That's the way I've seen it. So I can't see it as a bad thing, because I think the origins are from people who had empowered women a long time ago.

This reversal of the typical claim that "feminism" is white then suggests that Native feminist politics is not necessarily similar to the feminist politics of other communities or that Native feminists necessarily see themselves in alliance with white feminists. In addition, the binary between feminist versus nonfeminist politics is false because Native activists have multiple and varied perspectives on this concept. For instance, consider one woman's use of "strategic" feminism with another woman's affirmation of feminist politics coupled with her rejection of the term "feminist." These women are not neatly categorized as feminists versus nonfeminists.

NATIVE FEMINISM AND SOVEREIGNTY

If we successfully decolonize, the argument goes, then we will necessarily eliminate problems of sexism as well. This sentiment can be found in the words of Ward Churchill. He contends that all struggles against sexism are of secondary importance because, traditionally, sexism did not exist in Indian nations. Churchill asks whether sexism exists in Indian country after Native peoples have

attained sovereignty? His reply, "Ask Wilma Mankiller," former principal chief of the Cherokee Nation.[4] Well, let's ask Mankiller. She says of her election campaign for deputy chief that she thought people might be bothered by her progressive politics and her activist background. "But I was wrong," she says:

No one challenged me on the issues, not once. Instead, I was challenged mostly because of one fact—I am female. The election became an issue of gender. It was one of the first times I had ever really encountered overt sexism . . . (people) said having a female run our tribe would make the Cherokees the laughing stock of the tribal world.[5]

Regardless of its origins in Native communities, then, sexism operates with full force today and requires strategies that directly address it. Before Native peoples fight for the future of their nations, they must ask themselves, who is included in the nation? It is often the case that gender justice is often articulated as being a separate issue from issues of survival for indigenous peoples. Such an understanding presupposes that we could actually decolonize without addressing sexism, which ignores the fact that it has been precisely through gender violence that we have lost our lands in the first place.[6] In my activist work, I have often heard the sentiment expressed in Indian country: we do not have time to address sexual/domestic violence in our communities because we have to work on "survival" issues first. However, Indian women suffer death rates because of domestic violence twice as high as any other group of women in this country.[7] They are clearly not surviving as long as issues of gender violence go unaddressed. Scholarly analyses of the impact of colonization on Native communities often minimize the histories of oppression of Native women. In fact, many scholars argue that men were disproportionately affected by colonization because the economic systems imposed on Native nations deprived men of their economic roles in the communities more so than women.[8] By narrowing our analyses solely to the explicitly economic realm of society, we fail to account for the multiple ways women have disproportionately suffered under colonization—from sexual violence to forced sterilization. As Paula Gunn Allen argues:

> Many people believe that Indian men have suffered more damage to their traditional status than have Indian women, but I think that belief is more a reflection of colonial attitudes toward the primacy of male experience than of historical fact. While women still play the traditional role of housekeeper, childbearer, and nurturer, they no longer enjoy the unquestioned positions of power, respect, and decision making on local and international levels that were not so long ago their accustomed functions.[9]

This tendency to separate the health and well-being of women from the health and well-being of our nations is critiqued in Winona LaDuke's 1994 call to not "cheapen sovereignty." She discusses attempts by men in her community to use the rhetoric of "sovereignty" to avoid paying child support payments.

> What is the point of an Indian Child Welfare Act when there is so much disregard for the rights and well being of the children? Some of these guys from White Earth are saying the state has no jurisdiction to exact child support payments from them. Traditionally, Native men took care of their own. Do they pay their own to these women? I don't think so. I know better. How does that equation better the lives of our children? How is that (real) sovereignty?

> The U.S government is so hypocritical about recognizing sovereignty. And we, the Native community, fall into the same hypocrisy. I would argue the Feds only recognize Indian sovereignty when a first Nation has a casino or a waste dump, not when a tribal government seeks to preserve ground water from pesticide contamination, exercise jurisdiction over air quality, or stop clear-cutting or say no to a nuclear dump. "Sovereignty" has become a politicized term used for some of the most demeaning purposes.[10]

Beatrice Medicine similarly critiques the manner in which women's status is often pitted against sovereignty, as exemplified in the 1978 Santa Clara Pueblo v. Martinez case. Julia Martinez sued her tribe for sex discrimination under the Indian Civil Rights Act because the tribe had dictated that children born from female tribal members who married outside the tribe lost tribal status whereas children born from male tribal members who married outside the tribe did not. The Supreme Court ruled that the federal government could not intervene in this situation because the determination of tribal membership was the sovereign right of the tribe. On the one hand, many white feminists criticized the Supreme Court decision without considering how the Court's affirmation of the right of the federal government to determine tribal membership would constitute a significant attack against tribal sovereignty.[11] On the other hand, as Medicine notes, many tribes take this decision as a signal to institute gender-discriminatory practices under the name of sovereignty.[12] For these difficult issues, it is perhaps helpful to consider how they could be addressed if we put American Indian women at the center of analysis. Is it possible to simultaneously affirm tribal sovereignty and challenge tribes to consider how the impact of colonization and Europeanization may impact the decisions they make and programs they pursue in a manner which may ultimately undermine their sovereignty in the long term? Rather than adopt the strategy of fighting for sovereignty first and then improving Native women's status second, as Jaimes suggests, we must understand that attacks on Native women's status are themselves attacks on Native sovereignty. Lee Maracle illustrates the relationship between colonization and gender violence in Native communities in her groundbreaking work, *I Am Woman* (1988):

> If the State won't kill us we will have to kill ourselves. It is no longer good etiquette to head hunt savages. We'll just have to do it ourselves. It's not polite to violate "squaws" We'll have to find an Indian to oblige us. It's poor form to starve an Indian We'll have to deprive our young ourselves Blinded by niceties and polite liberality We can't see our enemy, so, we'll just have to kill each other.[13]

It has been through sexual violence and through the imposition of European gender relationships on Native communities that Europeans were able to colonize Native peoples in the first place. If we maintain these patriarchal gender systems in place, we are then unable to decolonize and fully assert our sovereignty.

NATIVE FEMINIST SOVEREIGNTY PROJECTS

Despite the political and theoretical straightjacket in which Native women often find themselves, there are several groundbreaking projects today that address both colonialism and sexism through an intersectional framework. One such attempt to tie indigenous sovereignty with the well-being of Native women is evident in the materials produced by the Sacred Circle, a national American Indian resource center for domestic and sexual violence based in South Dakota. Their brochure Sovereign Women Strengthen Sovereign Nations reads:

Tribal Sovereignty *All Tribal Nations Have an Inherent Right to:*	*Native Women's Sovereignty* *All Native Women Have an Inherent Right to:*
1) A land base: possession and control is unquestioned and honored by other nations. To exist without fear, but with freedom.	1) Their body and path in life: the possession and control is unquestioned and honored by others. To exist without fear, but without freedom.
2) Self-governance: the ability and authority to make decisions regarding all matters concerning the Tribe without the approval or agreement of others. This includes the ways and methods of decision-making in social, political and other areas of life.	2) Self-governance: the ability and authority to make decisions regarding all matters concerning themselves, without others' approval or agreement. This includes the ways and methods of decision-making in social, political and other areas of life.
3) An economic base and resources: the control, use and development of resources, businesses or industries the Tribe chooses. This includes resources that support the Tribal life way, including the practice of spiritual ways.	3) An economic base and resources: the control, use and development of resources, businesses or industries that Native women choose. This includes resources that support individual Native women's chosen life ways, including the practice of spiritual ways.
4) A distinct language and historical and cultural identity: Each tribe defines and describes its history, including the impact of colonization and racism, tribal culture, worldview and traditions.	4) A distinct identity, history and culture: Each Native woman defines and describes her history, including the impact of colonization, racism and sexism, tribal women's culture, worldview and traditions.
***	***
Colonization and violence against Native people means that power and control over Native people's life way and land have been stolen. As Native people, we have the right and responsibility to advocate for ourselves and our relatives in supporting our right to power and control over our tribal life way and land tribal sovereignty.	*Violence against women, and victimization in general, means that power and control over an individual's life and body have been stolen. As relatives of women who have been victimized, it is our right and responsibility to be advocates supporting every woman's right to power and control over her body and life—personal sovereignty.*

Another such project is the Boarding School Healing Project, which seeks to build a movement to demand reparations for U.S. boarding school abuses. This project, founded in 2002, is a coalition of indigenous groups across the United States, such as the American Indian Law Alliance, Incite! Women of Color against Violence, Indigenous Women's Network, and Native Women of Sovereign Nations of the South Dakota Coalition against Domestic Violence and Sexual Assault. In Canada, Native peoples have been able to document the abuses of the residential school system and demand accountability from the Canadian government and churches. The same level of documentation has not taken place in the United States. The Boarding School Healing Project is documenting these abuses to build a movement for reparations and accountability. However, the strategy of this project is not to seek remedies on the individual level, but to demand collective remedy by developing links with other reparations struggles that fundamentally challenge the colonial and capitalist status quo. In addition, the strategy of this project is to organize around boarding schools as a way to address gender violence in Native communities.

That is, one of the harms suffered by Native peoples through state policy was sexual violence perpetrated by boarding school officials. The continuing effect of this human rights violation has been the internalization of sexual and other forms of gender violence within Native American communities. Thus, the question is, how can we form a demand around reparations for these types of continuing effects of human rights violations that are evidenced by violence within communities, but are nonetheless colonial legacies. In addition, this project attempts to organize against interpersonal gender violence and state violence simultaneously by framing gender violence as a continuing effect of human rights violations perpetrated by state policy. Consequently, this project challenges the mainstream anti-domestic/sexual violence movement to conceptualize state-sponsored sexual violence as central to its work. As I have argued elsewhere, the mainstream antiviolence movement has relied on the apparatus of state violence (in the form of the criminal justice system) to address domestic and sexual violence without considering how the state itself is a primary perpetrator of violence.[14] The issue of boarding schools forces us to see the connections between state violence and interpersonal violence. It is through boarding schools that gender violence in our communities was largely introduced. Before colonization, Native societies were, for the most part, not male dominated. Women served

as spiritual, political, and military leaders. Many societies were matrilineal and matrilocal. Violence against women and children was infrequent or unheard of in many tribes.[15] Native peoples did not use corporal punishment against their children. Although there existed a division of labor between women and men, women's and men's labor was accorded similar status.[16] In boarding schools, by contrast, sexual/physical/emotional violence proliferated. Particularly brutalizing to Native children was the manner in which school officials involved children in punishing other children. For instance, in some schools, children were forced to hit other children with the threat that if they did not hit hard enough, they themselves would be severely beaten. Sometimes perpetrators of the violence were held accountable, but generally speaking, even when teachers were charged with abuse, boarding schools refused to investigate. In the case of just one teacher, John Boone at the Hopi school, FBI investigations in 1987 found that he had sexually abused more than 142 boys, but that the principal of that school had not investigated any allegations of abuse.[17] Despite the epidemic of sexual abuse in boarding schools, the Bureau of Indian Affairs did not issue a policy on reporting sexual abuse until 1987 and did not issue a policy to strengthen the background checks of potential teachers until 1989. Although not all Native peoples see their boarding school experiences as negative, it is generally the case that much if not most of the current dysfunctionality in Native communities can be traced to the boarding school era.

The effects of boarding school abuses linger today because these abuses have not been acknowledged by the larger society. As a result, silence continues within Native communities, preventing Native peoples from seeking support and healing as a result of the intergenerational trauma. Because boarding school policies are not acknowledged as human rights violations, Native peoples individualize the trauma they have suffered, thus contributing to increased shame and self-blame. If both boarding school policies and the continuing effects from these policies were recognized as human rights violations, then it might take away the shame from talking about these issues and thus provide an opportunity for communities to begin healing.

Unfortunately, we continue to perpetuate this colonial violence through domestic/sexual violence, child abuse, and homophobia. No amount of reparations will be successful if we do not address the oppressive behaviors we have internalized. Women of color have for too long been presented with the choices of either prioritizing racial justice or gender justice. This dualistic analysis fails to recognize that it is precisely through sexism and gender violence that colonialism and white supremacy have been successful. A question to ask ourselves then is, what would true reparations really look like for women of color who suffer state violence and interpersonal gender violence simultaneously? The Boarding School Healing Project provides an opportunity to organize around the connections between interpersonal gender violence and state violence that could serve as a model for the broader antiviolence movement.

In addition, this project makes important contributions to the struggle for reparations as a whole. That is, a reparations struggle is not necessarily radical if its demands do not call into question the capitalist and colonial status quo. What is at the heart of the issue is that no matter how much financial compensation the United States may give, such compensation does not ultimately end the colonial relationship between the United States and indigenous nations. What is at the heart of the struggle for native sovereignty is control over land and resources rather than financial compensation for past and continuing wrongs. If we think about reparations less in terms of financial compensation for social oppression and more about a movement to transform the neocolonial economic relationships between the United States and people of color, indigenous peoples, and Third World countries, we see how critical this movement

could be to all of us. The articulation of reparations as a movement to cancel the Third World debt, for instance, is instructive in thinking of strategies that could fundamentally alter these relations.

NATIVE FEMINISM AND THE NATION STATE

Native feminist theory and activism make a critical contribution to feminist politics as a whole by questioning the legitimacy of the United States specifically and the nation-state as the appropriate form of governance generally. Progressive activists and scholars, although prepared to make critiques of the U.S. government, are often not prepared to question its legitimacy. A case in point is the strategy of many racial justice organizations in the United States to rally against hate crimes resulting from the attacks of 9/11 under the banner, "We're American too." However, what the analysis of Native women activists suggests is that this implicit allegiance to "America" legitimizes the genocide and colonization of Native peoples, as there could be no "America" without this genocide. Thus by making anticolonial struggle central to feminist politics, Native women make central to their organizing the question of what is the appropriate form of governance for the world in general. Does self-determination for indigenous peoples equal aspirations for a nation-state, or are there other forms of governance we can create that are not based on domination and control?

Questioning the United States, in particular, and questioning the nation-state as the appropriate form of governance for the world, in general, allow us to free our political imagination to begin thinking of how we can begin to build a world we would actually want to live in. Such a political project is particularly important for colonized peoples seeking national liberation because it allows us to differentiate "nation" from "nation-state." Helpful in this project of imagination is the work of Native women activists who have begun articulating notions of nation and sovereignty that are separate from nation-states.

Whereas nation-states are governed through domination and coercion, indigenous sovereignty and nationhood is predicated on interrelatedness and responsibility. As Crystal Ecohawk states:

> Sovereignty is an active, living process within this knot of human, material and spiritual relationships bound together by mutual responsibilities and obligations. From that knot of relationships is born our histories, our identity, the traditional ways in which we govern ourselves, our beliefs, our relationship to the land, and how we feed, clothe, house and take care of our families, communities and Nations.[18]

It is interesting to me . . . how often non-Indians presume that if Native people regained their landbases, that they would necessarily call for the expulsion of non-Indians from those landbases. Yet, it is striking that a much more inclusive vision of sovereignty is articulated by Native women activists. For instance, this activist describes how indigenous sovereignty is based on freedom for all peoples:

> If it doesn't work for one of us, it doesn't work for any of us. The definition of sovereignty [means that] . . . none of us are free unless all of us are free. We can't, we won't turn anyone away. We've been there. I would hear stories about the Japanese internment camps . . . and I could relate to it because it happened to us. Or with Africans with the violence and rape, we've been there too. So how could we ever leave anyone behind.

This analysis mirrors much of the work currently going on in women of color organizing in the United States and in other countries. Such models rely on this dual strategy of what Sista II Sista (Brooklyn) describes as "taking power" and "making power."[19] That is, it is necessary to engage in oppositional politics to corporate and state power ("taking power"). However, if we only engage in the politics of taking power, we will have a tendency to replicate the hierarchical structures in our movements. Consequently, it is also important to "make power" by creating those structures within our organizations, movements, and communities that model the world we are trying to create. Many groups in the United States often try to create separatist communities based on egalitarian ideals. However, if we "make power" without also trying to "take power" then we ultimately support the political status quo by failing to dismantle those structures of oppression that will undermine all our attempts to make power. The project of creating a new world governed by an alternative system not based on domination, coercion, and control does not depend on an unrealistic goal of being able to fully describe a utopian society for all at this point in time. From our position of growing up in a patriarchal, colonial, and white supremacist world, we cannot even fully imagine how a world not based on structures of oppression could operate. Nevertheless, we can be part of a collective, creative process that can bring us closer to a society not based on domination. To quote Jean Ziegler from the 2003 World Social Forum held in Porto Alegre, Brazil: "We know what we don't want, but the new world belongs to the liberated freedom of human beings. 'There is no way; you make the way as you walk.' History doesn't fall from heaven; we make history."

NOTES

1. Quotes that are not cited come from interviews conducted in Rapid City, New York City, Santa Cruz, Minneapolis, and Bemidji in 2001. These interviews are derived primarily from women involved in Women of All Red Nations (WARN) and the American Indian Movement (AIM). All are activists today.

2. M. Annette Jaimes and Theresa Halsey, "American Indian Women: At the Center of Indigenous Resistance in North America," in *State of Native America*, ed. M. Annette Jaimes (Boston: South End Press, 1992), 330–31.

3. Janet McCloud, "The Backbone of Everything," *Indigenous Woman* 1, no. 3 (n.d.): 50.

4. Ward Churchill, *Struggle for the Land* (Monroe, Maine: Common Courage Press, 1993), 419.

5. Wilma Mankiller, *Mankiller* (New York: St. Martin's Press, 1993), 241.

6. Andrea Smith, "Sexual Violence and American Indian Genocide," in *Remembering Conquest: Feminist/Womanist Perspectives on Religion, Colonization, and Sexual Violence*, ed. Nantawan Lewis and Marie Fortune (Binghamton, N.Y.: Haworth Press, 1999), 31–52.

7. Callie Rennison, "Violent Victimization and Race, 1993–1998" (Washington, D.C.: Bureau of Justice Statistics, 2001).

8. Lucy Eldersveld Murphy, "Autonomy and the Economic Roles of Indian Women of the Fox-Wisconsin Riverway Region, 1763–1832," in *Negotiators of Change: Historical Perspectives on Native American Women,* ed. Nancy Shoemaker (New York: Routledge Press, 1995), 72–89; Theda Purdue, "Women, Men, and American Indian Policy: The Cherokee Response to "Civilization," in *Negotiators of Change,* 90–114.

9. Paula Gunn Allen, *The Sacred Hoop* (Boston: Beacon Press, 1986), 202.

10. Winona LaDuke, "Don't Cheapen Sovereignty," *American Eagle* 4 (May 1996): n.d. www.alphacdc.com/eagle/op0596.html.

11. Catherine MacKinnon, *Feminism Unmodified* (Cambridge: Harvard University Press, 1987), 63–69.

12. Beatrice Medicine, "North American Indigenous Women and Cultural Domination," *American Indian Culture and Research Journal* 17, no. 3 (1993): 121–30.

13. Lee Maracle, *I Am Woman* (North Vancouver: Write-On Press Publishers, 1988).

14. Smith, "Sexual Violence and American Indian Genocide," 31–52.

15. Paula Gunn Allen, "Violence and the American Indian Woman," *The Speaking Profit Us* (Seattle: Center for the Prevention of Sexual and Domestic Violence, n.d.), 5–7. See also *A Sharing: Traditional Lakota Thought and Philosophy Regarding Domestic Violence* (South Dakota: Sacred Shawl Women's Society, n.d.); and *Sexual Assault Is Not an Indian Tradition* (Minneapolis: Division of Indian Work Sexual Assault Project, n.d.).

16. See Jaimes and Halsey, "American Indian Women," 311–44; and Allen, *The Sacred Hoop.*

17. "Hello New Federalism, Goodbye BIA," *American Eagle* 4, no. 6(1994):19.

18. Crystal Echohawk, "Reflections on Sovereignty," *Indigenous Woman* 3, no. 1(1999):21–22.

19. Personal conversations with Sista II Sista members, ongoing from 2001–2005.

Introduction to Reading 50

R. W. Connell's article traces the emergence of a worldwide discussion of men and gender-equality reform and assesses the prospects of reform strategies involving men. Connell does so by locating recent policy discussions in the wider context of the cultural problematization of men and boys, the politics of "men's movements," the divided interests of men and boys in gender relations, and the increasing research evidence about the changing and conflict-ridden social construction of masculinities. Connell's analysis ranges from local to global, but the primary concern is with the global nature of debate about the role of men and boys in relation to gender equality.

1. Why is research on diverse social constructions of masculinity critical to worldwide efforts on behalf of achieving gender equality?

2. Connell states that men have a lot to lose from pursuing gender equality. But Connell also argues that men's advantages are conditions for the price they pay for their benefits. Discuss.

3. What are the "grounds for optimism" and the "grounds for pessimism" set out in this reading?

CHANGE AMONG THE GATEKEEPERS

MEN, MASCULINITIES, AND GENDER EQUALITY IN THE GLOBAL ARENA

R. W. Connell

Equality between women and men has been a doctrine well recognized in international law since the adoption of the 1948 Universal Declaration of Human Rights (United Nations 1958), and as a principle it enjoys popular support in many countries. The idea of gender equal rights has provided the formal basis for the international discussion of the position of women since the 1975–85 UN Decade for Women, which has been a key element in the story of global feminism (Bulbeck 1988). The idea that men might have a specific role in relation to this principle has emerged only recently.

The issue of gender equality was placed on the policy agenda by women. The reason is obvious: it is women who are disadvantaged by the main patterns of gender inequality and who therefore have the claim for redress. Men are, however, necessarily involved in gender-equality reform. Gender inequalities are embedded in a multidimensional structure of relationships between women and men, which, as the modern sociology of gender shows, operates at every level of human experience, from economic arrangements, culture, and the state to interpersonal relationships and individual emotions (Holter 1997; Walby 1997; Connell 2002). Moving toward a gender-equal society involves profound institutional change as well as change in everyday life and personal conduct. To move far in this direction requires widespread social support, including significant support from men and boys.

Further, the very gender inequalities in economic assets, political power, and cultural authority, as well as the means of coercion, that gender reforms intend to change, currently mean that men (often specific groups of men) control most of the resources required to implement women's claims for justice. Men and boys are thus in significant ways gatekeepers for gender equality. Whether they are willing to open the gates for major reforms is an important strategic question.

In this article, I will trace the emergence of a worldwide discussion of men and gender-equality reform and will try to assess the prospects of reform strategies involving men. To make such an assessment, it is necessary to set recent policy discussions in the wider context of the cultural problematization of men and boys, the politics of "men's movements," the divided interests of men and boys in gender relations, and the growing research evidence about the changing and conflict-ridden social construction of masculinities.

In an article of this scope, it is not possible to address particular national agendas in detail. I will refer to a number of texts where these stories can be found. Because my primary concern is with the global character of the debate, cussions in UN forums. These discussions culminated in the 2004 meeting of the UN Commission on the Status of Women, which produced the first world-level policy document on the role of men and boys in relation to gender equality (UN Commission on the Status of Women 2004.)

MEN AND MASCULINITIES IN THE WORLD GENDER ORDER

In the last fifteen years, in the "developed" countries of the global metropole, there has been a great deal of popular concern with issues about men and boys. Readers in the United States may recall a volume by the poet Robert Bly, *Iron John: A Book about Men* (1990), which became a huge best seller in the early 1990s, setting off a wave of imitations. This book became popular because it offered, in prophetic language, simple solutions to problems that were increasingly troubling the culture. A therapeutic movement was then developing in the United States, mainly though not exclusively among middle-class men, addressing problems in relationships, sexuality, and identity (Kupers 1993; Schwalbe 1996).

More specific issues about men and boys have also attracted public attention in the developed countries. Men's responses to feminism, and to gender-equality measures taken by government, have long been the subject of debate in Germany and Scandinavia (Metz-Göckel and Müller 1985; Holter 2003). In anglophone countries there has been much discussion of "the new fatherhood" and of supposed changes in men's involvement in families (McMahon 1999). There has been public agonizing about boys' "failure" in school, and in Australia there are many proposals for special programs for boys (Kenway 1997; Lingard 2003). Men's violence toward women has been the subject of practical interventions and extensive debate (Hearn 1998). There has also been increasing debate about men's health and illness from a gender perspective (Hurrelmann and Kolip 2002).

Accompanying these debates has been a remarkable growth of research about men's gender identities and practices, masculinities and the social processes by which they are constructed, cultural and media images of men, and related matters. Academic journals have been founded for specialized research on men and masculinities, there have been many research conferences, and there is a rapidly growing international literature.

We now have a far more sophisticated and detailed scientific understanding of issues about men, masculinities, and gender than ever before (Connell 2003a).

This set of concerns, though first articulated in the developed countries, can now be found worldwide (Connell 2000; Pease and Pringle 2001). Debates on violence, patriarchy, and ways of changing men's conduct have occurred in countries as diverse as Germany, Canada, and South Africa (Hagemann-White 1992; Kaufman 1993; Morrell 2001a). Issues about masculine sexuality and fatherhood have been debated and researched in Brazil, Mexico, and many other countries (Arilha, Unbehaum Ridenti, and Medrado 1998; Lerner 1998). A men's center with a reform agenda has been established in Japan, where conferences have been held and media debates about traditional patterns of masculinity and family life continue (Menzu Senta 1997; Roberson and Suzuki 2003). A "traveling seminar" discussing issues about men, masculinities, and gender equality has recently been touring in India (Roy 2003). Debates about boys' education, men's identities, and gender change are active from New Zealand to Denmark (Law, Campbell, and Dolan 1999; Reinicke 2002). Debates about men's sexuality, and changing sexual identities, are also international (Altman 2001).

The research effort is also worldwide. Documentation of the diverse social constructions of masculinity has been undertaken in countries as far apart as Peru (Fuller 2001), Japan (Taga 2001), and Turkey (Sinclair-Webb 2000). The first large-scale comparative study of men and gender relations has recently been completed in ten European countries (Hearn et al. 2002). The first global synthesis, in the form of a world handbook of research on men and masculinities, has now appeared (Kimmel, Hearn, and Connell 2005).

The rapid internationalization of these debates reflects the fact—increasingly recognized in feminist thought (Bulbeck 1998; Marchand and Runyan 2000)—that gender relations themselves have an international dimension. Each of the substructures of gender relations can be shown to have a global dimension, growing out of the history of imperialism and seen in the contemporary process of globalization (Connell 2002). Change in gender relations occurs on a world scale, though not always in the same direction or at the same pace.

The complexity of the patterns follows from the fact that gender change occurs in several different modes. Most dramatic is the direct colonization of the gender order of regions beyond the metropole. There has also been a more gradual recomposition of gender orders, both those of the colonizing society and the colonized, in the process of colonial interaction. The hybrid gender identities and sexualities now much discussed in the context of postcolonial societies are neither unusual nor new. They are a feature of the whole history of imperialism and are visible in many contemporary studies (e.g., Valdés and Olavarría 1998).

Imperialism and globalization change the conditions of existence for gender orders. For instance, the linking of previously separate production systems changes the flow of goods and services in the gendered division of labor, as seen in the impact of industrially produced foods and textiles on household economies. Colonialism itself often confronted local patriarchies with colonizing patriarchies, producing a turbulent and sometimes very violent aftermath, as in southern Africa (Morrell 1998). Pressure from contemporary Western commercial culture has destabilized gender arrangements, and models of masculinity, in Japan (Ito 1992), the Arab world (Ghoussoub 2000), and elsewhere.

Finally, the emergence of new arenas of social relationship on a world scale creates new patterns of gender relations. Transnational corporations, international communications systems, global mass media, and international state structures (from the United Nations to the European Union) are such arenas. These institutions have their own gender regimes and may form the basis for new configurations of masculinity, as has recently been argued for transnational business (Connell 2000) and the international relations system (Hooper 2001). Local gender orders now interact not only with the gender orders of other local societies but also with the gender order of the global arena.

The dynamics of the world gender order affect men as profoundly as they do women, though this fact has been less discussed. The best contemporary research on men and masculinity, such as Matthew C. Gutmann's (2002) ethnographic work in Mexico, shows in fine detail how the lives of particular groups of men are shaped by globally acting economic and political dynamics.

Different groups of men are positioned very differently in such processes. There is no single formula that accounts for men and globalization. There is, indeed, a growing polarization among men on a world scale. Studies of the "super-rich" (Haseler 2000) show a privileged minority reaching astonishing heights of wealth and power while much larger numbers face poverty, cultural dislocation, disruption of family relationships, and forced renegotiation of the meanings of masculinity.

Masculinities, as socially constructed configurations of gender practice, are also created through a historical process with a global dimension. The old-style ethnographic research that located gender patterns purely in a local context is inadequate to the reality. Historical research, such as Robert Morrell's (2001b) study of the masculinities of the colonizers in South Africa and T. Dunbar Moodie's (1994) study of the colonized, shows how a gendered culture is created and transformed in relation to the international economy and the political system of empire. There is every reason to think this principle holds for contemporary masculinities.

SHIFTING GROUND: MEN AND BOYS IN GENDER-EQUALITY DEBATES

Because of the way they came onto the agenda of public debate, gender issues have been widely regarded as women's business and of little concern to men and boys. In almost all policy discussions, to adopt a gender perspective substantially means to address women's concerns.

In both national and international policy documents concerned with gender equality, women are the subjects of the policy discourse.

The agencies or meetings that formulate, implement, or monitor gender policies usually have names referring to women, such as Department for Women, Women's Equity Bureau, Prefectural Women's Centre, or Commission on the Status of Women. Such bodies have a clear mandate to act for women. They do not have an equally clear mandate to act with respect to men. The major policy documents concerned with gender equality, such as the UN Convention on the Elimination of all Forms of Discrimination against Women (United Nations [1979] 1989), often do not name men as a group and rarely discuss men in concrete terms.

However, men are present as background throughout these documents. In every statement about women's disadvantages, there is an implied comparison with men as the advantaged group. In the discussions of violence against women, men are implied, and sometimes named, as the perpetrators. In discussions of gender and HIV/AIDS, men are commonly construed as being "the problem," the agents of infection. In discussions of women's exclusion from power and decision making, men are implicitly present as the power holders.

When men are present only as a background category in a policy discourse about women, it is difficult to raise issues about men's and boys' interests, problems, or differences. This could be done only by falling into a backlash posture and affirming "men's rights" or by moving outside a gender framework altogether.

The structure of gender-equality policy, therefore, created an opportunity for antifeminist politics. Opponents of feminism have now found issues about boys and men to be fertile ground. This is most clearly seen in the United States, where authors such as Warren Farrell (1993) and Christina Hoff Sommers (2000), purporting to speak on behalf of men and boys, bitterly accuse feminism of injustice. Men and boys, they argue, are the truly disadvantaged group and need supportive programs in education and health, in situations of family breakup, and so forth. These ideas have not stimulated a social movement, with the exception of a small-scale (though active and

sometimes violent) "father's rights" movement in relation to divorce. The arguments have, however, strongly appealed to the neoconservative mass media, which have given them international circulation. They now form part of the broad neoconservative repertoire of opposition to "political correctness" and to social justice measures.

Some policy makers have attempted to straddle this divide by restructuring gender-equality policy in the form of parallel policies for women and men. For instance, some recent health policy initiatives in Australia have added a "men's health" document to a "women's health" document (Schofield 2004). Similarly, in some school systems a "boys' education" strategy has been added to a "girls' education" strategy (Lingard 2003).

This approach acknowledges the wider scope of gender issues. But it also risks weakening the equality rationale of the original policy. It forgets the relational character of gender and therefore tends to redefine women and men, or girls and boys, simply as different market segments for some service. Ironically, the result may be to promote more gender segregation, not less. This has certainly happened in education, where some privileged boys' schools have jumped on the "gender equality" bandwagon and now market themselves as experts in catering to the special needs of boys.

On the other hand, bringing men's problems into an existing framework of policies for women may weaken the authority that women have so far gathered in that policy area. In the field of gender and development, for instance, some specialists argue that "bringing men in"—given the larger context in which men still control most of the wealth and institutional authority—may undermine, not help, the drive for gender equality (White 2000).

The role of men and boys in relation to gender equality emerged as an issue in international discussions during the 1990s. This development crystallized at the Fourth World Conference on Women, held in Beijing in 1995. Paragraph 25 of the Beijing Declaration committed participating governments to "encourage men to participate fully in all actions towards equality" (United Nations 2001). The detailed "Platform for Action" that accompanied the declaration prominently restated the principle of shared power and responsibility between men and women and argued that women's concerns could be addressed only "in partnership with men" toward gender equality (2001, pars. 1, 3). The "Platform for Action" went on to specify areas where action involving men and boys was needed and was possible: in education, socialization of children, child care and housework, sexual health, gender-based violence, and the balancing of work and family responsibilities (2001, pars. 40, 72, 83b, 107c, 108e, 120, 179).

Participating member states followed a similar approach in the twenty-third special session of the UN General Assembly in the year 2000, which was intended to review the situation five years after the Beijing conference. The "Political Declaration" of this session made an even stronger statement on men's responsibility: "[Member states of the United Nations] emphasise that men must involve themselves and take joint responsibility with women for the promotion of gender equality" (United Nations 2001, par. 6). It still remained the case, in this and the accompanying "Outcome Document," that men were present on the margins of a policy discourse concerned with women.

The role of men and boys has also been addressed in other recent international meetings. These include the 1995 World Summit on Social Development, its review session in 2000, and the special session of the General Assembly on HIV/AIDS in 2001. In 1997 the UN Educational, Scientific, and Cultural Organization (UNESCO) convened an expert group meeting about "Male Roles and Masculinities in the Perspective of a Culture of Peace," which met in Oslo and produced studies on the links among personal violence, war, and the construction of masculinities (Breines, Connell, and Eide 2000).

International meetings outside the UN system have addressed similar issues. In 1997 the Nordic Council of Ministers adopted the Nordic Action Plan for Men and Gender Equality. In the same year the Council of Europe conducted a seminar on equality as a common issue for men and women and made the role of men in promoting equality a theme at a ministerial conference. In 1998 the Latin American Federation of Social Science (FLACSO) began a series of conferences about masculinities, boys, and men across Latin America and the Caribbean. The first conference in this series had the specific theme of gender equity (Valdés and Olavarría 1998). The European Commission has recently funded a research network on men and masculinities.

DIVIDED INTERESTS: SUPPORT AND RESISTANCE

There is something surprising about the worldwide problematizing of men and masculinities, because in many ways the position of men has not greatly changed. For instance, men remain a very large majority of corporate executives, top professionals, and holders of public office. Worldwide, men hold nine out of ten cabinet-level posts in national governments, nearly as many of the parliamentary seats, and most top positions in international agencies. Men, collectively, receive approximately twice the income that women receive and also receive the benefits of a great deal of unpaid household labor, not to mention emotional support, from women (Gierycz 1999; Godenzi 2000; Inter-Parliamentary Union 2003).

The UN Development Program (2003) now regularly incorporates a selection of such statistics into its annual report on world human development, combining them into a "gender-related development index" and a "gender empowerment measure." This produces a dramatic outcome, a league table of countries ranked in terms of gender equality, which shows most countries in the world to be far from gender-equal. It is clear that, globally, men have a lot to lose from pursuing gender equality because men, collectively, continue to receive a patriarchal dividend.

But this way of picturing inequality may conceal as much as it reveals. There are multiple dimensions in gender relations, and the patterns of inequality in these dimensions may be qualitatively different. If we look separately at each of the substructures of gender, we find a pattern of advantages for men but also a linked pattern of disadvantages or toxicity (Connell 2003c).

For instance, in relation to the gender division of labor, men collectively receive the bulk of income in the money economy and occupy most of the managerial positions. But men also provide the workforce for the most dangerous occupations, suffer most industrial injuries, pay most of the taxation, and are under heavier social pressure to remain employed. In the domain of power men collectively control the institutions of coercion and the means of violence (e.g., weapons). But men are also the main targets of military violence and criminal assault, and many more men than women are imprisoned or executed. Men's authority receives more social recognition (e.g., in religion), but men and boys are underrepresented in important learning experiences (e.g., in humanistic studies) and important dimensions of human relations (e.g., with young children).

One could draw up a balance sheet of the costs and benefits to men from the current gender order. But this balance sheet would not be like a corporate accounting exercise where there is a bottom line, subtracting costs from income. The disadvantages listed above are, broadly speaking, the conditions of the advantages. For instance, men cannot hold state power without some men becoming the agents of violence. Men cannot be the beneficiaries of women's domestic labor and "emotion work" without many of them losing intimate connections, for instance, with young children.

Equally important, the men who receive most of the benefits and the men who pay most of the costs are not the same individuals. As the old saying puts it, generals die in bed. On a global scale, the men who benefit from corporate wealth, physical security, and expensive health care are a very different group from the men who provide the workforce of developing countries. Class, race, national, regional, and generational differences cross-cut the category "men,"

spreading the gains and costs of gender relations very unevenly among men. There are many situations where groups of men may see their interest as more closely aligned with the women in their communities than with other men. It is not surprising that men respond very diversely to gender-equality politics.

There is, in fact, a considerable history of support for gender equality among men. There is certainly a tradition of advocacy by male intellectuals. In Europe, well before modern gender-equality documents were written, the British philosopher John Stuart Mill published "The Subjection of Women" (1912), which established the presumption of equal rights; and the Norwegian dramatist Henrik Ibsen, in plays like A Doll's House ([1923] 1995), made gender oppression an important cultural theme. In the following generation, the pioneering Austrian psychoanalyst Alfred Adler established a powerful psychological argument for gender equality (Connell 1995). A similar tradition of men's advocacy exists in the United States (Kimmel and Mosmiller 1992).

Many of the historic gains by women's advocates have been won in alliance with men who held organizational or political authority at the time. For instance, the introduction of equal employment opportunity measures in New South Wales, Australia, occurred with the strong support of the premier and the head of a reform inquiry into the public sector, both men (Eisenstein 1991). Sometimes men's support for gender equality takes the form of campaigning and organizing among men. The most prominent example is the U.S. National Organization of Men against Sexism (NOMAS), which has existed for more than twenty years (Cohen 1991). Men's groups concerned with reforming masculinity, publications advocating change, and campaigns among men against violence toward women are found widely, for instance, in the United Kingdom, Mexico, and South Africa (Seidler 1991; Zingoni 1998; Peacock 2003).

Men have also been active in creating educational programs for boys and young men intended to support gender reform. Similar strategies have been developed for adult men, sometimes in a religious and sometimes in a health or therapeutic context. There is a strong tradition of such work in Germany, with programs that combine the search for self-knowledge with the learning of antisexist behavior (Brandes and Bullinger 1996). Work of the same kind has developed in Brazil, the United States, and other countries (Denborough 1996; Lyra and Medrado 2001).

These initiatives are widespread, but they are also mostly small-scale. What of the wider state of opinion? European survey research has shown no consensus among men either for or against gender equality. Sometimes a third/third/third pattern appears, with about one-third of men supporting change toward equality, about one-third opposing it, and one-third undecided or intermediate (Holter 1997, 131–34). Nevertheless, examinations of the survey evidence from the United States, Germany, and Japan have shown a long-term trend of growing support for change, that is, a movement away from traditional gender roles, especially among members of the younger generation (Thornton 1989; Zulehner and Volz 1998; Mohwald 2002).

There is, however, also significant evidence of men's and boys' resistance to change in gender relations. The survey research reveals substantial levels of doubt and opposition, especially among older men. Research on workplaces and on corporate management has documented many cases where men maintain an organizational culture that is heavily masculinized and unwelcoming to women. In some cases there is active opposition to gender-equality measures or quiet undermining of them (Cockburn 1991; Collinson and Hearn 1996). Research on schools has also found cases where boys assert control of informal social life and direct hostility against girls and against boys perceived as being different. The status quo can be defended even in the details of classroom life, for instance, when a particular group of boys used misogynist language to resist study of a poem that questioned Australian gender stereotypes (Kenworthy 1994; Holland et al. 1998).

Some men accept change in principle but in practice still act in ways that sustain men's dominance of the public sphere and assign domestic labor and child care to women. In strongly gender segregated societies, it may be difficult for men to recognize alternatives or to understand women's experiences (Kandiyoti 1994; Fuller 2001; Meuser 2003). Another type of opposition to reform, more common among men in business and government, rejects gender-equality measures because it rejects all government action in support of equality, in favor of the unfettered action of the market.

The reasons for men's resistance include the patriarchal dividend discussed above and threats to identity that occur with change. If social definitions of masculinity include being the breadwinner and being "strong," then men may be offended by women's professional progress because it makes men seem less worthy of respect. Resistance may also reflect ideological defense of male supremacy. Research on domestic violence suggests that male batterers often hold very conservative views of women's role in the family (Ptacek 1988). In many parts of the world, there exist ideologies that justify men's supremacy on grounds of religion, biology, cultural tradition, or organizational mission (e.g., in the military). It is a mistake to regard these ideas as simply outmoded. They may be actively modernized and renewed.

GROUNDS FOR OPTIMISM: CAPACITIES FOR EQUALITY AND REASONS FOR CHANGE

The public debates about men and boys have often been inconclusive. But they have gone a long way, together with the research, to shatter one widespread belief that has hindered gender reform. This obstacle is the belief that men cannot change their ways, that "boys will be boys," that rape, war, sexism, domestic violence, aggression, and self-centeredness are natural to men.

We now have many documented examples of the diversity of masculinities and of men's and boys' capacity for equality. For instance, life-history research in Chile has shown that there is no unitary Chilean masculinity, despite the cultural homogeneity of the country. While a hegemonic model is widely diffused across social strata, there are many men who depart from it, and there is significant discontent with traditional roles (Valdés and Olavarriá 1998). Though groups of boys in schools often have a dominant or hegemonic pattern of masculinity, there are usually also other patterns present, some of which involve more equal and respectful relations with girls.

Research in Britain, for instance, shows how boys encounter and explore alternative models of masculinity as they grow up (Mac an Ghaill 1994; O'Donnell and Sharpe 2000). Psychological and educational research shows personal flexibility in the face of gender stereotypes. Men and boys can vary, or strategically use, conventional definitions of masculinity. It is even possible to teach boys (and girls) how to do this in school, as experiments in Australian classrooms have shown (Davies 1993; Wetherell and Edley 1999).

Changes have occurred in men's practices within certain families, where there has been a conscious shift toward more equal sharing of housework and child care. The sociologist Barbara J. Risman (1998), who has documented such cases in one region of the United States, calls them "fair families." It is clear from her research that the change has required a challenge to traditional models of masculinity. In the Shanghai region of China, there is an established local tradition of relative gender equality, and men are demonstrably willing to be involved in domestic work. Research by Da Wei Wei (Da 2004) shows this tradition persisting among Shanghai men even after migration to another country.

Perhaps the most extensive social action involving men in gender change has occurred in Scandinavia. This includes provisions for paternity leave that have had high rates of take-up, among the most dramatic of all demonstrations of men's willingness to change gender practices. Øystein Holter sums up the research and practical experience: "The Nordic 'experiment' has shown that a majority of men can change their practice when circumstances are favorable. . . . When reforms or support policies are well-designed and targeted towards an ongoing cultural

process of change, men's active support for gender-equal status increases" (1997, 126). Many groups of men, it is clear, have a capacity for equality and for gender change. But what reasons for change are men likely to see?

Early statements often assumed that men had the same interest as women in escaping from restrictive sex roles (e.g., Palme 1972). Later experience has not confirmed this view. Yet men and boys often do have substantial reasons to support change, which can readily be listed.

First, men are not isolated individuals. Men and boys live in social relationships, many with women and girls: wives, partners, mothers, aunts, daughters, nieces, friends, classmates, workmates, professional colleagues, neighbors, and so on. The quality of every man's life depends to a large extent on the quality of those relationships. We may therefore speak of men's relational interests in gender equality. For instance, very large numbers of men are fathers, and about half of their children are girls. Some men are sole parents and are then deeply involved in caregiving—an important demonstration of men's capacity for care (Risman 1986). Even in intact partnerships with women, many men have close relationships with their children, and psychological research shows the importance of these relationships (Kindler 2002). In several parts of the world, young men are exploring more engaged patterns of fatherhood (Olavarría 2001). To make sure that daughters grow up in a world that offers young women security, freedom, and opportunities to fulfill their talents is a powerful reason for many men to support gender equality.

Second, men may wish to avoid the toxic effects that the gender order has for them. James Harrison long ago issued a "Warning: The Male Sex Role May Be Dangerous to Your Health" (1978). Since then health research has documented specific problems for men and boys. Among them are premature death from accident, homicide, and suicide; occupational injury; higher levels of drug abuse, especially of alcohol and tobacco; and in some countries at least, a relative unwillingness by men to seek medical help when it is needed. Attempts to assert a tough and dominant masculinity sustain some of these patterns (Sabo and Gordon 1995; Hurrelmann and Kolip 2002).

Social and economic pressures on men to compete in the workplace, to increase their hours of paid work, and sometimes to take second jobs are among the most powerful constraints on gender reform. Desire for a better balance between work and life is widespread among employed men. On the other hand, where unemployment is high the lack of a paid job can be a damaging pressure on men who have grown up with the expectation of being breadwinners. This is, for instance, an important gender issue in post-Apartheid South Africa. Opening alternative economic paths and moving toward what German discussions have called "multioptional masculinities" may do much to improve men's well-being (Widersprüche 1998; Morrell 2001a).

Third, men may support gender change because they see its relevance to the well-being of the community they live in. In situations of mass poverty and underemployment, for instance in cities in developing countries, flexibility in the gender division of labor may be crucial to a household that requires women's earnings as well as men's. Reducing the rigidity of masculinities may also yield benefits in security. Civil and international violence is strongly associated with dominating patterns of masculinity and with marked gender inequality in the state. Movement away from these patterns makes it easier for men to adopt historically "feminine" styles of nonviolent negotiation and conflict resolution (Zalewski and Parpart 1998; Breines, Connell, and Eide 2000; Cockburn 2003). This may also reduce the toxic effects of policing and incarceration (Sabo, Kupers, and London 2001).

Finally, men may support gender reform because gender equality follows from their political or ethical principles. These may be religious, socialist, or broad democratic beliefs. Mill argued a case based on classical liberal principles a century and a half ago, and the idea of equal human rights still has purchase among large groups of men.

GROUNDS FOR PESSIMISM: THE SHAPE OF MASCULINITY POLITICS

The diversity among men and masculinities is reflected in a diversity of men's movements in the developed countries. A study of the United States found multiple movements, with different agendas for the remaking of masculinity. They operated on the varying terrains of gender equality, men's rights, and ethnic or religious identities (Messner 1997). There is no unified political position for men and no authoritative representative of men's interests.

Men's movements specifically concerned with gender equality exist in a number of countries. A well-known example is the White Ribbon Campaign, dedicated to mobilizing public opinion and educating men and boys for the prevention of men's violence against women. Originating in Canada, in response to the massacre of women in Montreal in 1989, the White Ribbon Campaign achieved very high visibility in that country, with support from political and community leaders and considerable outreach in schools and mass media. More recently, it has spread to other countries. Groups concerned with violence prevention have appeared in other countries, such as Men against Sexual Assault in Australia and Men Overcoming Violence (MOVE) in the United States. These have not achieved the visibility of the White Ribbon Campaign but have built up a valuable body of knowledge about the successes and difficulties of organizing among men (Lichterman 1989; Pease 1997; Kaufman 1999).

The most extensive experience of any group of men organizing around issues of gender and sexual politics is that of homosexual men, in antidiscrimination campaigns, the gay liberation movement, and community responses to the HIV/AIDS pandemic. Gay men have pioneered in areas such as community care for the sick, community education for responsible sexual practices, representation in the public sector, and overcoming social exclusion, which are important for all groups of men concerned with gender equality (Kippax et al. 1993; Altman 1994).

Explicit backlash movements also exist but have not generally had a great deal of influence. Men mobilizing as men to oppose women tend to be seen as cranks or fanatics. They constantly exaggerate women's power. And by defining men's interests in opposition to women's, they get into cultural difficulties, since they have to violate a main tenet of modern patriarchal ideology—the idea that "opposites attract" and that men's and women's needs, interests, and choices are complementary.

Much more important for the defense of gender inequality are movements in which men's interests are a side effect—nationalist, ethnic, religious, and economic movements. Of these, the most influential on a world scale is contemporary neoliberalism—the political and cultural promotion of free-market principles and individualism and the rejection of state control.

Neoliberalism is in principle gender neutral. The "individual" has no gender, and the market delivers advantage to the smartest entrepreneur, not to men or women as such. But neoliberalism does not pursue social justice in relation to gender. In Eastern Europe, the restoration of capitalism and the arrival of neoliberal politics have been followed by a sharp deterioration in the position of women. In rich Western countries, neoliberalism from the 1980s on has attacked the welfare state, on which far more women than men depend; supported deregulation of labor markets, resulting in increased casualization of women workers; shrunk public sector employment, the sector of the economy where women predominate; lowered rates of personal taxation, the main basis of tax transfers to women; and squeezed public education, the key pathway to labor market advancement for women. However, the same period saw an expansion of the human-rights agenda, which is, on the whole, an asset for gender equality.

The contemporary version of neoliberalism, known as neoconservatism in the United States, also has some gender complexities. George W. Bush was the first U.S. president to place a woman in the very heart of the state security apparatus, as national security adviser to the president. And some of the regime's actions,

such as the attack on the Taliban regime in Afghanistan, were defended as a means of emancipating women.

Yet neoconservatism and state power in the United States and its satellites such as Australia remain overwhelmingly the province of men—indeed, men of a particular character: power oriented and ruthless, restrained by little more than calculations of likely opposition. There has been a sharp remasculinization of political rhetoric and a turn to the use of force as a primary instrument in policy. The human rights discourse is muted and sometimes completely abandoned (as in the U.S. prison camp for Muslim captives at Guantanamo Bay and the Australian prison camps for refugees in the central desert and Pacific islands).

Neoliberalism can function as a form of masculinity politics largely because of the powerful role of the state in the gender order. The state constitutes gender relations in multiple ways, and all of its gender policies affect men. Many mainstream policies (e.g., in economic and security affairs) are substantially about men without acknowledging this fact (Nagel 1998; O'Connor, Orloff, and Shaver 1999; Connell 2003b).

This points to a realm of institutional politics where men's and women's interests are very much at stake, without the publicity created by social movements. Public-sector agencies (Jensen 1998; Mackay and Bilton 2000; Schofield, forthcoming), private-sector corporations (Marchand and Runyan 2000; Hearn and Parkin 2001), and unions (Corman et al. 1993; Franzway 2001) are all sites of masculinized power and struggles for gender equality. In each of these sites, some men can be found with a commitment to gender equality, but in each case that is an embattled position. For gender-equality outcomes, it is important to have support from men in the top organizational levels, but this is not often reliably forthcoming.

One reason for the difficulty in expanding men's opposition to sexism is the role of highly conservative men as cultural authorities and managers. Major religious organizations, in Christianity, Islam, and Buddhism, are controlled by men who sometimes completely exclude women, and these organizations have often been used to oppose the emancipation of women. Transnational media organizations such as Rupert Murdoch's conglomerate are equally active in promoting conservative gender ideology.

A specific address to men is found in the growing institutional, media, and business complex of commercial sports. With its overwhelming focus on male athletes; its celebration of force, domination, and competitive success; its valorization of male commentators and executives; and its marginalization and frequent ridicule of women, the sports/business complex has become an increasingly important site for representing and defining gender. This is not traditional patriarchy. It is something new, welding exemplary bodies to entrepreneurial culture. Michael Messner (2002), one of the leading analysts of contemporary sports, formulates the effect well by saying that commercial sports define the renewed centrality of men and of a particular version of masculinity.

On a world scale, explicit backlash movements are of limited importance, but very large numbers of men are nevertheless engaged in preserving gender inequality. Patriarchy is defended diffusely. There is support for change from equally large numbers of men, but it is an uphill battle to articulate that support. That is the political context with which new gender-equality initiatives have to deal.

WAYS FORWARD: TOWARD A GLOBAL FRAMEWORK

Inviting men to end men's privileges, and to remake masculinities to sustain gender equality, strikes many people as a strange or utopian project. Yet this project is already under way. Many men around the world are engaged in gender reforms, for the good reasons discussed above.

The diversity of masculinities complicates the process but is also an important asset. As this diversity becomes better known, men and boys can more easily see a range of possibilities for their own lives, and both men and women are less likely to think of gender inequality as

unchangeable. It also becomes possible to identify specific groups of men who might engage in alliances for change.

The international policy documents discussed above rely on the concept of an alliance between men and women for achieving equality. Since the growth of an autonomous women's movement, the main impetus for reform has been located in women's groups. Some groups within the women's movement, especially those concerned with men's violence, are reluctant to work with men or are deeply skeptical of men's willingness to change. Other feminists argue that alliances between women and men are possible, even crucial. In some social movements, for instance, environmentalism, there is a strong ideology of gender equality and a favorable environment for men to support gender change (Connell 1995; Segal 1997).

In local and central government, practical alliances between women and men have been important in achieving equal-opportunity measures and other gender-equality reforms. Even in the field of men's violence against women, there has been cooperation between women's groups and men's groups, for instance, in prevention work. This cooperation can be an inspiration to grassroots workers and a powerful demonstration of women and men's common interest in a peaceful and equal society (Pease 1997; Schofield, forthcoming). The concept of alliance is itself important, in preserving autonomy for women's groups, in preempting a tendency for any one group to speak for others, and in defining a political role for men that has some dignity and might attract widespread support.

Given the spectrum of masculinity politics, we cannot expect worldwide consensus for gender equality. What is possible is that support for gender equality might become hegemonic among men. In that case it would be groups supporting equality that provide the agenda for public discussion about men's lives and patterns of masculinity.

There is already a broad cultural shift toward a historical consciousness about gender, an awareness that gender customs came into existence at specific moments in time and can always be transformed by social action (Connell 1995).

What is needed now is a widespread sense of agency among men, a sense that this transformation is something they can actually share in as a practical proposition. This is precisely what was presupposed in the "joint responsibility" of men invoked by the General Assembly declaration of the year 2000.[1]

From this point of view, the recent meeting of the UN Commission on the Status of Women (CSW) is profoundly interesting. The CSW is one of the oldest of UN agencies, dating from the 1940s. Effectively a standing committee of the General Assembly, it meets annually, and its current practice is to consider two main themes at each meeting. For the 2004 meeting, one of the defined themes was "the role of men and boys in achieving gender equality." The section of the UN secretariat that supports the CSW, the Division for the Advancement of Women, undertook background work. The division held, in June–July 2003, a worldwide online seminar on the role of men and boys, and in October 2003 it convened an international expert group meeting in Brasilia on the topic.

At the CSW meetings, several processes occur and (it is to be hoped) interact. There is a presentation of the division's background work, and delegations of the forty-five current member countries, UN agencies, and many of the nongovernmental organizations (NGOs) attending make initial statements. There is a busy schedule of side events, mainly organized by NGOs but some conducted by delegations or UN agencies, ranging from strategy debates to practical workshops. And there is a diplomatic process in which the official delegations negotiate over a draft document in the light of discussions in the CSW and their governments' stances on gender issues.

This is a politicized process, inevitably, and it can break down. In 2003 the CSW discussion on the issue of violence against women reached deadlock. In 2004 it was clear that some participating NGOs were not happy with the focus on men and boys, some holding to a discourse representing men exclusively as perpetrators of violence. Over the two weeks of negotiations, however, the delegations did reach consensus on a statement of "Agreed Conclusions."

Balancing a reaffirmation of commitment to women's equality with a recognition of men's and boys' potential for action, this document makes specific recommendations across a spectrum of policy fields, including education, parenthood, media, the labor market, sexuality, violence, and conflict prevention. These proposals have no force in international law—the document is essentially a set of recommendations to governments and other organizations. Nevertheless, it is the first international agreement of its kind, treating men systematically as agents in gender-equality processes, and it creates a standard for future gender-equality discussions. Most important, the CSW's "Agreed Conclusions" change the logic of the representation of men in gender policy. So far as the international discourse of gender-equality policy is concerned, this document begins the substantive presentation of gender equality as a positive project for men.

Here the UN process connects with the social and cultural possibilities that have emerged from the last three decades of gender politics among men. Gender equality is an undertaking for men that can be creative and joyful. It is a project that realizes high principles of social justice, produces better lives for the women whom men care about, and will produce better lives for the majority of men in the long run. This can and should be a project that generates energy, that finds expression in everyday life and the arts as well as in formal policies, and that can illuminate all aspects of men's lives.

NOTE

1. Twenty-third special session, UN General Assembly, "Political Declaration," par. 6.

REFERENCES

Altman, Dennis. 1994. *Power and Community: Organizational and Cultural Responses to AIDS.* London: Taylor & Francis.

———. 2001. *Global Sex.* Chicago: University of Chicago Press.

Arilha, Margareth, Sandra G. Unbehaum Ridenti, and Benedito Medrado, eds. 1998. *Homens e Masculinidades: Outras Palavras.* Sao Paulo: ECOS/Editora 34.

Bly, Robert. 1990. *Iron John: A Book about Men.* Reading, MA: Addison-Wesley.

Brandes, Holger, and Hermann Bullinger, eds. 1996. *Handbuch Männerarbeit.* Weinheim, Germany: Psychologic Verlags Union.

Breines, Ingeborg, Robert Connell, and Ingrid Eide, eds. 2000. *Male Roles, Masculinities and Violence: A Culture of Peace Perspective.* Paris: UNESCO.

Bulbeck, Chilla. 1988. *One World Women's Movement.* London: Pluto.

———. 1998. *Re-orienting Western Feminisms: Women's Diversity in a Postcolonial World.* Cambridge: Cambridge University Press.

Cockburn, Cynthia. 1991. *In the Way of Women: Men's Resistance to Sex Equality in Organizations.* Ithaca, NY: ILR Press.

———. 2003. *The Line: Women, Partition and the Gender Order in Cyprus.* London: Zed.

Cohen, Jon. 1991. "NOMAS: Challenging Male Supremacy." *Changing Men* (Winter/Spring): 45–46.

Collinson, David L., and Jeff Hearn, eds. 1996. *Men as Managers, Managers as Men: Critical Perspectives on Men, Masculinities and Managements.* London: Sage.

Connell, R. W. 1995. *Masculinities.* Berkeley: University of California Press.

———. 2000. *The Men and the Boys.* Sydney: Allen & Unwin Australia.

———. 2002. *Gender.* Cambridge: Polity.

———. 2003a. "Masculinities, Change and Conflict in Global Society: Thinking about the Future of Men's Studies." *Journal of Men's Studies* 11(3): 249–66.

———. 2003b. "Men, Gender and the State." In *Among Men: Moulding Masculinities,* ed. Søren Ervø and Thomas Johansson, 15–28. Aldershot: Ashgate.

———. 2003c. "Scrambling in the Ruins of Patriarchy: Neo-liberalism and Men's Divided Interests in Gender Change." In *Gender—from Costs to Benefits,* ed. Ursula Pasero, 58–69. Wiesbaden: Westdeutscher.

Corman, June, Meg Luxton, D. W. Livingstone, and Wally Seccombe. 1993. *Recasting Steel Labour: The Stelco Story.* Halifax: Fernwood.

Da Wei Wei. 2004. "A Regional Tradition of Gender Equity: Shanghai Men in Sydney." *Journal of Men's Studies* 12(2): 133–49.

Davies, Bronwyn. 1993. *Shards of Glass: Children Reading and Writing beyond Gender Identities.* Sydney: Allen & Unwin Australia.

Denborough, David. 1996. "Step by Step: Developing Respectful and Effective Ways of Working with Young Men to Reduce Violence." In *Men's Ways of Being,* ed. Chris McLean, Maggie Carey, and Cheryl White, 91–115. Boulder, CO: Westview.

Eisenstein, Hester. 1991. *Gender Shock: Practising Feminism on Two Continents.* Sydney: Allen & Unwin Australia.

Farrell, Warren. 1993. *The Myth of Male Power: Why Men Are the Disposable Sex.* New York: Simon & Schuster.

Franzway, Suzanne. 2001. *Sexual Politics and Greedy Institutions.* Sydney: Pluto.

Fuller, Norma. 2001. "The Social Constitution of Gender Identity among Peruvian Men." *Men and Masculinities* 3(3): 316–31.

Ghoussoub, Mai. 2000. "Chewing Gum, Insatiable Women and Foreign Enemies: Male Fears and the Arab Media." In *Imagined Masculinities: Male Identity and Culture in the Middle East,* ed. Mai Ghoussoub and Emma Sinclair-Webb, 227–35. London: Saqi.

Gierycz, Dorota. 1999. "Women in Decision-Making: Can We Change the Status Quo?" In *Towards a Women's Agenda for a Culture of Peace,* ed. Ingeborg Breines, Dorota Gierycz, and Betty A. Reardon, 19–30. Paris: UNESCO.

Godenzi, Alberto. 2000. "Determinants of Culture: Men and Economic Power." In Breines, Connell, and Eide 2000, 35–51. Paris: UNESCO.

Gutmann, Matthew C. 2002. *The Romance of Democracy: Compliant Defiance in Contemporary Mexico.* Berkeley: University of California Press.

Hagemann-White, Carol. 1992. *Strategien gegen Gewalt im Geschlechterverhältnis: Bestandsanalyse und Perspektiven.* Pfaffenweiler, Ger.: Centaurus.

Harrison, James. 1978. "Warning: The Male Sex Role May Be Dangerous to Your Health." *Journal of Social Issues* 34(1): 65–86.

Haseler, Stephen. 2000. *The Super-Rich: The Unjust New World of Global Capitalism.* London: Macmillan.

Hearn, Jeff. 1998. *The Violences of Men: How Men Talk about and How Agencies Respond to Men's Violence to Women.* Thousand Oaks, CA: Sage.

Hearn, Jeff, and Wendy Parkin. 2001. *Gender, Sexuality, and Violence in Organizations: The Unspoken of Organization Violations.* Thousand Oaks, CA: Sage.

Hearn, Jeff, Keith Pringle, Ursula Müller, Elzbeieta Oleksy, Emmi Lattu, Janna Chernova, Harry Ferguson, et al. 2002. "Critical Studies on Men in Ten European Countries: (1) The State of Academic Research." *Men and Masculinities* 4(4): 380–408.

Holland, Janet, Caroline Ramazanoglu, Sue Sharpe, and Rachel Thomson. 1998. *The Male in the Head: Young People, Heterosexuality and Power.* London: Tufnell.

Holter, Øystein Gullvåg. 1997. *Gender, Patriarchy and Capitalism: A Social Forms Analysis.* Oslo: Work Research Institute.

———. 2003. *Can Men Do It? Men and Gender Equality—the Nordic Experience.* Copenhagen: Nordic Council of Ministers.

Hooper, Charlotte. 2001. *Manly States: Masculinities, International Relations, and Gender Politics.* New York: Columbia University Press.

Hurrelmann, Klaus, and Petra Kolip, eds. 2002. *Geschlecht, Gesundheit und Krankheit: Männer und Frauen im Vergleich.* Bern: Hans Huber.

Ibsen, Henrik. (1923) 1995. *A Doll's House.* Cambridge: Cambridge University Press.

Inter-Parliamentary Union. 2003. "Women in National Parliaments: Situation at 30 December 2003." Available online at http://www.ipu.org/wmn–e/world.htm.

Ito, Kimio. 1992. "Cultural Change and Gender Identity Trends in the 1970s and 1980s." *International Journal of Japanese Sociology* 1(1): 79–98.

Jensen, Hanne Naxø. 1998. "Gender as the Dynamo: When Public Organizations Have to Change." In *Is There a Nordic Feminism? Nordic Feminist Thought on Culture and Society,* ed. Drude von der Fehr, Bente Rosenberg, and Anna G. Jóasdóttir, 160–75. London: UCL Press.

Kandiyoti, Deniz. 1994. "The Paradoxes of Masculinity: Some Thoughts on Segregated Societies." In *Dislocating Masculinity: Comparative Ethnographies,* ed. Andrea Cornwall and Nancy Lindisfarne, 197–213. London: Routledge.

Kaufman, Michael. 1993. *Cracking the Armour: Power, Pain and the Lives of Men.* Toronto: Viking.

———, ed. 1999. "Men and Violence." Special issue, *International Association for Studies of Men Newsletter* 6, no. 2.

Kenway, Jane, ed. 1997. *Will Boys Be Boys? Boys' Education in the Context of Gender Reform.* Canberra: Australian Curriculum Studies Association.

Kenworthy, Colin. 1994. "'We want to resist your resistant readings': Masculinity and Discourse in the English Classroom." *Interpretations* 27(2): 74–95.

Kimmel, Michael S., Jeff Hearn, and R. W. Connell, eds. 2005. *Handbook of Studies on Men and Masculinities.* Thousand Oaks, CA: Sage.

Kimmel, Michael S., and Thomas E. Mosmiller. 1992. *Against the Tide: Pro-feminist Men in the United States, 1776–1990: A Documentary History.* Boston: Beacon.

Kindler, Heinz. 2002. *Väter und Kinder.* Weinheim, Germany: Juventa.

Kippax, Susan, R. W. Connell, G. W. Dowsett, and June Crawford. 1993. *Sustaining Safe Sex: Gay Communities Respond to AIDS.* London: Falmer.

Kupers, Terry. 1993. *Revisioning Men's Lives: Gender, Intimacy, and Power.* New York: Guilford.

Law, Robin, Hugh Campbell, and John Dolan, eds. 1999. *Masculinities in Aotearo/New Zealand.* Palmerston North, NZ: Dunmore.

Lerner, Susana, ed. 1998. *Varones, sexualidad y reproducción: Diversas perspectivas teórico-metodológicas y hallazgos de investigación.* El Colegio de México, México.

Lichterman, Paul. 1989. "Making a Politics of Masculinity." *Comparative Social Research* 11:185–208.

Lingard, Bob. 2003. "Where to in Gender Policy in Education after Recuperative Masculinity Politics?" *International Journal of Inclusive Education* 7(1): 33–56.

Lyra, Jorge, and Benedito Medrado. 2001. "Constructing an Adolescent Father in Brazil." Paper presented at the Third International Fatherhood Conference, Atlanta, May 28–30.

Mac an Ghaill, Mairtin. 1994. *The Making of Men: Masculinities, Sexualities and Schooling.* Buckingham: Open University Press.

Mackay, Fiona, and Kate Bilton. 2000. *Learning from Experience: Lessons in Mainstreaming Equal Opportunities.* Edinburgh: Governance of Scotland Forum.

Marchand, Marianne H., and Anne Sisson Runyan, eds. 2000. *Gender and Global Restructuring: Sightings, Sites and Resistances.* London: Routledge.

McMahon, Anthony. 1999. *Taking Care of Men: Sexual Politics in the Public Mind.* Cambridge: Cambridge University Press.

Menzu Senta (Men's Center Japan). 1997. *Otokotachi no watashisagashi* (How are men seeking their new selves?). Kyoto: Kamogawa.

Messner, Michael A. 1997. *The Politics of Masculinities: Men in Movements.* Thousand Oaks, CA: Sage.

———. 2002. *Taking the Field: Women, Men and Sports.* Minneapolis: University of Minnesota Press.

Metz-Göckel, Sigrid, and Ursula Müller. 1985. *Der Mann: Die Brigitte–Studie.* Hamburg: Beltz.

Meuser, Michael. 2003. "Modernized Masculinities? Continuities, Challenges, and Changes in Men's Lives." In *Among Men: Moulding Masculinities,* vol. 1, ed. Søren Ervø and Thomas Johansson, 127–48. Aldershot: Ashgate.

Mill, John Stuart. 1912. "The Subjection of Women." In his *On Liberty; Representative Government; The Subjugation of Women: Three Essays,* 427–548. London: Oxford University Press.

Mohwald, Ulrich. 2002. *Changing Attitudes towards Gender Equality in Japan and Germany.* Munich: Iudicium.

Moodie, T. Dunbar. 1994. *Going for Gold: Men, Mines and Migration.* Johannesburg: Witwatersrand University Press.

Morrell, Robert. 1998. "Of Boys and Men: Masculinity and Gender in Southern African Studies." *Journal of Southern African Studies* 24(4): 605–30.

———, ed. 2001a. *Changing Men in Southern Africa.* Pietermaritzburg, S.A.: University of Natal Press.

———. 2001b. *From Boys to Gentlemen: Settler Masculinity in Colonial Natal, 1880–1920.* Pretoria: University of South Africa Press.

Nagel, Joane. 1998. "Masculinity and Nationalism: Gender and Sexuality in the Making of Nations." *Ethnic and Racial Studies* 21(2): 242–69.

Nordic Council of Ministers. 1997. *Nordic Action Plan for Men and Gender Equality, 1997–2000.* Copenhagen: Nordic Council of Ministers.

O'Connor, Julia S., Ann Shola Orloff, and Sheila Shaver. 1999. *States, Markets, Families: Gender, Liberalism and Social Policy in Australia, Canada, Great Britain, and the United States.* Cambridge: Cambridge University Press.

O'Donnell, Mike, and Sue Sharpe. 2000. *Uncertain Masculinities: Youth, Ethnicity and Class in Contemporary Britain.* London: Routledge.

Olavarría, José. 2001. *Y todos querian ser (buenos) padres: Varones de Santiago de Chile en conflicto.* Santiago: FLACSO-Chile.

Palme, Olof. 1972. "The Emancipation of Man." *Journal of Social Issues* 28(2): 237–46.

Peacock, Dean. 2003. "Building on a Legacy of Social Justice Activism: Enlisting Men as Gender Justice Activists in South Africa." *Men and Masculinities* 5(3): 325–28.

Pease, Bob. 1997. *Men and Sexual Politics: Towards a Profeminist Practice.* Adelaide: Dulwich Centre.

Pease, Bob, and Keith Pringle, eds. 2001. *A Man's World? Changing Men's Practices in a Globalised World.* London: Zed.

Ptacek, James. 1988. "Why Do Men Batter Their Wives?" In *Feminist Perspectives on Wife Abuse,* ed. Kersti Yllö and Michele Bograd, 133–57. Newbury Park, CA: Sage.

Reinicke, Kenneth. 2002. *Den Hele Mand: Manderollen i forandring.* Aarhus, Denmark: Schønberg.

Risman, Barbara J. 1986. "Can Men 'Mother'? Life as a Single Father." *Family Relations* 35(1): 95–102.

———. 1998. *Gender Vertigo: American Families in Transition.* New Haven, CT: Yale University Press.

Roberson, James E., and Nobue Suzuki, eds. 2003. *Men and Masculinities in Contemporary Japan: Dislocating the Salaryman Doxa.* London: Routledge.

Roy, Rahul. 2003. "Exploring Masculinities—a Travelling Seminar." Unpublished manuscript.

Sabo, Donald, and David Frederick Gordon, eds. 1995. *Men's Health and Illness: Gender, Power, and the Body.* Thousand Oaks, CA: Sage.

Sabo, Donald, Terry A. Kupers, and Willie London, eds. 2001. *Prison Masculinities.* Philadelphia: Temple University Press.

Schofield, Toni. 2004. *Boutique Health? Gender and Equity in Health Policy.* Sydney: Australian Health Policy Institute.

———. Forthcoming. "Gender Regimes in Public Policy Making." Unpublished manuscript, Faculty of Health Sciences, University of Sydney.

Schwalbe, Michael. 1996. *Unlocking the Iron Cage: The Men's Movement, Gender, Politics, and American Culture.* New York: Oxford University Press.

Segal, Lynne. 1997. *Slow Motion: Changing Masculinities, Changing Men.* 2nd ed. London: Virago.

Seidler, Victor T., ed. 1991. *The Achilles Heel Reader: Men, Sexual Politics and Socialism.* London: Routledge.

Sinclair-Webb, Emma. 2000. "'Our bülent is now a commando': Military Service and Manhood in Turkey." In *Imagined Masculinities: Male Identity and Culture in the Modern Middle East,* ed. Mai Ghoussoub and Emma Sinclair-Webb, 65–92. London: Saqi.

Sommers, Christina Hoff. 2000. *The War against Boys: How Misguided Feminism Is Harming Our Young Men.* New York: Simon & Schuster.

Taga, Futoshi. 2001. *Dansei no Jendâ Keisei: "Otoko-Rashisa" no Yuragi no Naka de* (The gender formation of men: Uncertain masculinity). Tokyo: Tôyôkan Shuppan-sha.

Thornton, Arland. 1989. "Changing Attitudes toward Family Issues in the United States." *Journal of Marriage and the Family 51*(4): 873–93.

United Nations. 1958. *Universal Declaration of Human Rights.* New York: Department of Public Information, United Nations.

———. (1979) 1989. *Convention on the Elimination of All Forms of Discrimination against Women.* New York: Department of Public Information, United Nations.

———. 2001. *Beijing Declaration and Platform for Action, with the Beijing +5 Political Declaration and Outcome Document.* New York: Department of Public Information, United Nations.

United Nations Commission on the Status of Women. 2004. *The Role of Men and Boys in Achieving Gender Equality: Agreed Conclusions.* Available online at http://www.un.org/womenwatch/daw/csw/csw48/ac-men-auv.pdf.

United Nations Development Program (UNDP). 2003. *Human Development Report 2003.* New York: UNDP and Oxford University Press.

Valdés, Teresa, and José Olavarría. 1998. "Ser hombre en Santiago de Chile: A pesar de todo, un mismo modelo." In their *Masculinidades y equidad de género en América Latina,* 12–36. Santiago: FLACSO/UNFPA.

Walby, Sylvia. 1997. *Gender Transformations.* London: Routledge.

Wetherell, Margaret, and Nigel Edley. 1999. "Negotiating Hegemonic Masculinity: Imaginary Positions and Psycho-Discursive Practices." *Feminism and Psychology 9*(3): 335–56.

White, Sara C. 2000. "Did the Earth Move? The Hazards of Bringing Men and Masculinities into Gender and Development." *IDS Bulletin 31*(2): 33–41.

Widersprüche. 1998. "Multioptionale Männlichkeiten?" Special issue, no. 67.

Zalewski, Marysia, and Jane Parpart, eds. 1998. *The "Man" Question in International Relations.* Boulder, CO: Westview.

Zingoni, Eduardo Liendro. 1998. "Masculinidades y violencia desde un programa de accíon en México." In *Masculinidades y equidad de género en America Latina,* ed. Teresa Valdés and José Olavarría, 130–36. Santiago: FLACSO/UNFPA.

Zulehner, Paul M., and Rainer Volz. 1998. *Männer im Aufbruch: Wie Deutschlands Männer sich Selbst und wie Frauen Sie Sehen.* Ostfildern, Ger.: Schwabenverlag.

❦ Topics for Further Examination ❧

- Look up research on men who participated in the first and second waves of feminism in the United States. Find and explore websites devoted to profeminist men's organizations in different countries around the world.
- Browse websites on women's organizations and gender issues such as Institute for Women's Policy Research (http://www.iwpr.org), Feminist Majority Foundation (http://www.feminist.org), WomenWatch (http://www.un.org/womenwatch/), and Women's International League for Peace and Freedom (http://www.wilpf.org).
- Locate articles on the impact of globalization on human rights. Go to the following websites: Amnesty International (www.amnesty.org/) and United Nations: Human Rights (www.un.org/rights/).

EPILOGUE

Possibilities

This book began with the metaphor of the kaleidoscope to aid in understanding the complex and dynamic nature of gender. Viewed kaleidoscopically, gender is not static. Gender patterns are social constructions, reconstructed as they intersect with multiple and changing social prisms such as race, ethnicity, culture, class, and sexuality. In concluding, we want to emphasize the dynamic nature of gender, underscoring the possibilities the future holds. No one can predict the future; therefore, we will illustrate changes in the institution of gender using stories of how changing gender patterns shaped our lives and the lives of many other people.

Reflecting on the course of our lives, we are struck by the depth and breadth of changes that have occurred in American culture, institutions, and social relationships since we were young girls in the 1950s. Many of these changes have been positive; patterns of oppression were reduced and the opportunity and power to participate meaningfully in America's social institutions were extended to more people. In the past 50 years, we have benefited from, and participated in, bringing about changes in the genderscape.

The cultural climate of the 1950s forged our early lives. Though romanticized in film and TV, that decade was in fact a deeply troubled time of blatant racism, sexism, and other forms of oppression. Civil rights had not yet been extended to people of color, women's rights were negligible, gay and lesbian Americans were largely closeted, poverty was ignored, political dissent was strongly discouraged, child abuse went unacknowledged or hidden, and an atomic war seemed ready to break out at any moment.

We didn't learn about the women's movement then, even though there had been significant organized social movements for gender change beginning almost 100 years before we were born, culminating in the right to vote in 1920. The second wave of feminism and subsequent women's movements began when we were very young, after World War II, inspired by books such as Simone de Beauvoir's *The Second Sex* (1952), first published in France in 1949 and Betty Friedan's *The Feminine Mystique* (1963). Although not widely recognized, the United Nations Charter of 1945 affirmed the equal rights of men and women and established the U.N. Commission on the Status of Women a few years later (Schneir, 1994). However, in many ways, women were still second-class citizens in the 1950s.

We grew up in families similar to those of many White Americans of the 1950s. Our parents held traditional views of proper roles for women and men. They tried to live up to those roles, and yet, like many, they often failed or fell short. They suffered with their failures in silence, behind the closed doors of the nuclear family of that era. For men and women, marriage and children came with the gender territory. Social sanctions in society maintained this territory. For example, people called women who didn't marry "old maids" pejoratively and looked at couples who didn't bear children suspiciously. Also, there were limited reproductive control options, and abortion, although widespread, was illegal. This left most women and many men with few options other than getting married and having children.

Jessie Bernard (1975) described men's and women's roles in White, middle-class families of that time as being destructive to adults and children alike. She spoke of "the work intoxicated father" and the "pathogenic mother" as the end result of the efforts to fulfill the cultural imperative for a traditional family. Bernard observed that middle-class, White family roles at that time were mostly stressful and unsatisfying. Men detached from their families as they struggled to earn enough for the household, while women shouldered the sole responsibility of raising perfect children and keeping a perfect home. Family and gender researchers (e.g., Bernard, 1972; Coontz, 1992, 1997; Rapp, 1982; Schwartz, 1994) found that this arrangement of distinct and separate roles did not foster full and loving relationships between men and women or parents and children. And, of course, by now you can guess that most people could not achieve this "perfect family."

However, television still reflected the image of the happy family behind the white picket fence, and for decades it stood as an ideal, even for those who failed to meet it. Marriages were supposed to be happy but often were not. Getting out of a conflict-ridden or abusive marriage was very difficult. There were divorces, but the courts granted these only if they decided there were "appropriate violations" of the marriage contract (Weitzman, 1985). As a result, many

marriages persisted, even when there was unbearable alienation, violence, and abuse.

Intensifying these struggles further, there was little recognition of domestic violence. Marital rape and rape in general were not taken seriously, legally or socially. For example, the police, when called to a domestic conflict, often ignored pleas of beaten or raped women, and the rules and procedures that guided police work made interventions almost meaningless. There was a great deal of resistance to changes in legislation relative to domestic violence and rape, including marital rape. The words of one U.S. Senator captured the general attitude at that time; he said, "If you can't rape your wife, who can you rape" (Russell, 1982). Thus, domestic violence and rape reforms took many years to implement.

As you can imagine, women in our mothers' cohort had few choices and opportunities. The "best" occupations most women could aspire to were limited to clerical or secretarial jobs, teaching, and nursing. Salaries were low, and women had a difficult time living independently, both financially and socially. There was no such legal concept as workplace sexual harassment, and equal pay for equal work was rarely considered. Married women who did work outside the home often had fragmented work lives, defined by their primary responsibility of caring for children and husbands.

The situation for White women was bad, but it was much worse for women of color and immigrant women. For example, most African American women worked outside the home but were confined to the lowest paying and most degrading jobs, such as domestic work. These jobs had even fewer protections against sexual harassment and workplace inequalities. Men of racial minority groups and immigrant men also endured considerable inequalities in the workplace, as well as in other domains of life.

Post–World War II saw a considerable increase in the number of people entering college; however, almost all new students were White men taking advantage of the G.I. Bill. Considerable gender segregation in higher education persisted throughout the 1950s, with many colleges and universities denying admittance to women and racial minorities. The proportion of women in higher education increased only slightly during the 1950s, from 31.6% in 1950 to 35.9% in 1959 (National Center for Education Statistics, 2005). And some of the most exclusive colleges and universities maintained gender-segregated spaces even after women were admitted. For example, although women were admitted to Harvard Law School in 1950, they were denied access to the only eating space at the law school until 1970 (Deckard, 1979). Harvard Law School even limited the days on which women could ask questions in classes (Deckard, 1979). Money was another resource denied to many women; there were few scholarships for females because administrators and faculty felt "men needed the money more" (Deckard, 1979, p. 130).

The decades of the 1960s and 1970s brought about the awakening of political consciousness and action by Americans from many walks of life. Early in this period, the civil rights movement resulted in the dismantling of many legal barriers to participation in American life for African Americans. In the 1960s, the second wave of feminism picked up steam, spawning several organized political movements around gender and race, ethnicity, nationality, and/or sexuality, as described in Chapter 10. These social movements focused attention on the social disadvantages faced by women and brought about considerable change, including greater legal, economic, political, educational, and familial equality. Other social movements emerged out of this culture of change: gay and lesbian rights, antiwar and peace, environmental, and children's rights movements.

We were fortunate to enter early adulthood during this time of positive social change. For example, Title IX (1972) opened up avenues in education previously closed to our mothers; attempts at pay equity made our labor somewhat more valuable than that of our mothers; the naming and litigation of sexual harassment, marital rape, and other forms of gender violence made

our lives somewhat safer than our mothers' lives; and the women's movement empowered us and helped us understand how we could contribute to a more just world. Our lives took us down different pathways, yet many of the same social change forces touched us deeply, and eventually our lives intersected.

Kay joined the ranks of one of the first waves of college-bound baby boomers in the mid-1960s. Her undergraduate years coincided with the civil rights movement, the height of the Vietnam War, the development of a strong political left, and the emergence of countercultural lifestyles. She found her intellectual passion in sociology, a home for her experimental self in the counterculture, and a political focus in the antiwar movement. With BA in hand, Kay entered the work world at the very moment the first of a series of economic recessions set in. She bounced from one unsatisfying, low-paying, female-type job to another and quickly found herself at an intellectual and emotional crossroads. Kay then chose a pathway that few women had gone down—graduate school.

In 1971, Kay joined the ranks of a rapidly growing number of women graduate students in departments of sociology across the United States. Although dominated by White men, this cohort contained more working-class White women and people of color than earlier generations. They moved through graduate school at the same time the second wave of feminism spawned organized movements for gender equality around the world. With these changes, Kay's consciousness expanded to embrace feminism. She took one of the first gender courses, sex roles, to be offered in any American institution of higher education. Feminism opened up a world of choices never before available to her. Empowered and exhilarated, Kay chose a nontraditional life course, as did many of the women in her graduate school cohort. Women postponed marriage and children. Others chose singlehood or cohabitating relationships. Still others chose child-free marriages. All pursued careers.

Of course, change is never smooth and even-handed. Although the women's movement was well under way during Kay's graduate school years, women students and professors had regular encounters with sexism both in and out of the classroom. Sexual harassment was built into the everyday educational experiences of women who pursued a PhD. Also, as the women of Kay's cohort entered the professional world of teaching and research, barriers to hiring, tenure, and promotion would prove to be part of their ongoing struggle for respect, security, and equality. The struggle for gender equality has continued in all domains of life in the United States, and although many barriers have been dismantled, sexism has taken on new, subtle, and covert forms that have proven difficult to target and eradicate. These subtle and covert patterns have emerged alongside global gender inequality as the center of the contemporary women's movement.

Joining the first wave of baby boomers, Kay retired from 32 years of college teaching in 2008. She marked that transition by setting off on solo journeys to various parts of the world. Retirement has opened up opportunities for Kay to reconnect with the political left and global feminist movements. It has also allowed her to develop new kinds of ties with professional associations, such as Sociologists for Women in Society and the American Sociological Association. Retirement has created space for Kay to pursue passions such as writing and traveling and to reflect carefully on her principles and practices.

But fair warning: Life is no nirvana for aging women in the United States (Calasanti, Slevin, & King, 2006). Kay's transition is also marked by the confluence of sexism and ageism in her life and the lives of similarly situated women. The experience of being "culturally disappeared" while at the same time observing aging men, especially those who are class privileged, experience enhanced status and value is unnerving and a stark reminder that gender equality has not been achieved. For Kay, carving out a life of resistance as she ages is centered on finding pathways that are an alternative to retreating into the limited roles and identities that are culturally approved and reserved for older women.

Meanwhile, unlike Kay, Joan was a "good girl." She went to a secretarial school and pursued a gender-appropriate job as a secretary. She became dissatisfied, though, because she was not receiving raises or being paid as well as others who had 2-year college degrees, so she went to a community college to earn that degree. One course in sociology was all Joan needed to become a student of understanding social processes. She married and had two children but continued on in school, moving from community college to university-level education.

In trying to understand the patterns of daily life, gender became a major explanatory framework for Joan. The isolation of women during child-rearing years and the lack of institutions to support raising children developed into major interests, along with the effects of work patterns on men and women. Despite this lack of support for women who chose to pursue family and profession, Joan pursued and received her PhD while rearing children. Her consciousness raising occurred more informally than Kay's, via books and one-on-one conversations with friends, often while caring for children.

Entry into professional sociology, while at first off-putting given the White, male dominance of the field, became a path to connect ideas with action and to form meaningful relationships with an array of women. It was through a relatively new organization, Sociologists for Women in Society, that we met one another and many others who taught and worked to improve the situation for women in society.

Together with another sociologist, Martha Cornwell, we started an Upstate New York chapter of Sociologists for Women in Society. We became involved in women's studies on our respective campuses and conducted research on women in the arts, work, family, education, and on women's bodily and emotional experiences.

Joan recently retired. She treasures the extra time, which she spends with friends and family, including five grandchildren, and she loves to travel. She continues to write and remains involved in Sociologists for Women in Society, the American Sociology Association, and the Eastern Sociological Society. She is just beginning her retirement journey, contemplating what paths to take, while looking forward to stepping out on new paths.

Today, we continue the journey toward a world that is more just and humane, a world in which people can live safe and satisfying lives unimpeded by the social prisms of difference and inequality described in this book.

Although it may seem that most of the work toward gender equality has been accomplished, as individuals and members of a global society, we have more work to do. For example, women still do not have equal pay for equal work; glass ceilings and sticky floors continue to keep women from high-paying jobs; only a few countries offer gender-equitable parental leaves; most women work a double day, in paid labor and in the home; violence against women remains a serious problem; heterosexist and homophobic beliefs and behaviors maintain restrictive gender patterns while oppressing gay men and lesbians; racism continues to degrade and diminish the lives of women and men of color; and hegemonic masculinity limits the life experiences of most men.

Although there is still more to be accomplished, the good news is that in a very short period of time—our lifetimes—much positive change has occurred in gender relations. A third wave of feminism has now emerged among young people (Baumgardner & Richards, 2000), and many of the new initiatives, including men's and global movements are now actively seeking changes in the genderscape across the globe. Clearly, more change is on the way. What possibilities for change do *you* see in your gendered future? How might you make a difference and contribute to the eradication of gender dichotomy and inequality?

REFERENCES

Baumgardner, J., & Richards, A. (2000). *Manifesta: Young women, feminism, and the future.* New York: Farrar, Straus & Giroux.

Bernard, J. (1972). *The future of marriage.* New York: World Publishing.

Bernard, J. (1975). *Women, wives, mothers.* Chicago: Aldine.

Calasanti, T., Slevin K., & King, N. (2006). Ageism and feminism: From "et cetera" to center. *NWSA Journal, 18*(1), 13–30.

Coontz, S. (1992). *The way we never were: Americans and the nostalgia trap.* New York: Basic Books.

Coontz, S. (1997). *The way we really are: Coming to terms with America's changing families.* New York: Basic Books.

de Beauvoir, S. (1952). *The second sex.* New York: Knopf.

Deckard, B. S. (1979). *The women's movement: Political, socioeconomic, and psychological issues.* New York: Harper & Row.

Friedan, B. (1963). *The feminine mystique.* New York: W. W. Norton.

National Center for Education Statistics. (2005). Table 170: Total fall enrollment in degree-granting institutions, by attendance status, sex of student, and control of institution: Selected years, 1947 through 2004. In *Digest of education statistics.* Retrieved from http://nces.ed.gov/programs/digest/d05/tables/dt05_170.asp

Rapp, R. (1982). Family and class in contemporary America. In B. Thorne (with M. Yalom) (Ed.), *Rethinking the family: Some feminist questions* (pp. 168–187). New York: Longman.

Russell, D. E. H. (1982). *Rape in marriage.* New York: Macmillan.

Schneir, M. (1994). *Feminism in our time: The essential writings, World War II to the present.* New York: Vintage Books.

Schwartz, P. (1994). *Peer marriage: How love between equals really works.* New York: Free Press.

Weitzman, L. J. (1985). *The divorce revolution: The unexpected social and economic consequences for women and children in America.* New York: Free Press.

ABOUT THE EDITORS

Joan Z. Spade is Professor Emeriti of sociology at The College at Brockport, State University of New York. She received her PhD from University at Buffalo, State University of New York, and her BA from State University of New York at Geneseo. In addition to courses on gender, Joan taught on education, family, research methods, and statistics. She published articles on rape culture in college fraternities and on work and family, including women's and men's orientations toward work. She has also coedited two books on education and published articles on education, including research on tracking and gender and education. Joan is active in Sociologists for Women in Society, Eastern Sociological Society, and the American Sociological Association. In addition to visiting her two children and five grandchildren, she enjoys the arts, travel, and being outdoors.

Catherine (Kay) G. Valentine is Professor Emerita of sociology at Nazareth College in Rochester, New York. She received her PhD from Syracuse University and her BA from the State University of New York at Albany. Kay taught a wide range of courses, such as sociology of gender, senior seminar in sociology, sociology of bodies and emotions, sociology of consumerism, and human sexuality. Her publications include articles on teaching sociology, on women's bodies and emotions, on gender and qualitative research, and on the sociology of art museums. She is the founding director of women's studies at Nazareth College and a longtime member of Sociologists for Women in Society. She has also served as president of the New York State Sociological Association. Kay and her life partner, Paul J. Burgett, University of Rochester vice president and professor of music, are devotees of the arts and world travel.

⑤SAGE research**methods**

The essential online tool for researchers from the world's leading methods publisher

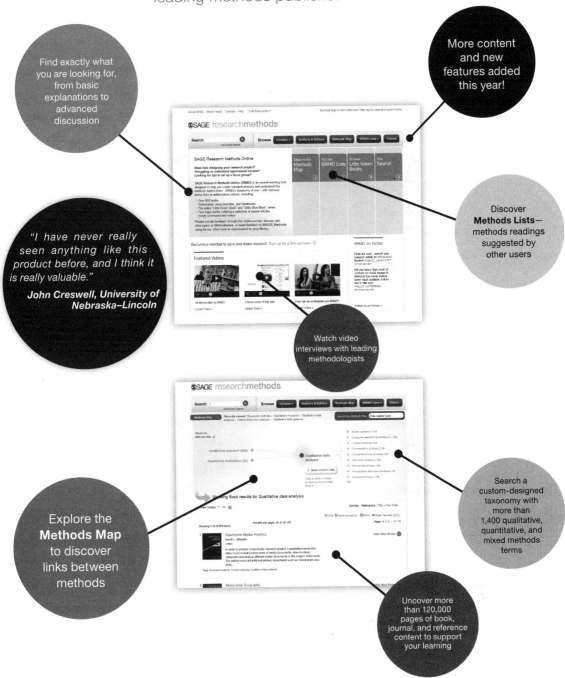

Find exactly what you are looking for, from basic explanations to advanced discussion

More content and new features added this year!

Discover **Methods Lists**— methods readings suggested by other users

"I have never really seen anything like this product before, and I think it is really valuable."

John Creswell, University of Nebraska–Lincoln

Watch video interviews with leading methodologists

Explore the **Methods Map** to discover links between methods

Search a custom-designed taxonomy with more than 1,400 qualitative, quantitative, and mixed methods terms

Uncover more than 120,000 pages of book, journal, and reference content to support your learning

Find out more at
www.sageresearchmethods.com